PAGE 54 **ON THE ROAD**

YOUR COMPLETE DESTINATION GUIDE
In-depth reviews, detailed listings
and insider tips

North Coast & Redwoods (p212)

Northern Mountains (p266)

Lake Tahoe (p363)

Napa & Sonoma Wine Country (p159)

Gold Country & Central Valley (p302)

San Francisco (p56)

Marin County & the Bay Area (p108)

Yosemite & the Sierra Nevada (p397)

Central Coast (p453)

Palm Springs & the Deserts (p651)

Disneyland & Orange County (p579)

Los Angeles (p527)

San Diego (p607)

PAGE 757 **SURVIVAL GUIDE**

VITAL PRACTICAL INFORMATION TO
HELP YOU HAVE A SMOOTH TRIP

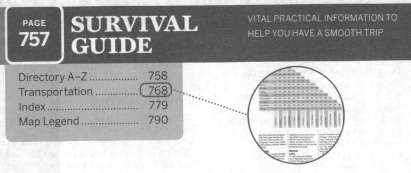

THIS EDITION WRITTEN AND RESEARCHED BY

Sara Benson

**Andrew Bender, Alison Bing, Nate Cavalieri, Bridget Gleeson, Beth Kohn,
Andrea Schulte-Peevers, John A Vlahides**

welcome to California

Natural Beauty

Don't be fooled by its perpetually fresh outlook and gung-ho attitude: California is older than it seems. Coastal bluffs and snow-capped peaks were created over millennia of tectonic upheavals that have threatened to shake California right off the continent. After unchecked 19th-century mining, logging and oil-drilling threatened to undermine the state's natural splendors, California's pioneering environmentalists rescued about 2.5 million acres of old-growth trees, aged from 150 to 5000 years old. Conservation initiatives by John Muir and his pioneering conservation group the Sierra Club resulted in the creation of Yosemite National Park and Red-wood National and State Parks. Unesco has named them World Heritage sites; visitors call them simply breathtaking.

Food & Drink

To start a conversation in California, don't bother opening with "Nice weather we've been having." Of course it's nice – this is California. Instead, walk into any crowd and ask, "Does anyone know where I can get a decent taco around here?" Now we're talking. Since California produces most of the fresh produce and specialty meats in the US, minor menu decisions have nation-wide impact. Every time they sit down to eat, Californians take trend-setting stands on mealtime moral dilemmas: certified

Everyone heads to the Golden State to find fame and fortune – but you can do better. Come for the landscape, stay for sensational meals, and glimpse the future in the making on America's creative coast.

(left) Surfer at Silver Strand beach (p622), near San Diego
(below) Wine tasting at Iron Horse Vineyards (p195) in Sebastopol, Sonoma County

organic versus spray-free, grass-fed versus grain-finished, farm-to-table versus urban-garden-grown, veganism versus humanely raised meats. But no matter what you order, it's likely to be local and creative, and it better be good – Californians compulsively share best and worst dining experiences via social media platforms Facebook Twitter, and Yelp, all created in California. For a chaser, try a stiff drink: California produces 99% of the nation's grapes and its most prestigious wines, and has three times more breweries than any other state.

Earth-Shaking Ideas

From the Gold Rush to the dot-com bubble, California has survived extreme booms and busts – and in the current US recession, Californians are once again getting by on their wits. Hollywood still single-handedly produces most of the world's movies and TV shows, fed by a vibrant performing arts scene on stages, in parks and balancing on barstools across the state. Trends are kick-started here not by moguls in offices, but by a motley crowd of surfers, artists and dreamers concocting the out-there ideas behind skateboarding, interactive art and biotechnology. The Creative Class research institute predicts that California has the talent, technology and tolerance to stage another stunning economic comeback – and if you linger in California galleries and cafes, you may actually see the future coming.

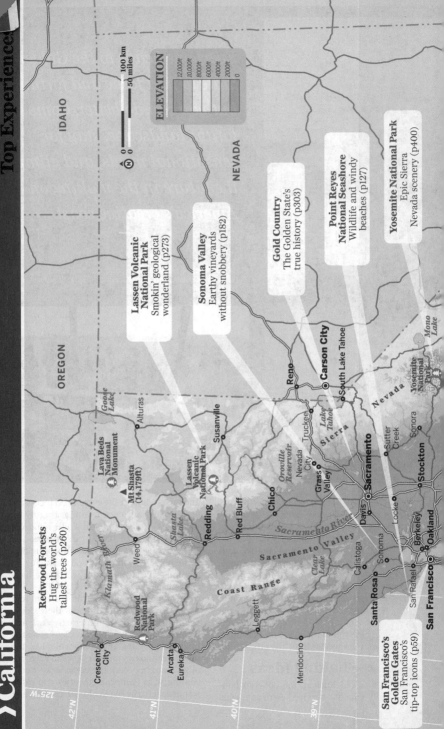

Redwood Forests
Hug the world's tallest trees (p260)

Lassen Volcanic National Park
Smokin' geological wonderland (p273)

Sonoma Valley
Earthy vineyards without snobbery (p182)

Gold Country
The Golden State's true history (p303)

Point Reyes National Seashore
Wildlife and windy beaches (p127)

Yosemite National Park
Epic Sierra Nevada scenery (p400)

San Francisco's Golden Gates
San Francisco's tip-top icons (p59)

ELEVATION

| 12,000ft |
| 10,000ft |
| 8000ft |
| 6000ft |
| 4000ft |
| 2000ft |
| 0 |

100 km
50 miles

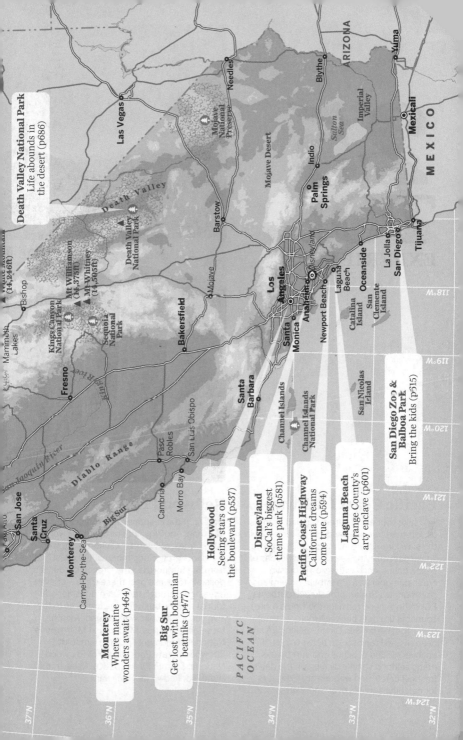

Death Valley National Park
Life abounds in the desert (p686)

Monterey
Where marine wonders await (p464)

Big Sur
Get lost with bohemian beatniks (p477)

Hollywood
Seeing stars on the boulevard (p537)

Disneyland
SoCal's biggest theme park (p581)

Pacific Coast Highway
California dreams come true (p594)

Laguna Beach
Orange County's arty enclave (p601)

San Diego Zoo & Balboa Park
Bring the kids (p515)

25 TOP EXPERIENCES

Pacific Coast Highway

1 Make your escape from tangled, traffic-jammed freeways and cruise the coast in the slow lane. California's coastal highways snake past dizzying sea cliffs and dozens of beach towns, each with its own idiosyncratic personality, from offbeat bohemian communities to glamorously rich outposts. PCH (the generic term for the whole route) connects the dots between major coastal cities, too: surfin' San Diego, rocking LA and beatnik San Francisco. In between, you'll uncover hidden beaches and surf breaks, rustic seafood shacks dishing up the day's freshest catch, and wooden seaside piers for catching sunsets over boundless Pacific horizons.

Redwood Forests

2 Ditch the cellphone and hug a tree, man. And why not start with the world's tallest trees, redwoods? California's towering giants grow along much of the coast, from Big Sur north to the Oregon border. It's possible to cruise past these trees – or even drive right through them at old-fashioned tourist traps – but nothing compares to the awe you'll feel while walking underneath these ancient ones. Meditate at Muir Woods National Monument (p123), Humboldt Redwoods State Park (p247) or Redwood National & State Parks (p260). Fallen tree in Humboldt Redwoods State Park

Sonoma Valley

3 As winemaking in the neighboring Napa Valley grows ever more dizzyingly upscale, here sun-dappled vineyards are surrounded by pastoral ranchlands. The uniqueness of *terroir* is valued most in this down-to-earth wine country, where you may taste new vintages straight from the barrel inside a tin-roofed shed while playing with the winemaker's pet dog. Who cares if it's not noon yet? Relax and enjoy your late-harvest zinfandel with a scoop of white-chocolate ice cream drizzled with organic olive oil. This is Sonoma; conventions need not apply.

Disneyland Resort

4 Where orange groves and walnut trees once grew, there Walt Disney built his dream, throwing open the doors of his Magic Kingdom in 1955. Today, Disneyland (p581) is SoCal's most-visited tourist attraction. Inside Anaheim's mega-popular theme parks, beloved cartoon characters waltz arm-in-arm down Main Street USA and fireworks explode over Sleeping Beauty's castle on hot summer nights. If you're a kid, or just hopelessly young at heart, who are we to say that Disneyland can't really be 'The Happiest Place on Earth'?

Indiana Jones Adventure ride (p586), Disneyland

Yosemite National Park

5 Welcome to what conservationist John Muir called his 'high pleasure-ground' and 'great temple.' At Yosemite National Park (p400), meander through wildflower-strewn meadows in valleys carved by glaciers, avalanches and earthquakes. Everything looks bigger here, whether you're getting splashed by thunderous waterfalls that tumble over sheer cliffs, staring up at granite domes or walking in ancient groves of giant sequoias, the planet's biggest trees. For the most sublime views, perch at Glacier Point on a full moon night or drive the high country's dizzying Tioga Rd in summer.

El Capitan (p401)

San Francisco's Golden Gates

6 Sashay out onto San Francisco's iconic bridge (p59) to spy on cargo ships threading through pylons painted 'International Orange,' then memorize 360-degree views of the rugged Marin Headlands, far-off downtown skyscrapers, and the speck that is Alcatraz Island (p79). Across town, you could spend days getting lost in Golden Gate Park (p75) without uncovering all of its secret haunts, like the paddleboat pond and Japanese teahouse, and delving into its eco-conscious science and innovative art museums. On Sundays, the park is closed to traffic, making it a pedestrian's paradise.

Ferry Building Marketplace

7 Other towns have their gourmet ghettos, but San Francisco puts its love – strike that, obsession – with food front and center at the Ferry Building (p59). Like a grand salute, the building's 240ft trademark clocktower has greeted millions of passengers since it opened in 1898. Today, with its airy shopping halls and waterfront tables with bay views, it's the perfect place to grab a bite of Northern California's locally grown bounty. Artisan cheeses, wine-country olive oil, organic veggies and even wild game all turn up at the thrice-weekly sidewalk farmers market. Organic carrots the farmers market

ARIADNE VAN ZANDBERGEN/LONELY PLANET IMAGES ©

Death Valley National Park

8 Just uttering the name brings up visions of broken-down pioneer wagon trains and parched lost souls crawling across desert sand dunes. But the most surprising thing about Death Valley (p686) is how full of life it really is. Spring wildflower blooms explode with a painter's palette of hues across camel-colored hillsides. Feeling adventurous? Twist your way up narrow canyons cluttered with geological oddities, stand atop volcanic craters formed by violent prehistoric explosions, or explore Wild West mining ghost towns where fortunes have been lost – and found.

San Diego Zoo & Balboa Park

9 Beautiful Balboa Park (p612) is where San Diegans come to play (when they're not at the beach). Bring the whole family and spend the day immersed in more than a dozen art, cultural and science museums, or marvel at the Spanish Revival architecture while sunning yourself along El Prado promenade. Glimpse exotic wildlife and ride the 'Skyfari' cable car at San Diego's world-famous zoo (p615), or take in a show at the Old Globe theater (p639), a faithful reconstruction of the Shakespearean original. Above: Polar Bear, San Diego Zoo

Santa Monica & Venice

10 Who needs LA traffic? Hit the beach instead. Posh Santa Monica (p547) can grant instant happiness. Learn to surf, ride a solar-powered Ferris wheel, dance under the stars on an old-fashioned pier, let the kids explore the aquarium's tidal touch pools or just dip your toes in the water and let your troubles float away. Did we mention jaw-dropping sunsets? Then join the parade of new agers, muscled bodybuilders, goth punks and hippie drummers at nearby Venice Beach (p547), where everyone lets their freak flag fly. Opposite top: Bodybuilders, Venice Beach

Hollywood

11 The movie and TV studios have all moved away, but Hollywood (p537) and its pink-starred Walk of Fame still attracts millions of wide-eyed visitors every year. Like an aging starlet making a comeback, this once-gritty urban neighborhood in LA is undergoing a rebirth of cool, blossoming with hip hotels, glittering restored movie palaces and glitzy velvet-roped bars and nightclubs. Snap a souvenir photo outside Grauman's Chinese Theatre or inside Hollywood & Highland's Babylon Court with the iconic Hollywood sign as a backdrop – go ahead, we know you can't resist. Right: Walk of Fame

California's Missions

12 If you road-trip along the coast between San Diego and Sonoma, you can't help but follow in the footsteps of early Spanish conquistadors and Catholic priests. Foremost among those colonists was Padre Junípero Serra, who founded many of California's 21 hauntingly historical missions in the late 18th century. Some missions today have been authentically restored, with gorgeous gardens, stone arcades, fountains, and chapels adorned with spiritual frescoes. Others are just the ruins of an era long past, where ghosts still pace the cloisters. Below: Mission Santa Barbara (p513)

Laguna Beach

13 In Orange County, Huntington Beach draws the hang-loose surfer crowd, while yachties play in the fantasyland of Newport Beach. But farther south, Laguna Beach (p601) beckons, with its sophisticated blend of money, culture and natural beauty: startling seascapes led an early-20th-century artists' colony to take root here. Laguna's bohemian past still peeks out in downtown's art galleries, historic arts-and-crafts bungalows tucked amongst multimillion-dollar mansions, and the annual Festival of Arts and Pageant of the Masters (p604). Right: Crescent Bay (p603)

12

13

14

15

Monterey

14 Northern California's fishing villages are made for heartier outdoors lovers – think John Steinbeck and his gritty novels of American realism. Hop aboard a whale-watching cruise out into Monterey Bay's national marine sanctuary (p464), some of whose denizens also swim in Cannery Row's ecologically sound aquarium (p464). Soak up the authentic maritime atmosphere at the West Coast's oldest lighthouse in Pacific Grove (p473), or downtown among flowering gardens and adobe-walled buildings from California's Mexican past. Top right: Jellyfish, Monterey Bay Aquarium

Coronado

15 Who says you can't turn back time? Speed over the two-mile bay bridge or board the ferry from San Diego to seaside Coronado (p622), a civilized escape back to a more genteel era. Revel in the late-19th-century socialite atmosphere at the palatial 'Hotel Del,' where royalty and presidents have bedded down, and Marilyn Monroe cavorted in the 1950s screwball classic *Some Like It Hot*. Then pedal past impossibly white beaches all the way down the peninsula's Silver Strand, stopping just long enough for ice cream and rainbow-colored cotton candy. Above: Hotel del Coronado (p622)

ig Sur

16 Nestled up against mossy, mysterious-looking redwood forests, the rocky Big Sur (p477) coast is a secretive place. Get to know it like the locals do, especially if you want to find hidden hot springs and beaches where the sand is tinged purple or where ginormous jade has been found. Time your visit for May, when waterfalls peak, or after summer–vacation crowds have left but sunny skies still rule. Don't forget to look skyward to catch sight of endangered California condors taking wing above the cliffs on thermal winds. Below: Mc-Way Falls, Julia Pfeiffer Burns State Park (p481)

Santa Barbara

17 Calling itself the 'American Riviera,' Santa Barbara (p513) is so idyllic you just have to sigh. Waving palm trees, sugar-sand beaches, boats bobbing by the harbor – it'd be a travel cliche if it wasn't the plain truth. California's 'Queen of the Missions' is a beauty, as are downtown's red-roofed, whitewashed adobe buildings all rebuilt in harmonious historical style after a devastating 1925 earthquake. Come escape just for the day, or maybe a wine-drenched weekend in the country. Bottom: State St, Downtown Santa Barbara

DAVID PEEVERS/LONELY PLANET IMAGES ©

STEPHEN SAKS/LONELY PLANET IMAGES ©

STEVE SHI/EV/ALAMY ©

Surfing

18 Even if you never set foot on a board – and we totally recommend that you do – there's no denying the influence of surfing on all aspects of California beach life, from fashion to street slang. With gnarly local waves, you won't need to jet over to Hawaii to experience the adrenaline rush for yourself. Pros ride world-class breaks off Malibu, San Diego, the OC's Huntington Beach (aka 'Surf City USA') and Santa Cruz, while newbies get schooled at 'surfari' camps along SoCal's sunny coast. Above left: Surfing in LA

Gold Country

19 'Go west, young man!' could have been the rallying cry of tens of thousands of immigrants who invaded during California's Gold Rush era, which kicked off back in 1848. Today, these rough-and-tumble Sierra Nevada foothills are a stronghold of Golden State history, thrillingly tainted by banditry, bordellos and bloodlust. Hwy 49, which slowly winds past sleepy townships and abandoned mines, is also a gateway to swimming holes and white-water rafting, downhill mountain-biking bomber runs and tasting the fruits of some of California's oldest vines. Top right: Panning for gold at Columbia State Historic Park (p323)

Coastin' on Amtrak

20 Evocatively named routes like *Coast Starlight* and *Pacific Surfliner* will tempt you to leave your car behind. South of San Luis Obispo, you can glimpse remote beaches from Amtrak's high-ceilinged observation cars. Blink and you're already in Santa Barbara, where you can hop off for wine tasting, then take a seaside swim at whistle-stop Carpinteria or Ventura before rolling into LA's architecturally imposing Union Station. Next up, historic Mission San Juan Capistrano and eclectic North County beach towns before finishing in San Diego. All aboard! Bottom right: Amtrak Pacific Surfliner

JOE MCBRIDE/GETTY ©

Lake Tahoe

21 High in the Sierra Nevada mountains, this all-seasons adventure base camp revolves around the USA's second-deepest lake. In summer, startlingly clear blue waters lead to splashing, kayaking or even scuba diving. Meanwhile, mountain-bikers careen down epic single-track runs and hikers stride along trails threading through thick forests. After fun in the sun, you can retreat to a cozy lakefront cottage and toast s'mores in the firepit. When the lake turns into a winter wonderland, gold-medal ski resorts keep downhill fanatics, punk snowboarders and Nordic traditionalists more than satisfied. Above left: Skiing at Lake Tahoe

Lassen Volcanic National Park

22 Anchoring the southernmost link in the Cascades Range volcanic chain, this alien landscape bubbles over with roiling mud pots, noxious sulfur vents and steamy fumaroles, not to mention its colorful cinder cones and crater lakes. You won't find the crowds of more famous national parks at this off-the-beaten-path destination, but Lassen (p273) still offers peaks to be conquered, azure waters to be paddled, forested campsites for pitching your tent and boardwalks through Bumpass Hell that will leave you awestruck. Top right: Boardwalk above fumaroles in Bumpass Hell

Palm Springs

23 A star-studded oasis in the Mojave ever since the retro days of Frank Sinatra's Rat Pack, 'PS' is a chic desert resort getaway. Do like A-list stars and hipsters do: lounge by your Mid-Century Modern hotel's swimming pool; go art-golfing, gallery hopping or vintage shopping, and then drink cocktails from sunset till dawn. Feeling less loungey? Break a sweat on hiking trails that wind through desert canyons across Native American tribal lands, or scramble to a summit in the San Jacinto Mountains, reached via a head-spinning aerial tramway (p653). Bottom right: Desert house and garden, Palm Springs

Mendocino

24 Mendocino (p223) is the North Coast's salt-washed sandcastle of dreams. Nothing restores the soul like a ramble out onto craggy headland cliffs and among berry brambles. In summer, fragrant bursts of lavender and jasmine drift on fog-laden winds. Churning surf is never out of earshot, and driftwood-littered beaches are potent reminders of the sea's power. Originally a 19th-century port built by New Englanders, Mendocino today belongs to bohemians who favor art and nature's outdoor temple for their religions. Below: Bowling Ball Beach (p220), Mendocino County

Point Reyes National Seashore

25 If one park could encapsulate Northern California, Point Reyes (p127) would get our vote. Step across the San Andreas fault, stand out by the lighthouse at what truly feels like land's end and peer through binoculars at migratory whales. Witness the raucous birthing and mating antics of elephant seals at Chimney Rock, then hike among herds of tule elk and drive out to windswept beaches, where the horizon stretches toward eternity. Bottom: Point Reyes Lighthouse (p128)

WES WALKER/LONELY PLANET IMAGES ©

EMILY RIDDELL/LONELY PLANET IMAGES ©

need to know

Currency
» US dollars ($)

Language
» English

When to Go

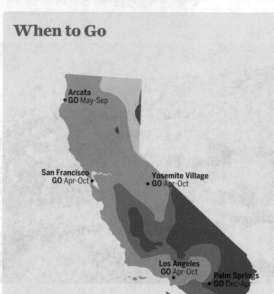

Arcata
• GO May-Sep

San Francisco
GO Apr-Oct •

Yosemite Village
• GO Apr-Oct

Los Angeles
GO Apr-Oct

Palm Springs
• GO Dec-Apr

Desert, dry climate
Dry climate
Warm to hot summers, mild winters
Warm to hot summers, cold winters

High Season
(Jun–Aug)

» Accommodation prices are up 50% to 100% on average.

» Major holidays are even busier and more expensive.

» Summer is low season in the desert, temperatures exceed 100°F (38°C).

Shoulder Season (Apr–May & Sep–Oct)

» Crowds and prices drop, especially along the coast and in the mountains.

» Mild temperatures and sunny, cloudless days.

» Typically wetter in spring, drier in autumn.

Low Season
(Nov–Mar)

» Accommodation rates drop by the coast.

» Chilly temperatures, frequent rainstorms and heavy snow falls in the mountains.

» Winter is peak season in SoCal's desert regions.

Your Daily Budget

Budget
less than $75

» Hostel dorm beds: $25–40

» Skip theme parks and hit 'free admission' days at museums

» Find farmers markets for cheap eats

Midrange
$75– 200

» Two-star motel or hotel double room: $75–150

» Rental car: from $30 per day, excluding insurance and gas

Top end
over $200

» Three-star lodging: from $150 per night in high season

» Three-course meal in top restaurant: $75 plus wine

Money

» ATMs are widely available. Credit cards are normally required for hotel reservations, car rentals and so on. Tipping is customary, not optional.

Visas

» Visas are generally not required for citizens of Visa Waiver Program (VWP) countries, but only with ESTA approval (apply online at least 72 hours in advance).

Cell Phones

» The only foreign phones that will work in the USA are GSM multiband models. Cell phone coverage can be spotty in remote areas (eg deserts, mountains).

Driving

» Traffic in cities and coastal areas can be nightmarish. Avoid commuter rush hours (roughly 7am to 10am and 3pm to 7pm from Monday to Friday).

Websites

California Travel and Tourism Commission (www.visitcalifornia. com) Multilingual trip-planning guides.

California State Parks (www.parks.ca.gov) Outdoor activities and free e-guides.

CalTrans (www.dot. ca.gov) Current highway conditions.

LA Times Travel (www. latimes.com/travel) Daily news, travel deals and blogs.

Lonely Planet (www. lonelyplanet.com/ california) Destination info, hotel bookings, travelers' forums and more.

Roadside America (www.roadsideamerica. com) Finding 'uniquely odd tourist attractions.'

Exchange Rates

Australia	A$1	$1.04
Canada	C$1	$1.05
Euro zone	€1	$1.33
China	Y10	$1.56
Japan	¥100	$1.29
Mexico	MXN10	$0.72
New Zealand	NZ$1	$0.76
UK	£1	$1.54

For current exchange rates see www.xe.com.

Important Numbers

All phone numbers have a three-digit area code followed by a seven-digit local number. For long-distance and toll-free calls, dial 1 plus all 10 digits.

Country code	⤹1
International dialing code	⤹011
Operator	⤹0
Emergency (ambulance, fire & police)	⤹911
Directory assistance (local)	⤹411

Arriving in California

» **Los Angeles International Airport** (LAX; see p573)
Taxis $30 to $55, 30 minutes to one hour
Door-to-door shuttles $16 to $25
Free Shuttle C to LAX Transit Center or Metro FlyAway bus ($7) to downtown LA

» **San Francisco International Airport** (SFO; see p106)
Taxis $35 to $50, 25 to 50 minutes
Door-to-door shuttles $15 to $20
Train – BART ($8.10, 30 minutes) every 20 minutes from 6am to 11:45pm

Pacific Coast Highway

Snaking over 1000 miles along dizzying sea cliffs and over landmark bridges, passing redwoods and beach towns, California's coastal highways connect the big cities (San Diego, Los Angeles and San Francisco) and Oregon to the north. 'Pacific Coast Highway (PCH)' refers to one stretch of Hwy 1 but loosely represents the entire coastal route. June through August, vacationing crowds descend on PCH and traffic often crawls. A thick, foggy layer descends in May and June along the NorCal coast. Sunny SoCal beaches beckon, especially during July and August. September and October are your best bets for sunny skies and avoiding the worst crowds. Winter brings coastal whale-watching opportunities, while spring sees wildflowers bloom.

what's new

For this new edition of California, our authors have hunted down the fresh, the revamped, the transformed, the hot and the happening. For up-to-the-minute reviews and recommendations, see lonelyplanet.com/usa/california.

Food Trucks

1 Sure, there have always been roadside taco trucks in California. But recently, a gourmands' street-food revolution has taken over, especially in Los Angeles and the San Francisco Bay Area. Whatever you're craving right now, from Korean BBQ to Indian dosa, haute grilled cheese to good ol' fried chicken, there's probably a restaurant-on-four-wheels driven by a rule-breaking urban chef to serve you. Track 'em all down on Twitter.

Disneyland

2 It's a Small World got dolled up, Captain EO returned, the Pixar Play Parade and World of Color spectacular debuted and Ariel's Undersea Adventure and Cars Land opened. See p581.

Downtown Los Angeles

3 Swing by the high-fidelity Grammy Museum (p536) at the new LA Live entertainment complex, then explore the city's Mexican-American heritage at La Plaza de Cultura y Artes (p532).

GLBT History Museum

4 San Francisco flies its rainbow-flag nation flag proudly at the USA's first stand-alone museum (p72) dedicated to the gay, lesbian, bisexual and transgender cultural experience.

Wine Country Goes 'Green'

5 Earthy cooking renews chefs' locavarian, grass-fed and organic roots, vineyards become solar-powered and biodynamic, and ever more boutique hotels jump on the eco-bandwagon too. See p159

San Diego's East Village

6 Popping up around Petco Park you'll find gastropubs, epicurean pizzerias, bistros and bars that are making stiff competition for the Gaslamp Quarter. See p610.

Half Dome Hiking Permits

7 Wanna summit Yosemite National Park's most iconic granite dome? Even day hikers now need permits (see p402), which sell out online months in advance – plan ahead, folks.

Shorebreak Hotel

8 Party animals still rule at Huntington Beach (p596), but this hip downtown boutique property is upping the sophistication ante with a 'surf concierge,' yoga studio and dog-friendly lodgings.

Outside-the-Box Tours

9 Go ziplining through redwood forests, dish over lunch with a Napa winemaker, step aboard Sausalito's charming houseboats, dig into foodie haunts in LA's ethnic neighborhoods and so much more.

California State Park Closures

10 Due to an ongoing fiscal crisis, 70 state parks (p754) are slated to shut their gates to the public in 2012. Visit www.parks.ca.gov for updates.

if you like...

Amazing Food

Infused by immigrant cultures for over 200 years, California cuisine is all about creatively mixing it up, from kim-chi tacos to vegan soul food. Even rock-star chefs are generous about sharing credit with local fishers, farmers, ranchers and wineries, emblazoning their names on menus like credits on a Hollywood blockbuster film.

Chez Panisse Chef Alice Waters revolutionized California cuisine back in the '70s with seasonal Bay Area locavarian cooking (p143)

French Laundry High-wattage kitchen mastered by Thomas Keller; the Wine Country's gastronomic highlight (p173)

Ferry Building Hit the thrice-weekly outdoor farmers market, or duck inside San Francisco's waterfront collection of artisan food vendors (p59)

LA's Food Trucks Food trucks may be everywhere now, but LA sparked the mobile gourmet revolution with Kogi BBQ – and over 200 out-of-the-box chefs on wheels followed (p559)

South Beach Bar & Grill Start your search for San Diego's perfect fish taco here (p634)

Microbreweries

Barrels from California's vineyards may steal the scene, but what's being brewed in big copper vats across the Golden State (maybe even in your neighbor's garage) is darn tasty too. Brewpubs are communal watering holes for grabbing a burger and a brew, then hashing out politics or bragging about that day's killer mountain-bike ride.

Lost Coast Brewery In Eureka, knock back a Downtown Brown while admiring the conceptual-art beer labels (p253)

Anderson Valley Brewing In Mendocino County's boondocks, this solar-powered Bavarian brewhouse lets you play disc golf with a bottle of amber ale or oatmeal stout in hand (p236)

Sierra Nevada Brewing Co A pioneer that's gotten too big for its microbrewery britches, but still offers tours and samples of its mega-popular pale ale in Chico (p339)

Stone Brewing Company A San Diego upstart not afraid to make Arrogant Bastard Ale and barleywine (p638)

Cities

It's a fact: six out of every 10 Californians lives within an hour's drive of the ocean. So it should come as no surprise that cities along this Pacific Coast dominate the state's multicultural and counter-cultural identities. Delve into what it really means to be Californian in these three kaleidoscopic megapolises.

San Francisco With fewer than a million people, the city with its head in the clouds has become a global capital of cuisine, technology, the arts, gay liberation and eco-consciousness (p56)

Los Angeles In California's biggest metro area, a perpetual influx of creative big dreamers, immigrant go-getters and wannabe-famous faces keep the energetic buzz going 24/7 (p527)

San Diego Sunny San Diego doesn't even have to try very hard to win over hearts and minds with its laid-back beach vibe, Mexican food and breweries (p607)

» Vintage boutique, San Francisco

Theme Parks

Southern California's theme parks are the best hands-down, ranking high among family favorites nationwide (who needs Orlando?). If visiting Disney's 'happiest place on earth,' getting a thrill from Hollywood's movie magic or just feeling a powerful need for speed on a rad roller coaster is on your itinerary, this is the place.

Disneyland Topping almost every family's must-do fun list is Walt Disney's 'imagineered' theme park, along with next-door Disney's California Adventure (p583)

Universal Studios Hollywood Cinematic theme park with a studio backlot tram tour, tame rides and live-action, special-effects shows (p550)

Six Flags Magic Mountain & Hurricane Harbor Hair-raising roller coasters will scare the bejeezus out of speed-crazed teens, who can cool off at the next-door water park (p574)

San Diego Zoo Safari Park Take a safari-style tram tour through an 'open-range' zoo (p614)

Legoland California Low-key theme park made of beloved building blocks for tots (p648)

Hiking

Lace up those hiking boots! It's time to hit the trail, anywhere you go. Ever since Native Americans made the first footpaths through the wilderness and gold-seeking pioneers trailblazed routes across mountain ranges, Californians have been walking. Oceanside rambles, desert palm oases, alpine peaks and verdant forest idylls await.

Sierra Nevada You could spend a lifetime trekking in Yosemite, Sequoia & Kings Canyon National Parks, or just a day summiting Mt Whitney (p397)

North Coast Hardy backpackers challenge the remote Lost Coast Trail, or ramble among old-growth redwood trees in fern-laden forests (p212)

Marin County Tawny headlands tempt hikers across San Francisco's Golden Gate Bridge, or step on the San Andreas Fault at wild, windblown Point Reyes National Seashore (p108)

Palm Springs & the Deserts Discover hidden palm-tree oases, stroll across salt flats or take a guided walk through Native American canyons (p651)

Small Towns

There's no denying that California, the most populous state in the nation, is a crowded place. If you get tired of never-ending freeway traffic, make your escape to these in-between places, whether by the beach, up in the mountains or just down the road from vineyards.

Calistoga For the blue-jeans and boots crowd in Napa Valley, where quaint downtown streets are speckled with mud-bath spas (p177)

Bolinas End-of-the-road hamlet in NorCal's Marin County is no longer a secret (p125)

San Luis Obispo Oprah called it 'the happiest place in America,' and with a bike-friendly downtown and fun farmers market, you might agree (p498)

Seal Beach Old-fashioned Orange County beach town with a cute main street and surf-worthy pier (p594)

Mammoth Lakes A jumping-off point for all-weather Eastern Sierra adventures (p436)

Julian Old West gold-mining history and apple pie in the hills east of San Diego (p679)

If you like... architecture, start in LA (p529), sheltering Arts-and-Crafts bungalows to postmodern sculptural edifices, then drive out to Palm Springs (p653), home of retro-chic Mid-Century Modern gems

Wilderness Parks

California's natural glories aren't only about those 1100-plus miles of beaches. Inland, jagged mountain peaks, high-country meadows and sand dunes beckon. Back at the coast, a chain of national and state parks protect an astonishing diversity of life zones, which extend offshore to wind-tossed islands.

Redwoods National & State Parks Get lost ambling among ancient groves of the world's tallest trees on the fog-laden North Coast (p260)

Yosemite National Park Ascend into the Sierra Nevada, where waterfalls tumble into glacier-carved valleys and wildflower meadows bloom (p400)

Death Valley National Park Uncover secret pockets of life in this austere desert landscape, peppered with geological oddities (p686)

Lassen Volcanic National Park Camp by northern alpine lakes and traipse around the boiling mud pots of Bumpass Hell (p273)

Channel Islands National Park Escape civilization on SoCal's isolated islands, nicknamed 'California's Galapagos' for their amazing biodiversity (p522)

Nightlife

You've seen the red carpet rolled out for movie-star premieres. Now it's your turn to step out in style at ultra-chic nightclubs. Oh, you're not a fan of velvet ropes and attitudinous bouncers? No problem. You'll find less exclusive, but equally entertaining watering holes all over California, from hipster bars in LA and the San Francisco Bay Area to San Diego surfer tiki bars and desert cocktail lounges.

Los Angeles Hip-hop to world beats, techno to trance, DJs spin it all in Hollywood's glam club scene, while nearby 'WeHo' is ground zero for LA's gay and lesbian scene (p566)

San Francisco Go beatnik in North Beach, hipster in the Mission or party with the rainbow-flag nation in the Castro (p96)

San Diego Go on a pub crawl in the Gaslamp Quarter, downtown's historic red-light district (p637)

Las Vegas, Nevada The Strip's high-powered nightclubs measure up to any fantasy (p705 & p706)

Shopping

From vintage clothing shops and deeply discounted outlet malls to high-end boutiques where celebrities casually drop thousands of dollars, California is a shoppers' nirvana. It doesn't matter where you roam, especially along the coast: there's a rack of haute couture or bargain finds begging to be stashed in your suitcase.

Los Angeles Forget Beverly Hills' Rodeo Dr: Mid-City's Robertson Blvd has LA's highest density of star-worthy boutiques per block, while Melrose Ave is fashion-forward (p569)

San Francisco Elevating thrift-store fashion to a high art, SF has tons of creative boutiques, from DIY paper-making shops to S&M toys, spread from the Marina to the Mission (p103)

Orange County Hit Costa Mesa's Camp and the Lab, both offbeat anti-malls for fashion mavens and indie souls, or browse trendy boutiques in Laguna Beach (p601)

Palm Springs Heaven for vintage and thrift-store shoppers looking for 20th-century gems and outlet shopping too (p664)

If you like... hot springs
Detour to Palm Springs (p653), the Eastern Sierra (p428), Big Sur (p477) or Calistoga (p177) to soak in natural-springs pools

Film & TV Locations

All California's a sound stage, it seems. The Industry shines its spotlight and sets up cameras in every corner of the state. If you want to see the magic in action, become a part of a live studio audience (p549) or tour a movie studio (p540) in LA.

Los Angeles Hollywood was born here, and today you can't throw a director's megaphone without hitting another celluloid sight, from Mulholland Drive to Malibu (p527)

San Francisco Bay Area Relive noir crime classics like the *Maltese Falcon* and Alfred Hitchcock's thrillers *Vertigo* and *The Birds* (p56 & p108)

Lone Pine Get misty-eyed over all those classic westerns filmed in the Alabama Hills of the Eastern Sierra (p446)

Mendocino For over a century, this little NorCal port town has starred in movies from *East of Eden* to *The Majestic* (p223)

Orange County Where soap operas, dramedies and reality TV hit their stride (p594)

Weird Stuff

A capital of freakdom, in California you'll encounter unique characters, odd places and bizarre experiences wherever you go. SoCal's deserts and the North Coast especially rope in kooks and offbeat souls, but even metro areas like loopy LA and bohemian SF are jam-packed with just plain weird stuff you won't want to miss.

Venice Boardwalk Gawk at the human zoo of chainsaw-jugglers and Speedo-clad snake-charmers (p547)

Kinetic Grand Championship Outrageously whimsical, artistic and human-powered sculptures race along the North Coast (p249)

Integratron With aliens' help, this giant rejuvenation and time machine stands in the middle of the Mojave (p666)

Madonna Inn Fantastically campy hotel with 110 bizarrely themed rooms, from 'Caveman' to 'Hot Pink' (p492)

Mystery Spot Santa Cruz's shamelessly kitschy 1940s tourist trap will turn your world upside down (p456)

Las Vegas, Nevada Exploding faux volcanoes, a mock Eiffel Tower and Egyptian pyramid – 'nuff said (p696)

Museums

Who says California only has pop culture? You could spend most of your trip inside mighty fine museums, forgetting all about theme parks. Get immersed in multimillion-dollar art galleries, interactive high-tech science exhibits, out-of-this-world planetariums and more.

Getty Center & Villa Art museums as beautiful as their ocean views in West LA (p544) and Malibu (p547)

LA County Museum of Art More than 150,000 works of art spanning the ages and crossing all borders (p542)

MH de Young Museum Copper-skinned temple to art from around the globe in San Francisco's Golden Gate Park (p74)

California Academy of Sciences SF's natural-history museum breathes 'green' in its eco-certified design, with a four-story rainforest and living roof (p74)

Balboa Park Go all-day museum-hopping in San Diego, diving into top-notch art, history and science exhibitions (p612)

Griffith Observatory No better place to see stars in Hollywood than at this hilltop planetarium (p541)

» Girl with snake on the Venice Boardwalk

History

Gold is usually the reason given for the madcap course of California's history, and abandoned mining ghost towns still litter the state. But Native American tribes, Spanish colonial *presidios* (forts), Catholic missions and Mexican *pueblos* (towns) have all left traces for you to dig deeper.

Mission San Juan Capistrano A painstakingly restored jewel along 'El Camino Real,' California's mission trail (p605)

Gold Country Follow in the tracks of Western pioneers and hard-scrabble miners, or pan for real gold yourself (p302)

Old Town San Diego Time travel on the site of California's first civilian Spanish colonial *pueblo* (p618)

El Pueblo de Los Angeles Get a feel for LA's earliest days along lively, adobe building–lined Olvera St (p532)

Bodie State Historic Park Haunting mining ghost town in the Eastern Sierra (p432)

Manzanar National Historic Site WWII Japanese American internment camp interprets a painful chapter of the USA's collective past (p446)

Water Sports

Like the Beach Boys sang in 1963, 'If everybody had an ocean/Across the USA/Then everybody'd be surfin'/like Californ-I-A.' You don't have to be a board rider to enjoy California's prime waterfront real-estate by paddling a sea kayak, donning a snorkel mask or scuba-diving wetsuit, or just taking a lazy shoreline dip.

Huntington Beach Ground zero for Orange County's surf culture, with beach volleyball courts and bonfires on the sand (p595)

La Jolla An eco-underwater park and cove draw scuba divers and snorkelers, while swimmers stroke at Torrey Pines and surfers tackle legendary Windansea (p626)

Channel Islands Visit Catalina (p575) or Channel Islands National Park (p522) for the sea-kayaking, snorkeling and diving experience of a lifetime

Sierra Nevada Challenge some of the wildest white-water rafting rivers in the USA (p407), or paddle into Lake Tahoe's 'Big Blue' (p363)

Bringing Your Dog

What fun is it to go on vacation and leave your four-legged family member at home? Although national and state parks have too many restrictions to be fun for pets, these outdoorsy destinations welcome them with open arms – or rather, paws!

Huntington Beach Southern California's biggest and best dog beach, where Fido can run off-leash for two miles (p595)

Lake Tahoe The Sierra Nevada's finest outdoor playground for pups, with dog-friendly hiking trails, beaches, campsites and cabins (p363)

Carmel-by-the-Sea On the Central Coast, everyone brings their pampered pooches to lunch, then lets them play off-leash in the surf (p474)

Big Bear Lake Bring your canine companions to the mountains near LA, where you'll find leashed hiking trails and pet-friendly cottages and camping (p576)

Fort Bragg Laid-back North Coast harbor town, with off-leash parks, leashed beaches, pet-friendly accommodations and even doggie kayaking (p229)

month by month

Top Events

1 **Tournament of Roses**, January

2 **Festival of Arts & Pageant of the Masters**, July

3 **Pride Month**, June

4 **Coachella Music & Arts Festival**, April

5 **Cinco de Mayo**, May

January

Typically the wettest month, January is a slow time for coastal travel. Mountain ski resorts are busy; so are Palm Springs and SoCal's deserts.

☆ Tournament of Roses

Before the Rose Bowl college football game, this famous New Year's parade of flower-festooned floats, marching bands and prancing equestrians draws over 100,000 spectators to Pasadena, a Los Angeles suburb.

✨ Chinese New Year

Firecrackers, parades, lion dances and street food celebrate the lunar new year, falling in late January or early February. Some of California's biggest celebrations happen in San Francisco and LA.

February

Another rainy month for coastal California, but mountain ski resorts stay busy. The low desert sees lots of visitors when wildflowers start blooming. Valentine's Day is booked solid at many restaurants and resort hotels.

Modernism Week

Do you dig Palm Springs' retro vibe, baby? Join other Mid-Century Modern aficionados in mid-February for more than a week of architectural tours, art shows, film screenings, expert lectures and swingin' cocktail parties.

🏃 Wildlife-Watching

Don't let winter storms drive you away from the coast! February is prime time for spotting migratory whales offshore, colonies of birthing and mating elephant seals, roosting monarch butterflies and hundreds of bird species along the Pacific Flyway.

March

Less rainy, so travelers head back to the coast, especially for spring break (exact dates vary, depending on school schedules and the Easter holiday). Desert tourism rises as wildflowers keep blooming. Ski season winds down.

✨ Festival of the Swallows

After wintering in South America, the swallows famously return to Mission San Juan Capistrano in Orange County around March 19. The historic mission town celebrates its Spanish and Mexican heritage with events all month long.

☆ Dinah Shore Weekend & White Party

Palm Springs' lesbian social event of the year sees pool parties, dancers and mixers coinciding with the LPGA golf tournament in late March or early April. For men, the four-day White Party gets crazy over Easter weekend.

April

Peak wildflower bloom in the high desert. Shoulder season in the mountains and along the coast means lower hotel prices, but not during spring break (varies, depending on when the Easter holiday falls).

⭐ Coachella Music & Arts Festival

Indie no-name rock bands, cult DJs and superstar rappers and pop divas all converge outside Palm Springs for a three-day musical extravaganza in mid-April. Bring lots of sunscreen, drink tons of water.

◉ Doo Dah Parade

Affectionately known as the twisted sister of Pasadena's world-famous Rose Parade, this offbeat, inventive and zany procession of artistically whimsical floats and unpredictable frolickers sashays down Colorado Blvd in late April.

⭐ San Francisco International Film Festival

Forget about seeing stars in Hollywood. The Americas' longest-running film festival has been lighting up San Francisco since 1957, with a slate of over 150 independent-minded films, including provocative premieres from around the globe in late April and early May.

May

Weather starts to heat up statewide, although some coastal areas remain blanketed by fog ('May grey'). The Memorial Day holiday weekend is the official start of summer, and one of the year's busiest travel times.

🎆 Cinco de Mayo

¡Viva Mexico! Margaritas, music and merriment commemorate the victory of Mexican forces over the French army at the Battle of Puebla on May 5, 1862. LA and San Diego really do it up in style.

◉ Calaveras County Fair & Jumping Frog Jubilee

Taking inspiration from Mark Twain's famous short story, this Gold Rush–era pioneer settlement offers good old-fashioned family fun over a long weekend in mid-May, with country-and-western musicians, rodeo cowboys and a celebrated frog-jumping contest.

🏃 Bay to Breakers

Jog costumed (although no longer naked or intoxicated) during San Francisco's annual pilgrimage from the Embarcadero to Ocean Beach on the third Sunday in May. Watch out for those participants dressed as salmon, who run 'upstream' from the finish line!

🏃 Kinetic Grand Championship

Over Memorial Day weekend, this 'triathlon of the art world' merits a three-day, 38-mile race from Arcata to Ferndale on the North Coast. Competitors outdo each other in inventing human-powered, self-propelled and sculptural contraptions to make the journey.

June

Once school lets out for the summer, almost everywhere in California gets busy, from beaches to mountain resorts. But in the deserts, it's just too darn hot. Some coastal fog lingers ('June gloom').

⭐ Pride Month

Out and proud since 1970, California's LGBTQ pride celebrations take place throughout June, with costumed parades, coming-out parties, live music, DJs and more. The biggest, bawdiest celebrations are in San Francisco and LA; San Diego celebrates in mid-July.

July

Beaches get into full swing, particularly in Southern California. Theme parks are mobbed by vacationing families, as are mountain resorts, but the deserts become deserted. July 4th holiday is the summer's peak travel weekend.

⭐ Reggae on the River

Come party with the 'Humboldt Nation' of hippies, Rastafarians, treehuggers and other beloved NorCal freaks for two days of live reggae bands, arts-and-crafts, barbecue, juggling, unicycling, camping and swimming in mid-July.

🎆 Festival of Arts & Pageant of the Masters

Exhibits by hundreds of working artists and a pageant of masterpiece paintings 're-created' by actors keep Orange County's Laguna Beach plenty busy during July and August.

◉ California State Fair

A million people come to ride the giant Ferris wheel, cheer on pie-eating contests and horseback jockeys, browse the blue-ribbon agricultural and arts-and-crafts exhibits, taste California wines and microbrews, and listen to live bands for two weeks in late July.

Comic-Con International

Affectionately known as 'Nerd Prom,' the alt-nation's biggest annual convention of comic book geeks, sci-fi and animation lovers, and pop-culture memorabilia collectors brings out-of-this-world costumed madness to San Diego in late July.

August

Warm weather and water temperatures keep beaches busy. School summer vacations come to an end, but everywhere (except for the hot, hot deserts) stays packed. Travel peaks over the weekend before the Labor Day holiday.

Old Spanish Days Fiesta

Santa Barbara celebrates its early Spanish, Mexican and American *rancho* culture with parades, rodeo events, crafts exhibits and live music and dance shows, all happening in early August.

Perseids

Peaking in mid-August, these annual meteor showers are the best time to catch shooting stars with your naked eye or a digital camera. Head away from urban light pollution to places like Joshua Tree and Death Valley National Parks in SoCal's deserts.

(Above) All dressed up for the Doo Dah Parade (p27)
(Below) Costumed participants in the Bay to Breakers race (p79), San Francisco

September

Summer's last hurrah is the Labor Day holiday weekend, which is extremely busy almost everywhere (except in the deserts). After kids go back to school, the beaches and cities start seeing fewer visitors.

✨ Monterey Jazz Festival

Cool trad-jazz cats, fusion magicians and world-beat drummers all line up to play at one of the world's longest-running jazz festivals, featuring outdoor concerts and more intimate shows on the Central Coast over a long weekend in mid-September.

October

Even with beautifully sunny and balmy weather, things quiet down just about everywhere during shoulder season. Travel deals abound along the coast and in cities, the mountains and the deserts as temperatures begin cooling off.

🍷 Vineyard Festivals

All month long under sunny skies, California's wine counties celebrate bringing in the harvest from the vineyards with star chef food-and-wine shindigs, grape-stomping 'crush' parties and barrel tastings, with some events starting earlier in September.

☆ Halloween

Hundreds of thousands of revelers come out to play in LA's West Hollywood LGBTQ neighborhood for all-day partying, dancing kids' activities and live entertainment. Over-the-top costumes must be seen to be believed.

November

Temperatures drop everywhere, with scattered winter rain and snowstorms just beginning. Coastal areas, cities and even the deserts are less busy for travelers, except around the Thanksgiving holiday. Ski season gets started.

✨ Día de los Muertos

Mexican communities honor dead ancestors on November 2 with costumed parades, sugar skulls, graveyard picnics, candlelight processions and fabulous altars. Join the colorful festivities in San Francisco, LA and San Diego.

◉ Death Valley '49ers

Take a trip back to California's hardy 19th-century Gold Rush days during this annual encampment at Furnace Creek, with old-timey campfire singalongs, cowboy poetry readings, horseshoe tournaments and a Western art show in early November.

December

Winter rains start to drench coastal areas, while travel to the typically sunny, dry desert regions picks up. Christmas and New Year's Eve are extremely crowded travel times, with a short-lived dip in tourism between them.

🏃 Mavericks

South of San Francisco, Half Moon Bay's monster big-wave surfing competition only takes place when winter swells top 50ft, usually between December and March. When the surf's up, invited pro surfers have 24 hours to fly in from around the globe.

◉ Parade of Lights

Spicing up the Christmas holiday season with nautical cheer, brightly bedecked and illuminated boats float through many harbors, notably Orange County's Newport Beach and San Diego. San Francisco and LA host winter-wonderland parades on land.

☆ New Year's Eve

Out with the old, in with the new: millions get drunk, resolve to do better, and the next day nurse hangovers while watching college football. Some cities and towns put on alternative, alcohol-free First Night street festivals.

itineraries

Whether you've got six days or 60, these itineraries provide a starting point for the trip of a lifetime. Want more inspiration? Head online to lonelyplanet.com/thorntree to connect with other travelers.

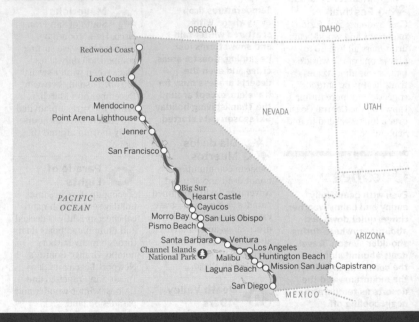

Two Weeks
Pacific Coastin'

Start your easy, breezy coastal tour in **San Diego**, if only to chow down on a few fish tacos first. Heading north, detour to **Mission San Juan Capistrano** before hitting art-haven **Laguna Beach** and **Huntington Beach**, aka 'Surf City USA.' Swoop down on **Los Angeles** for stargazing and clubby, cosmopolitan style.

Cruise north through celeb-happy **Malibu**. **Ventura** launches boats to offshore **Channel Islands National Park**, while idyllic **Santa Barbara** has a neighboring wine country. North of retro **Pismo Beach** and collegiate **San Luis Obispo**, Hwy 1 curves past laid-back little beach towns such as **Morro Bay** and **Cayucos**, as well as **Hearst Castle**, to soul-stirring **Big Sur** and the counter-cultural capital of **San Francisco**.

Over the Golden Gate Bridge, Hwy 1 skirts rocky shores, secluded coves and wind-tossed beaches. The lonely stretch between **Jenner** and Victorian-era **Mendocino** is especially scenic – don't miss **Point Arena Lighthouse**. Hwy 1 hooks inland to merge with Hwy 101, then passes turnoffs to the remote **Lost Coast** and a string of state and national parks along the iconic **Redwood Coast**.

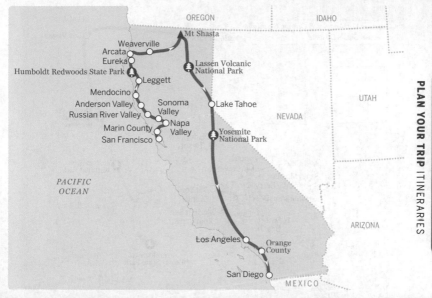

Three to Four Weeks
California Classics

Kick off with a dose of big-city culture in **San Francisco**, sitting proudly on its often foggy bay. Bite into inspiring California cooking at the Ferry Building Marketplace, then hop a boat over to infamous Alcatraz prison, aka 'the Rock.' For panoramic bay views, it's all aboard a cable car before getting lost in verdant Golden Gate Park.

Head north over the arched Golden Gate Bridge into outdoorsy **Marin County**. California's most famous grapes grow nearby in the rustic **Russian River Valley**, burgeoning **Sonoma Valley** and chichi **Napa Valley**. Detour west through the boondocks of the hidden **Anderson Valley**, jumping on Hwy 1 north to **Mendocino**, a postcard-perfect Victorian oceanfront town.

Work your way north to rejoin Hwy 101 at **Leggett**, where your magical mystery tour of the Redwood Coast really begins. In **Humboldt Redwoods State Park**, encounter some of the tallest trees on earth along the 'Avenue of the Giants.' Relax in harborfront **Eureka**, with its candy-colored Victorian architecture, or its radical northern neighbor, **Arcata**.

Turn east on Hwy 299 for a long, scenic trip through Gold Rush–era **Weaverville**, skirting around the lake-studded Trinity Alps. Keep trucking east, then head north on I-5 to **Mt Shasta**. Pay your respects to this majestic mountain, then cut southeast on Hwy 89 to unearthly **Lassen Volcanic National Park**, a hellishly beautiful world in the volcanic Cascade Range.

Keep trucking southeast on Hwy 89 to **Lake Tahoe**, a four-seasons outdoor playground and mountain resort. Roll down the Eastern Sierra's Hwy 395, taking the back-door route via high-country Tioga Rd (closed in winter and spring) into **Yosemite National Park**. Gape at waterfalls tumbling over soaring granite cliffs, then wander among groves of giant sequoias, the world's biggest trees.

Make the five-hour drive south to **Los Angeles**, with its legendary beaches, diverse neighborhoods and hot cuisine scene. Pound the pavement in a vibrantly reborn Hollywood, then kick back by the beach in chic Santa Monica or crazy Venice. Cruise south past the beautiful beaches of oh-so stylish **Orange County** and onward to laid-back **San Diego**. End your epic road trip with a wild night out in the Gaslamp Quarter or meet the city's famous wild things at the zoo.

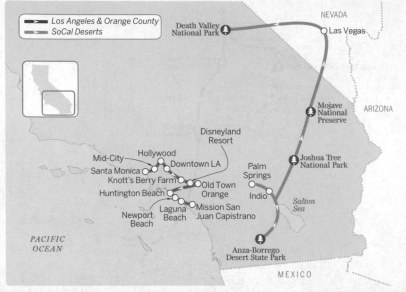

Five Days to One Week
LA & Orange County

Kick things off in **Los Angeles**, where top-notch attractions, bodacious beaches and tasty food form an irresistible trifecta. After you've traipsed along the star-studded sidewalks of **Hollywood**, dived into the arts and cultural scenes **Downtown**, and browsed the many museums of **Mid-City**, sophisticated seaside **Santa Monica** beckons with a carnival pier, creative restaurants and boutique shops.

Make a date with Mickey at perfectly 'imagineered' **Disneyland park**. Next door, **Disney California Adventure** celebrates the Golden State. Both parks, part of **Disneyland Resort**, are in Anaheim. Not far is Old West-themed **Knott's Berry Farm**, and time-warped **Old Town Orange**, clustered with antiques stores.

Head west toward the Pacific and take a day off in **Huntington Beach**, aka 'Surf City USA.' Rent a board, play beach volleyball, build a bonfire – kick back and chill. Make a quick stop in **Newport Beach** for people-watching by the piers, then roll south to **Laguna Beach** a former artists' colony with over two dozen public beaches. Slingshot back toward the I-5, stopping off at **Mission San Juan Capistrano** for a taste of Spanish colonial and Mexican rancho history.

One Week to 10 Days
SoCal Deserts

Start your desert road trip in glam **Palm Springs**, the retro-hip celeb hangout and a masterpiece of Mid-Century Modern architecture. Sip mojitos poolside, hike to palm-studded canyons, tour a wind farm and ride a revolving cable car up into cool pine-scented mountains.

Drive through the Coachella Valley past the date farms of **Indio** and along the shores of the mirage-like **Salton Sea**, then turn west into wild **Anza-Borrego Desert State Park**. See bighorn sheep, wind-sculpted caves and Old West stagecoach stops.

Boomerang north to **Joshua Tree National Park**, with its piles of giant boulders and twisted namesake trees. Take time to absorb the stark beauty of the lanscape, then continue north into the **Mojave National Preserve**, a little-visited land of 'singing' sand dunes, volcanic cinder cones and the world's largest Joshua-tree forest.

Ready for a change of pace? Drive straight to **Las Vegas**, baby. Before you gamble away your life savings at the Strip's casinos, hop back in the car and drive west to **Death Valley National Park**, where mysteriously moving boulders, otherworldly salt flats and mosaic-marbled canyons rank among the amazing all-natural attractions.

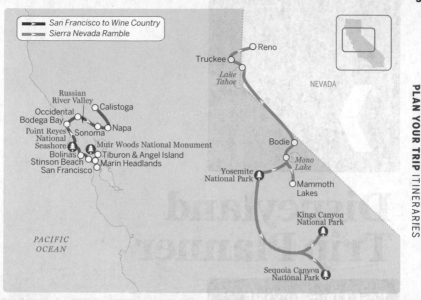

Key:
- San Francisco to Wine Country
- Sierra Nevada Ramble

Reno
Truckee
Lake Tahoe
NEVADA
Russian River Valley
Calistoga
Occidental
Bodega Bay
Napa
Point Reyes National Seashore
Sonoma
Muir Woods National Monument
Bolinas
Tiburon & Angel Island
Stinson Beach
Marin Headlands
San Francisco
Bodie
Mono Lake
Yosemite National Park
Mammoth Lakes
Kings Canyon National Park
PACIFIC OCEAN
Sequoia Canyon National Park

Five Days to One Week
SF to Wine Country

In the hilly 7-sq-mile peninsula that is innovative and ever-evolving **San Francisco**, uncover the alleyways of **Chinatown** and wander the mural-adorned **Mission District**, then brave the fog on a cruise over to **Alcatraz** or lose yourself on a sunny day in **Golden Gate Park**, where hippies danced during 1967's 'Summer of Love.'

Escape the city via the landmark **Golden Gate Bridge** to hike across the **Marin Headlands** or take the ferry from **Tiburon** over to **Angel Island** to go kayaking, hiking and mountain-biking. Meander north along the Marin County coast, passing the tall redwood trees of **Muir Woods National Monument**, small-town **Stinson Beach** and quirky **Bolinas** on your way to wildly beautiful **Point Reyes National Seashore**. Beyond **Bodega Bay**, country roads wind through **Occidental** and **Russian River Valley** vineyards. Truck east across Hwy 101, then turn south into the heart of Northern California's renowned **Wine Country**, orbiting stylish **Napa** and its countrified, still-chic cousin **Sonoma**. Soak your road-weary bones in a mud bath in **Calistoga** before looping back to San Francisco.

One Week to 10 Days
Sierra Nevada Ramble

Nothing can prepare you for off-the-charts **Yosemite National Park**, with its thunderous waterfalls, eroded granite monoliths, wildflower meadows and alpine lakes. To gaze in awe up at the world's biggest trees and down at a gorge deeper than the Grand Canyon, take extra time to detour south to **Sequoia & Kings Canyon National Parks**.

Soar over the Sierra Nevada's snowy rooftop on Yosemite's high-elevation **Tioga Rd**, which is usually open between June and October only. Relive the rough-and-tumble Gold Rush era in the ghost town of **Bodie**, sitting in a state of arrested decay on a wind-battered plain just north of **Mono Lake**, where you can paddle past odd-looking tufa formations. It's a quick trip south on Hwy 395 to **Mammoth Lakes**, an all-seasons resort town for serious adrenaline junkies.

Jump north to **Lake Tahoe**, a deep-blue jewel cradled by jutting peaks crisscrossed with rugged hiking trails, hot springs and the slopes of world-famous ski resorts. From the whistle-stop railroad town of **Truckee**, take I-80 east over the Nevada state line to **Reno**, 'the Biggest Little City in the World,' for casino nightlife.

Disneyland Trip Planner

Best Times to Visit

Mid-April–mid-May Miss both spring-break and summer-vacation crowds but still have a good chance of sunny weather.

Mid- to late September Summer vacationers depart after Labor Day and temperatures cool down, but it's still sunny.

Late November–early December As visitation dips between Thanksgiving and Christmas, holiday decorations spruce up the parks.

Weekdays Year-round, they're less busy than weekends.

Top Rides & Attractions

Disneyland park Pirates of the Caribbean, Indiana Jones Adventure, Haunted Mansion, Space Mountain, Finding Nemo Submarine Voyage, It's a Small World, Fantasmic show

Disney California Adventure Soarin' Over California, Cars Land, Twilight Zone Tower of Terror, California Screamin', Grizzly River Run, the Little Mermaid – Ariel's Sea Adventure, World of Color show

The happiest place on earth? It might not seem like it when you're trying to make sense of all the park information, and calculating just how much it's all going to cost. Not to worry – Walt Disney had a master plan! The parks are designed for family fun and, now more than ever, Disneyland Resort runs like clockwork. All you need to do before you go is read up on some advance-planning tips and strategies. Then you can just show up and let the Disney cast do their thing.

For in-depth coverage of both of the resort's theme parks, Disneyland park (Disneyland) and Disney's California Adventure (DCA), including reviews of rides and attractions, lodgings, dining and shopping, see p591.

Timing Your Visit

» Both theme parks, Disneyland and DCA, are open 365 days a year. Be sure to check the current schedule (recorded info ☎714-781-4565, live assistance ☎714-781-7290; www.disneyland.com) in advance. Park hours vary, depending on forecast attendance, and are subject to change at any time.

» During peak summer season (roughly mid-June to early September), Disneyland's hours are usually 8am to midnight; the rest of the year, hours are 10am to 8pm or 10pm. DCA closes at 10pm or 11pm in summer, earlier in the off season.

» If you visit off season, some attractions and shows may not be running, such as Disneyland's evening fireworks, so check the website in advance to avoid disappointment.

» Concerned about getting stuck waiting for a ride or attraction at closing time? Don't worry! The parks stay open until the last guest in line has had their fun.

Beating the Crowds

» Disneyland Resort parking lots and ticket booths open an hour before the theme parks' official opening times, so if you want to get in right away, show up early.

» The busiest time of day in the parks is between 11am and 4pm, making that a great time to go back to your hotel for a midday swim (and nap!), then return after dinner.

» To find out about the Disneyland and DCA FASTPASS system, which can cut your wait time significantly for some rides and attractions, see p582.

» For smartphone apps that may also help you avoid long queues in the parks, see p592.

Buying Tickets

» Tickets never sell out, but buying them in advance will save you time waiting in line at the park and probably some money, too.

» Remember that ticket prices increase annually. See the latest prices at p592.

» Some 'Park Hopper' bonus tickets include one 'Magic Morning' early-bird admission to select attractions on certain days, based on availability (show up 75 minutes before the theme park opens to the general public).

Discounts & Deals

» Disneyland Park sometimes makes promotional ticket offers available, such as five-day 'Park Hopper' tickets for the regular three-day price; check for specials online.

» If you're a resident of Southern California, you're eligible for discounted theme-park admission tickets.

» You might save substantially by booking your trip through the **Walt Disney Travel Company** (☑714-520-5060, 800-225-2024; www.disneytravel.com), which sells vacation packages that include air, hotel and theme-park tickets.

Bringing the Kids

You're never too young or too old for Disneyland. You'll see huge, multi-generational families enjoying the park's rides and attractions together, from mothers with newborn babes in arms to elderly great-grandparents.

Infants & Toddlers

» Stroller rentals are available (p592), but rental strollers can only be used in the theme parks, not Downtown Disney. Bringing your own stroller will save time and money.

» Strollers are not allowed on escalators or the parking lot tram. You need to fold up strollers before bringing them on the monorail.

» Baby centers, including diaper-changing and nursing facilities with comfy rocking chairs, are available at Disneyland (Main Street, USA) and DCA (Pacific Wharf).

» Day lockers are available. The daily rental fee runs from $7 to $15, depending on the locker size. Lockers can be found at the following locations: Main Street, USA (Disneyland), Sunshine Plaza (DCA) and outside main entrances to both parks.

Kids & Tweens

» Tell your kids that if they get lost, they should contact the nearest Disney staff, who will escort them to a 'lost children' center (on Disneyland's Main Street, USA or Pacific Wharf at DCA).

» Study the online minimum-height charts for rides and attractions in advance, to avoid disappointment when you get to the parks.

» Kids aged nine years and under may wear costumes inside the parks (but no masks, toy weapons or other sharp objects). During Halloween time, preteens may also wear costumes.

» Note for sensitive children: many kids' rides – including Roger Rabbit's Car Toon Spin and Mr. Toad's Wild Ride – can be surprisingly scary.

Teens

» Tell your teens that if their cell phones don't work, they can leave a message for 'lost parents' at City Hall, just inside Disneyland's entrance.

» Clothing or tattoos with any language, graphics or designs deemed offensive are prohibited, as is displaying what Disneyland deems an 'excessive' amount of bare skin (eg bikini tops).

DISNEYLAND TO-DO LIST

A Month or More in Advance

☐ Make area hotel reservations or book a Disneyland vacation package.

☐ Sign up online for Disney Fans Insider e-newsletters and resort updates.

A Week or Two Ahead

☐ Check the parks' opening hours and live show and entertainment schedules online.

☐ Make dining reservations for sit-down restaurants or special meals with Disney characters.

☐ If you haven't already, buy print-at-home tickets and passes online.

The Day or Night Before

☐ Recheck the next day's park opening hours and Anaheim or hotel shuttle schedules.

☐ Pack a small day pack with sunscreen, hat, sunglasses, swimwear, an extra change of clothes, a jacket or hoodie, a lightweight plastic rain poncho, and extra batteries and memory cards for digital and video cameras.

☐ Make sure your electronic devices (including cameras and phones) are fully charged.

☐ If you have a smartphone, consider downloading a Disneyland app (p592).

Where to Sleep

Disneyland Resort

» For the full-on Disney experience, stay in one of the resort's three **hotels** (reservations ☎714-956-6425, 800-225-2024; www.disneyland.com). For hotel reviews, see p588).

» Resort hotel guests usually get bonus perks, from early admission to the parks' attractions to preferred seating for live shows and parades.

» One-night stays at Disneyland Resort's hotels are comparatively expensive, but you might save money by booking multinight stays or vacation packages.

Outside the Parks

» Many Anaheim area motels and hotels offer packages combining lodging with theme-park tickets; most have family rooms or suites that sleep four to six people.

» Some local accommodations operate complimentary guest shuttles to the parks Otherwise, consider staying within walking distance, or along Anaheim's public shuttle route (see p592).

Dining & Drinking

» Technically, you can't bring any food or drinks into the parks, but security-inspection staff usually look the other way if you're just carrying small water bottles and a few snacks.

» If you haven't made restaurant reservations, plan on eating at off-peak times (eg outside the noon to 3pm lunch rush, and before 6pm or after 9pm for dinner).

» For good-value eats and fresher menu options, exit the parks and walk to Downtown Disney (p590).

» Drinking fountains are everywhere, so bring a refillable water bottle.

Reservations & Special Meals

» If you want to do any sit-down dining in the parks or at resort hotels, reservations are essential, especially during peak season. For restaurant reviews, see p590. For both parks, call **Disney Dining** (☎714-781-3463) if you have dietary restrictions, need to make dining reservations or want to inquire about character dining.

California Camping & Outdoors

Best Times to Go

Camping May–Sep

Cycling, mountain-biking Jun–Oct

Hiking Apr–Oct

Kayaking, snorkeling, diving Jun–Oct

Rock climbing Apr–Oct

Surfing Sep–Nov

Swimming Jul–Aug

Whale-watching Jan–Mar

White-water rafting Apr–Oct

California's Ultimate Outdoor Experiences

Backpacking the John Muir Trail

Cycling the Pacific Coast Highway

Rock climbing in Yosemite Valley

Sea kayaking and whale-watching in Channel Islands National Park

Snorkeling or scuba diving at La Jolla

Surfing Mavericks, Malibu or Santa Cruz

White-water rafting Cherry Creek on the Upper Tuolumne River

The Golden State is an all-seasons outdoor playground. Here you can go hiking among desert wildflowers in spring, swimming in the Pacific kissed by the summer sun, mountain-biking among fall foliage or celebrate winter by schussing through deep powder. For bigger thrills, launch a glider off ocean bluffs, climb granite walls and go bouldering in a wonderland of rocks or hook a kite onto a surfboard and launch yourself over foamy waves. Whatever your adrenaline fix, you'll find it here.

Camping

Throughout California, campers are absolutely spoiled for choice. Pitch a tent beside alpine lakes and streams with views of snaggletoothed Sierra Nevada peaks, along gorgeous strands of Southern California sand or take shelter underneath redwoods, the tallest trees on earth, from Big Sur north to the Oregon border. Inland SoCal deserts are also magical places to camp next to sand dunes on full-moon nights. If you didn't bring your own tent, you can rent or buy camping gear in most cities and some towns.

Campground Types & Amenities

Primitive campsites Usually have fire pits, picnic tables and access to drinking water and vault toilets; most common in national forests (United States Forest Service; USFS) and on Bureau of Land Management (BLM) land.

Developed campgrounds Typically found in state and national parks, with more amenities, including flush toilets, barbecue grills and occasionally hot showers and a coin-op laundry.

Camping in California

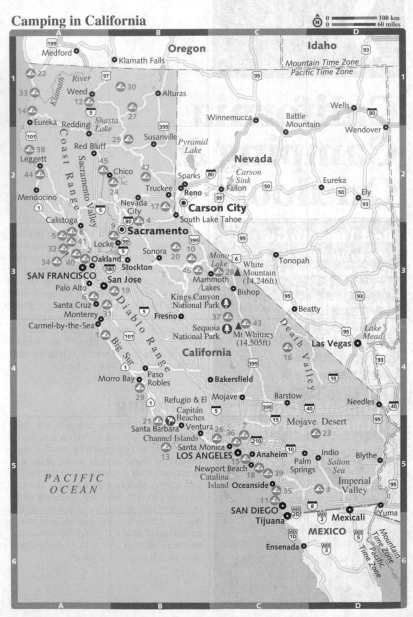

RV (recreational vehicle) hookups and **dump stations** Available at many privately owned campgrounds, but only a few public-lands campgrounds.
Private campgrounds Cater mainly to RVers and offer hot showers, swimming pools, wi-fi and family camping cabins; tent sites may be few and uninviting.
Walk-in (environmental) sites Providing more peace and privacy; a few public-lands campgrounds reserve these for long-distance hikers and cyclists.

Seasons, Rates & Reservations

Many campgrounds, especially in the mountains and in Northern California, are closed from late fall through early spring. Opening and closing dates vary each year, depending on weather conditions. Private campgrounds are often open year-round, especially those closest to cities, beaches and major highways.

Many public and private campgrounds accept reservations for all or some of their sites, while a few are strictly first-come, first-served. Overnight rates range from free for the most primitive campsites to $45 or more for pull-through RV sites with full hookups.

These agencies let you search for campground locations and amenities, check availability and reserve campsites online:

Recreation.gov (☎518-885-3639, 877-444-6777; www.recreation.gov) Camping and cabin reservations for national parks, national forests, BLM land, etc.

ReserveAmerica (☎916-638-5883, 800-444-7275; www.reserveamerica.com) Reservations for California state parks, East Bay and Orange County regional parks and some private campgrounds.

Kampgrounds of America (KOA; http://koa.com) National chain of reliable but more expensive private campgrounds offering full facilities, including for RVs.

Camping in California

🛌 Sleeping

Cycling & Mountain-Biking

Strap on that helmet! California is outstanding cycling territory, no matter whether you're off for a leisurely spin along the beach, an adrenaline-fueled mountain ride or a multiday bike-touring coastal adventure. The cycling season runs year-round in most coastal areas, but avoid the mountains in winter and the desert in summer.

Road Rules

» In national and state parks, bicycles are usually limited to paved and dirt roads and are not allowed on trails or in designated wilderness areas.

» Most national forests and BLM lands are open to mountain bikers. Stay on already established tracks and always yield to hikers and horseback riders.

» For road-cycling rules, rental rates, purchase tips, emergency roadside assistance and transporting your bike, see p771.

Best Places to Cycle

» Even heavily trafficked urban areas may have some good cycling turf, especially in Southern California. Take, for example, the beachside South Bay Bicycle Trail (p553) in Los Angeles or the oceanfront recreational path in Santa Barbara (p517).

» In Northern California's bike-friendly San Francisco, you can cruise through Golden Gate Park (p75) and over the Golden Gate Bridge, then hop the ferry back across the bay from Sausalito.

» South along the Central Coast, the waterfront Monterey Peninsula Recreational Trail (p468) and the famously scenic 17-Mile Drive (p475) entice cyclists of all skill levels.

NO RESERVATIONS?

If you can't get a reservation, plan to show up at the campground between 10am and noon, when other campers are leaving. Don't be too choosy or you may end up with no site at all, especially during summer holidays or spring wildflower blooms in the deserts. Park rangers, visitor centers and campground hosts can often tell you where spaces may still be available, if there are any; otherwise, ask about overflow camping and dispersed camping areas nearby.

» NorCal's Wine Country offers some beautiful bike tours, although nothing surpasses coastal Hwy 1, especially the dizzying stretch through Big Sur.

» Up north at Humboldt Redwoods State Park, ride among the world's tallest trees on the winding Avenue of the Giants (p247).

» In the Sierra Nevada, Yosemite National Park (p406) has mostly level, paved recreational paths through a glacier-carved valley overhung by waterfalls.

Best Mountain-Biking Areas

» Just north of San Francisco, the Marin Headlands (p122) offers a bonanza of trails for fat-tire fans, while Mt Tamalpais (p122) lays claim to being the sport's birthplace.

» Top-rated single-track rides near Lake Tahoe include Mr Toad's Wild Ride (p374) and the Flume Trail (p396). In the neighboring Gold Country, Downieville (p311) offers an enormous downhill rush.

» Speed freaks also sing the praises of the Eastern Sierra's Mammoth Mountain (p437), whose summer-only bike park beckons with 70 miles of dirt single-track.

» More ski areas that open trails and chairlifts to mountain-bikers in summer include Big Bear Lake (p577) outside LA and some resorts at Lake Tahoe (p374).

» SoCal's Joshua Tree (p668) and Death Valley National Parks (p689) have miles of backcountry roads for mountain-biking; so does Anza-Borrego Desert State Park (p676) outside San Diego and the Santa Monica Mountains (p553) north of LA.

» State parks especially popular with mountain-bikers include NorCal's Prairie Creek Redwoods (p261), Andrew Molera in Big Sur, San Luis Obispo's Montaña de Oro and Orange County's Crystal Cove.

Maps & Online Resources

Local bike shops can supply you with more cycling route ideas, maps and advice.

» **California Association of Bicycling Organizations** (www.cabobike.org) offers free bicycle touring and freeway access information.

» **California Bicycle Coalition** (www.calbike. org) links to free online cycling maps, bike-sharing programs and community bike shops.

» **Adventure Cycling Association** (www. adventurecycling.org) sells long-distance cycling

» (above) Camping along the John Muir trail, Ansel Adams Wilderness Area (p438), Sierra Nevada
» (left) White-water rafting on the Kern River (p353)

route guides and touring maps, including of the Pacific Coast Highway (PCH).

» **League of American Bicyclists** (www.bikeleague.org) can help you find bicycle specialty shops, local cycling clubs, group rides and other special events.

» For online forums and reviews of mountain-biking trails in California, search **DirtWorld.com** (http://dirtworld.com) and **MTBR.com** (www.mtbr.com).

Hiking

Got wanderlust? With epic scenery, California is perfect for exploring on foot. That's true whether you have your heart set on peak-bagging in the Sierra Nevada, trekking to SoCal desert oases, rambling among the world's tallest, largest and most ancient trees, or simply walking on the beach by booming surf. During spring and early summer, a painter's palette of wildflowers blooms on coastal hillsides, in mountain meadows, on damp forest floors and across endless desert sands.

Best Places to Hike

No matter where you find yourself in California, you're never far from a trail, even in busy metropolitan areas. For jaw-dropping scenery, head to national and state parks to choose from a staggering variety of trails, from easy nature walks negotiable by wheelchairs and strollers to multiday backpacking routes through rugged wilderness.

» **Sierra Nevada** In Yosemite (p403), Sequoia & Kings Canyon National Parks (p418), clamber toward waterfalls, wildflower meadows and alpine

lakes, tackle mighty granite domes and peaks, or wander among the world's biggest trees – giant sequoias.

» **San Francisco Bay Area** The Marin Headlands (p111), Muir Woods, Mt Tamalpais (p122), Point Reyes National Seashore and Big Basin Redwoods State Park (p463), all within a 90-minute drive of San Francisco, are crisscrossed by dozens of superb trails.

» **SoCal Deserts** Best hiked in spring and fall, Death Valley (p690) and Joshua Tree National Parks (p667), the Mojave National Preserve and Anza-Borrego Desert State Park (p690) offer trails leading to palm-canyon oases and mining ghost towns, up volcanic cinder cones and across sand dunes and salt flats.

» **Los Angeles** Ditch your car in the Santa Monica Mountains National Recreation Area, where many movies and TV shows have been filmed, or head out to the cooler climes of Big Bear Lake (p576) or Mt San Jacinto State Park near Palm Springs.

» **Northern Mountains** Summiting Mt Shasta is a spiritually uplifting experience, while Lassen Volcanic National Park is a bizarre world of smoking fumaroles, cinder cones and craters.

» **North Coast** Redwood National and State Parks offer misty walks through groves of old-growth redwoods, or tackle the truly wild beaches of the challenging Lost Coast Trail (p246).

Fees & Wilderness Permits

» Most California state parks charge a daily parking fee of $5 to $15; there's often no charge if you walk or bike into these parks.

» National park entry averages $10 to $20 per vehicle for seven consecutive days; some national parks are free.

» For unlimited admission to national parks, national forests and other federal recreation lands, buy an 'America the Beautiful' annual pass (see p760).

» Often required for overnight backpackers and extended day hikes, wilderness permits are issued at ranger stations and park visitor centers. Daily quotas may be in effect during peak periods, usually late spring through early fall.

» Some wilderness permits may be reserved ahead of time, and very popular trails (eg Half Dome, Mt Whitney) may sell out several months in advance.

» You'll need a National Forest Adventure Pass ($5 per day, $30 per year) to park in some of SoCal's national forests. Buy passes from USFS ranger stations and select local vendors such as sporting-goods stores.

TAKE A (REALLY LONG) HIKE

Famous long-distance trails that wind through California include the 2650-mile **Pacific Crest National Scenic Trail** (PCT; www.pcta.org), which takes hikers from Mexico to Canada. Running mostly along the PCT, the 211-mile John Muir Trail links Yosemite Valley and Mt Whitney via the Sierra Nevada high country. Or enjoy inspirational views of Lake Tahoe while tracing the footsteps of early pioneers and Native Americans along the 165-mile **Tahoe Rim Trail** (www.tahoerimtrail.org).

CALIFORNIA'S BEST WHITE-WATER RAFTING

NAME	CLASS	SEASON	DESCRIPTION
American River	Class II, IV	Apr, Oct	The South Fork (p313) is ideal for families and rafting virgins looking to get their feet wet, while the more challenging Middle and North Forks (p305) carve through deep gorges in the Gold Country.
Kern River	Class II, V	Apr, Sep	Near Bakersfield, the Upper and Lower Forks (p353) offer some of the southern Sierra's best white water.
Kaweah River	Class IV+	Apr, Jul	Steeply dropping through Sequoia National Park, this fast, furious ride is for experienced paddlers.
Kings River	Class III, IV	Apr, Jul	One of California's most powerful rivers cuts a groove deeper than the Grand Canyon; trips begin outside Kings Canyon National Park.
Merced River	Class III, IV	Apr, Jul	Starting outside Yosemite National Park, this canyon (p416) run is the Sierra's best one-day intermediate trip.
Stanislaus River	Class II, IV	Apr, Oct	In Gold Country, the North Fork provides rafting trips for all, from novices to the more adventure minded.
Truckee River	Class II, IV	Apr, Aug	Near Lake Tahoe, this river (p390) is a great beginner's run, with a white-water park for kayakers on the river in downtown Reno (p449).
Tuolumne River	Class IV, V	Apr, Sep	Experienced paddlers may prefer ferocious runs on 'the T'; in summer, experts-only Cherry Creek is a legendary Sierra Nevada run.

Maps & Online Resources

» There are bulletin boards showing basic trail maps and other information at most major trailheads in national, state and regional parks.

» For short, established hikes, free maps from visitor centers or ranger stations are usually sufficient.

» A more detailed topographical map may be necessary for longer backcountry hikes. Topo maps are sold at park bookstores, visitor centers, ranger stations and outdoor-gear shops including **REI** (www.rei.com).

» **US Geological Survey** (USGS; www.store. usgs.gov) offers free downloadable topographic maps, or you can order print copies online.

» **Trails.com** (www.trails.com) lets you search for hundreds of multi-sport trails throughout California (trail summary overviews are free).

» **Coastwalk** (www.coastwalk.org) advocates for a long-distance trail along California's 12,100-plus miles of shoreline. Join a group hike, or volunteer to do beach cleanup or trail maintenance.

» Learn how to minimize your impact on the environment while traipsing through the wilderness by visiting **Leave No Trace Center** (www.lnt.org).

Beaches & Swimming

» With miles and miles of wide, sandy beaches, you won't find it hard to get wet and wild, especially between Santa Barbara and San Diego.

» The mind-bogglingly detailed *California Coastal Access Guide* (University of California Press, 2003) has comprehensive beach driving directions and maps.

» Ocean temperatures in Southern California become tolerable by May or June, peaking in July and August. NorCal beaches remain chilly year-round – bring or rent a wetsuit!

» Popular beaches have lifeguards, but can still be dangerous places to swim. Obey all posted warning signs and ask about local conditions before venturing out.

» Water quality varies from beach to beach, and day to day. Stay out of the ocean for at least three days after a major rainstorm due to toxic pollutants being flushed out to sea through storm drains. For current water-safety conditions statewide, check the **Beach Report Card** (http://brc.healthebay.org).

» For safety tips about riptides, see p765.

Best Swimming Beaches

» **San Diego** La Jolla, Coronado, Mission and Pacific Beaches, Torrey Pines

» **Orange County** Newport Beach, Laguna Beach, Crystal Cove and Doheny Beach State Parks

» **Los Angeles** Santa Monica, South Bay, Malibu, Leo Carrillo State Beach

» **Central Coast** Ventura, Carpinteria, Santa Barbara, El Capitan and Refugio State Beaches

Scuba Diving & Snorkeling

All along the coast, rock reefs, shipwrecks and kelp beds teem with sea creatures ready for their close-up, especially in the warmer waters of Southern California.

If you already have your PADI certification, you can rent one-tank dive outfits for $65 to $100, while two-tank boat dives cost over $100; reserve at least a day in advance. **LA Diver** (http://ladiver.com) has encyclopedic listings of dive sites and shops, certification programs, safety resources and weather conditions for the LA area, with links to sites for Southern, Central and Northern California.

Snorkel kits can be rented from most dive shops for around $15 to $40 per day. If you're going to take the plunge more than once or twice, it's probably worth buying your own mask and fins. Remember not to touch anything while you're out snorkeling, don't snorkel alone and always wear a T-shirt or sunblock on your back!

Best Scuba Diving & Snorkeling Spots

» San Diego's La Jolla Underwater Park (p629) is a great place for beginning divers, while La Jolla Cove (p626) attracts snorkelers.

» More experienced divers and snorkelers might want to steer towards Orange County's Crystal Cove State Park (p599) and Diver's Cove (p603).

» Offshore from LA and Ventura, Catalina Island (p577) and Channel Islands National Park (p523) are major diving and snorkeling destinations.

» With its national marine sanctuary, Monterey Bay (p468) offers world-renowned diving and snorkeling, although you'll need to don a wet suit.

» Further south, Point Lobos State Natural Reserve (p476) is another gem for scuba divers (snorkeling prohibited); permit reservations required.

Surfing

Surf's up! The most powerful swells arrive along the coast during late fall and winter. May and June are generally the flattest months, although they do bring warmer water. Speaking of temperature, don't believe all those images of hot blonds surfing in skimpy bikinis; without a wetsuit, you'll likely freeze your butt off except at the height of summer, especially in NorCal.

Crowds can be a problem at many surf spots, as can an overly territorial surfers. Befriend a local surfer for an introduction before hitting Cali's most famous waves. Sharks do inhabit California waters but attacks are rare. Most take place in the so-called 'Red Triangle' between Monterey on the Central Coast, Tomales Bay north of San Francisco and the offshore Farallon Islands.

Top Surf Spots for Pros

California comes fully loaded with easily accessible world-class surf spots, the lion's share of which are in SoCal:

» Huntington Beach (p595) in Orange County may have the West Coast's most consistent waves, with miles of breaks centered on the pier.

» The OC's Trestles (p606) is a premier summer spot with big but forgiving waves, a fast ride and both right and left breaks.

» San Diego's Windansea Beach (p627) is a powerful reef break, while nearby Big Rock churns out gnarly tubes.

» Malibu's Surfrider Beach (p546) is a clean right break that just gets better with bigger waves.

» Santa Barbara's Rincon Point in Carpinteria is another legendary right point-break that peels forever.

» Santa Cruz's Steamers Lane (p456) has glassy point-breaks and rocky reef-breaks.

» Half Moon Bay's Mavericks (p155; www.maverickssurf.com) is world-famous for big-wave surfing, topping 50 feet when the most powerful winter swells arrive.

Best Breaks for Beginners

The best spots to learn to surf are at beach breaks of long, shallow bays where waves are small and rolling. Try the following:

» **San Diego** Mission Beach, Pacific Beach, Oceanside

» **Orange County** Seal Beach, Newport Beach, Dana Point

» **Los Angeles** Santa Monica, Manhattan Beach

» **Central Coast** Santa Cruz, Santa Barbara, Cayucos

Rentals & Lessons

You'll find board rentals on just about every patch of sand where surfing is possible. Expect to pay about $20 per half-day for a board, with wetsuit rental another $10.

Two-hour group lessons for beginners start around $75 per person, while private, two-hour instruction costs over $100. If you're ready to jump in the deep end, many surf schools offer pricier weekend surf clinics and week-long 'surfari' camps.

Stand-up paddle surfing (SUP) is easier to learn, and it's skyrocketing in popularity. You'll find similarly priced board-and-paddle rentals and lessons all along the coast, from San Diego to north of San Francisco Bay.

Books, Maps & Online Resources

» Browse the comprehensive atlas, live webcams and surf reports at **Surfline** (www.surfline.com) for the low-down from San Diego to Santa Barbara.

» Orange County-based *Surfer* magazine's website (www.surfermag.com) has travel reports, gear reviews, newsy blogs and videos.

» Plan a coastal surfing adventure using **SurfMaps** (www.surfmaps.net), which even details seasonal weather and water temperatures.

» Enlightened surfers can join up with **Surfrider** (www.surfrider.org), a nonprofit organization that aims to protect the coastal environment.

White-Water Rafting

California has dozens of kick-ass rivers, and feeling their surging power is like taking a thrilling ride on nature's rollercoaster. Paddling giant white-water rapids swelled by the snowmelt that rips through sheer canyons, your thoughts are reduced to just two simple words: 'survive' and 'damn!' Too much for you? Myriad opportunities are suited to the abilities of any wannabe river rat, even beginning paddlers.

California Whitewater Rafting (www.c-w-r.com) covers all of California's prime river-running spots, with links to outfitters and river conservation groups. Most of the premier river runs are in the Sierra Nevada and the Gold Country, but the Northern Mountains also offer some rollicking rides, including on the Klamath, Trinity, Sacramento, Smith and California Salmon Rivers.

White-water trips are not without danger, and it's not unusual for participants to fall out of the raft in rough conditions. Serious injuries are rare, however, and most trips are without incident. No prior experience is needed for guided river trips up to Class III, but for Class IV you want to be in good shape and an excellent swimmer, with some paddling experience under your life-jacket belt.

Seasons, Rates & Reservations

Commercial outfitters run a variety of trips, from short, inexpensive morning or afternoon floats to overnight outings and multi-day expeditions. Expect to pay from $100 for a guided all-day trip. Reservations are recommended, especially for overnight trips.

The main river-running season is from April to October, although the exact months depend on which river you're rafting and the year's spring snowmelt runoff from the mountains. You'll be hurtling along either in large rafts for a dozen or more people, or smaller ones seating half a dozen; the latter tend to be more exhilarating because they can tackle rougher rapids and everyone paddles.

Whale-Watching

» During their annual migration, gray whales can be spotted off the California coast from December to April, while blue, humpback and sperm whales pass by in summer and fall (see also p751.)

» You can try your luck whale-watching (eg from lighthouses) while staying shore-bound – it's free, but you're less likely to see whales and you'll be removed from all the action.

» Just about every port town worth its sea salt along the coast offers whale-watching boat excursions, especially during winter. Bring binoculars!

» Half-day boat trips cost from $30 to $45, while all-day trips average $65 to $100; make reservations at least a day ahead.

BUT WAIT, THERE'S MORE!

ACTIVITY	LOCATION	REGION	PAGE
Bird-watching	Klamath Basin NWR	Northern Mountains	p294
	Mono Lake	Yosemite & the Sierra Nevada	p434
	Salton Sea	Palm Springs & the Deserts	p680
Caving	Lava Beds National Monument	Northern Mountains	p293
	Crystal Cave	Yosemite & the Sierra Nevada	p425
	Pinnacles National Monument	Central Coast	p495
Fishing*	Dana Point	Disneyland & Orange County	p606
	San Diego	San Diego	p630
	Bodega Bay	North Coast & Redwoods	p215
	Klamath River	North Coast & Redwoods	p261
Golf	Palm Springs & Coachella Valley	Palm Springs & the Deserts	p658
	Pebble Beach	Central Coast	p475
	Torrey Pines	San Diego	p628
Hang-gliding & paragliding	Torrey Pines	San Diego	p631
	Santa Barbara	Central Coast	p517
Horseback riding	Yosemite National Park	Yosemite & the Sierra Nevada	p407
	Wild Horse Sanctuary	Northern Mountains	p276
	Point Reyes National Seashore	Marin County & the Bay Area	p128

*For fishing licenses, regulations and location information, consult the **California Department of Fish & Game website** (www.dfg.ca.gov).

» Better tour boats limit numbers and have a trained naturalist or marine biologist on board.

» Some tour companies will let you go again for free if you don't spot any whales on your first trip.

» Choppy seas can be nauseating. To avoid seasickness, sit outside on the boat's second level – but not too close to the diesel fumes in back.

Snow Sports

High-speed modern ski lifts, mountains of fresh powder, a cornucopia of trails from easy-peasy 'Sesame Street' to black-diamond 'Death Wish,' skyscraping alpine scenery, luxury mountain cabins – they're all hall-marks of a California vacation in the snow. The Sierra Nevada offers the best slopes and trails for skiers and snowboarders, not to mention the most reliable conditions.

Season, Rates & Lessons

Ski season generally runs from late November or early December until late March or early April. All resorts have ski schools and equipment-rental facilities and offer a variety of lift tickets, including half-day, all-day and multiday versions. Prices vary, from $25 to $95 per day for adults. Discounts for children, teens, students and seniors are typi-

ACTIVITY	LOCATION	REGION	PAGE
Hot-air ballooning	Del Mar	San Diego	p645
	Temecula	San Diego	p645
	Napa	Napa & Sonoma Wine Country	p173
Kiteboarding & windsurfing	San Francisco Bay	San Francisco	p77
	Lake Tahoe	Lake Tahoe	p390
	Long Beach	Los Angeles	p549
	Mission Bay	San Diego	p629
Rock climbing	Yosemite National Park	Yosemite & the Sierra Nevada	p406
	Joshua Tree National Park	Palm Springs & the Deserts	p669
	Pinnacles National Monument	Central Coast	p495
	Bishop	Yosemite & the Sierra Nevada	p443
	Truckee	Lake Tahoe	p391
Kayaking	Channel Islands National Park	Central Coast	p522
	Morro Bay	Central Coast	p489
	Elkhorn Slough	Central Coast	p464
	Tomales Bay	Marin County & the Bay Area	p127
	Santa Barbara	Central Coast	p517
	Bodega Bay	North Coast & the Redwoods	p216
	Mission Bay	San Diego	p623

cally available. 'Ski & stay' lodging packages may offer the best value.

Best Places for Snow Sports

For sheer variety, the dozen-plus downhill skiing and snowboarding resorts ringing Lake Tahoe are unbeatable. Alongside such world-famous places as Squaw Valley (p366) and Heavenly (p366), you'll find scores of smaller operations, many of them with lower ticket prices, smaller crowds and great runs for beginners and families. Royal Gorge (p367), west of Lake Tahoe, is North America's largest cross-country ski resort. For family-friendly sno-parks that offer sledding and snow play, visit http://ohv.parks.ca.gov/?page_id=1233.

Mammoth Mountain (p436) is another darling of downhill devotees and usually has the longest season. June Mountain (p434) is Mammoth's quieter neighbor.

In the western Sierra Nevada, Badger Pass (p407) is ideal for beginners and families, and good for cross-country skiing and snowshoe walks. Kids love the snow-tubing hill. At Sequoia & Kings Canyon National Parks, you can tramp or cross-country ski among giant sequoia trees.

In Northern California, Mt Shasta Board & Ski Park (p283) is the most popular. Southern Californians get in on the snow action at Big Bear Lake (p577).

Travel with Children

Best Regions for Kids

Los Angeles

See stars in Hollywood and get behind the movie magic at Universal Studios, then hit the beaches and Griffith Park for SoCal fun in the sun. What, it's raining? Dive into the city's kid-friendly museums instead.

San Diego, Disneyland & Orange County

Think theme parks galore: Disneyland, Knott's Berry Farm, the San Diego Zoo Wild Animal Park and more. Oh, and those beaches just couldn't be more beautiful.

Marin County & the Bay Area

Explore hands-on, whimsical and 'Wow!' science museums, hear the barking sea lions at Pier 39, then traipse through Golden Gate Park and atop that famous bridge.

Yosemite & the Sierra Nevada

Watch your kids gawk at Yosemite's waterfalls and granite domes and go hiking in ancient groves of giant sequoias, the world's biggest trees. Mammoth is a four-seasons family adventure base camp.

California is a tailor-made destination for traveling with kids. They'll already be begging to go to Southern California's theme parks. Get those over with (you may well enjoy them too!) and then introduce them to many other worlds, big and small.

Sunny skies lend themselves to outdoor activities of all kinds. Here's a start (big breath!): swimming, bodysurfing, snorkeling, bicycling, kayaking, hiking, horseback riding and more. Many outdoor outfitters and tour operators have dedicated kids' activities. If it's cold and rainy, foggy or snowing outside, you'll find museums and indoor entertainment galore.

Sometimes no organized activity is needed. We've seen young kids thrill at their first glimpse of a palm tree, and teens bliss out over their first taste of heirloom tomatoes at a farmers market. The bottom line: if the kids are having a good time, you will be too.

California for Kids

There's not too much to worry about when traveling in California with your kids, as long as you keep them covered in sunblock.

Children's discounts are available for everything from museum admission and movie tickets to bus fares and motel stays. The definition of a 'child' varies – from 'under 18' to age six. At amusement parks, some rides may have minimum-height requirements, so let younger kids know about this in advance, to avoid disappointment and tears.

It's fine to bring kids along to casual restaurants, which often have high chairs. Many diners and family restaurants break out paper place mats and crayons for drawing. Ask about children's menus too. At theme parks, pack a cooler in the car and have a picnic in the parking lot to avoid ballpark prices. On the road, local supermarkets have wholesome, ready-to-eat takeout dishes.

Baby food, infant formula, soy and cow's milk, disposable diapers (nappies) and other necessities are widely available in drugstores and supermarkets. Most women are discreet about breastfeeding in public. Many public toilets have a baby-changing table, and gender-neutral private 'family' bathrooms may be available at airports, museums and so on.

Children's Highlights

It's easy to keep kids entertained no matter where you travel in California. Throughout this book, look for family attractions and other fun activities, all marked with the child-friendly icon (🐾). At national and state parks, be sure to ask at visitor centers about ranger-led activities and self-guided 'Junior Ranger' programs, in which kids earn themselves a badge after completing an activity. To explore California's urban jungles, see the special 'City for Children' sections in the regional chapters in this book.

Theme Parks

» **Disneyland Park & Disney's California Adventure** All ages of kids, even teens, and the eternally young at heart adore the 'Magic Kingdom'.

» **Knott's Berry Farm** Near Disney, SoCal's original theme park offers thrills a minute, especially during spooky haunted Halloween nights.

» **Legoland** North of San Diego, this fantasyland of building blocks is made for tots and youngsters.

» **Universal Studios Hollywood** Enjoy movie-themed action rides, special-effects shows and a working studio backlot tram tour.

» **Six Flags Magic Mountain & Hurricane Harbor** Outside LA, it's high-adrenaline roller coasters, thrill rides and water slides.

Aquariums & Zoos

» **Monterey Bay Aquarium** Get acquainted with the denizens of the deep next door to the Central Coast's biggest marine sanctuary.

» **San Diego Zoo & Safari Park** Journey around the world and go on safari at California's best and biggest zoo.

» **Aquarium of the Pacific** Long Beach's high-tech aquarium houses critters from balmy Baja California to the chilly north Pacific, including a shark lagoon.

» **Living Desert** Outside Palm Springs, this educational zoo with real heart hosts a walk-through animal hospital, story hours and family camp-outs under the stars.

» **Seymour Marine Discovery Center** Santa Cruz's university-run aquarium makes interactive science fun, with tide pools for exploring nearby at the beach.

Beaches

» **Los Angeles** Carnival fun and an aquarium at Santa Monica Pier, or Malibu's perfect beaches just up Hwy 1.

» **Orange County** Newport Beach with its kiddie-sized Balboa Pier rides, Laguna Beach's miles of million-dollar sands, Huntington Beach (aka 'Surf City USA') and old-fashioned Seal Beach.

» **San Diego** Head over to Coronado's idyllic Silver Strand, play in Mission Bay by SeaWorld, lap up La Jolla and kick back in surf-style North County beach towns.

» **Central Coast** Laze on Santa Barbara's unmatched beaches, then roll all the way north to Santa Cruz's famous boardwalk and pier.

» **Lake Tahoe** In summer, it's California's favorite high-altitude beach escape: a sparkling diamond tucked in the craggy Sierra Nevada mountains.

Parks

» **Yosemite National Park** Get a juicy slice of Sierra Nevada scenery, with gushing waterfalls, alpine lakes, glacier-carved valleys and peaks.

» **Redwood National & State Parks** A string of nature preserves on the North Coast protect magnificent wildlife and the planet's tallest trees.

» **Lassen Volcanic National Park** This off-the-beaten path destination in the Northern Mountains has otherworldly volcanic scenery and lakeside camping and cabins.

» **Griffith Park** Bigger than NYC's Central Park, this LA green space has tons of fun for younger kids, from miniature train rides and a merry-go-round to planetarium shows.

» **Channel Islands National Park** Sail to California's Galapagos for wildlife watching, kayaking, hiking and camping adventures.

Museums

» **San Francisco** The city is a mind-bending classroom for kids, especially at the interactive Exploratorium, multimedia San Francisco's

Children's Creativity Museum and eco-friendly California Academy of Sciences.

» **Los Angeles** See stars (the real ones) at the Griffith Observatory, dinosaur bones at the Natural History Museum of LA County and the Page Museum at La Brea Tar Pits, then get hands-on at the amusing California Science Center.

» **San Diego** Balboa Park is jam-packed with museums and a world-famous zoo, too. Or take younger kids to the engaging New Children's Museum.

» **Orange County** Bring budding lab geeks to the Discovery Science Center, or get a pint-sized dose of arts and culture in the Kidseum at the Bowers Museum, both near Disneyland.

» **Northern Mountains** The Turtle Bay Exploration Park in Redding is an indoor-outdoor family attraction that combines an eco-museum with an arboretum, and botanical and butterfly gardens along the Sacramento River.

Planning
When to Go

For tips on the best times to visit and setting your family's trip budget, see p18. For a calendar of California's festivals and events, many of which are family-friendly, see p26.

A word of advice: Don't pack your schedule too tightly. Traveling with kids always takes longer than expected, especially when navigating metro areas such as LA and San Francisco, where you'll want to allow extra time for traffic jams and getting lost.

Accommodations

Motels and hotels typically have rooms with two beds or an extra sofa bed, ideal for families. They may also have roll-away beds or cots that can be added, typically for a surcharge. Some offer 'kids stay free' promotions, although this may apply only if no extra bedding is required. Some B&Bs don't allow children; ask when booking.

Resorts may have drop-off day camps for kids or babysitting services. At other hotels, the front-desk staff or concierge might help you make arrangements. Be sure to ask whether babysitters are licensed and bonded, what they charge per hour per child, whether there's a minimum fee and if they charge extra for transportation and meals.

Transportation

Airlines usually allow infants (up to age two) to fly for free – bring proof of age – while older children requiring a seat of their own qualify for reduced fares. Children receive substantial discounts on Amtrak trains and Greyhound buses. In cars, any child under age six or weighing less than 60lb must be buckled up in the back seat in a child or infant safety seat. Most car-rental agencies rent these for about $10/$50 per day/trip, but you must specifically book them in advance. Rest stops on freeways are few and far between, and gas stations and fast-food bathrooms are frequently icky. However, you're usually never far from a shopping mall, which generally have well-kept restrooms.

What to Pack

Sunscreen. And bringing sunscreen will remind you to bring hats, bathing suits, flip-flops and goggles. If you like beach umbrellas and sand chairs, pails and shovels, you'll probably want to bring your own or buy them at local supermarkets and drugstores. At many beaches, you can rent bicycles and watersports gear (eg snorkel sets).

For outdoor vacations, bring broken-in hiking shoes and your own camping equipment. Outdoor gear can be purchased or sometimes rented from outdoor outfitters and specialty shops. But remember Murphy's Law dictates that wearing brand-new hiking shoes always results in blisters, and setting up a new tent in the dark ain't easy.

If you forget some critical piece of equipment, **Baby's Away** (www.babysaway.com) rents cribs, strollers, car seats, high chairs, backpacks, beach gear and more.

Before You Go

» Lonely Planet's *Travel with Children* is loaded with valuable tips and amusing anecdotes, especially for new parents and kids who haven't traveled before.

» **Lonelyplanet.com** (www.lonelyplanet.com): ask questions and get advice from other travelers in the Thorn Tree's 'Kids to Go' and 'USA' forums.

» The state's official visitor website, **California Travel & Tourism** (www.visitcalifornia.com), lists family-friendly attractions, activities and more – just search for 'Family Fun' and 'Events'.

» **Family Travel Files** (www.thefamilytravelfiles.com/locations/california) is an info-packed site for vacation-planning articles, tips and discounts for both Northern and Southern California.

» **Parents Connect** (www.parentsconnect.com/family-travel) is a virtual encyclopedia of everything first-time family travelers need to know.

regions at a glance

A mosaic of Old and New Worlds, California's cities have more flavors than a jar of jellybeans. Start from San Francisco, equal parts earth-mother and geek-chic, or Los Angeles, where nearly 90 independent cities are rolled into one multicultural mosaic, then drift down the coast, past perfect beaches, to surf-style San Diego.

Or escape to the peaceful Sierra Nevada mountains, detour to soulful SoCal deserts, cruise agricultural heartland valleys and lose yourself in northern redwood forests. On sunny days when the coastal fog lifts, over 1100 miles of Pacific Ocean beaches await. And no matter where you go, vineyards never seem far away.

San Francisco

Food ✓✓✓
Culture ✓✓✓
Museums ✓✓✓

California's 'Left Coast' reputation rests on SF, where DIY self-expression, sustainability and spontaneity are the highest virtues. Free thinkers, top-tier museums and groundbreaking arts scenes thrive here.

p56

Marin County & the Bay Area

Hiking & Cycling ✓✓✓
Agrotourism ✓✓✓
Food ✓✓

Outdoors nuts adore Marin County, with its beaches, wildlife watching, hiking and cycling trails. There's also a fertile garden of ecotourism experiences, including at farms that inspire chefs all around the Bay Area.

p108

Napa & Sonoma Wine Country

Wineries ✓✓✓
Food ✓✓✓
Cycling & Canoeing ✓✓

Amid fruit orchards and ranch lands, these sunny valleys kissed by cool coastal fog have made Napa, Sonoma and the Russian River into California's premier wine-growing region – and also a showcase for bountiful farm-to-table cuisine.

p159

North Coast & Redwoods

Wildlife ✓✓✓
Hiking ✓✓✓
Beaches ✓✓

Primeval redwood forests are the prize along NorCal's foggy, rocky and wildly dramatic coastline. Let loose your inner hippie or Rastafarian in Humboldt County, or explore bootstrap fishing villages from Bodega Bay to Eureka.

p212

Northern Mountains

Mountains ✓✓✓
Lakes ✓✓✓
Scenic Drives ✓✓

Sacred Mt Shasta has brought together Native Americans, ice-axe-wielding alpinists, and new-age poets. Wilder places also await, from Lassen's volcanic Bumpass Hell to back-country byways and lakes.

p266

Gold Country & Central Valley

History ✓✓✓
Museums ✓✓
Outdoor Activities ✓✓

The state capital, Sacramento, is an unbeatable place to start digging up California's roots. Then spread out across the river delta into the foothills to find a rich vein of Wild West history in gold-mining country.

p302

Lake Tahoe

Winter Sports ✓✓✓
Water Sports ✓✓
Cabins & Camping ✓✓

North America's largest alpine lake is a four-seasons outdoor adventure land. Come for Olympic-worthy skiing in winter, or some serious beach time in summer. Nevada's casinos are a bonus attraction.

p363

Yosemite & the Sierra Nevada

Scenery ✓✓✓
Wildlife ✓✓✓
Hiking ✓✓✓

Granite peaks, alpine meadows, North America's deepest canyon, and shaggy forests of giant sequoias grace California's iconic mountain range. Summer is prime-time for all kinds of outdoor pursuits.

p397

Central Coast

Wildlife ✓✓✓
Beaches ✓✓✓
Scenic Drives ✓✓✓

Hike Big Sur's redwood forests, where waterfalls spring to life; hop aboard a whale-watching boat in Monterey Bay; surf from Santa Cruz to Santa Barbara; or kayak the Channel Islands, California's Galapagos.

p453

Los Angeles

Nightlife ✓✓✓
Food ✓✓✓
Beaches ✓✓✓

There's more to life in La La Land than just sunny beaches and air-kissing celebs. Get a dose of culture downtown, then dive into LA's diverse neighborhoods, from historic Little Tokyo to red-carpet Hollywood.

p527

Disneyland & Orange County

Theme Parks ✓✓✓
Beaches ✓✓✓
Surfing ✓✓✓

The OC's beaches are often packed bronze-shoulder-to-shoulder with surfers, beach-volleyball nuts and soap-opera-esque beauties. Inland, take the kids and grandparents – heck, load up the whole minivan – to Disney's Magic Kingdom.

p579

San Diego

Beaches ✓✓✓
Mexican Food ✓✓✓
Museums ✓✓✓

With a near-perfect year-round climate, lucky residents of California's southernmost city always seem to be slacking off – and who can blame them? Take a permanent vacation in SD's laid-back beach towns while scarfing down fish tacos.

p607

Palm Springs & the Deserts

Hiking ✓✓✓
Wildflowers ✓✓✓
Resorts & Spas ✓✓

A retro resort playground, Palm Springs has experienced a rebirth of Rat Pack–era cool. Or go get dirty by rock climbing in Joshua Tree, then test your 4WD mettle in Death Valley, where spring wildflowers bloom.

p651

> **Every listing is recommended by our authors, and their favourite places are listed first**

> **Look out for these icons:**

TOP CHOICE Our author's top recommendation

A green or sustainable option

FREE No payment required

On the Road

San Francisco

Best Places to Eat

» Coi (p87)

» Benu (p90)

» La Taquería (p90)

» Frances (p93)

» Aziza (p95)

Best Places to Stay

» Orchard Garden Hotel (p80)

» Hotel Vitale (p84)

» Hotel Bohème (p82)

» Inn San Fransisco (p84)

» Argonaut Hotel (p83)

Why Go?

Get to know the world capital of weird from the inside out, from mural-lined alleyways named after poets to clothing-optional beaches on a former military base. But don't be too quick to dismiss San Francisco's wild ideas. Biotech, gay rights, personal computers, cable cars and organic fine dining were once considered outlandish too, before San Francisco introduced these underground ideas into the mainstream decades ago. San Francisco's morning fog erases the boundaries between land and ocean, reality and infinite possibility.

Rules are never strictly followed here, but bliss is. Golden Gate Bridge and Alcatraz are entirely optional – San Franciscans mostly admire them from afar – leaving you free to pursue inspiration through Golden Gate Park, past flamboyantly painted Victorian homes and through Mission galleries. Just don't be late for your sensational, sustainable dinner: in San Francisco, you can find happiness and eat it too.

When to Go
San Francisco

Jan–Mar Low-season rates, brisk but rarely cold days, and the colorful Lunar New Year parade.

May–Aug Farmers markets and festivals make up for high-season rates and chilly afternoon fog.

Sep–Nov Blue skies, free concerts, bargain hotel rates and flavor-bursting harvest cuisine.

Cable Cars

Groaning brakes and clanging brass bells only add to the thrills of San Francisco's cable cars, which have hardly changed since their introduction here in 1873. Cable cars still can't move in reverse, and require burly gripmen (and one buff gripwoman) to lean hard on hand-operated brakes to keep from careening downhill. The city receives many applicants for this job, but 80% fail the strenuous tests of upper-body strength and hand–eye coordination, and rarely try again. Today the cable car seems more like a steampunk carnival ride than modern transport, but it remains the killer app to conquer San Francisco's breakneck slopes. There are no seat belts, child seats or air bags on board – just jump onto the wooden sideboard, grab a strap, and enjoy the ride of your life.

DON'T MISS...

» **Saloons** The Barbary Coast is roaring back to life with historically researched whiskey cocktails and staggering absinthe concoctions in San Francisco's great Western saloon revival (p96).

» **Foraged fine dining** No SF tasting menu is complete without wild chanterelles, miner's lettuce from Berkeley hillsides or SF-backyard nasturtium flowers, from **Commonwealth** (p90) to **Coi** (p87)

» **Green everything** Recent reports rank San Francisco as the greenest city in North America, with its LEED-certified green hotels, pioneering citywide composting laws and America's biggest stretch of urban greenery: **Golden Gate Park** (p57).

» **Showtime** Bewigged satire, world premiere opera, year-round film festivals, Grammy-winning symphonies and legendary, jawdropping drag: no one puts on a show like San Francisco, and the cheering, back-talking local audiences demand encores in no uncertain terms.

SF's Best Free...

» **Music** Golden Gate Park (p57) hosts free concerts summer through fall, from opera to Hardly Strictly Bluegrass (p80).

» **Speech** City Lights Bookstore (p63) won a landmark free speech case over the publication of Allen Ginsberg's magnificent, incendiary *Howl*; take a seat in the designated Poet's Chair and celebrate your right to read freely.

» **Love** Pride (p79) fills San Francisco streets with free candy, free condoms, and over a million people freely smooching total strangers under rainbow flags.

» **Spirits** Anywhere within city limits, at any time – consider yourself warned.

capita than ... any other US city.

Fast Facts

» **Population** 805,235
» **Area** 7 square miles
» **Telephone area code** 415

Planning Your Trip

» **Three weeks before** Book Alcatraz trips and dinner at Coi or Frances.

» **Two weeks before** Build stamina for downtown hills, South of Market (SoMa) galleries and Mission bars.

» **One week before** Score tickets to San Francisco Symphony or Opera, and assemble your costume – SF throws parades whenever.

Resources

» **SF Bay Guardian** (www.sfbg.com) Hot tips on local entertainment, arts, politics.

» **SFGate** (www.sfgate.com) News and event listings.

San Francisco Highlights

1 Make yourself at home where the buffalo roam in **Golden Gate Park** (p57)

2 Reach new artistic heights at the **San Francisco Museum** of **Modern Art** (p68) rooftop sculpture garden

3 Watch fog dance atop the deco towers of the **Golden Gate Bridge** (p59)

4 Graze the **Ferry Building** (p59), SF's local, sustainable foodie destination

5 Plot your escape from **Alcatraz** (p79), SF's notorious island prison

6 Discover unlikely urban marine life along **Fisherman's Wharf** (p64): sea lions, sharks, and a WWII submarine

7 Unwind in Japanese baths and catch film screenings in **Japantown** (p65)

8 Get br... climb, mura... views at **Coit To...**

9 Wander throu... of California history in ... topped **Chinatown** (p61)

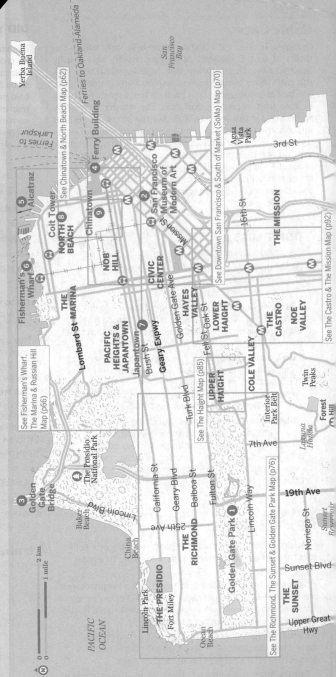

History

Oysters and acorn bread were prime dinner options in the Mexico-run Ohlone settlement of San Francisco circa 1848 – but a year and some gold nuggets later, Champagne and chow mein were served by the bucket. Gold found in the nearby Sierra Nevada foothills had turned a waterfront village of 800 into a port city of 100,000 prospectors, con artists, prostitutes and honest folk trying to make an honest living – good luck telling which was which. That friendly bartender might drug your drink, and you'd wake up a mile from shore, shanghaied into service on some ship bound for Argentina.

By 1850, California was nabbed from Mexico and fast-tracked for US statehood, and San Francisco attempted to introduce public order to 200 saloons and untold numbers of brothels and gambling dens. Panic struck when Australia glutted the market with gold in 1854, and ire turned irrationally on SF's Chinese community, who from 1877 to 1945 were restricted to living and working in Chinatown by anti-Chinese laws. The main way out of debt was dangerous work building railroads for the city's robber barons, who dynamited, mined and clear-cut their way across the Golden West, and built grand Nob Hill mansions above Chinatown.

The city's lofty ambitions and 20-plus theaters came crashing down in 1906, when earthquake and fire left 3000 dead, 100,000 homeless and much of the city reduced to rubble - including almost every mansion on Nob Hill. Theater troupes and opera divas performed for free amid smoldering ruins downtown, establishing SF's tradition of free public performances in parks.

Ambitious public works projects continued through the 1930s, when Diego Rivera, Frida Kahlo and federally funded muralists began the tradition of leftist politics in paint visible in some 400 Mission murals.

WWII brought seismic shifts to San Francisco's community as women and African Americans working in San Francisco shipyards created a new economic boom, and President Franklin Delano Roosevelt's Executive Order 9066 mandated the internment of the city's historic Japanese American community. A 40-year court battle ensued, ending in an unprecedented apology from the US government. San Francisco became a testing ground for civil rights and free speech, with Beat poet Lawrence Ferlinghetti and City Lights Bookstore winning a landmark 1957 ruling against book banning over the publication of Allen Ginsberg's splendid, incendiary *Howl and Other Poems*.

The Central Intelligence Agency (CIA) hoped an experimental drug called LSD might turn San Francisco test subject Ken Kesey into the ultimate fighting machine, but instead the author of *One Flew Over the Cuckoo's Nest* slipped some into Kool-Aid and kicked off the psychedelic '60s. The Summer of Love meant free food, love and music in The Haight until the '70s, when enterprising gay hippies founded an out-and-proud community in the Castro. San Francisco witnessed devastating losses from AIDS in the 1980s, but the city rallied to become a model for disease treatment and prevention.

Geeks and cyberpunks converged on SF in the mid-1990s, spawning the Web and dot-com boom – until the bubble popped in 2000. But risk-taking SF continues to float new ideas, and as recession hits elsewhere, social media, mobile apps and biotech are booming in San Francisco. Congratulations: you're just in time for San Francisco's next wild ride.

◉ Sights

THE BAY & THE EMBARCADERO

TOP CHOICE Golden Gate Bridge BRIDGE
(Map p58; ☎415-921-5858; www.goldengate.org; Fort Point Lookout, Marine Dr; southbound car $6, carpools free) San Franciscans have passionate perspectives on every subject, but especially their signature landmark. Cinema buffs believe Hitchcock had it right: seen from below at **Fort Point**, the 1937 bridge induces a thrilling case of *Vertigo*. Fog aficionados prefer the north-end lookout at Marin's **Vista Point**, to watch gusts billow through bridge cables like dry ice at a Kiss concert. Hard to believe the Navy almost nixed the soaring art deco design of architects Gertrude and Irving Murrow and engineer Joseph B Strauss in favor of a hulking concrete span painted with caution-yellow stripes.

To see both sides of the Golden Gate debate, hike or bike the 2-mile span. MUNI buses 28 and 29 run to the toll plaza, and pedestrians and cyclists can cross the bridge on the east side; Golden Gate Transit buses head back to SF from Marin.

Ferry Building HISTORIC BUILDING
(Map p70; www.ferrybuildingmarketplace.com; Embarcadero) Slackers have the right idea at the Ferry Building, the transport hub

NEIGHBORHOODS IN A NUTSHELL

North Beach & the Hills Poetry and parrots, top-of-the-world views, Italian gossip and opera on the jukebox.

Embarcadero & the Piers Gourmet treats, sea-lion antics, 19th-century video games, and getaways to and from Alcatraz.

Downtown & the Financial District The notorious Barbary Coast has gone legit with banks and boutiques, but reveals its wild side in provocative art galleries.

Chinatown Pagoda roofs, mahjong, and fortunes made and lost in historic alleyways.

Hayes Valley, Civic Center & the Tenderloin Grand buildings and great performances, dive bars and cable cars, foodie finds and local designs.

SoMa Where high technology meets higher art, and everyone gets down and dirty on the dance floor.

Mission A book in one hand, a burrito in the other, and murals all around.

Castro Out and proud with samba whistles, rainbow flags and policy platforms.

Haight Flashbacks and fashion-forwardness, free thinking, free music and pricey skateboards.

Japantown, the Fillmore & Pacific Heights Sushi in the fountains, John Coltrane over the altar, and rock at the Fillmore.

Marina & the Presidio Boutiques, organic dining, peace and public nudity at a former army base.

Golden Gate Park & the Avenues SF's mile-wide wild streak, surrounded by gourmet hangouts for hungry surfers.

turned gourmet emporium where no one's in a hurry to leave. Boat traffic tapered off after the grand hall and clock tower were built in 1898, and by the 1950s the building was literally overshadowed by a freeway overpass. But after the freeway collapsed in the 1989 Loma Prieta Earthquake, the city revived the Ferry Building as a tribute to San Francisco's monumental good taste. On weekends the **Ferry Building Farmers Market** (see the boxed text p88) fans out around the south end of the building like a fabulous garnish.

UNION SQUARE

Powell St Cable Car Turnaround   CABLE CAR
(Map p70) Pause at Powell and Market to notice operators leap out of a century-old cable car, and slooowly turn it around on a revolving wooden platform by hand. As technology goes, this seems pretty iffy. Cable cars can't go in reverse, emit mechanical grunts on uphill climbs and require burly operators to lean hard on the handbrake to keep from careening down Nob Hill. For a city of risk-takers, this steampunk transport is the perfect joyride.

Folk Art International   CULTURAL BUILDING
(Map p70; ☎415-392-9999; www.folkartintl.com; 140 Maiden Lane; ☺10am-6pm Tue-Sat) Squeeze the Guggenheim into a brick box with a sunken Romanesque archway, and there you have Frank Lloyd Wright's 1949 Circle Gallery Building, which since 1979 has been the home of the **Xanadu Gallery**.

FINANCIAL DISTRICT

14, 49 and 77 Geary   GALLERIES
(Map p70; www.sfada.com; ☺most galleries 10:30am-5:30pm Tue-Fri, 11am-5pm Sat) Eccentric art collectors descend from hilltop mansions for First Thursday gallery openings of unpredictable art among outspoken crowds. Look for conceptual art at **Gallery Paule Anglim** at 14 Geary; four floors of contemporary art at 49 Geary, from installations by jailed Chinese artist Ai Weiwei at **Haines Gallery** to conceptual photography at **Fraenkel Gallery**; and at 77 Geary, Taravat Talepasand's Iranian-American superheroine portraits at **Marx & Zavattero Gallery** and Vik Muniz's collaged masterworks at **Rena Bransten Gallery**.

Transamerica Pyramid
LANDMARK

(Map p70; 600 Montgomery St) Below the 1972 concrete rocketship that defines San Francisco's skyline, a half-acre redwood grove has taken root in the remains of old whaling ships. The building is off-limits to visitors, but the grove is open for daytime picnics on the site of a saloon frequented by Mark Twain and the newspaper office where Sun Yat-sen drafted his Proclamation of the Republic of China.

CIVIC CENTER & THE TENDERLOIN

TOP CHOICE Asian Art Museum
MUSEUM

(Map p70; 415-581-3500; www.asianart.org; 200 Larkin St; adult/student \$12/7; 10am-5pm Tue, Wed, Fri-Sun, to 9pm Thu;) Civic Center may be landlocked, but it has an unrivalled view of the Pacific thanks to this museum. Cover 6000 years and thousands of miles here in under an hour, from racy ancient Rajasthan miniatures to futuristic Japanese manga (graphic novels) via priceless Ming vases and even a Bhutan collection. The Asian has worked diplomatic wonders with a rotating collection of 17,000 treasures that bring Taiwan, China and Tibet together, unite Pakistan and India, and strike a harmonious balance among Japan, Korea and China. Stick around for outstanding educational events, from shadow-puppet shows and yoga for kids to First Thursday MATCHA nights from 5pm to 9pm, when soju cocktails flow, DJs spin Japanese hip-hop and guest acupuncturists assess visitors' tongues.

City Hall
HISTORIC BUILDING

(Map p70; 415-554-4000, tour info 415-554-6023, art exhibit line 415-554-6080; www.ci.sf.ca.us/cityhall; 400 Van Ness Ave; 8am-8pm Mon-Fri, tours 10am, noon & 2pm;) From its Gilded Age dome to the avant-garde art in the basement, City Hall is quintessentially San Franciscan. Rising from the ashes of the 1906 earthquake, this Beaux Arts building has seen historic firsts under its splendid Tennessee pink marble and Colorado limestone rotunda: America's first sit-in on the grand staircase in 1960, protesting red-baiting McCarthy hearings; the 1977 election and 1978 assassination of openly gay Supervisor Harvey Milk; and 4037 same-sex marriages performed in 2004, until the state intervened. Intriguing art shows downstairs showcase local artists; weekly Board of Supervisors meetings are open to the public at 2pm on Tuesdays.

FREE Luggage Store Gallery
GALLERY

(Map p70; 415-255-5971; www.luggagestoregallery.org; 1007 Market St; noon-5pm Wed-Sat) A dandelion pushing through cracks in the sidewalk, this plucky nonprofit gallery has brought signs of life to one of the toughest blocks in the Tenderloin for two decades. Streetwise art gets its due above an ex-luggage store in this second-floor gallery, which helped launch street satirists Barry McGee, Clare Rojas and Rigo. You'll recognize the place by its graffitied door and the rooftop mural by Brazilian duo Osgemeos of a defiant kid holding a lit firecracker. With such oddly touching works, poetry nights and monthly performing-arts events, this place puts the tender in the Tenderloin.

Glide Memorial United Methodist Church
CHURCH

(Map p70; 415-674-6090; www.glide.org; 330 Ellis St; 9am & 11am Sun) On Sundays, 1500 people add their voices to the electrifying gospel services at this GLBT-friendly (and just plain friendly) church. After the celebration ends in hearty handshakes and hugs, the radical Methodist congregation gets to work, providing one million free meals a year and homes for 52 formerly homeless families.

CHINATOWN

Chinese Historical Society of America Museum
MUSEUM

(Map p62; 415-391-1188; www.chsa.org; 965 Clay St; adult/child \$5/2, first Tue of month free; noon-5pm Tue-Fri, 11am-4pm Sat) Picture what it was like to be Chinese in America during the Gold Rush, the transcontinental railroad construction or in the Beat heyday at the nation's largest Chinese American historical institute. There are rotating exhibits across the courtyard in CHSA's graceful red-brick, green-tile-roofed landmark building, built as Chinatown's YWCA in 1932 by Julia Morgan, chief architect of Hearst Castle.

Chinese Culture Center
CULTURAL CENTER

(Map p62; 415-986-1822; www.c-c-c.org; 3rd fl, Hilton Hotel, 750 Kearny St; gallery free, donation requested; 10am-4pm Tue-Sat) You can see all the way to China on the 3rd floor of the Hilton inside this cultural center, which hosts exhibits of traditional Chinese arts; Xian Rui (Fresh & Sharp) cutting-edge art installations, such as Stella Zhang's discomfiting toothpick-studded pillows; and Art at Night, showcasing Chinese-inspired art, jazz, and food. Check the center's online

Chinatown & North Beach

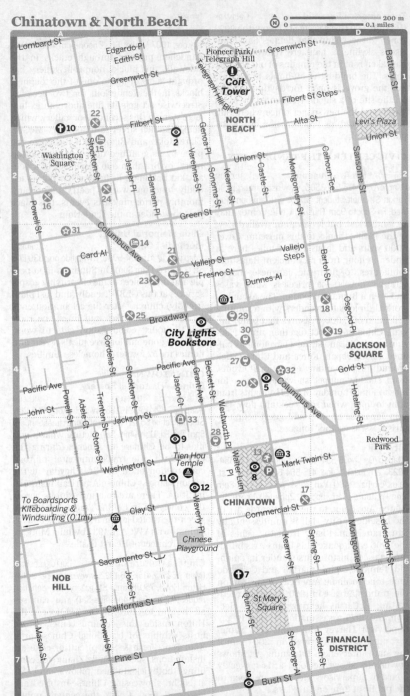

Chinatown & North Beach

schedule for concerts, hands-on arts workshops, Mandarin classes, genealogy services and Chinatown arts festivals.

Dragon Gate   LANDMARK
(Map p62; at Bush St & Grant Ave) Enter the Dragon Gate donated by Taiwan in 1970, and you're on the once-notorious street known as Dupont in its red-light heyday. Forward-thinking Chinatown businessmen headed by Look Tin Ely pooled funds in the 1920s to reinvent the area as the tourist attraction you see today, hiring architects to create a signature 'Chinatown Deco' look with pagoda-style roofs and dragon lanterns lining Grant Ave.

Old St Mary's Church   CHURCH
(Map p62; ☑415-288-3800; www.oldsaintmarys. org; 660 California St) For decades after its 1854 construction, the Catholic archdiocese valiantly tried to give this brothel district some religion. The 1906 fire destroyed one of the district's biggest bordellos directly across from the church, making room for St Mary's Sq, where skateboarders now ride handrails while Beniamino Bufano's 1929 **Sun Yat-sen statue** keeps a lookout.

Portsmouth Square   SQUARE
(Map p62) Chinatown's outdoor living room is named after John B Montgomery's sloop that docked nearby in 1846, but the presiding deity at this people's park is the **Goddess of Democracy**, a bronze replica of the plaster statue made by Tiananmen Sq protesters in 1989. Historical markers dot the perimeter of the historic square, noting the site of San Francisco's first bookshop and newspaper, and the bawdy Jenny Lind Theater, which with a few modifications became San Francisco's first City Hall. A **night market** is held here from 6pm to 11pm each Saturday from July to October.

NORTH BEACH

🏆 **City Lights**
Bookstore   CULTURAL BUILDING
Map p62; www.citylights.com; 261 Columbus Ave; ⊙10am-midnight) Ever since manager Shigeyoshi Murao and founder and Beat poet Lawrence Ferlinghetti successfully defended their right to 'willfully and lewdly print' Allen Ginsberg's magnificent *Howl and Other Poems* in 1957, this bookstore has been a landmark. Celebrate your freedom to read freely in the designated Poet's Chair upstairs overlooking Jack Kerouac Alley, load up on 'zines on the mezzanine or entertain radical

THREE CHINATOWN ALLEYS THAT MADE HISTORY

» **Waverly Place** (Map p62) After the 1906 earthquake and fire devastated Chinatown, developers schemed to relocate Chinatown residents left homeless to less desirable real estate outside the city. But representatives from the Chinese consulate and several gun-toting merchants marched back to Waverly Place, holding temple services amid the rubble at still-smoldering altars. The alley is also the namesake for the main character in Amy Tan's bestselling *The Joy Luck Club*.

» **Spofford Alley** (Map p62) Sun Yat-sen plotted the overthrow of China's last emperor at No 36 and the 1920s brought bootleggers' gun battles to this alley, but Spofford has mellowed with age. In the evenings you'll hear the shuffling of mahjong tiles and an *erhu* (two-stringed Chinese fiddle) warming up at local senior centers.

» **Ross Alley** (Map p62) Alternately known as Manila, Spanish and Mexico St after the working girls who once worked this block, mural-lined Ross Alley is occasionally pimped out for Hollywood productions, including *Karate Kid II* and *Indiana Jones and the Temple of Doom*.

ideas downstairs in the Muckracking and Stolen Continents sections.

Beat Museum   MUSEUM
(Map p62; ☏1-800-537-6822; www.thebeatmuseum.org; 540 Broadway; admission $5; ⊙10am-7pm Tue-Sun) For the complete Beat experience, stop by to check out City Lights' banned edition of Allen Ginsberg's *Howl*, Beat-era documentary footage in a makeshift theater, and tributes to authors who expanded the American outlook to include the margins – including a $10.18 check Jack Kerouac wrote for liquor.

Columbus Tower   BUILDING
(Map p62; 916 Kearny St) Shady political boss Abe Ruef had only just finished this copper-clad building in 1905 when it was hit by the 1906 earthquake, and he restored it right before he was convicted of bribery and bankrupted in 1907. The Kingston Trio bought the building in the 1960s, and recorded reggae and the Grateful Dead in the basement. Since 1970 the building has belonged to film-maker Francis Ford Coppola, who leases the top floors to fellow filmmakers Sean Penn and Wayne Wang and sells Italian fare and his own-label Napa wine at ground-level Café Niebaum-Coppola. Our advice: skip the pasta, take the cannoli.

Bob Kauffman Alley   STREET
(Map p62; off Grant Ave near Filbert St) Enjoy a moment of profound silence courtesy of the Beat-bebop-jazz-poet-anarchist-voodoo-Jewish-biracial-African-all-American-streetcorner-prophet who refused to speak for 12 years after the assassination of John F Kennedy. The day

the Vietnam War ended, he broke his silence by walking into a cafe and reciting his poem 'All Those Ships That Never Sailed'.

Saints Peter & Paul Church   CHURCH
(Map p62; ☏415-421-0809; www.stspeterpaul.san-francisco.ca.us; 666 Filbert St; ⊙7:30am-4pm) Wedding-cake cravings are to be expected upon sight of this 1924 church, the frosting-white triple-decker cathedral where Joe Di Maggio and Marilyn Monroe famously posed for wedding photos (since they were both divorced, they were denied a church wedding here). The church overlooks Washington Sq, the North Beach park where non-agenarian *nonnas* (Italian grandmothers) feed wild parrots by the 1897 **Ben Franklin statue**.

FISHERMAN'S WHARF
Aquatic Park Bathhouse   HISTORIC BUILDING
(Map p66; ☏415-447-5000; www.nps.gov/safr; 499 Jefferson at Hyde; adult/child $5/free; ⊙10am-4pm) A monumental hint to sailors in need of a scrub, this recently restored, ship-shape 1939 Streamline Moderne landmark is decked out with WPA art treasures: playful seal and frog sculptures by Beniamino Bufano, Hilaire Hiler's surreal underwater dreamscape murals and recently uncovered wood reliefs by Richard Ayer. Acclaimed African American artist Sargent Johnson created the stunning carved green slate marquee doorway and the veranda's mesmerizing aquatic mosaics, which he deliberately left unfinished on the east side to protest plans to include a private restaurant in this public facility. Johnson won: the east wing is now a maritime museum office.

FREE Musée Mecanique   MUSEUM

(Map p66; 415-346-2000; www.museemeca
nique.org; Pier 45, Shed A; 10am-7pm Mon-Fri,
to 8pm Sat & Sun;) A few quarters let you
start bar brawls in coin-operated Wild West
saloons, peep at belly-dancers through a vintage Mutoscope, save the world from Space
Invaders and get your fortune told by an
eerily lifelike wooden swami at this vintage
arcade.

USS Pampanito   HISTORIC SITE

(Map p66; 415-775-1943; www.maritime.org; Pier
45; adult/child $10/4; 9am-5pm) Explore a
restored WWII submarine that survived six
tours of duty, while listening to submariners'
tales of stealth mode and sudden attacks in a
riveting audio tour ($2) that makes surfacing
afterwards a relief (caution claustrophobes).

Pier 39   LANDMARK

(Map p66; 415-981-1280; www.pier39.com; Beach
St & Embarcadero;) Ever since they first
hauled out here in 1990, 300 to 1300 sea
lions have spent winter through summer
bellyflopped on these yacht docks. While
bulls jostle for prime sunning location on
the piers, boardwalk B-boyers compete for
street-dance supremacy and kids wage battles of the will with parents over souvenir
teddy bears.

RUSSIAN HILL & NOB HILL

Grace Cathedral   CHURCH

(Map p66; 415-749-6300; www.gracecathedral.
org; 1100 California St; suggested donation adult/
child $3/2; 7am-6pm Mon-Fri, 8am-6pm Sat,
8am-7pm Sun, services with choir 8:30am & 11am
Sun) Rebuilt three times since the Gold Rush,

and still this progressive Episcopal church
keeps pace with the times. Additions include
the AIDS Interfaith Memorial Chapel, which
features a bronze Keith Haring altarpiece;
stained-glass 'Human Endeavor' windows
that illuminate Albert Einstein in a swirl of
nuclear particles; and pavement labyrinths
offering guided meditation for restless souls.

San Francisco Art Institute   GALLERY

(SFAI; Map p66; 415-771-7020; www.sfai.edu; 800
Chestnut St; 9am-7:30pm) Founded during the
1870s, SFAI was the centre of the Bay Area's
figurative art scene in the 1940s and '50s,
turned to Bay Area Abstraction in the '60s and
conceptual art in the '70s, and since the '90s
has championed new media art in its Walter
and McBean Gallery (11am-6pm Mon-Sat).
Also on campus, the Diego Rivera Gallery
features Rivera's 1931 mural *The Making of a
Fresco Showing a Building of a City,* a fresco
within a fresco showing the back of the artist
himself, as he pauses to admire the constant
work in progress of San Francisco.

JAPANTOWN & PACIFIC HEIGHTS

Japan Center   CULTURAL BUILDING

(off Map p66; www.sfjapantown.org; 1625 Post St;
10am-midnight) Still looks much the way
it did when it opened in 1968, with indoor
wooden pedestrian bridges, *ikebana* (flower-
arranging) displays and *maneki-neko* (waving cat) figurines beckoning from restaurant
entryways.

Haas-Lilienthal House   HISTORIC BUILDING

(Map p66; 415-441-3004; 2007 Franklin St; adult/
child $8/5; noon-3pm Wed & Sat, 11am-4pm Sun)
An 1882 Queen Anne with decor that looks

WORTH A TRIP

COIT TOWER

Adding an exclamation mark to San Francisco's landscape, Coit Tower (Map p62; 415-
362-0808; Telegraph Hill; admission free, elevator rides $5; 10am-6pm) offers views worth
shouting about – especially after you climb the giddy, steep Filbert St or Greenwich St
steps to the top of Telegraph Hill. This 210ft, peculiar projectile is a monument to San
Francisco firefighters financed by eccentric heiress Lillie Hitchcock Coit. Lillie could
drink, smoke and play cards as well as any off-duty firefighter, rarely missed a fire or a
firefighter's funeral and even had the firehouse emblem embroidered on all her
bedsheets.

When Lillie's totem was completed in 1934, the worker-glorifying, Diego Rivera–style
WPA murals lining the lobby were denounced as Communist, as were the 25 artists who
worked on them. Now protected as historic landmarks, the lobby murals broaden world-
views just as surely as the 360-degree views of downtown from the tower-top viewing
platform. To see more murals hidden inside Coit Tower's stairwell, take one of the free
guided tours at 11am on Saturdays.

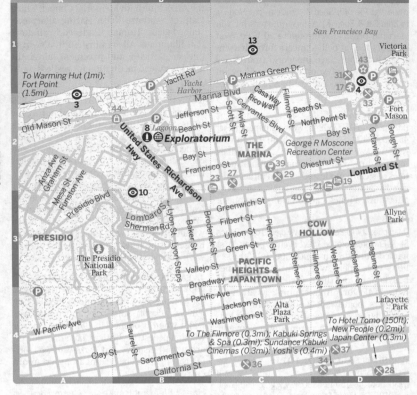

like a murder-mystery setting, including a dark-wood ballroom, red-velvet parlor and spooky stairways. One-hour tours are led by volunteers devoted to Victoriana.

Peace Pagoda   MONUMENT
(off Map p70; Peace Plaza) San Francisco's sister city of Osaka in Japan gifted Yoshiro Taniguchi's striking minimalist concrete pagoda to the people of San Francisco in 1968.

THE MARINA

TOP CHOICE Exploratorium   MUSEUM
(Map p66; ☎415-561-0360; www.exploratorium.edu; 3601 Lyon St; adult/child $15/10, incl. Tactile Dome $20; ⏰10am-5pm Tue-Sun; 🚻) Budding Nobel Prize winners swarm this hands-on discovery museum that's been blowing minds since 1969, answering the questions you always wanted to ask in science class: does gravity apply to skateboarding, do robots have feelings and do toilets flush counterclockwise in

Australia? One especially far-out exhibit is the **Tactile Dome**, a pitch-black space that you can crawl, climb and slide through (advance reservations required). It's moving to Piers 15 and 17 in 2013.

Palace of Fine Arts   MONUMENT
(Map p66; www.lovethepalace.org; Palace Dr) When San Francisco's 1915 Panama-Pacific expo was over, SF couldn't bear to part with this Greco-Roman plaster palace. California Arts and Crafts architect Bernard Maybeck's artificial ruin was recast in concrete, so that future generations could gaze up at the rotunda relief to glimpse Art under attack by Materialists, with Idealists leaping to her rescue.

Wave Organ   MONUMENT
(Map p66) Another intriguing Exploratorium project, this sound system of PVC tubes, concrete pipes and found marble from San Francisco's old cemetery was installed into the Marina Boat Harbor jetty by artist Peter

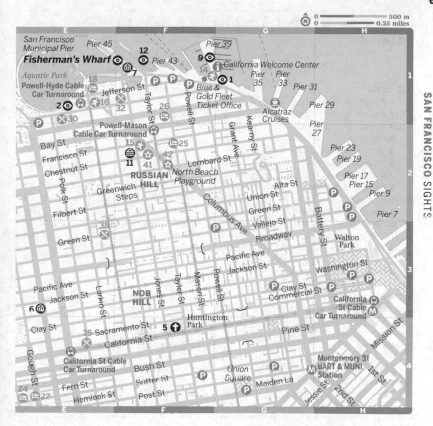

Richards in 1986. Depending on the waves, winds and tide, the tones emitted by the organ can sound like nervous humming, a gurgling baby or prank-call heavy breathing.

Fort Mason　　　　　　　　HISTORIC SITE
(Map p66; ☎415-345-7500; www.fortmason.org) Army sergeants would be scandalized by the frolicking at this former military outpost, including comedy improv workshops, vegetarian brunches at Greens (p89) and Off the Grid (p89), where gourmet trucks circle like pioneer wagons.

THE PRESIDIO

Presidio Visitors Center　　　HISTORIC BUILDING
(Map p66; ☎415-561-4323; www.nps.gov/prsf; cnr Montgomery St & Lincoln Blvd; ☺9am-5pm) San Francisco's official motto is still 'Oro in Paz, Fierro in Guerra' (Gold in Peace, Iron in War), but its main base hasn't seen much military action since it was built by conscripted Ohlone as a Spanish *presidio* (mili-

tary post) in 1776. Jerry Garcia began and ended his ignominious military career here by going AWOL nine times in eight months and getting court-martialed twice before co-founding the Grateful Dead.

The Presidio's military role ended in 1994, when the 1480-acre plot became part of the Golden Gate National Recreation Area. The Visitors Center can direct you towards the Pet Cemetery off Crissy Field Ave, where handmade tombstones commemorate military hamsters who've completed their final tour of duty. Today the only wars waged around here are interstellar ones in George Lucas' screening room in the Letterman Digital Arts Center, right by the Yoda statue.

Crissy Field　　　　　　　　　　PARK
(Map p66; www.crissyfield.org; 603 Mason St; ☺sunrise-sunset, Center 9am-5pm) War is now officially for the birds at this former military airstrip, restored as a tidal marsh and

Fisherman's Wharf, The Marina & Russian Hill

reclaimed by knock-kneed coastal birds. On blustery days, bird-watch from the shelter of Crissy Field Center, which has a cafe counter facing the field with binoculars. Join joggers and puppies romping beachside trails that were once oil-stained asphalt, and on foggy days stop by the certified green **Warming Hut** (off Map p66; 983 Marine Dr; ☺9am-5pm) to thaw out with Fair Trade coffee, browse field guides and sample honey made by Presidio honeybees.

Fort Point   HISTORIC BUILDING
(off Map p66; ☑415-561-4395; www.nps.gov/fopo; Marine Dr; ☺10am-5pm Thu-Mon) Despite its impressive guns, this Civil War fort saw no action – at least until Alfred Hitchcock shot scenes from *Vertigo* here, with stunning views of the Golden Gate Bridge from below.

Baker Beach   BEACH
The city's best beach, with windswept pines uphill, craggy cliffs and a whole lot of ex-posed goosebumps on the breezy, clothing-optional north end.

SOUTH OF MARKET (SOMA)

TOP
CHOICE **San Francisco Museum
of Modern Art**   MUSEUM
(SFMOMA; Map p70; ☑415-357-4000; www.sf moma.org; 151 3rd St; adult/student/child $18/11/ free, first Tue of month free; ☺11am-6pm Fri-Tue, to 9pm Thu) Swiss architect Mario Botta's light-filled brick box leans full-tilt toward the horizon, with curators similarly inclined to take forward-thinking risks on Matthew Barney's poetic videos involving industrial quantities of Vaseline and Olafur Eliasson's outer-space light installations. SFMOMA has arguably the world's leading photography collection, with works by Ansel Adams, Daido Moriyama, Diane Arbus, Edward Weston, William Eggleston and Dorothea Lange, and since its 1995 grand reopening coincided with the tech boom, SFMOMA

became an early champion of new media art. Sculpture sprouts from the new rooftop garden, and a $480 million expansion is underway to accommodate 1100 major modern works donated by the Fisher family (local founders of Gap). Go Thursday nights after 6pm for half-price admission and the most artful flirting in town.

Contemporary Jewish Museum   MUSEUM
(Map p70; ☑415-655-7800; www.jmsf.org; 736 Mission St; adult/child $10/8/free; ☺11am-5:30pm Fri-Tue, 1-8:30pm Thu) In 2008, architect Daniel Liebskind reshaped San Francisco's 1881 power plant with a blue steel extension to form the Hebrew word *l'chaim* ('to life'). Inside this architectural statement are lively shows, ranging from a retrospective of modern art instigator and Bay Area native Gertrude Stein to Linda Ellia's *Our Struggle: Artists Respond to Mein Kampf*, for which 600 artists from 17 countries were invited to alter one page of Hitler's book.

Cartoon Art Museum   MUSEUM
(Map p70; ☑415-227-8666; www.cartoonart.org; 655 Mission St; adult/student $7/5, 'pay what you wish' first Tue of month; ☺11am-5pm Tue-Sun; ☻) Comics fans need no introduction to the museum founded on a grant from Bay Area cartoon legend Charles M Schultz (of *Peanuts* fame). International and noteworthy local talent includes longtime Haight resident R Crumb and East Bay graphic novelists Daniel Clowes *(Ghostworld)*, Gene Yang *(American Born Chinese)* and Adrian Tomine *(Optic Nerve)*. Lectures and openings are rare opportunities to mingle with comics legends, Pixar studio heads and obsessive collectors.

Museum of the African Diaspora   MUSEUM
(MoAD; Map p70; ☑415-358-7200; www.moadsf.org; 685 Mission; adult/student $10/5; ☺11am-6pm Wed-Sat, noon-5pm Sun; ☻) An international cast of characters tell the epic story of the diaspora, from Ethiopian painter Qes Adamu Tesfaw's three-faced icons to quilts by India's Siddi community, descended from 16th-century African slaves. Themed interactive displays vary in interest and depth, but don't miss the moving video of slave narratives voiced by Maya Angelou.

Museum of Craft and Folk Art   MUSEUM
(Map p70; ☑415-227-4888; www.mocfa.org; 51 Yerba Buena Lane; adult/child $5/free; ☺11am-5pm Tue-Sun) Intricate handiwork with fascinating personal backstories, from sublime Shaker women's woodworking to contemporary Korean *bojagi* (wrapping textiles).

FREE **Catharine Clark Gallery**   GALLERY
(Map p70; ☑415-399-1439; www.cclarkgallery.com; 150 Minna St; ☺11am-6pm Tue-Sat) No material is too political or risqué at San Francisco's most cutting-edge gallery: Masami Teraoka paints geishas and goddesses as superheroines fending off wayward priests, and Packard Jennings offers instructional pamphlets for converting cities into wildlife refuges.

THE MISSION

Mission Dolores   CHURCH
(Map p92; ☑415-621-8203; www.missiondolores.org; cnr Dolores & 16th Sts; adult/child $5/3; ☺9am-4pm) The city's oldest building and its namesake, the whitewashed adobe Misión San Francisco de Asis was founded in 1776 and rebuilt in 1782 with conscripted Ohlone and Miwok labor in exchange – note the ceiling patterned after Native baskets. In the cemetery beside the adobe mission, a replica Ohlone hut is a memorial to the 5000 Ohlone and Miwok who died in 1814 and 1826 measles epidemics. The mission is overshadowed by the adjoining ornate 1913 basilica, where stained-glass windows commemorate the 21 original California missions, from Santa Cruz to San Diego.

826 Valencia   CULTURAL BUILDING
(Map p92; ☑415-642-5905; www.826valencia.com; 826 Valencia St; ☺noon-6pm; ☻) A mural by comic-artist Chris Ware graces the storefront housing this nonprofit youth writing program and purveyor of essential pirate supplies: eye patches, tubs of lard and tall tales for long nights at sea. Stop by the Fish Theater to see pufferfish immersed in Method acting. He's no Sean Penn, but as it says on the sign: 'Please don't judge the fish.' Check the website for workshops for kids and adults on scripting video games and starting up magazines, taught by industry experts.

Creativity Explored   GALLERY
(Map p92; ☑415-863-2108; www.creativityexplored.org; 3245 16th St; donations welcome; ☺10am-3pm Mon-Fri, until 7pm Thu, 1-6pm Sat) Fresh perspectives on themes ranging from superheroes to architecture by critically acclaimed, developmentally disabled artists – don't miss joyous openings with the artists, their families and fans.

Downtown San Francisco & South of Market (SoMa)

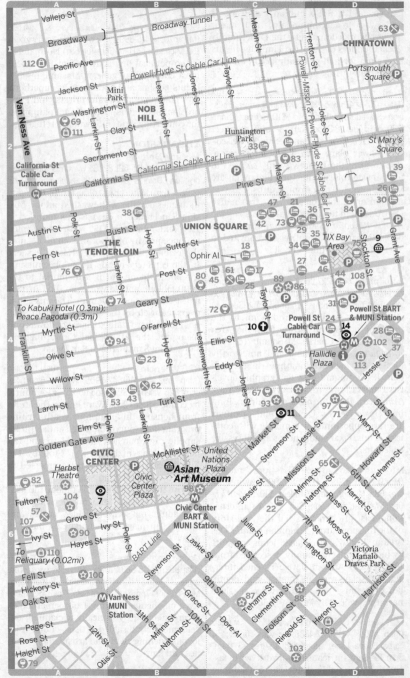

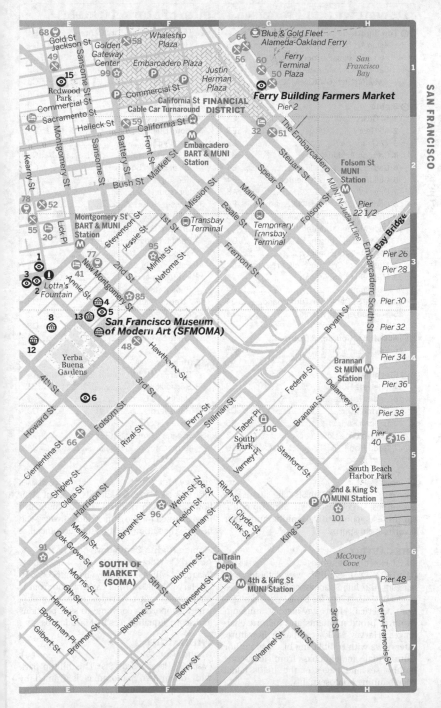

Gold St
Jackson St
68
49
Golden
Gateway
58
Whaleship
Plaza
64
Blue & Gold Fleet
Alameda-Oakland Ferry
Center
56
60
Ferry
Terminal
Plaza
San
Francisco
Bay
15
99
Embarcadero Plaza
Justin
Herman
Plaza
50
Redwood
Park
Commercial St
Commercial St
California St
FINANCIAL
DISTRICT
Ferry Building Farmers Market
40
Sacramento St
Cable Car Turnaround
Pier 2
Halleck St
59
California St
32
51
The Embarcadero
Folsom St
MUNI
Station
Embarcadero
BART & MUNI
Station
Steuart St
Pier
22 1/2
Bay Bridge
78
52
Bush St
Mission St
Beale St
Spear St
Main St
Folsom St MUNI N-Judah Line
Pier 26
55
20
Montgomery St
BART & MUNI
Station
Transbay
Terminal
Temporary
Transbay
Terminal
Pier 28
1
95
Fremont St
Embarcadero South St
Pier 30
3
41
77
Minna St
Natoma St
Pier 32
2
Lotta's
Fountain
4
85
8
13
5
San Francisco Museum
of Modern Art (SFMOMA)
Bryant St
Pier 34
Brannan
St MUNI
Station
Pier 36
12
48
Hawthorne St
Yerba
Buena
Gardens
Federal St
Pier 38
4th St
3rd St
Pier
40
16
6
Delancey St
Brannan St
Howard St
Folsom St
Rizal St
Perry St
Stillman St
Taber Pl
106
South
Park
South Beach
Harbor Park
66
Stanford St
Varney St
2nd & King St
MUNI Station
101
Clementina St
Shipley St
Clara St
Harrison St
Welsh St
Zoe St
Ritch St
Clyde St
Lusk St
King St
96
Freelon St
Brannan St
McCovey
Cove
91
Oak Grove St
Merlin St
Bryant St
Bluxome St
SOUTH OF
MARKET
(SOMA)
5th St
CalTrain
Depot
4th & King St
MUNI Station
Pier 48
Morris St
6th St
Townsend St
4th St
3rd St
Terry Francois St
Harriet St
Boardman Pl
Brannan St
Gilbert St
Bluxome St
Channel St
Berry St

Downtown San Francisco & South of Market (SoMa)

Dolores Park PARK

(Map p92; cnr Dolores & 18th Sts) The site of soccer games, street basketball, nonstop political protests, competitive tanning and other favorite local sports.

THE CASTRO

GLBT History Museum MUSEUM

(Map p92; ☎415-621-1107; www.glbthistory.org/museum; 4127 18th St; admission $5, free first Wed of month; ◷11am-7pm Tue-Sat & noon-5pm Sun-Mon) America's first gay-history museum captures proud moments and historic challenges: Harvey Milk's campaign literature, interviews with trailblazing bisexual author Gore Vidal, matchbooks from long-gone bathhouses and pages of the 1950s penal code banning homosexuality.

Harvey Milk Plaza LANDMARK

(Map p92; cnr Market & Castro Sts) A giant rainbow flag greets arrivals on Muni to this Castro plaza, named for the camera store owner who became the nation's first openly gay official.

**Human Rights Campaign
Action Center** HISTORIC SITE

(Map p92; ☎415-431-2200; www.hrc.org; 600 Castro St) Harvey Milk's former camera storefront is now home to the civil rights advocacy group, where supporters converge to sign petitions and score 'Equality' tees by Marc Jacobs.

THE HAIGHT

Alamo Square PARK

(Map p92; Hayes & Scott Sts) This hilltop park with downtown panoramas is framed by picturesque 'Painted Ladies' – the flamboyantly painted and outrageously ornamented Victorian homes that took San Franciscan liberties with the regal English style. The gingerbread-trimmed houses of Postcard Row facing the park along Steiner have been disappointingly repainted in innocuous neutrals, but stroll around the square between Steiner and Scott and you'll spot Painted Ladies with drag-diva color palettes.

Zen Center   HISTORIC BUILDING
(Map p92; www.sfzc.org; 300 Page St) Find a moment of Zen at the largest Buddhist community outside Asia, headquartered in an elegant building designed by Julia Morgan.

THE RICHMOND
California Palace of the Legion of Honor   MUSEUM
(Map p76; ☎415-750-3600; http://legionofhonor.famsf.org; 100 34th Ave; adult/child $10/6, $2 discount with Muni ticket, 1st Tue of month free; ⊙9:30am-5:15pm Tue-Sun) A nude sculptor's model who married well and collected art with a passion, 'Big Alma' de Bretteville Spreckels gifted this museum to San Francisco. Featured artworks range from Monet waterlilies to John Cage soundscapes, Iraqi ivories to R Crumb comics – part of the Legion's Achenbach Collection of 90,000 graphic artworks.

Cliff House   HISTORIC BUILDING
(Map p76; www.cliffhouse.com; 1090 Point Lobos Ave) Built by populist millionaire Adolph Sutro in 1863 as a workingman's resort, Cliff House is now in its fourth incarnation as an upscale (overpriced) restaurant. Three of the resort's attractions remain: hiking trails around the splendid ruins of Sutro Baths, wintertime views of sea lions frolicking

MISSION MURALS

Inspired by visiting artist Diego Rivera and the WPA murals and outraged by US foreign policy in Central America, Mission *muralistas* set out in the 1970s to transform the political landscape, one alley at a time. Precita Eyes (p77) restores historic murals, commissions new ones, and offers muralist-led tours. Several of the most noteworthy Mission murals can be found in three locations:

» **Balmy Alley** (Map p92; www.balmyalley.com; off 24th St) Between Treat Ave and Harrison St, historic early works transform garage doors into artistic and political statements, from an early memorial for El Salvador activist Archbishop Òscar Romero to a homage to the golden age of Mexican cinema.

» **Clarion Alley** (Map p92; btwn 17th & 18th Sts, off Valencia St) Only the strongest street art survives in Clarion, where lesser works are peed on or painted over. Very few pieces have lasted years, such as Andrew Schoultz's mural of gentrifying elephants displacing scraggly birds, and topical murals like the new one honoring the Arab Spring usually go up on the west end.

» **Women's Building** (Map p92; ☑415-431-1180; www.womensbuilding.org; 3543 18th St) San Francisco's biggest mural is the 1994 *MaestraPeace*, a show of female strength painted by 90 *muralistas* that wraps around the Women's Building, with icons of female strength from Mayan and Chinese goddesses to modern trailblazers, including Nobel Peace Prize winner Rigoberta Menchu, poet Audre Lorde and former US Surgeon-General Dr Jocelyn Elders.

on **Seal Rock,** and the **Camera Obscura** (admission $2; ☺11am-sunset), a Victorian invention projecting sea views inside a small building.

INSIDE GOLDEN GATE PARK
California Academy of Sciences   AQUARIUM, WILDLIFE RESERVE
(Map p76; ☑415-321-8000; www.calacademy.org; 55 Concourse Dr; adult/child $30/25, $3 discount with Muni ticket, 6-10pm Thu over 21s $10; ☺9:30am-5pm Mon-Sat, 11am-5pm Sun; ⓘ) Architect Renzo Piano's 2008 landmark LEED-certified green building houses 38,000 weird and wonderful animals in a four-story rainforest and split-level aquarium under a 'living roof' of California wildflowers. After the penguins nod off to sleep, the wild rumpus starts at kids'-only Academy Sleepovers and over-21 NightLife Thursdays, when rainforest-themed cocktails encourage strange mating rituals among shy Internet daters.

MH de Young Memorial Museum   MUSEUM
(Map p76; ☑415-750-3600; www.famsf.org/deyoung; 50 Hagiwara Tea Garden Dr; adult/child $10/free, $2 discount with Muni ticket, 1st Tue of month free; ☺9:30am-5:15pm Tue-Sun, until 8:45pm Fri) Follow sculptor Andy Goldsworthy's artificial fault-line in the sidewalk into Herzog & de Meuron's sleek, copper-clad building that's oxidizing to green, blending into the park. Don't be fooled by the de Young's cam-ouflaged exterior: shows here boldly broaden artistic horizons from Oceanic ceremonial masks and Balenciaga gowns to sculptor Al Farrow's cathedrals built from bullets. Access to the tower viewing room is free, and worth the wait for the elevator.

Conservatory of Flowers   GARDEN
(Map p76; ☑15-666-7001; www.conservatoryofflowers.org; Conservatory Dr West; adult/child $7/2; ☺10am-4pm Tue-Sun) Flower power is alive inside the newly restored 1878 Victorian conservatory, where orchids sprawl out like Bohemian divas, lilies float contemplatively and carnivorous plants reek of insect belches.

Strybing Arboretum & Botanical Gardens   GARDEN
(Map p76; ☑415-661-1316; www.strybing.org; 1199 9th Ave; admission $7; ☺9am-6pm Apr-Oct, 10am-5pm Nov-Mar) There's always something blooming in these 70-acre gardens. The Garden of Fragrance is designed for the visually impaired, and the California native plant section explodes with color when the native wildflowers bloom in early spring, right off the redwood trail.

Japanese Tea Garden   GARDEN
(Map p76; http://japaneseteagardensf.com; Hagiwara Tea Garden Dr; adult/child $7/5, Mon, Wed, Fri before 10am free; ☺9am-6pm; ⓘ) Mellow out

in the Zen Garden, admire doll-sized trees that are pushing 100, and sip toasted-rice green tea under a pagoda in this picturesque 5-acre garden founded in 1894.

Stow Lake
LAKE

(Map p76; http://sfrecpark.org/StowLake.aspx; paddleboats/canoes/rowboats/bikes per hr $24/20/19/8; ☺rentals 10am-4pm) Huntington Falls tumble down 400ft Strawberry Hill into the lake, near a romantic Chinese pavilion and a 1946 boathouse offering boat and bike rentals.

Ocean Beach
BEACH

(Map p76; ☏415-561-4323; www.parksconservancy. org; ☺sunrise-sunset) The park ends at this blustery beach, too chilly for bikini-clad clambakes but ideal for wet-suited pro surfers braving rip tides (casual swimmers beware). Bonfires are permitted in designated fire-pits only; no alcohol allowed. One mile south of Ocean Beach, hang-gliders leap off 200ft cliffs and shorebirds nest in defunct Nike missile silos near the parking lot of **Fort Funston** (Skyline Blvd); follow the Great Hwy south, turn right onto Skyline Blvd and the entrance to the park is past Lake Merced on the right-hand side.

🏃 Activities

Cycling & Skating

Avenue Cyclery
BICYCLE RENTAL

(Map p76; ☏415-387-3155; www.avenuecyclery. com; 756 Stanyan St; per hr/day $8/30; ☺10am-6pm Mon-Sat, to 5pm Sun) Just outside Golden Gate Park in the Upper Haight; bike rental includes a helmet.

Blazing Saddl
(Map p66; ☏41.
com; 2715 Hyde S
☺8am-7:30pm, we
this bike rental
outposts, cyclists
Bridge and take the

Golden Gate Park Bike & Skate
(Map p76; ☏415-668-
bikeandskate.com; 3038 F   …ay skates
from $5/20, bikes from $⌐⌐⌐; ☺10am-6pm; ⊕)
To make the most of Golden Gate Park, rent wheels – especially Sundays and summer Saturdays, when JFK Dr is closed to vehicular traffic. Call ahead weekdays to make sure they're open if the weather's dismal.

Wheel Fun Rentals
CYCLING, SKATING

(Map p76; ☏415-668-6699; www.wheelfunrentals. com; per hr/day skates $6/20, bikes $8/25, tandems $12/40; ☺9am-7pm) Glide around Golden Gate and dip into the Sunset on a reasonable rental. To cruise the waterfront, head to its second location in the Marina at Fort Mason.

Sailing, Kayaking, Windsurfing & Whale-Watching

Spinnaker Sailing
SAILING

(Map p70; ☏415-543-7333; www.spinnaker-sailing. com; Pier 40; lessons $375; ☺10am-5pm) Experienced sailors can captain a boat from Spinnaker and sail into the sunset, while landlubbers can charter a skippered vessel or take classes.

City Kayak
KAYAKING

(☏415-357-1010; http://citykayak.com; South Beach Harbor; kayak rentals per hr $35-65, 3hr

---

DON'T MISS

GOLDEN GATE PARK

When San Franciscans refer to 'the park,' there's only one that gets the definite article. Everything that San Franciscans hold dear is in Golden Gate Park: free spirits, free music, redwoods, Frisbee, protests, fine art, bonsai and buffalo. An 1870 competition to design the park was won by 24-year-old William Hammond Hall, who spent the next two decades tenaciously fighting casino developers, theme-park boosters and slippery politicians to transform the 1017 acres of dunes into the world's largest developed park. Sporty and not-so-sporty types will appreciate the park's range of outdoor activities, with 7.5 miles of bicycle trails, 12 miles of equestrian trails, an archery range, baseball and softball diamonds, fly-casting pools, lawn bowling greens, four soccer fields and 21 tennis courts. There are places in and around the park to rent bicycles and skates.

Park information is available from **McLaren Lodge** (Map p76; ☏415-831-2700; cnr Fell & Stanyan Sts; ☺8am-5pm Mon-Fri), and free park walking tours are organized by **Friends of Recreation & Parks** (☏415-263-0991).

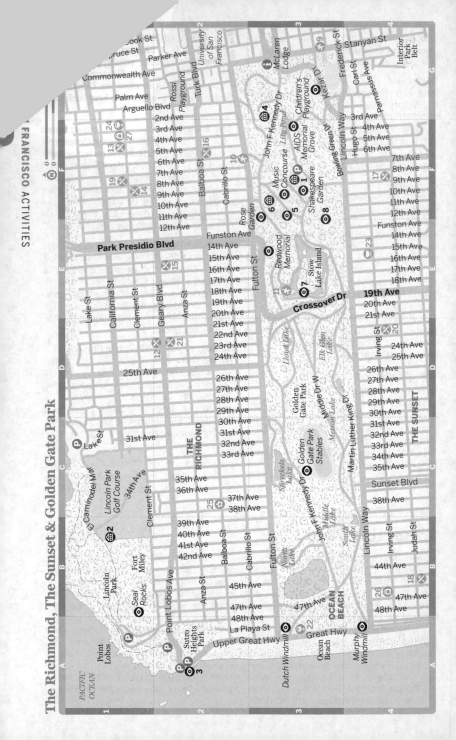

The Richmond, The Sunset & Golden Gate Park

The Richmond, The Sunset & Golden Gate P...

lesson & rental package $59, tours $65-75) Experienced paddlers hit the choppy waters beneath the Golden Gate Bridge or take a moonlit group tour, while newbies venture calm waters near the Bay Bridge.

Adventure Cat SAILING
(Map p66; ☑415-777-1630; www.adventurecat. com; Pier 39; adult/child $35/15, sunset cruise $50) Three daily catamaran cruises depart March-October; weekends only November-February.

Boardsports Kiteboarding & Windsurfing WINDSURFING
(off Map p62; ☑415-385-1224; www.boardsports school.com; 1200 Clay St; 1.5-2hr lessons $50-220;⊙by appointment) Offers kiteboarding and windsurfing rentals and lessons; experienced windsurfers take on the bay at the beach off Crissy Field. Most beginner classes are held east across the bay in Alameda.

Oceanic Society WHALE-WATCHING
(Map p66; ☑415-474-3385; www.oceanic-society. org; per person $100-120; ⊙office 8:30am-5pm Mon-Fri, trips Sat & Sun) Whale sightings aren't a fluke on naturalist-led, ocean-going weekend boat trips during mid-October through December migrations. In the off-season, trips run to the Farallon Islands, 27 miles west of San Francisco.

Spas

Kabuki Springs & Spa SPA
(off Map p66; ☑415-922-6000; www.kabukisprings. com; 1750 Geary Blvd; admission $22-25; ⊙10am-9:45pm) Soak muscles worked by SF's 43 hills in these Japanese baths for the ultimate cultural immersion experience. Men and women alternate days, and bathing suits are required on coed Tuesdays.

☞ Tours

Precita Eyes Mural Tours WALKING
(Map p92; ☑415-285-2287; www.precitaeyes.org; 2981 24th St; adult/child $12-15/5; ⊙11am, noon, 1:30pm Sat & Sun) Muralists lead two-hour tours on foot or bike covering 60 to 70 murals in a 6 to 10 block radius of mural-bedecked Balmy Alley; proceeds fund mural upkeep.

Chinatown Alleyways Tours WALKING
(Map p62; ☑415-984-1478; www.chinatownal leywaytours.org; adult/child $18/5/; ⊙11am Sat & Sun) Neighborhood teens lead two-hour tours for up-close-and-personal peeks into Chinatown's past (weather permitting). Book five days ahead or pay double for Saturday walk-ins; cash only. Tour meeting points vary.

[FREE] **Public Library City Guides** WALKING
(www.sfcityguides.org) Volunteer local historians lead tours by neighborhood and theme: Art

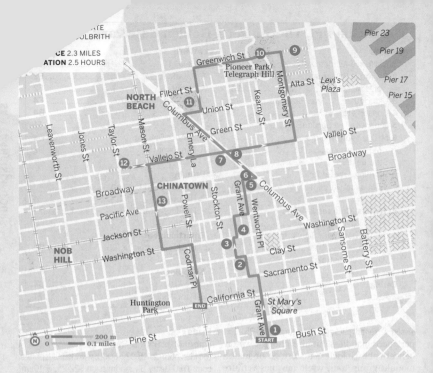

Walking Tour
San Francisco Hilltops

❭ Conquer San Francisco's three most famous hills – Telegraph, Russian and Nob – for views that are pure poetry.

Enter ❶ **Dragon Gate** and walk up dragon-lamp-lined Grant Ave to Sacramento St, where you'll turn left half a block up, then right onto ❷ **Waverly Place**, where prayer flags grace painted temple balconies. At Clay St, jog left and right again onto ❸ **Spofford Alley**, where Sun Yat-sen plotted revolution. At the end of the block on Washington, take a right and an immediate left onto ❹ **Ross Alley**, once San Francisco's bordello street.

Turn right down Jackson to Grant, then take the right-hand turnoff from Grant onto ❺ **Jack Kerouac Alley**, where the pavement echoes Kerouac's ode to San Francisco: 'The air was soft, the stars so fine, and the promise of every cobbled alley so great...' Ahead is literary landmark ❻ **City Lights**: head upstairs to Poetry, and read one poem.

Head left up Columbus to the corner of Vallejo and stop at ❼ **Molinari**, where you can get panini sandwiches for a picnic atop Telegraph Hill. Cross Columbus, veer right one block up Vallejo and fuel up with an espresso at ❽ **Caffe Trieste**, where Francis Ford Coppola drafted his script for *The Godfather*. Walk up Vallejo and scale the steps to Montgomery St. Go left three blocks, and turn left onto cottage-lined ❾ **Greenwich Street Steps** to summit Telegraph Hill. Inside ❿ **Coit Tower**, enjoy once-controversial murals downstairs and panoramic views of the bay up top.

Head downhill, past parrot-feeding *nonnas* (Italian grandmothers) at ⓫ **Washington Square**. Turn left on Columbus, right on Vallejo, up three blocks and another picturesque stairway path to ⓬ **Ina Coolbrith Park**. Any breath you have left will be taken away by sweeping views to Alcatraz. Summit your last hill of the day the easy way: catch the ⓭ **Mason-Powell Cable Car** up Nob Hill.

ALCATRAZ

Almost 150 years before Guantanamo, a rocky island in the middle of San Francisco Bay became the nation's first military prison: **Alcatraz** (Map p58; ☎415-981-7625; www.alcatrazcruises.com, www.nps.gov/alcatraz; adult/child day $26/16, night $33/19.50; ☺call center 8am-7pm, ferries depart Pier 33 every 30min 9am-3:55pm, plus 6:10pm & 6:45pm). Civil War deserters were kept in wooden pens along with Native American 'unfriendlies,' including 19 Hopis who refused to send their children to government boarding schools where Hopi religion and language were banned.

In 1934 the Federal Bureau of Prisons took over Alcatraz to make a public example of bootleggers and other gangsters. 'The Rock' only averaged 264 inmates, but its A-list criminals included Chicago crime boss Al Capone, Harlem poet-mafioso 'Bumpy' Johnson, and Morton Sobell, found guilty of Soviet espionage along with Julius and Ethel Rosenberg. Though Alcatraz was considered escape-proof, in 1962 the Anglin brothers and Frank Morris floated away on a makeshift raft and were never seen again.

Since importing guards and supplies cost more than putting up prisoners at the Ritz, the prison was closed in 1963. Native American leaders occupied the island from 1969–71 to protest US occupation of Native lands; their standoff with the FBI is commemorated in a dockside museum and 'This is Indian Land' water-tower graffiti.

Ferries depart for Alcatraz behind the Pier 33 ticket booth, but book tickets online at least two weeks ahead in summer. Day visits include captivating audio tours with prisoners and guards recalling cellhouse life, while popular, creepy twilight tours are led by park rangers.

Deco Marina, Gold Rush Downtown, Pacific Heights Victorians, North Beach by Night and more. See website for upcoming tours.

Haight-Ashbury Flower Power Walking Tour
WALKING
(Map p85; ☎415-863 1621; www.haightashburytour.com; adult/under 9yr $20/free; ☺9:30am Tue & Sat, 2pm Thu, 11am Fri) Take a long, strange trip through 12 blocks of hippie history, following in the steps of Jimi, Jerry and Janis – if you have to ask for last names, you really need this tour, man. Tours meet at the corner of Stanyan and Waller Sts and last about two hours; reservations required. Meeting points vary.

Victorian Home Walk
WALKING
(Map p70; ☎415-252-9485; www.victorianwalk.com; Westin St Francis Hotel, cnr Powell & Post Sts; per person $25; ☺11am) Learn to tell your Queen Annes from your Sticks with prime examples in Pacific Heights. Tours last about 2½ hours; meeting points vary.

🎊 Festivals & Events

February
Lunar New Year
CULTURAL
(www.chineseparade.com) Firecrackers, legions of tiny-tot martial artists and a 200ft dancing dragon make this parade at the end of February the highlight of San Francisco winters.

April & May
Cherry Blossom Festival
CULTURAL
(www.nccbf.org) Celebrate spring mid-April with scrumptious food-stall yakitori, raucous taiko drums and origami flower kits from the street crafts fair.

San Francisco International Film Festival
FILM
(www.sffs.org) Pace yourself: the nation's longest-running film fest is a marathon event, with 325 films, 200 directors and sundry actors and producers over two weeks from late April.

Bay to Breakers
QUIRKY
(www.baytobreakers.com; race registration $44-48) Run costumed or naked from Embarcadero to Ocean Beach the third Sunday in May, while joggers dressed as salmon run upstream.

Carnaval
CULTURAL
(www.carnavalsf.com) Shake your tail feathers through the Mission on Memorial Day weekend in late May.

June
Other towns have a gay day, but SF goes all out for **Pride Month**, better known elsewhere as the month of June.

ⓘ DEALS AND HIDDEN COSTS

San Francisco is the birthplace of the boutique hotel, offering stylish rooms for a price: $100 to $200 rooms midrange, plus 15.5% hotel tax (hostels exempt) and $35-50 for overnight parking. For vacancies and deals, check San Francisco Visitor Information Center's **reservation line** (☎800-637-5196, 415-391-2000; www.onlyinSanFrancisco.com), **Bed & Breakfast SF** (☎415-899-0060; www.bbsf.com) and **Lonely Planet** (http://hotels. lonelyplanet.com).

Gay and Lesbian Film Festival   FILM
(www.frameline.org) Here, queer and ready for a premiere: the world's oldest, biggest GLBT film fest launches new talents from 30 countries, with 200 film screenings over the last half of June.

Dyke March & Pink Saturday   PARADE
(www.dykemarch.org & www.sfpride.org) Around 50,000 lesbian, bisexual and transgender women converge in Dolores Park at 7:30pm and head to Castro St to show some coed Pride at the Pink Saturday street party on the last Saturday in June.

Lesbian, Gay, Bisexual and Transgender Pride Parade   PARADE
(www.sfpride.org) No one does Pride like San Francisco on the last Sunday in June: 1.2 million people, seven stages, tons of glitter, ounces of bikinis and more queens for the day than anyone can count.

September

SF Shakespeare Fest   CULTURAL
(www.sfshakes.org; ⏰7:30pm Sat, 2:30pm Sun) The play's the thing in the Presidio, outdoors and free of charge on sunny September weekends.

Folsom Street Fair   QUIRKY
(www.folsomstreetfair.com) Enjoy public spankings for local charities on the last Sunday in September. To answer the obvious question in advance: yes, people do actually get pierced there, but it's best not to stare unless you're prepared to strip down and compare.

October & November

Jazz Festival   MUSIC
(www.sfjazz.org) Old schoolers and hot new talents jam around the city in late October.

Litquake   CULTURAL
(www.litquake.org) Authors tell stories at the biggest lit fest in the West and spill trade secrets over drinks at the legendary Lit Crawl during the second week in October.

Hardly Strictly Bluegrass   MUSIC
(www.strictlybluegrass.com) SF celebrates Western roots with three days of free Golden Gate Park concerts and headliners ranging from Elvis Costello to Gillian Welch in early October.

Día de los Muertos   CULTURAL
(Day of the Dead; www.dayofthedeadsf.org) Zombie brides, Aztec dancers and toddler Frida Kahlos with drawn-on unibrows lead the parade honoring the dead down 24th St on November 2.

🛏 Sleeping

UNION SQUARE

TOP CHOICE **Orchard Garden Hotel**   BOUTIQUE HOTEL $$
(Map p70; ☎415-399-9807; www.theorchardgardenhotel.com; 466 Bush St; r $179-249;❄@🖵) SF's first all-green-practices hotel has soothingly quiet rooms with luxe touches, like Egyptian-cotton sheets, plus an organic rooftop garden.

Hotel Rex   BOUTIQUE HOTEL $$
(Map p70; ☎415-433-4434; www.jdvhotels.com; 562 Sutter St; r $169-279; P❄@🖵) Noir-novelist chic, with 1920s literary lounge and compact rooms with hand-painted lampshades, local art and sumptuous beds piled with down pillows.

🖋 **Hotel Palomar**   BOUTIQUE HOTEL $$$
(Map p70; ☎415-348-1111, 866-373-4941; www. hotelpalomar-sf.com; 12 4th St; r $199-299; ❄@🖵) The sexy Palomar is decked out with crocodile-print carpets, chocolate-brown wood and cheetah-print robes in the closet. Beds have feather-light down comforters and Frette linens, and there's floor space for in-room yoga (request mats and DVD at check-in). Smack downtown, but rooms have soundproof windows.

Hotel Triton
BOUTIQUE HOTEL **$$**

(Map p70; ☑415-394-0500, 800-800-1299; www.hotel-tritonsf.com; 342 Grant Ave; r $169-239; ❋@⊚) The lobby looks straight out of a comic book, and rooms are whimsically designed and ecofriendly; least-expensive rooms are tiny and celeb suites are named after Carlos Santana and Jerry Garcia. Don't miss tarot-card readings and chair massages during nightly happy hour.

Hotel Abri
BOUTIQUE HOTEL **$$**

(Map p70; ☑415-392-8800, 866-823-4669; www.hotel-abri.com; 127 Ellis St; r $149-229; ❋@⊚) Snazzy boutique hotel with bold black-and-tan motifs and ultra-mod cons: iPod docking stations, pillow-top beds, flat-screen TVs and rainfall showerheads.

Hotel des Arts
QUIRKY **$$**

(Map p70; ☑415-956-3232; www.sfhoteldesarts.com; 447 Bush St; r $139-199, without bath $99-149; ⊚) A budget hotel for art freaks, with specialty rooms painted by underground artists – it's like sleeping inside an art installation. Standard rooms are less exciting, but clean and good value; bring earplugs.

White Swan Inn
BOUTIQUE HOTEL **$$**

(Map p70; ☑415-775-1755, 800-999-9570; www.jdvhotels.com; 845 Bush St; r $159-199; P@⊚) An English country inn downtown, with cabbage-rose wallpaper, red-plaid flannel bedspreads and colonial-style furniture. Hipsters may find it stifling, but if you love Tudor style, you'll feel right at home. Every room has a gas fireplace.

Hotel Adagio
BOUTIQUE HOTEL **$$**

(Map p70; ☑415-775-5000, 800-228-8830; www.thehoteladagio.com; 550 Geary St; r $159-249; ❋@⊚) Huge rooms set the Adagio apart, along with the snappy style; chocolate-brown and off-white leather furnishings with bright-orange splashes. Sumptuous beds have Egyptian-cotton sheets and feather pillows; bathrooms are disappointing. Still, it's a hot address for a fair price – great bar, too.

Westin St Francis Hotel
HISTORIC HOTEL **$$$**

(Map p70; ☑415-397-7000, 800-228-3000; www.westin.com; 335 Powell St; r $209-369; ❋@⊚) One of the city's most famous hotels, the St Francis lords over Union Sq. Tower rooms have stellar views, but feel generic; we prefer the original building's old-fashioned charm, with its high ceilings and crown moldings. The Westin's beds set the industry standard for comfort.

Hotel Frank
BOUTIQUE HOTEL **$$**

(Map p70; ☑415-986-2000, 800-553-1900; www.hotelfranksf.com; 386 Geary St; r $169-299; ❋⊚) A block off Union Square, Frank has a snappy, swinging design aesthetic, with big black-and-white houndstooth rugs and faux-alligator headboards. The baths are tight, but extras like plasma-screen TVs compensate.

Larkspur Hotel
BOUTIQUE HOTEL **$$**

(Map p70; ☑415-421-2865, 866-823-4669; www.larkspurhotelunionsquare.com; 524 Sutter St; r $169-199; @⊚) Built in 1915 and overhauled in 2008, the understatedly fancy Larkspur has a monochromatic, earth-tone color scheme and simple, clean lines. Baths are tiny but have fab rainfall showerheads.

Golden Gate Hotel
HOTEL **$$**

(Map p70; ☑415-392-3702, 800-835-1118; www.goldengatehotel.com; 775 Bush St; r $165, without bath $105; @⊚) A homey Edwardian hotel with kindly owners, homemade cookies and a cuddly cat, safely uphill from the Tenderloin. Most rooms have private baths, some with clawfoot tubs.

Petite Auberge
B&B **$$**

(Map p70; ☑415-928-6000, 800-365-3004; www.jdvhotels.com; 863 Bush St; r $169-219; ⊚) French provincial charmer; some rooms have fireplaces.

Stratford Hotel
HOTEL **$**

(Map p70; ☑415-397-7080; hotelstratford.com; 242 Powell St; r incl breakfast $89-149; @⊚) Simple, smallish, clean rooms with rainfall showers; request rooms facing away from clanging Powell St cable cars.

Kensington Park Hotel
BOUTIQUE HOTEL **$$$**

(Map p70; ☑415-788-6400; www.kensingtonparkhotel.com; 450 Post St; r $189-269; ❋@⊚) Stellar location for shopping trips; great beds, stylish rooms.

Andrews Hotel
HOTEL **$$**

(Map p70; ☑415-563-6877, 800-926-3739; www.andrewshotel.com; 624 Post St; r incl breakfast $109-199; ⊚) Folksy character, great rates, good location.

Inn at Union Square
HOTEL **$$$**

(Map p70; ☑415-397-3510, 800-288-4346; www.unionsquare.com; 440 Post St; r $229-289; ste

$309-359; ✳@☎) Quiet, conservative elegance steps from Union Sq.

Hotel Union Square
HOTEL $$

(Map p70; ☑415-397-3000, 800-553-1900; www.hotelunionsquare.com; 114 Powell St; r $150-220; ✳@☎) Swank design touches such as concealed lighting, mirrored walls and plush fabrics complement the original brick walls, compensating for small, dark rooms. Convenient location near public transport; not all rooms have air-con.

Adelaide Hostel
HOSTEL $

(Map p70; ☑415-359-1915, 877-359-1915; www.adelaidehostel.com; 5 Isadora Duncan Lane; dm $30-35, r $70-90, incl breakfast; @☎) The 22-room Adelaide sets the standard for SF hostels, with up-to-date furnishings, marble-tiled bathrooms and optional $5 dinners and group activities. Private rooms may be in the nearby Dakota or Fitzgerald Hotels; request the Fitzgerald.

USA Hostels
HOSTEL $

(Map p70; ☑415-440-5600, 877-483-2950; www.usahostels.com; 711 Post St; dm $30-34, r $73-83; ☎) Built in 1909, this former hotel was recently converted into a spiffy hostel with great service. Private rooms sleep 3-4; on-site cafe serves inexpensive cafeteria-style dinners.

FINANCIAL DISTRICT
Palace Hotel
HISTORIC HOTEL $$$

(Map p70; ☑415-512-1111, 800-325-3535; www.sfpalace.com; 2 New Montgomery St; r $199-329; ✳@☎✖) The landmark Palace stands as a monument to turn-of-the-20th-century grandeur, aglow with century-old Austrian crystal chandeliers. Cushy (if staid) accommodations cater to expense-account travelers, but prices drop weekends. Even if you're not staying here, drop into the opulent Garden Court to sip tea.

✎ Galleria Park
BOUTIQUE HOTEL $$

(Map p70; ☑415-781-3060, 800-738-7477; www.jdvhotels.com; 191 Sutter St; r $189-229; ✳@☎) A restyled 1911 hotel with contemporary art, Frette linens, high-end bath amenities, free evening wine hour, and – most importantly – good service. Rooms on Sutter St are noisier, but get more light; interior rooms are quietest.

Pacific Tradewinds Guest House
HOSTEL $

(Map p70; ☑415-433-7970, 888-734-6783; www.Sanfranciscohostel.org; 680 Sacramento St; dm $29.50; @☎) San Francisco's smartest-looking all-dorm hostel has a blue-and-white nautical theme, fully equipped kitchen and spotless glass-brick showers. The nearest BART station is Embarcadero, and you'll have to haul your bags up four flights – but service is terrific.

CIVIC CENTER & THE TENDERLOIN
Phoenix Motel
MOTEL $$

(Map p70; ☑415-776-1380, 800-248-9466; www.jdvhospitality.com; 601 Eddy St; r $119-169 incl breakfast; P☎✖) The city's rocker crash pad draws artists and hipsters to a vintage-1950s motor lodge with tropical décor in the gritty Tenderloin. Check out the shrine to actor Vincent Gallo, opposite Room 43, and happening lounge Chambers. Bring earplugs. Parking is free, as is weekday admission to Kabuki Springs & Spa (p77).

HI San Francisco City Center
HOSTEL $

(Map p70; ☑415-474-5721; www.sfhostels.com; 685 Ellis St; dm incl breakfast $25-30, r $85-100; @☎) A converted seven-story 1920s apartment building, this hostel sports 262 beds and 11 private rooms, all with private baths. The neighborhood is grim, but cheap eats and good bars are nearby.

NORTH BEACH
TOP CHOICE Hotel Bohème
BOUTIQUE HOTEL $$

(Map p62; ☑415-433-9111; www.hotelboheme.com; 444 Columbus Ave; r $174-194; @☎) Like a love letter to the jazz era, the Bohème has moody 1950s orange, black and sage-green color schemes. Inverted Chinese umbrellas hang from ceilings and photos from the Beat years decorate the walls. Rooms are smallish, and some front on noisy Columbus Ave, but the hotel is smack in the middle of North Beach's vibrant street scene.

San Remo Hotel
HOTEL $

(Map p66; ☑415-776-8688, 800-352-7366; www.sanremohotel.com; 2237 Mason St; d $65-99; @☎) One of the city's best values, the 1906 San Remo has old-fashioned charm. Rooms are simply done with mismatched turn-of-the-century furnishings, and all share bathrooms. Note: least-expensive rooms have windows onto the corridor, not the outdoors; no elevator.

Washington Square Inn
B&B $$$

(Map p62; ☑415-981-4220, 800-388-0220; www.wsisf.com; 1660 Stockton St; r $179-329 incl breakfast; @☎) On a leafy, sun-dappled park, this European-style inn has tasteful rooms and a few choice antiques, including carved-wooden armoires; least-expensive rooms are tiny. Wine and cheese each evening, and breakfast in bed.

FISHERMAN'S WHARF

TOP CHOICE Argonaut Hotel HOTEL $$$
(Map p66; ✆415-563-0800, 866-415-0704; www.argonauthotel.com; 495 Jefferson St; r $205-325; P❋🐾🛜📶) Built as a cannery in 1908, the nautical-themed Argonaut has century-old wooden beams, exposed brick walls, and porthole-shaped mirrors. All rooms have ultra-comfy beds and CD players, but some are tiny and get limited sunlight; pay extra for mesmerizing bay views.

Tuscan Inn HOTEL $$
(Map p66; ✆415-561-1100, 800-648-4626; www.tuscaninn.com; 425 North Point St; r $169-279; P❋🐾🛜📶) Way more character than the Wharf's other tourist hotels, with bold colors and mixed patterns – who says stripes and checks don't match? Managed by fashion-forward Kimpton Hotels, with character, spacious rooms, in-room Nintendo and wine hour for parents.

HI San Francisco Fisherman's Wharf HOSTEL $
(Map p66; ✆415-771-7277; www.sfhostels.com; Bldg 240, Fort Mason; dm $25-30, r $65-100; P🐾🛜📶) Trade downtown convenience for a lush, green setting. Dorms range from four to 22 beds; some are coed. No curfew, and no heat on during the day in winter: bring warm clothes. Limited free parking.

NOB HILL

Huntington Hotel LUXURY HOTEL $$$
(Map p70; ✆415-474-5400, 800-227-4683; www.huntingtonhotel.com; 1075 California St; r from $325; ❋@🛜🏊) The go-to address of society ladies who prefer the comfort of tradition over the garishness of style. Book a refurbished room and an appointment at on-site Nob Hill Spa, one of the city's best.

Fairmont HISTORIC HOTEL $$$
(Map p70; ✆415-772-5000, 800-441-1414; www.fairmont.com; 950 Mason St; r $219-339; ❋@🛜) The historic lobby is decked out with crystal chandeliers and towering yellow-marble columns, and rooms are comfortably business-class; for maximum character, book a room in the original 1906 building. Tower rooms have stupendous views, but look generic.

Nob Hill Hotel HOTEL $$
(Map p70; ✆415-673-6080; www.nobhillinn.com; 1000 Pine St; r $125-165, ste $195-275; 🛜) A 1906 hotel dressed up in Victorian style, with brass beds and floral-print carpet. The look borders on grandma-lives-here, but it's definitely not cookie cutter. Rooms on Hyde St are loud; book in back. Friendly service. Wi-fi in lobby.

JAPANTOWN & PACIFIC HEIGHTS

Kabuki Hotel HOTEL $$
(off Map p70; ✆415-922-3200, 800-333-3333; www.radisson.com; 1625 Post St; r $189-249; ❋@🛜) Shoji (rice-paper) screens, platform beds, deep Japanese soaking tubs and adjoining showers liven up boxy '60s architecture. Bonuses: bonsai garden and free weekday passes to Kabuki Springs & Spa (p77).

Hotel Tomo HOTEL $$
(of Map p66; ✆415-921-4000, 888-822-8666; www.jdvhotels.com/tomo; 1800 Sutter St; r $119-189; P❋@🛜📶) Japanese pop culture makes a splash in minimalist, blond-wood rooms that look like cool college dorms, with *anime* murals and beanbags.

Hotel Majestic HOTEL $$
(Map p66; ✆415-441-1100, 800-869-8966; www.thehotelmajestic.com; 1500 Sutter St; r $100-175; @🛜) Traditional elegance c 1902, with Chinese porcelain lamps beside triple-sheeted beds. Standard rooms are small and need updating, but good value; don't miss the clubby lobby bar.

Queen Anne Hotel B&B $$
(Map p66; ✆415-441-2828, 800-227-3970; www.queenanne.com; 1590 Sutter St; r incl breakfast

$123-169, ste $203-255; (P@☎) The Queen Anne Hotel occupies a lovely former Victorian girls' school, built in 1890, with frills galore. Comfortable (if sometimes tiny) rooms are antique-filled; some have wood-burning fireplaces.

THE MARINA & COW HOLLOW

Hotel Del Sol   MOTEL $$
(Map p66; ☑415-921-5520; www.thehoteldelsol. com; 3100 Webster St; d $149-199; P✳@☎✜♿) A colorful, revamped 1950s motor lodge, with heated outdoor pool, board games, and family suites with bunk-beds.

Marina Motel   MOTEL $$
(Map p66; ☑415-928-1000; www.marinainn.com; 3110 Octavia Blvd; r $79-109; ☎) The Marina is a bougainvillea-bedecked 1939 motor court, offering some rooms with kitchens ($10 extra) and free parking. Request quiet rooms in back.

Coventry Motor Inn   MOTEL $
(Map p66; ☑415-567-1200; www.coventrymotorinn. com; 1901 Lombard St; r $95-145; P✳☎♿) Of the motels lining Lombard St, the generic Coventry has the highest overall quality-to-value ratio, with spacious rooms and covered parking.

SOUTH OF MARKET (SOMA)

TOP CHOICE Hotel Vitale   HOTEL $$$
(Map p70; ☑415-278-3700, 888-890-8688; www. hotelvitale.com; 8 Mission St; d $239-379; ✳@☎) Behind that skyscraper exterior is a soothing spa-hotel, with silky-soft 450-thread-count sheets and rooftop hot tubs; upgrade to bayview rooms.

Good Hotel   MOTEL $$
(Map p70; ☑415-621-7001; www.thegoodhotel.com; 112 7th St; r $109-169; P@☎✜) A revamped motor lodge that places a premium on green, with reclaimed wood headboards, light fixtures of repurposed bottles, and fleece bedspreads made of recycled soda bottles. The vibe is upbeat and there's a pool across the street and bikes for rent, but the neighborhood is sketchy.

Mosser Hotel   HOTEL $$
(Map p70; ☑415-986-4400, 800-227-3804; www. themosser.com; 54 4th St; r $129-159, with shared bath $69-99; @☎) Tiny rooms and tinier bathrooms, but with stylish details and central location.

THE MISSION

Inn San Francisco   B&B $$
(Map p92; ☑415-641-0188; www.innsf.com; 943 S Van Ness Ave; r incl breakfast $175-285, with shared bath $120-145, cottage $335; P@☎) Impeccably maintained and packed with antiques, this 1872 Italianate-Victorian mansion has a redwood hot tub in the English garden, genteel guestrooms with fresh-cut flowers and featherbeds and limited parking.

THE CASTRO

Parker Guest House   B&B $$
(Map p92; ☑415-621-3222; www.parkerguesthouse. com; 520 Church St; r incl breakfast $149-229; P@☎) SF's best gay B&B has cushy rooms with super-comfortable beds and down comforters in adjoining Edwardian mansions, plus a steam room and garden.

Belvedere House   B&B $$
(off Map p92; ☑415-731-6654; www.belvederehouse.com; 598 Belvedere St; r incl breakfast $125-190; @☎) Castro's romantic getaway on a leafy side street, with vintage chandeliers and eclectic art in six cozy rooms. Though primarily for gay guests, all are welcome – kids get child-sized bathrobes. No elevator.

Inn on Castro   B&B $$
(Map p92; ☑415-861-0321; www.innoncastro.com; 321 Castro St; r $165-195, without bath $125-155, breakfast incl; self-catering apt $165-220; ☎) A portal to the Castro's disco heyday, this Edwardian townhouse is decked out with top-end '70s-mod furnishings, and the patio has a flower-festooned private deck. Breakfasts are exceptional – the owner is a chef. Also rents out nearby apartments.

Willows   B&B $$
(Map p92; ☑415-431-4770; www.willowssf.com; 710 14th St; r $110-140; ☎) Homey comforts of a B&B, without the frills or fuss. None of the 12 rooms has a private bathroom; all have sinks. Shared kitchenette. Rooms on 14th St are sunnier and have good street views, but they're noisier. No elevator.

THE HAIGHT & HAYES VALLEY

The Parsonnage   B&B $$$
(Map p92; ☑415-863-3699, 888-763-7722; www. theparsonage.com; 198 Haight St; r incl breakfast $200-250; @☎) A 23-room Italiante-Victorian with original rose-brass chandeliers and Carrera-marble fireplaces, close to Market St. Spacious, airy rooms have oriental rugs and period antiques; some have wood-burning

The Haight

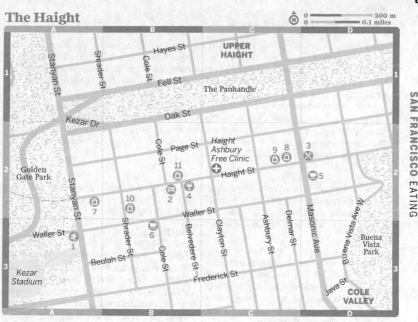

The Haight

fireplaces. Don't miss brandy and chocolates before bed.

Chateau Tivoli INN $$
(off Map p92; ☎415-776-5462, 800-228-1647; www. chateautivoli.com; 1057 Steiner St; r $140-200, r

without bathroom $100-130, ste $250-290; 🛜) The glorious turreted chateau has faded since the days when Mark Twain and Isadora Duncan visited, and rooms are modest, but the place is full of soul, character and – rumor has it – the ghost of a Victorian opera diva. Wi-fi in lobby.

Red Victorian QUIRKY $$
(Map p85; ☎415-864-1978; www.redvic.net; 1665 Haight St; r $149-229, without bath $89-129, incl breakfast; 🛜) The '60s live on at the tripped-out Red Vic. The 18 rooms have themes such as Sunshine, Flower Children and the Summer of Love; only four have baths, but all come with breakfast in the organic cafe. Wi-fi in the lobby; no elevator.

Metro Hotel HOTEL $
(Map p92; ☎415-861-5364; www.metrohotelsf.com; 319 Divisadero St; r $76-120; 🛜) No-frills rooms in the center of The Haight, with good pizza and a garden downstairs and bars and shopping just outside. Rooms in back are quietest.

✕ Eating
THE EMBARCADERO

Slanted Door VIETNAMESE, CALIFORNIAN $$
(Map p70; ☎415-861-8032; www.slanteddoor.com; 1 Ferry Bldg; lunch/dinner mains $13-24/$18-36; ⊙lunch & dinner) California ingredients, Con-

SF MEALS AND DEALS

Hope you're hungry – there are 10 times more restaurants per capita in San Francisco than in any other US city. Check out the recommendations below and foodie sites such as **www.chowhound.com** and **http://sf.eater.com**, then scan for deals at **www.black boardeats.com** and **www.opentable.com** – and since SF's top restaurants are quite small, reserve now.

Prices are often more reasonable than you might expect for organic, sustainable fare, though you might notice some restaurants now tack on a 4% surcharge to cover city-mandated healthcare for SF food workers – a tacky way to pass along basic business costs, especially for upscale restaurants. Factor in 9.5% tax on top of your meal price, plus a tip ranging from 15% to 25%.

tinental influences and Vietnamese flair with a sparkling bay outlook, from award-winning chef/owner Charles Phan. Reserve ahead or picnic on takeout from the Open Door stall.

Hog Island Oyster Company SEAFOOD $$
(Map p70; 415-391-7117; www.hogislandoysters. com; 1 Ferry Bldg; oyster samplers $15-30; 11:30am-8pm Mon-Fri, 11am-6pm Sat & Sun) Sustainably farmed, local Tomales Bay oysters served raw or cooked to perfection, with superb condiments and a glass of Sonoma bubbly. From 5pm to 7pm on Mondays and Thursdays, oysters are half-price and pints are $4.

Mijita MEXICAN $
(Map p70; 415-399-0814; www.mijitasf.com; No 44, 1 Ferry Bldg; small plates $2-9; 10am-7pm Mon-Wed, to 8pm Thu-Sat, 10am-4pm Sun;) Sustainable fish tacos reign supreme and *agua fresca* (fruit punch) is made with fresh juice at chef Traci des Jardins' thoughtful tribute to her Mexican grandmother's cooking, with bay views to be savored from your leather stool.

Boulette's Larder CALIFORNIAN $$
(Map p70; 415-399-1155; www.bouletteslarder. com; 1 Ferry Bldg; breakfast $7.50-16.50, lunch $9-20, brunch $7-22; breakfast Mon-Fri, lunch Mon-Sat, brunch Sun) Dinner theater doesn't get better than brunch at Boulette's communal table, amid the swirl of chefs preparing for dinner service. Inspired by the truffled eggs and beignets? Get spices and mixes at the counter.

Il Cane Rosso CALIFORNIAN $$
(Map p70; 415-391-7599; http://canerossosf.com; 1 Ferry Bldg; mains $13; breakfast, lunch & dinner) Farm-fresh breakfasts and lunches and soul-

satisfying three-course dinners for $25 from 5pm to 9pm in a Ferry Building hallway or outdoor bistro table.

UNION SQUARE
Michael Mina CALIFORNIAN $$$
(Map p70; 415-397-9222; www.michaelmina.net; 252 California St; lunch menus/dinner mains $49-59/$35-42; lunch Mon-Fri, dinner nightly) The James Beard Award winner has reinvented his posh namesake restaurant as a lighthearted take on French-Japanese cooking – there's still caviar and lobster, but also foie gras PB&J and lobster pot pie. Reservations essential, or grab bar bites and cocktails at the bar.

farmerbrown MODERN AMERICAN, ORGANIC $$
(Map p70; 415-409-3276; www.farmerbrownsf. com; 25 Mason St; mains $12-23; 6-10:30pm Tue-Sun, weekend brunch 11am-2pm) A rebel from the wrong side of the block, dishing up seasonal watermelon margaritas with a cayenne-salt rim, ribs that stick to yours and coleslaw with kick. Chef-owner Jay Foster works with local organic and African American farmers to provide food with actual soul, in a shotgun-shack setting with live funk bands.

Millennium VEGETARIAN, VEGAN $$$
(Map p70; 415-345-3900; www.millennium restaurant.com; 580 Geary St; menus $39-72; dinner;) Three words you're not likely to hear together outside these doors sum up the menu: opulent vegan dining. GMO-free and proud of it, with wild mushrooms and organic produce in succulent seasonal concoctions. Book ahead for aphrodisiac dinners and vegetarian Thanksgiving.

FINANCIAL DISTRICT
Kokkari GREEK $$$
(Map p70; 415-981-0983; www.kokkari.com; 200 Jackson St; mains $21-35; lunch Mon-Fri,

dinner nightly; 🍴) This is one Greek restaurant where you'll want to lick your plate instead of break it, with starters such as grilled octopus with lemon-oregano zing, and a lamb and eggplant moussaka rich as the Pacific Stock Exchange. Reserve ahead, or make a meal of appetizers at the bar.

Bocadillos   MEDITERRANEAN $$
(Map p70; ☎415-982-2622; www.bocasf.com; 710 Montgomery St; dishes $9-15; ⊙7am-10pm Mon-Fri, 5-10:30pm Sat) Lunchtime fine dining that won't break the bank or pop buttons, with just-right Basque bites of lamb burger, snapper ceviche with Asian pears, Catalan sausages and wines by the glass.

Gitane   MEDITERRANEAN $$
(Map p70; ☎415-788-6686; www.gitanerestaurant.com; 6 Claude Lane; mains $15-25; ⊙5:30pm-midnight Tue-Sat, bar to 1am; 🍴) Slip out of the Financial District and into something more comfortable at this boudoir-styled bistro, featuring Basque and Moroccan-inspired stuffed squash blossoms, silky pan-seared scallops, herb-spiked lamb tartare and craft cocktails.

Boxed Foods   SANDWICHES $
(Map p70; www.boxedfoodscompany.com; 245 Kearny St; dishes $8-10; ⊙8am-3pm Mon-Fri; 🍴) The SF salad standard is set here daily, with organic greens topped by tart goat cheese, smoked bacon, wild strawberries and other local treats. Grab hidden seating in back, or get yours to go to the Transamerica Pyramid redwood grove.

CIVIC CENTER & THE TENDERLOIN

TOP CHOICE **Jardinière**   CALIFORNIAN $$$
(Map p70; ☎415-861-5555; www.jardiniere.com; 300 Grove St; mains $18-38; ⊙dinner) Opera arias can't compare to the high notes hit by James Beard Award winner, Iron Chef and Top Chef Master Traci des Jardins, who lavishes braised oxtail ravioli with summer truffles and stuffs crispy pork belly with salami and Mission figs. Go Mondays, when $45 scores three market-inspired, decadent courses with wine pairings, or enjoy post-SF Opera meals in the bar downstairs.

Brenda's French Soul Food   CREOLE $
(Map p70; ☎415-345-8100; www.frenchsoulfood.com; 652 Polk St; mains $8-12; ⊙8am-3pm Sun-Tue, 8am-10pm Wed-Sat) Chef-owner Brenda Buenviaje combines Creole cooking with French technique in hangover-curing Hangtown fry (omelette with cured pork and corn-breaded

oysters), shrimp-stuffed po' boys, and fried chicken with collard greens and hot-pepper jelly – all worth inevitable waits on a sketchy stretch of sidewalk.

Saigon Sandwich Shop   VIETNAMESE $
(Map p70; ☎415-475-5698; 560 Larkin St; sandwiches $3.50; ⊙6.30am-5:30pm) Might as well order two of those roast-pork *banh mi* (Vietnamese sandwiches) with housemade pickled vegetables now, so you don't have to wait in line on this sketchy sidewalk again.

Bar Jules   CALIFORNIAN $$
(Map p92; ☎415-621-5482; www.barjules.com; 609 Hayes St; mains $10-26; ⊙6-10pm Tue, 11:30am-3pm & 6-10pm Wed-Sat, 11am-3pm Sun) Small and succulent is the credo at this dinky bistro, where the short daily menu packs a wallop of local flavor – think Sonoma duck breast with cherries, almonds and arugula, Napa wines and the dark, sinister 'chocolate nemesis.' Waits are a given, but so is unfussy, tasty food.

CHINATOWN

City View   CHINESE $
(Map p62; ☎415-398-2838; 662 Commercial St; small plates $3-5; ⊙11am-2:30pm Mon-Fri, 10am-2:30pm Sat & Sun) Take your seat in a sunny dining room and your pick from carts loaded with delicate shrimp and leek dumplings, tender black-bean asparagus and crisp Peking duck and other tantalizing, ultrafresh dim sum.

Yuet Lee   CHINESE, SEAFOOD $$
(Map p62; ☎415-982-6020; 1300 Stockton St; ⊙11am-3am Wed-Mon; 🌶) That brash fluorescent lighting isn't especially kind on dates, but if you're willing to share Yuet Lee's legendary crispy salt-and-pepper crab or smoky-sweet roast duck with your booth mate, it must be love.

House of Nanking   CHINESE $$
(Map p62; ☎415-421-1429; 919 Kearny St; starters $5-8, mains $9-15; ⊙11am-10pm Mon-Fri, noon-10pm Sat, noon-9pm Sun) Bossy service with bravura cooking. Supply the vaguest outlines for your dinner – maybe seafood, nothing deep-fried, perhaps some greens – and within minutes you'll be devouring pan-seared scallops, sautéed pea shoots and garlicky noodles.

NORTH BEACH

TOP CHOICE **Coi**   CALIFORNIAN $$$
(Map p62; ☎415-393-9000; http://coirestaurant.com; 373 Broadway; set menu $145 per person;

TOP 5 SF FARMERS MARKETS

» **Fancy foods** Ferry Building (www.cuesa.org) showcases California-grown, organic produce, artisan meats and gourmet prepared foods at moderate-to premium prices at markets held Tuesday, Thursday and Saturday mornings year-round.

» **Best value and selection** City-run Alemany (www.sfgov.org/site/alemany) has offered bargain prices on local and organic produce every Saturday year-round since 1943, plus stalls with ready-to-eat foods.

» **Most convenient** Sundays and Wednesdays from 7am to 5pm in UN Plaza, Heart of the City (www.hocfarmersmarket.org) offers local produce (some organics) at good prices and prepared-food stalls for downtown lunches at UN Plaza, which on other days is an obstacle course of skateboarders, Scientologists and raving self-talkers, plus a few crafts stalls.

» **Best for families** Inner Sunset (parking lot btwn 8th & 9th Ave, off Irving St; ☺9am-1pm) has local and some organic produce and artisan foods at moderate prices, plus kids' programs on Sundays April–September.

» **Best evening market** Castro farmers market (Market St at Noe St; ☺4-8pm Mar-Dec) has local and organic produce and artisan foods at moderate prices, cooking demos and live folk music.

☺6-10pm Tue-Fri, 5:30-10pm Fri & Sat; ☑) Chef Daniel Patterson's wild tasting menu featuring foraged morels, wildflowers and Pacific seafood is like licking the California coastline. Black and green noodles are made from clams and Pacific seaweed, and purple ice-plant petals are strewn atop Sonoma duck's tongue, wild-caught abalone and just-picked arugula. Only-in-California flavors and intriguing wine pairings ($95; pours generous enough for two to share) will keep you California dreaming.

Cotogna ITALIAN $$
(Map p62; ☑415-775-8508; www.cotognasf.com; 470 Pacific Av; mains $14-24; ☺noon-3pm & 7-10pm Mon-Sat; ☑) No wonder chef-owner Michael Tusk won the 2011 James Beard Award: his rustic Italian pastas and toothsome pizzas magically balance a few pristine, local flavors. Book ahead; the $24 prix-fixe is among SF's best dining deals.

Ideale ITALIAN $$
(Map p62; ☑415-391-4129; 1315 Grant Ave; ☺5:30-10:30pm Mon-Sat, 5-10pm Sun) SF's most authentic Italian restaurant, with a Roman chef that grills a mean fish and whips up gorgeous truffled zucchini – but order anything with bacon or meat and Tuscan-staff-recommend wine, and everyone goes home happy.

Liguria Bakery ITALIAN, BAKERY $
(Map p62; ☑415-421-3786; 1700 Stockton St; focaccia $3; ☺8am-1pm Mon-Fri, 7am-1pm Sat,

7am-noon Sun) Bleary-eyed art students and Italian grandmothers are in line by 8am for the cinnamon-raisin focaccia, leaving 9am dawdlers a choice of tomato or classic rosemary, and noontime arrivals out of luck.

Cinecittà PIZZA $
(Map p62; ☑415-291-8830; 663 Union St; ☺noon-10pm Sun-Thu, to 11pm Fri & Sat;☑🍴) Squeeze in at the counter for your thin-crust pie and Anchor Steam on draft with a side order of sass from Roman owner Romina. Go with the two standouts: wild mushroom with sundried tomato for vegetarians, or the omnivore's delight with artichoke hearts, olives, prosciutto and egg.

Molinari ITALIAN, SANDWICHES $
(Map p62; ☑415-421-2337; 373 Columbus Ave; sandwiches $5-8; ☺9am-5:30pm Mon-Fri, 7:30am-5:30pm Sat) Grab a number and wait your turn ogling Italian wines and cheeses, and by the time you're called, the scent of house-cured salami dangling from the rafters and Parma prosciutto will have made your choice for you.

Tony's Coal-Fired Pizza
Slice House PIZZA, SANDWICHES $
(Map p62; ☑415-835-9888; www.tonyspizzanapoletana.com; 1556 Stockton St; ☺noon-11pm Wed-Sun) Get a meatball sub or cheesy, thin-crust slice to go from nine-time world champ pizza-slinger Tony Gemignani, and take that slice to sunny Washington Square Park to savor amid wild parrots.

FISHERMAN'S WHARF

Crown & Crumpet   DESSERTS, SANDWICHES **$$**
(Map p66; ☑415-771-4252; www.crownandcrumpet.
com; 207 Ghirardelli Square; dishes $8-12; ☺10am-
9pm Mon-Fri, 9am-9pm Sat, 9am-6pm Sun; ⊛)
Designer style and rosy cheer usher teatime
into the 21st century: dads and daughters
clink teacups with crooked pinkies, Lolita
Goth teens nibble cucumber sandwiches
and girlfriends rehash dates over scones and
champagne. Reservations recommended
weekends.

In-N-Out Burger   BURGERS **$**
(Map p66; ☑800-786-1000; www.in-n-out.com; 333
Jefferson St; burgers $3-6; ☺10:30am-1am Sun-
Thu, to 1:30am Fri & Sat; ⊛) Serving burgers for
60 years the way California likes them: with
prime chuck ground onsite, fries and shakes
made with pronounceable ingredients,
served by employees paid a living wage.

RUSSIAN HILL & NOB HILL

Swan Oyster Depot   SEAFOOD **$$**
(Map p66; ☑415-673-1101; 1517 Polk St; dishes $10-
20; ☺8am-5:30pm Mon-Sat) Superior freshness
without the superior attitude of most seafood restaurants. Order yours to go, browse
nearby boutiques and breeze past the line to
pick up your crab salad and oysters with mi-
gnonette (wine and shallot) picnic.

Za   PIZZA **$**
(Map p66; ☑415-771-3100; www.zapizzasf.com;
1919 Hyde St; ☺noon-10pm Sun-Wed, to 11pm Thu-
Sat) Pizza lovers brave the uphill climb for
cornmeal-dusted, thin-crust pizza by the
slice piled with fresh ingredients, a pint of
Anchor Steam and a cozy bar setting with
highly flirtatious pizza-slingers – all for under 10 bucks.

JAPANTOWN & PACIFIC HEIGHTS

Tataki   SUSHI **$$**
(Map p66; ☑415-931-1182; www.tatakisushibar.
com; 2815 California St; dishes $12-20; ☺11:30am-
2pm & 5:30-10:30pm Mon-Fri, 5-11:30pm Sat,
5-9:30pm Sun) Rescue dinner dates and the
oceans with sensational, sustainable sushi:
silky arctic char drizzled with yuzu-citrus
and capers replaces dubious farmed salmon,
and the Golden State Roll is a local hero
with spicy line-caught scallop, Pacific tuna,
organic apple slivers and edible gold.

Out the Door   VIETNAMESE **$$**
(Map p66; ☑415-923 9575; www.outthedoors.com;
2232 Bush St; lunch/dinner mains $12-18/$18-28;
☺8am-4:30pm & 5:30-10pm Mon-Fri, 8am-3pm

& 5:30pm-10pm Sat & Sun) Stellar French beignets and Vietnamese coffee, or salty-sweet
dungeness-crab frittatas at this offshoot of
famous Slanted Door (p85). Lunchtime's rice
plates and noodles are replaced at dinner
with savory clay-pot meats and fish.

Benkyodo   JAPANESE, SANDWICHES **$**
(Map p66; ☑415-922-1244; www.benkyodocom
pany.com; 1747 Buchanan St; sandwiches $3-4;
☺8am-5pm Mon-Sat) The perfect retro lunch
counter cheerfully serves old-school egg
salad and pastrami sandwiches, plus $1
chocolate-filled strawberry and green-tea
mochi made in-house.

The Grove   AMERICAN **$**
(Map p66; ☑415-474-1419; 2016 Fillmore St; dishes
$8-12; ☺7am-11pm; ☺⊛) Rough-hewn recy-
cled wood and a stone fireplace give this
Fillmore St cafe ski-lodge coziness for made-
to-order breakfasts, working lunches with
salads, sandwiches and wi-fi, and chat sessions with warm-from-the-oven cookies and
hot cocoa.

THE MARINA & COW HOLLOW

Off the Grid   FOOD TRUCKS **$**
(Map p66; http://offthegridsf.com; Fort Mason parking lot; dishes under $10; ☺5-10pm Fri; ⊛) Some
30 food trucks circle their wagons at SF's
largest mobile-gourmet hootenanny (other
nights/locations attract less than a dozen
trucks; see website). Arrive before 6:30pm
or expect 20-minute waits for Chairman
Bao's clamshell buns stuffed with duck and
mango, Roli Roti's free-range herbed roast
chicken, or dessert from The Crème Brûlée
Man. Cash only; take dinner to nearby docks
for Golden Gate Bridge sunsets.

Blue Barn Gourmet   SANDWICHES **$**
(Map p66; ☑415-441-3232; www.bluebarngourmet.
com; salads & sandwiches $8-10; 2105 Chestnut
St; ☺11am-8:30pm Sun-Thu, to 7pm Fri & Sat; ⊛)
Toss aside thoughts of ordinary salads with
organic produce, heaped with fixings: artisan cheeses, caramelized onions, heirloom
tomatoes, candied pecans, pomegranate
seeds, even Meyer grilled sirloin. For something hot, try the toasted panini oozing with
Manchego cheese, fig jam and salami.

Greens   VEGETARIAN **$$**
(Map p66; ☑415-771-6222; www.greensrestau-
rant.com; Fort Mason Center, bldg A; mains $7-20;
☺noon-2:30pm Tue-Sat, 5:30-9pm Mon-Sat, 9am-
4pm Sun; ⊛) In a converted army barracks,
enjoy Golden Gate views, smoky-rich black

bean chili with pickled jalapeños and roasted eggplant panini. All Greens' dishes are meat-free and organic, mostly raised on a Zen farm in Marin – sure beats army rations.

A16
ITALIAN $$

(Map p66; ☎415-771-2216; www.a16sf.com; 2355 Chestnut St; pizza $12-18, mains $18-26; ⊙lunch Wed-Fri, dinner nightly) SF's James Beard Award–winning Neapolitan pizzeria requires reservations, then haughtily makes you wait in the foyer like a high-maintenance date. The housemade mozzarella burata and chewy-but-not-too-thick-crust pizza topped with kicky calamari makes it worth your while.

🖊 Warming Hut
CAFE

(off Map p66; Crissy Field; pastries $2-4; ⊙9am-5pm) When the fog rolls into Crissy Field, head here for Fair Trade coffee, organic pastries and organic hot dogs within walls insulated with recycled denim; all purchases support Crissy Field conservation.

SOUTH OF MARKET (SOMA)

TOP CHOICE Benu
CALIFORNIAN, FUSION $$$

(Map p70; ☎415-685-4860; www.benusf.com; 22 Hawthorne St; mains $25-40; ⊙5:30-10pm Tue-Sat) SF has refined fusion cuisine over 150 years, but no one rocks it quite like chef Corey Lee, who remixes local fine-dining staples and Pacific Rim flavors with a SoMa DJ's finesse. Velvety Sonoma foie gras with tangy, woodsy yuzu-sake glaze makes tastebuds bust wild moves, while Dungeness crab and black truffle custard bring such outsize flavor to faux-shark's fin soup, you'll swear there's Jaws in there. The tasting menu is steep ($160) and beverage pairings add $110, but you won't want to miss star-sommelier Yoon Ha's flights of fancy – including a rare 1968 Madeira with your soup.

Boulevard
CALIFORNIAN $$$

(Map p70; ☎415-543-6084; www.boulevardrestaurant.com; 1 Mission St; lunch $17-25, dinner $29-39; ⊙lunch Mon-Fri, dinner daily) Belle epoque decor adds grace notes to this 1889 building that once housed the Coast Seamen's Union, but chef Nancy Oakes has kept the menu honest with juicy pork chops, enough soft-shell crab to satisfy a sailor and crowd-pleasing desserts.

Zero Zero
PIZZA $$

(Map p70; ☎415-348-8800; www.zerozerosf.com; 826 Folsom St; pizzas $12-17; ⊙noon-2:30pm & 5:30-10pm Sun-Thu, to 11pm Fri & Sat) The name is a throw-down of Neapolitan pizza credentials – '00' flour is used exclusively for Naples' puffy-edged crust – and these pies deliver, with inspired SF-themed toppings. The Geary is piled with Manila clams, bacon and chillis, but the real crowd-pleaser is the Castro, turbo-loaded with house-made sausage.

Juhu Beach Club
INDIAN $

(Map p92; ☎415-298-0471; www.facebook.com/JuhuBeachClub; 320 11th St; dishes $4-8 ⊙11:30am-2:30pm Mon-Fri) SoMa's gritty streets are looking positively upbeat ever since reinvented *chaat* (Indian street snacks) popped up inside Garage Café, serving lunchtime pork vindaloo buns, aromatic grilled Nahu chicken salad, and the aptly named, slow-cooked shredded steak 'holy cow' sandwich.

Sentinel
SANDWICHES $

(Map p70; ☎415-284-9960; www.thesentinelsf.com; 37 New Montgomery St; sandwiches $8.50-9; ⊙7:30am-2:30pm Mon-Fri) Rebel SF chef Dennis Leary takes on the classics: tuna salad gets radical with chipotle mayo, and corned beef crosses borders with Swiss cheese and housemade Russian dressing. Menus change daily; come prepared for about a 10-minute wait, since sandwiches are made to order.

Split Pea Seduction
SANDWICHES $

(Map p70; ☎415-551-2223; www.splitpeaseduction.com; 138 6th St; lunches $6-9.75; ⊙8am-5pm Mon-Fri; 🖊) Right off Skid Row are unexpectedly healthy, homey soup-and-sandwich combos, including seasonal soups such as potato with housemade pesto and a signature *crostata* (open-faced sandwich), such as cambozola cheese and nectarine drizzled with honey.

THE MISSION

TOP CHOICE La Taquería
MEXICAN $

(Map p92; ☎415-285-7117; 2889 Mission St; burritos $6-8; ⊙11am-9pm Mon-Sat, 11am-8pm Sun) No debatable tofu, saffron rice, spinach tortilla or mango salsa here: just classic tomatillo or mesquite salsa, marinated, grilled meats and flavorful beans inside a flour tortilla – optional housemade spicy pickles and sour cream highly recommended.

🖊 Commonwealth
CALIFORNIAN $$

(Map p92; ☎415-355-1500; www.commonwealthsf.com; 2224 Mission St; small plates $5-16; ⊙5:30-10pm Tue-Thu & Sun, to 11pm Fri & Sat; 🖊) Califor-

VEGETARIANS: TURNING THE TABLES IN SF

San Francisco offers far more than grilled cheese and veggie burgers for vegetarians and vegans.

» **Vegan** Three organic vegan options could convert even committed carnivores: **Millennium** (p86), **Greens** (p89) and **Samovar Tea Lounge** (p99).

» **Vegetarian prix-fixe** Multicourse options featuring local, seasonal produce are offered at fancy restaurants like **Michael Mina** (p86) and **Benu** (p90).

» **Ethnic vegetarian** Omnivores veer to the vegetarian side of the menu at ethnic specialty joints like Ethiopian **Axum Café** (p94), Mexican **Pancho Villa** (p91), and Indian **Udupi Palace** (p91).

» **Vegetarian power lunches** Organic soup/salad/sandwich joints downtown offer fresh perspectives on lunch: **Boxed Foods** (p87), **Split Pea Seduction** (p90)

nia's most imaginative farm-to-table dining isn't in some quaint barn, but the converted cinderblock Mission dive where chef Jason Fox serves crispy hen with toybox carrots cooked in hay (yes, hay), and sea urchin floating on a bed of farm egg and organic asparagus that looks like a tidepool and tastes like a dream. Savor the $65 prix-fixe knowing $10 is donated to charity.

Locanda
ITALIAN $$

(Map p92; ☑415-863-6800; www.locandasf.com; 557 Valencia St; share plates $10-24; ☺5:30pm-midnight) The vintage Duran Duran Rome concert poster in the bathroom is your first clue that Locanda is all about cheeky, streetwise Roman fare. Scrumptious tripe melting into rich tomato-mint sauce is a must, piazza bianco with figs and prosciutto creates obsessions, and Roman fried artichokes and sweetbreads mean authenticity minus the airfare.

Pizzeria Delfina
PIZZA $$

(Map p92; ☑415-437-6800; www.delfinasf.com; 3611 18th St; pizzas $11-17; ☺11:30am-10pm Tue-Thu, to 11pm Fri, noon-11pm Sat & Sun, 5.30-10pm Mon; ☑) One bite explains why SF is obsessed with pizza lately: Delfina's thin crust supports the weight of fennel sausage and fresh mozzarella without drooping or cracking, while white pizzas let chefs freestyle with Cali-foodie ingredients like maitake mushrooms, broccoli rabe and artisan cheese. No reservations; sign up on the chalkboard and wait with wine at Delfina bar next door.

Range
CALIFORNIAN $$

(Map p92; ☑415-282-8283; www.rangesf.com; 842 Valencia St; mains $20-28; ☺5:30-10pm Sun-Thu, to 11pm Fri & Sat; ☑) Inspired American dining is alive and well within Range. The menu is

seasonal Californian, prices are reasonable and the style is repurposed industrial chic – think coffee-rubbed pork shoulder served with microbrewed beer from the blood-bank refrigerator.

Bi-Rite Creamery
ICE CREAM $$

(Map p92; ☑415-626-5600; http://biritecreamery. com; 3692 18th St; ice cream $3.25-7; ☺11am-10pm Sun-Thu, to 11pm Fri & Sat) Velvet ropes at clubs seem pretentious in laid-back San Francisco, but at organic Bi-Rite Creamery they make perfect sense: lines wrap around the corner for legendary salted-caramel ice cream with housemade hot fudge. For a quick fix, get balsamic strawberry soft serve at the soft-serve window (☺1-9pm).

Pancho Villa
MEXICAN $

(Map p92; ☑415-864-8840; www.sfpanchovilla. com; 3071 16th St, burritos $7-8.50; ☺10am-midnight; ☑) The hero of the downtrodden and burrito-deprived, delivering tinfoil-wrapped meals the girth of your forearm and a worthy condiments bar. The line moves fast, and as you leave the door is held open for you and your Pancho's paunch.

Udupi Palace
INDIAN $

(Map p92, ☑415-970-8000; www.udupipalaceca. com; 1007 Valencia St; mains $8-10; ☺11am-10pm Mon-Thu, to 10:30pm Fri-Sun; ☑) Tandoori in the Tenderloin is for novices – SF foodies swoon over the bright, clean flavors of South Indian *dosa,* a light, crispy pancake made with lentil flour dipped in mildly spicy vegetable *sambar* (soup) and coconut chutney.

Mission Chinese
CALIFORNIAN, CHINESE $$

(Map p92; Lung Shan; ☑415-863-2800; www. missionchinesefood.com; 2234 Mission St; dishes

The Castro & The Mission

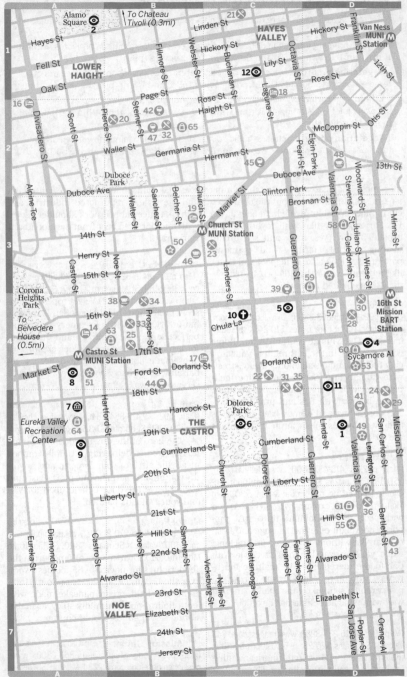

$9-16; ☺11:30am-10:30pm Mon-Tue & Thu-Sun)
Lovers of spicy food, Chinese takeout and
sustainable meat converge on this gourmet
dive. Creative, meaty mains such as tingly
lamb noodles are big enough for two – if not
for the salt-shy – and $0.75 from each main
is donated to San Francisco Food Bank.

Tartine
BAKERY $

(Map p92; ☎415-487-2600; www.tartinebakery.
com; 600 Guerrero St; pastries $2-5; ☺8am-7pm
Mon-Wed, to 8pm Thu-Sat, 9am-8pm Sun) Lines
out the door for pumpkin tea bread, Valrho-
na chocolate cookies and open-face *croques
monsieurs* (toasted ham-and-cheese sandwiches) – all so loaded with butter that you
feel fatter and happier just looking at them.

THE CASTRO

TOP CHOICE Frances
CALIFORNIAN $$

(Map p92; ☎415-621-3870; www.frances-sf.com;
3870 17th St; mains $14-27; ☺5-10.30pm Tue-Sun)
Chef and owner Melissa Perello earned a
Michelin star for fine dining, then ditched
downtown to start this market-inspired
neighborhood bistro. Daily menus showcase
bright, seasonal flavors and luxurious tex-
tures: cloud-like sheep's milk ricotta gnocchi
with crunchy breadcrumbs and broccolini,
grilled calamari with preserved Meyer lem-
on, and artisan wine served by the ounce,
directly from Wine Country.

Chilango
MEXICAN $$

(Map p92; ☎415-552-5700; chilangorestaurantsf.
com; 235 Church St; dishes $8-12; ☺11am-10pm)
Upgrade from to-go *taquerías* (Mexican
fast-food restaurants) to organic *chilango*
(Mexico City native) dishes worthy of a sit-
down dinner, including grassfed filet mignon tacos, sustainable pork carnitas and
sensational freerange chicken mole.

Starbelly
CALIFORNIAN $$

(Map p92; ☎415-252-7500; www.starbellysf.com;
3583 16th St; dishes $6-19; ☺11:30am-11pm, to
midnight Fri & Sat) Reclaimed wood décor
to match the food: market-fresh salads,
scrumptious paté, roasted mussels with
house-made sausage and juicy grassfed
burgers. Reserve ahead to lounge amid flow-
ering herbs on the heated patio, or join the
communal table.

Sushi Time
SUSHI $

(Map p92; ☎415-552-2280; www.sushitime-sf.com;
2275 Market St; rolls $4-10; ☺dinner Mon-Sat) De-
vour sashimi and Barbie, GI Joe and Hello

The Castro & The Mission

Kitty rolls in the tiny glassed-in patio like a shark in an aquarium. Happy-hour specials run from 5pm to 6:30pm.

THE HAIGHT & HAYES VALLEY

Rosamunde Sausage Grill　　SANDWICHES $
(Map p92; ☎415-437-6851; 545 Haight St; sausages $4-6; ⊙11:30am-10pm) Here's what they serve at baseball games in heaven: divine duck, spicy lamb or wild boar sausages, fully loaded with your choice of roasted peppers,

grilled onions, mango chutney or wasabi mustard, washed down with microbrews at Toronado (p99).

Axum Café　　ETHIOPIAN $
(Map p92; ☎415-252-7912; www.axumcafe.com; 698 Haight St; $7-14; ⊙dinner; 🖉) When you've got a hot date with a vegan, a marathoner's appetite and/or the salary of an activist, Axum's vegetarian platter for two is your saving grace: lip-tingling red lentils, fiery

mushrooms and mellow yellow chickpeas, scooped up with spongy *injera* bread.

Magnolia Brewpub   CALIFORNIAN $$

(Map p85; ☎415-864-7468; www.magnoliapub. com; 1398 Haight St; mains $11-20; ⊙noon-midnight Mon-Thu, until 1am Fri, 10am-1am Sat, 10am-midnight Sun) Organic pub grub and homebrew samplers keep conversation flowing at communal tables, while grass-fed Prather Ranch burgers satisfy stoner appetites in side booths – it's like the Summer of Love is back, only with better food.

THE RICHMOND

TOP CHOICE Aziza   CALIFORNIAN, NORTH AFRICAN $$

(Map p76; ☎415-752-2222; www.azizasf.com; 5800 Geary Blvd; mains $16-29; ⊙5:30-10:30pm Wed-Mon; ⊘) Mourad Lahlou's inspiration is Moroccan and his produce organic Californian, but his flavors are out of this world: Sonoma duck confit melts into caramelized onion in flaky pastry *basteeya* (savory phyllo pastry), while sour cherries rouse slow-cooked local lamb shank from its barley bed.

Namu   KOREAN, CALIFORNIAN $$

(Map p76; ☎415-386-8332; www.namusf.com; 439 Balboa St; small plates $8-16; ⊙6-10:30pm Sun-Tue, 6pm-midnight Wed-Sat, 10:30am-3pm Sat & Sun) Organic ingredients, Silicon Valley inventiveness and Pacific Rim roots are showcased in Korean-inspired soul food, including housemade kimchee, umami-rich shitake mushroom dumplings and NorCal's definitive *bibimbap:* organic vegetables, grassfed steak and Sonoma farm egg served in a sizzling stone pot.

Ton Kiang   DIM SUM $

(Map p76; ☎415-387-8273; www.tonkiang.net; 5821 Geary Blvd; dim sum $3-7; ⊙10am-9pm Mon-Thu, 10am-9:30pm Fri, 9:30am-9:30pm Sat, 9am-9pm Sun; ⊛) Don't bother asking what's in those bamboo steamers: choose some on aroma alone and ask for the legendary *gao choy gat* (shrimp and chive dumplings), *dao miu gao* (pea tendril and shrimp dumplings) and *jin doy* (sesame balls) by name.

Kabuto   CALIFORNIAN, SUSHI $$

(Map p76; ☎415-752-5652; www.kabutosushi.com; 5121 Geary Blvd; sushi $2-7, mains $9-13; ⊙dinner Tue-Sun) Innovative sushi served in a converted vintage hot-dog drive-in: nori-wrapped sushi rice with foie gras and ollalieberry reduction, *hamachi* (yellowtail) with pear and wasabi mustard, and – eureka! – the 49er

oyster with sea urchin, caviar, a quail's egg and gold leaf, chased with rare sake.

Spices   CHINESE $

(Map p76; ☎415-752-8884; http://spicesrestaurantonline.com; 294 8th Ave; mains $7-13; ⊙lunch & dinner) The menu reads like an oddly dubbed Hong Kong action flick, with dishes labeled 'explosive!!' and 'stinky!', but the chefs can call zesty pickled Napa cabbage, silky ma-po tofu and brain-curdling spicy chicken whatever they want – it's all worthy of exclamation. Cash only.

Halu   JAPANESE $

(Map p76; ☎415-221-9165; 312 8th Ave; yakitori $2.50-4, ramen $10-11; ⊙5-10pm Tue-Sat) Dinner at this surreal, snug yakitori joint covered with Beatles memorabilia feels like stowing away on the Yellow Submarine. Small bites crammed onto sticks and barbecued, including bacon-wrapped scallops, quail eggs and mochi – and if you're up for offal, have a heart.

Genki   DESSERT, SELF-CATERING $

(Map p76; ☎415-379-6414; www.genkicrepes.com; 330 Clement St; crepes $5; ⊙2-10:30pm Mon, 10:30am-10:30pm Tue-Thu & Sun, 10am-11:30pm Fri & Sat) A teen mob scene for French crepes by way of Tokyo with green-tea ice cream and Nutella, and tropical fruit tapioca bubble tea. Stock up in the beauty supply and Pocky aisle to satisfy sudden snack or hair-dye whims.

THE SUNSET

TOP CHOICE Outerlands   CALIFORNIAN $

(Map p76; ☎415-661-6140; http://outerlandssf. com; 4001 Judah St; sandwiches & small plates $8-9; ⊙11am-3pm & 6-10pm Tue-Sat, 10am-2:30pm Sun) Drift into this beach-shack bistro for organic California comfort food: lunch means a $9 grilled artisan cheese combo with seasonal housemade soup, and dinner brings slow-cooked pork shoulder slouching into green-garlic risotto. Arrive early and sip wine outside until seats open up indoors.

Nanking Road Bistro   CHINESE $

(Map p76; ☎415-753-2900; 1360 9th Ave; mains $7-12; ⊙11:30am-10pm Mon-Fri, noon-10pm Sat & Sun; ⊘⊛) Northern regional Chinese food is underrepresented in historically Cantonese SF, but the breakaway stars of Nanking Road's menu are clamshell *bao* (bun) folded over crispy Beijing duck and a definitive *kung pao* chicken lunch special ($7), with the right ratio of chili to roast peanuts.

Sunrise Deli   MIDDLE EASTERN $
(Map p76; ☑415-664-8210; 2115 Irving St; dishes $4-7; ☺9am-9pm Mon-Sat, 10am-8pm Sun; ✐) A hidden gem in the fog belt, Sunrise dishes up what is arguably the city's best smoky baba ghanoush, *mujeddrah* (lentil-rice with crispy onions), garlicky *foul* (fava bean spread) and crispy falafel, either to go or to enjoy in the old-school cafe atmosphere.

🍷 Drinking

DOWNTOWN & SOUTH OF MARKET (SOMA)

Emporio Rulli Caffè   CAFE
(Map p70; www.rulli.com; 333 Post St; ☺7:30am-7pm) Ideal people-watching atop Union Sq, with excellent espresso and pastries to fuel up for shopping, plus wine by the glass afterward.

Bar Agricole   BAR
(Map p92; www.baragricole.com; 355 11th St; 6-10pm Sun-Wed, til late Thu-Sat) Drink your way to a history degree with well-researched cocktails: Bellamy Scotch Sour with egg whites passes the test, but Tequila Fix with lime, pineapple gum, and hellfire bitters earns honors.

Sightglass Coffee   CAFE
(Map p70; http://sightglasscoffee.com; 270 7th St; ☺7am-6pm Mon-Sat, 8am-6pm Sun) San Francisco's newest cult coffee is roasted in a SoMa warehouse – follow the wafting aromas of Owl's Howl Espresso, and sample their family-grown, high-end 100% Bourbon-shrub coffee.

Bloodhound   BAR
(Map p70; www.bloodhoundsf.com; 1145 Folsom St; ☺4pm-2am) The murder of crows painted on the ceiling is definitely an omen: nights at Bloodhound assume mythic proportions with top-shelf booze served in Mason jars and pool marathons. SF's best food trucks often park out front; ask the barkeep to suggest a pairing.

House of Shields   BAR
(Map p70; 39 New Montgomery St; ☺2pm-2am Mon-Fri, from 7pm Sat) Flash back a hundred years at this recently restored mahogany bar, with original c 1908 chandeliers hanging from high ceilings and old-fashioned cocktails without the frippery.

Blue Bottle Coffee Company   CAFE
(Map p70; www.bluebottlecoffee.net; 66 Mint St; ☺7am-7pm Mon-Fri, 8am-6pm Sat, 8am-4pm Sun) The microroaster with the crazy-looking $20,000 coffee siphon for superior Fair Trade organic drip coffee is rivaled only by the bittersweet mochas and cappuccinos with ferns drawn in the foam. Expect a wait and $4 for your fix.

UNION SQUARE

Rickhouse   BAR
(Map p70; www.rickhousebar.com; 246 Kearny St; ☺Mon-Sat) Like a shotgun shack plunked downtown, Rickhouse is lined with repurposed whisky casks imported from Kentucky, and backbar shelving from an Ozark Mountains nunnery that once secretly brewed hooch. The emphasis is on bourbon, but authentic Pisco Punch (Peruvian-liquor citrus cocktail) is served in garage-sale punchbowls.

🖋Barrique   BAR
(Map p70; www.barriquesf.com; 461 Pacific Ave; ☺3pm-10pm Tue-Sat) Roll out the barrel: get your glass of high-end small-batch vino straight from the cask, directly from the vineyard. Settle into white-leather sofas in back, near the casks, with artisan cheese and charcuterie plates.

Irish Bank   PUB
(Map p70; www.theirishbank.com; 10 Mark Lane; ☺11:30am-2am) Perfectly pulled pints, thick-cut fries with malt vinegar and juicy sausages served in a hidden alleyway or church pews indoors. Irish owner Ronin bought the place from his boss, and is now every working stiff's close and personal friend.

Tunnel Top Bar   BAR
(Map p70; www.tunneltop.com; 601 Bush St; ☺Mon-Sat) Chill two-story bar with exposed beams, beer-bottle chandelier, and a balcony where you can spy on the crowd below, grooving to hip-hop. Cash only.

Cantina   BAR
(Map p70; www.cantinasf.com; 580 Sutter St; ☺Mon-Sat) Latin-inspired cocktails made with fresh juice – there's not even a soda gun behind the bar – make this a go-to bar for off-duty bartenders; DJs spin weekends.

CIVIC CENTER & THE TENDERLOIN

Hemlock Tavern   BAR
(Map p70; www.hemlocktavern.com; 1131 Polk St; ☺4pm-2am) Cheap drinks at the oval bar,

pogo-worthy punk rock in the back room, a heated smoking area and free peanuts in the shell to eat and throw at literary events.

Edinburgh Castle
BAR

(Map p70; www.castlenews.com; 950 Geary St; ⊙7pm-1am) Photos of bagpipers, the *Trainspotting* soundtrack on the jukebox, dart boards and a service delivering vinegary fish and chips in newspaper are all the Scottish authenticity you could ask for, short of haggis.

Rye
BAR

(Map p70; www.ryesf.com; 688 Geary St; ⊙5:30pm-2am Mon-Fri, 7pm-2am Sat & Sun) Polished cocktails with herb-infused spirits and fresh-squeezed juice in a sleek dark-wood setting. Come early, drink something challenging involving dark rum or juniper gin, and leave before the smoking cage overflows.

Bourbon & Branch
BAR

(Map p70; ☑415-346-1735; www.bourbonandbranch.com; 501 Jones St; ⊙Wed-Sat by reservation) 'Don't even think of asking for a cosmo' reads one of many House Rules at this revived speakeasy, complete with secret exits from its Prohibition-era heyday. For top-shelf gin and bourbon cocktails in the Library, use the buzzer and the password 'books.'

CHINATOWN

Li Po
BAR

(Map p62; 916 Grant Ave; ⊙2pm-2am) Enter the grotto doorway and get the once-over by the dusty Buddha as you slide into red vinyl booths beloved of Beats for beer or Chinese Mai Tai, made with *baiju* (rice liquor).

NORTH BEACH

TOP CHOICE Caffe Trieste
CAFE

(Map p62; www.caffetrieste.com; 601 Vallejo St; ⊙6:30am-11pm Sun-Thu, 6:30am-midnight Fri & Sat; ☜) Look no further for inspiration: Francis Ford Coppola drafted *The Godfather* here under the mural of Sicily, and Poet Laureate Lawrence Ferlinghetti still swings by en route to City Lights. With opera on the jukebox and weekend accordion jam sessions, this is North Beach at its best since 1956.

Specs'
BAR

(Map p62; 12 William Saroyan Pl; ⊙5pm-2am) A saloon that doubles as a museum of nautical memorabilia gives neighborhood characters license to drink like sailors, tell tall tales to gullible newcomers and plot mutinies against last call.

Comstock Saloon
BAR

(Map p62; 155 Columbus Ave; ⊙11:30am-2am Mon-Fri, 2pm-2am Sat) A Victorian saloon with period-perfect Pisco Punch with real pineapple gum and Hop Toads with Jamaican rum, bitters and apricot brandy – plus beef shank and bone marrow pot pie and maple bourbon cake in the adjacent restaurant.

Tosca Cafe
COCKTAIL BAR

(Map p62; http://toscacafesf.com; 242 Columbus Ave; ⊙5pm-2am Tue-Sun) Come early for your pick of opera on the jukebox and red circular booths, and stay late for Irish coffee nightcap crowds and chance sightings of Sean Penn, Bono or Robert De Niro.

NOB HILL

Bigfoot Lodge
BAR

(Map p70; ☑415-440-2355; www.bigfootlodge.com; 1750 Polk St; ⊙3pm-2am) Cure cabin fever at this log-cabin bar with happy hours in the shadow of an 8ft Sasquatch, getting nicely toasted on Toasted Marshmallows – vanilla vodka, Bailey's and a flaming marshmallow.

Top of the Mark
BAR

(Map p70; www.topofthemark.com; 999 California St; cover $5-15; ⊙5pm-midnight Sun-Thu, 4pm-1am Fri & Sat) Sashay across the dance floor and feel on top of the world overlooking SF. Cocktails will set you back $15 plus cover, but watch the sunset and then try to complain.

THE MARINA

California Wine Merchant
WINE BAR

(Map p66; www.californiawinemerchant.com; 2113 Chestnut St; ⊙10am-midnight Mon-Wed, to 1:30am Thu-Sat, 11am-11pm Sun) Pair local wines by the glass with mild flirting in this wine cave, and be surprised by the subtleties of Central Coast pinots and playboys improving their game.

MatrixFillmore
LOUNGE

(Map p66; 3138 Fillmore St; ⊙6pm-2am) The one bar in town where the presumption is that you're straight and interested. Modern and sleek, if a little sharp around the edges – and the same can be said of the crowd.

GAY/LESBIAN/BI/TRANS SAN FRANCISCO

Singling out the best places to be queer in San Francisco is almost redundant. Though the Castro is a gay hub and the Mission is a magnet for lesbians, the entire city is gay-friendly – hence the number of out elected representatives in City Hall at any given time. New York Marys may label SF the retirement home of the young – indeed, the sidewalks roll up early – but for sexual outlaws and underground weirdness, SF trounces New York. Dancing queens and slutty boys head South of Market (SoMa), the location of most thump-thump clubs. In the 1950s, bars euphemistically designated Sunday afternoons as 'tea dances,' appealing to gay crowds to make money at an otherwise slow time. The tradition now makes Sundays one of the busiest times for SF's gay bars. Top GLBT venues include:

The Stud (Map p70; ☎415-252-7883; www.studsf.com; 399 9th St; admission $5-8; ☺5pm-3am) Rocking the gay scene since 1966, and branching out beyond leather daddies with rocker-grrrl Mondays, Tuesday drag variety shows, raunchy comedy/karaoke Wednesdays, Friday art-drag dance parties, and performance-art cabaret whenever hostess/DJ Anna Conda gets it together.

Lexington Club (Map p92; ☎415-863-2052; 3464 19th St; ☺3pm-2am) Odds are eerily high you'll develop a crush on your ex-girlfriend's hot new girlfriend here over strong drink, pinball and tattoo comparisons – go on, live dangerously at SF's most famous/notorious full-time lesbian bar.

Rebel Bar (Map p70; ☎415-431-4202; 1760 Market St; admission varies; ☺5pm-3am Mon-Thu, to 4am Fri, 11am-4am Sat & Sun) Funhouse southern biker disco, complete with antique mirrored walls, Hell's Angel cocktails (Bulleit bourbon, Chartreuse, OJ) and exposed pipes. The crowd is mostly 30-something, gay and tribally tattooed; on a good night, poles get thoroughly worked.

Aunt Charlie's (Map p70; ☎415-441-2922; www.auntcharlieslounge.com; 133 Turk St; ☺9am-2am) Total dive, with the city's best classic drag show Fridays and Saturdays at 10pm. Thursday nights, art-school boys freak for bathhouse disco at Tubesteak ($5).

Endup (Map p70; ☎415-646-0999; www.theendup.com; 401 6th St; admission $5-20; ☺10pm-4am Mon-Thu, 11pm-11am Fri, 10pm Sat to 4am Mon) Home of Sunday 'tea dances' (gay dance parties) since 1973, though technically the party starts Saturday – bring a change of clothes and EndUp watching the sunrise Monday over the freeway on-ramp.

Sisters of Perpetual Indulgence (Map p70; ☎415-820-9697; www.thesisters.org) For guerrilla antics and wild fundraisers, check in with the self-described 'leading-edge order of queer nuns,' a charitable organization and San Francisco institution.

THE MISSION

TOP CHOICE Zeitgeist   BAR
(Map p92; www.zeitgeistsf.com; 199 Valencia St; ☺9am-2am) When temperatures tip over 70°F (21°C), bikers and hipsters converge on Zeitgeist's huge outdoor beer garden (minus the garden) for 40 brews on tap pulled by SF's toughest lady barkeeps and late-night munchies courtesy of the Tamale Lady.

Elixir   BAR
(Map p92; www.elixirsf.com; 3200 16th St; ☺3pm-2am Mon-Fri, noon-2am Sat & Sun) Drinking is good for the environment at SF's first certified green bar, with your choice of organic, green and even biodynamic cocktails – *ayiyi*, those peach margaritas with ancho-chili-infused tequila. Mingle over darts and a killer jukebox.

Homestead   BAR
(Map p92; 2301 Folsom St; ☺5pm-1am) Your friendly Victorian corner dive c 1893, complete with carved-wood bar, roast peanuts in the shell, cheap draft beer and Victorian tin-stamped ceiling.

Make-Out Room
BAR

(Map p92; www.makeoutroom.com; 3225 22nd St) Between the generous pours and Pabst beer specials, the Make-Out has convinced otherwise sane people to leap onstage and read from their teen journals for Mortified nights, sing along to punk-rock fiddle and flail to '80s one-hit-wonder DJ mashups.

Ritual Coffee Roasters
CAFE

(Map p92; www.ritualroasters.com; 1026 Valencia St; ⊙6am-10pm Mon-Fri, 7am-10pm Sat, 7am-9pm Sun; ☏) Cults wish they inspired the same devotion as Ritual, where lines head out the door for house-roasted cappuccino with ferns in the foam and deliberately limited electrical outlets to encourage conversation.

THE CASTRO

Café Flore
CAFE

(Map p92; 2298 Market St; ⊙7am-1am; ☏) The see-and-be-seen, glassed-in corner cafe at the center of the gay universe. Eavesdrop on blind dates with bracing cappuccino or knee-weakening absinthe.

Thorough Bread
CAFE, BAKERY

(Map p92; www.thoroughbreadandpastry.com; 248 Church St; ⊙7am-7pm Tue-Sat, to 3pm Sun) Pedigreed pastries and excellent breads from San Francisco Baking Institute chefs, plus powerful drip coffee.

Samovar Tea Lounge
TEAHOUSE

(Map p92; 498 Sanchez St; ⊙10am-11pm; ☏) Iron pots of tea with scintillating side dishes, from savory pumpkin dumplings to chocolate brownies with green-tea mousse.

The Mint
THEME BAR

(Map p92; www.themint.net; 1942 Market St; ⊙4pm-2am) Show tunes are serious stuff at karaoke sessions starting at 9pm nightly, where it takes courage and a vodka gimlet to attempt Barbra Streisand. Prepare to be upstaged by a banker with a boa and a mean falsetto.

THE HAIGHT & HAYES VALLEY

Cole Valley Café
CAFE

(Map p85; www.colevalleycafe.com; 701 Cole St; ⊙6:30am-8:30pm Mon-Fri, 6:30am-8pm Sat & Sun; ☏) Powerful coffee and chai, free wi-fi, and hot gourmet sandwiches that are a bargain at any price, let alone $6 for lip-smacking thyme-marinated chicken with lemony avocado spread or the smoky roasted eggplant with goat cheese and sundried tomatoes.

Coffee to the People
CAFE

(Map p85; www.coffeetothepeople.squarespace. com; 1206 Masonic Ave; ⊙6am-8pm Mon-Fri, to 9pm Sat & Sun; ☏☒☖) The people, united, will never be decaffeinated at this utopian coffee shop with free wireless, 3% pledged to coffee-growers' nonprofits, a radical reading library and enough Fair Trade coffee to revive the Sandinista movement.

⭐TOP CHOICE Smuggler's Cove
THEME BAR

(Map p70; http://smugglerscovesf.com; 650 Gough St; ⊙5pm-2am) Yo-ho-ho and a bottle of rum...or make that 200 at this Barbary Coast shipwreck of a tiki bar. With tasting flights and 70 historic cocktail recipes gleaned from rum-running around the world, you won't be dry-docked for long.

⭐TOP CHOICE Toronado
BAR

(Map p92; www.toronado.com; 547 Haight St; ⊙6pm-1am) Bow before the chalkboard altar listing 50 microbrews and hundreds more bottled, including spectacular seasonal microbrews. Bring cash, come early and stay late, with a sausage from Rosamunde next door to accompany seasonal ales.

Aub Zam Zam
LOUNGE

(Map p85; 1633 Haight St; ⊙3pm-2am) Arabesque arches, jazz on the jukebox and enough paisley to make Prince feel right at home pay homage to the purist Persian charm of dearly departed cocktail fascist Bruno, who'd throw you out for ordering a vodka martini.

THE RICHMOND

Beach Chalet Brewery
BREWERY

(Map p76; www.beachchalet.com; 1000 Great Hwy; ⊙9am-10pm Sun-Thu, to 11pm Fri & Sat) Brews with views: sunsets over the Pacific, a backyard bar, and recently restored 1930s WPA frescoes downstairs showing a condensed history of San Francisco.

Plough & Stars
PUB

(Map p76; www.theploughandstars.com; 116 Clement St; ⊙3pm-2am Mon-Thu, 2pm-2am Fri-Sun, showtime 9pm) The Emerald Isle by the Golden Gate. Jigs are to be expected after the first couple of rounds and rousing Irish fiddle tunes are played most nights by top Celtic talent.

THE SUNSET

Hollow
CAFE

(Map p76; http://hollowsf.com; 1493 Irving St; ⊙8am-5pm Mon-Fri, 9am-5pm Sat & Sun) Between

HOT TICKETS

Big events sell out fast in SF. Scan the free weeklies, the *San Francisco Bay Guardian* and the *SF Weekly,* and see what half-price and last-minute tickets you can find at **TIX Bay Area** (Map p70; ☑415-433-7827; Union Sq at 251 Stockton St; ⏲11am-6pm Tue-Thu, to 7pm Fri & Sat). Tickets are sold on the day of the performance for cash only. For tickets to theater shows and big-name concerts in advance, call **Ticketmaster** (☑415-421-8497) or **BASS** (☑415-478-2277).

simple explanations and Golden Gate Park, there's Hollow: cultish Ritual coffee and Guiness cupcakes served amid art-installation displays of magnifying glasses, tin pails, and monster etchings.

☆ Entertainment

Nightclubs

El Rio   CLUB
(off Map p92; ☑415-282-3325; www.elriosf.com; 3158 Mission St; admission $3-8) Free-form funky grooves worked by regulars of every conceivable ethnicity and orientation. 'Salsa Sundays' are legendary – arrive at 3pm for lessons – and other nights feature oyster happy hours, eclectic music, and shameless flirting on the garden patio.

Cat Club   CLUB
(Map p70; www.catclubsf.com; 1190 Folsom St; admission $5 after 10pm; ⏲Tue-Sun) Thursday's '1984' is a euphoric straight/gay/bi/whatever party scene from a lost John Hughes movie; other nights vary from Saturday power pop to Bondage-a-Go-Go.

AsiaSF   CLUB
(Map p70; ☑415-255-2742; www.asiasf.com; 201 9th St; $35 minimum per person; ⏲Wed-Sun) Cocktails and Asian-inspired dishes are served with a tall order of sass and one little secret: your servers are drag stars. Your hostesses rock the bar/runway hourly – but once inspiration and drinks kick in, everyone mixes it up on the downstairs dance floor. The three-course 'Menage á Trois Menu' runs $39, cocktails around $10, and honey, those tips are well-earned.

DNA Lounge   CLUB
(Map p92; www.dnalounge.com; 375 11th St; admission $3-25) SF's mega-club hosts live bands and big-name DJs. Second and fourth Saturdays bring Bootie, the kick-ass original mashup party; Monday's Goth Death Guild means shuffle-dancing and free tea service.

Harlot   CLUB
(Map p70; www.harlotsf.com; 46 Minna St; admission $10-20, free 5-9pm Wed-Fri; ⏲Wed-Sat) Aptly named after 10pm, when the bordello-themed lounge cuts loose to house Thursdays, indie-rock Wednesdays, and women-only Fem Bar parties.

111 Minna   CLUB
(Map p70; www.111minnagallery.com; 111 Minna St) Street-wise art gallery by day, after-work lounge and club after 9pm, when '90s and '80s dance parties take the back room by storm.

Live Music

☆ The Fillmore   LIVE MUSIC
(off Map p66; www.thefillmore.com; 1805 Geary Blvd; tickets from $20) Hendrix, Zeppelin, Janis – they all played the Fillmore. The legendary venue that launched the psychedelic era has the posters to prove it upstairs, and hosts arena acts in a 1250-seat venue where you can squeeze in next to the stage.

Slim's   LIVE MUSIC
(www.slims-sf.com; 333 11th St; tickets $11-28) Guaranteed good times by Gogol Bordello, Tenacious D, and AC/DShe (the hard-rocking female tribute band) fill the bill at this mid-sized club, where Prince and Elvis Costello have shown up to play sets unannounced.

Yoshi's   JAZZ
(off Map p66; www.yoshis.com; 1300 Fillmore St; tickets $12-50) San Francisco's definitive jazz club draws the world's top talent to the historic African and Japanese American Fillmore jazz district, and serves pretty good sushi besides.

Mezzanine   LIVE MUSIC
(Map p70; www.mezzaninesf.com; 444 Jessie St; admission $10-40) The best sound system in SF bounces off the brick walls at breakthrough hiphop shows by Quest Love, Method Man, Nas and Snoop Dogg, plus throwback alt-

classics like the Dandy Warhols and Psych-edelic Furs.

Warfield
LIVE MUSIC

(Map p70; www.thewarfieldtheatre.com; 982 Market St) Originally a vaudeville theater but now an obligatory stop for marquee acts from Beastie Boys and PJ Harvey to Furthur (formerly the Grateful Dead).

Great American Music Hall
LIVE MUSIC

(Map p70; www.musichallsf.com; 859 O'Farrell St; admission $12-35) Previously a bordello and a dance hall, this ornate venue now hosts rock, country, jazz and world music artists. Arrive early to stake your claim to front-row balcony seats with a pint and a passable burger.

Bottom of the Hill
LIVE MUSIC

(off Map p92; www.bottomofthehill.com; 1233 17th St; admission $5-12; ⊘Tue-Sat) Top of the list for breakthrough bands, from notable local alt-rockers like Deerhoof to newcomers worth checking out by name alone (Yesway, Strip-mall Architecture, Excuses for Skipping) in *Rolling Stone*'s favorite SF venue; cash only.

Bimbo's 365 Club
LIVE MUSIC

(Map p66; www.bimbos365club.com; 1025 Columbus Ave; tickets from $20) Anything goes behind these vintage-1931 speakeasy velvet curtains, lately including live shows by the likes of Cibo Matto, Ben Harper and Coldplay. Cash only, and bring something extra to tip the ladies' powder room attendant – this is a classy joint.

Hotel Utah
LIVE MUSIC

(Map p70; www.thehotelutahsaloon.com; 500 4th St; bar admission free, shows $5-10) Whoopi Goldberg and Robin Williams broke in the stage of this historic Victorian hotel back in the '70s, and the thrill of finding SF's hidden talents draws crowds to singer-songwriter Open Mic Mondays, indie-label debuts and local favorites like Riot Earp, Saucy Monkey and The Dazzling Strangers.

Cafe du Nord
LIVE MUSIC

(Map p92; www.cafedunord.com; 2170 Market St; admission $7-15) A 1930s downstairs speak-casy in the basement of the Swedish-American Hall serves 'em short and strong and glam-rocks, afrobeats, retro-rockabillies and indie-record-release parties almost nightly – plus pulled-on-stage performances by off-duty musicians and novelists.

Elbo Room
LIVE MUSIC

(Map p92; www.elbo.com; 647 Valencia St; admission $5-8) Funny name, because there isn't much to speak of upstairs on show nights with crowd-favorite funk, dancehall dub, and offbeat indie bands like Uni and Her Ukelele.

Rickshaw Stop
LIVE MUSIC

(Map p70; www.rickshawstop.com; 155 Fell St; admission $5-35) Noise-poppers, eccentric rockers and crafty DJs cross-pollinate hemispheres with something for everyone: bad-ass banghra nights, Latin explosion bands, lesbian disco, and mainstay Thursday 18+ Popscene.

Amnesia
LIVE MUSIC

(Map p92; www.amnesiathebar.com; 853 Valencia St) A teensy bar featuring nightly local music acts that may be playing in public for the first time, so show hardworking bands some love and buy that shy rapper a drink.

Theater

Musicals and Broadway spectaculars play at a number of downtown theaters. SHN (☑415-512-7770; www.shnsf.com) hosts touring Broadway shows at opulent Orpheum Theatre (Map p70; 1192 Market St), Curran Theatre (Map p70; 445 Geary St), and 1920s Golden Gate Theatre (Map p70; 1 Taylor St). But the pride of SF is its many indie theaters that host original, solo and experimental shows, including the following.

TOP CHOICE American Conservatory Theater
THEATER

(Map p70; ACT; ☑415-749-2228; www.act-sf.org; 415 Geary St) San Francisco's most famous mainstream venue has put on original landmark productions of Tony Kushner's *Angels in America* and Robert Wilson's *Black Rider,* with a libretto by William S Burroughs and music by the Bay Area's own Tom Waits.

Beach Blanket Babylon
COMEDY, CABARET

(Map p62; ☑415-421-4222; www.beachblanket babylon.com; 678 Green St; seats $25-78) San Francisco's longest-running comedy caba-ret keeps the belly laughs coming with giant hats, killer drag and social satire with bite. Spectators must be 21-plus, except at matinees.

Magic Theatre
THEATER

(Map p66; ☑415-441-8822; www.magictheatre.org; Fort Mason, Bldg D) Risk-taking original productions from major playwrights, including Sam Shepard, Edna O'Brien and Terrence McNally, starring actors like Ed Harris and Sean Penn, plus staged works written by teenagers.

Cobb's Comedy Club
COMEDY

(Map p66; ☎415-928-4320; www.cobbscomedy club.com; 915 Columbus Ave; admission $13-33 plus 2-drink minimum) Bumper-to-bumper shared tables make for an intimate (and vulnerable) audience for stand-up acts, from new talent to HBO's Dave Chapelle and NBC's Tracy Morgan.

Exit Theater
THEATER

(Map p70; ☎415-673-3847; http://theexit.org; 156 Eddy St; admission $15-20) Hosts the SF Fringe Festival and avant-garde productions year-round.

Intersection for the Arts
LIVE MUSIC, THEATER

(Map p92; ☎415-626-2787; www.theintersection. org; 446 Valencia; admission $5-20) Ambidextrous nonprofit art space with famous playwrights-in-residence, a major jazz showcase and a provocative upstairs gallery program since 1965.

Marsh
THEATER

(Map p92; ☎415-826-5750; www.themarsh.org; 1062 Valencia St; tickets $15-35) Choose your seat wisely: you'll spend the evening on the edge of it, with one-acts, monologues and works-in-progress that involve the audience.

Punch Line
COMEDY

(Map p70; ☎415-397-4337; www.punchlinecomedy club.com; 444 Battery St; admission $12-23, plus 2-drink minimum; ⊗Tue-Sun) Turns unknown comics into known names – Chris Rock, Ellen DeGeneres and David Cross, to name a few.

Purple Onion
COMEDY

(Map p62; ☎415-956-1653; www.caffemacaroni. com; 140 Columbus Ave; admission $10-15) Woody Allen, Robin Williams and Phyllis Diller clawed their way up from underground at this grotto nightclub, and Zach Galifianakis shot an excruciatingly funny comedy special here.

Classical Music, Opera & Dance

TOP CHOICE Davies Symphony Hall
CLASSICAL MUSIC

(Map p70; ☎415-864-6000; www.sfsymphony.org; 201 Van Ness Ave) Home of nine-time Grammy-

winning SF Symphony, conducted with verve by Michael Tilson Thomas from September to May here – don't miss Beethoven.

War Memorial Opera House
OPERA

(Map p70; ☎415-864-3330; www.sfopera. com; 301 Van Ness Ave) Rivaling City Hall's grandeur is the 1932 home to **San Francisco Opera** (www.sfopera.com) from June through December and the **San Francisco Ballet** (www.sfballet.org) from January through May. Student tickets and standing-room tickets go on sale two hours before performances.

TOP CHOICE ODC Theater
DANCE

(Map p92; ☎415-863-9834; www.odctheater.org; 3153 17th St) For 40 years, redefining dance with risky, raw performances and the sheer joy of movement with performances September through December, and 200 dance classes a week.

Cinemas

TOP CHOICE Castro Theatre
CINEMA

(Map p92; www.thecastrotheatre.com; 429 Castro St; adult/child $10/7.50) Showtunes on a Wurlitzer are the overture to independent cinema, silver-screen classics and unstoppable audience participation.

Sundance Kabuki Cinema
CINEMA

(off Map p66; www.sundancecinemas.com/kabuki. html; 1881 Post St; adult/child $10-14) Trendsetting green multiplex with GMO-free popcorn, reserved seating in cushy recycled-fiber seats and the frankly brilliant Balcony Bar, where you can slurp seasonal cocktails during your movie.

Roxie Cinema
CINEMA

(Map p92; www.roxie.com; 3117 16th St; adult/ child $10/6.50) Independent gems, insightful documentaries and rare film noir you won't find elsewhere, in a landmark 1909 cinema recently upgraded with Dolby sound.

Balboa Theater
CINEMA

(Map p76; www.balboamovies.com; 3630 Balboa St; double-features adult/child $10/7.50) Double-features perfect for foggy weather, including film fest contenders selected by the director of the Telluride Film Festival, in a renovated 1926 art deco cinema.

Sports

San Francisco Giants
BASEBALL

(Map p70; http://Sanfrancisco.giants.mlb.com; AT&T Park; tickets $5-135; ⊗season Apr-Oct)

SAN FRANCISCO FOR CHILDREN

Imaginations come alive in this storybook city, with wild parrots squawking indignantly at passersby near **Coit Tower** (p65) on Telegraph Hill and sunning sea lions gleefully nudging one another off the docks at **Pier 39** (p65). For thrills, try rickety, seatbelt-free **cable cars** (p103), or pick up a dragon kite in Chinatown souvenir shops to fly at **Crissy Field** (p67) – just be sure to bundle up for the wind. Kids will find playmates in playgrounds at **Golden Gate Park** (p57) and **Portsmouth Square** (p63).

For organized activities, try these kid-friendly attractions:

» **Children's Creativity Museum** (Map p70; ✆415-820-3320; www.zeum.org; 221 4th St; admission $10; ⏰11am-5pm Tue-Sun; 🚸) Technology that's too cool for school: robots, live-action video games, DIY music videos, and 3D animation workshops with Silicon Valley innovators. The vintage 1906 Loof Carousel out front operates until 6pm daily ($3 for two rides).

» **Aquarium of the Bay** (Map p66; www.aquariumofthebay.com; Pier 39; adult/child $17/8; ⏰9am-8pm summer, 10am-6pm winter; 🚸) Glide through glass tubes underwater on conveyer belts as sharks circle and manta rays flutter overhead.

» **Fire Engine Tours** (Map p66; ✆415-333-7077; www.fireenginetours.com; Beach St at the Cannery; adult/child $50/30; ⏰tours depart 1pm; 🚸) Hot stuff: a 75-minute, open-air vintage fire engine ride over Golden Gate Bridge.

See also: the **Exploratorium** (p66), **California Academy of Sciences** (p74), **Cartoon Art Museum** (p69), **Musée Mecanique** (p65) and **826 Valencia** (p69).

Watch and learn how the World Series is won – bushy beards, women's underwear and all. The city's National League baseball team draws crowds to AT&T Park and its solar-powered scoreboard; the Waterfront Promenade offers a free view of right field.

San Francisco 49ers FOOTBALL
(www.49ers.com; Candlestick Park; tickets from $59; ⏰season Aug-Dec) For NFL football, beer and garlic-fries, head to Candlestick Park. Lately they've been in a slump, but the '49ers are one of the most successful teams in National Football League history, with no fewer than five Super Bowl championships. Home games are played at cold and windy Candlestick Park, off Hwy 101 south of the city.

🛍 Shopping

San Francisco has big department stores and name-brand boutiques around Union Sq, including **Macy's** (Map p70; www.macys.com; 170 O'Farrell Street) and the sprawling new **Westfield Shopping Centre** (Map p70; www.westfield.com/SanFrancisco; 865 Market St; ⏰9:30am-9pm Mon-Sat, 10am-7pm Sun), but special, only-in-SF scores are found in the Haight, the Castro, the Mission and Hayes Valley (west of Civic Center).

TOP CHOICE **Adobe Books & BackRoom Gallery** BOOKS
(Map p92; http://adobebookshackroomgallery.blogspot.com; 3166 16th St; ⏰11am-midnight) Come here for every book you never knew you needed used and cheap, plus 'zine launch parties, poetry readings, and BackRoom Gallery – but first you have to navigate the obstacle course of sofas, cats, art books and German philosophy.

TOP CHOICE **Under One Roof** GIFTS
(Map p92; www.underoneroof.org; 518a Castro St; ⏰10am-8pm Mon-Sat, 11am-7pm Sun) AIDS service organizations receive 100% of the proceeds from goods donated by local designers and retailers, so show volunteer salespeople some love for raising $11 million to date.

Reliquary CLOTHING, ACCESSORIES
(off Map p70; http://reliquarysf.com; 537 Octavia Blvd; ⏰11am-7pm Tue-Sat, noon-6pm Sun) Owner Leah Bershad was once a designer for Gap, but the folksy jet-set aesthetic here is the exact opposite of khaki-and-fleece global domination: Santa Fe woollen blankets, silver jewelry banged together by Humboldt hippies, Majestic tissue-tees and Clare Vivier pebble-leather clutches.

Piedmont Boutique   ACCESSORIES
(Map p85; 1452 Haight St; 11am-7pm) Glam up or get out at this supplier of drag fabulousness: pleather hot pants, airplane earrings and a wall of feather boas.

Amoeba Records   MUSIC
(Map p85; www.amoeba.com; 1855 Haight St; 10:30pm-10pm Mon-Sat, 11am-9pm Sun) Bowling-alley-turned-superstore of new and used records in all genres, plus 'free in-store concerts and Music We Like 'zine for great new finds.

MAC   CLOTHING
(Map p70; http://modernappealingclothing.com; 387 Grove St; 11am-7pm Mon-Sat, noon-6pm Sun) Impeccably structured looks for men from Belgian minimalist Dries Van Noten and Tsumori Chisato's Japanese luxe for the ladies; superb 40% to 75% off sales rack.

Velvet da Vinci   JEWELRY
(Map p70; www.velvetdavinci.com; 2015 Polk St; 11am-6pm Tue-Sat, to 4pm Sun) Ingenious jewelry by local and international artisans: Julia Turner's satellite-dish ring, Ben Neubauer's cage earrings, a drinking flask bracelet by William Clark.

Nancy Boy   BEAUTY
(Map p70; www.nancyboy.com; 347 Hayes St; 11am-7pm Mon-Fri, to 6pm Sat & Sun) Wear these highly effective moisturizers, pomades and sun balms with pride, all locally made with plant oils and tested on boyfriends, never animals.

New People   CLOTHING, GIFTS
(off Map p66; www.newpeopleworld.com; 1746 Post St) An eye-popping three-story emporium devoted to Japanese art and pop culture, with contemporary art, Lolita fashions, traditional Japanese clothing with contemporary graphics, and *kawaii* (Japanese for all things cute).

Gravel & Gold   HOUSEWARES, GIFTS
(Map p92; gravelandgold.com; 3266 21st St; noon-7pm Tue-Sat, noon-5pm Sun) A gallery/boutique celebrating the 1960s-1970s hippie homesteader movement, from stoneware teapots to hand-dyed smocked dresses – which you can try on among psychedelic murals behind a patched curtain.

Goorin Brothers Hats   ACCESSORIES
(Map p85; www.goorin.com; 1446 Haight St; 11am-7pm Sun-Fri, to 8pm Sat) Peacock feathers, high crowns and local-artist-designed embellishments make it easy to withstand the fog while standing out in a crowd in SF-designed fedoras, caps and cloches.

Accident & Artifact   GIFTS, ACCESSORIES
(Map p92; www.accidentandartifact.com; 381 Valencia St; noon-6pm Thu-Sun) A most curious curiosity shop, even by Mission standards: decorative dried fungi, vintage Okinawan indigo textiles, artfully redrawn topographical maps and fur-covered televisions with antlers.

Dema   CLOTHING
(Map p92; www.godemago.com; 1038 Valencia St; 11am-7pm Mon-Fri, noon-6pm Sat & Sun) Wear-everywhere shifts in vintage-inspired prints by local designer Dema, plus clever cardigans and Orla Kiely tees.

Madame S & Mr S Leather   CLOTHING
(Map p70; www.madame-s.com; 385 8th St; 11am-7pm) S&M superstore, with such musts as leashes, dungeon furniture and for that special someone, a chrome-plated codpiece.

Wasteland   VINTAGE, CLOTHING
(Map p85; www.thewasteland.com; 1660 Haight St; 11am-8pm Mon-Sat, noon-7pm Sun) The catwalk of thrifting: psychedelic Pucci maxi-skirts, barely worn Marc Jacobs smocks and a steady supply of go-go boots.

Jeremy's   CLOTHING, ACCESSORIES
(Map p70; www.jeremys.com; 2 South Park St; 11am-6pm Mon-Sat, to 5pm Sun) Window displays, photo shoot ensembles and department store customer returns translate to jaw-dropping bargains on major designers for men and women.

Park Life   ARTWORK, BOOKS
(Map p76; www.parklifestore.com; 220 Clement St; 11am-8pm) Design store, indie publisher and art gallery with gift options: tees with drawn-on pockets, Park Life's catalog of graffiti artist Andrew Schoultz, and Ian Johnson's portrait of Miles Davis radiating prismatic thought waves.

Sui Generis   VINTAGE, CLOTHING
(Map p92; men's shop 2231 Market St, women's shop 2265 Market St; noon-7pm Tue-Thu, to 8pm Fri & Sat, to 4pm Sun) Straight-off-the-runway, lightly worn scores from Prada, Zegna, Armani & Co, some in the double-digit range.

Studio GIFTS
(Map p70; www.studiogallerysf.com; 1815 Polk St; ☺11am-8pm Wed-Fri, to 6pm Sat & Sun) Winsome locally made arts and crafts at bargain prices, including Chiami Sekine's collages of boxing bears, SF architectural etchings by Alice Gibbons, and Monique Tse's fat-free glass cupcakes.

Golden Gate Fortune Cookie Company FOOD & DRINK
(Map p62; 56 Ross Alley; admission free; ☺8am-7pm) Make a fortune in San Francisco at this bakery, where cookies are stamped out on old-fashioned presses and folded over your customized message (50c each). Cash only; 50c tip for photo requested.

Sports Basement OUTDOOR EQUIPMENT
(Map p66; www.sportsbasement.com; 610 Mason St; ☺9am-8pm Mon-Fri, 8am-7pm Sat & Sun) There's 70,000 sq ft of sports and camping equipment housed in the Presidio's former US Army PX; free coffee and hot cider while you shop.

Community Thrift CLOTHING, HOUSEWARES
(Map p92; www.communitythriftsf.org; 623 Valencia St; ☺10am-6:30pm) Vintage home furnishing scores and local retailer overstock, all sold to benefit local charities.

SFO Snowboarding & FTC Skateboarding OUTDOOR EQUIPMENT
(Map p85; 1630 Haight St; ☺11am-7pm) State-of-the-art gear, snowboards and skateboards, some with designs by local artists.

Mollusk OUTDOOR EQUIPMENT
(Map p76; www.mollusksurfshop.com; 4500 Irving St; ☺10am-6:30pm) For locally designed surf gear.

❶ Information

Dangers & Annoyances

Keep your city smarts and wits about you, especially at night in SoMa, the Mission and the Haight. Unless you know where you're going, avoid the sketchy, depressing Tenderloin (bordered east–west by Powell and Polk Sts and north–south by O'Farrell and Market Sts), Skid Row (6th St between Market and Folsom Sts) and Bayview-Hunters Point. To cut through the Tenderloin, take Geary or Market Sts – still seedy, but tolerable. Panhandlers and homeless people are a fact of life in the city. People will probably ask you for spare change, but donations to local non-profits stretch further. For safety, don't engage with panhandlers at night or around ATMs. Otherwise, a simple 'I'm sorry,' is a polite response.

Emergency & Medical Services

San Francisco General Hospital (☑emergency room 415-206-8111, main 415-206-8000; www.sfdph.org; 1001 Potrero Ave) 24-hour care.

Walgreens (☑415-861-3136; www.walgreens.com 498 Castro St; ☺24hr) Pharmacy and over-the-counter meds; dozens of locations citywide.

Internet Access

SF has free wi-fi hot spots citywide – locate one nearby with **www.openwifispots.com**. Connect for free in Union Sq and most cafes and hotel lobbies.

Apple Store (☑415-392-0202; www.apple.com/retail/SanFrancisco; 1 Stockton St; ☺9am-9pm Mon-Sat, 10am-8pm Sun; 🖥) Free wi-fi access and internet terminal usage.

Main Library (http://sfpl.org; 100 Larkin St; ☺10am-6pm Mon & Sat, 9am-8pm Tue-Thu, noon-5pm Fri & Sun; 🖥) Free 15-minute Internet terminal usage; spotty wi-fi access.

Brain Wash (www.brainwash.com; 1122 Folsom St; per wash from $2; ☺7am-10pm Mon-Thu, to 11pm Fri & Sat, 8am-10pm Sun; 🖥) Come with laundry, stay for lunch, beer, live entertainment, pinball, free wi-fi and internet terminals ($3 per 20 minutes).

Money

Bank of America (www.bankamerica.com; One Market Plaza; ☺9am-6pm Mon-Fri)

Post

Rincon Center post office (Map p70; www.usps.com; 180 Steuart St; ☺8am-6pm Mon-Fri, 9am-2pm Sat) Postal services plus historic murals.

Union Square post office (Map p70; www.usps.com; 170 O'Farrell St; ☺10am-5:30pm Mon-Sat, 11am-5pm Sun) In the basement of Macy's department store.

Tourist Information

California Welcome Center (Map p66; ☑415-981-1280; www.visitcwc.com; Pier 39, Bldg P, ste 241b; ☺10am-5pm) Handy for travel information, brochures, maps and help booking accommodations.

San Francisco Visitors Information Center (Map p70; ☑415-391-2000; www.onlyinSanFrancisco.com; lower level, Hallidie Plaza; ☺9am-5pm Mon-Fri, 9am-3pm Sat & Sun) Maps, guidebooks, brochures, accommodations help.

Websites

http://sfbay.craigslist.org Events, activities, partners, freebies and dates.

http://sf.eater.com SF food, nightlife and bars.

www.flavorpill.com Live music, lectures, art openings and movie premieres.

www.urbandaddy.com Bars, shops, restaurants and events.

❶ Getting There & Away

Air

The Bay Area has three major airports: **San Francisco International Airport** (SFO; www.flysfo.com), 14 miles south of downtown SF, off Hwy 101; Oakland International Airport (see p136), a few miles across the bay; and San José International Airport (p136), at the southern end of the bay. The majority of international flights use SFO. Travelers from other US cities may find cheaper flights into Oakland on discount airlines such as JetBlue and Southwest.

Improvements over the last decade include a new international terminal, LEED-certified green Terminal 2 and a BART extension directly to the airport. All three SFO terminals have ATMs and information booths on the lower level, and **Travelers' Aid information booths** (◷9am-9pm) on the upper level. The airport paging and information line is staffed 24 hours; call from any white courtesy phone.

Bus

Until the new terminal is complete in 2017, SF's intercity hub remains the **Temporary Transbay Terminal** (Map p70; Howard & Main Sts), where you can catch buses on **AC Transit** (www.actransit.org) to the East Bay, **Golden Gate Transit** (http://goldengatetransit.org) north to Marin and Sonoma Counties, and **SamTrans** (www.samtrans.com) south to Palo Alto and the Pacific coast. **Greyhound** (☏800-231-2222; www.greyhound.com) buses leave daily for Los Angeles ($56.50, eight to 12 hours), Truckee near Lake Tahoe ($33, 5½ hours), and other destinations.

Car & Motorcycle

All major car-rental operators (Alamo, Avis, Budget, Dollar, Hertz, Thrifty) are represented at the airports, and many have downtown offices.

Ferry

For Alcatraz Cruises, see p79.

Blue & Gold Fleet Ferries (Map p70; www.blueandgoldfleet.com) The Alameda-Oakland Ferry runs from the Ferry Building to Jack London Sq in Oakland ($6.25, 30 minutes). Ferries to Tiburon, Sausalito and Angel Island run from Pier 41 at Fisherman's Wharf.

Golden Gate Ferries (Map p70; ☏415-923-2000; www.goldengateferry.org; ◷6am-10pm Mon-Fri, 10am-6pm Sat & Sun) Regular services run from the Ferry Building to Larkspur and Sausalito in Marin County. Transfers are available to MUNI bus services, and bicycles permitted.

Vallejo Ferries (Map p70; ☏415-773-1188; one way adult/child $15/7.50) Get to Napa car-free, with departures from Ferry Building docks about every hour from 6:30am through 7pm weekdays and every two hours from 11am through 7:30pm on weekends; bikes are permitted. From the Vallejo Ferry Terminal, take Napa Valley Vine bus 10 to downtown Napa, Yountville, St Helena or Calistoga. Also connects to Six Flags Marine World theme park in Vallejo.

Train

CalTrain (Map p70; www.caltrain.com; cnr 4th & King Sts) links San Francisco to the South Bay, including Palo Alto (Stanford University) and San Jose.

Amtrak (☏800-872-7245; www.amtrakcalifornia.com) offers low-emission, leisurely travel to and from San Francisco. *Coast Starlight*'s spectacular 35-hour run from Los Angeles to Seattle stops in Oakland, and the *California Zephyr* takes its sweet time (51 hours) traveling from Chicago through the Rockies to Oakland. Both have sleeping cars and dining/lounge cars with panoramic windows. Amtrak runs free shuttle buses to San Francisco's Ferry Building and CalTrain station.

❶ Getting Around

For Bay Area transit options, departures and arrivals, check ☏511 or www.511.org.

To/From the Airport

» **BART** (Bay Area Rapid Transit; www.bart.gov; one-way $8.10) offers a fast, direct ride to downtown San Francisco.

» **SamTrans** (www.samtrans.com; one-way $5) express bus KX gets you to Temporary Transbay Terminal in about 30 minutes.

» **SuperShuttle** (☏800-258-3826; www.supershuttle.com; one-way $17) door-to-door vans depart from baggage-claim areas, taking 45 minutes to most SF locations.

» **Taxis** to downtown San Francisco cost $35-50.

Bicycle

San Francisco is cyclable, but traffic downtown can be dangerous; bicycling is best east of Van Ness Ave and across the bay. For bike shops and rentals, see p75. Bicycles can be carried on BART, but not in the commute direction during weekday rush hours.

Car & Motorcycle

If you can, avoid driving in San Francisco: street parking is harder to find than true love, and meter readers are ruthless. Convenient downtown parking lots are at Embarcadero Center, 5th and Mission Sts, Union Sq, and Sutter and Stockton Sts. National car-rental agencies have airport and downtown offices.

Before you set out to any bridge or other traffic choke-point, call ☑511 toll-free for a traffic update. Members of the **American Automobile Association** (AAA; ☑415-773-1900, 800-222-4357; www.aaa.com; 160 Sutter St; ☺8.30am-5:30pm Mon-Fri) can call the 800 number any time for emergency road service and towing. AAA also provides travel insurance and free road maps of the region.

Parking authorities are quick to tow cars. If this should happen to you, you'll have to retrieve your car at **Autoreturn** (☑415-865-8200; www. autoreturn.com; 450 7th St; ☺24hr). Besides at least $73 in fines for parking violations, you'll also have to fork out a towing and storage fee ($392.75 for the first four hours, $61.75 for the rest of the first day, $61.75 for every additional day, plus a $25.50 transfer fee if your car is moved to a long-term lot). Cars are usually stored at 415 7th St, corner of Harrison St.

Some of the cheaper downtown parking garages are **Sutter-Stockton Garage** (Map p70; ☑415-982-7275, cnr Sutter & Stockton Sts), **Ellis-O'Farrell Garage** (Map p70; ☑415-986-4800; 123 O'Farrell St) and **Fifth & Mission Garage** (Map p70; ☑415-982-8522; 833 Mission St), near Yerba Buena Gardens. The parking garage under Portsmouth Sq in Chinatown is reasonably priced for shorter stops; ditto for the **St Mary's Square Garage** (☑415-956-8106; California St), under the square, at Grant and Kearny Sts. Daily rates range between $20 and $35.

BART

Bay Area Rapid Transit (BART; ☑415-989-2278; www.bart.gov; ☺4am-midnight Mon-Fri, 6am-midnight Sat, 8am-midnight Sun) is a subway system linking SFO, the Mission District, downtown, San Francisco and the East Bay. The fastest link between Downtown and the Mission District also offers transit to SF airport, Oakland ($3.20) and Berkeley ($3.75). Within SF, one-way fares start at $1.75.

MUNI

MUNI (Municipal Transit Agency; www.sfmuni. com) operates bus, streetcar and cable-car lines. Two cable-car lines leave from Powell and Market Sts; a third leaves from California and Markets Sts. A detailed *MUNI Street & Transit Map* is available free online and at the Powell MUNI kiosk ($3). Standard fare for buses or streetcars is $2, and tickets are good on buses or streetcars (not BART or cable cars) for 90 minutes; cable-car fare is $6 for a single ride.

Tickets are available on board, but you'll need exact change. Hang onto your ticket – if you're caught without one, you're subject to a $75 fine.

A **MUNI Passport** (one-/three-/seven-days $14/21/27) allows unlimited travel on all MUNI transport, including cable cars; it's sold at San Francisco's Visitor Information Center (p80) and at the TIX Bay Area kiosk at Union Sq and from a number of hotels. A seven-day **City Pass** (adult/child $69/39) covers Muni and admission to five attractions.

Key MUNI routes include:

» F Fisherman's Wharf and Embarcadero to Castro

» J Downtown to Mission/Castro/Noe Valley

» K, L, M Downtown to Castro

» N Caltrain and SBC Ballpark to Haight, Golden Gate Park and Ocean Beach

» T Embarcadero to Caltrain and Bayview

Taxi

Fares run about $2.25 per mile, plus 10% tip (starting at $1); meters start at $3.50. Major cab companies include:

Green Cab (☑415-626-4733; www.626green. com) Fuel-efficient hybrids; worker-owned collective.

DeSoto Cab (☑415-970-1300)

Luxor (☑415-282-4141)

Yellow Cab (☑415-333-3333)

Marin County & the Bay Area

Includes »

Best Places to Eat

» Chez Panisse (p143)

» Fish (p116)

» Bakesale Betty (p133)

» Duarte's Tavern (p156)

» Gather (p142)

Best Places to Stay

» Cavallo Point (p113)

» Mountain Home Inn (p120)

» Hotel Shattuck Plaza (p142)

» Pigeon Point Lighthouse Hostel (p156)

» East Brother Light Station (p147)

Why Go?

The region surrounding San Francisco encompasses a bonanza of natural vistas and wildlife. Cross the Golden Gate Bridge to Marin and visit wizened ancient redwoods body-blocking the sun and herds of elegant tule elk prancing along the bluffs of Tomales Bay. Gray whales show some fluke off the cape of wind-scoured Point Reyes, and hawks surf the skies in the pristine hills of the Marin Headlands.

On the cutting edge of intellectual thought, Stanford University and the University of California at Berkeley draw academics and students from around the world. The city of Berkeley sparked the locavore food movement and continues to be on the forefront of environmental and left-leaning political causes. South of San Francisco, Hwy 1 traces miles of undeveloped coastline and sandy pocket beaches.

When to Go
Berkeley

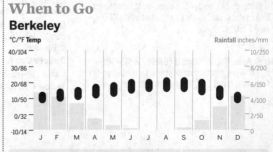

Dec–Mar Elephant seal pupping season and the peak of gray whale migrations.

Mar–Apr Wildflowers hit their peak on trails throughout the region.

Jun–Sep Farmers markets overflow with sweet seasonal fruit.

ⓘ Getting Around

Visitors taking multiple forms of public transportation throughout the Bay Area should note that the regional **Clipper card** (www.clippercard.com) can be used on the Caltrain, BART, SamTrans, VTA, Golden Gate Transit and the Golden Gate Ferry systems. It can be a handy way to avoid buying multiple tickets, and offers some small discounts, plus almost 50% off on the Golden Gate Ferry system.

MARIN COUNTY

If there's a part of the Bay Area that consciously attempts to live up to the California dream, it's Marin County. Just across the Golden Gate Bridge from San Francisco, the region has a wealthy population that cultivates a seemingly laid-back lifestyle. Towns may look like idyllic rural hamlets, but the shops cater to cosmopolitan and expensive tastes. The 'common' folk here eat organic, vote Democrat and drive hybrids.

Geographically, Marin County is a near mirror image of San Francisco. It's a south-pointing peninsula that nearly touches the north-pointing tip of the city, and is surrounded by ocean and bay. But Marin is wilder, greener and more mountainous. Redwoods grow on the coast side of the hills, the surf crashes against cliffs, and hiking and cycling trails crisscross the blessed scenery of Point Reyes, Muir Woods and Mt Tamalpais. Nature is what makes Marin County such an excellent day trip or weekend escape from San Francisco.

Busy Hwy 101 heads north from the Golden Gate Bridge ($6 toll when heading back into San Francisco), spearing through Marin's middle; quiet Hwy 1 winds its way along the sparsely populated coast. In San Rafael, Sir Francis Drake Blvd cuts across west Marin from Hwy 101 to the ocean.

Hwy 580 comes in from the East Bay over the Richmond-San Rafael bridge ($5 toll for westbound traffic) to meet Hwy 101 at Larkspur.

Frequent Marin Airporter (📞415-461-4222; www.marinairporter.com; fare $20) buses connect from Marin stops to the San Francisco International Airport from 4am until about 10:30pm; SFO-Marin service departs every 30 minutes.

The Marin Convention & Visitors Bureau (📞415-925-2060, 866-925-2060; www.visitmarin.org; 1 Mitchell Blvd, San Rafael; ⊙9am-5pm Mon-Fri) provides tourist information for the entire county.

Marin Headlands

The headlands rise majestically out of the water at the north end of the Golden Gate Bridge, their rugged beauty all the more striking given the fact that they're only a few miles from San Francisco's urban core. A few forts and bunkers are left over from a century of US military occupation – which is, ironically, the reason they are protected parklands today and free of development. It's no mystery why this is one of the Bay Area's most popular hiking and cycling destinations. As the trails wind through the headlands, they afford stunning views of the sea, the Golden Gate Bridge and San Francisco, leading to isolated beaches and secluded spots for picnics.

⊙ Sights

After crossing the Golden Gate Bridge, exit immediately at Alexander Ave, then dip left under the highway and head out west for the expansive views and hiking trailheads. Conzelman Rd snakes up into the hills, where it eventually forks. Conzelman Rd continues west, becoming a steep, one-lane road as it descends to Point Bonita. From here it continues to Rodeo Beach and Fort Barry. McCullough Rd heads inland, joining Bunker Rd toward Rodeo Beach.

Hawk Hill   HILL
About 2 miles along Conzelman Rd is Hawk Hill, where thousands of migrating birds of prey soar along the cliffs from late summer to early fall.

Point Bonita Lighthouse   LIGHTHOUSE
(www.nps.gov/goga/pobo.htm; ⊙12:30-3:30pm Sat-Mon) At the end of Conzelman Rd, this light-

---

FAST FACTS

Population of Berkeley 112,500

Average temperature low/high in Berkeley Jan 43/56°F, Jul 54/70°F

Downtown Berkeley to Sacramento 80 miles, 1½ hours

San Jose to San Francisco 45 miles, one hour

San Francisco to Point Reyes Lighthouse 55 miles, 2½ hours

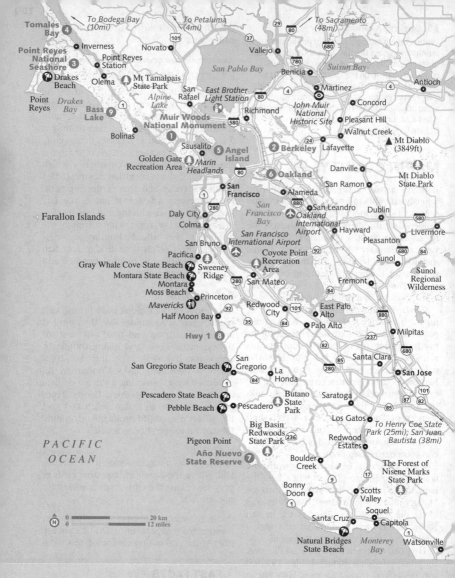

Marin County & the Bay Area Highlights

1 Gaze up at the majestic redwood canopy at **Muir Woods National Monument** (p123)

2 Feast your way through the delectable **Gourmet Ghetto** (p139) in Berkeley

3 Cavort with elk and gray whales at the **Point Reyes National Seashore** (p127)

4 Kayak **Tomales Bay** (p127) amid harbor seals and splendid shorelines

5 Hike or cycle the perimeter of panoramic **Angel Island** (p119)

6 Head to Oakland's **Chabot Space & Science Center** (p132) to marvel at the stars

7 Spy on the elephant seals at **Año Nuevo State Reserve** (p157)

8 Tour the beach cove coastline along **Hwy 1** (p154) from Pacifica to Santa Cruz

9 Cool off with a cannonball splash at blissful **Bass Lake** (p125)

house is a breathtaking half-mile walk from a small parking area. From the tip of Point Bonita, you can see the distant Golden Gate Bridge and beyond it the San Francisco skyline. It's an uncommon vantage point of the bay-centric city, and harbor seals haul out nearby in season. To reserve a spot on one of the free monthly full-moon tours of the promontory, call ☑415-331-1540.

FREE **Nike Missile Site SF-88** HISTORIC SITE (☑415-331-1453; www.nps.gov/goga/nike-missile-site.htm; ⊙12:30-3:30pm Wed-Fri & 1st Sat of month) File past guard shacks with uniformed mannequins to witness the area's not-too-distant military history at this fascinating Cold War museum staffed by veterans. Watch them place a now-warhead-free missile into position, then ride a missile elevator to the cavernous underground silo to see the multikeyed launch controls that were thankfully never set in motion.

FREE **Marine Mammal Center** ANIMAL RESCUE CENTER (☑415-289-7325; www.marinemammalcenter.org; ⊙10am-5pm; ⊞) Set on the hill above Rodeo Lagoon, the newly expanded Marine Mammal Center rehabilitates injured, sick and orphaned sea mammals before returning them to the wild, and has educational exhibits about these animals and the dangers they face. During the spring pupping season the center can have up to several dozen orphaned seal pups on site and you can often see them before they're set free.

Headlands Center for the Arts ARTS CENTER (☑415-331-2787; www.headlands.org) In Fort Barry, refurbished barracks converted into artist work spaces host open studios with its artists-in-residence, as well as talks, performances and other events.

🏃 Activities

Hiking
At the end of Bunker Rd sits Rodeo Beach, protected from wind by high cliffs. From here the Coastal Trail meanders 3.5 miles inland, past abandoned military bunkers, to the Tennessee Valley Trail. It then continues 6 miles along the blustery headlands all the way to Muir Beach.

All along the coastline you'll find cool old battery sites – abandoned concrete bunkers dug into the ground with fabulous views. Evocative Battery Townsley, a half-mile walk or bike ride up from the Fort Cronkite parking lot, opens for free subterranean tours from noon to 4pm on the first Sunday of the month.

Mountain-Biking
The Marin Headlands have some excellent mountain-biking routes, and it's an exhilarating ride across the Golden Gate Bridge to reach them (see the boxed text, p117).

For a good 12-mile dirt loop, choose the Coastal Trail west from the fork of Conzelman and McCullough Rds, bumping and winding down to Bunker Rd where it meets Bobcat Trail, which joins Marincello Trail and descends steeply into the Tennessee Valley parking area. The Old Springs Trail and the Miwok Trail take you back to Bunker Rd a bit more gently than the Bobcat Trail, though any attempt to avoid at least a couple of hefty climbs is futile.

Horseback Riding
For a ramble on all fours, Miwok Livery Stables (☑415-383-8048; www.miwokstables.com; 701 Tennessee Valley Rd; trail ride $75) offers hillside trail rides with stunning views of Mt Tam and the ocean.

🛏 Sleeping

There are four small campgrounds in the headlands, and two involve hiking (or cycling) in at least 1 mile from the nearest parking lot. Hawk, Bicentennial and Haypress campgrounds are inland, with free camping, but sites must be reserved through the Marin Headlands Visitors Center (p112).

🌿 **Marin Headlands Hostel** HOSTEL $ (☑415-331-2777; www.norcalhostels.org/marin; Bldg 941, Fort Barry, Marin Headlands; dm $22-26, r $72-92; @) Wake up to grazing deer and dew on the ground at this spartan 1907 military compound snuggled in the woods. It has comfortable beds and two well-stocked kitchens, and guests can gather round a fireplace in the common room, shoot pool or play ping-pong. Most importantly, the Hostelling International (HI) hostel is surrounded by hiking trails.

Kirby Cove Campground CAMPGROUND $ (☑877-444-6777; www.recreation.gov; tent sites $25; ⊙Apr-Oct) In a spectacular shady nook near the entrance to the bay, there's a small beach with the Golden Gate Bridge arching over the rocks nearby. At night you

WHY IS IT SO FOGGY?

When the summer sun's rays warm the air over the chilly Pacific, fog forms and hovers offshore; to grasp how it moves inland requires an understanding of California's geography. The vast agricultural region in the state's interior, the Central Valley, is ringed by mountains like a giant bathtub. The only substantial sea-level break in these mountains occurs at the Golden Gate, to the west, which happens to be the direction from which prevailing winds blow. As the inland valley heats up and the warm air rises, it creates a deficit of air at surface level, generating wind that gets sucked through the only opening it can find: the Golden Gate. It happens fast and it's unpredictable. Gusty wind is the only indication that the fog is about to roll in. But even this is inconsistent: there can be fog at the beaches south of the Golden Gate and sun a mile to the north. Hills block fog – especially at times of high atmospheric pressure, as often happens in summer. Because of this, weather forecasters speak of the Bay Area's 'microclimates.' In July it's not uncommon for inland areas to reach 100°F (38°C), while the mercury at the coast barely reaches 70°F (21°C).

can watch the phantom shadows of cargo ships passing by (and sometimes be lulled to sleep by the dirge of a fog horn). Reserve far ahead.

❶ Information

Information is available from the **Golden Gate National Recreation Area** (GGNRA; ☑415-561-4700; www.nps.gov/goga) and the **Marin Headlands Visitors Center** (☑415-331-1540; www.nps.gov/goga/marin-headlands.htm; ◎9:30am-4:30pm), in an old chapel off Bunker Rd near Fort Barry.

❶ Getting There & Away

By car, take the Alexander Ave exit just after the Golden Gate Bridge and dip left under the freeway. Conzelman Rd, to the right, takes you up along the bluffs; you can also take Bunker Rd, which leads to the headlands through a one-way tunnel. It's also a snap to reach these roads from the bridge via bicycle.

Golden Gate Transit (☑415-455-2000, 511; www.goldengatetransit.org) bus 2 runs a limited weekday commuter service from the corner of Pine and Battery Sts in San Francisco's Financial District to Sausalito and the Headlands ($4.25). On Sunday and holidays **MUNI** (☑415-701-2311, 511; www.sfmta.com) bus 76 runs from the 4th St Caltrain depot in San Francisco to the Marin Headlands Visitors Center and Rodeo Beach.

Sausalito

Perfectly arranged on a secure little harbor on the bay, Sausalito is undeniably lovely. Named for the tiny willows that once populated the banks of its creeks, it's a small settlement of pretty houses that tumble neatly down a green hillside into a well-heeled downtown. Much of the town affords the visitor uninterrupted views of San Francisco and Angel Island, and due to the ridgeline at its back, fog generally skips past it.

Sausalito began as a 19,000-acre land grant to an army captain in 1838. When it became the terminus of the train line down the Pacific coast, it entered a new stage as a busy lumber port with a racy waterfront. Dramatic changes came in WWII when Sausalito became the site of Marinship, a huge shipbuilding yard. After the war a new bohemian period began, with a resident artists' colony living in 'arks' (houseboats moored along the bay). You'll still see dozens of these floating abodes.

Sausalito today is a major tourist haven, jam-packed with souvenir shops and costly boutiques. It's the first town you encounter after crossing the Golden Gate Bridge from San Francisco, so daytime crowds turn up in droves and make parking difficult. Ferrying over from San Francisco makes a more relaxing excursion.

◉ Sights

Sausalito is actually on Richardson Bay, a smaller bay within San Francisco Bay. The commercial district is mainly one street, Bridgeway Blvd, on the waterfront.

FREE **Bay Model Visitor Center**　MUSEUM
(☑415-332-3871; www.spn.usace.army.mil/bmvc; 2100 Bridgeway Blvd; ◎9am-4pm Tue-Fri, plus 10am-5pm Sat & Sun in summer; 👶) One of the coolest things in town, fascinating to both

kids and adults, is the Army Corps of Engineers' visitor center. Housed in one of the old Marinship warehouses, it's a 1.5-acre hydraulic model of San Francisco Bay and the delta region. Self-guided tours take you over and around it as the water flows.

Bay Area Discovery Museum MUSEUM
(☎415-339-3900; www.baykidsmuseum.org; adult/child $10/8; ⊙9am-4pm Tue-Fri, 10am-5pm Sat & Sun; ⊕) Just under the north tower of the Golden Gate Bridge, at East Fort Baker, this excellent hands-on activity museum is specifically designed for children. Permanent (multilingual) exhibits include a wave workshop, a small underwater tunnel and a large outdoor play area with a shipwreck to romp around. A small cafe has healthy nibbles.

Plaza de Viña Del Mar PARK
Near the ferry terminal, the plaza has a fountain flanked by 14ft-tall elephant statues from the 1915 Panama–Pacific Exposition in San Francisco.

🏃 Activities

Sausalito is great for bicycling, whether for a leisurely ride around town, a trip across the Golden Gate Bridge or a longer-haul journey. From the ferry terminal, an easy option is to head south on Bridgeway Blvd, veering left onto East Rd toward the Bay Area Discovery Museum. Another nice route heads north along Bridgeway Blvd, then crosses under Hwy 101 to Mill Valley. At Blithedale Ave, you can veer east to Tiburon; a bike path parallels parts of Tiburon Blvd.

Sea Trek KAYAKING
(☎415-488-1000; www.seatrek.com; Schoonmaker Point Marina; single/double kayaks per hr $20/35) On a nice day, Richardson Bay is irresistible. Kayaks and stand-up paddleboards can be rented here, near the Bay Model Visitor Center. No experience is necessary, and lessons and group outings are also available.

Also on offer are guided kayaking excursions around Angel Island (see p119) from $75 per person, including overnight camping ($140). Tours include equipment and instructions. May through October is the best time to paddle.

Mike's Bikes BICYCLE RENTAL
(☎415-332-3200; 1 Gate 6 Rd; 24hr $40) At the north end of Bridgeway Blvd near Hwy 101, this shop rents out road and mountain bikes. Supplies are limited and reservations aren't accepted.

🛏 Sleeping

All of the lodgings below charge an additional $15 to $20 per night for parking.

Cavallo Point HOTEL $$$
(☎415-339-4700; www.cavallopoint.com; 601 Murray Circle, Fort Baker; r from $280; ❄⛺@🐾🐕) Spread out over 45 acres of the Bay Area's most scenic parkland, Cavallo Point is a buzz-worthy lodge that flaunts a green focus, a full-service spa and easy access to outdoor activities. Choose from richly renovated rooms in the landmark Fort Baker officers' quarters or more contemporary solar-powered accommodations with exquisite bay views (including a turret of the Golden Gate Bridge).

Inn Above Tide INN $$$
(☎415-332-9535, 800-893-8433; www.innabovetide.com; 30 El Portal; r incl breakfast $320-595, ste $695-1100; ❄@🐕) Next to the ferry terminal, ensconce yourself in one of the 29 modern and spacious rooms – most with private decks and wood burning fireplaces – that practically levitate over the water. With envy-inducing bay views from your window, scan the horizon with the in-room binoculars. Free loaner bicycles available.

Gables Inn INN $$$
(☎415-289-1100; www.gablesinnsausalito.com; 62 Princess St; r incl breakfast $185-445; @🐕) Tranquil and inviting, this inn has nine guest rooms in a historic 1869 home, and six in a newer building. The more expensive rooms have Jacuzzi baths, fireplaces and balconies with spectacular views, but even the smaller, cheaper rooms are stylish and tranquil. Evening wine is included.

Hotel Sausalito HISTORIC HOTEL $$
(☎415-332-0700; www.hotelsausalito.com; 16 El Portal; r $155-195, ste $265-285; ❄🐕) Steps away from the ferry in the middle of downtown, this grand 1915 hotel has loads of period charm, paired with modern touches like MP3-player docking stations. Each guest room is decorated in Mediterranean hues, with sumptuous bathrooms and park or partial bay views.

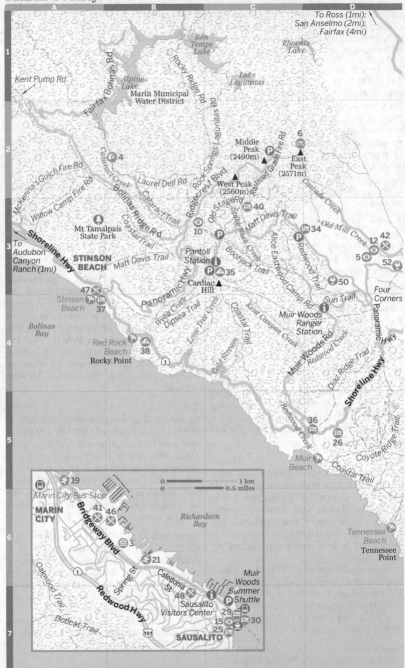

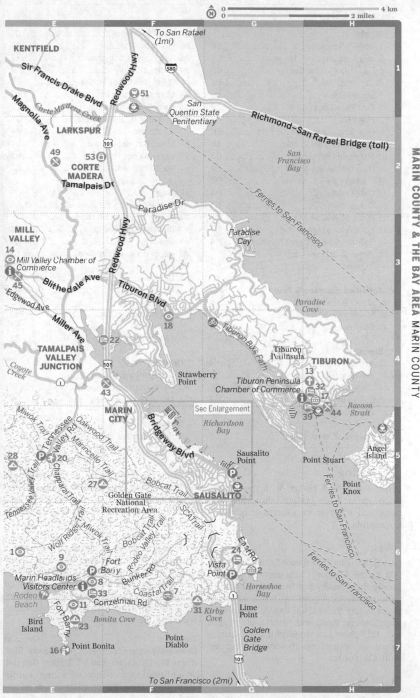

Marin County

✕ Eating

Bridgeway Blvd is packed with moderately priced cafes, a few budget ethnic food options and some more expensive bay-view restaurants.

Fish   SEAFOOD $$

(www.331fish.com; 350 Harbor Dr; mains $13-25; ◷11:30am-8:30pm; ⛶) Chow down on seafood sandwiches, oysters and Dungeness crab roll with organic local butter at redwood picnic tables facing Richardson Bay. A local leader in promoting fresh and sustainably caught fish, this place has wonderful wild salmon in season, and refuses to serve the farmed stuff. Cash only.

Murray Circle   AMERICAN $$

(☏415-339-4750; www.cavallopoint.com/dine.html; 601 Murray Circle, Fort Baker; mains $17-29; ◷7-11am & 11:30am-2pm Mon-Fri, to 2:30pm Sat & Sun, 5:30-10pm Sun-Thu, to 11pm Fri & Sat) At the Cavallo Point lodge, dine on locally sourced meats, seafood and produce, like grass-fed organic burgers or Dungeness crab BLT, in a clubby dining room topped by a pressed-tin ceiling. Reservations recommended for lunch and dinner, especially for seating on the panoramic-view balcony. Save room for the butterscotch soufflé.

Avatar's   INDIAN $$

(www.enjoyavatars.com; 2656 Bridgeway Blvd; mains $10-17; ◷11am-3pm & 5-9:30pm Mon-Sat; ⛶⛶) Boasting a cuisine of 'ethnic confusion,' the Indian fusion dishes here incorporate Mexican, Italian and Caribbean ingredients and will bowl you over with their flavor and creativity. Think Punjabi enchilada with curried sweet potato or spinach and mushroom ravioli with mango and rose petal alfredo sauce. All diets (vegan, gluten-free, etc) are graciously accommodated.

Sushi Ran   SUSHI **$$**
(☑415-332-3620; www.sushiran.com; 107 Caledonia St; sushi $4-19) Many Bay Area residents claim this place is the best sushi spot around. A wine and sake bar next door eases the pain of the long wait for a table.

❶ Information

The **Sausalito Visitors Center** (☑415-332-0505; www.sausalito.org; 780 Bridgeway Blvd; ⊙11:30am-4pm Tue-Sun) has local information. There's also an information kiosk at the ferry terminal.

❶ Getting There & Away

Driving to Sausalito from San Francisco, take the Alexander Ave exit (the first exit after the Golden Gate Bridge) and follow the signs into Sausalito. There are five municipal parking lots in town, and street parking is difficult to find.

Golden Gate Transit (☑415-455-2000; www.goldengatetransit.org) bus 10 runs daily to Sausalito from downtown San Francisco ($4.25).

The ferry is a fun and easy way to travel to Sausalito. **Golden Gate Ferry** (☑415-455-2000; www.goldengateferry.org; one-way $9.25) operates to and from the San Francisco Ferry Building six to nine times daily and takes

30 minutes. The **Blue & Gold Fleet** (☑415-705-8200; www.blueandgoldfleet.com; Pier 41, Fisherman's Wharf; one-way $10.50) sails to Sausalito four to five times daily from the Fisherman's Wharf area in San Francisco. Both ferries operate year-round and transport bicycles for free.

Tiburon

At the end of a small peninsula pointing out into the center of the bay, Tiburon is blessed with gorgeous views. The name comes from the Spanish *Punta de Tiburon* (Shark Point). Take the ferry from San Francisco, browse the shops on Main St, grab a bite to eat and you've seen Tiburon. The town is also a jumping-off point for nearby Angel Island (see p119).

◉ Sights & Activities

The central part of town is comprised of Tiburon Blvd, with Juanita Lane and charming Main St arcing off. Main St, which is also known as Ark Row, is where the old houseboats have taken root on dry land and metamorphosed into classy shops and boutiques.

FREE **Railroad & Ferry Depot Museum**   MUSEUM
(1920 Paradise Drive; www.landmarks-society.org; ⊙1-4pm Wed, Sat & Sun Mar-Oct) Formerly the terminus for a 3000-person ferry to San Francisco and a railroad that once reached north to Ukiah, this late 19th century building showcases a scale model of Tiburon's commercial hub, circa 1909. The restored

HIKING & CYCLING THE BRIDGE

Walking or cycling across the Golden Gate Bridge to Sausalito is a fun way to avoid traffic, get some great ocean views and bask in that refreshing Marin County air. It's a fairly easy journey, mostly flat or downhill when heading north from San Francisco (cycling back to the city involves one big climb out of Sausalito). You can also simply hop on a ferry back to SF (see p117).

The trip is about 4 miles from the south end of the bridge and takes less than an hour. Pedestrians have access to the bridge's east walkway between 5am and 9pm daily (until 6pm in winter). Cyclists generally use the west side, except on weekdays between 5am and 3:30pm, when they must share the east side with pedestrians (who have the right-of-way). After 9pm (6pm in winter), cyclists can still cross the bridge on the east side through a security gate. Check the bridge website (http://goldengatebridge.org/bikes bridge/bikes.php) for changes.

For more ambitious cyclists, the reopening of the Cal Park Hill Tunnel means a safe subterranean passage from Larkspur (another ferry terminus) to San Rafael.

More information and resources are available at the websites of the **San Francisco Bicycle Coalition** (www.sfbike.org) and the **Marin County Bicycle Coalition** (www.marinbike.org).

stationmaster's quarters can be visited upstairs.

Angel Island–Tiburon Ferry CRUISE
(☑415-435-2131; www.angelislandferry.com; adult/child $20/10) Runs sunset cruises on Friday and Saturday evenings from May through October. Reservations recommended.

Old St Hilary's Church CHURCH
(201 Esperanza; ☑1-4pm Sun Apr-Oct) There are great views from the lovely hillside surrounding this fine 19th-century example of Carpenter Gothic.

Richardson Bay Audubon Center NATURE RESERVE
(☑415-388-2524; www.tiburonaudubon.org; 376 Greenwood Beach Rd; ☑9am-5pm Mon-Sat) Off Tiburon Blvd, this center is home to a huge variety of water birds.

🛏 Sleeping

Water's Edge Hotel HOTEL $$
(☑415-789-5999; www.watersedgehotel.com; 25 Main St; r incl breakfast $169-499; ✳@🐾) This hotel, with its deck extending over the bay, is exemplary for its tasteful modernity. Rooms have an elegant minimalism that combines comfort and style, and all afford an immediate view of the bay. The rooms with rustic, high wood ceilings are quite romantic.

Lodge at Tiburon HOTEL $$
(☑415-435-3133; www.larkspurhotels.com/collection/tiburon; 1651 Tiburon Blvd; r from $135; ✳🐕@🐾🐾) Now a stylish and comfortable contemporary hotel with a grill restaurant, the concrete hallways and staircases testify to the more basic motel it once was. The best value in town, it's a short stroll to anywhere – including the ferry – and there's a pool, DVD library, free parking and a rooftop deck with fireplace and heady Mt Tamalpais views.

🍴 Eating

Sam's Anchor Cafe SEAFOOD $$
(www.samscafe.com; 27 Main St; mains $17-28; ☑11am-10pm Mon-Fri, from 9:30am Sat & Sun) Sam's has been slinging seafood and burgers since 1920, and though the entrance looks like a shambling little shack, the area out back has unbeatable views. On a warm afternoon, you can't beat a cocktail or a tasty plate of sautéed prawns on the deck.

Caprice AMERICAN $$$
(☑415-435-3400; www.thecaprice.com; 2000 Paradise Dr; mains $18-49; ☑5-10pm Tue-Sun, plus 11am-3pm Sun) Splurge-worthy and romantic, book a table here at sunset for riveting views of Angel Island, the Golden Gate Bridge and San Francisco. Caprice mostly features seafood, though other standouts include the artichoke bisque and the filet mignon. Take a peek at the fireplace downstairs – it's constructed into the coast bedrock. A three-course midweek dinner ($25) is easier on the wallet.

Guaymas MEXICAN $$
(www.guaymasrestaurant.com; 5 Main St; mains $15-25; ☑11am-9pm Sun-Thu, 11am-10pm Fri & Sat) Steps from the ferry, noisy Guaymas packs in a fun, boisterous crowd. Margaritas energize the place, and solid Mexican seafood dishes help keep people upright.

ℹ Information
The **Tiburon Peninsula Chamber of Commerce** (☑415-435-5633; www.tiburonchamber.org; 96b Main St) can provide information about the area.

ℹ Getting There & Away
Golden Gate Transit (☑415-455-2000; www.goldengatetransit.org) commute bus 8 runs direct between San Francisco and Tiburon ($4.25) during the week.

On Hwy 101, look for the off-ramp for Tiburon Blvd, E Blithedale Ave and Hwy 131; driving east, it leads into town and intersects with Juanita Lane and Main St.

Blue & Gold Fleet (☑415-705-8200; one-way $10.50) sails daily from either Pier 41 or the Ferry Building in San Francisco to Tiburon; ferries dock right in front of the Guaymas restaurant on Main St. You can transport bicycles for free. From Tiburon, ferries also connect regularly to Angel Island.

Mill Valley
Nestled under the redwoods at the base of Mt Tamalpais, tiny Mill Valley is one of the Bay Area's most picturesque hamlets. Mill Valley was originally a logging town, its name stemming from an 1830s sawmill – the first in the Bay Area to provide lumber. Though the 1892 Mill Valley Lumber Company still greets motorists on Miller Ave, the town's a vastly different place today, packed with wildly expensive homes, fancy cars and pricey boutiques.

DON'T MISS

ANGEL ISLAND

Angel Island (📞415-435-5390; www.parks.ca.gov/?page_id=468), in San Francisco Bay, has a mild climate with fresh bay breezes, which make it pleasant for hiking and cycling. For a unique treat, picnic in a protected cove overlooking the close but distant urban surroundings. The island's varied history – it was a hunting and fishing ground for the Miwok people, served as a military base, an immigration station, a WWII Japanese internment camp and a Nike missile site – has left it with some evocative old forts and bunkers to poke around in. There are 12 miles of roads and trails around the island, including a hike to the summit of 781ft **Mt Livermore** (no bicycles) and a 5-mile perimeter trail.

The **Immigration Station**, which operated from 1910 to 1940, was the Ellis Island of the west coast. But this facility was primarily a screening and detention center for Chinese immigrants, who were at that time restricted from entering the US under the Chinese Exclusion Act. Many detainees were held here for long periods before ultimately being returned home, and one of the most unusual sights on the island is the sad and longing Chinese poetry etched into the barrack walls. A **visitor center** (www.aiisf.org/visit; ⏱usually 11am-3pm Wed-Sun) contains interpretive exhibits, and more extensive **tours** (📞415-435-3522, adult/child $7/5) can be reserved ahead or purchased at the cafe near the ferry dock.

Sea Trek (see p113) runs **kayaking** excursions around the island. You can rent **bicycles** at Ayala Cove (per hour/day $10/35), and there are **tram tours** ($13.50) around the island. Schedules vary seasonally; go to www.angelisland.com for more information.

You can camp on the island, and when the last ferry sails off for the night, the place is your own – except for the very persistent raccoons. The dozen hike-, bicycle- or kayak-in **campsites** (📞800-444-7275; www.reserveamerica.com; tent sites $30) are usually reserved months in advance. Near the ferry dock, there's a **cafe** that specializes in barbecued oysters.

From San Francisco, take a **Blue & Gold Fleet** (📞415-705-8200; www.blueandgoldfleet.com) ferry from Pier 41 or the Ferry Building. From May to September there are three ferries a day on weekends and two on weekdays; during the rest of the year the schedule is reduced. Round-trip tickets cost $16 for adults and $9 for children.

From Tiburon, take the **Angel Island–Tiburon Ferry** (📞415-435-2131; www.angelislandferry.com; round trip $13.50, plus $1 for bicycles).

Mill Valley also served as the starting point for the scenic railway that carried visitors up Mt Tamalpais (see p122). The tracks were removed in 1940, and today the Depot Bookstore & Cafe occupies the space of the former station.

👁 Sights & Activities

Old Mill Park   PARK
Several blocks west of downtown along Throckmorton Ave is Old Mill Park, perfect for a picnic. Here you'll also find a replica of the town's namesake sawmill. Just past the bridge at Old Mill Creek, the **Dipsea Steps** mark the start of the Dipsea Trail.

Mill Valley Film Festival   FILM FESTIVAL
(www.mvff.com) Each October the Mill Valley Film Festival presents an innovative, internationally regarded program of independent films.

Tennessee Valley Trail   HIKING
In the Marin Headlands, this trail offers beautiful views of the rugged coastline and is one of the most popular hikes in Marin (expect crowds on weekends), especially for families. It has easy, level access to the cove beach and ocean, and is a short 3.8-mile round trip. From Hwy 101, take the Mill Valley–Stinson Beach–Hwy 1 exit and turn left onto Tennessee Valley Rd from the Shoreline Hwy; follow it to the parking lot and trailhead.

TOP CHOICE Dipsea Trail   HIKING
A beloved though more demanding hike is the 7-mile Dipsea Trail, which climbs over the coastal range and down to Stinson Beach, cutting through a corner of Muir Woods. This classic trail starts at Old Mill Park with a climb up 676 steps in three separate flights, and includes a few more ups

and downs before reaching the ocean. **West Marin Stagecoach** (www.marintransit.org/stage.html) route 61 runs from Stinson Beach to Mill Valley, making it a doable one-way day hike.

Outdoor Art Club   HISTORIC SITE
(www.outdoorartclub.org; cnr W Blithedale & Throckmorton Aves) Said to have been founded by 35 Mill Valley women determined to preserve the local environment, this private club is housed in a landmark 1904 building designed by prominent architect Bernard Maybeck.

🛏 Sleeping

Mountain Home Inn   INN $$$
(☑415-381-9000; www.mtnhomeinn.com; 810 Panoramic Hwy; r incl breakfast $195-345; 🛜) Set amid redwood, spruce and pine trees on a ridge of Mt Tamalpais, this retreat is both modern and rustic. The larger (more expensive) rooms are rugged beauties, with unfinished timbers forming columns from floor to ceiling, as though the forest is shooting up through the floor. Smaller rooms are cozy dens for two. A lack of TVs and the positioning of a good local trail map on the dresser make it clear that it's a place to breathe and unwind.

Acqua Hotel   BOUTIQUE HOTEL $$
(☑415-380-0400, 888-662-9555; www.marinhotels.com; 555 Redwood Hwy; r incl breakfast from $169; ❉@🛜🐾) With views of the bay and Mt Tamalpais, and a lobby with a soothing fireplace and fountain, the Acqua doesn't lack for pleasant eye candy. Contemporary rooms are sleekly designed with beautiful fabrics.

🍴 Eating & Drinking

Depot Bookstore & Cafe   CAFE $
(www.depotbookstore.com; 87 Throckmorton Ave; meals under $10; ⊙7am-7pm; 🛜) Smack in the town center, Depot serves cappuccinos, sandwiches and light meals. The bookstore sells lots of local publications, including trail guides.

Buckeye Roadhouse   AMERICAN $$
(☑415-331-2600; www.buckeyeroadhouse.com; 15 Shoreline Hwy; mains $15-33; ⊙11:30am-10:30pm Mon-Sat, 10:30am-10pm Sun) Originally opened as a roadside stop in 1932, the Buckeye is a Marin County gem, and its upscale American cuisine is in no danger of being compared to truck-stop fare. Stop off for chili-lime 'brick' chicken, baby back ribs or oysters Bingo and

a devilish wedge of s'more pie before getting back on the highway.

Mill Valley Beerworks   PUB
(www.millvalleybeerworks.com; 173 Throckmorton Ave; sandwiches & small plates $9-14; ⊙11am-midnight) With 100 bottled varieties of brew and a few of its own on tap, beer lovers can giddily explore new frontiers while chewing on house-made pretzels. The setting is stark and stylish, with unfinished wood tables and a pressed-tin wall.

Avatar's Punjabi Burritos   INDIAN $
(www.enjoyavatars.com; 15 Madrona St; mains $6.50-9; ⊙11am-8pm Mon-Sat, to 7pm Sun; 🥗) For a quick bite, try a tasty burrito of lamb and curry or spicy veggies.

ℹ Information

Visitor information is available from the **Mill Valley Chamber of Commerce** (☑415-388-9700; www.millvalley.org; 85 Throckmorton Ave; ⊙9am-5pm Mon-Fri).

ℹ Getting There & Away

From San Francisco or Sausalito, take Hwy 101 north to the Mill Valley–Stinson Beach–Hwy 1 exit. Follow Hwy 1 (also called the Shoreline Hwy) to Almonte Blvd (which becomes Miller Ave), then follow Miller Ave into downtown Mill Valley.

From the north, take the E Blithedale Ave exit from Hwy 101, then head west into downtown Mill Valley.

Golden Gate Transit (☑415-455-2000; www.goldengatetranist.org) bus 4 runs directly from San Francisco to Mill Valley ($4.25) on weekdays.

Sir Francis Drake Blvd & Around

The towns along and nearby the Sir Francis Drake Blvd corridor – including Larkspur, Corte Madera, Ross, San Anselmo and Fairfax – evoke charmed small-town life, even though things get busy around Hwy 101.

Starting from the eastern section in **Larkspur**, window-shop along Magnolia Ave or explore the redwoods in nearby Baltimore Canyon. On the east side of the freeway is the hulking mass of **San Quentin State Penitentiary**, California's oldest and most notorious prison, founded in 1852. Johnny Cash recorded an album here in 1969 after scoring a big hit with his live *Folsom Prison* album a few years earlier.

Take the bicycle and pedestrian bridge from the ferry terminal across the road to the **Marin Brewing Company** (www.marinbrewing.com; 1809 Larkspur Landing Cir, Marin Country Mart, Bldg 2, Larkspur; mains $10-15; ☺11:30am-midnight Sun-Thu, to 1am Fri & Sat) brewpub, where you can see the glassed-in kettles behind the bar. The head brewer, Arne Johnson, has won many awards, and the Mt Tam Pale Ale complements the menu of pizza, burgers and hearty sandwiches.

The **Tavern at Lark Creek** (☏415-924-7766; 234 Magnolia Ave, Larkspur; mains $13-29; ☺5:30-9:30pm Mon-Thu, to 10pm Fri & Sat, 10am-2pm & 5-9:30pm Sun; ☏) is in a lovely spot and offers a fine-dining experience. It's housed in an 1888 Victorian house tucked away in a redwood canyon, and the rotating farm-fresh American food (like the macaroni-and-cheese croquettes, pork loin chop and rainbow trout in brown butter) is gratifying.

Just south, **Corte Madera** is home to one of the Bay Area's best bookstores, **Book Passage** (☏415-927-0960; www.bookpassage.com; 51 Tamal Vista Blvd), in the Marketplace shopping center. It has a strong travel section, plus frequent author appearances.

Continuing west along Sir Francis Drake, **San Anselmo** has a cute, small downtown area along San Anselmo Ave, including several antique shops. The attractive center of neighboring **Fairfax** has ample dining and shopping options, and cyclists congregate at **Gestalt Haus Fairfax** (28 Bolinas Rd, Fairfax) for the indoor bicycle parking, board games, European draft beers and sausages of the meaty or vegan persuasion.

🍴 **Arti** (www.articafe.com; 7282 Sir Francis Drake Blvd, Lagunitas; mains $9-14; ☺noon-9:30pm Tue-Sun; ☏), between Hwys 1 and 101 in the tiny hamlet of Lagunitas, is a tempting stop for organic Indian fare. There's a cozy casual dining room and an outdoor patio for warm days, and folks from miles around adore its sizzling chicken tikka platter.

Golden Gate Ferry (☏415-455-2000; www.goldengateferry.org) runs a daily ferry service ($8.75, 50 minutes) from the Ferry Building in San Francisco to Larkspur Landing on E Sir Francis Drake Blvd, directly east of Hwy 101. You can take bicycles on the ferry.

San Rafael

The oldest and largest town in Marin, San Rafael is slightly less upscale than most of its neighbors but doesn't lack atmosphere.

It's a common stop for travelers on their way to Point Reyes. Just north of San Rafael, Lucas Valley Rd heads west to Point Reyes Station, passing George Lucas' Skywalker Ranch. Fourth St, San Rafael's main drag, is lined with cafes and shops. If you follow it west out of downtown San Rafael, it meets Sir Francis Drake Blvd and continues west to the coast.

◉ Sights & Activities

Mission San Rafael Arcángel   MISSION
(1104 5th Ave) The town began with this mission, founded in 1817, which served as a sanitarium for Native Americans suffering from European diseases. The present building is a replica dating from 1949.

China Camp State Park   PARK
(☏415-456-0766; parking $5) About 4 miles east of San Rafael, this is a pleasant place to stop for a picnic or short hike. From Hwy 101, take the N San Pedro Rd exit and continue 3 miles east. A Chinese fishing village once stood here, and a small museum exhibits its interesting artifacts from the settlement. At press time, the future of this state park was uncertain.

Rafael Film Center   CINEMA
(☏415-454-1222; www.cafilm.org/rfc; 1118 4th St) A restored downtown cinema offering innovative art-house programming on three screens in state-of-the-art surroundings.

🛏 Sleeping & Eating

Panama Hotel   B&B $$
(☏415-457-3993; www.panamahotel.com; 4 Bayview St; r $120-195; ❀🐾) The 10 artsy rooms at this B&B, in a building dating from 1910, each have their own unique style and charming decor – like crazy quilts and vibrant accent walls. The hotel restaurant has an inviting courtyard patio.

TOP CHOICE **Sol Food Puerto Rican Cuisine**   PUERTO RICAN $$
(☏415-451-4765; www.solfoodrestaurant.com; Lincoln Ave & 3rd St; mains $7.50-16; ☺7am-midnight Mon-Thu, to 2am Fri, 8am-2am Sat, to midnight Sun) Lazy ceiling fans, a profusion of tropical plants and the pulse of Latin rhythms create a soothing atmosphere for delicious dishes like a *jíbaro* sandwich (thinly sliced steak served on green plantains) and other island-inspired meals concocted with *plátanos,* organic veggies and free range meats.

WORTH A TRIP

GERMAN TOURIST CLUB

A private club that occasionally shares its sudsy love, the **German Tourist Club** (☎415-388-9987; www.touristclubsf. org; ◷1-5pm 1st, 3rd & 4th weekends of the month), or Nature Friends (*Die Naturefreunde*), has a gorgeous beer garden patio overlooking Muir Woods and Mt Tamalpais that's a favored spot for parched Marin hikers. By car, turn onto Ridge Ave from Panoramic Hwy, park in the gravel driveway at the end of the road and start the 0.3-mile walk downhill. You can also hike in on the Sun Trail from Panoramic – a half-hour of mostly flat trail with views of the ocean and Muir Woods.

China Camp State Park   CAMPGROUND **$**
(☎800-444-7275; www.reserveamerica.com; tent sites $35; ⛺) The park has 30 walk-in campsites with pleasant shade.

ⓘ Getting There & Away

Numerous **Golden Gate Transit** (☎415-455-2000; www.goldengatetransit.org) buses operate between San Francisco and the San Rafael Transit Center at 3rd and Hetherton Sts ($5.25, one hour).

Mt Tamalpais State Park

Standing guard over Marin County, majestic Mt Tamalpais (Mt Tam) has breathtaking 360-degree views of ocean, bay and hills rolling into the distance. The rich, natural beauty of the 2571ft mountain and its surrounding area is inspiring – especially considering it lies within an hour's drive from one of the state's largest metropolitan areas.

Mt Tamalpais State Park was formed in 1930, partly from land donated by congressman and naturalist William Kent (who also donated the land that became Muir Woods National Monument in 1907). Its 6300 acres are home to deer, foxes, bobcats and many miles of hiking and cycling trails.

Mt Tam was a sacred place to the coastal Miwok people for thousands of years before the arrival of European and American settlers. By the late 19th century, San Franciscans were escaping the bustle of the city with all-day outings on the mountain, and in 1896 the 'world's crookedest railroad' (281

turns) was completed from Mill Valley to the summit. Though the railroad was closed in 1930, Old Railroad Grade is today one of Mt Tam's most popular and scenic hiking and cycling paths.

⊙ Sights

Panoramic Hwy climbs from Mill Valley through the park to Stinson Beach. From Pantoll Station, it's 4.2 miles by car to **East Peak Summit**; take Pantoll Rd and then panoramic Ridgecrest Blvd to the top. Parking is $8 (good for the entire park) and a 10-minute hike leads to a fire lookout at the very top and awesome sea-to-bay views.

Mountain Theater   THEATER
(☎415-383-1100; www.mountainplay.org) The park's natural-stone, 4000-seat theater hosts the annual 'Mountain Play' series on a half dozen weekend afternoons between mid-May and late June. Free shuttles are provided from Mill Valley. Free monthly **astronomy programs** (☎415-455-5370; www. mttam.net/astronomy.html; ◷Apr-Oct) also take place here on Saturday nights around the new moon.

🏃 Activities

Hiking

The park map is a smart investment, as there are a dozen worthwhile hiking trails in the area. From Pantoll Station, the **Steep Ravine Trail** follows a wooded creek on to the coast (about 2.1 miles each way). For a longer hike, veer right (northwest) after 1.5 miles onto the **Dipsea Trail**, which meanders through trees for 1 mile before ending at Stinson Beach. Grab some lunch, then walk north through town and follow signs for the **Matt Davis Trail**, which leads 2.7 miles back to Pantoll Station, making a good loop. The Matt Davis Trail continues on beyond Pantoll Station, wrapping gently around the mountain with superb views.

Another worthy option is **Cataract Trail**, which runs along Cataract Creek from the end of Pantoll Rd; it's approximately 3 miles to Alpine Lake. The last mile is a spectacular rooty staircase as the trail descends alongside **Cataract Falls**.

Mountain-Biking

Cyclists must stay on the fire roads (and off the single-track trails) and keep to speeds under 15mph. Rangers are prickly about these rules, and a ticket can result in a steep fine.

The most popular ride is the **Old Railroad Grade**. For a sweaty, 6-mile, 2280ft climb, start in Mill Valley at the end of W Blithedale Ave and cycle up to East Peak. It takes about an hour to reach the West Point Inn (see below) from Mill Valley. For an easier start, begin partway up at the Mountain Home Inn (see p120) and follow the **Gravity Car Grade** to the Old Railroad Grade and the West Point Inn. From the Inn, it's an easy half-hour ride to the summit.

From just west of Pantoll Station, cyclists can either take the **Deer Park fire road**, which runs close to the Dipsea Trail, through giant redwoods to the main entrance of Muir Woods, or the southeastern extension of the **Coastal Trail**, which has breathtaking views of the coast before joining Hwy 1 about 2 miles north of Muir Beach. Either option requires a return to Mill Valley via Frank Valley/Muir Woods Rd, which climbs steadily (800ft) to Panoramic Hwy and then becomes Sequoia Valley Rd as it drops toward Mill Valley. A left turn on Wildomar and two right turns at Mill Creek Park lead to the center of Mill Valley.

For further information on bicycle routes and rules, contact the **Marin County Bicycle Coalition** (415-456-3469; www.marinbike. org), whose Marin Bicycle Map is the gold standard for local cycling.

🛏 Sleeping & Eating

TOP CHOICE **Steep Ravine** CABINS, CAMPGROUND **$**
(800-444-7275; www.reserveamerica.com; campsites/cabins $25/100; ⊙closed Oct) Just off Hwy 1, about 1 mile south of Stinson Beach, this jewel has seven beachfront campsites and nine rustic five-person cabins with wood stoves overlooking the ocean. Both options are booked out months in advance and reservations can be made up to seven months ahead.

West Point Inn INN **$**
(inn 415-388-9955, reservations 415-646-0702; www.westpointinn.com; per person r or cabin $50; ⊙closed Sun & Mon night) Load up your sleeping bag and hike in to this rustic 1904 hilltop hideaway built as a stopover for the Mill Valley and Mt Tamalpais Scenic Railway. Rates drop to $35 per person Tuesday through Thursday from mid-September until the end of May. It also hosts monthly pancake breakfasts ($10) on Sundays during the summer.

Pantoll Station Campground CAMPGROUND **$**
(415-388-2070; tent sites $25; ❸) From the parking lot it's a 100yd walk or bicycle ride to the campground, with 16 first-come, first-served tent sites but no showers.

ℹ Information

Pantoll Station (415-388-2070; 801 Panoramic Hwy; ❸) is the park headquarters. Detailed park maps are sold here. The **Mt Tamalpais Interpretive Association** (www.mttam. net; ⊙11am-4pm Sat & Sun) staffs a small visitor center at East Peak.

ℹ Getting There & Away

To reach Pantoll Station by car, take Hwy 1 to the Panoramic Hwy and look for the Pantoll signs. **West Marin Stagecoach** (415-526-3239; www.marintransit.org/stage.html) route 61 runs daily minibuses ($2) from Marin City (via Mill Valley; plus weekend and holiday service from the Sausalito ferry) to both the Pantoll Station and Mountain Home Inn.

Muir Woods National Monument

Walking through an awesome stand of the world's tallest trees is an experience to be had only in Northern California and a small part of southern Oregon. The old-growth redwoods at **Muir Woods** (415-388-2595; www.nps.gov/muwo; adult/child under 16 $5/free; ⊙8am-sunset), just 12 miles north of the Golden Gate Bridge, is the closest redwood stand to San Francisco. The trees were initially eyed by loggers, and Redwood Creek, as the area was known, seemed ideal for a dam. Those plans were halted when congressman and naturalist William Kent bought a section of Redwood Creek and, in 1907, donated 295 acres to the federal government. President Theodore Roosevelt made the site a national monument in 1908, the name honoring John Muir, naturalist and founder of environmental organization the Sierra Club.

Muir Woods can become quite crowded, especially on weekends. Try to come midweek, early in the morning or late in the afternoon, when tour buses are less of a problem. Even at busy times, a short hike will get you out of the densest crowds and onto trails with huge trees and stunning vistas. A lovely cafe serves local and organic goodies and hot drinks that hit the spot on foggy days.

Activities

The 1-mile Main Trail Loop is a gentle walk alongside Redwood Creek to the 1000-year-old trees at Cathedral Grove; it returns via Bohemian Grove, where the tallest tree in the park stands 254ft high. The Dipsea Trail is a good 2-mile hike up to the top of aptly named Cardiac Hill.

You can also walk down into Muir Woods by taking trails from the Panoramic Hwy, such as the Bootjack Trail from the Bootjack picnic area, or from Mt Tamalpais' Pantoll Station campground, along the Ben Johnson Trail.

ⓘ Getting There & Away

The parking lot fills up during busy periods, so consider taking the summer shuttle operated by Marin Transit (www.marintransit.org; round trip adult/child $3/1; ☺weekends & holidays late-May–Sep). The 40-minute shuttle connects with four Sausalito ferries arriving from San Francisco.

To get there by car, drive north on Hwy 101, exit at Hwy 1 and continue north along Hwy 1/Shoreline Hwy to the Panoramic Hwy (a right-hand fork). Follow that for about 1 mile to Four Corners, where you turn left onto Muir Woods Rd (there are plenty of signs).

The Coast

MUIR BEACH

The turnoff to Muir Beach from Hwy 1 is marked by the longest row of mailboxes on the North Coast. Muir Beach is a quiet little town with a nice beach, but it has no direct bus service. Just north of Muir Beach there are superb views up and down the coast from the Muir Beach Overlook; during WWII, watch was kept from the surrounding concrete lookouts for invading Japanese ships.

Pelican Inn (☎415-383-6000; www.pelicaninn.com; 10 Pacific Way; r incl breakfast $190-265; ☏) is the only commercial establishment in Muir Beach. The downstairs restaurant and pub (mains $9 to $34) is an Anglophile's dream and perfect for pre- or post-hike nourishment.

Green Gulch Farm & Zen Center (☎415-383-3134; www.sfzc.org; 1601 Shoreline Hwy; s $90-135, d $160-205, d cottage $300-350, all with 3 meals; @☏🖉) is a Buddhist retreat in the hills above Muir Beach. The center's accommodations are elegant, restful and modern, and delicious buffet-style vegetarian meals are included. A hilltop retreat cottage is 25 minutes away by foot.

STINSON BEACH

Positively buzzing on warm weekends, Stinson Beach is 5 miles north of Muir Beach. The town flanks Hwy 1 for about three blocks and is densely packed with galleries, shops, eateries and B&Bs. The beach itself is often blanketed with fog, and when the sun's shining it's blanketed with surfers, families and gawkers. There are views of Point Reyes and San Francisco on clear days, and the beach is long enough for a vigorous stroll. From San Francisco it's nearly an hour's drive, though on weekends plan for toe-tapping traffic delays.

Three-mile-long Stinson Beach is a popular surf spot, but swimming is advised from late May to mid-September only; for updated weather and surf conditions call ☑415-868-1922. The beach is one block west of Hwy 1.

Around 1 mile south of Stinson Beach is Red Rock Beach. It's a clothing-optional beach that attracts smaller crowds, probably because it can only be accessed by a steep trail from Hwy 1.

Audubon Canyon Ranch (☑415-868-9244; www.egret.org; donations requested; ☺10am-4pm Sat, Sun & holidays mid-Mar–mid-Jul) is about 3.5 miles north of town on Hwy 1, in the hills above the Bolinas Lagoon. A major nesting ground for great blue herons and great egrets, viewing scopes are set up on hillside blinds where you can watch these magnificent birds congregate to nest and hatch their chicks in tall redwoods. At low tide, harbor seals often doze on sand bars in the lagoon.

Just off Hwy 1 and a quick stroll to the beach, the ten comfortable rooms of the Sandpiper (☑415-868-1632; www.sandpiperstinsonbeach.com; 1 Marine Wy; r $140-210; ☏) have gas fireplaces and kitchenettes, and are ensconced in a lush garden and picnic area. Prices dip from November through March.

Parkside Cafe (☑415-868-1272; www.parksidecafe.com; 43 Arenal Ave; mains $9-25; ☺7:30am-9pm Mon-Fri, from 8am Sat & Sun) is famous for its hearty breakfasts and lunches, and noted far and wide for its excellent coastal cuisine. Reservations are recommended for dinner.

West Marin Stagecoach (☑415-526-3239; www.marintransit.org/stage.html) route 61 runs daily minibuses ($2) from Marin City, and weekend and holiday services to the Sausalito ferry; the 62 route runs three days a week from San Rafael.

BOLINAS

For a town that is so famously unexcited about tourism, Bolinas offers some fairly tempting attractions for the visitor. Known as Jugville during the Gold Rush days, the sleepy beachside community is home to writers, musicians and fisherfolk, and deliberately hard to find. The highway department used to put signs up at the turnoff from Hwy 1; locals kept taking them down, so the highway department finally gave up.

◉ Sights & Activities

FREE **Bolinas Museum** MUSEUM
(☑415-868-0330; www.bolinasmuseum.org; 48 Wharf Rd; ◎4-7pm Wed, 1-5pm Fri, noon-5pm Sat & Sun) This courtyard complex of five galleries exhibits local artists and showcases the region's history. Look for the weathered Bolinas highway sign affixed to the wall, since you certainly didn't see one on your way into town.

2 Mile Surf Shop SURFING
(☑415-868-0264; 22 Brighton Ave) Surfing's popular in these parts, and this shop behind the post office rents boards and wet suits and also gives lessons. Call ☑415-868-2412 for the surf report.

Agate Beach BEACH
There are tide pools along some 2 miles of coastline at Agate Beach, around the end of Duxbury Point.

PRBO Conservation Science BIRD-WATCHING
(☑415-868-0655; www.prbo.org) Off Mesa Rd west of downtown and formerly known as the Point Reyes Bird Observatory, the Palomarin Field Station of PRBO has bird-banding and netting demonstrations, a visitors center and nature trail. Banding demonstrations are held in the morning every Tuesday to Sunday from May to late November, and on Wednesday, Saturday and Sunday the rest of the year. Check its website for information on monthly bird walks held throughout the region.

HIKING

Beyond the observatory is the Palomarin parking lot and access to various walking trails in the southern part of the Point Reyes National Seashore (see p127), including the easy (and popular) 3-mile trail to lovely Bass Lake. A sweet inland spot buffered by tall trees, this small lake is perfect for a pastoral swim on a toasty day. You can dive in wearing your birthday suit (or not), bring an inner tube to float about, or do a long lap all the way across.

If you continue 1.5 miles northwest, you'll reach the unmaintained trail to Alamere Falls, a fantastic flume plunging 50ft off a cliff and down to the beach. But sketchy beach access makes it more enjoyable to walk another 1.5 miles to Wildcat Beach and then backtrack a mile on sand.

🛏 Sleeping & Eating

Smiley's Schooner Saloon & Hotel MOTEL $
(☑415-868-1311; www.smileyssaloon.com; 41 Wharf Rd; r $89-109; ☜) A crusty old place dating back to 1851, Smiley's has simple but decent rooms, and last-minute weekday rates can go down to $60. The bar, which serves some food, has live bands Thursday through Saturday and is frequented by plenty of salty dogs and grizzled deadheads.

Coast Café AMERICAN $$
(www.bolinascafe.com; 46 Wharf Rd; mains $10-22; ◎11:30am-3pm & 5-8pm Tue & Wed, to 9pm Thu & Fri, 8am-3pm & 5-9pm Sat, to 8pm Sun; ☑🚴🐕🍴) The only 'real' restaurant in town, everyone jockeys for outdoor seats among the flowerboxes for fish and chips, barbecued oysters, or buttermilk pancakes with damn good coffee.

Bolinas People's Store MARKET $
(14 Wharf Rd; ◎8:30am-6:30pm; ☑) An awesome little co-op grocery store hidden behind the community center, the People's Store serves Fair Trade coffee and sells organic produce, fresh soup and excellent tamales. Eat at the tables in the shady courtyard, and have a rummage through the Free Box, a shed full of clothes and other waiting-to-be-reused items.

ℹ Getting There & Away

Route 61 of the **West Marin Stagecoach** (☑415-526-3239; www.marintransit.org/stage.html) goes daily ($2) from the Marin City transit hub (weekend and holiday service from the Sausalito ferry) to downtown Bolinas; the 62 route runs three days a week from San Rafael. By car, follow Hwy 1 north from Stinson Beach and turn west (left) for Bolinas at the first road north of the lagoon. At the first stop sign, take another left onto Olema-Bolinas Rd and follow it 2 miles to town.

WORTH A TRIP

LOCAL AG ROADTRIP

Along the border of Marin and Sonoma County, make a detour for these two local favorites.

At **Marin French Cheese** (www.marinfrenchcheese.com; 7500 Red Hill Rd, Novato; ☺8:30am-5pm), stop to picnic beside the languid pond of this 150-year-old cheese producer. Sample its soft cheeses, watch the cheesemaking process at one of its four daily tours, and savor the rolling green hills over a baguette with triple crème brie.

Continue north 9 miles on the Petaluma-Point Reyes Rd to Petaluma Blvd and turn left to the stately **Petaluma Seed Bank** (http://rareseeds.com/petaluma-seed-bank; 199 Petaluma Blvd N, Petaluma; ☺9:30am-5:30pm Sun-Fri, shorter winter hrs). Formerly the Sonoma County National Bank, the soaring windows and carved ceiling of the 1925 building make it a stately place to peruse the 1200 varieties of heirloom seeds.

OLEMA & NICASIO

About 10 miles north of Stinson Beach near the junction of Hwy 1 and Sir Francis Drake Blvd, **Olema** was the main settlement in West Marin in the 1860s. Back then, there was a stagecoach service to San Rafael and there were *six* saloons. In 1875, when the railroad was built through Point Reyes Station instead of Olema, the town's importance began to fade. In 1906 it gained distinction once again as the epicenter of the Great Quake.

The **Bolinas Ridge Trail**, a 12-mile series of ups and downs for hikers or bikers, starts about 1 mile west of Olema, on Sir Francis Drake Blvd. It has great views.

About a 15-minute drive inland from Olema, at the geographic center of Marin County, is **Nicasio**, a tiny town with a low-key rural flavor and a cool saloon and music venue. It's at the west end of Lucas Valley Rd, 10 miles from Hwy 101.

🍴 **Olema Inn & Restaurant** (☎415-663-9559; www.theolemainn.com; cnr Sir Francis Drake Blvd & Hwy 1; r incl breakfast Mon-Thu $174-198, Fri & Sat $198-222; restaurant ☺9am-9pm; ☎☀) is a very stylish and peaceful country retreat. Its six rooms retain some of the building's antiquated charm, but are up to modern standards of comfort. The almost-entirely organic **restaurant** (mains $22-30) can set you up with Hog Island oysters, a small plate meal or something from the extensive list of smaller-scale California wineries.

Six miles east of Olema on Sir Francis Drake Blvd, **Samuel P Taylor State Park** (☎415-488-9897; www.reserveamerica.com; tent & RV sites $35; ☎☀) has beautiful, secluded campsites in redwood groves. It's also located on the **Cross Marin bike path**, with miles of creekside landscape to explore

along a former railroad grade. At press time, the future of this state park was uncertain and subject to closure or reduced services.

In the town center, **Rancho Nicasio** (☎415-662-2219; www.ranchonicasio.com; mains $17-23; ☺11:30am-3pm & 5-9pm Mon-Thu, to 10pm Fri, 11am-3pm & 5-10pm Sat, to 9pm Sun) is the local fun spot. It's a rustic saloon that regularly attracts local and national blues, rock and country performers.

Route 68 of the **West Marin Stagecoach** (☎415-526-3239; www.marintransit.org/stage.html) runs daily to Olema and Samuel P Taylor State Park from the San Rafael Transit Center ($2).

POINT REYES STATION

Though the railroad stopped coming through in 1933 and the town is small, Point Reyes Station is nevertheless the hub of West Marin. Dominated by dairies and ranches, the region was invaded by artists in the 1960s. Today it's an interesting blend of art galleries and tourist shops. The town has a rowdy saloon and the occasional smell of cattle on the afternoon breeze.

🛏 Sleeping & Eating

Cute little cottages, cabins and B&Bs are plentiful in and around Point Reyes. The **West Marin Chamber of Commerce** (☎415-663-9232; www.pointreyes.org) has numerous listings, as does the **Point Reyes Lodging Association** (www.ptreyes.com).

Holly Tree Inn   INN, COTTAGES **$$**
(☎415-663-1554, 800-286-4655; www.hollytreeinn.com; Silver Hills Rd; r incl breakfast $130-180, cottages $190-265) The Holly Tree Inn, off Bear Valley Rd, has four rooms and three private cottages in a beautiful country setting. The

Sea Star Cottage is a romantic refuge at the end of a small pier on Tomales Bay.

Bovine Bakery   BAKERY $
(11315 Hwy 1; ⏱6:30am-5pm Mon-Thu, 7am-5pm Sat & Sun) Don't leave town without sampling something buttery from possibly the best bakery in Marin. A bear claw (a large sweet pastry) and an organic coffee are a good way to kick off your morning.

🍽**Pine Cone Diner**   DINER $$
(www.pineconediner.com; 60 4th St; mains $9-13; ⏱8am-2:30pm; 🌱🦞) The Pine Cone serves big breakfasts and lunches inside a cute retro dining room and at shaded al fresco picnic tables. Try the buttermilk biscuits, the chorizo or tofu scramble, or the fried oyster sandwich.

🍽**Osteria Stellina**   ITALIAN $$
(☎415-663-9988; www.osteriastellina.com; 11285 Hwy 1; mains $15-25; ⏱11:30am-2:30pm & 5-9pm; 🌱) This place specializes in rustic Italian cuisine, with pizza and pasta dishes and Niman Ranch meats. Head over Tuesday nights for lasagna and live music, and definitely make reservations for the weekend.

🍽**Tomales Bay Foods and Cowgirl Creamery**   MARKET $$
(☎415-663-9335; www.cowgirlcreamery.com; 80 4th St; ⏱10am-6pm Wed-Sun; 🌱) A local market in an old barn selling picnic items, including gourmet cheeses and organic produce. Reserve a spot in advance for the small-scale artisanal cheesemaker's demonstration and tasting ($5), where you can watch the curd-making and cutting, then sample a half dozen of the fresh and aged cheeses. All of the milk is local and organic, with vegetarian rennet in all its soft cheeses.

☆ **Entertainment**

The lively community center, **Dance Palace** (☎415-663-1075; www.dancepalace.org; 503 B St), has weekend events, movies and live music. The **Old Western Saloon** (☎415-663-1661; cnr Shoreline Hwy & 2nd St) is a rustic 1906 saloon with live bands and cool tables emblazoned with horseshoes. Prince Charles stopped in here for an impromptu pint during a local visit in 2006.

❶ **Getting There & Away**

Hwy 1 becomes Main St in town, running right through the center. Route 68 of the **West Marin Stagecoach** (☎415-526-3239; www.marintran-sit.org/stage.html) runs here daily from the San Rafael Transit Center ($2), and the 62 route goes south to Bolinas and Stinson Beach on Tuesday, Thursday and Saturday.

INVERNESS

This tiny town, the last outpost on your journey westward, is spread along the west side of Tomales Bay. It's got good places to eat and, among the surrounding hills and picturesque shoreline, multiple rental cottages and quaint B&Bs. Several great beaches are only a short drive north.

Blue Waters Kayaking (☎415-669-2600; www.bwkayak.com; kayak rental 2/4hr $50/60), at the Tomales Bay Resort and across the bay in Marshall (on Hwy 1, eight miles north of Point Reyes Station), offers various Tomales Bay tours, or you can rent a kayak and paddle around secluded beaches and rocky crevices on your own; no experience necessary.

Formerly the Golden Hinde Inn, the bayside **Tomales Bay Resort** (☎415-669-1389; www.tomalesbayresort.com; 12938 Sir Francis Drake Blvd; r $120-225; 🐾🛜🏊) has 36 recently renovated motel rooms, a pool (unheated) and a restaurant. When rates drop – Sunday through Thursday and in the winter – it's one of the best bargains around.

🍽**Inverness Valley Inn** (☎415-669-7250, 800-416-0405; www.invernessvalleyinn.com; 13275 Sir Francis Drake Blvd; r $149-219; 🐾🛜🎾🏊) is a family-friendly place hidden away in the woods, just a mile from town. It offers clean, modern kitchenette rooms in A-frame structures, and has a tennis court, horseshoe pitches, barbecue pits and in-room DVD players. There's a large garden and a few farm animals on site, and guests receive free eggs from the inn's chickens. It's past the town, on the way down the Pt Reyes Peninsula.

From Hwy 1, Sir Francis Drake Blvd leads straight into Inverness. Route 68 of the **West Marin Stagecoach** (☎415-526-3239; www.marintransit.org/stage.html) makes daily stops here from San Rafael ($2).

POINT REYES NATIONAL SEASHORE

The windswept peninsula Point Reyes is a rough-hewn beauty that has always lured marine mammals and migratory birds as well as scores of shipwrecks. It was here in 1579 that Sir Francis Drake landed to repair his ship, the *Golden Hind*. During his five-week stay he mounted a brass plaque near the shore claiming this land for England. Historians believe this occurred at **Drakes Beach** and there is a marker there today. In

1595 the first of scores of ships lost in these waters, the *San Augustine,* went down. She was a Spanish treasure ship out of Manila laden with luxury goods, and to this day bits of her cargo wash up on shore. Despite modern navigation, the dangerous waters here continue to claim the odd boat.

Point Reyes National Seashore has 110 sq miles of pristine ocean beaches, and the peninsula offers excellent hiking and camping opportunities. Be sure to bring warm clothing, as even the sunniest days can quickly turn cold and foggy.

◉ Sights & Activities

For an awe-inspiring view, follow the Earthquake Trail from the park headquarters at Bear Valley. The trail reaches a 16ft gap between the two halves of a once-connected fence line, a lasting testimonial to the power of the 1906 earthquake that was centered in this area. Another trail leads from the visitors center a short way to Kule Loklo, a reproduction of a Miwok village.

Limantour Rd, off Bear Valley Rd about 1 mile north of Bear Valley Visitor Center, leads to the Point Reyes Hostel (p128) and Limantour Beach, where a trail runs along Limantour Spit with Estero de Limantour on one side and Drakes Bay on the other. The Inverness Ridge Trail heads from Limantour Rd up to Mt Vision (1282ft), from where there are spectacular views of the entire national seashore. You can drive almost to the top of Mt Vision from the other side.

About 2 miles past Inverness, Pierce Point Rd splits off to the right from Sir Francis Drake Blvd. From here you can get to two nice swimming beaches on the bay: Marshall Beach requires a mile-long hike from the parking area, while Hearts Desire, in Tomales Bay State Park (whose future was uncertain at press time), is accessible by car.

Pierce Point Rd continues to the huge windswept sand dunes at Abbotts Lagoon, full of peeping killdeer and other shorebirds. At the end of the road is Pierce Point Ranch, the trailhead for the 3.5-mile Tomales Point Trail through the Tule Elk Reserve. The plentiful elk are an amazing sight, standing with their big horns against the backdrop of Tomales Point, with Bodega Bay to the north, Tomales Bay to the east and the Pacific Ocean to the west.

Five Brooks Stables   HORSEBACK RIDING
(☏415-663-1570; www.fivebrooks.com; trail rides from $40; ⊕) Explore the landscape on horseback with a trail ride. Take a slow amble through a pasture or ascend over 1000ft to Inverness Ridge for views of the Olema Valley. If you can stay in the saddle for six hours, ride along the coastline to Alamere Falls (see p125) via Wildcat Beach.

TOP
CHOICE **Point Reyes Lighthouse**   LIGHTHOUSE
(☏415-669-1534; ⊕10am-4:30pm Thu-Mon) At the very end of Sir Francis Drake Blvd, with wild terrain and ferocious winds, this spot feels like the ends of the earth and offers the best whale-watching along the coast. The lighthouse sits below the headlands; to reach it requires descending over 300 stairs. Nearby Chimney Rock is a fine short hike, especially in spring when the wildflowers are blossoming. A nearby viewing area allows you to spy on the park's elephant seal colony.

Keep back from the water's edge at the exposed North Beach and South Beach, as people have been dragged in and drowned by frequent rogue waves.

⏢ Sleeping & Eating

Wake up to deer nibbling under a blanket of fog at one of Point Reyes' four very popular hike-in campgrounds (☏415-663-8054; www.nps.gov/pore/planyourvisit/campgrounds. htm; tent sites $15), each with pit toilets, water and tables. Reservations accepted up to three months in advance, and weekends go fast. Reaching the campgrounds requires a 2- to 6-mile hike or bicycle ride, or you can try for a permit to kayak camp on the beach in Tomales Bay.

Point Reyes Hostel   HOSTEL $
(☏415-663-8811;   www.norcalhostels.org/reyes; dm/r $24/68; ⊕) Just off Limantour Rd, this rustic HI property has bunkhouses with warm and cozy front rooms, big-view windows and outdoor areas with hill vistas, and a brand new LEED-certified building with four more private rooms in the works. It's in a beautiful secluded valley 2 miles from the ocean and surrounded by lovely hiking trails.

Drakes Bay Oyster Company   SEAFOOD $$
(☏415-669-1149; www.drakesbayoyster.com; 17171 Sir Francis Drake Blvd, Inverness; 1 dozen oysters to go/on the half shell $15/24; ⊕8:30am-4:30pm) Drakes Bay and nearby Tomales Bay are famous for excellent oysters. Stop by to do some on-the-spot shucking and slurping, or pick some up to grill later.

ⓘ Information

The park headquarters, **Bear Valley Visitor Center** (☑415-464-5100; Bear Valley Rd; ⏰9am-5pm Mon-Fri, from 8am Sat & Sun), is near Olema and has information and maps. You can also get information at the Point Reyes Lighthouse and the **Ken Patrick Center** (☑415-669-1250; ⏰10am-5pm Sat, Sun & holidays) at Drakes Beach. All visitor centers have slightly longer hours in summer.

ⓘ Getting There & Away

By car you can get to Point Reyes a few different ways. The curviest is along Hwy 1, through Stinson Beach and Olema. More direct is to exit Hwy 101 in San Rafael and follow Sir Francis Drake Blvd all the way to the tip of Point Reyes. For the latter route, take the Central San Rafael exit and head west on 4th St, which turns into Sir Francis Drake Blvd. By either route, it's about 1½ hours to Olema from San Francisco.

Just north of Olema, where Hwy 1 and Sir Francis Drake Blvd come together, is Bear Valley Rd; turn left to reach the Bear Valley Visitor Center. If you're heading to the further reaches of Point Reyes, follow Sir Francis Drake Blvd through Point Reyes Station and out onto the peninsula (about an hour's drive).

West Marin Stagecoach (☑415-526-3239; www.marintransit.org/stage.html) route 68 makes daily stops at the Bear Valley Visitor Center from San Rafael ($2).

EAST BAY

Berkeley and Oakland, collectively and affectionately called the 'five and dime,' after their 510 area code, are what most San Franciscans think of as the East Bay, though the area includes numerous other suburbs that swoop up from the bayside flats into exclusive enclaves in the hills. While many residents of the 'West Bay' would like to think they needn't ever cross the Bay Bridge or take a BART train under water, a wealth of museums, universities, excellent restaurants, woodsy parklands and better weather are just some of attractions that lure travelers from San Francisco.

Oakland

Named for the grand oak trees that once lined its streets, Oakland is to San Francisco what Brooklyn is to Manhattan. To some degree a less expensive alternative to the nearby city of hills, it's often where bohemian refugees have fled to escape pricey San Francisco housing

---

ⓘ POINT REYES SHUTTLE

On good-weather weekends and holidays from late December through mid-April, the road to Chimney Rock and the lighthouse is closed to private vehicles. Instead you must take a shuttle ($5, children under 17 free) from Drakes Beach.

---

costs. An ethnically diverse city, Oakland has a strong African American community and a long labor union history. Urban farmers raise chickens in their backyard or occupy abandoned lots to start community gardens, families find more room to stretch out, and self-satisfied residents thumb their noses at San Francisco's fog while basking in a sunnier Mediterranean climate.

◉ Sights & Activities

Broadway is the backbone of downtown Oakland, running from Jack London Sq at the waterfront all the way north to Piedmont and Rockridge. Telegraph Ave branches off Broadway at 15th St and heads north straight to Berkeley via the Temescal neighborhood (located between 40th St and 51st St). San Pablo Ave also heads north from downtown into Berkeley. Running east from Broadway is Grand Ave, leading to the Lake Merritt commercial district.

Downtown BART stations are on Broadway at both 12th and 19th Sts; other stations are near Lake Merritt, Rockridge and Temescal (MacArthur station).

DOWNTOWN

Oakland's downtown is full of historic buildings and a growing number of colorful local businesses. With such easy access from San Francisco via BART and the ferry, it's worth spending part of a day exploring here – and nearby Chinatown and Jack London Sq – on foot or by bicycle.

The pedestrianized **City Center**, between Broadway and Clay St, 12th and 14th Sts, forms the heart of downtown Oakland. The twin towers of the **Ronald Dellums Federal Building** are on Clay St, just behind it. **City Hall**, at 14th & Clay Sts, is a beautifully refurbished 1914 beaux arts hall.

Continuing north of the City Center, the **Uptown** district contains many of the city's art deco beauties and a proliferating arts

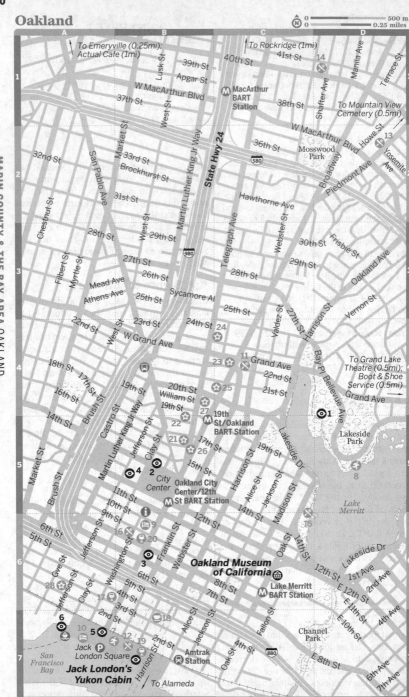

and restaurant scene. The area stretches roughly between Telegraph and Broadway, bounded by Grand Ave to the north.

Old Oakland, along Washington St between 8th and 10th Sts, is lined with historic buildings dating from the 1860s to the 1880s. The buildings have been restored and the area has a lively restaurant and after-work scene. The area also hosts a lively farmers market every Friday morning.

East of Broadway and bustling with commerce, **Chinatown** centers on Franklin and Webster Sts, as it has since the 1870s. It's much smaller than the San Francisco version.

JACK LONDON SQUARE

The area where writer and adventurer Jack London once raised hell now bears his name, and recent spasms of redevelopment have added a new cinema complex, condo development, excellent restaurants and some eclectic watering holes. The pretty waterfront location is worth a stroll, especially when the Sunday farmers market (⊘10am-2pm) takes over, or get off your feet and kayak around the harbor. Catch a ferry from San Francisco – a worthwhile excursion in and of itself – and you'll land just paces away.

Jack London's Yukon Cabin   LANDMARK
A replica of Jack London's Yukon cabin stands at the eastern end of the square. It's

partially built from the timbers of a cabin London lived in during the Yukon gold rush. Oddly, people throw coins inside as if it's a fountain. Another interesting stop, adjacent to the tiny cabin, is Heinold's First & Last Chance Saloon (see p135).

USS Potomac   HISTORIC SHIP
(☑510-627-1215; www.usspotomac.org; admission $10; ⊘11am-3pm Wed, Fri & Sun) Franklin D Roosevelt's 'floating White House,' the 165ft USS Potomac, is moored at Clay and Water Sts by the ferry dock, and is open for dockside tours. Two-hour history cruises (adult/child $45/25) are also held several times a month from May through October.

LAKE MERRITT

An urban respite, Lake Merritt is a popular place to stroll or go running (a 3.5-mile track circles the lake). The two main commercial streets skirting Lake Merritt are Lakeshore Ave on the eastern edge of the lake and Grand Ave, running along the north shore.

TOP CHOICE **Oakland Museum of California**   MUSEUM
(☑510-238-2200; www.museumca.org; 1000 Oak St; adult/child 9-17/child under 9 $12/6/free; ⊘11am-5pm Wed-Sun, to 9pm Fri; ▣) Near the southern end of the lake and one block from the Lake Merritt BART sta-

MARIN COUNTY & THE BAY AREA OAKLAND

Oakland

tion, this museum has rotating exhibitions on artistic and scientific themes, and excellent permanent galleries dedicated to the state's diverse ecology and history, as well as California art.

Children's Fairyland AMUSEMENT PARK
(☑510-238-6876; www.fairyland.org; admission $8; ⊙10am-4pm Mon-Fri, to 5pm Sat & Sun summer, 10am-4pm Wed-Sun spring & fall, Fri-Sun winter; ⊛) Lakeside Park, at the northern end of the saltwater lake, includes this 10-acre attraction, which dates from 1950 and has charming fairy-tale-themed train, carousel and mini Ferris-wheel rides.

Lake Merritt Boating Center BOAT HIRE
(☑510-238-2196; ⊙Sat & Sun Nov-Feb, daily Mar-Oct; ⊛) Rents canoes, rowboats, kayaks, pedal boats and sailboats for $10 to $18 per hour.

PIEDMONT AVE & ROCKRIDGE

North of downtown Oakland, Broadway becomes a lengthy strip of car dealerships called Broadway Auto Row. Just past that is Piedmont Ave, wall-to-wall with antique stores, coffeehouses, fine restaurants and an art cinema.

One of Oakland's most popular shopping areas is Rockridge, a lively, upscale neighborhood. It is centered on College Ave, which runs from Broadway all the way to the UC Berkeley Campus. College Ave is lined with clothing boutiques, good bookstores, a vintage record shop, several pubs and cafes, and quite a few upscale restaurants – maybe the largest concentration in the Bay Area. BART at the Rockridge station puts you in the thick of things.

Mountain View Cemetery CEMETERY
(www.mountainviewcemetery.org; 5000 Piedmont Ave) At the end of Piedmont Ave; perhaps the most serene and lovely artificial landscape in all the East Bay. Designed by Frederic Law Olmstead, the architect of New York City's Central Park, it's great for walking and the views are stupendous.

OAKLAND HILLS

The large parks of the Oakland Hills are ideal for day hiking and challenging cycling, and the East Bay Regional Parks District (www.ebparks.org) manages over 1200 miles of trails in 65 regional parks, preserves and recreation areas in the Alameda and Contra Costa counties.

Off Hwy 24, Robert Sibley Volcanic Regional Preserve is the northernmost of the Oakland Hills parks. It has great views of the Bay Area from its Round Top Peak (1761ft). From Sibley, Skyline Blvd runs south past Redwood Regional Park and adjacent Joaquin Miller Park to Anthony Chabot Regional Park. A hike or mountain-bike ride through the groves and along the hilltops of any of these sizable parks will make you forget you're in an urban area. At the southern end of Chabot Park is the enormous Lake Chabot, with an easy trail along its shore and canoes, kayaks and other boats for rent from the Lake Chabot marina (☑510-247-2526; www.norcalfishing.com/chabot).

**Chabot Space &
Science Center** SCIENCE CENTER
(☑510-336-7300; www.chabotspace.org; 10000 Skyline Blvd, Oakland; adult/child $15/11; ⊙10am-5pm Wed & Thu, to 10pm Fri & Sat, 11am-5pm Sun, plus 10am-5pm Tue summer; ⊛) Stargazers will go gaga over this science and technology center in the Oakland Hills with loads of exhibits on subjects such as space travel and eclipses, as well as cool planetarium shows. When the weather's good, check out the free Friday and Saturday evening viewings using a 20in refractor telescope.

🛏 Sleeping

If you like B&Bs, the Berkeley and Oakland Bed & Breakfast Network (www.bbonline. com/ca/berkeley-oakland) lists private homes that rent rooms, suites and cottages; prices start from $100 per night and many have a two-night-minimum stay. Reservations recommended.

Claremont Resort and Spa RESORT $$$
(☑510-843-3000, 800-551-7266; www.claremon tresort.com; 41 Tunnel Rd; r $189-309; ❋⊛☀@⊜) Oakland's classy crème de la crème, the Claremont is a glamorous white 1915 building with elegant restaurants, a fitness center, swimming pools, tennis courts and a full-service spa (room/spa packages are available). The bay view rooms are superb. It's located at the foot of the Oakland Hills, off Hwy 13 (Tunnel Rd) near Claremont Ave.

Waterfront Hotel BOUTIQUE HOTEL $$
(☑510-836-3800; www.waterfronthoteloakland.com; 10 Washington; r $149-269; ❋⊛☀@⊜☀) Paddle-printed wallpaper and lamps fashioned from faux lanterns round out the playful nautical theme of this bright and cheerful hotel at

harbor's edge. A huge brass-topped fireplace warms the foyer, and comfy rooms include MP3-player docking stations and coffeemakers, plus microwaves and fridges upon request. Unless you're an avid trainspotter, water-view rooms are preferred, as freight trains rattle by on the city side.

Washington Inn   HISTORIC HOTEL $$

(📞510-452-1776; www.thewashingtoninn.com; 495 10th St; r incl breakfast $89-149; ✵@🛜) Small and modern with a boutique feel, this historic downtown lodging offers updated comfort and character, with a lobby and guest rooms that project snazz and efficient sophistication. The carved lobby bar is perfect for a predinner cocktail, and you're spoiled for choice with several fine restaurants within a few block radius.

Anthony Chabot
Regional Park   CAMPGROUND $

(📞510-639-4751; www.ebparks.org/parks/anthony_ chabot; tent sites $22, RV sites with hookups $22-28; ✵) This 5000-acre park has 75 campsites open year-round and hot showers. Reservations ($8 service charge) at 📞888-327-2757 or www.reserveamerica.com.

✗ Eating

Oakland has seen a restaurant renaissance, with scores of fun and sophisticated new eateries opening up all over town.

DOWNTOWN & JACK LONDON SQUARE

TOP CHOICE **Bakesale Betty**   BAKERY $
(www.bakesalebetty.com; 2228 Broadway; pastries from $2, sandwiches $6.50-9; ✵11am-2pm Tue-Fri; 📋) An Aussie expat and Chez Panisse alum, Betty Barakat (in signature blue wig) has patrons licking their lips and lining up out the door for her heavenly scones, strawberry shortcake and scrumptious fried chicken sandwiches. Rolling pins dangle from the ceiling, and blissed-out locals sit down at ironing-board sidewalk tables to savor buttery baked goods and seasonal specialties like sticky date pudding. Free cookie if there's a line!

Bocanova   LATIN AMERICAN $$

(📞510-444-1233; www.bocanova.com; 55 Webster St; mains $12-28; ✵11:30am-10pm Mon-Thu, 11am-11pm Fri & Sat, to 10pm Sun) A new addition to Jack London Square, you can people-watch from the outdoor patio or eat in a chic industrial dining room lit by hanging glass lamps. The focus here is Pan-American cuisine, and standouts include the Dungeness crab deviled eggs, scallops in Brazilian curry sauce, and the sweet potato and chipotle gratin. Reservations recommended on Wednesday – when wine bottles are half-price – and weekends.

Ratto's   DELI $

(www.rattos.com; 821 Washington St; sandwiches from $6; ✵9am-5:30pm Mon-Fri, 10am-3pm Sat; 📋) If you want to eat outside on a sunny day, grab a sandwich from Ratto's, a vintage Oakland grocery (since 1897) with a deli counter that attracts a devoted lunch crowd.

Plum   ORGANIC $$

(📞510-444-7586; www.plumoakland.com; 2214 Broadway; dishes $10-22; ✵11:30am-2pm & 5:30pm-1am Mon-Fri, 10am-2pm & 5pm-1am Sat & Sun; 📋) Foodies and design fans pack the communal tables at this minimalist gallery-like space with bruise-black walls and sustainable entrees.

LAKE MERRITT

Lake Chalet   SEAFOOD $$

(📞510-208-5253; www.thelakechalet.com; 1520 Lakeside Dr; mains $13-28; ✵11am-10pm Mon-Thu, to 11pm Fri, 10am-11pm Sat, to 10pm Sun) Whether you stop by the long pump house view bar for a martini and oysters during the buzzing happy hour (3pm to 6pm and 9pm to close), feast on a whole roasted crab by a window seat in the formal dining room, or cruise Lake Merritt on a Venetian-style gondola (www.gondolaservizio.com; per couple from $40), this 100-year-old former park office and boathouse is an enjoyable destination restaurant. Weekend reservations recommended.

🍴 Boot & Shoe Service   PIZZERIA $$

(📞510-763-2668; www.bootandshoeservice.com; 3308 Grand Ave; pizza from $10; ✵5:30-10pm Tue-Thu, 5-10:30pm Fri & Sat, to 10pm Sun) The occasional old-timer comes in looking for the long-gone cobbler shop, but the current patrons pack this place for its wood-fired pizzas, original cocktails and creative antipasti made from sustainably sourced fresh ingredients. Seating is mostly at shared tables, under the watch of anthropomorphic footwear paintings.

Arizmendi   BAKERY $

(http://lakeshore.arizmendi.coop; 3265 Lakeshore Ave; pizza slices $2.50; ✵7am-7pm Tue-Sat, to 6pm Sun, to 3pm Mon; 📋) Great for breakfast or lunch but beware – this bakery co-op is not for the weak-willed. The gourmet vegetarian pizza, yummy fresh breads and amazing scones are mouthwateringly addictive.

PIEDMONT AVE & ROCKRIDGE

Wood Tavern   AMERICAN $$$

(510-654-6607; www.woodtavern.net; 6317 College Ave; lunch mains $10-19, dinner mains $19-32; 11:30am-10pm Mon-Thu, to 10:30pm Fri & Sat, 5-9pm Sun) With a knock-out cheese board and charcuterie – the restaurant cures meats and makes its own salami – and a constantly changing menu of local and organic California cuisine featuring fish, pork and beef dishes with French and Italian influences, Wood Tavern has established itself as the local favorite for upscale food in a comfortable environment. The formal wood bar serves absinthe drinks and other elegant cocktails and the high-ceiling dining room is cozy enough that weekend dinner reservations are recommended.

À Côté   MEDITERRANEAN $$

(510-655-6469; www.acoterestaurant.com; 5478 College Ave; dishes $8-18; 5:30-10pm Sun-Tue, to 11pm Wed & Thu, to midnight Fri & Sat) This small plates eatery with individual and friendly communal tables is one of the best restaurants along College Ave. What the menu calls 'flatbread' is actually pizza for the gods. Mussels with Pernod is a signature dish.

Commis   CALIFORNIAN $$$

(510-653-3902; www.commisrestaurant.com; 3859 Piedmont Ave; 5-course dinner $68; from 5:30pm Wed-Sat, from 5pm Sun;) The only Michelin-starred restaurant in the East Bay, the signless and discreet dining room counts a minimalist decor and some coveted counter real estate (reservable by phone only) where patrons can watch chef James Syhabout and his team piece together creative and innovative dishes. Reservations highly recommended.

TEMESCAL & EMERYVILLE

Emeryville is a separate bite-sized city, wedged between Oakland and south Berkeley on I-80.

Homeroom   AMERICAN $

(510-597-0400; www.homeroom510.com; 400 40th St; mains $7.50-10; 11am-2pm Tue-Sat, plus 5-9pm Sun-Thu & 5-10pm Fri & Sat;) Follow the instructions to fold your menu into a paper airplane at this quirky mac-n-cheese restaurant modeled after a school. A handy

chalkboard caricature of California pinpoints the source of its regionally focused food, and the cheese choices – including cheddar, chèvre, vegan and firehouse jack – are more gourmet than anything Mom packed for your lunchbox.

Emeryville Public Market   INTERNATIONAL $

(www.emerymarket.com; 5959 Shellmound St, Emeryville; mains under $10; 7am-9pm Mon-Thu, from 9am Fri & Sat, 9am-8pm Sun) To satisfy a group of finicky eaters, cross the Amtrak tracks to the indoor and choose from dozens of ethnic food stalls dishing out a huge range of international cuisines.

Drinking

TOP CHOICE Beer Revolution   BEER HALL

(www.beer-revolution.com; 464 3rd St) Go ahead and drool. With almost 50 beers on tap, and over 500 in the bottle, there's a lifetime of discovery ahead, so kick back on the sunny deck or park yourself at that barrel table embedded with bottle caps. Bonuses include no distracting TVs and a punk soundtrack played at conversation-friendly levels. Check the website for special events like the Wednesday night meet-the-brewer sessions and Sunday barbecues.

Actual Café   CAFE

(www.actualcafe.com; 6334 San Pablo Ave; mains $4-7; 7am-8pm Mon-Thu, to 10pm Fri, 8am-10pm Sat, to 8pm Sun;) Known for its wi-fi-free weekends and inside bicycle parking, the Actual promotes sustainability and face-to-face community while keeping folks well fed with its housemade baked goods and sandwiches. Weekly movies (with free popcorn!) and live music promote mingling at its long wooden tables.

Blue Bottle Coffee Company   CAFE

(www.bluebottlecoffee.net; 300 Webster St; pastries $2-3; 7am-5pm Mon-Fri, from 8am Sat & Sun) The java gourmands queue up here for single-origin espressos and what some consider the best coffee in the country. The all-organic and very origin-specific beans are roasted on site, with compostable cups if you're taking your drink to go.

Trappist   PUB

(www.thetrappist.com; 460 8th St) So popular that it busted out of its original brick-and-wood-paneled shoebox and expanded into a second storefront and back terrace, the specialty here is Belgian ales. More than two dozen drafts rotate through the taps – with serving sizes varying based on alcohol content and special glasses for each brew – and tasty stews and sandwiches ($8 to $14) make it easy to linger.

Punchdown   WINE BAR
(www.punchdownwine.com; 2212 Broadway; ☺4-9pm Tue-Thu, to 10pm Fri, 5-1pm Sat) A super-new 'natural' wine bar, Punchdown seeks out organic, sustainably created and biodynamic producers. Playful flights include an 'adventurous orange' – whites with extended grape skin contact – and a blind flight that's free if you guess the three selections. There's an attractive outdoor area plus charcuterie and cheese board options.

Heinold's First & Last Chance Saloon BAR
(48 Webster St) An 1883 bar constructed from wood scavenged from an old whaling ship, you really have to hold on to your beer here. Keeled to a severe slant during the 1906 earthquake, the building's 20% grade might make you feel self-conscious about stumbling before you even order. Its big claim to fame is that author Jack London was a regular patron.

☆ Entertainment

Art
On the first Friday evening of the month, gallery-hop through downtown and Temescal as part of the **Oakland Art Murmur** (www.oaklandartmurmur.com; ☺6-10pm). One fun place to check out is the crafty DIY art space of the **Rock Paper Scissors Collective** (www.rpscollective.com; 2278 Telegraph Ave).

Music

TOP
CHOICE **Café Van Kleef**   LIVE MUSIC, BAR
(www.cafevankleef.com; 1621 Telegraph Ave) Order a greyhound (with fresh-squeezed grapefruit juice) and take a gander at the profusion of antique musical instruments, fake taxidermy heads, sprawling formal chandeliers and bizarro ephemera clinging to every surface possible here. Quirky, kitschy and evocative even *before* you get lit, the decade-old Café Van Kleef features live blues, jazz and the occasional rock band from Thursday through Saturday ($5 cover).

Uptown   LIVE MUSIC
(www.uptownnightclub.com; 1928 Telegraph Ave) For an eclectic calendar of indie, punk and experimental sounds, a weekly burlesque show and fun DJ dance parties, this club hits the spot. Come for a good mix of national acts and local talent, and the easy two-block walk to BART.

Yoshi's   JAZZ
(☎510-238-9200; www.yoshis.com/oakland; 510 Embarcadero W; shows $12-40) Yoshi's has a solid jazz calendar, with talent from around the world passing through on a near-nightly basis. Often, touring artists will stop in for a stand of two or three nights. It's also a Japanese restaurant, so you might enjoy a sushi plate before the show.

Mama Buzz Café   LIVE MUSIC
(www.mamabuzzcafe.com; 2318 Telegraph Ave; ☎♫) This low-key hipster cafe and alternative arts space has an eclectic roster of free music shows most nights. It serves simple vegetarian fare as well as beer.

Luka's Taproom & Lounge   DJ
(www.lukasoakland.com; 2221 Broadway) Go Uptown to get down. DJs spin nightly at this popular restaurant and lounge, with a soulful mix of hip-hop, reggae, funk and house. There's generally a $10 cover on Fridays and Saturdays after 11pm.

Theaters & Cinemas
The 2009 reopening of the Fox Theater has contributed to a groundswell of new restaurants and evening activity in the Uptown district.

Fox Theater   THEATER
(www.thefoxoakland.com; 1807 Telegraph Ave) A phoenix arisen from the urban ashes, this 1928 art deco stunner was recently restored, adding dazzle to downtown and a corner-

---

PINBALL WIZARDS, UNITE!

Put down that video game console, cast aside your latest phone app, and return to the bygone days of pinball play. Lose yourself in bells and flashing lights at **Pacific Pinball Museum** (☎510-769-1349; www.pacificpinball.org; 1510 Webster St, Alameda; adult/child $15/7.50; ☺2-9pm Tue-Thu, to midnight Fri, 11am-midnight Sat, to 9pm Sun; ☗), a pinball parlor with almost 100 games dating from the 1930s to the present, and vintage jukeboxes playing hits from the past. Take AC Transit bus 51A from downtown Oakland.

stone to the happening Uptown theater district. It's now a popular concert venue.

Paramount Theatre　　　　　THEATER
(☎510-465-6400; www.paramounttheatre.com; 2025 Broadway) This massive 1931 art deco masterpiece shows classic films a few times each month and is also home to the Oakland East Bay Symphony (www.oebs.org) and Oakland Ballet (www.oaklandballet.org). It periodically books big-name concerts. Tours ($5) are given at 10am on the first and third Saturdays of the month.

Grand Lake Theatre　　　　　CINEMA
(☎510-452-3556; www.renaissancerialto.com; 3200 Grand Ave) In Lake Merritt, this 1926 beauty lures you in with its huge corner marquee (which sometimes displays left-leaning political messages) and keeps you coming with a fun balcony and a Wurlitzer organ playing the pipes on weekends.

Sports

Sports teams play at **Overstock.com Coliseum** or the **Oracle Arena** off I-880 (Coliseum/Oakland Airport BART station). Cheer on the **Golden State Warriors**, the Bay Area's NBA basketball team, the **Oakland A's**, the Bay Area's American League baseball team, and the **Raiders**, Oakland's NFL team.

❶ Information

Oakland's daily newspaper is the *Oakland Tribune*. The free weekly *East Bay Express* (www.eastbayexpress.com) has good Oakland and Berkeley listings.

Oakland Convention & Visitors Bureau (☎510-839-9000; www.visitoakland.org; 463 11th St; ☉9am-5pm Mon-Fri) Between Broadway and Clay St.

❶ Getting There & Away

Air

Oakland International Airport (www.flyoakland.com) is directly across the bay from San Francisco International Airport, and it's usually less crowded and less expensive to fly here. Southwest Airlines has a large presence.

BART

Within the Bay Area, the most convenient way to get to Oakland and back is by **BART** (☎510-465-2278, 511; www.bart.gov). Trains run on a set schedule from 4am to midnight on weekdays, 6am to midnight on Saturday and 8am to midnight on Sunday, and operate at 15- or 20-minute intervals on average.

To get to downtown Oakland, catch a Richmond or Pittsburg/Bay Point train. Fares to the 12th or 19th St stations from downtown San Francisco are $3.10. From San Francisco to Lake Merritt ($3.10) or the Oakland Coliseum/Airport station ($3.80), catch a BART train that is heading for Fremont or Dublin/Pleasanton. Rockridge ($3.50) is on the Pittsburg/Bay Point line. Between Oakland and downtown Berkeley you can catch a Fremont-Richmond train ($1.75).

For AC Transit connections, take a transfer from the white AC Transit machines in the BART station to save 25¢ off the bus fare.

Bus

Regional company **AC Transit** (☎510-817-1717, 511; www.actransit.org) runs convenient buses from San Francisco's Transbay Temporary Terminal at Howard and Main Streets to downtown Oakland and Berkeley, and between the two East Bay cities. Scores of buses go to Oakland from San Francisco during commute hours ($4.20), but only the 'O' line runs both ways all day and on weekends; you can catch the 'O' line at the corner of 5th and Washington Sts in downtown Oakland.

After BART trains stop, late-night transportation between San Francisco and Oakland is with the 800 line, which runs hourly from downtown Market St and the Transbay Temporary Terminal in San Francisco to the corner of 14th St and Broadway.

Between Berkeley and downtown Oakland ($2.10) on weekdays, take the fast and frequent 1R bus along Telegraph Ave between the two city centers. Alternatively, take bus 18 that runs via Martin Luther King Jr Way daily.

Greyhound (☎510-832-4730; www.greyhound.com; 2103 San Pablo Ave) operates direct buses from Oakland to Vallejo, San Jose, Santa Rosa and Sacramento. The station is pretty seedy.

Car & Motorcycle

From San Francisco by car, cross the Bay Bridge and enter Oakland via one of two ways: I-580, which leads to I-980 and drops you near the City Center; or I-880, which curves through West Oakland and lets you off near the south end of Broadway. I-880 then continues to the Coliseum, the Oakland International Airport and, eventually, San Jose.

Driving to San Francisco, the bridge toll is $4 to $6, depending on the time and day of the week.

Ferry

With splendid bay views, ferries are the most enjoyable way of traveling between San Francisco and Oakland, though also the slowest and most expensive. From San Francisco's Ferry Building, the **Alameda–Oakland ferry** (☏510-522-3300; www.eastbayferry.com) sails to Jack London Sq (one-way $6.25, 30 minutes, about 12 times a day on weekdays and six to nine times a day on weekends). Ferry tickets include a free transfer, which you can use on AC Transit buses from Jack London Sq.

Train

Oakland is a regular stop for Amtrak trains operating up and down the coast. From Oakland's **Amtrak station** (☏800-872-7245; www.amtrak.com; 245 2nd St) in Jack London Sq, you can catch AC Transit bus 72 to downtown Oakland (and on weekdays the free Broadway Shuttle), or take a ferry across the bay to San Francisco.

Amtrak passengers with reservations on to San Francisco need to disembark at the **Emeryville Amtrak station** (5885 Horton St), one stop away from Oakland. From there, an Amtrak bus shuttles you to San Francisco's Ferry Building stop. The free **Emery Go Round** (www.emerygoround.com) shuttle runs a circuit that includes the Emeryville Amtrak station and MacArthur BART.

❶ Getting Around

To/From the Airport

BART is the cheapest and easiest transportation option. AirBART buses connect between the airport and the Coliseum/Oakland Airport BART station every 10 minutes until midnight. Tickets cost $3 with exact change or a BART ticket of that value.

SuperShuttle (☏800-258-3826; www.supershuttle.com) is one of many door-to-door shuttle services operating out of Oakland International Airport. One-way service to San Francisco destinations costs about $27 for the first person and $10 for the second. East Bay service destinations are also served. Reserve ahead.

A taxi from Oakland International Airport to downtown Oakland costs about $30; to downtown San Francisco about $60.

Bus

AC Transit (☏510-817-1717, 511; www.actransit.org) has a comprehensive bus network within Oakland. Fares are $2.10 and exact change is required.

On weekdays, the free new **Broadway Shuttle** (www.meetdowntownoak.com/shuttle.php; ⏱7am-7pm Mon-Fri) runs down Broadway between Jack London Square and Lake Merritt, stopping at Old Oakland/Chinatown, the downtown BART stations and the Uptown district. The lime-green buses arrive every 10 to 15 minutes.

Berkeley

As the birthplace of the Free Speech and disability rights movements, and the home of the hallowed halls of the University of California, Berkeley is no bashful wallflower. A national hotspot of (mostly left-of-center) intellectual discourse and one of the most vocal activist populations in the country, this infamous college town has an interesting mix of graying progressives and idealistic undergrads. It's easy to stereotype 'Beserkeley' for some of its recycle-or-else PC crankiness, but the city is often on the forefront of environmental and political issues that eventually go mainstream.

WATERSPORTS ON THE BAY

The San Francisco Bay makes a lovely postcard or snapshot, and there are myriad outfits to help you play in it.

California Canoe & Kayak (☏510-893-7833; www.calkayak.com; 409 Water St; rental per hr s/d kayak $15/25, canoe $25, stand-up paddleboard $15) Rents kayaks, canoes and stand-up paddleboards at Oakland's Jack London Square.

Cal Adventures (☏510-642-4000; www.recsports.berkeley.edu; 124 University Ave; ♿) Run by the UC Berkeley Aquatic Center and located at the Berkeley Marina, Cal offers sailing, surfing and sea kayaking classes and rentals for adults and youth.

Cal Sailing Club (www.cal-sailing.org) An affordable membership-based and volunteer-run nonprofit with sailing and windsurfing programs. Also based at the Berkeley Marina.

Boardsports School & Shop (http://boardsportsschool.com) Offers lessons and rentals for kiteboarding, windsurfing and stand-up paddleboarding from its three locations in San Francisco, Alameda (East Bay) and Coyote Point (p148).

Sea Trek (p113) Has kayaking and stand-up paddleboards, and a fabulous full moon paddle tour. Located in Sausalito.

Berkeley is also home to a large South Asian community, as evidenced by an abundance of sari shops on University Ave and a large number of excellent Indian restaurants.

◉ Sights & Activities

Approximately 13 miles east of San Francisco, Berkeley is bordered by the bay to the west, the hills to the east and Oakland to the south. I-80 runs along the town's western edge, next to the marina; from here University Ave heads east to downtown and the campus.

Shattuck Ave crosses University Ave one block west of campus, forming the main crossroads of the downtown area. Immediately to the south is the downtown shopping strip and the downtown Berkeley BART station.

UNIVERSITY OF CALIFORNIA, BERKELEY

The Berkeley campus of the University of California (UCB, called 'Cal' by both students and locals) is the oldest university in the state. The decision to found the college was made in 1866, and the first students arrived in 1873. Today UCB has over 35,000 students, more than 1500 professors and more Nobel laureates than you could point a particle accelerator at.

From Telegraph Ave, enter the campus via Sproul Plaza and Sather Gate, a center for people-watching, soapbox oration and pseudotribal drumming. Or you can enter from Center St and Oxford Lane, near the downtown BART station.

UC Berkeley Art Museum   MUSEUM
(☑510-642-0808; www.bampfa.berkeley.edu; 2626 Bancroft Way; adult/student $10/7, 1st Thu each month free; ☺11am-5pm Wed-Sun) The museum has 11 galleries showcasing a huge range of works, from ancient Chinese to cutting-edge contemporary. The complex also houses a bookstore, cafe and sculpture garden. The museum and the much-loved Pacific Film Archive (see p144) are scheduled to move to a new home on Oxford St between Addison and Center Streets by 2014.

Campanile   TOWER
(elevator rides $2; ☺10am-4pm Mon-Fri, to 5pm Sat, to 1:30pm & 3-5pm Sun) Officially called Sather Tower, the Campanile was modeled on St Mark's Basilica in Venice. The 328ft spire offers fine views of the Bay Area, and at the top you can stare up into the carillon of 61 bells, ranging from the size of a cereal bowl to that of a Volkswagen. Recitals take place daily at 7:50am, noon and 6pm, with a longer piece performed at 2pm on Sunday.

FREE Museum of Paleontology   MUSEUM
(☑510-642-1821; www.ucmp.berkeley.edu; ☺8am-10pm Mon-Thu, to 5pm Fri, 10am-5pm Sat, 1-10pm Sun) Housed in the ornate Valley Life Sciences Building (and primarily a research facility that's closed to the public), you can see a number of fossil exhibits in the atrium, including a *Tyrannosaurus rex* skeleton.

Bancroft Library   LIBRARY
(☑510-642-3781; http://bancroft.berkeley.edu; ☺10am-5pm Mon-Fri) The Bancroft houses, among other gems, the papers of Mark Twain, a copy of Shakespeare's First Folio and the records of the Donner Party (see the boxed text, p390). Its small public exhibits of historical Californiana include the surprisingly small gold nugget that sparked the 1849 Gold Rush. You must register to use the library and, to do so, you need to be 18 years of age (or to have graduated from high school) and present two forms of identification (one with a photo). Stop by the registration desk on your way in.

FREE Phoebe Hearst Museum of Anthropology   MUSEUM
(☑510-643-7649; http://hearstmuseum.berkeley.edu; ☺10am-4:30pm Wed-Sat, noon-4pm Sun) South of the Campanile in Kroeber Hall, this museum includes exhibits from indigenous cultures around the world, including ancient Peruvian, Egyptian and African items. There's also a large collection highlighting native Californian cultures.

SOUTH OF CAMPUS
Telegraph Ave   STREET
Telegraph Ave has traditionally been the throbbing heart of studentville in Berkeley, the sidewalks crowded with undergrads, postdocs and youthful shoppers squeezing their way past throngs of vendors, buskers and homeless people. Numerous cafes and budget food options cater to students, and most of them are very good.

The frenetic energy buzzing from the university's Sather Gate on any given day is a mixture of youthful posthippies reminiscing about days before their time and young hipsters and punk rockers who sneer at tie-dyed nostalgia. Panhandlers press you for change, and street stalls hawk everything from crystals to bumper stickers to self-published tracts.

People's Park
PARK

This park, just east of Telegraph, between Haste St and Dwight Way, is a marker in local history as a political battleground between residents and the city and state government in the late 1960s. The park has since served mostly as a gathering spot for Berkeley's homeless. A publicly funded restoration spruced it up a bit, and occasional festivals do still happen here, but it's rather run-down.

Elmwood District
DISTRICT

South along College Ave is the Elmwood District, a charming nook of shops and restaurants that offers a calming alternative to the frenetic buzz around Telegraph Ave. Continue further south and you'll be in Rockridge.

First Church of Christ Scientist
CHURCH

(www.friendsoffirstchurch.org; 2619 Dwight Way; ⊗services Sun) Bernard Maybeck's impressive 1910 church uses concrete and wood in its blend of Arts and Crafts, Asian and Gothic influences. Maybeck was a professor of architecture at UC Berkeley and designed San Francisco's Palace of Fine Arts, plus many landmark homes in the Berkeley Hills. Free tours happen the first Sunday of every month at 12:15pm.

Julia Morgan Theatre
THEATER

(☑510-845-8542; 2640 College Ave) To the southeast of People's Park is this beautifully understated, redwood-infused 1910 theater, a performance space (formerly a church) created by Bay Area architect Julia Morgan. She designed numerous Bay Area buildings and, most famously, the Hearst Castle (see p485).

DOWNTOWN

Berkeley's downtown, centered on Shattuck Ave between University Ave and Dwight Way, has far fewer traces of the city's tie-dyed reputation. The area has emerged as an exciting arts district with numerous shops and restaurants and restored public buildings. At the center are the acclaimed thespian stomping grounds of the Berkeley Repertory Theatre (see p144) and the Aurora Theatre Company (see p145) and live music at the Freight & Salvage Coffeehouse (see p144); a few good movie houses are also nearby.

NORTH BERKELEY

Not too far north of campus is a neighborhood filled with lovely garden-front homes, parks and some of the best restaurants in California. The popular **Gourmet Ghetto** stretches along Shattuck Ave north of University Ave for several blocks, anchored by Chez Panisse (see p143). Northwest of here, **Solano Ave**, which crosses from Berkeley into Albany, is lined with lots of funky shops and more good restaurants.

On Euclid Ave just south of Eunice St is the **Berkeley Rose Garden** and its eight terraces of colourful explosions. Here you'll find quiet benches and a plethora of almost perpetually blooming roses arranged by hue. Across the street is a picturesque park with a children's playground (including a very fun concrete slide, about 100ft long).

THE BERKELEY HILLS

Tilden Regional Park
PARK

(www.ebparks.org/parks/tilden) This 2079-acre park, in the hills east of town, is Berkeley's crown jewel. It has more than 30 miles of trails of varying difficulty, from paved paths to hilly scrambles, including part of the magnificent Bay Area Ridge Trail. Other attractions include a miniature steam train ($2), a children's farm, a wonderfully wild-looking botanical garden, an 18-hole **golf course** (☑510-848-7373) and environmental education center. **Lake Anza** is a favorite area for picnics, and from spring through late fall you can swim here for $3.50. AC Transit bus 67 runs to the park on weekends and holidays from the downtown BART station, but only stops at the entrances on weekdays.

UC Botanical Garden
GARDENS

(☑510-643-2755; http://botanicalgarden.berkeley.edu; 200 Centennial Dr; adult/child 13-17/child 5-12 $9/5/2, 1st Thu of month free; ⊗9am-5pm, closed 1st Tue of month) This is another great find in the hills, in Strawberry Canyon. With 34 acres and more than 12,000 species of plants, the garden is one of the most varied collections in the USA. It can be reached via the Bear Transit shuttle H line.

The nearby fire trail is a woodsy walking loop around Strawberry Canyon that has great views of town and the off-limits Lawrence Berkeley National Laboratory. Enter at the trailhead at the parking lot on Centennial Dr just southwest of the Botanical Garden; you'll emerge near the Lawrence Hall of Science.

Central Berkeley

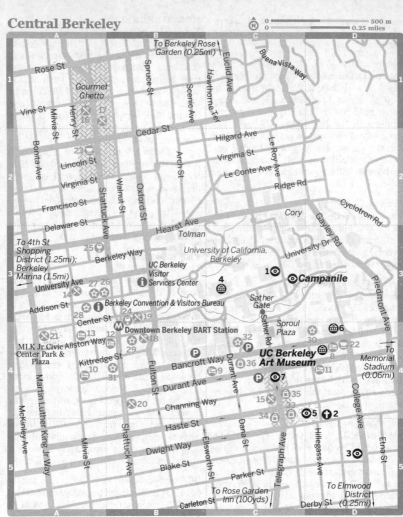

Lawrence Hall of Science SCIENCE CENTER
(☎510-642-5132; www.lawrencehallofscience.org;
Centennial Dr; adult/senior & child 7-8/child 3-6
$12/9/6; ☺10am-5pm daily; ⌖) Near Grizzly
Peak Blvd, the science hall is named after
Ernest Lawrence, who won the Nobel Prize
for his invention of the cyclotron particle
accelerator. He was a key member of the
WWII Manhattan Project, and he's also the
name behind the Lawrence Berkeley and
Lawrence Livermore laboratories. The Hall
of Science has a huge collection of interactive exhibits for kids and adults on subjects
ranging from earthquakes to nanotechnology, and outside there's a 60ft model of a DNA
molecule. AC Transit bus 65 runs to the hall
from the downtown BART station. You can
also catch the university's Bear Transit shuttle (H line) from the Hearst Mining Circle.

WEST BERKELEY

San Pablo Ave STREET
Formerly US Rte 40, this was the main thoroughfare from the east before I-80 came
along. The area north of University Ave is
still lined with a few older motels, diners
and atmospheric dive bars with neon signs.
South of University Ave are pockets of trend-

Central Berkeley

MARIN COUNTY & THE BAY AREA BERKELEY

iness, such as the short stretch of gift shops and cafes around Dwight Way.

4th St Shopping District DISTRICT
Hidden within an industrial area near I-80 lies a three-block area offering shaded sidewalks for upscale shopping or just strolling, and a few good restaurants.

Berkeley Marina MARINA
At the west end of University Ave is the marina, frequented by squawking seagulls, silent types fishing from the pier, unleashed dogs and, especially on windy weekends, lots of colorful kites. Construction of the marina began in 1936, though the pier has much older origins. It was originally built in the 1870s, then replaced by a 3-mile-long ferry pier in 1920 (its length was dictated by the extreme shallowness of the bay). Part of the original pier is now rebuilt, affording visitors sweeping bay views.

Adventure Playground PLAYGROUND
(☑510-981-6720; www.cityofberkeley.info/marina; ⊙11am-4pm Sat & Sun, closed last week of year; ♿) At the marina is one of the coolest play spaces in the country – a free outdoor park

encouraging creativity and cooperation where supervised kids of any age can help build and paint their own structures. Dress the tykes in play clothes, because they *will* get dirty.

FREE **Takara Sake** MUSEUM
(www.takarasake.com; 708 Addison St; ⊙noon-6pm) Stop in to see the traditional wooden tools used for making sake and a short video of the brewing process. Tours of the factory aren't offered, but you can view elements of modern production and bottling through a window. Flights ($5) are available in a spacious tasting room constructed with reclaimed wood and floor tiles fashioned from recycled glass.

🛏 Sleeping

Lodging rates spike during special university events like graduation (mid-May) and home football games. A number of older motels along University Ave can be handy during peak demand. For B&B options, see the Berkeley & Oakland Bed & Breakfast Network (p132).

TOP CHOICE **Hotel Shattuck Plaza** BOUTIQUE HOTEL $$$
(☎510-845-7300; www.hotelshattuckplaza.com; 2086 Allston Way; r $219-59; ❄@📶) Peace is quite posh following a $15 million renovation and greening of this 100-year-old downtown jewel. A foyer of red Italian glass lighting, flocked Victorian-style wallpaper – and yes, a peace sign tiled into the floor – leads to comfortable rooms with down comforters, and an airy and columned restaurant serving all meals. Accommodations off Shattuck are the quietest, and Cityscape rooms boast bay views.

Hotel Durant BOUTIQUE HOTEL $$
(☎510-845-8981; www.hoteldurant.com; 2600 Durant Ave; r from $134; @📶🐾) Located a block from campus, this classic 1928 hotel has been cheekily renovated to highlight the connection to the university. The lobby is adorned with embarrassing yearbook photos and a ceiling mobile of exam books, and smallish rooms have dictionary-covered shower curtains and bongs repurposed into bedside lamps.

Berkeley City Club HISTORIC HOTEL $$
(☎510-848-7800; www.berkeleycityclub.com; 2315 Durant Ave; r/ste incl breakfast from $145/235; 🏊@📶) Designed by Julia Morgan, the architect of Hearst Castle (see p485), the 36 rooms and dazzling common areas of this refurbished 1929 historic landmark building (which is also a private club) feel like a glorious time warp into a more refined era. The hotel contains lush and serene Italianate courtyards, gardens and terraces, and a stunning indoor pool. Elegant Old-World rooms contain no TVs, and those with numbers ending in 4 and 8 have to-die-for views of the bay and the Golden Gate Bridge.

Bancroft Hotel HISTORIC HOTEL $$
(☎510-549-1000, 800-549-1002; www.bancrofthotel.com; 2680 Bancroft Way; r incl breakfast $129-149; @📶) A gorgeous 1928 Arts and Crafts building that was originally a women's club, the Bancroft is just across the street from campus and two blocks from Telegraph Ave. It has 22 comfortable, beautifully furnished rooms (number 302 boasts a lovely balcony) and a spectacular bay-view rooftop, though no elevator.

YMCA HOSTEL $
(☎510-848-6800; www.ymca-cba.org/downtown-berkeley; 2001 Allston Way; s/d $49/81; 🏊@📶) Recently remodeled with new bedding and carpet, the 100-year-old downtown Y building is still the best budget option in town. Rates for the austere private rooms (all with shared bathroom) include use of the sauna, pool and fitness center, and kitchen facilities, and wheelchair accessible rooms are available as well. Corner rooms 310 and 410 boast enviable bay views. Entrance on Milvia St.

Downtown Berkeley Inn MOTEL $
(☎510-843-4043; www.downtownberkeleyinn.com; 2001 Bancroft Way; r $89-109; ❄📶) A 27-room budget boutique-style motel with good-sized rooms and correspondingly ample flat-screen TVs.

Rose Garden Inn INN $$
(☎510-549-2145, 800-922-9005; www.rosegardeninn.com; 2740 Telegraph Ave; r incl breakfast $98-185; @📶) The decor flirting with flowery, this cute place is a few blocks south from the Telegraph Ave action and very peaceful, with two old houses surrounded by pretty gardens.

Eating

Telegraph Ave is packed with cafes, pizza counters and cheap restaurants, and Berkeley's Little India runs along the University Ave corridor. Many more restaurants can be found downtown along Shattuck Ave near the BART station. The section of Shattuck Ave north of University Ave is the 'Gourmet Ghetto,' home to lots of excellent eating establishments.

DOWNTOWN & AROUND CAMPUS

Gather AMERICAN $$
(☎510-809-0400; www.gatherrestaurant.com; 2200 Oxford St; lunch mains $10-17, dinner mains $14-19; ⏲11:30am-2pm Mon-Fri, 10am-2:30pm Sat & Sun, & 5-10pm daily; 🖉) When vegan foodies and passionate farm-to-table types dine out together, they often end up here. Inside a salvaged wood interior punctuated by green vines streaking down over an open kitchen, patrons swoon over dishes created from locally sourced ingredients and sustainably raised meats. Reserve for dinner.

TOP CHOICE **Ippuku** JAPANESE $$
(☎510-665-1969; www.ippukuberkeley.com; 2130 Center St; small plates $5-18; ⏲5-11pm) Specializing in *shochu* (flights $12), a distilled alcohol made from rice, barley or sweet potato, Japanese expats gush that Ippuku reminds

them of *izakayas* (pub-style restaurants) back in Tokyo. Choose from a menu of skewered meats and settle in at one of the traditional wood platform tables (no shoes, please) or cozy booth perches. Reservations essential.

La Note
FRENCH **$$**

(☎510-843-1535; www.lanoterestaurant.com; 2377 Shattuck Ave; mains $10-17; ⏱8am-2:30pm Mon-Fri, to 3pm Sat & Sun, & 6-10pm Thu-Sat) A rustic country-French bistro downtown, La Note serves excellent breakfasts. Wake up to a big bowl of café au lait, paired with oatmeal raspberry pancakes or lemon gingerbread pancakes with poached pears. Anticipate a wait on weekends.

Café Intermezzo
CAFETERIA **$**

(2442 Telegraph Ave; sandwiches & salads $6.50) Mammoth salads draw a constant crowd, and we're not talking about delicate little rabbit food plates. Bring a friend, or you might drown while trying to polish off a Veggie Delight heaped with beans, hard-boiled egg and avocado.

Au Coquelet Café
CAFE **$**

(www.aucoquelet.com; 2000 University Ave; mains $6-9; ⏱6am-1am Sun-Thu, to 1:30am Sat & Sun; 🛜) Open till late, Au Coquelet is a popular stop for postmovie meals or late-night studying. The front section serves coffee and pastries while the skylit and spacious back room does a big range of omelets, pastas, sandwiches, burgers and salads.

Berkeley Farmers Market
MARKET **$**

(⏱10am-3pm Sat) Pick up some organic produce or tasty prepared food at the downtown farmers market, operating year-round, at Center St and MLK Way, and sit down to munch at MLK Park across from city hall.

NORTH BERKELEY

TOP CHOICE Chez Panisse
AMERICAN **$$$**

(☎restaurant 510-548-5525, cafe 510-548-5049; www.chezpanisse.com; 1517 Shattuck Ave; restaurant mains $60-95, cafe mains $18-29; ⏱restaurant dinner Mon-Sat, cafe lunch & dinner Mon-Sat) Foodies come to worship here at the church of Alice Waters, the inventor of California cuisine. The restaurant is as good and popular as it ever was, and despite its fame the place has retained a welcoming atmosphere. It's in a lovely Arts and Crafts house in the Gourmet Ghetto, and you can choose to pull all the stops with a prix-fixe meal downstairs, or go less expensive and a tad less formal in the cafe upstairs. [...] ahead.

Cheese Board Collective
(☎510-549-3183; www.cheeseb[...] 1504 & 1512 Shattuck Ave; piz[...] Stop in to take stock of the [...] available at this worker-owned busin[...] scoop up some fresh bread to make a picnic lunch. Or sit down for a slice of the fabulously crispy one-option-per-day veggie pizza just next door, where live music's often featured.

WEST BERKELEY

Vik's Chaat Corner
INDIAN **$**

(www.vikschaatcorner.com; 2390 4th St; dishes $5-7; ⏱11am-6pm Mon-Thu, to 8pm Fri-Sun; 🍴) This longtime and very popular *chaat* house has moved to a larger space but still gets mobbed at lunchtime by regulars that include an equal number of hungry office workers and Indian families. Try a *cholle* (spicy garbanzo curry) or one of the many filling *dosas* (savory crepes) from the weekend menu. It's on the corner of Channing Way, one block east of the waterfront.

Bette's Oceanview Diner
DINER **$**

(☎510-644-3230; www.bettesdiner.com; 1807 4th St; mains $7-11; ⏱6:30am-2:30pm Mon-Fri, to 4pm Sat & Sun) A buzzing breakfast spot, especially on the weekends, serving yummy baked soufflé pancakes and German-style potato pancakes with applesauce, plus eggs and sandwiches. Superfresh food and a nifty diner interior make it worth the wait. It's about a block north of University Ave.

🍷 Drinking

Guerilla Café
CAFE

(☎510-845-2233; www.guerillacafe.com; 1620 Shattuck Ave) Exuding a 1970s flavor, this small and sparkling cafe has a creative political vibe, with polka-dot tiles on the counter handmade by one of the artist-owners, and order numbers spotlighting guerillas and liberation revolutionaries. Organic and Fair Trade ingredients feature in the breakfasts and panini sandwiches, and locally roasted Blue Bottle coffee is served. Occasional film screenings and pop-up cuisine nights pack the place.

Caffe Strada
CAFE

(2300 College Ave; 🛜) A popular, student-saturated hangout with an inviting shaded patio and strong espressos. Try the signature white chocolate mocha.

Jupiter
(www.j[...]
dow[...]
b[...]

PUB

...piterbeer.com; 2181 Shattuck Ave) This ...town pub has loads of regional micro-...ws, a beer garden, good pizza and live bands most nights. Sit upstairs for a bird's-eye view of bustling Shattuck Ave.

Casa Vino
WINE BAR

(www.casavinobistro.com; 3136 Sacramento St) A few blocks west of Ashby BART, this unpretentious and somewhat nondescript wine bar serves an eyebrow-raising 95 wines by the glass. Relax on the outdoor patio during warm nights.

Albatross
PUB

(www.albatrosspub.com; 1822 San Pablo Ave; ☻) A block north of University Ave, Berkeley's oldest pub is one of the most inviting and friendly in the entire Bay Area. Some serious darts are played here, and boardgames will be going on around many of the worn-out tables. Sunday is Pub Quiz night.

Triple Rock Brewery & Ale House
BREWERY

(1920 Shattuck Ave) Opened in 1986, Triple Rock was one of the country's first brewpubs. The house beers and pub grub are quite good, and the antique wooden bar and rooftop sun deck are delightful.

☆ Entertainment

The arts corridor on Addison St between Milvia and Shattuck Sts anchors a lively downtown entertainment scene.

Live Music

Berkeley has plenty of intimate live music venues. Cover charges range from $5 to $20, and a number of venues are all-ages or 18-and-over.

924 Gilman
PUNK ROCK

(www.924gilman.org; 924 Gilman St; ⊘Fri-Sun) This volunteer-run and booze-free all-ages space is a West Coast punk rock institution. Take AC Transit bus 9 from Berkeley BART.

Freight & Salvage Coffeehouse
FOLK, WORLD

(☑510-644-2020; www.thefreight.org; 2020 Addison St; ♿) This legendary club has over 40 years of history and recently relocated to the downtown arts district. It still features great traditional folk and world music and welcomes all ages, with half price tickets for patrons under 21.

Shattuck Down Low
CLUB

(☑510-548-1159; www.shattuckdownlow.com; 2284 Shattuck Ave) A fun multiethnic crowd fills this basement space that sometimes books big-name bands. Locals love the Tuesday karaoke nights and the smokin' all-levels-welcome salsa on Wednesdays.

La Peña Cultural Center
WORLD

(☑510-849-2568; www.lapena.org; 3105 Shattuck Ave) A few blocks east of the Ashby BART station, this cultural center and Chilean cafe presents dynamic musical and visual arts programming with a peace and justice bent. Look for the vibrant mural on its facade.

Ashkenaz
FOLK, WORLD

(☑510-525-5054; www.ashkenaz.com; 1317 San Pablo Ave; ♿) Ashkenaz is a 'music and dance community center' attracting activists, hippies and fans of folk, swing and world music who love to dance (lessons offered).

Cinemas

Pacific Film Archive
CINEMA

(☑510-642-1124; www.bampfa.berkeley.edu; 2575 Bancroft Way; adult/student & senior $9.50/6.50) A world-renowned film center with an ever-changing schedule of international and classic films, cineastes should seek this place out. The spacious theater has seats that are comfy enough for hours-long movie marathons.

Theater & Dance

Zellerbach Hall
PERFORMING ARTS

(☑510-642-9988; http://tickets.berkeley.edu) On the south end of campus near Bancroft Way and Dana St, Zellerbach Hall features dance events, concerts and performances of all types by national and international artists. The onsite Cal Performances Ticket Office sells tickets without a handling fee.

Berkeley Repertory Theatre
THEATER

(☑510-647-2949; www.berkeleyrep.org; 2025 Addison St) This highly respected company has produced bold versions of classical and modern plays since 1968.

California Shakespeare Theater
THEATER

(☑510-548-9666; www.calshakes.org; box office 701 Heinz Ave) Headquartered in Berkeley, with a fantastic outdoor amphitheater further east in Orinda, 'Cal Shakes' is a warm-weather tradition of al fresco Shakespeare (and other classic) productions, with a season that lasts from about June through September.

Aurora Theatre Company THEATER
(☎510-843-4822; www.auroratheatre.org; 2081 Addison St) An intimate downtown theater, it performs contemporary and thought-provoking plays staged with a subtle chamber-theater aesthetic.

Marsh PERFORMING ARTS
(☎510-704-8291; www.themarsh.org; 2120 Allston Way) The 'breeding ground for new performance' now has a Berkeley toehold for eclectic solo and comedy acts.

Shotgun Players THEATER
(☎510-841-6500; www.shotgunplayers.org; 1901 Ashby Avenue) The country's first all-solar-powered theater company stages exciting and provocative work in an intimate space. Across from the Ashby BART station.

Sports
Memorial Stadium, which dates from 1923, is the university's 71,000-seat sporting venue, and the Hayward Fault runs just beneath it. On alternate years, it's the site of the famous football frenzy between the UC Berkeley and Stanford teams.

The Cal Athletic Ticket Office (☎800-462-3277; www.calbears.com) has ticket information on all UC Berkeley sports events. Keep in mind that some sell out weeks in advance.

🛍 Shopping
Branching off the UC campus, Telegraph Ave caters mostly to students, hawking a steady dose of urban hippie gear, handmade sidewalk-vendor jewelry and head-shop paraphernalia. Audiophiles will swoon over the music stores. Other shopping corridors include College Ave in the Elmwood District, 4th St (north of University Ave) and Solano Ave.

Amoeba Music MUSIC
(☎510-549-1125; 2455 Telegraph Ave) If you're a music junkie, you might plan on spending a few hours at the original Berkeley branch of Amoeba Music, packed with massive quantities of new and used CDs, DVDs, tapes and records (yes, lots of vinyl).

Moe's BOOKS
(☎510-849-2087; 2476 Telegraph Ave) A long-standing local favorite, Moe's offers four floors of new, used and remaindered books for hours of browsing.

University Press Books BOOKS
(☎510-548-0585; 2430 Bancroft Way) Across the street from campus, this academic and scholarly bookstore stocks works by UC Berkeley professors and other academic and museum publishers.

Down Home Music MUSIC
(☎510-525-2129; 10341 San Pablo Ave, El Cerrito) North of Berkeley in El Cerrito, this world-class store for roots, blues, folk, Latin and world music is affiliated with the Arhoolie record label, which has been issuing landmark recordings since the early 1960s.

Rasputin MUSIC
(☎800-350-8700; 2401 Telegraph Ave) Another large music store full of new and used releases.

Marmot Mountain Works OUTDOOR EQUIPMENT
(☎510-849-0735; 3049 Adeline St) Has climbing, ski and backpacking equipment for sale and for rent. Located one block north of Ashby BART station.

North Face Outlet OUTDOOR EQUIPMENT
(☎510-526-3530; cnr 5th & Gilman Sts) Discount store for the well-respected Bay Area-based brand of outdoor gear. It's a few blocks west of San Pablo Ave.

REI OUTDOOR EQUIPMENT
(☎510-527-4140; 1338 San Pablo Ave) This large and busy co-op lures in active folks for camping and mountaineering rentals, sports clothing and all kinds of nifty outdoor gear.

ℹ Information
Alta Bates Summit Medical Center (☎510-204-4444; 2450 Ashby Ave) 24-hour emergency services.

Berkeley Convention & Visitors Bureau (☎510-549-7040, 800-847-4823; www.visit berkeley.com; 2030 Addison St; ⊙9am-1pm & 2-5pm Mon-Fri) This helpful bureau has a free visitors guide.

UC Berkeley Visitor Services Center (☎510-642-5215; http://visitors.berkeley.edu; 101 Sproul Hall) Campus maps and information available. Free 90-minute campus tours are given at 10am Monday to Saturday and 1pm Sunday; reservations required.

ℹ Getting There & Away
BART
The easiest way to travel between San Francisco, Berkeley, Oakland and other East Bay points is on **BART** (☎510-465-2278, 511; www.bart. gov). Trains run approximately every 10 minutes

SHAKE, RATTLE & ROLL

Curious to find a few places where the earth shook? Visit these notorious spots in and around the Bay Area:

» **Earthquake Trail** (p128) at Point Reyes National Seashore shows the effects of the big one in 1906.

» Forty-two people died when the Cypress Freeway collapsed in West Oakland, one of the most horrifying and enduring images of the 1989 Loma Prieta quake. The **Cypress Freeway Memorial Park** at 14th St and Mandela Parkway commemorates those who perished and those who helped rescue survivors.

» Near Aptos in Santa Cruz County, a sign on the Aptos Creek Trail in the **Forest of Nisene Marks State Park** (☎831-763-7062; www.parks.ca.gov) marks the actual epicenter of the Loma Prieta quake, and on the Big Slide Trail a number of fissures can be spotted.

» The Hayward Fault runs just beneath **Memorial Stadium** (p145) at UC Berkeley.

from 4am to midnight on weekdays, with limited service from 6am on Saturday and from 8am on Sunday.

To get to Berkeley, catch a Richmond-bound train to one of three BART stations: Ashby (Adeline St and Ashby Ave), Downtown Berkeley (Shattuck Ave and Center St) or North Berkeley (Sacramento and Delaware Sts). The fare ranges from $3.50 to $3.85 between Berkeley and San Francisco; $1.75 between Berkeley and downtown Oakland. After 8pm on weekdays, 7pm on Saturday and all day Sunday, there is no direct service operating from San Francisco to Berkeley; instead, catch a Pittsburg/Bay Point train and transfer at 19th St station in Oakland.

A **BART-to-Bus** transfer ticket, available from white AC Transit machines near the BART turnstiles, reduces the connecting bus fare by 25¢.

Bus

The regional company **AC Transit** (☎510-817-1717, 511; www.actransit.org) operates a number of buses from San Francisco's **Transbay Temporary Terminal** (Howard & Main Sts) to the East Bay. The F line leaves from the Transbay Temporary Terminal to the corner of University and Shattuck Aves approximately every half-hour ($4.20, 30 minutes).

Between Berkeley and downtown Oakland ($2.10) on weekdays, take the fast and frequent 1R bus along Telegraph Ave between the two city centers, or bus 18 that runs daily via Martin Luther King Jr Way. Bus 51B travels along University Ave from Berkeley BART to the Berkeley Marina.

Car & Motorcycle

With your own wheels you can approach Berkeley from San Francisco by taking the Bay Bridge and then following either I-80 (for University Ave, downtown Berkeley and the UCB campus)

or Hwy 24 (for College Ave and the Berkeley Hills).

Driving to San Francisco, the bridge toll is $4 to $6, depending on the time and day of the week.

Train

Amtrak does stop in Berkeley, but the shelter is not staffed and direct connections are few. More convenient is the nearby **Emeryville Amtrak station** (☎800-872-7245; www.amtrak.com; 5885 Horton St), a few miles south.

To reach the Emeryville station from downtown Berkeley, take a Transbay F bus or ride BART to the MacArthur station and then take the free Emery Go Round bus (Hollis route) to Amtrak.

ⓘ Getting Around

Public transportation, cycling and walking are the best options for getting around central Berkeley.

BICYCLE Cycling is a popular means of transportation, and safe and well-marked 'bicycle boulevards' with signed distance information to landmarks make crosstown journeys very easy. Just north of Berkeley, **Solano Avenue Cyclery** (☎510-524-1094; 1554 Solano Ave, Albany; ☺Mon-Sat) has 24-hour mountain- and road-bike rentals for $35 to $45.

BUS AC Transit operates public buses in and around Berkeley, and UC Berkeley's **Bear Transit** (http://pt.berkeley.edu/around/transit/routes) runs a shuttle from the downtown BART station to various points on campus ($1). From its stop at the Hearst Mining Circle, the H Line runs along Centennial Dr to the higher parts of the campus.

CAR & MOTORCYCLE Drivers should note that numerous barriers have been set up to prevent car traffic from traversing residential streets at high speeds, so zigzagging is necessary in some neighborhoods.

Mt Diablo State Park

Collecting a light dusting of snowflakes on the coldest days of winter, at 3849ft Mt Diablo is more than 1000ft higher than Mt Tamalpais in Marin County. On a clear day (early on a winter morning is a good bet) the views from Diablo's summit are vast and sweeping. To the west you can see over the bay and out to the Farallon Islands; to the east you can see over the Central Valley to the Sierra Nevada.

The Mt Diablo State Park (925-837-2525; www.mdia.org; per vehicle $6-10; 8am-sunset) has 50 miles of hiking trails, and can be reached from Walnut Creek, Danville or Clayton. You can also drive to the top, where there's a visitors center (10am-4pm). The park office is at the junction of the two entry roads. Of the three campgrounds (800-444-7275; www.reserveamerica.com; tent & RV sites $30), Juniper has showers, though all can be closed during high fire danger.

John Muir National Historic Site

Less than 15 miles north of Walnut Creek, the John Muir residence (925-228-8860; www.nps.gov/jomu; 4202 Alhambra Ave, Martinez; adult/child $3/free; 10am-5pm Wed-Sun) sits in a pastoral patch of farmland in bustling, modern Martinez. Though he wrote of sauntering the High Sierra with a sack of tea and bread, it may be a shock for those familiar with the iconic Sierra Club founder's ascetic weather-beaten appearance that the house (built by his father-in-law) is a model of Victorian Italianate refinement, with a tower cupola, a daintily upholstered parlor and splashes of fussy white lace. His 'scribble den' has been left as it was during his life, with crumbled papers overflowing from wire wastebaskets and dried bread balls – his preferred snack – resting on the mantelpiece. Acres of his fruit orchard still stand, and visitors can enjoy seasonal samples. The grounds include the 1849 Martinez Adobe, part of the rancho on which the house was built.

The park is just north of Hwy 4, and accessible by County Connection (http://cccta.org) buses from Amtrak and BART.

Vallejo

For one week in 1852 Vallejo was officially the California state capital – but the fickle legislature changed its mind. It tried Vallejo a second time in 1853, but after a month moved on again (to Benicia). That same year, Vallejo became the site of the first US naval installation on the West Coast (Mare Island Naval Shipyard, now closed). Vallejo Naval & Historical Museum (707-643-0077; www.vallejomuseum.org; 734 Marin St; admission $5; noon-4pm Tue-Sat) tells the story.

The town's biggest tourist draw, though, is Six Flags Discovery Kingdom (707-643-6722; www.sixflags.com/discoverykingdom; adult/child under 4ft $50/36; approx 10:30am-6pm Fri-Sun spring & fall, to 8pm or 9pm daily summer, variable weekend & holiday hr Dec), a modern wildlife and theme park offering mighty coasters and other rides alongside animal shows featuring sharks and a killer whale. Significant discounts are available on the park's website. Exit I-80 at Hwy 37 westbound, 5 miles north of downtown Vallejo. Parking is $15.

Operated by Blue & Gold Fleet, Vallejo Baylink Ferry (877-643-3779; www.baylinkferry.com; one way adult/child $13/6.50) runs ferries from San Francisco's Pier 41 at Fisherman's Wharf and the Ferry Building to Vallejo; the

WORTH A TRIP

EAST BROTHER LIGHT STATION

Most Bay Area residents have never heard of this speck of an island off the East Bay city of Richmond, and even fewer know that the East Brother Light Station (510-233-2385; www.ebls.org; d incl breakfast & dinner $355-415; Thu-Sun) is a extraordinary five-room Victorian B&B. Spend the night in the romantic lighthouse or fog signal building (the foghorn is used from October through March), where every window has stupendous bay views and harbor seals frolic in the frigid currents. Resident innkeepers serve afternoon hors d'oeuvres and champagne, and between gourmet meals you can stroll around the breezy one-acre islet and rummage through historical photos and artifacts journey takes one hour. Discount admission and transportation packages for Six Flags are available from San Francisco.

Vallejo is also somewhat of a gateway to the Wine Country. See p161 and p167.

THE PENINSULA

South of San Francisco, squeezed tightly between the bay and the coastal foothills, a vast swath of suburbia continues to San Jose and beyond. Dotted within this area are Palo Alto, Stanford University and Silicon Valley, the center of the Bay Area's immense tech industry. West of the foothills, Hwy 1 runs down the Pacific coast via Half Moon Bay and a string of beaches to Santa Cruz. Hwy 101 and I-280 both run to San Jose, where they connect with Hwy 17, the quickest route to Santa Cruz. Any of these routes can be combined into an interesting loop or extended to the Monterey Peninsula.

And don't bother looking for Silicon Valley on the map – you won't find it. Because silicon chips form the basis of modern microcomputers, and the Santa Clara Valley – stretching from Palo Alto down through Mountain View, Sunnyvale, Cupertino and Santa Clara to San Jose – is thought of as the birthplace of the microcomputer, it's been dubbed 'Silicon Valley.' The Santa Clara Valley is wide and flat, and its towns are essentially a string of shopping centers and industrial parks linked by a maze of freeways. It's hard to imagine that even after WWII this area was still a wide expanse of orchards and farms.

San Francisco to San Jose

South of the San Francisco peninsula, I-280 is the dividing line between the densely populated South Bay area and the rugged and lightly populated Pacific Coast. With sweeping views of hills and reservoirs, I-280 is a more scenic choice than crowded Hwy 101, which runs through miles of boring business parks. Unfortunately, these parallel north-south arteries are both clogged with traffic during commute times and often on weekends.

A historic site where European explorers first set eyes on San Francisco Bay, Sweeney Ridge (www.nps.gov/goga/planyourvisit/upload/sb-sweeney-2008.pdf), straddles a prime spot between Pacifica and San Bruno, and offers hikers unparalleled ocean and bay views. From I-280, exit at Sneath Lane and follow it 2 miles west until it dead ends at the trailhead.

Right on the bay at the northern edge of San Mateo, 4 miles south of San Francisco International Airport, is Coyote Point Recreation Area (per vehicle $5; 📷), a popular park and windsurfing destination. The main attraction – formerly known as the Coyote Point Museum – is CuriOdyssey (☑650-342-7755; www.curiodyssey.org; adult/child $8/4; ☺10am-5pm Tue-Sat, noon-5pm Sun, free 1st Sun of month; 📷), with innovative exhibits for kids and adults concentrating on ecological and environmental issues. Exit Hwy 101 at Coyote Point Dr.

San Jose

Though culturally diverse and historic, San Jose has always been in San Francisco's shadow, awash in Silicon Valley's suburbia. Founded in 1777 as El Pueblo de San José de Guadalupe, San Jose is California's oldest Spanish civilian settlement. Its downtown is small and scarcely used for a city of its size, though it does bustle with 20-something clubgoers on the weekends. Industrial parks, high-tech computer firms and look-alike housing developments have sprawled across the city's landscape, taking over where farms, ranches and open spaces once spread between the bay and the surrounding hills.

◉ Sights

Downtown San Jose is at the junction of Hwy 87 and I-280. Hwy 101 and I-880 complete the box. Running roughly north-south along the length of the city, from the old port town of Alviso on the San Francisco Bay all the way downtown, is 1st St; south of I-280, its name changes to Monterey Hwy.

San Jose State University is immediately east of downtown, and the SoFA district, with numerous nightclubs, restaurants and galleries, is on a stretch of S 1st St south of San Carlos St.

TOP CHOICE History Park   PARK
(☑408-287-2290; www.historysanjose.org; cnr Senter Rd & Phelan Ave; ☺11am-5pm Tue-Sun) Historic buildings from all over San Jose have been brought together in this open-air history museum, southeast of the city center in Kelley Park. The centerpiece is a dramatic half-scale

STANFORD UNIVERSITY

Sprawled over 8200 leafy acres in Palo Alto, Stanford University (www.stanford.edu) was founded by Leland Stanford, one of the Central Pacific Railroad's 'Big Four' founders and a former governor of California. When the Stanfords' only child died of typhoid during a European tour in 1884, they decided to build a university in his memory. Stanford University was opened in 1891, just two years before Leland Stanford's death, but the university grew to become a prestigious and wealthy institution. The campus was built on the site of the Stanfords' horse-breeding farm and, as a result, Stanford is still known as 'The Farm.'

Auguste Rodin's *Burghers of Calais* bronze sculpture marks the entrance to the Main Quad, an open plaza where the original 12 campus buildings, a mix of Romanesque and Mission revival styles, were joined by the Memorial Church (also called MemChu) in 1903. The church is noted for its beautiful mosaic-tiled frontage, stained-glass windows and four organs with over 8000 pipes.

A campus landmark at the east of the Main Quad, the 285ft-high Hoover Tower (adult/child $2/1; ☺10am-4pm, closed during final exams, breaks btwn sessions & some holidays) offers superb views. The tower houses the university library, offices and part of the right-wing Hoover Institution on War, Revolution & Peace (where Donald Rumsfeld caused a university-wide stir by accepting a position after he resigned as Secretary of Defense).

The Cantor Center for Visual Arts (http://museum.stanford.edu; 328 Lomita Dr; admission free; ☺11am-5pm Wed & Fri-Sun, to 8pm Thu) is a large museum originally dating from 1894. Its collection spans works from ancient civilizations to contemporary art, sculpture and photography, and rotating exhibits are eclectic in scope.

Immediately south is the open-air Rodin Sculpture Garden, which boasts the largest collection of bronze sculptures by Auguste Rodin outside of Paris, including reproductions of his towering *Gates of Hell*. More sculpture can be found around campus, including pieces by Andy Goldsworthy and Maya Lin.

The Stanford Visitor Center (www.stanford.edu/dept/visitorinfo; 295 Galvez St) offers free one-hour walking tours of the campus daily at 11am and 3:15pm, except during the winter break (mid-December through early January) and some holidays. Specialized tours are also available.

Stanford University's free public shuttle, Marguerite (http://transportation.stanford.edu/marguerite), provides service from Caltrain's Palo Alto and California Ave stations to the campus, and has bicycle racks. Parking on campus is expensive and trying.

MARIN COUNTY & THE BAY AREA SAN JOSE

replica of the 237ft-high 1881 Electric Light Tower. The original tower was a pioneering attempt at street lighting, intended to illuminate the entire town center. It was a complete failure but was left standing as a central landmark until it toppled over in 1915 because of rust and wind. Other buildings include an 1888 Chinese temple and the Pacific Hotel, which has rotating exhibits inside. The Trolley Restoration Barn restores historic trolley cars to operate on San Jose's light-rail line. Check the website for when you can ride a trolley along the park's own short line.

Tech Museum   MUSEUM
(☎408-294-8324; www.thetech.org; 201 S Market St; museum & 1 IMAX theater admission $10; ☺10am-5pm Mon-Wed, to 8pm Thu-Sun; ⊞) This excellent technology museum, opposite Plaza de Cesar Chavez, examines subjects from robotics to space exploration to genetics. The museum also includes an IMAX dome theater, which screens different films throughout the day.

San Jose Museum of Art   MUSEUM
(☎408-271-6840; www.sjmusart.org; 110 S Market St; adult/student & senior $8/5; ☺11am-5pm Tue-Sun) With a strong permanent collection of 20th-century works and a variety of imaginative changing exhibits, the city's central art museum is one of the Bay Area's finest. The main building started life as the post office in 1892, was damaged by the 1906 earthquake and became an art gallery in 1933. A modern wing was added in 1991.

Rosicrucian Egyptian Museum MUSEUM
(☏408-947-3635; www.egyptianmuseum.org; 1342 Naglee Ave; adult/child/student $9/5/7; ⏰9am-5pm Wed-Fri, 10am-6pm Sat & Sun) West of downtown, this unusual and educational Egyptian Museum is one of San Jose's more interesting attractions, with an extensive collection that includes statues, household items and mummies. There's even a two-room, walk-through reproduction of an ancient subterranean tomb. The museum is the centerpiece of Rosicrucian Park (cnr Naglee & Park Aves), west of downtown San Jose.

FREE MACLA GALLERY
(Movimiento de Arte y Cultura Latino Americana; ☏408-998-2783; www.maclaarte.org; 510 S 1st St; ⏰noon-7pm Wed & Thu, noon-5pm Fri & Sat) A cutting-edge gallery highlighting themes by both established and emerging Latino artists, MACLA is one of the best community arts spaces in the Bay Area, with open-mic performances, hip-hop and other live music shows, experimental theater and well-curated and thought-provoking visual arts exhibits. It's also a hub for the popular South First Fridays (www.southfirstfridays.com) art walk and street fair.

Plaza de Cesar Chavez PLAZA
This leafy square in the center of downtown, which was part of the original plaza of El Pueblo de San José de Guadalupe, is the oldest public space in the city. It's named after Cesar Chavez – founder of the United Farm Workers, who lived part of his life in San Jose – and is surrounded by museums, theaters and hotels.

Cathedral Basilica of St Joseph CHURCH
(80 S Market St) At the top of the plaza, the pueblo's first church. Originally constructed of adobe brick in 1803, it was replaced three times due to earthquakes and fire; the present building dates from 1877.

Santana Row MARKET
(www.santanarow.com; Stevens Creek & Winchester Blvds) An upscale Main St-style mall, Santana Row is a mixed-use space west of downtown with shopping, dining and entertainment along with a boutique hotel, lofts and apartments. Restaurants spill out onto sidewalk terraces, and public spaces have been designed to invite loitering and promenading. On warm evenings, the Mediterranean-style area swarms with an energetic crowd.

San Jose for Children

Children's Discovery Museum MUSEUM
(☏408-298-5437; www.cdm.org; 180 Woz Way; admission $10; ⏰10am-5pm Tue-Sat, from noon Sun; ♿) Downtown, this science and creativity museum has hands-on displays incorporating art, technology and the environment, with plenty of toys, and very cool play-and-learn areas. The museum is on Woz Way, which is named after Steve Wozniak, the cofounder of Apple.

Great America AMUSEMENT PARK
(☏408-986-5886; www.cagreatamerica.com; adult/child under 48in $55/35; 4701 Great America Pkwy, Santa Clara; ⏰Apr-Oct; ♿) If you can handle the shameful product placements, kids love the roller coasters and other thrill rides. Note that online tickets cost much less than walk-up prices listed here; parking costs $12 but it's also accessible by public transportation.

Raging Waters AMUSEMENT PARK
(☏408-238-9900; www.rwsplash.com; 2333 South White Rd; adult/child under 48in $34/24, parking $6; ⏰May-Sep; ♿) A water park inside Lake Cunningham Regional Park, Raging Waters has fast water slides, a tidal pool and a nifty water fort.

🛏 Sleeping

Conventions and trade shows keep the downtown hotels busy year-round, and midweek rates are usually higher than weekends.

TOP CHOICE Sainte Claire Hotel HISTORIC HOTEL $$
(☏408-295-2000, 866-870-0726; www.thesainteclaire.com; 302 S Market St; r weekend/midweek from $95/169; ✴@☎🐕) Stretched leather ceilings top off the drop-dead beautiful lobby at this 1926 landmark hotel overlooking Plaza de Cesar Chavez. Guest rooms, while smallish, are modern and smartly designed, and bathrooms have hand-painted sky murals, dark wood vanities and restored tile floors.

Hotel De Anza HOTEL $$
(☏408-286-1000, 800-843-3700; www.hoteldeanza.com; 233 W Santa Clara St; r $149-229; ✴@☎🐕) This downtown hotel is a restored art deco beauty, although contemporary stylings overwhelm the place's history. Guest rooms offer plush comforts (the ones facing south are a tad larger) and full concierge service is available.

WHAT THE...?

An odd structure purposefully commissioned to be so by the heir to the Winchester rifle fortune, the **Winchester Mystery House** (☎408-247-2101; www.winchestermysteryhouse.com; 525 S Winchester Blvd; adult/senior/child 6-12 $30/27/20; ⏲9am-5pm Oct-Mar, 8am-7pm Apr-Sep) is a ridiculous Victorian mansion with 160 rooms of various sizes and little utility, with dead-end hallways and a staircase that runs up to a ceiling all jammed together like a toddler playing architect. Apparently, Sarah Winchester spent 38 years constructing this mammoth white elephant because the spirits of the people killed by Winchester rifles told her to. No expense was spared in the construction and the extreme results sprawl over 4 acres. Tours start every 30 minutes, and the standard hour-long guided mansion tour includes a self-guided romp through the gardens as well as entry to an exhibition of guns and rifles. It's west of central San Jose and just north of I-280, across the street from Santana Row.

Hotel Valencia BOUTIQUE HOTEL **$$$**
(☎408-551-0010, 866-842-0100; www.hotelvalencia-santanarow.com; 355 Santana Row; r incl breakfast $199-309; ❄@📶🏊) A burbly lobby fountain and deep-red corridor carpeting set the tone for this tranquil 212-room contemporary hotel in the Santana Row shopping complex. In-room minibars and bathrobes and an outdoor pool and hot tub create an oasis of luxury with European and Asian design accents.

Henry Coe State Park CAMPGROUND **$**
(☎408-779-2728, reservations 800-444-7275 or www.reserveamerica.com; www.coepark.org; sites $20) southeast of San Jose near Morgan Hill, this huge state park has 20 drive-in campsites at the top of an open ridge overlooking the hills and canyons of the park's backcountry. There are no showers. You can't make reservations less than two days in advance, though it rarely fills up except on spring and summer holidays and weekends.

Eating

Original Joe's ITALIAN **$$**
(www.originaljoes.com; 301 S 1st St; mains $14-34; ⏲11am-1am) Waiters in bow ties flit about this busy 1950s San Jose landmark, serving standard Italian dishes to locals and conventioneers. The dining room is a curious but tasteful hodgepodge of '50s brick, contemporary wood paneling and 5ft-tall Asian vases. Expect a wait.

Amber India INDIAN **$$**
(☎408-248-5400; www.amber-india.com; No 1140, 377 Santana Row; dinner mains $14-24) The cooking at this upscale Indian restaurant is superb, offering a full complement of kebabs, curries and tandooris. Presentation is highly styled, with artsy china and groovy paintings on the walls. Whet your whistle with an exotic cocktail as you feast on the delectable butter chicken.

Arcadia STEAKHOUSE **$$$**
(☎408-278-4555; www.michaelmina.net/restaurants; 100 W San Carlos St; lunch mains $11-16, dinner mains $24-42) This fine New American steakhouse restaurant in the Marriott Hotel is run by Chef Michael Mina, one of San Francisco's biggest celebrity chefs. It's not the daring, cutting-edge style Mina is known for, but it's slick, expensive and, of course, very good.

Tofoo Com Chay VEGETARIAN **$**
(www.tofoocomchay.com; 388 E Santa Clara St; mains $6.50; ⏲9am-9pm Mon-Fri, 10am-6pm Sat; 🌱) Conveniently located on the border of the San Jose State University campus, students and vegetarians queue up for the Vietnamese dishes like the fake-meat *pho* and the heaped combo plates.

Drinking

TOP CHOICE **singlebarrel** COCKTAIL BAR
(www.singlebarrelsj.com; 43 W San Salvador St; ⏲Tue-Sun) A new speakeasy-style lounge, where bartenders sheathed in tweed vests artfully mix custom cocktails ($10 to $11) tailored to customer's preferences, with some recipes dating back to before Prohibition. There's often a line out the door, but you'll be whisked downstairs as soon as they're ready to craft you a drink.

Caffe Trieste CAFE
(www.caffetrieste.com; 315 S 1st St; ⏲7am-10pm Mon-Thu, to midnight Fri, 8am-midnight Sat, to 9pm Sun; 📶) Photos of local theater folks line

PSYCHO DONUTS? QU'EST QUE C'EST?

Who knew that a sugary confection with a hole could induce such devious giggles and fiendish delight? Saunter on over to **Psycho Donuts** (www.psycho-donuts.com; 288 S 2nd St; ⊙7am-10pm Mon-Thu, to midnight Fri, 8am-11pm Sat, to 10pm Sun; ⓐ), where counter staff dressed in saucy medical garb hand out bubble wrap to pop as patrons choose from twisted flavors like Cereal Killer (topped with marshmallows and Cap'n Crunch breakfast cereal), Headbanger (death-metal visage oozing red jelly) and the too-true-to-life Hamburger (sesame seed donut with bacon strips).

the walls at this high-ceilinged outpost of San Francisco's North Beach treasure (p97). Linger over a cappuccino with a pastry or panini, and stop by for live music on Thursday, Friday and Saturday nights. Opera performances rattle the cups the first Friday of each month.

Trials Pub   PUB
(www.trialspub.com; 265 N 1st St) If you seek a well-poured pint in a supremely comfortable atmosphere, Trials Pub, north of San Pedro Sq, has many excellent ales on tap (try a Fat Lip), all served in a warm and friendly room with no TVs. There's good pub food and a fireplace in the back room.

Hedley Club Lounge   LOUNGE
(www.hoteldeanza.com/hedley_club.asp; 233 W Santa Clara St) Also downtown, inside the elegant 1931 Hotel De Anza, Hedley Club is a good place for a quiet drink in swanky art deco surroundings. Jazz combos play Thursday through Saturday night.

☆ Entertainment

Clubs

The biggest conglomeration of clubs is on S 1st St, aka SoFA, and around S 2nd at San Fernando. Raucous young clubgoers pack the streets on Friday and Saturday nights.

South First Billiards   POOL HALL
(420 S 1st St; www.sofapool.com) It's a great place to shoot some stick, and a welcoming club to boot. Free rock shows on Friday and Saturday always draw a fun crowd.

Blank Club   LIVE MUSIC
(44 S Almaden; www.theblankclub.com; ⊙Tue-Sat) A small club near the Greyhound station and off the main party streets. Live bands jam on a stage cascading with silver tinsel, and a glittering disco ball presides over fun retro dance parties.

Fahrenheit Ultra Lounge   LOUNGE
(☎408-998-9998; www.fahrenheitsj.com; 99 E San Fernando St) Expect short party dresses, velvet ropes and clubbers enjoying bottle service and small-plates menu at this buzzing dance club. DJs play a mix and mash-ups of top 40, house and hip-hop, and bartenders pour drinks with flair.

Theaters

California Theatre   THEATER
(☎408-792-4111; http://californiatheatre.sanjose. org; 345 S 1st St) The absolutely stunning Spanish interior of this landmark entertainment venue is cathedral-worthy. The theater is home to Opera San José, Symphony Silicon Valley, and is a venue for the city's annual film festival, **Cinequest** (www.cinequest. org), held in late February or early March.

San Jose Repertory Theatre   THEATER
(☎408-367-7255; www.sjrep.com; 101 Paseo de San Antonio) Steaming ahead into its third decade, this company offers a full season of top-rated productions in a contemporary 525-seat venue downtown.

Sports

HP Pavilion   STADIUM
(☎408-287-9200; www.hppsj.com; cnr Santa Clara & N Autumn Sts) The fanatically popular San Jose Sharks, the city's NHL (National Hockey League) team, plays at the HP Pavilion, a massive glass-and-metal stadium. The NHL season runs from September to April.

Buck Shaw Stadium   STADIUM
(www.sjearthquakes.com; 500 El Camino Real, Santa Clara) Located at Santa Clara University, this is the home of the San Jose Earthquakes Major League Soccer team; games run from February through October.

ⓘ Information

To find out what's happening and where, check out the free weekly *Metro* (www.metroactive. com) newspaper or the Friday 'eye' section of

the daily *San Jose Mercury News* (www.mercu
rynews.com).

San Jose Convention & Visitors Bureau
(☎408-295-9600, 800-726-5673; www.
sanjose.org; 150 W San Carlos St; ⊗8am-
5pm Mon-Fri) Inside the San Jose Convention
Center.

Santa Clara Valley Medical Center (☎408-
885-5000; 751 S Bascom Ave; ⊗24hr)

❶ Getting There & Away

Air

Two miles north of downtown, between Hwy 101
and I-880, is **Mineta San José International
Airport** (www.flysanjose.com). The airport
has grown busier as the South Bay gets more
crowded, with numerous domestic flights at two
terminals and free wi-fi.

BART

To access the BART system in the East Bay, **VTA**
(☎408-321-2300; www.vta.org) bus 181 runs
daily between the Fremont BART station and
downtown ($4).

Bus

Greyhound buses to San Francisco ($10, 90
minutes) and Los Angeles ($42 to $60, seven
to 10 hours) leave from the **Greyhound station**
(☎408-295-4151; www.greyhound.com; 70
Almaden Ave).

The VTA Hwy 17 Express bus (route 970) plies
a handy daily route between Diridon Station and
Santa Cruz ($5, one hour)

Car & Motorcycle

San Jose is right at the bottom end of the San
Francisco Bay, about 40 miles from Oakland (via
I-880) or San Francisco (via Hwy 101 or I-280).
Expect lots of traffic at all times of the day on
Hwy 101. Although I-280 is slightly longer, it's
much prettier and usually less congested. Head-
ing south, Hwy 17 leads over the hill to Santa
Cruz.

Many downtown retailers offer two-hour
parking validation, and on weekends until 6pm
parking is free in city-owned lots and garages
downtown. Check www.sjdowntownparking.com
for details.

Train

A double-decker commuter rail service that
operates up and down the Peninsula between
San Jose and San Francisco, **Caltrain** (☎800-
660-4287; www.caltrain.com) makes over
three dozen trips daily (fewer on weekends); the
60-minute (on the Baby Bullet commuter trains)
to 90-minute journey costs $8.50 each way and
bicycles can be brought on designated cars.
It's definitely your best bet, as traffic can be
crazy any day of the week. San Jose's terminal,

Diridon Station (off 65 Cahill St) is just south of
the Alameda.

Diridon Station also serves as the terminal for
Amtrak (☎408-287-7462; www.amtrak.com),
serving Seattle, Los Angeles and Sacramento,
and **Altamont Commuter Express** (ACE; www.
acerail.com), which runs to Great America,
Livermore and Stockton.

VTA runs a free weekday shuttle (known as the
Downtown Area Shuttle or DASH) from the station to downtown.

❶ Getting Around

VTA buses run all over Silicon Valley. From the
airport, VTA Airport Flyer shuttles (route 10)
run every 10 to 15 minutes to the Metro/Airport
Light Rail station, where you can catch the San
Jose light rail to downtown San Jose. The route
also goes to the Santa Clara Caltrain station.
Fares for buses (except express lines) and light-
rail trains are $2 for a single ride and $6 for a
day pass.

The main San Jose light-rail line runs 20 miles
north-south from the city center. Heading south
gets you as far as Almaden and Santa Teresa.
The northern route runs to the Civic Center,
the airport and Tasman, where it connects with
another line that heads west past Great America
to downtown Mountain View.

San Francisco to Half Moon Bay

One of the real surprises of the Bay Area is
how fast the urban landscape disappears
along the rugged and largely undeveloped
coast. The 70-mile stretch of coastal Hwy 1
from San Francisco to Santa Cruz is one of
the most beautiful motorways anywhere.
For the most part a winding two-lane blacktop, it passes small farmstands and beach
after beach, many of them little sandy coves
hidden from the highway. Most beaches
along Hwy 1 are buffeted by wild and unpredictable surf, making them more suitable for sunbathing (weather permitting)
than swimming. The state beaches along the
coast don't charge an access fee, but parking
can cost a few dollars.

A cluster of isolated and supremely scenic HI hostels, at Point Montara (22 miles
south of San Francisco) and Pigeon Point
(36 miles), make this an interesting route
for cyclists, though narrow Hwy 1 itself can
be stressful, if not downright dangerous, for
the inexperienced.

WORTH A TRIP

NERDS' NIRVANA

Now touted as the largest computer history exhibition in the world, a $19 million remodel has launched the **Computer History Museum** (☑650-810-1010; www.computerhistory.org; 1401 N Shoreline Blvd, Mountain View; adult/student & senior $15/12; ⏱10am-5pm Wed-Sun) into a new league. Artifacts range from the abacus to the iPod, including Cray-1 supercomputers and the first Google server. Rotating exhibits draw from its 100,000-item collection and will keep you exploring this place for hours.

PACIFICA & DEVIL'S SLIDE

Pacifica and Point San Pedro, 15 miles from downtown San Francisco, signal the end of the urban sprawl. South of Pacifica is Devil's Slide, an unstable cliff area through which Hwy 1 winds and curves. Drive carefully, especially at night and when it is raining, as rock and mud slides are frequent. Heavy winter storms often lead to the road's temporary closure. A tunnel will soon bypass this dramatic stretch of the highway.

In Pacifica, collecting a suntan or catching a wave are the main attractions at **Rockaway Beach** and the more popular **Pacifica State Beach** (also known as Linda Mar Beach), where the nearby **NorCal Surf Shop** (☑650-738-9283; 5460 Coast Hwy) rents surfboards ($18 per day) and wet suits ($16).

GRAY WHALE COVE TO MAVERICKS

One of the coast's popular 'clothing-optional' beaches is **Gray Whale Cove State Beach** (☑650-726-8819), just south of Point San Pedro. Park across the road and cross Hwy 1 to the beach *very* carefully. **Montara State Beach** is just a half-mile south. From the town of Montara, 22 miles from San Francisco, trails climb up from the Martini Creek parking lot into **McNee Ranch State Park**, which has hiking and cycling trails aplenty, including a strenuous ascent to the panoramic viewpoint of Montara Mountain.

Point Montara Lighthouse Hostel (☑650-728-7177; www.norcalhostels.org/montara; cnr Hwy 1 & 16th St; dm $29, r $78; ⏻🖥📶) started

life as a fog station in 1875. The hostel is adjacent to the current lighthouse, which dates from 1928. This very popular hostel has a living room, kitchen facilities and an international clientele. There are a few private rooms for couples or families. Reservations are a good idea anytime, but especially on weekends during summer. From Monday through Friday, SamTrans bus 294 will let you off at the hostel if you ask nicely; bus 17 runs daily and stops across the highway (a ten minute walk).

Montara has a few B&Bs, including the historic **Goose & Turrets B&B** (☑650-728-5451; www.gooseandturretsbandb.com; 835 George St; r $145-190; 📶), with a lovely garden area, afternoon tea and bright red cannons out front to greet you.

TOP CHOICE **Fitzgerald Marine Reserve** (☑650-728-3584; 🖐), south of the lighthouse at Moss Beach, is an extensive area of natural tidal pools and a habitat for harbor seals. Walk out among the pools at low tide – wearing shoes that you can get wet – and explore the myriad crabs, sea stars, mollusks and rainbow-colored sea anemone. Note that it's illegal to remove any creatures, shells or even rocks from the marine reserve. From Hwy 1 in Moss Beach, turn west onto California Ave and drive to the end. SamTrans buses 294 and 17 stop along Hwy 1.

Moss Beach Distillery (☑650-728-5595; www.mossbeachdistillery.com; cnr Beach Way & Ocean Blvd; mains $15-33; ⏱noon-9pm Mon-Sat, from 11am Sun; 🖥) is a 1927 landmark overlooking the ocean. In fair weather the deck here is the best place for miles around to have a leisurely cocktail or glass of vino. Reservations recommended.

South of here is a hamlet named Princeton, with a stretch of coast called Pillar Point. Fishing boats bring in their catch at the Pillar Point Harbor, some of which gets cooked up in a bevy of seafront restaurants. In the harbor, **Half Moon Bay Kayak** (☑650-773-6101; www.hmbkayak.com) rents kayaks and offers guided trips of Pillar Point and the Fitzgerald Marine Reserve. **Half Moon Bay Brewing Company** (www.hmbbrewinco.com; 390 Capistrano Rd; mains $11-21; ⏱11:30am-8:30pm, longer hr on weekends) serves seafood, burgers and a tantalizing menu of local brews from a sheltered and heated outdoor patio looking out over the bay, complemented by live music on the weekends.

At the western end of Pillar Point is **Mavericks**, a serious surf break that attracts the world's top big-wave riders to battle its huge, steep and very dangerous waves. The annual Mavericks surf contest, called on a few days' notice when the swells get huge, is usually held between December and March.

Half Moon Bay

Developed as a beach resort back in the Victorian era, Half Moon Bay is the main coastal town between San Francisco (28 miles north) and Santa Cruz (40 miles south). Its long stretches of beach still attract rambling weekenders and hearty surfers. Half Moon Bay spreads out along Hwy 1 (called Cabrillo Hwy in town), but despite the development it's still relatively small. The main drag is a five-block stretch called Main St lined with shops, cafes, restaurants and a few upscale B&Bs. Visitor information is available from the **Half Moon Bay Coastside Chamber of Commerce** (650-726-8380; www.halfmoonbaychamber.org; 235 Main St; 9am-5pm Mon-Fri).

Pumpkins are a major deal around Half Moon Bay, and the pre-Halloween harvest is celebrated in the annual **Art & Pumpkin Festival** (www.miramarevents.com/pumpkinfest). The mid-October event kicks off with the World Championship Pumpkin Weigh-Off, where the bulbous beasts can bust the scales at more than 1000lb.

Around 1 mile north of the Hwy 92 junction, **Sea Horse Ranch** (650-726-9903; www.seahorseranch.org) offers daily horseback rides along the beach. A two-hour ride is

$75; an early-bird special leaves at 8am and cost just $50.

Sleeping & Eating

San Benito House HISTORIC HOTEL $$$
(650-726-3425; www.sanbenitohouse.com; 356 Main St; r incl breakfast with shared bath $80-100, r incl breakfast $130-200;) Supposedly a former bordello, this traditional Victorian inn has creaky wood floors and 11 neatly antiquated rooms without TVs. The saloon downstairs has live music a few nights a week, but doesn't stay open too late.

Pasta Moon ITALIAN $$
(650-726-5125; www.pastamoon.com; 315 Main St; mains $12-32; 11:30am-2:30pm & 5:30-9pm) If you're in the mood for romantic Italian, come here for yummy housemade pasta, organic produce, locally sourced ingredients and all-Italian wine list. Reservations recommended on weekends.

Getting There & Away

SamTrans (800-660-4287; www.samtrans.com) bus 294 operates from the Hillsdale Caltrain station to Half Moon Bay, and up the coast to Moss Beach and Pacifica, weekdays until about 7:30pm ($2).

Half Moon Bay to Santa Cruz

With its long coastline, mild weather and abundant fresh water, this area has always been prime real estate. When Spanish missionaries set up shop along the California coast in the late 1700s, it had been Ohlone

SCENIC DRIVE: HIGHWAY 84

Inland, large stretches of the hills are protected in a patchwork of parks that, just like the coast, remain remarkably untouched despite the huge urban populations only a short drive to the north and east. Heading east toward Palo Alto, Hwy 84 winds its way through thick stands of redwood trees and several local parks with mountain biking and hiking opportunities.

A mile in from San Gregorio State Beach on Hwy 1, kick off your shoes and stomp your feet to live bluegrass, Celtic and folk music on the weekends at the landmark **San Gregorio General Store** (www.sangregoriostore.com), and check out the wooden bar singed by area branding irons.

Eight miles east is the tiny township of **La Honda**, former home to *One Flew Over the Cuckoo's Nest* author Ken Kesey, and the launching spot for his 1964 psychedelic bus trip immortalized in Tom Wolfe's *The Electric Kool-Aid Acid Test*. Housed in an old blacksmith's shop, **Apple Jack's Inn** (650-747-0331) is a rustic, down-home bar offering live music on weekends and lots of local color.

Indian territory for thousands of years. Pescadero was formally established in 1856, when it was mostly a farming and dairy settlement, although its location along the stagecoach route – now called Stage Rd – transformed it into a popular vacation destination. The Pigeon Point promontory was an active whaling station until 1900, when Prohibition-era bootleggers favored the isolated regional beaches for smuggling booze.

PESCADERO

A foggy speck of coastside crossroads between the cities of San Francisco and Santa Cruz, 150-year-old Pescadero is a close-knit rural town of sugar-lending neighbors and community pancake breakfasts. But on weekends the tiny downtown strains its seams with long-distance cyclists panting for carbohydrates and day trippers dive-bombing in from the ocean-front highway. They're all drawn to the winter vistas of emerald-green hills parched to burlap brown in summer, the wild Pacific beaches populated by seals and pelicans, and the food at a revered destination restaurant. With its cornucopia of tide-pool coves and parks of sky-blotting redwood canopy, city dwellers come here to slow down and smell the sea breeze wafting over fields of bushy artichokes.

◉ Sights & Activities

A number of pretty sand beaches speckle the coast, though one of the most interesting places to stop is Pebble Beach, a tide pool jewel a mile and a half south of Pescadero Creek Rd. As the name implies, the shore is awash in bite-sized eye candy of agate, jade and carnelians, and sandstone troughs are pockmarked by groovy honeycombed formations called tafoni. Bird-watchers enjoy Pescadero Marsh Reserve, across the highway from Pescadero State Beach, where numerous species feed year-round.

TOP CHOICE Pigeon Point
Light Station   LIGHTHOUSE
(☑650-879-2120; www.parks.ca.gov/?page_id=533) Five miles south along the coast, the 115ft Light Station is one of the tallest lighthouses on the West Coast. The 1872 landmark had to close access to the Fresnel lens when chunks of its cornice began to rain from the sky, but the beam still flashes brightly and the bluff is a prime though blustery spot to scan for breaching gray whales. The hostel here is one of the best in the state.

Butano State Park   PARK
(☑650-879-2040; parking fee $10) About 5 miles south of Pescadero, bobcats and full-throated coyotes reside discreetly in a dense redwood canyon. The hiking is also excellent further down the coast at Big Basin Redwoods State Park (p463) with the easiest access from Santa Cruz. Camping ($35 per site) is available at both parks.

🛏 Sleeping & Eating

🍴 Pescadero Creek Inn B&B   B&B $$
(☑888-307-1898; www.pescaderocreekinn.com; 393 Stage Rd; r $170-255; 🖥) Unwind in the private two-room cottage or one of the spotless Victorian rooms in a restored 100-year-old farmhouse. Afternoon wine and cheese features wine bottled by the owners, and organic ingredients from the creekside garden spice up a hot breakfast.

🍴 Pigeon Point Lighthouse
Hostel   HOSTEL $
(☑650-879-0633; www.norcalhostels.org/pigeon; dm $24-26, r $72-98; @🖥) Not your workaday HI outpost, this highly coveted coastside hostel is all about location. Check in early to snag a spot in the outdoor hot tub, and contemplate roaring waves as the lighthouse beacon races through a starburst sky.

🍴 Costanoa Lodge   RESORT $$
(☑650-879-1100, 877-262-7848; www.costanoa.com; 2001 Rossi Rd; tent cabin $89-145, cabin $189-199, lodge r $179-279; 🖥📶) Even though the resort includes a campground (☑800-562-9867; www.koa.com/campgrounds/santa-cruz-north; tent site $22-52, RV site from $65), no one can pull a straight face to declare they're actually roughing it here. Down bedding swaddles guests in cushy canvas tent cabins, and chill-averse tent campers can use communal 'comfort stations' with 24-hour dry saunas, fireside patio seating, heated floors and hot showers. Lodge rooms with private fireplaces and hot tub access fulfill the whims of those without such spartan delusions. There's a restaurant (dinner mains $15-27) and spa on site; bicycle rentals and horseback riding are available as well.

TOP CHOICE Duarte's Tavern   AMERICAN $$
(☑650-879-0464; www.duartestavern.com; 202 Stage Rd; mains $11-40) You'll rub shoulders with fancy-pants foodies, spandex-swathed cyclists and dusty cowboys in spurs at this casual and surprisingly unpretentious

THE CULINARY COAST

Pescadero is renowned for Duarte's Tavern (see opposite page), but loads of other scrumptious tidbits are very close by.

Phipps Country Store (2700 Pescadero Creek Rd; 🚹) Peek inside the shop, known universally as 'the bean store,' to marvel at whitewashed bins overflowing with dried heirloom varieties with names like Eye of the Goat, Painted Lady and Desert Pebble.

Arcangeli Grocery/Norm's Market (287 Stage Rd; sandwiches $6-8.50) Create a picnic with made-to-order deli sandwiches, homemade artichoke salsa and a chilled bottle of California wine. And don't go breezing out the door without nabbing a crusty loaf of the famous artichoke garlic herb bread, fresh-baked almost hourly.

Harley Farms Cheese Shop (☑650-879-0480; www.harleyfarms.com; 250 North St; 🚹) Follow the cool wooden cut-outs of the goat and the Wellington-shod girl with the faraway eyes. Another local food treasure with creamy artisanal goat cheeses festooned with fruit, nuts and a rainbow of edible flowers. Weekend farm tours by reservation. Splurge for a seat at one of the monthly five-course farm dinners in the restored barn's airy hayloft.

Pie Ranch (www.pieranch.org; 2080 Cabrillo Hwy; ⊙noon-6pm Sat & Sun Mar-Oct; 🚹) Hit the brakes for this roadside farmstand in a wooden barn, and pick up fresh produce, eggs and coffee, plus amazing pies made with the fruit grown here. The historic pie-shaped farm is a nonprofit dedicated to leadership development and food education for urban youth. Check the website for details on its monthly farm tours and barn dances. Located 11 miles south of Pescadero Creek Rd.

Swanton Berry Farm (☑650-469-8804; www.swantonberryfarm.com; Coastways Ranch, 640 Cabrillo Hwy) To get a better appreciation of the rigors and rewards of farm life, smoosh up your shirtsleeves and harvest some fruit at this organic pick-your-own farm near Año Nuevo. It's a union outfit (operated by Cesar Chavez's United Farm Workers), with buckets of seasonal kiwis and olallieberries ripe for the plucking. Its farm stand and strawberry u-pick is 8.5 miles further south near Davenport.

fourth-generation family restaurant. Duarte's (pronounced DOO-arts) is the culinary magnet of Pescadero, and for many the town and eatery are synonymous. Feast on crab cioppino and a half-and-half split of the cream of artichoke and green chili soups, and bring it home with a wedge of olallieberry pie. Except for the unfortunate lull of Prohibition, the wood-paneled bar has been hosting the locals and their honored guests since 1894. Reservations recommended.

❶ Getting There & Away

By car, the town is 3 miles east from Hwy 1 on Pescadero Creek Rd, south of San Gregorio State Beach. On weekdays, **SamTrans** bus 17 runs to/from Half Moon Bay twice a day.

AÑO NUEVO STATE RESERVE

More raucous than a full-moon beach rave, thousands of boisterous elephant seals party down year-round on the dunes of Año Nuevo point, their squeals and barks reaching fever pitch during the winter pupping season. The beach is 5 miles south of Pigeon Point and 27 miles north of Santa Cruz. Check out the park's live **SealCam** (www.parks.ca.gov/popup/main.asp).

Elephant seals were just as fearless two centuries ago as they are today, but unfortunately, club-toting seal trappers were not in the same seal-friendly category as camera-toting tourists. Between 1800 and 1850, the elephant seal was driven to the edge of extinction. Only a handful survived around the Guadalupe Islands off the Mexican state of Baja California. With the availability of substitutes for seal oil and the conservationist attitudes of more recent times, the elephant seal has made a comeback, reappearing on the Southern California coast from around 1920. In 1955 they returned to Año Nuevo Beach.

In the midwinter peak season, during the mating and birthing time from December 15 to the end of March, you must plan well ahead if you want to visit the reserve, because visitors are only permitted access through heavily booked guided tours. For the busiest period, mid-January to mid-February, it's recommended you book eight weeks ahead. If you haven't booked, bad weather can sometimes lead to last-minute cancellations.

The rest of the year, advance reservations aren't necessary, but visitor permits from the entrance station are required; arrive before 3pm from September through November and by 3:30pm from April through August.

Although the **park office** (☎650-879-2025, recorded information 650-879-0227; www. parks.ca.gov/?page_id=523) can answer general questions, high season tour bookings must be made at ☎800-444-4445 or http://anon-uevo.reserveamerica.com. When required, these tours cost $7, and parking is $10 per car year-round. From the ranger station it's a 3- to 5-mile round-trip hike on sand, and a visit takes two to three hours. No dogs are al-lowed on-site, and visitors aren't permitted for the first two weeks of December.

There's another, more convenient viewing site further south in Piedras Blancas.

Napa & Sonoma Wine Country

Why Go?

America's premier viticulture region has earned its reputation among the world's best. Despite hype about Wine Country style, it's from the land that all Wine Country lore springs. Rolling hills, dotted with century-old oaks, turn the color of lion's fur under the summer sun and swaths of vineyards carpet hillsides as far as the eye can see. Where they end, lush redwood forests follow serpentine rivers to the sea.

There are over 600 wineries in Napa and Sonoma Counties, but it's quality, not quantity, that sets the region apart – especially in Napa, which competes with France and doubles as an outpost of San Francisco's top-end culinary scene. Sonoma prides itself on agricultural diversity, with goat-cheese farms, you-pick-em orchards and roadside fruit stands. Plan to get lost on back roads, and, as you picnic atop sun-dappled hillsides, grab a hunk of earth and know firsthand the thing of greatest meaning in Wine Country.

Best Places to Eat

» Zazu (p207)
» Oxbow Public Market (p171)
» Fremont Diner (p189)
» Madrona Manor (p210)

Best Places to Stay

» Beltane Ranch (p192)
» Cottages of Napa Valley (p170)
» Mountain Home Ranch (p178)
» El Bonita Motel (p175)
» Auberge du Soleil (p174)

When to Go

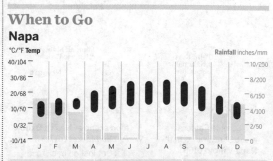

Jan Bright-yellow flowers carpet the valleys during the off-season; room rates plummet.

May Before summer holidays, the weather is perfect for touring, with long days and hot sun.

Sep–Oct 'Crush' time is peak season, when wine-making operations are in full force.

Wine Tasting

To help you discover the real Wine Country, we've mostly avoided factories and listed family-owned boutique houses (producing fewer than 20,000-annual cases) and midsized houses (20,000- to 60,000-annual cases). Why does it matter? Think of it. If you were to attend two dinner parties, one for 10 people, one for 1000, which would have the better food? Small wineries maintain tighter control. Also, you won't easily find these wines elsewhere.

Tastings are called 'flights' and include four-to-six different wines. Napa wineries charge $10 to $50. In Sonoma Valley, tastings cost $5 to $15, refundable with purchase. In Sonoma County, tastings are free or $5 to $10. You must be 21 to taste.

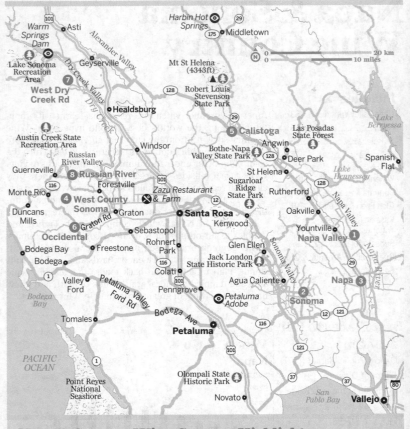

Napa & Sonoma Wine Country Highlights

① Sample California's greatest red wines in the **Napa Valley** (p163)

② Picnic in sun-dappled shade on the state's largest town square, **Sonoma Plaza** (p185)

③ Bite into the artisinal food scene at Napa's **Oxbow Public Market** (p171)

④ Get lost on back roads in **West County Sonoma** (p193)

⑤ Submerge yourself in a volcanic-ash mud bath in **Calistoga** (p177)

⑥ Chill with locals at the **Occidental Farmers Market** (p199)

⑦ Pedal between wineries along pastoral **West Dry Creek Rd** (p196)

⑧ Float in a canoe or kayak down the **Russian River** (p194)

Do not drink and drive. The curvy roads are dangerous, and police monitor traffic, especially on Napa's Hwy 29.

To avoid burnout, visit no more than three wineries per day. Most open daily from 10am or 11am to 4pm or 5pm, but call ahead if you've got your heart set, or absolutely want a tour, especially in Napa, where law requires that some wineries accept visitors only by appointment. If you're buying, ask if the winery has a wine club, which is often free to join and provides discounts, but you'll have to agree to buy a certain amount annually.

High Season vs Low

Many Wine Country restaurants and hotels diminish operations in wintertime. We list high-season hours and rates. Make reservations, especially in summer, or you may not eat. Hotel rates increase during September and October's grape-crushing season – the most popular time to come.

❶ Getting There & Away

Napa and Sonoma counties each have an eponymous city and valley. So, the town of Sonoma is in Sonoma County, at the southern end of Sonoma Valley. The same goes for the city, county and valley of Napa.

From San Francisco, public transportation gets you to the valleys, but it's insufficient for vineyard-hopping. For public-transit information, dial ✆511 from Bay Area telephones, or look online at www.transit.511.org.

Both valleys are 90 minutes' drive from San Francisco. Napa, the farther inland, has over 400 wineries and attracts the most visitors (expect heavy traffic summer weekends). Sonoma County has 260 wineries, 40 in Sonoma Valley, which is less commercial and less congested than Napa. If you have time to visit only one, choose Sonoma for ease.

Bus

Evans Transportation (✆707-255-1559; www.evanstransportation.com) Shuttles ($29) to Napa from San Francisco and Oakland Airports.

Golden Gate Transit (✆415-923-2000; www.goldengate.org) Bus 70/80 from San Francisco to Petaluma ($9.25) and Santa Rosa ($10.25); board at 1st and Mission Sts. Connect with Sonoma County Transit buses (p161).

Greyhound (✆800-231-2222; www.greyhound.com) San Francisco to Santa Rosa ($22 to $30) and Vallejo ($17 to $23); transfer for local buses.

Napa Valley Vine (✆800-696-6443, 707-251-2800; www.nctpa.net) Operates bus 10 from

the Vallejo Ferry Terminal and Vallejo Transit bus station, via Napa, to Calistoga ($2.90).

Sonoma County Airport Express (✆707-837-8700, 800-327-2024; www.airportexpressinc.com) Shuttles ($34) between Sonoma County Airport (Santa Rosa) and San Francisco and Oakland Airports.

Sonoma County Transit (✆707-576-7433, 800-345-7433; www.sctransit.com) Buses from Santa Rosa to Petaluma ($2.35, 70 minutes), Sonoma ($2.90, 1¼ hours) and western Sonoma County, including Russian River Valley towns ($2.90, 30 minutes).

Car

From San Francisco, take Hwy 101 north over the Golden Gate Bridge, then Hwy 37 east to Hwy 121 north; continue to the junction of Hwys 12/121. For Sonoma Valley, take Hwy 12 north; for Napa Valley, take Hwy 12/121 east. Plan 70 minutes in light traffic, two hours during weekday commute times.

Hwy 12/121 splits south of Napa: Hwy 121 turns north and joins with Hwy 29 (aka St Helena Hwy); Hwy 12 merges with southbound Hwy 29 toward Vallejo. Hwy 29 backs up weekdays 3pm to 7pm, slowing returns to San Francisco.

From the East Bay (or from downtown San Francisco), take I-80 east to Hwy 37 west (north of Vallejo), then northbound Hwy 29.

From Santa Rosa, take Hwy 12 east to access the northern end of Sonoma Valley. From Petaluma and Hwy 101, take Hwy 116 east.

Ferry

Baylink Ferry (✆877-643-3779; www.baylinkferry.com) Downtown San Francisco to Vallejo (adult/child $13/6.50, 60 minutes); connect with Napa Valley Vine Bus 10 (p161).

Trains

Amtrak (✆800-872-7245; www.amtrak.com) trains travel to Martinez (south of Vallejo), with connecting buses to Napa (45 minutes), Santa Rosa (1¼ hours) and Healdsburg (1¾ hours).

BART trains (✆415 989-2278; www.bart.gov) run from San Francisco to El Cerrito del Norte ($4.05, 30 minutes). Transfer to **Vallejo Transit** (✆707-648-4666; www.vallejotransit.com) for Vallejo ($5, 30 minutes), then take Napa Valley Vine buses to Napa and Calistoga.

❶ Getting Around

You'll need a car to winery-hop. Alternatively visit tasting rooms in downtown Napa or downtown Sonoma.

Bicycle

Touring Wine Country by bicycle is unforgettable. Stick to back roads. We most love pastoral West Dry Creek Rd, northwest of Healdsburg, in

NAPA OR SONOMA?

Napa and Sonoma valleys run parallel, a few miles apart, separated by the narrow, imposing Mayacamas Mountains. The two couldn't be more different. It's easy to mock aggressively sophisticated Napa, its monuments to ego, trophy homes and trophy wives, $1000-a-night inns, $40+ tastings and wine-snob visitors, but Napa makes some of the world's best wines. Constrained by its geography, it stretches along a single valley, so it's easy to visit. Drawbacks are high prices and heavy traffic, but there are 400 nearly side-by-side wineries. And the valley is gorgeous.

Sonoma County is much more down-to-earth and politically left leaning. You'll see lots more rusted-out pick-ups. Though becoming gentrified, Sonoma lacks Napa's chic factor (Healdsburg notwithstanding), and locals like it that way. The wines are more approachable, but the county's 260 wineries are spread out (see boxed text p186). If you're here on a weekend, head to Sonoma (County or Valley), which gets less traffic, but on a weekday, see Napa, too. Ideally schedule two to four days: one for each valley, and one or two additional for western Sonoma County.

Spring and fall are the best times to visit. Summers are hot, dusty and crowded. Fall brings fine weather, harvest time and the 'crush,' the pressing of the grapes, but lodging prices skyrocket. For cost-saving tips on lodging in Napa, see p167.

Sonoma County. Through Sonoma Valley, take Arnold Dr instead of Hwy 12; through Napa Valley, take the Silverado Trail instead of Hwy 29.

Cycling between wineries isn't demanding – the valleys are mostly flat – but crossing between Napa and Sonoma Valleys is intense, particularly via steep Oakville Grade and Trinity Rd (between Oakville and Glen Ellen).

Bicycles, in boxes, can be checked on Greyhound buses for $30 to $40; bike boxes cost $10 (call ahead). You can transport bicycles on Golden Gate Transit buses, which usually have free racks available (first-come, first-served). For rentals, see Tours (this page).

Car

Napa Valley is 30-miles long and 5-miles wide at its widest point (the city of Napa), 1 mile at its narrowest (Calistoga). Two roads run north–south: Hwy 29 (St Helena Hwy) and the more scenic Silverado Trail, a mile east. Drive up one, down the other.

The American Automobile Association determined Napa Valley to be America's 8th most congested rural vacation destination. Summer and fall weekend traffic is unbearable, especially on Hwy 29 between Napa and St Helena. Plan accordingly.

Cross-valley roads that link Silverado Trail with Hwy 29 – including Yountville, Oakville and Rutherford crossroads – are bucolic and get less traffic. For scenery, the Oakville Grade and rural Trinity Rd (which leads southwest to Hwy 12 in Sonoma Valley) are narrow, curvy and beautiful – but treacherous in rainstorms. Mt Veeder Rd leads through pristine countryside west of Yountville.

Note: Police watch like hawks for traffic violators. *Don't drink and drive.*

Shortcuts between Napa and Sonoma Valleys: from Oakville, take Oakville Grade to Trinity Rd; from St Helena, take Spring Mountain Rd into Calistoga Rd; from Calistoga, take Petrified Forest Rd to Calistoga Rd.

Public Transportation

Napa Valley Vine (☎800-696-6443, 707-251-2800; www.nctpa.net) Bus 10 from downtown Napa to Calistoga ($2.15, 1¼ hours).

Sonoma County Transit (☎707-576-7433, 800-345-7433; www.sctransit.com) Buses from Santa Rosa to Petaluma ($2.35, 70 minutes), Sonoma ($2.90, 1¼ hours) and western Sonoma County, including Russian River Valley towns ($2.90, 30 minutes).

Train

A cushy, if touristy, way to see Wine Country, the **Napa Valley Wine Train** (☎707-253-2111, 800-427-4124; www.winetrain.com; adult/child from $89/55) offers three-hour daily trips in vintage Pullman dining cars, from Napa to St Helena and back, with an optional winery tour. Trains depart from McKinstry St near 1st St.

☞ Tours

For balloons and airplane rides, see the boxed text, p173.

Bicycle

Guided tours start around $90 per day including bikes, tastings and lunch. Daily rentals cost $25 to $85; make reservations.

Backroads (☎800-462-2848; www.backroads.com) All-inclusive guided biking and walking.

Calistoga Bike Shop (☎707-942-9687, 866-942-2453; www.calistogabikeshop.com; 1318 Lincoln Ave, Calistoga) Wine-tour rental package ($80) includes wine pickup.

Getaway Adventures (☎707-568-3040, 800-499-2453; www.getawayadventures.com) Great guided tours, some combined with kayaking, of Napa, Sonoma, Calistoga, Healdsburg and Russian River. Single- and multi-day trips.

Good Time Touring (☎707-938-0453, 888-525-0453; www.goodtimetouring.com) Tours of Sonoma Valley, Dry Creek and West County Sonoma.

Napa River Vélo (☎707-258-8729; www.naparivervelo.com; 680 Main St, rear of Bldg, Napa) Daily rentals and weekend tours with wine pickup.

Napa Valley Adventure Tours (☎707-259-1833, 877-548-6877; www.napavalleyadventuretours.com; Oxbow Public Market, 610 1st St, Napa) Guides tours between wineries, off-road trips, hiking and kayaking. Daily rentals.

Napa Valley Bike Tours (☎707-944-2953, 800-707-2453; www.napavalleybiketours.com; 6488 Washington St, Yountville) Daily rentals; easy and moderately difficult tours.

Sonoma Valley Cyclery (Map p184; ☎707-935-3377; www.sonomacyclery.com; 20093 Broadway, Sonoma) Daily rentals; Sonoma Valley tours.

Spoke Folk Cyclery (☎707-433-7171; www.spokefolk.com; 201 Center St, Healdsburg) Daily rentals near Dry Creek Valley.

Jeeps

Wine Country Jeep Tours (☎707-546-1822, 800-539-5337; www.jeeptours.com; 3hr tour $75) Tour Wine Country's back roads and boutique wineries by Jeep, year-round at 10am and 1pm. Also operates tours of Sonoma Coast.

Limousine

Antique Tours Limousine (☎707-226-9227; www.antiquetours.net) Hit the road in style in a 1947 Packard convertible; tours cost $130 per hour (minimum five hours).

Beau Wine Tours (☎707-938-8001, 800-387-2328; www.beauwinetours.com) Winery tours in sedans and stretch limos; charges $60 to $95 per hour (3-hour minimum weekdays, 6 hours weekends).

Beyond the Label (☎707-363-4023; www.btlnv.com; per person $299) Personalized tours, including lunch at home with a vintner, guided by a Napa native.

Flying Horse Carriage Company (☎707-849-8989; www.flyinghorse.org; 4hr tours per person $145) Clippety-clop through Alexander Valley by horse-drawn carriage. Includes picnic.

Magnum Tours (☎707-753-0088; www.magnumwinetours.com) Sedans and specialty limousines from $65 to $125 per hour (four-hour minimum, five hours Saturdays). Exceptional service.

NAPA VALLEY

The birthplace of modern-day Wine Country is famous for regal cabernet sauvignons, château-like wineries and fabulous food. Napa Valley attracts more than four million visitors a year, each expecting to be wined, dined, soaked in hot-springs spas and tucked between crisp linens.

Just a few decades ago, this 5-by-35-mile strip of former stagecoach stops seemed forgotten by time. Grapes had grown here since the Gold Rush, but grape-sucking phylloxera bugs, Prohibition and the Great Depression reduced 140 wineries, in the 1890s, to around 25 by the 1960s.

In 1968, Napa was declared the 'Napa Valley Agricultural Preserve', effectively blocking future valley development for non-agricultural purposes. The law stipulated no subdivision of valley-floor land under 40 acres. This succeeded in preserving the valley's natural beauty, but when Napa wines earned top honors at a 1976 blind tasting in Paris, the wine-drinking world took note and land values shot through the roof. Only the very rich could afford to build. Hence, so many architecturally jaw-dropping wineries. Independent, family-owned wineries still exist – we highlight a number of them – but much of Napa Valley is now owned by global conglomerates.

The city of Napa anchors the valley, but the real work happens up-valley. Napa isn't as pretty as other towns, but has some noteworthy sights, among them Oxbow Public Market (p168). Scenic towns include St Helena, Yountville and Calistoga – the latter more famous for water than wine.

Napa Valley Wineries

Cab is king in Napa. No varietal captures imaginations like the fruit of the cabernet sauvignon vine – Bordeaux is the French equivalent – and no wine fetches a higher price. Napa farmers can't afford *not* to grow cabernet. Other heat-loving varietals, such as sangiovese and merlot, also thrive here.

Napa's wines merit their reputation among the world's finest – complex, with

NAPA & SONOMA WINE COUNTRY NAPA VALLEY WINERIES

luxurious finishes. Napa wineries sell many 'buy-and-hold' wines, versus Sonoma's 'drink-now' wines.

Artesa Winery
WINERY

(Map p164; ☎707-224-1668; www.artesawinery.com; 1345 Henry Rd; nonreserve/reserve tastings $10/15; ☺10am-4:30pm) Begin or end the day with a glass of bubbly or pinot at Artesa, southwest of Napa. Built into a mountainside, the ultramodern Barcelona-style architecture is stunning, and you can't beat the top-of-the-world vistas over San Pablo Bay. Free tours leave 11am and 2pm. Bottles cost $20 to $60.

Vintners' Collective
TASTING ROOM

(Map p169; ☎707-255-7150; www.vintnerscollective.com; 1245 Main St; Napa tasting $25; ☺11am-6pm) Ditch the car and chill in downtown Napa at this super-cool tasting bar – inside a former 19th-century brothel – that represents 20 high-end boutique wineries too small to have their own tasting rooms.

Ceja
WINERY

(Map p164; ☎707-226-6445; www.cejavineyards.com; 1248 First St; tasting $10; ☺11am-6pm Sun-Wed, 11am-8pm Thu-Sat; ☻) Ceja was founded by former vineyard workers, who now craft superb pinot noir and unusual blends, including a great pinot-syrah-cabernet for $20. The tasting room stays open late, and features interesting art, including Maceo Montoya's mural celebrating winemaking's roots. Bottles cost $20 to $50.

Twenty Rows
WINERY

(off Map p169; ☎707-287-1063; www.vinoce.com; 880 Vallejo St, Napa; tasting $10; ☺11am-5pm Tue-Sat) Downtown Napa's only working winery crafts light-on-the-palate cabernet sauvignon for a mere $20 a bottle. Taste in the barrel room – a chilly garage with plastic furniture – with fun dudes who know wine. Good sauvignon blanc, too.

Hess Collection
WINERY

(Map p164; ☎707-255-1144; www.hesscollection.com; 4411 Redwood Rd; tastings $10; ☺10am-4pm; ☻) Art lovers: don't miss Hess Collection, whose galleries display mixed-media and large-canvas works, including pieces by Francis Bacon and Louis Soutter. In the cave-like tasting room, you can find well-known cabernet and chardonnay, but also try the viognier. Hess overlooks the valley, so be prepared to drive a winding road. (NB: Hess Collection is not be be confused

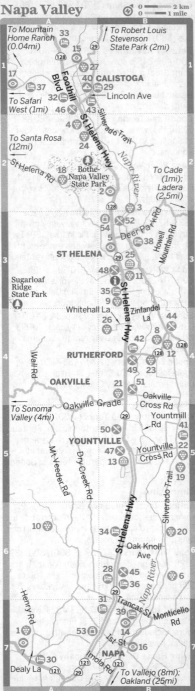

Napa Valley

NAPA & SONOMA WINE COUNTRY NAPA VALLEY WINERIES

with Hess Select, the grocery-store brand.) Bottles cost $15 to $60. Reservations are recommended.

Darioush WINERY
(Map p164; ☏707-257-2345; www.darioush.com; 4240 Silverado Trail; tastings $18-35; ⏰10:30am-5pm) Like a modern-day Persian palace, Darioush ranks high on the fabulosity scale,

with towering columns, Le Corbusier furniture, Persian rugs and travertine walls. Though known for cabernet, Darioush also bottles chardonnay, merlot and shiraz, all made with 100% of their respective varietals. Call about wine-and-cheese pairings. Bottles cost $40 to $80.

BOOKING APPOINTMENTS

Because of strict county zoning laws, many Napa wineries cannot legally receive drop-in visitors; unless you've come strictly to buy, you'll have to call ahead. This is *not* the case with all wineries. We recommend booking one appointment and planning your day around it.

Regusci
WINERY

(Map p164; ☑707-254-0403; www.regusciwinery. com; 5584 Silverado Trail, Napa; tasting $15-25; ☺10am-5pm; ☒) One of Napa's oldest, unfussy Regusci dates to the late 1800s, with 173 acres of vineyards unfurling around a century-old stone winery that makes Bordeaux-style blends on the valley's quieter eastern side – good when traffic up-valley is bad. No appointment necessary; lovely oak-shaded picnic area. Bottles run $36 to $125.

Robert Sinskey
WINERY

(Map p164; ☑707-944-9090; www.robertsinskey. com; 6320 Silverado Trail; tastings $25; ☺10am-4:30pm) For hilltop views and food-friendly wines, visit chef-owned Robert Sinskey, whose discreetly dramatic tasting room of stone, redwood and teak resembles a small cathedral. The winery specializes in organically grown pinot, merlot and cabernet, great Alsatian varietals, *vin gris,* cabernet franc and dry rosé. Small bites accompany the vino. Tasting fees are discounted with a two-bottle purchase – a rarity in Napa. Call about special culinary tours. Bottles cost $22 to $95.

Quixote
WINERY

(Map p164; ☑707-944-2659; www.quixotewinery. com; 6126 Silverado Trail; tastings $25; ☺by appointment) Famed architect Friedensreich Hundertwasser (1928–2000) designed whimsical Quixote. The exterior is a riot of color, with the architect's signature gold-leaf onion dome crowning the building. No two windows are alike, no lines straight, no surfaces perfectly level. Tour it, by appointment only, on weekdays. Weekends, you can only glimpse it while sampling pretty-good, 100% organic petite sirah and cabernet. Bottles cost $40 to $60.

Robert Mondavi
WINERY

(Map p164; ☑888-766-6328; www.robertmondavi. com; 7801 Hwy 29, Oakville; tour $25) This huge, corporate-owned winery draws oppressive crowds, but if you know nothing about wine, the worthwhile tours provide excellent insight into wine-making. Otherwise, skip it – unless you're here for one of the wonderful summer **concerts,** ranging from classical and jazz to R&B and Latin; call for schedules. Bottles run $19 to $150.

Tres Sabores
WINERY

(Map p164; ☑707-967-8027; www.tressabores.com; 1620 South Whitehall Lane, St Helena; tour/tasting $20; ☺by appointment; ☒) At the valley's westernmost edge, where sloping vineyards meet wooded hillsides, Tres Sabores is a portal to old Napa – no fancy tasting room, no snobbery, just great wine in a spectacular setting. Bucking the cabernet custom, Tres Sabores crafts elegantly structured, Burgundian-style zinfandel, and spritely sauvignon blanc, which the *New York Times* dubbed a Top 10. Guinea fowl and sheep control pests on the 35-acre estate, while golden labs chase butterflies through gnarled old vines. Reservations essential, and include a tour. Afterward, linger at olive-shaded picnic tables and drink in gorgeous valley views. Bottles cost $22 to $80.

Mumm Napa
WINERY

(Map p164; ☑800-686-6272; www.mummnapa. com; 8445 Silverado Trail, Rutherford; tasting $7-25; ☺10am-4:45pm; ☒) The valley views are spectacular at Mumm, which makes respectable sparkling wines that you can sample while seated on a vineyard-view terrace – ideal when you want to impress conservative parents-in-law. No appointment necessary; dodge crowds by paying $5 extra for the reserve-tasting terrace. Check website for discounted-tasting coupons.

Round Pond
WINERY

(Map p164; ☑888-302-2575; www.roundpond. com; 875 Rutherford Rd, Rutherford; tastings $25; ☺by appointment) Fantastic food pairings on a vineyard-view stone patio. We especially love the olive-oil and wine-vinegar tastings, included with guided tours of the olive mill ($25). Bottles $24 to $95.

TOP CHOICE Frog's Leap
WINERY

(Map p164; ☑707-963-4704, 800-959-4704; www. frogsleap.com; 8815 Conn Creek Rd; tours & tastings $20, ☺by appointment; ☒☒) Meandering paths wind through magical gardens and fruit-bearing orchards – pick peaches in July – surrounding an 1884 barn and farmstead with cats and chickens. But more than anything, it's the vibe that's wonderful: casual and down-to-earth, with a major emphasis on *fun*. Sauvignon blanc is its best-known wine, but the merlot merits attention. There's also a dry, restrained cabernet, atypical in Napa. All are organic. Appointments required. Bottles cost $18 to $42.

Hall
WINERY

(Map p164; ☏707-967-2626; www.hallwines.com; 401 St Helena Hwy, St Helena; tastings $15-25; ☺10am-5:30pm; ☒) Owned by Clinton's former ambassador to Austria, Hall specializes in cabernet franc, sauvignon blanc, merlot and cabernet sauvignon. There's a cool abstract-sculpture garden, a lovely picnic area shaded by mulberry trees (with wines by the glass), and a LEED-gold-certified winery – California's first (tours $45, including barrel tastings). Bottles cost $22 to $80.

Elizabeth Spencer
TASTING ROOM

(Map p164; ☏707-963-6067; www.elizabethspencerwines.com; 1165 Rutherford Rd, Rutherford; tastings $20; ☺10am-6pm; ☒) Taste inside an 1872 railroad depot or an outdoor garden. Small-lot wines include monster-sized pinot noir, and a well-priced grapefruity sauvignon blanc. Bottles $20 to $85.

Long Meadow Ranch
TASTING ROOM

(Map p164; ☏707-963-4555; www.longmeadowranch.com; 738 Main St, St Helena; tastings $10-30; ☺11am-6pm) Excellent olive-oil tastings (free) and fine cabernet and sauvignon blanc (bottles $19-35), served inside an 1874 farmhouse surrounded by lovely gardens.

Pride Mountain
WINERY

(Map p164; ☏707-963-4949; www.pridewines.com; 4026 Spring Mountain Rd, St Helena; tastings $10; ☺by appointment; ☒☒) High atop Spring Mountain, cult-favorite Pride straddles the Napa-Sonoma border and bottles vintages under both appellations. The well-structured cabernet sauvignon and heavy-hitting merlot are the best-known wines, but there are also elegant viognier (perfect with oysters) and standout cab franc, available only at the winery. Picnicking here is spectacular (choose Viewpoint for drop-dead vistas, or Ghost Winery for shade and historic ruins of a 19th-century winery), but you *must* first reserve a tasting appointment. Bottles cost $37 to $85.

Cade
WINERY

(Map p164; ☏707-965-2746; www.cadewinery.com; 360 Howell Mtn Rd, Angwin; tasting $20; ☺by appointment) Ascend Mt Veeder for drop-dead vistas, 1800ft above the valley floor, at Napa's oh-so-swank, first-ever organically farmed, LEED gold-certified winery, owned in part by former San Francisco Mayor Gavin Newsom. Hawks ride thermals at eye level as you sample bright sauvignon blanc and luscious cabernet sauvignon that's more Bordelaise in style than Californian. Reservations required. Bring your camera.

Casa Nuestra
WINERY

(Map p164; ☏707-963-5783; www.casanuestra.com; 3451 Silverado Trail, St Helena; tastings $10, refundable with purchase; ☺by appointment; ☒☒) A peace flag and a portrait of Elvis greet you in the tasting barn at this old-school, '70s-vintage, mom-and-pop winery, which produces unusual blends and interesting varietals (including good chenin blanc) and 100% cabernet franc. Vineyards are all-organic and the sun provides the power. Best of all, you can picnic free (call ahead and buy a bottle) beneath weeping willows, beside two happy goats. Bottles cost $20 to $55.

Ladera
WINERY

(Map p164; ☏707-965-2445, 866-523-3728; www.laderavineyards.com; 150 White Cottage Rd S, Angwin; tastings $15; ☺by appointment) High atop Howell Mountain, Ladera makes wonderful,

ℹ CUTTING COSTS IN NAPA

To avoid overspending on tasting fees, it's perfectly acceptable to pay for one tasting to share between two people. Ask in advance if fees are applicable to purchase (they usually aren't). Tour fees, by contrast, cannot be split. Ask at your hotel for free- or discounted-tasting coupons. If you can't afford the valley's hotels, try western Sonoma County, but if you want to be nearer Napa, try the suburban towns of Vallejo and American Canyon, about 20 minutes from downtown Napa. Both have motels for about $75 to $125 in high season. Also find chains 30 minutes away in Fairfield, off I-80 exits 41 (Pittman Rd) and 45 (Travis Blvd).

little-known, estate-grown cabernet sauvignon and sauvignon blanc. Make an appointment to visit this well-off-the-beaten-path 1886 stone-walled winery, one of Napa's oldest. Tasting fees refunded with two-bottle purchase. Bottles run $25 to $70.

Schramsberg
WINERY

(Map p164; 707-942-4558; www.schramsberg. com; 1400 Schramsberg Rd; tastings $45; by appointment) Napa's second-oldest winery, Schramsberg makes some of California's best brut sparkling wines, and in 1972 was the first domestic wine served at the White House. Blanc de blancs is the signature. The appointment-only tasting and tour (book well ahead) is expensive, but you'll sample all the *tête de cuvées*, not just the low-end wines. Tours include a walk through the caves; bring a sweater. Located off Peterson Dr. Bottles cost $22 to $100.

Castello di Amorosa
WINERY

(Map p164; 707-967-6272; www.castellodiamo rosa.com; 4045 Hwy 29, Calistoga; tasting $10-15, tour adult/child $32/22; by appointment;) It took 14 years to build this perfectly replicated 12th-century Italian castle, complete with moat, hand-cut stone walls, ceiling frescoes by Italian artisans, Roman-style cross-vault brick catacombs, and a torture chamber with period equipment. You can taste without an appointment, but this is one tour worth taking. Oh, the wine? Some respectable Italian varietals, including a velvety Tuscan blend, and a merlot blend that goes great with pizza. Bottles cost $20 to $125.

Vincent Arroyo
WINERY

(Map p164; 707-942-6995; www.vincentarroyo. com; 2361 Greenwood Ave, Calistoga; tastings free; by appointment;) The tasting room at Vincent Arroyo is a garage, where you may even meet Mr Arroyo, known for his all-estate-grown petite sirah and cabernet sauvignon. These wines are distributed nowhere else and are so consistently good that 75% of production is sold before it's bottled. Tastings are free, but appointments required. Bottles cost $22 to $45.

Lava Vine
TASTING ROOM

(Map p164; 707-942-9500; www.lavavine.com; 965 Silverado Trail, Calistoga; tasting $10 waived with purchase; 10am-5pm, appointment suggested;) Breaking ranks with Napa snobbery, the party kids at Lava Vine take a lighthearted approach to their seriously good

wines, all paired with small bites, including some hot off the barbecue. Children and dogs play outside, while you let your guard down in the tiny tasting room and tap your toe to James Brown. Bring a picnic. Reservations recommended.

Napa

The valley's workaday hub was once a nothing-special city of storefronts, Victorian cottages and riverfront warehouses, but booming real-estate values caused an influx of new money that has transformed Napa into a growing city of arts and food.

Sights & Activities

Napa lies between Silverado Trail and St Helena Hwy/Hwy 29. For downtown, exit Hwy 29 at 1st St and drive east. Napa's main drag, 1st St, is lined with shops and restaurants.

Oxbow Public Market
COVERED MARKET

(Map p169; 707-226-6529; www.oxbowpublicmar ket.com; 610 1st St; 9am-7pm Mon-Sat, to 8pm Tue, 10am-6pm Sun;) Showcasing all things culinary – from produce stalls to kitchen stores to fantastic edibles – Oxbow is foodie central, with an emphasis on seasonal-regional ingredients, grown sustainably. For more, see p171.

di Rosa Art & Nature Preserve
GALLERY, NATURE RESERVE

(Map p164; 707-226-5991; www.dirosapreserve. org; 5200 Carneros Hwy 121; gallery 9:30am-3pm Wed-Fri, by appointment Sat) West of downtown, scrap-metal sheep graze Carneros vineyards at 217-acre di Rosa Preserve, a stunning collection of Northern California art, displayed indoors in galleries and outdoors in sculpture gardens. Reservations recommended for tours.

Sleeping

Summer demand exceeds supply. Weekend rates skyrocket. Also try Calistoga (p178).

TOP CHOICE Carneros Inn
RESORT $$$

(Map p164; 707-299-4900; www.thecarnerosinn. com; 4048 Sonoma Hwy; r Mon-Fri $485-570, Sat & Sun $650-900;) Carneros Inn's snappy aesthetic and retro small-town agricultural theme shatters the predictable Wine Country mold. The semidetached, corrugated-metal cottages look like itinerant housing, but

Napa

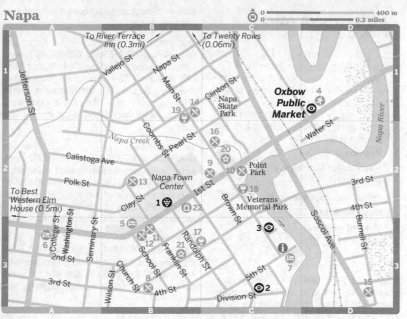

To River Terrace Inn (0.3mi)
To Twenty Rows (0.06mi)
To Best Western Elm House (0.5mi)

Napa

inside they're snappy and chic, with cherry-wood floors, ultrasuede headboards, wood-burning fireplaces, heated-tile bathroom floors, giant tubs and indoor-outdoor showers. Splurge on a vineyard-view room. Linger by day at the hilltop swimming pool, and by

night at the bar's outdoor fireplaces. Two excellent onsite restaurants.

Milliken Creek Inn   INN $$$
(Map p164; ☏707-255-1197, 888-622-5775; www.millikencreekinn.com; 1815 Silverado Trail; r incl

A LOVELY SPOT FOR A PICNIC

Unlike Sonoma, there aren't many places to picnic legally in Napa. Here's a short list, in south-to-north order, but call ahead and remember to buy a bottle (or glass, if available) of your host's wine. If you don't finish it, California law forbids driving with an uncorked bottle in the car (keep it in the trunk).

» **Regusci** (p166)
» **Napa Valley Museum** (p172)
» **Hall** (p167)
» **Pride Mountain Vineyards** (p167)
» **Casa Nuestra** (p167)
» **Vincent Arroyo** (p168)
» **Lava Vine** (p168)

breakfast $275-650; ✳@🏠) Understatedly elegant Milliken Creek combines small-inn charm, fine-hotel service and B&B intimacy. The impeccably styled, English Colonial rooms have top-flight amenities, fireplaces, ultrahigh-thread-count linens, and breakfast in bed. Book a river-view room.

Cottages of Napa Valley   BUNGALOWS $$$
(Map p164; 📞707-252-7810; www.napacottages. com; 1012 Darns Lane; d $395-500, q $475-575; ✳🏠) Originally constructed in the 1940s and rebuilt with top-end amenities in 2005, these eight cottages are ideal for a romantic hideaway, with extra-long soaking tubs, gas fireplaces, and outdoor fire pits beneath towering pines. Cottages 4 and 8 have private porches and swinging chairs. The only drawback is traffic noise, but interiors are silent.

Avia Hotel   HOTEL $$
(Map p169; 📞707-224-3900; www.aviahotels.com; 1450 1st St, Napa; r $149-249; ✳@🏠) Downtown Napa's newest hotel opened in 2009 and feels like a big-city hotel, with business-class-fancy rooms, styled in sexy retro-70s chic. Walkable to restaurants and bars.

Napa River Inn   HOTEL $$$
(Map p169; 📞707-251-8500, 877-251-8500; www. napariverinn.com; 500 Main St; r include breakfast $229-349; ✳@🏠🐾) Beside the river, in the 1884 Hatt Building, the inn has upper-midrange rooms in three satellite buildings, ranging from Victoriana to modern. Walk-

able to restaurants and bars. Dogs get special treatment.

Best Western Ivy Hotel   HOTEL $$
(Map p164; 📞707-253-9300, 800-253-6272; www. ivyhotelnapa.com; 4195 Solano Ave, Napa; r $149-249; ✳@🏠🐾) Redone in 2011, this smart-looking motel, on the suburban strip north of Napa, has extras like fridge, microwave and onsite laundry. Good value when under $200.

John Muir Inn   HOTEL $$
(Map p164; 📞707-257-7220, 800-522-8999; www. johnmuirnapa.com; 1998 Trower Ave; r incl breakfast Mon-Fri $130-155, Sat & Sun $170-240; ✳@🏠🐾) Request a remodeled room at this excellent-value hotel, north of downtown. Some have kitchenettes ($5 extra). Hot tub, great service.

Chablis Inn   MOTEL $$
(Map p164; 📞707-257-1944, 800-443-3490; www. chablisinn.com; 3360 Solano Ave, Napa; r weekday/ weekend $89-109/$159-179; ✳@🏠🐾) A good-value, well-kept motel near the highway. Hot tub.

River Terrace Inn   HOTEL $$$
(📞707-320-9000, 866-627-2386; www.riverter raceinn.com; 1600 Soscol Ave; r $189-289; ✳🏠🐾) An upmarket chain-style hotel, fronting on the Napa River. Heated outdoor pool.

Casita Bonita   BUNGALOW $$$
(📞707-259-1980, 707-738-5587; www.lacasitaboni ta.com; q $375; ✳🏠🐾) Smartly decorated two-bedroom cottage with full kitchen and veggie garden – kids love the chickens. Perfect for two couples or a family.

Best Western Elm House   INN $$
(off Map p169; 📞707-255-1831; www.bestwester nelmhouseinn.com; 800 California Blvd; r include breakfast $149-229; ✳@🏠) Impeccably kept rooms with generic furnishings in soft pastels. Ideal for conservative travelers. Ten minute walk to downtown; easy highway access. Hot tub.

Blackbird Inn   B&B $$$
(Map p169; 📞707-226-2450, 888-567-9811; www. blackbirdinnnapa.com; 1775 1st St; r incl breakfast $185-300; ✳🏠) Gorgeous, eight-room Arts and Crafts–style B&B, but anticipate traffic noise.

Napa Valley Redwood Inn   MOTEL $$
(📞707-257-6111, 877-872-6272; www.napavalleyred woodinn.com; 3380 Solano Ave; r Mon-Fri $90-110,

Sat & Sun $140-150; ❋🤙❋) Generic freeway-side motel.

✖ Eating

Make reservations when possible. July to mid-August, look for the peach stand at Deer Park Rd and Silverado Trail (across Deer Park Rd from Stewart's farmstand) for juicy-delicious heirloom varieties.

Oxbow Public Market — COVERED MARKET $
(Map p169; www.oxbowpublicmarket.com; 610 & 644 First St, Napa; ⊙9am-7pm Mon-Sat, 10am-5pm Sun; 🤙🖉) Graze your way through this gourmet market and plug into the Northern California food scene. Look for Hog Island oysters (six for $15); comfort cooking at celeb-chef Todd Humphries' Kitchen Door (mains $13 to $20); Pica Pica's Venezuelan cornbread sandwiches ($8); standout Cal-Mexican at Casa (tacos $4 to $8); pastries at Ca'Momi ($1.50); and Three Twins certified-organic ice cream ($3.65 single cone). Tuesday is locals night, with many discounts. Tuesday and Saturday mornings, there's a farmers market. Friday nights bring live music. Some stalls remain open till 9pm, even on Sundays, but many close earlier.

Ubuntu — VEGETARIAN $$
(Map p169; ☑707-251-5656; www.ubuntunapa.com; 1140 Main St, Napa; dishes $14-18; ⊙dinner nightly, lunch Sat & Sun; 🖉) The Michelin-starred, seasonal, vegetarian menu features artfully presented natural wonders from the biodynamic kitchen garden, satisfying hearty eaters with four-to-five inspired small plates, and eco-savvy drinkers with 100-plus sustainably produced wines.

Boon Fly Café — AMERICAN $$
(Map p164; ☑707-299-4870; www.theboonflycafe.com; 4048 Sonoma Hwy; mains $10-20; ⊙7am-9pm) For New American comfort food done well, make a beeline to Boon Fly – but avoid peak meal times unless you've made reservations. At breakfast, try homemade doughnuts or brioche French toast; at lunch and dinner, grilled Reubens, roasted chicken, and spinach salads. Save room for warm chocolate-chip cookies.

Pearl Restaurant — NEW AMERICAN $$
(Map p169; ☑707-224-9161; www.therestaurantpearl.com; 1339 Pearl St; mains $14-19; ⊙Tue-Sat 5:30-9pm; ❋) Meet locals at this dog-friendly bistro with red-painted concrete floors, pinewood tables and open-rafter ceilings. The winning down-to-earth cooking includes double-cut pork chops, chicken verde with polenta, steak tacos and the specialty, oysters.

Oenotri — ITALIAN $$
(☑707-252-1022; www.oenotri.com; 1425 First St, Napa; mains $15-25; ⊙dinner, lunch hours vary) Housemade salumi and pastas, and wood-fired Naples-style pizzas are the stars at always-busy Oenotri, which draws bon vivants for its daily-changing lineup of locally sourced, rustic-Italian cooking, served in a cavernous brick-walled space.

Bistro Don Giovanni — ITALIAN $$$
(Map p164; ☑707-224-3300; www.bistrodongiovanni.com; 4110 Howard Lane at Hwy 29; mains $19-26) This long-running favorite roadhouse cooks up modern-Italian pastas, crispy pizzas and wood-roasted meats. Reservations essential. Weekends get packed – and loud. Request a vineyard-view table (good luck).

Bounty Hunter Wine Bar — AMERICAN $$
(Map p169; www.bountyhunterwine.com; 975 1st St; dishes $14-24; ⊙11am-10pm; ❋) Inside an 1888 grocery store, Bounty Hunter has an old West vibe and superb barbecue, made with house-smoked meats. The standout whole chicken is roasted over a can of Tecate. Ten local beers and 40 wines by the glass.

Bistro Sabor — LATIN AMERICAN $
(Map p169; ☑707-252-0555; www.bistrosabor.com; 1126 1st St; dishes $8-11; ⊙11:30am-11pm Tue-Thu, 11:30am-1:30am Fri & Sat; ❋) Not your typical Mexican joint, this order-at-the-counter downtowner makes super-fresh Latin American street foods, including ceviches, papusas and chile rellenos. Save room for churros.

Alexis Baking Co — CAFE $
(Map p169; ☑707-258-1827; www.alexisbakingcompany.com; 1517 3rd St; dishes $6-10; ⊙Mon-Fri 7:30am-3pm, Sat 7am-3pm, Sun 8am-2pm; 🤙🖉) Our fave spot for scrambles, granola, focaccia sandwiches, big cups of joe and boxed lunches to go.

Pizza Azzuro — PIZZERIA $$
(Map p169; ☑707-255-5552; www.azzurropizzeria.com; 1260 Main St; mains $12-16; 🤙🖉) This Napa classic gets deafeningly loud, but the tender-crusted pizzas and salad-topped 'manciata'

bread make the noise worth bearing. Good Caesar salad and pastas.

Norman Rose Tavern   PUB $$
(☎707-258-1516; normanrosenapa.com; 1401 1st St; mains $10-20; ◉11:30am-10pm ⌨) This happening gastropub, styled with reclaimed wood and tufted-leather banquettes, is good for a burger and beer. Great fries. Beer and wine only.

Soscol Café   DINER $
(Map p169; ☎707-252-0651; 632 Soscol Av; dishes $6-9; ◉6am-2pm Mon-Sat, 7am-1pm Sun) The ultimate greasy-spoon diner, Soscol makes massive huevos rancheros, and chicken-fried steak and eggs. Not a high heel in sight.

⚲ Drinking & Entertainment

Silo's Jazz Club   LIVE MUSIC
(Map p169; ☎707-251-5833; www.silosjazzclub.com; 530 Main St; cover varies; ◉Wed-Thu 4-10pm, Fri & Sat to midnight) A cabaret-style wine-and-beer bar, Silo's hosts jazz and rock acts Friday and Saturday nights; Wednesday and Thursdays it's good for drinks. Reservations recommended weekends.

Salsa Saturdays at Bistro Sabor   DANCE
(Map p169; www.bistrosabor.com; 1126 1st St; admission free; ◉10pm-1:30am Sat) DJs spin salsa and merengue at this happening Saturday-night restaurant dance party.

Billco's Billiards & Darts   SPORTS BAR
(Map p169; www.billcos.com; 1234 3rd St; ◉noon-1am) Dudes in khakis swill craft beers, shoot pool and throw darts.

Downtown Joe's   SPORTS BAR, BREWERY
(Map p169; www.downtownjoes.com; 902 Main St at 2nd St; ☎) Live music Thursday to Sunday, TV sports nightly. Often packed, sometimes messy.

Napa Valley Opera House   THEATER
(Map p169; ☎707-226-7372; www.nvoh.org; 1030 Main St) Restored vintage-1880s opera house; straight plays, comedy and major acts.

Uptown Theatre   THEATER
(Map p169; ☎707-259-0333; www.uptowntheatrenapa.com; 1350 3rd St) Big name acts play this restored 1937 theater.

🛍 Shopping

Betty's Girl   WOMEN'S CLOTHING, VINTAGE
(☎707-254-7560; 1144 Main St) Hollywood costume designer Kim Northrup fits women

with fabulous vintage cocktail dresses, altering and shipping for no additional charge.

Napa General Store   GIFTS
(☎707-259-0762; www.napageneralstore.com; 540 Main St) Finally, clever Wine Country souvenirs that are reasonably priced. The on-site wine bar is convenient for non-shopping husbands.

❶ Information

Napa Valley Welcome Center (☎707-260-0107; www.legendarynapavalley.com; 600 Main St; ◉9am-5pm) Spa deals, wine-tasting passes and comprehensive winery maps.

Napa Library (☎707-253-4241; www.countyofnapa.org/Library; 580 Coombs St; ◉10am-9pm Mon-Thu, 10am-6pm Fri & Sat; @) Email connections.

Queen of the Valley Medical Center (☎707-252-4411; 1000 Trancas St) Emergency medical.

❶ Getting Around

Pedi cabs park outside downtown restaurants – especially at the foot of Main St, near the NV Welcome Center – in summertime.

Yountville

This onetime stagecoach stop, 9 miles north of Napa, is now a major foodie destination, with more Michelin stars per capita than any other American town. There are some good inns here, but it's deathly boring at night. You stay in Yountville to drink with dinner without having to drive afterward. St Helena and Calistoga make better bases. Most businesses are on Washington St.

Ma(i)sonry (☎707-944-0889; www.maisonry.com; 6711 Washington St; ◉9am-10pm) occupies a 1904 stone house, now transformed into a rustic-modern showplace for furniture, art and wine; the garden is a swank post-dinner fireside gathering spot for vino.

Yountville's modernist 40,000-sq-ft **Napa Valley Museum** (☎707-944-0500; www.napavalleymuseum.org; 55 Presidents Circle; adult/child $5/2.50; ◉10am-5pm Wed-Mon), off California Dr, chronicles cultural history and showcases local paintings. Good picnicking outside.

The only worthwhile shop at V Marketplace is TV-chef Michael Chiarello's **Napa Style** (www.napastyle.com; 6525 Washington St), but it's overpriced.

FLYING & BALLOONING

Wine Country is stunning from the air – a multihued tapestry of undulating hills, deep valleys and rambling vineyards. Make reservations.

The **Vintage Aircraft Company** (Map p184; ☎707-938-2444; www.vintageaircraft.com; 23982 Arnold Dr) flies over Sonoma in a vintage biplane with an awesome pilot who'll do loop-de-loops on request (add $50). Twenty-minute tours cost $175/270 for one/two adults.

Napa Valley's signature hot-air balloon flights leave early, around 6am or 7am, when the air is coolest; they usually include a champagne breakfast on landing. Adults pay about $200 to $250, and kids $130 to $150. Call **Balloons above the Valley** (☎707-253-2222, 800-464-6824; www.balloonrides.com) or **Napa Valley Balloons** (☎707-944-0228, 800-253-2224; www.napavalleyballoons.com), both in Yountville.

🛏 Sleeping

🌿 Bardessono LUXURY HOTEL **$$$**
(☎707-204-6000, 877-932-5333; www.bardessono.com; 6524 Yount St; r $600-800, ste from $800; ✳@🛜🏊) The outdoors flows indoors at California's first-ever LEED-platinum-certified green hotel, made of recycled everything, styled in Japanese-led austerity, with neutral tones and hard angles that feel exceptionally urban for farm country. Glam pool deck and onsite spa. Tops for a splurge.

Poetry Inn INN **$$$**
(☎707-944-0646; www.poetryinn.com; 6380 Silverado Trail; r incl breakfast $650-1400; ✳🛜🏊) There's no better view of Napa Valley than from this understatedly chic, three-room inn, high on the hills east of Yountville. Rooms are decorated in Arts and Crafts-inspired style, and have private balconies, wood-burning fireplaces, 1000-thread-count linens and enormous baths with indoor-outdoor showers. Bring a ring.

Maison Fleurie B&B **$$$**
(☎707-944-2056, 800-788-0369; www.maisonfleurienapa.com; 6529 Yount St; r incl breakfast $145-295; ✳🛜🏊) Rooms at this ivy-covered country inn are in a century-old home and carriage house, decorated in French-provincial style. There's a big breakfast, and afternoon wine and *hors d'oeuvres*. Hot tub.

Napa Valley Lodge HOTEL **$$$**
(☎707-944-2468, 888-944-3545; www.napavalleylodge.com; 2230 Madison St; r $300-455; ✳🛜🏊) It looks like a condo complex, but rooms are spacious and modern, some with fireplaces. Hot tub, sauna and exercise room.

Petit Logis INN **$$$**
(☎707-944-2332, 877-944-2332; www.petitlogis.com; 6527 Yount St, r Mon-Fri $195-255, Sat & Sun $235-285; ✳🛜) This cedar-sided inn has five individually decorated rooms. Think white wicker furniture and dusty-rose fabric. Add $20 for breakfast for two.

Napa Valley Railway Inn THEME INN **$$**
(☎707-944-2000; www.napavalleyrailwayinn.com; 6523 Washington St, Yountville; r $125-260; ✳@🛜🏊) Sleep in a converted railroad car, part of two short trains parked at a central platform. They've little privacy, but are moderately priced. Bring earplugs.

🍴 Eating

Make reservations or you might not eat. **Yountville Park** (cnr Washington & Madison Sts) has picnic tables and barbecue grills, you'll find groceries across from the post office, and there's a great **taco truck** (6764 Washington St).

French Laundry CALIFORNIAN **$$$**
(☎707-944-2380; www.frenchlaundry.com; 6640 Washington St; prix fixe incl service charge $270; ☺dinner, lunch Sat & Sun) The pinnacle of California dining, Thomas Keller's French Laundry is epic, a high-wattage culinary experience on par with the world's best. Book two months ahead at 10am sharp, or log onto OpenTable.com precisely at midnight. Avoid tables before 7pm; first-service seating moves faster than the second – sometimes too fast.

Bouchon FRENCH **$$$**
(☎707-944-8037; www.bouchonbistro.com; 6534 Washington St; mains $17-36; ☺11:30am-12:30am) At celeb-chef Thomas Keller's French brasserie, everything from food to decor is so authentic, from zinc bar to white-aproned

waiters, you'd swear you were in Paris – even the Bermuda-shorts-clad Americans look out of place. On the menu: oysters, onion soup, roasted chicken, leg of lamb, trout with almonds, runny cheeses and profiteroles for dessert, impeccably prepared.

TOP CHOICE Ad Hoc
NEW AMERICAN $$$

(☎707-944-2487; www.adhocrestaurant.com; 6476 Washington St, Yountville; menu $48; ☺Wed-Mon dinner, Sun 10:30am-2pm) Another winning formula by Yountville's culinary oligarch, Thomas Keller, Ad Hoc serves the master's favorite American home cooking in four-course family-style menus, with no variations except for dietary restrictions. Monday is fried-chicken night, which you can also sample weekend lunchtime, take-out only, behind the restaurant at Keller's latest venture, Addendum (☺11am-2pm Thu-Sat), which also serves barbecue; get the daily menu on Twitter at @AddendumatAdHoc.

Étoile
CALIFORNIAN $$$

(Map p164; ☎707-944-8844; www.chandon.com; 1 California Dr; lunch/dinner mains $26-31/$32-36; ☺11:30am-2:30pm & 6-9pm Thu-Mon) Within Chandon winery, Michelin-starred Étoile's is perfect for a lingering white-tablecloth lunch in the vines; ideal when you want to visit a winery and eat a good meal with minimal driving.

Bistro Jeanty
FRENCH $$$

(☎707-944-0103; www.bistrojeanty.com; 6510 Washington St; mains $18-29) A true French bistro serves comfort food to weary travelers, and that's exactly what French-born chef-owner Philippe Jeanty does, with succulent cassoulet, coq au vin, *steak-frites,* braised pork with lentils, and scrumptious tomato soup.

Paninoteca Ottimo
SANDWICHES, CAFE $

(☎707-945-1229; www.napastyleottimocafe.com; 6525 Washington St; dishes $8-10; ☺10am-6pm Mon-Sat, 10am-5pm Sat) TV-chef Michael Chiarello's cafe makes stellar salads and delish paninos (try the slow-roasted pork) that pair well with his organically produced wines. Tops for picnic supplies.

Bouchon Bakery
BAKERY $

(☎707-944-2253; www.bouchonbakery.com; 6528 Washington St; dishes $3-9; ☺7am-7pm) Bouchon makes perfect French pastries and strong coffee. Order at the counter and sit outside, or pack a bag to go.

Mustards Grill
CALIFORNIAN $$$

(Map p164; ☎707-944-2424; www.mustardsgrill.com; 7399 St Helena Hwy; mains $22-27; ☻) The valley's original roadhouse whips up wood-fired California comfort food – roasted meats, lamb shanks, pork chops, hearty salads and sandwiches. Great crowd-pleaser.

Drinking & Entertainment

Pancha's
DIVE BAR

(6764 Washington St) Swill tequila with vineyard workers early, restaurant waiters late.

Lincoln Theater
THEATER

(Map p164; ☎707-944-1300, 866-944-9199; www.lincolntheater.org; 100 California Dr) Various artists play this 1200-seat theater, including the Napa Valley Symphony.

Oakville & Rutherford

But for its famous grocery, you'd drive through Oakville (pop 71) and never know you'd missed it. This is the middle of the grapes – vineyards sprawl in every direction. Rutherford (pop 164) is more conspicuous, but the wineries put these towns on the map.

Sleeping & Eating

There's no budget lodging here.

Auberge du Soleil
LUXURY HOTEL $$$

(Map p164; ☎707-963-1211, 800-348-5406; www.aubergedusoleil.com; 180 Rutherford Hill Rd; r $650-975, ste $1400-2200; ❋☎❋) The top splurge for a no-holds-barred romantic weekend, Auberge's hillside cottages are second to none. Less-expensive rooms feel comparatively cramped; book a suite. Excellent guests-only spa. Auberge's dining room (mains breakfast $16-19, lunch $29-42, 3-/4-/6-course prix-fixe dinner $98/115/140) showcases an expertly prepared Euro-Cal menu, among the valley's best. Come for a fancy breakfast, lazy lunch or will-you-wear-my-ring dinner. Valley views are mesmerizing from the terrace – *don't* sit inside. Make reservations; arrive before sunset.

Rancho Caymus
HOTEL $$$

(☎707-963-1777, 800-845-1777; www.ranchocaymus.com; 1140 Rutherford Rd, Rutherford; r $175-285; ❋☎❋) Styled after California's missions, this hacienda-style inn scores high marks for its tiled fountain courtyard, and rooms' kiva-style fireplaces, oak-beamed ceilings and wood floors, but the furniture looks tired.

La Luna Market & Taqueria
MARKET $

(Map p164; 707-963-3211; 1153 Rutherford Rd, Rutherford; dishes $4-6; 9am-5pm May-Nov) Look no further for honest burritos with homemade hot sauce.

Rutherford Grill
AMERICAN $$

(707-963-1792; www.hillstone.com; 1180 Rutherford Rd, Rutherford; mains $15-30) Yes, it's a chain (Houston's), but to rub shoulders with winemakers, snag a stool for lunch at the bar. The food is consistent – ribs, rotisserie chicken, outstanding grilled artichokes – and there's no corkage, so bring that bottle you just bought down the road.

Oakville Grocery & Cafe
DELI $$

(Map p164; 707-944-8802; www.oakvillegrocery.com; 7856 Hwy 29, Oakville; 8am-5:30pm) The once-definitive Wine Country deli has gotten ridiculously overpriced, with less variety than in previous years, but still carries excellent cheeses, charcuterie, bread, olives and wine. There are tables outside, but ask where to picnic nearby.

St Helena

You'll know you're arriving when traffic halts. St Helena (ha-lee-na) is the Rodeo Dr of Napa, with fancy boutiques lining Main St (Hwy 29). The historic downtown is good for a stroll, with great window-shopping, but parking is next-to-impossible summer weekends.

The **St Helena Welcome Center** (707-963-4456, 800-799-6456; www.sthelena.com; 657 Main St; 9am-5pm Mon-Fri) has information and lodging assistance.

Sights & Activities

FREE **Silverado Museum**
MUSEUM

(Map p164; 707-963-3757; www.silveradomuseum.org; 1490 Library Lane; noon-4pm Tue-Sat) Contains a fascinating collection of Robert Louis Stevenson memorabilia. In 1880, the author – then sick, penniless and unknown – stayed in an abandoned bunkhouse at the old Silverado Mine on Mt St Helena (p181) with his wife, Fanny Osbourne; his novel *The Silverado Squatters* is based on his time there. To reach Library Lane, turn east off Hwy 29 at the Adams St traffic light and cross the railroad tracks.

Culinary Institute of America at Greystone
COOKING SCHOOL

(Map p164; 707-967-2320; www.ciachef.edu/california; 2555 Main St; mains $25-29, cooking demonstration $20; restaurant 11:30am-9pm, cooking demonstrations 1:30pm Sat & Sun) An 1889 stone chateau houses a gadget- and cookbook-filled **culinary shop**; fine **restaurant**; weekend **cooking demonstrations**; and **wine-tasting classes** by luminaries in the field, including Karen MacNeil, author of *The Wine Bible*.

Farmers market
MARKET

(www.sthelenafarmersmkt.org; 7:30am-noon Fri May-Oct) Meets at Crane Park, half a mile south of downtown.

Sleeping

Meadowood
RESORT $$$

(Map p164; 707-963-3646, 800-458-8080; www.meadowood.com; 900 Meadowood Lane; r from $600;) Hidden in a wooded dell with towering pines and miles of hiking, Napa's grandest resort has cottages and rooms in satellite buildings surrounding a croquet lawn. We most like the hillside fireplace cottages; lawn-view rooms lack privacy but are good for families, with room to play outside. The vibe is country club, with white-clapboard buildings reminiscent of New England. Wear linen and play *Great Gatsby*. Kids love the mammoth pool.

Harvest Inn
INN $$$

(707-963-9463, 800-950-8466; www.harvestinn.com; 1 Main St; r incl breakfast $329-549;) If you can't swing Meadowood, this former estate, with sprawling gardens and rooms in satellite buildings, is a lovely backup. The new building is generic; book the vineyard-view rooms, with their private hot tubs.

El Bonita Motel
MOTEL $$

(Map p164; 707-963-3216, 800-541-3284; www.elbonita.com; 195 Main St, St Helena; $119-179;) Book in advance to secure a room at this sought-after motel, with up-to-date rooms (quietest are in back), attractive grounds, hot tub and sauna.

Hotel St Helena
HISTORIC HOTEL $$

(707-963-4388; www.hotelsthelena.net; 1309 Main St; r with/without bath $125-235/$105-165;) Decorated with period furnishings, this frayed-at-the-edges 1881 hotel sits right downtown. Rooms are tiny, but good value, especially those with shared bathroom. No elevator.

✗ Eating

Make reservations where possible. If you're just after something quick, consider Gillwood's Cafe (www.gillwoodscafe.com; 1313 Main St; dishes $8-12; 7am-3pm) for an all-day breakfast; Sunshine Foods (www.sunshinefoodsmarket.com; 1115 Main St; 7:30am-8:30pm), the town's best grocery and deli; Model Bakery (www.themodelbakery.com; 1357 Main St; dishes $5-10; 7am-6pm Tue-Sun, 8am-4pm Sun) for great scones, muffins, salads, gelato, pizzas, sandwiches and strong coffee; or Armadillo's (1304 Main St; mains $8-12) for respectable and reasonable Mexican eats.

Gott's Roadside (Taylor's Auto Refresher)   BURGERS $$
(707-963-3486; www.gottsroadside.com; 933 Main St; dishes $8-15; 10:30am-9pm; 🖪) Wiggle your toes in the grass and feast on all-natural burgers, Cobb salads and fried calamari at this classic roadside drive-in, whose original name, 'Taylor's Auto Refresher,' is still listed on the roadside sign. Avoid big weekend waits by calling in your order. There's another branch at Oxbow Public Market (p171).

Napa Valley Olive Oil Mfg Co   MARKET $
(707-963-4173; www.oliveoilsainthelena.com; 835 Charter Oak St; 8am-5:30pm) Before the advent of fancy-food stores, this ramshackle Italian market introduced Napa to Italian delicacies – succulent prosciutto and salami, meaty olives, fresh bread, nutty cheeses and, of course, olive oil. Yellowed business cards from 50 years ago adorn the walls, and the owner knows everyone in town. He'll lend you a knife and a board to make a picnic at the rickety wooden tables outside in the grass. Cash only.

Cook   CAL-ITALIAN $$
(707-963-7088; www.cooksthelena.com; 1310 Main St; lunch mains $12-21, dinner mains $17-25; 11:30am-10pm Mon-Sat, 5-10pm Sun) Locals crowd the counter at this tiny storefront bistro, much loved for its earthy cooking – homemade pasta, melt-off-the-bone ribs and simple-delicious burgers. Try the butter-braised Brussels sprouts – fantastic. Expect a wait, even with reservations.

Market   NEW AMERICAN $$
(707-963-3799; www.marketsthelena.com; 1347 Main St; mains $13-24; 11:30am-9pm) We love the big portions of simple, fresh American

cooking at Market. Maximizing the season's best produce, the chef creates enormous, inventive salads and soul-satisfying mains like buttermilk fried chicken. The stone-walled dining room dates to the 19th century, as does the ornate backbar, where cocktails are muddled to order.

Cindy's Backstreet Kitchen   NEW AMERICAN $$
(707-963-1200; www.cindysbackstreetkitchen.com; 1327 Railroad Ave; mains $17-25) The inviting retro-homey decor complements the menu's Cal-American comfort food, like avocado-and-papaya salad, wood-fired duck, steak with French fries, and the simple grilled burger. The bar makes a mean mojito.

Farmstead   NEW AMERICAN $$$
(707-963-9181; www.farmsteadnapa.com; 738 Main St; mains $16-26; 11:30am-9pm) A cavernous open-truss barn with big leather booths and rocking-chair porch, Farmstead grows many of its own ingredients – including grass-fed beef – for its earthy menu that highlights wood-fired cooking.

Terra   CALIFORNIAN $$$
(707-963-8931; www.terrarestaurant.com; 1345 Railroad Ave; 3-/4-/5-/6-course menus $57/66/81/92; 6-9pm Wed-Sun) Inside an 1884 stone building, Terra wows diners with seamlessly blended Japanese, French and Italian culinary styles. The signature is broiled sake-marinated black cod with shrimp dumplings in shiso broth. Perfect. The bar serves small bites, but the dining room's the thing.

Restaurant at Meadowood   CALIFORNIAN $$$
(Map p164; 707-967-1205; www.meadowood.com; 900 Meadowood Lane; 4-/9-course menu $125/225; 5:30-10pm Mon-Sat) If you couldn't score reservations at French Laundry, fear not: the clubby Restaurant at Meadowood – the valley's only other Michelin-three-star restaurant – has a more sensibly priced menu, elegant but unfussy forest-view dining room, and lavish haute cuisine that's never too esoteric. Auberge has better views, but Meadowood's food and service far surpass the former.

Silverado Brewing Co   BREWPUB $$
(Map p164; 707-967-9876; www.silveradobrewingcompany.com; 3020 Hwy 29; mains $12-18; 11:30am-1am; 🖪) Silverados' microbrews

measure up to Napa's wines – Brewmaster Ken Mee's Certifiable Blonde has organic ingredients and crazy-tasty malts, and competes for top choice with the hopped-up Amber Ale. Food is typical pub grub that keeps your buzz in check.

Shopping

Main St is lined with high-end boutiques (think $100 socks), but some mom-and-pop shops remain. Also see p182.

Woodhouse Chocolates FOOD
(www.woodhousechocolate.com; 1367 Main St) Woodhouse looks more like Tiffany & Co than a candy shop, with chocolates similarly priced, but they're made in town and their quality is beyond reproach.

Napa Soap Company DEAUTY
(www.napasoap.com; 651 Main St) Hand-crafted eco-friendly bath products, locally produced.

Lolo's Consignment VINTAGE
(www.loloconsignment.com; 1120 Main St) Groovy dresses and cast-off cashmere.

Main Street Books BOOKS
(1315 Main St; Mon-Sat) Good used books.

Calistoga

The least gentrified town in Napa Valley feels refreshingly simple, with an old-fashioned main street lined with shops, not boutiques, and diverse characters wandering the sidewalks. Bad hair? No problem. Fancy-pants St Helena couldn't feel farther away. Most tourists don't make it this far north. You should.

Famed 19th-century author Robert Louis Stevenson said of Calistoga: 'the whole neighborhood of Mt St Helena is full of sulfur and boiling springs...Calistoga itself seems to repose on a mere film above a boiling, subterranean lake.'

Indeed, it does. Calistoga is synonymous with the mineral water bearing its name, bottled here since 1924. Its springs and geysers have earned it the nickname the 'hot springs of the West.' Plan to visit one of the town's spas, where you can indulge in the local specialty: a hot-mud bath, made of the volcanic ash from nearby volcanic Mt St Helena.

The town's odd name comes from Sam Brannan, who founded Calistoga in 1859, believing it would develop like the New York spa town of Saratoga. Apparently Sam liked his drink and at the founding ceremony tripped on his tongue, proclaiming it the 'Cali-stoga' of 'Sara-fornia.' The name stuck.

Sights

Hwys 128 and 29 run together from Rutherford through St Helena; in Calistoga, they split. Hwy 29 turns east and becomes Lincoln Ave, continuing across Silverado Trail, toward Clear Lake. Hwy 128 continues north as Foothill Blvd (not St Helena Hwy). Calistoga's shops and restaurants line Lincoln Ave.

Old Faithful Geyser GEYSER
(Map p164; 707-942-6463; www.oldfaithfulgeyser.com; 1299 Tubbs Lane; adult/child $10/free; 9am-6pm summer, to 5pm winter;) Calistoga's mini-version of Yellowstone's Old Faithful shoots boiling water 60ft to 100ft into the air, every 30 minutes. The vibe is pure roadside Americana, with folksy hand-painted interpretive exhibits, picnicking and a little petting zoo, where you can come nose-to-nose with llamas. It's 2 miles north of town, off Silverado Trail. Look for discount coupons around town.

Sharpsteen Museum MUSEUM
(707-942-5911; www.sharpsteen-museum.org; 1311 Washington St; adult/child $3/free; 11am-4pm;) Across from the picturesque 1902 City Hall (which was originally an opera house), the Sharpsteen Museum was created by an ex-Disney animator (whose Oscar is on display) and houses a fabulous diorama of the town in the 1860s, big Victorian dollhouse, full-size horse-drawn carriage, cool taxidermy and a restored cottage from Brannan's original resort. (The only Brannan cottage still at its

TOP KID-FRIENDLY WINERIES

» **Kaz** (p184) Play-Doh, playground and grape juice
» **Benziger** (p183) Open-air tram ride and peacocks
» **Frog's Leap** (p166) Cats, chickens and croquet.
» **Casa Nuestra** (p167) Playful goats.
» **Castello di Amorosa** (p168) Historical-imagination sparker.
» **Lava Vine** (p168) Mellow vibe, grassy play area.

original site is at 106 Wapoo Ave, near the Brannan Cottage Inn.)

🏃 Activities

Hardcore mountain bikers can tackle **Oat Hill Mine Trail**, one of Northern California's most technically challenging trails, just outside town. Find information and rentals at **Calistoga Bike Shop** (☎707-942-9687, 866-942-2453; www.calistogabikeshop.com; 1318 Lincoln Ave), which rents full-suspension mountain bikes (per day $75) and hybrids (per hour/day $10/35). Wine-touring packages (per day $80) include wine-rack baskets and free wine pickup.

SPAS

Calistoga is famous for hot-spring spas and mud-bath emporiums, where you're buried in hot mud and emerge feeling supple, detoxified and enlivened. (The mud is made with volcanic ash and peat; the higher the ash content, the better the bath.)

Packages take 60 to 90 minutes and cost $70 to $90. You start semi-submerged in hot mud, then soak in hot mineral water. A steam bath and blanket-wrap follow. The treatment can be extended with a massage, increasing the cost to $130 and up.

Baths can be taken solo or, at some spas, as couples. Variations include thin, painted-on clay-mud wraps (called 'fango' baths, good for those uncomfortable sitting in mud), herbal wraps, seaweed baths and various massage treatments. Discount coupons are sometimes available from the visitors center. Book ahead, especially on summer weekends. Reservations essential at all spas.

The following spas in downtown Calistoga offer one-day packages. Some also offer discounted spa-lodging packages.

TOP CHOICE Indian Springs SPA
(☎707-942-4913; www.indianspringscalistoga.com; 1712 Lincoln Ave; ⊙8am-9pm) The longest continually operating spa and original Calistoga resort has concrete mud tubs and mines its own ash. Treatments include use of the huge, hot-spring-fed pool. Great cucumber body lotion.

Spa Solage SPA
(Map p164; ☎707-226-0825; www.solagecalistoga.com; 755 Silverado Trail; ⊙8am-8pm) Chichi, austere, top-end spa, with couples' rooms and a fango-mud bar for DIY paint-on treatments. Also has zero-gravity chairs for blanket wraps, and a clothing-optional pool.

Dr Wilkinson's Hot Springs SPA
(☎707-942-4102; www.drwilkinson.com; 1507 Lincoln Ave; ⊙8:30am-5:30pm) Fifty years running; 'the doc' uses more peat in its mud.

Mount View Spa SPA
(☎707-942-6877, 800-816-6877; www.mountviewhotel.com; 1457 Lincoln Ave; ⊙9am-9pm) Traditional full-service, 12-room spa, good for clean-hands gals who prefer painted-on mud to submersion.

Lavender Hill Spa SPA
(Map p164; ☎707-942-4495; www.lavenderhillspa.com; 1015 Foothill Blvd; ⊙10am-6pm, to 8pm Fri & Sat) Small, cute, two-room spa that uses much-lighter, less-icky lavender-infused mud; offers couples' treatments.

Golden Haven Hot Springs SPA
(☎707-942-8000; www.goldenhaven.com; 1713 Lake St; ⊙8am-8pm) Old-school and unfussy; offers couples' mud baths and couples' massage.

Calistoga Spa Hot Springs SPA
(☎707-942-6269, 866-822-5772; www.calistogaspa.com; 1006 Washington St; ⊙appointments 8:30am-4:30pm Tue-Thu, to 9pm Fri-Mon; 👪) Traditional mud baths and massage at a motel complex with two huge **swimming pools** (⊙10am-9pm) where kids can play while you soak (pool passes $25).

🛏 Sleeping

Also see Safari West (p182).

TOP CHOICE Mountain Home Ranch LODGE, B&B $$
(off Map p164; ☎707-942-6616; www.mountainhomeranch.com; 3400 Mountain Home Ranch Rd; r $109-119, cabin with/without bath $119-144/$69; ❀🛜🏊👪🐾) In continuous operation since 1913, this 340-acre homestead ranch is a flashback to old California. Doubling as a retreat center, the ranch has simple lodge rooms and rustic freestanding cabins, some with kitchens and fireplaces, ideal for families, but you may be here during someone else's family reunion or spiritual quest. No matter. With miles of oak-woodland trails, a hilltop swimming pool, private lake with canoeing and fishing, and hike-to warm springs in a magical fault-line canyon, you may hardly notice – and you may never make it to a single winery. Breakfast included, but you'll have to drive 15 minutes to town for dinner. Pack hiking boots, not high heels.

Solage
RESORT $$$

(Map p164; ☑707-226-0800, 866-942-7442; www.solagecalistoga.com; 755 Silverado Trail; r $510-625; ❄🖥🐕🏊) The latest addition to Calistoga's spa-hotels ups the style factor, with Cali-chic semidetached cottages and a glam palm-tree-lined pool. Rooms are austere, with vaulted ceilings, zillion-thread-count linens and pebble-floor showers. Cruiser bikes included.

Indian Springs Resort
RESORT $$$

(☑707-942-4913; www.indianspringscalistoga.com; 1712 Lincoln Ave; motel r $229-299, bungalow $259-349, 2-bedroom bungalow $359-419; ❄🖥🐕🏊) The definitive old-school Calistoga resort, Indian Springs has bungalows facing a central lawn with palm trees, shuffleboard, bocce, hammocks and Weber grills – not unlike a vintage Florida resort. Some bungalows sleep six. There are also top-end motel-style rooms. Huge hot-springs-fed swimming pool.

Chateau De Vie
B&B $$$

(Map p164; ☑707-942-6446, 877-558-2513; www.cdvnapavalley.com; 3250 Hwy 128; r incl breakfast $229-429; ❄🖥🐕🏊) Surrounded by vineyards, with gorgeous views of Mt St Helena, CDV has five modern B&B rooms with top-end amenities. The house is elegantly decorated, with zero froufrou. Charming owners serve wine every afternoon on the sun-dappled patio, then leave you alone. Hot tub, big pool. Gay-friendly.

Meadowlark Country House
B&B $$$

(Map p164; ☑707-942-5651, 800-942-5651; www.meadowlarkinn.com; 601 Petrified Forest Rd; r incl breakfast $195-275, ste $285; ❄🖥🐕🏊) On 20 acres west of town, Meadowlark has luxury rooms decorated in contemporary style, most with decks and Jacuzzis. Outside there's a hot tub, sauna and clothing-optional pool. The truth-telling innkeeper lives in another house, offers helpful advice, then vanishes when you want privacy. There's a fabulous cottage for $450. Gay-friendly.

Mount View Hotel & Spa
HISTORIC HOTEL $$$

(☑707-942-6877, 800-816-6877; www.mountviewhotel.com; 1457 Lincoln Ave; r $179-329; ❄🖥🐕) Smack in the middle of town, this 1917 Mission Revival hotel was redone in 2009 in vaguely mod-Italian style, sometimes at odds with the vintage building, but clean and fresh-looking nonetheless. Gleaming bathrooms, on-site spa, year-round heated pool, but no elevator.

Eurospa Inn
MOTEL $$

(☑707-942-6829; www.eurospa.com; 1202 Pine St, Calistoga; r $139-189; ❄🖥🐕) Immaculate single-story motel on a quiet side street, with extras like gas-burning fireplaces, afternoon wine and small on-site spa. Wonderful service, but tiny pool.

Brannan Cottage Inn
B&B $$$

(☑707-942-4200; www.brannancottageinn.com; 109 Wapoo Ave; r incl breakfast $195-230, ste $230-270; ❄🖥🐕) Sam Brannan built this 1860 cottage, listed on the National Register of Historic Places. Long on folksy charm and friendly service, it's decorated with floral-print fabrics and simple country furnishings, but walls are thin and floors creak. Suites sleep four. Guests use the pool at Golden Haven motel.

Dr Wilkinson's Motel & Hideaway Cottages
MOTEL, COTTAGES $$

(☑707-942-4102; www.drwilkinson.com; 1507 Lincoln Ave; r $149-255, cottages w/kitchens $165-270; ❄🖥🐕) This good-value vintage-1950s motel has well-kept rooms facing a swimming-pool courtyard. No hot tub, but three pools (one indoors) and mud baths. Doc Wilkinson's also rents simple stand-alone cottages, with kitchens, at the affiliated Hideaway Cottages.

Chanric
B&B $$$

(Map p164; ☑707-942-4535; www.thechanric.com; 1805 Foothill Blvd; r incl breakfast $229-349; ❄🖥🐕) A converted Victorian close to the road, this B&B has smallish rooms with modern furnishings, but the affable owners compensate with a lavish three-course breakfast. Gay-friendly.

Aurora Park Cottages
COTTAGES $$$

(Map p164; ☑707-942-6733, 877-942-7700; www.aurorapark.com; 1807 Foothill Blvd; cottages incl breakfast $259-289; ❄🖥) Six immaculately kept, sunny-yellow cottages – with polished-wood floors, featherbeds and sundeck – stand in a row beside flowering gardens, and though close to the road, they're quiet by night. The innkeeper couldn't be nicer.

Calistoga Spa Hot Springs
MOTEL $$

(Map p164; ☑707-942-6269, 866-822-5772; www.calistogaspa.com; 1006 Washington St; r $132-252; ❄🖥🐕) Great for families, who jam the place weekends, this motel-resort has slightly scuffed generic rooms, with kitchenettes, and fantastic pools – two full-size, a kiddie-pool with miniwaterfall and a huge

NAPA & SONOMA WINE COUNTRY CALISTOGA

adults-only Jacuzzi. Outside are barbecues and snack bar. Wi-fi in lobby.

Golden Haven Hot Springs MOTEL $$
(707-942-8000; www.goldenhaven.com; 1713 Lake St; r $149-219; ❄🌐🏊) This motel-spa has mudbath-lodging packages and well-kept rooms; some have Jacuzzis.

Calistoga Inn & Brewery INN $
(707-942-4101; www.calistogainn.com; 1250 Lincoln Ave; r Mon-Fri/Sat & Sun $69/$119; 🌐) For no-fuss bargain-hunters, this inn, upstairs from a busy bar, has 18 clean, basic rooms with shared bath. No TVs. Bring earplugs.

Bothe-Napa Valley State Park CAMPGROUND $
(707-942-4575, reservations 800-444-7275; www.reserveamerica.com; tent & RV sites $35; 🏊) Three miles south, Bothe has shady camping near redwoods, coin-operated showers, and gorgeous hiking, but call ahead to confirm it's open. Sites 28 to 36 are most secluded.

Napa County Fairgrounds & RV Park CAMPGROUND $
(Map p164; 707-942-5221; www.napacountyfair.org; 1435 Oak St; tent sites $20, RV sites w/hookups $33-36; 🌐) A dusty RV park northwest of downtown.

Cottage Grove Inn BUNGALOWS $$$
(707-942-8400, 800-799-2284; www.cottagegrove.com; 1711 Lincoln Ave; cottages $250-425; ❄🌐) Romantic cottages for over-40s, with wood-burning fireplaces, two-person tubs and rocking-chair front porches.

Chelsea Garden Inn B&B $$$
(707-942-0948; www.chelseagardeninn.com; 1443 2nd St; r incl breakfast $195-275; ❄🌐🏊) On a quiet street, five floral-print rooms with private entrances. Pretty gardens, but the pool looked dingy at our last inspection.

Wine Way Inn B&B $$
(Map p164; 707-942-0680, 800-572-0679; www.winewayinn.com; 1019 Foothill Blvd; r $180-220; ❄🌐) A small B&B, in a 1910-era house, close to the road; friendly owners.

✕ Eating

🌱 Jolé CALIFORNIAN $$
(707-942-5938; www.jolerestaurant.com; 1457 Lincoln Ave, Calistoga; mains $15-20; ⏱5-9pm Sun-Thu, to 10pm Fri & Sat) The earthy and inventive farm-to-table small plates at chef-owned Jolé evolve seasonally, and may include such dishes as local sole with tangy miniature Napa grapes, caramelized Brussels sprouts with capers, and organic Baldwin apple strudel with burnt-caramel ice cream. Four courses cost $50. Reservations essential.

🌱 Solbar CALIFORNIAN $$$
(Map p164; 707-226-0850; www.solagecalistoga.com; 755 Silverado Trail; lunch/dinner mains $15-19/$30-37; ⏱7am-11am, 11:30am-3pm, 5:30-9pm) The ag-chic look at this superb restaurant is spare, with concrete floors, exposed-wood tables and soaring ceilings. Maximizing seasonal produce, each dish is elegantly composed, some with tongue-in-cheek playfulness. The menu is divided into light and hearty, so you can mind calories. Reservations essential.

🌱 All Seasons Bistro NEW AMERICAN $$$
(707-942-9111; www.allseasonsnapavalley.net; 1400 Lincoln Ave; lunch mains $10-15, dinner mains $16-22; ⏱noon-2pm & 5:30-8:30pm Tue-Sun) The dining room looks like a white-tablecloth soda fountain, but All Seasons makes some very fine meals, from simple steak-*frites* to composed dishes like cornmeal-crusted scallops with summer succotash. Good lobster bisque.

Buster's Southern BBQ BARBECUE $
(Map p164; 707-942-5605; www.busterssouthernbbq.com; 1207 Foothill Blvd; dishes $8-11; ⏱10am-7:30pm Mon-Sat, 10:30am-6:30pm Sun; 🍴) The sheriff eats lunch at this indoor-outdoor barbecue joint, which serves smoky ribs, chicken, tri-tip steak and burgers, but closes early at dinnertime. Beer and wine.

Calistoga Inn & Brewery AMERICAN $$
(707-942-4101; www.calistogainn.com; 1250 Lincoln Ave; lunch/dinner mains $9-13/$14-26; ⏱11:30am-3pm & 5:30-9pm) Locals crowd the outdoor beer garden Sundays. Midweek we prefer the country dining room and its big oakwood tables, a homey spot for pot roast and other simple American dishes. There's live music summer weekends.

🍷 Drinking

🌱 Yo El Rey CAFE
(707-942-1180; www.yoelrey.com; 1217 Washington St; ⏱6:30am-8pm) Meet the hip kids at this micro-roastery cafe and living room, which brews superb small-batch fair-trade coffee.

Hydro Grill BAR
(707-942-9777; 1403 Lincoln Ave) Live music plays weekend evenings at this hoppin' corner bar-restaurant.

Solbar   BAR
(Map p164; ☑707-226-0850; www.solagecalistoga. com; 755 Silverado Trail) Sip cocktails and wine on cane sofas beside outdoor fireplaces and a palm-lined pool. Wear white.

Brannan's Grill   BAR
(☑707-942-2233; www.brannansgrill.com; 1374 Lincoln Ave) Calistoga's most handsome restaurant; the mahogany bar is great for martinis and microbrews, especially weekends, when jazz combos sometimes play.

Susie's Bar   DIVE BAR
(☑707-942-6710; 1365 Lincoln Ave) Turn your baseball cap sideways, do shots and play pool while the juke box blares classic rock and country and western.

🔒 Shopping

Wine Garage   WINE
(☑707-942-5332; www.winegarage.net; 1020 Foothill Blvd) Every bottle costs under $25 at this winning wine store, formerly a service station.

Mudd Hens   BEAUTY
(☑707-942-0210; www.muddhens.com; 1348 Lincoln Ave) Recreate mud baths at home with mineral-rich Calistoga Mud ($27/pound) and volcanic-ash soap from this cute bath shop.

Calistoga Pottery   CERAMICS
(☑707-942-0216; www.calistogapottery.com; 1001 Foothill Blvd) Winemakers aren't the only artisans in Napa. Watch potters throw vases, bowls and plates, all for sale.

Coperfield's Bookshop   BOOKS
(☑707-942-1616; 1330 Lincoln Ave) Great indie bookshop, with local maps and guides.

ℹ️ Information

Chamber of Commerce & Visitors Center (☑707-942-6333, 866-306-5588; www.calistogavisitors.com; 1133 Washington St; ⊙9am-5pm)

Around Calistoga

◎ Sights & Activities

Bale Grist Mill & Bothe-Napa Valley State Parks   HISTORIC PARK $
There's good weekend picnicking at Bale Grist Mill State Historic Park (☑707-963-2236; adult/child $3/2; ⊙10am-5pm Sat & Sun 🚹), which features a 36ft water-powered mill wheel dating from 1846 – the largest still operating in North America. Watch it grind corn and wheat into flour Saturdays and Sundays; call for times. In early October, look for the living-history festival, Old Mill Days.

A mile-long trail leads to adjacent Bothe-Napa Valley State Park (Map p164; ☑707-942-4575; parking $8; ⊙8am-sunset; 🚹), where there's a swimming pool (adult/child $5/2; ⊙summer only) and lovely hiking through redwood groves.

Admission to one park includes the other. If you're more than three, go to Bothe first, and pay $8 instead of the per-head charge at Bale Grist Mill.

The mill and both parks are on Hwy 29/128, midway between St Helena and Calistoga.

FREE Robert Louis Stevenson State Park   MOUNTAIN
(off Map p164; ☑707-942-4575; www.parks.ca.gov) The long-extinct volcanic cone of Mt St Helena marks the valley's end, 8 miles north of Calistoga. The undeveloped state park on Hwy 29 often gets snow in winter.

It's a strenuous 5-mile climb to the peak's 4343ft summit, but what a view – 200 miles on a clear winter's day. Check conditions before setting out. Also consider 2.2-mile one-way Table Rock Trail (go south from the summit parking area) for drop-dead valley views. Temperatures are best in wildflower season, February to May; fall is prettiest, when the vineyards change colors.

The park includes the site of the Silverado Mine where Stevenson and his wife honeymooned in 1880.

Petrified Forest   FOREST
(Map p164; ☑707-942-6667; www.petrifiedforest. org; 4100 Petrified Forest Rd; adult/child $10/5; ⊙9am-7pm summer, to 5pm winter) Three million years ago, a volcanic eruption at nearby Mt St Helena blew down a stand of redwoods between Calistoga and Santa Rosa. The trees fell in the same direction, away from the blast, and were covered in ash and mud. Over the millennia, the mighty giants' trunks turned to stone; gradually the overlay eroded, exposing them. The first stumps were discovered in 1870. A monument marks Robert Louis Stevenson's 1880 visit. He describes it in *The Silverado Squatters*.

It's 5 miles northwest of town, off Hwy 128. Check online for 10%-off coupons.

Safari West WILDLIFE RESERVE
(off Map p164; 707-579-2551, 800-616-2695; www.safariwest.com; 3115 Porter Creek Rd; adult/child $68/30;) Giraffes in Wine Country? Whadya know! Safari West covers 400 acres and protects zebras, cheetahs and other exotic animals, which mostly roam free. See them on a guided three-hour safari in open-sided jeeps; reservations required. You'll also walk through an aviary and lemur condo. The reservations-only cafe serves lunch and dinner. If you're feeling adventurous, stay overnight in nifty canvas-sided **tent cabins** (cabins incl breakfast $200-295), right in the preserve.

SONOMA VALLEY

We have a soft spot for Sonoma's folksy ways. Unlike in fancy Napa, nobody cares if you drive a clunker and vote Green. Locals call it 'Slow-noma.' Anchoring the bucolic 17-mile-long Sonoma Valley, the town of Sonoma makes a great jumping-off point for exploring Wine Country – it's only an hour from San Francisco – and has a marvelous sense of place, with storied 19th-century historical sights surrounding the state's largest town square. Halfway up-valley, tiny Glen Ellen is right out of a Norman Rockwell painting, in stark contrast to the valley's northernmost town, Santa Rosa, the workaday urban center best known for its traffic. If you have more than a day, explore Sonoma's quiet, rustic side along the Russian River Valley (p194) and work your way to the sea.

Sonoma Hwy/Hwy 12 is lined with wineries and runs from Sonoma to Santa Rosa, then to western Sonoma County; Arnold Dr has less traffic (but few wineries) and runs parallel, up the valley's western side to Glen Ellen.

Sonoma Valley Wineries

Rolling grass-covered hills rise from 17-mile-long Sonoma Valley. Its 40 wineries get less attention than Napa's, but many are equally good. If you love zinfandel and syrah, you're in for a treat.

Picnicking is allowed at Sonoma wineries. Get maps and discount coupons in the town of Sonoma (p191) or, if you're approaching from the south, the **Sonoma Valley Visitors Bureau** (Map p184; 707-935-4747; www.sonomavalley.com; Cornerstone Gardens, 23570 Hwy 121; 10am-4pm) at Cornerstone Gardens (p187).

Plan at least five hours to visit the valley from bottom to top. For other Sonoma County wineries, see the Russian River Valley section.

Homewood WINERY
(Map p184; 707-996-6353; www.homewoodwinery.com; 23120 Burndale Rd at Hwy 121/12; tastings free; 10am-4pm;) A stripy rooster named Steve chases dogs in the parking lot of this down-home winery, where the tasting room is a garage, and the winemaker crafts standout ports and Rhône-style grenache, mourvèdre and syrah – 'Da redder, da better.' Ask about 'vertical tastings,' and sample wines from the same vineyards, but different years. Dogs welcome, but you've been warned. Bottles cost $18 to $32.

Nicholson Ranch WINERY
(707-938-8822; www.nicholsonranch.com; 4200 Napa Rd; tastings $10; 10am-6pm) Unfiltered pinot noir and non-buttery chardonnay in a hilltop tasting room; lovely for picnicking.

Robledo WINERY
(Map p184; 707-939-6903; www.robledofamilywinery.com; 21901 Bonness Rd, of Hwy 116; tastings $5-10; by appointment only) Sonoma Valley's feel-good winery, Robledo was founded by a former grape-picker from Mexico who worked his way up to vineyard manager, then land owner, now vintner. His kids run the place. The wines – served at hand-carved Mexican furniture in a windowless tasting room – include a no-oak sauvignon blanc,

jammy syrah, spicy cabernet, and bright-fruit pinot noir. Bottles cost $18 to $45.

Gundlach-Bundschu
WINERY

(Map p184; ☎707-938-5277; www.gunbun.com; 2000 Denmark St; tastings $10; ☉11am-4:30pm) One of Sonoma Valley's oldest and prettiest, Gundlach-Bundschu looks like a storybook castle. Founded in 1858 by Bavarian immigrant Jacob Gundlach, it's now at the cutting edge of sustainability. Signature wines are rieslings and gewürztraminers, but 'Gun-Bun' was the first American winery to produce 100% merlot. Tours of the 2000-barrel cave ($20) are available by reservation. Down a winding lane, it's a good bike-to winery, with picnicking, hiking and a small lake. Bottles cost $22 to $40.

Bartholomew Park Winery
WINERY, MUSEUM

(Map p184; ☎707-939-3026; www.bartpark.com; 1000 Vineyard Lane; tasting $5-10; museum & park entry free; ☉tasting room & museum 11am-4:30pm) Gundlach-Bundschu also runs nearby Bartholomew Park Winery (another good bike-to destination), a 400-acre preserve with vineyards originally cultivated in 1857 and now certified-organic, yielding citrusy sauvignon blanc and smoky merlot. Bottles cost $22 to $40.

Hawkes
TASTING ROOM

(Map p188; ☎707-938-7620; www.hawkeswine.com; 383 1st St W; tasting $10, waived with purchase over $30; ☉noon-6pm) When you're in downtown Sonoma and don't feel like fighting traffic, Hawke's refreshingly unfussy tasting room showcases meaty merlot and cabernet sauvignon, never blended with other grape varietals. Bottles cost $20 to $60.

Little Vineyards
WINERY

(Map p184; ☎707-996-2750; www.littlevineyards.com; 15188 Sonoma Hwy, Glen Ellen; tastings $5; ☉11am-4:30pm Thu-Mon; ▣) The name fits at this family-owned small-scale winery, long on atmosphere, with a lazy dog to greet you and a weathered, cigarette-burned tasting bar, which Jack London drank at (before it was moved here). The tiny tasting room is good for shy folks who dislike crowds. If you're new to wine, consider the $20 introductory class (call ahead). Good picnicking on the vineyard-view terrace. The big reds include syrah, petite sirah, zin, cab and several delish blends. Bottles cost $17 to $35. Also rents a cottage in the vines.

BR Cohn
WINERY

(Map p184; ☎707-938-4064; www.brcohn.com; 15000 Sonoma Hwy, Glen Ellen; tasting $10, applicable to purchase; ☉10am-5pm) Picnic like a rock star at always-busy BR Cohn, whose founder managed '70s superband the Doobie Brothers before moving on to make outstanding organic olive oils and fine wines – including excellent cabernet sauvignon, unusual in Sonoma. In autumn, he throws benefit concerts, amid the olives, by the likes of Skynyrd and the Doobies. Bottles cost $16 to $55.

Arrowood
WINERY

(Map p184; ☎707-935-2600; www.arrowoodvineyards.com; 14347 Sonoma Hwy; tastings $5-10; ☉10am-4:30pm) Excellent cabernet and chardonnay; stunning views.

Benziger
WINERY

(Map p184; ☎888-490-2739; www.benziger.com; 1883 London Ranch Rd, Glen Ellen; tasting $10-20, tram tour adult incl tasting/child $15/5; ☉10am-5pm; ▣) If you're new to wine, make Benziger your first stop for Sonoma's best crash course in wine-making. The worthwhile, non-reservable tour includes an open-air tram ride through biodynamic vineyards, and a four-wine tasting. Kids love the peacocks. The large-production wine's OK (head for the reserves); the tour's the thing. Bottles cost $15 to $80.

Imagery Estate
WINERY

(Map p184; ☎877-550-4278; www.imagerywinery.com; 14355 Sonoma Hwy; tastings $10-15; ☉10am-4:30pm) Obscure varietals, biodynamically grown, with artist-designed labels.

Loxton
WINERY

(Map p184; ☎707-935-7221; www.loxtonwines.com; 11466 Dunbar Rd, Glen Ellen; tastings free) Say g'day to Chris, the Aussie winemaker, at Loxton, a no-frills winery with million-dollar views. The 'tasting room' is actually a small warehouse, where you can taste wonderful syrah and zinfandel; non-oaky, fruit-forward chardonnay; and good port. Bottles cost $15 to $25.

Wellington
WINERY

(Map p184; ☎707-939-0708; www.wellingtonvineyards.com; 11600 Dunbar Rd, Glen Ellen; tastings $5) Known for port (including a white) and meaty reds, Wellington makes great zinfandel, one from vines planted in 1892 – wow, what color! The noir de noir is a cult favorite. Alas, servers have vineyard views, while you face the warehouse. Bottles cost $15 to $30.

Family Wineries   TASTING ROOM

(Map p184; ☏707-433-0100; www.familywines.com; 9380 Sonoma Hwy at Laurel Ave; tastings $5-10; ☺10:30am-5pm) Several labels under one roof. Standout: David Noyes pinot noir.

TOP
CHOICE **Kaz**   WINERY

(Map p184; ☏707-833-2536; www.kazwinery.com; 233 Adobe Canyon Rd, Kenwood; tastings $5; ☺11am-5pm Fri-Mon; 🚻🐾) Sonoma's cult favorite, supercool Kaz is about blends: whatever's in the organic vineyards goes into the wine – and they're blended at crush, not during fermentation. Expect lesser-known varietals like Alicante Bouchet and Lenoir, and a worthwhile cabernet-merlot blend. Kids can sample grape juice, then run around the playground out back, while you sift through LPs and pop your favorites onto the turntable. Crazy fun. Dogs welcome. Bottles cost $20 to $48.

Sonoma & Around

Fancy boutiques may lately be replacing hardware stores, but Sonoma still retains an old-fashioned charm, thanks to the plaza – California's largest town square – and its surrounding frozen-in-time historic buildings. You can legally drink on the plaza, a rarity in California parks.

Sonoma has rich history. In 1846 it was the site of a second American revolution, this time against Mexico, when General Mariano Guadalupe Vallejo deported all foreigners from California, prompting outraged American frontiersmen to occupy the Sonoma Presidio and declare independence. They dubbed California the Bear Flag Republic after the battle flag they'd fashioned.

The republic was short-lived. The Mexican-American War broke out a month later, and California was annexed by the US. The revolt gave California its flag, which remains emblazoned with the words 'California Republic' beneath a muscular brown bear. Vallejo was initially imprisoned, but ultimately returned to Sonoma and played a major role in the region's development.

◉ Sights

Sonoma Hwy (Hwy 12) runs through town. Sonoma Plaza, laid out by General Vallejo

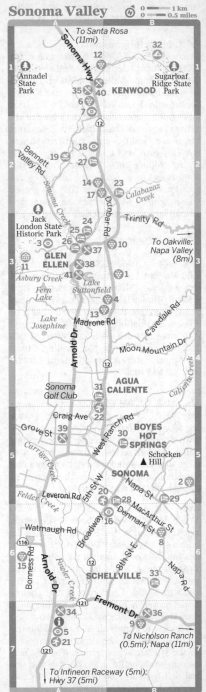

Sonoma Valley

in 1834, is the heart of downtown, lined with hotels, restaurants and shops. Pick up a walking-tour brochure from the visitors bureau. Immediately north along Hwy 12, expect a brief suburban landscape before the valley's pastoral gorgeousness begins, outside town.

SONOMA PLAZA & AROUND
Sonoma Plaza SQUARE
(Map p188) Smack in the center of the plaza, the Mission-revival-style **city hall**, built 1906–08, has identical facades on four sides, reportedly because plaza businesses all demanded City Hall face their direction. At the plaza's northeast corner, the **Bear Flag Monument** marks Sonoma's moment of revolutionary glory. The town shows up for the **farmers market** (⏱5:30-8pm Tue, Apr-Oct), where you can sample Sonoma's exquisite produce.

Sonoma State Historic Park HISTORIC BUILDINGS
(☏707-938-1519; www.parks.ca.gov; adult/child $3/2; ⏱10am-5pm Tue-Sun) The park is comprised of multiple sites. The **Mission San Francisco Solano de Sonoma** (Map p188; E Spain St), at the plaza's northeast corner, was built in 1823, in part to forestall the Russian coastal colony at Fort Ross from moving inland. The mission was the 21st and final California mission, and the only one built during the Mexican period (the rest were founded by the Spanish). It marks the northernmost point on El Camino Real. Five of the mission's original rooms remain. The not-to-be-missed chapel dates from 1841.

The adobe **Sonoma Barracks** (Map p188; E Spain St; ⏱daily) was built by Vallejo between 1836 and 1840 to house Mexican troops, but it became the capital of a rogue nation on June 14, 1846, when American settlers, of

A WINE COUNTRY PRIMER

When people talk about Sonoma, they're referring to the *whole* county, which unlike Napa is huge. It extends all the way from the coast, up the Russian River Valley, into Sonoma Valley and eastward to Napa Valley; in the south it stretches from San Pablo Bay (an extension of San Francisco Bay) to Healdsburg in the north. It's essential to break Sonoma down by district.

West County refers to everything west of Hwy 101 and includes the **Russian River Valley** and the coast. **Sonoma Valley** stretches north-south along Hwy 12. In northern Sonoma County, **Alexander Valley** lies east of Healdsburg, and **Dry Creek Valley** lies north of Healdsburg. In the south, **Carneros** straddles the Sonoma–Napa border, north of San Pablo Bay. Each region has its own particular wines; what grows where depends upon the weather.

Inland valleys get hot; coastal regions stay cool. In West County and Carneros, night-time fog blankets the vineyards. Burgundy-style wines do best, particularly pinot noir and chardonnay. Further inland, Alexander, Sonoma and much of Dry Creek Valleys (as well as Napa Valley) are fog-protected. Here, Bordeaux-style wines thrive, especially cabernet sauvignon, sauvignon blanc, merlot and other heat-loving varieties. For California's famous cabernets, head to Napa. Zinfandel and Rhône-style varieties, such as syrah and viognier, grow in both regions, warm and cool. In cooler climes, resultant wines are lighter, more elegant; in warmer areas they are heavier and more rustic.

For a handy-dandy reference on the road, pick up a copy of Karen MacNeil's *The Wine Bible* (2001, Workman Publishing) or Jancis Robinson's *Concise Wine Companion* (2001, Oxford University Press) to carry in the car.

varying sobriety, surprised the guards and declared an independent 'California Repub-lc' [sic] with a homemade flag featuring a blotchy bear. The US took over the republic a month later, but abandoned the barracks during the Gold Rush, leaving Vallejo to turn then into (what else?) a winery in 1860. Today, displays describe life during the Mexican and American periods.

Next to the Sonoma Barracks, **Toscano Hotel** (Map p188; 20 E Spain St) opened as a store and library in the 1850s, then became a hotel in 1886. Peek into the lobby from 10am to 5pm; except for the traffic outside, you'd swear you'd stepped back in time. Free tours 1pm through 4pm, weekends and Mondays.

A half-mile northwest, the lovely **Vallejo Home** (Map p188; 363 3rd St W), otherwise known as Lachryma Montis (Latin for 'Tears of the Mountain'), was built 1851–52 for General Vallejo. It's named for the spring on the property; the Vallejo family later made a handy income piping water to town. The property remained in the family until 1933, when the state of California purchased it, retaining much of its original furnishings. A bike path leads to the house from downtown.

Admission here includes entry to the **Petaluma Adobe** (Map p160; ☎707-762-4871; www.petalumaadobe.com; 3325 Adobe Rd, Petaluma; ⏰10am-5pm Sat & Sun), a historic ranch 15 miles northwest in suburban Petaluma.

La Haye Art Center ARTS CENTER
(Map p188; ☎707-996-9665; www.lahayeartcenter.com; 148 E Napa St; ⏰11am-5pm) At this collective in a converted foundry, you can tour a storefront gallery and meet the artists – sculptor, potter and painters – in their garden studios. Beverly Prevost's asymmetrical ceramic dinnerware is featured next door at Café La Haye (p189).

Sonoma Valley Museum of Art MUSEUM
(Map p188; ☎707-939-7862; www.svma.org; 551 Broadway; adult/family $5/8; ⏰11am-5pm Wed-Sun) Though this 8000-sq-ft museum presents compelling work by local and international artists, such as David Hockney, the annual standout is October's Día de los Muertos exhibition.

BEYOND SONOMA PLAZA

FREE **Bartholomew Park** PARK
(Map p184; ☎707-935-9511; www.bartholomewparkwinery.com; 1000 Vineyard Lane) The top close-to-town outdoors destination is 375-acre Bartholomew Park, off Castle Rd, where you can picnic beneath giant oaks and hike three miles of trails, with hilltop vistas to San Francisco. There's also a good winery

(p186) and small museum. The Palladian Villa, at the park's entrance, is a turn-of-the-20th-century replica of Count Haraszthy's original residence, open noon to 3pm, Saturdays and Sundays, operated by the **Bartholomew Foundation** (☎707-938-2244).

FREE **Cornerstone Gardens** GARDENS
(Map p184; ☎707-933-3010; www.cornerston egardens.com; 23570 Arnold Dr; ⊙10am-4pm; ⊞) There's nothing traditional about Cornerstone Gardens, which showcase the work of 19 renowned avant-garde landscape designers. We especially love Pamela Burton's 'Earth Walk,' which descends into the ground; and Planet Horticulture's 'Rise,' which exaggerates space. Let the kids run around while you explore top-notch garden shops and gather information from the onsite **Sonoma Valley Visitors Bureau** (☎707-935-4747; www.sonomavalley.com; ⊙10am-4pm), then refuel at the on-site cafe. Look for the enormous blue chair at road's edge.

Traintown AMUSEMENT PARK
(Map p184; ☎707-938-3912; www.traintown.com; 20264 Broadway; ⊙10am-5pm daily summer, Fri-Sun only mid-Sep-late May) Little kids adore Traintown, one mile south of the plaza. A miniature steam engine makes 20-minute loops ($4.75), and there are vintage amusement-park rides ($2.75 per ride), including a carousel and a Ferris wheel.

🏃 Activities

Many local inns provide bicycles.

Sonoma Valley Cyclery BICYCLE RENTAL
(Map p184; ☎707-935-3377; www.sonomacyclery. com; 20091 Broadway/Hwy 12; bikes from $25 per day; ⊙10am-6pm Mon-Sat, to 4pm Sun; ⊞) Sonoma is ideal for cycling – not too hilly – with multiple wineries near downtown. Book ahead weekends.

Willow Stream Spa at Sonoma Mission Inn SPA
(Map p184; ☎707-938-9000; www.fairmont.com/ sonoma; 100 Boyes Blvd; ⊙7:30am-8pm) Few Wine Country spas compare with glitzy Sonoma Mission Inn, where two treatments – or $89 – allows use of three outdoor and two indoor mineral pools, gym, sauna, and herbal steam room at the Romanesque bathhouse. No children.

Triple Creek Horse Outfit HORSEBACK RIDING
(☎707-887-8700; www.triplecreekhorseoutfit.com; 1-/2hr rides $60/100; ⊙Wed-Mon) Hit the trail

for stunning vistas of Sonoma Valley. Reservations required.

🎓 Courses

Ramekins Sonoma Valley Culinary School COOKING SCHOOL
(Map p188; ☎707-933-0450; www.ramekins.com; 450 W Spain St; ⊞) Offers excellent demonstrations and hands-on classes for home chefs. Also runs weekend 'culinary camps' for both adults and kids.

🛏 Sleeping

Off-season rates plummet. Reserve ahead. Ask about parking; some historic inns have no lots. Also consider Glen Ellen (p192) and, if counting pennies, Santa Rosa (p206)

Sonoma Chalet B&B, COTTAGES $$
(Map p184; ☎707-938-3129; www.sonomachalet. com; 18935 5th St W; r without bath $125, r with bath $140-180, cottages $190-225; ❀) An old farmstead surrounded by rolling hills, Sonoma Chalet has rooms in a Swiss chalet-style house adorned with little balconies and country-style bric-a-brac. We love the free-standing cottages; Laura's has a wood-burning fireplace. Breakfast is served on a deck overlooking a nature preserve. No aircon in rooms with shared bath. No phones, no internet.

Sonoma Hotel HISTORIC HOTEL $$
(Map p188; ☎707-996-2996; www.sonomahotel. com; 110 W Spain St; r incl breakfast $170-200; ❀🛜) Long on charm, this spiffy vintage 1880s hotel is decked with Spanish-colonial and American-country-crafts furnishings. No elevator or parking lot.

El Dorado Hotel HOTEL $$$
(Map p188; ☎707-996-3030, 800-289-3031; www. eldoradosonoma.com; 405 1st St W; r weekday/ weekend $195/225; ❀🛜❄) Stylish touches like high-end linens make up for the rooms' compact size, as do private balconies overlooking the plaza or the rear courtyard (we prefer the plaza view, despite the noise). No elevator.

Swiss Hotel HISTORIC HOTEL $$
(Map p188; ☎707-938-2884; www.swisshotel-sonoma.com; 18 W Spain St; r incl breakfast Mon-Fri $150-170, Sat & Sun $200-240; ❀🛜) It opened in 1905, so you'll forgive the wavy floors. Think knotty pine and wicker. In the morning sip coffee on the shared plaza-view balcony. Downstairs there's a raucous bar and restaurant. No parking lot or elevator.

Sonoma

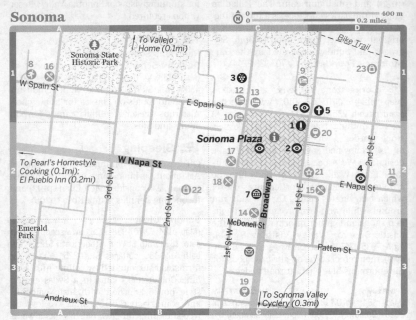

To Vallejo Home (0.1mi)

To Pearl's Homestyle Cooking (0.1mi); El Pueblo Inn (0.2mi)

To Sonoma Valley Cyclery (0.3mi)

NAPA & SONOMA WINE COUNTRY SONOMA & AROUND

Sonoma

◎ **Top Sights**
Sonoma Plaza...C2

◎ **Sights**
1 Bear Flag Monument...........................C2
2 City Hall...C2
3 Hawkes...C1
4 La Haye Art Center.............................D2
5 Mission San Francisco Solano de
   Sonoma...D1
6 Sonoma Barracks................................C1
7 Sonoma Valley Museum of Art...........C2
Toscano Hotel...............................(see 6)

✦ **Activities, Courses & Tours**
8 Ramekins Sonoma Valley
   Culinary School...............................A1

▣ **Sleeping**
9 Bungalows 313.....................................C1
10 El Dorado Hotel...................................C1
11 Hidden Oak Inn D2
12 Sonoma Hotel.....................................C1
13 Swiss Hotel C1

✕ **Eating**
14 599 Thai Cafe.......................................C2

Café la Haye...................................(see 4)
15 Della Santina's.....................................D2
El Dorado Corner Cafe................(see 10)
16 Estate A1
girl & the fig..................................(see 12)
17 Harvest Moon Cafe C2
18 Red Grape C2
Taste of the Himalayas...............(see 20)

◉ **Drinking**
Enoteca Della Santina..................(see 15)
19 Hopmonk Tavern C3
20 Murphy's Irish Pub...............................D2
Steiner's..(see 17)
Sunflower Caffé & Wine Bar........(see 10)
Swiss Hotel ....(see 13)

◉ **Entertainment**
21 Sebastiani Theater...............................D2

◉ **Shopping**
Chanticleer Books & Prints ....(see 4)
22 Chateau Sonoma B2
Readers' Books .... (see 4)
Sign of the Bear............................(see 17)
Tiddle E Winks ....(see 15)
23 Vella Cheese Co D1

El Pueblo Inn
MOTEL **$$**

(Off Map p188; ☎707-996-3651, 800-900-8844; www.elpuebloinn.com; 896 W Napa St; r incl breakfast $169-289; ❋@❀☎♠) One mile west of downtown, family-owned El Pueblo has surprisingly cushy rooms with great beds. The big lawns and the heated pool are perfect for kids; parents appreciate the 24-hour hot tub.

Sonoma Creek Inn
MOTEL **$$**

(Map p184; ☎707-939-9463, 888-712-1289; www.sonomacreekinn.com; 239 Boyes Blvd; r $139-199; ❋☎♠) This cute-as-a-button motel has cheery, retro-Americana rooms, with primary colors and country quilts. It's not downtown; valley wineries are a short drive.

Les Petites Maisons
COTTAGES **$$$**

(Map p184; ☎707-933-0340, 800-291-8962; www.lespetitesmaisons.com; 1190 E Napa St; cottages $165-295; ❋♠♠☎) A mile east of the plaza, each of these four colorful, inviting cottages has a bedroom, living room, kitchen and barbecue, with comfy furniture, stereos, DVDs and bicycles.

Windhaven Cottage
COTTAGE **$$**

(Map p184; ☎707-938-2175, 707-483-1856; www.windhavencottage.com; 21700 Pearson Ave; cottage $155-165; ❋☎) Great-bargain Windhaven has two units: a hideaway cottage with vaulted wooden ceilings and a fireplace, and a handsome 800-sq-ft studio. We prefer the romantic cottage. Both have hot tubs. Tennis facilities, bicycles and barbecues sweeten the deal.

Bungalows 313
BUNGALOWS **$$$**

(Map p188; ☎707-996-8091; www.bungalows313.com; 313 1st St E; d $229-329, q $379-469; ❋☎♠) Century-old brick farmhouse and bungalows with kitchens. Gorgeous gardens. Perfect for couples.

MacArthur Place
INN **$$$**

(Map p184; ☎707-938-2929, 800-722-1866; www.macarthurplace.com; 29 E MacArthur St; r from $350, ste from $425; ❋@☎♠) Sonoma's top full-service inn; built on a former estate, with century-old gardens.

Hidden Oak Inn
B&B **$$$**

(Map p184; ☎707-996-9863, 877-996-9863; www.hiddenoakinn.com; 214 E Napa St; r incl breakfast $195-245; ❋☎♠) A B&B built c 1914.

Sugarloaf Ridge State Park
CAMPGROUND **$**

(Map p184; ☎707-833-5712, reservations 800-444-7275; www.reserveamerica.com; 2605 Adobe Canyon Rd; sites $30) Sonoma's nearest camping is north of Kenwood at this lovely hilltop park, with 50 drive-in sites, clean coin-operated showers, and great hiking.

✖ Eating

Also see Glen Ellen, p192. There's creek-side picnicking, with barbecue grills, up-valley at **Sugarloaf Ridge State Park** (2605 Adobe Canyon Rd; per car $8). Find late-night taco trucks on Hwy 12, between Boyes Blvd and Aqua Caliente.

✎ Fremont Diner
AMERICAN **$**

(Map p184; ☎707-938-7370; 2698 Fremont Dr/Hwy 121; mains $8-11; ☻8am-3pm Mon-Fri, 7am-4pm Sat & Sun; ♠) Lines snake out the door weekends at this order-at-the-counter, farm-to-table roadside diner. Snag a table indoors or out and feast on ricotta pancakes with real maple syrup, chicken and waffles, oyster po' boys and finger-licking barbecue. Arrive early to beat the line.

✎ Café La Haye
NEW AMERICAN **$$$**

(Map p188; ☎707-935-5994; www.cafelahaye.com; 140 E Napa St; mains $15-25; ☻5:30-9pm Tue-Sat) One of Sonoma's top tables for earthy New American cooking, made with produce sourced from within 60 miles, La Haye's tiny dining room gets packed cheek-by-jowl and service can border on perfunctory, but the clean simplicity and flavor-packed cooking make it many foodies' first choice. Reserve well ahead.

✎ Harvest Moon Cafe
NEW AMERICAN **$$**

(Map p188; ☎707-933-8160; www.harvestmooncafesonoma.com; 487 1st St W; dinner/brunch mains $18-25/$10-15; ☻5:30-9pm Wed-Mon, 10am-2pm Sun) Inside a cozy 1836 adobe, this casual bistro uses local ingredients in its changing menu, with simple soul-satisfying dishes like duck risotto with Bellwether Farms ricotta. Book a garden table.

✎ Estate
ITALIAN-CALIFORNIAN **$$**

(Map p188; ☎707-933-3633; www.estate-sonoma.com; 400 W Spain St; pizzas $10-14, dinner/brunch mains $21-24/$11-14; ☻from 5pm nightly, 10am-3pm Sun) Sonoma's landmark mansion features earthy Cal-Italian cooking, on-site produce garden and lovely outdoor porch. Come before 6:30pm (6:15 Fri & Sat) for pizza and a glass of pinot noir for $15. Nightly four-course dinners cost $26. Great Sunday brunch. Make reservations.

girl & the fig
FRENCH-CALIFORNIAN **$$$**

(Map p188; 707-938-3634; www.thegirlandthefig.com; 110 W Spain St; lunch mains $10-15, dinner mains $18-26) For a festive evening, book a garden table at this French-provincial bistro. We like the small plates ($11 to $14), especially the steamed mussels with matchstick fries, and duck confit with lentils. Weekday three-course prix-fixe costs $34; add $10 for wine. Stellar cheeses. Reservations essential.

Della Santina's
ITALIAN **$$**

(Map p188; 707-935-0576; www.dellasantinas.com; 135 E Napa St; mains $11-17) The waiters have been here forever, and the 'specials' never change, but Della Santina's Italian-American cooking – linguini pesto, veal parmigiana, rotisserie chickens – is consistently good. The brick courtyard is charming on warm evenings.

El Dorado Corner Cafe
CAFE **$$**

(Map p188; 707-996-3030; www.eldoradosonoma.com; 405 1st St W; dishes $9-15; 7am-10pm) Little sister to El Dorado Kitchen (whose chef had just left at the time of writing, hence the non-review of this noteworthy restaurant), the Corner Cafe has more affordable cooking – pizzas, sandwiches, and salads – all made with artisinal local produce and served continuously throughout the day. Save room for house-made ice cream.

Juanita Juanita
MEXICAN **$$**

(Map p188; 707-935-3981; 19114 Arnold Dr; mains $8-15; Wed-Mon 11am-8pm;) Dig the crazy mural outside this drive-in Mexican, which makes winning tostadas, garlic-garlic burritos and fiery *chile verde* (green chili stew with pork or chicken). Dog-friendly patio. Beer and wine.

Red Grape
PIZZA **$$**

(Map p188; 707-996-4103; www.theredgrape.com; 529 1st St W; mains $11-15; 11:30am-8:30pm;) A reliable spot for an easy meal, Red Grape serves good thin-crust pizzas and big salads in a cavernous, echoey space. Good for takeout, too.

Pearl's Homestyle Cooking
DINER **$**

(Map p188; 707-996-1783; 561 5th St W; mains $7-10; 7am-2:30pm;) Across from Safeway's west-facing wall, Pearl's serves giant American breakfasts, including succulent bacon and waffles (the secret is melted vanilla ice cream in the batter).

Angelo's Wine Country Deli
DELI **$**

(Map p184; 707-938-3688; 23400 Arnold Dr; sandwiches $6; 9am-5pm Tue-Sun) Look for the cow on the roof of this roadside deli, south of town, a fave for fat sandwiches and homemade jerky. In springtime, little lambs graze outside.

Taste of the Himalayas
INDIAN, NEPALESE **$$**

(Map p188; 707-996-1161; 464 1st St E; mains $10-20; 11am-10pm) Spicy curries, luscious lentil soup and sizzle-platter meats – a refreshing break from the usual French-Italian Wine Country fare.

599 Thai Cafe
THAI **$**

(Map p188; 707-938-8477; 599 Broadway; mains $7-10; 11am-9pm Mon-Sat;) Reliably good, tiny Thai cafe.

Sonoma Market
DELI, MARKET **$**

(Map p188; 707-996-3411; www.sonoma-glenellenmkt.com; 500 W Napa St; sandwiches $7) Sonoma's best groceries and deli sandwiches.

Drinking

Murphy's Irish Pub
PUB

(Map p188; 707-935-0660; www.sonomapub.com; 464 1st St E) Don't ask for Bud – only *real* brews here. Good hand-cut fries and shepherd's pie, too. Live music Thursday through Sunday evenings.

Swiss Hotel
BAR

(Map p188; 18 W Spain St) Locals and tourists crowd the 1909 Swiss Hotel for afternoon cocktails. There's OK food, but the bar's the thing.

Hopmonk Tavern
BREWERY

(Map p188; 707-935-9100; www.hopmonk.com; 691 Broadway; dishes $12-22; 11:30am-10pm) This happening gastro-pub and beer garden takes its brews seriously, with 16 on tap, served in type-appropriate glassware. Live music Friday through Sunday.

Enoteca Della Santina
WINE BAR

(Map p188; www.enotecadellasantina.com; 127 E Napa St; 2-10pm Wed-Fri, noon-11pm Sat, 4-10pm Tue & Sun) Thirty global vintages by the glass let you compare what you're tasting in California with the rest of the world's wines.

Steiner's
BAR

(Map p188; 456 1st St W) Sonoma's oldest bar gets crowded Sunday afternoons with cyclists and motorcyclists. Dig the taxidermy mountain lions.

Sunflower Caffé & Wine Bar CAFE $$
([☎]707-996-6845; www.sonomasunflower.com; 421 1st St W; dishes $9-14; ⊙7am-8pm; ⊠) The big back garden at this local hangout is a good spot for breakfast, a no-fuss lunch, or an afternoon glass of wine.

☆ Entertainment

Free jazz concerts happen on the plaza every second Tuesday, June to September, 6pm to 8:30pm; arrive early and bring a picnic.

Sebastiani Theatre CINEMA
(Map p188; [☎]707-996-2020; sebastianitheatre. com; 476 1st St E) The plaza's gorgeous 1934 Mission-revival cinema screens art house and revival films, and sometimes live theater.

🛍 Shopping

Vella Cheese Co FOOD
(Map p188; [☎]707-928-3232; www.vellacheese.com; 315 2nd St E) Known for its dry-jack cheeses (made here since the 1930s), Vella also makes good Mezzo Secco with cocoa powder–dusted rind. Staff will vacuum-pack for shipping.

Tiddle E Winks TOYS
(Map p188; [☎]7070-939-6993; www.tiddleewinks. com; 115 E Napa St; ⊞) Vintage five-and-dime, with classic, mid-20th-century toys.

Sign of the Bear HOMEWARES
(Map p188; [☎]707-996-3722; 435 1st St W) Kitchen-gadget freaks: make a beeline to this indie cookware store.

Chateau Sonoma HOMEWARES, GIFTS
(Map p188; [☎]707-935-8553; www.chateausonoma. com; 153 W Napa St) Provence meets Sonoma in a one-of-a-kind gifts and arty home decor.

Chanticleer Books & Prints BOOKS
(Map p188; [☎]707-996-7613; chanticleerbooks.com; 127 E Napa St; ⊙Wed-Sun) Rare books, first editions and California history.

Readers' Books BOOKS
(Map p188; [☎]707-939-1779; readers.indiebound. com; 130 E Napa St) Independent bookseller.

ℹ Information

Sonoma Post Office ([☎]800-275-8777; www. usps.com; 617 Broadway; ⊙Mon-Fri)

Sonoma Valley Hospital ([☎]707-935-5000; 347 Andrieux St)

Sonoma Valley Visitors Bureau ([☎]707-996-1090; www.sonomavalley.com; 453 1st St E; ⊙9am-6pm Jul-Sep, to 5pm Oct-Jun) Arranges accommodations; has a good walking-tour pamphlet and information on events. There's another location at Cornerstone Gardens (p187).

Glen Ellen & Around

Sleepy Glen Ellen is a snapshot of old Sonoma, with white picket fences, tiny cottages and 19th-century brick buildings beside a poplar-lined creek. When downtown Sonoma is jammed, you can wander quiet Glen Ellen and feel far away. It's ideal for a leg-stretching stopover between wineries or a romantic overnight – the nighttime sky blazes with stars.

Arnold Dr is the main drag and the valley's back-way route. Kenwood is just north, along Hwy 12, but has no town center like Glen Ellen's. For services, drive 8 miles south to Sonoma.

Glen Ellen's biggest draws are Jack London State Historic Park (p193) and Benziger winery (p183); several interesting shops line Arnold Dr.

Two family-friendly alternatives to wine tasting: **Figone's Olive Oil** (Map p184; [☎]707-282-9092; www.figoneoliveoil.com; 9580 Sonoma Hwy), in Kenwood, presses its own extra-virgin olive oil – including lovely Meyer lemon-infused oil – which you can taste; in Glen Ellen, compare chocolates of varying percentages of cacao at **Wine Country Chocolates Tasting Bar** (Map p184; [☎]707-996-1010; www.winecountrychocolates.com; 14301 Arnold Dr).

Gardeners: don't miss **Wildwood Farm and Sculpture Garden** (Map p184; [☎]707-833-1161, 888-833-4181; www.wildwoodmaples.com; 10300 Sonoma Hwy, Kenwood; ⊙10am-4pm Wed-Sun, 10am-3pm Tue), where abstract outdoor sits between exotic plants and Japanese maples.

There's fantastic hiking (when it's not blazingly hot) at **Sugarloaf Ridge State Park** (Map p184; [☎]707-833-5712; www.parks. ca.gov; 2605 Adobe Canyon Rd, Kenwood; per car

$8). On clear days, Bald Mountain has drop-dead views to the sea, while Bushy Peak Trail peers into Napa Valley. Both are moderately strenuous; plan four hours round-trip.

On hot days, families cool off in mineral-spring-fed swimming pools at **Morton's Warm Springs Resort** (Map p184; ☎707-833-5511; www.mortonswarmsprings.com; 1651 Warm Springs Rd; adult/child $8/7, reserved picnic & BBQ sites per person $11; ☺10am-6pm Sat & Sun May & Sep, Tue-Sun Jun-Aug, closed Oct-Apr; ▨♿). From Sonoma Hwy in Kenwood, turn west on Warm Springs Rd.

For shopping, stop by **Kenwood Farmhouse** (Map p184; 9255 Sonoma Hwy, Kenwood; ☺10:30am-7pm), a co-op of vendors selling artisinal crafts and gifts.

🛏 Sleeping

Jack London Lodge   MOTEL $$
(Map p184; ☎707-938-8510; http://jacklondon lodge.com; 13740 Arnold Dr; r Mon-Fri/Sat & Sun $120/180; ▨♷☎♨♿) An old-fashioned wood-sided motel, with well-kept rooms decorated with a few antiques, this is a weekday bargain – and the manager will sometimes negotiate rates. Outside there's a hot tub; next door there's a saloon.

TOP CHOICE Beltane Ranch   INN $$
(Map p184; ☎707-996-6501; www.beltaneranch. com; 11775 Hwy 12; r incl breakfast $150-240; ☎) Surrounded by horse pastures, Beltane is a throwback to 19th-century Sonoma. The cheerful, lemon-yellow 1890s ranch house occupies 100 acres and has double porches lined with swinging chairs and white wicker. Though technically a B&B, each unfussy, country-Americana-style room has a private entrance – nobody will make you pet the cat. Breakfast in bed. No phones or TVs mean zero distraction from pastoral bliss.

ℹ **WHAT'S CRUSH?**

Crush is harvest, the most atmospheric time of year, when the vine's leaves turn brilliant colors, and you can smell fermenting fruit on the breeze. Farmers throw big parties for the vineyard workers to celebrate their work. Everyone wants to be here. That's why room rates skyrocket. If you can afford it, come during autumn. To score party invitations, join your favorite winery's wine club.

Gaige House   INN $$$
(Map p184; ☎707-935-0237, 800-935-0237; www. gaige.com; 13540 Arnold Dr, Glen Ellen; r $249-299, ste $299-599; ▨♨☎♿) Sonoma's chicest inn serves lavish breakfasts. An 1890 house contains five of the 22 rooms, decked out in Euro-Asian style. But best are the Japanese-style 'spa suites,' with requisite high-end bells and whistles, including freestanding tubs made from hollowed-out granite boulders. Fabulous.

Kenwood Inn & Spa   INN $$$
(Map p184; ☎707-833-1293, 800-353-6966; www.kenwoodinn.com; 10400 Sonoma Hwy, Kenwood; r incl breakfast $425-850, ste $850-1375; ▨@☎♿) Lush gardens surround ivy-covered bungalows at this gorgeous inn, which feels like a Mediterranean château. Two hot tubs (one with a waterfall) and an on-site spa make this ideal for lovers: leave the kids home. Book an upstairs balcony room.

Glen Ellen Cottages   BUNGALOWS $$
(Map p184; ☎707-996-1174; www.glenelleninn. com; 13670 Arnold Dr; cottage Mon-Fri/Sat & Sun $149/239; ♨) Hidden behind Glen Ellen Inn, these five creek-side cottages are designed for romance, with oversized jetted tubs, steam showers and gas fireplaces.

🍴 Eating

🌿 fig café & winebar   CALIFORNIAN, FRENCH $$
(☎707-938-2130; www.thefigcafe.com; 13690 Arnold Dr, Glen Ellen; mains $15-20; ☺5:30-9pm daily, 10am-2:30pm Sat & Sun) It's worth a trip to Glen Ellen for the fig's earthy California-Provençal comfort food, like flash-fried calamari with spicy-lemon aioli, duck confit and *moules-frites* (mussels and French fries). Good wine prices and weekend brunch give reason to return.

🌿 Vineyards Inn Bar & Grill   SPANISH, TAPAS $$
(Map p184; ☎707-833-4500; www.vineyardsinn. com; 8445 Sonoma Hwy 12, Kenwood; mains $8-20; ☺11:30am-9:30pm; ♪) Though nothing fancy, this roadside tavern's food is terrific – succulent organic burgers, line-caught seafood, paella, ceviche, and biodynamic produce from the chef's ranch. Full bar.

Cafe Citti   ITALIAN $$
(☎707-833-2690; www.cafecitti.com; 9049 Sonoma Hwy; mains $8-15; ☺11am-3:30pm, 5-9pm; ♿) Locals flock to this mom-and-pop Italian

American deli-trattoria, where you order at the counter then snag a seat on the deck. Standouts include roasted chicken, homemade gnocchi and ravioli; at lunchtime, there's also pizza and housebaked focacciabread sandwiches.

Glen Ellen Village Market   MARKET $
(Map p184; www.sonoma-glenellenmkt.com; 13751 Arnold Dr; ☺6am-9pm) Fantastic market, perfect for picnics.

🖋 Olive & Vine   NEW AMERICAN $$$
(Map p184; ☎707-996-9152; oliveandvinerestaurant.com; 14301 Arnold Dr; mains $17-28; ☺5:30-9pm Wed-Sat) Part catering kitchen, part restaurant, with great seasonal flavors; make reservations.

Yeti   INDIAN $$
(Map p184; ☎707-996-9930; www.yetirestaurant.com; 14301 Arnold Dr; mains $10-18; ☺11:30am-2:30pm & 5-9pm) Indian on a creek-side patio. Great naan.

Glen Ellen Inn   AMERICAN $$
(Map p184; ☎707-996-6409; www.glenelleninn.com; 13670 Arnold Dr; mains $13-23; ☺11:30am-9pm) Oysters, martinis and grilled steaks. Lovely garden, full bar.

Garden Court Cafe   CAFE $
(Map p184; ☎707-935-1565; www.gardencourtcafe.com; 13647 Arnold Dr; mains $9-12; ☺7:30am-2pm Wed-Mon) Basic breakfasts, sandwiches and salads.

Mayo Winery Reserve Room   WINERY $$
(Map p184; ☎707-833-5544; www.mayofamilywinery.com; 9200 Sonoma Hwy, Kenwood; 7-course menu $35; ☺11am-5pm, by reservation) Snag a seven-course small-plates menu, paired with seven wines, for just $35 at this roadside wine-tasting room.

Jack London State Historic Park

Napa has Robert Louis Stevenson, but Sonoma's got Jack London. This 1400-acre park (Map p184; ☎707-938-5216; www.jacklondonpark.com; 2400 London Ranch Rd, Glen Ellen; parking $8; ☺10am-5pm Thu-Mon; 🖨) traces the last years of the author's life.

Changing occupations from Oakland fisherman to Alaska gold prospector to Pacific yachtsman – and novelist on the side – London (1876–1916) ultimately took up farming. He bought Beauty Ranch in 1905 and moved there in 1910. With his second wife, Charmian, he lived and wrote in a small cottage while his mansion, Wolf House, was under construction. On the eve of its completion in 1913, it burned down. The disaster devastated London, and although he toyed with rebuilding, he died before construction got underway. His widow, Charmian, built the House of Happy Walls, which has been preserved as a museum. It's a half-mile walk from there to the remains of Wolf House, passing London's grave along the way. Other paths wind around the farm to the cottage where he lived and worked. Miles of hiking trails (some open to mountain bikes) weave through oak-dotted woodlands, between 600ft and 2300ft elevation. Watch for poison oak. NB: State budget cuts may temporarily close this park; call ahead.

RUSSIAN RIVER AREA

Lesser-known West Sonoma County was formerly famous for its apple farms and vacation cottages. Lately vineyards are replacing the orchards, and the Russian River has now taken its place among California's important wine appellations for superb pinot noir.

'The River,' as locals call it, has long been a summertime weekend destination for Northern Californians, who come to canoe, wander country lanes, taste wine, hike redwood forests and live at a lazy pace. In winter the river floods, and nobody's here.

The Russian River begins in the mountains north of Ukiah, in Mendocino County, but the most famous sections lie southwest of Healdsburg, where it cuts a serpentine course toward the sea. Just north of Santa Rosa, River Rd, the lower valley's main artery, connects Hwy 101 with coastal Hwy 1 at Jenner. Hwy 116 heads northwest from Cotati through Sebastopol and on to Guerneville. Westside Rd connects Guerneville and Healdsburg. West County's winding roads get confusing; carry a map.

Russian River Area Wineries

Outside Sonoma Valley, Sonoma County's wine-growing regions encompass several diverse areas, each famous for different reasons (see A Wine Country Primer, p186). Pick up the free, useful *Russian River Wine*

Russian River Area

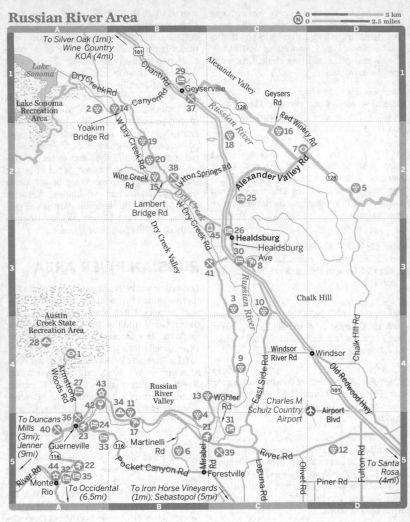

Road map (www.wineroad.com) in tourist-brochure racks.

RUSSIAN RIVER VALLEY

Nighttime coastal fog drifts up the Russian River Valley, then usually clears by midday. Pinot noir does beautifully here, as does chardonnay, which also grows in hotter regions, but prefers the longer 'hang time' of cooler climes. The highest concentration of wineries is along **Westside Rd**, between Guerneville and Healdsburg.

Hartford Family Winery WINERY
(Map p194; ☎707-887-8030; www.hartfordwines.com; 8075 Martinelli Rd, Forestville; tastings $5-15, applicable to purchase; ⊙10am-4:30pm; ☺) Surprisingly upscale for West County, Hartford sits in a pastoral valley surrounded by redwood-forested hills, on one of the area's prettiest back roads. It specializes in fine single-vineyard pinot (eight kinds), chardonnay and zinfandel, some from old-vine fruit. Umbrella-shaded picnic tables dot the garden. Bottles cost $35 to $70.

Russian River Area

Sophie's Cellars   WINE SHOP $
(Map p194; ☎707-865-1122; www.sophiescellars.com; 20293 Hwy 116; ⏰11am-7pm Thu-Tue) Stellar wine shop, with many hard-to-find local cult labels; the owner-connoisseur can help direct you to good wineries. Also stocks Sonoma cheeses, good for picnics. Find it across the road from Rio Villa Beach Resort.

Korbel   WINERY
(Map p194; ☎707-824-7316, 707-824-7000; www.korbel.com; 13250 River Rd; tastings free; ⏰10am-5pm; 🅿) Gorgeous rose gardens (April to October) and stellar on-site deli make Korbel worth a stop, but the champagne's just OK.

Iron Horse Vineyards   WINERY
(Map p160; ☎707-887-1507; www.ironhorsevineyards.com; 9786 Ross Station Rd, Sebastopol; tastings $10-20, refundable with purchase; ⏰10am-4:30pm; 🅿) Atop a hill with drop-dead views over the county, Iron Horse is known for pinot noir and sparkling wines, which the White House often pours. The outdoor tasting room is refreshingly unfussy; when you're done with your wine, pour it in the grass. Located off Hwy 116. Bottles cost $20 to $85.

Marimar   WINERY
(Map p160; ☎707-823-4365; www.marimarestate.com; 11400 Graton Rd, Sebastopol; tastings $10;

⊗11am-4pm; 🥾) Middle-of-nowhere Marimar specializes in all-organic pinot – seven different kinds – and chardonnay. The Spanish-style hilltop tasting room has a knockout vineyard-view terrace, lovely for picnics. Also consider tapas-and-wine pairings ($35). Bottles cost $29 to $52.

Gary Farrell
WINERY

(Map p194; ☎707-473-2900; www.garyfarrell wines.com; 10701 Westside Rd; tastings $10-15; ⊗10:30am-4:30pm; 🥾) High on a hilltop, overlooking the Russian River, Gary Farrell's tasting room sits perched among second-growth redwoods. The elegant chardonnay and long-finish pinot, made by a big-name winemaker, score high marks for consistency. Bottles cost $32 to $60.

🍷Porter Creek
WINERY

(Map p194; ☎707-433-6321; www.portercreekvine yards.com; 8735 Westside Rd; tastings free; 🥾) Inside a vintage 1920s garage, Porter Creek's tasting bar is a former bowling-alley lane, plunked atop barrels. Porter is old-school Northern California and an early pioneer in biodynamic farming. High-acid, food-friendly pinot noir and chardonnay are specialties, but there's silky zinfandel and other Burgundian- and Rhône-style wines, too. Check out the aviary and yurt. Bottles cost $24 to $65.

Hop Kiln Winery
WINERY

(Map p194; ☎707-433-6491; www.hopkilnwinery. com; 6050 Westside Rd; tastings $5-7; ⊗10am-5pm) Photogenic, historic landmark, with busy redwood tasting barn; the excellent artisinal vinegars make great $10 gifts.

De La Montaña
WINERY

(Map p194; ☎707-433-3711; www.dlmwine.com; 2651 Westside Rd at Foreman Lane; tastings $5, refundable with purchase; ⊗Mon-Thu call ahead, Fri-Sun 11am-4:30pm; 🥾) On weekends, meet the practical-joker winemaker at this tiny winery, known for 17 small-batch varieties made with estate-grown fruit. Viognier, primitivo, pinot and cabernet are signatures; the 'summer white' and gewürztraminer are great back-porch wines. Apple-shaded picnic area and bocce ball, too. Bottles $20 to $60.

Martinelli
WINERY

(Map p194; ☎707-525-0570; www.martinelliwin ery.com; 3360 River Rd, Windsor; tastings $5-15; ⊗10am-5pm; 🥾) Celeb winemaker Helen Turley makes the top-end pinot; there's also good syrah, sauvignon blanc and chardonnay in the gift shop-tasting barn.

🍷 J Winery
WINERY

(Map p194; ☎707-431-3646; www.jwine.com; 11447 Old Redwood Hwy; tastings $20; ⊗11am-5pm) Crafts crisp sparkling wines – some of Wine Country's best – but tastings are overpriced. Buy it in local shops.

DRY CREEK VALLEY

Hemmed in by 2000ft-high mountains, Dry Creek Valley is relatively warm, ideal for sauvignon blanc and zinfandel, and in some places cabernet sauvignon. It's west of Hwy 101, between Healdsburg and Lake Sonoma. Dry Creek Rd is the fast-moving main thoroughfare. Parallel-running West Dry Creek Rd is an undulating country lane with no center stripe – one of Sonoma's great back roads, ideal for cycling.

🍷Bella Vineyards
WINERY

(Map p194; ☎707-473-9171; www.bellawinery. com; 9711 W Dry Creek Rd; tasting $5-10; ⊗11am-4:30pm; 🥾) Atop the valley's north end, always-fun Bella has caves built into the hillside. The estate-grown grapes include 110-year-old vines from the Alexander Valley. The focus is on big reds – zin and syrah – but there's terrific rosé (good for barbecues), and late-harvest zin (great with brownies). The wonderful vibe and dynamic staff make Bella special. Bottles cost $25 to $40.

🍷Preston Vineyards
WINERY

(Map p194; ☎707-433-3372; www.prestonvine yards.com; 9282 W Dry Creek Rd; tasting $10, refundable with purchase; ⊗11am-4:30pm; 🐕) An early leader in organics, Lou Preston's 19th-century farm feels like old Sonoma County. Weathered picket fencing frames the 19th-century farmhouse-turned-tasting room, with candy-colored walls and tongue-in-groove ceilings setting a country mood. The signature is citrusy sauvignon blanc, but try the Rhône varietals and small-lot wines: mourvèdre, viognier, cinsault and cult-favorite barbera. Preston also bakes good bread; have a picnic in the shade of the walnut tree. Monday to Friday there's bocce ball. Bottles cost $24 to $38.

🍷Truett-Hurst
WINERY

(Map p194; ☎707-433-9545; www.truetthurst.com; 5610 Dry Creek Rd; tastings $5, refundable with purchase; ⊗10am-5pm; 🥾) Pull up an Adirondack chair and picnic creekside at Truett-Hurst. Dry Creek's newest biodynamic winer

Sample terrific old-vine zins, standout petite sirah and Russian River pinots at the handsome contemporary tasting room, then meander through fragrant butterfly gardens to the creek, where salmon spawn in autumn. Ever-fun weekends, with food-and-wine pairings and live music (◎1-5pm Sat & Sun).

Unti Vineyards
WINERY

(Map p194; ☎707-433-5590; www.untivineyards. com; 4202 Dry Creek Rd; tastings $5, waived with purchase; ◎by appointment 10am-4pm; ◉) Inside a fluorescent-lit windowless garage, Unti makes all estate-grown reds – Châteauneuf-du-Pape–style grenache, compelling syrah, and superb sangiovese – favored by oenophiles for their structured tannins and concentrated fruit. If you love artisinal wines, don't miss Unti. Bottles cost $22 to $35.

Quivira
WINERY

(Map p194; ☎707-431-8333; www.quivirawine.com; 4900 W Dry Creek Rd; tastings $5, waived with purchase; ◎11am-5pm; ◉◉) Sunflowers, lavender and crowing roosters greet your arrival at this winery and biodynamic farm, with self-guided garden tours and picnic grove beside the vineyards. The kids can scan the grapes for the football-sized feral sow – the winery's mascot – while you sample Rhône varietals and unusual blends, including lip-smacking sauvignon blanc-gewürztztraminer. Bottles cost $18 to $45.

ALEXANDER VALLEY

Bucolic Alexander Valley flanks the Mayacamas Mountains, with postcard-perfect vistas and wide-open vineyards. Summers are hot, ideal for cabernet sauvignon, merlot and warm-weather chardonnays, but there's also fine sauvignon blanc and zinfandel. For events info, visit www.alexandervalley.org.

Stryker Sonoma
WINERY

(Map p194; ☎707-433-1944; www.stryker-sonoma.com; 5110 Hwy 128; tastings $10, refundable with purchase; ◎10:30am-5pm; ◉) Wow, what a view from the hilltop concrete-and-glass tasting room at Stryker Sonoma. The standouts are fruit-forward zinfandel and sangiovese, which you can't buy anywhere else. Good picnicking. Bottles cost $20 to $50.

Hawkes
TASTING ROOM

(Map p194; ☎707-433-4295; www.hawkeswine. com; 6734 Hwy 128; tastings $10, refundable with purchase; ◎10am-5pm; ◉) Funky teapots grace the walls at friendly Hawkes', an easy roadside stopover while you're exploring the valley. The single-vineyard cab is damn good, as is the blend; there's also a clean-and-crisp, non-malolactic chardonnay. Bottles cost $20 to $70.

Hanna
WINERY

(Map p194; ☎707-431-4310, 800-854-3987; http:// hannawinery.com; 9280 Hwy 128; tastings $10; ◎10am-4pm; ◉) Abutting oak-studded hills, Hanna's tasting room has lovely vineyard views and good picnicking. At the bar, find estate-grown merlot and cabernet, and big-fruit zins and syrah. Sit-down wine-and-cheese tastings available ($25). Bottles cost $15 to $48.

Silver Oak
WINERY

(off Map p194; ☎800-273-8809; www.silveroak. com; 24625 Chianti Rd; tastings $20, partially applicable to purchase; ◎9am-4pm Mon-Sat) Sister to the legendary Napa winery; the Alexander Valley cabernet is similarly luxurious. Bottles start at $70.

Trentadue
WINERY

(Map p194; ☎707-433-3104, 888-332-3032; www. trentadue.com; 19170 Geyserville Ave; port tastings $5; ◎10am-5pm) Specializes in ports (ruby, not tawny); the chocolate port makes a great gift.

Sebastopol

Grapes have replaced apples as the new cash crop, but Sebastopol's farm-town identity remains rooted in the apple – evidence the much-heralded summertime Gravenstein Apple Fair. The town center feels suburban because of traffic, but a hippie tinge gives it color. This is the refreshingly unfussy side of Wine Country, and makes a good-value home base for exploring the area.

Hwy 116 splits downtown; southbound traffic uses Main St, northbound traffic Petaluma Ave. North of town, it's called Gravenstein Hwy N and continues toward Guerneville; south of downtown, it's Gravenstein Hwy S, which heads toward Hwy 101 and Sonoma.

◉ Sights & Activities

Around Sebastopol, look for family-friendly farms, gardens, animal sanctuaries and pick-your-own orchards. For a countywide list, check out the Sonoma County Farm Trails Guide (www.farmtrails.org).

Farmers market　　　　　　　　MARKET
(cnr Petaluma & McKinley Aves; ⊙10am-1:30pm Sun Apr–mid-Dec) Meets at the downtown plaza.

Sturgeon's Mill　　　　　　　　MILL
(www.sturgeonsmill.com; 2150 Green Hill Rd; ⊕) A historic steam-powered sawmill, open for demonstrations several weekends a year; check the website.

✷ Festivals & Events

Apple Blossom Festival　　　CULTURAL
(www.sebastopol.org) April

Gravenstein Apple Fair　　　FOOD
(www.farmtrails.org/gravenstein-apple-fair) August

⌂ Sleeping

Sebastopol is good for get-up-and-go travelers exploring Russian River Valley and the coast.

Sebastopol Inn　　　　　　MOTEL $$
(☎707-829-2500, 800-653-1082; www.sebastopolinn.com; 6751 Sebastopol Ave; r $119-179; ❀❂❋⊕) We like this independent, non-cookie-cutter motel for its quiet, off-street location, usually reasonable rates and good-looking if basic rooms. Outside are grassy areas for kids and a hot tub.

Vine Hill Inn　　　　　　　B&B $$
(☎707-823-8832; www.vine-hill-inn.com; 3949 Vine Hill Rd; r incl breakfast $170; ❀❂❋⊕) Mature landscaping surrounds this four-room 1897 Victorian farmhouse, with gorgeous vineyard views, just north of town off Hwy 116. Breakfast is made with eggs from the barn's chickens. Two rooms have Jacuzzis.

Raccoon Cottage　　　　COTTAGE $$
(☎707-545-5466; www.raccooncottage.com; 2685 Elizabeth Ct; cottage incl breakfast $130-150) A small B&B cottage, off Vine Hill Rd, amid oaks, fruit trees and gardens.

Fairfield Inn & Suites　　　HOTEL $$
(☎707-829-6677, 800-465-4329; www.winecountryhi.com; 1101 Gravenstein Hwy S; r $129-209; ❀@❂❋⊕) Generic, but modern, with in-room refrigerators, coffee makers and hot tub.

✕ Eating

Gourmet **food trucks** (⊙11:30am-2:30pm Thu) gather in the parking lot at **O'Reilly Media** (1050 Gravenstein Hwy N).

K&L Bistro　　　　　　　FRENCH $$$
(☎707-823-6614; www.klbistro.com; 119 S Main St; lunch $14-20, dinner $19-29; ⊙11:30am-2:30pm & 5:30-9pm Mon-Sat) Sebastopol's top restaurant serves down-to-earth provincial Cal-French bistro cooking in a convivial – if loud – room, with classics like mussels and French fries, and grilled steaks with red-wine reduction. Tables are tight, but the crowd is friendly. Reservations essential.

Hopmonk Tavern　　　　　PUB $$
(☎707-829-7300; www.hopmonk.com; 230 Petaluma Ave; mains $10-20; ⊙11:30am-9pm) Inside a converted 1903 railroad station, Hopmonk's competent cooking is designed to pair with beer – 76 varieties – served in type-specific glassware. Good burgers, fried calamari, charcuterie platters and salads.

East-West Cafe　　　MEDITERRANEAN $
(☎707-829-2822; www.eastwestcafesebastopol.com; 128 N Main St; meals $9-12; ⊙8am-9pm Mon-Sat, 8am-8pm Sun; ❋⊕) This unfussy cafe serves everything from grass-fed burgers to macrobiotic wraps, stir-fries to *huevos rancheros* (corn tortilla with fried egg and chili-tomato sauce). Good blue-corn pancakes at breakfast.

Slice of Life　　　　　VEGETARIAN $
(☎707-829-6627; www.thesliceoflife.com; 6970 McKinley St; mains under $10; ⊙11am-9pm Tue-Fri, 9am-9pm Sat & Sun; ❋) This terrific vegan-vegetarian kitchen doubles as a pizzeria. Breakfast all day. Great smoothies and date shakes.

Mom's Apple Pie　　　　DESSERTS $
(☎707-823-8330; www.momsapplepieusa.com; 4550 Gravenstein Hwy N; whole pies $7-15; ⊙10am-6pm; ❋⊕) Pie's the thing here – and yum, that flaky crust. Apple is predictably good, especially in autumn, but the blueberry is our fave, made better with vanilla ice cream.

Viva Mexicana　　　　　MEXICAN $
(☎707-823-5555, 707-829-5555; 841 Gravenstein Hwy S; mains $8-10; ⊙8am-8pm; ❋) A tiny roadside *taquería* with outdoor tables and good vegetarian choices.

Fiesta Market　　　　　MARKET $
(☎707-823-9735; fiestamkt.com; 550 Gravenstein Hwy N; ⊙8am-8pm) The town's best groceries and picnics.

Screamin' Mimi　　　　DESSERT $
(☎707-823-5902; www.screaminmimisicecream.com; 6902 Sebastopol Ave; ⊙11am-10pm) Delish homemade ice cream.

Drinking & Entertainment

Hardcore Espresso CAFE
(707-823-7588; 1798 Gravenstein Hwy S; 6am-7pm;) Meet local hippies and art freaks over coffee and smoothies at this classic Nor-Cal off-the-grid, indoor-outdoor coffeehouse that's essentially a corrugated-metal-roofed shack surrounded by umbrella tables. The organic coffee is the town's best.

Hopmonk Tavern PUB
(707-829-7300; www.hopmonk.com; 230 Petaluma Ave; 11:30am-10pm, later weekends) Always-fun beer garden with 76 craft brews, several housemade. Live music most nights; Tuesday is open mic.

Aubergine After Dark CABARET
(707-861-9190; aubergineafterdark.com; 755 Petaluma Ave; 4pm-midnight Sun-Thu, to 1am Sat & Sun) Various acts play weekends at this cool cafe with a bohemian bent, adjoining a vintage-thrift shop; full bar, snacks, and coffee drinks.

Jasper O'Farrell's BAR
(707-823-1389; 6957 Sebastopol Ave; Tue-Sun) Busy bar with billiards and live bands Wednesday nights; good drink specials.

Coffee Catz CAFE
(707-829-6600; www.coffeecatz.com; 6761 Sebastopol Ave; 7am-10pm Fri & Sat, to 6pm Sun-Thu) Early-evening and afternoon acoustic music, Thursday to Sunday, at a cafe in an historic rail barn (Gravenstein Station).

Shopping

Antique shops line Gravenstein Hwy S toward Hwy 101.

Renga Arts ARTS & CRAFTS, GIFTS
(707-823-9407; www.rengaarts.com; 11am-5pm Thu-Mon) Reduce, reuse, rejoice at Renga Arts, a functional-art shop, where every ingenious item is made with repurposed, reclaimed goods, from bottle-cap necklaces to birdhouses. Owner Joe is an excellent resource on all things West County Sonoma. Say hello.

Aubergine VINTAGE CLOTHING
(707-827-3460; www.aubergineafterdark.com; 755 Petaluma Ave, Sebastopol) Vast vintage emporium, specializing in cast-off European thrift-shop clothing.

Sumbody BEAUTY
(707-823-2053; www.sumbody.com; 118 N Main St; 10am-7pm Mon-Sat, 10am-5pm Sun) Eco-friendly bath products made with all-natural ingredients. Also offers well-priced facials ($49) and massages ($75) at small on-site spa.

Toyworks TOYS
(707-829-2003; www.sonomatoyworks.com; 6940 Sebastopol Ave;) Indie toy-seller with phenomenal selection of quality games for kids.

Antique Society ANTIQUES
(707-829-1733; www.antiquesociety.com; 2661 Gravenstein Hwy S) Antiques vendors, 125 of them, under one roof.

Beekind FOOD, HOMEWARES
(707-824-2905; www.beekind.com; 921 Gravenstein Hwy S) Local honey and beeswax candles.

Copperfield's Books BOOKS
(707-823-2618; www.copperfields.net; 138 N Main St) Indie bookshop with literary events.

Incredible Records MUSIC
(707-824-8099; 112 N Main St) A legendary record store.

Midgley's Country Flea Market MARKET
(707-823-7874; mfleamarket.com; 2200 Gravenstein Hwy S; 6:30am-4:30pm Sat & Sun) The region's largest flea market.

Information

Sebastopol Area Chamber of Commerce & Visitors Center (707-823-3032, 877-828-4748; www.visitsebastopol.org; 265 S Main St; 10am-4pm Mon-Fri) Maps, information and exhibits.

Occidental

Our favorite West County town is a haven of artists, back-to-the-landers and counter-culturalists. Historic 19th-century buildings line a single main street, easy to explore in an hour; continue north by car and you'll hit the Russian River, in Monte Rio. Check out **Bohemian Connection** (www.bohemianconnection.com) for information. At Christmastime, Bay Area families flock to Occidental to buy trees. The town decorates to the nines, and there's weekend cookie-decorating and caroling at the Union Hotel's Bocce Ballroom.

◉ Sights & Activities

Meet the whole community at the detour-worthy **farmers market** (www.occidentalfarmersmarket.com; ⊘4pm-dusk Fridays, Jun-Oct), with musicians, craftspeople and – the star attraction – **Gerard's Paella** (www.gerardspaella.com) of TV-cooking-show fame.

Sonoma Canopy Tours
ECOTOUR
(☏888-494-7868; www.sonomacanopytours.com; 6250 Bohemian Hwy; adult $79-89, child $49) North of town, fly through the redwood canopy on seven interconnected ziplines, ending with an 80ft-rappel descent; reservations required.

Osmosis Enzyme Bath & Massage
BATH HOUSE
(☏707-823-8231; www.osmosis.com; 209 Bohemian Hwy; ⊘9am-9pm) Three miles south in Freestone, tranquility prevails at this Japanese-inspired place, which indulges patrons with dry-enzyme baths of aromatic cedar fibers (bath-and-blanket wrap $85), lovely tea-and-meditation gardens, plus outdoor massages. Make reservations.

⊨ Sleeping

Inn at Occidental
INN $$$
(☏707-874-1047, 800-522-6324; www.innatoccidental.com; 3657 Church St; r incl breakfast $229-339; ❉@❡❄) This beautifully restored 18-room Victorian inn – one of Sonoma's finest – is filled with collectible antiques; rooms have gas fireplaces and cozy feather beds.

Valley Ford Hotel
INN $$
(☏707-876-1983; www.vfordhotel.com; r $115-165) Surrounded by pastureland in the nearby tiny town of Valley Ford, this 19th-century six-room inn has good beds, soft linens, and great rates. Downstairs there's a terrific roadhouse restaurant.

Occidental Hotel
MOTEL $$
(☏707-874-3623, 877-867-6084; www.occidentalhotel.com; 3610 Bohemian Hwy; r $130-160, 2-bedroom q $180-200; ❉❡❄❄) Fresh-looking motel rooms.

✗ Eating

Bohemian Market (☏707-874-3312; 3633 Main St; ⊘8am-9pm) has the best groceries. In Freestone, **Wild Flour Bakery** (☏707-874-3928; www.wildflourbread.coml 140 Bohemian Hwy; ⊘8:30am-6pm Fri-Mon) makes hearty artisinal brick-oven breads, scones and coffee.

Bistro des Copains
FRENCH-CALIFORNIAN $$$
(☏707-874-2436; www.bistrodescopains.com; 3728 Bohemian Hwy; mains $23-25, 3-course menu $38-42; ⊘5-9pm Wed-Mon) Worth a special trip, this bistro draws bon vivants for its Cal-French country cooking, like steak-*frites* and roast duck. Great wines; $10 corkage for Sonoma vintages. Make reservations.

Howard Station Cafe
CAFE $
(☏707-874-2838; www.howardstationcafe.com; 3811 Bohemian Hwy; mains $8-11; ⊘7am-2:30pm; ❡❄) Makes big plates of comfort cooking and fresh-squeezed juices.

Barley & Hops
PUB $$
(☏707-874-9037; barleyandhopstavern.blogspot.com; 3688 Bohemian Hwy; mains $10-15; ⊘4-9:30pm Mon-Fri, from 11am Sat & Sun; ❡) Serves over 100 beers, sandwiches, giant salads and lamb stew.

Union Hotel
ITALIAN $$
(☏707-874-3555; www.unionhoteloccidental.com; 3703 Bohemian Hwy; meals $15-25; ❡) Occidental has two old-school American Italian restaurants that serve family-style meals. Of the two, the Union is slightly better than

---

SCENIC DRIVE: COLEMAN VALLEY ROAD

Wine Country's most scenic drive isn't through the grapes, but along these 10 miles of winding West County byway, from Occidental to the sea. It's best late morning, after the fog has cleared. Drive west, not east, with the sun behind you and the ocean ahead. First you'll pass through redwood forests and lush valleys where Douglas firs stand draped in sphagnum moss – an eerie sight in the fog. The real beauty shots lie further ahead, when the road ascends 1000ft hills, dotted with gnarled oaks and craggy rock formations, with the vast blue Pacific unfurling below. The road ends at coastal Hwy 1, where you can explore Sonoma Coast State Beach, then turn left and find your way to the tiny town of Bodega (not Bodega Bay) to see locales where Hitchcock shot his 1963 classic, *The Birds*.

VALLEY FORD

Valley Ford (population 147) is a tableau of rural California, with rolling hills dotted with grazing cows and manure lingering on the breeze – the forced sophistication of other Wine Country locales couldn't feel further away. It's ideal for an affordable one-nighter, or a lazy meal while exploring back roads.

West County Design (☑707-875-9140; 14390 Hwy 1; ☺Thu-Sun) houses a stonemason's and custom furniture–builder's shops, giving a glimpse of contemporary California home-furnishings styles. 'Round back there's a man who builds birdhouses.

We love the flavor-rich cooking at **Rocker Oysterfeller's** (☑707-876-1983; www.rockeroysterfellers.com; 14415 Hwy 1; mains $14-22; ☺Wed-Fri 4:30pm-8:30pm, 10am-8:30pm Sat & Sun), with its barbecued oysters, local crab cakes, steaks and fried chicken. Great wine bar, too. Or snag a picnic table at **Fish Bank** (☑707-876-3473; www.sonomacoastfishbank.com; 14435 Hwy 1; ☺Wed-Sun 11:30am-6pm) for crab rolls, fish salads, chowder, cheese and bread – good picnic fixings if you're continuing to the coast. Stay the night at the Valley Ford Hotel (p200), with simple country B&B rooms.

Negri's (neither is great), and has a hard-to-beat lunch special in its 1869 saloon – whole pizza, salad and soda for $12. At dinner, sit in the fabulous Bocce Ballroom.

Negri's ITALIAN **$$**
(☑707-823-5301; www.negrisrestaurant.com; 3700 Bohemian Hwy; meals $15-25; ⊞) Serves multi-course family-style dinners.

🛍 **Shopping**

Verdigris HOMEWARES
(☑707-874-9018; www.1lightartlamps.com; 72 Main St; ☺Thu-Mon) Crafts gorgeous art lamps.

Hand Goods CERAMICS
(☑707-874-2161; www.handgoods.net; 3627 Main St) A collective of ceramicists and potters.

Guerneville & Around

The Russian River's biggest vacation-resort town, Guerneville gets busy summer weekends with party hardy gay boys, sun-worshipping lesbians and long-haired beer-drinking Harley riders, earning it the nickname 'Groin-ville.' The gay scene has died back since the unfortunate closure of Fife's, the world's first gay resort, but fun-seeking crowds still come to canoe, hike redwoods and hammer cocktails poolside.

Downriver, some areas are sketchy (due to drugs). The local chamber of commerce has chased most of the tweakers from Main St in Guerneville, but if some off-the-beaten-path areas feel creepy – especially campgrounds – they probably are.

Four miles downriver, tiny Monte Rio has a sign over Hwy 116 declaring it 'Vacation Wonderland' – an overstatement, but the dog-friendly beach is a hit with families. Further west, idyllic Duncans Mills is home to a few dozen souls, but has picture-ready historic buildings. Upriver, east of Guerneville, Forestville is where agricultural country resumes.

👁 **Sights & Activities**

Look for sandy beaches and swimming holes along the river; there's good river access east of town at **Sunset Beach** (Map p194; www.sonoma-county.org/parks; 11403 River Rd, Forestville; per car $6). Fishing and watercraft outfitters operate mid-May to early October, after which winter rains dangerously swell the river. A **farmers market** meets downtown on Wednesdays June through September, from 4pm to 7pm. On summer Saturdays, there's also one at Monte Rio Beach, 11am to 2pm.

Armstrong Redwoods State Reserve NATURE RESERVE
(Map p194; www.parks.ca.gov; 17000 Armstrong Woods Rd; day use per vehicle $8) A magnificent redwood forest 2 miles north of Guerneville, the 805-acre Armstrong Redwoods State Reserve was set aside by a 19th-century lumber magnate. Walk or cycle in for free; you pay only to park. Short interpretive trails lead into magical forests; beyond lie 20 miles of backcountry trails, through oak woodlands, in adjoining **Austin Creek State Recreation Area**, one of Sonoma County's

few-remaining wilderness areas (although State budget cuts may temporarily close this park).

Burke's Canoe Trips
CANOEING, KAYAKING

(Map p194; ☎707-887-1222; www.burkesca noetrips.com; 8600 River Rd, Forestville; canoes $60; ⚑) You can't beat Burke's for a day on the river. Self-guided canoe and kayak trips include shuttle back to your car. Make reservations; plan four hours. Camping in its riverside redwood grove costs $10 per person.

Pee Wee Golf & Arcade
GOLF, BICYCLING

(Map p194; ☎707-869-9321; 16155 Drake Rd at Hwy 116; 18/36 holes $8/12; ◷11am-10pm Memorial Day-Labor Day, Sat & Sun Sep; ⚑) Flashback to 1948 at this impeccably kept retro-kitsch 36-hole miniature golf course, just south of the Hwy 116 bridge, with brilliantly painted obstacles, including T Rex and Yogi Bear. Bring your own cocktails; also rents gas barbecue grills ($20) and bicycles ($30).

Armstrong Woods Pack Station
HORSEBACK RIDING

(☎707-887-2939; www.redwoodhorses.com) Leads year-round 2½-hour trail rides ($80), full-day rides and overnight treks. Reservations required.

Johnson's Beach
BOATING

(☎707-869-2022; www.johnsonsbeach.com; end of Church St, Guerneville) Canoe, paddleboat and watercraft rental (from $30).

King's Sport & Tackle
FISHING, KAYAKING, CANOEING

(☎707-869-2156; www.kingsrussianriver.com; www.guernevillesport.com; 16258 Main St, Guerneville) *The* local source for fishing and river-condition information. Also rents kayaks ($35 to $55) and canoes ($55).

Northwood Golf Course
GOLF

(Map p194; ☎707-865-1116; www.northwoodgolf. com; 19400 Hwy 116, Monte Rio) Vintage-1920s Alistair MacKenzie-designed, par-36, nine-hole course.

✵ Festivals & Events

Monte Rio Variety Show
MUSIC

(www.monterioshow.org) Members of the elite, secretive Bohemian Grove (Google it) perform publicly, sometimes showcasing unannounced celebrities; July.

Lazy Bear Weekend
CULTURAL

(www.lazybearweekend.com) Read: heavy, furry gay men; August.

Russian River Jazz & Blues Festival
MUSIC

(www.omegaevents.com/russianriver) September. A day of jazz, followed by a day of blues, with occasional luminaries like BB King.

🛌 Sleeping

Russian River has few budget sleeps, although prices drop midweek. On weekends and holidays, book ahead. Many places have no TVs. Because the river sometimes floods, some lodgings have cold linoleum floors, so pack slippers.

GUERNVILLE

The advantage of staying downtown is you can walk to dinner and bars. At this writing, the long-running gay hotel and disco, Russian River Resort (aka Triple R), had closed, but may re-open. Check with the chamber of commerce.

Applewood Inn
INN $$$

(Map p194; ☎707-869-9093, 800-555-8509; www. applewoodinn.com; 13555 Hwy 116; r incl breakfast $195-345; ❀@☎⛱) A former estate on a wooded hilltop south of town, cushy Applewood has marvelous Arts and Crafts-era detail, with dark wood and heavy furniture. Rooms sport Jacuzzis, couples' showers and top-end linens; some have fireplaces. Great hideaway. Small onsite spa.

Fern Grove Cottages
CABINS $$

(☎707-869-8105; www.ferngrove.com; 16650 River Rd; cabins incl breakfast $159-219, with kitchen $199-269; @☎⛱) Downtown Guerneville's cheeriest resort, Fern Grove has vintage-1930s pine-paneled cabins, tucked beneath redwoods and surrounded by lush flowering gardens. Some have Jacuzzis and fireplaces. The pool uses salt, not chlorine; the lovely English innkeeper provides concierge service; and breakfast includes homemade scones.

🍃 Boon Hotel & Spa
INN $$$

(Map p194; ☎707-869-2721; www.boonhotels.com; 14711 Armstrong Woods Rd; r $180-225; ☎⛱) Rooms surround a swimming-pool courtyard (with Jacuzzi) at this mid-century-modern, 14-room motel, gussied up in minimalist style. The look is austere but fresh, with organic-cotton linens and spacious rooms; most have wood-burning fireplaces. Drive to town, or ride the free bicycles.

Santa Nella House B&B $$
(Map p194; ☑707-869-9448; www.santanellahouse.
com; 12130 Hwy 116; r incl breakfast $179-199; @🐾)
All four spotless rooms at this 1871 Victo-
rian, south of town, have wood-burning
fireplaces and frilly Victorian furnishings.
Upstairs rooms are biggest. Outside there's
a hot tub and sauna. Best for travelers who
appreciate the B&B aesthetic.

Highlands Resort CABINS, CAMPGROUND $$
(☑707-869-0333; www.highlandsresort.com;
14000 Woodland Dr; tent sites $20-25; r with/
without bathroom $90-100/70-80, cabins $120-
205; 🐾🐾) Guerneville's mellowest all-gay
resort sits on a wooded hillside, walkable
to town, and has simply furnished rooms
and little cottages with porches. The large
pool and hot tub are clothing-optional
(weekday/weekend day use $5/10). There's
camping, too.

Riverlane Resort CABINS $$
(☑707-869-2323, 800-201-2324; www.riverlan
eresort.com; 16320 1st St; cabins $90-150; 🐾🐾)
Right downtown, Riverlane has cabins with
kitchens, decorated with mismatched fur-
niture, but they're very clean and all have
decks with barbecues. Best for no-frills
travelers or campers wanting an upgrade.
Friendly service, heated pool, private beach
and hot tub.

Johnson's Beach Resort CABINS, CAMPGROUND $
(☑707-869-2022; www.johnsonsbeach.com; 16241
1st St; tent sites $25, RV sites from $25-35, cabins
$50, per week $300) On the river in Guernev-
ille, Johnson's has rustic, but clean, thin-
walled cabins on stilts; all have kitchens.
Bring earplugs. There's camping, too, but it's
loud. No credit cards.

Bullfrog Pond CAMPGROUND $
(Map p194; www.parks.ca.gov; tent sites $25)
Reached via a steep road from Armstrong
Redwoods, Bullfrog Pond has forested camp-
sites, with cold water, and primitive hike-in
and equestrian backcountry campsites. All
are first-come, first-served. Budget cuts may
limit operation to summer only.

**Schoolhouse Canyon
Campground** CAMPGROUND $
(Map p194; ☑707-869-2311; www.school
housecanyon.com; 12600 River Rd; tent sites
$30; 🐾🐾) Two miles east of Guerneville,
Schoolhouse's tent sites lie beneath tall
trees, across the road from the river. Coin-

operated hot showers, clean bathrooms,
quiet location.

FORESTVILLE

Raford Inn B&B $$
(Map p194; ☑707-887-9573, 800-887-9503; www.
rafordhouse.com; 10630 Wohler Rd, Healdsburg; r
$160-260; 🐾@🐾) We love this 1880 Victorian
B&B's secluded hilltop location, surrounded by tall palms and rambling vineyards.
Rooms are big and airy, done with lace and
antiques; some have fireplaces. And wow,
those sunset views.

Farmhouse Inn INN $$$
(Map p194; ☑707-887-3300, 800-464-6642; www.
farmhouseinn.com; 7871 River Rd; r $325-695;
🐾@🐾🐾) Think love nest. The area's premier
inn has spacious rooms and cottages, styled
with cushy amenities like saunas, steam-
showers and wood-burning fireplaces. Small
on-site spa and top-notch restaurant (p204).
Check in early to maximize time.

MONTE RIO
Village Inn INN $$
(Map p194; ☑707-865-2304; www.villageinn-ca.
com; 20822 River Blvd; r $145-235; @🐾) A retired
concierge owns this cute, old-fashioned 11-
room inn, beneath towering trees, right on
the river. Some rooms have river views; all
have fridge and microwave.

Rio Villa Beach Resort INN $$
(Map p194; ☑707-865-1143, 877-746-8455; www.ri
ovilla.com; 20292 Hwy 116; r with kitchen $149-209,
r without kitchen $139-189; 🐾🐾🐾) Landscaping
is lush at this small riverside resort with ex-
cellent sun exposure (you see redwoods, but
you're not under them). Rooms are well kept
but simple (request a quiet room, not by the
road); the emphasis is on the outdoors, evi-
dent by the large riverside terrace, outdoor
fireplace and barbecues.

Highland Dell INN $$
(Map p194; ☑707-865-2300; highlanddell.com;
21050 River Blvd; r $109-179; 🐾🐾) Built in 1906
in grand lodge style, redone in 2007, the inn
fronts right on the river. Above the giant dining room are 12 bright, fresh-looking rooms
(carpet stains notwithstanding) with comfy
beds.

DUNCANS MILLS
Casini Ranch CAMPGROUND $
(☑707-865-2255, 800-451-8400; www.casiniranch.
com; 22855 Moscow Rd, Duncans Mills; tent sites
$38-45, RV sites partial/full hookups $40-51/46-49;

🛶📶🐕) In quiet Duncans Mills, beautifully set on riverfront ranchlands, Casini is an enormous, well-run campground. Amenities include kayaks and paddleboats (day use $3); bathrooms are spotless.

🍴 Eating

GUERNEVILLE

There's a good **taco truck** (16451 Main St), in the Safeway parking lot.

🌱**Boon Eat + Drink**   NEW AMERICAN $$$
(☎707-869-0780; www.eatatboon.com; 16248 Main St; lunch/dinner mains $10-12/$20-24; ⊙11am-3pm & 5-9pm) Locally sourced ingredients inform the seasonal, Cali-smart cooking at this tiny, always-packed New American bistro, with cheek-by-jowl tables that fill every night. Make reservations or expect to wait.

Applewood Inn Restaurant   CALIFORNIAN $$$
(Map p194; ☎707-869-9093, www.dineatap plewood.com; 13555 Hwy 116; mains $20-28; ⊙5:30-8:30pm Wed-Sun) Cozy by the fire in the treetop-level dining room and sup on Michelin-starred Euro-Cal cooking that maximizes seasonal produce, with dishes like rack of lamb with minted *chimichuri* (garlic-parsley vinaigrette) and smoked trout with corn and crayfish. Reservations essential.

Coffee Bazaar   CAFE $
(☎707-869-9706; www.mycoffeeb.com; 14045 Armstrong Woods Rd; dishes $5-9; ⊙6am-8pm; 📶) Happening cafe with salads, sandwiches and all-day breakfasts; adjoins a good used bookstore.

Garden Grill   BARBECUE $
(☎707-869-3922; www.gardengrillbbq.com; 17132 Hwy 116, Guernewood Park; mains $6-12; ⊙8am-8pm) The Garden Grill is a roadhouse barbecue joint, with a redwood-shaded patio, one mile west of Guerneville; good house-smoked meats, but the fries could be better. Breakfast till 3pm.

Andorno's Pizza   PIZZERIA $
(☎707-869-0651; www.andornospizza.com; 16205 1st St; ⊙11:30am-9pm; 🍴) Downtown pizzeria with river-view terrace.

Taqueria La Tapatia   MEXICAN $
(☎707-869-1821; 16632 Main St; mains $7-14; ⊙11am-9pm) Reasonable choice for traditional Mexican.

🌱**Big Bottom Market**   MARKET $
(☎707-604-7295; www.bigbottommarket.com; 16228 Main St) Gourmet deli and wine shop, with grab-and-go picnic supplies.

🌱**Food for Humans**   MARKET $
(☎707-869-3612; 16385 1st St; ⊙9am-8pm; 🍴) Organic groceries; better alternative than neighboring Safeway, but no meat.

FORESTVILLE

🌱**Farmhouse Inn**   NEW AMERICAN $$$
(Map p194; ☎707-887-3300; www.farmhouseinn. com; 7871 River Rd; 3-/4-course dinner $69/89; ⊙dinner Thu-Sun) Special-occasion worthy, Michelin-starred Farmhouse changes its seasonal Euro-Cal menu daily, using locally raised, organic ingredients like Sonoma lamb, wild salmon and rabbit – the latter is the house specialty. Details are impeccable, from aperitifs in the garden to tableside cheese service. Make reservations.

MONTE RIO

Highland Dell   GERMAN $$
(Map p194; ☎707-865-2300; http://highlanddell. com; 21050 River Blvd; lunch mains $9-15, dinner mains $16-26; ⊙5-9pm Mon, Tue, Fri & Sat, 1-7pm Sun; closed Oct-May) A dramatic three-story-high chalet-style dining room with a riverview deck, Highland Dell makes pretty good German food – steaks, schnitzel, sauerbraten and sausage. Full bar.

Village Inn   AMERICAN $$$
(Map p194; ☎707-865-2304; www.villageinn-ca. com; 20822 River Blvd; mains $19-26; ⊙5-8:30pm Wed-Sun) The straightforward steaks-and-seafood menu is basic American and doesn't distract from the wonderful river views. Great local wine list, full bar.

Don's Dogs   SNACK BAR $
(Map p194; ☎707-865-4190; cnr Bohemian Hwy & Hwy 116; ⊙9am-5pm Wed-Sun) Gourmet hot dogs and coffee, behind the Rio Theater.

🍸 Drinking & Entertainment

Stumptown Brewery   BREWERY
(Map p194; www.stumptown.com; 15045 River Rd; ⊙11am-midnight Sun-Thu, 11-2am Fri & Sat) Guerneville's best straight bar is gay-friendly and has a foot-stompin' jukebox, billiards, riverside beer garden, and several homemade brews. Pretty good pub grub, including house-smoked barbecue.

Rio Theater CINEMA
(Map p194; ☑707-865-0913; www.riotheater.com; cnr Bohemian Hwy & Hwy 116, Monte Rio; adult/child $7/5; ☺Fri-Sun) Dinner and a movie take on new meaning at this vintage-WWII Quonset hut converted to a cinema in 1950, with a concession stand serving gourmet hot dogs ($7). It's freezing inside on cool nights, but they supply blankets. Charming. Call to confirm showtimes, especially off-season.

Rainbow Cattle Company GAY
(www.queersteer.com; 16220 Main St) The stalwart gay watering hole.

Guerneville River Theater LIVE MUSIC, DJS
(www.rivertheater.biz; 16135 Main St; ☺Wed, Fri & Sat) Former movie theater, now a honky-tonk club, with town's biggest dance floor. Live bands weekends, open mic Wednesdays. Very DIY feeling. Beer and wine only.

Rio Nido Roadhouse BAR, LIVE MUSIC
(www.rionidoroadhouse.com; 14540 Canyon Two, off River Rd) Raucous roadhouse bar with eclectic lineup of live bands. Shows start 6pm Saturdays and sometimes Fridays and Sundays, too; check website.

Main Street Station CABARET
(☑707-869-0501; www.mainststation.com; 16280 Main, Guerneville; cover $3-6) Live acoustic-only jazz, blues and cabaret nightly in summer, weekends in winter. Suggest reservations, but you can normally walk in. Also an Italian-American restaurant.

🖉 Kaya Organic Espresso CAFE
(16626 Main St, Guerneville; ☺7am-2pm) Hippie kids strum guitars and play hackie sack outside this coffee shack.

Wine Tasting of Sonoma County WINE BAR $
(☑707-865-0565; winetastingofsonomacounty. com; 25179 Hwy 116, Duncans Mills; wine tastings $5; ☺noon-5pm Fri-Mon) Local vino and cheeses alfresco.

❶ Information

Get information and lodging referrals:

Russian River Chamber of Commerce & Visitor Center (☑707-869-9000, 877-644-9001; www.russianriver.com; 16209 1st St, Guerneville; ☺10am-5pm Mon-Sat, to 4pm Sun)
Russian River Visitor Information Center (☑707-869-4096; ☺10am-3:45pm) At Korbel Cellars.

Santa Rosa

Wine Country's biggest city, and the Sonoma County seat, Santa Rosa is known for traffic and suburban sprawl. It lacks small-town charm, but has reasonably priced accommodations and easy access to Sonoma County and Valley.

Santa Rosa claims two famous native sons – a world-renowned cartoonist and a celebrated horticulturalist – and you'll find enough museums, gardens and shopping for an afternoon. Otherwise, there ain't much to do, unless you're here in July during the Sonoma County Fair (www.sonomacountyfair. com), at the fairgrounds on Bennett Valley Rd.

◎ Sights & Activities

The main shopping stretch is 4th St, which abruptly ends at Hwy 101 but reemerges on the other side at historic Railroad Sq. Downtown parking garages ($0.75/hour, $8 max) are cheaper than street parking. East of town, 4th St turns into Hwy 12 to Sonoma Valley.

FREE **Luther Burbank Home & Gardens** GARDENS
(☑707-524-5445; www.lutherburbank.org; ☺8am-dusk) Pioneering horticulturist Luther Burbank (1849–1926) developed many hybrid plant species at his 19th-century Greek-revival home, at Santa Rosa and Sonoma Aves, including the Shasta daisy. The extensive gardens are lovely. The house and adjacent **Carriage Museum** (guided tour adult/child $7/free, self-guided cell-phone tour free ☺10am-3:30pm Tue-Sun Apr-Oct) have displays on Burbank's life and work. Across the street from Burbank's home, Julliard Park has a playground.

OLIVE-OIL TASTING

When you weary of wine tasting, pop in to one of the following olive-oil mills (all free except Round Pond) and dip some crusty bread. The harvest and pressing happen in November.

» **BR Cohn** (p205)
» **Long Meadow Ranch** (p167)
» **Round Pond** (p166) Ninety-minute mill tour and tasting $25.
» **Figone's Olive Oil** (p191)

Charles M Schulz Museum — MUSEUM

(✆707-579-4452; www.schulzmuseum.org; 2301 Hardies Lane; adult/child $10/5; ◷11am-5pm Mon-Fri, 10am-5pm Sat & Sun, closed Tue Sep-May; ♿) Charles Schulz, creator of *Peanuts* cartoons, was a long-term Santa Rosa resident. Born in 1922, he published his first drawing in 1937, introduced the world to Snoopy and Charlie Brown in 1950, and produced Peanuts cartoons until just before his death in 2000.

At the museum a glass wall overlooks a courtyard with a Snoopy labyrinth. Exhibits include Peanuts-related art and Schulz's actual studio. Skip Snoopy's Gallery gift shop; the museum has the good stuff.

Redwood Empire Ice Arena — SKATING

(✆707-546-7147; www.snoopyshomeice.com; adult/child incl skates $12/10; ♿) This skating rink was formerly owned and deeply loved by Schulz. It's open most afternoons (call for schedules). Bring a sweater.

Farmers Markets — MARKET

Sonoma County's largest farmers market meets Wednesday, 5pm to 8:30pm, mid-May through August, at 4th and B Sts. A year-round market meets Saturdays at the Santa Rosa Veterans Building, 8:30am to 1pm, 1351 Maple Ave.

🛏 Sleeping

Look for hotels near Railroad Square. Nothing-special motels line Cleveland Ave, fronting Hwy 101's western side, between Steele Lane and Bicentennial Lane exits; skip the Motel 6. Also consider nearby Windsor, which has two chain hotels off Hwy 101 at the Central Windsor exit.

Hotel La Rose — HISTORIC HOTEL $$

(✆707-579-3200; www.hotellarose.com; 308 Wilson St; r weekday/weekend $129-189/$199-219; ❋🛜) At Railroad Sq, this charming 1907 hotel has rooms with marble baths, sitting areas with thick carpeting and wing chairs, and supercomfy mattresses with feather beds. Great for a moderate splurge. Rooftop hot tub.

Vintners Inn — INN $$$

(✆707-575-7350, 800-421-2584; www.vintnersinn.com; 4350 Barnes Rd; r $225-495; ❋@🛜) Built in the 1980s, Vintners Inn sits on the rural outskirts of town (near River Rd) and appeals to the gated-community crowd. Rooms' amenities are business-class fancy.

Jacuzzi, but no pool. Check for last-minute specials.

Flamingo Resort Hotel — HOTEL $$

(✆707-545-8530, 800-848-8300; www.flamingoresort.com; 2777 4th St; r $99-219; ❋@🛜🛆♿) Sprawling over 11 acres, this mid-century modern hotel doubles as a conference center. Rooms are motel-generic, but what a gigantic pool – and it's 82 degrees year-round. Kids love it. On-site health-club and gym. Prices double summer weekends.

Hillside Inn — MOTEL $

(✆707-546-9353; www.hillside-inn.com; 2901 4th St, Santa Rosa; s/d Nov-Mar $70/82, Apr-Oct $74/86; 🛜🛆♿) One of Santa Rosa's best-kept motels, Hillside is close to Sonoma Valley; add $4 for kitchens. Furnishings are dated, but everything is scrupulously maintained. Adjoins an excellent breakfast cafe.

Best Western Garden Inn — MOTEL $$

(✆707-546-4031, 888-256-8004; www.thegardeninn.com; 1500 Santa Rosa Ave; r $119-149; ❋@🛜🛆♿) Book a room in back for quiet, up front for privacy, at this well-kept cookie-cutter motel, south of downtown. The street gets seedy by night, but the hotel is secure, clean and comfortable.

Spring Lake Park — CAMPGROUND $

(✆707-539-8092, reservations 707-565-2267; www.sonoma-county.org/parks; 5585 Newanga Ave; sites $28; ◷daily May-Sep, weekends only Oct-Apr; 🛆) Lovely lakeside park, 4 miles from downtown; make reservations ($7 fee) 10am to 3pm weekdays. The park is open year-round, with lake swimming in summer; campground operates May to September, weekends October to April. Take 4th St eastbound, turn right on Farmer's Lane, pass the first Hoen St and turn left on the *second* Hoen St, then left on Newanga Ave.

Best Western Wine Country Inn & Suites — HOTEL $$

(✆707-545-9000, 800-780-7234; www.winecountryhotel.com; 870 Hopper Ave; r weekday/weekends $120/170; ❋@🛜🛆🛆) Generic chain hotel, off Cleveland Ave.

Sandman Hotel — MOTEL $

(✆707-544-8570; www.sandmansantarosa.com; 3421 Cleveland Ave; $83-102 ❋🛜🛆) Cleveland Ave's reliable budget choice.

✕ Eating

TOP CHOICE Zazu
CALIFORNIAN, ITALIAN $$

(☏707-523-4814; 3535 Guerneville Rd, Santa Rosa; brunch mains $11-15, dinner mains $18-26; ⊙5:30-8:30pm Wed-Mon, 9am-2pm Sun) The cooking at Zazu is an expression of the land: if it's in the garden, it's on the plate. Husband-and-wife team Duske Estes and John Stewart use only local ingredients from within 30 miles of their little roadhouse restaurant, 10 miles west of downtown Santa Rosa. John raises heirloom pigs, which he transforms into gorgeous salumi. Duske fashions homemade pasta, using eggs from their own hens. Dishes skew Italian-country, using few ingredients that let the dynamic flavors sparkle. One of Sonoma's top tables for seasonal-regional cooking. Great brunch, too. Wednesday, Thursday and Sunday are pizza-and-pinot nights, with wine flights paired for pizza. For true farm-to-table cooking, don't miss Zazu.

Rosso Pizzeria & Wine Bar
PIZZERIA $$

(☏707-544-3221; 53 Montgomery St, Creekside Shopping Centre; pizzas $12-15; ⊙11am-10pm; ✦) Crispy brick-oven pizzas – some of NorCal's best – along with inventive salads and a standout wine list make Rosso worth seeking out.

🍴 Jeffrey's Hillside Cafe
AMERICAN $

(www.jeffreyshillsidecafe.com; 2901 4th St; dishes $8-12; ⊙7am-2pm; ✦) East of downtown, near the top of Sonoma Valley, chef-owned Jeffrey's is excellent for breakfast or brunch before wine tasting.

Taqueria Las Palmas
MEXICAN $

(☏707-546-3091; 415 Santa Rosa Ave; dishes $4-7; ⊙9am-9pm; ✦) For Mexican, this is the real deal, with standout *carnitas* (barbecued pork), homemade salsas and veggie burritos.

Pho Vietnam
VIETNAMESE $

(☏707-571-7687; No 8, 711 Stony Point Rd; dishes $6-8; ⊙10am-8:30pm Mon-Sat, to 7:30pm Sun) Fantastic noodle bowls and rice plates at a hole-in-the-wall shopping-center restaurant, just off Hwy 12, west of downtown.

Willi's Wine Bar
TAPAS $$$

(☏707-526-3096; www.williswinebar.net; dishes $10-15; ⊙11am-9:30pm Wed-Sat, 5-9pm Sun & Mon) Stellar small plates.

Traverso's Gourmet Foods
DELI $

(☏707-542-2530; www.traversos.com; 2097 Stagecoach Rd; ⊙10am-6pm Mon-Sat) Excellent Italian deli and wine shop.

Mac's Delicatessen
DELI $

(☏707-545-3785; 630 4th St; dishes under $10; ⊙7am-5pm Mon-Fri, 7am-4pm Sat) Downtown Kosher-style deli.

🍷 Drinking

Third Street Aleworks
BREWERY

(thirdstreetaleworks.com; 610 3rd St; ☎) This giant brew pub gets packed weekends and game days. Great garlic fries and half-a-dozen pool tables.

🍴 Aroma Roasters
CAFE

(www.aromaroasters.com; 95 5th St, Railroad Sq; ☎) Town's hippest café; serves no booze; acoustic music Friday and Saturday evenings.

Russian River Brewing Co
BREWERY

(www.russianriverbrewing.com; 729 4th St) Locally crafted brews.

ℹ Information

Aroma Roasters (☏707-576-7765, 95 5th St, Railroad Sq; per 15min $1.50; ⊙6am-11pm Mon-Thu, 7am-midnight Fri & Sat, 7am-10pm Sun; @☎) Internet access. No electrical outlets for laptops.

California Welcome Center & Santa Rosa Visitors Bureau (☏707-577-8674, 800-404-7673; www.visitsantarosa.com; 9 4th St; ⊙9am-5pm Mon-Sat, 10am-5pm Sun) At Railroad Sq, west of Hwy 101; take the downtown Santa Rosa exit off Hwy 12 or Hwy 101.

Santa Rosa Memorial Hospital (☏707-935-5000; 347 Andrieux St)

Healdsburg

Once a sleepy ag town best known for its Future Farmers of America parade, Healdsburg has emerged as northern Sonoma County's culinary capital. Foodie-scenester restaurants and cafes, wine-tasting rooms and fancy boutiques line Healdsburg Plaza, the town's sun-dappled central square (bordered by Healdsburg Ave and Center, Matheson and Plaza Sts). Traffic grinds to a halt summer weekends, when second-home-owners and tourists jam downtown. Old-timers aren't happy with the Napa-style gentrification, but at least Healdsburg retains its historic look, if not its once-quiet summers. It's best visited weekdays – stroll tree-lined streets, sample locavore cooking and soak up the NorCal flavor.

◉ Sights

Tasting rooms surround the plaza. Free summer concerts play Tuesday afternoons.

Healdsburg Museum
MUSEUM

(☎707-431-3325; www.healdsburgmuseum.org; 221 Matheson St; donation requested; ◷11am-4pm Thu-Sun) East of the plaza, worth a visit for a glimpse of Healdsburg's past. Exhibits include compelling installations on northern Sonoma County history. Pick up a walking-tour pamphlet.

Locals Tasting Room
TASTING ROOM

(Map p194; ☎707-857-4900; www.tastelocalwines.com; tastings free; Geyserville Ave & Hwy 128; ◷10am-6pm) Eight miles north, photo-ready one-block-long Geyserville is home to this indie tasting room, which represents ten small-production wineries.

Farmers Markets
MARKET

(www.healdsburgfarmersmarket.org) Meet locals and discover the region's agricultural abundance at the **Tuesday market** (cnr Vine & North Sts; ◷4-7pm Tue Jun-Oct) and **Saturday market** (one block west of the plaza; ◷9am-noon Sat May-Nov).

🏃 Activities

The more active you are in Healdsburg, the more you can eat. After you've walked around the plaza, there isn't much to do in town. Go wine tasting in Dry Creek Valley (p196) or Russian River Valley (p194). Bicycling on winding West Dry Creek Rd is brilliant, as is paddling the Russian River, which runs through town. You can swim at **Healdsburg Veterans Memorial Beach** (Map p194; ☎707-433-1625; www.sonoma-county.org/parks; 13839 Healdsburg Ave; parking $7; 🅿); lifeguards are on duty daily in summer (call ahead). If you're squeamish, confirm current water quality online (www.sonoma-county.org/health/eh/russian_river.htm).

Russian River Adventures
CANOEING

(Map p194; ☎707-433-5599; www.rradventures.info; 20 Healdsburg Ave; adult/child $50/25; 🅿🚼) Paddle a secluded stretch of river, in quiet inflatable canoes, stopping for rope swings, swimming holes, gravel beaches, and bird-watching. This ecotourism outfit points you in the right direction and shuttles you back at day's end. Or they'll guide your kids

downriver while you go wine-tasting (guides $120/day). Self-guided departures leave 10am sharp; reservations required.

Getaway Adventures
CYCLING, KAYAKING

(☎707-763-3040, 800-499-2453; www.getaway adventures.com) Guides spectacular morning vineyard cycling in Dry Creek Valley, followed by lunch and optional kayaking on Russian River ($150 to $175).

River's Edge Kayak & Canoe Trips
BOATING

(Map p194; ☎707-433-7247; www.riversedgekay akandcanoe.com; 13840 Healdsburg Ave) Rents hard-sided canoes ($70/85 per half/full day) and kayaks ($40/55). Self-guided rentals include shuttle. Guided trips – by reservation – originate upriver in Alexander Valley, and end in town.

Healdsburg Spoke Folk Cyclery
BICYCLE RENTAL

(☎707-433-7171; www.spokefolk.com; 201 Center St) Rents touring, racing and tandem bicycles. Great service.

Relish Culinary Adventures
COOKING COURSE

(☎707-431-9999, 877-759-1004; www.relishculi nary.com; 14 Matheson St; ◷by appointment) Plug into the locavore food scene with culinary day trips, demo-kitchen classes or winemaker dinners.

✨ Festivals & Events

Russian River Wine Road Barrel Tasting
WINE

(www.wineroad.com) March

Future Farmers Parade
CULTURAL

(www.healdsburgfair.org) May

Wine & Food Affair
FOOD

(www.wineroad.com/events) November

🛏 Sleeping

Healdsburg is expensive and demand exceeds supply. Rates drop winter to spring, but not by that much. Guerneville (p202) is much less expensive, and only 20 minutes away.

Most Healdsburg inns are within walking distance of the plaza; several B&Bs are in surrounding countryside. Two older motels lie south of the plaza, two to the north at Hwy 101's Dry Creek exit.

Hotel Healdsburg
HOTEL $$$

(☎707-431-2800, 800-889-7188; www.hotelhealds burg.com; 25 Matheson St; r incl breakfast $335-585; 🅿@🛜🏊) Smack on the plaza, the chic

HH has a coolly minimalist style. Wear Armani and blend in. The ultracushy rooms, all hard angles and muted colors, have delicious beds and extra-deep tubs. Downstairs there's a full-service spa.

🌿 H2 Hotel
HOTEL **$$$**

(☎707-431-2202, 707-922-5251; www.h2hotel.com; 219 Healdsburg Ave; r incl breakfast weekday $255-455, weekend $355-555; ❀@🛜⊛) Little sister to Hotel Healdsburg, H2 has the same angular concrete style, but was built LEED-gold-certified from the ground up, with a living roof, reclaimed everything, and fresh-looking rooms with cush organic linens. Tiny pool, free bikes.

Madrona Manor
HISTORIC INN **$$$**

(Map p194; ☎707-433-4231, 800-258-4003; www.madronamanor.com; 1001 Westside Rd; r & ste $270-390; ❀🛜⊛) The first choice of lovers of country inns and stately manor homes, the regal 1881 Madrona Manor exudes Victorian elegance. Surrounded by eight acres of woods and gorgeous century-old gardens, the hilltop mansion is decked out with many original furnishings. A mile west of downtown, it's convenient to Westside Rd wineries.

Belle de Jour Inn
B&B **$$$**

(Map p194; ☎707-431-9777; www.belledejourinn.com; 16276 Healdsburg Ave; r $225-295, ste $355; ❀🛜) Belle de Jour's sunny, uncomplicated, lovely rooms have American-country furnishings, with extras like sun-dried sheets, hammocks and CD players. The manicured gardens are perfect for a moonlight tryst.

Healdsburg Inn on the Plaza
INN **$$$**

(☎707-433-6991, 800-431-8663; www.healdsburginn.com; 110 Matheson St; r $295-375; ❀🛜⊛) The spiffy, clean-lined rooms, conservatively styled in khaki and beige, feel bourgeois summer-house casual, with fine linens and gas fireplaces; some have jetted double tubs. The plaza-front location explains the price.

Best Western Dry Creek Inn
MOTEL **$$**

(Map p194; ☎707-433-0300, 800-222-5784; www.drycreekinn.com; 198 Dry Creek Rd, Healdsburg; weekday/weekend r $59-129/199-259; ❀@🛜⊛) Town's top motel has good service and an outdoor hot tub. New rooms have jetted tubs and gas fireplaces. Check for weekday discounts.

Geyserville Inn
MOTEL **$$**

(Map p194; ☎707-857-4343, 877-857-4343; www.geyservilleinn.com; 21714 Geyserville Ave, Geyserville; r weekday $119-169, weekend $189-249; ❀🛜⊛) Eight miles north of Healdsburg, this immaculately kept upmarket motel is surrounded by vineyards. Rooms have unexpectedly smart furnishings, like overstuffed side chairs and fluffy feather pillows. Request a remodeled room. Hot tub.

Honor Mansion
INN **$$$**

(☎707-433-4277, 800-554-4667; www.honormansion.com; 891 Grove St; r incl breakfast $300-550; ❀🛜) Victorian mansion c 1883; spectacular grounds.

Camellia Inn
B&B **$$$**

(☎707-433-8182, 800-727-8182; www.camelliainn.com; 211 North St; r $139-329; ❀🛜⊛) Italianate 1869 house; one room accommodates families.

George Alexander House
B&B **$$$**

(☎707-433-1358, 800-310-1358; www.georgealexanderhouse.com; 423 Matheson St; r $180-350; ❀🛜) Queen Anne c 1905, with Victorian and Asian antiques; also a sauna.

Haydon Street Inn
B&B **$$$**

(☎707-433-5228, 800-528-3703; www.haydon.com; 321 Haydon St; r $195-325, cottage $425; ❀🛜) Two-story Queen Anne with big front porch and cottage out back.

Piper Street Inn
INN **$$$**

(☎707-433-8721, 877-703-0370; www.piperstreetinn.com; 402 Piper St; r $195-265; ❀🛜⊛) Two rooms: homey bedroom, garden cottage.

L&M Motel
MOTEL **$$**

(Map p194; ☎707-433-6528; www.landmmotel.com; 70 Healdsburg Ave, Healdsburg; r incl breakfast $100-140; ⊛❀🛜) Simple, clean old-fashioned motel; big lawns and barbecue grills, great for families. Dry sauna and Jacuzzi.

Cloverdale Wine Country KOA
CAMPGROUND **$**

(☎707-894-3337, 800-368-4558; www.winecountrykoa.com; 1166 Asti Ridge Rd, Cloverdale; tent/RV sites from $42/60, 1-/2-bedroom cabins $80/90; 🛜⊛) Six miles from Central Cloverdale exit off Hwy 101; hot showers, pool, hot tub, laundry, paddleboats and bicycles.

🍴 Eating

Healdsburg is the gastronomic capital of Sonoma County. Your hardest decision will be choosing where to eat. Reservations essential.

Cyrus
FRENCH-CALIFORNIAN $$$

(☎707-433-3311; www.cyrusrestaurant.com; 29 North St, Healdsburg; fixed-price menu $102-130; ☺dinner Thu-Mon, lunch Sat) Napa's venerable French Laundry has stiff competition in swanky Cyrus, an ultrachic dining room in the great tradition of the French country auberge. The emphasis is on luxury foods, expertly prepared with a French sensibility and flavored with global spices, as in the signature Thai marinated lobster. The staff moves as if in a ballet, ever intuitive of your pace and tastes. From the caviar cart to the cheese course, Cyrus is a meal to remember.

TOP CHOICE Madrona Manor
CALIFORNIAN $$$

(Map p194; ☎707-433-4231, 800-258-4003; www.madronamanor.com; 1001 Westside Rd; 4-/5-/6-course menu $73/82/91; ☺6-9pm Wed-Sun) You'd be hard-pressed to find a lovelier place to pop the question than this retro-formal Victorian mansion's garden-view veranda – though there's nothing old-fashioned about the artful Californian haute cuisine: the kitchen churns its own butter, each course comes with a different variety of still-warm house-baked bread, lamb and cheese originate down the road, and deserts include ice cream flash-frozen tableside. Reserve a pre-sunset table.

Scopa
ITALIAN $$

(☎707-433-5282; www.scopahealdsburg.com; 109-A Plaza St, Healdsburg; mains $12-26; ☺5:30-10pm Tue-Sun) Space is tight inside this converted barbershop, but it's worth cramming in for perfect thin-crust pizza and rustic Italian home cooking, like Nonna's slow-braised chicken, with sautéed greens, melting into toasty polenta. A lively crowd and good wine prices create a convivial atmosphere.

Bovolo
ITALIAN, CAFE $$

(☎707-431-2962; www.bovolorestaurant.com; 106 Matheson St, Healdsburg; dishes $6-14; [☺9am-4pm Mon, Weds, Thu, 9am-8pm Tue, Fri, Sat, 9am-6pm Sun; ⊞) Fast food gets a slow-food spin at this order-at-the-counter Cal-Ital bistro – little sister to Zazu (p207) – that serves farm-fresh egg breakfasts, just-picked salads, and hand-thrown pizzas topped with house-cured meats from heirloom pigs. Sit outside and save room for hand-turned gelato. Enter through the bookstore.

Healdsburg Bar & Grill
PUB $$

(☎707-433-3333; www.healdsburgbarandgrill.com; 245 Healdsburg Ave; mains $9-15; ☺11:30am-9pm) Great when you're famished but don't want to fuss, HBG does gastropub cooking right – mac-n-cheese, pulled-pork sandwiches, top-end burgers and truffle-parmesan fries. Sit in the garden, or watch the game at the bar.

Zin
NEW AMERICAN $$

(☎707-473-0946; www.zinrestaurant.com; 344 Center St; lunch mains $10-20, dinner mains $76-27; ☺11:30am-2:30pm Mon-Fri, dinner nightly; ⊞) Reliable zin makes hearty Cal-American comfort food, designed to pair with zinfandel and other local varietals. Think pot roast and apple pie. Fun wine bar, good service.

Oakville Grocery
DELI $$

(☎707-433-3200; www.oakvillegrocery.com; 124 Matheson St; sandwiches $10; ☺8am-7pm) Luxurious smoked fish and caviar, fancy sandwiches and grab-and-go gourmet picnics. It's overpriced, but the plaza-view fireside terrace is ever-fun for scouting Botox blonds, while nibbling cheese and sipping vino.

Diavola
ITALIAN $$

(Map p194; ☎707-814-0111; www.diavolapizzera.com; 21021 Geyserville Ave, Geyserville; pizzas $12-15; ☺11:30am-9pm Wed-Mon; ⊞) Ideal for lunch while wine tasting in Alexander Valley, Diavola makes excellent salumi and thin-crust pizzas, served in an Old West brick-walled space, loud enough to drown out the kids.

Barndiva
CALIFORNIAN $$$

(☎707-431-0100; www.barndiva.com; 231 Center St; brunch mains $16-22, dinner mains $25-34; ☺noon-11pm Wed-Sun) Impeccable seasonal-regional cooking, happening bar, beautiful garden, but service sometimes misses.

Ravenous
NEW AMERICAN $$

(☎707-431-1770; www.theravenous.com; 420 Center St; mains $13-17) Chalkboard-scrawled menu, with California comfort cooking and excellent burgers, served (s-l-o-w-l-y) inside a former cottage. Sit outside with Healdsburg's hipper half. $10 corkage.

Flaky Cream Coffee Shop
DINER $

(☎707-433-3895; Healdsburg Shopping Center, 441 Center St; dishes $5-9; ☺6am-2pm) Bacon-and-egg breakfasts, yummy doughnuts.

Self-Catering

Dry Creek General Store
DELI $

(Map p194; ☎707-433-4171; www.dcgstore.com; 3495 Dry Creek Rd; sandwiches $8-10; ☺6am-6pm) Before wine tasting in Dry Creek Valley, make a pit stop at this vintage general store, where locals and bicyclists gather for coffee on the creaky front porch. Perfect picnics supplies include Toscano-salami-and-manchego sandwiches on chewy-dense ciabatta.

Jimtown Store — DELI $

(Map p194; 707-433-1212; www.jimtown.com; sandwiches $8-11; 6706 Hwy 128; ⊙7.30am-4pm) One of our favorite Alexander Valley stopovers, Jimtown is great for picnic supplies and sandwiches made with housemade condiment spreads.

Downtown Bakery & Creamery — BAKERY $

(707-431-2719; www.downtownbakery.net; 308a Center St; ⊙7am-5:30pm) Healdsburg's finest bakery makes scrumptious pastries.

Costeaux French Bakery & Cafe — BAKERY $

(707-433-1913; www.costeaux.com; 417 Healdsburg Ave; ⊙7am-4pm Mon-Sat, to 1pm Sun) Fresh bread and good boxed lunches.

Cheese Shop — CHEESE $

(707-433-4998; www.doraliceimports.com; 423 Center St; ⊙Mon-Fri 11am-6pm, Sat 10am-6pm) Top-notch imported and local cheeses.

Shelton's Natural Foods — MARKET, DELI $

(707-431-0530; www.sheltonsmarket.com; 428 Center S; ⊙8am-8pm) Indie alternative for groceries and picnic supplies more reasonably priced than Oakville Grocery.

🍷 Drinking & Entertainment

Flying Goat Coffee — CAFE

(www.flyinggoatcoffee.com; 324 Center St; ⊙7am-6pm) See ya later, Starbucks. Flying Goat is what coffee should be – fair-trade and house-roasted – and locals line up for it every morning.

Bear Republic Brewing Company — BREWERY

(www.bearrepublic.com; 345 Healdsburg Ave; ⊙11:30am-late) Bear Republic features handcrafted award-winning ales, non-award-winning pub grub and live music weekends.

Barndiva — COCKTAIL BAR

(707-431-0100; www.barndiva.com; 231 Center St; ⊙noon-11pm Wed-Sun) Swanky seasonal cocktails, like blood-orange margaritas, with a pretty crowd.

Raven Theater & Film Center — THEATER

(707-433-5448; www.raventheater.com; 115 N Main St) Hosts concerts, events and first-run art-house films.

🛍 Shopping

Arboretum — CLOTHING

(707-433-7033; www.arboretumapparel.com; 332 Healdsburg Ave; ⊙Wed-Mon) Lending fresh meaning to 'fashion-conscious,' this eco-boutique features fair trade and US designers, with great finds like organic-cotton pants for men and ultra-soft bamboo-fiber cardigans for gals.

Jimtown Store — GIFTS

(Map p194; 707-433-1212; www.jimtown.com; 6706 Hwy 128) Forage antique bric-a-brac, candles and Mexican oilcloths at this roadside deli and store in Alexander Valley.

Baksheesh — GIFTS, HOMEWARES

(707-473-0880; www.baksheeshfairtrade.com; 106B Matheson St) Household goods with a global outlook: everything sourced from fair-trade collectives, from Alpaca shawls to Vietnamese trivets.

Gardener — HOMEWARES

(Map p194; 707-431-1063; www.thegardener.com; 516 Dry Creek Rd) Garden-shop lovers; don't miss this rural beauty.

Studio Barndiva — GIFTS, HOMEWARES

(707-431-7404; www.studiobarndiva; 237 Center St) Reclaimed ephemera never looked so chic: thousand-dollar *objets d'art*.

Copperfield's Books — BOOKS

(707-433-9270; copperfieldsbooks.com; 104 Matheson St) Good general-interest books.

Levin & Company — BOOKS, MUSIC

(707-433-1118; 306 Center St) Fiction and CDs; co-op art gallery.

ℹ Information

Healdsburg Chamber of Commerce & Visitors Bureau (707-433-6935, 800-648-9922; www.healdsburg.org; 217 Healdsburg Ave; ⊙9am-5pm Mon-Fri, to 3pm Sat, 10am-2pm Sun) A block south of the plaza. Has winery maps and information on hot-air ballooning, golf, tennis, spas and nearby farms (get the *Farm Trails* brochure); 24-hour walk-up booth.

Healdsburg Public Library (707-433-3772; www.sonoma.lib.ca.us; cnr Piper & Center Sts; ⊙10am-6pm Mon & Wed, to 8pm Tue & Thu-Sat; @⊕) One-hour free internet access (bring ID). Wine Country's leading oenology-reference library.

NAPA & SONOMA WINE COUNTRY HEALDSBURG

North Coast & Redwoods

Best Places to Eat

» Café Beaujolais (p227)

» Six Rivers Brewery (p256)

» Ravens (p227)

» Franny's Cup & Saucer (p222)

» Table 128 (p237)

Best Places to Stay

» Mar Vista (p220)

» Victorian Gardens (p222)

» Apple Farm (p236)

» Andiron (p225)

» Redwood National Park (p260)

Why Go?

The craggy cliffs, towering redwoods and windswept bluffs of the north have little in common with California's other coastline. This is no Beach Boys' song; there are no bikinis and few surfboards. The jagged edge of the continent is wild, scenic and even slightly foreboding, where spectral fog and outsider spirit have fostered the world's tallest trees, most potent weed and a string of idiosyncratic two-stoplight towns. Visitors explore hidden coves with a blanket and bottle of local wine, scan the horizon for migrating whales and retreat at night to fire-warmed Victorians. The further north you travel on the region's winding two-lane blacktop, the more dominant the landscape becomes, with valleys of redwood, wide rivers and mossy, overgrown forests. Befitting this dramatic clash of land and water are its unlikely mélange of residents: timber barons and tree huggers, pot farmers and political radicals of every stripe.

When to Go
Eureka

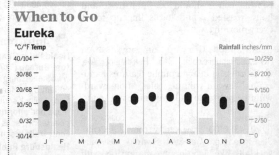

Jun–Jul The driest season in the Redwoods is spectacular for day hikes and big views.

Aug–Oct Warm weather and clear (or clearer) skies are the best for hiking the Lost Coast.

Dec–Apr Whales migrate off the coast. In early spring look for mothers and calves.

Getting Around

Although Hwy 1 is popular with cyclists and there are bus connections, you will almost certainly need a car to explore this region. Those headed to the far north and on a schedule should take Hwy 101, the faster, inland route and then cut over to the coast. Windy Hwy 1 hugs the coast, then cuts inland and ends at Leggett, where it joins Hwy 101. Neither Amtrak nor Greyhound serve cities on coastal Hwy 1.

Amtrak (📞800-872-7245; www.amtrakcalifornia.com) operates the *Coast Starlight* between Los Angeles and Seattle (see p776). From LA, buses connect to several North Coast towns including Leggett ($82, 11 hours, two daily) and Garberville ($84, 11½ hours, two daily).

Brave souls willing to piece together bus travel through the region will face a time-consuming headache, but connections are possible to almost every town in the region. **Greyhound** (📞800-231-2222; www.greyhound.com) runs buses from San Francisco to Santa Rosa ($22, 1¾ hours, one daily), Ukiah, ($40, three hours, one daily) Willits ($40, 3½ hours, one daily), Rio Dell (near Fortuna, $52.50, six hours, one daily), Eureka ($52.50, 6¾ hours, one daily) and Arcata ($52.20, seven hours, one daily). In Santa Rosa, **Golden Gate Transit** (📞707-541-2000; www.goldengatetransit.org) bus 80 serves San Rafael ($5.55, 1½ hours) and San Francisco ($8.80, 1¼ hours, 19 times daily), **Sonoma County Transit** (📞800-345-7433; www.sctransit.com) serves Sonoma County, and **Sonoma County Airport Express** (📞707-837-8700, 800-327-2024; www.airportexpressinc.com) operates buses to San Francisco ($32, 2¼ hours, 15 daily) and Oakland ($34, 2¼ hours, 10 daily) airports.

The **Mendocino Transit Authority** (MTA; 📞707-462-1422, 800-696-4682; www.4mta.org; fares $3.25-7.75) operates bus 65, which travels between Mendocino, Fort Bragg, Willits, Ukiah and Santa Rosa daily, with an afternoon return. Bus 95 runs between Point Arena and Santa Rosa, via Jenner, Bodega Bay and Sebastopol. Bus 54 connects Ukiah and Hopland on weekdays. Bus 75 heads north every weekday from Gualala to the Navarro River junction at Hwy 128, then runs inland through the Anderson Valley to Ukiah, returning in the afternoon. The North Coast route goes north from Navarro River junction to Albion, Little River, Mendocino and Fort Bragg, Monday to Friday. The best long distance option is a daily ride from Fort Bragg south to Santa Rosa via Willits and Ukiah ($21, three hours).

North of Mendocino County, the **Redwood Transit System** (📞707-443-0826; www.hta.org) operates buses ($2.75) Monday through Saturday between Scotia and Trinidad (2½ hours), stopping en route at Eureka (1¼ hours) and Arcata (1½ hours). **Redwood Coast Transit** (📞707-464-9314; www.redwoodcoasttransit.org) runs buses Monday to Saturday between Crescent City, Klamath ($1.50, one hour, five daily) and Arcata ($25, two hours, three time daily), with numerous stops along the way.

FAST FACTS

» **Population of Mendocino** 1000

» **Average temperature low/high in Mendocino** Jan 47/60°F, Jul 50/71°F

» **Mendocino to San Francisco** 155 miles, 3¼ hours

» **Mendocino to Los Angeles** 530 miles, nine hours

» **Mendocino to Eureka** 145 miles, three hours

COASTAL HIGHWAY 1

Down south it's called the 'PCH,' or Pacific Coast Hwy, but North Coast locals simply call it 'Hwy 1.' However you label it, get ready for a fabulous coastal drive, which cuts a winding course on isolated cliffs high above the crashing surf. Compared to the famous Big Sur coast, the serpentine stretch of Hwy 1 up the North Coast is more challenging, more remote and more *real*; passing farms, fishing towns and hidden beaches. Drivers use roadside pull-outs to scan the hazy Pacific horizon for migrating whales and explore a coastline dotted with rock formations that are relentlessly pounded by the surf. The drive between Bodega Bay and Fort Bragg takes four hours of daylight driving without stops. At night in the fog, it takes steely nerves and much, much longer. The most popular destination is the cliffside charmer of Mendocino.

Considering their proximity to the Bay Area, Sonoma and Mendocino counties remain unspoiled, and the austere coastal bluffs are some of the most spectacular in the country. But the trip north gets more rewarding and remote with every mile. By the time Hwy 1 cuts inland to join Hwy 101, the land along the Pacific – called the Lost Coast – the highway disappears and offers the state's best-preserved natural gifts.

Coastal accommodations (including campgrounds) can fill from Memorial Day to Labor Day and on fall weekends, and often require two-night stays, so reserve ahead. Try to visit

North Coast & Redwoods Highlights

1 Explore the largest stands of old growth redwood in **Humboldt Redwoods State Park** (p247)

2 Hike the remote and wild **Lost Coast** (p245)

3 Backpack under giants along **Redwood Creek** (p260)

4 Find a hidden cove on the **Sonoma Coast** (p217)

5 Get pampered at **Mendocino's B&Bs** (p225)

6 Drink the sampler at **Six Rivers Brewery** (p256), NorCal's best brewpub

7 Rent a canoe to float down the **Big River** (p225)

8 Visit immaculate botanical gardens in **Fort Bragg** (p229)

9 Tour the vineyards of the **Anderson Valley** (p236)

10 Stay at **Mar Vista** (p220), a plush and sustainable retreat

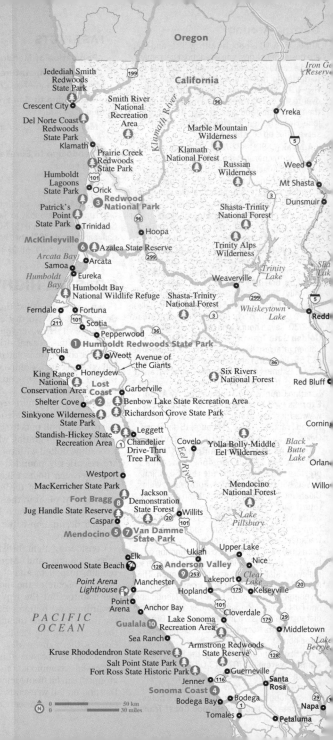

during spring or fall, especially in September and October; when the fog lifts, the ocean sparkles and most other visitors have gone home.

Bodega Bay

Bodega Bay is the first pearl in a string of sleepy fishing towns that line the North Coast and was the setting of Hitchcock's terrifying 1963 avian psycho-horror flick *The Birds*. The skies are free from bloodthirsty gulls today (though you best keep an eye on the picnic); it's Bay Area weekenders who descend en masse for extraordinary beaches, tide pools, whale-watching, fishing, surfing and seafood. Mostly a few restaurants, hotels and shops on both sides of Hwy 1, the downtown is not made for strolling, but it is a great base for exploring the endless nearby coves of the Sonoma Coast State Beach (p217).

Originally inhabited by the Pomo people, the bay takes its name from Juan Francisco de la Bodega y Quadra, captain of the Spanish sloop *Sonora,* which entered the bay in 1775. The area was then settled by Russians in the early 19th century, and farms were established to grow wheat for the Russian fur-trapping empire, which stretched from Alaska all the way down the coast to Fort Ross. The Russians pulled out in 1842, abandoning fort and farms, and American settlers moved in.

Hwy 1 runs through town and along the east side of Bodega Bay. On the west side, a peninsula resembling a crooked finger juts out to sea, forming the entrance to Bodega Harbor.

Sights & Activities

Surfing, beach combing and sportfishing are the main activities here – the latter requires advance booking. From December to April, the fishing boats host whale-watching trips, which are also good to book ahead. The excellent *Farm Trails* (www.farmtrails.org) guide at the Sonoma Coast Visitor Center has suggestions for tours of local ranches, orchards, farms and apiaries.

Bodega Head LOOKOUT
At the peninsula's tip, Bodega Head rises 265ft above sea level. To get there (and see the open ocean), head west from Hwy 1 onto Eastshore Rd, then turn right at the stop sign onto Bay Flat Rd. It's great for whale-watching. Landlubbers enjoy hiking above the surf, where several good trails include a 3.75-mile trek to Bodega Dunes Campground and a 2.2-mile walk to Salmon Creek Ranch. Candy & Kites (10am-5pm) is right along Hwy 1 in the middle of town – you can't miss it – selling kites to take advantage of all that wind.

Bodega Marine Laboratory & Reserve SCIENCE CENTER
(707-875-2211; www.bml.ucdavis.edu; 2099 Westside Rd; admission free; 2-4pm Fri) Run by University of California (UC) Davis, this spectacularly diverse teaching and research reserve surrounds the functioning research lab, which has studied Bodega Bay since the 1920s. The 263-acre reserve hosts many marine environments, including rocky intertidal coastal areas, mudflats and sandflats, salt marsh, sand dunes and freshwater wetlands. On most Friday afternoons docents give tours of the lab and its aquaria.

Ren Brown Collection Gallery GALLERY
(www.renbrown.com; 1781 Hwy 1; 10am-5pm Wed-Sun) The renowned collection of modern Japanese prints and California works at this small gallery is a tranquil escape from the elements.

Chanslor Riding Stables HORSEBACK RIDING
(707-875-3333; www.chanslor.com; 2660 Hwy 1, group rides $40-125) Just north of town, this friendly outfit leads horseback expeditions along the coastline and the rolling inland hills. Ron, the trip leader, is an amiable, sun-weathered cowboy straight from central casting; he recommends taking the Salmon Creek ride or calling ahead for weather-permitting moonlight rides. The 90-minute beach rides are donation based, and support a horse rescue program. Overnight trips in simple platform tents, which are excellent for families, can also be arranged. If you book a ride, you can park your RV at the ranch for free.

Bodega Bay Sportfishing Center FISHING, WHALE-WATCHING
(707-875-3344; www.bodegacharters.com; 1410 Bay Flat Rd) Beside the Sandpiper Cafe, this outfit organizes full-day fishing trips ($135) and whale-watching excursions (three hours adult/child $35/25). It also sells bait, tackle and fishing licenses. Call ahead to ask about recent sightings.

BLOODTHIRSTY BIRDS OF BODEGA BAY

Bodega Bay has the enduring claim to fame as the setting for Alfred Hitchcock's *The Birds*. Although special effects radically altered the actual layout of the town, you still get a good feel for the supposed site of the farm owned by Mitch Brenner (played by Rod Taylor). The once-cozy Tides Restaurant, where much avian-caused havoc occurs in the movie, is still there but since 1962 it has been transformed into a vast restaurant complex. Venture 5 miles inland to the tiny town of Bodega and you'll find two icons from the film: the schoolhouse and the church. Both stand just as they did in the movie – a crow overhead may make the hair rise on your neck.

Coincidentally, right after production of *The Birds* began, a real-life bird attack occurred in Capitola, the sleepy seaside town south of Santa Cruz. Thousands of seagulls ran amok, destroying property and attacking people.

Bodega Bay Surf Shack   SURFING, KAYAKING
(www.bodegabaysurf.com; 1400 N Hwy 1; surfboards per day $15, kayaks per 4hr single/double $45/65 ⊙10am-6pm Mon-Fri, 9am-7pm Sat & Sun) If you want to get on the water, this easygoing one-stop shop has all kinds of rentals, lessons and good local information.

✦ Festivals & Events

Bodega Seafood, Art & Wine Festival   FOOD, WINE
(www.winecountryfestivals.com) In late August, this festival of food and drink brings together the best beer- and wine-makers of the area, tons of seafood and activities for kids.

Bodega Bay Fishermen's Festival   CULTURAL
(www.bbfishfest.org) At the end of April, this festival culminates in a blessing of the fleet, a flamboyant parade of vessels, an arts-and-crafts fair, kite-flying and feasting.

⊨ Sleeping

There's a wide spread of options – RV and tent camping, quaint motels and fancy hotels. All fill up early during peak seasons. Campers should consider heading just north of town to the state-operated sites.

Bodega Bay Lodge & Spa   LODGE $$$
(☎707-875-3525, 888-875-2250; www.bodegabaylodge.com; 103 Hwy 1; r $300-470; @🛜🐾) Bodega's plushest, this small oceanfront resort has indulgent accommodations and a price tag to match. There is an ocean-view swimming pool, a whirlpool and a state-of-the-art fitness club. In the evenings it hosts wine tastings. The more expensive rooms have commanding views, but all have balconies, high-thread-count sheets, feather pillows and the usual amenities of a full-service hotel. The other pluses on-site include a golf course, Bodega

Bay's best spa and a fine-dining restaurant, the **Duck Club** (☎707-875-3525; mains $16-37; ⊙7:30-11am & 6-9pm), which is the fanciest dining in town.

Bodega Harbor Inn   MOTEL $$
(☎707-875-3594; www.bodegaharborinn.com; 1345 Bodega Ave; r $90-155; 🛜🐾) Half a block inland from Hwy 1, surrounded by grassy lawns and furnished with both real and faux antiques, this modest blue-and-white shingled motel is the town's most economical option. Pets are allowed in some rooms for a fee of $15 plus a security deposit of $50. Freestanding cottages have BBQs.

Chanslor Guest Ranch   RANCH $$
(☎707-875-2721; www.chanslorranch.com; 2660 Hwy 1; furnished tents & eco-cabins $75-125, r $350) A mile north of town, this working horse ranch has three rooms and options for upscale camping. Wildlife programs and guided horse tours make this one sweet place, with sweeping vistas across open grasslands to the sea. If you take a horse ride, you can negotiate a great deal for camping in your own tent.

Sonoma County Regional Parks   CAMPGROUND $
(☎707-565-2267; www.sonoma-county.org/parks; tent 7 RV sites without hookups $30) There are a few walk-in sites at the **Doran Regional Park** (201 Doran Beach Rd), at the quiet Miwok Tent Campground, and **Westside Regional Park** (2400 Westshore Rd), which is best for RVs. It caters primarily to boaters and has windy exposures, beaches, hot showers, fishing and boat ramps. Both are heavily used. Excellent camping is also available at the Sonoma Coast State Beach (p217).

✖ Eating & Drinking

For the old-fashioned thrill of seafood by the docks there are two options: **Tides Wharf & Restaurant** (835 Hwy 1; breakfast $6-12, lunch $12-22, dinner $15-25; ⊙7:30am-9:30pm Mon-Thu, 7:30am-10pm Fri, 7am-10pm Sat, 7am-9:30pm Sun; ⊕) and **Lucas Wharf Restaurant & Bar** (595 Hwy 1; mains $14-25; ⊙11:30am- 9pm Mon-Fri, 11am-10pm Sat; ⊕). Both have views and similar menus of clam chowder, fried fish and coleslaw and markets for picnic supplies. Tides boasts a great fish market, though Lucas Wharf feels less like a factory. Don't be surprised if a bus pulls up outside either of them.

Spud Point Crab Company　　SEAFOOD $
(www.spudpointcrab.com; 1860 Bay Flat Rd; mains $4-10; ⊙9am-5pm Thu-Tue; ⊕) In the classic tradition of dockside crab shacks, Spud Point serves salty-sweet crab cocktails and *real* clam chowder, served at picnic tables overlooking the marina. Take Bay Flat Rd to get here.

Terrapin Creek Cafe & Restaurant　　CALIFORNIAN $$
(⊙707-875-2700, www.terrapincreekcafe.com; 1580 Eastshore Dr; mains $18-20; ⊙11am-2pm & 4:30-9pm Thu-Sun; ⊕) Bodega Bay's most exciting upscale restaurant is run by a husband-wife team who espouse the slow food movement and serve local dishes sourced from the surrounding area. Modest comfort-food offerings like the pulled pork sandwich are artfully executed, while the Dungeness crab salad is fresh, briny and perfect. Jazz and warm light complete the atmosphere.

Sandpiper Restaurant　　SEAFOOD $$
(www.sandpiperrestaurant.com; 1410 Bay Flat Rd; mains $13-26; ⊙8am-8pm Sun-Thu, to 8:30pm Fri & Sat) Popular with the locals, Sandpiper serves breakfast, straightforward seafood and chowder that can be ordered in a formidable 'Viking Bowl' (downing two of these wins you a free t-shirt).

Dog House　　AMERICAN $
(573 Hwy 1; dishes $5-9; ⊙11am-6pm) Load up on Vienna beef dogs, hand-cut fries and shakes made with hand-scooped ice cream. There's even a view.

Gourmet Au Bay　　WINE BAR $$
(⊙11am-6pm Thu-Tue) The back deck of this wine bar offers a salty breeze with local zinfandel.

ⓘ Information

Sonoma Coast Visitor Center (⊙707-875-3866; www.bodegabay.com; 850 Hwy 1; ⊙9am-5pm Mon-Thu & Sat, 9am-6pm Fri, 10am-5pm Sun) Opposite the Tides Wharf. The best reason to stop by is for a copy of the *North Coaster*, a small-press indie newspaper of essays and brilliant insight on local culture.

Sonoma Coast State Beach

Stretching 17 miles north from Bodega Head to Vista Trail, the glorious **Sonoma Coast State Beach** (⊙707-875-3483) is actually a series of beaches separated by several beautiful rocky headlands. Some beaches are tiny, hidden in little coves, while others stretch far and wide. Most of the beaches are connected by vista-studded coastal hiking trails that wind along the bluffs. Exploring this area makes an excellent day-long adventure, so bring a picnic. Be advised however: the surf is often too treacherous to wade, so keep an eye on children. While this system of beaches and parks has some camping, you can't just pitch a tent anywhere; most are for day-use only.

⊙ Sights & Activities

Beaches

The following beaches are listed from south to north.

Salmon Creek Beach　　BEACH
Situated around a lagoon, this has 2 miles of hiking and good waves for surfing.

Portuguese Beach & Schoolhouse Beach　　BEACH
Both are very easy to access and have sheltered coves between rocky outcroppings.

Duncan's Landing　　BEACH
Small boats unload near this rocky headland in the morning. A good place to spot wild flowers in the spring.

Shell Beach　　BEACH
A boardwalk and trail leads out to a stretch perfect for tide-pooling and beachcombing.

Goat Rock　　BEACH
Famous for its colony of harbor seals, lazing in the sun at the mouth of the Russian River.

🛏 Sleeping

Bodega Dunes　　CAMPGROUND $
(⊙800-444-7275; www.reserveamerica.com; 3095 Hwy 1, Bodega Bay; tent & RV sites $35, $8

day use) The largest campground in the Sonoma Coast State Beach system of parks, it is also closest to Bodega Bay. It gets a lot of use. Sites are in high dunes and have hot showers but be warned – the fog horn sounds all night.

Wright's Beach Campground CAMPGROUND $

(☏800-444-7275; www.reserveamerica.com; tent & RV sites $35, $8 day use) Of the few parks that allow camping along Sonoma Coast State Beach, this is the best, even though sites lack privacy. Sites can be booked six months in advance, and numbers 1–12 are right on the beach. There are BBQ pits for day use and it's a perfect launch for sea kayakers. Everyone else, stay out of the water; according to camp hosts the treacherous rip tides claim a life every season.

Willow Creek Environmental Campground CAMPGROUND $

(tent sites $20) The beautiful environmental campground is under a cathedral-like grove of second-growth redwoods on Willow Creek Rd, inland from Hwy 1 on the southern side of the Russian River Bridge. To reach the sites, walk the Pomo Canyon trail and emerge into wildflower-studded meadows with exquisite views of the Russian River and vistas that extend south as far as Pt Reyes on a clear day. Note that Willow Creek has no running water, though it is possible to filter water from the river. It is usually open April to November.

Jenner

Perched on the hills looking out to the Pacific and above the mouth of the Russian River, tiny Jenner offers access to the coast and the Russian River wine region (see p193). A harbor-seal colony sits at the river's mouth and pups are born here from March to August. There are restrictions about getting too close to the chubby, adorable pups – handling them can be dangerous and cause the pups to be abandoned by their mothers. Volunteers answer questions along the roped-off area where day trippers can look on at a distance. The best way to see them is by kayak and most of the year you will find a truck renting kayaks at the rivers edge. Heading north on Hwy 1 you will begin driving on one of the most beautiful, windy stretches of California highway. You'll also probably lose cell-phone service – possibly a blessing.

🛏 Sleeping & Eating

Jenner Inn & Cottages INN $$

(☏707-865-2377; www.jennerinn.com; 10400 Hwy 1; r incl breakfast creekside $118-178, ocean-view $178-278, cottages $228-278; @) It's difficult to sum up this collection of properties dispersed throughout Jenner – some are in fairly deluxe ocean-view cottages with kitchen and ready-to-light fireplaces, others are small upland near a creek. All have the furnishings of a stylish auntie from the early 1990s.

TOP CHOICE River's End CALIFORNIAN $$$

(☏707-865-2484; www.rivers-end.com; 11048 Hwy 1; lunch mains $13-26, dinner mains $25-39; ⊙noon-3pm & 5-8:30pm Thu-Mon; 🖉) Unwind in style at this picture-perfect restaurant, perched on a cliff overlooking the river's mouth and the grand sweep of the Pacific Ocean. It serves world-class meals at world-class prices, but the real reward is the view. Its ocean-view cottages (r & cottages $120-200) are wood paneled and have no TVs, wi-fi or phones. Children under 12 are not recommended.

Café Aquatica CAFE $

(www.cafeaquatica.com; 11048 Hwy 1; sandwiches $10-13; 🛜) This is the kind of North Coast coffee shop you've been dreaming of: fresh pastries, fog-lifting coffee and chatty locals. The expansive view of the Russian River from the patio and strangely appropriate new-age tunes are bonuses.

Fort Ross State Historic Park

A curious glimpse into Tsarist Russia's exploration of the California coast, the salt-washed buildings of Fort Ross State Historic Park offer a fascinating insight into the pre-American Wild West. It's a quiet, picturesque place with a riveting past.

In March 1812, a group of 25 Russians and 80 Alaskans (including members of the Kodiak and Aleutian tribes) built a wooden fort here, near a Kashaya Pomo village. The southernmost outpost of the 19th-century Russian fur trade on America's Pacific coast, Fort Ross was established as a base for sea-otter hunting operations and trade with Alta California, and for growing crops for Russian settlements in Alaska. The Russians dedicated the fort in August 1812 and occupied it until 1842, when it was abandoned because the sea otter population had been decimated and agricultural production had never taken off.

Fort Ross State Historic Park (☎707-847-3286; www.fortrossstatepark.org; 19005 Hwy 1; per car $8; ☑10am-4:30pm), an accurate reconstruction of the fort, is 11 miles north of Jenner on a beautiful point. The original buildings were sold, dismantled and carried off to Sutter's Fort during the Gold Rush. The **visitor center** (☎707-847-3437) has a great museum with historical displays and an excellent bookshop on Californian and Russian history. Ask about hikes to the Russian cemetery.

On **Fort Ross Heritage Day**, the last Saturday in July, costumed volunteers bring the fort's history to life; check the website www.parks.ca.gov or call the visitor center for other special events.

Timber Cove Inn (☎707-847-3231, 800-987-8319; www.timbercoveinn.com; 21780 N Hwy 1; r from $155, ocean-view from $183) is a dramatic and quirky '60s-modern seaside inn that was once a top-of-the-line luxury lodge. Though the price remains high, it has slipped a bit. The rustic architectural shell is still stunning, though, and a duet of tinkling piano and crackling fire fills the lobby. The quirky rooms facing the ocean have a tree house feel, with rustic redwood details, balconies, fireplaces and lofted beds. Even those who don't bunk here should wander agape in the shadow of Benny Bufano's 93ft peace statue, a spectacular totem on the edge of the sea. The expensive restaurant on-site is nothing to write home about.

Stillwater Cove Regional Park (☑reservations 707-565-2267; www.sonoma-county.org/parks; 22455 N Hwy 1; tent & RV sites $28), 2 miles north of Timber Cove, has hot showers and hiking under Monterey pines. Sites 1, 2, 4, 6, 9 and 10 have ocean views.

Salt Point State Park

If you stop at only one park along the Sonoma Coast, make it 6000-acre **Salt Point State Park** (☎707-847-3221; per car $8), where sandstone cliffs drop dramatically into the kelp-strewn sea and hiking trails crisscross windswept prairies and wooded hills, connecting pygmy forests and coastal coves rich with tidepools. The 6-mile-wide park is bisected by the San Andreas Fault – the rock on the east side is vastly different from that on the west. Check out the eerily beautiful

tafonis, honeycombed-sandstone formations, near Gerstle Cove. For a good roadside photo op, there's a pullout at mile-marker 45, with views of decaying redwood shacks, grazing goats and headlands jutting out to the sea.

Though many of the day use areas have been closed off due to budget cuts, trails lead off Hwy 1 pull-outs to views of the pristine coastline. The platform overlooking **Sentinel Rock** is just a short stroll from the Fisk Mill Cove parking lot at the park's north end. Further south, seals laze at **Gerstle Cove Marine Reserve**, one of California's first underwater parks. Tread lightly around tidepools and don't lift the rocks: even a glimpse of sunlight can kill some critters. If it's springtime, you *must* see **Kruse Rhododendron State Reserve**. Growing abundantly in the forest's filtered light, magnificent, pink rhododendrons reach heights of over 30ft, making them the tallest species in the world; turn east from Hwy 1 onto Kruse Ranch Rd and follow the signs.

Two campgrounds, **Woodside** and **Gerstle Cove** (☎800-444-7275; www.reserveamerica.com; tent & RV sites $35), both signposted off Hwy 1, have campsites with cold water. Inland Woodside is well protected by Monterey pines. Gerstle Cove's trees burned over a decade ago and have only grown halfway back, giving the gnarled, blackened trunks a ghostly look when the fog twirls between the branches.

Sea Ranch

Though not without its fans, the exclusive community of Sea Ranch might well be termed Stepford-by-the-Sea. The ritzy subdivision that sprawls 10 miles along the coast is connected with a well-watched network of private roads. Approved for construction prior to the existence of the watchdog Coastal Commission, the community was a precursor to the concept of 'slow growth,' with strict zoning laws requiring that houses be constructed of weathered wood only. According to *The Sea Ranch Design Manual:* 'This is not a place for the grand architectural statement; it's a place to explore the subtle nuances of fitting in...' Indeed. Though there are some lovely and recommended short-term rentals here, don't break any community rules – like throwing wild parties – or security will come knockin'. For supplies and gasoline, go to Gualala.

After years of litigation, public throughways onto private beaches have been legally mandated and are now well marked. Hiking trails lead from roadside parking lots to the sea and along the bluffs, but don't dare trespass on adjacent lands. **Stengel Beach** (Hwy 1 Mile 53.96) has a beach-access staircase, **Walk-On Beach** (Hwy 1 Mile 56.53) provides wheelchair access and **Shell Beach** (Hwy 1 Mile 55.24) also has beach-access stairs; parking at all three areas costs $6. For hiking details, including maps, contact the **Sea Ranch Association** (www.tsra.org).

Sea Ranch Lodge (707-785-2371, www.searanchlodge.com; 60 Sea Walk Dr; r incl breakfast from $212;), a marvel of '60s-modern California architecture, has spacious, luxurious, minimalist rooms, many with dramatic views to the ocean; some have hot tubs and fireplaces. For the past few years the entire lodge was slated for a decadent stem-to-stern renovation, but the last update was that they couldn't find a bank to float the loan. The fine contemporary **restaurant** (lunch mains $12-16, dinner mains $22-35; 8am-9pm) has a menu for discerning guests; expect everything from duck breast to local fish tacos. North of the lodge you'll see Sea Ranch's iconic nondenominational **chapel**; it's on the inland side of Hwy 1, mileage marker 55.66. For those short on time or on a budget, this is the best reason to pull over in Sea Ranch.

Depending on the season, it can be surprisingly affordable to rent a house in Sea Ranch; contact **Rams Head Realty** (www.ramshead-realty.com), **Sea Ranch Rentals** (www.searanchrentals.com), or **Sea Ranch Escape** (www.searanchescape.com).

Gualala & Anchor Bay

At just 2½ hours north of San Francisco, Gualala – pronounced by most locals as 'Wah-la-la' – is northern Sonoma coast's hub for a weekend getaway as it sits square in the middle of the 'Banana Belt,' a stretch of coast known for unusually sunny weather. Founded as a lumber town in the 1860s, the downtown stretches along Hwy 1 with a bustling commercial district that has a great grocery store and some cute, slightly upscale shops. Just north, quiet Anchor Bay has several inns, a tiny shopping center and, heading north, a string of secluded, hard-to-find beaches. Both are excellent jumping-off points for exploring the area.

Sights & Activities

Gualala Arts Center   ARTS CENTER
(707-884-1138; www.gualalaarts.org; 9am-4pm Mon-Fri, noon-4pm Sat & Sun) Inland along Old State Rd, at the south end of town and beautifully built entirely by volunteers, this center hosts changing exhibitions, organizes the Art in the Redwoods Festival in late August and has loads of info on local art.

Adventure Rents   CANOEING, KAYAKING
(707-884-4386, 888-881-4386; www.adventurerents.com) In the summer, a sand spit forms at the mouth of the river, cutting it off from the ocean and turning it into a warm-water lake. This outfit rents **canoes** (2 hours/half-day/full day $70/80/90) and **kayaks** (2 hours/half-day/full day $35/40/45) and provides instruction.

Seven miles north of Anchor Bay, pull off at mileage marker 11.41 for **Schooner Gulch**. A trail into the forest leads down cliffs to a sandy beach with tidepools. Bear right at the fork in the trail to reach iconic **Bowling Ball Beach**, where low tide reveals rows of big, round rocks resembling bowling balls. Consult tide tables for Arena Cove. The forecast low tide must be lower than +1.5ft on the tide chart for the rocks to be visible.

Sleeping & Eating

Of the two towns, Gualala has more services and is a more practical hub for exploring – there are a bunch of good motels and a pair of nice grocery stores. Get fresh veggies at the **farmers market** (Gualala Community Center; 10am-12:30pm Sat Jun-Oct) and organic supplies and local wine at the **Anchor Bay Village Market** (35513 S Hwy 1).

TOP CHOICE **Mar Vista Cottages**   COTTAGES $$$
(707-884-3522, 877-855-3522; www.marvistamendocino.com; 35101 S Hwy 1, Anchor Bay; cottages from $155;) The elegantly renovated 1930s fishing cabins of Mar Vista is a simple, stylish seaside escape with a vanguard commitment to sustainability. The harmonious environment, situated in the sunny 'Banana Belt' of the North Coast, is the result of pitch perfect details: linens are line-dried over lavender, guests browse the organic vegetable garden to harvest their own dinner and chickens cluck around the grounds laying

the next morning's breakfast. It often requires two-night stays.

North Coast Country Inn B&B **$$**
(☎707-884-4537, 800-959-4537; www.northcoast
countryinn.com; 34591 S Hwy 1; r incl breakfast $195-225; @✖) Perched on an inland hillside beneath towering trees, surrounded by lovely gardens, the perks of this place begin with the gregarious owner and a hot tub. The six spacious country-style rooms are decorated with lovely prints and boast exposed beams, fireplaces, board games and private entrances.

Gualala Point Regional Park CAMPGROUND **$**
(www.sonoma-county.org/parks; 42401 S Hwy 1, Gualala; tent & RV sites $28) Shaded by a stand of redwoods and fragrant California Bay Laurel trees, a short trail connects this creekside campground to the windswept beach. The quality of sites, including several secluded hike-in spots, makes it the best drive-in camping on this part of the coast.

St Orres Inn INN **$$**
(☎707-884-3303; www.saintorres.com; 36601 Hwy 1; B&B $95-135, cottages from $140; ✖) Famous for its unusual Russian-inspired architecture: dramatic rough-hewn timbers and copper domes, there's no place quite like St Orres. On the property's 90 acres, hand-built cottages range from rustic to luxurious. The inn's fine **restaurant** (☎707-884-3335; dinner mains $40-50) serves inspired Californian cuisine in one of the coast's most romantic rooms. Decidedly spendy, sure, but the Andouille-stuffed pheasant with mushroom risotto is *so* worth it.

Gualala River Redwood Park COUNTY CAMPGROUND **$**
(☎707-884-3533; www.gualalapark.com; day use $6, tent & RV sites $22-42; ☀Memorial Day-Labor Day) Another excellent Sonoma County Park. Inland along Old State Rd, you can camp and do short hikes along the river.

Laura's Bakery & Taqueria MEXICAN **$**
(☎707-884-3175; 38411 Robinson Reef Rd at Hwy 1; mains $7-12; ☀7am-7pm Mon-Sat; ✖) Laura's is a refreshing, low-key break from Hwy 1 upscale dining. The menu's taqueria staples are fantastic (the Baja style fish tacos are a steal) but the fresh *mole* dishes and distant ocean view are the real surprises.

Bones Roadhouse BBQ **$$**
(www.bonesroadhouse.com; 39350 S Hwy 1, Gualala; mains $10-20; ☀11:30am-9pm Sun-Thu, to 10pm Fri & Sat) Savory smoked meats make this Gualala's best lunch. On weekends, a codgerly blues outfit may be growling out 'Mustang Sally.'

❶ Information

Redwood Coast Chamber of Commerce (www.redwoodcoastchamber.com) In Gualala; has local information.

Point Arena

This laid-back little town combines creature comforts with relaxed, eclectic California living and is the first town up the coast where the majority of residents don't seem to be retired Bay Area refugees. Sit by the docks a mile west of town at Arena Cove and watch surfers mingle with fishermen and hippies.

Point Arena Lighthouse LIGHTHOUSE
(www.pointarenalighthouse.com; adult/child $7.50/1; ☀10am-3:30pm winter, to 4:30pm summer) Two miles north of town, this 1908 lighthouse stands 10 stories high and is the only lighthouse in California you can ascend. Check in at the museum, then climb the 145 steps to the top and see the Fresnel lens and the jaw-dropping view. After $1.5-million renovations, the building and adjoining fog signal building are looking fantastic. True lighthouse buffs should look into staying at the plain three-bedroom former **Coast Guard homes** (☎707-882-2777; houses $125-300) onsite. They're a quiet, wind-swept retreat.

Stornetta Public Lands NATURE AREA
For fabulous bird-watching, hiking on terraced rock past sea caves and access to hid-

TOP WHALE-WATCHING SPOTS

Watch for spouts, sounding and breaching whales and pods. Anywhere coastal will do, but the following are some of the north coast's best:

» Bodega Head (p215)
» Mendocino Headlands State Park (p225)
» Jug Handle State Reserve (p228)
» MacKerricher State Park (p232)
» Shelter Cove & The Lost Coast (p246)
» Trinidad Head Trail (p257)
» Klamath River Overlook (p261)

den coves, head 1 mile down Lighthouse Rd from Hwy 1 and look for the Bureau of Land Management (BLM) signs on the left indicating these 1132-acre public lands.

🛏 Sleeping & Eating

Wharf Master's Inn HOTEL $$$
(☎707-882-3171, 800-932-4031; www.wharfmasters.com; 785 Port Rd; r $105-255; 🛜🐾) This is a cluster of small, modern rooms on a cliff overlooking fishing boats and a stilting pier. Tidy and very clean, rooms have the character of a chain hotel.

Coast Guard House Inn INN $$
(☎707-882-2442; www.coastguardhouse.com; 695 Arena Cove; r $105-225) Come here if you want to soak up old-world ocean side charm and are willing to deal with historic plumbing. It's a 1901 Cape Cod–style house and cottage, with water-view rooms.

TOP CHOICE Franny's Cup & Saucer PATISSERIE $
(☎707-882-2500; www.frannyscupandsaucer.com; 213 Main St; pastries $1-5; ⊙8am-4pm Wed-Sat; 🐾🍴) The cutest patisserie on this stretch of coast is run by Franny and her mother, Barbara (a veteran of Chez Panisse). The fresh berry tarts and rich chocolaty desserts seem too beautiful to eat, until you take the first bite and immediately want to order another. Several times a year they pull out all the stops for a Sunday garden brunch ($28).

Pizzas N Cream PIZZA $
(www.pizzasandcream.com; 790 Port Rd; pizzas $10-18; ⊙11:30am-9pm; 🐾🛜) In Arena Cove, this friendly place whips up exquisite pizzas and fresh salads, and serves beer and ice cream.

🍴 Arena Market ORGANIC DELI $
(www.arenaorganics.org; 183 Main St; ⊙7:30am-7pm Mon-Sat, 8:30am-6pm Sun; 🍴🛜) The deli in front of this fully stocked organic grocer makes excellent to-go veg options, often sourced from local farms.

🍷 Drinking & Entertainment

215 Main BAR
(www.facebook.com/215Main; 215 Main; ⊙2pm-2am Tue-Sun) Head to this open, renovated historic building to drink local beer and wine. There's jazz on the weekends.

Arena Cinema CINEMA
(www.arenatheater.org; 214 Main St) shows mainstream, foreign and art films in a beautifully restored movie house. Sue, the ticket seller, has been in that booth for 40 years. Got a question about Point Arena? Ask Sue.

ℹ Information

Public library (☎707-882-3114; 225 Main St; ⊙noon-6pm Mon-Fri, to 3pm Sat) Free internet access.

Manchester

Follow Hwy 1 for about 7 miles north of Point Arena, through gorgeous rolling fields dropping down from the hills to the blue ocean, and a turnoff leads to Manchester State Beach, a long, wild stretch of sand. The area around here is remote and beautiful (only one grocery store), but it's a quick drive to Point Arena for more elaborate provisions.

Ross Ranch (☎707-877-1834; www.elkcoast.com/rossranch) at Irish Beach, another 5 miles to the north, arranges two-hour horseback beach ($60) and mountain ($50) rides; reservations recommended.

TOP CHOICE Victorian Gardens (☎707-882-3606; www.innatvictoriangardens.com; 14409 S Hwy 1; r $240-310) is wihout doubt the finest B&B on the coast. This lovingly restored 1904 farmhouse (smartly expanded by the owner, an architect) sits on 92 exquisitely situated acres just north of Manchester. Every detail here is picture perfect: the spacious gardens that provide fresh flowers and vegetables for gourmet meals, the rustic green house dining room which opens to the sea breeze and comfortable common spaces, decorated with a discerningly elegant mix of antique pieces and modern furniture. There's even a Picasso. For larger groups, the owners can prepare five-course authentic Italian dinners with carefully paired wines.

Mendocino Coast KOA (☎707-882-2375, www.manchesterbeachkoa.com; tent/RV sites from $35/50, cabins $68-78; 🐾🛜🐾) is an impressive private campground with tightly packed campsites beneath enormous Monterey pines, a cooking pavilion, hot showers, a hot tub and bicycles. The cabins are a great option for families who want to get the camping experience without roughing it.

A quarter-mile west, the sunny, exposed campground at Manchester State Park (tent & RV sites $25-35) has cold water and quiet right by the ocean. Sites are non-reservable. Budget cuts have all but eliminated ranger service.

Elk

Thirty minutes north of Point Arena, itty-bitty Elk is famous for its stunning cliff-top views of 'sea stacks,' towering rock formations jutting out of the water. There is *nothing* to do after dinner, so bring a book – and sleeping pills if you're a night owl. And you can forget about the cell phone, too; reception here is nonexistent. Elk's visitor center (5980 Hwy 1; ☉11am-1pm Sat & Sun mid-Mar–Oct) has exhibits on the town's logging past. At the southern end of town, Greenwood State Beach sits where Greenwood Creek meets the sea. Force 10 (☎707-877-3505; www.force10tours.com) guides ocean-kayaking tours ($115).

Tucked into a tiny clapboard house looking across the road to the ocean, the Elk Studio Gallery & Artist's Collective (www.artists-collective.net; 6031 S Hwy 1; ☉10am-5pm) is cluttered with tons of local art – everything from carvings and pottery to photography and jewelry.

Several upmarket B&Bs take advantage of the views. Harbor House Inn (☎707-877-3203, 800-720-7474; www.theharborhouseinn.com; 5600 S Hwy 1; r & cottages incl breakfast & dinner $360-490; ☎), located in a 1915 Arts and Crafts–style mansion built by the town's lumber baron, has gorgeous cliff-top gardens and a private beach. The view from the Lookout, Oceansong and Shorepine rooms are the best. Rates include a superb four-course dinner for two in the ocean view room with a lauded wine list.

Griffin House (☎707-877-3422; www.griffinn.com; 5910 S Hwy 1; cottages $130-160, ocean-view cottages $145-325; ☎☎) is an unpretentious cluster of simple, powder-blue bluffside cottages with wood-burning stoves.

A new-agey feel pervades the Buddha-dotted grounds and ocean-view cottages at Greenwood Pier Inn (☎707-877-9997; www.greenwoodpierinn.com; 5928 S Hwy 1; d incl breakfast $185-335; ☎☎). If you can look past the trippy art work, the rooms have fireplaces and private decks. Its cafe is open for lunch and dinner.

Everyone swears by excellent Queenie's Roadhouse Cafe (☎707-877-3285; 6061 S Hwy 1; dishes $6-10; ☉8am-3pm Thu-Mon; ☎) for a creative range of breakfast (try the wild rice waffles) and lunch treats. Sweet, little Bridget Dolan's (☎707-877-1820; 5910 S Hwy 1; mains $10-15; ☉4:30-8pm) serves straight-forward cookin' like pot pies, and bangers and mash.

Van Damme State Park

Three miles south of Mendocino, this gorgeous 1831-acre park (☎707-937-5804; www.parks.ca.gov; day use $6) draws divers, beachcombers and kayakers to its easy-access beach. It's also known for its pygmy forest, where the acidic soil and an impenetrable layer of hardpan just below the surface create a bonsai forest with decades-old trees growing only several feet high. A wheelchair-accessible boardwalk provides access to the forest. To get there, turn east off Hwy 1 onto Little River Airport Rd, a half-mile south of Van Damme State Park, and drive for 3 miles. Alternatively, hike or bike up from the campground on the 3.5-mile Fern Canyon Scenic Trail, which crosses back and forth over Little River.

The visitor center (☎707-937-4016; ☉10am-3pm Fri-Sun) has nature exhibits, videos and programs; a half-hour marsh loop trail starts nearby.

Two pretty campgrounds (☎800 444-7275; www.reserveamerica.com, tent & RV sites $35; ☎) are excellent for family car camping. They both have hot showers: one is just off Hwy 1, the other is in a highland meadow, which has lots of space for kids to run around. Nine environmental campsites (tent sites $25) lie just a 1¼-mile hike up Fern Canyon; there's untreated creek water.

For sea-cave kayaking tours ($50), contact Lost Coast Kayaking (☎707-937-2434; www.lostcoastkayaking.com).

Mendocino

Leading out to a gorgeous headland, Mendocino is the North Coast's salt-washed gem, with B&Bs surrounded by rose gardens, white-picket fences and New England–style redwood water towers. Bay Area weekenders walk along the headland among berry bramble and wildflowers, where cypress trees stand over dizzying cliffs. Nature's power is evident everywhere, from driftwood-littered fields and cave tunnels to the raging surf. The town itself is full of cute shops – no chains – and has earned the nickname 'Spendocino,' for its upscale goods. In summer, fragrant bursts of lavender and jasmine permeate the foggy wind, tempered by salt air from the churning surf, which is never out of earshot.

Built by transplanted New Englanders in the 1850s, Mendocino thrived late into the

Mendocino

19th century, with ships transporting redwood timber from here to San Francisco. The mills shut down in the 1930s, and the town fell into disrepair until it was rediscovered in the 1950s by artists and bohemians. Today the culturally savvy, politically aware, well-traveled citizens welcome visitors, but eschew corporate interlopers – don't look for a Big Mac or try to use your cell phone. To avoid crowds, come midweek or in the low season, when the vibe is mellower – and prices more reasonable.

◎ Sights

Mendocino is lined with all kinds of interesting galleries, which hold openings on the second Saturday of each month from 5pm to 8pm.

Mendocino Art Center GALLERY
(www.mendocinoartcenter.org; 45200 Little Lake St; ⊙10am-5pm Apr-Oct, to 4pm Tue-Sat Nov-Mar) Behind a yard of twisting iron sculpture, the city's art center takes up a whole tree-filled block, hosting exhibitions, the 81-seat Helen Schonei Theatre and nationally renowned art classes. This is also where to pick up the *Mendocino Arts Showcase* brochure, a quarterly publication listing all the happenings and festivals in town.

Kelley House Museum MUSEUM
(www.mendocinohistory.org; 45007 Albion St; admission $2; ⊙11am-3pm Thu-Tue Jun-Sep, Fri-Mon Oct-May) With a research library and changing exhibits on early California and Mendocino, the 1861 museum hosts seasonal, two-hour walking tours for $10; call for times.

Point Cabrillo Lighthouse LIGHTHOUSE
(www.pointcabrillo.org; Point Cabrillo Dr; admission free; ⊙11am-4pm Sat & Sun Jan & Feb, daily Mar-Oct, Fri-Mon Nov & Dec) Restored in 1909, this lighthouse stands on a 300-acre wildlife preserve north of town, between Russian Gulch and Caspar Beach. The head lighthouse keeper's home is now a simple lodging (p226). Guided walks of the preserve leave at 11am on Sundays from May to September.

Kwan Tai Temple TEMPLE
(www.kwantaitemple.org; 45160 Albion St) Peering in the window of this 1852 temple reveals an old altar dedicated to the Chinese god of war. Tours are available by appointment.

🏃 Activities

Wine tours, whale watching, shopping, hiking, cycling: there's more to do in the area than a thousand long weekends could accom-

Mendocino

plish. For navigable river and ocean kayaking, launch from tiny Albion, which hugs the north side of the Albion River mouth, 5 miles south of Mendocino.

TOP CHOICE Catch A Canoe & Bicycles, Too! BICYCLE & CANOE RENTAL
(www.stanfordinn.com; Comptche-Ukiah Rd & Hwy 1; ⏰9am-5pm) This friendly riverside outfit south of town rents bikes, kayaks and stable outrigger canoes for trips up the 8-mile Big River tidal estuary, the longest undeveloped estuary in Northern California. No highways or buildings, only beaches, forests, marshes, streams, abundant wildlife and historic logging sites. Bring a picnic and a camera to enjoy the ramshackle remnants of century-old train trestles and majestic blue herons.

Mendocino Headlands State Park COASTAL PARK
A spectacular park surrounds the village, with trails crisscrossing the bluffs and rocky coves. Ask at the visitor center about guided weekend walks, including spring wildflower walks and whale-watching.

✹ Festivals & Events

For a complete list of Mendocino's many festivals, check with the visitor center or www.gomendo.com.

Mendocino Whale Festival WHALE-WATCHING
(www.mendowhale.com) Early March, with wine and chowder tastings, whale-watching and music.

Mendocino Music Festival MUSIC
(www.mendocinomusic.com) Mid-July, with orchestral and chamber music concerts on the headlands, children's matinees and open rehearsals.

Mendocino Wine & Mushroom Festival FOOD, WINE
(www.mendocino.com) Early November, guided mushroom tours and symposia.

🛏 Sleeping

Standards are high and so are prices; two-day minimums often crop up on weekends. Fort Bragg, 10 miles north, has cheaper lodgings (see p230). All B&B rates include breakfast; only a few places have TVs. For a range of cottages and B&Bs, contact **Mendocino Coast Reservations** (☎707-937-5033, 800-262-7801; www.mendocinovacations.com; 45084 Little Lake St; ⏰9am-5pm).

TOP CHOICE Andiron COTTAGES $$
(☎800-955-6478; www.theandiorn.com; 6051 N Hwy 1, Mendocino; r $99-149; 🛜🐾🎬) Styled with hip vintage decor, this cluster of 1950s roadside cottages is a refreshingly playful option amid the stuffy cabbage-rose and

lace aesthetic of Mendocino. Each cabin houses two rooms with complementing themes: 'Read' has old books, comfy vintage chairs, and hip retro eyeglasses while the adjoining 'Write' features a huge chalkboard and ribbon typewriter. A favorite for travelers? 'Here' and 'There,' themed with old maps, 1960s airline paraphernalia and collectables from North Coast's yesteryear.

MacCallum House Inn
B&B $$$

(☎707-937-0289, 800-609-0492; www.maccallumhouse.com; 45020 Albion St; r from $204; @🛜🐾🐕) The finest B&B option in the center of town. When the weather is warm, the gardens surrounding the refurbished 1882 barn are a riot of color. There are bright and cheerful cottages, and a modern luxury home, but the most memorable space here is within one of Mendocino's iconic historic water towers – where living quarters fill the ground floor, a sauna is on the second and there's a view of the coast from the top. All accommodations have cushy extras like robes, DVD players, stereos and plush linens.

Stanford Inn by the Sea
INN $$

(☎707-937-5615, 800-331-8884; www.stanfordinn.com; cnr Hwy 1 & Comptche-Ukiah Rd; r $195-305; @🛜🐾🐕) This masterpiece of a lodge standing on 10 lush acres has wood-burning fireplaces, original art, stereos and top-quality mattresses in every room. Figure in a stroll in the organic gardens, where they harvest food for the excellent on-site restaurant, the solarium-enclosed pool and the hot tub, and it's a sublime getaway.

Brewery Gulch Inn
B&B $$$

(☎800-578-4454; www.brewerygulchinn.com; 9401 N Hwy 1, Mendocino; r $210-450; 🛜) Just south of Mendocino, this fresh place has 10 modern rooms (all with flat-screen televisions, iPod docs, gas fireplaces and spa bathtubs), and guests enjoy luxury touches like feather beds and leather reading chairs. The hosts pour heavily at the complimentary wine hour and leave out sweets for midnight snacking. Made-to-order breakfast is served in a small dining room overlooking the distant water.

Sea Gull Inn
B&B $$

(☎707-937-5204, 888-937-5204; www.seagullbb.com; 44960 Albion St; r $130-165, barn $185; 🐕🛜) With pristine white bedspreads, organic breakfasts and a flowering garden, this cute, converted motel is extremely comfortable, fairly priced, and right in the thick of the action.

Mendocino Hotel
HISTORIC HOTEL $$

(☎707-937-0511, 800-548-0513; www.mendocinohotel.com; 45080 Main St; r with bath $135-295, without bath $95-125, ste $325-395; P🛜) Built in 1878 as the town's first hotel, this is like a piece of the Old West. The modern garden suites sit behind the main building and don't have a shade of old-school class, but are modern and serviceable. Some wheelchair accessible.

Packard House
B&B $$$

(☎707-937-2677, 888-453-2677; www.packardhouse.com; 45170 Little Lake St; r $190-275) Decked out in contemporary style, this place is Mendocino's sleekest B&B choice – chic and elegant, with beautiful fabrics, colorful minimalist paintings and limestone bathrooms.

Alegria
B&B $$

(☎707-937-5150, 800-780-7905; www.oceanfrontmagic.com; 44781 Main St; r $159-189, r with ocean view $239, cottages $179-269) Perfect for a romantic hideaway, rooms have oceanview decks and wood-burning fireplaces; outside a gorgeous path leads to a private beach. Ever-so-friendly innkeepers rent simpler rooms in a 1900s Arts and Crafts place across the street.

Headlands Inn
B&B $$$

(☎707-937-4431; www.headlandsinn.com; cnr Albion & Howard Sts; r $139-249) Homey saltbox with featherbeds and fireplaces. Quiet dorm rooms have sea views and staff will bring you the gourmet breakfast in bed.

Lighthouse Inn at Point Cabrillo
HISTORIC B&B $$

(☎707-937-6124; 866-937-6124; www.pointcabrillo.org; Point Cabrillo Dr; r $152-279) On 300 acres, in the shadow of Point Cabrillo Lighthouse, the lightkeeper's house and several cottages have been turned into B&B rooms. Rates include a private night tour of the lighthouse and a five-course breakfast.

Joshua Grindle Inn
B&B $$$

(☎707-937-4143, 800-474-6353; www.joshgrin.com; 44800 Little Lake Rd; r $189-299) Mendocino's oldest B&B has bright, airy, uncluttered rooms in an 1869 house, a weathered saltbox cottage and water tower. Enjoy goodies like fluffy muffins, warm hospitality and gorgeous gardens.

Glendeven
B&B $$$

(☑707-937-0083; www.glendeven.com; 8205 N Hwy 1; r $135-320; 🐾) Elegant estate 2 miles south of town with organic gardens.

Russian Gulch State Park
CAMPGROUND $

(☑reservations 800-444-7275; www.reserveamerica.com; tent & RV sites $35) In a wooded canyon 2 miles north of town, with secluded drive-in sites, hot showers, a small waterfall and the Devil's Punch Bowl (a collapsed sea arch).

✖ Eating

With quality to rival Napa Valley, the influx of Bay Area weekenders have fostered an excellent dining scene that enthusiastically espouses organic, sustainable principles. Make reservations. Gathering picnic supplies is easy at the central markets and the **farmers market** (Howard & Main St; ☑noon-2pm Fri May-Oct).

[TOP CHOICE] Café Beaujolais
CALIFORNIAN, FUSION $$

(☑707-937-5614; www.cafebeaujolais.com; 961 Ukiah St; mains lunch $9-16, dinner $24-36; ☑11:30am-2:30pm Wed-Sun, dinner from 5:30pm nightly) Mendocino's iconic, beloved country-Cal–French restaurant occupies an 1896 house restyled into a monochromatic urban-chic dining room, perfect for holding hands by candlelight. The refined, inspired cooking draws diners from San Francisco, who make this the centerpiece of their trip. The locally sourced menu changes with the seasons, but the Petaluma duck breast served with crispy skin is a gourmand's delight.

Ravens
CALIFORNIAN $$$

(☑707-937-5615; www.ravensrestaurant.com; Stanford Inn, Comptche-Ukiah Rd; breakfast $11-15, mains $22-35; ☑8-10:30am Mon-Sat, to noon Sun, dinner 5:30-10pm; 🖋) Ravens brings haute-contemporary concepts to a completely vegetarian and vegan menu. Produce comes from the inn's own idyllic organic gardens, and the bold menu takes on everything from sea-palm strudel and portabella sliders to decadent (guilt-free) deserts.

MacCallum House Restaurant
CALIFORNIAN $$$

(☑707-937-0289; www.maccallumhouse.com; 45020 Albion St; cafe dishes $12-16, mains $25-42; ☑8:15-10am Mon-Fri, to 11am Sat & Sun, 5:30-9pm daily; 🖋) Sit on the veranda or fireside for a romantic dinner of all-organic game, fish or risotto primavera. Chef Alan Kantor makes

everything from scratch and his commitment to sustainability and organic ingredients is nearly as visionary as his menu. The cafe menu, served at the Grey Whale Bar, is one of Mendocino's few four-star bargains.

Garden Bakery
BAKERY $

(☑707-937-0282; 10450 Lansing; baked goods $3-6; ☑9am-4pm) Nearly every corner of Mendocino gets explored by hordes, but this little garden-side bakery still feels like a hidden gem. To describe the quality of the baked goods would invite hyperbole: they are *a-ma-zing*. The menu changes with the seasons and the baker's whim; one day, you're trying not to inhale the savory, cabbage-stuffed German pastry (a family recipe), on another you'll find apple cheddar croissants. If you show up early enough you'll get a taste of their renowned bear claw. If you don't find this place at first, keep looking: the bakery is located off the street, accessible by sidewalks that cut through the block.

Mendocino Cafe
CALIFORNIAN, FUSION $$

(www.mendocinocafe.com; 10451 Lansing St; lunch mains $12-15, dinner mains $12-24; ☑11:30am-8pm; 🖋) One of Mendocino's few midpriced dinner spots also serves lovely alfresco lunches on its ocean-view deck surrounded by roses. Try the fish tacos or the Thai burrito. At dinner there's grilled steak and seafood.

Patterson's Pub
PUB $$

(www.pattersonspub.com; 10485 Lansing St; mains $10-15 ☑11am-11pm Mon-Fri, brunch 10am-2pm Sat & Sun) If you pull into town late and you're hungry, you'll thank your lucky stars for this place; it serves quality pub grub – fish and chips, huge burgers and dinner salads – with cold beer. The only spoiler to the traditional Irish pub ambience is the plethora of flat-screen TVs.

Moosse Cafe
CALIFORNIAN $$

(☑707-937-4323; www.themoosse.com; 390 Kasten St; lunch mains $12-16, dinner mains $22-28; ☑noon-2:30pm & 5:30-8:30pm; 🖋) The blond woodwork and starched linen napkins set a relaxed yet elegant tone for top-notch Cal-French cooking. Try the cioppino in saffron-fennel-tomato broth at dinner; lunch is more casual. Note that it keeps variable hours in the winter and on slow weekdays.

Ledford House
MEDITERRANEAN $$

(☑707-937-0282; www.ledfordhouse.com; 3000 N Hwy 1, Albion; mains $19-30; ☑5-8pm Wed-Sun;

☑) Watch the water pound the rocks and the sun set out of the Mendocino hubbub (8 miles south) at this friendly Cal-Med bistro. Try the cassoulet or the gnocchi. It's a local hangout and gets hoppin' with live jazz most nights.

✑**Mendosa's**   MARKET $
(www.harvestmarket.com; 10501 Lansing St; ☑8am-9pm) The town's biggest grocery store has legit organic credentials, an excellent cold food bar and great cheese and meat.

Mendocino Market   DELI $
(45051 Ukiah St; sandwiches $6-9; ☺11am-5pm Mon-Fri, to 4pm Sat & Sun; ☎) Pick up huge deli sandwiches and picnics here.

✑**Lu's Kitchen**   INTERNATIONAL $
(☑707-937-4939; 45013 Ukiah St; mains $8-10; ☑11:30am-5:30pm; ☑☀) Rustles up fab organic veggie burritos in a tiny shack; outdoor-only tables.

☉ Drinking

Have cocktails at the **Mendocino Hotel** (45080 Main St) or the **Grey Whale Bar** (45020 Albion St)at the MacCallum House Inn.

Patterson's Pub   PUB
(www.pattersonspub.com; 10485 Lansing St) This boisterous, inviting, Irish-style bar has a friendly staff and a good vibe.

Dick's Place   DIVE BAR
(45080 Main St) A bit out of place among the fancy-pants shops downtown, but an excellent spot to check out the *other* Mendocino and do shots with rowdy locals.

Moody's Coffee Bar   COFFEE SHOP
(10450 Lansing St; ☺6am-8pm; ☎) Moody's covers the essentials: strong coffee, wi-fi and the *New York Times*.

⛏ Shopping

Mendocino's walkable streets are great for shopping, and the ban on chain stores ensures unique, often upscale gifts. There are many small galleries in town where one-of-a-kind artwork is for sale.

Compass Rose Leather   LEATHER GOODS
(45150 Main St) From hand-tooled belts and leather bound journals to purses and peg-secured storage boxes, the craftsmanship here is unquestionable.

Out Of This World   OUTDOOR & SCIENCE SUPPLIES
(45100 Main St) Birders, astronomy buffs and science geeks head directly to this telescope, binocular and science-toy shop.

Village Toy Store   TOYS
(10450 Lansing St) Get a kite to fly on Bodega head or browse the old-world selection of wooden toys and games that you won't find in the chains – hardly anything requires batteries.

Gallery Bookshop   BOOKS
(www.gallerybookshop.com; 319 Kasten St) Stocks a great selection of books on local topics, titles from California's small presses and specialized outdoor guides.

Twist   CLOTHING
(45140 Main St) Twist stocks ecofriendly, natural-fiber clothing and lots of locally made clothing and toys.

Moore Used Books   SECONDHAND BOOKS
(990 Main St) An excellent bad weather hideout, the stacks here have over 10,000 used titles. The shop is in an old house at the far east end of Main Street.

ⓘ Information

Ford House Visitor Center & Museum (☑707-937-5397; www.gomendo.com; 735 Main St; suggested donation $2; ☺11am-4pm) Maps, books, information and exhibits, including a scale model of 1890 Mendocino.

Mendocino Coast Clinics (☑707-964-1251; 205 South St; ☺9am-5pm Mon-Fri, to 8pm Wed, 9am-1pm Sat) Nonemergencies.

Jug Handle State Reserve

Between Mendocino and Fort Bragg, Jug Handle preserves an **ecological staircase** that you can view on a 5-mile (round trip) self-guided nature trail. Five wave-cut terraces ascend in steps from the seashore, each 100ft and 100,000 years removed from the previous one, and each with its own distinct geology and vegetation. One of the terraces has a pygmy forest, similar to the better-known example at Van Damme State Park (p223). Pick up a printed guide detailing the area's geology, flora and fauna from the parking lot. The reserve is also a good spot to stroll the headlands, whale-watch or lounge on the beach. It's easy to miss the entrance; watch for the turnoff, just north of Caspar.

Jug Handle Creek Farm & Nature Center (☎707-964-4630; www.jughandlecreekfarm.com; tent sites $12, r & cabins adult $40-50, child $15, student $28-33; ☀) is a nonprofit 39-acre farm with rustic cabins and hostel rooms in a 19th-century farmhouse. Call ahead about work-stay discounts. Drive 5 miles north of Mendocino to Caspar; the farm is on the east side of Hwy 1. Take the second driveway after Fern Creek Rd.

Fort Bragg

In the past, Fort Bragg was Mendocino's ugly stepsister, home to a lumber mill, a scrappy downtown and blue-collar locals who gave a cold welcome to outsiders. Since the mill closure in 2002, the town has started to re-invent itself, slowly warming to a tourism-based economy. What to do with the seaside mill site is the talk of the town, running the gamut from progressive ideas like a marine research center or university to disastrous ones like a condo development, a world-class golf course or (gasp!) another mill. Regardless, the effect on Fort Bragg is likely to be profound. Follow the progress at www.fortbraggmillsite.com.

In the meantime, Fort Bragg's downtown continues to develop as an unpretentious alternative to Mendocino, even if the *entire* southern end of town is hideous. Unlike the *entire* franchise-free 180-mile stretch of Coastal Hwy 1 between here and the Golden Gate, southern Fort Bragg is blighted by McDonalds, Starbucks and other Anywhere, USA chain stores polluting the coastal aesthetic. Put on blinkers and don't stop till you're downtown, where you'll find better hamburgers and coffee, old-school architecture and residents eager to show off their little town.

Twisting Hwy 20 provides the main access to Fort Bragg from the east, and most facilities are near Main St, a 2-mile stretch of Hwy 1. Franklin St runs parallel, one block east.

◉ Sights & Activities

Fort Bragg has the same banner North Coast activities as Mendocino – beach combing, surfing, hiking – but basing yourself here is much cheaper and a little less quaint. The wharf lies at Noyo Harbor – the mouth of the Noyo River – south of downtown where you can find whale-watching cruises and deep-sea fishing trips.

NORTH COAST BEER TOUR

The craft breweries of the North Coast don't mess around – bold hop profiles, Belgium-style ales and smooth lagers are regional specialties, and they're produced with style. Some breweries are better than others, but the following tour makes for an excellent long weekend of beer tasting in the region.

» Ukiah Brewing Company (p238), Ukiah

» Anderson Valley Brewing Company (p236), Boonville.

» North Coast Brewing Company (p231), Fort Bragg

» Six Rivers Brewery (p256), McKinleyville

» Eel River Brewing (p248), Fortuna

TOP CHOICE Skunk Train   HISTORIC TRAIN
(☎707-964-6371, 866-866-1690; www.skunktrain.com; adult/child $49/24) Fort Bragg's pride and joy, the vintage train got its nickname in 1925 for its stinky gas-powered steam engines, but today the historic steam and diesel locomotives are odorless. Passing through redwood-forested mountains, along rivers, over bridges and through deep mountain tunnels, the trains run from both Fort Bragg and Willits (p240) to the midway point of Northspur, where they turn around (if you want to go to Willits, plan to spend the night). The depot is downtown at the foot of Laurel St, one block west of Main St.

Mendocino Coast Botanical Gardens   GARDENS
(☎707-964-4352; www.gardenbythesea.org; 18220 N Hwy 1; adult/child/senior $14/5/10; ⊙9am-5pm Mar-Oct, to 4pm Nov-Feb; ☀) This gem of Northern California displays native flora, rhododendrons and heritage roses. The succulent display alone is amazing and the organic garden is harvested by volunteers to feed area residents in need. The serpentine paths wander along 47 seafront acres south of town. Primary trails are wheelchair-accessible.

Glass Beach   BEACH
Named for (what's left of) the sea-polished glass in the sand, remnants of its days as a city dump, this beach is now part of MacKerricher State Park where visitors comb

the sand for multicolored glass. Take the headlands trail from Elm St, off Main St, but leave the glass; as a part of the park system, visitors are not supposed to pocket souvenirs.

All-Aboard Adventures
FISHING, WHALE-WATCHING

(☏707-964-1881; www.allaboardadventures.com; 32400 N Harbor Dr) Captain Tim leads crabbing and salmon fishing trips (five hours, $80) and whale watching during the whale migration (two hours, $35).

Northcoast Artists Gallery
GALLERY

(www.northcoastartists.org; 362 N Main St; ⊙10am-6pm) An excellent local arts cooperative that has the useful *Fort Bragg Gallery & Exhibition Guide,* which directs you to other galleries around town. Openings are the first Fridays of the month. Antique and book stores line Franklin St, one block east.

FREE Triangle Tattoo & Museum
MUSEUM

(www.triangletattoo.com; 356B N Main St; admission free; ☑noon-7pm) Shows multicultural, international tattoo art.

Guest House Museum
MUSEUM

(☏707-964-4251; www.fortbragghistory.org; 343 N Main St; admission $2; ⊙1-3pm Mon, 11am-2pm Tue-Fri, 10am-4pm Sat-Sun May-Oct, 11am-2pm Thu-Sun) A majestic Victorian structure built in 1892, displays historical photos and relics of Fort Bragg's history. As hours vary, call ahead.

Pudding Creek Trestle
BOARDWALK

The walk along the Pudding Creek Trestle, north of downtown, is fun for the whole family.

☆ Festivals & Events

Fort Bragg Whale Festival
WILDLIFE

(www.mendowhale.com) Held on the third weekend in March, with microbrew tastings, crafts fairs and whale-watching trips.

Paul Bunyan Days
COMMUNITY FESTIVAL

(www.paulbunyandays.com) Held on Labor Day weekend in September, celebrate California's logging history with a logging show, square dancing, parade and fair.

⌁ Sleeping

Fort Bragg's lodging is cheaper than Mendocino's, but most of the motels along noisy Hwy 1 don't have air-conditioning, so you'll hear traffic through your windows. Most B&Bs do not have TVs and they all include breakfast. The usual chains abound.

Shoreline Cottages
COTTAGES $$

(☏707-964-2977; www.shoreline-cottage.com; 18725 N Hwy 1; r $120-155; 🌐📶🐾) Low-key and pet-friendly four-person rooms and cottages with kitchens surround a central tree-filled lawn. The family rooms are a good bargain, and suites feature modern art work and clean sight lines. All rooms have docks for your iPod, snacks and access to a library of DVDs.

Country Inn
B&B $

(☏707-964-3737; www.beourguests.com; 18725 N Hwy 1; r $90-145; 🌐📶) This unpretentious bed & breakfast is right in the middle of town and is an excellent way to dodge the chain motels for a good value stay. The lovely family hosts are welcoming and easy going, and can offer good local tips. Breakfast can be delivered to your room and at night you can soak in a hot tub out back.

Weller House Inn
B&B $$

(☏707-964-4415, 877-893-5537; www.wellerhouse.com; 524 Stewart St; r $130-195; 🌐) Rooms in this beautifully restored 1886 mansion have down comforters, good mattresses and fine linens. The water tower is the tallest structure in town – and it has a hot tub at the top! Breakfast is in the massive redwood ballroom.

Grey Whale Inn
B&B $$

(☏707-964-0640, 800-382-7244; www.greywhaleinn.com; 615 N Main St; r $100-195; 📶🌐) Situated in a historic building on the north side of town, this comfortable, family-run inn has simple, straightforward rooms that are good value – especially for families.

California Department of Forestry
CAMPING $

(☏707-964-5674; 802 N Main St; ⊙8am-4:30pm Mon, to noon Tue-Thu) Come here for maps, permits and camping information for the Jackson State Forest, east of Fort Bragg, where camping is free.

✖ Eating

Similar to the lodging scene, the food in Fort Bragg is less spendy than Mendocino's, and there are a number of good options. Self-caterers should try the **farmers market** (cnr Laurel & Franklin Sts; ⊙3:30-6pm Wed May-Oct) downtown or the **Harvest Market** (☏707-

964-7000; cnr Hwys 1 & 20; ☺5am-11pm) for the best groceries.

Piaci Pub & Pizzeria
PIZZA $

(www.piacipizza.com; 120 W Redwood Ave; pizza $8-12; ☺11am-4pm Mon-Fri, 4-9pm Sun-Thu, 4-10pm Fri & Sat) Fort Bragg's must-visit pizzeria is the place to chat up locals while enjoying microbrews and a menu of fantastic wood-fired, brick-oven, 'adult' pizzas (a sight more sophisticated than your average Dominos pie). The 'Gustoso' – an immaculate selection with Chevre, pesto and seasonal pears – speaks to the carefully orchestrated thin-crust pies. It's tiny, loud and fun, but expect to wait at peak times.

Mendo Bistro
AMERICAN $$

(☎707-964-4924; www.mendobistro.com; 301 N Main St; mains $14-25; ☺5-9pm; ⊞) This dining option gets packed with a young crowd on the weekend, offering a choose-your-own-adventure menu, where you select a meat, a preparation and an accompanying sauce from a litany of options. The loud, bustling 2nd-story room is big enough for kids to run around and nobody will notice.

Chapter & Moon
AMERICAN $

(32150 N Harbor Dr; mains $8-18; ☎8am-8pm) Overlooking Noyo Harbor, this small cafe serves blue-plate American cooking: chicken and dumplings, meatloaf melts, and fish with yam chips. Save room for fruit cobbler.

North Coast Brewing Company
BREWPUB $$

(www.northcoastbrewing.com; 444 N Main St; mains $8-25; ☺7am-9:30pm Sun-Thu, to 10pm Fri & Sat) Though thick, rare slabs of steak and a list of specials demonstrate that they take the food as seriously as the bevvies, it's burgers and garlic fries that soak up the fantastic selection of handcrafted brews.

Headlands Coffeehouse
DELI $

(www.headlandscoffeehouse.com; 120 E Laurel St; dishes $4-8; ☺7am-10pm Mon-Sat, to 7pm Sun; ⊞) The town's best cafe is in the middle of the historic downtown, with high ceilings and lots of atmosphere. The menu gets raves for the Belgian waffles, homemade soups, veggie-friendly salads, panini and lasagna.

Living Light Café
VEGAN, RAW $

(☎707-964-2420; 444 N Main St; mains $5-11; ☺8am-5:30pm Mon-Sat, to 4pm Sun; ⊞) As an extension of the renowned Living Light Cu-

linary Institute, one of the nation's leading raw food schools, this bright cafe serves a tasty to-go menu that's a sight better than bland crudités, like the Sicilian-style pizza on a spouted seed crust, raw desserts and tangy cold soups.

Eggheads
BREAKFAST $

(www.eggheadsrestaurant.com; 326 N Main St; mains $8-13; ☺7am-2pm) Enjoy the *Wizard of Oz* theme as you tuck into one of 50 varieties of omelet, crepe or burrito, some with local Dungeness crab.

La Playa
MEXICAN $

(542 N Main St; mains $6-12; ☺10am-9pm Mon-Sat) Down-home, no-frills Mexican cookin' right by the train tracks – try the *carne asada* (seasoned, roasted beef).

Cap'n Flint's
SEAFOOD $$

(32250 N Harbor Dr; mains $11; ☺11am-9pm) Skip the overpriced Wharf Restaurant (aka Silver's), and head next door to this unpretentious place to eat the same fried fish for less.

Drinking & Entertainment

Caspar Inn
LIVE MUSIC

(www.casparinn.com; 14957 Caspar Rd; cover $3-25 Tue-Sat) Square in the middle of Mendocino and Fort Bragg, off Hwy 1, this jumpin' roadhouse rocks out the reggae, hip-hop, rockabilly, jam bands and international acts. The best live music venue on this stretch of the coast, it's worth checking out the calendar, which is posted on bulletin boards and public spaces throughout the area. Hours vary according to the events and the season.

North Coast Brewing Company
DREWERY

(www.northcoastbrewing.com; 444 N Main St) Of all the many breweries up the coast, this might be the most *serious,* with an arsenal of handcrafted, bold brews. If you order the sampler, designate a driver.

Gloriana Opera Company
THEATER COMPANY

(www.gloriana.org; 721 N Franklin St) Stages musical theater and operettas.

Shopping

There's plenty of window-shopping in Fort Bragg's compact downtown, including a string of antique shops along Franklin St.

Outdoor Store
OUTDOOR EQUIPMENT

(www.mendooutdoors.com; 247 N Main St) If you're planning on camping on the coast or exploring the Lost Coast, this is the best outfitter in the region, stocking detailed maps of the region's wilderness areas, fuel for stoves and high-quality gear.

Mendocino Vintage ANTIQUES
(www.mendocinovintage.com; 344 N Franklin St) Of the antique shops on Franklin, this is the hippest by a long shot, with a case full of vintage estate jewelry, antique glassware and old local oddities.

❶ Information

Fort Bragg-Mendocino Coast Chamber of Commerce (www.fortbragg.com, www.men\docinocoast.com; 332 N Main St; per 15min $1; ☺9am-5pm Mon-Fri, to 3pm Sat) Internet access.

Mendocino Coast District Hospital (☎707-961-1234; 700 River Dr; ☺24hr) Emergency room.

❶ Getting There & Around

Fort Bragg Cyclery (☎707-964-3509; www.fortbraggcyclery.com; 221a N Main St) Rents bicycles.

Mendocino Transit Authority (MTA; ☎707-462-1422, 800-696-4682; www.4mta.org) Runs local route 5 'BraggAbout' buses between Noyo Harbor and Elm St, north of downtown ($1). Service runs throughout the day.

Mackerricher State Park

Three miles north of Fort Bragg, the **Mac-Kerricher State Park** (☎707-964-9112; www.parks.ca.gov) preserves 9 miles of pristine rocky headlands, sandy beaches, dunes and tidepools.

The **visitor center** (☺10am-4pm Mon-Fri & 9am-6pm Sat & Sun summer, 9am-3pm rest of year) sits next to the whale skeleton at the park entrance. Hike the **Coastal Trail** along dark-sand beaches and see rare and endangered plant species (tread lightly). **Lake Cleone** is a 30-acre freshwater lake stocked with trout and visited by over 90 species of birds. At nearby **Laguna Point** an interpretive disabled-accessible boardwalk overlooks harbor seals and, from December to April, migrating whales. **Ricochet Ridge Ranch** (☎707-964-7669; www.horse-vacation.com; 24201 N Hwy 1) offers horseback-riding trips through redwoods or along the beach ($45 for 90 minutes).

Popular **campgrounds** (☎800-444-2725; www.reserveamerica.com; tent & RV sites $35), nestled in pine forest, have hot showers and water; the first-choice reservable tent sites are numbers 21 to 59. Ten superb, secluded walk-in tent sites (numbers 1 to 10) are first-come, first-served.

Westport

If sleepy Westport feels like the peaceful edge of nowhere, that's because it is. The last hamlet before the Lost Coast, on a twisting 15-mile drive north of Fort Bragg, it is the last town before Hwy 1 veers inland on the 22-mile ascent to meet Hwy 101 in Leggett. For details on accessing the Lost Coast's southernmost reaches from Westport, see p246.

Head 1.5 miles north of town for the ruggedly beautiful **Westport-Union Landing State Beach** (☎707-937-5804; tent sites $25), which extends for 3 miles on coastal bluffs. A rough hiking trail leaves the primitive campground and passes by tidepools and streams, accessible at low tide. Bring your own water.

Simple accommodations in town include the blue-and-red, plastic-flower-festooned **Westport Inn** (☎707-964-5135; 37040 N Hwy 1; r incl breakfast from $77).

TOP CHOICE **Westport Hotel & Old Abalone Pub** (☎877-964-3688; www.westporthotel.us; Hwy 1; r $90-165, ste $125-200, cabins $140-195; ☏) has been elegantly refashioned under new proprietors; the place is quiet enough to have a motto which brags 'You've finally found nowhere.' The rooms are bright and beautiful – feather duvets, hardwood furniture, simple patterns – and enjoy excellent views. The classy historic pub downstairs is the only option for dinner, so be thankful it's a delicious sampling of whimsical California fusions (like turduken sausage and buttermilk potatoes and rock shrimp mac and cheese) and hearty, expertly presented pub food.

Howard Creek Ranch (☎707-964-6725; www.howardcreekranch.com; 40501 N Hwy 1; r $90-165, ste $125-200, cabins $75-200; ☏), sitting on 60 stunning acres of forest and farmland abutting the wilderness, has accommodations in an 1880s farmhouse or a carriage barn, whose way-cool redwood rooms have been expertly handcrafted by the owner. Rates include full breakfast. Bring hiking boots, not high heels.

ALONG HIGHWAY 101

To get into the most remote and wild parts of the North Coast on the quick, eschew winding Hwy 1 for inland Hwy 101, which runs north from San Francisco as a freeway, then as a two- or four-lane highway north of Sonoma County, occasionally pausing under the traffic lights of small towns.

Know that escaping the Bay Area at rush hour (weekdays between 4pm and 7pm) ain't easy. You might sit bumper-to-bumper through Santa Rosa or Willits, where trucks bound for the coast turn onto Hwy 20.

Although Hwy 101 may not look as enticing as the coastal route, it's faster and less winding, leaving you time along the way to detour into Sonoma and Mendocino counties' wine regions (Mendocino claims to be the greenest wine region in the country), explore pastoral Anderson Valley, splash about Clear Lake or soak at hot-springs resorts outside Ukiah – time well spent indeed!

Hopland

Cute Hopland is the gateway to Mendocino County's wine country. Hops were first grown here in 1866, but Prohibition brought the industry temporarily to a halt. Today, booze drives the local economy again with wine tasting as the primary draw.

Sights & Activities

For an excellent weekend trip, use Hopland as a base for exploring the regional wineries. More information about the constantly growing roster of wineries is available at www.destinationhopland.com. Find a map to the wine region at www.visitmendocino. com.

Real Goods Solar Living Center   SOLAR ENERGY CENTER
(www.solarliving.org; 13771 S Hwy 101; ⏰9am-5pm; ♿) The progressive, futuristic 12-acre campus at the south end of town is largely responsible for the areas bold green initiates. There's no charge but the suggested donation is $3 to $5.

SIP! Mendocino   TASTING ROOM
(www.sipmendocino.com; 13420 S Hwy 101; ⏰11am-6pm) In central Hopland, this is a friendly place to get your bearings, pick up a map to the region and taste several wines without navigating all the back roads. Ami-

able proprietors guide you through a tour of 18 wines with delectable appetizer pairings and a blossom-filled courtyard.

Saracina   WINERY
(www.saracina.com; 11684 S Hwy 101; ⏰10am-5pm) The highlight of a tour here is the descent into the cool caves. Sensuous whites are all biodynamcially and sustainably farmed.

Fetzer Vineyards Organic Gardens   WINERY
(www.fetzer.com; 13601 Eastside Rd; ⏰9am-5pm) Fetzer's sustainable practices have raised the bar, and their gardens are lovely. The wines are excellent value.

Brutocao Schoolhouse Plaza   TASTING ROOM
(www.brutocaoschoolhouseplaza.com; 13500 S Hwy 101; ⏰11am-8pm) In central Hopland, this place has bocce courts and bold reds – a perfect combo.

Graziano Family of Wines   WINERY
(www.grazianofamilyofwines.com; 13251 S Hwy 101; ⏰10am-5pm) Specializes in 'Cal-Ital' wines – nebbiolo, dolcetto, barbera and sangiovese – at some great prices.

Sleeping & Eating

Hopland Inn   HISTORIC HOTEL $$
(☎707-744-1890, 800-266-1891; www.hoplandinn. com; 13401 S Hwy 101; r $180; ❉❂❄) If you're spending the night in town, your only choice is a good one: the 1890 inn in the middle of town. Enjoy bevvies from the full bar downstairs in the cozy, wood-paneled library.

Bluebird Cafe   AMERICAN $
(☎707-744-1633; 13340 S Hwy 101; breakfast & lunch $5-12, dinner $12-17; ⏰7am-2pm Mon-Thu, to 7pm Fri-Sun; ♿) For conservative tastes, this classic American diner serves hearty breakfasts, giant burgers and homemade pie (the summer selection of peach-blueberry pie is dreamy). For a more exciting culinary adventure, try the wild game burgers, including boar with apple chutney and elk with a bite of horseradish.

Clear Lake

With over 100 miles of shoreline, Clear Lake is the largest naturally occurring freshwater lake in California (Tahoe is bigger, but crosses the Nevada state line). In summer the warm water thrives with algae, giving it a murky green appearance and creating a

TOP CLEAR LAKE WINERIES

From north to south, the following four wineries are the best; some offer tours by appointment.

» **Ceago Vinegarden** (www.ceago.com; 5115 E Hwy 20, Nice; ☉10am-6pm) Ceago (cee-ay-go) occupies a spectacular spot on the north shore, and pours biodynamic, fruit-forward wines.

» **Wildhurst Vineyards** (www.wildhurst.com; 3855 Main St, Kelseyville; ☉10am-5pm) The best wine on the lake, but lacks atmosphere. Try the sauvignon blanc.

» **Ployez Winery** (1171 S Hwy 29, Lower Lake; ☉11am-5pm) Above-average *méthode champenoise* sparkling wines; surrounded by farmland.

» **Langtry Estate Vineyards** (21000 Butts Canyon Rd, Middletown; ☉11am-5pm) The most beautiful vineyard. Try the port.

fabulous habitat for fish – especially bass – and tens of thousands of birds. Mt Konocti, a 4200ft-tall dormant volcano, lords over the scene. Alas, the human settlements don't always live up to the grandeur and thousands of acres near the lake remain scarred from wildfires in 2008.

⊙ Sights & Activities

Locals refer to the northwest portion as 'upper lake' and the southeast portion as 'lower lake.' **Lakeport** (population 5240) sits on the northwest shore, a 45-minute drive east of Hopland along Hwy 175 (off Hwy 101); **Kelseyville** (population 3000) is 7 miles south. **Clearlake**, off the southeastern shore, is the biggest (and ugliest) town.

Hwy 20 links the north-shore hamlets of **Nice** (the northernmost town) and **Lucerne**, 4 miles southeast. **Middletown**, a cute village, lies 20 miles south of Clearlake at the junction of Hwys 175 and 129, 40 minutes north of Calistoga.

Many outfits rent boats, including **On the Waterfront** (☎707-263-6789; 60 3rd St, Lakeport, six person boats per 3hr/day $185/350) and Konocti Harbor Resort & Spa in Kelseyville (p234).

Clear Lake State Park   STATE PARK
(☎707-279-4293; 5300 Soda Bay Rd, Kelseyville; per car $8) Six miles from Lakeport, on the lake's west shore, the park is idyllic and gorgeous, with hiking trails, fishing, boating and camping. The **bird-watching** is extraordinary. The **visitor center** has geological and historical exhibits.

Redbud Audubon Society   BIRD WATCHING
(www.redbudaudubon.org) In Lower Lake, this conservation group leads birding walks.

🛏 Sleeping & Eating

Make reservations on weekends and during summer, when people flock to the cool water.

LAKEPORT & KELSEYVILLE

There are a number of motels along the main drag in Kelseyville and Lakeport, but if you want fresh air, Clear Lake State Park has four **campgrounds** (☎800-444-7275; www.reserveamerica.com; tent & RV sites $35) with showers. The weekly **farmers market** (Hwy 29 & Thomas Rd; ☉8:30am-noon Sat May-Oct) is in Kelseyville.

Lakeport English Inn   B&B $$
(☎707-263-4317; www.lakeportenglishinn.com; 675 N Main St, Lakeport; r $159-210, cottages $210; ✳🛜) The finest B&B at Clear Lake is an 1875 Carpenter Gothic with 10 impeccably furnished rooms, styled with a nod to the English countryside. Weekends take high tea (public welcome by reservation) – with real Devonshire cream.

Konocti Harbor Resort & Spa   RESORT $$
(☎707-279-4281, 800-660-5253; www.konoctiharbor.com; 8727 Soda Bay Rd, Konocti Bay; r $89-199, apt & beach cottages $199-349, ste $259-399; 🛜🏊) On Konocti Bay, 4 miles from Kelseyville, this gargantuan resort, famous for huge concerts, includes four pools, a fitness center, tennis, golf, marina and spa. Rates spike on concert nights.

Mallard House   MOTEL $
(☎707-262-1601; www.mallardhouse.com; 970 N Main St, Lakeport; r with kitchen $69-149, without $49-99; ✳🛜) Waterfront motels with boat slips include this cottage-style place, which is a fantastic value during the week.

TOP CHOICE Saw Shop
Gallery Bistro
CALIFORNIAN **$$$**

(☎707-278-0129; www.sawshopbistro.com; 3825 Main St, Kelseyville; small plates $10-12, mains $18-30; ☑dinner Tue-Sat) The best restaurant in Lake County serves a Californian-cuisine menu of wild salmon and rack of lamb, as well as a small plates menu of sushi, lobster tacos, Kobe-beef burgers and flatbread pizzas. Laid-back atmosphere, too.

Molly Brennan's
PUB **$**

(www.mollybrennans.com; 175 Main St, Lakeport; mains $9-20; ☺11am-11pm Mon, Wed & Thu, to 2am Fri-Sun) Big mirrors and dark wood, pints of Guinness and bangers and mash make Molly Brennan's a quality pub. You'd be remiss to leave without trying the more ambitious menu items, like the lamb stew or pistachio-crusted salmon.

Bigg's 155
DINER **$**

(155 Park St, Lakeport; mains $5-12) It may look like a humble diner, but the menu is adventuresome (Shrimp Po' Boys?) and the ice cream treats are enormous.

NORTH SHORE

🖋 Tallman Hotel
HISTORIC HOTEL **$$**

(☎707-274-0200, 888-880-5253; www.tallmanhotel.com; 4057 E Hwy 20, Nice; cottages $159-229; ❄🖗☀) The centerpiece may be the smartly renovated historic hotel – tile bathrooms, warm lighting, thick linens – but the rest of the property's lodging, including several modern, sustainably built cottages, are equally peaceful. The shaded garden, walled-in swimming pool, brick patios and big porches exude a timeless elegance. Garden rooms come with Japanese soaking tubs, all heated and cooled by an energy-efficient geothermal-solar system.

Featherbed Railroad Co
HOTEL **$$**

(☎707-274-8378, 800-966-6322; www.featherbedrailroad.com; 2870 Lakeshore Blvd, Nice; cabooses incl breakfast $140-190; ❄☀) A treat for train buffs and kids, Featherbed has 10 comfy, real cabooses on a grassy lawn. Some of the cabooses straddle the border between kitschy and tacky (the 'Easy Rider' has a Harley Davidson headboard and a mirrored ceiling), but they're great fun if you keep a sense of humor. There's a tiny beach across the road.

Sea Breeze Resort
COTTAGES **$$**

(☎707-998-3327; www.seabreezeresort.net; 9595 Harbor Dr, Glenhaven; cottages with kitchen $130-150, without $100; ☑Apr-Oct; ❄🖗) Just south of Lucerne on a small peninsula, gardens surround seven spotless lakeside cottages. All have barbecues.

MIDDLETOWN

Harbin Hot Springs
SPA **$$**

(☎707-987-2377, 800-622-2477; www.harbin.org; Harbin Hot Springs Rd; tent & RV sites midweek/weekend $25/35, dm $35/50, s midweek $60-75, weekend $95-120, d midweek $90-190, weekend $140-260) Harbin is classic Northern California. Originally a 19th-century health spa and resort, it now has a retreat-center vibe and people come to unwind in silent, clothing-optional hot- and cold-spring pools. This is the birthplace of Watsu (floating massage) and there are wonderful body therapies as well as yoga, holistic-health workshops and 1100 acres of hiking. Accommodations are in Victorian buildings (which could use sprucing up) and share a common vegetarian-only kitchen. Food is available at the market, cafe and restaurant. Day-trippers are welcome; day rates are $25 and require one member of your group to purchase a membership (one month $10).

The springs are 3 miles off Hwy 175. From Middletown, take Barnes St, which becomes Big Canyon Rd, and head left at the fork.

☆ Entertainment

Library Park, in Lakeport, has free lakeside Friday-evening summer concerts, with blues and rockabilly tunes to appeal to middle-aged roadtrippers. Harbin Hot Springs (p235) presents a surprising lineup of world music and dances. The Konocti Harbor Resort & Spa (p234) hosts national acts (recent guests include Los Lonely Boys and Lyle Lovett) in an outdoor amphitheater and indoor concert hall.

ⓘ Information

Lake County Visitor Information Center
(www.lakecounty.com; 6110 E Hwy 120, Lucerne; ☺9am-5pm Mon-Sat, noon-4pm Sun) Has complete information and an excellent website, which allows potential visitors to narrow their focus by interests.

ⓘ Getting Around

Lake Transit (☎707-263-3334, 707-994-3334; www.laketransit.org) operates weekday routes between Middletown and Calistoga ($3.50, 35 minutes, three daily); on Thursday it connects through to Santa Rosa. Buses serve Ukiah ($3.50, two hours, four daily), from Clearlake via

TOP ANDERSON VALLEY WINERIES

The valley's cool nights yield high-acid, fruit-forward, food-friendly wines. Pinot noir, chardonnay and dry gewürtztraminer flourish. Most wineries (www.avwines.com) sit outside Philo. Many are family-owned and offer tastings, some give tours. The following are particularly noteworthy.

» **Navarro** (www.navarrowine.com; 5601 Hwy 128; ⊙10am-6pm) The best option, and picnicking is encouraged.

» **Esterlina** (www.esterlinavineyards.com) For big reds, pack a picnic and head high up the rolling hills; call ahead.

» **Husch** (www.huschvineyards.com; 4400 Hwy 128; ⊙10am-5pm) Husch serves exquisite tastings inside a rose-covered cottage.

Lakeport ($2.25, 1¼ hours, seven daily). Since piecing together routes and times can be difficult, it's best to phone ahead.

Anderson Valley

Rolling hills surround pastoral Anderson Valley, famous for apple orchards, vineyards, pastures and quiet. Visitors come primarily to winery-hop, but there's good hiking and bicycling in the hills, and the chance to escape civilization. Traveling through the valley is the most common route to Mendocino from San Francisco.

◉ Sights & Activities

Boonville (population 1370) and **Philo** (population 1000) are the valley's principal towns. From Ukiah, winding Hwy 253 heads 20 miles south to Boonville. Equally scenic Hwy 128 twists and turns 60 miles between Cloverdale on Hwy 101, south of Hopland, and Albion on coastal Hwy 1.

Apple Farm   ORCHARD
(☎707-895-2333; www.philoapplefarm.com; 18501 Greenwood Rd, Philo; ⊙daylight) For the best fruit, skip the obvious roadside stands and head to this gorgeous farm for organic preserves, chutneys, heirloom apples and pears. It also hosts cooking classes with some of the Wine Country's best chefs. You can make a weekend out of it by staying in one of the orchard cottages (p236).

Anderson Valley Brewing Company   BREWERY, FRISBEE GOLF
(☎707-895-2337; www.avbc.com; 17700 Hwy 253; tours $5; ⊙11am-6pm) East of the Hwy 128 crossroads, this solar-powered brewery crafts award-winning beers in a Bavarian-style brewhouse. You can also toss around a

disc on the course while enjoying the brews but, be warned, the sun can take its toll. Tours leave at 1:30pm and 3pm daily (only Tuesday and Wednesday in winter); call ahead.

Anderson Valley Historical Society Museum   MUSEUM
(www.andersonvalleymuseum.org; 12340 Hwy 128; ⊙1-4pm Fri-Sun Feb-Nov) In a recently renovated little red schoolhouse west of Boonville, this museum displays historical artifacts.

✪ Festivals & Events

Pinot Noir Festival   WINE
(www.avwines.com) One of Anderson Valley's many wine celebrations.

Sierra Nevada World Music Festival   MUSIC
(www.snwmf.com) In June, the sounds of reggae and roots fill the air, co-mingling with the scent of Mendocino county's *other* cash crop.

California Wool & Fiber Festival   CRAFT
(www.fiberfestival.com) Events with names like 'Angora Rabbit Demonstration' bring out the natural-fiber fanatics from around the state.

Mendocino County Fair   FAIR
(www.mendocountyfair.com) A county classic in mid-September.

⌂ Sleeping

Accommodations fill on weekends.

TOP CHOICE Apple Farm   COTTAGES $$$
(☎707-895-2333; www.philoapplefarm.com; 18501 Greenwood Rd, Philo; r midweek/weekend $175/250) Set within the orchard, guests of Philo's bucolic Apple Farm choose from four exquisite cottages, each built with reclaimed materials. With bright, airy spaces, polished

plank floors, simple furnishings and views of the surrounding trees, each one is an absolute dream. Red Door cottage is a favorite because of the bathroom – you can soak in the slipper tub, or shower on the private deck under the open sky. The cottages often get booked with participants of the farm's **cooking classes**, so book well in advance. For a swim, the Navarro River is within walking distance.

Boonville Hotel BOUTIQUE HOTEL $$
(☏707-895-2210; www.boonvillehotel.com; 14040 Hwy 128; r $125-200, ste $225) Decked out in a contemporary American-country style with sea-grass flooring, pastel colors and fine linens that would make Martha Stewart proud, this historic hotel's rooms are safe for urbanites who refuse to abandon style just because they've gone to the country.

Hendy Woods State Park CAMPGROUND $
(☏707-937-5804, reservations 800-444-7275; www.reserveamerica.com; tent & RV sites $35, cabins $50) Bordered by the Navarro River on Hwy 128, west of Philo, the park has hiking, picnicking and a forested campground with hot showers.

Other Place COTTAGES $$
(☏707-895-3979; www.sheepdung.com; cottages $140-200; ☎🐕🐾) Outside of town, 500 acres of ranch land surrounds private hilltop cottages.

✗ Eating & Drinking

Boonville restaurants seem to open and close as they please, so expect variations in the hours listed below based on season and whimsy. There are several places along Hwy 128 which can supply a picnic with fancy local cheese and fresh bread.

Table 128 NEW AMERICAN $$
(☏707-895-2210; www.boonvillehotel.com; 14040 Hwy 128; 3-/4-course prix fixe $40/50; ☎5-9pm Thu-Mon) Food-savvy travelers love the constantly changing New American menu here, featuring simple dishes done well, like roasted chicken, grilled local lamb and strawberry shortcake. The family-style service makes dinner here a freewheeling, elegant social affair, with big farm tables and soft lighting.

Paysenne ICE CREAM $
(14111 Hwy 128; ice cream cone $3; ☎10am-3pm Thu-Mon) Booneville's new ice-cream shop serves the innovative flavors of Three Twins Ice Cream, whose delightful flavors include Lemon Cookie and Strawberry Je Ne Sais Quoi (which has a hint of balsamic vinegar).

Boonville General Store DELI $
(17810 Farrer Lane; dishes $5-8; ☎7:30am-3pm Mon-Fri from 8:30am Sat & Sun, pizza night Fri 5:30-8pm) Opposite the Boonville Hotel, this deli is good to stock up for picnics, offering sandwiches on homemade bread, thin-crust pizzas and organic cheeses.

Lauren's AMERICAN $$
(www.laurensgoodfood.com; 14211 Hwy 128, Boonville; mains $8-14; ☎5-9pm Tue-Sat; 🚗🍴) Locals pack Lauren's for eclectic homemade cookin' and a good wine list. Musicians sometimes jam on the stage by the front window.

ℹ Information

Anderson Valley Chamber of Commerce
(☏707-895-2379; www.andersonvalleychamber.com) Has tourist information and a complete schedule of annual events.

Ukiah

As the county seat and Mendocino's largest city, Ukiah is mostly a utilitarian stop for travelers to refuel the car and get a bite. But, if you have to stop here for the night, you could do much worse: the town is a friendly place, there are a plethora of cookie-cutter hotel chains, some cheaper midcentury motels and a handful of good dining options. The coolest attractions, a pair of thermal springs and a sprawling campus for Buddhist studies, lie outside the city limits.

> ## BOONTLING
>
> Boonville is famous for its unique language, 'Boontling,' which evolved about the turn of the 20th century when Boonville was very remote. Locals developed the language to *shark* (stump) outsiders and amuse themselves. You may hear *codgie kimmies* (old men) asking for a horn of *zeese* (a cup of coffee) or some *bahl gorms* (good food). If you are really lucky, you'll spot the tow truck called Boont Region De-arkin' Moshe (literally 'Anderson Valley Unwrecking Machine').

⊙ Sights

**Grace Hudson Museum-
Sun House** MUSEUM
(www.gracehudsonmuseum.org; 431 S Main St;
donation $2; ⊙10am-4:30pm Wed-Sat, from noon
Sun) One block east of State St, the collection's mainstays are paintings by Grace Hudson (1865–1937). Her sensitive depictions of Pomo people complement the ethnological work and Native American baskets collected by her husband, John Hudson.

✺ Festivals & Events

Redwood Empire Fair COUNTY FAIR
(www.redwoodempirefair.com) On the second weekend of August.

Ukiah Country PumpkinFest CULTURAL
(www.cityofukiah.com) In late October, with an arts-and-crafts fair, children's carnival and fiddle contest.

⊨ Sleeping

Every imaginable chain resort is here, just off the highway. For something with more personality, resorts and campgrounds cluster around Ukiah (see p239).

Sanford House B&B B&B $$
(☎707-462-1653; www.sanfordhouse.com; 306 S Pine St; s/d $95/175; ✴) This well-preserved Victorian is situated among a lovely garden. The rooms fit the standard of northern California's other Victorian B&Bs – lace curtains, wicker chairs, floral wallpaper and brass beds. The sweet owners offer an organic breakfast.

Sunrise Inn MOTEL $
(☎707-462-6601; www.sunriseinn.net; 650 S State St; r $58-78; ✴🐾) Request one of the remodeled rooms at Ukiah's best budget motel. All have microwaves and refrigerators.

Discovery Inn Motel MOTEL $
(☎707-462-8873; www.discoveryinnukiahca.com; 1340 N State St; r $55-95; ✴🐾🏊) Clean, but dated with a 75ft pool and several Jacuzzis.

✗ Eating

It'd be a crime to eat the fast food junk located off the highway; Ukiah has a lot of affordable, excellent eateries.

TOP CHOICE Oco Time JAPANESE $$
(☎707-462-2422; www.ocotime.com; 111 W Church St; lunch mains $7-10, dinner mains $8-16;
⊙11:15am-2:30pm Tue-Fri, 5:30-8:30pm Mon-Sat; ✎) Shoulder your way through the locals to get Ukiah's best sushi, noodle bowls and *oco* (a delicious mess of seaweed, grilled cabbage, egg and noodles). The 'Peace Café' has a great vibe, a friendly staff and interesting special rolls. Downside? The place gets mobbed, so reservations are a good idea.

Patrona NEW AMERICAN $$
(☎707-462-9181; www.patronarestaurant.com; 130 W Standley St; lunch mains $10-15, dinner mains $15-28; ⊙11am-3pm & 5-9pm Tue-Sat; ✎) Foodies flock to excellent Patrona for earthy, flavor-packed, seasonal and regional organic cooking. The unfussy menu includes dishes like roasted chicken, brined-and-roasted pork chops, housemade pasta and local wines. Make reservations and ask about the prix fixe.

Ukiah Brewing Company BREWPUB $$
(www.ukiahbrewingco.com; 102 S State St, Ukiah; dinner mains $15-25; ⊙11:30am-9pm Sun-Thu, to 10pm Fri-Sat; 🍺) The brews might outshine the food – barely – but there's no question that the dance floor is the most happening spot downtown. When it gets rowdy to live music on the weekend, this place is a blast. The menu has a strong organic and sustainable bent, with plenty of vegan and raw options.

Schat's Courthouse Bakery & Cafe CAFE $
(www.schats.com; 113 W Perkins St; lunch mains $3-7, dinner mains $8-14; ⊙5:30am-6pm Mon-Fri, to 5pm Sat) Founded by Dutch bakers, Schat's makes a dazzling array of chewy, dense breads, sandwiches, wraps, big salads, dee-lish hot mains and homemade pastries.

Kilkenny Kitchen CAFE $
(www.kilkennykitchen.com; 1093 S Dora St; lunch $7-10; ⊙10am-3pm Mon-Fri; ✎) Tucked into a neighborhood south of downtown, county workers love this chipper yellow place for the fresh rotation of daily soups and sandwich specials (a recent visit on a blazing hot day found a heavenly, cold cucumber dill soup). The salads – like the pear, walnut and blue cheese – are also fantastic.

Himalayan Cafe HIMALAYAN $
(www.thehimalayancafe.com; 1639 S State St; mains lunch $9-13, dinner $10-17; ✎) South of

downtown, find delicately spiced Nepalese cooking – tandoori breads and curries.

Ukiah farmers market   MARKET
(cnr School & Clay Sts; ☺8:30am-noon Sat May-Oct, 3-6pm Tue Jun-Oct) The market offers farm-fresh produce, crafts and entertainment.

Drinking & Entertainment
Dive bars and scruffy cocktail lounges line State St. Ask at the chamber of commerce about cultural events, including Sunday summer concerts at Todd Grove Park, which have a delightfully festive atmosphere, and local square dances.

Ukiah Brewing Co   BREWERY
(www.ukiahbrewingco.com; 102 S State St; ☎) A great place to drink, this local brewpub makes organic beer and draws weekend crowds.

Coffee Critic   COFFEE SHOP
(www.thecoffeecritic.com; 476 N State St; ☎) Drop in for fair trade espresso, ice cream and occasional live music.

Shopping
Ukiah has a pleasant, walkable shopping district along School St near the courthouse.

Nomad's World   JEWELRY, HOMEWARES
(www.nomads-world.com; 111 S School St; ☺Mon-Sat) Step inside for cool jewelry and home furnishings.

Ruby Slippers   VINTAGE
(110 N School St; ☺Wed-Sat) Take turns trying on vintage drag.

Mendocino Book Co   BOOKS
(www.mendocinobookcompany.com; 102 S School St; ☺Mon-Sat) The best bookstore in town.

Information
Running north–south, west of Hwy 101, State St is Ukiah's main drag. School St, near Perkins St, is also good for strolling.
Bureau of Land Management (☎707-468-4000; 2550 N State St) Maps and information on backcountry camping, hiking and biking in wilderness areas.
Greater Ukiah Chamber of Commerce (☎707-462-4705; www.gomendo.com; 200 S School St; ☺9am-5pm Mon-Fri) One block west of State St; information on Ukiah, Hopland and Anderson Valley.

Around Ukiah
UKIAH WINERIES
You'll notice the acres of grapes stretching out in every direction on your way into town. Winemakers around Ukiah enjoy much of the same climatic conditions that made Napa so famous. Pick up a wineries map from the Ukiah chamber of commerce (p239).

Parducci Wine Cellars   WINERY
(www.parducci.com; 501 Parducci Rd, Ukiah; ☺10am-5pm) Sustainably grown, harvested and produced, 'America's Greenest Winery' produces affordable, bold, earthy reds. The tasting room, lined in brick and soft light, is a perfect little cave-like environment to get out of the summer heat, sip wine and chat about sustainability practices.

Fife   WINERY
(☎707-485-0323; www.fifevineyards.com; 3621 Ricetti Lane, Redwood Valley; ☺10am-5pm) Fruit-forward reds include a peppery zinfandel and petite sirah, both affordable and food-friendly. And oh, the hilltop views! Bring a picnic.

Germain-Robin   DISTILLERY
(☎707-462-0314; Unit 35, 3001 S State St; ☺by appointment) Makes some of the world's best brandy, which is handcrafted by a fifth-generation brandy-maker from the Cognac region of France. It's just a freeway-side warehouse, but if you're into cognac, you gotta come.

VICHY HOT SPRINGS RESORT
Opened in 1854, Vichy is the oldest continuously operating mineral-springs spa in California. The water's composition perfectly matches that of its famous namesake in Vichy, France. A century ago, Mark Twain, Jack London and Robert Louis Stevenson traveled here for the water's restorative properties, which ameliorate everything from arthritis to poison oak.

Today, the beautifully maintained historic **resort** (☎707-462-9515; www.vichysprings.com; 2605 Vichy Springs Rd, Ukiah; lodge s/d $135/195, creekside r $195/245, cottages from $280; ❀☎☎☎) has the only warm-water, naturally carbonated mineral baths in North America. Unlike others, Vichy requires swimsuits (rentals $2). Day use costs $30 for two hours, $50 for a full day.

Facilities include a swimming pool, outdoor mineral hot tub, 10 indoor and outdoor tubs with natural 100°F waters, and a grotto for sipping the effervescent waters. Massages and facials are available. Entry includes use of the 700-acre grounds, abutting Bureau of Land Management (BLM) lands; hiking trails lead to a 40ft waterfall, an old cinnabar mine and 1100ft peaks – great for sunset views.

The resort's suite and two cottages, built in 1854, are Mendocino County's three oldest structures. The cozy rooms have wooden floors, top-quality beds, breakfast and spa privileges, and no TVs.

From Hwy 101, exit at Vichy Springs Rd and follow the state-landmark signs east for 3 miles. Ukiah is five minutes, but a world, away.

ORR HOT SPRINGS

A clothing-optional resort that's beloved by locals, back-to-the-land hipsters, backpackers and liberal-minded tourists, **springs** (☎707-462-6277; tent sites $45-50, d $140-160, cottages $195-230; ☺10am-10pm; ⊠) has private tubs, a sauna, spring-fed rock-bottomed swimming pool, steam, massage and magical gardens. Day use costs $25, $20 on Mondays.

Accommodation includes use of the spa and communal kitchen; some cottages have kitchens. Reservations are essential.

To get there from Hwy 101, take N State St exit, go north a quarter of a mile to Orr Springs Rd, then 9 miles west. The steep, winding mountain road takes 30 minutes to drive.

MONTGOMERY WOODS STATE RESERVE

Two miles west of Orr, this 1140-acre **reserve** (Orr Springs Rd) protects five old-growth redwood groves, and some of the best groves within a day's drive from San Francisco. A 2-mile loop trail crosses the creek, winding through the serene groves, starting near the picnic tables and toilets. It's out of the way, so visitors are likely to have it mostly to themselves. Day use only; no camping.

LAKE MENDOCINO

Amid rolling hills, 5 miles northeast of Ukiah, this tranquil 1822-acre artificial lake fills a valley, once the ancestral home of the Pomo people. On the lake's north side, **Pomo Visitor Center** (☎707-467-4200) is modeled after a Pomo roundhouse, with exhibits on tribal culture and the dam. The center was closed indefinitely for upgrades at the time of update, but was still offering information via phone about camping.

Coyote Dam, 3500ft long and 160ft high, marks the lake's southwest corner; the lake's eastern part is a 689-acre protected wildlife habitat. The **Army Corps of Engineers** (www.spn.usace.army.mil/mendocino; 1160 Lake Mendocino Dr; ☺8am-4pm Mon-Fri) built the dam, manages the lake and provides recreation information. Its office is inconveniently located on the lower lake.

There are 300 **tent and RV sites** (☎877-444-6777; www.reserveusa.com; $20-22), most with hot showers and primitive boat-in sites ($8).

CITY OF TEN THOUSAND BUDDHAS

Three miles east of Ukiah, via Talmage Rd, the **site** (☎707-462-0939; www.cttbusa.org; 2001 Talmage Rd; ☺8am-6pm) used to be a state mental hospital. Since 1976 it has been a lush, quiet 488-acre Chinese-Buddhist community. Don't miss the temple hall, which really does have 10,000 Buddhas. As this is a place of worship, please be respectful of those who use the grounds for meditating. Stay for lunch in the vegetarian Chinese **restaurant** (4951 Bodhi Way; mains $10; ☺noon-3pm; ☑).

Willits

Twenty miles north of Ukiah, Willits mixes NorCal dropouts with loggers and ranchers (the high school has a bull-riding team). Lamp posts of the main drag are decorated with bucking broncos and cowboys, but the heart of the place is just as boho. Though ranching, timber and manufacturing may be its mainstays, tie-dye is de rigueur. For visitors, Willits' greatest claim to fame is as the eastern terminus of the Skunk Train. Fort Bragg is 35 miles away on the coast; allow an hour to navigate twisty Hwy 20.

◉ Sights & Activities

Ten miles north of Willits, **Hwy 162/Covelo Rd** makes for a superb drive following the route of the Northwestern Pacific Railroad along the Eel River and through the Mendocino National Forest. The trip is only about 30 miles, but plan on taking at least an hour on the winding road, passing exquisite river canyons and rolling hills. Eventually, you'll reach **Covelo**, known for its unusual round valley.

Skunk Train
HISTORIC TRAIN

(☎707-964-6371, 866-866-1690; www.skunktrain.com; adult/child $49/24) The depot is on E Commercial St, three blocks east of Hwy 101. Trains run between Willits and Fort Bragg (p229).

Mendocino County Museum
MUSEUM

(www.mendocinomuseum.org; 400 E Commercial St; adult/child $4/1; ⓒ10am-4:30pm Wed-Sun) Among the best community museum's in the northern half of the state, this puts the lives of early settlers in excellent historical context – much drawn from old letters – and there's an entire 1920s soda fountain and barber shop inside. You could spend an hour perusing Pomo and Yuki basketry and artifacts, or reading about local scandals and countercultural movements. Outside, the Roots of Motive Power (www.rootsofmotivepower.com) exhibit occasionally demonstrates steam logging and machinery.

Ridgewood Ranch
RANCH

(☎reservations 707-459-7910; www.seabiscuitheritage.com; 16200 N Hwy 101; tours $15-25) Willits' most famous resident was the horse Seabiscuit, which grew up here. Ninety-minute tours operate on Monday, Wednesday and Friday (June to September); once a month on Saturday there's a three-hour tour by reservation.

Jackson Demonstration State Forest
HIKING

Fifteen miles west of Willits on Hwy 20, the forest offers day-use recreational activities, including educational hiking trails and mountain-biking. You can also camp here (see p241).

✖ Festivals & Events

Willits Frontier Days & Rodeo
RODEO

(www.willitsfrontierdays.com) Dating from 1926, Willits has the oldest continuous rodeo in California, occurring the first week in July.

Willits Renaissance Faire
CULTURAL

(www.willitsfaire.com) Held in August, featuring Highland Scottish games, food, music, jugglers, arts and crafts.

🛏 Sleeping

Some of the in-town motels – and there seems to be about a hundred of them – are dumps, so absolutely check out the room before checking in. Ask about Skunk Train packages. There are a couple crowded, loud RV parks on the edges of town for only the most desperate campers.

Baechtel Creek Inn & Spa
BOUTIQUE HOTEL $$

(☎707-459-9063, 800-459-9911; www.baechtelcreekinn.com; 101 Gregory Lane; d incl breakfast $100-130; ❄@☀) As Willits' only upscale option, this place draws an interesting mix: Japanese bus tours, business travelers and wine trippers. The standard rooms are nothing too flashy, but they have top knotch linens, iPod docks and tasteful art. Custom rooms come with local wine and more space. The immaculate pool and lovely egg breakfast on the patio are perks.

Best Value Inn Holiday Lodge
MOTEL $

(☎707-459-5361, 800-835-3972; www.bestvalueinn.com; 1540 S Main St; d from $63; ❄🛜☀) It's a bit of a draw between the 1950s motels that line Willits' main drag, but this is our favorite because of the kind staff and relatively quiet rooms.

Jackson Demonstration State Forest
CAMPGROUND $

(☎707-964-5674; sites free) Campsites have barbecue pits and pit toilets, but no water. Get a permit from the on-site host, or from a self-registration kiosk.

✖ Eating

TOP CHOICE Zaza's Bakery, Bistro & Gallery
BAKERY, CAFE $

(35 E Commercial St; pastries $2-4, sandwiches $8; ⓒ9am-2pm) So far, little Zaza's is the only bakery in California to sell a bagel that could be mistaken for one baked in New York. And that's only where the delightful surprises begin: a delicious, delicate soup menu that changes every day (last visit it was red snapper, corn and coconut chowder), a bright atmosphere completed by good artwork, jazz on the radio and hearty sandwiches on nutty, multigrain bread.

🌿 Purple Thistle
FUSION $$

(☎707-459-4750; 50 S Main St; mains $13-25; ⓒ5-9pm) Willits' best fine dining; cooks up Cajun- and Japanese-inspired 'Mendonesian' cuisine, using fresh organic ingredients. Make reservations, and expect it to be a bit crowded.

Loose Caboose Cafe
SANDWICHES $

(10 Woods St; sandwiches $7-10; ⓒ7:30am-3pm) People tend to get a bit flushed when talking about the sandwiches at the Loose Caboose,

which gets jammed at lunch. The Reuben and Sante Fe Chicken sandwiches are two savory delights.

Burrito Exquisito MEXICAN $
(42 S Hain St; mains $7; ⊘11am-7pm) A cute hippie burrito shop dishes out big burritos, which you can eat in the back garden.

Ardella's Kitchen DINER $$
(35 E Commercial St; mains $5-11; ⊘6am-noon Tue-Sat) For quick eats, this tiny place is tops for breakfast – and is *the* place for gossip.

Mariposa Market GROCERIES $
(600 S Main St) Willits natural food outlet.

🍷 Drinking & Entertainment

Shanachie Pub BAR
(50B S Main St; ⊘Mon-Sat) Sharing the garden with Burrito Exquisito, this is a friendly little dive with tons on tap.

Willits Community Theatre THEATER
(www.willitstheatre.org; 212 S Main St) Stages award-winning plays, poetry readings and comedy.

🛍 Shopping

JD Redhouse & Co CLOTHING, HOMEWARES
(212 S Main St; ⊘10am-6pm) Family-owned and operated, this central mercantile is a good reflection of Willits itself, balancing cowboy essentials – boots and grain, tools and denim – with treats for the weekend tourist. The ice cream counter is a good place to cool off when the heat on the sidewalk gets intense.

Book Juggler BOOKS
(50B S Main St; ⊘10am-7pm Mon-Thu, to 8pm Fri, 10am-6pm Sat, noon-5pm Sun) Has dense rows of new and used books, music books and local papers (pick up the weird, locally printed *Anderson Valley Advertiser* here).

SOUTHERN REDWOOD COAST

There's some real magic in the loamy soil and misty air 'beyond the redwood curtain'; it yields the tallest trees and most potent herb on the planet. North of Fort Bragg, Bay Area weekenders and antique-stuffed B&Bs give way to lumber wars, pot farmers and an army of carved bears. The 'growing' culture here is palpable and the huge profit it brings to the region has evi-

dent cultural side effects – an omnipresent population of transients who work the harvests, a chilling respect for 'No Trespassing' signs and a political culture that is an uneasy balance between gun-toting libertarians, ultra-left progressives and typical college-town chaos. Nevertheless, the reason to visit is to soak in the magnificent landscape, which runs through a number of pristine, ancient redwood forests.

❶ Information

Redwood Coast Heritage Trails (www.red woods.info) Gives a nuanced slant on the region with itineraries based around lighthouses, Native American culture, the timber and rail industries, and maritime life.

Leggett

Leggett marks the redwood country's beginning and Hwy 1's end. There ain't much but an expensive gas station, pizza joint and two markets.

Visit 1000-acre **Standish-Hickey State Recreation Area** (69350 Hwy 101; day use $8), 1.5 miles to the north, for picnicking, swimming and fishing in the Eel River and hiking trails among virgin and second-growth redwoods. Year-round **campgrounds** (⊘800-444-7275; www.reserveamerica.com; tent & RV sites $35) with hot showers book up in summer. Avoid highway-side sites.

Chandelier Drive-Thru Tree Park (www.drivethrutree.com; Drive-Thru Tree Rd; per car $5; ⊘8am-dusk) has 200 private acres of virgin redwoods with picnicking and nature walks. And yes, there's a redwood with a square hole carved out, which cars can drive through. Only in America.

The 1949 tourist trap of **Confusion Hill** (www.confusionhill.com; 75001 N Hwy 101; adult/child Gravity House $5/4, train rides $8.50/6.50; ⊘9am-6pm May-Sep, 10am-5pm Oct-Apr; 🚻) is an enduring curiosity and the most elaborate of the old-fashioned stops that line the route north. The Gravity House challenges queasy visitors to keep their balance while standing at a 40-degree angle (a rad photo op). Kids and fans of kitsch go nuts for the playhouse quality of the space and the narrow-gauge train rides are exciting for toddlers.

For basic supplies, visit **Price's Peg House** (⊘707-925-6444; 69501 Hwy 101; ⊘8am-9pm).

Richardson Grove State Park

Fifteen miles to the north, and bisected by the Eel River, serene **Richardson Grove** (Hwy 101; per car $8) occupies 1400 acres of virgin forest. Many trees are over 1000 years old and 300ft tall, but there aren't many hiking trails. In winter, there's good fishing for silver and king salmon. At the time of research, CalTrans was considering widening the road through Richardson Grove, which sparked an intense protest.

The **visitor center** (☎707-247-3318; ⊙9am-2pm) sells books inside a 1930s lodge, which often has a fire going during cool weather. The park is primarily a **campground** (☎reservations 800-444-7275; www.reserveamerica.com; tent & RV sites $35) with three separate areas with hot showers; some remain open year-round. Summer-only Oak Flat on the east side of the river is shady and has a sandy beach.

Benbow Lake

On the Eel River, 2 miles south of Garberville, the 1200-acre **Benbow Lake State Recreation Area** (☎summer 707-923-3238, winter 707-923-3318; per car $8) exists when a seasonal dam forms the 26-acre Benbow Lake, mid-June to mid-September. In mid-August, avoid swimming in the lake or river until two weeks after the Reggae on the River festival (p244), when 25,000 people use the river as a bathtub. The water is cleanest in early summer. The year-round riverside **campground** (☎reservations 800-444-7275; www.reserveamerica.com; tent & RV sites $35) is subject to wintertime bridge closures due to flooding. This part of the Eel has wide banks and is also excellent for swimming and sunbathing. You can avoid the day use fee by parking near the bridge and walking down to the river. According to a ranger, you can float from here all the way through the redwood groves along the Avenue of the Giants.

Benbow Inn (☎707-923-2124, 800-355-3301; www.benbowinn.com; 445 Lake Benbow Dr; r $90-305, cottage $395-595; ❋🐾🖥) is a monument to 1920s rustic elegance; the Redwood Empire's first luxury resort is a national historic landmark. Hollywood's elite once frolicked in the Tudor-style resort's lobby, where you can play chess by the crackling fire, and enjoy complimentary afternoon

tea and evening hors d'oeuvres. Rooms have top-quality beds and antique furniture. The window-lined dining room (breakfast and lunch $10 to $15, dinner mains $22 to $32) serves excellent meals and the rib eye earns raves.

Southern Redwood Coast

NORTH COAST & REDWOODS RICHARDSON GROVE STATE PARK

Garberville

The main supply center for southern Humboldt County is the primary jumping-off point for both the Lost Coast, to the west, and the Avenue of the Giants, to the north. There's an uneasy relationship between the old-guard loggers and the hippies, many of whom came in the 1970s to grow sinsemilla (potent, seedless marijuana) after the feds chased them out of Santa Cruz. At last count, the hippies were winning the culture wars, but it rages on: a sign on the door of a local bar reads simply: 'Absolutely NO patchouli oil!!!' Two miles west, Garberville's ragtag sister, Redway, has fewer services. Garberville is about four hours north of San Francisco, one hour south of Eureka.

✯✯✯ Festivals & Events

The **Mateel Community Center** (www.mateel.org), in Redway, is the nerve center for many of the area's long-running annual festivals, which celebrate everything from hemp to miming.

Reggae on the River/Reggae Rising MUSIC (www.reggaeontheriver.com) In mid-July, drawing huge crowds for reggae, world music, arts and craft fairs, camping and swimming in the river.

Avenue of the Giants Marathon MARATHON (www.theave.org) Among the nation's most picturesque marathons, held in May.

Harley-Davidson Redwood Run MOTORCYCLE RALLY (www.redwoodrun.com) The redwoods rumble with the sound of hundreds of shiny bikes in June.

🛏 Sleeping

Garberville is lined with motels, and many of them are serviceable, if uninspiring. South of town, Benbow Inn (p243) blows away the competition. For cheaper lodging, there are two satisfactory motels. First try **Sherwood Forest** (☎707-923-2721; www.sherwoodforestmotel.com; 814 Redwood Dr; r $66-84; ❄ 🐾📶), then **Humboldt Redwoods Inn** (☎707-923-2451; www.humboldtredwoodsinn.com; 987 Redwood Dr; r $59-95; ❄ 📶), though the desk clerks are hardly ever there, so call ahead.

🍴 Eating & Drinking

Woodrose Café BREAKFAST $ (www.woodrosecafe.com; 911 Redwood Dr; meals $7-11; ⏰7am-1pm; 🚗📶) Garberville's beloved cafe serves organic omelettes, veggie scrambles and buckwheat pancakes with *real* maple syrup in a cozy room. Lunch brings crunchy salads, sandwiches with all-natural meats and good burritos. No credit cards.

Cecil's New Orleans Bistro CAJUN $$$ (www.cecilsrestaurant.com; 733 Redwood Dr; dinner mains $20-26; ⏰6-10pm Thu-Mon) This 2nd story eatery overlooks Main St and serves ambitious dishes that may have minted the California-Cajun style. Start with fried green tomatoes before launching into the smoked boar gumbo.

Mateel Café AMERICAN $$ (3342-3344 Redwood Dr, Redway; mains lunch $8-12, dinner $20-26; ⏰11:30am-9pm Mon-Sat) The big, diverse menu of this Redway joint includes a rack of lamb, stone-baked pizzas and terrific salads. There's pleasant patio seating out back.

Chautauqua Natural Foods HEALTH FOOD $ (436 Church St; sandwiches & lunch plates $5-10; ⏰10am-6pm Mon-Sat) Sells natural groceries. It has a small dining area and a great bulletin board.

Nacho Mama MEXICAN $ (375 Sprowel Creek Rd; meals under $6; ⏰11am-7pm Mon-Sat) A tiny shack on the corner of Redwood Dr with organic fast-food Mexican.

Calico's Deli & Pasta ITALIAN $ (808 Redwood Dr; dishes $6-13; ⏰11am-9pm; 📶) Calico's has house-made pasta and sandwiches, and is good for kids.

Branding Iron Saloon BAR $ (744 Redwood Dr) Craft beer, nice locals and a hopping pool table. We'll forgive the stripper pole in the middle of the room.

ℹ Information

Garberville-Redway Area Chamber of Commerce (www.garberville.org; 784 Redwood Dr; ⏰10am-4pm May-Aug, Mon-Fri Sep-Apr) Inside the Redwood Dr Center.

KMUD FM91 (www.kmud.org) Find out what's really happening by tuning in to community radio.

Lost Coast

The North Coast's superlative backpacking destination is a rugged, mystifying stretch of coast where narrow dirt trails ascend rugged coastal peaks and volcanic beaches of black sand and ethereal mist hovers above the roaring surf as majestic Roosevelt elk graze the forests. Here, the rugged King Range boldly rises 4000ft within 3 miles of the coast between where Hwy 1 cuts inland north of Westport to just south of Ferndale. The coast became 'lost' when the state's highway system deemed the region impassable in the early 20th century.

The best hiking and camping is within the King Range National Conservation Area and the Sinkyone Wilderness State Park, which make up the central and southern stretch of the region. The area north of the King Range is more accessible, if less dramatic.

In autumn, the weather is clear and cool. Wildflowers bloom from April through May and gray whales migrate from December through April. The warmest, driest months are June to August, but days are foggy. Note that the weather can quickly change.

Hiking

The best way to see the Lost Coast is to hike, and the best hiking is through the southern regions within the Sinkyone and Kings Range Wilderness areas. Some of the best trails start from Mattole Campground, just south Petrolia, which is on the northern border of the Kings Range. It's at the ocean end of Lighthouse Rd, 4 miles from Mattole Rd (sometimes marked as Hwy 211), southeast of Petrolia.

The Lost Coast Trail follows 24.7 miles of coastline from Mattole Campground in the north to Black Sands Beach at Shelter Cove in the south. The prevailing northerly winds make it best to hike from north to south; plan for three or four days. In October and November, and April and May, the weather is iffy and winds can blow south to north, depending on whether there's a low-pressure system overhead. The best times to come are summer weekdays in early June, at the end of August, September and October. The trail will often have hikers; busiest times are Memorial Day, Labor Day and summer weekends. Only two shuttles have permits to transport backpackers through the area, Lost Coast Trail Transport Services (☑707-986-9909; www.lostcoast trail.com) or the more reliable Lost Coast Shuttle (☑707-223-1547; www.lostcoastshuttle. com). Neither is cheap; prices for the ride between Mattole and Black Sands Beach start at $100 per person with a two-person minimum.

Highlights include an abandoned lighthouse at Punta Gorda, remnants of early shipwrecks, tidepools and abundant wildlife including sea lions, seals and some 300 bird species. The trail is mostly level, passing beaches and crossing over rocky outcrops. Along the Lost Coast Trail, Big Flat is the most popular backcountry destination. Carry a tide table, lest you get trapped: from Buck Creek to Miller Creek, you can only hike during an outgoing tide.

A good day hike starts at the Mattole Campground trailhead and travels 3 miles south along the coast to the Punta Gorda lighthouse (return against the wind).

People have discovered the Lost Coast Trail. To ditch the crowds, take any of the (strenuous) upland trails off the beach toward the ridgeline. For a satisfying, hard 21-mile-long hike originating at the Lost Coast Trail, take Buck Creek Trail to King Crest Trail to Rattlesnake Ridge Trail. The 360 degree views from King Peak are stupendous, particularly with a full moon or during a meteor shower. Note that if you hike up, it can be hellishly hot on the ridges, though the coast remains cool and foggy; wear removable layers. Carry a topographical map and a compass: signage is limited.

Both Wailaki and Nadelos have developed campgrounds (tent sites $8) with toilets and water. There are another four developed campgrounds around the range, with toilets but no water (except Honeydew, which has purifiable creek water). There are multiple primitive walk-in sites. You'll need a bear canister and backcountry permit, both available from BLM offices.

ⓘ Information

Aside from a few one-horse villages, Shelter Cove, the isolated unincorporated town 25 long miles west of Garberville, is the option for services. Get supplies in Garberville, Fort Bragg, Eureka or Arcata. The area is a patchwork of government-owned land and private property; visit the Bureau of Land Management office (p257) for information, permits and maps. There are few circuitous routes for hikers, and rangers can advise on reliable (if expensive) shuttle services in the area. A few words of caution: lots of weed is grown around here and it's wise to stay on trail to and respect no trespassing signs, lest you find yourself at the business end of someone's right to bear arms. And pot farmers don't pose the only threat: you'll want to check for ticks (Lyme disease is common) and keep food in bear-proof containers, which are required for camping.

SINKYONE WILDERNESS STATE PARK

Named for the Sinkyone people who once lived here, this 7367-acre wilderness extends south of Shelter Cove along pristine coastline. The Lost Coast Trail continues here for another 22 miles, from Whale Gulch south to Usal Beach Campground, taking at least three days to walk as it meanders along high ridges, providing bird's-eye views down to deserted beaches and the crashing surf (side trails descend to water level). Near the park's northern end, the (haunted!) Needle Rock Ranch (☎707-986-7711; tent sites $35) serves as a remote visitor center. Register here for the adjacent campsites ($25 to $35). This is the only source of potable water. For information on when the ranch is closed (most of the time), call Richardson Grove State Park (☎707-247-3318).

To get to Sinkyone, drive west from Garberville and Redway on Briceland-Thorn Rd, 21 miles through Whitethorn to Four Corners. Turn left (south) and continue for 3.5 miles down a very rugged road to the ranch house; it takes 1½ hours.

There's access to the Usal Beach Campground (tent sites $25) at the south end of the park from Hwy 1 (you can't make reservations). North of Westport, take the unpaved County Rd 431 beginning from Hwy 1's Mile 90.88 and travel 6 miles up the coast to the campground. The road is graded yearly in late spring and is passable in summer via two-wheel-drive vehicles. Most sites are past the message board by the beach. Use bear canisters or keep food in your trunk. Look for giant elk feeding on the tall grass – they live behind sites No 1 and 2 – and osprey by the creek's mouth.

North of the campground, Usal Rd (County Rd 431) is much rougher and recommended only if you have a high-clearance 4WD and a chainsaw. Seriously.

KING RANGE NATIONAL CONSERVATION AREA

Stretching over 35 miles of virgin coastline, with ridge after ridge of mountainous terrain plunging to the surf, the 60,000-acre area tops out at namesake King's Peak (4087ft). The wettest spot in California, the range receives over 120 inches – and sometimes as much as 240 inches – of annual rainfall, causing frequent landslides; in winter, snow falls on the ridges. (By contrast, nearby sea-level Shelter Cove gets only 69 inches of rain and no snow.) Two-thirds of the area is awaiting wilderness designation.

Nine miles east of Shelter Cove, the Bureau of Land Management (BLM; ☎707-986-5400, 707-825-2300; 768 Shelter Cove Rd; ☻8am-4:30pm Mon-Sat Memorial Day-Labor Day, 8am-4:30pm Mon-Fri May-Sep) has maps and directions for trails and campsites; they're posted outside after hours. For overnight hikes, you'll need a backcountry-use permit. Don't turn left onto Briceland-Thorn Rd to try to find the 'town' of Whitethorn; it doesn't exist. Whitethorn is the BLM's name for the *general* area. To reach the BLM office from Garberville/Redway, follow signs to Shelter Cove; look for the roadside information panel, 0.25 miles past the post office. Information and permits are also available from the BLM in Arcata (p257).

Fire restrictions begin July 1 and last until the first soaking rain, usually in November. During this time, there are no campfires allowed outside developed campgrounds.

NORTH OF THE KING RANGE

Though it's less of an adventure, you can reach the Lost Coast's northern section year-round via paved, narrow Mattole Rd. Plan three hours to navigate the sinuous 68 miles from Ferndale in the north to the coast at Cape Mendocino, then inland to Humboldt Redwoods State Park and Hwy 101. Don't expect redwoods; the vegetation is grassland and pasture. It's beautiful in spots - lined sweeping vistas and wildflowers that are prettiest in spring.

You'll pass two tiny settlements, both 19th-century stage-coach stops. Petrolia has an all-in-one store (☎707-629-3455; ☻9am-5pm) which rents bear canisters and sells supplies for the trail, good beer and gasoline. Honeydew also has a general store. The drive is enjoyable, but the Lost Coast's wild, spectacular scenery lies further south in the more remote regions.

SHELTER COVE

The only sizable community on the Lost Coast, Shelter Cove is surrounded by the King Range National Conservation Area and abuts a large south-facing cove. It's a tiny

DRIVE-THRU TREES

Three carved-out (but living) redwoods await along Hwy 101, a bizarre holdover from a yesteryear road trip.

Chandelier Drive-Thru Tree Fold in your mirrors and inch forward, then cool off in the uberkitschy gift shop; in Leggett.

Shrine Drive-Thru Tree Look up to the sky as you roll through, on the Ave of the Giants in Myers Flat. The least impressive of the three.

Tour Thru Tree Take exit 769 in Klamath, squeeze through a tree and check out an emu.

seaside subdivision with an airstrip in the middle – indeed, many visitors are private pilots. Fifty years ago, Southern California swindlers subdivided the land, built the airstrip and flew in potential investors, fast-talking them into buying seaside land for retirement. But they didn't tell buyers that a steep, winding, one-lane dirt road provided the *only* access and that the seaside plots were eroding into the sea.

Today, there's still only one route, but now it's paved. Cell phones don't work here: this is a good place to disappear. The town is a mild disappointment, with not much to do, but stunning **Black Sands Beach** stretches for miles northward.

🛏 Sleeping

Shelter Cove has some plain motels and decent inns, but camping is far and away the best way to spend the night here.

TOP CHOICE **Tides Inn** INN $$
(☎707-986-7900, 888-998-4377; www.shelter covetidesinn.com; 59 Surf Point Rd; r from $155; 🛜🐾) Perched above tidepools teeming with starfish and sea urchins, this is the top-choice indoor sleeping in Shelter Cove. The squeaky clean rooms offer excellent views (go for the mini suites on the 3rd floor). The suite options are good for families, and kids are greeted warmly by the innkeeper with an activity kit.

Inn of the Lost Coast INN $$
(☎707-986-7521, 888-570-9676; www.innofthelost coast.com; 205 Wave Dr; r $160-250; 🛜🐾) After a big overhaul, this renovated inn has breath-taking ocean views and clean, fireplace rooms. Downstairs there's a serviceable take-out pizza place and Shelter Cove's only breakfast joint, an espresso stand named Fish Tanks.

Oceanfront Inn & Lighthouse INN $$
(☎707-986-7002; www.sheltercoveoceanfront inn.com; 10 Seal Court; r $135-165, ste $195) The tidy, modern rooms here have microwaves, refrigerators and balconies overlooking the sea. The decor is spartan so as not to detract from the view. Splurge on a kitchen suite; the best is upstairs, with its peaked ceiling and giant windows.

Shelter Cove RV Park, Campground & Deli CAMPGROUND $
(☎707-986-7474; 492 Machi Rd; tent/RV sites $33/43) The services may be basic, but the fresh gusts of ocean air can't be beat – the deli has good fish and chips.

🍴 Eating

The first-choice place to eat, **Cove Restaurant** (☎707-986-1197; 10 Seal Court; mains $6-19; ⊙5-9pm Thu-Sun), has everything from veggie stir-fries to New York steaks. For those who are self-catering, **Shelter Cove General Store** (☎707-986-7733; 7272 Shelter Cove Rd) is 2 miles beyond town. Get groceries and gasoline here.

Humboldt Redwoods State Park & Avenue of the Giants

Don't miss this magical drive through California's largest redwood park, **Humboldt Redwoods State Park** (www.humboldtred woods.org), which covers 53,000 acres – 17,000 of which are old-growth – and contains some of the world's most magnificent trees. It also boasts three-quarters of the world's tallest 100 trees. Tree huggers take note: these groves rival (and many say surpass) those in Redwood National Park, which is a long drive further north.

Exit Hwy 101 when you see the 'Avenue of the Giants' sign, take this smaller alternative to the interstate; it's an incredible, 32-mile, two-lane stretch. You'll find free driving guides at roadside signboards at both the avenue's southern entrance, 6 miles north of Garberville, near Phillipsville, and at the northern entrance, south of Scotia, at Pepperwood; there are access points off Hwy 101.

South of Weott, a volunteer-staffed **visitor center** (☏707-946-2263; ☺9am-5pm May-Sep, 10am-4pm Oct-Apr) shows videos and sells maps.

Three miles north, the **California Federation of Women's Clubs Grove** is home to an interesting four-sided hearth designed by renowned San Franciscan architect Julia Morgan in 1931 to commemorate 'the untouched nature of the forest.'

Primeval **Rockefeller Forest**, 4.5 miles west of the avenue via Mattole Rd, appears as it did a century ago. You quickly walk out of sight of cars and feel like you have fallen into the time of the dinosaurs. It's the world's largest contiguous old-growth redwood forest, and contains about 20% of all such remaining trees. Check out the subtly variegated rings (count one for each year) on the cross sections of some of the downed giants that are left to mulch back into the earth over the next few hundred years.

In **Founders Grove**, north of the visitor center, the **Dyerville Giant** was knocked over in 1991 by another falling tree. A walk along its gargantuan 370ft length, with its wide trunk towering above, helps you appreciate how huge these ancient trees are.

The park has over 100 miles of trails for hiking, mountain-biking and horseback riding. Easy walks include short nature trails in Founders Grove and Rockefeller Forest and **Drury-Chaney Loop Trail** (with berry picking in summer). Challenging treks include popular **Grasshopper Peak Trail**, south of the visitor center, which climbs to the 3379ft fire lookout.

🛏 Sleeping & Eating

If you want to stay along the avenue, several towns have simple lodgings of varying calibers and levels of hospitality, but camping at Humboldt Redwoods is by far the best option.

Humboldt Redwoods State Park Campgrounds CAMPGROUND **$**
(☏reservations 800-444-7275; www.reserveamerica.com; tent & RV sites $20-35) The park runs three campgrounds, with hot showers, two environmental camps, five trail camps, a hike/bike camp and an equestrian camp. Of the developed spots, **Burlington Campground** is open year-round beside the visitor center and near a number of trailheads. **Hidden Springs Campground**, 5 miles south, and **Albee Creek Campground**, on

Mattole Rd past Rockefeller Forest, are open mid-May to early fall.

Miranda Gardens Resort RESORT **$$**
(☏707-943-3011; www.mirandagardens.com; 6766 Ave of the Giants, Miranda; cottages with kitchen $165-275, without $115-175; ✖ ☂ ☃) The best indoor stay along the avenue. The cozy, slightly rustic cottages have redwood paneling, some with fireplaces, and are spotlessly clean. The grounds – replete with outdoor ping pong and a play area for kids and swaying redwoods – have wholesome appeal for families.

Riverbend Cellars TASTING ROOM **$$**
(www.riverbendcellars.com; 12990 Ave of the Giants, Myers Flat; ☺11am-5pm) For something a bit more posh, pull over here. The El Centauro red – named for Pancho Villa – is an excellent estate-grown blend.

Groves NEW AMERICAN **$$**
(13065 Ave of the Giants, Myers Flat; ☺5-9pm) This is the most refined eating option within miles, despite an aloof staff. The menu turns out simple, brick oven pizzas, but spicy prawns and fresh salads are all artfully plated.

Chimney Tree AMERICAN **$**
(1111 Ave of the Giants, Phillipsville; burgers $7-11; ☺10am-7pm May-Sep) If you're just passing through and want something quick, come here. It raises its own grass-fed beef. Alas, the fries are frozen, but those burgers... mmm-mmm!

Scotia

For years, Scotia was California's last 'company town,' entirely owned and operated by the Pacific Lumber Company, which built cookie-cut houses and had an open contempt for long-haired outsiders who liked to get between their saws and the big trees. The company recently went belly up, sold the mill to another redwood company and, though the town still has a creepy *Twilight Zone* vibe, you no longer have to operate by the company's posted 'Code of Conduct.' A history of the town awaits at the **Scotia Museum & Visitor Center** (www.townofscotia.com; cnr Main & Bridge Sts; ☺8am-4:30pm Mon-Fri Jun-Sep), at the town's south end. The museum's **fisheries center** (admission free) is remarkably informative – ironic, considering that logging destroys fish habitats – and houses the largest freshwater aquarium on the North Coast.

There are dingy motels and diners in **Rio Dell** (aka 'Real Dull'), across the river. Back in the day, this is where the debauchery happened: because it wasn't a company town, Rio Dell had bars and hookers. In 1969, the freeway bypassed the town and it withered.

As you drive along Hwy 101 and see what appears to be a never-ending redwood forest, understand that this 'forest' sometimes consists of trees only a few rows deep – called a 'beauty strip' – a carefully crafted illusion for tourists. Most old-growth trees have been cut. **Bay Area Coalition for Headwaters Forest** (www.headwaterspreserve. org) helped preserve over 7000 acres of land with public funds through provisions in a long-negotiated agreement between the Pacific Lumber Company and state and federal agencies.

Up Hwy 101 there's a great pit stop at **Eel River Brewing** (www.eelriverbrewing.com; 1777 Alamar Way, Fortuna; ⊙11am-11pm Mon-Sun), where a breezy beer garden and excellent burgers accompany all-organic brews.

Ferndale

The North Coast's most charming town is stuffed with impeccable Victorians – known locally as 'butterfat palaces' because of the dairy wealth that built them. There are so many, in fact, that the entire place is a state and federal historical landmark. Dairy farmers built the town in the 19th century and it's still run by the 'milk mafia': you're not a local till you've lived here 40 years. A stroll down Main St offers galleries, old-world emporiums and soda fountains. Although Ferndale relies on tourism, it has avoided becoming a tourist trap – and has no chain stores. Though a lovely place to spend a summer night, it's dead as a doornail in winter.

◉ Sights & Activities

Half a mile from downtown via Bluff St, enjoy short tramps through fields of wildflowers, beside ponds, past redwood groves and eucalyptus trees at 110-acre **Russ Park**. The **cemetery**, also on Bluff St, is amazingly cool with graves dating to the 1800s and expansive views to the ocean. Five miles down Centerville Rd, **Centerville Beach** is one of the few off-leash dog beaches in Humboldt County.

FREE Kinetic Sculpture
Museum MUSEUM, GALLERY
(580 Main St; ⊙10am-5pm Mon-Sat, noon-4pm Sun; 🚗) This warehouse holds the fanciful, astounding, human-powered contraptions used in the town's annual Kinetic Grand Championship. Shaped like giant fish and UFOs, these colorful piles of junk propel racers over roads, water and marsh in the May event.

Fern Cottage HISTORIC BUILDING
(☎707-786-4835; www.ferncottage.org; Centerville Rd; group tours $10 per person; ⊙by appointment) This 1866 Carpenter Gothic grew to a 32-room mansion. Only one family ever lived here, so the interior is completely preserved.

Gingerbread Mansion HISTORIC BUILDING
(400 Berding St) An 1898 Queen Anne-Eastlake, this is the town's most photographed building. It held guests as a B&B for years, but has recently closed.

★ Festivals & Events

This wee town has a packed social calendar, especially in the summer. If you're planning a visit, check the events page at www.victorianferndale.com.

Tour of the Unknown Coast BICYCLE RACE
(www.tuccycle.org) A challenging event in May, in which participants of the 100 mile race climb nearly 10,000 feet.

Humboldt County Fair FAIR
(www.humboldtcountyfair.org) Held in mid-August, the longest running county fair in California.

🛏 Sleeping

Shaw House B&B $$
(☎707-786-9958, 800-557-7429; www.shawhouse. com; 703 Main St; r $145-175, ste $225-275; 🛜) Shaw House, an emblematic 'butterfat palace,' was the first permanent structure in Ferndale, completed by founding father Seth Shaw in 1866. Today, it's California's oldest B&B, set back on extensive grounds. Original details remain, including painted wooden ceilings. Most of the rooms have private entrances, and three have private balconies over a large garden.

Francis Creek Inn MOTEL $
(☎707-786-9611; www.franciscreekinn.com; 577 Main St; r from $85; 🛜) White picket balconies stand in front of this sweet little downtown motel, which is family owned and operated

(you check in at the Red Front convenience store, right around the corner). Spartan rooms are basic, clean and furnished simply, and the value is outstanding.

Hotel Ivanhoe   HISTORIC HOTEL **$$**
(☎707-786-9000; www.ivanhoe-hotel.com; 315 Main St; r $95-145) Ferndale's oldest hostelry opened in 1875. It has four antique-laden rooms and an Old West–style 2nd-floor gallery, perfect for morning coffee. The adjoining saloon, with dark wood and lots of brass, is an atmospheric place for a nightcap.

Victorian Inn   HISTORIC HOTEL **$$**
(☎707-786-4949, 888-589-1808; www.victorianvillageinn.com; 400 Ocean Ave; r $105-225; ☎) The bright, sunny rooms inside this venerable 1890 two-story, former bank building, are comfortably furnished with thick carpeting, good linens and antiques.

Humboldt County Fairgrounds   CAMPGROUND **$**
(☎707-786-9511; www.humboldtcountyfair.org; 1250 5th St; tent/RV sites $10/20) Turn west onto Van Ness St and go a few blocks for lawn camping with showers.

✖ Eating

A **farmers market** (400 Ocean Ave; ◷10:30am-2pm Sat May-Oct) has locally grown veggies and locally produced dairy – including the freshest cheese you'll find anywhere. Main St has lots of cafe options for eating, as well as white table cloth spots in both historic hotels.

Lotus Asian Bistro & Tea Room   PAN-ASIAN **$**
(www.lotusasianbistro.com; 619 Main St; mains $7-14; ◷11:30am-9pm Sat, Sun & Tue, 4-9pm Mon & Fri) Cherry glazed beef, crispy scallion pancakes with pulled duck and udon bowls spiced with a ginger broth – the menu at this excellent Asian fusion bistro offers welcome diversity to Ferndale's lunch and dinner options.

No Brand Burger Stand   BURGERS **$**
(989 Milton St; burgers $7; ◷11am-5pm) Sitting near the entrance to town, this hole-in-the-wall turns out a juicy jalapeño double cheese burger that ranks easily as the North Coast's best burger. The shakes – so thick your cheeks hurt from pulling on the straw – are about the only other thing on the menu.

Poppa Joe's   AMERICAN **$**
(409 Main St; mains $5-7; ◷11am-8:30pm Mon-Fri, 6am-noon Sat & Sun) You can't beat the atmosphere at this diner, where trophy heads hang from the wall, the floors slant at a precarious angle and old men play poker all day. The American-style breakfasts are good, too – especially the pancakes.

Sweetness & Light   CANDY **$**
(554 Main St; confections $2-3) The house-made, gooey Moo bars are this antique candy shop's flagship. It also serves great ice cream and espresso.

☆ Entertainment

Ferndale Repertory Theatre   THEATER
(☎707-786-5483; www.ferndale-rep.org; 447 Main St) This top-shelf community company produces excellent contemporary theatre in the historic Hart Theatre Building.

🔒 Shopping

Blacksmith Shop & Gallery   METAL GOODS
(☎707-786-4216; www.ferndaleblacksmith.com; 455 & 491 Main St) From wrought-iron art to hand-forged furniture, this is the largest collection of contemporary blacksmithing in America.

Abraxas Jewelry & Leather Goods JEWELRY
(505 Main St) The pieces of locally forged jewelry here are extremely cool and moderately priced. The back room is filled with tons of hats.

Farmer's Daughter   CLOTHING
(358 Main; ◷11am-5pm Tue-Sat, noon-4pm Sun) An actual dairy farmer's daughter owns this cute Western boutique.

Humboldt Bay National Wildlife Refuge

This pristine **wildlife refuge** (☎707-733-5406; ◷sunrise-sunset) protects wetland habitats for more than 200 species of birds migrating annually along the Pacific Flyway. Between the fall and early spring, when Aleutian geese descend en masse to the area, more than 25,000 geese might be seen in a cackling gaggle outside the visitor center.

The peak season for waterbirds and raptors runs September to March; for black brant geese and migratory shorebirds mid-March to late April. Gulls, terns, cormorants, pelicans, egrets and herons come year-round. Look for harbor seals offshore; bring binoculars. If it's open, drive out South Jetty Rd to the mouth of Humboldt Bay for a stunning perspective.

Pick up a map from the **visitor center** (1020 Ranch Rd; ☺8am-5pm). Exit Hwy 101 at Hookton Rd, 11 miles south of Eureka, turn north along the frontage road, on the freeway's west side. In April, look for the **Godwit Days** festival.

Eureka

One hour north of Garberville, on the edge of the giant Humboldt Bay, lies Eureka, the largest bay north of San Francisco. With strip-mall sprawl surrounding a lovely historic downtown, it wears its role as the county seat a bit clumsily. Despite a diverse and interesting community of artists, writers, pagans and other free-thinkers, Eureka's wild side slips out only occasionally – the **Redwood Coast Dixieland Jazz Festival** (www.redwoodcoastmusicfestivals.org) is a rollicking festival with events all over town, and summer concerts rock out the F Street Pier – but mostly, it goes to bed early. Make for Old Town, a small district with colorful Victorians, good shopping and a revitalized waterfront. For night life, head to Eureka's trippy sister up the road, Arcata.

👁 Sights

The free *Eureka Visitors Map,* available at tourist offices, details walking tours and scenic drives, focusing on architecture and history. **Old Town**, along 2nd and 3rd Sts from C St to M St, was once down-and-out, but has been refurbished into a buzzing pedestrian district. The F Street Plaza and Boardwalk run along the waterfront at the foot of F St. Gallery openings fall on the first Saturday of every month.

Blue Ox Millworks & Historic Park   MILL
(www.blueoxmill.com; adult/child 6-12yr $7.50/3.50; ☺9am-4pm Mon-Sat; 🖈) One of only seven of its kind in America, antique tools and mills are used to produce authentic gingerbread trim for Victorian buildings; one-hour self-guided tours take you through the mill and historical buildings, including a blacksmith shop and 19th-century skid camp. Kids love the oxen.

Romano Gabriel Wooden Sculpture Garden   ART INSTALLATION
(315 2nd St) The coolest thing to gawk at downtown is this collection of whimsical outsider art that's enclosed by glass. For 30 years, wooden characters in Gabriel's front yard delighted locals. After he died in 1977, the city moved the collection here.

Clarke Historical Museum   MUSEUM
(www.clarkemuseum.org; 240 E St; admission $1; ☺11am-4pm Wed-Sat) The best community historical museum on this stretch of the coast houses a set of typically musty relics – needlework hankies and paintings of the area's history-making notables (in this case Ulysses Grant, who was once dismissed from his post at Fort Humboldt for drunkenness). Its best collection is that of intricately woven baskets from local tribes. One look at the scenes of animals and warriors that unfold in the weave and you'll quickly understand the Pomo saying that 'every basket tells a story.'

Carson Mansion   HISTORIC BUILDING
(134 M St) Of Eureka's fine Victorian buildings the most famous is the ornate 1880s home of lumber baron William Carson. It took 100 men a full year to build. Today it's a private men's club. The **pink house** opposite, at 202 M St, is an 1884 Queen Anne Victorian designed by the same architects and built as a wedding gift for Carson's son.

Sequoia Park   PARK
(www.sequoiaparkzoo.net; 3414 W St; park free, zoo adult/child $5.50/3.50; ☺zoo 10am-5pm May-Sep, Tue-Sun Oct-Apr; 🖈) A 77-acre old-growth redwood grove is a surprising green gem in the middle of a residential neighborhood. It has biking and hiking trails, a children's playground and picnic areas, and a small zoo.

Morris Graves Museum of Art   MUSEUM
(www.humboldtarts.org; 636 F St; suggested donation $4; ☺noon-5pm Thu-Sun) Across Hwy 101, the excellent museum shows rotating Californian artists and hosts performances inside the 1904 Carnegie library, the state's first public library.

Discovery Museum   MUSEUM
(www.discovery-museum.org; 517 3rd St; admission $4; ☺10am-4pm Tue-Sat, from noon Sun; 🖈) A hands-on kids' museum.

🏃 Activities

Harbor Cruise   HARBOR CRUISE
(www.humboldtbaymaritimemuseum.com; 75-minute narrated tour cruise adult/child $18/10, 1-hour cocktail cruise $10) Board the 1910 *Madaket,* America's oldest continuously operating passenger vessel, and learn the history of Humboldt Bay. Located at the foot of C St, it originally ferried

mill workers and passengers until the Samoa Bridge was built in 1972. The $10 sunset cocktail cruise serves from the smallest licensed bar in the state.

Hum-Boats Sail, Canoe & Kayak Center
BOAT RENTAL

(www.humboats.com; Startare Dr; ⏰9am-5pm Mon-Fri, 9am-6pm Sat & Sun Apr-Oct, 9am-2:30pm Nov-Mar) At Woodley Island Marina, this outfit rents kayaks and sailboats, offering lessons, tours, charters, sunset sails and full-moon paddles.

🛏 Sleeping

Every brand of chain hotel is along Hwy 101. Room rates run high midsummer; you can sometimes find cheaper in Arcata, to the north, or Fortuna, to the south. There are also a handful of motels which cost from $60 to $100 and have no air-conditioning; choose places set back from the road. The cheapest are south of downtown on the suburban strip.

Hotel Carter & Carter House Victorians
HOTEL, B&B $$$

(☎707-444-8067, 800-404-1390; www.carterhouse.com; 301 L St; r incl breakfast $159-225, ste incl breakfast $304-385; 🛜🏊) For those with a few extra bucks, the Hotel Carter and its associated Victorian rentals bear the standard for North Coast luxury. Recently constructed in period style, the hotel is a Victorian look-alike, holding rooms with top-quality linens and modern amenities; suites have in-room whirlpools and marble fireplaces. The same owners operate three sumptuously decorated houses: a single-level 1900 house, a honeymoon-hideaway cottage and a replica of an 1880s San Francisco mansion, which the owner built himself, entirely by hand. Unlike elsewhere, you won't see the innkeeper unless you want to. Guests have an in-room breakfast or can eat at the understated, elegant restaurant.

Eagle House Inn
HISTORIC INN $$

(☎707-444-3344; www.eaglehouseinn.com; 139 2nd St; r $105-205; 🛜📶) This hulking Victorian hotel in Old Town has 24 rooms above a turn-of-the-century ballroom perfect for hide-and-seek. Rooms aren't overly stuffed with precious period furniture – carved headboards, floral-print carpeting and antique armoires – but some have bizarre touches (like the bright red spa tub that would fit in on an '80s adult film set). The coolest rooms are in the corner and have sitting areas in turrets looking over the street.

Abigail's Elegant Victorian Mansion
B&B $$

(☎707-444-3144; www.eureka-california.com; 1406 C St; r $145-215) Inside this National Historic Landmark that's practically a living-history museum, the sweet-as-could-be innkeepers lavish guests with warm hospitality.

Daly Inn
B&B $$

(☎707-445-3638, 800-321-9656; www.dalyinn.com; 1125 H St; r with bathroom $170-185, without bathroom $130) This impeccably maintained 1905 Colonial Revival mansion has individually decorated rooms with turn-of-the-20th-century European and American antiques. Guest parlors are trimmed with rare woods; outside are century-old flowering trees.

Bayview Motel
MOTEL $

(☎707-442-1673, 866-725-6813; www.bayviewmotel.com; 2844 Fairfield St; r $109; 🛜🏊) Spotless rooms are of the chain motel standard; some have patios overlooking Humboldt Bay.

Eureka Inn
HISTORIC HOTEL $

(☎707-497-6903, 877-552-3985; www.eurekainn.com; cnr 7th & F St; r $65-90, ste $85-130; 🛜) This enormous historic hotel, long dormant, has found a new owner. While rooms are bland, they're cheap and the structure itself is magnificent.

Ship's Inn
B&B $$

(☎707-443-7583, 877-443-7583; www.shipsinn.net; 821 D St; r $130-175, cottages $160; 🛜) Warmly modern furnishings with nautical themes, kind hosts and a full breakfast make this three-room inn a favorite for return guests.

🍴 Eating

Eureka is blessed with two excellent natural food grocery stores – **Eureka Co-op** (cnr 5th & L Sts) and **Eureka Natural Foods** (1626 Broadway) – and two weekly farmers markets – at the corner of **2nd & F Sts** (⏰10am-1pm Tue Jun-Oct) and the **Henderson Center** (⏰10am-1pm Thu Jun-Oct). The vibrant dining scene is focused in the Old Town district.

Kyoto
JAPANESE $$

(☎707-443-7777; 320 F St; sushi $4-6, mains $15-25; ⏰5:30-9:30pm Wed-Sat) New owners have had big shoes to fill by taking over a place renowned as the best sushi in Humboldt County, but the quality has not slipped and the atmosphere – in a tiny, packed room, where conversation with the neighboring table is inevitable – is as fun as ever. A menu of sushi and sashimi is rounded out by grilled scallops and fern tip salad. North coast travelers who absolutely need sushi should phone ahead for a reservation.

Hurricane Kate's
TAPAS $$

(www.hurricanekates.com; 511 2nd St; lunch mains $9-15, dinner mains $16-26; ⊙11am-2:30pm & 5-9pm; 🖉) The favorite spot of local *bon vivants*, Kate's open kitchen pumps out pretty good, eclectic, tapas-style dishes and roast meats, but the wood-fired pizzas are the standout option. There is a full bar.

🖉 Restaurant 301
CALIFORNIAN $$$

(☎707 444 8062; www.carterhouse.com; 301 L St; breakfast $11, dinner mains $20-35, 4-course menu $62; ⊙7:30-10am & 6-9pm) Eureka's top table, romantic, sophisticated 301 serves a contemporary Californian menu, using produce from its organic gardens (tours available). Mains are pricey, but the prix-fixe menu is a good way to taste local food in its finest presentation. The eight-course Chef's Grand Menu ($92) is only worthy of *really* special occasions.

Waterfront Café Oyster Bar
SEAFOOD $$

(102 F St; mains lunch $8-13, dinner $13-20; ⊙9am-9pm) With a nice bay view and baskets of steamed clams, fish and chips, oysters and chowder, this is a solid bay-side lunch. A top spot for Sunday brunch, with jazz and Ramos fizzes.

La Chapala
MEXICAN $

(201 2nd St; mains $6-14; ⊙11am-8pm) For Mexican, family-owned La Chapala makes strong margaritas and homemade flan.

Ramone's
BAKERY, DELI $

(2223 Harrison St; mains $6-10; ⊙7am-6pm Mon-Sat, 8am-4pm Sun) For grab-and-go sandwiches, fresh soups and wraps.

🍷 Drinking

Lost Coast Brewery
BREWERY

(☎707-445-4480; 617 4th St; 🛜) The roster of the regular brews at Eureka's colorful brewery might not knock the socks off a serious beer snob (and can't hold a candle to some of the others on the coast), but highlights include the Downtown Brown Ale, Great White and Lost Coast Pale Ale. After downing a few pints, the fried pub grub starts to look pretty tasty.

Shanty
DIVE BAR

(213 2nd St; ⊙noon-2am; 🛜) The coolest spot in town is grungy and fun. Play pool, Donkey Kong, Ms Pac Man or Ping Pong, or kick it on the back patio with local 20- and 30-something hipsters.

321 Coffee
COFFEE SHOP

(321 3rd St; ⊙8am-9pm; 🛜) Students sip French-press coffee and play chess at this living-room-like coffeehouse. Good soup.

🔒 Shopping

Eureka's streets lie on a grid; numbered streets cross lettered streets. For the best window-shopping, head to the 300, 400 and 500 blocks of 2nd St, between D and G Sts. The town's low rents and cool old spaces harbor lots of indie boutiques.

Shipwreck
VINTAGE

(430 3rd St) The quality of vintage goods here – *genuinely* distressed jeans and leather jackets, 1940s housedresses and hats – is complimented by hand-made local jewelry and paper products.

Going Places
TRAVELGOODS, BOOKS

(www.goingplacesworld.com; 1328 2nd St) Guidebooks, travel gear and international goods are certain to give a thrill to any vagabond. It's one of three excellent book shops in Old Town.

☆ Entertainment

Morris Graves Museum of Art
PERFORMANCE SPACE

(www.humboldtarts.org; 636 F St; suggested donation $4; ⊙noon-5pm Thu-Sun) Hosts performing-arts events between September and May, usually on Saturday evenings and Sunday afternoons.

Arkley Center for the Performing Arts
ARTS CENTER

(www.arkleycenter.com; 412 G St) Home to the Eureka Symphony and North Coast Dance, and stages musicals and plays.

Club Triangle at The Alibi
CLUB

(535 5th St) On Sunday nights this place becomes the North Coast's gay dance club. For gay events, log onto www.queerhumboldt.com.

ℹ Information

Eureka Chamber of Commerce (☎707-442-3738, 800-356-6381, www.eurekachamber.com; 2112 Broadway; ⊙8:30am-5pm Mon-Fri)

The main visitor information center is on Hwy 101.

Pride Enterprises Tours (☑707-445-2117, 800-400-1849) Local historian Ray Hillman leads outstanding history tours. He's also licensed to guide in the national parks.

Six Rivers National Forest Headquarters (☑707-442-1721; 1330 Bayshore Way; ⊙8am-4:30pm Mon-Fri) Maps and information.

❶ Getting There & Around

The Arcata/Eureka airport (ACV) is a small, expensive airport which connects regionally. See p257 for more information. The Greyhound station is in Arcata; see p257).

Eureka Transit Service (☑707-443-0826; www.eurekatransit.org) operates local buses ($1.30), Monday to Saturday.

Samoa Peninsula

Grassy dunes and windswept beaches extend along the half-mile-wide, 7-mile long Samoa Peninsula, Humboldt Bay's western boundary. Stretches of it are spectacular, particularly the dunes, which are part of a 34-mile-long dune system – the largest in Northern California – and the wildlife viewing is excellent. The shoreline road (Hwy 255) is a backdoor route between Arcata and Eureka.

At the peninsula's south end, **Samoa Dunes Recreation Area** (⊙sunrise-sunset) is good for picnicking and fishing. For wildlife, head to **Mad River Slough & Dunes**; from Arcata, take Samoa Blvd west for 3 miles, then turn right at Young St, the Manila turn-off. Park at the community center lot, from where a trail passes mudflats, salt marsh and tidal channels. There are over 200 species of birds: migrating waterfowl in spring and fall, songbirds in spring and summer, shorebirds in fall and winter, and waders year-round.

These undisturbed dunes reach heights of over 80ft. Because of the environment's fragility, access is by guided tour only. **Friends of the Dunes** (www.friendsofthedunes.org) leads free guided walks; register via email through the website. Check online for departure locations and information.

The lunch place on the peninsula is the **Samoa Cookhouse** (☑707-442-1659; www.samoacookhouse.net; off Samoa Blvd; breakfast/lunch/dinner $12/13/16; ⊞), the last surviving lumber camp cookhouse in the West, where you can shovel down all-you-can-eat family meals at long red-checkered tables. Kids eat for half-price. The cookhouse is five minutes northwest of Eureka, across the Samoa Bridge; follow the signs. From Arcata, take Samoa Blvd (Hwy 255).

Arcata

The North Coast's most progressive town, Arcata surrounds a tidy central square that fills with college students, campers, transients and tourists. Sure, it occasionally reeks of patchouli and its politics lean far left (in 2003, the city outlawed voluntary compliance with the USA Patriot Act, in 2006 it spearheaded a coalition of cities to impeach conservative president George W Bush), but its earnest embrace of sustainability has fostered some of the most progressive civic action in America. Here, garbage trucks run on biodiesel, recycling gets picked up by tandem bicycle, wastewater gets filtered clean in marshlands and almost every street has a bike lane.

Founded in 1850 as a base for lumber camps, today Arcata is defined as a magnate for 20-somethings looking to expand their minds: either at Humboldt State University (HSU), and/or on the highly potent marijuana which grows around here like, um, weeds. After a 1996 state proposition legalized marijuana for medical purposes, Arcata became what one *New Yorker* article referred to as the 'heartland of high grade marijuana.' The economy of the regions has become inexorably tied to the crop since.

Roads run on a grid, with numbered streets traveling east–west and lettered streets going north–south. G and H Sts run north and south (respectively) to HSU and Hwy 101. The plaza is bordered by G and H and 8th and 9th Sts.

❍ Sights

Around **Arcata Plaza** are two National Historic Landmarks: the 1857 **Jacoby's Storehouse** (cnr H & 8th Sts) and the 1915 **Hotel Arcata** (cnr G & 9th Sts). Another great historic building is the 1914 **Minor Theatre** (1013 10th St), which some local historians claim is the oldest theater in the US built specifically for showing film.

Humboldt State University   UNIVERSITY
(HSU; www.humboldt.edu) The University on the northeastern side of town holds the Campus Center for Appropriate Technology (CCAT), a

world leader in developing sustainable technologies; on Fridays at 2pm you can take a self-guided tour of the **CCAT House**, a converted residence that uses only 4% of the energy of a comparably sized dwelling.

Arcata Marsh & Wildlife Sanctuary
WILDLIFE SANCTUARY

On the shores of Humboldt Bay, this has 5 miles of walking trails and outstanding birding. The **Redwood Region Audubon Society** (www.rras.org; donation welcome) offers guided walks Saturdays at 8:30am, rain or shine, from the parking lot at I St's south end. Friends of Arcata Marsh offer guided tours Saturdays at 2pm from the **Arcata Marsh Interpretive Center** (☎707-826-2359; 569 South G St; tours free; ☺9am-5pm).

🏃 Activities

TOP CHOICE Finnish Country Sauna & Tubs
HOT TUBS, SAUNA

(☎707-822-2228, www.cafemokkaarcata.com; cnr 5th & J Sts; ☺noon-11pm Sun-Thu, to 1am Fri & Sat) Like some kind of Euro-crunchy bohemian dream, these private, open-air redwood hot tubs (half-hour/hour $9/17) and sauna are situated around a small frog pond, perfect for the sore legs of hikers or weary travelers up Hwy 101. The rates are reasonable, the staff is easygoing, and the facility is relaxing, simple and clean. Reserve ahead, especially on weekends.

HSU Center Activities
OUTDOOR ACTIVITIES

(www.humboldt.edu/centeractivities) An office on the 2nd floor of the University Center, beside the campus clock tower, sponsors myriad workshops, outings and sporting-gear rentals; nonstudents welcome.

Arcata Community Pool
SWIMMING

(ww.arcatapool.com; 1150 16th St; adult/child $7/5.25; ☺5:30am-9pm Mon-Fri, 9am-6pm Sat, 1-4pm Sun; ☺) Has a coed hot tub, sauna and exercise room.

Adventure's Edge
OUTDOOR GEAR RENTAL

(www.adventuresedge.com; 650 10th St; ☺9am-6pm Mon-Sat, 10am-5pm Sun) Rents, sells and services outdoor equipment.

✯ Festivals & Events

Kinetic Grand Championship
RACE

(www.kineticgrandchampionship.com) Arcata's most famous event is held Memorial Day weekend: people on amazing self-propelled contraptions travel 38 miles from Arcata to Ferndale.

Arcata Bay Oyster Festival
FOOD FESTIVAL

(www.oysterfestival.net) A magical celebration of oysters and beer happens in June.

North Country Fair
FAIR

(www.sameoldpeopl.org) A fun September street fair, where bands with names like The Fickle Hillbillies jam.

🛏 Sleeping

Arcata has affordable but limited lodgings. A cluster of hotels – Comfort Inn, Hamption Inn, etc – is just north of town, off Hwy 101's Giuntoli Lane. There's cheap camping further north at Clam Beach (p258).

Hotel Arcata
HISTORIC HOTEL $$

(☎707-826-0217, 800-344-1221; www.hotelarcata.com; 708 9th St; r $96-156; ☎) Anchoring the plaza, the renovated 1915 brick landmark has friendly staff, high ceilings and comfortable, old-world rooms of mixed quality. The rooms in front are an excellent perch for people-watching on the square, but the quietest face the back.

Lady Anne Inn
B&B $$

(☎707-822-2797; www.ladyanneinn.com; 902 14th St; r $125-140) Roses line the walkway to this 1888 mansion full of Victorian bric-a-brac. The frilly rooms are pretty, but there's no breakfast.

Arcata Stay
VACATION RENTALS $$

(☎707-822-0935, 877-822-0935; www.arcatastay.com; apt from $165) A network of excellent

---

MONEY TREES: ECONOMICS OF HUMBOLDT HERB

» Estimated percentage of Humboldt residents (18–65) with income partially tied to cultivating marijuana: 50

» Estimated wholesale value of one pound of 'Humboldt Kush': $3000

» Number of plants allowed per Proposition 215 card holder: 99

» Number of pounds produced by one high-yield plant: 1

» Estimated cost of production, one ounce: $100–180

» Estimated street value, one ounce: $300–600

apartment and cottage rentals. There is a two-night minimum.

Fairwinds Motel MOTEL $
(☎707-822-4824; www.fairwindsmotelarcata.com; 1674 G St; s $70-75, d $80-90; ☎) Serviceable rooms in this standard-issue motel, with some noise from Hwy 101.

✗ Eating

Great food abounds in restaurants throughout Arcata, almost all casual.

There are fantastic **farmers markets**, at the **Arcata Plaza** (☺9am-2pm Sat Apr-Nov) and in the parking lot of **Wildberries Market** (☺3:30-6:30pm Tue Jun-Oct). Even at other times, **Wildberries Marketplace** (www.wildberries.com; 747 13th St; ☺7am-11pm), has a deli counter and a great selection of natural foods. The gigantic **North Coast Co-op** (cnr 8th & I Sts; ☺6am-9pm) carries organic foods and is a community staple; check the kiosk out front. Just a few blocks north of downtown, there is a cluster of the town's best restaurants on G St.

🌿 Folie Douce NEW AMERICAN $$$
(☎707-822-1042; www.holyfolie.com; 1551 G St; dinner mains $27-36; ☺5:30-9pm Tue-Thu, to 10pm Fri-Sat; 🍽) Just a slip of a place, but with an enormous reputation. The short but inventive menu features seasonally inspired bistro cooking, from Asian to Mediterranean, with an emphasis on local organics. Wood-fired pizzas ($14 to $19) are renowned. Sunday brunch, too. Reservations essential.

Jambalaya LATIN AMERICAN FUSION $$
(915 H St; mains lunch $7-9, dinner $15-20; ☺5pm-2am Mon-Tue & Thu-Fri, from 9pm Wed, from 10am Sat-Sun) Probably the most vibrant dining option on the square, Jambalaya serves a mishmash of Caribbean-influenced dishes – at lunch Cuban sandwiches, at dinner wild salmon and (of course) jambalaya. The drink menu also shines, with fresh fruit cocktails and a great beer selection. As if this wasn't fun enough, it also hosts Arcata's best live music scene.

3 Foods Cafe FUSION $$
(www.cafeattheendoftheuniverse.com; 835 J St; mains brunch $8-14, dinner $10-30; ☺5:30am-10pm Tue-Thu, to 11pm Fri & Sat, to 9pm Sun; 🍽) A perfect fit with the Arcata dining scene: whimsical, creative, worldly dishes (think Korean beef in a spicy chili sauce) at moderate prices (a prix fixe is sometimes available for $20). The lavender-infused cocktails start things off on the right foot. The mac and cheese is the crowd favorite.

Wildflower Cafe & Bakery CAFE $$
(☎707-822-0360; 1604 G St; breakfast & lunch $5-8, dinner mains $15-16; ☺8am-8pm Sun-Wed; 🍽) Tops for vegetarians, this tiny storefront serves fab frittatas, pancakes and curries, and big crunchy salads.

Japhy's Soup & Noodles NOODLES $
(1563 G St; mains $5-8; ☺11:30am-8pm Mon-Fri) Big salads, tasty coconut curry, cold noodle salads and homemade soups – and cheap!

Stars Hamburgers BURGERS $
(1535 G St; burgers $3-5; ☺11am-8pm Mon-Thu, to 9pm Fri, to 7pm Sat, noon-6pm Sun; ♿) Uses grass-fed beef to make fantastic burgers.

Don's Donuts FAST FOOD $
(933 H St; donuts $0.80-1.35, sandwiches from $6; ☎24hr) Get a southeast-Asian sandwich.

🍷 Drinking

Dive bars and cocktail lounges line the plaza's northern side. Arcata is awash in coffeehouses.

TOP CHOICE Six Rivers Brewery BREWPUB
(www.sixriversbrewery.com; 1300 Central Ave, McKinleyville; mains $11-18; ☺11:30am-midnight Tue-Sun, from 4pm Mon) One of the first female-owned breweries in California, the 'brew with a view' kills it in every category: great beer, amazing community vibe, occasional live music and delicious hot wings. The spicy chili pepper ale is amazing. At first glance the menu might seem like ho-hum pub grub, but the batter crusted halibut is a golden treat and the salads are fresh and huge. They also make a helluva pizza.

Humboldt Brews BAR
(www.humbrews.com; 856 10th St; pub grub $5-10) This popular beer house has been elegantly remodeled and has a huge selection of carefully selected beer taps, fish tacos and buffalo wings. Live music nightly.

Cafe Mokka COFFEE SHOP
(www.cafemokkaarcata.com; cnr 5th & J Sts; snacks $4) Bohos head to this cafe at Finnish Country Sauna & Tubs (p255) for a mellow, old-world vibe, good coffee drinks and homemade cookies.

⭐ Entertainment

Arcata Theatre CINEMA
(www.arcatatheater.com; 1036 G St) An exquisite remodeling has revived this classic movie house, which shows art films, rock documentaries, silent films and more. Plus, it serves beer.

Center Arts ARTS CENTER
(tickets 707-826-3928; www.humboldt.edu/centerarts/) Hosts events on campus and you'd be amazed at who shows up: from Diana Krall and Dave Brubeck to Lou Reed and Ani Difranco. The place to buy tickets is at the University Ticket Office in the HSY Bookstore on the 3rd floor of the University Center.

ℹ Information

Arcata Eye (www.arcataeye.com) Free newspaper listing local events; the 'Police Log' column is hysterical.
Bureau of Land Management (BLM; 707-825-2300; 1695 Heindon Rd) Has information on the Lost Coast.
California Welcome Center (707-822-3619; www.arcatachamber.com; 1635 Heindon Rd; 9am 5pm) Two miles north of town, off Giuntoli Lane, Hwy 101's west side. Operated by the Arcata Chamber of Commerce. Provides local and statewide information. Get the free *Official Map Guide to Arcata*.
Tin Can Mailman (www.tincanbooks.com; 1000 HSt) Used volumes on two floors; excellent for hard-to-find books.

ℹ Getting There & Around

Horizon Air (www.alaskaair.com) and **United** (www.united.com) make regional connections (which are predictably expensive) to the Arcata/Eureka airport.
   Greyhound (www.greyhound.com) serves Arcata; from San Francisco budget $53 and seven hours. **Redwood Transit buses** (www.hta.org) serve Arcata and Eureka on the Trinidad–Scotia routes ($2.50, 2½ hours), which don't run on Sunday.
   Arcata city buses (707-822-3775; Mon-Sat) stop at the **Arcata Transit Center** (707-825-8934; 925 E St at 9th St). For shared rides, read the bulletin board at the North Coast Co-op (p256).
   Revolution Bicycle (www.revolutionbicycle.com; 1360 G St) and **Life Cycle Bike Shop** (www.lifecyclearcata.com; 1593 G St; Mon-Sat) rent, service and sell bicycles.
   Only in Arcata: borrow a bike from **Library Bike** (www.arcata.com/greenbikes; 865 8th St) for a $20 deposit, which gets refunded when you return the bike – up to six months later! They're beaters, but they ride.
   Though hitchhiking is still fairly rare and safety concerns should be taken seriously, a culture of hippies of all ages and transient marijuana harvesters makes this the easiest region in California to thumb a ride.

NORTHERN REDWOOD COAST

Congratulations, traveler, you've reached the middle of nowhere, or at least the top of the middle of nowhere. Here, the trees are so large that the tiny towns along the road seem even smaller. The scenery is pure drama: cliffs and rocks, native lore, legendary salmon runs, mammoth trees, redneck towns and RVing retirees. It's certainly the *weirdest* part of the California Coast. Leave time to dawdle and bask in the haunting grandeur of it all and, even though there are scores of mid-century motels, you simply must make an effort to sleep outdoors if possible.

Trinidad

Cheery Trinidad perches prettily on the side of the ocean, combining upscale homes with a mellow surfer vibe. Somehow it feels a bit off-the-beaten-path even though tourism augments fishing to keep the economy going. Trinidad gained its name when Spanish sea captains arrived on Trinity Sunday in 1775 and named the area La Santisima Trinidad (the Holy Trinity). It didn't boom, though, until the 1850s, when it became an important port for miners.

◉ Sights & Activities

Trinidad is small: approach via Hwy 101 or from the north via Patrick's Point Dr (which becomes Scenic Dr further south). To reach town, take Main St.
   The free town map at the information kiosk shows several fantastic hiking trails, most notably the **Trinidad Head Trail** with superb coastal views; excellent for whale-watching (December to April). Stroll along an exceptionally beautiful cove at **Trinidad State Beach**; take Main St and bear right at Stagecoach, then take the second turn left (the first is a picnic area) into the small lot.
   Scenic Dr twists south along coastal bluffs, passing tiny coves with views back

Northern Redwood Coast

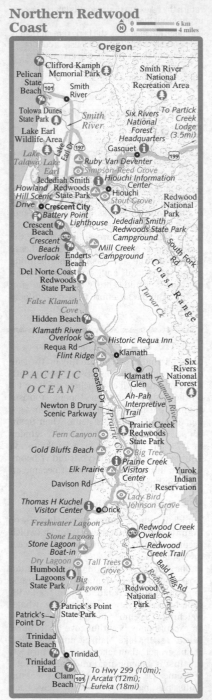

NORTH COAST & REDWOODS TRINIDAD

toward the bay. It peters out before reaching the broad expanses of **Luffenholtz Beach** (accessible via the staircase) and serene white-sand **Moonstone Beach**. Exit Hwy 101 at 6th Ave/Westhaven to get there. Further south Moonstone becomes **Clam Beach County Park**.

Surfing is good year-round, but potentially dangerous: unless you know how to judge conditions and get yourself out of trouble – there are no lifeguards here – surf in better-protected Crescent City.

FREE **HSU Telonicher**
Marine Laboratory   SCIENCE CENTER
(☏707-826-3671; www.humboldt.edu/marinelab; Ewing St; ◷9am-4:30pm Mon-Fri, noon-4pm Sat Sep–mid-May; ♿) Near Edwards St, has a touch tank, several aquariums (look for the giant Pacific octopus), an enormous whale jaw and a cool three-dimensional map of the ocean floor. You can also join a naturalist on tide pooling expeditions (90 minutes, $3); call ahead to ask about conditions.

🛏 Sleeping

Many of the inns line Patrick's Point Dr, north of town. **Trinidad Retreats** (www.trinidadretreats.com) and **Redwood Coast Vacation Rentals** (www.enjoytrinidad.com) handle local property rentals.

TOP CHOICE **Trinidad Bay B&B**   B&B $$$
(☏707-677-0840; www.trinidadbaybnb.com; 560 Edwards St; r incl breakfast from $200; ☎) Opposite the lighthouse, this gorgeous light-filled Cape Cod overlooks the harbor and Trinidad Head. Breakfast is delivered to your uniquely styled room and in the afternoon the house fills with the scent of freshly baked cookies. Each room also comes with a loaner iPad to use, loaded up with apps focused on local events and activities.

Clam Beach   CAMPGROUND $
(tent sites per vehicle $10) South of town off Hwy 101, has excellent camping, but can get very crowded. Pitch your tent in the dunes (look for natural windbreaks). Facilities include pit toilets, cold water, picnic tables and fire rings.

View Crest Lodge   LODGE $$
(☏707-677-3393; www.viewcrestlodge.com; 3415 Patrick's Point Dr; sites $32, 1-bedroom cottages $95-170; ☎) On a hill above the ocean on the inland side, some of the well-maintained, modern cottages have views and Jacuzzis;

most have kitchens. Also a good campground.

Trinidad Inn
INN $

(707-677-3349; www.trinidadinn.com; 1170 Patrick's Point Dr; r $75-115; 🐾) Sparklingly clean and attractively decorated rooms (many with kitchens) fill this upmarket, gray-shingled motel under tall trees.

Bishop Pine Lodge
LODGE $$

(707-677-3314; www.bishoppinelodge.com; 1481 Patrick's Point Dr; cottages with/without kitchen from $150/110; 🐾) It feels like summer camp: rent free-standing redwood cottages in a grassy meadow. Expect woodsy charm and unintentionally retro-funky furniture.

Lost Whale Inn
B&B $$$

(707-677-3425; www.lostwhaleinn.com; 3452 Patrick's Point Dr; r all incl breakfast $200-285, ste all incl breakfast $375; 🐾) Perched atop a grassy cliff, high above crashing waves and braying sea lions, this spacious, modern, light-filled B&B has jaw-dropping views out to the sea. The lovely gardens have a 24-hour hot tub.

✗ Eating & Drinking

TOP CHOICE Larrupin Cafe
CALIFORNIAN $$$

(707-677-0230; www.larrupin.com; 1658 Patrick's Point Dr; mains $20-30; 5-9pm Thu-Tue) Everybody loves Larrupin, where Moroccan rugs, chocolate brown walls, gravity-defying floral arrangements and deep-burgundy Oriental carpets create a moody atmosphere perfect for a lovers' tryst. On the menu, expect consistently good mesquite-grilled seafood and meats. In the summer, book a table on the garden patio. No credit cards.

Kahish's Catch Café
FAST FOOD $

(707-677-0390; 355 Main St; mains $6-9; 11am-7pm Tue-Sun; 🐾) Across from the Chevron, this fun little hippie joint makes good food fast, using mostly organic ingredients – from pizzettas and grass-fed burgers to brown rice and veggies. Order at the counter and then sit outside.

Moonstone Grill
SEAFOOD $$$

(Moonstone Beach; mains $20-32; 5:30-8:30pm Wed-Sun) Enjoy drop-dead sunset views over a picture-perfect beach while supping on the likes of oysters on the half-shell, Pacific wild king salmon or spice-rubbed rib eye. If the high price tag is a bit out-of-budget, drop in for a glass of wine.

Katy's Smokehouse & Fishmarket
SEAFOOD $

(www.katyssmokehouse.com; 740 Edwards St; 9am-6pm) Makes its own chemical-free smoked and canned fish, using line-caught sushi-grade seafood.

Beachcomber Café
CAFE $

(707-677-0106; 363 Trinity St; 7am-4pm Mon-Fri, 9am-4pm Sat & Sun) Head here for the best homemade cookies and to meet locals. Friday rocks live music.

❶ Information

Beachcomber Cafe (707-677-0106; 363 Trinity St; per hr $5; 7am-4pm Mon-Thu, to 9pm Fri, 9am-4pm Sat & Sun) Internet access.

Information kiosk (cnr Patrick's Point Dr & Main St) Just west of the freeway. The pamphlet *Discover Trinidad* has an excellent map.

Trinidad Chamber of Commerce (707-667-1610; www.trinidadcalif.com) Information on the web, but no visitor center.

Patrick's Point State Park

Coastal bluffs jut out to sea at 640-acre **Patrick's Point** (707-677-3570; 4150 Patrick's Point Dr; day use $8; 🐾), where sandy beaches abut rocky headlands. Five miles north of Trinidad, with supereasy access to dramatic coastal bluffs, it's a best-bet for families. Stroll scenic overlooks, climb giant rock formations, watch whales breach, gaze into tidepools, or listen to barking sea lions and singing birds from this manicured park.

Sumêg is an authentic reproduction of a Yurok village, with hand-hewn redwood buildings where Native Americans gather for traditional ceremonies. In the native plant garden you'll find species for making traditional baskets and medicines.

On **Agate Beach** look for stray bits of jade and sea-polished agate. Follow the signs to tidepools, but tread lightly and obey regulations. The 2-mile **Rim Trail**, a former Yurok trail around the bluffs, circles the point with access to huge rocky outcroppings. Don't miss **Wedding Rock**, one of the park's most romantic spots. Other trails lead around unusual formations like **Ceremonial Rock** and **Lookout Rock**.

The park's three well-tended **campgrounds** (reservations 800-444-7275; www.reserveamerica.com; tent & RV sites $35) have coin-operated hot showers and very clean bathrooms. Penn Creek and Abalone campgrounds are more sheltered than Agate Beach.

Humboldt Lagoons State Park

Stretching out for miles along the coast, Humboldt Lagoons has long, sandy beaches and a string of coastal lagoons. Big Lagoon and the even prettier Stone Lagoon are both excellent for kayaking and bird-watching. Sunsets are spectacular, with no manmade structures in sight. Picnic at Stone Lagoon's north end. The Stone Lagoon Visitor Center, on Hwy 101, has closed due to staffing shortages, but there's a toilet and a bulletin board displaying information.

A mile north, Freshwater Lagoon is also great for birding. South of Stone Lagoon, tiny Dry Lagoon (a freshwater marsh) has a fantastic day hike. Park at Dry Lagoon's picnic area and hike north on the unmarked trail to Stone Lagoon; the trail skirts the southwestern shore and ends up at the ocean, passing through woods and marshland rich with wildlife. Mostly flat, it's about 2.5 miles one way – and nobody takes it because it's unmarked.

All campsites are first-come, first-served. The park runs two environmental campgrounds (tent sites $20; ☺Apr-Oct); bring water. Stone Lagoon has six boat-in environmental campsites; Dry Lagoon has six walk-in campsites. Check in at Patrick's Point State Park, at least 30 minutes before sunset.

Humboldt County Parks (☎707-445-7651; tent sites $20) operates a lovely cypress-grove picnic area and campground beside Big Lagoon, a mile off Hwy 101, with flush toilets and cold water, but no showers.

Redwood National & State Parks

A patchwork of public lands jointly administered by the state and federal governments, the Redwood National & State Parks include Redwood National Park, Prairie Creek Redwoods State Park (p261), Del Norte Coast Redwoods State Park (p262) and Jedediah Smith Redwoods State Park (p265). A smattering of small towns break up the forested area, making it a bit confusing to get a sense of the parks as a whole. Prairie Creek and Jedediah Smith parks were originally land slated for clear-cutting, but in the '60s

activists successfully protected them and today all these parks are an International Biosphere Reserve and World Heritage Site. At one time the national park was to absorb at least two of the state parks, but that did not happen, and so the cooperative structure remains.

Little-visited compared to their southern brethren, the world's tallest living trees have been standing here for time immemorial, predating the Roman Empire by over 500 years. Prepare to be impressed.

The small town of Orick (population 650), at the southern tip of the park, in a lush valley, is barely more than a few storefronts and a vast conglomeration of woodcarving.

◉ Sights & Activities

Just north of the southern visitor center, turn east onto Bald Hills Rd and travel 2 miles to Lady Bird Johnson Grove, one of the park's most spectacular groves, accessible via a gentle 1-mile loop trail. Continue for another 5 miles up Bald Hills to Redwood Creek Overlook. On the top of the ridgeline at 2100ft get views over the forest and the entire watershed – provided it's not foggy. Just past the overlook lies the gated turnoff for Tall Trees Grove, the location of several of the world's tallest trees. Rangers issue only 50 vehicle permits per day, but they rarely run out. Pick one up, along with the gate-lock combination, from the visitor centers. Allow four hours for the round-trip, which includes a 6-mile drive down a rough dirt road (speed limit 15mph) and a steep 1.3-mile one-way hike, which descends 800ft to the grove.

Several longer trails include the awe-inspiring Redwood Creek Trail, which also reaches Tall Trees Grove. You'll need a free backcountry permit to hike and camp (highly recommended, as the best backcountry camping in on the North Coast), but the area is most accessible from Memorial Day to Labor Day, when summer footbridges are up. Otherwise, getting across the creek can be perilous or impossible.

❶ Information

Unlike most national parks, there are no fees and no highway entrance stations at Redwood National Park, so it's imperative to pick up the free map at the park headquarters (p264) in Crescent City or at the Redwood Information Center (Kuchel Visitor Center;

707-464-6101; www.nps.gov/redw; Hwy
101; 9am-6pm June-Aug, to 5pm Sept-Oct &
March-May, to 4pm Nov-Feb) in Orick. Rangers
here issue permits to visit Tall Trees Grove and
loan bear-proof containers for backpackers. For
in-depth redwood ecology, buy the excellent
official park handbook. The **Redwood Parks
Association** (www.redwoodparksassociation.
org) provides good information on its website,
including detailed descriptions of all the parks
hikes.

Prairie Creek Redwoods State Park

Famous for virgin redwood and unspoiled
coastline, this 14,000-acre section of Redwood National & State Parks has spectacular
scenic drives and 70 miles of hiking trails,
many of which are excellent for children.
Pick up maps and information and sit by the
river-rock fireplace at **Prairie Creek Visitor
Center** (707-464-6101; 9am-5pm Mar-Oct,
10am-4pm Nov-Feb;). Kids will love the taxidermy dioramas with push-button, light-up
displays. Outside, elk roam grassy flats.

Sights & Activities

**Newton B Drury Scenic
Parkway**   SCENIC DRIVE
Just north of Orick is the turn off for the
8-mile parkway, which runs parallel to Hwy
101 through untouched ancient redwood forests. It's worth the short detour off the freeway to view the magnificence of these trees.
Numerous trails branch off from roadside
pullouts, including family- and ADA (American Disabilities Act) -friendly trails including Big Tree and Revelation Trail.

Hiking & Mountain-Biking
There are 28 mountain-biking and hiking trails through the park, from simple to
strenuous. Only a few of these will appeal
to hard core hikers, who should take on the
Del Norte Coast Redwoods. Those tight on
time or with mobility impairments should
stop at **Big Tree**, an easy 100yd walk from
the car park. Several other easy nature trails
start near the visitor center, including **Revelation Trail** and **Elk Prairie Trail**. Stroll
the recently reforested logging road on the
Ah-Pah Interpretive Trail at the park's
north end. The most challenging hike in this
corner of the park is the truly spectacular
11.5-mile **Coastal Trail** which goes through
primordial redwoods.

Just past the **Gold Bluffs Beach Campground** the road dead ends at **Fern Canyon**,
where 60ft fern-covered sheer-rock walls
can be seen from Steven Spielberg's *Jurassic
Park 2: The Lost World*. This is one of the
most photographed spots on the North Coast
– damp and lush, all emerald green – and *totally* worth getting your toes wet to see.

Sleeping

Welcome to the great outdoors: without
any motels or cabins, the only choice here
is to pitch a tent in the campgrounds at the
southern end of the park.

Gold Bluffs Beach   CAMPGROUND $
(no reservations; tent sites $35) This camp
ground sits between 100ft cliffs and wide-
open ocean, but there are some windbreaks
and solar-heated showers. Look for sites up
the cliff under the trees.

Elk Prairie Campground   CAMPGROUND $
(reservations 800-444-7275; www.reserveameri
ca.com; tent & RV sites $35) Elk roam this popu-
lar campground, where you can sleep under
redwoods or at the prairie's edge. There are
hot showers, some hike-in sites and a shallow creek to splash in. Sites 1-7 and 69–76
are on grassy prairies and get full sun; sites
8–68 are wooded. To camp in a mixed redwood forest, book sites 20–27.

Klamath

Giant metal-cast golden bears stand sentry
at the bridge across the Klamath River, an-
nouncing Klamath, one of the tiny settlements that break up Redwood National &
State Parks. With a gas station/market, a
great diner and a casino, Klamath is basically a wide spot in the road. The Yurok
Tribal Headquarters is here and the entire
town and much of the surrounding area is
the tribe's ancestral land. Klamath is roughly
an hour north of Eureka.

Sights & Activities

The mouth of the **Klamath River** is a dramatic sight. Marine, riparian, forest and
meadow ecological zones all converge and
the birding is exceptional. For the best
views, head north of town to Requa Rd and
the **Klamath River Overlook** and picnic on
high bluffs above driftwood-strewn beaches. On a clear day, this is one of the most
spectacular viewpoints on the North Coast,
and one of the best whale-watching spots

in California. For a good hike, head north along the Coastal Trail. You'll have the sand to yourself at **Hidden Beach**; access the trail at the northern end of Motel Trees.

Just south of the river, on Hwy 101, follow signs for the scenic **Coastal Drive**, a narrow, winding country road (unsuitable for RVs and trailers) atop extremely high cliffs over the ocean. Come when it's not foggy, and mind your driving. Though technically in Redwood National Park, it's much closer to Klamath.

Klamath Jet Boat Tours   BOAT TOURS
(www.jetboattours.com; 2hr tours adult/child $42/22) Book jet-boat excursions and fishing trips.

🛏 Sleeping & Eating

Woodsy Klamath is cheaper than Crescent City, but there aren't as many places to eat or buy groceries, and there's nothing to do at night but play cards. There are ample private RV parks in the area.

TOP CHOICE **Historic Requa Inn**   HISTORIC HOTEL $
(☏707-482-1425; www.requainn.com; 451 Requa Rd, Klamath; r $85-155; ☏) A woodsy country lodge on bluffs overlooking the mouth of the Klamath, the 1914 Requa Inn is one of our North Coast favorites and – a cherry on top – it's a carbon neutral facility. Many of the charming country-style rooms have mesmerizing views over the misty river, as does the dining room, where guests have breakfast.

Ravenwood Motel   MOTEL $$
(☏707-482-5911, 866-520-9875; www.ravenwood motel.com; 131 Klamath Blvd; r/ste with kitchen $75/115) The spotlessly clean rooms are bet-

ter than anything in Crescent City and individually decorated with furnishings and flair you'd expect in a city hotel, not a small-town motel.

FREE **Flint Ridge Campground**   CAMPGROUND
(☏707-464-6101) Four miles from the Klamath River Bridge via Coastal Dr, this tent-only, hike-in campground sits among a wild, overgrown meadow of ghostly, overgrown ferns and moss. It's a 10-minute walk east, uphill from the dirt parking area. There's no water, plenty of bear sightings (bear boxes on site) and you have to pack out trash. But, hey, it's free.

Klamath River Cafe   AMERICAN $
(☏707-482-1000;mains $8-12; ☺7:30am-2pm) With excellent homemade baked goods, a daily pie special and excellent breakfast food, this shiny new place is the best diner food within miles. The breakfasts are killer. Seasonal hours vary, so call ahead. If you arrive around dinner time, cross your fingers – it's open sporadically for dinner.

Del Norte Coast Redwoods State Park

Marked by steep canyons and dense woods, half the 6400 acres of this **park** (vehicle day-use $8) are virgin redwood forest, crisscrossed by 15 miles of hiking trails. Even the most cynical of redwood-watchers can't help but be moved.

Pick up maps and inquire about guided walks at the Redwood National & State Parks Headquarters (p264) in Crescent City or the Redwood Information Center in Orick (p260).

Hwy 1 winds in from the coast at rugged, dramatic **Wilson Beach**, and traverses the dense forest, with groves stretching off as far as you can see.

Picnic on the sand at **False Klamath Cove**. Heading north, tall trees cling precipitously to canyon walls that drop to the rocky, timber-strewn coastline, and it's almost impossible to get to the water, except via gorgeous but steep **Damnation Creek Trail** or **Footsteps Rock Trail**.

Between these two, serious hikers will be most greatly rewarded by the Damnation Creek Trail. It's only 4 miles long, but the 1100-foot elevation change and cliff-side redwood makes it the park's best hike. The

---

WHAT THE...?

It's hard to miss the giant statues of Paul Bunyan and Babe the Blue Ox towering over the parking lot at **Trees of Mystery** (☏707-482-2251; www. treesofmystery.net; 15500 Hwy 101; adult/ child & senior $14/7; ☺8am-7pm Jun-Aug, 9am-4pm Sep-May; 🖑), a shameless tourist trap with a gondola running through the redwood canopy. The **End of the Trail Museum** located behind the Trees of Mystery gift shop has an outstanding collection of Native American arts and artifacts, and it's *free*.

SMITH RIVER NATIONAL RECREATION AREA

West of Jedediah Smith Redwoods, the Smith River, the state's last remaining undammed waterway, runs right beside Hwy 199. Originating high in the Siskiyou Mountains, its serpentine course cuts through deep canyons beneath thick forests. Chinook salmon and steelhead trout annually migrate up its clear waters. Camp, hike, raft and kayak here, but check regulations if you want to fish. Stop by the **Six Rivers National Forest Headquarters** (☎707-457-3131; www.fs.fed.us/r5/sixrivers; 10600 Hwy 199, Gasquet; ⊗8am-4:30pm daily May-Sep, 8am-4:30pm Mon-Fri Oct-Apr) to get your bearings. Pick up pamphlets for the **Darlingtonia Trail** and **Myrtle Creek Botanical Area**, both easy jaunts into the woods, where you can see rare plants and learn about the area's geology.

unmarked trailhead starts from a parking area off Hwy 101 at mile mark 16.

Crescent Beach Overlook and picnic area has superb wintertime whale-watching. At the park's north end, watch the surf pound at **Crescent Beach**, just south of Crescent City via Enderts Beach Rd.

Mill Creek Campground (☎800-444-7275; www.reserveamerica.com; tent & RV sites $35) has hot showers and 145 sites in a redwood grove, 2 miles east of Hwy 101 and 7 miles south of Crescent City. Sites 1-74 are woodsier; sites 75-145 sunnier. Hike-in sites are prettiest.

Crescent City

Though Crescent City was founded as a thriving 1853 seaport and supply center for inland gold mines, the town's history was quite literally washed away in 1964, when half the town was swallowed by a tsunami. Of course, it was rebuilt (though mostly with the utilitarian ugliness of ticky-tacky buildings), but its marina was devastated by the 2011 Japan earthquake and tsunami, when the city was evacuated. Crescent City remains California's last big town north of Arcata, though the constant fog (and sounding fog horn) and damp, '60s sprawl makes it about as charming as a wet bag of dirty laundry. The economy depends heavily on shrimp and crab fishing, hotel tax and on Pelican Bay maximum-security prison, just north of town, which adds tension to the air and lots of cops on the streets.

◉ Sights & Activities

Hwy 101 splits into two parallel one-way streets, with the southbound traffic on L St, northbound on M St. To see the major sights, turn west on Front St toward the lighthouse. Downtown is centered along 3rd St.

If you're in town in August, the **Del Norte County Fair** features a rodeo, and lots of characters.

🐾 North Coast Marine Mammal Center
SCIENCE CENTER
(☎707-465-6265; www.northcoastmmc.org; 424 Howe Dr; by donation; ⊗10am-5pm; 🚸) Just east of Battery Point, this is the ecologically minded foil to the garish Ocean World: the clinic treats injured seals, sea lions and dolphins and releases them back into the wild (donation requested).

Battery Point Lighthouse
LIGHTHOUSE
(www.delnortehistory.org/lighthouse) The 1856 lighthouse, at the south end of A St, still operates on a tiny, rocky island that you can easily reach at low tide. From April to September, tour the **museum** (adult/child $3/1; ⊗10am-4pm Mon-Sat May-Sep); hours vary with tides and weather.

Beachfront Park
PARK
(Howe Dr; 🚸) Between B and H Sts, this park has a harborside beach with no large waves, making it perfect for little ones. Further east on Howe Dr, near J St, you'll come to **Kidtown**, with slides and swings and a make-believe castle.

🛏 Sleeping

Most people stop here for one night while traveling; motels are overpriced, but you'll pass a slew of hotels on the main arteries leading into and out of town. The county operates two excellent reservable **campgrounds** (☎707-464-7230; tent & RV sites $10) just outside of town. **Florence Keller Park** (3400 Cunningham Lane) has 50 sites in a beautiful grove of young redwoods (take Hwy 101 north to Elk Valley Cross Rd and follow the signs). **Ruby Van Deventer Park** (4705 N Bank Rd) has 18 sites along the Smith River, off Hwy 197. Both of these are an excellent bargain.

TOP CHOICE **Curly Redwood Lodge** MOTEL $
(☎707-464-2137; www.curlyredwoodlodge.com; 701 Hwy 101 S; r $68-73; ❄✿) The Redwood Lodge is a marvel: it's entirely built and paneled from a single curly redwood tree which measured over 18-in thick in diameter. Progressively restored and polished into a gem of mid-century kitsch, the inn is a delight for retro junkies. Rooms are clean, large and comfortable (request one away from the road). For truly modern accommodations, look elsewhere.

Bay View Inn HOTEL $
(☎800-742-8439; www.bayviewinn.net; 2844 Fairfield; r $74-89; ❄✿) Bright, modern, updated rooms with microwaves and refrigerators fill this centrally located independent hotel. It may seem a bit like better-than-average highway exit chain, but colorful bead spreads and warm hosts add necessary homespun appeal. The rooms upstairs in the back have views of the lighthouse and the harbor.

Crescent Beach Motel MOTEL $
(☎707-464-5436; www.crescentbeachmotel.com; 1455 Hwy 101 S; r $70-100; ❄✿) Just south of town, this basic, old-fashioned motel is the only place in town to stay right on the beach, offering views that distract you from the somewhat plain indoor environs. Try here first, but skip rooms without a view.

Anchor Beach Inn HOTEL $
(☎707-464-2600; www.anchorbeachinn.com; 880 Hwy 101 S; r $85-105; ❄✿✿) Microwave, DSL, soundproof walls and personality-free.

✕ Eating & Drinking

Beacon Burger BURGERS $
(160 Anchor Way; burgers $6-10; ☉11:30am-8:30pm Mon-Sat) This scrappy little one-room burger joint has been here forever, square in the middle of a parking lot overlooking the South Bay. It looks like it might invite a health inspector's scorn, but you'll quickly forgive it after ordering a burger – perfectly greasy and mysteriously wonderful. They come sided with potato gems and a menu of thick shakes.

Wing Wah Restaurant CHINESE $
(383 M St; mains $7-11; ☉11:30am-9pm Sun-Thu, to 9:30 Fri & Sat) Tucked into a shopping center, Wing Wah serves Crescent City's best Chinese food; savory pork and beef dishes are fresh and come quickly to the table.

Good Harvest Café AMERICAN $
(575 Hwy 101 S; mains $7-10; ☉7am-9pm Mon-Sat, from 8am Sun; ✸) This popular local cafe recently moved into a spacious new location across from the harbor. It also added a dinner menu on par with the quality salads, smoothies and sandwiches that made it so popular in the first place. Good beers, a crackling fire and loads of vegetarian options make this the best dining spot in town.

Chart Room SEAFOOD $
(130 Anchor Way; dinner mains $9-23; ☉6:30am-7pm Sun-Thu, to 8pm Fri & Sat; ✸) At the tip of the South Harbor pier, this joint is renowned far and wide for its fish and chips: batter-caked golden beauties which deliver on their reputation. It's often a hive of families, retirees, Harley riders and local businessmen, so grab a beer at the small bar and wait for a table.

Tomasini's CAFE $
(960 3rd St; mains $4-8; ☉7:30am-2pm; ✐) Stop in for salads, sandwiches or jazz on weekend nights. Hands down the most happening place downtown.

❶ Information

Crescent City-Del Norte Chamber of Commerce (☎707-464-3174, 800-343-8300; www.northerncalifornia.net; 1001 Front St; ☉9am-5pm May-Aug, 9am-5pm Mon-Fri Sep-Apr) Local information.

Redwood National & State Parks Headquarters (☎707-464-6101; 1111 2nd St; ☉9am-5pm Oct-May, to 6pm Jun-Sep) On the corner of K St; rangers and information about all four parks under its jurisdiction.

❶ Getting There & Around

United Express (☎800-241-6522) flies into tiny **Crescent City Airport** (CEC), north of town. **Redwood Coast Transit** (www.redwoodcoast transit.org) serves Crescent City with local buses ($1), and runs buses Monday to Saturday to Klamath ($1.50, one hour, two daily) and Arcata ($20, two hours, two daily) with stops in between.

Tolowa Dunes State Park & Lake Earl Wildlife Area

Two miles north of Crescent City, this **state park and wildlife area** (☎707-464-6101, ext 5112; ☉sunrise-sunset) encompasses 10,000 acres of wetlands, dunes, meadows and two lakes, **Lake Earl** and **Lake Tolowa**. This major stopover on the Pacific Flyway route brings over 250 species of birds. Listen for the whistling, warbling chorus. On land, look for coyotes and deer, Angle for trout, or hike or ride 20 miles of trails; at sea, spot whales, seals and sea lions.

The park and wildlife area is a patchwork of lands administered by California State Parks and the Department of Fish and Game (DFG). The DFG focuses on single-species management, hunting and fishing; the State Parks' focus is on ecodiversity and recreation. You might be hiking a vast expanse of pristine dunes, then suddenly hear a shotgun or a whining 4WD. Strict regulations limit where and when you can hunt and drive; trails are clearly marked.

Register for two primitive, nonreservable campgrounds (tent sites $20) at Jedediah Smith or Del Norte Coast Redwoods State Park campgrounds. The mosquitoes are plentiful in the spring and early summer.

Jedediah Smith Redwoods State Park

The northern-most park in the system of Redwood National & State Parks, the dense stands at Jedediah Smith (day use $8) are 10 miles northeast of Crescent City (via Hwy 101 east to Hwy 197). The redwood stands are so thick that few trails penetrate the park, but the outstanding 11-mile Howland Hill scenic drive cuts through otherwise inaccessible areas (take Hwy 199 to South Fork Rd; turn right after crossing two bridges). It's a rough road, impassable for RVs, but if you can't hike, it's the best way to see the forest.

Stop for a stroll under enormous trees in Simpson-Reed Grove. If it's foggy at the coast it may be sunny here. There's a swimming hole and picnic area near the park entrance. An easy half-mile trail, departing from the far side of the campground, crosses the Smith River via a summer-only footbridge, leading to Stout Grove, the park's most famous grove. The visitor center (☎707-464-6101; ⊙10am-4pm daily Jun-Aug, 10am-4pm Sat & Sun Sep-Oct & Apr-May) sells hiking maps and nature guides. If you wade in the river, be careful in the spring when currents are swift and the water cold.

The popular campground (☎reservations 800-444-7275; www.reserveamerica.com; tent & RV sites $35) has gorgeous sites tucked through the redwoods beside the Smith River.

If you don't camp, try the renovated Hiouchi Motel (☎707-458-3041, 888-881-0819; www.hiouchimotel.com; 2097 Hwy 199; s $50, d $65-70; @☎) offering clean, straightforward motel rooms.

Pelican Beach State Park

Never-crowded Pelican State Beach (☎707-464-6101, ext 5151) occupies five coastal acres on the Oregon border. There are no facilities, but it's great for kite flying; pick one up at the shop just over the border in Oregon.

The best reason to visit is to stay at secluded, charming Casa Rubio (☎707-487-4313; www.casarubio.com; 17285 Crissey Rd; r $108-168; @☎☎), where three of the four ocean-view rooms have kitchens.

Pitch a tent by the ocean (no windbreaks) at Clifford Kamph Memorial Park (☎707-464-7230; 15100 Hwy 101; tent sites $10); no RVs. It's a steal for the beachside location and, even though sites are exposed in a grassy area and there isn't much privacy, all have BBQs.

Northern Mountains

Best Places to Eat

» Jack's Grill (p269)
» Red Onion Grill (p277)
» Café Le Coq (p281)
» Trinity Café (p287)
» Vivify (p287)

Best Places to Stay

» McCloud River Mercantile Hotel (p292)
» Houseboat on Shasta Lake (p272)
» Bidwell House B&B (p277)
» Feather Bed B&B (p280)
» Feather River Canyon Campgrounds (p280)

Why Go?

The northeast corner is the remote, rugged, refreshingly pristine backyard of a state better known for sunny cities, sandy beaches and foggy groves of redwoods. This is California's wild frontier, where vast expanses of wilderness – some 24,000 protected acres – are divided by rivers and streams, dotted with cobalt lakes, horse ranches and alpine peaks. Much of it doesn't even look the way people envision California – the topography more resembles the older mountains of the Rockies than the relatively young granite Goliaths in Yosemite. Don't come here for the company (the towns are hospitable but tiny, with virtually no urban comforts); come to get lost in vast remoteness. Even the two principal attractions, Mt Shasta and Lassen Volcanic National Park, remain uncrowded (and sometimes snow-covered) at the peak of the summer.

When to Go
Lassen National Park

Jul–Sep Warm weather and snow-free passes are ideal for backcountry camping.

Oct–Nov & Apr–May Shoulder seasons; scattered showers and snow at the high elevations.

Nov–Jan Skiing Mt Shasta is the main draw. Prices drop outside of ski areas.

REDDING & AROUND

North of Red Bluff the dusty central corridor along I-5 starts to give way to panoramic mountain ranges on either side. Redding is the last major outpost before the small towns of the far north, and the surrounding lakes make for easy day trips or overnight camps. If you get off the highway – way off – this can be an exceptionally rewarding area of the state to explore.

Redding

Originally called Poverty Flats during the Gold Rush for its lack of wealth, Redding today has a whole lot of tasteless new money – malls, big-box stores and large housing developments surround its core. A tourist destination it is not, though it is the major gateway city to the northeast corner of the state and a useful spot for restocking before long jaunts into the wilderness. Recent constructions like the Sundial Bridge and Turtle Bay Exploration Park are enticing lures and worth a visit...but not a long one. Downtown is bordered by the Sacramento River to the north and east. Major thoroughfares are Pine and Market Sts.

Sights & Activities

Sundial Bridge   BRIDGE
Resembling a beached cruise ship, the shimmering-white 2004 Sundial Bridge spans the river and is one of Redding's marquee attractions, providing an excellent photo op. The glass-deck pedestrian overpass connects the Turtle Bay Exploration Park to the north bank of the Sacramento River and was designed by renowned Spanish architect Santiago Calatrava. The bridge/sundial attracts visitors from around the world, who come to marvel at this unique feat of engineering artistry. It is accessed from the park and connects to the Sacramento River Trail system.

Turtle Bay Exploration Park   SCIENCE CENTER
(www.turtlebay.org; 840 Auditorium Dr; adult/child 4-12yr $14/10; ☺9am-5pm May-Sep, 9am-4pm Wed-Sat & 10am-4pm Sun Oct-Apr; ⊞) Situated on 300 meandering acres, this is an artistic, cultural and scientific center for visitors of all ages, with an emphasis on the Sacramento River watershed. The complex houses art and natural science museums, fun interactive exhibits for kids (a recent show was 'Grossology', a study of the human

body's less-delicate biology). There are also extensive arboretum gardens, a butterfly house and a 22,000-gallon, walk-through river aquarium full of regional aquatic life (yes, including turtles). The on-site Café at Turtle Bay (meals $12) serves excellent gourmet coffee and great light meals.

Redding Aquatic Center   WATER PARK
(www.reddingaquaticcenter.com; adult/child $5/3; ☺1-5pm summer, with seasonal variations) Further west in Caldwell Park, this hugely popular center contains an Olympic-size pool, another vast recreation pool and a 160ft-long water slide. Also in Caldwell Park, you can pick up the Sacramento River Trail (www.reddingtrails.com), a paved walking and cycling path that meanders along the river for miles.

Cascade Theatre   HISTORIC BUILDING
(www.cascadetheatre.org; 1733 Market St) Try to catch some live music downtown at this refurbished 1935 art deco theater. Usually it hosts second-tier national acts but, if nothing else, take a peek inside; this is a neon-lit gem.

Sleeping

Redding's many motels and hotels huddle around noisy thoroughfares, though a few rooms can be found on less busy N Market St. A couple of motel rows lie close to I-5 at the southern end of town: just west of the freeway close to the Cypress Ave exit on Bechelli Lane, and on the east side of the freeway on Hilltop Dr. The chain hotels – and there are plenty of them – are all off I-5 and you can get great last-minute deals on the internet. The best tent camping is just up the road at Whiskeytown Lake (p271) or Shasta Lake (p271).

Northern Mountains Highlights

1 Stand agape at geothermal spectacles in **Lassen Volcanic National Park** (p273)

2 Wander the cute mountainside community of **Mt Shasta City** (p284)

3 Explore the many caves of **Lava Beds National Monument** (p293)

4 Look overhead at the bird superhighway at **Tule Lake** (p294)

5 Get lost in **Modoc** (p295), California's most remote national forest

6 Hide out and wade in the trout-filled water near **Weaverville** (p296)

7 Camp along the shores of gorgeous **Eagle Lake** (p279)

8 Hit the dramatic slopes of **Shasta** (p283)

9 Float with a dozen pals on a **Shasta Lake houseboat** (p272)

10 Kick up your heels at **McCloud's famous dance hall** (p292)

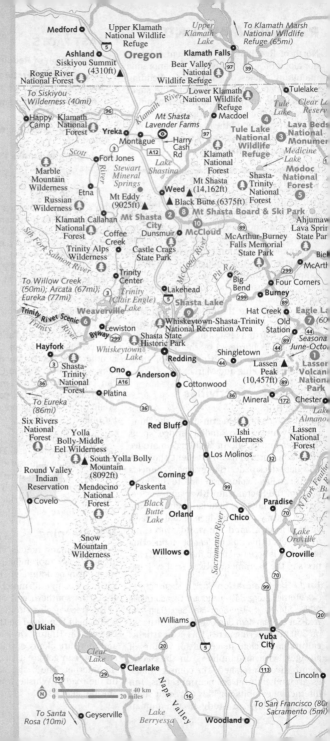

Apples' Riverhouse B&B
B&B $$

(☎530-243-8440; www.applesriverhouse.com; 201 Mora Ct; r $95-110) Just steps from the Sacramento River Trail, this modern, ranch-style home has three comfortable upstairs rooms, two with decks. It's a bit suburban, but it's the best independent stay in Redding. In the evening the sociable hosts invite you for cheese and wine. Bikes are yours to borrow and the proximity to the trail is inviting.

Tiffany House B&B Inn
B&B $$

(☎530-244-3225; www.tiffanyhousebb.com; 1510 Barbara Rd; r $110-120, cottage $170; ☀) In a quiet cul-de-sac, a mile north of the river, this Victorian cottage has an expansive garden with sweeping views. Cozy rooms are packed with antiques, rosebuds and ruffles. Affable hosts make a big yummy to-do over breakfast.

✖ Eating & Drinking

If you want Redding's best food, it's essential that you get off the highway and into the downtown area.

Carnegie's
CALIFORNIAN $$

(1600 Oregon St; meals $12; ☺10am-3pm Mon & Tue, to 11pm Wed-Fri; ✏) This hip and homey, split-level cafe serves up healthy food – big fresh salads, garlicky prawns and pasta and homemade tomato soup. There's a good selection of beer and wine, too. Friday nights get a little rowdy, and there can be a wait.

Jack's Grill
STEAKHOUSE $$$

(www.jacksgrillredding.com; 1743 California St; mains $15-31; ☺5-11pm, bar from 4pm Mon-Sat) This funky little old-time place doesn't look so inviting – the windows are blacked out and it's dark as a crypt inside – but the popularity with locals starts with its stubborn ain't-broke-don't-fix-it ethos and ends with its steak – a big, thick, charbroiled decadence. Regulars start lining up for dinner at 4pm, when cocktail hour begins. There are no reservations, so it easily takes an hour to get a seat.

🌱 Grilla Bites
SANDWICHES $

(www.grillabites.com; 1427 Market St; meals $5-10; ☺11am-8pm Mon-Thu, to 9pm Fri & Sat, to 4pm Sun; ☎✏) It doesn't get much simpler than this menu of grilled sandwiches and pay-by-the-pound salad bar but, to Grilla's credit, the food is fresh, locally sourced and the sandwiches are punched up with fresh herbs and global fusions. The grilled Italian Veggie sandwich is a savory melt of pesto and cheese, and the Thai Tuna is a local favorite.

ℹ DETOUR AROUND THE I-5 DOLDRUMS

A good alternative for travelers heading north and south on I-5 is to drive along Hwy 3 through the Scott Valley, which rewards with world-class views of the Trinity Alps. Compared to rushing along the dull highway, this scenic detour will add an additional half a day of driving.

Thai Cafe
THAI $$

(www.thaicafeofredding.com; 820 Butte St; mains $10-15; ☺11am-9pm Mon-Sat) To mix it up after days of camp-stove cooking on the trail, hit this excellent Thai place with an extensive menu. The seafood mains (so far from the sea) are surprisingly fresh, and the tom yum soup – with lemongrass, cilantro and the right amount of sourness – is spot on.

Gironda's Chicago Style Italian Restaurant
ITALIAN $$

(www.2girondas.com; 1100 Center St; mains $10-20; ☺11:30am-9pm Mon-Thu, to 10pm Sat; ✏) It's a little pricey and finding the place is a bit of a chore (it hides near the Eureka Way rail overpass, just off downtown), but the plates of Chicago-style deep dish, fresh pastas and relaxed family vibe are a nice break from the highway-side chains. Start with the crispy calamari.

Buz's Crab
SEAFOOD $

(www.buzscrab.com; 2159 East St; meals $5-12; ☺11am-9pm) There's zero pretension to Buz's; it's just a low-slung crab shack along the busy central district of Redding. The menu has fish and chips alongside healthier choices like grilled trout and salmon. It comes sided with garlic bread on 'almost famous' sourdough and slaw. The attached market has lobster and good advice about what to grill for a picnic.

Alehouse Pub
BAR

(www.reddingalehouse.com; 2181 Hilltop Dr; ☺3pm-midnight Mon-Thu, to 1:30am Fri & Sat) Too bad for fans of the cheap stuff, this local pub keeps a selection of highly hopped beers on tap and sells T-shirts emblazoned with 'No Crap on Tap.' It's a fun local place that gets packed after Redding's young professionals get out of work.

Breaking New Grounds
CAFE

(☎530-246-4563; 1320 Yuba St; ☺6am-7pm Mon-Thu, to 10pm Fri, 7am-4pm Sat; ☎) With a sort

Redding

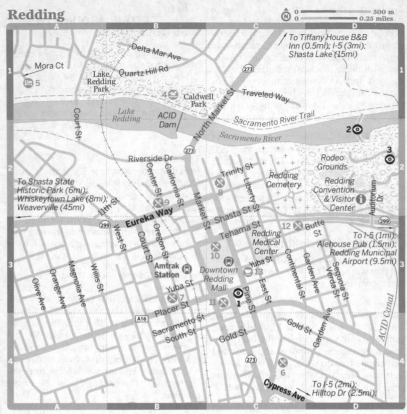

of relaxed living-room feel, this wi-fi cafe attracts a cross section of local folks. Live acoustic music is featured on Friday nights.

ℹ Information

California Welcome Center (☏530-365-1180; www.shastacascade.org; 1699 Hwy 273, Anderson; ◷9am-6pm Mon-Sat, from 10am Sun) About 10 miles south of Redding, in Anderson's Prime Outlets Mall. It's an easy stop for northbound travelers who are likely to pass it on the I-5 approach. It stocks maps for hiking and guides to outdoor activities, and the website has an excellent trip planning section for the region.

Redding Convention & Visitor Center (☏530-225-4100; www.visitredding.com; 777 Auditorium Dr; ◷9am-6pm Mon-Fri, 10am-5pm Sat) Near Turtle Bay Exploration Park.

Shasta-Trinity National Forest Headquarters (☏530-226-2500; 3644 Avtech Pkwy; ◷8am-4:30pm Mon-Fri) South of town, in the USDA Service Center near the airport. Has maps and

free camping permits for all seven national forests in Northern California.

ℹ Getting There & Around

Redding Municipal Airport (RDD; www.ci.redding.ca.us; 6751 Woodrum Circle, ☏) is 9.5 miles southeast of the city, just off Airport Rd. United Express flies to San Francisco.

The **Amtrak station** (www.amtrak.com; 1620 Yuba St), one block west of the Downtown Redding Mall, is not staffed. For the *Coast Starlight* service, make advance reservations by phone or via the website, then pay the conductor when you board the train. Amtrak travels once daily to Oakland ($62, six hours), Sacramento ($47, four hours) and Dunsmuir ($22, 1¾ hours).

The **Greyhound bus station** (1321 Butte St), adjacent to the Downtown Redding Mall, never closes. Destinations include San Francisco ($41, 8½ hours, four daily) and Weed ($24.50, 1½ hours, three daily). The **Redding Area Bus Authority** (RABA; www.rabaride.com) has a dozen city routes operating until around 6pm

Redding

◉ **Sights**

➕ **Activities, Courses & Tours**

🛏 **Sleeping**

✖ **Eating**

🍷 **Drinking**

Monday to Saturday. Fares start at $1.50 (exact change only).

Around Redding

SHASTA STATE HISTORIC PARK

On Hwy 299, 6 miles west of Redding, this **state historic park** (☉sunrise-sunset) preserves the ruins of an 1850s Gold Rush mining town called Shasta – not to be confused with Mt Shasta City (p284). When the Gold Rush was at its heady height, everything and everyone passed through this Shasta. But when the railroad bypassed it to set up in Poverty Flats (present-day Redding), poor Shasta lost its raison d'être. Shopkeepers packed up shingle and moved to Redding – literally. They moved many of Shasta's businesses brick by brick.

An 1861 courthouse contains the excellent **museum** (☎530-243-8194; admission $2; ☉10am-5pm Wed-Sun; 🐾), the best in this part of the state. With its amazing gun collection, spooky holograms in the basement and a gallows out back, it's a thrill ride. There's also a fantastic collection of art. Pick up walking-tour pamphlets from the information desk and follow trails to the Catholic cemetery, brewery ruins and many other historic sites. At the time of writing, the future of this state park was uncertain and it was subject to closure.

WHISKEYTOWN LAKE

Two miles further west on Hwy 299, sparkling **Whiskeytown Lake** (☎530-242-3400; www.nps.gov/whis; day use per vehicle $5) takes its name from an old mining camp. When the lake was created in the 1960s by the construction of a 263ft dam, designed for power generation and Central Valley irrigation, the few remaining buildings of old Whiskeytown were moved and the camp was submerged. John F Kennedy was present at the dedication ceremony, less than two months before his assassination. Today folks descend on the lake's serene 36 miles of forested shoreline to camp, swim, sail, mountain bike and pan for gold.

The **visitors center** (☎530-246-1225; ☉9am-6pm May-Sep, 10am-4pm Oct-Apr), on the northeast point of the lake, just off Hwy 299, provides free maps and information on Whiskeytown and Whiskeytown-Shasta-Trinity National Recreation Area from knowledgeable and agreeable staff. Look for ranger-led interpretive programs and guided walks. The hike from the visitors center to roaring **Whiskeytown Falls** (3.4 miles round trip) follows a former logging road and is a good quick trip.

On the southern shore of the lake, **Brandy Creek** is ideal for swimming. Just off Hwy 299, on the northern edge of the lake, **Oak Bottom Marina** (☎530-359-2269) rents boats. On the western side of the lake, the **Tower House Historic District** contains the El Dorado mine ruins and the pioneer Camden House, open for summer tours. In winter, when the trees are bare, it's an atmospheric, quiet place to explore.

Oak Bottom Campground (☎800-365-2267; tent/RV sites $20/22) is a privately run place with RV and tent camping. It's a bit tight, but nicer than most private campgrounds, with lots of manzanita shade. Most attractive are the walk-in sites right on the shore. **Primitive campsites** (summer/winter $10/5) surround the lake. The most accessible of these is the one at **Crystal Creek** which doesn't have water, but has nice views.

Shasta Lake

About 15 minutes north of Redding, the largest reservoir in California, **Shasta Lake** (www.shastalake.com), is home to the state's biggest population of nesting bald eagles. Surrounded by hiking trails and campgrounds, the lake gets packed in summer. The lake is also home to more than 20 different kinds of fish, including rainbow trout.

The **ranger station** (☎530-275-1589; 14250 Holiday Rd; ◷8am-4:30pm daily May-Sep, Mon-Fri Oct-Apr) offers free maps and information about fishing, boating and hiking. To get here take the Mountaingate Wonderland Blvd exit off I-5, about 9 miles north of Redding, and turn right.

◉ Sights & Activities

Shasta Dam
DAM

On scale with the enormous natural features of the area, this colossal, 15-million-ton dam is second only in size to Hoover Dam in Nevada. It's at the south end of the lake on Shasta Dam Blvd (Hwy 151). Built between 1938 and 1945, its 487ft spillway is as high as a 60-story building – three times higher than Niagara Falls. Woody Guthrie wrote 'This Land is Your Land' while he was here working on the dam. The **Shasta Dam visitors center** (☎530-275-4463; ◷8:30am-4:30pm) offers fascinating free guided tours of the structure's rumbling interior.

Lake Shasta Caverns
CAVE TOUR

(www.lakeshastacaverns.com; adult/child 3-11yr $22/13; ◷tours 9am-4pm; 🚻) High in the limestone megaliths at the north end of the lake hide these prehistoric caves. Tours of the crystalline caves operate daily and include a boat ride across Lake Shasta, and the office has a spacious play area for kids. The Cathedral Room is particularly stunning. Bring a sweater for the tours, as the temperature inside is 58°F (14°C) year-round. To get there take the Shasta Caverns Rd exit from I-5, about 15 miles north of Redding, and follow the signs for 1.5 miles.

🛏 Sleeping & Eating

Hike-in camping and RV parks are sprinkled around the shores of the lake and houseboats are a wildly popular option. Most houseboats require a two-night minimum stay. Make reservations as far in advance as possible, especially in the summer months. Boats usually sleep 10 to 16 adults and cost around $1400 to $8400 per week. The RV parks are often crowded and lack shade, but they have on-site restaurants. If you want to explore the area on a day trip, stay in Redding (p267).

US Forest Service (USFS) campgrounds
CAMPGROUNDS $

(☎877-444-6777; www.reserveusa.com; tent sites $6-26) About half of the USFS campgrounds around the lake are open year-round. The lake's many fingers have a huge range of camping, with lake and mountain views, and some of them are very remote. Free boat-in sites are first-come, first-served. Camping outside organized campgrounds requires a campfire permit from May to October, available free from any USFS office.

Holiday Harbor Resort
HOUSEBOATS & CAMPGROUND $

(☎530-238-2383; www.lakeshasta.com; Holiday Harbor Rd; tent & RV sites $36, houseboats for 2 nights from $920; 📶🚻) Primarily an RV campground, it also rents houseboats and the busy marina offers parasailing and fishing-boat rentals. A little **cafe** (◷8am-3pm) sits lakefront. It's off Shasta Caverns Rd, next to the lake.

Antlers RV Park & Campground
CAMPGROUND & CABINS $

(☎530-238-2322; www.shastalakevacations.com; 20679 Antlers Rd; tent & RV sites $17-35, cabins from $179; 🚻🏕) East of I-5 in Lakehead, at the north end of the lake, this family-oriented campground has cabins, a country store and a marina renting watercraft and houseboats.

Lakeshore Inn & RV
CAMPGROUND $

(☎530-238-2003; www.shastacamping.com; 20483 Lakeshore Dr; RV sites $20-33, cabins from $95; 📶🚻🏕) On the western side of I-5, this lakeside vacation park has a restaurant and tavern, horseshoes and basic cabins.

MT LASSEN & AROUND

The dramatic crags, volcanic formations and alpine lakes of Lassen Volcanic National Park seem surprisingly untrammeled when you consider they are only a few hours from the Bay Area. Snowed in through most of winter, the park blossoms in late spring. While it is only 50 miles from Redding, and thus close enough to be enjoyed on a day trip, to really do it justice you'll want to invest a few days exploring the area along its scenic, winding roads. From Lassen Volcanic National Park you can take one of two very picturesque routes: Hwy 36, which heads east past Chester, Lake Almanor and historic Susanville; or Hwy 89, which leads southeast to the cozy mountain town of Quincy.

Lassen Volcanic National Park

The dry, smoldering, treeless terrain within this 106,000-acre national park stands in stunning contrast to the cool, green conifer forest that surrounds it. That's the summer; in winter tons of snow ensures you won't get too far inside its borders. Still, entering the park from the southwest entrance is to suddenly step into another world. The lavascape offers a fascinating glimpse into the earth's fiery core. In a fuming display the terrain is marked by roiling hot springs, steamy mud pots, noxious sulfur vents, fumaroles, lava flows, cinder cones, craters and crater lakes.

In earlier times the region was a summer encampment and meeting point for Native American tribes – namely the Atsugewi, Yana, Yahi and Maidu. They hunted deer and gathered plants for basket-making here. Some indigenous people still live nearby and work closely with the park to help educate visitors on their ancient history and contemporary culture.

◉ Sights & Activities

Lassen Peak, the world's largest plug-dome volcano, rises 2000ft over the surrounding landscape to 10,457ft above sea level. Classified as an active volcano, its most recent eruption was in 1917, when it spewed a giant cloud of smoke, steam and ash 7 miles into the atmosphere. The national park was created the following year to protect the newly formed landscape. Some areas destroyed by the blast, including the aptly named **Devastated Area** northeast of the peak, are recovering impressively. You can hike the **Lassen Peak Trail**, which has been under renovation for some time; check in with rangers before attempting to get to the top. An easy 1.3 mile hike partway up, to the Grandview viewpoint, is suitable for families. The 360-degree view from the top is stunning, even if the weather is a bit hazy.

Hwy 89, the road through the park, wraps around Lassen Peak on three sides and provides access to dramatic geothermal formations, pure lakes, gorgeous picnic areas and remote hiking trails.

In total, the park has 150 miles of **hiking trails**, including a 17-mile section of the Pacific Crest Trail. Experienced hikers can attack the Lassen Peak Trail; it takes at least 4½ hours to make the 5-mile round trip. Early in the season you'll need snow and ice-climbing equipment to reach the summit. Near the Kom Yah-mah-nee visitor facility, a gentler 2.3-mile trail leads through meadows and forest to **Mill Creek Falls**. Further north on Hwy 89 you'll recognize the road side **sulfur works** by its bubbling mud pots, hissing steam vent, fountains and fumaroles. At **Bumpass Hell** a moderate 1.5-mile trail and boardwalk lead to an active geothermal area, with bizarrely colored pools and billowing clouds of steam.

The road and trails wind through cinder cones, lava and lush alpine glades, with views of Juniper Lake, Snag Lake and the plains beyond. Most of the lakes at higher elevations remain partially and beautifully frozen in summer. Leave time to fish, swim or boat on **Manzanita Lake**, a slightly lower emerald gem near the northern entrance.

⌂ Sleeping & Eating

If you're coming to Lassen Volcanic National Park from the north on Hwy 89, you won't see many gas/food/lodgings signs after Mt Shasta City and your best option is to stock up en route and camp.

The park has eight developed **campgrounds** (☎877-444-6777; www.recreation.gov; tent & RV sites $10-18), and there are many more in the surrounding Lassen National Forest. Campgrounds in the park are open from late May to late October, depending on snow conditions. Manzanita Lake is the only one with hot showers, but the two Summit Lake campgrounds, in the middle of the park, are also

ⓘ KNOW ABOUT THE SNOW

Rangers tell rueful stories about people who drive across the country in their RVs to find the roads of Lassen Volcanic National Park impassable; don't let it happen to you. The road through the park is usually only open from June to October, though it has been closed due to snow (as much as 40ft of it) well into July at times. Travelers need to call ahead or check the park website (www.nps.gov/lavo; click 'Current Conditions') to get weather conditions before considering a visit during all but a couple of months of the year – the only safe bets are August and September. A slow melt or freak storm can close major parts of the park at any other time of year.

Lassen Volcanic National Park

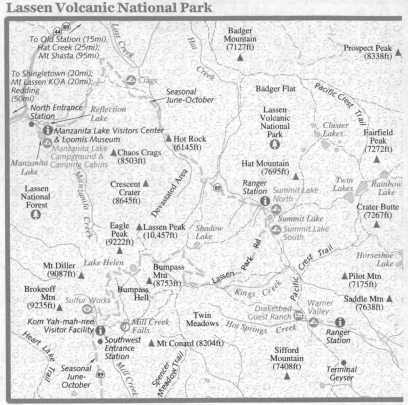

To Old Station (15mi);
Hat Creek (25mi);
Mt Shasta (95mi)

Badger
Mountain
(7127ft)

Prospect Peak
(8338ft)

To Shingletown (20mi);
Mt Lassen KOA (20mi);
Redding
(50mi)

Crags

Seasonal
June-October

Badger Flat

Pacific Crest Trail

North Entrance
Station

Reflection
Lake

Lassen
Volcanic
National
Park

Cluster
Lakes

Fairfield
Peak
(7272ft)

Manzanita Lake Visitors Center
& Loomis Museum

Hot Rock
(6145ft)

Manzanita Lake
Campground &
Camping Cabins

Chaos Crags
(8503ft)

Hat Mountain
(7695ft)

Manzanita
Lake

Lassen
National
Forest

Crescent
Crater
(8645ft)

Devastated Area

Ranger
Station

Summit Lake
North

Twin
Lakes

Rainbow
Lake

Crater Butte
(7267ft)

Summit Lake

Eagle
Peak
(9222ft)

Lassen Peak
(10,457ft)

Shadow
Lake

Summit Lake
South

Horseshoe
Lake

Mt Diller
(9087ft)

Lake Helen

Bumpass
Mtn
(8753ft)

Lassen Park Rd

Pacific Crest Trail

Pilot Mtn
(7175ft)

Brokeoff
Mtn
(9235ft)

Sulfur Works

Bumpass
Hell

Kings Creek

Warner
Valley

Saddle Mtn
(7638ft)

Kom Yah-mah-nee
Visitor Facility

Mill Creek
Falls

Twin
Meadows

Drakesbad
Guest Ranch

Hot Springs Creek

Ranger
Station

Heart Lake Trail

Southwest
Entrance
Station

Mt Conard (8204ft)

Sifford
Mountain
(7408ft)

Terminal
Geyser

Seasonal
June-
October

Mill Creek

Spencer Meadow Trail

popular. Reservations are permitted at Butte Lake in the northeast corner of the park, Manzanita Lake in the northwest, Summit Lake North and Summit Lake South.

If you don't want to camp, the nearest place to stay is Chester (p276), which accesses the south entrance of the park. There are some basic services near the split of Hwy 88 and Hwy 44, in the north.

NORTH ENTRANCE OF THE PARK

Manzanita Lake Camping Cabins
CABINS & CAMPGROUND $

(winter 530-200-4578; summer 530-335-7557; www.lassenrecreation.com; Hwy 89, near Manzanita Lake; tent & RV sites $18, r $57-81;) These freshly built log cabins enjoy a lovely position on one of Lassen's lakes and they come in one- and two-bedroom options and slightly more basic bunk configurations, which are a bargain for groups. They all have bear boxes and fire rings. Those who want to get a small taste of Lassen's more

rustic comforts can call ahead to arrange a 'Camper Package,' which includes basic supplies for a night under the stars (starting at $100, it includes a s'mores kit).

Hat Creek Resort & RV Park
CABINS, CAMPGROUND $

(800-568-0109; www.hatcreekresortrv.com; 12533 Hwy 44/89; ten & RV sites without/with hookups $22/39, r $90-180;) Outside the park Old Station makes a decent stop before entering and is a good second choice after Manzanita Lake Camping Cabins, sitting along a fast-moving, trout-stocked creek. Some simple motel rooms and cabins have full kitchens. Stock up at the convenience store and deli, then eat on a picnic table by the river.

SOUTH ENTRANCE OF THE PARK

Drakesbad Guest Ranch
RANCH $$$

(530-529-1512, ext 120; www.drakesbad.com; Warner Valley Rd; r per person $176-190; Jun-early Oct;) Seventeen miles northwest of Ches-

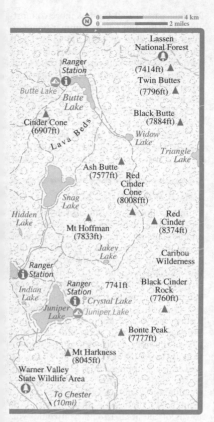

Map labels: Lassen National Forest, Ranger Station, (7414ft), Twin Buttes (7796ft), Butte Lake, Butte Lake, Cinder Cone (6907ft), Black Butte (7884ft), Lava Beds, Widow Lake, Triangle Lake, Ash Butte (7577ft), Red Cinder Cone (8008ft), Snag Lake, Hidden Lake, Mt Hoffman (7833ft), Red Cinder (8374ft), Jakey Lake, Caribou Wilderness, Ranger Station, Ranger Station, 7741ft, Black Cinder Rock (7760ft), Indian Lake, Crystal Lake, Juniper Lake, Juniper Lake, Bonte Peak (7777ft), Mt Harkness (8045ft), Warner Valley State Wildlife Area, To Chester (10mi)

Mt Lassen KOA

CAMPGROUND $

(530-474-3133; www.koa.com; 7749 KOA Rd; tent sites $28, RV sites from $40, cabins $57-140; mid-Mar–Nov;) Enjoy all the standard KOA amenities: a playground, a deli and laundry facilities. It's off Hwy 44 in Shingletown, about 20 miles west of the park.

Information

Whether you enter at the north or southwest entrance, you'll be given a free map with general information.

Kom Yah-mah-nee visitor facility (530-595-4480; 9am-6pm Jun-Sep, hr vary Oct-May) About half a mile north of the park's southwest entrance, this handsome new center is certified at the highest standard by the US Green Building Council. Inside there are educational exhibits (including a cool topographical volcano), a bookstore, an auditorium, a gift shop and a restaurant. Visitor information and maps available.

Manzanita Lake Visitors Center & Loomis Museum (530-595-4480; 9am-5pm Jun-Sep) Just past the entrance-fee station at the park's northern boundary, you can see exhibits and an orientation video inside this museum. During summer, rangers and volunteers lead programs on geology, wildlife, astronomy and local culture. Visitor information and maps available.

Park headquarters (530-595-4444; www.nps.gov/lavo; 38050 Hwy 36; 8am-4:30pm daily Jun-Sep, 8am-4:30pm Mon-Fri Oct-May) About a mile west of the tiny town of Mineral, it's the nearest stop for refueling and supplies.

Getting There & Away

There's virtually no way to visit this park without a car, though all the two-lane roads around the park and the ample free national forest camping options make for excellent, if fairly serious, cycle touring.

The park has two entrances. The northern entrance, at Manzanita Lake, is 50 miles east of Redding via Hwy 44. The southwest entrance is on Hwy 89, about 5 miles north of the junction with Hwy 36. From this junction it is 5 miles west on Hwy 36 to Mineral and 44 miles west to Red Bluff. Heading east on Hwy 36, Chester is 25 miles away and Susanville about 60 miles. Quincy is 65 miles southeast from the junction on Hwy 89.

Mt Lassen Transit (530-529-2722; www.mtlassentransit.com) buses between Red Bluff and Susanville ($25) run via Mineral ($15), which is the stop closest to the park. There's no public transportation within the park or on the 5 miles between Hwy 36 and the park entrance. Call ahead to arrange pick-up.

ter, this fabulously secluded place lies inside the park's southern boundary. Guests, many of whom are faithful repeat visitors, use the hot-springs-fed swimming pool or go horseback riding. Except in the main lodge, there's no electricity here (the kerosene lamps and campfires give things a lovely glow). Rates include country-style meals (vegetarian options available) and campfire barbecues every Wednesday. This is one of the few places in the region to book up solidly, so make advance reservations as soon as possible.

Childs Meadow Resort

CABINS $$

(530-595-3383; www.childsmeadowresort.com; 41500 E Hwy 36, Mill Creek; d $60-70, cabins $75-150;) Rustic cabins – some of them more like permanently parked RV trailers – sit at the edge of a spectacularly lush mountain meadow 9 miles outside the park's southwest entrance. Don't expect the Ritz; it's an old-fashioned, very rustic, mountain resort experience, but it's very close to the park.

WILD HORSE SANCTUARY

Since 1978 the **Wild Horse Sanctuary** (☑530-335-2241; www.wildhorses anctuary.com; Shingletown; admission free; ⊙9am-4pm Wed & Sat) has been sheltering horses and burros that would otherwise have been destroyed. You can visit its humble visitors center on Wednesdays and Saturdays to see these lovely animals or even volunteer for a day, with advance arrangement. To see them on the open plains, take a two- to three-day weekend pack trip in spring or summer (from $435 per person). Shingletown lies 20 miles to the west of Lassen Volcanic National Park.

Lassen National Forest

The vast **Lassen National Forest** (www.fs.fed. us/r5/lassen) surrounding Lassen Peak and Lassen Volcanic National Park, is so big that it's hard to comprehend: it covers 1.2 million acres (1875 sq miles) of wilderness in an area called the Crossroads, where the granite Sierra, volcanic Cascades, Modoc Plateau and Central Valley meet. It's largely unspoiled land, though if you wander too far off the byways surrounding the park, you'll certainly see evidence of logging and mining operations that still happen within its borders.

The forest has some serious hikes, with 460 miles of **trails**, ranging from the brutally challenging (120 miles of the Pacific Crest Trail), to ambitious day hikes (the 12-mile Spencer Meadows National Recreation Trail), to just-want-to-stretch-the-legs-a-little trails (the 3.5-mile Heart Lake National Recreation Trail). Near the intersection of Hwys 44 and 89, visitors to the area will find one of the most spectacular features of the forest, the pitch-black 600yd **Subway Cave** lava tube. Other points of interest include the 1.5-mile volcanic **Spattercone Crest Trail**, **Willow Lake** and **Crater Lake**, 7684ft **Antelope Peak**, and the 900ft-high, 14-mile-long **Hat Creek Rim** escarpment.

For those seeking to get far off the beaten trail, the forest has three wilderness areas. Two high-elevation wilderness areas are the **Caribou Wilderness** and **Thousand Lakes Wilderness**, best visited from mid-June to mid-October. The **Ishi Wilderness**, at a much lower elevation in the Central Valley

foothills east of Red Bluff, is more comfortable in spring and fall, as summer temperatures often climb to over 100°F (37°C). It harbors California's largest migratory deer herd, which can be upwards of 20,000 head.

The Lassen National Forest supervisor's office is in Susanville (p278). Other ranger offices include **Eagle Lake Ranger District** (☑530-257-4188; 477-050 Eagle Lake Rd, Susanville), **Hat Creek Ranger District** (☑530-336-5521; 43225 E Hwy 299, Fall River Mills) and **Almanor Ranger District** (☑530-258-2141; 900 E Hwy 36, Chester), about a mile west of Chester.

Lake Almanor Area

Calm, turquoise Lake Almanor lies south of Lassen Volcanic National Park via Hwys 89 and 36. This man-made lake is a crystalline example of California's sometimes awkward conservation and land-management policy: the lake was created by the now-defunct Great Western Power Company and is now ostensibly owned by the Pacific Gas & Electric Company. The lake is surrounded by lush meadows and tall pines and was once little-visited. Now, a 3000-acre ski resort sits on the hills above, with properties continually being developed near its shore and power boats zipping across its surface.

The main town near the lake, Chester (population 2500, elevation 4528ft), is a sight better than some of the dreary little towns of the area. Though you could whiz right by and dismiss it as a few blocks of nondescript roadside storefronts, don't – it's not. This robust little community has a fledgling art scene, decent restaurants and some comfy places to stay.

🛏 Sleeping & Eating

The best sleeping options for campers are in the surrounding national forest.

CHESTER

Along Chester's main drag you'll find a scattering of '50s-style inns, some chain motels and a few chain lodgings (the nicest of which is the fairly overpriced Best Western Rose Quartz Inn). Many of these places keep seasonal hours and, when you live in a place where it can snow in mid-June, the season is short.

St Bernard Lodge   B&B **$**
(☑530-258-3382; www.stbernardlodge.com; 44801 E Hwy 36, Mill Creek; d with shared bath $99; ☎) Located 10 miles west of Chester, at Mill Creek

this old-world charmer has seven B&B rooms with views to the mountains and forest. All have knotty-pine paneling and quilted bedspreads. There are stables on site where those travelling with a horse can board them and have access to the nearby network of Lassen's trails. The tavern is good too – serving meaty American lunches and dinner.

Bidwell House B&B
B&B $$

(530-258-3338; www.bidwellhouse.com; 1 Main St; r with shared bath $85, r with private bath $115-165, cottage $175; 🛜) Set back from the street, this historic summer home of pioneers John and Annie Bidwell, is packed with antiques. The classic accommodations come with all the modern amenities (including a spa in some rooms) – no roughing it here. Enjoy goodies like a three-course breakfast, home-baked cookies and afternoon sherry.

Cinnamon Teal Inn
VACATION RENTAL $$

(530-258-3993; www.cinnamontealinn.net; 227 Feather River Dr; r from $140) You can rent out just one room or the entire large home, a half-block back from Main St. There's a more intimate option on the property – perfect for three people – with the small nearby cottage. All have river access from the gardens. Fluffy feather beds dominate each wood-paneled room. The cottage has a full kitchen.

TOP CHOICE Red Onion Grill
NEW AMERICAN $$$

(www.redoniongrill.com; 384 Main St; meals $10-25; 11am-9pm) Hand's-down the finest dining that Chester has on offer, the upscale New American cuisine has generous Italian influ-ences (like the simply prepared rock shrimp and crab Alfredo) and bar food that's executed with real panache. The setting is casual and fun – wall lanterns and a crackling fire – made all the more warm by the best wine list in town.

Knotbumper Restaurant
AMERICAN $

(274 Main St; meals $8-10; 11am-8pm Tue-Sat) The Knotbumper is unlikely to dish up your most memorable meal, but it has a generous deli menu, including tamale pies, shrimp salad sandwiches and other eclectic selections. On summer days, eat on the lively front porch and watch the trucks rumble by. This place virtually closes down in the winter.

AROUND THE LAKE
Book ahead for lakefront lodgings in summer. There are restaurants at the resorts.

Federal campgrounds
CAMPGROUNDS $

(reservations 877-444-6777; www.reserveusa.com; tent sites $12-20) These campgrounds lie within the surrounding Lassen and Plumas National Forests on the lake's southwest shore. Sites tend to be more tranquil than the RV-centric private campgrounds that are right on the water. A favorite for tents and RVs, **Rocky Point Campground** is right on the lake, with some sites basically on the beach. For something more remote, try the **Cool Springs Campground** at the Butt Reservoir (try to say that with a straight face!). It's at the south end of the lake, at the end of Prattville Butt Reservoir Rd.

NORTHERN MOUNTAINS LAKE ALMANOR AREA

SCENIC DRIVE: LASSEN SCENIC BYWAY

Even in the peak of summer, you'll have the uncrowded byways of the Lassen Scenic Byway mostly to yourself. The long loop though Northern California wilderness skirts the edge of Lassen Volcanic National Park (p273) and circles Lassen Peak (p273) one of the largest dormant volcanoes on the planet. It mostly covers the big green patches on the map: expansive areas perfect for hiking, fishing, camping or just getting lost. This is a place where few people venture, and those who do come back with stories.

The launching point for this big loop could be either Redding (p267) or Sacramento (p326), but there are few comforts for travelers along this course. The only cities in this neck of the woods – little places like Chester (p276) and Susanville (p278) – aren't all that exciting on their own; they're mostly just places to gas up, buy some beef jerky and enjoy the week's only hot meal. But the banner attractions are visible in every direction – the ominous, dormant volcanic peak of Lassen, the wind-swept high plains and the seemingly endless wilderness of the Lassen and Plumas National Forests.

This loop is formed by Hwy 36, Hwy 44 and Hwy 89. (You can see the map and some of the highlights at www.byways.org/explore/byways/2195.) Its best to do the drive between late June through mid-October. Other times of the year some of these roads close due to snow.

North Shore Campground
CABINS, CAMPGROUND $

(☎530-258-3376; www.northshorecampground.com; tent sites $35, RV sites $39-51, cabins $150-230; ☎) Two miles east of Chester on Hwy 36, these expansive, forested grounds stretch for a mile along the water, but they get filled up with mostly RVs. Ranch-style cabins have full kitchens and are a good option for families. This place is fine if you want to spend all your time waterskiing on the lake, but those seeking the solitude of nature should look elsewhere.

Knotty Pine Resort & Marina
CABINS $$

(☎530-596-3348; www.knottypine.net; 430 Peninsula Dr; weekly RV sites $175, 2-bedroom cabins with kitchen $155, r $195; ☎) This full-service lakeside alternative, 7 miles east of Chester, has simple cabins and rents boats, kayaks and canoes.

❶ Information

Rent boats and water-sports equipment at many places around the lake.

Bodfish Bicycles & Quiet Mountain Sports (☎530-258-2338; www.bodfishbicycles.com; 152 Main St, Chester) This outfit rents bicycles ($40 per day), cross-country skis and snowshoes, and sells canoes and kayaks. It's a great source of mountain-biking and bicycle-touring advice. If you want just a taste of the lovely rides possible in this part of the state, make this a priority stop.

Chester & Lake Almanor Chamber of Commerce (☎530-258-2426; www.chester-lakealmanor.com; 529 Main St, Chester; ☉9am-4pm Mon-Fri) Get information about lodging and recreation around the lake, in Lassen National Forest and in Lassen Volcanic National Park.

Lassen National Forest Almanor ranger station (☎530-258-2141; 900 E Hwy 36; ☉8am-4:30pm Mon-Fri) About a mile west of Chester, with similar information to the chamber of commerce.

Susanville

Though it sits on a lovely high desert plateau, the Lassen County seat (population 17,974) isn't so much of a charmer; it's a resupply post with a Wal-Mart, a few stop lights and two prisons. Not a tourist destination in itself, it does provide basic services for travelers passing through. It lies 35 miles east of Lake Almanor and 85 miles northwest of Reno – and is home to a couple of modest historic sites. Despite the fact that it recently ranked 29th as a place for hunt-

ers and fishermen to live in *Outdoor Life* magazine, chances are this will be a place to stop on the way to somewhere else. The best event in town is the **Lassen County Fair** (☎530-251-8900; www.lassencountyfair.org), which swings into gear in July.

For local information about the town visit the **Lassen County Chamber of Commerce** (☎530-257-4323; www.lassencountychamber.org; 84 N Lassen St; ☉9am-4pm Mon-Fri), while the **Lassen National Forest supervisor's office** (☎530-257-2151; 2550 Riverside Dr; ☉8am-4:30pm Mon-Fri) has maps and recreation information for getting into the surrounding wilds.

The restored **Susanville Railroad Depot**, south of Main St, off Weatherlow St, sits beside the terminus of the Bizz Johnson Trail (see the boxed text, p279). The **visitors center** (☎530-257-3252; 601 Richmond Rd; ☉10am-4pm May-Oct) rents bicycles and has brochures on mountain-biking trails in the area.

The town's oldest building, **Roop's Fort** (1853), is named after Susanville's founder, Isaac Roop. The fort was a trading post on the Nobles Trail, a California emigrant route. The town itself was named after Roop's daughter, Susan. Beside the fort is the freshly built **Lassen Historical Museum** (75 N Weatherlow St; admission by donation; ☉10am-4pm Mon-Fri May-Oct), which has well-presented displays of clothing and memorabilia from the area that's worth a 20-minute visit.

Motels along Main St, none of them exceptional, average $50 to $75 per night. Try **Roseberry House B&B** (☎530-257-5675; www.roseberryhouse.com; 609 North St; r/ste $110/135; ☎) for more character. This sweet 1902 Victorian house is two blocks north of Main St. Striking dark-wood antique headboards and armoires combine with rosebuds and frill. There are nice little touches, like bath salts and candy dishes. In the morning, expect homemade muffins and jam as part of the full breakfast turned out by Richard, a culinary-school grad.

For simple, quick lunches and dinners, the best bet is the standout **Happy Garden** (1960 Main St; mains $6-13; ☉11am-7pm), which serves steaming plates of noodles and a big lunch combo that comes with soup, an egg roll and rice for $7. The serviceable Chinese food is served in a light-filled, centrally located former diner.

The other option for food is the historic **Pioneer Café** (724 Main St), the oldest surviving watering hole on Main St. One saloon or another has been operating on this site since 1862 and today it's a combination bar, billiards room and inexpensive eatery. At the time of research it was closed.

Mt Lassen Transit (☏530-529-2722) buses leave Red Bluff at 8:30am Monday to Saturday ($25, 4½ hours) and return from Susanville at 2pm. **Susanville City Buses** (☏530-252-7433) make a circuit around town (fare $1).

Eagle Lake

Those who have the time to get all the way out to Eagle Lake, California's second-largest natural lake, are rewarded with one of the most striking sites in the region: a stunningly blue jewel on the high plateau. From late spring until fall this lovely lake, about 15 miles northwest of Susanville, attracts a smattering of visitors who come to cool off, swim, fish, boat and camp. On the south shore, you'll find a pristine 5-mile **recreational trail** and several busy **campgrounds** (☏reservations 877-444-6777; www.recreation.gov; tent sites $20, RV sites $29-33) administered by Lassen National Forest and the **Bureau of Land Management** (BLM; ☏530-257-5381). Campgrounds for tent camping include Merrill, Aspen, Christie and Eagle. Most of them are fairly scrubby, considering how lovely the lake is, though there are some highly sought-after lakeside sites in Merrill. Merrill and Eagle also have RV sites. Nearby **Eagle Lake Marina** (www.eaglelakerecreationarea.com) offers hot showers, laundry and boat rentals. It also can help you get out onto the lake with a fishing license.

Eagle Lake RV Park (☏530-825-3133; www.eaglelakeandrv.com; 687-125 Palmetto Way; tent/RV sites $25/37, cabins $115-170; 🛜), on the western shore, and **Mariners Resort** (☏530-825-3333; Stones Landing; RV sites $37-40, cabins $115-185), on the quieter northern shore, both rent boats.

Quincy

Idyllic Quincy (population 1738) is one of the Northern Mountains three mountain communities, which teeter on the edge of becoming an incorporated town (the other two are Burney, in Shasta County, and Weaverville). It's no metropolis, but it does have a large grocery store and two of the three fast-food franchises in the entirety of Plumas County. Nestled in a high valley in the northern Sierra, southeast of both

WORTH A TRIP

WESTWOOD & THE BIZZ JOHNSON TRAIL

A few miles east of Chester is Westwood, a tiny speck of a town that marks the beginning of the **Bizz Johnson Trail**, an extremely picturesque route that runs the remote 25.5 miles from Westwood to Susanville. Once part of the old Southern Pacific right-of-way, the wooden bridges and serenely crossing-free trail are traversable by foot, mountain bike, horseback or cross-country skis (no motorized vehicles allowed!). Do the trail in the Westwood–Susanville direction, as it's mostly downhill that way. Get trail guides at the chamber of commerce in Chester (p278) or at the Susanville Railroad Depot (p278).

Lassen Volcanic National Park and Lake Almanor via Hwy 89, it is a lovely little place, endowed with just enough edge by the student population of the local Feather River College. Nearby Feather River, Plumas National Forest, Tahoe National Forest and their oodles of open space make Quincy an excellent base from which to explore.

Once in town Hwy 70/89 splits into two one-way streets, with traffic on Main St heading east, and traffic on Lawrence St heading west. Jackson St runs parallel to Main St, one block south, and is another main artery. Just about everything you need is on, near or between these three streets, making up Quincy's low-key commercial district.

Sights & Activities

Pick up free walking and driving tour pamphlets from the visitors center to guide you through the gorgeous surrounding **American Valley**. The Feather River Scenic Byway (Hwy 70) leads into the Sierra. In summer the icy waters of county namesake **Feather River** (*plumas* is Spanish for feathers) are excellent for swimming, kayaking, fishing and floating in old inner tubes. The area is also a wonderland of winter activities, especially at Bucks Lake (p281).

Plumas County Museum   MUSEUM
(www.plumasmuseum.org; 500 Jackson St, at Coburn St; adult/child $2/1; ⊙9am-4:30pm Tue-Sat; 🅿) In the block behind the courthouse, this excellent multifloor county museum has

flowering gardens, as well as hundreds of historical photos and relics from the county's pioneer and Maidu days, its early mining and timber industries, and construction of the Western Pacific Railroad. Unlike most other Northern Mountains community museums, it's not easy to see this all within an hour.

Plumas County Courthouse
HISTORIC BUILDING

(Main St) Pop into the 1921 Plumas County Courthouse, at the west end of Main St, to see enormous interior marble posts and staircases, and a 1-ton bronze-and-glass chandelier in the lobby.

Sierra Mountain Sports
OUTDOORS

(www.sierramountainsports.net; 501 W Main St) Across from the courthouse, rent cross-country ski gear and snowshoes here.

Big Daddy's Guide Service
FISHING TRIPS

(www.bigdaddyfishing.com) Captain Bryan Roccucci is Big Daddy, the only fishing guide in Northeast California. He knows the lakes well and leads trips for all levels (starting at $150 per person).

✦✦ Festivals & Events

TOP CHOICE High Sierra Music Festival
MUSIC

(www.highsierramusic.com) On the first weekend in July, quiet Quincy is host to this blowout festival, renowned statewide. The four-day extravaganza brings a five-stage smorgasbord of art and music from a spectrum of cultural corners (indie rock, classic blues, folk and jazz). Local national acts include My Morning Jacket, Gillian Welch, former James Brown saxophonist Maceo Parker and Neko Case. Sure, a curmudgeonly local might call it the Hippie Fest, but it's pretty tame in comparison to some of Northern California's true fringe festivals. If you plan to attend, reserve a room or campsite a couple of months in advance. For those who don't want to camp in nearby national forest land, Susanville (p278), one hour away, will have the largest number of rooms.

🛏 Sleeping

TOP CHOICE Quincy Courtyard Suites
VACATION RENTAL $$

(530-283-1401; www.quincycourtyardsuites.com; 436 Main St; apt $129-159; 🛜) Staying in this beautifully renovated 1908 Clinch building, overlooking the small main drag of Quincy's downtown, feels just right, like renting the village's cutest apartment. The warmly decorated rooms are modern – no fussy clutter – and apartments have spacious, modern kitchens, claw-foot tubs and gas fireplaces.

Feather Bed B&B
B&B $$

(530-283-0102; www.featherbed-inn.com; 542 Jackson St, at Court St; d from $150, cottages $179-190; 🚲) Just behind the courthouse, this frilly pink 1893 Queen Anne home is all antiques and cuteness – a teddy bear adorns every quilted bed (just one reason this is a family-friendly B&B). The buildings share space on a block of wide lawns and big old trees. Gracious hosts make afternoon tea with cookies, killer breakfasts (fresh fruit smoothies, eggs and sausage) and guests can borrow bikes. The cottage is accessible for travelers with disabilities.

Feather River Canyon Campgrounds
CAMPGROUNDS $

(reservations 877-444-6777; www.recreation.gov; tent & RV sites $15-20) Area campgrounds are administered through the Mt Hough Ranger District Office. They are in a cluster along the north fork of the Feather River west of Quincy – five are no-fee, but also have no piped water.

Ada's Place
B&B $$

(530-283-1954; www.adasplace.com; 562 Jackson St; cottages $100-145; 🛜) Even though it has the feel of a B&B, it's a bit of a misnomer. Without breakfast, Ada's is just an excelent B. No problem, as each of the three brightly painted garden units has a full kitchen. Ada's Cottage is worth the slight extra charge, as its skylights offer an open feel. It's very quiet and private, with a DSL internet connection.

Pine Hill Motel
MOTEL $

(530-283-1670; www.pinehillmotel.com; 42075 Hwy 70; s/d/cabin from $69/75/150; ❄🛜) A mile west of downtown Quincy, this little hotel is protected by an army of statues and surrounded by a big lawn. The units are nothing fancy, but they're clean and in a constant state of renovation. Each is equipped with a microwave, coffeemaker and refrigerator; some cabins have full kitchens.

Greenhorn Guest Ranch
RANCH $$$

(800-334-6939; www.greenhornranch.com; 2116 Greenhorn Ranch Rd; per person per day incl trail rides from $290; ⊘May-Oct; ❄🚲) Not a 'dude' ranch but rather a 'guest' ranch: instead of shoveling stalls, guests are pampered with mountain trail rides, riding lessons, even rodeo practice. Or you can just fish, hike, square dance and attend evening bonfires, cookouts and frog races – think of it like a cowboy version of the getaway resort in *Dirty Dancing*. Before you raise an eyebrow at the price, note that meals and riding are all included.

✖ Eating & Drinking

Quincy is a good supply point for those headed into or out of the wilderness. There are some good restaurants, a big grocery store, and a sprawling **farmers market** (cnr Church & Main Sts; ⊙5-8pm Thu mid-Jul–mid-Sep).

Café Le Coq   FRENCH $$

(☎530-283-0114; www.cafelecoq.biz; 189 Main St; prix fixe menu lunch/dinner $17/32; ⊙11:30am-1:30pm Mon-Wed & 5-8pm Tue-Sat) The French chef/owner, Michel LeCoq, flutters about this cute little Victorian; on a leisurely (perfectly French) lunch, he'll amble out to explain the specials (the $10 prix fixe lunch is a steal), help guide you in the right direction, cook them and check in when it's done. Delicious gourmet French meals, including house-cured meats, are served in a homey dining area or on the wraparound porch in summer.

🍴 Pangaea Café & Pub   CAFE $

(www.pangaeapub.com; 461 W Main St; mains $8-12; ⊙11am-9pm Mon-Thu, to 10pm Fri @🛜🐾) Like a stranger you feel you've met before, this earthy spot feels warmly familiar, all the more lovable when you consider its commitment to serving produce from local farmers. The specialty is panini, which come in flavorful, mostly veggie combinations. The beer list has lots of interesting choices, too. The little nook in the back has a computer and it has live music most weekends.

Morning Thunder Café   BREAKFAST $$

(557 Lawrence St; meals $9-15; ⊙7am-2pm; 🐾) Homey and hip, this is the best place in town for breakfast and the vine-shaded patio is a lovely way to start the day. The menu is mainly, though not exclusively, vegetarian. Try the vegetaters: roasted veg and potatoes smothered in cheese, the chicken avocado 'thunder melt,' or the 'drunken pig,' which brilliant balances savory pork and pineapple.

Moon's   ITALIAN $$

(☎530-283-0765; 497 Lawrence St; mains $11-24; ⊙5-8:30pm Tue-Sun) Follow the aroma of ~arlic to this welcoming little chalet with a ~arming ambience. Dig into choice steaks

and Italian-American classics, including excellent pizza and rich lasagna.

Sweet Lorraine's   CALIFORNIAN $$

(384 Main St; meals $12-22; ⊙lunch Mon-Fri, dinner Mon-Sat) On a warm day – or, better yet, evening – the patio here is especially sweet. The menu features light Californian cuisine (fish, poultry, soups and salads), but it's also known for its award-winning St Louis ribs. Finish things off with the whiskey bread pudding.

Drunk Brush   WINE BAR

(www.facebook.com/TheDrunkBrush; 438 Main St) A sweet little courtyard wine bar pours 25 wines and a few beers. Sample delicious appetizer pairings in a welcoming, arty atmosphere.

❶ Information

Mt Hough Ranger District Office (☎530-283-0555; 39696 Hwy 70; ⊙8am-4:30pm Mon-Fri) Five miles west of town. Has maps and outdoors information.

Plumas County visitors center (☎530-283-6345; www.plumascounty.org; 550 Crescent St; ⊙8am-5pm Mon-Sat) Half a mile west of town.

Plumas National Forest headquarters (☎530-283-2050; 159 Lawrence St; ⊙8am-4:30pm Mon-Fri) For maps and outdoors information.

Bucks Lake

This clear mountain lake is cherished by locals in the know. Surrounded by pine forests, it's excellent for swimming, fishing and boating. It's about 17 miles southwest of Quincy, via the white-knuckle roads of Bucks Lake Rd (Hwy 119). The region is lined with beautiful **hiking trails**, including the Pacific Crest Trail, which passes through the adjoining 21,000-acre Bucks Lake Wilderness in the northwestern part of Plumas National Forest. In winter, the last 3 miles of Bucks Lake Rd are closed by snow, making it ideal for cross-country skiers.

Bucks Lake Lodge (☎530-283-2262; www.buckslakelodge.com; 16525 Bucks Lake Rd; d & cabins $109-119; 🐾) rents boats and fishing tackle in summer and cross-country skis in winter. The **restaurant** (mains $7-16) is popular with locals. **Haskins Valley Inn** (☎530-283-9667; www.haskinsvalleyinn.com; 1305 Haskins Circle; r from $149; 🛜) is actually a lakefront B&B with cozily overstuffed furnishings, woodsy paintings, Jacuzzis, fireplaces and a deck. The bold southwestern rugs and heavy rough timber bed post of the Cowboy Room is a favorite.

Five first-come, first-served **campgrounds** (sites $20-25) are open from June to September. Get a map at the Plumas National Forest Headquarters or the ranger station, both in Quincy (see p281).

MT SHASTA & AROUND

'Lonely as God, and white as a winter moon, Mount Shasta starts up sudden and solitary from the heart of the great black forests of Northern California,' wrote poet Joaquin Miller on the sight of this lovely mountain. A sight of it is so awe-inspiring that the new age prattle about its power as an 'energy vortex' begins to sound plausible after a few days in its shadow. There are a million ways to explore the mountain and surrounding Shasta-Trinity National Forest, depending on the season – you can take scenic drives or get out and hike, mountain-bike, raft, ski or snowshoe. At Mt Shasta's base sit three excellent little towns: Dunsmuir, Mt Shasta City and McCloud. Each community has a distinct personality but all share a wild-mountain sensibility and first-rate restaurants and places to stay. In the same dramatic vicinity rise the snaggle-toothed peaks of Castle Crags, just 6 miles west of Dunsmuir.

Northeast of Mt Shasta, a long drive and a world away, is remote, eerily beautiful Lava Beds National Monument, a blistered badland of petrified fire. The contrasting cool wetlands of Klamath Basin National Wildlife Refuges are just west of Lava Beds.

Further east, high desert plateaus give way to the mountains of the northern Sierra. Folks in this remote area are genuinely happy to greet a traveler, even if they're a bit uncertain why you've come.

Mt Shasta

'When I first caught sight of it I was 50 miles away and afoot, alone and weary. Yet all my blood turned to wine, and I have not been weary since,' wrote naturalist John Muir of Mt Shasta in 1874. Mt Shasta's beauty is intoxicating, and the closer you get to her the headier you begin to feel. Dominating the landscape, the mountain is visible for more than 100 miles from many parts of Northern California and southern Oregon. Though not California's highest peak (at 14,162ft it ranks fifth), Mt Shasta is especially magnificent because it rises alone on the horizon, unrivaled by other mountains.

Mt Shasta is part of the vast volcanic Cascade chain that includes Lassen Peak to the south and Mt St Helens and Mt Rainier to the north in Washington state. The presence of thermal hot springs indicates that Mt Shasta is dormant, not extinct. Smoke was seen puffing out of the crater on the summit in the 1850s, though the last eruption was about 200 years ago. The mountain has two cones: the main cone has a crater about 200yd across; the younger, shorter cone on the western flank, called Shastina, has a crater about half a mile wide.

The mountain and surrounding Shasta-Trinity National Forest (www.fs.fed.us/r5/shastatrinity) are crisscrossed by trails and dotted with alpine lakes. It's easy to spend days or weeks here, camping, hiking, river rafting, skiing, mountain-biking and boating.

The story of the first settlers here is a sadly familiar one: European fur trappers arrived in the area in the 1820s, encountering several Native American tribes, including the Shasta, Karuk, Klamath, Modoc, Wintu and Pit River people. By 1851, hordes of Gold Rush miners had arrived and steamrolled the place, destroying the tribes' traditional life and nearly causing their extinction. Later the newly completed railroad began to import workers and export timber for the booming lumber industry. And since Mt Shasta City (called Sisson at the time) was the only non-dry town around, it became *the* bawdy, good-time hangout for lumberjacks.

The lumberjacks have now been replaced by middle-aged mystics and outdoor sports enthusiasts. While the slopes have immediate appeal for explorers, spiritual seekers are attracted to the peak's reported cosmic properties. In 1987, about 5000 believers from around the world convened here for the Harmonic Convergence, a communal meditation for peace. Reverence for the mountain is nothing new; for centuries Native Americans have honored the mountain as sacred, considering it to be no less than the Great Spirit's wigwam.

Many use Redding (p267) as a base since there are plenty of chain options along the highway, but Mt Shasta City (p285) is the best balance of convenience, value and personality. For food, there are satisfying restaurants at all the mountain towns, though consider having snacks on hand in the car as the winding drives from the woods to the lunch counter are time-consuming.

⊙ Sights & Activities

THE MOUNTAIN

You can drive almost the whole way up the mountain via the Everitt Memorial Hwy (Hwy A10) and see exquisite views at any time of year. Simply head east on Lake St from downtown Mt Shasta City, then turn left onto Washington Dr and keep going. **Bunny Flat** (6860ft), which has a trailhead for Horse Camp and the Avalanche Gulch summit route, is a busy place with parking spaces, information signboards and a toilet. The section of highway beyond Bunny Flat is only open from about mid-June to October, depending on snow, but if it's clear, it's worth the trouble. This road leads to **Lower Panther Meadow**, where trails connect the campground to a Wintu sacred spring, in the upper meadows near the **Old Ski Bowl** (7800ft) parking area. Shortly thereafter is the highlight of the drive, **Everitt Vista Point** (7900ft), where a short interpretive walk from the parking lot leads to a stone-walled outcrop affording exceptional views of Lassen Peak to the south, the Mt Eddy and Marble Mountains to the west and the whole Strawberry Valley below.

Climbing the summit is best done between May and September, preferably in spring and early summer, when there's still enough snow on the southern flank to make footholds easier on the nontechnical route. Although the elements are occasionally volatile and the winds are incredibly strong, the round trip could conceivably be done in one day with 12 or more hours of solid hiking. A more enjoyable trip takes at least two days with one night on the mountain. How long it actually takes depends on the route selected, the physical condition of the climbers and weather conditions (for weather information call the recorded message of the Forest Service Mt Shasta climbing advisory on ☎530-926-9613).

The hike to the summit from Bunny Flat follows the **Avalanche Gulch Route**. Although it is only about 7 miles, the vertical climb is more than 7000ft, so acclimatizing to the elevation is important – even hearty hikers will be short of breath. Additionally this route requires crampons, an ice ax and a helmet, all of which can be rented locally. Rock slides, while rare, are also a hazard. If

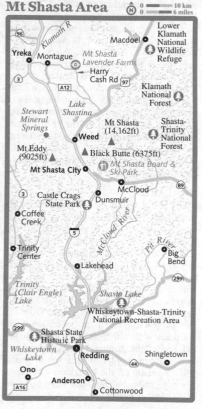

Mt Shasta Area

you want to make the climb without gear, the only option is the **Clear Creek Route** to the top, which leaves from the east side of the mountain. In late summer, this route is usually manageable in hiking boots, though there's still loose scree, and it should be done as an overnight hike. Novices should contact the Mt Shasta ranger station for a list of available guides.

There's a charge to climb beyond 10,000ft - a three-day summit pass costs $20; an annual pass is $30. Contact the ranger station for details. You must obtain a free wilderness permit any time you go into the wilderness, whether on the mountain or in the surrounding area.

Mt Shasta Board & Ski Park SNOW SPORTS (☎snow reports 530-926-8686; www.skipark.com; full-day lift tickets adult/child $39/20; ◷9am-9pm Thu-Sat, to 4pm Sun-Tue) On the south slope of Mt Shasta, off Hwy 89 heading toward McCloud, this winter skiing and snowboarding park opens depending on snowfall. The park has a 1390ft vertical drop, over two dozen alpine runs and 18 miles of cross-country trails. These are all exceptionally good for beginner and intermediate skiers, and the area makes a less-crowded alternative to the slopes around Lake Tahoe. Rentals, instruction and weekly specials are available. It's Northern California's largest night-skiing operation. There are lots of inexpensive options for skiing half a day or just at night, when hitting the slopes and taking in a full moon can be enchanting.

In summer, the park occasionally hosts mountain-biking events.

THE LAKES

There are a number of pristine mountain lakes near Mt Shasta. Some of them are accessible only by dirt roads or hiking trails and are great for getting away from it all.

The closest lake to Mt Shasta City is Lake Siskiyou (also the largest), 2.5 miles southwest on Old Stage Rd, where you can peer into Box Canyon Dam, a 200ft-deep chasm. Another 7 miles up in the mountains, southwest of Lake Siskiyou on Castle Lake Rd, lies Castle Lake, an unspoiled gem surrounded by granite formations and pine forest. Swimming, fishing, picnicking and free camping are popular in summer; in winter folks ice-skate on the lake. Lake Shastina, about 15 miles northwest of town, off Hwy 97, is another beauty.

ℹ Information

Peak tourist season is from Memorial Day through Labor Day and weekends during ski season (late November to mid-April). The ranger station and visitors center are in Mt Shasta City (p288).

Mt Shasta City

No town, no matter how lovely – and Mt Shasta City (population 3394) is lovely – could compete with the surrounding natural beauty here. Understandably most visitors don't make a pilgrimage here to visit the fish hatchery, they come to meet the mountain. Still, downtown itself is charming; you can spend hours poking around bookstores, galleries and boutiques. Orienting yourself is easy with Mt Shasta looming over the east side of town. The downtown area is a few blocks east of I-5. Take the Central Mt Shasta exit, then drive east on Lake St past the visitors center, up to the town's main intersection at Mt Shasta Blvd, the principal drag.

◉ Sights & Activities

To head out hiking on your own, first stop by the ranger station or the visitors center for excellent free trail guides, including several access points along the Pacific Crest Trail. Gorgeous Black Butte, a striking, treeless, black volcanic cone, rises almost 3000ft. The 2.5-mile trail to the top takes at least 2½ hours for the round trip. It's steep and rocky in many places, and there is no shade or water, so don't hike on a hot summer day. Wear good, thick-soled shoes or hiking boots and bring plenty of water. If you want an easier amble, try the 10-mile Sisson-Callahan National Recreation Trail, a partially paved trail that affords great views of Mt Shasta and the jagged Castle Crags, following a historic route established in the mid-1800s by prospectors, trappers and cattle ranchers to connect the mining town of Callahan with the town of Sisson, now called Mt Shasta City.

Mt Shasta City Park &
Sacramento River Headwaters   PARK
(Nixon Rd) Off Mt Shasta Blvd, about a mile north of downtown, the headwaters of the Sacramento River gurgle up from the ground in a large, cool spring. It's about as pure as water can get – so bring a bottle and have a drink. The park also has walking trails, picnic spots, sports fields and courts and a children's playground.

Sisson Museum   MUSEUM
(www.mountshastasissonmuseum.org; 1 Old Stage Rd; admission $1; ◷10am-4pm Mon-Sat, 1-4pm Sun Jun-Sep, 1-4pm Fri-Sun Oct-Dec, 1-4pm daily Apr & May) A half-mile west of the freeway, this former hatchery headquarters is full of curious mountaineering artifacts and old pictures. The changing exhibitions highlight history – geological and human – but also occasionally showcase local artists. Next door, the oldest operating hatchery in the West maintains outdoor ponds teeming with thousands of rainbow trout that will eventually be released into lakes and rivers.

Shastice Park   SKATING
(www.msrec.org; adult/child $10/5; cnr Rockfellow & Adams Drs; ◷10am-5pm Mon-Thu, to 9pm Fri & Sat, 1:30-5pm Sun) East of downtown the immense outdoor skating rink is open to ice-skaters in winter and in-line skaters on summer weekends.

River Dancers Rafting & Kayaking
RAFTING

(☑530-926-3517; www.riverdancers.com; 302 Terry Lynn Ave) Excellent outfit run by active environmentalists who guide one- to five-day whitewater rafting excursions down the area's rivers: the Klamath, Sacramento, Salmon, Trinity and Scott. Prices start with a half-day on the nearby Sacramento River for $75.

Shasta Mountain Guides
CLIMBING

(www.shastaguides.com) Offers two-day guided climbs of Mt Shasta between April and September, with all gear and meals included, for around $500. The experienced mountaineers have operated in Shasta for 30 years.

Shasta Valley Balloons
BALLOONING

(☑530-926-3612; 316 Pony Trail; rides $200) Live a dream by seeing the area from a hot-air balloon.

🎓 Courses

Osprey Outdoors Kayak School
MOUNTAINEERING

(www.ospreykayak.com; 2925 Cantara Loop Rd) Owner and instructor Michael Kirwin has a reputation for quality classes on high mountain lakes and rivers. Expect to pay around $80 to $100 per adult per day.

Mt Shasta Mountaineering School
CLIMBING

(www.swsmtns.com; 210a E Lake St) Conducts clinics and courses for serious climbers, or those looking to get serious. A two-day summit climb of Mt Shasta costs $450.

👉 Tours

Note that hiking Mt Shasta doesn't require an operator, but those wanting one have plenty of options. For information on summiting the mountain on your own, see p283.

Shasta Vortex Adventures
SPIRITUAL

(www.shastavortex.com; 400 Chestnut St) For a uniquely Mt Shasta outdoor experience, Shasta Vortex offers low-impact trips accented with the spiritual quest as much as the physical journey. The focus of the trips includes guided meditation and an exploration of the mountain's metaphysical power. Full-day tours for two people cost $456; larger groups get a slight discount.

🛏 Sleeping

Shasta really has it all – from free rustic camping to plush boutique B&Bs. If you are intent on staying at the upper end of he spectrum you should make reservations well in advance, especially on weekends and holidays and during ski season.

Camping & Cabins

Camping in the area is excellent and the visitors center has details on over two dozen campgrounds around Mt Shasta. Check with the Mt Shasta and McCloud ranger stations about USFS campgrounds in the area. As long as you set up camp at least 200ft from the water and get a free campfire permit from a ranger station, you can camp near many mountain lakes. Castle Lake (6450ft) and Gumboot Lake (6000ft) have free tent camping (purify your own drinking water) but are closed in winter. Lovely Toad Lake (7060ft), 18 miles from Mt Shasta City, isn't a designated camping area, but you may camp there if you follow the regulations. To get there go down the 11-mile gravel road (4WD advised) and walk the last quarter-mile.

TOP CHOICE Historic Lookout & Cabin Rentals
CABIN $

(☑530-994-2184; www.fs.fed.us/r5/shastatrinity; up to 4 people from $35) What better way to rough it in style than to bunk down in a restored fire lookout on the slopes of Little Mt Hoffman or Girard Ridge? Built from the 1920s to '40s, they come with cots, tables and chairs, have panoramic views and can accommodate four people. You can find a listing of them on the national forest website.

Panther Meadows
CAMPGROUND $

(tent sites free) Ten walk-in tent sites (no drinking water) sit at the timberline, right at the base of the mountain. They're a few miles up the mountain from other options, but are still easily accessible from Everitt Memorial Hwy. No reservations; arrive early to secure a site.

McBride Springs
CAMPGROUND $

(tent sites $10) Easily accessible from Everitt Memorial Hwy, this campground has running water and pit toilets, but no showers. It's near mile-marker 4, at an elevation of 5000ft. It's no beauty – a recent root disease killed many of the white fir trees that shaded the sites – but it's convenient. Arrive early in the morning to secure a spot (no reservations).

Horse Camp
ALPINE HUT $

(per person without/with tent $3/5) This 1923 alpine lodge run by the Sierra Club is a 2-mile hike uphill from Bunny Flat, at 8000ft. The stone construction and natural setting are lovely. Caretakers staff the hut from May to September only.

WEED & STEWART MINERAL SPRINGS

Just outside of Weed, **Stewart Mineral Springs** (☎530-938-2222; www.stewartmineral springs.com; 4617 Stewart Springs Rd; mineral baths $28, sauna $18; ⓧ10am-6pm Sun-Wed, to 7pm Thu-Sat) is a popular alternative (read clothing-optional) hangout on the banks of a clear mountain stream. Locals come for the day and visitors from afar come for weeks. Henry Stewart founded these springs in 1875 after Native Americans revived him from a near-death experience. He attributed his recovery to the healthful properties of the mineral waters, said to draw toxins out of the body.

Today you can soak in a private claw-foot tub or steam in the dry-wood sauna. Other perks include massage, body wraps, meditation, a Native American sweat lodge and a riverside sunbathing deck. You'll want to call ahead to be sure there is space in the steam and soaking rooms, especially on busy weekends. Dining and **accommodations** (tent & RV sites $35, tipis $45, r $65-85) are available. To reach the springs, go 10 miles north of Mt Shasta City on I-5, past Weed to the Edgewood exit, then turn left at Stewart Springs Rd and follow the signs.

While in the area, tickle your other senses at the **Mt Shasta Lavender Farms** (www. mtshastalavenderfarms.com), 16 miles northwest of Weed, off Hwy A12, on Harry Cash Rd. You can harvest your own sweet French lavender in the June and July blooming season. Or drink up the tasty porter at the **Weed Mt Shasta Brewing Company** (www.weed ales.com; 360 College Ave, Weed). The rich, amber-colored Mountain High IPA is delicious, but watch out – at 7% ABV it has real kick.

Lake Siskiyou Camp-Resort RV PARK $
(☎530-926-2618; www.lakesis.com; 4239 WA Barr Rd; tent/RV sites from $20/29, cabins $100-145; ☒) Tucked away on the shore of Lake Siskiyou, this sprawling campus has a summer-camp feel (there's an arcade and ice-cream stand). Hardly rustic, it has a swimming beach, and kayak, canoe, fishing boat and paddle boat rentals. Lots of amenities make it a good option for families on an RV trip.

Bed & Breakfasts, Hotels & Motels
Many modest motels stretch along S Mt Shasta Blvd. All have hot tubs, wi-fi and rooms cost between $60 and $140 in peak season. As many of them were built in the '50s, the cost difference is basically based on how recently they were remodeled. Many motels offer discount ski packages in winter and lower midweek rates year-round.

Shasta MountInn TOP CHOICE B&B $$
(☎530-926-1810; www.shastamountinn.com; 203 Birch St; r without/with fireplace $130/175; @☎) Only antique on the outside, inside this bright Victorian farmhouse is all relaxed minimalism, bold colors and graceful decor. Each airy room has a designer mattress and exquisite views of the luminous mountain. Enjoy the expansive garden, wraparound deck and outdoor sauna. Not relaxed enough yet? There are also a couple of perfectly placed porch swings and on-site massage.

Dream Inn B&B $$
(☎530-926-1536; www.dreaminnmtshastacity. com; 326 Chestnut St; r with shared bath $80-110, ste $120-160; @☎) Made up of two houses in the center of town: one is a meticulously kept Victorian cottage stuffed with fussy knickknacks; the other a Spanish-style two-story with chunky, raw-wood furniture and no clutter. A rose garden with a koi pond joins the two properties. A hefty breakfast is included.

Finlandia Motel MOTEL $$
(☎530-926-5596; www.finlandiamotel.com; 1612 S Mt Shasta Blvd; r $60-120, with kitchen $89-150) An excellent deal, the standard rooms are... standard – clean and simple. The suites get a little chalet flair with vaulted pine-wood ceilings and mountain views. There's an outdoor hot tub and the Finnish sauna is available by appointment.

Woodsman Cabins & Lodge MOTEL $
(☎530-926-3411; 1121 S Mt Shasta Blvd; r $89-139; ☒☎) Owned by the same folks who have the Strawberry Valley Inn across the street, the cluster of renovated mid-century buildings that make up the Woodsman is the mannish alternative. Taxidermy looks over the reception area, where a fire keeps things warm in

the winter. At the time of writing there was a plan to open a casual restaurant on site.

Strawberry Valley Inn
B&B $$
(530-926-2052; 1142 S Mt Shasta Blvd; d from $139;) The understated rooms surround a garden courtyard, allowing you to enjoy the intimate feel of a B&B without the pressure of having to chat with the darling newlyweds around the breakfast table. A full vegetarian breakfast is included. In the evenings there's complimentary wine.

Mt Shasta Resort
RESORT $$
(530-926-3030; www.mountshastaresort.com; 1000 Siskiyou Lake Blvd; r from $90, 1-/2-bedroom chalets from $154/193) Divinely situated away from town, this upscale golf resort and spa has Arts and Crafts–style chalets nestled in the woods around the shores of Lake Siskiyou. They're a bit soulless, but immaculate, and each has a kitchen and gas fireplace. Basic lodge rooms are near the golf course, which boasts some challenging greens and offers amazing views of the mountain. The restaurant has excellent views as well and serves Californian cuisine with a large selection of steaks.

Evergreen Lodge
MOTEL $
(530-926-2143; www.evergreenlodgemtshasta.com; 1312 S Mt Shasta Blvd; r $70;) The economy rooms up front are a bit rundown, but the rooms in back are newer with high ceilings and good light. The small fee for the sauna? Worth it.

Swiss Holiday Lodge
MOTEL $
(530-926-3446; www.swissholidaylodge.com; 2400 S Mt Shasta Blvd; d $60;) Don't think of the furnishings as old…they're vintage.

✗ Eating

Trendy restaurants and cafes here come and go with the snowmelt. Most of the following are tried and true, favored by locals and visitors alike. A farmers market (3:30-6pm Mon) sets up on Mt Shasta Blvd during summer.

TOP CHOICE Trinity Café
CALIFORNIAN $$
(530-926-6200; 622 N Mt Shasta Blvd; mains $17-28; 5-9pm Tue-Sat) Trinity has long rivaled the Bay Area's best. The owners, who hail from Napa, infuse the bistro with a Wine Country feel and an extensive, excellent wine selection. The organic menu ranges from delectable, perfectly cooked teaks, savory roast game hen to creamy-

on-the-inside, crispy-on-the-outside polenta. The warm, mellow mood makes for an overall delicious experience.

Mount Shasta Pastry
BAKERY $
(610 S Mt Shasta Blvd; mains $17-28; 6am-2:30pm Mon-Sat, 7am-1pm Sun) Walk in hungry and you'll be plagued with an existential breakfast crisis: the potato and egg frittata topped with red peppers, ham and melted cheese, or the smoky breakfast burrito? The flaky croissants or peach cobbler? It also serves terrific sandwiches and gourmet pizza.

Vivify
JAPANESE $$
(530-926-1345; www.vivifyshasta.com; 531 Chestnut St; meals $9-15; 5:30-10pm Wed-Mon) Bowls of udon and ramen accompany a long list of rolls at Shasta's reigning sushi place. But the food goes a lot deeper than Japanese basics, with hearty savory dishes (a roast rack of local lamb quinoa and curry) and light raw and wheat-free options. Be warned, it's popular and the dining room gets crowded.

Poncho & Lefkowitz
FOOD CART $
(401 S Mt Shasta Blvd; meals $4-10; 11am-4pm Tue-Sat;) Surrounded by picnic tables, this classy, wood-sided food cart – sort of a cafe on wheels – turns out juicy Polish sausage, big plates of nachos and veggie burritos. It's a good bet for food on the go.

Lily's
BREAKFAST $$
(www.lilysrestaurant.com; 1013 S Mt Shasta Blvd; breakfast & lunch mains $9-15, dinner mains $15-22; 8am-4pm Mon-Fri, 4-10pm Sat & Sun;) Enjoy quality Californian cuisine – Asian- and Mediterranean-touched salads, fresh sandwiches and all kinds of veg options – in a cute, white, clapboard house. Outdoor tables overhung by flowering trellises are almost always full, especially for breakfast.

Berryvale Grocery & Deli
MARKET $
(www.berryvale.com; 305 S Mt Shasta Blvd; mains $9; 8:30am-7pm Mon-Sat, 10am-6pm Sun;) This market sells groceries and organic produce to the health conscious. The excellent deli cafe serves good coffee and an array of tasty – mostly veggie – salads, sandwiches and burritos.

Andaman Healthy Thai Cuisine
THAI $
(313 N Shasta Blvd; mains $8; 11am-9pm Mon, Tue, Thu & Fri, from 4pm Sat & Sun) The food is great, but the kitchen and the staff can't keep up with the crowds. If it's full, look elsewhere.

Black Bear Diner   DINER **$**
(401 W Lake St; mains $8; ⊘breakfast, lunch & dinner) Part of a cute bear-themed chain; it's right off the highway and enjoys a nice view.

🍷 Drinking & Entertainment

The Goats Tavern   BAR
(www.thegoatmountshasta.com; 107 Chestnut St; ⊘7am-6pm; 🛜) Come here first to drink – it has 12 taps rotating some of the best microbrewed beer in the country – and then tuck into a 'wino burger,' which comes topped with peppered goat cheese, thick sliced bacon and a red-wine reduction sauce. It's a friendly place with an affable staff, surly regulars and a great summer patio.

**Stage Door Coffeehouse
& Cabaret**   LIVE MUSIC
(www.stagedoorcabaret.com; 414 N Mt Shasta Blvd; ⊘7am-6pm, longer during performances; 🛜🎵) The menu at this popular cafe-bar and theater features espresso, microbrews, wine and lots of veggie dishes. On Wednesday nights there are indie films; on weekends, live music – anything from Celtic punk to bluegrass.

Has Beans Coffeehouse   COFFEE
(www.hasbeans.com; 1011 S Mt Shasta Blvd; ⊘5:30am-7pm; @🛜) This snug little hangout serves organic, locally roasted coffee. One computer is tucked away in the back corner (internet $3 per hour). There's live acoustic music some evenings.

🛍 Shopping

Looking for an imported African hand drum, some prayer flags or a nice crystal? You've come to the right place. The downtown shopping district has a handful of cute little boutiques to indulge a little shopping for the spiritual seeker. Both **Village Books** (320 N Mt Shasta Blvd) and **Golden Bough Books** (219 N Mt Shasta Blvd) carry fascinating volumes about Mt Shasta, on topics from geology and hiking to folklore and mysticism, as does the Sisson Museum shop (p284).

A favorite outdoor store in Shasta, **Fifth Season Sports** (www.thefifthseason.com; 300 N Mt Shasta Blvd, at Lake St) rents camping, mountain-climbing and backpacking gear and has staff familiar with the mountain (a three-day rental of crampons and an ice ax to summit Shasta costs $24). It also rents skis, snowshoes and snowboards.

ℹ Information

Mt Shasta ranger station (☎530-926-4511; 204 W Alma St; ⊘8am-4:30pm) One block west of Mt Shasta Blvd. Issues wilderness and mountain-climbing permits, good advice, weather reports and all you need for exploring the area. It also sells topographic maps.

Mt Shasta visitors center (☎530-926-4865; www.mtshastachamber.com; 300 Pine St; ⊘9am-5:30pm Mon-Sat, to 4:30pm Sun summer, 10am-4pm daily winter) Detailed information on recreation and lodging across Siskiyou County.

ℹ Getting There & Around

Greyhound (www.greyhound.com) buses heading north and south on I-5 stop opposite the Vet's Club (406 N Mt Shasta Blvd) and at the **depot** (628 S Weed Blvd) in Weed, 8 miles north on I-5. Services include Redding ($27.50, one hour and 20 minutes, three daily), Sacramento ($63, 5½ hours, three daily) and San Francisco ($80.50, 10½ hours, two or three times daily).

The **STAGE bus** (☎530-842-8295; www.co.siskiyou.ca.us) includes Mt Shasta City in its local I-5 corridor route (fares $1.50 to $8, depending on distance), which also serves McCloud, Dunsmuir, Weed and Yreka several times each weekday. Other buses connect at Yreka (see p301).

The **California Highway Patrol** (CHP; ☎530-842-4438) recorded report gives weather and road conditions for Siskiyou County.

Dunsmuir

Built by Central Pacific Railroad, Dunsmuir (population 1650) was originally named Pusher, for the auxiliary 'pusher' engines that muscled the heavy steam engines up the steep mountain grade. In 1886 Canadian coal baron Alexander Dunsmuir came to Pusher and was so enchanted that he promised the people a fountain if they would name the town after him. The fountain stands in the park today. Stop there to quench your thirst; it could easily be – as locals claim – 'the best water on earth.'

Dunsmuir might have aptly been named Phoenix. Rising from the ashes, this town has survived one cataclysmic disaster after another – avalanche, fire, flood, even a toxic railroad spill in 1991. Long since cleaned up, the river has been restored to pristine levels and the community has a notably plucky spirit, though today a number of empty storefronts attest to the community's greatest challenge: the Global Economic Crisis.

Still, it's home to a spirited set of artists, naturalists, urban refugees and native Dunsmuirians who are rightly proud of the pristine rivers around their little community. Its downtown streets – once a bawdy Gold Rush district of five saloons and three brothels – hold cafes, restaurants and galleries, and the town's reputation is still inseparable from the trains.

◉ Sights & Activities

The chamber of commerce stocks maps of **cycling trails** and **swimming holes** on the Upper Sacramento River.

Ruddle Cottage   GALLERY
(www.ruddlecottage.net; 5815 Sacramento Ave; ⊙10am-4pm May-Oct, 11am-4pm Nov-Apr) Behind a shaded garden, cluttered with eclectic sculptures, Jayne Bruck-Fryer's colorful gallery feels a bit like something from a fairy tale. Fryer makes each and every ingenious creation – from sculptures to jewelry – from recycled materials. The pretty fish hanging in the window? Dryer lint!

California Theater   HISTORIC BUILDING
(5741 Dunsmuir Ave) At downtown's north end stands what was once the town's pride. In a grassroots community effort, this longdefunct, once-glamorous venue is being carefully restored to its original glory. First opened in 1926 the theater hosted stars such as Clark Gable, Carole Lombard and the Marx Brothers. Today the lineup includes films, musical performances, theater groups and comedians.

Dunsmuir City Park & Botanical Gardens   PARK
(www.dunsmuirparks.org; admission free; ⊙dawn to dusk) As you follow winding Dunsmuir Ave north over the freeway, look for this park with its local native gardens and a **vintage steam engine** in front. A forest path from the riverside gardens leads to a small waterfall, but **Mossbrae Falls** are the larger and more spectacular of Dunsmuir's waterfalls. To get there from Dunsmuir Ave, turn west onto Scarlett Way, passing under an archway marked 'Shasta Retreat.' Park by the railroad tracks (there's no sign), then walk north along the right-hand side of the tracks for a half-hour until you reach a railroad bridge built in 1901. Backtracking slightly from the bridge, you'll find a little path going down through the trees to the river and the falls. Be *extremely careful* of trains as you walk by the tracks – the river's sound can make it impossible to hear them coming.

⌶ Sleeping

Railroad Park Resort   BOUTIQUE HOTEL $$
(☎530-235-4440; www.rrpark.com; 100 Railroad Park Rd, tent/RV sites $27/35, caboose & boxcar ste $115-120; ☀) About a mile south of town, off I-5, visitors can spend the night inside vintage railroad cars and cabooses that have been refitted from a number of the area's historic operators. The grounds are fun for kids, who can run around the iron engines and plunge in a centrally situated pool. The deluxe boxcars are furnished with antiques and claw-foot tubs, although the cabooses are simpler and a bit less expensive. You get tremendous views of Castle Crags, a peaceful creekside setting and tall pines shading the adjoining campground.

Dunsmuir Lodge   MOTEL $
(☎530-235-2884; www.dunsmuirlodge.net; 6604 Dunsmuir Ave; r $79-153; ☎☀) Toward the south entrance of town, the simple but tastefully renovated rooms have hardwood floors, big chunky blond-wood bed frames and tiled baths. A grassy communal picnic area overlooks the canyon slope. It's a peaceful little place and very good value.

Cave Springs Resort   MOTEL $
(☎530-235-2721; www.cavesprings.com; 4727 Dunsmuir Ave; r $56-76; ❄☀☀) These creek-side cabins seem unchanged since the 1950s, and they are rustic – *very* rustic – but their location is sublime. Nestled on a piney crag above the Sacramento River, the river is right outside the backdoor and ideal for anglers. Though mostly frequented by anglers, the place has romantic appeal if you can handle the cobwebs: at night there's nothing but the sound of rushing water and the haunting whistle of trains. The motel rooms are bland, but they're up to modern standards and have more amenities.

Dunsmuir Inn & Suites   MOTEL $
(☎530-235-4395; www.dunsmuirinn.com; 5400 Dunsmuir Ave; r $69-159; ☎☀) Straightforward, immaculately clean motel rooms make a good, no-fuss option.

✕ Eating & Drinking

⌷TOP⌷ CHOICE⌿ **Café Maddalena**   MEDITERRANEAN $$$
(☎530-235-2725; 5801 Sacramento Ave; mains $17-25; ⊙5-10pm Thu-Sun) Simple and elegant, this cafe put Dunsmuir on the foodie map.

NORTHERN BITES

Northern California was propelled into culinary stardom by the Bay Area and Wine Country's fine restaurants, not by the mountain region's greasy spoons. Still, the area doesn't suffer from foodie famine. Don't expect concentrations of fine bistros here, but enjoy the sprinkling (like a fine dusting of cocoa powder over tiramisu) of exceptional restaurants you do find.

Try the area's top recommended spots:

Café Maddalena (p289) Dunsmuir

Trinity Café (p287) Mt Shasta City

La Grange Café (p297) Weaverville

Vivify (p287) Mt Shasta City

The menu was designed by chef Bret LaMott (of Trinity Café fame, p287) and changes weekly to feature dishes from southern Europe and north Africa. Some highlights include seared scallops with orange glaze, or fresh angel hair with heirloom tomatoes. The wine bar is stocked with rare Mediterranean labels, including a great selection of Spanish varietals.

Dunsmuir Brewery Works   BREWPUB $$
(☎530-235-1900; www.dunsmuirbreweryworks.info; 5701 Dunsmuir Ave; mains $11-20; ◌11am-9pm Tue-Sun; ☎) It's hard to describe this little microbrew pub without veering into hyperbole. Start with the beer: the crisp ales and chocolate porter are perfectly balanced and the IPA is apparently pretty good too, because patrons are always drinking it dry. Soak it up with the short menu of awesome bar food – a warm potato salad, bratwurst or a thick Angus burger. The atmosphere, with a buzzing patio and aw-shucks staff, completes a perfect picture.

**Sengthongs Restaurant &
Blue Sky Room**   ASIAN $$
(☎530-235-4770; www.sengthongs.com; 5843 Dunsmuir Ave; mains $11-20; ◌11am-8pm Mon-Fri, with seasonal variations) This funky joint serves up sizzling Thai, Lao and Vietnamese food and books first-rate jazz, reggae, salsa or blues most nights. Many dishes are simply heaping bowls of noodles, though the meat dishes – flavored with ginger, scallions and spices – are more complex and uniformly delicious.

Cornerstone Bakery & Café   CAFE $
(5759 Dunsmuir Ave; mains $8-9; ◌8am-2pm Thu-Mon; ☎) Smack in the middle of town, it serves smooth, strong coffee, espresso and chai. All the baked goods – including thick, gooey cinnamon rolls – are warm from the oven. Creative omelets include cactus. The wine list is extensive, as is the dessert selection.

Brown Trout Café & Gallery   CAFE $$
(☎530-235-0754; 5841 Sacramento Ave; mains $10; ◌7am-5pm Mon-Sat, from 8am Sun; ☎☎) This casual, high-ceilinged, brick-walled hangout (formerly the town mercantile) serves strong fair-trade coffee and light snacks. There's also a short wine and microbrew list.

Railroad Park Dinner House   CALIFORNIAN $$
(☎530-235-4440; Railroad Park Resort, 100 Railroad Park Rd; mains $15-25; ◌5-9pm Fri & Sat Apr-Nov) Set inside a vintage railroad car, this popular restaurant-bar offers trainloads of dining-car ambience and Californian cuisine.

ⓘ Information

The **Dunsmuir Chamber of Commerce** (☎530-235-2177; www.dunsmuir.com; Suite 100, 5915 Dunsmuir Ave; ◌10am-3:30pm Tue-Sat) has free maps, walking-guide pamphlets and excellent information on outdoor activities.

ⓘ Getting There & Away

Dunsmuir's **Amtrak station** (www.amtrak.com; 5750 Sacramento Ave) is the only train stop in Siskiyou County and it is not staffed. Buy tickets for the north–south *Coast Starlight* on board the train, but only after making reservations by phone or via the website. The *Coast Starlight* runs once daily to Redding ($22, 1¾ hours), Sacramento ($60, 5¾ hours) and Oakland ($79, eight hours).

The **STAGE bus** (☎530-842-8295) includes Dunsmuir in its local I-5 corridor route, which also serves Mt Shasta City ($2, 20 minutes), Weed ($3.50, 30 minutes) and Yreka ($5, 1¼ hours) several times each weekday. The bus runs on Dunsmuir Ave.

Castle Crags State Park

The stars of this glorious state park alongside Castle Crags Wilderness Area are its soaring spires of ancient granite formed some 225 million years ago, with elevations ranging from 2000ft along the Sacramento River to more than 6500ft at the peaks. The crags are similar to the granite formations of the eastern Sierra, and Castle Dome resembles Yosemite's famous Half Dome.

Rangers at the **park entrance station** (☎530-235-2684; day use per vehicle $8) have information and maps covering nearly 28 miles of **hiking trails**. There's also **fishing** in the Sacramento River at the picnic area on the opposite side of I-5.

If you drive past the campground you'll reach **Vista Point**, near the start of the strenuous 2.7-mile **Crags Trail**, which rises through the forest past the Indian Springs spur trail, then clambers up to the base of **Castle Dome**. You're rewarded with unsurpassed views of Mt Shasta, especially if you scramble the last 100yd or so up into the rocky saddle gap. The park also has gentle **nature trails** and 8 miles of the **Pacific Crest Trail**, which passes through the park at the base of the crags.

The **campground** (☎reservations 800-444-7275; www.reserveamerica.com; sites $35) is one of the nicer public campgrounds in this area, and very easily accessible from the highway. It has running water, hot showers, and three spots that can accommodate RVs but have no hookups. Sites are shady, but suffer from traffic noise. You can camp anywhere in the Shasta-Trinity National Forest surrounding the park if you get a free campfire permit, issued at park offices. At the time of writing the future of this state park was uncertain because of budget issues.

McCloud

This tiny, historic mill town (population 1101) sits at the foot of the south slope of Mt Shasta, and is an alternative to staying in Mt Shasta City. Quiet streets retain a simple, easygoing charm, centered around the enormous McCloud Mercantile, which has enjoyed a vibrant revitalization and hosts the town's best hotel, a cute store and a couple of good places to eat. It's the closest settlement to Mt Shasta Board & Ski Park (p283) and is surrounded by abundant natural beauty. Hidden in the woods upriver are woodsy getaways for the Western aristocracy, including mansions owned by the Hearst and Levi Strauss estates.

The town made some press during a recent battle against the Nestlé corporation, which announced a plan for a water bottling facility on the site of the defunct mill. Fearing the damage to the local watershed, a cadre of residents organized to oppose the factory. By 2009 they succeeded in sufficiently entangling the multinational giant in red tape and bad publicity, and Nestlé scuttled the project. Still, for a little town hungry for job creation, the situation brought neighbor-against-neighbor politics to a fever pitch. Things have settled down, and curious visitors can wander around the eerily quiet site of the McCloud lumber mill, which would have been home to the plant. The mill's main building is as big as an airplane hangar, and completely empty.

◉ Sights & Activities

The **McCloud River Loop**, a gorgeous, 6-mile, partially paved road along the Upper McCloud River, begins at Fowlers Camp, 5.5 miles east of town on Hwy 89, and re-emerges about 11 miles east of McCloud. Along the loop, turn off at **Three Falls** for a pretty trail that passes...yep, three lovely falls and a riparian habitat for bird-watching in the Bigelow Meadow. The loop can easily be done by car, bicycle or on foot, and has five first-come, first-served campgrounds.

Other good hiking trails include the **Squaw Valley Creek Trail** (not to be confused with the ski area near Lake Tahoe), an easy 5-mile loop trail south of town, with options for swimming, fishing and picnicking. Also south of town, **Ah-Di-Na** is the remains of a Native American settlement and historic homestead once owned by the William Randolph Hearst family. Sections of the **Pacific Crest Trail** are accessible from Ah-Di-Na Campground, off Squaw Valley Rd, and also up near Bartle Gap, offering head-spinning views.

Fishing and swimming are popular on remote **Lake McCloud** reservoir, 9 miles south of town on Squaw Valley Rd, which is signposted in town as Southern. You can also go fishing on the Upper McCloud River (stocked with trout) and at the Squaw Valley Creek.

The huge **McCloud Mercantile** (www.mccloudmercantile.com; ⊙8am-6pm) anchors the downtown. There's a hotel upstairs and it hosts a couple of restaurants (p292) that warrant a longer stay, but those just passing though can get a bag of licorice at the old-world candy counter or browse the main floor. The collection of dry goods is very woodsy and very NorCal: Woolrich blankets, handmade soap and interesting gifts for the gardener, outdoors person or chef.

A tiny **historical museum** (admission free; ⊙11am-3pm Mon-Sat, 1-3pm Sun) sits opposite the depot and could use a bit of organization – it has the feel of a cluttered, messy thrift store – but tucked in the nooks and crannies are plenty of worthwhile curiosities from the town's past.

🛏 Sleeping

Lodging in McCloud is taken seriously – all are excellent and reservations are recommended. For camping go to the McCloud ranger district office for information on the half-dozen campgrounds nearby. Fowlers Camp is the most popular. The campgrounds have a range of facilities, from primitive (no running water and no fee) to developed (hot showers and fees of up to $20 per site). Ask about nearby fire-lookout cabins for rent – they give amazing, remote views of the area.

TOP CHOICE **McCloud River Mercantile Hotel** BOUTIQUE HOTEL $$
(☑530-964-2330; www.mccloudmercantile.com; 241 Main St; r $129-250; 🖥) Stoll up the stairs to the 2nd floor of McCloud's central Mercantile and try not to fall in love; it's all high ceilings, exposed brick and a perfect marriage of preservationist class and modern panache. The rooms with antique furnishings are situated within open floor plans. Guests are greeted with fresh flowers and can drift to sleep on feather beds after soaking in claw-foot tubs. Certainly the best hotel in the Northern Mountains.

McCloud Hotel HISTORIC HOTEL $$
(☑530-964-2822; www.mccloudhotel.com; 408 Main St; r $100-235; 🖥) Regal, butter-yellow and a whole block long, the grand hotel opposite the depot first opened in 1916 and has been a destination for Shasta's visitors ever since. The elegant historic landmark has been restored to a luxurious standard, and the included breakfast has gourmet flair. Many rooms have Jacuzzi tubs; one room is accessible for travelers with disabilities.

Stoney Brook Inn HOTEL $
(☑530-964-2300; www.stoneybrookinn.com; 309 W Colombero Dr; s & d with shared bath $79, with private bath $94, ste with kitchen $99-156) Smack in the middle of town, under a stand of pines, this alternative B&B also sponsors group retreats. Creature comforts include an outdoor hot tub, a sauna, a Native American sweat lodge and massage by appointment. Downstairs rooms are nicest. Vegetarian breakfast available.

McCloud River Lodge LODGE $
(☑530-964-2700; www.mccloudlodge.com; 140 Squaw Valley Rd; d $89-113, 🖥🖥) Tidy, new log cabins surround a lush central grassy area. Simple rooms have homey, plush, quilted beds and many have fireplaces and Jacuzzis. Accessible rooms for travelers with disabilities are available.

McCloud River Inn B&B $$
(☑530-964-2130; www.mccloudriverinn.com; 325 Lawndale Ct; r $115-199; 🖥) Rooms in this rambling, quaint Victorian are fabulously big – the bathrooms alone could sleep two. In the morning look out for the frittatas; in the evening enjoy a couple of glasses of wine in the cute downstairs wine bar. The relaxed and familial atmosphere guarantees that it books up quickly.

McCloud Dance Country RV Park CAMPGROUND $
(☑530-964-2252; www.mccloudrvpark.com; 480 Hwy 89, at Southern Ave; tent sites $14-24, RV sites $21-37, cabins $85-120; 🖥) Chock-full of RVs, with sites under the trees and a small creek, this is a good option for families. The view of the mountain is breathtaking and there's a large, grassy picnic ground. Cabins are basic but clean.

🍴 Eating

McCloud's eating options are few. For more variety, make the 10-mile trip over to Mt Shasta City.

Mountain Star Cafe VEGETARIAN $
(241 Main St; mains $7-9; ⊗8am-3pm) Deep within the creaking Mercantile, this sweet lunch counter is a surprise, serving vegetarian specials made from locally sourced, organic produce. Some options on the menu during a recent visit included the morale biscuits and gravy, a garlicky tempeh Ruben, roast vegetable salad and a homemade oat and veggie burger.

White Mountain Fountain Cafe AMERICAN $
(241 Main St; mains $8; ⊗8am-4pm) In the window-lined corner of the Mercantile, this old-fashioned little soda fountain serves burgers and shakes. The one coyly called 'Not the Dolly Varden' is an excellent vegetarian sandwich with roasted zucchini, red peppers and garlic aioli.

☆ Entertainment

McCloud Dance Country DANCEHALL
(www.mcclouddancecountry.com; cnr Broadway & Pine Sts; per couple $20; ⊗7pm Fri & Sat) Dust it up on the 5000-sq-ft maple dance floor in the

1906 Broadway Ballroom. Square dancing, round dancing, ballroom dancing – they do it all. Starting at $289 per couple, multiday packages include lessons and evening dances. It's a worthwhile centerpiece to a weekend getaway. Visit the website to see what's on and whether you need a reservation for the event.

ⓘ Information

McCloud Chamber of Commerce (☑530-964-3113; www.mccloudchamber.com; 205 Quincy St; ☺10am-4pm Mon-Fri)

McCloud ranger district office (☑530-964-2184; Hwy 89; ☺8am-4:30pm Mon-Sat summer, 8am-4:30pm Mon-Fri rest of year) A quarter-mile east of town. Detailed information on camping, hiking and recreation.

McArthur-Burney Falls Memorial State Park

This beautiful state park (☑530-335-2777; www.parks.ca.gov; day use per vehicle $8) lies southeast of McCloud, near the crossroads of Hwys 89 and 299 from Redding. The 129ft falls cascade with the same volume of water – 100 million gallons per day – and at the same temperature – 42°F (5°C) – year-round. Clear, lava-filtered water surges over the top and also from springs in the waterfall's face. Teddy Roosevelt loved this place; he called it the 'Eighth Wonder of the World.'

A lookout point beside the parking lot also has trails going up and down the creek from the falls. (Be careful of your footing here; in 2011 there was a fatality in the park when someone slipped on the rocks.) The nature trail heading downstream leads to Lake Britton; other hiking trails include a portion of the Pacific Crest Trail. The scenes in the film *Stand By Me* (1986) where the boys dodge the train were shot on the Lake Britton Bridge trestle in the park.

The park's **campgrounds** (☑530-335-2777, summer reservations 800-444-7275; www.reserveamerica.com; day use $8, sites $35) have hot showers and are open year round.

About 10 miles northeast of McArthur-Burney Falls, the 6000-acre **Ahjumawi Lava Springs State Park** is known for its abundant springs, aquamarine bays, islets, and jagged flows of black basalt lava. It can only be reached by boats that are launched from Rat Farm, 3 miles north of the town of McArthur along a graded dirt road. Arrangements for primitive camping can be made by calling McArthur-Burney Falls Memorial State Park.

Lava Beds National Monument

A wild landscape of charred volcanic rock and rolling hills, this remote **national monument** (☑530-667-8100; www.nps.gov/labe; 7-day entry per vehicle/hiker/cyclist $10/5/5, cash only) is reason enough to visit the region. Off Hwy 139, immediately south of Tule Lake National Wildlife Refuge, it's a truly remarkable 72-sq-mile landscape of volcanic features – lava flows, craters, cinder cones, spatter cones, shield volcanoes and amazing lava tubes.

Lava tubes are formed when hot, spreading lava cools and hardens when the surfaces get exposed to the cold air. The lava inside is thus insulated and stays molten, flowing away to leave an empty tube of solidified lava. Nearly 400 such tubular caves have been found in the monument, and many more are expected to be discovered. About two dozen or so are currently open for exploration by visitors.

On the south side of the park, the **visitors center** (☑530-667-2282, ext 230; ☺8am-6pm, shorter hrs in winter) has free maps, activity books for kids and information about the monument and its volcanic features and history. Rangers loan flashlights, rent helmets and kneepads for cave exploration and lead summer interpretive programs, including campfire talks and guided cave walks. To explore the caves it's essential you use a high-powered flashlight, wear good shoes and long sleeves (lava is sharp), and do not go alone.

Near the visitors center, a short, one-way **Cave Loop** drive provides access to many lava-tube caves. **Mushpot Cave**, the one nearest the visitors center, has lighting and information signs and is a good introductory hike. There are a number of caves that are a bit more challenging, including Labyrinth, Hercules Leg, Golden Dome and Blue Grotto. Each one of these caves has an interesting history – visitors used to ice-skate by lantern light in the bottom of Merrill Cave, and when Ovls Cave was discovered, it was littered with bighorn sheep skulls. There are good brochures with details about each cave available from the visitors center. Rangers are stern with their warnings for new cavers though, so be sure to check in with the visitors center before exploring to avoid harming the fragile geological and biological resources in the park.

The tall black cone of **Schonchin Butte** (5253ft) has a magnificent outlook accessed via a steep 1-mile hiking trail. Once you reach the top, you can visit the fire-lookout staff between June and September. **Mammoth Crater** is the source of most of the area's lava flows.

The weathered Modoc **petroglyphs** at the base of a high cliff at the far northeastern end of the monument, called Petroglyph Point, are thousands of years old. At the visitors center, be sure to take the leaflet explaining the origin of the petroglyphs and their probable meaning. Look for the hundreds of nests in holes high up in the cliff face, which provide shelter for birds that sojourn at the wildlife refuges nearby.

Also at the north end of the monument, be sure to go to the labyrinthine landscape of **Captain Jack's Stronghold**. A brochure will guide you through the breathtaking Stronghold Trail.

Indian Well Campground (tent & RV sites $10), near the visitors center at the south end of the park, has water and flush toilets, but no showers. The campsites are lovely and have broad views of the surrounding valleys. The nearest place to buy food and camping supplies is on Hwy 139 in the nearby town of Tulelake, but the place is pretty rugged – just a couple of bars, a bunch of boarded-up buildings and a pair of gas stations.

Klamath Basin National Wildlife Refuges

Of the six stunning national wildlife refuges in this group, Tule Lake and Clear Lake refuges are wholly within California, Lower Klamath refuge straddles the California–Oregon border, and the Upper Klamath, Klamath Marsh and Bear Valley refuges are across the border in Oregon. Bear Valley and Clear Lake (not to be confused with the Clear Lake just east of Ukiah) are closed to the public to protect their delicate habitats, but the rest are open during daylight hours.

These refuges provide habitats for a stunning array of birds migrating along the Pacific Flyway (see the boxed text, p295). Some stop over only briefly; others stay longer to mate, make nests and raise their young. The refuges are always packed with birds, but during the spring and fall migrations, populations can rise into the hundreds of thousands.

The **Klamath Basin National Wildlife Refuges visitors center** (☎530-667-2231; http://klamathbasinrefuges.fws.gov; 4009 Hill Rd, Tulelake; ☻8am-4:30pm Mon-Fri, 10am-4pm Sat & Sun) sits on the west side of the Tule Lake refuge, about 5 miles west of Hwy 139, near the town of Tulelake. Follow the signs from Hwy 139 or from Lava Beds National Monument. The center has a bookstore and interesting video program, as well as maps, information on recent bird sightings and updates on road conditions. It rents photo blinds. Be sure to pick up the excellent, free *Klamath Basin Birding Trail* brochure for detailed lookouts, maps, color photos and a species checklist.

The spring migration peaks during March, and in some years more than a million birds fill the skies. In April and May the songbirds, waterfowl and shorebirds arrive, some to stay and nest, others to build up their energy before they continue north. In summer ducks, Canada geese and many other waterbirds are raised here. The fall migration peaks in early November. In cold weather the area hosts the largest wintering concentration of bald eagles in the lower 48 states, with 1000 in residence at times from December to February. The Tule Lake and Lower Klamath refuges are the best places to see eagles and other raptors.

The Lower Klamath and Tule Lake refuges attract the largest numbers of birds year-round, and **auto trails** (driving routes) have been set up; a free pamphlet from the visitors center shows the routes. Self-guided **canoe trails** have been established in three of the refuges. Those in the Tule Lake and Klamath Marsh refuges are usually open from July 1 to September 30; no canoe rentals are available. Canoe trails in the Upper Klamath refuge are open year-round. Here, canoes can be rented at **Rocky Point Resort** (☎541-356-2287; 28121 Rocky Point Rd, Klamath Falls, OR; canoe, kayak & paddle boat rental per hr/half-day/day $15/30/40), on the west side of Upper Klamath Lake.

Camp at nearby Lava Beds National Monument (p293). A couple of RV parks and budget motels cluster along Hwy 139 near the tiny town of Tulelake (4035ft), including the friendly **Ellis Motel** (☎530-667-5242; 2238 Hwy 139; d without/with kitchen $75/95). Comfortable **Fe's B&B** (☎877-478-0184; www.fesbandb.com; 660 Main St; s/d with shared bath $60/70) has four simple rooms, with a big breakfast included.

THE AVIAN SUPERHIGHWAY

California is on the Pacific Flyway, a migratory route for hundreds of species of birds heading south in winter and north in summer. There are birds to see year-round, but the best viewing opportunities are during the spring and fall migrations. Flyway regulars include everything from tiny finches, hummingbirds, swallows and woodpeckers to eagles, hawks, swans, geese, ducks, cranes and herons. Much of the flyway route corresponds with I-5 (or Fly-5 in the birds' case), so a drive up the interstate in spring or fall is a show: great Vs of geese undulate in the sky and noble hawks stare from roadside perches.

In Northern California, established wildlife refuges safeguard wetlands used by migrating waterfowl. The Klamath Basin National Wildlife Refuges (p294) offer extraordinary year-round bird-watching.

Modoc National Forest

It's nearly impossible to get your head around this enormous national forest (www.fs.usda.gov/modoc) – it covers almost two million spectacular, remote acres of California's northeastern corner. Travelers through the remote northeast of the state will be passing in and out of its borders constantly. Fourteen miles south of Lava Beds National Monument, on the western edge of the forest, Medicine Lake is a stunning crater lake in a caldera (collapsed volcano) surrounded by pine forest, volcanic formations and campgrounds. The enormous volcano that formed the lake is the largest in area in California. When it erupted it ejected pumice followed by flows of obsidian, as can be seen at Little Glass Mountain, east of the lake.

Pick up the *Medicine Lake Highlands: Self-Guided Roadside Geology Tour* pamphlet from the McCloud ranger district office (p293) to find and learn about the glass flows, pumice deposits, lava tubes and cinder cones throughout the area. Roads are closed by snow from around mid-November to mid-June, but the area is still popular for winter sports, and accessible by cross-country skiing and snowshoeing.

Congratulations are in order for travelers who make it all the way to the Warner Mountains. This spur of the Cascade Range in the east of the Modoc National Forest is probably the least visited range in California. With extremely changeable weather, it's also not so hospitable; there have been snowstorms here in every season of the year. The range divides into the North Warners and South Warners at Cedar Pass (elevation 6305ft), east of Alturas. Remote Cedar Pass Snow Park (☎530-233-3323; all day T-bar adult/child under 6yr/6-18yr $15/5/12, all-day rope

tow $5; ☺10am-4pm Sat, Sun & holidays during ski season) offers downhill and cross-country skiing. The majestic South Warner Wilderness contains 77 miles of hiking and riding trails. The best time to use them is from July to mid-October.

Maps, campfire permits and information are all available at the Modoc National Forest supervisor's headquarters (☎530-233-5811; 800 W 12th St; ☺8am-5pm Mon-Fri) in Alturas.

If you are heading east into Nevada from the forest, you'll pass through Alturas, the fairly uninspiring seat of Modoc County. The town was founded by the Dorris family in 1874 as a supply point for travelers, and it serves the same function today, providing basic services, motels and family-style restaurants. If you are looking for supplies yourself, seek out the Four Corners Market (1077 N Main St), a bright and friendly grocery with a handful of specialty items and surprisingly fresh produce.

WEST OF I-5

The wilderness west of I-5 is right in the sweet spot: here are some of the most rugged towns and seductive wilderness areas in the entire state of California – just difficult enough to reach to discourage big crowds.

The Trinity River Scenic Byway (Hwy 299) winds spectacularly along the Trinity River and beneath towering cliffs as it makes its way from the plains of Redding to the coastal redwood forests around Arcata. It provides a chance to cut through some of the Northern Mountains' most pristine wilderness and passes through the vibrant Gold Rush town of Weaverville.

Heavenly Hwy 3 (a highly recommended – although slower and windier – alternative

WHAT THE...?

Pop over to the **Willow Creek China Flat Museum** (☎530-629-2653; www.bigfootcountry.net; Hwy 299, Willow Creek; admission free, donations accepted; ☺10am-4pm Wed-Sun May-Sep, 11am-4pm Fri & Sat, noon-4pm Sun Oct-Apr) to take in its persuasive Bigfoot collection. Footprints, handprints, hair...it has all kinds of goodies to substantiate the ole boy's existence. In fact, namesake Bigfoot Scenic Byway (Hwy 96) starts here and heads north, winding through breathtaking mountain and river country.

route to I-5) heads north from Weaverville. This mountain byway transports you through the Trinity Alps – a stunning granite range dotted with azure alpine lakes – past the shores of Lewiston and Trinity Lakes, over the Scott Mountains and finally into emerald, mountain-rimmed Scott Valley. Rough-and-ready Yreka awaits you at the end of the line.

Weaverville

In 1941 a reporter interviewed James Hilton, the British author of *Lost Horizon*. 'In all your wanderings,' the journalist asked, 'what's the closest you've found to a real-life Shangri-La?' Hilton's response? 'A little town in northern California. A little town called Weaverville.'

Cute as a button, Weaverville's streets are lined with flower boxes in the summer and banks of snow in the winter. The seat of Trinity County, it sits amid an endless tract of mountain and forest area that's 75% federally owned. With its almost 3300 sq miles, the county is roughly the size of Delaware and Rhode Island together, yet has a total population of only 13,700 and not one traffic light, freeway or parking meter.

Weaverville (population 3600) is a small gem of a town on the National Register of Historic Places and has a laid-back, gentle bohemian feel (thanks in part to the young back-to-landers and marijuana-growing subculture). You can easily spend a day here just strolling around the quaint storefronts and visiting art galleries, museums and historic structures.

◉ Sights & Activities

TOP CHOICE **Joss House State Historic Park**   TEMPLE
(☎530-623-5284; cnr Hwy 299 & Oregon St; admission $3; ☺10am-5pm Sat winter, 10am-5pm Wed-Sun rest of year) Of all California's historic parks, these are the walls that actually talk – they're papered inside with 150-year-old donation ledgers from the once-thriving Chinese community, a testament to the rich culture of immigrants who built Northern California's infrastructure, a culture that has all but disappeared. It's an unexpected surprise that the oldest continuously used Chinese temple in California, dating to the 1870s, is in little Weaverville. The rich blue-and-gold Taoist shrine contains an ornate altar, more than 3000 years old, which was brought here from China. The adjoining schoolhouse was the first to teach Chinese students in California. Tours depart from 10am until 4pm, on the hour. Sadly, state budget issues have made the future of this park uncertain.

JJ Jackson Memorial Museum & Trinity County Historical Park   MUSEUM
(www.trinitymuseum.org; 508 Main St; donation requested; ☺10am-5pm daily May-Oct, noon-4pm daily Apr & Nov-Dec 24, noon-4pm Tue & Sat Dec 26-Mar) Next door to the Joss House you'll find gold-mining and cultural exhibits, plus vintage machinery, memorabilia, an old miner's cabin and a blacksmith shop.

Highland Art Center   GALLERY
(www.highlandartcenter.org; 691 Main St; ☺10am-5pm Mon-Sat, 11am-4pm Sun) Stroll through galleries showcasing local artists.

Coffee Creek Ranch   OUTFITTER
(☎530-266-3343; www.coffeecreekranch.com) In Trinity Center, these guys lead fishing and fully outfitted pack trips into the Trinity Alps Wilderness and week-long fishing excursions.

⌱ Sleeping

The ranger station has information on many USFS campgrounds in the area, especially around Trinity Lake. Commercial RV parks, some with tent sites, dot Hwy 299.

TOP CHOICE **Weaverville Hotel**   HISTORIC HOTEL $$
(☎800-750-8957; www.weavervillehotel.com; 203 Main St; r $100-260; ❄🕾) Play like you're in the Old West at this upscale hotel and historic landmark, refurbished in grand Victorian style. It's luxurious but not stuffy, and

the very gracious owners take great care in looking after you. Guests may use the local gym, and breakfast at a neighboring cafe is on the house.

Red Hill Motel & Cabins MOTEL $
(☎530-623-4331; 116 Red Hill Rd; d $42, cabins without/with kitchen $48/59) This very quiet and simple motel is tucked under ponderosa pines at the west end of town, just off Main St, next to the library. It's a set of red wooden cabins built in the 1940s and the kitchenettes and mini refrigerators make it a good option for people who are on a longer stay. It's nothing fancy, but the rooms are simple, clean and very good value.

Whitmore Inn HISTORIC INN $$
(☎530-623-2509; www.whitmoreinn.com; 761 Main St; r $100-165; ❀🐾) Settle into plush, cozy rooms in this downtown Victorian with a wraparound deck and abundant gardens. One room is accessible for travelers with disabilities.

🍴 Eating

Downtown Weaverville is ready to feed hungry hikers – in the summer the main drag has many cheap, filling options. There's also a fantastic **farmers market** (⊙4:30-7:30pm Wed May Oct), which takes over Main St in the warmer months. In winter the tourist season dries up and opening hours get very short.

TOP CHOICE La Grange Café CALIFORNIAN $$
(☎530-623-5325; 315 N Main St; mains $15-30; ⊙11:30am-9pm Mon-Thu, to 10pm Fri-Sun, with seasonal variations) Spacious yet intimate, this celebrated multistar restaurant serves exceptional light, fresh and satisfying fare. Chef and owner Sharon Heryford knows how to do dining without a whiff of pretension: apple-stuffed red cabbage in the fall, and brightly flavored chicken enchiladas in the summer, plus game dishes and seasonal vegetables. Exposed brick and open sight lines complement the exceedingly friendly atmosphere. A seat at the bar is great when the tables are full, which they often are. The all-you-can-eat soup and salad is a stroke of genius.

Trinideli DELI $
(201 Trinity Lakes Blvd, at Center St; sandwiches $5-7; ⊙6am-4pm Mon-Fri) Cheerful staff prepare decadent sandwiches stuffed with fresh goodness. The 'Peasant's Pleasure' with Braunschweiger, horseradish and pickles is satisfying

for brave palates, and simple turkey and ham standards explode with fresh veggies and tons of flavor. The suite of breakfast burritos are perfect for a quick pre-hike fill up.

Noelle's Garden Café CAFE $
(☎530-623-2058; 252 Main St; mains $9; ⊙breakfast & lunch; 🐾) *The* best place for breakfast. Sit inside the cheery white clapboard house, or out on the adjoining vine-trellised deck when the weather is fair. Lunch on soups, sandwiches and salads – with lots of veggie options.

Johnny's Pizza PIZZA $$
(227 Main St; pizzas $10-15; ⊙11am-8pm) A small-town pizza joint with a good vibe, rock and roll on the stereo and friendly staff.

La Casita MEXICAN $
(570 Main St; mains $9; ⊙11am-7pm) Tucked next door to Noelle's, low-ceilinged little La Casita serves passable Mexican classics.

Mountain Marketplace MARKET $
(222 S Main St; ⊙9am-6pm Mon-Fri, 10am-5pm Sat; 🐾) Stock up on natural foods or hit its juice bar and vegetarian deli.

🍷 Drinking & Entertainment

Mamma Llama COFFEE SHOP
(www.mammallama.com; 208 N Main St; ⊙6am-6pm Mon-Fri, 7am-6pm Sat, 7am-3pm Sun; 🐾) A local institution, this coffeehouse is a roomy and relaxed chill spot under the white arcade. The espresso is well made, there's a selection of books and CDs, and there are couches for lounging. The small menu does wraps and sandwiches. Live folk music (often including a hand drum) takes over occasionally.

Red House COFFEE SHOP
(www.vivalaredhouse.com; 218 S Miner St; ⊙6:30am 5:30pm Mon-Fri, 7:30am-1pm Sun) This airy, light and bamboo-bedecked spot serves a wide selection of teas, light snacks and organic, fair-trade, shade-grown coffee. The daily food specials include a delicious chicken-and-rice soup on Mondays. If you're in a hurry (rare in Weaverville) there's a drive-through window.

Trinity Theatre CINEMA
(310 Main St) Plays first-run movies.

ℹ Information

Trinity County Chamber of Commerce
(☎530-623-6101; www.trinitycounty.com; 215 Main St; ⊙10am-4pm) Knowledgeable staff with lots of useful information.

Weaverville ranger station (☎530-623-2121; 210 N Main St; ⏰8am-4:30pm Mon-Fri) Maps, information and permits for all lakes, national forests and wilderness areas in and near Trinity County.

ℹ Getting There & Away

A local **Trinity Transit** (☎530-623-5438; www.trinitytransportation.org; fares 50¢) bus makes a Weaverville–Lewiston loop via Hwy 299 and Hwy 3 from Monday to Friday. Another one runs between Weaverville and Hayfork, a small town about 30 miles to the southwest on Hwy 3.

Lewiston Lake

Pleasant little **Lewiston** (www.lewistonca.com) is little more than a collection of buildings beside a crossroad, 26 miles west of Redding, around 5 miles off Hwy 299 on Trinity Dam Blvd and a few miles south of Lewiston Lake. It's right beside the Trinity River, and the locals here are in tune with the environment – they know fishing spots on the rivers and lakes, where to hike and how to get around.

The lake is about 1.5 miles north of town and is a serene alternative to the other area lakes because of its 10mph boat speedlimit. The water is kept at a constant level, providing a nurturing habitat for fish and waterfowl. Migrating bird species sojourn here – early in the evening you may see ospreys and bald eagles diving for fish. The **Trinity River Fish Hatchery** (⏰sunrise-sunset) traps juvenile salmon and steelhead and holds them until they are ready to be released into the river. The only marina on the lake, **Pine Cove Marina** (www.pine-cove-marina.com; 9435 Trinity Dam Blvd), has free information about the lake and its wildlife, boat and canoe rentals, potluck dinners and guided off-road tours.

If you're just passing through town, make a stop at the **Country Peddler** (4 Deadwood Rd), a drafty old barn that sits behind a field of red poppies and is filled with cool antiques, rusting road signs and antique collectibles that seem like they were pulled out of some long-lost uncle's hunting cabin. The owners, avid outdoor enthusiasts, know the area like the back of their hand.

🛏 Sleeping & Eating

Several commercial campgrounds dot the rim of the lake. For information on USFS campgrounds, contact the ranger station in Weaverville (p298). Two of these are right on the lake: the wooded **Mary Smith**, which is more private; and the sunny **Ackerman** (sites $11), which has more grassy space for families. If there's no host, both have self-registration options. There are all kinds of RV parks, cabins for rent and motels in Lewiston.

Lewiston Hotel HISTORIC HOTEL **$**
(☎530-778-3823; www.lewistonhotel.net; 125 Deadwood Rd; r $69-89; 🐾) Squarely in the center of town, this 1862 hotel was recently reopened to guests and the rooms – with quilts, historic photos and river views – have tons of character. The pizza place onsite, **Trinity Dam Good Pizza** (mains $8-10; ⏰11am-7pm, with seasonal variations), serves a helluva tuna melt, gooey pizza and stiff drinks. This is also the best place to hang out after dark. If you're lucky, there may be live music and dancing.

Old Lewiston Inn B&B B&B **$$**
(☎530-778-3385; www.theoldlewistoninn.com; Deadwood Rd; r $110-125; ❄) In town, beside the river, this B&B is in an 1875 house and serves country-style breakfasts. Enjoy the hot tub, or ask about all-inclusive fly-fishing packages.

Lewiston Valley Motel MOTEL **$**
(☎530-778-3942; www.lewistonvalleymotel.com; 4789 Trinity Dam Blvd; RV sites $20, r $60; ❄🐾) This simple, plain-Jane motel has an RV park and sits next to a gas station and convenience store.

Old Lewiston Bridge RV Resort RV PARK **$**
(☎530-778-3894; www.lewistonbridgerv.com; 8460 Rush Creek Rd, at Turnpike Rd; tent/RV sites $15/28) A pleasant place to park the RV, with campsites beside the river bridge.

Lakeview Terrace Resort CABINS, RV PARK **$**
(☎530-778-3803; www.lakeviewterraceresort.com; RV sites $30, cabins $80-135; ❄🐾) Five miles north of Lewiston, this is a woodsy Club Med, which rents boats.

Trinity (Clair Engle) Lake

Placid Trinity Lake, California's third-largest reservoir, sits beneath dramatic snowcapped alps north of Lewiston Lake. In the off season it is serenely quiet, but it attracts multitudes in the summer, who come for swimming, fishing and other water sports. Most of the campgrounds, RV parks, motels, boat rentals and restaurants line the west side of the lake.

The Pinewood Cove Resort (☎530-286-2201; www.pinewoodcove.com; 45110 Hwy 3; tent/RV sites $28/40, cabins $126-147; ❋), on the waterfront, is a popular place to stay, but doesn't provide bed linens.

The east side of the lake is quieter, with more secluded campgrounds, some accessible only by boat. The Weaverville ranger station (p298) has information on USFS campgrounds.

Klamath & Siskiyou Mountains

A dense conglomeration of rugged coastal mountains gives this region the nickname 'the Klamath Knot.' Wet, coastal, temperate rain forest gives way to moist inland forest, creating an immense diversity of habitats for many species, some found nowhere else in the world. Around 3500 native plants live here. Local fauna includes the northern spotted owl, the bald eagle, the tailed frog, several species of Pacific salmon and carnivores like the wolverine and the mountain lion. One theory for the extraordinary biodiversity of this area is that it escaped extensive glaciation during recent ice ages. This may have given species refuge and longer stretches of relatively favorable conditions during which to adapt.

The region also includes the largest concentration of wild and scenic rivers in the US: the Salmon, Smith, Trinity, Eel and Klamath, to name a few. The fall color change is magnificent.

Five main wilderness areas dot the Klamath Knot. The Marble Mountain Wilderness in the north is marked by high rugged mountains, valleys and lakes, all sprinkled with colorful geological formations of marble and granite, and a huge array of flora. The Russian Wilderness is 8000 acres of high peaks and isolated, beautiful mountain lakes. The Trinity Alps Wilderness, west of Hwy 3, is one of the area's most lovely regions for hiking and backcountry camping, and has more than 600 miles of trails that cross passes over its granite peaks and head along its deep alpine lakes. The Yolla Bolly-Middle Eel Wilderness in the south is little-visited, despite its proximity to the Bay Area, and so affords spectacular, secluded backcountry experiences. The Siskiyou Wilderness, closest to the coast, rises to heights of 7300ft, from where you can see the ocean. An extensive trail system crisscrosses the wilderness, but it is difficult to make loops.

WORTH A TRIP

ALPEN CELLARS

Jaunt over to little-known, utterly picturesque Alpen Cellars (☎530-266-9513; www.alpencellars.com; ☉10am-4pm summer, by appointment Oct-May). Specializing in riesling, gewürtztraminer, chardonnay and pinot noir, the vineyard is open for tours, tastings and picnicking on idyllic riverside grounds. To get there from Weaverville, take Hwy 3 for about 35 miles to the north end of Trinity Lake (5 miles past Trinity Center), then turn right on East Side Rd; 8 miles further, head left on East Fork Rd and continue for 2 miles.

The Trinity River Scenic Byway (Hwy 299) follows the rushing Trinity River to the Pacific coast and is dotted with lodges, RV parks and blink-and-you'll-miss-'em burgs. There's river rafting at Willow Creek, 55 miles west of Weaverville. Bigfoot Rafting Company (☎530-629-2263; www.bigfootrafting.com) leads guided trips (from $79) and also rents rafts and kayaks (from $38 per day).

Scott Valley

North of Trinity Lake, Hwy 3 climbs along the gorgeous eastern flank of the Trinity Alps Wilderness to Scott Mountain Summit (5401ft) and then drops gracefully down into verdant Scott Valley, a bucolic agricultural area nestled between towering mountains. There are good opportunities for hiking, cycling and mountainbiking, or taking horse trips to mountain lakes. For a bit of history, pick up the *Trinity Heritage Scenic Byway* brochure from the Weaverville ranger station (p298) before taking this world-class drive.

Etna (population 737), toward the north end of the valley, is known by its residents as 'California's Last Great Place' and they might be right. It hosts a fantastic Bluegrass Festival at the end of July and the tiny Etna Brewing Company (www.etnabrew.net; 131 Callahan St; brewery tours free; ☉pub 11am-4pm Tue, to 8pm Wed & Thu, to 9pm Fri & Sat, to 7pm Sun, tours by appointment) offers delicious beers and pub grub. If you're sticking around try the immaculate 10-room Motel Etna (☎530-467-5338; 317 Collier Way; d $55). Scott Valley Drug (www.scottvalleydrug.com; 511 Main St; ☉Mon-Sat) serves up old-fashioned ice-cream sodas.

THE STATE OF JEFFERSON

Welcome to the State of Jefferson (www.jeffersonstate.com). When you first notice the billboards and bumper stickers ('Jefferson: A State of Mind') endorsing the proposed 51st state it might seem like a joke, but as you travel the two-lane blacktop in Northern California and Southern Oregon, the cultural differences of the states' border region start to make more sense. The State of Jefferson was originally proposed in 1941 by a band of well-armed locals, who were exceptionally pissed off about the terrible conditions of local roads. Jefferson's original draft included a good chunk of Northern California – including Del Norte, Siskiyou, Modoc, Humboldt, Trinity, Shasta and Lassen Counties – and several more in Southern Oregon. But just as the movement was gaining momentum, the Japanese bombing of Pearl Harbor brought a swell of US nationalism, and plans for the 51st state were scuttled. Today Jefferson feels alive and well in the libertarian spirit of the locals, and you can tune into news of the area by listening to Jefferson Public Radio (www.ijpr.org), transmitting on KNCA 89.7 FM from Redding and KNSQ 88.1 FM from Mt Shasta.

Beyond Etna Fort Jones (population 839) is just 18 miles from Yreka. The visitors center (☑530-468-5442; 11943 Main St; ☾10am-5pm Tue-Sat, noon-4pm Sun) sits at the back of the Guild Shop mercantile. Down the street, a small museum (www.fortjonesmuseum.com; 11913 Main St; donation requested; ☾Mon-Sat Memorial Day-Labor Day) houses Native American artifacts.

Yreka

Inland California's northernmost town, Yreka (wy-*ree*-kah; population 7400) was once a booming Gold Rush settlement. Most travelers only pass through en route to Oregon. Yreka, especially the quaint historic downtown, makes a good spot to stretch, eat and refuel before heading out into the hinterlands of the Scott Valley or the northeastern California wilderness.

⊙ Sights & Activities

About 25 miles north of Yreka, on I-5, just across the Oregon border, Siskiyou Summit (elevation 4310ft) often closes in winter – even when the weather is just fine on either side. Call ☑530-842-4438 to check.

Siskiyou County Museum   MUSEUM
(www.siskiyoucountyhistoricalsociety.org; 910 S Main St; admission $3; ☾9am-3pm Tue-Thu, 10am-4pm Sat) Several blocks south of the downtown grid, this exceptionally well-curated museum brings together pioneer and Native American history. An outdoor section contains historic buildings brought from around the county.

Siskiyou County
Courthouse   HISTORIC BUILDING
(311 4th St) This hulking downtown building was built in 1857 and has a collection of gold nuggets, flakes and dust in the foyer.

Yreka Creek Greenway   WALKING, CYCLING
(www.yrekagreenway.org) Behind the museum, the Yreka Creek Greenway has walking and cycling paths winding through the trees.

Blue Goose Steam Excursion
Train   TRAIN RIDE
(www.yrekawesternrr.com; adult/child 2-12yr $20/12) This train hisses and chugs along a 100-year-old track. The schedule is sporadic; look at the website for current information. It's one of the last remaining railroads of California's quickly vanishing historic rail network.

🛏 Sleeping & Eating

Motels, motels and more motels: budget travelers can do lots of comparison shopping along Yreka's Main St. There are mid-century motels galore. Many chains hotels are set up along the highway to help catch travelers rushing along I-5; there's a cluster off exit 773 south of town. Klamath National Forest runs several campgrounds; the supervisor's office (p301) has information. RV parks cluster on the edge of town.

Third Street Inn   B&B $$
(☑530-841-1120; www.yrekabedandbreakfast.com; 326 Third St; d $105-120) The cute little cottage is the best deal for privacy, but the other three rooms in this family-run Victorian B&B are immaculate and exude homespun charm.

NORTHERN MOUNTAINS YREKA

Klamath Motor Lodge
MOTEL $

(☎530-842-2751; www.klamathmotorlodge.net; 1111 S Main St; d $70; 🛜🅿️) Folks at this motor court are especially friendly, the rooms are clean and – bonus for those headed in from the wilderness – it has an on-site laundry. Of all the motels in Yreka, this is tops.

The Audacity & Cafe
CAFE & WINE BAR $

(http://theaudacitycafe.wordpress.com; 200 W Miner St; sandwiches $7-10; �9am-5pm Mon-Thu, to 10pm Sat; 🛜) This mother-daughter venture is Yreka's most-happening place on a Saturday night, when the little stage comes alive with local folk and rock acts and people sip wine and sit back on the comfortable couches. The food is simple – wraps and fresh salads, smoothies and sandwiches.

Klander's Deli
DELI $

(211 S Oregon St; sandwiches $6; �8am-2pm Mon-Fri) Local to the core, the long list of yummy sandwiches is named after regulars. Bob is a favorite, named for the first owner and stacked with ham, turkey, roast beef and Swiss.

Nature's Kitchen
NATURAL FOODS $

(☎530-842-1136; 412 S Main St; dishes $7; �8am-5pm Mon-Sat; 🅿️) Friendly natural-foods store and bakery, serving healthy and tasty vegetarian dishes, fresh juices and good espresso.

The adjoining store has all kinds of fairies, herbal supplements and new-agey trinkets.

Grandma's House
AMERICAN $

(123 E Center St; mains $8-15; �7am-8pm) Home-style platters include a killer open-faced turkey sandwich and rib-sticking breakfast dishes. Look for the cutesy gingerbread house east of downtown between Main St and I-5.

ℹ Information

Klamath National Forest supervisor's office
(☎530-842-6131; 1312 Fairlane Rd, at Oberlin Rd; �8am-4:30pm Mon-Fri) At the south edge of town, with the lowdown on recreation and camping. This place is enormous; you can see it from the highway.

Yreka Chamber of Commerce (☎530-842-1649; www.yrekachamber.com; 117 W Miner St; �9am-5pm, with seasonal variations; 🛜)

ℹ Getting There & Away

STAGE (☎530-842-8295; fares from $1.75) buses run throughout the region from a few different stops in Yreka. There are several daily services on weekdays along the I-5 corridor to Weed, Mt Shasta, McCloud and Dunsmuir. Other buses depart daily for Fort Jones (25 minutes), Greenview (35 minutes) and Etna (45 minutes) in the Scott Valley. On Monday and Friday only, buses go out to Klamath River (40 minutes) and Happy Camp (two hours).

Gold Country & Central Valley

Includes »

Best Places to Eat

» Noriega Hotel (p352)

» Dusty Buns Bistro Bus
(p348)

» Treats (p309)

» V Restaurant (p322)

» Mulvaney's Building and
Loan (p332)

Best Places to Stay

» Padre Hotel (p351)

» Citizen Hotel (p330)

» Outside Inn (p308)

» Lure Resort (p311)

» Camino Hotel (p317)

Why Go?

Gold Country is where it all began – the drowsy hill towns and oak-lined byways of today's quiet road trip belie the wild chaos of California's founding. Shortly after a sparkle caught James Marshall's eye in 1848, the rush for gold brought a stampede of 300,000 '49ers to the Sierra foothills. Today, fading historical markers tell tales of bloodlust and banditry, while the surviving boom towns survive on antiques, ice cream, wine and gold-rush ephemera. This 400-mile-long green strip of the Central Valley, in the center of the state, is the most agriculturally productive region in America. Many travelers hardly hit the brakes while rushing between California's coasts and mountains, or cities of the south and the Bay Area, but those who slow down long enough are rewarded with fresh farm stands, twangy country music traditions and, naturally, wine.

When to Go
Sacramento

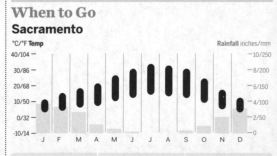

Jul When temperatures are scorching, plunge into a Gold Country swimming hole.

Oct & Nov The trees explode with color and fall fairs happen throughout the region.

Apr–Jun The Central Valley's spring crops bring food festivals galore.

NEVADA COUNTY & NORTHERN GOLD COUNTRY

The '49ers hit it big in Nevada County – the richest score of the mother lode – and the wealth built one of the most picturesque and well-preserved boomtowns, Nevada City. Get out of town and you'll find lovely, remote wilderness areas, a clutch of historic parks and rusting relics of the long-gone miners. This is also a magnet for adrenaline junkies looking to fly down single-track mountain-bike lanes or plunge into icy swimming holes that are remote enough for skinny-dipping.

Auburn

Look for the big man: a 45-ton effigy of pioneer gold panner Claude announces the visitor's arrival in Gold Country. The hallmarks of Gold Country – ice-cream shops, strollable historic districts, antiques, curious historical sites – are all here. A major stop on the Central Pacific's transcontinental route, Auburn is busy with trains on the Union Pacific's main line to the east and a popular stop for those rushing along I-80 between the Bay Area and Lake Tahoe. You'll have to venture along Hwy 49 for a deeper taste of Gold Country, but those who want just a sample will be rewarded in this accessible town.

Sights & Activities

The fact that Auburn has minted itself the 'Endurance Sport Capital of the World' will give you a sense of how good the area is for cycling, trail running and other gut-busting athletics. See www.auburnendurancecapital.com for a complete list of events.

FREE **Placer County Museum** MUSEUM
(101 Maple St; admission free; ⊙10am-4pm) The 1st floor of the monumental 1898 **Placer County Courthouse** (⊙8am-5pm) has Native American artifacts and displays of Auburn's transportation heritage. It's the easiest museum to visit and gives a good overview of area history; there's also the impressive bling of the museum's gold collection.

Bernhard Museum Complex MUSEUM
(☎530-888-6891; 291 Auburn-Folsom Rd; donation requested; ⊙11am-4pm Tue-Sun) At the south end of High St, this museum was built in 1851 as the Traveler's Rest Hotel. The museum has displays depicting the typical life of a 19th-century farm family, and at times volunteers in period garb ham it up.

FREE **Gold Country Museum** MUSEUM
(1273 High St; admission free; ⊙11am-4pm Tue-Sun) Those with a taste for exploring history should hit this museum, which is toward the back of the fairgrounds, where you can walk through a reproduced mining tunnel and try panning for gold for a small fee.

Sleeping & Eating

Upper Lincoln Way toward the Chamber of Commerce has several restaurants popular with locals, but there's plenty of sunny outdoor eating right off the highway. For a place to sleep look to the highway exits where there's every brand of chain hotel.

Auburn Ale House BREWPUB $
(www.auburnalehouse.com; 289 Washington; mains $7-17; ⊙11am-10pm Sun-Thu, to 11pm weekends) One of those rare brewpubs that offers excellent craft beer *and* excellent food; patrons dig into burgers, sweet potato fries, 'adult mac and cheese' and sweet-and-savory salads (the walnut gorgonzola is delicious). The beer sampler is a great deal, and a must for beer fans, as Auburn brings home tons of festival medals for their spread of ales and pilsners. Hand over the keys before trying too many of the PU240 Imperial IPAs, its flavor profile sporting a 'weapons grade hop bomb.'

Ikedas BURGERS, GROCERY $
(www.ikedas.com; 13500 Lincoln Way; burgers $9-12; ⊙8am-7pm, to 8pm weekends) If you're cruising this part of the state without time to explore, the best pit stop is off I-80 at exit 121. This place feeds Tahoe-bound travelers

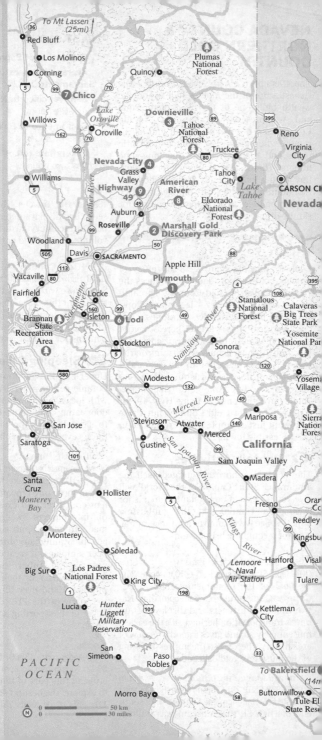

Gold Country & Central Valley Highlights

1 Touring Amador County's unpretentious vineyards in the hills around **Plymouth** (p317)

2 Discovering the birthplace of California at **Marshall Gold Discovery Park** (p314)

3 Rumbling down California's best single-track trails at **Downieville** (p311)

4 Wandering the historic streets of Gold Country's gem, **Nevada City** (p308)

5 Honkytonking with **Bakersfield's** (p350) twanging musical icons

6 Uncorking **Lodi's** (p343) emerging wine scene

7 Tubing through the icy rivers of **Chico** (p338)

8 Running the white-water of the **American River** (p305)

9 Hunting for antiques and ice cream on **Highway 49**

thick, grass-fed burgers, homemade pies and snacks. The seasonal fresh peach shake is deliriously good.

Awful Annie's
AMERICAN $

(www.awfulannies.com; 321 Spring St; mains $9-15; ☻8am-3pm) Huge breakfast scrambles and a sunny patio keep Annie's packed. Worth the wait.

Katrina's
BREAKFAST $

(www.katrinascafe.com; 456 Grass Valley Hwy; mains $10-15; ☻7am-2:30pm Wed-Sat, to 1:30pm Sun) Lemon pancakes, Tuscan scrambles and a homey atmosphere; this place is legit.

Tsuda's Old Town Eatery
DELI $

(www.tsudas.com; 103 Sacramento; mains $8; ☻7am-6pm Mon-Thu, to 9pm Fri & Sat, 8am-6pm Sun; ☻☻☻☻) An organic deli with something for every dietary consideration (gluten-free, veg, etc), an excellent kid's menu (with organic fruit leather) and a brick patio welcoming to dogs.

ⓘ Information

Auburn Area Chamber of Commerce (☎530-885-5616; www.auburnchamber.net; 601 Lincoln Way; ☻9am-5pm Mon-Fri) Housed in the old Southern Pacific railroad depot at the north end of Lincoln Way, it has lots of useful local info. There's a nearby monument to the first transcontinental railroad.

California Welcome Center (☎530-887-2111; www.visitplacer.com; 13411 Lincoln Way; ☻9am-4:30pm Mon-Sat, 11am-4pm Sun) Right off I-80 at the Foresthill exit; there is oodles of information for those entering the state from the east.

ⓘ Getting There & Away

BUS **Amtrak** (☎800-872-7245; www.amtrak.com) runs several buses a day linking Auburn with Sacramento ($15, one hour) where you can connect to Bay Area and Central Valley trains. There are usually two buses daily east to Reno (2½ hours).

The **Gold Country Stage** (www.goldcountrystage.com) links Auburn with Grass Valley and Nevada City several times a day. Weekends have a slightly more limited schedule. Adult fare between the cities is $3 and the trip takes about 50 minutes.

TRAIN Amtrak's *California Zephyr* stops in Auburn on its daily runs between the Bay Area and Chicago via Reno and Denver. The trip between Auburn and San Francisco takes just over three hours and costs $32.

Auburn State Recreation Area

The deep gorges of this popular **park** (☎530-885-4527; www.parks.ca.gov, day use fee for some areas $10) were cut by the rushing waters of the North and Middle Forks of the **American River**, which converge below a bridge on Hwy 49, about 4 miles south of Auburn. In the early spring, when waters are high, this is immensely popular for white-water rafting, as the rivers offer a range of difficulty levels. Later in the summer the waters get a bit quieter, perfect for sunning and swimming. Numerous trails in the area are shared by hikers, mountain-bikers and horses.

The best tour of the area is offered by **All-Outdoors California Whitewater Rafting** (☎800-247-2387; www.aorafting.com), a family-run outfit that was the first on the remote Middle Fork. It is one of the few to lead adventuresome two-day wilderness ventures that break up the trip with waterfall-lined hikes and historically significant sightseeing on the canyon. On the two-day trips they haul your camping gear and feed you. The burrito lunch might be worth the trip alone. All-Outdoors also operates excellent tours on other rivers throughout the area.

One of the most popular trails is the **Western States Trail**, which connects Auburn State Recreation Area to Folsom Lake State Recreation Area and Folsom Lake. It's the site of the **Western States 100 Mile Endurance Run** (www.ws100.com). For more information check the website.

The **Quarry Trail** takes a level path from Hwy 49, just south of the bridge, along the Middle Fork of the American. Several side trails go down to the river.

WHAT THE...?

Floating along any of the rivers in Gold Country, you're bound to pass someone still trying to get rich on the gold of the Sierras using a suction dredge – a floating contraption that sucks up rocks from the river bed and sorts the gold. Even though the dredging season is short and tightly regulated by the state, prospecting pays off – locals claim to average around $50,000 a year.

Gold Country

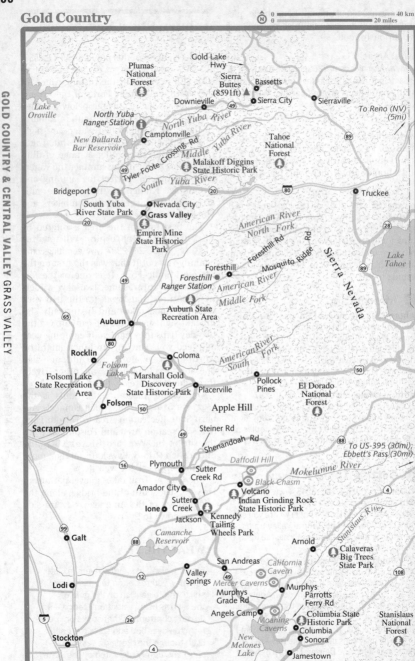

0   40 km
0   20 miles

Plumas
National
Forest

Gold Lake
Hwy

Sierra
Buttes
(8591ft)
Bassetts

Downieville
Sierra City
Sierraville

To Reno (NV)
(5mi)

Lake
Oroville

North Yuba
Ranger Station

North Yuba River

Camptonville

New Bullards
Bar Reservoir

Middle Yuba River

Tahoe
National
Forest

Tyler Foote Crossing Rd

Malakoff Diggins
State Historic Park

South Yuba River

Bridgeport

Truckee

South Yuba
River State Park

Nevada City

Grass Valley

American River
North Fork

Lake
Tahoe

Empire Mine
State Historic
Park

Foresthill Rd

Mosquito Ridge Rd

Foresthill

Foresthill
Ranger Station

American River
Middle Fork

Sierra Nevada

Auburn State
Recreation Area

Auburn

Rocklin

American River
South Fork

Coloma

Folsom
Lake

Folsom Lake
State Recreation
Area

Marshall Gold
Discovery
State Historic Park

Placerville

Pollock
Pines

El Dorado
National
Forest

Folsom

Apple Hill

Sacramento

Steiner Rd

Shenandoah Rd

To US-395 (30mi);
Ebbett's Pass (30mi)

Plymouth

Daffodil Hill

Mokelumne River

Sutter
Creek Rd

Black Chasm

Amador City

Volcano

Indian Grinding Rock
State Historic Park

Sutter
Creek

Ione

Jackson

Kennedy
Tailing
Wheels Park

Camanche
Reservoir

Galt

Arnold

Stanislaus River

Calaveras
Big Trees
State Park

Lodi

Valley
Springs

San Andreas

California
Cavern

Mercer Caverns

Murphys
Grade Rd

Murphys

Parrotts
Ferry Rd

Stockton

Angels Camp

Moaning
Caverns

Columbia State
Historic Park

Columbia

Sonora

Stanislaus
National
Forest

New
Melones
Lake

Jamestown

To Manteca
(5mi)

Hwy 120

To Yosemite
National Park
(41mi)

For camping, there are some basic sites on a sweeping bend of the Middle Fork at the blackberry-dotted Ford's Bar. It's accessible only by a 2-mile hike or half-day raft. A hike begins at the end of Ruck-A-Chucky Rd. Permits to this and other government-operated camping areas are available from Foresthill Ranger Station (☎530-367 2224; www.fs.fed.us; 22830 Foresthill Rd, Foresthill) for $25 to $35.

Grass Valley

From the margins, Grass Valley, with its Anywhere, USA, chain stores, is the ugly utilitarian sister to Nevada City – where people come to buy groceries, get oil changes and groom their pets. But if you get under the surface by driving to the historic business district, the little gem at the center of the sprawl is another rich Gold Country downtown.

The mines in Grass Valley – some of the first shaft mines in the state – were hugely profitable, and the first to flaunt the benefits of lode-mining techniques. Nearly 400 miles of shaft made up the Empire Mine, now a state park.

Grass Valley's main thoroughfares of Mill St and W Main St are the heart of the historic district, which boasts an old-time movie theater, cafes and bars. E Main St goes north to shopping centers and mini-malls, continuing north into Nevada City, while S Auburn St divides E and W Main St.

On Thursday nights in July and August, Mill St is closed to car traffic with farmstead food, arts and crafts and music.

◉ Sights & Activities

Empire Mine State Historic Park PARK
(www.empiremine.org; 10791 E Empire St; adult/child $7/3; ⊙10am-5pm) Situated atop miles of mine shafts is Gold Country's best-preserved gold quartz–mining operation – worth a solid half-day's exploration. From 1850 to 1956 the mines produced six million ounces of gold (about four billion modern dollars' worth). The mine yard is littered with massive mining equipment and buildings constructed from waste rock. There are docent-led tours and sunny hiking. There are plans to open the main mine shaft, next to the largest head frame (a structure that held the pulleys, which once hoisted the plunder up from underground) in the yard, for subterranean tours.

Around the side of the visitors center you'll find stately buildings that belonged to the Bourne family, who ran the mine. They did it in style too, apparent in the elegant country club, English manor home, gardener's house and rose garden. Take a guided tour; check the visitors center for schedules.

Hiking trails begin near the old stamp mill in the mine yard and pass abandoned mines and equipment. A trail map is available at the visitors center. The park is 2 miles east of Grass Valley via the Empire St exit off Hwy 49.

🛏 Sleeping & Eating

The quality of food here is proportional to how much you hunt for it: there are several good eateries and bars around downtown, and every imaginable chain lurks among the strip malls by the highway.

Holbrooke Hotel HISTORIC HOTEL $$
(☎530-273-1353; www.holbrooke.com, 212 W Main St; r $119-239; ✴@⑤) The register in this 1862 hotel boasts the signatures of Mark Twain and Ulysses Grant and well-appointed rooms are named after other presidents who slept there. The bistro (mains $10 to $20) serves casual fare in the ornate dining room or on the shaded patio. The bar has tables overlooking the Main St action.

Cousin Jack Pasties PASTIES $
(100 S Auburn St; meals $4-10; ⊙11am-7pm) Cousin Jack and his kin have been serving flaky pasties – a meat-and-potato- stuffed pastry beloved by Cornish miners – for five generations. The pies – pesto lamb, steak and ale and several vegetarian options – are all made from local meat and vegetables.

Tofanelli's ITALIAN $$
(www.tofanellis.com; 302 W Main St; meals $13-26) Hugely popular with those locals in the know, this creative restaurant has everything from salads to hearty steaks with seasonal accents like summer squash ravioli. Portions are burly, prices are small and the patio is a treat.

Dorado Chocolates SWEETS $
(104 E Main St; snacks $3; ⊙10am-5pm Tue-Sat) Ken Kossoudji's handmade chocolates are made to savor slowly, and when the snow falls the hot chocolate is divine.

GOLD COUNTRY & CENTRAL VALLEY NEVADA CITY

ℹ Information

Grass Valley/Nevada County Chamber of Commerce (☏530-272-8315; www.grassvalleychamber.com; 248 Mill St; ◷9am-5pm Mon-Fri) In the former Mill St home of enchantress Lola Montez. It has some very good maps and brochures. Be sure to pick up a copy of the historic walking-tour brochure.

ℹ Getting There & Away

Gold Country Stage bus service (www.goldcountrystage.com) Links Nevada City with Grass Valley (adult $1.50, adult one-day pass $4.50, 30 minutes) at least hourly from 7am to 5pm. It also offers information about using the bus for sightseeing in gold country on its website and day passes to all points between Auburn and Nevada City for $7.50.

Nevada City

Maybe it's all those prayer flags, or new-agey Zen goodies that clutter the sandalwood-scented gift shops, but, like a yogi in the lotus position, Nevada City is all about *balance*. The city has the requisite Victorian Gold Rush tourist attractions – an elegantly restored town center, an informative local history museum, girlishly decorated bed-and-breakfasts by the dozen – and a proud contemporary identity, with a small but thriving independent arts and culture scene. Perch on a bar stool in any of the area watering holes and the person next to you might just as easily be a crusty old-timer, a sun-pink tourist or a mystical folk artist.

Spending a couple days here, you'll soak up distinctly rural NorCal culture – with theater companies, alternative film houses, bookstores and live music performances almost every night. Nevada City's streets, best navigated on foot, are jammed with pedestrians by day, especially in the summer. Broad St is the main drag, reached by the Broad St exit off Hwy 49/20. Just north of town on Hwy 49, look for dusty pull-outs at the trailheads to icy swimming holes. In December the blankets of snow and twinkling lights are something out of a storybook.

◉ Sights & Activities

The main attraction is the town itself – its restored buildings, all brick and wrought-iron trimmings, wear their history proudly. There are curious (if pricey) boutiques, galleries and places for food and drink everywhere, all with exhaustive information about the town's history.

Firehouse Museum   MUSEUM
(www.nevadacountyhistory.org; 214 Main St; admission by donation; ◷1-4pm Tue-Sun, varies seasonally) History buffs flock to this museum. Run by the Nevada Country Historical Society, the museum's shady interior smells of old wood and features an impressive collection from Chinese laborers who often built but seldom profited from the mines.

Nevada City Winery   WINERY
(☏530-265-9463; 321 Spring St; ◷11am-5pm Mon-Sat, noon-5pm Sun) This popular winery bottles two regional varietals, syrah and zinfandel, which you can savor while overlooking the production facility. It's a good place to get information on touring the surrounding wine region.

🛏 Sleeping

During weekends, Nevada City fills up with urban refugees who inevitably weigh themselves down with real-estate brochures. There are frilly B&Bs everywhere, but the cheapest options are the National Forest campgrounds, just outside of town in any direction.

TOP CHOICE Broad Street Inn   B&B $$
(☏530-265-2239; www.broadstreetinn.com; 517 E Broad St, Nevada City; r $110-120; ✳🖧) It seems as if there are a million bed-and-breakfasts in town, but this six-room inn is a favorite because it keeps it simple. (No weird old dolls, no yellowing lace doilies.) The rooms are modern, brightly furnished and elegant. The delicious breakfast adds to the amazing value.

Outside Inn   MOTEL $
(☏530-265-2233; www.outsideinn.com; 575 E Broad St, Nevada City; r $75-150; ✳🖧🐾) The best option for active explorers, this is an exceptionally friendly and fun motel, with 14 individually named and decorated rooms and a staff that loves the outdoors. Some rooms have a patio overlooking a small creek; all of them have nice quilts, access to BBQ grills and excellent information about hiking in the area. It's a 10-minute walk from downtown.

Red Castle Historic Lodgings   B&B $$
(☏530-265-5135; www.redcastleinn.com; 109 Prospect St; r $120-185; ✳🖧) In a city chock-

full of B&Bs this is the granddaddy of them all – the first in Nevada City and one of the oldest in the state. The historic red-brick building combines a Gothic Revival exterior with a well-appointed Victorian interior. Every detail is faithful to 19th century Victorian – even the selection of breakfast foods, and elevated beds. It sits atop a hill a short walk from town and is surrounded by shady walking paths. The Garden Room is the most private.

Northern Queen Inn   MOTEL, CABINS **$$**
(📞530-265-3720;   www.northernqueeninn.com; 400 Railroad Ave; r $99-154; ✻@🛜🐾) With a wide range of options – from basic queen rooms to two-story chalets – this hotel might be a bit dated, but the cabins, with small kitchens, are a good deal for small groups and families.

✕ Eating

TOP CHOICE **Treats**   ICE CREAM **$**
(www.treatsnevadacity.com; 110 York St; meals $7-21; ⊙noon-8pm Sun-Thu, to 10pm Fri & Sat) It's a crowded contest for Gold Country's best ice-cream shop, but this cute little place – the brilliant second career of avuncular scooper Bob Wright – wins in a walk. The organic flavors are sourced from ripe local fruit, highlights are the rhubarb strawberry, rose and salt caramel but the natural mint and dark chocolate chip is like reinventing the wheel.

Sopa Thai   THAI **$$**
(www.sopathai.net; 312 Commercial St; meals $7-21; ⊙11am-3pm & 5-9:30pm Mon-Fri) Mango red curry, steamed mussels and springs rolls are all excellent at Nevada City's best and most popular Thai restaurant. The interior is furnished with lovely imported carvings and silk, and the patio seating in back is a busy scene midday. The $10 lunch special is a great value.

Café Mekka   CAFE **$**
(237 Commercial St; meals $5-15; ⊙7am-10pm Mon-Thu, to midnight Fri, 8am-midnight Sat, to 10pm Sun) Decorated in a style best described as 'whorehouse baroque,' this charmer serves coffee and beer through the day, along with sandwiches, pizzas and famous desserts. Listen for live folk music on some nights.

Ike's Quarter Cafe   CAJUN, BREAKFAST **$$**
(www.ikesquartercafe.com; 401 Commercial St; meals $8-19; ⊙8am-8pm Wed-Mon) Ike's serves

splendid Cajun fare with a sassy charm that leaves the blue hairs pink-cheeked. The creative menu features banana and pecan pancakes, jambalaya and more. It's an excellent place to get the 'Hangtown Fry' – a cornmeal crusted mess of oysters, bacon, caramelized onions and spinach. This is right out of the Garden District in New Orleans.

📷 New Moon Café   CALIFORNIAN **$$**
(www.thenewmooncafe.com; 230 York St; mains $13-20; ⊙11:30-2pm Tue-Fri & 5-8:30pm Tue-Sun) Pure elegance, Peter Selaya's regularly changing menu keeps an organic, local bent. If you visit during the peak of the summer keep to the aquatic theme by trying the wild, line-caught fish or seared duck, prepared with a French-Asian fusion.

☆ Entertainment

There's always something going on in Nevada City – this little village has a vibrant scene for the arts. The Arts section of the *Union* newspaper comes out on Thursday, with a listing of what's going on around the area.

Nevada Theater   THEATRE, CINEMA
(www.nevadatheatre.com; 401 Broad St) This brick fortress is one of California's first theaters (1865) and has welcomed the likes of Jack London and Mark Twain to its stage. Now it's used for productions of the top-notch **Foothill Theater Company** (📞530-265-8587; www.foothilltheatre.com), as well as off-beat movie screenings.

Magic Theatre   CINEMA
(www.themagictheatrenc.com; 107 Argall Way) This fantastic theater screens a matchless line-up of unusual films and is about a mile south of downtown Nevada City. Enjoy bowls of fresh popcorn, coffee in real mugs and hot brownies at intermission.

ⓘ Information

Nevada City Chamber of Commerce (📞530-265-2692, 800-655-6569; www.nevadacitychamber.com; 132 Main St; ⊙9am-5pm Mon-Sat, 11am-4pm Sun) Ideally located at the east end of Commercial St, this has two welcome comforts for the traveler – an immaculate public toilet and expert local advice.

Tahoe National Forest USFS Headquarters (📞530-265-4531; 631 Coyote St; ⊙8am-5pm Mon-Sat) A useful and friendly resource for trail and campground information, covering the area from here to Lake Tahoe. It sells topographical maps.

ⓘ Getting There & Away

Gold Country Stage bus service (☏530-477-0103; www.goldcountrystage.com) Links Nevada City with Grass Valley at least hourly from 7am to 5pm. Serves the Amtrak station in Auburn several times a day ($1.50).

South Yuba River State Park

Icy swimming holes are fed by rushing rapids in this 11,000-acre plot along the South Yuba River, a combination of state land and acres of federal jurisdiction. This area has a growing network of trails, including the wheelchair-accessible **Independence Trail**, which starts from the south side of the South Yuba River bridge on Hwy 49 and continues for a couple miles with canyon overlooks. June is the best time, when the rivers are rushing and the wildflowers are out.

The longest, single-span, wood-truss **covered bridge** in the USA, all 251ft of it, crosses the South Yuba River at Bridgeport (not to be confused with the Eastern Sierra town of the same name). It's easy to spend a whole day hiking and swimming in this wild area, where crowds can be left behind with little effort. The **Buttermilk Bend Trail** skirts the South Yuba for 1.4 miles, offering river access and wonderful wildflower-viewing around April.

Maps and park information are available from the **state park headquarters** (☏530-432-2546; ⊙11am-4pm) in Bridgeport, or from the Tahoe National Forest USFS (United States Forest Service) Headquarters in Nevada City. At press time, the future of this state park was uncertain due to budget cuts, though it is under the watchful protection the **South Yuba Citizen's league** (www.yubariver.org), a great source for information.

Malakoff Diggins State Historic Park

A bizarre testament to the mechanical determination of the gold hunt, **Malakoff Diggins** (admission per car $8; ⊙sunrise-sunset) is a place to get lost on fern-lined trails and take in the surprising beauty of the recovering landscape. The red stratified cliffs and small mountains of tailings are curiously beautiful, and all part of the deeply scarred landscape left behind from hydraulic mining.

Water cannons designed specifically for hydraulic mining cut a 200ft canyon through ancient bedrock during the 1850s to reach gold veins. Rubble washed down into the Yuba River and this often-toxic waste was filled with heavy metals, many of which remain in the Sacramento Valley floor. By the 1860s, 20ft mud glaciers blocked rivers and caused severe flooding during the snowmelt. After a year of heated courtroom (and bar-room) debate between farmers and miners, the 1884 court case (known as the Sawyer Decision) makes a profoundly timely statement today: a destructive, profitable industry can be stopped for public good. No longer able to reap profits from blasting down the hills with hydraulic cannons, the fortune-hunting game was over. North Bloomfield, the mining community at the center of Malakoff's operation, packed up the shingle shortly after, and what remains is an eerily quiet ghost town within the park's limits.

The **Park Headquarters and Museum** (☏530-265-2740; admission per vehicle $6; ⊙9am-5pm) offers tours at 1:30pm daily and the chance to see some impressive gold nuggets. The one-mile **Digging Loop Trail** is the quick way to get a glimpse of the scarred moonscape.

You can reach Tyler Foote Crossing Rd, the turnoff for the park, 10 miles northwest of Nevada City on Hwy 49. At press time the future of the park was uncertain due to budget issues.

North Yuba River

The northernmost segment of Hwy 49 follows the North Yuba River through some stunning, remote parts of the Sierra Nevada, known for a tough, short season of white water and great fly-fishing. An entire lifetime could hardly cover the trails that are crossed every season by hikers, mountain-bikers and skiers. Even in summer, snow is likely at the highest elevations and many places have roaring fireplaces year-round.

The best source of trail and camping information is the **North Yuba Ranger Station** (☏530-288-3231; 15924 Hwy 49; ⊙8am-4:30pm Mon-Fri) in Camptonville.

DOWNIEVILLE

Downieville is the biggest town in the remote Sierra County, located at the junction of the North Yuba and Downie Rivers. With a reputation that quietly rivals Moab, Utah (before it got big), the town is the premiere place for mountain-bike riding in the state, and a staging area for true wilderness adventures.

Like most Gold Rush survivors it wasn't always fun and games: its first justice of the peace was the local barkeep, and the only woman to ever hang in California did so from Downieville's gallows in what was an allegedly racially motivated punishment. (It's a town that seems to have a grisly affection for frontier justice; a reconstructed gallows is across the river, by the civic building.)

◎ Sights & Activities

Brave souls bomb down the **Downieville Downhill**, a molar-rattling 5000ft vertical descent, which is rated among the best mountain-bike routes in the USA. It hosts the annual Downieville Classic, drawing world-class athletes. Slightly more casual riders get shuttled to the top, which can be arranged from outfitters in town.

Yuba Expeditions (☑530-289-3010; www.yubaexpeditions.com; 105 Commercial St; bike rentals $65-85; ⊙9am-5pm Thu-Mon) is a center of the summer trail-bike scene. The other option for a bike rental and shuttle is **Downieville Outfitters** (☑530-289-3010; www.downievilleoutfitters.com; 114 Main St; bike rentals from $65, shuttles $20; ⊙shuttles 10am, 2pm weekdays, every 2hr weekends).

Favorite hikes in the area include the **Chimney Rock Trail** and **Empire Creek Trail**. Both are a bit tricky to reach, so pick up a trail guide at the North Yuba Ranger Station or the USFS Headquarters in Nevada City.

⌂ Sleeping

Downtown Downieville has several places to stay where the rustle of the rapids lull weary bikers to sleep. The town's charming streets boast several vintage bars and eateries, some with river views.

Lure Resort   CABINS, CAMPGROUND **$$**
(☑800-671-4084; www.lureresort.com; camping cabins $75, housekeeping cabins $135-260; ☎⧌☒) The best option if you want to come with biking buddies or a family, this tidy place has modern log cabins along a sublime stretch of river, and big green lawns where kids can play games and adults can lounge in the sun. The spare camping cabins, which have campfire rings instead of a kitchen and a shared bathroom, are a basic, affordable option.

Riverside Inn   INN **$**
(☑530-289-1000; www.downieville.us; 206 Commercial St; r $97-120; ☎☒) Has 11 stove-warmed rooms that are the first choice in Downieville. Some rooms have balconies that overlook the river and all have a secluded, rustic charm, with warm comforters and a homey breakfast area. Riverside rooms are best; you can open the screen door and listen to the water run by. They also have excellent information about hiking and biking in the area, and in winter they lend snowshoes.

Tahoe National Forest campgrounds   CAMPGROUND **$**
(☑530-993-1410; tent sites $21) Just west of town Hwy 49 has a number of beautiful sites at this campground. Most have vault toilets, running water and unreserved sites along the Yuba River. Of these, the prettiest is **Fiddlecreek**, which has tent-only sites right on the river.

Carriage House Inn   INN **$**
(☑530-289-3573; www.downievillecarriagehouse.com; 110 Commercial St; r $55-100; ☎☒) This homelike inn has country-style charms, which include rockers and river views. Some have private baths and TVs.

Sierra Shangri-La   CABINS, HOTEL **$$**
(☑530-289-3455; www.sierrashangrila.com; r $115, cabins $160-260) Near Lure and also a secluded option, this is 3 miles east of Downieville on Hwy 49. In July and August the cabins are usually booked with standing reservations, but rooms – each with a balcony overlooking the river – are often available.

SIERRA CITY & THE LAKES BASIN

Sierra City is the primary supply station for people headed to the **Sierra Buttes**, a rugged, rocky shock of mountains that are probably the closest thing to the Alps you'll find in California without hoisting a backpack. It's also the last supply point for people headed into the remote and lovely fishing paradise of the Lakes Basin. There's information about lodging and area activities at www.sierracity.com.

◎ Sights & Activities

There's a vast network of trails, including access to the famous **Pacific Crest Trail**, which is ideal for backpacking and casual hikes. The **Sierra Country Store** (☑530-862-1181; Hwy 49; ⊙9am-7pm; ☎) is about the only consistently open place in town, and it welcomes Pacific Crest Trail refugees with its laundromat and deli.

To reach the Buttes, and many lakes and streams nearby, take Gold Lake Hwy north from Hwy 49 at Bassetts, 9 miles northeast of Sierra City. An excellent hiking trail leads 1.5 miles to **Haskell Peak** (8107ft), where you can see from the Sierra Buttes right to Mt Shasta and beyond. To reach the trailhead, turn right from Gold Lake Hwy at Haskell Peak Rd (Forest Rd 9) and follow it for 8.5 miles.

🛏 Sleeping

One of several USFS campgrounds recommended for camping north of Hwy 49 is **Salmon Creek campground** (☑530-993-1410; tent & RV sites without hook-ups $21), 2 miles north of Bassetts on Gold Lake Hwy. It has vault toilets, running water and first-come, first-served sites for RVs and tents, but no hook-ups. This site has the most dramatic view of the Sierra Buttes. Sites 16 and 20 are separated from the rest by a creek.

Going east from Sierra City along Hwy 49 are Wild Plum, Sierra, Chapman Creek and Yuba Pass **USFS campgrounds** (☑530-993-1410; tent sites $21). They have vault water and running water (Sierra has river water only), and first-come, first-served sites. Wild Plum (47 sites) is the most scenic.

In the heart of Sierra City, the small **Buttes Resort** (☑530-862-1170, 800-991-1170; www.sierracity.com; 230 Main St; cabins $75-145) occupies a lovely spot overlooking the river and is a favorite with hikers looking to recharge. Most cabins have a private deck and barbecue, some have full kitchens. You can borrow bikes and games from the kind owners.

🍴 Eating

Red Moose Cafe CAFE $
(☑530-862-1502; 224 Main St; mains $6-12; ⊙breakfast & lunch Tue-Sun) A local institution that's been serving rib-sticking fare since 1940. Anything with 'Red Moose' in

---

GOING FOR THE GOLD

California's Gold Rush started in 1848 when James Marshall was inspecting the fatefully sited lumber mill he was building for John Sutter near present-day Coloma. He saw a sparkle in the mill's tailrace water and pulled out a nugget 'roughly half the size of a pea.' Marshall hightailed it to Sacramento and consulted Sutter, who tested the gold by methods described in an encyclopedia. But Sutter wanted to finish his mill so made a deal with his laborers, allowing them to keep gold they found in their spare time if they kept working. Before long, word of the find leaked out.

Sam Brannan, for example, went to Coloma to investigate the rumors just a few months after Marshall's find. After finding 6oz of gold in one afternoon, he returned to San Francisco and paraded through the streets proclaiming, 'There's gold in the Sierra foothills!' Convinced there was money to be made, he bought every piece of mining equipment in the area – from handkerchiefs to shovels. When gold seekers needed equipment for their adventure, Brannan sold them goods at a 100% markup and was a rich man by the time the first folks hit the foothills.

By the time the mill's construction was finished in the spring of 1848, gold seekers had begun to arrive, the first wave coming from San Francisco. Only a few months later, San Francisco was almost depleted of able-bodied men, while towns near the 'diggins,' as the mines were called, swelled with thousands of people. News of the Gold Rush spread around the world, and by 1849 more than 60,000 people (who became widely known as '49ers) rushed to California. They were looking for the mother lode: the mythical big deposit that miners believed was the source of all the gold found in the streams and riverbeds.

Most prospectors didn't stick around after the initial diggings petered out; gold-extraction processes became increasingly complex and invasive. It culminated in the practice of hydraulic mining, by which miners drained lakes and rivers to power their water cannons and blast away entire hillsides (see Malakoff Diggins State Historic Park, p310). People downstream who were inundated by the muck sued, and eventually the environmental cost was too great to justify staying in business.

the name comes with chili, be it omelet or burger. The scent of their fresh cinnamon wafts down Main St every morning.

Big Springs Gardens BRUNCH $$$
(☎530-862-1333; www.bigspringsgardens.com; 32163 Hwy 49; mains incl price of admission $37-39; ⊙buffet meals at noon & 6pm Fri, 1pm Sat, 10:30pm Sun, reservations required) Offers the perfect brunch of berries from the surrounding hills and trout fresh from the pond, served in an open-air dining area. The hiking trails pass the 'Wild Garden,' a waterfall-laced natural area with views well worth the heart-pumping hike.

EL DORADO & AMADOR COUNTIES

In the heart of the pine- and oak-covered Sierra foothills, this is where gold was first discovered – Spanish-speaking settlers appropriately named El Dorado County after a mythical city of riches. Today, SUVs en route to South Lake Tahoe pull off Hwy 50 to find a rolling hillside dotted with the historic towns, sun-soaked terraces and rocky soil of one of California's underdog wine regions. If you make the stop, don't leave without toasting a glass of regional zinfandel, which, like the locals, is packed with earthy attitude and regional character. It's also worth the detour to pause a few minutes at the shore where a glint of gold caught James Marshall's eye and gave birth to the Golden State.

Traveling through much of the central part of Gold Country requires a car, as the public transportation is unreliable between the towns. The good news? This stretch of Hwy 49 makes an excellent road trip.

Coloma

Coloma is the nearest town to Sutter's Mill (the site of California's first gold discovery) and Marshall Gold Discovery State Historic Park (p314). There's little here – just a ramshackle strip of wooden historic buildings and an obligatory blacksmith shop – but it is also a great launching pad for **rafting** operations. The **South Fork of the American River** gets the most traffic, since it features exciting rapids, but is still manageable for beginners. Adrenaline junkies who have never rafted before should try the Middle Fork (p305).

Half-day rafting trips usually begin at the Chile Bar and end close to the state park. Full-day trips put in at the Coloma Bridge and take out at Salmon Falls, near Folsom Lake. The half-day options start in Class III rapids and are action-packed (full-day trips start out slowly, then build up to Class III as a climax). Full-day trips include a lavish lunch. The season usually runs from May to mid-October, depending on snow melts. Prices are generally lower on weekdays.

Whitewater Connection (☎530-622-6446, 800-336-7238; www.whitewaterconnection. com; half-day trips $89-109, full-day trips $109-129) is typical of the area's operators, with knowledgeable guides and excellent food.

Don't want to get wet? Watch people navigate the **Trouble Maker Rapids**, upstream from the bridge next to Sutter's Mill in the state park.

🛏 Sleeping & Eating

If you're looking for a basic hotel and don't mind the blandness of a highway motel, Auburn is a better bet.

Coloma Country Inn B&B $$
(☎530-622-6919; www.colomacountryinn.com; 345 High St; r $125-195; @🛜🏊) The four-room B&B is situated in a historic farmhouse and the hosts offer good advice about area rafting. The rooms are bright and lovely, as are the hosts. If you're not in a rush, try the quiet cottage suite, where you can spend an afternoon floating on the pond.

American River Resort CAMPGROUND, CABINS $
(☎530-622-6700; www.americanriverresort.com; 6019 New River Rd; tent & RV sites $30-35, cabins $170-280; 🏊🐾) Only a quarter mile off Hwy 49, just south of the state park. The site is more cushy than most other area campgrounds: there's a restaurant and bar, a playground, a pond and farm animals. The sites are basic, but some are right on the river. The most spacious and pretty oak-shaded sites are 14 to 29.

Coloma Resort CAMPGROUND, CABINS $
(☎530-621-2267; www.colomaresort.com; 6921 Mt Murphy Rd; tent & RV sites $45-49, tent cabins & on-site RV rentals $125-165; 🛜🏊🐾) Another long-established riverside campground, this is better for RVs. It comes with a full range of activities, playgrounds and wireless internet. With lots of family activities, this has the feel of a summer camp.

Coloma Club Cafe & Saloon   BAR & GRILL $
(☎530-626-6390; 7171 Hwy 49; ⊘restaurant 6:30am-9pm, bar 10am-2am) North of Marshall SHP, the patio at this rowdy hangout comes alive with guides and river rats when the water is high.

Marshall Gold Discovery State Historic Park

Compared to the stampede of gun-toting, hill-blasting, hell-raising settlers that populate tall tales along Hwy 49, the **Marshall Gold Discovery State Historic Park** (admission per car $5; ⊘8am-7pm; 🛜) is a place of bucolic tranquillity, with two tragic heroes in John Sutter and James Marshall. Sutter, who had a fort in Sacramento, partnered with Marshall to build a sawmill on a swift stretch of the American River in 1847. It was Marshall who discovered gold here on January 24, 1848, and though the men tried to keep their findings secret, it eventually brought a chaotic rush of prospectors from around the world. In one of the great tragic ironies of the Gold Rush, the men who made this discovery died nearly penniless.

If there aren't a million school kids squealing around, the pastoral park is quietly befitting of this legacy, with a grassy area bordered on the east by the river. Follow a simple dirt path to the place along the bank where Marshall found gold and started the revolutionary birth of the 'Golden State.'

The park's quiet charms are mostly experienced outdoors, strolling past the carefully reconstructed mill and taking in the grounds. There's also a humble **Visitor Information Center & Museum** (☎530-622-3470; Bridge St; ⊘10am-4pm Tue-Sun) with a tidy shop where you can buy kitsch from the frontier days.

On a hill overlooking the park is the **James Marshall Monument**, where he was buried in 1885, a ward of the state. You can drive a circuit but it's much better to meander the many trails around the park, past old mining artifacts and pioneer cemeteries.

Panning for gold is popular – you can pay $7 for a quick training session and 45 minutes of gold panning, or pan for free if you have your own.

Placerville

Placerville has always been a travelers' town: it was originally a destination for fortune hunters who reached California by following the South Fork of the American River. In 1857 the first stagecoach to cross the Sierra Nevada linked Placerville to Nevada's Carson Valley, which eventually became part of the nation's first transcontinental stagecoach route. Today, Placerville is a place to gas up, stretch your legs and get a bite while traveling between Sacramento and Tahoe on Hwy 50. It has a thriving and well-preserved downtown with antique shops and bars, where local wags cherish the wild reputation of 'Hangtown' – a name earned when a handful of men swung from the gallows in the mid-1800s. Among the many other awesome local legends is 'Snowshoe' John A Thompson, a postal carrier who carried some 80lbs of mail on skis from Placerville over the Sierra to Carson Valley during the winter.

⊙ Sights & Activities

Main St is the heart of downtown Placerville and runs parallel to Hwy 50 between Canal St and Cedar Ravine Rd. Hwy 49 meets Main St at the west edge of downtown. Looking like a movie set, most buildings along Main St are false fronts and sturdy brick structures from the 1850s, dominated by the spindly **Bell Tower**, a relic from 1856 that once rallied volunteer firemen.

Gold Bug Park   HISTORIC SITE
(www.goldbugpark.org; ⊘10am-4pm Apr-Oct, noon-4pm Sat & Sun Nov-Mar) The best museum in Placerville, about 1 mile north of town on Bedford Ave. The park stands over the site of four mining claims that yielded gold from 1849 to 1888; you can descend into the self-guided Gold Bug Mine, do some gold panning ($2) and explore the grounds and picnic area for free.

FREE **El Dorado County Historical Museum**   MUSEUM
(☎530-621-5865; 104 Placerville Dr; admission free; ⊘10am-4pm Wed-Sat, noon-4pm Sun) On the El Dorado County Fairgrounds west of downtown (exit north on Placerville Dr from Hwy 50), is an extensive complex of restored buildings, mining equipment and re-created businesses.

🍽 Sleeping & Eating

Chain motels and fast-food places can be found at either end of the historic center of Placerville along Hwy 50.

Cary House Hotel   HISTORIC HOTEL $$
(📞530-622-4271; www.caryhouse.com; 300 Main St; r from $114; ❋@🛜) This historic hotel is centrally located in the middle of downtown Placerville and has a large, comfortable lobby with back-lit stained glass depicting scenes from the region's history. Once a bordello, it's said to be haunted, though modern rooms (some with kitchenettes) with tasteful period decor and drop ceilings in the hallways belie its rich history. Ask for a room at the back of the hotel overlooking the courtyard to avoid street noise, or for room 212, which is rumored to be a supernatural hangout.

National 9 Inn   MOTEL $
(📞530-622-3884, 1500 Broadway; r $50-89; ❋🛜) This mid-century motel, recently renovated by a young couple, is the best bargain in Placerville, even if it lies at the lonely north end of town. The building's exterior is ho-hum, but the rooms are sparkling, bathrooms are remodeled and all come with refrigerators and microwaves. It's a great option for travelers who want a clean, no-frills stay and to support independent business.

Albert Shafsky House B&B   B&B $$
(📞530-642-2776; www.shafsky.com; 2942 Coloma St; r $145-185; ❋🛜) Of all the Victorian bed-and-breakfast options in Placerville, Albert's proximity to downtown, ornate period furnishings and luxurious bedding make this cozy three-room option a favorite.

Heyday Café   CAFE $
(www.heydaycafe.com; 325 Main St; mains $9-24; ⏱11am-8pm Tue-Sun) Fresh, and well-executed, the menu here leans toward simple Italian comfort food, made all the more comfortable by the wood-and-brick interior. The wine list is long on area vineyards and locals rave about its lunch menu.

Z-Pie   AMERICAN $
(www.z-pie.com; 3182 Center St; mains $5-6; ⏱11am-9pm) With its whimsical take on the all-American comfort food staple, this casual stop across from City Hall stuffs flaky, butter-crusted pot pies with a gourmet flourish (steak cabernet! Thai chicken! black bean chili and tofu!). California beers are on tap and the four-beer sampler ($9) is ideal for the undecided.

Sweetie Pie's   BREAKFAST $
(www.sweetiepies.biz; 577 Main St; mains $5-12; ⏱breakfast & lunch Tue-Sun) Ski bunnies and bums fill this diner and bakery counter on the weekends en route to Tahoe slopes, filling up with egg dishes and top-notch homemade baked goods. Breakfast is its specialty, but it also does a capable lunch, with sandwiches and salads. The cinnamon rolls alone are worth a stop.

📷 Cozmic Cafe   CAFE $
(www.ourcoz.com; 594 Main St; meals $6-10; ⏱breakfast, lunch & dinner; 🖊) In the historic Placerville Soda Works building, the menu is organic and boasts vegetarian and healthy fare backed by fresh smoothies. There's a good selection of microbrews and live music on weekends, when it is often open late.

🍷 Drinking

The wines of El Dorado County are rising in profile, and several tasting rooms dot the main street offering earthy, elegant zins of the region (see p316 for more on wineries). Placerville's bars, on the other hand, are akin to the neighborhood watering holes in the Midwest: they open around 6am, get an annual cleaning at Christmas and are great for people who want to chew the fat with a colorful cast of locals.

Liars' Bench   BAR
(📞530-622-0494; 255 Main St) With the closure of the shady Hangman's Tree dive bar, the Liar's Bench survives at the town's classic watering hole under a neon martini sign that beckons after dark.

🛍 Shopping

🏆 TOP CHOICE Gothic Rose
Antiques   ANTIQUES, CURIOSITIES
(www.gothicroseantiques.com; 484 Main St) This artfully designed curiosity shop likely frightens the wigs off the other antique dealers in town, with its collection of haute gothic house wares, antique occult goods and flawlessly macabre sensibility. Browsing the antique medical instruments, taxidermy, 19th-century photos of corpses and – just for fun – a few garments of latex and lace, is titillating. The most interesting

antique store in Gold Country? It's a dead ringer.

Placerville Hardware
HARDWARE

(www.placervillehardware.com; 441 Main St) The 1852 building, an anchor of Placerville's main drag, is the oldest continuously operating hardware store west of the Mississippi and one of many places along Main St to pick up a brochure for a self-guided tour of the town. The store has a smattering of Gold Country bric-a-brac but most of the goods that clutter the place are bona fide dry goods, like hammers and buckets, all unusually curious within the tight aisles.

Placerville Antiques
ANTIQUES

(448 Main St) Of Placerville's many antique shops, the collection of dealers in this brightly lit space is a favorite. Reasonably priced mid-century dishware is a particular strength.

Bookery
BOOKS

(326 Main St; ⊙10am-5:30pm Mon-Thu, to 7pm Fri & Sat, to 4pm Sun) A great used-book store to stock up on vacation pulp.

ⓘ Information

El Dorado County Chamber of Commerce (www.eldoradocounty.org; 542 Main St; ⊙9am-5pm Mon-Fri) Has decent maps and local information.

Placerville News Co (www.pvillenews.com; 409 Main St; ⊙8am-6:30pm Mon-Thu, to 7pm Fri & Sat, to 5:30pm Sun) This plank-floored shop has a wealth of excellent maps, history and local interest books.

ⓘ Getting There & Away

Amtrak (☎800-872-7245; www.capitolcorridor.org) Runs several buses daily to Sacramento ($15, one hour 20 minutes), though some require train connections to points further along the Capital Corridor route.

El Dorado Transit (www.eldoradotransit.com) Operates weekday commuter buses to Sacramento ($5, one hour 30 minutes) out of the **Placerville Transit Station** (2984 Mosquito Rd), a charming covered bus stop with benches and restrooms. It's about half a mile from downtown, on the north side of Hwy 50.

Placerville Wineries

The region's high heat and rocky soil produces excellent wines, which frequently appear on California menus. Oenophiles could spend a long afternoon rambling through the welcoming vineyards of El Dorado Country alone (though a full weekend of tasting could be had if it was coupled with adjoining Amador County). Details can be found at the **El Dorado Winery Association** (☎800-306-3956; www.eldoradowines.org) or **Wine Smith** (www.thewinesmith.com; 346 Main St; ⊙11am-8pm), a local shop with just about everything grown in the area.

Some noteworthy wineries, all north of Hwy 50, include **Lava Cap Winery** (www.lavacap.com; 2221 Fruitridge Rd; ⊙11am-5pm), which has an on-hand deli for picnic supplies and **Boeger Winery** (www.boegerwinery.com; 1709 Carson Rd; ⊙10am-5pm). Both have free tastings.

Amador County Wine Region

Amador County might be something of an underdog among California's winemaking regions, but a thriving circuit of family wineries, Gold Rush history and local characters make for excellent wine touring without a whiff of pretension. The region lays claim to the oldest zinfandel vines in the United States and the surrounding country has a lot in common with this celebrated variety – bold and richly colored, earthy and constantly surprising.

The region has two tiny towns, Plymouth and Amador City, which offer a range of services aimed at those on the wine circuit. To begin the circuit of Amador wineries, leave Hwy 49 in Plymouth and follow Shenandoah Rd, which takes you through rows of vines basking in the heat. You'll see hill after rolling hill covered with rocky rows of neatly pruned vines, soaking up gallons of too-bright sun. Tastings at the family-operated wineries around the county have little in common with those in the Napa Valley – most hosts are welcoming and helpful, offering free tastes and information about their operations.

Maps are available at the wineries, and from the **Amador Vintners Association** (www.amadorwine.com).

Drytown Cellars
WINERY

(www.drytowncellars.com; 16030 Hwy 49; ⊙11am-5pm Fri-Sun) This is the most fun tasting room in Amador County, thanks to Allan, a gregarious host and an array of stunning reds.

Deaver Vineyards
WINERY

(www.deavervineyard.com; 12455 Steiner Rd; ⊙10:30am-4pm) A true family affair where nearly everyone's last name seems to match the one on the bottles.

Sobon Estate
WINERY
(www.sobonwine.com; 14430 Shenandoah Rd; ☺10am-5pm) Founded in 1856, it's home to the Shenandoah Valley Museum featuring wine-related memorabilia.

Wildrotter
WINERY
(www.wildrottervineyard.com; 19890 Shenandoah School Rd; ☺10am-5pm Fri-Sun, 11am-4pm Mon & Thu) This winery brought home prestigious honors for California's best red at a recent State Fair.

PLYMOUTH & AMADOR CITY

Two small, sunny villages make equally decent bases for exploring Amador County's wine region. The first, Plymouth, is where the region's Gold Rush history is evident in its original name, Pokerville. Few card sharks haunt the slumbering town today; it wakes late when the tiny main street fills with the smell of barbecue, a few strolling tourists and the odd rumble of a motorcycle posse. Amador City was once home to the Keystone Mine – one of the most prolific gold producers in California – but the town lay deserted from 1942 (when the mine closed) until the 1950s, when a family from Sacramento bought the dilapidated buildings and converted them into antique shops.

FREE Amador Whitney Museum (www.amador-city.com; Main St, Amador City; admission free; ☺noon-4pm Fri-Sun) is the only sight of any note. It has a covered wagon and a replica school house scene and mineshaft. It's worth the 15-minute stop.

TOP CHOICE Imperial Hotel (☎209-267-9172; www.imperialamador.com; 14202 Main St, Amador City; r $120-145; ❋☎) is the nicest place to stay. Built in 1879, it's one of the area's most inventive updates to the typical antique-cluttered hotels, with sleek deco touches accenting the usual gingerbread flourish, a genteel bar and an excellent seasonally minded restaurant (dinner $20 to $30). On weekends during the summer, expect a two-night minimum.

Book a table at Taste (☎209-245-3463; 9402 Main St, Plymouth; mains $31-50; ☺5-9pm Thu-Mon & 11:30-2pm Sat), where excellent Amador wines are paired with a four-star menu of California fusions. Pull on the over-sized fork-shaped door handle to be greeted by smells of fresh, seasonally changing dishes, all artfully presented.

Tired of wine? Hit the Drytown Club (www.drytownclub.com; 15950 Hwy 49), the kind of rowdy roadhouse where people start drinking a little too early and soak it up with weekend BBQ. The bands on the weekend are bluesy, boozy and sometimes brilliant. The dance floor of this place has seen the death of many visitors' inhibitions.

Sutter Creek

Perch on the balcony of one of the gracefully restored buildings on Main St and view Sutter Creek, a gem of a Gold Country town with raised, arcaded sidewalks and high-balconied buildings with false fronts that are perfect examples of California's 19th-century architecture. This is an excellent place to stay

WORTH A TRIP

APPLE HILL

In 1860, a miner planted a Rhode Island Greening apple tree on a hill just up the way from Placerville and with it the foundation for bountiful Apple Hill, a 20-sq-mile area east of Placerville and north of Hwy 50 where there are more than 60 orchards. Apple growers sell directly to the public, usually from August to December, and some let you pick your own. Other fruits are available during different seasons.

A decent map of Apple Hill is available at the Apple Hill Visitors Center (☎530-644-7692; www.applehill.com) in the Camino Hotel, near the Camino exit off Hwy 50. If you'd rather do it yourself, there's a good map of 'El Dorado County Farm Trails' at www.visiteldorado.com.

The Camino Hotel (☎530-644-1800; www.caminohotel.com; r incl breakfast $75-125; ❋) is a former lumberjack bunkhouse – every bit as creaky and crooked as you'd hope – with rooms that have been recently redone. The rates are a steal (as low as $50 on weekdays) and room 4 is perfect for families with two rooms adjoined by a central sitting room. The breakfast is made to order. A great spot to hunker down while touring Apple Hill's farms.

when visiting Amador and El Dorado County wineries.

Begin the visit at volunteer-operated **Sutter Creek Visitor Center** (☎209-267-1344; www.suttercreek.org; 25 Eureka St; ⊙hours vary) to collect a walking-tour map of town or an excellent, free driving-tour guide to local gold mines. The website has seasonal suggestions for day trippers.

◉ Sights & Activities

FREE **Monteverde General Store**   HISTORIC BUILDING
(☎209-267-0493; admission free; ⊙by appointment) Next door to the visitor center, this building goes back in time to when the general store was the center of the town's social and economic life, represented by the chairs that circle the potbelly stove and the detailed historic scale. Senior docents lead fun tours by appointment.

Knight Foundry   MINE
(www.knightfoundry.org; 81 Eureka St) In its prime, Sutter Creek was Gold Country's main supply center. Three foundries operating in 1873 made pans and rock crushers. This foundry operated until 1996 as the last water-powered foundry and machine shop in the US. You can still see the workings of the foundry, and on some days volunteers can explain how everything worked while they toil to put the foundry back into production.

Sutter Creek Theatre   PERFORMING ARTS
(www.suttercreektheater.com; 44 Main St) One of several excellent Gold Country arts groups, it has nearly a 100-year-long history of presenting live drama, films and other cultural events.

⏢ Sleeping & Eating

Eureka Street Inn   B&B $$
(☎209-267-5500; www.eurekastreetinn.com; 55 Eureka St; r $145; ❀⧉) Each of the four rooms in this 1914 Arts-and-Crafts–style home has unique decor and gas fireplaces. Once the home of a wealthy stagecoach operator, the inn is on a quiet street close to everything and serves a delicious breakfast with strong coffee and fresh fruit.

Sutter Creek Inn   B&B $$
(☎209-267-5606; www.suttercreekinn.com; 75 Main St; r $90-195; ❀) The 17 rooms and cottages here vary in decor and amenities (antiques, fireplaces, sunny patios) but all have private bathrooms. Guests can snooze

in the hammock by the gardens or sprawl out on the large lawn, which is dotted with comfy chairs for curling up in with a book. Of course it's jammed with knickknacks, including a spectacular collection of cow-shaped coffee creamers.

Sutter Creek Ice Cream Emporium   SWEETS $
(51 Main St; ⊙11am-6pm Thu-Sun) The sugared environment of this shop of sweets gets downright enchanted when Stevens Price, the man behind the counter, takes to the 1919 Milton Piano and plays ragtime. Price also organizes the Sutter Creek Ragtime Festival each August.

Pizza Plus   PIZZA $
(20 Eureka St; pizzas $14; ⊙11am-9pm; ⧉) Crisp, chewy thin-crust pizza and pitchers of beer make this a favorite; it's the perfect place to hang out and chat up the locals. Special topping combinations like the BBQ pizza put it over the top.

Thomi's Coffee & Eatery   AMERICAN $
(40 Hanford St; meals $7-12; ⊙8am-3pm Fri-Wed; ⧉) A real star in a galaxy of them, Thomi serves classic griddle breakfasts, huge salads to prime rib dinners. The brick dining room is welcoming in winter; in summer there's a sunny little patio.

Sutter Creek Cheese   MARKET $
(www.suttercreekcheese.com; 33 Main St; ⊙11am-5pm) A stop for cheese from California and Europe.

Volcano

One of the many fading plaques in Volcano accurately calls it a place of 'quiet history,' and even though the little L-shaped village on the bank of Sutter Creek yielded tons of gold and a Civil War battle, today it slumbers away in remote solitude. Now only a scattering of greening bronze monuments attest to Volcano's lively past.

Large sandstone rocks line Sutter Creek, which skirts the center of town. The rocks, now flanked by picnic tables, were blasted from surrounding hills by a hydraulic process before being scraped clean of gold-bearing dirt. The process had dire environmental consequences, but at its peak miners made nearly $100 a day.

The winding 12-mile drive from Sutter Creek is along lovely Sutter Creek Rd.

◉ Sights & Activities

Daffodil Hill
FLOWER FARM

(donations accepted; ⊘daily mid-Mar–mid-Apr) This hilltop farm, 2 miles northeast of Volcano, is blanketed with more than 300,000 daffodils. The McLaughlin and Ryan families have operated the farm since 1887 and keep hyacinths, tulips, violets, lilacs and the occasional peacock among the daffodils.

Black Chasm
CAVE TOUR

(☑888-762-2837; www.caverntours.com; 15701 Pioneer Volcano Rd; adult/child $14.75/7.50; ⊘9am-5pm) A quarter of a mile east of Volcano, this has the whiff of a tourist trap, but one look at the helictite crystals – rare, sparkling white formations that look like enlarged snowflakes – makes the crowd more sufferable. The tour guides are all experienced cavers.

Indian Grinding Rock State Historic Park
HISTORIC SITE

(☑209-296-7488; Pine Grove-Volcano Rd; admission per vehicle $8) Two miles southwest of Volcano is a sacred area for the local Miwok people. There's a limestone outcrop that's covered with petroglyphs – 363 originals and a few modern additions – and over 1000 mortar holes called *chaw'ses* used for grinding acorns into meal.

Volcano Theatre Company
PERFORMING ARTS

(☑209-223-4663; www.volcanotheatre.org; adult/child $16/11) On weekends between April and November, this highly regarded company produces live dramas in the restored Cobblestone Theater.

🛏 Sleeping & Eating

Volcano Union Inn
HISTORIC HOTEL $$

(☑209-296-4458; www.volcanounion.com; 16104 Main St, Volcano; r incl breakfast $109-129; ❊@☎) The preferred of two historic hotels in Volcano, there are four lovingly updated rooms with crooked floors: two have street-facing balconies. Flat-screen TVs and modern touches are a bit incongruous with the old building, but it's a comfortable place to stay and the on-site Union Pub has a superb menu and will host the occasional old-time fiddler.

St George Hotel
HISTORIC HOTEL $$

(☑209-296-4458; www.stgeorgehotel.com; 16104 Main St; r $80-190) Up the crooked stairs of this charming, creaky hotel are 20 rooms which vary in size and amenity and are free of clutter. The restaurant (open for dinner Thursday to Sunday, brunch Sunday) has a menu anchored by steak, but the best place to hang out is in the accompanying bar, where the local concoction of 'Moose Milk' (a whisky-and-dairy-based inebriant) is worthy of the bartender's playful warning.

Indian Grinding Rock State Historic Park
CAMPGROUND $

(www.reserveamerica.com; tent and RV sites $25) The beautiful campground at Indian Grinding Rock State Historic Park has fresh water, plumbing and 23 unreserved sites set among the trees, with tent sites and hookups for RVs.

Jackson

Jackson has some historic buildings and a small downtown, but it ain't much to look at; standing at the junction of Hwy 49 and Hwy 88 it's probably the least attractive Gold Rush hub. Hwy 88 turns east from Hwy 49 here and heads over the Sierra near the Kirkwood ski resort (see p366).

◉ Sights

Kennedy Tailing Wheels Park
HISTORIC SIGHT

One mile from downtown Jackson via North Main St, Kennedy Tailing Wheels Park doesn't look like much at first glance, but the four iron and wood wheels, 58ft in diameter (which look like fallen carnival rides), transported tailings from the Eureka Mine over two low hills and are marvelous examples of engineering and craftsmanship. Be sure to climb to the top of the hill behind the wheels to see the impounding dam.

Mokelumne Hill
HISTORIC AREA

Somewhat undiscovered Mokelumne Hill, which lies 7 miles south of Jackson just off Hwy 49, was settled by French trappers in the early 1840s. It's a good place to see historic buildings without the common glut of antique stores and gift shops.

🛏 Sleeping & Eating

National Hotel
HISTORIC HOTEL $

(☑209-223-0500; www.national-hotel.com; 2 Water St; r $75-195) This is Jackson's historic hotel, though the rooms, decorated with themed flair from pop icons, don't jibe with the historic facade. The rooms are worn, and there's plenty of sound from the nearby highway and locals who gather on the bar's balcony below, so light sleepers should look elsewhere.

Mel's and Faye's Diner   AMERICAN $$

(www.melandfayesdiner.com; 205 N Hwy 49; meals $5-12; ⊙4am-10pm Mon-Thu, to 11pm Fri-Sun) A local institution near Hwy 88. It serves up excellent diner fare that includes breakfasts that could feed a small family, classic burgers (try the chili-soaked 'Miner') and – to balance the divine grease binge – a decent salad bar.

ⓘ Information

Amador County Chamber of Commerce
(☑209-223-0350, www.amadorcountychamber.com; 125 Peek St; ⊙9am-4pm Mon-Fri) On the corner of Hwys 49 and 88. Has enough brochures to fill several recycling bins.

ⓘ Getting There & Away

The only way to reliably travel through this area is with your own wheels. Placer Country runs its (fairly pathetic) bus system out of Jackson, but good luck catching it – the buses are few and far between. **Amador Transit** (209-267-9395; www.amadortransit.com) is a bit better. It makes two daily connections to Sacramento ($1, one hour) and, if you have enough patience, you can connect to Calaveras County and southern Gold Country. By car, Jackson is 2½ hours from San Francisco and just over one hour to the ski resorts of S Lake Tahoe.

CALAVERAS COUNTY & SOUTH GOLD COUNTRY

The southern region of Gold Country is hot as blazes in the summer so cruising through its historic Gold Rush hubs will demand more than one stop for ice cream. The tall tales of yesteryear come alive here through the region's infamous former residents: author Mark Twain, who got his start writing about a jumping frog contest in Calaveras County, and Joaquin Murrieta, a Robin Hood figure who somehow seems to have frequented every old bar and hotel in the area.

Angels Camp

On the southern stretch of Hwy 49 one figure looms over all others: literary giant Mark Twain, who got his first big break with the story of *The Celebrated Jumping Frog of Calaveras County*, written and set in Angels Camp. There are differing claims as to when or where Twain heard this tale, but Angels Camp makes the most of it. There are gentlemanly Twain impersonators, statues and dozens of bronze frogs embedded in the sidewalk of Main St celebrating amphibious champions of the past 80 years. Look for the plaque of Rosie the Riveter, who set an impressive 21ft record in 1986. Today the town is an attractive mix of buildings from the Gold Rush to art deco periods.

Calaveras County Visitors Bureau (☑209-736-0049; www.gocalaveras.com; 1192 S Main St; ⊙9am-5pm Mon-Sat, 11am-3pm Sun; ☎) has a walking and driving tour of Angels Camp, history books and lots more information for your trip.

⊙ Sights & Activities

Angels Camp makes the most of the Twain connection; hosting the **Jumping Frog Jubilee** the third weekend in May (in conjunction with the county fair and something of a Harley rally) and **Mark Twain Days** over the Fourth of July weekend.

Moaning Cavern   CAVE TOURS
(☑209-736-2708; www.caverntours.com; adult/child $14.75/7.50; ⊙10am-5pm) Though nearby California Cavern offers roomier digs with more impressive natural formations this cave has more thrills by allowing visitors to rappel down the 165ft shaft to the bottom ($65). They also have an above-ground zip line and self-guided nature walk. A pile of bones found at the bottom were some of the oldest human remains ever found in the United States. In winter, they host caroling (amazing considering the cave's acoustics) and a rappelling Santa Claus.

✖ Eating

Strung out along Hwy 49 are a number of motels, fast-food joints and places to fill up the gas tank.

Sidewinders   CAL-MEX $
(1251 S Main St; mains $8-12; ⊙11am-8pm Tue-Sat; ⊛) The guacamole-dressed white panko fish tacos are excellent. When the sun pounds down on Angels Camp, the cool stone walls and pints of regional California beer are soothing.

Crusco's   ITALIAN $$
(www.cruscos.com; 1240 S Main St; mains $14-26; ⊙11am-3pm & 5-9pm Thu-Mon) The class act in downtown Angels Camp puts out a serious,

WORTH A TRIP

CALAVERAS BIG TREES STATE PARK

From Angels Camp, Hwy 4 ascends into the High Sierra, eventually cresting at Ebbetts Pass (8730ft) and then descending to junctions with Hwys 89 and 395. Along the way the road passes through the workmanlike town of Arnold, which has a few cafes and motels strung along the roadside. But the real reason for taking Hwy 4 is 2 miles east of Arnold and 15 miles east of Murphys: a chance to commune with the largest living things on the planet.

Calaveras Big Trees State Park (209-795-2334; admission per vehicle $6) is home to giant sequoia redwood trees. Reaching as high as 325ft and with trunk diameters up to 33ft, these leftovers from the Mesozoic era are thought to weigh upwards of 3000 tons, or close to 20 blue whales.

The redwood giants are distributed in two large groves, one of which is easily seen from the North Grove Big Trees Trail, a 1.5-mile self-guided loop, near the entrance, where the air is fresh with pine and rich soil. A 4-mile trail that branches off from the self-guided loop climbs out of the North Grove, crosses a ridge and descends 1500ft to the Stanislaus River.

It's possible to find giant trees throughout the park's 6000 acres, though the largest are in fairly remote locations. The visitor center (9am-4pm) can offer maps and lots of good advice on the miles of trails. It also has good exhibits about the trees and how a few dedicated individuals fought for decades to save them from becoming so many thousands of picnic tables.

Camping is popular and reservations (800-444-7275; www.parks.ca.gov; tent & RV sites $35) are essential. North Grove Campground is near the park entrance; less crowded is Oak Hollow Campground, 4 miles further on the park's main road. Most atmospheric are the hike-in environmental sites.

---

authentic northern Italian menu. Each year the owners travel to Italy in search of new recipes and bring home treats like polenta Castellana (creamy corn meal with garlic and parsley).

ℹ️ Getting There & Away

Calaveras Transit (209-754-4450; www.calaverastransit.com) operates the most reliable public transportation system in the region from the **Government Center** (891 Mountain Ranch Rd) in downtown San Andreas. You can use it to connect to Angels Camp ($2, 30 minutes, several times daily) and other surrounding towns. To connect via public transportation to the rest of California is tough – you have to take Route 1 to the Mokelumne Hill and transfer to Amador County Transit.

Murphys

With its white picket fences and old world charm, Murphys is one of the most picturesque towns along the southern stretch of Gold Country, befitting its nickname as 'Queen of the Sierra.' It lies 8 miles east of Hwy 49 on Murphys Grade Rd, and is named for Daniel and John Murphy, who

founded a trading post and mining operation on Murphy Creek in 1848, in conjunction with the local Maidu people. John was apparently very friendly with the tribe and eventually married the chief's daughter. The town's Main St is refined with tons of wine-tasting rooms, boutiques, galleries and good strolling. For information and a town overview, look to www.visitmurphys.com.

👁️ Sights & Activities

Even more than frogs, wine touring is a consistent draw in Calaveras County, and Murphys is the hub of it – a couple new tasting rooms seem to pop up downtown every summer.

California Cavern CAVE TOURS
(209-736-2708; www.caverntours.com; adult/child $14.75/7.50; 10am-5pm Apr-Oct;) In Cave City, 12 winding miles north of Murphys (take Main St to Sheep Ranch Rd to Cave City Rd), is another natural cavern, which John Muir described as 'graceful flowing folds deeply placketed like stiff silken drapery.' Regular tours take 60 to 90 minutes. For $148 you can try a Middle Earth Expedition, which lasts five hours and includes

CAVES AT A GLANCE

» **California Cavern** Large variety of tours, lengthy adventure trips.

» **Moaning Cavern** Allows rapelling down the tallest public shaft in California, above ground zip line.

» **Black Chasm** Quiet self-guided Zen Garden walk above ground, rare helictite crystals.

» **Lake Shasta Caverns** Sublime natural setting, tours include boat ride.

» **Lava Beds National Monument** Very remote and stunning natural area, no touristy vibe.

» **Crystal Cave** In Sequoia National Park, with large marble rooms, only 3 miles from giant sequoias.

serious spelunking (note that these happen in the dry summer season only). The lakes walking tour, available only in the wet season, is magical.

Ironstone Vineyards   WINERY
(www.ironstonevineyards.com; 1894 Six Mile Rd; ⊗10am-5pm; ⊕) We love everything *but* the wine at Ironstone – there's a natural spring waterfall, a mechanical pipe organ, frequent exhibits by local artists, and blossoming grounds. The large winery is particularly distinct for its family-friendly atmosphere, a deli and a museum which displays the world's largest crystalline gold leaf specimen (it weighs 44lb and was found in Jamestown in 1992). While crowds are frequent, the wine-tasting room is spacious. Ironstone is 1 mile south of town via Six Mile Rd, and other wineries cluster nearby.

Murphys Old Timers Museum   MUSEUM
(☎209-728-1160; donation requested; ⊗11am-4pm Fri-Sun) The name is a good hint that this place approaches history with a whimsical touch. Housed in an 1856 building, it holds a photograph of so-called Mexican Robin Hood, Joaquin Murrieta (p324), and the excellent 'Wall of Relative Ovation.' Guided tours leave from the museum every Saturday at 10am.

🛏 Sleeping

Most accommodations in Murphys are top-end B&Bs. Check nearby Angels Camp or Arnold for cheaper alternatives.

Victoria Inn   B&B $$
(☎209-728-8933; www.victoriainn-murphys.com; 402 Main St; r $125-350; ☎) This newly built B&B is thankfully free of dusty antique clutter. Its elegantly furnished rooms and well-appointed common spaces have a chic country-modern appeal with claw foot slipper tubs, sleigh beds and balconies. (Opi's Cabin – with its iron bed and exposed beams – is the most interesting of the basic rooms.) There's a long veranda where you can enjoy good tapas and wines from the long list at the bar (mains $6-12; ⊗noon-10pm Wed-Sun).

Murphys Historic Hotel & Lodge   B&B $$
(☎209-728-3444, 800-532-7684; www.murphyshotel.com; 457 Main St; r $89-125) Dating back to either 1855 or 1856 (you have your pick of plaques out front), Murphys anchors Main St. A must-stop on the Twain tour of the area (he was a guest here, as was the bandit Black Bart), the original structure is a little rough around the edges, but has a bar that blends locals and 1850s decor. The adjoining building has bland, if modern rooms. The dining room's menu (mains $8 to $35) goes deep into game dishes like elk, duck and wild boar.

Murphys Inn Motel   MOTEL $$
(☎209-728-1818, 888-796-1800; www.centralsierralodging.com; 76 Main St; r $129-149; ❄@☎☎) Just off Hwy 4, half a mile from the center of town, this option has clean and modern motel rooms with a small pool. Not much by way of personality, but a solid choice.

🍴 Eating

V Restaurant   MEDITERRANEAN $$
(☎209-728-0107; 402 Main St; mains $10-25; ⊗11:30am-9pm Thu-Sun, from 5pm Wed) Attached to the Victoria Inn, Murphys' most elegant dinner spot offers Mediterranean small and large plates and a creative cocktail list. Options start with excellent tapas (deep-fried anchovy-stuffed olives!) and end with a commanding rib eye – rubbed in cumin and served with scientific perfection. The room fills up on weekends with wine tourists, so call ahead for a reservation.

Fire Wood   PIZZA $
(www.firewoodeats.com; 420 Main St; meals $9-15; ⊗11am-9pm) A rarity in a town with so much historical frill, Fire Wood's exposed concrete walls and corrugated metal offers the feel of a minimalist urban loft. When the weather's

nice and the front wall is opened onto the street, the space has a casual al fresco atmosphere. There are wines by the glass, half a dozen beers on tap and basic pub fare, but the wood-fired pizzas are their hallmark.

Grounds BISTRO $

(☎209-728-8663; www.groundsrestaurant.com; 402 Main St; meals $8-24; ☉7am-3pm, from 8am Sun, to 9pm Wed-Sun; ☑) Casual and refined, Grounds does everything competently – expert breakfast foods, a roster of light lunch mains and weekend dinners of steaks and fresh fish. The herbal ice tea and fresh vegetarian options are key when the temperatures rise.

Alchemy Market & Café MARKET $

(www.alchemymarket.com; 191 Main St; meals $7-15; ☉11am-7pm with seasonal variations) For fancy picnic supplies. The adjoining cafe has a small fusion menu to enjoy on the patio.

Columbia State Historic Park

More than any other place in Gold Country, Columbia blurs the lines between present and past with a carefully preserved Gold Rush town – complete with volunteers in authentic dress – at the center of a modern community. In 1850 Columbia was founded over the 'Gem of the Southern Mines,' and the center of the town (which was taken over by the state parks system) looks almost exactly as it did then. The authenticity of the old Main St is only shaken a bit by the sugared fragrance of the fudge and the occasional play-acting '49er who forgets to remove his digital watch. On the fringe of these blocks are homes and businesses that blend in so well that it becomes hard to tell what's park and what's not.

The blacksmith's shop, theater, old hotels and authentic bar are a carefully framed window into history, completed by gold panning and breezy picnic spots.

Looking rather like dinosaur bones, limestone and granite boulders are noticeable around town. These were washed out of the surrounding hills by hydraulic mining and scraped clean by prospectors. There's a fascinating explanation of this technique at the renovated **Columbia Museum** (☎209-532-4301; cnr Main & State Sts; admission free; ☉10am-4:30pm). For information and snacks, stop at the friendly **Columbia Mercantile** (☎209-

532-7511; cnr Main & Jackson Sts; ☉9am-6pm), which also has a wide variety of groceries.

After most shops and attractions close around 5pm, you can have the atmospheric town to yourself, which makes staying here an attractive option.

Among the many elegant hotel restorations in the area, the **City Hotel** (☎20 9-532-1479; www.cityhotel.com; r $126-148; ❋☞) is the most thoughtful, and rooms overlook a shady stretch of street and open on lovely sitting rooms. The acclaimed **restaurant** (meals $14-30) is frequented by a Twain impersonator and the adjoining What Cheer Saloon is one of those atmospheric Gold Country saloons with oil paintings of lusty ladies and stripped wallpaper.

Fallon Hotel (☎209-532-1470; www.cityho tel.com; cnr Washington St & Broadway; r $90-148; ❋☞) is just as refined and has wider options. It also hosts the most professional theater troupe in the region, the **Sierra Repertory Theatre** (☎209-532-3120; www. sierrarep.org), who mix chestnuts of the stage (*Romeo & Juliet, South Pacific*) with popular reviews.

Sonora & Jamestown

Settled in 1848 by miners from Sonora, Mexico, this area was once a cosmopolitan center of commerce and culture with parks, elaborate saloons and the Southern Mines' largest concentration of gamblers, drunkards and gold. Racial unrest drove the Mexican settlers out and their European immigrant replacements got rich on the Big Bonanza Mine, where Sonora High School now stands. That mine yielded 12 tons of gold in two years (including a 28lb nugget).

Today, people en route to Yosemite National Park use Sonora as a staging area, wandering though its pubs for refreshment or grabbing quick eats at the chain restaurants and stores that have cropped up on its periphery. Fortunately, the historic center is well preserved (so much so that it's a frequent backdrop in films, including *Unforgiven* and *Back to The Future III*).

Little Jamestown is 3 miles south of Sonora, just south of the Hwy 49/108 junction. Founded around the time of Tuolumne County's first gold strike in 1848 it has suffered the ups and downs of the region's roller-coaster development, and today it limps along on

JOAQUIN MURRIETA: AVENGER OR TERRORIST?

In a land where tall tales tower, none casts a darker shadow than Joaquin Murrieta, the rakish immigrant miner long celebrated as the Robin Hood of the Gold Rush, whose inscrutable portrait gazes out from a tin type (an early method of photography) at the Murphys Old Timers Museum (p322). Stories of the bloodthirsty Murrieta are as ubiquitous as they are incongruous: he was born in either Sonora, Mexico or Quillota, Chile and, after immigrating to California seeking gold in 1850, he became either a treacherous villain or a folk avenger for brutally persecuted Mexicans in Gold Country. In the soft focus of historical hindsight, the fiery wrath of Joaquin Murrieta – real or not – has forged Gold Country's most intriguing antihero.

Consolidating 'Once upon a time' stories goes like this: Murrieta and his brother had a claim near Hangtown (now known, somewhat blandly, as Placerville). They had some luck, but refused to pay a newly established 'foreign miners tax' levied by the state in response to the overwhelming success of experienced Mexican and Chileno prospectors. To force Murrieta off his claim, a mob of jealous Anglo miners whipped Murrieta and raped his wife. With no recourse in the justice system, Murrieta formed a posse to kill his assaulters and began a life of banditry that left a trail of slashed throats and purloined gold. His band of highwaymen, known as the Five Joaquins, terrorized the countryside between 1850 and 1853.

Governor John Bigler put a large price on Murrieta's head, and in July of 1853 a Texas bounty hunter named Harry Love produced a jar containing the severed head of a man he claimed was Murrieta. Love toured cities of Northern California charging audiences $1 to see his trophy but, even in death, Murrieta's legend grew: a woman claiming to be his sister disputed the kill and sightings of the bandit continued long after his supposed death. Joaquin Murrieta was celebrated as a peoples' hero by many Latin Americans who were enraged by the oppressive, racist laws of the Gold Rush, which are largely unmentioned today, and his legend is a centerpiece of Gold Rush folklore.

tourism and antiques. It has its charm, but is only a few blocks long.

◉ Sights & Activities

Two highways cross the Sierra Nevada east of Sonora and connect with Hwy 395 in the Eastern Sierra: Hwy 108 via Sonora Pass and Hwy 120 via Tioga Pass. Note that the section of Hwy 120 traveling through Yosemite National Park is only open in summer (see the boxed text, p403).

The center of downtown Sonora is the T-shaped intersection of Washington and Stockton Sts, with Washington as the main thoroughfare. There are boutiques, shops, cafes, bars and more. If you're looking to get out of town, try a short hike through the oaks on the newly developed **Dragoon Gulch Trail**, which can be found just northwest of the main drag on Alpine Lane.

Sonora is also a base for white-water rafting: the Tuolumne River is known for Class IV rapids and its population of golden eagles and red-tailed hawks, while the Stanislaus River is more accessible and better for novices. **Sierra Mac River Trips** (☎209-532-1327; www.sierramac.com; trips from $225) and **All-**

Outdoors (☎800-247-2387; www.aorafting.com) both have good reputations and run trips of one day or more.

TOP CHOICE **Railtown 1897 State Historic Park**   HISTORIC RAILYARD
(☎209-984-3953; www.railtown1897.org; 5th Ave, Jamestown; admission $5, train ride $8; ⏱9:30am-4:30pm; ⛟) Five blocks south of Jamestown's Main St, this 26-acre collection of trains and railroad equipment is the little sister to the huge rail museum in Sacramento, though the surrounding hills have made it the backdrop for countless films and TV shows including *High Noon* and *Back to the Future*. There's a lyrical romance to the place, where an explosion of orange poppies grow among the rusting shells of steel goliaths. On some weekends and holidays you can ride the narrow-gauge railroad that once transported ore, lumber and miners, though today it has been shortened to a quick 3-mile circuit. Still, it's the best train ride in Gold Country, with the air spiced with creosote, campfire and pine, and green views. The state-operated park is staffed by

passionate volunteers and includes a restored station, engine house and bookstore.

Gold Prospecting Adventures GOLD PANNING (www.goldprospecting.com; 18170 Main St, Jamestown) Gold-finding outings involving pans and sluices start at $30. It even offers a three-day college-accredited gold-prospecting course ($595). Look for the (disturbing!) hanging dummy on Jamestown's main drag.

FREE **Tuolumne County Museum** HISTORY MUSEUM (www.tchistory.org; 158 W Bradford St, Sonora; admission free; ⏰10am-4pm) In the former 1857 Tuolumne County Jail, two blocks west of Washington St is this interesting museum with a fortune's worth of gold on display.

Sleeping & Eating

Gunn House Hotel HISTORIC HOTEL $ (☎209-532-3421; www.gunnhousehotel.com; 286 S Washington St, Sonora; r $79-115; P❄🅿🐾🛁) For a lovable alternative to Gold Country's cookie-cut chains, this historic hotel hits the sweet spot. Rooms feature period decor and guests take to rocking chairs on the wide porches in the evening. Stuffed bears, a nice pool and a big breakfast also make it a hit with families.

Bradford Place Inn B&B $$ (☎209-532-2400; www.bradfordplaceinn.com; 56 W Bradford St, Sonora; r $130-245; ❄@🅿) Gorgeous gardens and inviting porch seats surround this four-room B&B, which emphasizes green living. With a two-person claw-foot tub, the Bradford Suite is the definitive, romantic B&B experience.

TOP CHOICE **Lighthouse Deli & Ice Cream Shop** CAJUN DELI $ (www.thelighthousedeli.com; 28 S Washington, Sonora; mains $7-9; ⏰10am-4pm Mon-Fri, 11am-3pm Sat, with seasonal variations) The flavors of 'N'Awlins' make this unassuming deli an unexpected delight. The muffeletta – a toasted piece of Cajun paradise that's stacked with ham, salami, cheese and olive tapenade – is the best sandwich within 100 miles.

Diamondback Grill MEDITERRANEAN $$ (www.thediamondbackgrill.com; 93 S Washington St, Sonora; meals $6-10; ⏰11am-9pm) With exposed brick and modern fixtures, the fresh menu and contemporary details at this cafe are a reprieve from occasionally overbearing Victorian frill. Sandwiches dominate the menu (the salmon and mozzarella eggplant are both excellent) and everything is homemade, but for the freshest fare try one of the six (count 'em – six!) daily specials scrawled on the chalkboard.

☆ Entertainment

The free and widely available weekend supplement of the *Union Democrat* comes out on Friday and lists movies, music, performance art and events for Tuolumne County.

Iron Horse Lounge BAR (☎209-532-4482; 97 S Washington St, Sonora) The most elaborate of the traditional old taverns in the center; bottles glitter like gold on the backlit bar.

Sierra Repertory Theatre PERFORMING ARTS (☎209-532-3120; www.sierrarep.com; 13891 Hwy 108, Sonora; tickets $18-32) In East Sonora, close to the Junction Shopping Center, is the same critically acclaimed company that performs in the Fallon Hotel in Columbia.

ℹ Information

Mi-Wuk Ranger District Office (☎209-586-3234; 24695 State Hwy 108; ⏰8am-4:30pm Mon-Fri) For information and permits for the Stanislaus National Forest.

Sierra Nevada Adventure Company (www.snacattack.com; 173 S Washington St, Sonora; ⏰9am-6pm Sun-Thu, to 7pm Fri & Sat) For maps, equipment rental and sales and friendly advice from guides with a passionate knowledge of the area.

Tuolumne County Visitors Bureau (☎209-533-4420; www.tcvb.com; 542 Stockton St, Sonora; ⏰9am-6pm Jun-Sep, 9am-6pm Mon-Sat Oct-May) More so than many other brochure-jammed chamber of commerce joints, the staff here offers helpful trip planning throughout Gold Country. It also covers Yosemite National Park and Stanislaus National Forest up in the Sierras on Hwy 108.

ℹ Getting There & Away

Like elsewhere in Southern Gold Country, you're in for trouble if you try to navigate this region on public transportation. Bus service to Sonora, the major town in the region, ended in 2005. Hwy 108 is the main access road and it links up with I-5, 55 miles west near Stockton. An entrance to Yosemite National Park is 60 scenic miles south on Hwy 120. Many Yosemite visitors stay in the Sonora area. There is a new **Historic Trolley Service** (www.historic49trolleyservice.com) which offers free rides between Sonora and Jamestown on weekends through Labor Day.

SACRAMENTO VALLEY

The labyrinth of waterways that makes up the Sacramento–San Joaquin River Delta feeds the San Francisco Bay and divides the Central Valley in half, with the Sacramento Valley in the north and the San Joaquin Valley in the south. The Sacramento River, California's largest, rushes out of the northern mountains from Shasta Lake before hitting the valley basin above Red Bluff. Then, it snakes south across grassy plains and orchards before lazily skirting the state capital, fanning across the delta and draining into the San Francisco Bay. Lined with fruit and nut orchards and huge tracts of grazing land, the valley is a subtle beauty, particularly in spring when orchards are in full blossom. In the summer, it's a place of wide horizons and punishing, relentless sunshine; the skies go gray in fall, when they are decorated with the Vs of migratory birds.

Travelers going through the valley are often on their way to or from some other destination – the Bay Area, Gold Country or Lake Tahoe being the popular neighbors – but the shady streets, gardens and stately marble buildings of Sacramento and the inviting college town of Davis warrant exploring.

Sacramento

Sacramento has become a city of head-scratching anomalies. It's a former cow town that gets choked with rush-hour traffic, with the polished sedans of state legislators idling next to muddy half-ton pickup trucks. It claims stunning racial diversity, yet its neighborhoods are homogenous pockets of single ethnicities. Square in the middle of the sweltering valley, Sacramento's downtown is couched by the confluence of two cool rivers – the American and the Sacramento – and its

Metropolitan Sacramento

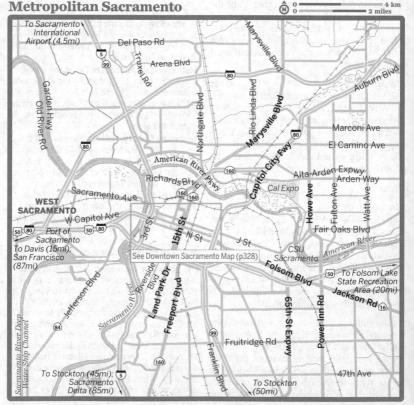

See Downtown Sacramento Map (p328)

streets are shushed by the leaves of huge oaks. Its sprawling suburbanization has recently turned around, placing lofts and upscale eateries next to abandoned mid-century shops in Midtown – an area called 'the Grid' for its uniformly square streets.

If you find yourself jammed on the roads that bypass Sacramento, jump off the highway for scoops at one of the city's vintage ice-cream parlors, or spend the evening in one of its elegantly preserved movie houses or friendly dive bars, where newcomers are welcomed with cheap drinks and sent off with slaps on the back.

The people of 'Sac' are an unpretentious lot, and have fostered small but thriving arts and nightlife scenes. They beam with pride about Second Saturday, the monthly Midtown gallery crawl that is emblematic of the city's cultural awakening. The summer is best: fat-tired cruisers meander around the Grid, people crack cold ones and chat with neighbors on the porches of high-water Victorians (built to resist the flooding rivers in the years before they were levied), and farmers markets dot the downtown parks every day of the week.

Remember not to bruise feelings of locals by comparing Sacramento to the Bay Area – their perspective on the bigger, prettier kid-sister city is colored with an underdog's dismissiveness. After you spend a few hours here, the Bay Area's bustle might start to seem jarring.

History

If you ask local historians, modern California was born here. Paleo-era peoples fished the rivers and lived in the area for generations before a hot-headed Swiss immigrant named John Sutter showed up. Realizing the strategic importance of the rivers, he built an outpost here, which quickly became a safe haven for traders. Sutter raised a militia of Native Americans and extended his operations to the surrounding area and it was at his lumber mill near Coloma that gold was discovered in 1848. Gold rushers flowed through the trading post, which was eventually handed over to Sutter's son, who christened the newly sprung town 'Sacramento.' Though plagued by fires and relentless flooding, the riverfront settlement prospered and became the state capital in 1850.

The transcontinental railroad was conceived in Sacramento by a quartet of local merchants known as the 'Big Four' – Leland Stanford, Mark Hopkins, Collis P Huntington and Charles Crocker – who are pictured in a fresco inside the Amtrak station. They founded the Central Pacific Railroad, which began construction in Sacramento in 1863 and connected with the Union Pacific in Promontory, Utah, in 1869.

◉ Sights

At the confluence of the Sacramento and American Rivers, Sacramento is roughly halfway between San Francisco and Lake Tahoe. The city is boxed in by four main highways: Hwy 99, which is the best route through the Central Valley, and I-5, which runs along its west side; I-80 skirts downtown on the city's northern edge, heading west to the Bay Area and east to Reno; and Hwy 50 runs along downtown's southern edge (where it's also called Business Route 80) before heading east to Lake Tahoe.

Downtown, numbered streets run from north to south and lettered streets run east to west (Capitol Ave replaces M St). One-way J St is a main drag east from Downtown to Midtown. The Tower District is south of downtown at the corner of Broadway and 16th St.

Cal Expo (Map p326), the site of the California State Fair every August, is east of I-80 from the Cal Expo exit.

THE GRID

Finding sights along the grid is easy – every road is in a straight line – but they are spread out.

TOP CHOICE **California Museum** MUSEUM
(Map p328; www.californiamuseum.org; 1020 O St; adult/child 6-13yr $8.50/7; ⊙10am-5pm Mon-Sat, noon-5pm Sun; ⓐ) A few blocks away from the brilliantly white capitol dome is the attractive, modern California Museum, home to the California Hall Of Fame – perhaps the only place to simultaneously encounter Cesar Chavez, Mark Zuckerburg and Amelia Earhart. Nary a dusty 19th-century relic lies in slumber among graceful modern exhibits, which tell an even-handed story of California's youth, by giving attention to typically underrepresented stories from the margins of history books. Perfect example: the newly opened exhibit *California Indians: Making A Difference* is the state's best view of the traditions and culture of California's first residents, past and present.

Downtown Sacramento

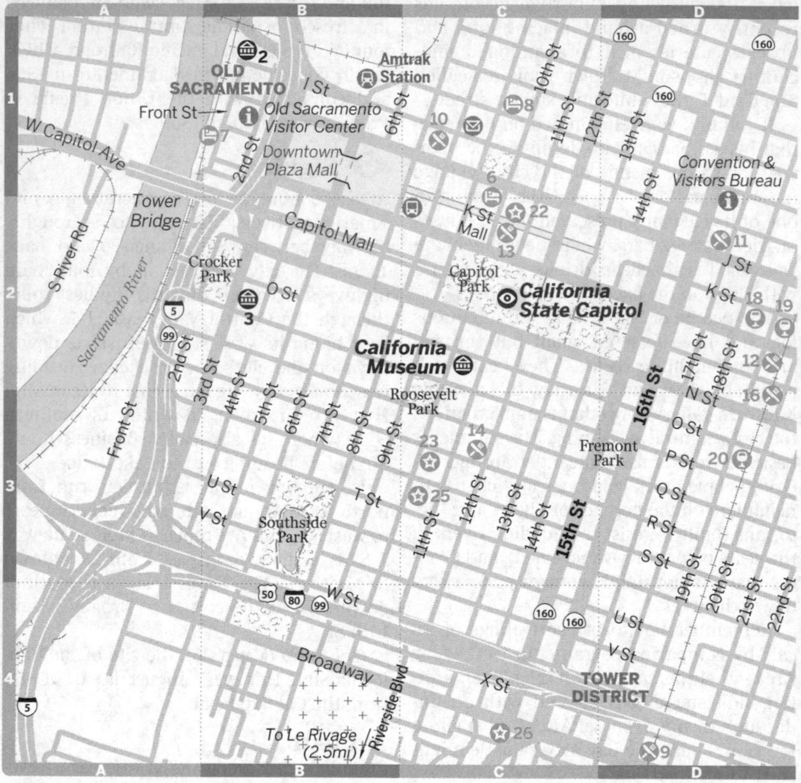

FREE **California State Capitol** HISTORIC BUILDING

(Map p328; ☎916-324-0333; cnr 10th & L Sts; ⏰9am-5pm) The California State Capitol is Sacramento's most recognizable structure. Built in the late 19th century, it underwent major reconstruction in the 1970s, and its marble halls offer a cool place for a stroll. There's a **bookstore** (⏰9:30am-4pm) in the basement, but the real attraction is in the west wing, where there is a painting of a Hollywood action hero posing as a governor. (Oh, wait a minute...) It could be argued that the 40 acres of garden surrounding the dome, **Capitol Park**, are better than the building itself. There are exotic trees from around the world, stern-looking statues of missionaries and a powerful Vietnam War Memorial. A quieter war commemoration is the Civil War Memorial Grove, which was planted in 1897 with saplings from famous battlefields.

Sutter's Fort State Historic Park HISTORIC SITE

(Map p328; www.parks.ca.gov/suttersfort; cnr 27th & L Sts; adult/child $5/3; ⏰10am-5pm) Originally built by John Sutter, the park was once the only trace of white settlement for hundreds of miles – hard to tell by the housing developments that surround the park today. California history buffs should carve out a couple hours to stroll within its walls, where original furniture, equipment and a working ironsmith are straight out of the 1850s.

California State Indian Museum MUSEUM

(Map p328; ☎916-324-0971; 2618 K St; adult/child $3/2; ⏰10am-2pm) It's with some irony that the humble structure of the State Indian Museum sits across the park in the shadow of the turrets of Sutter's Fort. The fascinating pieces of Native American handicrafts – including immaculate weaving that once thrived in the area – were all but lost during the Gold Rush.

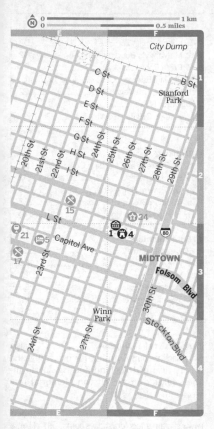

OLD SACRAMENTO

Though the art and culture of Midtown have challenged the conventional perception of Sacramento's visitors attractions as lackluster, this historic river port, adjacent to downtown, is the city's stalwart tourist draw. The pervasive scent of salt-water taffy and the somewhat garish restoration give Sacramento the vibe of a second-rate Frontierland, but it's good for a stroll on summer evenings, when boomers rumble though the brick streets on Harleys, and tourists and dolled-up legislative aides stroll the elevated sidewalks. It has California's largest concentration of buildings on the National Register of Historic Places (most of which now peddle Gold Rush trinkets and fudge) and a couple of quality attractions. Unfortunately, the restaurant scene is a bust – to eat and drink, head to Midtown.

California State Railroad Museum
MUSEUM

(Map p328; www.californiastaterailroadmuseum. org; 125 I St; adult/child 6-17yr $9/4; ⊙10am-5pm) At Old Sac's north end is this excellent museum, the largest of its kind in the US. It has an impressive collection of railcars, locomotives, toy models and memorabilia, and a fully outfitted Pullman sleeper and vintage diner cars to induce joy in railroad enthusiasts. Tickets include entrance to the restored **Central Pacific Passenger Depot**, across the plaza from the museum entrance. On weekends from April to September, you can board a steam-powered passenger train from the depot (adult/child $10/5) for a 40-minute jaunt along the riverfront.

Crocker Art Museum
ART MUSEUM

(Map p328; www.crockerartmuseum.org; 216 O St; adult/student $10/5, 3rd Sun of each month by donation; ⊙10am-5pm Tue-Sun, to 9pm Thu) Housed in a pair of side-by-side Victorians, the Crocker Art Museum is stunning as much for its outrageous stairways and beautiful tile floors as it is for its fine collection. There are some fine early California paintings and stellar drawings by European masters. The curatorial passion really comes through in its enthusiastic presentation of modern art.

Discovery Museum
CHILDREN'S MUSEUM

(Map p328; www.thediscovery.org; 101 I St; adult/ child $5/3; ⊙10am-5pm Jun-Aug, Tue-Sun Sep-May; ⋒) Next door to the railroad museum, this place has hands-on exhibits and Gold Rush displays for the kids. A major expansion is in the works.

TOWER DISTRICT

South of Midtown, Tower District is dominated by Tower Theatre, a beautiful 1938 art deco movie palace (see p333), which you'll probably spot on the way into town. From the theater, head east on Broadway to pass a stretch of the city's most eclectic and affordable ethnic eateries – including an excellent pair of side-by-side Thai restaurants. The **Tower Records** chain started here, and the original neon sign survives, though the retailer itself closed its doors in 2006, a casualty of the digital music revolution.

🏃 Activities

The **American River Parkway** (Map p326), a 23-mile river system on the north bank of the American River, is surely Sacramento's most appealing geographic feature. It's one of the most extensive riparian habitats in the continental US, lined by a network of well-marked and maintained trails and picnic areas. It's accessible from Old Sacramento by taking Front St north until it becomes Jiboom St and crosses the river, or by taking the Jiboom St exit off I-5/Hwy 99. The parkway includes a lovely bicycle and jogging path called the **Jedediah Smith National Recreation Trail**, which stretches over 30 miles from Old Sac to Folsom.

✿ Festivals & Events

In the summer, when the Central Valley's harvest is in full swing, Sacramento has an excellent farmers market nearly every day. Check www.california-grown.com for listings.

Second Saturday   STREET
(www.2nd-sat.com) Every second Saturday the galleries and shops in midtown draw people of all ages to the streets, where open-air music and culture events abound. It has rightly become a major point of civic pride and helped revitalize Sacramento's once-fading Midtown grid.

Jazz Festival & Jubilee   MUSIC
(www.sacjazz.com) Running for over 30 years, this festival of Dixieland and jazz performances takes over the city on Memorial Day weekend.

Gold Rush Days   HISTORICAL
(www.sacramentogoldrushdays.com; 👪) Horse races and historical costumes, music and kids' events make Old Sacramento particularly festive each Labor Day weekend.

🛏 Sleeping

The capital is a magnet for business travelers, so Sacramento doesn't suffer a lack of hotels – many of which sport good deals during the legislative break. Unless you're in town for the California State Fair or something else at Cal Expo, stay Downtown or in Midtown, where there's plenty to do within walking distance. If you're into cheap and kitschy motor lodges of the 1950s, cross the river into West Sac and look for 'Motel Row' on Rte 40.

TOP CHOICE **Citizen Hotel**   BOUTIQUE HOTEL $$
(Map p328; ☎916-492-4460; 926 J St; r $159, ste from $215; 🛜) With an elegant, ultra-hip upgrade by the Joie de Vivre group, the long-vacant Citizen has suddenly become one

of the coolest stays in this part of the state. Rooms are lovely with luxurious linen, bold patterned fabrics and stations for your iPod. The little touches make a big impression too: vintage political cartoons adorning the walls, loaner bikes and a nightly wine reception. There's an upscale farm-to-table restaurant on the ground floor (a daily menu of seasonal mains starts around $25).

Sacramento HI Hostel
HOSTEL $

(Map p328; ☑916-443-1691, www.norcalhostels. org/sac; 925 H St; dm $28, r $56; [P][@][🛜]) In a grand Victorian mansion, this hostel offers impressive trimmings at rock-bottom prices. It's within walking distance of the capitol, Old Sac and the train station and has a piano in the parlor and large dining room. It attracts an international crowd and is a useful place to find rides to San Francisco and Lake Tahoe.

Amber House
B&B $$

(Map p328; ☑916-444-8085, 800-755-6526; www.amberhouse.com; 1315 22nd St; r $149-259; [❄][@][🛜]) This Dutch Colonial home in Midtown has been transformed into an elegant bed and breakfast, where rooms named for composers and writers come with Jacuzzi baths and fireplaces. Breakfast is served in the rooms – this is best enjoyed in Mozart, which boasts a private balcony.

Le Rivage
BOUTIQUE HOTEL $$$

(off Map p328; ☑916-443-8400; www.lerivagehotel.com; 4800 Riverside Blvd; from r $199; [❄][@][🛜][🏊])

From the outside, this hotel has a lot in common with much of Sacramento architecture: enormous, new, with vaguely pre-fab Mediterranean touches. Inside, the rich linens and lovely views are a different story. Add a riverfront location and lovely spa, and this independent luxury option is excellent for the speedboat set.

Delta King
RIVERBOAT $$

(Map p328; ☑916-444-5464, 800-825-5464; www.deltaking.com; 100 Front St; r $113-163; [❄][@][🛜]) If you stay near Old Town, you can't beat the experience of sleeping aboard the *Delta King*, a docked 1927 paddlewheeler that lights up like a Christmas tree at night.

Folsom Lake State Recreation Area
CAMPGROUND $

(off Map p326; ☑916-988-0205; www.parks.ca.gov; 7806 Folsom-Auburn Rd; tent & RV sites without/with hookups $25/55; ☉office 6am-10pm summer, 7am-7pm winter) Sacramento is a good staging area before going into the Sierras, and this campground, while hardly picturesque, is the best option for testing out your gear before heading into the mountains. It's not ideal – the rangers can be overbearing, the sites rocky and the lake overrun by powerboats, but the only other nearby camping is a KOA west of town on I-80.

✖ Eating

Skip the overpriced fare in Old Sacramento or near the capitol and go to Midtown or the Tower District for higher-quality food at a

---

GETTING AROUND THE CENTRAL VALLEY

Although the Central Valley's main artery is connected with bus and Amtrak, much of the region is most easily traveled by car. The main routes through this part of California are Hwy 99 and I-5. I-80 meets Hwy 99 in Sacramento, and I-5 meets Hwy 99 south of Bakersfield. Amtrak also intersects the state with two lines – the *San Joaquin* route through the Central Valley and the *Pacific Surfliner* between the Central Coast and San Diego (see p776 for more information). The *San Joaquin* service stops in just about every town covered here. **Greyhound** (☑800-229-9424) stops in all of the Central Valley towns and cities covered in this chapter. Trips between Sacramento and Bakersfield take about 6½ hours and cost around $50.

The Central Valley has lots of long, straight byways for those making the trip on bikes, and the **American River Parkway** (p329) is a veritable human-powered expressway for commuters between Downtown Sacramento and Auburn.

Still, the transportation talk in the Central Valley these days is all about high speed rail. California voters gave a green light to start work on a network of super fast trains that would eventually connect San Francisco to Los Angeles at speeds of up to 220 miles per hour (it would make the trip just over 2½ hours). The total price tag is estimated at a whopping $50 billion, but the beginning is comically humble; the first stage will connect two tiny farm towns in the Central Valley, Borden and Concordion.

lower price. A cruise up J St or Broadway will pass a number of hip, affordable restaurants where tables sprawl out onto the sidewalks in the summer.

TOP CHOICE La Bonne Soupe Cafe   SANDWICHES $
(Map p328; www.labonnesoupe.com; 920 8th St; $8-10; ⊘11am-3pm Mon-Fri) Chef Daniel Pont assembles his divine sandwiches with such loving, affectionate care that the line of downtown lunchers snakes out the door. If you're in a hurry, skip it; Pont's humble lunch counter is focused on quality that predates drive-through haste. If you do have time, consider yourself lucky and ponder: smoky duck breast or apples and brie? Braised pork or smoked salmon? And the creamy soups made from scratch prove the restaurant's name is a painful understatement.

Andy Nguyen's   VEGETARIAN, THAI $$
(Map p328; www.andynguyenvegetarianrestaurant. com; 2007 Broadway; meals $8-16; ⊘11:30am-9pm Sun-Mon, to 9:30pm Tue-Thu, to 10pm Fri & Sat; ⏏) The best vegetarian fare in all of California might be at this tranquil Buddhist Thai diner. Try the steaming curries and artful fake meat dishes (the 'chicken' leg has a little wooden bone).

Shoki II Ramen House   JAPANESE $$
(⏏916-441-0011; 1201 R St; meals $8-16; ⊘11am-10pm Mon-Fri, from noon Sat, 11am-8pm Sun) In their old location, Shoki would get cheek-to-jowl with noodle-slurping dinner guests, but their new Midtown location has more space and the same amazing handmade noodles. The methodical technique, evident in walls covered in notes about the broths and the strict ban on to-go orders, are the work of noodle masters.

Mulvaney's Building
and Loan   MODERN AMERICAN $$$
(Map p328; ⏏916-443-1189; 2726 Capitol Ave; mains $20-40; ⊘dinner Wed-Sun) With an obsessive flourish for seasonality, the menu here changes every single day. Patrick Mulvaney flutters between the kitchen and the dining room, offering delicate pasta dishes and buttery braised meats.

Zelda's Original Gourmet Pizza   PIZZA $$
(Map p328; www.zeldasgourmetpizza.com; 1415 21st St; mains $10-20; ⊘lunch Mon-Fri, dinner daily) Zelda's roughshod windowless exterior doesn't look like much, but through the doors of this Nixon-era pizza dive, a troupe of gruff veteran waitresses sling a magical, messy variation of doughy Chicago deep-dish. It can take a while to come out of the kitchen, so occupy yourself with cheap little glasses of Bud at the bar. And no, you can't get the dressing on the side.

Sugar Plum Vegan   VEGAN $
(Map p328; www.sugarplumvegan.com; 2315 K St; $8-11; ⊘10am-9pm Wed-Sun; ⏏) This is an excellent vegan option in a restored Victorian with a back garden and creaking floors. The vegan tacos are good, but the baked goods – including a dark chocolate cup cake with almond paste – are simply decadent.

Pizza Rock   PIZZA $
(Map p328; www.pizzarocksacramento.com; 1020 K St; meals $8-18; ⊘11am-10pm Sun-Tue, to midnight Wed, to 3am Thu-Sat) An anchor of the newly renovated K Street Mall area, this loud, enormous pizza joint has fun, kitschy rock 'n roll themes, DJs and a staff who are cheerful and absolutely covered in tattoos. Pizza Chef Tony Gemignani scored an underdog win in the 2007 Pizza Cup in Naples, Italy for his dead-simple Margherita.

Water Boy   CALIFORNIAN $$
(Map p328; ⏏916-498-9891; www.waterboyrestaurant.com; 2000 Capitol Ave; mains $15-40; ⊘11:30am-9pm Thu-Mon, to 10pm Fri & Sat) The wicker and palms in the windowed dining room reflect the French colonial spin of the menu's California fusions. The seasonal menu soars from the briny oyster starter through the crispy skin of the poultry and smoky fresh catches. If it's too steep, look across the street for comfort food at Jack's Urban Eats.

Kitchen Restaurant   CALIFORNIAN $$
(⏏916-568-7171; www.thekitchenrestaurant.com; No 101, 2225 Hurley Way; prix-fixe dinner $125; ⊘5-10pm Wed-Sun) The cozy dining room of husband-and-wife team Randall Selland and Nancy Zimmer is the pinnacle of Sacramento's foodie world. Their demonstration dinners focus on local, organic foods, immaculately prepared before your eyes. Book well in advance, and brace yourself. Reservations are absolutely essential. Just when you thought it was perfect, consider the location: it's in the northeast suburbs. To get here, take I-80 east and exit at Exposition Blvd Exit. Take a left on Howe Ave and a right on Hurley Way.

Lucca
ITALIAN $$
(Map p328; ☎916-669-5300; 1615 J St; meals $8-18; ⊙11:30am-10pm Mon-Thu, to 11pm Fri, noon-11pm Sat, 4-9pm Sun) Within a stroll of the convention center is this quality Italian eatery. The escargot – wrapped in a buttery, flaky dough crust – is the way to start.

Gunther's
ICE CREAM $
(www.gunthersicecream.com; 2801 Franklin Blvd; shakes $4; ⊙10am-10pm) A beautiful vintage soda fountain that makes its own excellent ice cream. South of Broadway and Hwy 50.

🍷 Drinking

Sacramento has a split personality when it comes to drinking – sleek upscale joints that serve a fruity rainbow of vodka drinks to dressed-up weekenders from the 'burbs, and sans-bullshit dive bars with vintage neons and menus that begin and end with a-shot-ana-beer. Both options dot the Midtown grid.

Rubicon Brewing Company
BREWPUB
(Map p328; www.rubiconbrewing.com; 2004 Capitol Ave; 🛜) These people take their hops *seriously*. Their heady selection is brewed on-site and crowned by Monkey Knife Fight Pale Ale, ideal to wash back platters of lip-tingling wings ($10 for one dozen).

📷 Temple Coffee House
COFFEE SHOP
(Map p328; www.templecoffee.com; 1014 10th St; ⊙6am-11pm; 🛜) The warm environs of this Downtown coffee shop still imbibe the comfy feel of the bookstore that used to be in this space. Hip young patrons nurse organic free-trade coffee and chai while tapping at their wi-fi connected laptops.

58 Degrees and Holding Co
WINE BAR
(Map p328; www.58degrees.com; 1217 18th St) A huge selection of California reds and a refined bistro menu make this a favorite for young professional singles on the prowl.

Old Tavern Bar & Grill
BAR
(Map p328; 1510 20th St) This friendly dive is a standout among Sacramento's many excellent workaday joints for their huge beer selection, tall pours and rowdy mix of tattooed bar hounds.

Head Hunters
CLUB
(Map p328; www.headhuntersonk.com; 1930 K St) Though wilder bars are within sight, start here before partying around the two-block radius of gay bars and clubs that locals coyly

CALIFORNIA STATE FAIR

For the last two weeks in August, the **California State Fair** (☎916-263-3000; 1600 Exposition Blvd, Sacramento; adult/child $10/6) fills the Cal Expo with a small city of cows, candied apples and carnival rides. It's likely the only place on earth where you can plant a redwood tree, watch a pig give birth, ride a roller coaster, catch some barrel racing, taste exquisite Napa vintages and eat a deep-fried Snickers bar within an (admittedly exhausting) afternoon. Put on some comfy sneakers and pencil in two whole days, making time to see some of the auctions ($500 for a dozen eggs!) and the interactive exhibits run by the University of California, Davis. Try to book a room at the hotels near Cal Expo, which run regular shuttles to the event.

call 'Lavender Heights.' You might be back at the end of the night; the kitchen stays open into the wee hours.

☆ Entertainment

Pick up a copy of the free weekly *Sacramento News & Review* (www.newsandreview.com) for a list of current happenings around town.

Harlow's
LIVE MUSIC
(Map p328; www.harlows.com; 2708 J St) A classy joint that's a solid bet for quality jazz, R&B and the occasional salsa or indie act...if you don't get lost on the potent martinis.

Old Ironsides
LIVE MUSIC
(Map p328; www.theoldironsides.com; 1901 10th St; cover $3-10) The tiny back room of this cool, somewhat crusty, venue hosts some of the best indie bands that come through town.

California Musical Theatre
PERFORMING ARTS
(www.calmt.com) A top-notch company holds court at a few venues around town, including the Music Circus and the Cosmopolitan Caberet.

Tower Theatre
CINEMA
(Map p328; ☎916-442-4700; www.thetowertheatre.com; 2508 Landpark Dr) Classic, foreign and indie films screen at this historic movie house. Call to check if your film is showing on the

main screen, rather than in a smaller side room.

Crest Theatre
CINEMA

(Map p328; www.thecrest.com; 1013 K St) Another classic old movie house that's been lovingly restored to its 1949 splendor, hosting indie and foreign films and the annual Trash Film Orgy.

Fox & Goose Pub
LIVE MUSIC

(Map p328; www.foxandgoose.com; 1001 R St) This spacious, fern-filled warehouse-pub has good beer on tap and a jovial open-mic scene.

ℹ️ Information

Convention & Visitors Bureau (Map p328; ☎916-264-7777; www.discovergold.org; 1608 I St; ⓒ8am-5pm Mon-Fri) Local information, including event and bus schedules.

Old Sacramento Visitor Center (Map p328; www.oldsacramento.com; 1002 2nd St; ⓒ10am-5pm) Also has local information, including event and bus schedules.

ℹ️ Getting There & Away

Amtrak Station (Map p328; cnr 5th & I Sts) Between downtown and Old Sac. This station is a major hub for connecting trains to all points east and west, as well as regional bus lines serving the Central Valley.

Greyhound (Map p328; ☎916-444-6858; cnr 7th & L Sts) Stops near the Capitol. Greyhound service between Sacramento and Colfax, in Gold Country, cost $20 and takes 1½ hours.

Sacramento International Airport (off Map p326; ☎916-929-5411; www.sacairports.org) This small but busy airport 15 miles north of Downtown off I-5 is serviced by all major airlines and offers some indirect flights to Europe. Flights in and out of here can be an amazingly good value, especially considering the easy rail connection to the Bay Area.

ℹ️ Getting Around

The regional **Yolobus** (☎916-371-2877; www.yolobus.com) route 42A costs $2 and runs hourly between the airport and Downtown (take the counter-clockwise loop) and also goes to West Sacramento, Woodland and Davis. Local **Sacramento Regional Transit** (RT; ☎916-321-2877; www.sacrt.com) buses cost $2.50 per ticket or $6 for a day pass. RT also runs a trolley between Old Sacramento and Downtown, as well as Sacramento's light-rail system, which is mostly used for commuting from outlying communities. Sacramento is also a fantastic city to cruise around on a bike. The best place to rent is **City Bicycle Works** (www.citybicycleworks.

com; 2419 K St; ⓒ10am-7pm Mon-Fri, to 6pm Sat, to 5pm Sun), which charges by the hour (from $5) or by the day (from $20).

Sacramento River Delta

The Sacramento Delta is a sprawling web of waterways and one-stoplight towns that feel plucked out of the 1930s – popular for locals who like to gun powerboats on glassy waterways and cruise winding levy roads. Its marshy area encompasses a huge patch of the state map – from the San Francisco Bay to Sacramento, and all the way south to Stockton. Travelers often zoom by on I-80 and I-5 without stopping to smell the mossy Delta breeze blowing off the conflux of the Sacramento and San Joaquin Rivers, which drain into the San Francisco Bay. If you have the time to take the unhurried route between San Francisco and Sacramento, travel across the rusting iron bridges and gracefully winding roads of Hwy 160, which lazily makes its way through a region of lush wetlands, vast orchards and little towns with long histories.

In the 1930s the Bureau of Reclamation issued an aggressive water-redirection program – the Central Valley and California State Water Projects – that dammed California's major rivers and directed 75% of their supply through the Central Valley (for agricultural use) and Southern California. The siphoning has affected the Sacramento Delta, its wetlands and estuaries, and has been a source of environmental, ecological and political debate ever since. No one knows about this more than the folks at the Hartland Nursery, home of **Delta Ecotours** (☎916-775-4545; www.hartlandnursery. com; 13737 Grand Island Rd, Walnut Grove; admission free, tours adult/child $45/20; ⓒSat by appointment). Led by Jeff Hart, the tours are ideal for land lubbers wanting to travel the channels and learn about the area's unique agricultural, environmental and historical concerns. The nursery is filled with regional plants and is a worthy stop even if the tours aren't happening

Locke (www.locketown.com) is the delta's most fascinating town, built by Chinese farmers after a fire wiped out Walnut Grove's Chinatown in 1912. In its time, Locke was the only free-standing Chinatown in the US and its unincorporated status kept it free of pesky lawmen, encouraging gambling houses and bootleg gin joints. Tucked below the highway and the levee, Locke's main street still has the feel of a Western ghost town, with weather-beaten buildings leaning into each other over the town's single street, all protected by the National Register of Historic Places. The handful of shops and galleries, worn by age and proximity to the water, are worth a stroll.

Keeping the town's heritage alive is the dusty but worthwhile **Dai Loy Museum** (www.locketown.com/museum; admission $1.25; ☾noon-4pm Sat & Sun), an old gambling hall filled with photos and relics of gaming operations, including betting tables and the antique safe.

Locke's unlikely centerpiece is **Al the Wop's** (meals $8-20), a wooden bar that's been pouring since 1934. The draw isn't the food – the special is a peanut-butter-slathered Texas toast – as much as it is the ambience. Below are creaking floorboards; above, the ceiling's covered in crusty dollar bills and more than one pair of erstwhile undies.

Hwy 160 passes through **Isleton**, so-called Crawdad Town USA, whose main street is lined with shops, restaurants, bars and buildings hinting at the region's Chinese heritage. Isleton's **Crawdad Festival**, at the end of June, draws folks from all over the state, but you can slurp down the fresh little crayfish all year long at **Isleton Joe's** (www.isletonjoes.com; mains $6-16; ☾8am-9pm).

Further west on Hwy 160 you'll see signs for the **Delta Loop**, a drive that passes boater bars and marinas where you can rent something to take on the water. At the end, you come to the **Brannan State Recreation Area** (☾Fri-Mon) a tidy state-run facility with boat-in, drive-in and walk-in **campsites** (☾Fri & Sat, sites $30-40) and picnic facilities galore.

Davis

Davis, home to a University of California school, is a sunny college town where bikes outnumber cars two-to-one (it boasts more bikes per capita than any other American city). With students comprising about half of the population, it's a progressive outpost amid the conservative farm towns of Sacramento Valley. Its vibrant cafe, pub and arts scene comes alive during the school year.

Dodging the bikes on a walk through downtown Davis you will pass a number of cute small businesses (the progressive city council has forbidden any store over 50,000 sq ft – sorry, Wal-Mart).

I-80 skirts the south edge of town, and you can reach downtown via the Richards Blvd exit. University of California, Davis (UCD) is southwest of downtown, bordered by A St, 1st St and Russell Blvd. The campus' main entrances are accessed from I-80 via Old Davis Rd or from downtown via 3rd St. East of the campus, Hwy 113 heads north 10 miles to Woodland, where it intersects with I-5; another 28 miles north it connects with Hwy 99.

⊙ Sights & Activities

Bicycling is popular here, probably because the only hill around is the bridge that crosses over the freeway. **Lake Berryessa**, around 30 miles west, is a favorite destination. See p337 for bike-rental information.

Pence Gallery   GALLERY
(www.pencegallery.org; 212 D St; ☾11:30am-5pm Tue-Sun) The impressive, purpose-built gallery exhibits contemporary California art and hosts lectures and art films.

UC Davis Arboretum   PARK
(http://arboretum.ucdavis.edu) For a short hike, there is a paved 2-mile trail through the peaceful arboretum.

🛏 Sleeping

Davis isn't a great town for hotels. Like most university towns, the rates are stable until graduation or special campus events, when they rise high and sell out fast. Worse, the trains that roll though the middle of town will infuriate a light sleeper. For a utilitarian (if bland) stay, look for chains along the highway.

University Park Inn & Suites   HOTEL **$$**
(☎530-756-0910; www.universityparkinn.com; 111 Richards Blvd; r $110-140; P❄@☎) Right off the highway and a short walk from campus and downtown, this independently operated hotel is not the Ritz, but is clean and has spacious suites.

Aggie Inn   HOTEL **$$**
(☎530-756-0352; www.aggieinn.com; 245 1st St; r from $129; ❄☎) Across from UCD's east entrance, the Aggie is neat, modern and unassuming. The hotel has a Jacuzzi and offers free coffee and pastries.

ℹ️ TULE FOG

Radiation or tule (*too*-lee) fog causes dozens of collisions each year on Central Valley roads, including Hwy 99 and I-5. As thick as the proverbial pea soup, the fog limits visibility to about 10ft, making driving nearly impossible. The fog is thickest from November to February, when cold mountain air settles on the warm valley floor and condenses into fog as the ground cools at night. The fog often lifts for a few hours during the afternoon, just long enough for the ground to warm back up and thus perpetuate the cycle.

If you end up on a fog-covered road, drive with your low beams on, keep a good distance from the car in front of you, stay at a constant speed, avoid sudden stops and never try to pass other cars.

✖️ Eating

College students love to eat and drink cheap, and downtown has no short supply of lively ethnic eateries gunning for the student dollar. The **Davis farmers market** (www.davisfarmersmarket.org; cnr 4th & C Sts; ⊙8am-noon Sat, 2-8.30pm Wed) features food vendors, street performers and live bands. There are a number of good options for self-catering.

Davis Noodle City　　　　　ASIAN $
(129 E St; mains $5-10; ⊙11am-9pm Mon-Sat, to 8:30pm Sun) Situated in the back of a courtyard behind Sophia's Thai Kitchen, the menu here has dishes from all over Asia, with homemade noodles and superb scallion pancakes. The pork-chop noodle soup – with thick noodles and slices of tender pork rubbed with Chinese five spice – is the best thing on the menu.

Delta of Venus Coffeehouse & Pub　CAFE $
(www.deltaofvenus.org; 122b St; meals $5-10; ⊙7:30am-10pm; 🖧) This converted Arts and Crafts bungalow has a very social shaded front patio. The chalkboard menu has breakfast items, salads, soups and sandwiches, including vegetarian and vegan options. At dinner time you can order jerk-seasoned Caribbean dishes and wash them down with a beer or wine. It comes alive with a hip folk scene at night.

Woodstocks　　　　　　PIZZA $
(www.woodstocksdavis.com; 219 G St; slice $2.50, pizzas $15-20; ⊙lunch & dinner) Woodstocks has Davis' most popular pizza, which is also sold by the slice for lunch. In addition to cheap and meaty favorites, the menu gets a touch more sophisticated with a variety of veggie and gourmet pies that come with a chewy wheat crust. Open until 2am Thursday to Saturday when school is in session.

Redrum　　　　　　BURGERS $
(☎530-756-2142; 978 Olive Dr; meals $5-10; ⊙10am-11pm Mon-Thu, to midnight Fri & Sat) Formerly known as Murder Burger, Redrum is popular with students and travelers for fresh, made-to-order beef, turkey and ostrich burgers, thick espresso shakes and crispy curly fries. The ZOOM – a gnarled, deep-fried pile of zucchini, onion rings and mushrooms – is the menu must.

☆ Entertainment

Major theater, music, dance and other performances take place at **Mondavi Center for the Performing Arts** (www.mondaviarts.org; 1 Shields Ave), a state-of-the-art venue on the UCD campus. **Varsity Theatre** (☎530-759-8724; 616 2nd St) also stages performances. For tickets and information on shows at either the Varsity or the Mondavi Center, you can also call the **UC Davis Ticket Office** (☎530-752-1915, 866-823-2787).

Just up the road in Winters, **Palm's Playhouse** (www.palmsplayhouse.com) books lots of rhythm 'n' blues, cover bands and blues.

ℹ️ Information

Davis Conference and Visitor Bureau (☎530-297-1900; www.davisvisitor.com; Suite 300, 105 E St; ⊙8:30am-4:30pm Mon-Fri) Has free maps and brochures. The exhaustive www.daviswiki.org is useful to peruse.

ℹ️ Getting There & Away

Amtrak (☎530-758-4220; 840 2nd St) Davis' station is on the southern edge of downtown. There are trains bound for Sacramento or San Francisco throughout the day. The fare to San Francisco is $25 and the trip takes about two hours.

Yolobus (☎530-666-2877; ⊙5am-11pm) Route 42A ($2) loops between Davis and the Sacramento airport. The route also connects Davis with Woodland and Downtown Sacramento.

ℹ️ Getting Around

When driving around – especially when you pull out from a parking space – be aware of bike traffic: it's the primary mode of transportation here.

Ken's Bike & Ski (www.kensbikeski.com; 650 G St) Rents basic bikes (from $19 per day) as well as serious road and mountain bikes.

Unitrans (☏530-752-2877; http://unitrans. ucdavis.edu; one-way fare $1) If you're not biking, this student-run outfit shuttles people around town and campus. Many buses are red double-deckers.

Oroville

Oroville has seen quite a reversal: the lust for gold initially attracted white settlers to the area, who displaced native tribes. Today, crowds flock to the thriving tribal casinos on the periphery of the town seeking riches. Aside from the slots, the economy leans on the plastic-bag factory on the outskirts of town and the tourists who mill though the throng of antique stores. Oroville's population boomed in recent years, with families fleeing the high-priced housing of the Bay Area, but the housing bubble's burst has hit these suburbs hard. Oroville's most enduring attraction, aside from the nearby lake, is an excellent museum left behind by a long-gone Chinese community.

Gold was discovered near here in 1848 by John Bidwell, and the booming little town took the name Ophir (Gold) City. Oroville was where Ishi, the last surviving member of the local Yahi tribe, was 'found' back in 1911 (p338).

◎ Sights & Activities

Chinese Temple   TEMPLE
(1500 Broderick St; adult/child $3/free; ⊙noon-4pm) A relatively quiet monument to the 10,000 Chinese people who once lived here, the temple is a compelling draw that exceeds expectations. The temple seved a Chinese community who worked to rebuild the area levees after a devastating 1907 flood wiped out Chinatown. During the 19th century, theater troupes from China toured a circuit of Chinatowns in California and Oroville was the end of the line. The troupes often left their sets, costumes and puppets here before returning to China, which has left the temple with an unrivaled collection of 19th-century Chinese stage finery. The temple itself is a beautifully preserved building bursting with religious shrines, festival tapestries, ancient lion masks and furniture. To keep everything in context, take advantage of docent-led tours, which can take an hour.

Sacramento National Wildlife Refuge   BIRD-WATCHING
Serious bird-watchers should head to the Sacramento National Wildlife Refuge during winter, where the migratory waterfowl are a spectacular sight. The **visitor center** (☏530-934-2801; www.fws.gov/sacramentovalleyrefuges; 752 County Rd, Willows; ⊙7:30am-4pm Mon-Fri) is off I-5 near Willows; a 6-mile driving trail ($3) and walking trails are open daily. The peak season to see birds is between October and late February, with large populations of geese in December and January.

Lake Oroville (www.lakeoroville.net), a popular summertime destination, sits 9 miles northeast of town behind **Oroville Dam**, the largest earthen dam in the US. The surrounding Lake Oroville State Recreation Area attracts boaters, campers, swimmers, bicyclists, hikers and fishing folk. Oroville is also a gateway to the gorgeous Feather River Canyon and the rugged northern reaches of the Sierra Nevada. The lake's **visitor center** (☏530-538-2219; 917 Kelly Ridge Rd; ⊙9am-5pm) has exhibits on the California State Water Project and local Native American history, plus a viewing tower and loads of recreational information.

The area surrounding Lake Oroville is full of hiking trails, and a favorite is the 7-mile round-trip walk to 640ft **Feather Falls**, which takes about four hours. The **Freeman Bicycle Trail** is a 41-mile off-road loop that takes cyclists to the top of 770ft Oroville Dam, then follows the Feather River back to the Thermalito Forebay and Afterbay storage reservoirs, east of Hwy 70. The ride is mostly flat, but the dam ascent is steep. Get a free map of the ride from the chamber of commerce. The **Forebay Aquatic Center** (www.aschico.com/forebayaquaticcenter; Garden Dr) rents watercraft to get out on the water.

Hwys 162 and 70 head northeast from Oroville into the mountains and on to Quincy. Hwy 70 snakes along the magnificent **Feather River Canyon**, an especially captivating drive during the fall.

🛏️ Sleeping & Eating

A launching pad for outdoorsy trips, there's plenty of camping in the area, which you can arrange through the chamber of com-

LONE YAHI FOUND IN OROVILLE

At daybreak on August 29, 1911, frantic dogs woke the butchers sleeping inside a slaughterhouse outside Oroville. When they came out, they found their dogs holding a man at bay – a Native American clad only in a loincloth, starving, exhausted and unable to speak English.

The stories of the discovery of a 'wild man' spread through California papers, eventually attracting Berkeley anthropologists Alfred L Kroeber and Thomas Talbot Waterman. They traveled to Oroville and, with scraps of nearly lost vocabulary from vanished native languages, eventually discovered the man belonged to the Yahi, the southernmost tribe of the Yana, who were believed to be extinct.

Waterman took 'Ishi,' meaning 'man' in the Yahi language, to the museum at the university, where he was cared for and brought back to health. Ishi spent his remaining years there, telling the anthropologists his life story and teaching them his tribal language, lore and ways.

Ishi's tribe had been virtually exterminated by settlers before he was born. In 1870, when he was a child, there were only 12 or 15 Yahi people left, hiding in remote areas in the foothills east of Red Bluff. By 1908 Ishi, his mother, sister and an old man were all who were left of the Yahi tribe. In that year the others died and Ishi was left alone. On March 25, 1916, Ishi died of tuberculosis at the university hospital and the Yahi disappeared forever.

The site where Ishi was found is east of Oroville along Oro-Quincy Hwy at Oak Ave, marked by a small monument. Part of the Lassen National Forest where Ishi and the Yahi people lived, is now called the Ishi Wilderness.

merce, the USFS office or the Lake Oroville visitor center. A strip of decent budget motels – mostly chains and some humble mid-century cheapies – are clustered on Feather River Blvd, between Hwy 162 to the south and Montgomery St to the north. There's not much of a chance that you'll be thrilled about the dining options in town, but aside from fast-food joints by the major eateries, there are some passable places in the small downtown offering plates of Mexican and pub grub.

**Lake Oroville State
Recreation Area**   CAMPGROUND $
(✆530-538-2219; www.parks.ca.gov; 917 Kelly Ridge Rd; tent/RV sites $20/40; 🛜) The wi-fi might be the first clue that this isn't the most rustic choice, but there are a variety of sites. There are good primitive sites if you're willing to hike, and – perhaps the coolest feature of the park – floating campsites on platforms that are accessible only by boat.

ⓘ Information

The office of the USFS **Feather River Ranger District** (✆530-534-6500; 875 Mitchell Ave; ⊙8am-4:30pm Mon-Fri) has maps and brochures. For road conditions, phone ✆800-427-7623.

ⓘ Getting There & Away

Although Greyhound buses stop at **Tom's Sierra Chevron** (✆530-533-1333; cnr 5th Ave & Oro Dam Blvd), a few blocks east of Hwy 70, a car is far and away the simplest and most cost effective way to reach the area. There are two buses daily between Oroville and Sacramento. The trip takes 1½ hours and costs $37.

Chico

With its huge population of students, Chico has the devil-may-care energy of a college kegger during the school year, and a lazy, lethargic hangover during the summertime. Its oak-shaded downtown and university attractions makes it one of Sacramento Valley's more attractive social and cultural hubs, where easygoing folks mingle late in the restaurants and bars, which open onto patios in the balmy summer evenings.

And though Chico wilts in the heat of the summer, the swimming holes in Bidwell Park take the edge off during the day, as does a tubing trip down the gentle Sacramento River. The fine pale ales produced at the Sierra Nevada Brewing Company, near downtown, are another of Chico's refreshing blessings.

There's a bit of irony in the fact a town so widely celebrated for its brews was founded by John Bidwell, the illustrious California pioneer who made a bid for US president with the Prohibitionist party. In 1868, Bidwell and his wife, Annie Ellicott Kennedy, moved to the new mansion he had built, now the Bidwell Mansion State Historic Park. After John died in 1900, Annie continued as a philanthropist until her death in 1918.

◉ Sights

Downtown is west of Hwy 99, easily reached via Hwy 32 (8th St). Main St and Broadway are the central downtown streets; from there, Park Ave stretches southward and the tree-lined Esplanade heads north.

🍃 Sierra Nevada Brewing Company
BREWERY

(www.sierranevada.com; 1075 E 20th St) Though too big to officially qualify as a 'microbrewery,' this hotspot draws hordes of beer snobs to the birthplace of their nationally distributed Sierra Nevada Pale Ale and Schwarber, a Chico-only black ale. Also for sale are the **'Beer Camp' brews** (www.sierrabeercamp.com), which are short-run boutique beers brewed by ultra beer nerds at invitation-only three-day summer seminars. The brewery is on the very cutting edge of sustainable business practices – their rooftop solar fields are among the largest privately owned solar fields in the US and they extended a spur of local railroad to increase transportation efficiency. Excellent tours are given at 2:30pm daily, and continuously from noon to 5pm on Saturdays. There's also a pub and restaurant (see p340).

Chico Creek Nature Center
NATURE CENTER

(www.bidwellpark.org; 1968 East 8th St; suggested donation $1; ⏰11am-4pm Tue-Sun; 🚼) If you plan on spending the afternoon in Bidwell Park, first stop at this sparkling new nature center, with great displays on local plants and animals and excellent hands-on science programs for families.

Chico State University
UNIVERSITY

Ask for a free map of the Chico State University campus, or ask about campus events and tours, at the **CSU Information Center** (☎530-898-4636; www.csuchico.edu; cnr Chestnut & W 2nd Sts), on the main floor of Bell Memorial Union. The attractive campus is infused with sweet floral fragrances in spring, and there's a rose garden at its center.

Honey Run Covered Bridge
HISTORIC SITE

The historic 1894 bridge is straight out of *The Legend of Sleepy Hollow* – and an unusual type of bridge in this part of the country. Take the Skyway exit off Hwy 99 on the southern outskirts of Chico, head east and go left on Honey Run-Humbug Rd; the bridge is 5 miles along, in a small park.

Bidwell Mansion State Historic Park
HISTORIC BUILDING

(☎530-895-6144; 525 Esplanade; adult/child $6/3; ⏰noon-5pm Wed-Fri, 11am-5pm Sat & Sun) Chico's most prominent landmark, the opulent Victorian home built for Chico's founders John and Annie Bidwell. The 26-room mansion was built between 1865 and 1868 and hosted many US presidents. Tours start every hour on the hour. Due to budget difficulty, this park was slated for closure in 2012.

🏃 Activities

Growing out of downtown, the 3670-acre **Bidwell Park** (www.bidwellpark.org) is the nation's third-largest municipal park. It stretches 10 miles northwest along Chico Creek with lush groves and miles of trails. The upper part of the park is fairly untamed, which is surprising to find smack dab in the middle of the city. Several classic movies have been shot here, including *The Adventures of Robin Hood* and parts of *Gone with the Wind*.

The park is full of hiking and mountain-biking trails and swimming spots, and has a nature center. You'll find pools at One-Mile and Five-Mile recreation areas and swimming holes (including Bear Hole, Salmon Hole and Brown Hole) in Upper Bidwell Park, north of Manzanita Ave. Don't be surprised if locals opt for birthday suits, not swimsuits.

In summer you'll want to cool off from the hike by **tubing** the Sacramento. Inner tubes can be rented at grocery stores and other shops along Nord Ave (Hwy 32) for around $6. Tubers enter at the Irvine Finch Launch Ramp on Hwy 32, a few miles west of Chico, and come out at the Washout, off River Rd.

🎉 Festivals & Events

With the students out of town, family-friendly outdoor events take over the town each summer. The **Thursday Night Market** fills several blocks of Broadway every Thursday evening from April to September. At City Plaza you'll find free **Friday Night Concerts** starting in

May. **Shakespeare in the Park** (☑530-891-1382; www.ensembletheatreofchico.com; admission free), at Cedar Grove in lower Bidwell Park, runs from mid-July to the end of August.

🛏 Sleeping

There's an abundance of well-kept independent motels with sparkling swimming pools, some of them along the shaded Esplanade north of downtown. Beware that Chico State's graduation and homecoming mania (in May and October, respectively) send prices through the roof.

TOP CHOICE **Hotel Diamond**   HISTORIC HOTEL $$$

(☑866-993-3100; www.hoteldiamondchico.com; 220 W 4th St; r from $189; ❋@🤶) This whitewashed 1904 building is the most luxurious place to lay your head in Chico, with high-thread-count linens, valet laundry and room service of comfort foods in California-fusion style like prawn-dressed macaroni and cheese. The Diamond Suite, with its balcony, original furnishings and spacious top-floor balcony is a-*maz*-ing.

Matador Motel   MOTEL $

(☑530-342-7543; 1934 Esplanade; r $47-51; ❋❋) This pleasant courtyard motel not far from downtown has simple rooms done up with old-fashioned Mission-style details. The buildings wrap around a beautiful tiled swimming pool shaded by palms.

The Grateful Bed   B&B $$

(☑530-342-2464; www.thegratefulbed.net; 1462 Arcadian Ave; r $105-160; ❋@) Well, obviously you're a bedhead if you stay here. Tucked in a residential neighborhood near downtown, it's a stately 1905 Victorian home with four sweetly decorated rooms with warm hosts. Breakfast is included.

Woodson Bridge State Recreation Area   CAMPGROUND $

(☑530-839-2112; tent sites $25) This shaded campground, adjacent to a huge native riparian preserve, has 46 tent sites on the banks of the Sacramento River. It's about 25 miles north of Chico on Hwy 99, then west toward Corning.

🍴 Eating

Downtown Chico is packed with fun places to eat, many of them catering to a student budget. The outdoor **farmers market** (cnr Wall & E 2nd Sts; ⊙7:30am-1pm Sat) draws from the plentiful surrounding valley.

Café Coda   BREAKFAST, BRUNCH $

(www.cafecoda.com; 265 Humboldt Ave; mains $6-10; ⊙7am-2pm Tue-Sun; 🤶) Café Coda is Chico's best breakfast for its expert Southwestern-influenced scrambles, sweet selections (like lemon poppyseed pancakes with mint butter) and thrifty Champagne brunch (all you can drink for only $4.50). Served by a chipper staff, all breakfasts come in half-portions upon request. Appropriate to their name, they host live music on some evenings.

Nobby's   BURGERS $

(1444 Park Ave; burgers $5-7; ⊙10:30am-9pm Tue-Sun) Simply put, the Nobby Burger, topped with a large fried disc of cheese and crispy, thick bacon, is a heart attack. Worth it? Probably. Note that the place is tiny and you'll likely have to stand. Cash only.

Sierra Nevada Taproom & Restaurant   BREWPUB $$

(www.sierranevada.com; 1075 E 20th St; meals $8-15; ⊙11am-9pm Sun-Thu, to 10pm Fri & Sat) The apple-malt pork loin is a standout at the Sierra Nevada Brewery's on-site restaurant, a genuine Chico destination. It's great to soak up the brews, but lacks ambience – the huge, loud dining room feels a bit like a factory cafeteria (which it kind of is). Still, it has better-than-average pub food, superb fresh ales and lagers on tap, some not available anywhere else.

5th Street Steakhouse   AMERICAN $$$

(☑530-899-8075; www.5thstreetsteakhouse.com; 345 W 5th Street; mains $16-37; ⊙from 4:30pm) This is the joint where college students take their visiting parents, featuring steaks tender enough to cut with a reproachful look, and occasional live jazz. The interior is stately, with exposed brick and crisp white tablecloths.

🗹 **Red Tavern**   FUSION $$$

(☑530-894-3463; www.redtavern.com; 1250 Esplanade; mains $15-29; ⊙from 4:30pm Mon-Sat) Slightly swanky, the Red Tavern is one of Chico's favorite fine-dining experiences, with a sophisticated menu that balances discriminatingly between Europe and Asia and uses local, seasonal organic food.

Celestino's Live from New York Pizza   PIZZA $

(101 Salem St; mains $3-7; ⊙10:30am-10pm Mon-Thu, to 11pm Fri & Sat) One of the best imitations of 'real' New York pizza in Northern California, they serve slices with a thin,

chewy crust and playfully themed variations like the meaty Godfather. The slice-n-a-soda lunch special for $4 is a good deal.

Sins of Cortez
CAFE $

(www.sinofcortez.com; 101 Salem St; mains $6-16; ⊙7am-9pm) The service won't win awards for speed, but this local favorite draws a mob for its burly breakfast plates. Order anything with the homemade chorizo.

Shubert's Ice Cream & Candy
ICE CREAM $

(178 E 7th St; ⊙9.30am-10pm Mon-Fri, 11am-10pm Sat & Sun) Having produced delicious homemade ice cream and chocolates for more than 60 years, this is a beloved Chico landmark.

El Pasia Taco Truck
MEXICAN $

(cnr 8th & Pine Sts; mains $1.50-5; ⊙11am-8pm) Debate about which of Chico's taco trucks is the best can quickly lead to fisticuffs – but the smoky *carnitas* (braised pork) tacos here are a broke college student's dream.

🍷 Drinking

As you might have guessed from Chico's party-school rep, you're unlikely to go thirsty. There's a strip of bars on Main St if you want to go hopping.

Madison Bear Garden
BAR

(www.madisonbeargarden.com; 316 W 2nd St; ⊙noon-2am; 🐾) This whimsically decorated student hangout is housed in a spacious brick building. It's the place to chat to students over thick burgers and cool beers. Toward the end of the night, the ramshackle disorder of the decor is a perfect match with the boozy, high-fiving co-eds in the big beer garden. They serve burgers to soak up the beers.

Panama Bar & Cafe
BAR

(128 Broadway; ⊙11am-10pm) The house specializes in variations of Long Island iced tea (most of which are priced around $3), so brace yourself. For a wild night out in Chico, the only way to consume more liquor would be with an IV drip.

Naked Lounge
COFFEE SHOP

(118 2nd St; ⊙10am-9pm Sun-Thu, to midnight Fri & Sat; 🐾) With its dark-red, enveloping interior and expertly drawn espresso drinks, this is Chico's best place to get caffeinated.

☆ Entertainment

For entertainment options, pick up the free weekly *Chico News & Review* (www.newsan dreview.com), available in newspaper boxes and businesses downtown. For theater, films, concerts, art exhibits and other cultural events at the CSU campus, contact the **CSU Box Office** (☑530-898-6333) or the **CSU Information Center** (☑530-898-4636) in the Bell Memorial Union.

LaSalle's
CLUB

(www.lasallesbar.com; 229 Broadway) This venue is open nightly for hip-hop, Top 40 and retro dance nights and live bands that play anything to pack people in – from reggae to hard rock.

Pageant Theatre
CINEMA

(www.pageantchico.com; 351 E 6th St) Screens international and alternative films. Monday is bargain night, with all seats just $3.

Chico Caberet
CABERET

(☑530-895-0245; www.chicocabaret.com; tickets $16) All fishnets and sass, this local theater troupe brings racy annual shows to Butte County theaters.

❶ Information

Chico Chamber of Commerce & Visitor Center (☑530-891-5559; www.chicochamber. com; 300 Salem St; ⊙9am-5pm Mon-Fri, 10am-3pm Sat) Offers local information.

❶ Getting There & Around

Greyhound (www.greyhound.com) buses stop at the **Amtrak station** (cnr W 5th & Orange Sts). The train station is unattended so purchase tickets in advance from travel agents or on board from the conductor. Trips between Chico and Sacramento on the *Coast Starlight* line are $26 (2½ hours, once daily). Amtrak also operates buses from the station multiple times daily for a similar fare.

B-Line (☑530-342-0221, www.blinetransit. com) handles all buses throughout Butte County, and can get you around Chico and down to Oroville (tickets $2, four times daily).

Bicycles can be rented from **Campus Bicycles** (www.campusbicycles.com; 330 Main St; mountain bikes half/full day $20/35).

Red Bluff

The smoldering streets of Red Bluff – one of California's hottest towns due to the hot air trap of the Shasta Cascades – are of marginal interest unto themselves, but looking to the mountain-dominated horizon offers a clue to the outdoor activities that bring most travelers through town. The agreeable tree-lined neighborhoods are full of restored

19th-century Victorian mansions and there are some historic storefronts in the business district filled with antiques and Western wear.

Peter Lassen laid out the town site in 1847 and it grew into a key port along the Sacramento River. Now it's more of a pit stop on the way to the national park that bears his name and other points along on I-5.

Cowboy culture is alive and well here. Catch it in action the third weekend of April at the **Red Bluff Round-Up** (www.red bluffroundup.com; tickets $10-20), a major rodeo event dating back to 1921, or in any of the dive bars where the jukeboxes are stocked with Nashville, and plenty of big-buckled cowboys belly up to the bar.

◉ Sights & Activities

Red Bluff Lake Recreation Area   PARK
A good break from the highway, the Red Bluff Lake Recreation Area, on the east bank of the Sacramento River, is a spacious park full of trees, birds and meadows. It offers numerous picnicking, swimming, hiking and camping opportunities and has interpretive trails, bicycle paths, boat ramps, a wildlife-viewing area with excellent bird-watching, a fish ladder (in operation between May and September) and a 2-acre native-plant garden.

**William B Ide Adobe State
Historic Park**   HISTORIC SITE
(☑530-529-8599; 21659 Adobe Rd; ☺sunrise-sunset) Set on a beautiful, shaded piece of land overlooking a languorous section of the Sacramento River, the park preserves the original adobe home and grounds of pioneer William B Ide, who 'fought' in the 1846 Bear Flag Revolt at Sonoma (p714) and was named president of the short-lived California Republic (though, even with the blacksmith shop and the gift shop, these are humble digs for a president). To get to the park, head about a mile north on Main St, turn east onto Adobe Rd and go another mile, following the signs. At press time, the future of this state park was uncertain and subject to closure.

**Sacramento River
Discovery Center**   SCIENCE CENTER
(1000 Sale Lane; ☺11am-4pm Tue-Sat; ⊞) The center has kid-friendly displays about the river, fairly subjective information about the benefits of cattle grazing and resources about the Diversion Dam just outside its

doors. From mid-May to mid-September, the dam diverts water into irrigation canals and in the process creates Red Bluff Lake, which is a popular swimming destination.

🛌 Sleeping & Eating

Over a dozen motels are found beside I-5 and south of town along Main St, and the historic residential neighborhood has some bed-and-breakfasts. The restaurant scene isn't thrilling – a lot of cheap take-out Chinese, pizza and stick-to-the-ribs grub that's straight from a can.

**Sycamore Grove
Camping Area**   CAMPGROUND $
(☑530-824-5196; www.recreation.gov; undeveloped/developed sites $16/$25) Beside the river in the Red Bluff Lake Recreation Area is this quiet, attractive USFS campground. Campsites for tents and RVs are on a first-come, first-served basis. It also has a large group campground, Camp Discovery, where cabins are available (reservations required).

Los Mariachis   MEXICAN $
(☑530-529-1217; 248 S Main St; mains $5-14 ☺9am-9pm; ⊞) This bright, friendly, family-run Mexican dinner spot is lined with windows looking over the central junction of Red Bluff, and is a perfect stop for families. They have great salsa and *molcajetes* (meat or seafood stew, served in a stone bowl) big enough to satisfy hungry campers – big enough to share otherwise. To get a feel for the locals, saddle up to the bright yellow bar (facing a taxidermy rattle snake) and order a couple cold ones, served in frosty mugs.

New Thai House   THAI $
(www.newthaihouse.com; 248 S Main St; mains $5-14; ☺11am-9pm Mon-Fri, from noon Sat, ☑) This is a remarkably good Thai restaurant, with excellent curries and tom yum soup.

Hal's Eat 'Em Up   DRIVE-IN $
(158 Main St) If the heat is raging, grab a root-beer float from Hal's, a great small-town drive-in just south of downtown.

ℹ Information

Red Bluff Chamber of Commerce (☑530-527-6220, www.redbluffchamber.com; 100 Main St; ☺8:30am-4pm Mon, to 5pm Tue-Thu, to 4:30pm Fri) To get your bearings and a stack of brochures, go south of downtown to this small place.

ⓘ Getting There & Away

Most visitors come to Red Bluff to take a break from the busy I-5. By the highway, the town is three hours north of San Francisco and 15 minutes north of Sacramento. **Greyhound** (www.greyhound.com) and **Amtrak** (www.amtrak.com) connect it with other California cities via bus. The station is east of town at the corner of Hwy 36 E.

SAN JOAQUIN VALLEY

The southern half of California's Central Valley – named for the San Joaquin River – sprawls from Stockton to the turbine-covered Tehachapi Mountains, southeast of Bakersfield. Everything stretches to the horizon in straight lines – railroad tracks, two-lane blacktop and long irrigation channels. Through the elaborate politics and machinery of water management, this once-arid region ranks among the most agriculturally productive places in the world, though the profits often go to agribusiness shareholders, not the increasingly displaced family farmer. While some of the tiny towns scattering the region, such as Gustine and Reedley, retain a classic Main Street Americana feel, many have adapted to the influx of Latino culture brought by enormous immigrant force that harvests these fields in unaccounted numbers. Many other towns are paved over with housing developments that are populated by families escaping the onerous housing prices of the Bay Area.

Today the San Joaquin Valley is beguiling for both travelers and locals, where intense heat and dubious reminders of history and the valley's development are evident through tract houses and rusting tractors, scrawling spray-painted gang signs and the arching spray of irrigation systems.

It's also a place of seismic, often contentious, development. High housing prices in the coastal cities have resulted in unchecked eastward sprawl – some half a million acres have been paved over in the last decade. Where there once were cattle ranches and vineyards there are now the nostalgically named developments of American anyplace: a big-box shopping complex named Indian Ranch, a tidy row of McMansions named Vineyard Estates.

To sink your teeth into the region, skip I-5 and travel on Hwy 99 – a road with nearly as long a history as the famous Route 66. It'll be hot – very hot – so put the windows down and crank up the twangy traditional country or the booming traditional *norteño* (an accordion-driven genre of folk music imported from Mexico). If you have the time, exit often for bushels of the freshest produce on earth and brushes with California's nearly forgotten past.

Many of the following towns are excellent launching points for Yosemite National Park, and Hwy 99 is lined with classic, affordable motor lodges and hotel chains.

Lodi

Although Lodi used to be the 'Watermelon capital of the world,' today, wine rules this patch of the valley. Breezes from the Sacramento River Delta soothe the area's hot vineyards, where more zinfandel grapes are grown than anywhere else in the world. Some particularly old vines have been tended by the same families for over a century. Lodi's diverse soil is sometimes rocky, sometimes a fine sandy loam, giving its zins a range of distinctive characteristics.

Get your first taste of Lodi's powerful, sun-soaked zins at the **Lodi Wine & Visitor Center** (☎209-365-0621; www.lodiwine.com; 2545 W Turner Rd; tastings $5; ◷10am-5pm), where 100 local vintages are sold by the glass at the solid-wood tasting bar. They'll provide maps to wineries of the region. Another stop to sip the region's boutique wines and experimental labels by more famous names is the Italian-style **Vino Piazza** (☎209-727-3270; 12470 Locke Rd, Lockeford) where you can park the car, order a bistro lunch and amble between tasting rooms. It is just east of town. Follow the signs from Hwy 12.

Given Lodi's love of the tipple, it's no surprise that they have a slew of festivals dedicated to wine, including the **Grape & Harvest Festival** in September and **Zinfest** in May.

Lodi's **Micke Grove Regional Park and Zoo** (☎209-953-8840; www.mgzoo.com; admission $2; 2545 W Turner Rd; ◷10am-5pm; ⚐) is a good stop for the seriously underage, with a water play area, hissing cockroaches and some barking sea lions. There's also a small children's amusement park, where rides cost a nominal extra fee.

🛏 Sleeping & Eating

Along Hwy 99, Lodi hosts a string of budget chain hotels. Though the rooms are bland, the competition ensures that they are all very clean; they can be a real bargain.

TOP LODI WINERIES

Low key and constantly improving, Lodi's vineyards make an easy escape from the Bay Area, and the quality of grapes will delight Napa veterans. It's also an incredibly easy wine area to navigate, as the roads are well marked. For a map, try the **Lodi Wine & Visitor Center** (www.lodiwine.com). Opinions on Lodi's best wineries tend to be as entangled as the vines, but these are some favorites. The region is easily accessed from I-5 or Hwy 99.

Jesse's Grove (www.jessiesgrovewinery.com; 1973 W Turner Rd; ⊘noon-5pm) With its 'Groovin' in the Grove' summer concert series and long family tradition of estate grown wines, this is an anchor of Lodi wine producers. The tasting room has a terrific collection of historic photos of Lodi. During events you can sometimes camp here.

Michael David (www.michaeldavidwinery.com; 4580 W Hwy 12; ⊘10am-5pm) With a cafe that serves platters of fresh food (count yourself lucky if you get here on taco Tuesday) and an old-fashioned dry goods store, Michael David produces a renowned zinfandel, 7 Deadly Zins.

Harney Lane (www.harneylane.com; 9010 E Harney Lane; ⊘noon-5pm Thu-Sun) A sweet family outfit that's been around Lodi forever, their tempranillo is an overachiever in wine competitions.

d'Art (www.dartwines.com; 13299 N Curry Ave; ⊘noon-5pm Thu-Sun) Helen and Dave Dart bring artisanal passion to their bold Cab. The tasting room is comfortable and fun.

Jeremy Wine Co (www.jeremywineco.com; 6 W Pine St; ⊘1-5pm Wed-Sun) For those who don't have time for a countryside tour, Jeremy's brass- and wood-fitted tasting room in central Lodi offers a good taste of the region's promise. The bright fruit-forward sangiovese is their best.

🍷 **Wine & Roses**　BOUTIQUE HOTEL **$$$**
(☎209-334-6988; www.winerose.com; 2505 W Turner Rd; r $169-269, ste from $325) Surrounded by a giant rose garden and deep green lawns, Wine & Roses is a surprisingly luxurious offering to spring up amid the blistering heat of Lodi's vineyards. Tasteful, modern and romantic, the rooms have slate bathrooms and high quality bath products, luxurious sheets and large sitting areas. Naturally each one has a pair of wine glasses too. The suites? Even more over-the-top; some open to private terraces. There's also an acclaimed spa and on-site restaurant.

Crush Kitchen & Bar　ITALIAN **$$**
(www.crushkitchen.com; 115 S School St; mains $17-23; ⊘11:30am-9:30pm Sun, Mon, Thu, to 11:30pm Fri & Sat, 5-9pm Wed) With an excellent, extremely long wine list and a menu that leans heavily Italian, Crush is several notches of sophistication ahead of anything else in town. The plates are expert, simple and rustic cooking: fresh tomato salad, gnocchi with a touch of truffle oil and duck confit. If you don't have time to sit, the accompanying market has all kinds of cured meat, artisanal cheese and local honey for a perfect picnic.

Cheese Central　MARKET **$**
(www.cheesecentrallodi.com; 11 N School St; ⊘10am-6pm Mon-Sat) Ask Cindy, the owner of this shop, for thoughtful pairings with Lodi's wine. If there's just two of you, check the 'mouse trap,' a cute little cheese board where excellent imported selections are offered in modest portions. If you want to make a weekend out of Lodi's wine region, the cooking classes here get rave reviews.

Stockton

Little Stockton looked down and out for a while there. What remained of its proud past as a major inland port was blighted by crime-ridden streets and crumbling facades. This not-so-distant past is evident in the city's outskirts, which are lined with slouching, sun-bleached houses, old doughnut shops, liquor stores and taco trucks – a sad fate for a major supply point for Gold Rushers, which was hit hard by a decline in its shipbuilding and commercial transportation industries. But the downtown and waterfront redevelopment is one of the valley's more promising turnarounds, warranting a short detour.

You'll know you've reached the good part of town when you see the modern white edifice of the **Weber Point Events Center** (221 Center St), standing in the middle of a grassy park looking rather like a pile of sailboats. The events center is where much of the action is, with the huge **Asparagus Festival** in April, a series of open-air concerts, and fountains where squealing children cool off during summer break. Nearby is the beautiful new **Banner Island Ballpark** (www.stocktonports.com; 404 W Fremont St), where the minor-league Stockton Seals play baseball (April to September). Also near is the **Haggin Museum** (www.hagginmuseum.org; 1201 N Pershing Ave; tickets $5; 1:30am-5pm Wed-Fri, noon-5pm Sat & Sun), which has an excellent collection of American landscape paintings and an Egyptian mummy.

Just across the channel is the Greater Stockton Chamber of Commerce's **Department of Tourism** (209-547-2770; www.visitstockton.org; Suite 220, 445 W Weber Ave; 9am-5pm Mon-Fri), with complete information about the goings-on in town.

Get lunch a few blocks north at **Manny's California Fresh Café** (209-463-6415; 1612 Pacific Ave; mains $6-15; 10am-9:45pm), where rotisserie meats and fried-chicken sandwiches burst with flavor. It's at the edge of the **Miracle Mile** district (a developing shopping stretch on Pacific Ave, north of downtown).

If you're spending the night here after a ball game, the best bet is the **University Plaza Waterfront Hotel** (209-944-1140; www.universityplazawaterfronthotel.com; 110 W Fremont St; r $99-109;), a place where work travelers mingle with students (the upper floors have student lofts). The very modern building overlooking the harbor and historic park, unlike the highway side chains, is walkable from other locations at the city center.

Modesto

Cruising was banned in Modesto in 1993, but the town still touts itself as the 'cruising capital of the world.' That notoriety stems mostly from hometown boy George Lucas' 1973 film *American Graffiti*. You'll still see hot rods and flashy wheels around town, but they won't be clogging thoroughfares on Friday night. The Ernest & Julio Gallo Winery, makers of America's best-selling jug wines, is among the town's biggest businesses. Old oaks arch over the city's attractive streets and you can eat well in the compact downtown. This is a good spot for getting off the dusty highway.

Downtown sits just east of Hwy 99 (avoid the area west of the freeway), centering on 10th and J Sts. From downtown, Yosemite Blvd (Hwy 132) runs east toward Yosemite National Park.

Many historic buildings have survived revitalization, including the 1934 **State Theatre** (www.thestate.org; 1307 J St), which hosts films and live music, and the old **SP depot**, a Mission-style beauty. The famous **Modesto Arch**, on the corner of 9th and I Sts, erected in 1912, stands at what was once the city's main entry point (see boxed text, p305). Classic car shows are held in **Graffiti Month** (June); for details, call the **chamber of commerce** (209-577-5757; 1114 J St; 8:30am-5pm Mon-Fri).

Amid all the '50s charm of Modesto, **Brighter Side** (www.brighter-side.com; cnr 13th & K Sts; mains $4-6; 11am-3:30pm Mon-Fri) is an earthy little sandwich shop that seems about a decade late to the party; housed in a wood-shingled former gas station, they make amazing sandwiches. The sandwiches all have personalized names, like the flavorful Larry (polish sausage, mushrooms, green onions on rye) or the crisp Christine, enjoyed on the sunny patio by a crowd of Modesto's downtown office workers.

Papachino's Greco-Roman Restaurant (www.mypapachinos.com; 1212t J St; mains

DON'T MISS

STOCKTON ASPARAGUS FESTIVAL

Of all the Central Valley food celebrations, none pay such creative respect to the main ingredient as the **Stockton Asparagus Festival** (www.asparagusfest.com), which brings together more than 500 vendors who serve the little green stalks in every presentation imaginable – more than 10 tons of it! – along 'Asparagus Alley.' It all unfolds along the lovely waterfront at the end of April.

$9-13, ⊙11am-8pm Mon-Sat; ✍) is another quick, quality meal in an equally eclectic setting – don't be put off by the trippy murals. The gyro plate is savory, garlicky and dressed in a brightly flavored dill sauce and the lamb is a favorite. The yogurt is homemade and there are lots of options for vegetarians. Lunches are served with a simple white bean soup.

A&W Drive-In (cnr 14th & G Sts; mains $3-9, ⊙10am-10pm) is a vintage burger stand (part of a chain founded in nearby Lodi) filled with poodle-skirt corniness, though roller-skating carhops, classic cars and ties to *American Graffiti* move a lot of root beer. (George Lucas supposedly cruised here as a youth.)

Merced

You can jog over to Yosemite from many of the small towns in this part of the valley, but this is the most convenient staging area, right on Hwy 140. The machine of progress has not been kind to Merced, as it suffers more than its share of strip malls, but at its core there are tree-lined streets, historic Victorian homes and a magnificent 1875 courthouse. The downtown business district is a work-in-progress, with 1930s movie theaters, antique stores and a few casual eateries undergoing constant renovation.

Merced is right in the midst of a population makeover, thanks to the newest University of California campus, opened in 2005. UC Merced's first freshman class numbered just 1000 students, but the school continues to grow with a diverse student body, which has begun to dramatically shape the city.

Downtown Merced is east of Hwy 99 along Main St, between R St and Martin Luther King Jr Way. The **California Welcome Center** (☎209-384-2791; 710 W 16th St), adjacent to the bus depot, has local maps and information on Merced and Yosemite.

The big attraction is the **Castle Air Museum** (☎209-723-2178; 5050 Santa Fe Dr; adult/child $10/5; ⊙9am-5pm) in Atwater, about 6 miles northwest of Merced. A squadron of restored military aircrafts from WWII, the Korean War and the Vietnam War sit eerily dormant across from a large hangar. Even the most conscientious of objectors stand agape at these streamlined killing machines.

In a grand old Colonial-style mansion, **Hooper House Bear Creek Inn** (☎209-723-3991; www.hooperhouse.com; 575 W North Bear Creek Dr; r $129-159; ✸🐾🌐) is a leisurely retreat. Rooms are large and beautifully furnished with hardwood furniture, soft beds and tiled bathrooms. A full breakfast is included, which you can have sent to your room.

The six-bed, family-style **HI Merced Home Hostel** (☎209-725-0407; dm $15-18; ⊙reception 5:30-10pm) is in the home of long-time Merced residents. The place is like staying at the home of long-lost aunt and uncle (think collectable spoons) who sit around the kitchen table at night to help lend sage advice for excursions into Yosemite. The hostel fills quickly, especially during summer weekends. Beds must be reserved in advance; call between 5:30pm and 10pm. The hostel is in a quiet residential neighborhood and doesn't give out its address, but it will pick up and drop off guests at the bus and train stations.

The **Branding Iron** (www.thebrandingiron -merced.com; 640 W 16th St; lunch mains $9-11, dinner mains $10-25; ⊙11am-9pm Mon-Fri, from 5pm Sat & Sun) roadhouse, a favorite of ranchers in the area, has been spruced up a bit for the tour buses, but folks dig the hearty steak platters and Western atmosphere. Presiding over the dining room is 'Old Blue,' a massive stuffed bull's head from a local dairy farm.

Yarts (☎209-388-9589, www.yarts.com) buses depart four times daily for Yosemite Valley from several Merced locations, including the **Merced Transpo Center** (cnr 16th & N Sts) and the **Amtrak station** (cnr 24th &

K Sts). The trip takes about 2½ hours and stops include Mariposa, Midpines and the Yosemite Bug Lodge & Hostel. Round-trip adult/child tickets cost $25/18 and include the park entrance fee (quite a bargain!). There's also space on the Yarts buses for bicycles, but space is limited, so show up early.

Greyhound (710 W 16th St) also operates from the Transpo Center.

Fresno

Bulging like a blister in the arid center of the state, Fresno is the biggest city in the San Joaquin Valley by far. The old brick warehouses lining the Santa Fe railroad tracks are an impressive sight, as are the many historic downtown buildings, such as the 1894 Fresno Water Tower and the 1928 Pantages (Warnors) Theatre. These compete for attention with newer structures, including the sprawling Convention Center and the modern ballpark, Chukchansi Park, for Fresno's Triple-A baseball team, the Grizzlies.

The biggest interest for a traveler is the Tower District, which boasts the only active alternative-culture neighborhood between Sacramento and Los Angeles. North of downtown, the Tower District has book and record stores, music clubs and a handful of stylish restaurants.

Like many valley towns, Fresno's huge diversity comes from Mexican, Basque and Chinese communities, which have been here for decades. More recently thousands of Hmong people have put down roots in the area. The longstanding Armenian community is most famously represented by author and playwright William Saroyan, who was born, lived and died in this city he loved dearly.

⊙ Sights & Activities

Downtown lies between Divisadero St, Hwy 41 and Hwy 99. Two miles north, the Tower District sits around the corner of E Olive Ave and N Fulton Ave.

Forestiere Underground Gardens
BOTANICAL GARDENS

(☏559-271-0734; www.undergroundgardens.info; 5021 W Shaw Ave; adult/child $12/7; ⊙tours 11am-2pm hourly Thu-Fri, 10am, 11am, noon, 1:30pm & 2:30pm Sat & Sun) If you see only one thing in Fresno, make it this, two blocks east of Hwy 99. The gardens are the singular result of Sicilian immigrant Baldasare Forestiere,

who dug out some 70 acres beneath the hardpan soil to plant citrus trees, starting in 1906. With a unique skylight system, he created a beautiful subterranean space for commercial crops and his own living quarters. Some fruit trees grow to full maturity with the sun only from the skylights. The tunnel system includes bedrooms, a library, patios, grottos and a fish pond, and is now a historic landmark. This utterly fantastical accomplishment took Forestiere some 40 years to complete and when he died in 1946 he left behind one of the Central Valley's most intriguing attractions.

Tower Theatre
HISTORIC BUILDING

(☏559-485-9050; www.towertheaterfresno.com; 815 E Olive Ave) Fresno's **Tower District** began as a shopping mecca during the 1920s, gaining its name from the Tower Theatre, a beautiful art deco movie house that opened in 1939. The theater is now used as a center for the performing arts. Surrounding it are bookstores, shops, high-end restaurants and coffeehouses, which cater to Fresno's gay and alternative communities. This is the city's best neighborhood for browsing and kicking back with an iced latte – even if the hipster quotient is tiny by comparison to that of, say, San Francisco's Mission District.

Fresno Art Museum
ART MUSEUM

(☏559-441-4221; www.fresnoartmuseum.org; 2233 N 1st St; adult/student $4/2, Tue admission free; ⊙11am-5pm Fri-Wed, to 8pm Thu) In Radio Park, this museum has rotating exhibits of contemporary art – including work by local artists – that are among the most intriguing in the valley.

Roeding Park   PARK

(per vehicle $3) On Olive Ave just east of Hwy 99, this large and shady park is home to the small **Chaffee Zoological Gardens** (☎559-498-2671; www.fresnochaffeezoo.com; adult/child $7/3.50; ☺9am-4pm; ☒). Adjacent to it are **Storyland** (☎559-264-2235; adult/child $4/3; ☺10am-5:30pm Sat & Sun, with seasonal variations; ☒), a kitschy children's fairytale world dating from 1962, and **Playland** (adult/child $5/3.50; ☒), which has kiddie rides and games.

🛏 Sleeping & Eating

Fresno has room to grow when it comes to world-class accommodations, but those using it as a launch pad for visiting Sequoia and Kings Canyon National Parks have plenty of options, either in slightly weathered midcentury structures on Hwy 99, a cluster of chains near the airport or a couple of high-rise offerings downtown. For food, the best stuff is found in the Tower District, though there's a strip of places catering to college students (read: insane beer and chicken-wing specials).

Piccadilly Inn Shaw   HOTEL $$

(☎559-226-3850; www.picadillyinn.com; 2305 W Shaw Ave; r $119-179; ☒@☒) This is Fresno's nicest option, with a lovely pool, big rooms and tons of amenities. Ask for a room with a fireplace to cuddle by in winter. If they are full, try one of their other properties in town: Piccadilly Inn University, the Piccadilly Inn Express and the Piccadilly Inn Airport.

TOP CHOICE **Dusty Buns Bistro Bus**   FOOD TRUCK $

(www.dustybuns.com, http://twitter.com/dusty bunsbistro; mains $7; ☺lunch Wed-Sun hours vary) This brightly painted bus dishes out organic, seasonal sandwiches which have single handedly actualized Fresno's would-be foodie culture. The young couple in the drivers' seat has made the business as exciting as their signature Dusty Bun (a brilliant little number of chipotle roast chicken and sesame cucumber summer slaw on a bun) by announcing the hours, location and menu via

---

BLOODLESS BULLFIGHTS

Bullfighting has been illegal in the USA since 1957, but there are exceptions to the rule. When Portuguese communities in the Central Valley have *festas* (religious festivals) they are permitted to stage bloodless bullfights. The *festas* are huge events, attracting as many as 25,000 Portuguese Americans, and the bullfights are generally the climax of several days of parades, food, music and beauty contests.

Portuguese fishermen and farmers, mostly from the Azores, began settling in California during the late 19th century. The communities grew, especially in the Central Valley, with steady immigration continuing until very recently. Many people in the valley still speak Portuguese fluently and attend the *festas* that are held up and down the state.

Festas are largely cultural events, typically to honor religious icons such as St Anthony or Our Lady of Fátima. Candlelight processions, folk dancing, blessing of the cows, performances of *pezinho* songs (sad melodies with a lilting violin accompaniment) and eating until you feel like a plump sausage are all part of the experience. The *festa* queen contests are taken very seriously by the contestants.

Festas are held throughout the summer, with major events in Hanford, Gustine (along Hwy 33, north of the junction of I-5 and Hwy 152) and Stevinson (east of Gustine). They're not well publicized and the relevant websites that go up are often temporary. The only reliable thing to do is search 'festas california' and see what comes up in English.

their Twitter feed. Seem like a highbrow lark doomed to wither in little ol' Fresno? There's plenty of time to ponder that question while waiting in the lines that stretch around the block.

📋 **Loving Hut** THAI $
(www.lovinghut.us; 1495 N Van Ness Ave; mains $7; ⏰11am-2pm & 5-8pm Wed-Sat; 🅿️📶) The star of this excellent vegan place, situated just off the Tower District in an old Craftsman house, is the 'Heavenly Rhelms,' a savory plate of BBQ fake-chicken drumsticks. The 'Ocean of Love' ain't half bad either, it's a vegan dish cooked in black pepper sauce, sided with rice and steamed veggies. Amid the valley's cow country, this place is a vegetarian's dream come true.

**Grand Marie's Chicken
Pie Shop** AMERICAN $
(☎559-237-5042; 2861 E Olive Ave; mains $5-12; ⏰breakfast & lunch daily, dinner Mon-Sat) With a ladle of gravy and a flaky crust, the beautiful chicken-stuffed pies at this chipper Tower District stalwart bear no resemblance to the frozen, soggy mess of your childhood. Breakfast is also supreme thanks to buttery biscuits.

Sam's Italian Deli & Market DELI $
(2415 N First St; mains $5-9; ⏰8:30am-6pm Mon-Sat) This Italian market and deli is the real deal, stacking up the 'New Yorker' pastrami and some mean prosciutto and mozzarella.

☆ **Entertainment**

**Tower Theatre for the
Performing Arts** PERFORMING ARTS
(www.towertheatrefresno.com; 815 E Olive Ave) In the center of Fresno's hippest neighborhood, it's hard to miss the neon phallus, a stunning deco palace that opens its stage to touring rock and jazz acts and ballet, and seasonal cultural events.

ℹ️ **Information**

Fresno Convention & Visitors Bureau (☎559-237-0988, 800-788-0836; www.fresnocvb.org; cnr Fresno & O Sts; ⏰10am-4pm Mon-Fri, 11am-3pm Sat) Inside the Fresno Water Tower.

ℹ️ **Getting There & Around**

Fresno Yosemite International Airport Just east of the center of town is this dreary if serviceable two-runway strip surrounded by chain hotels. The 'Yosemite' and 'International' elements of the name are generous – it's a two-hour drive to the interior of the park and the only air service outside the States is to Mexico City.

Fresno Area Express (FAX; ☎559-488-1122; one-way fare $1.25) The local service that has daily bus services to the Tower District (bus 22 or 26) and Forestiere Underground Gardens (bus 20, transfer to bus 9) from the downtown transit center at Van Ness Ave and Fresno St.

Greyhound (☎559-268-1829; 1033 Broadway) Stops downtown near the new ballpark. One-way trips to or from Los Angeles are $39. One way between Fresno and San Francisco is $29.50 (five hours, five daily).

Visalia

Its agricultural prosperity and well-maintained downtown make Visalia one of the valley's most charming places to stay en route to Sequoia and Kings Canyon National Parks or the Sierra Peaks. Bypassed a century ago by the railroad, the city is 5 miles east of Hwy 99, along Hwy 198. Its downtown has great old buildings and makes for a nice stroll.

◎ **Sights & Activities**

The original Victorian and Arts-and-Crafts–style homes in Visalia are architectural gems worth viewing on foot. Get information about a self-guided walking tour from the **Visalia Chamber of Commerce & Visitor Center** (www.visaliatourism.com; 720 W Mineral King Ave; ⏰8:30am-5pm Mon-Fri). The tour leads north of Main St on both N Willis and Encina Sts.

Kaweah Oak Preserve NATURE PRESERVE
About 7 miles east of Visalia is Kaweah Oak Preserve, home to 324 acres of valley oak trees, which once stretched from the Sierras to (long-gone) Tulare Lake in the valley. Nice for a short hike, it's a rare glimpse into the valley's past before orchards and vineyards took over. From Hwy 198, turn north onto Rd 182; the park is about a half-mile along on your left.

Cellar Door LIVE MUSIC
(www.cellardoorvisalia.com; cnr W Main & Court Sts) Visalia is blessed with this great small venue, which snags touring indie acts from well beyond the Central Valley. They also have a big wine list and host open mic nights.

SCENIC DRIVE: THE BLOSSOM TRAIL

When the Central Valley's trees blossom, the roads surrounding Visalia make for a stunning, leisurely afternoon drive past citrus and vineyards. The 62-mile **Blossom Trail** (www.gofresnocounty.com) is an excellent scenic drive between February and March, when everything is flowering (those with allergies beware). You a get a map of the route at the Fresno City & County Convention and Visitors Bureau, but a DIY trip can be just as pretty. Pull out a roadmap and start navigating back roads between Reedley, Orange Cove, Selma and Kingsburg.

The last of these is another Central Valley town with a striking ethnic heritage – the town was founded by Swedish farmers and its Main St is decked out with bright red and yellow Dala Horses, Swedish gift shops and buttery bakeries.

Fox Theatre   LIVE MUSIC
(☎ box office 559-625-1369; www.foxvisalia.org; cnr W Main & Encina Sts) The gloriously restored 1930 theater hosts concerts, classic films and special events.

🛏 Sleeping & Eating

There are tons of dining options, including a spread of ethnic food, in the middle of town. If you want to follow your nose just wander down Main St between Floral and Bridge Sts.

Spalding House   B&B $
(☎ 559-739-7877; www.thespaldinghouse.com; 631 N Encina St; r $95; ❀) This B&B has three classy suites, each with an antique bed, a sitting room and a modern bathroom. The full-on breakfasts will get you going in the morning, and you can tickle the keys of the 1923 Steinway piano in the parlor all evening.

TOP CHOICE **Brewbaker's Brewing Company**   BREWPUB $
(www.brewbakersbrewingco.com; 219 E Main St; mains $6-12; ⏰ 11:30am-10pm; 🐾) A wait is normal on busy weekends at Brewbaker's, but the microbrews are worth it, particularly the smooth flagship Sequoia Red or chocolatey Possum Porter. The atmosphere is downright classy – brightly polished copper tanks and Tiffany-style stained-glass fixtures – which is befitting of the well-executed pub food.

The Vintage Press   CALIFORNIAN $$$
(☎ 559-733-3033; www.thevintagepress.com; 216 N Willits; mains $12-29; ⏰ 11:30am-2pm & 5:30pm-10pm Mon-Sat, 10am-9pm Sun) Red leather booths, stained glass and dark woods suggest the fairly buttoned-up Continental fare at this long-running Central Valley fine-dining destination. It hasn't gotten hip to the local eating trend – the menu includes an Australian lobster, New Zealand lamb rack and Hawaiian fish – but it's grilled and sautéed to the delight of the moneyed ranchers who come here to celebrate anniversaries.

❶ Getting There & Away

Amtrak (www.amtrak.com) Shuttles connect with the station in Hanford by reservation only. From Hanford, riders can connect to all other Amtrak routes in the state, including the *San Joaquin*, which travels north to Sacramento ($31, four hours, two direct services daily) or south to Bakersfield ($16, 1½ hours, six trains daily).

Bakersfield

Nearing Bakersfield, the landscape is dotted with evidence of California's *other* gold rush: rusting rigs alongside the route burrow into Southern California's vast oil fields. Oil was discovered here in the late 1800s, and Kern County, the southernmost county on Hwy 99, still pumps more than some OPEC countries. (This is the setting of Upton Sinclair's *Oil!*, which was adapted into the 2007 Academy Award–winning film, *There Will Be Blood*.) In the 1930s the oil attracted a stream of 'Okies' – farmers who migrated out of the dusty Great Plains – to work the derricks (see boxed text, p352). The children of these tough-as-nails roughnecks minted the 'Bakersfield Sound' in the mid-1950s, with heroes Buck Owens and Merle Haggard waving a defiant middle finger to the silky Nashville establishment (see boxed text, p351 for a Bakersfield roadtrip soundtrack).

As Bakersfield tries to become all sophisticated like some of its valley neighbors, it has an uneasy relationship with the rhinestone-studded country pluckers of its past. Much of the twangy Bakersfield sound went to the grave with Buck Owens, who passed away in 2006.

Though some parts of town are rather shabby, downtown holds some real surprises in its upbeat mix of restored buildings, county offices, restaurants and antique shops, such as the **Five and Dime** (cnr 19th & K Sts; ☉10am-5pm Mon-Sat, noon-5pm Sun) inside an original Woolworth's building. The 1930 **Fox Theater** hosts regular performances; Merle Haggard was on the marquee during a recent visit.

◉ Sights

The Kern River flows along Bakersfield's northern edge, separating it from its blue-collar neighbor, Oildale, and a host of oil fields. Truxtun and Chester Aves are the main downtown thoroughfares. Though currently suffering from a bit of neglect, Old Town Kern, located east of downtown around Baker and Sumner Sts, was once a bustling centre. It certainly makes for an interesting view into the region's decaying past. The **Bakersfield Historic Preservation Commission** (www.bakersfieldcity.us/edcd/historic/) has downloadable maps of walking tours covering Old Town Kern and Bakersfield's historic downtown.

Kern County Museum & Lori Brock Children's Discovery Center   MUSEUM
(www.kcmuseum.org; 3801 Chester Ave; adult/student $10/9; ☉10am-5pm Wed-Sun, ♿) This museum has a pioneer village with more than 50 restored and replicated buildings. The musty main structure has a large (and fairly disturbing) display of the area's taxidermied wildlife. On the 2nd floor waits a collection of pristine memorabilia from Bakersfield's musical heyday.

California Living Museum   ZOO
(www.calmzoo.org; 10500 Alfred Harrell Hwy; adult/child $9/5; ☉9am-5pm; ♿) A half-hour northeast of town, the zoo and botanical gardens have a menagerie of native animals, including black bear and bald eagles. Kids will squirm in the rattlesnake house, which has every type of rattler in the state. It's about a 20-minute drive from downtown Bakersfield.

🛏 Sleeping & Eating

Chain motels line the highways near Bakersfield like weeds. Old-school budget motels, starting from about $35, line Union Ave heading south from Hwy 178, though some are pretty shady. Bakersfield is blessed with a clutch of traditional Basque restaurants, where food is served family-style in a series of courses including soup, salad, beans and thin slices of tangy beef tongue. All this comes *before* the main course, so arrive hungry.

Padre Hotel   TOP CHOICE   BOUTIQUE HOTEL $$
(☎661-427-4900; www.thepadrehotel.com; 1702 8th St; r $89-199, ste from $500; ♨) After standing vacant for years, this historic tower found long-sought investors and opened with a blindingly stylish facelift, including an upscale restaurant and pair of bars that instantly became *the* place for cocktails in Bakersfield. The standard rooms have lush details: foam beds, thick sheets and designer furniture. The two themed suites – the 'Oil Baron' and 'Farmer's Daughter' – are *way* over the top, with velvet wallpaper, leather couches and showers for two. Did

KINGS OF BAKERSFIELD SOUND

Driving down Hwy 99 requires getting on a first-name basis with Bakersfield's two drawling titans: Merle and Buck. Masters of twanging Telecasters and hayseed heartbreak, they're country kings of the Central Valley.

» 'I'm Gonna Break Every Heart I Can' – Merle Haggard
» 'I've Got A Tiger by the Tail' – Buck Owens
» 'Okie from Muskogee' – Merle Haggard
» 'Second Fiddle' – Buck Owens
» 'The Bottle Let Me Down' – Merle Haggard
» 'Under Your Spell Again' – Buck Owens
» 'Swinging Doors' – Merle Haggard
» 'The Streets of Bakersfield' – Buck Owens and Dwight Yoakam

we mention the suite with the 'stripper pole' in the shower?

TOP CHOICE Noriega Hotel
BASQUE $$

(☑661-322-8419; www.noriegahotel.com; 525 Sumner St; lunch $14, dinner $20; ☺Tue-Sun) Surly Basque gentlemen pat their ample stomachs, joke in several languages and pass around the communal bottles of zinfandel at Bakersfield's last remaining family-style Basque institution. Join diners at a long communal table for a rotating offering of silky oxtail stew, pork chops and veal. The ambience is simply magic – long tables and checkered floors, black-and-white photos of the multigenerational owners – all of which likely helped them to win a prestigious James Beard award. Note that dining hours are strict (breakfast 7am to 9am, lunch at noon, dinner at 7pm).

Dewar's Candy Shop
ICE CREAM $

(www.dewarscandy.com; 1120 Eye St; ice cream $3-10; ☺11am-9pm Mon-Thu, to 10pm Fri & Sat) Perched on the pastel stools at the counter, families dig into homemade ice cream with ingredients sourced from surrounding farms. Dreamy flavors like lemon flake and cotton candy change seasonally.

Luigi's
ITALIAN $

(www.shopluigis.com; 725 E 19th St; mains $6-12; ☺lunch Tue-Sat) Lined with black-and-white photos of sporting legends, this amazing lunch spot has been around over 100 years. The stuffed chicken melts in your mouth and the excellent bakery turns out soft, buttery rolls and an amazingly rich Butterfinger

Pie. Vegetarian options include a mushroom ravioli in sage butter sauce.

Jake's Original Tex Mex Cafe
SOUTHWESTERN $

(www.jakestexmex.com; 1710 Oak E St; mains $7-14; ☺lunch & dinner Mon-Sat) More Tex than Mex, this excellent cafeteria packs in city workers for smoky slow-roasted pit beef. The chili fries are a messy delight, and Herb's Belcher Spuds are as decadent as the name suggests.

Wool Growers
BASQUE $

(☑661-327-9584; www.woolgrowers.net; 620 E 19th St; mains $7-20; ☺lunch & dinner Mon-Sat) Another simple Basque eating hall loaded with character. A fried chicken dinner will leave you full for a week.

☆ Entertainment

TOP CHOICE Buck Owens' Crystal Palace
LIVE MUSIC

(☑661-328-7560; www.buckowens.com; 2800 Buck Owens Blvd) For fans of the city's plucky musical heritage, this is the first stop – hard to miss thanks to the huge neon sign in the shape of Buck's famous red, white and blue guitar. Part music museum, part honky-tonk, part steakhouse, the Palace has a top-drawer country act on stage every night, and locals in meticulous snap-button shirts, shiny boots and pressed jeans tear up the dance floor.

Trout's & the Blackboard Stage
HONKY-TONK

(www.troutsblackboard.com; 805 N Chester Ave at Decatur St) The legendary Trout's, in neigh-

---

WORTH A TRIP

WEEDPATCH LABOR CAMP

In the years following the Depression, Kern County boasted California's highest proportion of poor white farm laborers from the South and the Great Plains. Called 'Okies' (whether they came from Oklahoma or not), they came with dreams of a new life in the fields the Golden State. The majority, though, found only migrant labor jobs and continued hardship.

Dating from 1935, this Farm Security Administration labor camp (the model for 'Weedpatch Camp' in *The Grapes of Wrath*) was one of about 16 in the US set up at the time to aid migrant workers – and it's the only one with any original buildings left. After some recent restoration, the camp sparkles with a surreal sheen, but it remains a fascinating vision into the past – and a wake-up call to the continuing dichotomy between corporate agribusiness and its strife with the migrant workforce. From Bakersfield, take Hwy 58 east to Weedpatch Hwy; head south for about 7 miles, past Lamont; then turn left on Sunset Blvd, driving another mile. The buildings (the sign reads 'Arvin Farm Labor Center') are on your right. **Dust Bowl Days** (www.weedpatchcamp.com) is a celebration of Okie history held here each October.

boring Oildale, is the only remaining honky-tonk in these parts, hobbling along after half a century as a testament to the hell-raisin' days gone by. Expect no Crystal Palace – the parking lot glistens only in broken glass and the bartender is one salty princess – but the live music comes from Bakersfield legends and their disciples. Monday is a memorable 'Seniors Night.'

ℹ Information

Greater Bakersfield Convention & Visitors Bureau (☑661-325-5051; www.bakersfieldcvb.org; 515 Truxtun Ave; ☺8:30am-5pm Mon-Fri) Carries maps and brochures.

ℹ Getting There & Around

Airport Bus of Bakersfield (☑805-395-0635; 2530 F St) Runs a shuttle seven times daily between Bakersfield and LAX ($32, 2½ hours).

Amtrak station (☑661-395-3175; 601 Truxtun Ave at S St) Trains head north from here to Sacramento ($43 to $77, five hours, two direct trains). Buses head to LA ($16 to $33), though only available in combination with a train ticket.

Golden Empire Transit (GET; www.getbus.org; basic fare 90¢) The local bus system. Route 2 runs north on Chester Ave to the Kern County Museum and Oildale.

Greyhound (☑661-327-5617; 1820 18th St) Depot is downtown near the Padre Hotel.

Kern River Area

A half-century ago the Kern River originated on the slopes of Mt Whitney and journeyed close to 170 miles before finally settling into Buena Vista Lake in the Central Valley. Now, after its wild ride from the high country – where the river drops an incredible 60ft per mile – it's dammed in several places and almost entirely tapped for agricultural use after hitting the valley floor. Its upper reaches, declared wild and scenic by the Secretary of the Interior, is nicknamed the 'Killer Kern' for its occasionally lethal force, but there's no denying it provides some of the best rafting in the Western US.

Hwy 178 follows the dramatic **Kern River Canyon**, making for a stunning drive through the lower reaches of Sequoia National Forest. East of the lake, Hwy 178 winds another 50 miles through a picturesque mixture of pine and Joshua trees before reaching Hwy 395.

There are two **USFS Ranger Stations** in the area; one in Kernville (☑760-376-3781; 105 Whitney Rd; ☺8am-4:30pm Mon-Fri) and another in Lake Isabella (☑760-379-5646; 4875 Ponderosa Dr; ☺8am-4:30pm). Both have hiking and camping information, maps and wilderness permits.

☉ Sights & Activities

This part of the state is all about the white water, and rafting is the banner attraction for visitors. The town of **Lake Isabella** is a dreary strip of local businesses on the south end of the lake, but Hwy 155 runs north, around the west side to **Kernville**, a cute little town straddling the Kern River. The town is the hub for rafting in the area. While the lake is popular for cooling off, note that the river's deceptively strong currents can be extremely dangerous.

The Upper Kern and Forks of the Kern (both sections of the river north of Kernville) yield Class IV and V rapids during spring runoff and offer some of the most awe-inspiring white-water trips in the country. You'll need experience before tackling these sections, though there are plenty more opportunities for novices. Below Lake Isabella, the Kern is tamer and steadier.

Currently five rafting companies are licensed to operate out of Kernville; all offer competitive prices and run trips from May to August, depending on conditions. Excursions include popular one-hour runs ($30), day-long Lower Kern trips ($150 to $190) and multiday Forks of the Kern wilderness experiences ($600 to $920). Walk-ups are welcome and experience is not necessary. Kids aged six and up can usually participate too.

Mountain & River Adventures RAFTING, OUTDOOR OUTFITTERS (☑800-861-6553, 760-376-6553; www.mtnriver.com; 11113 Kernville Rd) Offers rafting trips, guided climbing and camping excursions.

Sierra South RAFTING (☑760-376-3745, 800-457-2082; www.sierrasouth.com; 11300 Kernville Rd)

Whitewater Voyages RAFTING (☑800-400-7238, 660-376-8806; www.whitewatervoyages.com)

🛏 Sleeping

Lake Isabella has motels, but Kernville is a nicer location with more reasonable rates.

Many of Kernville's motels have two-day minimum stays on weekends.

USFS campgrounds CAMPGROUND $
(☎877-444-6677; developed/undeveloped sites $12/16) These campgrounds line the 10-mile stretch between Lake Isabella and Kernville, and several more lie north of Kernville on Mtn 99. Rangers recommend the Fairview and Limestone sites for their seclusion. Any campground without running water and electricity is free.

Whispering Pines Lodge B&B $$$
(☎760-376-3733; www.kernvalley.com/whispering pines; 13745 Sierra Way; r $219-299; ☒) This secluded B&B, blending rustic character with luxurious comfort, is just north of town.

Best of the Golden State

California Cuisine »
Wine Countries »
Scenic Drives »
Beaches »

Mustard and grape vines at a vineyard in the Napa Valley (p163)

JERRY ALEXANDER/LONELY PLANET IMAGES ©

California Cuisine

Slow food, artisan producers and a year-round harvest mean you can eat your way through California and never be sated. From taquerías and fusion food trucks to urban kitchens and roadside fruit and veggie stands, take time to taste the Golden State.

Central Valley

1 Along rural Hwy 99, this is America's basket of fruit and vegetables. Irrigated fields of strawberries, lettuce, raisins, artichokes and tomatoes lie near orchards of heritage peaches and apricots. See p326.

Wine Country

2 Get straight to the source at farm-to-table restaurants, such as Thomas Keller's renowned French Laundry (p173) restaurant in Napa Valley. Chefs mix the best of what's in season with cutting-edge foodie fashions from around the world. See p725.

Los Angeles

3 Forget about star chefs' tables in stuffy Beverly Hills. LA's truest eating delights are its authentic ethnic foods (p560) served up at hole-in-the-wall kitchens in neighborhoods from Thai Town to 'Tehrangeles.'

San Francisco Bay Area

4 Whether it's a Mission-style burrito or fresh Marin oysters, San Franciscans are fanatics about finding the best local food. Just step inside the market in the Ferry Building (p59) to be amazed by NorCal's cornucopia.

San Luis Obispo

5 In the state where the term 'locavarian' was invented, take a peek behind the scenes on organic farm and vineyard tours, buy fresh seafood straight off the docks and pick your own orchard apples, lemons and avocados straight off the trees. See p498.

Clockwise from top left
1. Fresh strawberries at a farmers market **2.** Ubuntu vegetarian restaurant (p171), Napa **3.** Micro green salad at a restaurant in LA

Wine Countries

Vineyards never feel very far away in California, where world-beating wines wait to be tasted. The pleasures of California's dozens of wine-producing regions include touring biodynamic farms, cycling along sunny country roads and dining at high-flying restaurants.

Napa & Sonoma Valleys

1 In Northern California's premier wine-growing region (p159), you can still unearth the uniqueness of *terroir,* where cult winemakers offer barrel tastings in their sun-dappled vineyards. Chardonnays and cabernet sauvignons are especially prized.

Santa Ynez & Santa Maria Valleys

2 North of Santa Barbara, the wine country (p508) just gets better the further away from the city you travel. Follow rural wine trails and chat with biodynamic, organic grape growers while tippling excellent pinot noir.

Paso Robles

3 Most famous for its fruity and brambly zinfandel vines, this hot, sunny wine country (p496) on the Central Coast spreads east and west along Hwy 46, tucked between horse ranches and rustic farmstands.

Mendocino County

4 Take a memorably winding drive via Hwy 128 through the Anderson Valley (p236), known for its delicate Alsatian-style whites, sparkling wines and pinot noir.

El Dorado County

5 In the Sierra Nevada foothills (p313) where gold miners tried their luck, the earth brings forth hearty grapes that absorb their unique character from the mineral-rich soil: bold, earthy and richly colored.

Clockwise from top left
1. Hot-air balloon over a vineyard, Napa Valley 2. Harvest time in the Santa Maria Valley 3. Stomping grapes in a barrel, Paso Robles 4. Glass of wine at Navarro Vineyards (p236), Anderson Valley

Scenic Drives

From towering redwoods to sun-kissed surf beaches, the scenery that unfurls along California's coastal highways is spectacular. Inland, epic highways ascend into the glacier-carved Sierra Nevada Mountains or dive into deep canyons.

Avenue of the Giants

1 This 32-mile, two-lane byway (p247) passes right by some of the tallest trees on earth. Go in the morning when sunlight glints off dew-laden ferns.

Pacific Coast Highway

2 Hwy 1 runs almost the entire length of the state, but it's the official stretch of the Pacific Coast Highway (PCH) in Orange County (p606) and north into LA past Santa Monica and Malibu that gets raves for its ocean panoramas.

Gold Country's Hwy 49

3 That highway number is no coincidence – it commemorates the '49ers who came seeking fame and fortune in California's original Gold Rush days. Today, the highway (p313) winds past ghostly Old West mines and Victorian inns in the Sierra Nevada foothills.

Kings Canyon Scenic Byway

4 This dizzying cliff-hugging route (p419) passes by the ancient trees of Kings Canyon National Park and the Giant Sequoia National Monument as it plunges into North America's deepest canyon.

Palms to Pines Scenic Byway

5 From the desert playground of Palm Springs east of LA, wind slowly up from the Sonoran Desert floor into cool pine-scented forests and past snow-capped peaks around the mountain hamlet of Idyllwild. See p667.

Clockwise from top left
1. Avenue of the Giants **2.** Pacific Coast Highway, Malibu (p546) **3.** Hwy 49, near Nevada City (p308) **4.** Kings River, Kings Canyon National Park (p419)

Beaches

California's nickname 'Golden State' dates from its Wild West mining era. But on sunny days when the coastal fog lifts, it might just as well describe California's more than 1100 miles of Pacific beaches. Whether you swim, surf or just lie on the sands, don't miss these seductive shoreline spots.

Coronado

1 San Diego's coastal beaches farther north might attract more crowds, but Coronado's quieter Silver Strand (p622), with its old-fashioned amusements and a paved cycling path, is a favorite with families.

Santa Cruz

2 Ride the 1920s Giant Dipper roller coaster on the beach boardwalk (p455), then check out the surfers at Steamer Lane (p456) and go tidepooling with the kids at Natural Bridges State Beach (p457).

Huntington Beach

3 Nowhere in Southern California is the Orange County lifestyle as real as in 'Surf City USA' (p595). Bounce around a beach volleyball, surf by the pier and build a bonfire on the beach after dark.

Malibu

4 Miles of white-sand beaches and rolling Pacific waves are backed by million-dollar oceanfront mansions in Malibu (p546). Luckily, those gorgeous strands favored by Hollywood celebrities are public-access up to the high tide line – as any good paparazzi photographer knows.

Trinidad

5 Had enough of beach blanket bingo in sunny SoCal? If you like your beaches natural and wild, come to this Northern California bay (p257), where hiking trails lead along spectacular coastal bluffs. Very chilly for swimming, though!

Right
1. Surfer at Huntington Beach 2. Santa Cruz Beach Boardwalk at dusk

Lake Tahoe

Best Places to Eat

» Moody's Bistro & Lounge (p392)

» Café Fiore (p379)

» Wild Goose (p394)

» Fire Sign Café (p385)

» Dockside 700 Wine Bar & Grill (p387)

Best Places to Stay

» Cedar House Sport Hotel (p391)

» Plumpjack Squaw Valley Inn (p388)

» Tahoma Meadows Bed & Breakfast Cottages (p384)

» Deerfield Lodge at Heavenly (p377)

» Clair Tappaan Lodge (p391)

Why Go?

Shimmering in myriad shades of blue and green, Lake Tahoe is the USA's second-deepest lake and, at 6255ft high, it's also one of the highest-elevation lakes in the country. Generally speaking, the north shore is quiet and upscale; the west shore, rugged and old-timey; the east shore, undeveloped; and the south shore, busy and tacky, with aging motels and flashy casinos. Driving around the lake's spellbinding 72-mile scenic shoreline will give you quite a workout behind the wheel.

The horned peaks surrounding the lake, which straddles the California–Nevada state line, are year-round destinations. The sun shines on Tahoe three out of four days in the year. Swimming, boating, kayaking, windsurfing, stand-up paddle boarding and other water sports take over in summer, as do hiking, camping and wilderness backpacking adventures. Winter brings bundles of snow, perfect for those of all ages to hit the slopes at Tahoe's top-tier ski and snowboard resorts.

When to Go

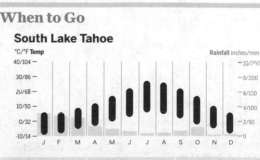

South Lake Tahoe

Jul–Aug Beach season; wildflowers bloom, and hiking and mountain-biking trails open.

Sep–Oct Cooler temperatures, colorful foliage and fewer tourists after Labor Day.

Dec–Mar Snow sports galore at resorts; storms bring hazardous roads.

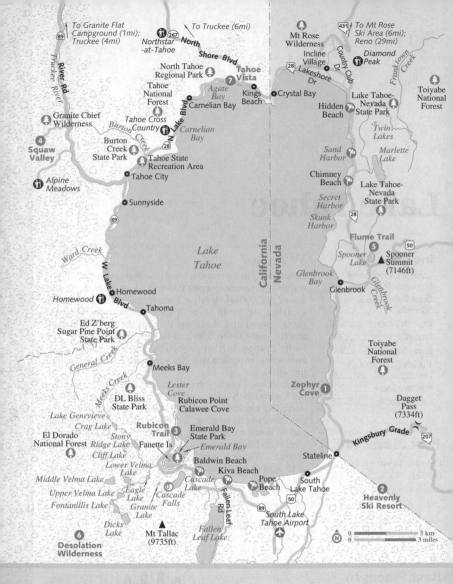

Lake Tahoe Highlights

❶ Surveying the shimmering expanse of Lake Tahoe aboard a kayak or from the sandy beach at **Zephyr Cove** (p373)

❷ Swooshing down the vertiginous double-black-diamond runs of **Heavenly ski resort** (p366)

❸ Trekking the **Rubicon Trail** (p383) from Vikingsholm

Castle on sparkling Emerald Bay, to DL Bliss State Park

❹ Swimming in an outdoor lagoon, or ice-skating above 8000ft atop the cable-car line in **Squaw Valley** (p388)

❺ Thundering down the **Flume Trail** (p396) on a mountain bike to tranquil Spooner Lake.

❻ Escaping summer crowds with an overnight backpack to alpine lakes and high-country meadows in the **Desolation Wilderness** (p374)

❼ Cozying up with your family around a lakefront beach firepit or inside a cozy cabin at **Tahoe Vista** (p393) on the no-fuss northern shore

Tahoe Ski, Snowboard & Snowshoe Areas

Lake Tahoe has phenomenal skiing, with thousands of acres of the white stuff beckoning at more than a dozen resorts. Winter-sports complexes range from the giant, jet-set slopes of Squaw Valley, Heavenly and Northstar-at-Tahoe, to the no less enticing insider playgrounds like Sugar Bowl and Homewood. Tahoe's simply got a hill for everybody, from kids to kamikazes.

Ski season generally runs November to April, although it can start as early as October, and last until the last storm whips through in May or even June. All resorts have ski schools, equipment rental and other facilities; check their websites for snow conditions, weather reports and ski-season shuttle buses from area lodgings.

Downhill Skiing & Snowboarding

Tahoe's downhill resorts are usually open every day from December through April, weather permitting. All of these resorts rent equipment and have places to warm up slopeside and grab a quick bite or après-ski beer. Most offer group ski and snowboard lessons for adults and children (a surcharge applies, but usually no reservations are required).

TRUCKEE & DONNER PASS

Northstar-at-Tahoe   SKIING, SNOWBOARDING
(☎530-562-1010, 800-466-6784; www.north starattahoe.com; 5001 Northstar Dr, off Hwy 267, Truckee; adult/child 5-12yr/youth 13-22yr $92/41/80; ☺8:30am-4pm; ⓓ) An easy 7 miles south of I-80, this hugely popular resort has great intermediate terrain. Northstar's relatively sheltered location makes it the second-best choice after Homewood when it's snowing, and the seven terrain parks and pipes are top-ranked. Advanced and expert skiers can look for tree-skiing challenges on the back of the mountain, reached via a new high-speed lift. Recent additions to Northstar's 'Village' are making it look a lot more like amenity-rich Squaw. Weekends get superbusy. Stats: 19 lifts, 2280 vertical feet, 93 runs.

Sugar Bowl   SKIING, SNOWBOARDING
(☎530-426-9000; www.sugarbowl.com; 629 Sugar Bowl Rd, off Donner Pass Rd, Truckee; adult/child 6-12yr/youth 13-22yr $71/23/59; ☺9am-4pm; ⓓ)

Cofounded by Walt Disney in 1939, this is one of the Sierra's oldest ski resorts and a miniature Squaw Valley in terms of variety of terrain, including plenty of exhilarating gullies and chutes. Views are stellar on sunny days, but conditions go downhill pretty quickly, so to speak, during stormy weather. It's 4 miles southeast of I-80 (exit Soda Springs/Norden). Stats: 13 lifts, 1500 vertical feet, 95 runs.

Boreal   SKIING, SNOWBOARDING
(☎530-426-3666; www.borealski.com; 19659 Boreal Ridge Rd, off I-80 exit Castle Peak/Boreal Ridge Rd, Truckee; adult/child 5-12yr/teen 13-19yr $49/15/39, night-skiing adult/child 5-12yr $25/12; ☺9am-9pm; ⓓ) Fun for newbies and intermediate skiers, Boreal is traditionally the first resort to open each year in the Tahoe area. For boarders, there are four terrain parks including a competition-level 450ft superpipe. Boreal is the only North Tahoe downhill resort besides Squaw that offers night skiing. Stats: nine lifts, 500 vertical feet, 41 runs.

Soda Springs   SKIING, SNOWBOARDING
(☎530-426-3901; www.skisodasprings.com; 10244 Soda Springs Rd, off I-80 exit Soda Springs/Norden, Soda Springs; adult/child under 18yr $35/25, snowmobiling $10, tubing $25; ☺9am-4pm Thu-Mon, daily during holidays; ⓓ) This cute little resort is a winner with kids, who can snow-tube, ride around in pint-sized snowmobiles, or learn to ski and snowboard. Stats: two lifts, 650 vertical feet, 16 runs.

Donner Ski Ranch   SKIING, SNOWBOARDING
(☎530-426-3635; www.donnerskiranch.com; 19320 Donner Pass Rd, Norden; adult/child 7-12yr/teen 13-19yr $42/13/34; ☺9am-4pm; ⓓ) Generations of skiers have enjoyed this itty-bitty family-owned resort. It's a great place to

---

FAST FACTS

» **Population of South Lake Tahoe** 21,403

» **Average temperature low/high in South Lake Tahoe** Jan 15/41°F, Jul 40/79°F

» **Reno, NV to Truckee** 35 miles, 40 to 60 minutes

» **Tahoe City to South Lake Tahoe/ Stateline, NV** 30 miles, 1 to 1½ hours

» **Truckee to San Francisco** 190 miles, 3½ to five hours

Tahoe Ski & Snowboard Areas

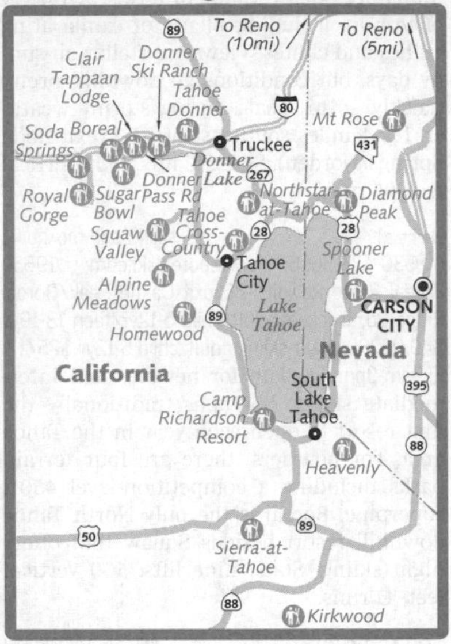

teach your kids how to ski, or for beginners to build skills. Prices drop after 12:30pm. It's 3.5 miles southeast of I-80, exit Soda Springs/Norden. Stats: six lifts, 750 vertical feet, 52 runs.

Tahoe Donner SKIING, SNOWBOARDING

(☎530-587-9444; www.skitahoedonner.com; 11603 Snowpeak Way, off I-80 exit Donner Pass Rd, Truckee; adult/child 7-12yr $39/19; ⌚9am-4pm; 👪) Small, low-key and low-tech, Tahoe Donner is a darling resort with family-friendly beginner and intermediate runs only. Stats: four lifts, 600 vertical feet, 14 runs.

TAHOE CITY & AROUND

TOP CHOICE **Squaw Valley** SKIING, SNOWBOARDING

(☎530-583-6985, 800-403-0206; www.squaw.com; 1960 Squaw Valley Rd, off Hwy 89, Olympic Valley; adult/child under 13yr/teen 13-19yr $88/10/64; ⌚9am-7pm Mon-Thu, to 9pm Fri-Sun) Few ski hounds can resist the siren call of this mega-sized, world-class, see-and-be-seen resort that hosted the 1960 Winter Olympic Games. Hardcore skiers thrill to white-knuckle cornices, chutes and bowls, while beginners practice their turns in a separate area on the upper mountain. Coming attractions: upgraded terrain parks, including a gnarly superpipe. The valley turn-off is 5 miles northwest of Tahoe City. Stats: 34 lifts, 2850 vertical feet, over 170 runs.

Alpine Meadows SKIING, SNOWBOARDING

(☎530-583-4232, 800-441-4423; www.skialpine.com; 2600 Alpine Meadows Rd, off Hwy 89, Tahoe City; adult/child 5-12yr/teen 13-19yr $69/15/54; ⌚9am-4pm) Alpine is a no-nonsense resort without the fancy village, attitude or crowds. It gets more snow than neighboring Squaw and its open-boundary policy makes it the most backcountry-friendly around. Boarders jib down the mountain in a terrain park designed by Eric Rosenwald. Also look for the adorable – and supersmart – ski patrol dogs. The turn-off is 4 miles northwest of Tahoe City. Stats: 13 lifts, 1800 vertical feet, 100 runs.

Homewood SKIING, SNOWBOARDING

(☎530-525-2992; www.skihomewood.com; 5145 Westlake Blvd, off Hwy 89; adult/child 5-12yr/teen 13-19yr Fri-Sun $61/15/42; ⌚9am-4pm; 👪) Larger than it looks from the road, this gem, 6 miles south of Tahoe City, proves that bigger isn't always better. Locals and in-the-know visitors cherish the awesome lake views, laid-back ambience, smaller crowds, tree-lined slopes, open bowls (including the excellent but expert 'Quail Face') and a high-speed quad that gets things moving. Families love the wide, gentle slopes. It's also the best place to ski during stormy weather. Stats: seven lifts, 1650 vertical feet, 60 runs.

SOUTH LAKE TAHOE

Heavenly SKIING, SNOWBOARDING

(☎775-586-7000, 800-432-8365; www.skiheavenly.com; 3860 Saddle Rd, South Lake Tahoe; adult/child 5-12yr/teen 13-19yr $90/50/78; ⌚9am-4pm Mon-Fri, 8:30am-4pm Sat, Sun & holidays) The 'mother' of all Tahoe mountains boasts the most acreage, the longest run (5.5 miles) and the biggest vertical drop around. Follow the sun by skiing on the Nevada side in the morning, moving to the California side in the afternoon. Views of the lake and the high desert are heavenly indeed. Five terrain parks won't strand snowboarders of any skill level, with the High Roller for experts only. Stats: 30 lifts, 3500 vertical feet, 94 runs.

Kirkwood SKIING, SNOWBOARDING

(☎209-258-6000; www.kirkwood.com; 1501 Kirkwood Meadows Dr, off Hwy 88, Kirkwood; adult/child 6-12yr/teen 13-19yr $79/20/62; ⌚9am-4pm) Off-the-beaten-path Kirkwood, set in a high-elevation valley, gets great snow and holds it longer than almost any other Tahoe resort. It has stellar tree-skiing, gullies, chutes and terrain parks, and is the only Tahoe resort with backcountry runs accessible by snowcats. Novice out-of-bounds skiers should sign up in advance for backcountry safety-skills clinics. It's 35 miles southwest of South Lake Tahoe via Hwy 89; ski-season shuttles are available (from $15). Stats: 14 lifts, 2000 vertical feet, 72 runs.

Sierra-at-Tahoe   SNOWBOARDING, SKIING
(☑530-659-7453; www.sierraattahoe.com; 1111 Sierra-at-Tahoe-Rd, off Hwy 50, Twin Bridges; adult/child 5-12yr/youth 13-22yr $75/18/65; ⊙9am-4pm Mon-Fri, 8:30am-4pm Sat, Sun & holidays; ⊞) About 18 miles southwest of South Lake Tahoe, this is snowboarding central, with five raging terrain parks and a 17ft-high superpipe. A great beginners' run meanders gently for 2.5 miles from the summit, but there are also gnarly steeps and chutes for speed demons. Kids get four 'adventure zones' while adults-only Huckleberry Gates tempts with steep-and-deep backcountry terrain for experts. Stats: 14 lifts, 2200 vertical feet, 46 runs.

NEVADA

Mt Rose   SKIING, SNOWBOARDING
(☑775-849-0704, 800-754-7673; www.mtrose.com; 22222 Mt Rose Hwy/Hwy 431, Reno; adult/child 6-12yr/teen 13-19yr $69/19/55; ⊙9am-4pm) Conveniently the closest ski resort to Reno, Mt Rose has Tahoe's highest base elevation (8260ft) and offers four terrain parks and good snow conditions well into spring. 'The Chutes' expert terrain delivers some screamers along its north-facing steeps. Crowds aren't too bad, but the mountain's exposure means it gets hammered in a storm and avalanche control may intermittently close runs. Stats: eight lifts, 1800 vertical feet, 60 runs.

Diamond Peak   SKIING, SNOWBOARDING
(☑775-832-1177, 877-468-4397; www.diamondpeak.com; 1210 Ski Way, off Hwy 28, Incline Village; adult/child 7-14yr/youth 15-17yr $49/18/39; ⊙9am-4pm; ⊞) This midsize mountain is a good place to learn, and boarders can romp around the terrain park, but experts get bored quickly. From the top you'll have a 360-degree panorama of desert, peaks and the lake. Free ski-season shuttle from Incline Village and Crystal Bay. Stats: six lifts, 1840 vertical feet, 30 runs.

Cross-Country Skiing & Snowshoeing

Tahoe's cross-country ski resorts are usually open daily from December through March, and sometimes into April. Most rent equipment and offer lessons; reservations typically aren't taken for either, so show up early in the morning for the best availability.

TRUCKEE & DONNER PASS

TOP CHOICE Royal Gorge   SKIING, SNOWSHOEING
(☑530-426-3871; www.royalgorge.com; 9411 Hillside Dr, off I-80 exit Soda Springs/Norden, Soda Springs; adult/child Sat & Sun $29/18, Mon-Fri $25/16; ⊙9am-5pm Mon Fri, 8:30am-5pm Sat & Sun; ⊞) Nordic skiing aficionados won't want to pass up a spin around North America's largest cross-country resort with its mind-boggling 205 miles of groomed track criss-crossing 9000 acres of terrain on 90 trails. It has great skating lanes and diagonal stride tracks and also welcomes telemark skiers and snowshoers. Group lessons are offered a few times daily, with ski camps for kids ages 6 to 12 (reservations recommended). Consider overnighting at one of the resort's two cozy lodges.

Tahoe Donner   SKIING, SNOWSHOEING
(☑530-587-9484; www.tdxc.com; 15275 Alder Creek Rd, off I-80 exit Donner Pass Rd, Truckee;

ℹ WINTER DRIVING AROUND LAKE TAHOE

From late fall through early spring, always pack snow chains in case a storm rolls in. Chains can also be purchased and installed in towns along I-80 and Hwy 50. Also stash some emergency supplies (eg blankets, water, flashlights) in the trunk, just in case your car breaks down, traffic gets tied up or roads close completely due to snowfall or avalanche danger.

Before hopping in the car and driving up to Tahoe, check road closures and conditions with:

California Department of Transportation (Caltrans; ☑800-427-7623; www.dot.ca.gov)

Nevada Department of Transportation (NDOT; ☑877-687-6237, 511 within Nevada; www.safetravelusa.com/nv)

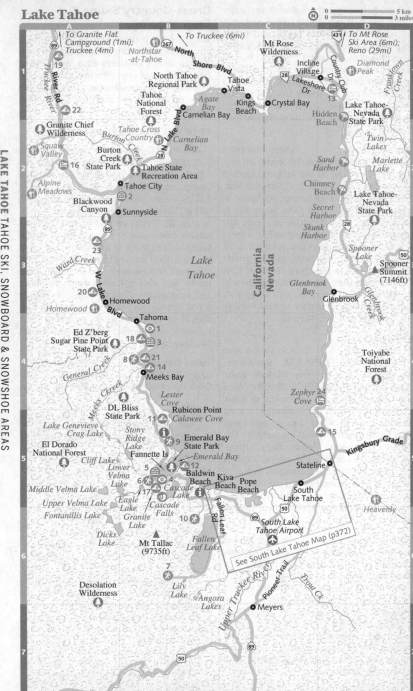

Lake Tahoe

adult/child under 13yr $24/free; ⏰8:30am-5pm, night skiing 5-7pm Wed; 🚗) Occupying 4800 acres of thick forest north of Truckee, Tahoe Donner has lovely and varied terrain with over 62 miles of groomed tracks that cover three track systems and 51 trails. The most beautiful spot is secluded Euer Valley, where a warm hut serves food on weekends. A 1.5-mile loop stays open for night skiing, usually on Wednesdays. Group lessons for beginners and 'Tiny Tracks,' a supervised kids' ski and snow-play camp, are available; reserve ahead for intermediate skills clinics.

Northstar-at-Tahoe SKIING, SNOWSHOEING
(☎530-562-3270, 800-466-6784; www.northstarat tahoe.com; 5001 Northstar Dr, off Hwy 267, Truckee; adult/child 5-12yr $25/13; ⏰9am-3pm Mon-Thu, 8:30am-4pm Fri-Sun & holidays; 🚗) Seven miles southeast of I-80, this mega ski resort has a highly regarded Nordic and telemark school, making it a great choice for novices. A package, which includes the trail fee, ski rental and a group lesson, costs $65. Afterwards you can explore the nearly 40km of groomed trails. Moonlight snowshoe tours and open-range biathlon-race and clinic days take place monthly.

Clair Tappaan Lodge SKIING, SNOWSHOEING
(☎530-426-3632; www.sierraclub.org/outings/ lodges/ctl; 19940 Donner Pass Rd, off I-80 exit Soda Springs/Norden, Norden; adult/child under 12yr $7/3.50; ⏰9am-5pm; 🚗) You can ski right out the door if you're staying at this rustic mountain lodge (see p391) near Donner Summit. Its 12km of groomed and tracked trails are great for beginners and intermediate skiers, and connect to miles of backcountry skiing (for overnight hut reservations, call ☎800-679-6775). Stop by the lodge for ski and snowshoe rentals, and value priced ski lessons at all skill levels (sign-up starts at 9am daily).

TAHOE CITY & AROUND

Tahoe Cross Country SKIING, SNOWSHOEING
(☎530-583-5475; www.tahoexc.org; 925 Country Club Dr, off N Lake Blvd/Hwy 28, Tahoe City; adult/ child under 10yr/youth 10-17yr $22/free/18; ⏰8:30am-5pm; 🚗🐕) Run by the nonprofit Tahoe Cross Country Ski Education Association, this center, about 3 miles north of Tahoe City, has 65km of groomed tracks (19 trails) that wind through lovely forest, suitable for all skill levels. Dogs are allowed on two trails. Group lessons come with good-value equipment-rental packages; half-day and twilight trail-pass discounts are also available. Ask about free skate clinics and beginners' cross-country mid-week lessons.

Squaw Valley SKIING, SNOWSHOEING
(☎530-583-6300, 800-403-0206; www.squaw. com; 1960 Squaw Valley Rd, off Hwy 89, Olympic Valley; adult/child under 13yr/youth 13-19yr $88/10/64; ⏰9am-5pm) Although downhill skiers rule the roost at this ex-Olympic resort, 11 miles of groomed track winding around an alpine meadow will keep beginner-level Nordic skiers busy too. Book ahead

TOP WAYS TO SKI TAHOE FOR LESS MONEY

Midweek and half-day afternoon discounts on lift tickets are usually available, but expect higher prices on weekends and holidays. Lift-ticket rates go up incrementally almost every year, too. Parents should ask about interchangeable 'Parent Predicament' lift tickets offered by some resorts, which let one parent ski while the other one babysits the kids, then switch off later.

The **Bay Area Ski Bus** (☎925-680-4386; www.bayareaskibus.com) allows you to leave the headache of driving I-80 to others. Round-trips start at $109 including lift tickets, with various add-on packages available. Pick-up locations include San Francisco and Sacramento.

Handy money-saving websites include:

» **Ski Lake Tahoe** (www.skilaketahoe.com) Portal for the seven biggest Tahoe resorts, with deals covering all.

» **Sliding on the Cheap** (www.slidingonthecheap.com) Homegrown website listing discounts and deals on lift tickets.

for monthly moonlight snowshoe tours high atop the mountain. To reach the trailheads at the Resort at Squaw Creek, which supplies cross-country ski, snowshoe and sled rentals, grab a free shuttle from the main downhill ski-area parking lot.

SOUTH LAKE TAHOE

Kirkwood SKIING, SNOWSHOEING
(☎209-258-7248; www.kirkwood.com; 1501 Kirkwood Meadows Dr, off Hwy 88, Kirkwood; adult/child under 10yr/child 11-12yr/youth 13-19yr $22/free/8/17; ⊙9am-4pm; ☷) Definitely not a jogging trail, this cross-country network has sections that are very challenging and where you can actually gain some elevation. Groomed track stretches for 80km with separate skating lanes and three trailside warming huts; the views from the higher slopes are phenomenal. Dogs are welcome on one ridgeline loop. Rentals, lessons and tours all available. It's at least an hour's drive south of Lake Tahoe.

Camp Richardson Resort SKIING, SNOWSHOEING
(☎530-542-6584; www.camprichardson.com; 1900 Jameson Beach Rd, off Emerald Bay Rd/Hwy 89, South Lake Tahoe; adult/child under 13yr/teen 13-19yr $20/free/14) At this woodsy resort with 21 miles of groomed track, you can ski lakeside or head for the solitude of the Desolation Wilderness. Locals turn out in droves for full-moon ski and snowshoe parties, which kick off at the resort's Beacon Bar & Grill.

NEVADA

Spooner Lake SKIING, SNOWSHOEING
(☎775-749-5349; www.spoonerlake.com; 3709 Hwy 28, Glenbrook, NV; adult/child under 13yr/youth 13-19yr $21/free/10; ⊙9am-5pm; ☷) This nature preserve, near the junction of Hwys 28 and 50 in Nevada, offers pretty trails – some around petite Spooner Lake, some through aspen and pine forest, and some through high country – with fabulous views. Altogether there are 50 miles of groomed trails for all levels of expertise and fitness. Equipment rentals, including snowshoes or sleds for kids, and group lessons are available, with midweek discounts and half-day and twilight trail passes. Make reservations for overnight stays in wilderness backcountry ski-in cabins.

South Lake Tahoe & Stateline

Highly congested and arguably overdeveloped, South Lake Tahoe is a chock-a-block commercial strip bordering the lake and framed by picture-perfect alpine mountains. At the foot of the world-class Heavenly mountain resort and buzzing from the gambling tables in the casinos just across the border in Stateline, Nevada, Lake Tahoe's south shore draws visitors with a cornucopia of activities and lodging and restaurant options, especially for summer beach access and tons of powdery winter snow.

⊙ Sights

FREE **Tallac Historic Site** HISTORIC SITE
(☎530-541-5227; www.fs.usda.gov; Tallac Rd, off Hwy 89/Emerald Bay Rd; tours adult/child 6-12yr $5/3; ⊙usually 10am-4:30pm mid-Jun–Sep, Fri

& Sat only late May–mid-Jun; 🅳) Sheltered by a pine grove and bordering a wide, sandy beach, this national historic site sits on the archaeologically excavated grounds of the former Tallac Resort, a swish vacation retreat for San Francisco's high society around the turn of the 20th century.

Inside the 1921 Baldwin Estate, the **Tallac Museum** (donation requested; ⊘11am-4pm late May–mid-Jun & early Sep–mid-Sep, 10:30am-4:30pm mid-Jun–early Sep) has exhibits on the history of the resort and its founder, Elias 'Lucky' Baldwin, who made a bundle off Nevada's Comstock Lode. Nearby is the 1894 **Pope Estate**, now used for art exhibits and open for guided tours (⊘daily except Wednesday). The boathouse of the **Valhalla Estate** functions as a theater venue – for tickets and schedules, call ☎530-541-4795. The 1923 Grand Hall contains an art gallery and gift shop.

Feel free to just amble or cycle around the breezy forested grounds, today transformed into a community arts hub, where leashed dogs are allowed. In summer, concerts, plays and other cultural events happen here, most notably the three-decade-old **Valhalla Festival of Arts, Music & Film** (www.valhallatahoe.com; ⊘July-Sep).

The parking lot is about 3 miles north of the 'Y' junction of Hwys 89 and 50.

FREE **Lake Tahoe Historical Society Museum**   MUSEUM
(www.laketahoemuseum.org; 3058 Lake Tahoe Blvd; ⊘11am-3pm Thu-Mon late May-early Sep) A small but interesting museum displays artifacts from Tahoe's pioneer past, including Washoe tribal baskets, vintage black-and-white films, hoary mining memorabilia and a model of a classic Lake Tahoe steamship. On summer Saturday afternoons, join a volunteer-led tour of the restored 1930s cabin out back.

🏃 Activities

For downhill skiing and snowboarding around South Lake Tahoe, see p366; for cross-country skiing and snowshoeing, see p370.

Heavenly Gondola   GONDOLA, ZIP LINE
(www.skiheavenly.com; Heavenly Village; adult/child 5-12yr/teen 13-19yr from $32/20/26; ⊘10am-5pm Jun-Aug, reduced off-season hr; 🅳) Soar to the top of the world as you ride this gondola, which sweeps you from Heavenly Village to some 2.4 miles up the mountain in just 12 minutes. From the observation deck at 9123ft, get gobstopping panoramic views of the entire Tahoe Basin, the Desolation Wilderness and Carson Valley. Then jump on the Tamarack Express chair lift to get all the way to the mountain summit, where the longest zip line in the continental US, **Heavenly Flyer** (per trip $40; ⊘11am-4pm), lets you speed through the air for a heady 3100ft.

Hiking

Many miles of summer hiking trails start from the top of the **Heavenly Gondola** (see p371), many with mesmerizing lake views. On the Nevada side of the state line, **Lam Watah Nature Trail** meanders for just over a mile each way across USFS land, winding underneath pine trees and beside meadows and ponds, on its way between Hwy 50 and Nevada Beach, starting from the community park off Kahle Dr.

Several easy kid- and dog-friendly hikes begin near the USFS Taylor Creek Visitor Center off Hwy 89. The mile-long, mostly flat **Rainbow Trail** loops around a creekside meadow, with educational panels about ecology and wildlife all along the way. On the opposite side of Hwy 89, the gentle, rolling one-mile **Moraine Trail** follows the shoreline of Fallen Leaf Lake; free trailhead parking is available near campsite No 75. Up at cooler elevations, the mile-long round-trip to **Angora Lakes** is another popular trek with kids, especially because it ends by a sandy swimming beach and a summer snack bar selling ice-cream treats. You'll find the trailhead on Angora Ridge Rd, off Tahoe Mountain Rd, accessed from Hwy 89.

For longer and more strenuous day hikes to alpine lakes and meadows, several major trailheads provide easy access to the evocatively named **Desolation Wilderness** (see p374): **Echo Lakes** (south of town); **Glen Alpine** (near Lily Lake, south of Fallen Leaf Lake), to visit a historic tourist resort and waterfall; and **Tallac** (opposite the entrance to Baldwin Beach). The latter two trailheads also lead to the peak of Mt Tallac (9735ft), a strenuous 10- to 12-mile day hike. Self-serve wilderness permits for day hikers only are freely available at trailheads; for overnight backpacking permits, which are subject to quotas, see the boxed text, p374.

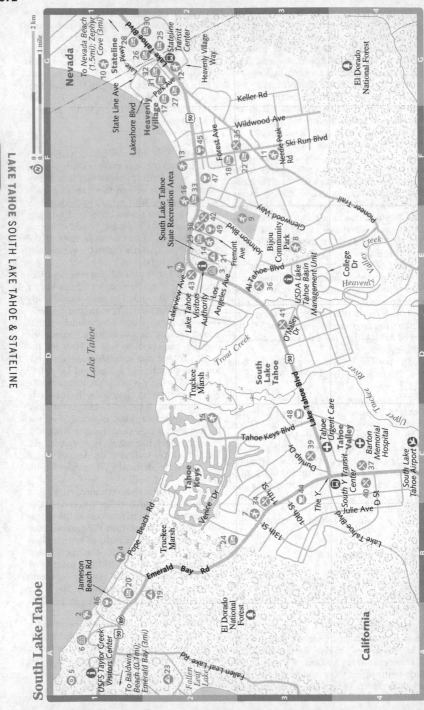

South Lake Tahoe

Lake Tahoe

Nevada

California

El Dorado National Forest

El Dorado National Forest

Tahoe Keys

Truckee Marsh

Truckee Marsh

Fallen Leaf Lake

Stateline

Heavenly Village

Stateline Transit Center

Heavenly Village Way

South Lake Tahoe State Recreation Area

Lake Tahoe Visitors Authority

South Lake Tahoe

USDA Lake Tahoe Basin Management Unit

Bijou Community Park

Heavenly

Tahoe Valley

Barton Memorial Hospital

South Lake Tahoe Airport

South Y Transit Center

The Y

Tahoe Urgent Care

To Nevada Beach (1.5mi); Zephyr Cove (3mi)

To Baldwin Beach (0.1mi); Emerald Bay (3mi)

USFS Taylor Creek Visitors Center

Lake Tahoe Blvd

Emerald Bay Rd

Pope-Beach Rd

Jameson Beach Rd

Fallen Leaf Lake Rd

Venice Dr

Dunlap Dr

13th St

10th St

11th St

D St

Julie Ave

Lake Tahoe Blvd

Tahoe Keys Blvd

Al Tahoe Blvd

O'Malley Dr

Glenwood Way

College Dr

Pioneer Trail

Needle Peak Rd

Ski Run Blvd

Wildwood Ave

Keller Rd

Forest Ave

Park Ave

Heavenly Village Way

Lakeshore Blvd

State Line Ave

Lake Tahoe Blvd

Johnson Blvd

Fremont Ave

Los Angeles Ave

Lakeview Ave

Trout Creek

Valley Creek

Upper Truckee River

2 km
1 mile

South Lake Tahoe

LAKE TAHOE SOUTH LAKE TAHOE & STATELINE

🏊 Beaches & Swimming

On the California side, the nicest strands are **Pope Beach** (www.fs.usda.gov/tahoe; per car $7; 🐕), **Kiva Beach** (🐕) and **Baldwin Beach** (www.fs.usda.gov/tahoe; per car $7; 🐕), each with picnic tables and barbecue grills; Kiva beach offers free parking and allows leashed dogs, too. They're all found along Emerald Bay Rd (Hwy 89), running west and east of Tallac Historic Site. Nearby, **Fallen Leaf Lake**, where scenes from the Hollywood flicks *The Bodyguard* and *City of Angels*

were filmed, is also good for summer swims. **El Dorado Beach** is a free public beach in town, just off Lake Tahoe Blvd.

Many folks prefer to head over to Stateline and keep driving north 2 miles to pretty **Nevada Beach** (www.fs.usda.gov/tahoe; per car $7), where the wind really picks up in the afternoons, or always-busy **Zephyr Cove** (www.zephyrcove.com; per car $8; 🐕), which has rustic resort and marina facilities along its sandy mile-long shoreline.

DON'T MISS

HIKING & BACKPACKING THE DESOLATION WILDERNESS

Sculpted by powerful glaciers eons ago, this relatively compact **wilderness area** (www.fs.fed.us/r5/eldorado/recreation/wild/deso/) spreads south and west of Lake Tahoe and is the most popular in the Sierra Nevada. It's a 100-sq-mile wonderland of polished granite peaks, deep-blue alpine lakes, glacier-carved valleys and pine forests that thin quickly at the higher elevations. In summer, wildflowers nudge out from between the rocks.

All this splendor makes for some exquisite backcountry exploration. Six major trailheads provide access from the Lake Tahoe side: Glen Alpine, Tallac, Echo Lakes (the southernmost trailhead), Bayview, Eagle Falls and Meeks Bay. Tallac and Eagle Falls get the most traffic, but solitude comes quickly once you've scampered past the day hikers.

Wilderness permits are required year-round for both day and overnight explorations. Day hikers can self-register at the trailheads, but overnight permits must be either reserved online (fee $6) at www.recreation.gov and printed at home, or picked up in person at the USFS Taylor Creek Visitor Center or USDA Lake Tahoe Basin Management Unit, both in South Lake Tahoe (see p381). Permits cost $5 per person for one night or $10 per person for two or more nights.

Quotas are in effect from late May through the end of September. Half of the permits for the entire season may be reserved online usually starting in late March or April; the other half are available on a first-arrival basis on the day of entry only.

Bearproof canisters are strongly advised in all wilderness areas (hanging your food in trees will not work – these bears are too smart!). Borrow canisters for free from the USFS Taylor Creek Visitors Center. Bring bug repellent as the mosquitoes can be merciless. Wood fires are a no-no, but portable stoves are OK. Dogs must be leashed at *all* times.

Boating & Water Sports

Ski Run Boat Company (☎530-544-0200; www.tahoesports.com; 900 Ski Run Blvd), at the Ski Run Marina, and **Tahoe Keys Boat & Charter Rentals** (☎530-544-8888; www.tahoesports.com; 2435 Venice Dr), at the Tahoe Keys Marina, both rent motorized powerboats, pontoons, sailboats and jet skis (rentals per hour $95 to $200), as well as human-powered kayaks, canoes, hydro bikes, paddleboats and paddleboard sets (per hour $15 to $35). If you want to go parasailing up to 1200ft above Lake Tahoe's waves, the Ski Run Marina branch can hook you up (rides $50 to $75). For summer boat dives, book ahead with **Scuba Mood** (☎916-420-9820; www.scubamood.com; Tahoe Keys Marina, 2435 Venice Dr East).

Kayak Tahoe   KAYAKING
(☎530-544-2011; www.kayaktahoe.com; rental kayaks $15-60, lessons & tours from $30; ⏰usually 9am-5:30pm Jul & Aug, shorter hr Jun & Sep) Rent a kayak, take a lesson or sign up for a guided tour, including sunset cove paddles, trips to Emerald Bay and explorations of the Upper Truckee River estuary and the eastern shore. Four seasonal locations at Timber Cove Marina and Baldwin, Pope and Nevada Beaches.

Zephyr Cove Resort & Marina   MARINA
(Map p368; ☎775-589-4901; www.zephyrcove.com; 760 Hwy 50, NV; ⏰9am-5pm) Rents powerboats, pedal boats, waverunners, jet skis, canoes, kayaks and stand-up paddleboards (SUP); also offers single and tandem parasailing flights ($59 to $129).

Camp Richardson Resort Marina   MARINA
(☎530-542-6570; www.camprichardson.com; 1900 Jameson Beach Rd) Rents powerboats, paddleboats, water skis, kayaks and SUP gear.

Mountain-Biking

For expert mountain-bikers, the classic **Mr Toad's Wild Ride**, with its steep downhill sections and banked turns reminiscent of a Disneyland theme-park ride, should prove sufficiently challenging. Usually open from June until October, the one-way trail along Saxon Creek starts off Hwy 89 south of town near Grass Lake and Luther Pass.

Intermediate mountain-bikers should steer towards the mostly single-track **Pow-**

erline Trail, which traverses ravines and creeks. You can pick up the trail off Ski Run Blvd near the Heavenly resort, from the western end of Saddle Rd. For a more leisurely outing over mostly level terrain, you can pedal around scenic Fallen Leaf Lake. Anyone with good lungs might try the **Angora Lakes Trail**, which is steep but technically easy and rewards you with sweeping views of Mt Tallac and Fallen Leaf Lake. It starts further east, off Angora Ridge and Tahoe Mountain Ridge Rds.

For shuttle service and mountain-bike rentals for Mr Toad's Wild Ride, the Tahoe Rim Trail and other downhill adventures, as well as family-friendly tours, talk to **Wanna Ride** (✆775-588-5800; www.wannaridetahoe. com). For mountain-biking trail conditions, race schedules, volunteer days and other special events, contact the **Tahoe Area Mountain Biking Association** (http://moun tainbiketahoe.org).

Cycling

The **South Lake Tahoe Bike Path** is a level, leisurely ride suitable for anyone. It heads west from El Dorado Beach, eventually connecting with the **Pope-Baldwin Bike Path** past Camp Richardson, Tallac Historic Site and the USFS Taylor Creek Visitor Center. Visitors centers carry the excellent Lake Tahoe bike route map, available online from the **Lake Tahoe Bicycle Coalition** (www.tahoebike.org), which has an info-packed website for cycling enthusiasts. **Anderson's Bike Rental** (✆530-541-0500, 877-720-2121; www.laketahoebikerental.com; 645 Emerald Bay Rd/Hwy 89; per hr $9; ⊛), about 1.5 miles north of the 'Y', rents hybrid bikes with helmets.

Golf

Edgewood Tahoe Golf Course   GOLF
(✆775-588-2787; www.edgewood-tahoe.com; 100 Lake Pkwy, Stateline; green fee $110-240) Stunning lakeside scenery is a major distraction at this challenging championship 18-hole course designed by George Fazio, a favorite for celebrity golf tournaments. Tee-time reservations are required; cart and club rentals available.

Bijou Golf Course   GOLF
(✆530-542-6097; www.cityofslt.us; 3464 Fairway Ave; green fee $19-37, club/cart rental $15/5; ⊗call for hr) So you don't know your putter from your 9-iron? That's OK at this laid-back, no-reservations municipal course with views of Heavenly Mountain. Built in the 1920s, it's

got just 9 holes, which you can play twice around.

FREE Kirkwood Disc-Wood   DISC GOLF
(✆209-258-7210; www.kirkwood.com; 1501 Kirkwood Meadows Dr, Kirkwood) Crazy terrain, tons of distance and high-elevation Sierra Nevada views from an epic 18 holes. Call ahead for directions and to check opening hours before making the hour-long drive southwest of South Lake Tahoe.

FREE Zephyr Cove Park   DISC GOLF
(Hwy 50 at Warrior Way, north of Stateline, NV) PDGA-approved 18-hole course is scenically set on the eastern shore, with kick-ass uphill and downhill shoots.

FREE Bijou Community Park   DISC GOLF
(Bijou Community Park, 1201 Al Tahoe Blvd) In town, these 27 holes will taunt even experts with loooong greens on a mostly flat, forested course (ahoy, trees!).

Horseback Riding

Both **Camp Richardson Corral & Pack Station** (✆530-541-3113, 877-541-3113; www. camprichardsoncorral.com; Emerald Bay Rd/Hwy 89; trail rides $40-90; ⊛) and **Zephyr Cove Stables** (✆775-588-5664; www.zephyrcovest able.com; Hwy 50, NV; trail rides $40-70; ⊛), about 4 miles north of Stateline casinos, offer daily horseback rides in summer, varying from one-hour kid-friendly trips through the forest, to extended treks with meadow and lake views (reservations required).

South Lake Tahoe for Children

FREE Stream Profile Chamber   HIKING
(✆530-543-2674; trailhead at USFS Taylor Creek Visitor Center, off Hwy 89; ⊗8am-4:30pm late May–mid-Jun & Oct, to 5:30pm mid-Jun–Sep) Along a family-friendly hiking trail, this submerged glass structure in a teeming creek lets you check out what plants and fish live below the waterline. The best time to visit is in October during the Kokanee salmon run, when the brilliant red beauties arrive to spawn.

Tahoe Bowl   BOWLING
(✆530-544-3700; http://tahoebowl.com; 1030 Fremont Ave; game per person $4.50, shoe rental $4.50; ⊗schedules vary; ⊛) For yucky-weather days or to tire out the tots by bedtime, this is a fun indoor haunt with 16

SLEDDING, TUBING & SNOW PLAY FOR KIDS

Major ski resorts such as Heavenly and Kirkwood around South Lake Tahoe, and Squaw Valley and Northstar-at-Tahoe near Truckee, offer sledding hills for the kiddos, some with tubing rentals and thrilling rope tows. Smaller ski mountains including Sierra-at-Tahoe outside South Lake Tahoe, and Boreal, Soda Springs and Tahoe Donner, all near Truckee, also offer child-friendly slopes.

To avoid the crowds, bring your own sleds to designated local snow-play areas at North Tahoe Regional Park in Tahoe Vista on the north shore, or to Nevada's Incline Village, Tahoe Meadows off the Mt Rose Hwy (Hwy 431) or Spooner Summit on Hwy 50, all along the east shore. Back in California, free DIY **Sno-Parks** (☏916-324-1222; www.parks. ca.gov/?page_id=1233) are found along Hwy 89 at Blackwood Canyon, 3 miles south of Tahoe City on the west shore, and Taylor Creek, just north of Camp Richardson at South Lake Tahoe. Coming from Sacramento or the San Francisco Bay Area, two Sno-Parks are along I-80 at Yuba Gap (exit 161) and Donner Summit (exit 176 Castle Peak/Boreal Ridge Rd); their parking lots often fill by 11am on winter weekends.

For private groomed sledding and tubing hills, swing by **Hansen's Resort** (Map p372; ☏530-577-4352; www.hansensresort.com; 1360 Ski Run Blvd; per person incl rental per hr $10; ⊗9am-5pm) in South Lake Tahoe or **Adventure Mountain** (☏530-577-4352; www.adven turemountaintahoe.com; 21200 Hwy 50; per car $15, rentals available; ⊗10am-4:30pm Mon-Fri, 9am-5pm Sat, Sun & holidays), south of town at Echo Summit.

bowling lanes and a pocket-sized pizza parlor and video arcade. Call ahead for open-play schedules.

Shops at Heavenly Village MINI-GOLF, SKATING (☏530-542-1215; www.theshopsatheavenly.com; 1001 Heavenly Way; ⊗seasonal hr vary; ⊛) If you don't feel like wandering far, this downtown outdoor mall sets up a little putt-putt golf course in summer, and opens an outdoor ice-skating rink in winter. Call for current schedules and prices.

👉 Tours

Lake Tahoe Cruises CRUISES (☏800-238-2463; www.zephyrcove.com; 2hr cruise adult/child from $45/15; ⊛) Two paddle wheelers ply Lake Tahoe's 'big blue' year-round with a variety of sightseeing, drinking, dining and dancing cruises, including a narrated two-hour daytime trip to Emerald Bay. The *Tahoe Queen* leaves from Ski Run Marina in town, while the MS *Dixie II* is based at Zephyr Cove Marina on the eastern shore in Nevada.

Woodwind Cruises CRUISES (☏775-588-1881; www.sailwoodwind.com; Zephyr Cove Marina, 760 Hwy 50, NV; 1hr cruise adult/ child 2-12yr from $34/15) Sunset champagne and happy-hour floats aboard this sailing catamaran are the perfect way to chill after a sunny afternoon lazing on the beach. Five

daily departures during summer; reservations recommended.

Action Watersports SPEEDBOAT TOURS (☏530-544-5387; www.action-watersports.com; Timber Cove Marina, 3411 Lake Tahoe Blvd; adult/ child under 13yr $60/30) In a hurry to get to Emerald Cove? Wanna avoid those near-constant traffic jams on Hwy 89? Jump on board the *Tahoe Thunder* speedboat, which zips across the lake – watch out, though, you'll get wet!

Lake Tahoe Balloons BALLOONING (☏530-544-1221, 800-872-9294; www.lake tahoeballoons.com; per person $250) From May through October (weather permitting), you can cruise on a catamaran launched from Tahoe Keys Marina, then clamber aboard a hot-air balloon launched right from the boat's upper deck. The lake and Sierra Nevada mountain views may take away what little breath you have left up at 10,000ft high.

🛏 Sleeping
SOUTH LAKE TAHOE

South Lake Tahoe has a bazillion choices for all budgets. Lodging options line Lake Tahoe Blvd (Hwy 50) between Stateline and Ski Run Blvd. Further west, closer to the 'Y,' at the intersection of Hwys 50 and 89 is a string of mostly budget motels ranging from barely adequate to inexcusable. Prices listed here are for peak season (generally winter ski season from December to March and summer from June to August). Some properties may impose minimum stays, especially on weekends and holidays. For more ski condos and hotel rooms near the slopes, contact **Heavenly** (☎775-586 7000, 800-432-8365; www.skiheavenly.com).

TOP CHOICE Deerfield Lodge at Heavenly

BOUTIQUE HOTEL **$$$**

(☎530-544-3337, 888-757-3337; http://tahoedeerfieldlodge.com; 1200 Ski Run Blvd; r/ste incl breakfast from $219/259; ❄🐾🛜♨) A small boutique hotel close to Heavenly ski resort, Deerfield has a dozen intimate rooms and spacious suites that each have a patio or balcony facing the green courtyard, along with a whirlpool tub, flickering gas fireplace and amusing coat racks crafted from skis and snowboards. Happy-hour party snacks and drinks are complimentary, and barbecue grills appear in summer. Pet fee $25.

Timber Lodge

HOTEL **$$**

(☎530-542-6600, 800-845-5279; www.marriott.com; 4100 Lake Tahoe Blvd; r $179-219, ste $219-299; ❄@🛜♨🐾) Don't let the Marriott chaingang brand put you off this modern ski lodge with an enviable position, where you can watch the Heavenly gondola whoosh by outside your window. Cookie-cutter hotel rooms have kitchenettes, while apartment-style 'vacation villa' suites come with full kitchens, gas fireplaces and deep soaking tubs for après-ski warm-ups.

🌿968 Park Hotel

BOUTIQUE MOTEL **$$**

(☎530-544-0968, 877-544-0968; www.968parkhotel.com; 968 Park Ave; r $109-309; @🛜♨) Critics cry 'Lipstick on a pig!', but this refashioned motel has serious hipster edge. Recycled, rescued and re-envisioned building materials have made this LEED-certified property an ecohaven near the lake, within walking distance of the Stateline border scene. In summer, unwind in a cabana by the sunny pool or in the zen garden, then sink into your dreamy Sterling bed.

Alder Inn

B&B **$$**

(☎530-544-4485; www.thealderinn.com; 1072 Ski Run Blvd; r $99-209; 🛜♨) Even better than staying at your best friend's house by the lake, this hospitable inn on the Heavenly ski-shuttle route charms with color schemes that really pop, pillow-top mattresses, organic bath goodies, mini-fridges, microwaves and flat-screen TVs. Dip your toes in the kidney-shaped pool in summer.

Fireside Lodge

INN **$$**

(☎530-544-5515; www.tahoefiresidelodge.com; 515 Emerald Bay Rd/Hwy 89, d incl breakfast $119-255; 🛜🐾♨) This woodsy cabin B&B wholeheartedly welcomes families, with free bikes and kayaks to borrow and evening s'mores. Kitchenette rooms and suites have river-rock gas fireplaces, cozy patchwork quilts and pioneer-themed touches like wagon wheels or vintage skis. Pet fee $20.

Paradice Inn

MOTEL **$$**

(☎530-544-6800; www.paradicemoteltahoe.com; 953 Park Ave; r $120-210; ❄🛜) Harried travelers will appreciate the hospitality at this small two-story motel property. Step outside your minimalist room bordered by flower boxes that overflow with geraniums, then stroll across the street to the Heavenly gondola. Families should ask about two-bedroom suites.

Tahoe Lakeshore Lodge & Spa

HOTEL **$$$**

(☎530-541-2180, 800-448-4577; www.tahoelakeshorelodge.com; 930 Bal Bijou Rd; d $169-319; ❄🛜♨🐾) It's all about the lakefront views at this centrally located conference hotel. Renovated rooms in the main lodge all share the same log-cabin decor, while nearby condos with full kitchens vary depending on the whims of their individual owners.

Inn by the Lake

HOTEL **$$$**

(☎530-542-0330, 800-877-1466; www.innbythelake.com; 3300 Lake Tahoe Blvd; r $170-270; ❄@🛜♨) Rooms here are disappointingly nondescript, although a bilevel outdoor hot tub, spa suites with kitchens, and bicycles and snowshoes to borrow are nifty. Rooms out back are cheaper and quieter, but then you'll miss the lake views.

Highland Inn

MOTEL **$$**

(☎530-544-4161, 800-798-7311; www.highlandlaketahoe.com; 3979 Lake Tahoe Blvd; r $59-159; ❄🛜🐾) Budget-conscious stylemongers will enjoy this older, two-story remodeled motel. Artsy prints, light wood floors and new plasma TVs make it an altogether fairly pleasant, if thin-walled place to bunk down. Pet fee $20.

Avalon Lodge

MOTEL **$$**

(☎530-544-2285, 888-544-7829; http://avalonlodge.com; 4075 Manzanita Ave; r $115-220;

🔊🐾🐕) A quiet, roomy two-story motor lodge off the main drag; pet fee $20.

Seven Seas Inn
MOTEL $

(☎530-544-7031, 800-800-7327; www.sevenseas tahoe.com; 4145 Manzanita Ave; r $50-100; 🔊🐕) Friendly, tidy, bargain-basement motel with a hot tub; pet fee $10.

Camping & Cabins

Spruce Grove Cabins
CABINS $$

(☎530-544-0549, 800-777-0914; http://spruce grovetahoe.com; 3599-3605 Spruce Ave; d $159-205; 🔊🐾🐕) Away from the Heavenly hub-bub, these tidy, private cabins are fenced off on a quiet residential street. The vintage look of these kitchen-equipped cabins, from knotty pine walls to the stone-bordered gas fireplaces, will make you feel like you're stay-ing lakeside. Let your dogs cavort in the yard while you swing in the hammock or soak in outdoor hot tubs. Cleaning fee $30; refund-able pet deposit $100.

Camp Richardson Resort
CABINS, CAMPGROUND $

(☎530-541-1801, 800-544-1801; www.campri chardson.com; 1900 Jameson Beach Rd; tent sites from $35, RV sites with partial/full hookups from $40/45, r $95-180, cabins $100-265; 🔊🐾) Removed from downtown's strip-mall aes-thetic, this sprawling family camp is a hectic place offering seasonal camping (expect ma-rauding bears all night long!), forested cab-ins rented by the week in summer, and so-so beachside hotel rooms. Sports gear and bicycle rentals available. Wi-fi in lobby only.

Fallen Leaf Campground
CABINS, CAMPGROUND $

(☑info 530-544-0426, reservations 877-444-6777; www.recreation.gov; Fallen Leaf Lake Rd; tent & RV sites $30, yurts $85; ⊙mid-May–mid-Oct; ❄) Near the north shore of stunning Fallen Leaf Lake, this is one of the biggest and most popular campgrounds on the south shore, with 180 wooded sites and newly built canvas-sided yurts that can sleep a family of five (bring your own sleeping bags).

Campground by the Lake
CAMPGROUND $

(☑530-542-6096; www.cityofslt.us; 1150 Rufus Allen Blvd; tent & RV sites without/with electric hookups from $29/40, cabins $51-69; ⊙Apr-Oct; 🔊🐕) Highway noise can be an around-the-clock irritant, though proximity to the city pool and ice rink make this wooded in-town campground with an RV dump station a de-cent choice. Basic sleeping-platform cabins are available between Memorial Day (late May) and Labor Day (early September).

STATELINE, NV
At Nevada's high-rise casino complexes, prices rise and fall like your luck at the slot machines. Season, day of the week and type of room are key. In winter ask about special ski-and-stay packages.

Harrah's
CASINO HOTEL $$$

(☎775-588-6611, 800-223-7277; www.harrahslake tahoe.com; 15 Hwy 50, Stateline; r $139-449; ❄@🔊🐕) Clad in an oddly tasteful forest-green facade, this buzzing casino hotel is Stateline's top contender. Let yourself be swallowed up by even standard 'luxury' rooms, which each have two bathrooms with their own mini TVs and telephones, or spring for a luxury suite with panoramic lake-vista windows. For more eye-popping views, snag a window table at one of Har-rah's upper-floor restaurants.

MontBleu
CASINO HOTEL $$

(☎775-588-3515, 888-829-7630; www.montb leuresort.com; 55 Hwy 50, Stateline; r $70-280; ❄@🔊🐕) The public areas may sport über-cool modern boutique decor, but rooms still have that classic, tacky casino hotel look (some of the marble-accented bathrooms come with hedonistic whirlpool tubs, how-ever). Unwind instead in the lavish indoor pool lagoon, accented by a rockscape and mini waterfalls.

Harvey's
CASINO HOTEL $$

(☎775-588-2411, 800-223-7277; www.harvey stahoe.com; 18 Hwy 50, Stateline; r $79-559; ❄@🔊🐕) Harvey's was South Lake Tahoe's first casino, and with 740 rooms, is also its biggest. Lake Tower rooms have fancy mar-ble bathrooms and oodles of space, but reno-vated Mountain Tower rooms are more chic and design-savvy. The heated outdoor pool is open year-round, for beach and snow bun-nies alike. Pet fee $40.

Horizon
CASINO HOTEL $$

(☎775-588-6211, 800-648-3322; www.horizoncasi no.com; 50 Hwy 50, Stateline; r $70-290; ❄🔊🐕🐾) Diehard Elvis fans can stay in the special suite where the star himself once boozed and snoozed at this otherwise generic prop-erty, formerly the Sahara. Family-friendly touches include Tahoe's largest outdoor summer pool, a huge game arcade and a multiplex movie theater.

Camping & Cabins

Zephyr Cove Resort & Marina
CABIN, CAMPGROUND $$$

(Map p368; ☎800-238-2463; www.zephyrcove.com; 760 Hwy 50, NV; tent & RV sites without/with hookups from $27/43, cabins $169-339; ⊗cabins year-round, camping May-Sep; ☎☀☒) On the Nevada side, about 4 miles north of Stateline, this family-oriented lakeside resort on USFS land has historic cabins scattered among the pines and similar campground facilities to Camp Richardson, including hot showers, coin-op laundry, barbecue grills and fire rings. Take your pick of 93 paved RV or 10 drive-in tent sites (a few dozen with lake views), or 47 walk-in tent sites tucked deeper into the shady forest. Leashed dogs allowed, except on the main beach.

Nevada Beach Campground
CAMPGROUND $

(Map p368; ☎info 775-588-5562, reservations 877-444-6777; www.recreation.gov; off Hwy 50, NV; tent & RV sites $28-34; ⊗mid-May–mid-Oct; ☀☒) Bed down on a carpet of pine needles at this tidy lakeside campground, about 3 miles north of Stateline, where 48 sites are nestled amid pines. Leashed dogs allowed at campsites, but not the beach.

✖ Eating

For late-night cravings, each of the big casinos in Stateline has a 24-hour coffee shop for hangover-helper and night-owl breakfasts. If you're just looking for filling pub grub or après-ski appetizers and cocktails, most bars and cafes also serve just-OK food, some with waterfront views and live music too.

TOP CHOICE Café Fiore
ITALIAN $$$

(☎530-541-2908; www.cafefiore.com; 1169 Ski Run Blvd; mains $16-31; ⊗5:30-9pm Sun-Thu, to 9:30pm Fri & Sat) Upscale Italian without pretension, this tiny romantic eatery pairs succulent pasta, seafood and meats with an award-winning 300-vintage wine list. Swoon over the rack of lamb, homemade white-chocolate ice cream and near-perfect garlic bread. With only seven tables (a baker's dozen in summer when the candle-lit outdoor patio opens), reservations are essential.

Freshie's
ECLECTIC $$

(☎530-542-3630; www.freshiestahoe.com; 3330 Lake Tahoe Blvd; mains $14-27; ⊗11:30am-9pm) From vegans to seafood lovers, nobody should have a problem finding a favorite on the extensive menu at this Hawaiian fusion joint with sunset upper-deck views.

Most of the produce is local and organic, and the blackened fish tacos are South Lake Tahoe's best. Service, although full of aloha, is slooow. Make reservations for dinner.

Blue Angel Cafe
CALIFORNIAN $$

(☎530 544-6544; www.theblueangelcafe.com; 1132 Ski Run Blvd; lunch $10-14, dinner $12-26; ⊗11am-9pm Sun-Thu, to 10pm Fri & Sat; ☒) Inside a cute wooden house on the way uphill to ski at Heavenly, this modern American kitchen churns out crispy kettle chips, club sandwiches, elaborate salads and flank steaks to stuff your belly. Turn up for happy hour or the blue-plate lunch and dinner specials.

Off the Hook Sushi
FUSION $$

(www.offthehooksushi.com; 2660 Lake Tahoe Blvd; mains $14-23; ⊗5-10pm) Sushi, so far from the ocean? Yup. Locals keep on coming back to this dynamite little sushi shack, where you can feast on bento boxes and *nigiri* combos, or big steaming bowls of floury udon noodles and pan-fried halibut steaks off the Japanese, Hawaiian and Californian menu.

Latin Soul
LATIN AMERICAN $$

(www.lakesideinn.com; 168 Hwy 50, Stateline; mains $8-24; ⊗8am-10pm) For something completely different, steal away to this little casino kitchen with a big, bold menu of spicy south-of-the-border flavors: Argentinean churrasco-grilled steak, Veracruz shrimp ceviche, goat *birria* (stew) and outrageously mixed mojitos.

Getaway Cafe
COMFORT FOOD $$

(www.getawaycafe.com; 3140 Hwy 50; mains breakfast & lunch $8-12, dinner $10-22; ⊗7am-2pm Mon & Tue, 7am-9pm Wed-Sun Jun-Aug, reduced off-season hr; ☒) On the outskirts of town, south of the airport, this place really lives up to its name: avoid the weekend crowds here. Friendly waitresses sling heaped-up buffalo chicken salads, barbecue burgers, chorizo quesadillas, coconut-crusted French toast and more.

Burger Lounge
AMERICAN $

(www.tahoeburgerlounge.com; 717 Emerald Bay Rd/Hwy 89; dishes $3-6; ⊗11am-8pm, to 9pm Jun-Aug; ☒) You can't miss that giant beer mug standing outside a shingled cabin. Step inside for the south shore's tastiest burgers, including the crazy 'Just a Jiffy' (with peanut butter, bacon and cheddar cheese) or the zingy pesto fries.

Sprouts

VEGETARIAN $

(3123 Harrison Ave; mains $6-9; ⊗8am-9pm; ⊘❄) Cheerful chatter greets you at this energetic, mostly organic cafe that gets extra kudos for its smoothies. A healthy menu will have you noshing happily on satisfying soups, rice bowls, sandwiches, burrito wraps, tempeh burgers and fresh salads.

Ernie's Coffee Shop

DINER $

(www.erniescoffeeshop.com; 1207 Emerald Bay Rd/Hwy 89; mains $7-11; ⊗6am-2pm; ❄) A sun-filled local institution, Ernie's dishes out filling four-egg omelets, hearty biscuits with gravy, fruity and nutty waffles, mix-your-own salads and bottomless cups of locally roasted coffee. Toddlers can happily munch the ears off the Mickey Mouse pancake.

Lake Tahoe Pizza Co

PIZZERIA $$

(www.laketahoepizzaco.com; 1168 Emerald Bay Rd/Hwy 89; pizzas $11-22; ⊗4-9:30pm, to 10pm Jun-Aug; ❄) Since the '70s, this classic pizza parlor has been hand rolling its house-made dough (cornmeal or whole wheat, anyone?), then piling the pizzas with crafty combos such as the meaty 'Barnyard Massacre' or vegan 'Green Giant.'

Self-caterers can stock up at:

Cork & More

DELI $

(http://thecorkandmore.com; 1032 Al Tahoe Blvd; ⊗10am-7pm) Specialty foods, gourmet deli (sandwiches, soups, salads) and picnic baskets to go.

Sugar Pine Bakery

BAKERY $

(3564 Lake Tahoe Blvd; ⊗8am-6pm Tue-Sat, 8am-4pm Sun) Crunchy baguettes, ooey-gooey cinnamon rolls, fruit tarts and choco-chunk cookies.

⊘ Grass Roots Natural Foods

GROCERY

(2040 Dunlap Dr; ⊗9am-7pm Mon-Sat, 10am-6pm Sun; ⊘) Organic produce and home-baked muffins, sandwiches and fresh pizzas.

Safeway

GROCERY

(www.safeway.com; 1020 Johnson Blvd; ⊗9am-8pm Mon-Fri, 9am-5pm Sat & Sun) Standard supermarket fare, with an in-house deli and bakery.

⛾ Drinking & Entertainment

The siren song of blackjack and slot machines calls the masses over to Stateline. It's no Vegas, but there are plenty of ways to help you part with a bankroll. Each of the major casinos has live entertainment and several bars and lounges for you to while away the night. Published on Thursdays, the free alt-weekly newspaper **Reno News & Review** (www.newsreview.com) has comprehensive Stateline entertainment and events listings. For what's going on around South Lake Tahoe, pick up a copy of the free weekly *Lake Tahoe Action,* published by the **Tahoe Daily Tribune** (www.tahoedailytribune.com).

Beacon Bar & Grill

BAR

(www.camprichardson.com; Camp Richardson Resort, 1900 Jameson Beach Rd; ⊗11am-10pm) Imagine all of Lake Tahoe is your very own front yard when you and your buddies sprawl across this big wraparound wooden deck. If you want to get schnockered, order the signature Rum Runner cocktail. Bands rock here in summer.

Brewery at Lake Tahoe

BREWPUB

(www.brewerylaketahoe.com; 3542 Lake Tahoe Blvd; ⊗opens at 11am daily, closing time varies) Crazy-popular brewpub pumps its signature Bad Ass Ale into grateful local patrons, who may sniff at bright-eyed out-of-towners. The barbecue is dynamite and a roadside patio opens in summer. Don't leave without a bumper sticker!

Macduffs Pub

PUB

(www.macduffspub.com; 1041 Fremont Ave; ⊗11:30am-2am) With Boddingtons on tap, fish-and-chips and full-on Scottish breakfasts on the menu, as well as a dart board on the wall, this dark and bustling pub wouldn't look out of place in Edinburgh. Sports fans and spirit drinkers, step right up.

Opal Ultra Lounge

NIGHTCLUB

(⊘775-586-2000; www.montbleuresort.com; MontBleu, 55 Hwy 50, Stateline; cover free-$10; ⊗10pm-3am Wed-Sat) With DJ booths and go-go dancers, this Top 40 and electro dance club draws a young party crowd that enjoys getting their bodies painted in-house. Ladies might get in free before midnight. On summer Sunday nights, hit up the casino's poolside DJ parties. Dress to impress.

Stateline Brewery

BREWPUB

(www.statelinebrewery.com; 4118 Lake Tahoe Blvd; ⊗11am-9pm Sun-Thu, to 10pm Fri & Sat) Seat yourself by the shiny industrial brewing vats at this subterranean spot. German, Scotch and American-style ales taste mighty good after a day of sunning yourself on the lakeshore or skiing Heavenly (the gondola swings nearby).

Fresh Ketch BAR
(http://thefreshketch.com; Tahoe Keys Marina, 2345 Venice Dr; ⊙11:30am-10pm) We know all you're really looking for is sunset drinks on the waterfront with blissful lake views, right? Kick back on the outdoor waterfront patio, or inside at the bar, where live blues, jazz and acoustic guitarists groove several nights a week.

Improv COMEDY CLUB
(www.harveystahoe.com; 18 Hwy 50, Stateline; tickets $25-30; ⊙usually 9pm Wed & Fri-Sun, 8 & 10pm Sat) Catch up-and-coming stand-up comedians doing their funny shtick at the intimate cabaret theater inside Harvey's old-school casino.

Mt Tallac Brewing Company MICROBREWERY
(2060 Eloise Ave; ⊙usually 5-7pm) Tiny mom-and-pop joint is so jammed with locals, it's practically standing-room only (and brrrr, cold in winter). Pints are cheap, the company chill and the brews – well, they're serious beer-geek heaven.

Après Wine Company WINE BAR
(http://apreswineco.com; Ski Run Center, 3668 Lake Tahoe Blvd; ⊙11am-10pm Mon-Sat, 2-9pm Sun) Tucked away, this teensy wine shop lures oenophiles with happy hours, sipper specials, tapas-sized bites and DIY enomatic wine dispensers.

For a jolt of java, tea or free wi-fi:

Alpina Coffee Café COFFEE SHOP
(822 Emerald Bay Rd/Hwy 89; ⊙6am-5pm; @🛜) Internet-connected laptops, plus locally roasted brews, toasted bagels and a summer garden patio.

Keys Café COFFEE SHOP
(www.tahoekeyscafe.com; 2279 Lake Tahoe Blvd; ⊙7am-4pm; 🛜) Butter-yellow roadside cabin for single-origin coffees, espresso, organic teas and fresh smoothies.

❶ Information

Barton Memorial Hospital (☏530-541-3420; www.bartonhealth.org; 2170 South Ave; ⊙24hr) Around-the-clock emergency room. Barton's urgent-care clinic is inside the Stateline Medical Center at 155 Hwy 50, Stateline, NV.

Explore Tahoe (☏530-542-2908; www.cityofslt.us; Heavenly Village Transit Center, 4114 Lake Tahoe Blvd; ⊙9am-5pm) Interpretive exhibits and recreational and transportation information at a multipurpose 'urban trailhead.'

Lake Tahoe Visitors Authority (☏800-288-2463; http://tahoesouth.com); Stateline (☏775-588-5900; 169 Hwy 50, Stateline, NV; ⊙9am-5pm Mon-Fri); South Lake Tahoe (☏530-544-5050; 3066 Lake Tahoe Blvd; ⊙9am-5pm) Tourist information, maps, brochures and money-saving coupons.

South Lake Tahoe Library (☏530-573-3185; www.eldoradolibrary.org/tahoe.htm; 1000 Rufus Allen Blvd; ⊙10am-8pm Tue-Wed, 10am-5pm Thu-Sat; @) First-come, first-served free internet terminals.

Tahoe Urgent Care (☏530-541-3277; 2130 Lake Tahoe Blvd; ⊙8am-6pm) Walk-in medical clinic for nonemergencies.

USDA Lake Tahoe Basin Management Unit (☏530-543-2600; www.fs.usda.gov/ltbmu; 35 College Dr; ⊙8am-4:30pm Mon-Fri) Wilderness permits and camping and outdoor recreation information.

USFS Taylor Creek Visitor Center (☏530-543-2674; Hwy 89; ⊙8am-4:30pm late May–mid-Jun & Oct, to 5:30pm mid-Jun–Sep) Outdoor information, wilderness permits and daily ranger-led walks and talks during July and August.

❶ Getting There & Away

From Reno-Tahoe International Airport (see p452), **South Tahoe Express** (☏866-898-2463; www.southtahoeexpress.com; adult/child 4-12yr one-way $27/15, round-trip $48/27) operates several daily shuttle buses to Stateline casinos; the journey takes 75 minutes up to two hours.

Amtrak (☏800-872-7245; www.amtrak.com) has a daily Thruway bus service between Sacramento and South Lake Tahoe ($34, 2½ hours), stopping at the South Y Transit Center.

❶ Getting Around

South Lake Tahoe's main transportation hubs are the **South Y Transit Center** (1000 Emerald Bay Rd/Hwy 89), just south of the 'Y' intersection of Hwys 50 and 89; and the more central **Heavenly Village Transit Center** (4114 Lake Tahoe Blvd).

BlueGO (☏530-541-7149; www.bluego.org; single-ride/day pass $2/5) local buses operate year-round from 6am to 11pm daily, stopping all along Hwy 50 between the two transit centers. BlueGO also operates a reservable on-demand shuttle anywhere within South Lake Tahoe ($4 to $6).

In summer, BlueGO's **Nifty Fifty Trolley** (single-ride/day pass $2/5; ⊙hourly from 9am or 10am to 5pm or 6pm daily Jul-early Sep, Sat & Sun only Jun & mid-Sep–early Oct) heads north from the South Y Transit Center along the western shore to Tahoma. During winter ski season, BlueGO provides free and frequent

NAVIGATING SOUTH LAKE TAHOE TRAFFIC

South Lake Tahoe's main east–west thoroughfare is a 5-mile stretch of Hwy 50 called Lake Tahoe Blvd. Most hotels and businesses hover around the California–Nevada state line and Heavenly Village. Casinos are located in Stateline, which is officially a separate city.

West of town, Hwy 50 runs into Hwy 89 at the 'Y' junction. Heavy snowfall sometimes closes Hwy 89 north of the Tallac Historic Site. The section of Hwy 89 between South Lake Tahoe and Emerald Bay is also known as Emerald Bay Rd.

Traffic all along Hwy 50 between the 'Y' junction and Heavenly Village gets jammed around lunchtime and again by 5pm Monday to Friday in both summer and winter, but Sunday afternoons when skiers head back down the mountain are the worst.

An alternate, less-crowded route through town is Pioneer Trail, which branches east off the Hwy 89/50 junction (south of the 'Y') and reconnects with Hwy 50 at Stateline.

shuttle service from Stateline and South Lake Tahoe to all Heavenly base operations every 30 minutes from stops along Hwy 50, Ski Run Blvd and Pioneer Trail.

Western Shore

Lake Tahoe's densely forested western shore, between Emerald Bay and Tahoe City, is idyllic. Hwy 89 sinuously wends past gorgeous state parks with swimming beaches, hiking trails, pine-shaded campgrounds and historic mansions. Several trailheads also access the rugged splendor of the Desolation Wilderness (see the boxed text, p374).

All campgrounds and many businesses shut down between November and May. Hwy 89 often closes after snowfall for plowing or due to imminent avalanche danger. Once you drive its torturous slopeside curves, you'll understand why. The further south you go, the more of a roller coaster it is, no matter the season – so grip that steering wheel!

EMERALD BAY STATE PARK

Sheer granite cliffs and a jagged shoreline hem in glacier-carved **Emerald Bay** (☎530-541-3030; www.parks.ca.gov; per car $8; ⊙late May-Sep), a teardrop cove that will have you digging for your camera. Its most captivating aspect is the water, which changes from cloverleaf green to light jade depending on the angle of the sun.

◉ Sights

You'll spy panoramic pullouts all along Hwy 89, including at **Inspiration Point**, opposite Bayview Campground. Just south, the road shoulder evaporates on both sides of a steep drop-off, revealing a postcard-perfect view of Emerald Bay to the north and Cascade Lake to the south.

The mesmerizing blue-green waters of the bay frame **Fannette Island**. This uninhabited granite speck, Lake Tahoe's only island, holds the vandalized remains of a tiny 1920s teahouse belonging to heiress Lora Knight, who would occasionally motorboat guests to the island from **Vikingsholm Castle** (tours adult/child 6-13yr $8/5; ⊙10am-4pm late May-Sep), her Scandinavian-style mansion on the bay. The focal point of the state park, Vikingsholm Castle is a rare example of ancient Scandinavian-style architecture. Completed in 1929, it has trippy design elements aplenty, including sod-covered roofs that sprout wildflowers in late spring. The mansion is reached by a steep 1-mile trail, which also leads to a visitors center.

🏃 Activities & Tours

HIKING

Vikingsholm Castle is the southern terminus of the famous Rubicon Trail (see p383).

Two popular trailheads lead into the Desolation Wilderness (see the boxed text, p374). From the Eagle Falls parking lot ($5), the **Eagle Falls Trail** travels one steep mile to Eagle Lake, crossing by Eagle Falls along the way. This scenic short hike often gets choked with visitors, but crowds disappear quickly as the trail continues up to the Tahoe Rim Trail and Velma, Dicks and Fontanillis Lakes (up to 10 miles round-trip).

From the back of Bayview Campground, it's a steep 1-mile climb to glacial Granite Lake or a moderate 1.5-mile round-trip to Cascade Falls, which rushes with snowmelt in early summer.

BOATING

Fannette Island is accessible by boat, except during Canada goose nesting season (typically February to mid-June). Rent boats at Meeks Bay or South Lake Tahoe; from the latter, you can also catch narrated bay cruises or speedboat tours.

🛏 Sleeping

Eagle Point Campground   CAMPGROUND $
(☑info 530-525-7277, reservations 800-444-7275; www.reserveamerica.com; Hwy 89; tent & RV sites $35; ☺mid-Jun–early Sep; 🚻) With over 90 sites perched on the tip of Eagle Point, this state-park campground provides flush toilets, hot pay showers, beach access and bay views. Another 20 scattered sites are reserved for boat-in campers.

USFS Bayview Campground   CAMPGROUND $
(Hwy 89; tent & RV sites $15; ☺Jun-Sep) This rustic, nay, primitive forest-service campground has 13 no-reservation sites and vault toilets, but its potable water supplies are often exhausted sometime in July. It's opposite Inspiration Point.

DL BLISS STATE PARK

Emerald Bay State Park spills over into **DL Bliss State Park** (☑530-525-7277, www.parks.ca.gov; per car $8; ☺late May-late Sep), which has the western shore's most alluring beaches at Lester Cove and Calawee Cove. A half-mile round-trip nature trail leads to **Balancing Rock**, a 130-ton chunk of granite perched on a natural pedestal. Pick up an interpretive trail guide to park ecology and wildlife from the **visitor center** (☺8am-5pm) near the entrance.

Near Calawee Cove is the northern terminus of the scenic one-way **Rubicon Trail**, which ribbons along the lakeshore for 4.5 mostly gentle miles from Vikingsholm Castle (add one mile for the downhill walk to the castle from Hwy 89) in Emerald Bay State Park. It leads past small coves perfect for taking a cooling dip, and treats you to great views along the way. Add an extra mile to loop around and visit the restored historic lighthouse, a square wood-enclosed beacon constructed by the Coast Guard in 1916. Poised above 6800ft, it's the USA's highest-elevation lighthouse.

The park's **campground** (☑800-444-7275; www.reserveamerica.com; tent & RV sites $35-45, hike-and-bike sites $7; ☺mid-May–Sep; 🚻) has 145 sites, including some coveted spots near the beach, along with flush toilets, hot pay showers, picnic tables, fire rings and an RV dump station.

The small visitor parking lot at Calawee Cove usually fills up by 10am, in which case it's a 2-mile walk from the park entrance to the beach. Alternatively, ask park staff at the entrance station about closer access points to the Rubicon Trail.

MEEKS BAY

With a wide sweep of shoreline, sleek and shallow **Meeks Bay** has warm water by Tahoe standards and is fringed by a beautiful, but busy, sandy beach. On the west side of the highway, a few hundred feet north of the fire station, is another **trailhead** for the Desolation Wilderness (see the boxed text, p374). A moderate, mostly level and nicely shaded path parallels Meeks Creek before kicking off more steeply uphill through the forest to **Lake Genevieve** (9 miles round-trip), **Crag Lake** (10 miles round-trip) and other backcountry ponds, all surrounded by scenic Sierra peaks.

🛏 Sleeping & Eating

Meeks Bay Resort   CABIN, CAMPGROUND $$
(☑530-525-6946, 877-326-3357; www.meeksbayresort.com; 7941 Emerald Bay Rd/Hwy 89; tent & RV sites without/with full hookups $25/45, cabins $125-400; ☺May-Oct; 🚻) The Washoe tribe offers various lodging options (cabins require minimum stays) plus kayak, canoe and paddleboat rentals. If you're hungry, swing by the fast-food snack bar or small market, which stocks limited groceries and

DON'T MISS

TAHOE RIM TRAIL

Partly paralleling the Pacific Crest Trail, the 165-mile **Tahoe Rim Trail** (www.tahoerimtrail.org) wraps around the lofty ridges and mountaintops of the Lake Tahoe Basin. Hikers, equestrians and – in some sections – mountain-bikers can enjoy inspirational views of the lake and the snowcapped Sierra Nevada while tracing the footsteps of early pioneers, Basque shepherds and Washoe tribespeople. Dozens of marked trailheads all around the lakeshore provide easy access points for hikers, bikers and horseback riders. The drone of car traffic can be an occasional nuisance, however.

DON'T MISS

SNOWSHOEING UNDER THE STARS

A crisp quiet night with a blazing glow across the lake. What could be more magical than a full-moon snowshoe tour? Reserve ahead, as ramblings at these places are very popular:

» Ed Z'Berg Sugar Pine Point State Park (p384)
» Squaw Valley (p369)
» Camp Richardson Resort (p370)
» Northstar-at-Tahoe (p369)
» Kirkwood (p370)

camping, fishing and beach gear, as well as Native American crafts and cultural books.

USFS Meeks Bay Campground
CAMPGROUND $

(✆info 530-525-4733, reservations 877-444-6777; www.recreation.gov; tent & RV sites $23-25; ☼mid-May–mid-Oct; ▣) This developed campground offers 36 reservable sites along the beach, and flush toilets, picnic tables and fire rings. For pay showers, head to Meeks Bay Resort next door.

ED Z'BERG SUGAR PINE POINT STATE PARK

About 10 miles south of Tahoe City, this woodsy **state park** (✆530-525-7982; www.parks.ca.gov; per car $8) occupies a promontory blanketed by a fragrant mix of pine, juniper, aspen and fir. It has a swimming beach, over a dozen miles of hiking trails and abundant fishing in General Creek. A paved cycling path travels north to Tahoe City. In winter, 12 miles of groomed cross-country trails await inside the park; book ahead for ranger-guided full-moon **snowshoe tours** (✆530-525-9920; adult/child under 13yr incl snowshoe rental $15/free).

Historic sights include the modest 1872 **cabin** of William 'General' Phipps, an early Tahoe settler, and the considerably grander 1903 Queen Anne–style **Hellman-Ehrman Mansion** (tours adult/child under 13yr $5/3; ☼usually 10am-3pm mid-Jun–Sep), an elegant lakefront house also known as Pine Lodge. Guided tours take in the richly detailed interior, including marble fireplaces, leaded-glass windows and period furnishings.

The park's secluded **USFS General Creek Campground** (✆800-444-7275; www.

reserveamerica.com; tent & RV sites $20-25; ☼late May–mid-Sep; ▣▣) has 110 fairly spacious, pine-shaded sites, plus flush toilets and hot pay showers.

TAHOMA

Another blink-and-you'll-miss-it lakeside outpost, Tahoma has a post office and a handful of places to stay and eat.

Cute but not too kitschy, the red cabins of **Tahoma Meadows Bed & Breakfast Cottages** (✆530-525-1553, 866-525-1533; www.tahomameadows.com; 6821 W Lake Blvd; cottages incl breakfast $109-199, with kitchen $159-395; ▣▣▣) dot a pine grove. Each has classy country decor, thick down comforters, a small TV, and bathrooms with clawfoot tubs. Pick up the in-room journal to record your impressions while you're toasting your feet by the gas-burning fireplace. Pet fee $20.

Nearby, the **PDQ Market** (6890 W Lake Blvd; ☼6:30am-10pm) has groceries and a deli. Laying claim to being Tahoe's oldest bar, lakeside **Chamber's Landing** (✆530-525-9190; 6400 W Lake Blvd; ☼usually noon-8pm Jun-Sep) sees the biggest crowds descend for drinks and appetizers in the all-day bar, especially during happy hour. Do yourself a favor and skip the 'Chamber's Punch,' though.

HOMEWOOD

This quiet hamlet is popular with summertime boaters and, in winter, skiers and snowboarders (see p366). **West Shore Sports** (✆530-525-9920; www.westshoresports.com; 5395 W Lake Blvd; ☼8am-5pm Sun-Fri, 7:30am-5:30pm Sat) rents bicycles, kayaks, stand-up paddle boarding (SUP) gear and snow-sports equipment (eg skis, snowboards, snowshoes).

🛏 Sleeping & Eating

West Shore Inn
INN $$$

(✆530-525-5200; www.skihomewood.com/westshorecafe/lodging; 5160 W Lake Blvd; r/ste incl breakfast from $249/349; ▣▣) Oriental rugs and Arts & Crafts decor give this luxurious six-room inn a classic, aged feel, and the lake's so close you feel like you could dive in. It's an upscale mountain lodge where crisp, modern suites feel decadent, and each has a fireplace and lake-view balcony. Rates include complimentary use of bicycles, kayaks and stand-up paddleboards.

USFS Kaspian Campground
CAMPGROUND $

(✆877-444-6777; www.recreation.gov; tent sites $17-19; ☼mid-May–mid-Oct), The closest campground is this nine-site, tent-only spot set among ponderosa and fir trees; amenities include flush toilets, picnic tables and fire rings.

West Shore Café
CALIFORNIAN $$$

(☎530-525-5200; www.skihomewood.com/westshorecafe; 5160 W Lake Blvd; mains $12-33; ◎11:30am-9:30pm late Jun-Sep, 5-9:30pm Oct–mid-Jun) At the inn's cozy restaurant, chef Rusty Johns whips up California cuisine using artisanal cheeses, fresh produce and ranched meats, from juicy burgers to buffalo rib-eye steaks accompanied by tender broccoli rabe. Dinner reservations recommended.

SUNNYSIDE

Sunnyside is yet another lakeshore hamlet that may be just a dot on the map, but has a couple of detour-worthy restaurants worth stopping for. To work off all that dang good eating, rent a bicycle from **Cyclepaths** (☎530-581-1171; www.cyclepaths.net; 1785 W Lake Blvd), where you can get the scoop on all sorts of local outdoor information. You can pedal all the way north to Tahoe City along the paved bike path, or rent a stand-up paddle boarding (SUP) set and hit the popular local beaches.

Sleeping & Eating

USFS William Kent Campground
CAMPGROUND $

(☎877-444-6777; www.recreation.gov; Hwy 89; tent & RV sites $23-25; ◎mid-May–mid-Oct) About 2 miles south of Tahoe City, this roadside campground offers over 85 nicely shaded, but cramped, sites that often fill up. Amenities include flush toilets, picnic tables and fire rings, along with swimming beach access.

Sunnyside Restaurant & Lodge
INN, CALIFORNIAN $$

(☎530-583-7200; www.sunnysidetahoe.com; 1850 W Lake Blvd; d incl breakfast $135-380, mains lunch $11-17, dinner $15-35; 🐾) Classic and innovative contemporary takes on steak and seafood – think porterhouse pork with cherry chutney, or roasted chicken with braised fennel – pervade the lakeside dining room. In summer you'll probably have more fun doing lunch – or drinks with the signature zucchini sticks – on the huge lakefront deck. Two dozen noisy roadside lodge rooms and suites spell Old Tahoe; some have river-rock gas fireplaces and lake views.

Fire Sign Café
DINER $

(☎530-583-0871; 1785 W Lake Blvd; mains $6-12; ◎7am-3pm; 🚲) For breakfast, everyone heads to the friendly Fire Sign for down-home omelets, blueberry pancakes, eggs Benedict with smoked salmon, fresh made-from-scratch pastries and other carbo-loading bombs, plus organic coffee. In summer, hit the outdoor patio. Lines are usually very long, so get there early.

❶ Getting There & Around

In summer, BlueGO's **Nifty Fifty Trolley** (☎530-541-7149; www.bluego.org; single/day pass $2/5; ◎9:15am-5:15pm daily Jul-early Sep, Sat & Sun only Jun & mid-Sep–early Oct) rolls along the western shore every hour, from South Lake Tahoe's South Y Transit Center north to Tahoma, stopping at Emerald Bay State Park (including Inspiration Point and Vikingsholm Castle parking lot), DL Bliss State Park, Ed Z'berg Sugar Pine Point State Park and Meeks Bay. From Tahoma, **Tahoe Area Rapid Transit** (TART; ☎530-550-1212, 800-736-6365; www.laketahoetransit.com; single/day pass $2/4; ◎10am-6pm) buses continue north every hour to Tahoe City, stopping at Homewood and Sunnyside; between June and September, TART also stops at Ed Z'berg Sugar Pine Point State Park.

Tahoe City

The north shore's commercial hub, Tahoe City straddles the junction of Hwys 89 and 28, making it almost inevitable that you'll find yourself breezing through here at least once during your 'round-the-lake sojourn. The town is handy for grabbing food and supplies and renting sports gear. It's also the closest lake town to Squaw Valley (p366). The main drag, N Lake Blvd, is chockablock with outdoor outfitters, touristy shops and cafes.

◉ Sights

Gatekeeper's Museum & Marion Steinbach Indian Basket Museum
MUSEUM

(☎530-583-1762; 130 W Lake Blvd/Hwy 89; adult/child under 13yr $3/1; ◎usually 10am-5pm Wed-Mon May-Sep, 11am-3pm Sat & Sun Oct-Apr) In a reconstructed log cabin close to town, this museum has a small but fascinating collection of Tahoe memorabilia, including Olympics history and relics from the early steamboat era and tourism explosion around the lake. In the museum's newer wing, uncover an exquisite array of Native

American baskets collected from over 85 indigenous California tribes.

Fanny Bridge   LANDMARK

Just south of the always-jammed Hwy 89/28 traffic stoplight junction, the Truckee River flows through dam floodgates and passes beneath this bridge, cutely named for the most prominent feature of people leaning over the railings to look at fish (in American slang, 'fanny' means your rear end).

Watson Cabin   MUSEUM

(☎530-583-8717; 560 N Lake Tahoe Blvd; admission by donation; ⊙noon-4pm Wed-Mon mid-Jun–early Sep) A few blocks east, this well-preserved 1908 settlers' cabin is one of the town's oldest buildings, built overlooking the beach.

🏃 Activities

Beaches & River Rafting

Though not an outstanding swimming area, **Commons Beach** is a small, attractive park with sandy and grassy areas, picnic tables, barbecue grills, a climbing rock and playground for kids, as well as free summer concerts and outdoor movie nights. Leashed dogs welcome.

The Truckee River itself is gentle and wide as it flows northwest from the lake – perfect for novice paddlers. **Truckee River Raft Rentals** (☎530-583-0123; www.truckeeriverraft.com; 185 River Rd; adult/child 6-12yr $30/25; ⊙8:30am-3:30pm Jun-Sep; 🚸) rents rafts for the 5-mile float from Tahoe City to the River Ranch Lodge, including transportation back to town. Reservations strongly advised.

Hiking

Explore the fabulous trails of the **Granite Chief Wilderness** north and west of Tahoe City. For maps and trailhead directions, stop by the visitors center. Recommended day hikes include the moderately strenuous **Five Lakes Trail** (over 4 miles round-trip), which starts from Alpine Meadows Rd off Hwy 89 heading toward Squaw Valley, and the easy trek to **Paige Meadows**, leading onto the Tahoe Rim Trail. Paige Meadows is also good terrain for novice mountain-bikers and for snowshoeing. Wilderness permits are not required, even for overnight trips, but free campfire permits are needed, even for gas stoves. Leashed dogs are allowed on these trails.

Cycling

The paved 4-mile **Truckee River Bike Trail** runs from Tahoe City toward Squaw Valley, while the multi-use **West Shore Bike Path** heads 9 miles south to Ed Z'berg Sugar Pine Point State Park, including highway shoulder and residential street sections. Both are fairly easy rides, but expect crowds on summer weekends. The whole family can rent bicycles from any of several shops along N Lake Blvd.

Winter Sports

Tahoe City is within easy reach of a half dozen downhill and cross-country skiing and snowboarding resorts (see p366). For winter sports equipment rentals, drop by:

Tahoe Dave's   OUTDOOR OUTFITTER

(☎530-583-6415/0400, 800-398-8915; www.tahoedaves.com; 590 N Lake Tahoe Blvd) Additional branches at Squaw Valley, Kings Beach and Truckee (rentals can be returned to any shop); reservations accepted.

Porters Tahoe   OUTDOOR OUTFITTER

(☎530-583-2314; www.porterstahoe.com; 501 N Lake Blvd; ⊙10am-6pm) First-come, first-served rentals only.

🛏 Sleeping

If you show up without reservations, dingy, last-resort budget motels are along N Lake Blvd. For camping, head north to USFS campgrounds off Hwy 89 (see p392) or south along Hwy 89 to state parks and small towns along the lake's western shore.

Mother Nature's Inn   INN $$

(☎530-581-4278, 800-558-4278; www.mothernaturesinn.com; 551 N Lake Blvd; r $60-135; 🐾) Right in town behind Cabin Fever knickknack boutique, this good-value option offers quiet motel-style rooms with a tidy country look, fridges, eclectic furniture and comfy pillowtop mattresses. It's within walking distance of Commons Beach. Pet fee $5.

Pepper Tree Inn   MOTEL $$

(☎530-583-3711, 800-624-8590; www.peppertreetahoe.com; 645 N Lake Blvd; r incl breakfast $90-199; 🐾📶) The tallest building in town, this somberly painted establishment redeems itself with some birds-eye lake views. Fairly comfortable modern rooms with that familiar log-cabin decor each have a microwave and mini fridge. Top-floor rooms with hot tubs are most in demand.

Granlibakken
LODGE **$$**

(☎530-583-4242, 800-543-3221; www.granlibakken.com; 725 Granlibakken Rd, off Hwy 89; r/ste from $130/230, 1/2/3 br townhome from $330/380/430; ☎) Sleep seriously old-school at this cross-country ski area and kitschy wedding and conference venue. Basic lodge rooms are spacious, but timeshare townhomes with kitchens, fireplaces and lofts can be a decent deal for families and groups.

River Ranch Lodge
INN **$$**

(☎530-583-4264, 866-991-9912; www.riverranchlodge.com; Hwy 89 at Alpine Meadows Rd; r incl breakfast $115-195; ☎) If it weren't for noise from traffic outside and the bar downstairs, you'd be drifting off to dreamland as the Truckee River tumbles below your window here. Rooms bulge with lodgepole-pine furniture; those upstairs have wistful balconies. Pet-friendly rooms available in summer only.

✗ Eating & Drinking

TOP
CHOICE **Dockside 700 Wine**
Bar & Grill
AMERICAN **$$**

(☎530-581-0303; www.dockside700.com; 700 N Lake Blvd; breakfast & lunch $5-10, dinner $13-29; ☺9am-9pm Mon-Fri, 8am-9pm Sat & Sun; ☎) On a lazy summer afternoon, grab a table on the back deck that overlooks the boats bobbing at Tahoe City Marina. On weekends, barbecue chicken, ribs and steak light a fire under dinner (reservations advised), alongside seafood pastas and pizzas. Caramelized praline French toast and build-your-own sandwiches show up earlier in the day.

River Ranch Lodge
NEW AMERICAN **$$$**

(☎530-583-4264; www.riverranchlodge.com; Hwy 89 at Alpine Meadows Rd; mains patio & cafe $8-15, restaurant $18-31; ☺lunch Jun-Sep, dinner year-round, call for seasonal hr) This riverside dining room is a popular stop, drawing rafters and bikers to its patio for summer barbecue lunches. Dinner is a meat-heavy affair, with filet mignon and roasted duck. However, the bar's eclectic cafe menu – anything from Hawaii-style ahi *poke* (marinated raw fish) to pulled-pork sliders – will leave you feeling less like you overpaid.

Fat Cat
CALIFORNIAN **$$**

(www.fatcattahoe.com; 599 N Tahoe Blvd; mains $10-15; ☺11am-9pm, bar till 2am; ☎) Hitting that happy Goldilocks median – not too expensive, but not too cheap – this casual, family-run restaurant with local art splashed on the walls does it all: from-scratch soups, heaped salads, sandwiches, pasta bowls and plenty of fried munchies for friends to share. Look for live indie music on Friday and Saturday nights.

Rosie's Cafe
DINER **$$**

(www.rosiescafe.com; 571 N Lake Blvd; breakfast & lunch $7-14, dinner $14-20; ☺7:30am-9:30pm Mon-Thu, 7:30am-10pm Fri, 7am-10pm Sat & Sun; ☎) With antique skis, shiny bikes and lots of pointy antlers belonging to stuffed wildlife mounted on the walls, this quirky place serves breakfast until 2:30pm. The all-American hodge-podge menu is all right, but the convivial atmosphere is a winner.

Tahoe House Bakery
BAKERY, TAKEOUT **$**

(www.tahoe-house.com; 625 W Lake Blvd; items $2-10; ☺6am-6pm, closing at 4pm Sun-Thu Oct-May) Before you take off down the western shore for a bike ride or hike, drop by this mom-and-pop shop that opened in the 1970s. Their motto: 'While you sleep, we loaf.' Sweet cookies, European pastries, fresh-baked deli sandwiches and homemade salads and soups will keep you going all afternoon on the trail.

Spoon
AMERICAN, TAKEOUT **$$**

(☎530-581-5400; www.spoontakeout.com; 1785 W Lake Blvd; mains $9-14; ☺3-9pm, closed Tue & Wed Oct-May; ☎) Call ahead for takeout, or squeeze yourselves into the cozy upstairs dining room at this little slat-sided cabin by the side of the highway. Barbecue tri-tip beef sandwiches, roasted veggies, baked pastas and chicken enchiladas are the comfort-food staples, with brownies and ice cream for dessert.

New Moon Natural Foods
GROCERY, TAKEOUT **$**

(505 W Lake Blvd; dishes $6-10; ☺9am-7pm Mon-Sat, 10am-6pm Sun; ☎) Tucked away in a tiny but well-stocked natural-foods store, this gem of a deli concocts scrumptious ethnic food to go, all packaged in biodegradable and compostable containers. Try the Thai salad with organic greens and spicy peanut sauce.

Dam Café
CAFE **$**

(55 W Lake Blvd; items $2-8; ☺7am-3:30pm) Right by the Truckee River dam and the Fanny Bridge, stash your bikes in the racks outside this cute cottage and walk inside for a breakfast burrito, ice-cream fruit smoothie or pick-me-up espresso.

Syd's Bagelry and Espresso CAFE $
(550 N Lake Blvd; items $2-10; ⊘6am-4pm; 🛜) A handy spot on the main drag serves bagels and locally roasted coffee, plus smoothies and fresh homemade soups (often vegan) made with organic produce.

Bridgetender Tavern BAR, GRILL $$
(www.tahoebridgetender.com; 65 W Lake Blvd; mains $8-12; ⊘11am-11pm, to midnight Fri & Sat) Après-ski crowds gather for beer, burgers and chili-cheese or garlic waffle fries at this woodsy bar. In summer, grab a seat on the open-air patio.

❶ Information

Tahoe City Downtown Association (www. visittahoecity.org) Free tourist information and online events calendar.

Tahoe City Library (📞530-583-3382; Boatworks Mall, 740 N Lake Blvd; ⊘10am-5pm Tue & Thu-Fri, noon-7pm Wed, 10am-2pm Sun; @🛜) Free wi-fi and walk-in internet terminals.

Tahoe City Visitors Information Center (📞530-581-6900, 888-434-1262; www.gota hoenorth.com; 380 N Lake Blvd; ⊘9am-5pm) North of the fire station.

Truckee Tahoe Medical Group (📞530-581-8864 ext 3; www.ttmg.net; Trading Post Center, 925 N Lake Blvd; ⊘9am-6pm Mon-Sat year-round, also 10am-5pm Sun early Jul-early Sep) Walk-in clinic for nonemergencies.

❶ Getting There & Around

With a saucy acronym and reliable service, **Tahoe Area Rapid Transit** (TART; 📞530-550-1212, 800-736-6365; www.laketahoetransit. com; single/day pass $2/4) runs buses along the north shore as far as Incline Village, down the western shore to Tahoma (continuing south to Ed Z'berg Sugar Pine Point State Park between June and September only), and north to Squaw Valley and Truckee via Hwy 89. The main routes typically run every 30 to 60 minutes from 6am or 7am until 5pm or 6pm daily.

Between June and September, TART also operates a night-time **Tahoe Trolley**, a free local bus service connecting Squaw Valley, Tahoe City, Carnelian Bay, Tahoe Vista, Kings Beach, Crystal Bay and Incline Village hourly from 7pm until 10pm, 11pm or midnight. Two more free nighttime summer-only trolley routes loop between Tahoe City and Tahoma via Sunnyside and Homewood, and between Northstar-at-Tahoe, Kings Beach and Crystal Bay, every hour from 6pm until 10:30pm daily.

Squaw Valley

The nirvana of the north shore, Squaw Valley played host to the 1960 Olympic Winter Games and still ranks among the world's top ski resorts (also see p366). The stunning setting amid granite peaks, though, makes it a superb destination in any season, and this deluxe family-friendly resort stays almost as busy in summer as in winter.

◉ Sights & Activities

Much of the summertime action centers on 8200ft **High Camp** (📞800-403-0206; www. squaw.com; cable-car adult/child under 13/youth 13-18yr $29/10/22, all-access pass $63/57/57; 🐾), reached by a dizzying cable car (leashed dogs OK). At the top you'll find a heated seasonal outdoor swimming lagoon (adult/child $14/7), 18-hole disc-golf course (free), two high-altitude tennis courts (racquet rentals and ball purchase available), a kids-only zip line ($12) and a roller-skating rink (adult/child $10/5) that doubles as an ice-skating rink in winter. Cable-car tickets include admission to the **Olympic Museum**, which relives those magic moments from 1960.

Several hiking trails radiate out from High Camp, or try the lovely, moderate **Shirley Lake Trail** (round-trip 5 miles), which follows a sprightly creek to waterfalls, granite boulders and abundant wildflowers. It starts at the mountain base, near the end of Squaw Peak Rd, behind the cable-car building. Leashed dogs are allowed.

Other fun activities down below include a ropes course, a climbing wall, mini golf and a Sky Jump (bungee trampoline), all operated by the **Squaw Valley Adventure Center** (📞530-583-7673; www.squawadventure. com). Golfers tee up at the 18-hole, par 71, Scottish-style links **Resort at Squaw Creek Golf Course** (📞530-581-6637; www.squawcreek. com; green fee incl cart $50-95); rental clubs are available.

🛏 Sleeping & Eating

For more resort hotel and condo lodging options, including ski-vacation packages, contact **Squaw Valley** (📞800-403-0206; www. squaw.com).

TOP CHOICE **PlumpJack Squaw Valley Inn** BOUTIQUE HOTEL $$$
(📞530-583-1576, 800-323-7666; www.plumpjack squawvalleyinn.com; 1920 Squaw Valley Rd, Olym-

pic Valley; r incl breakfast $169-349; ✽@🛜🖥🐾) Bed down at this artsy boutique hotel in the village, where every room has mountain views and extra-comfort factors like plush terry-cloth robes and slippers. Ski-in, ski-out access doesn't hurt either, but a $150 pet fee will. The chic **PlumpJack Cafe** (mains $23-31; ⊙6pm-9pm, bar 11:30am-10pm), with its crisp linens and plush banquettes, serves seasonally inspired California cuisine with ace wines.

Le Chamois & Loft Bar   PIZZERIA, PUB $$
(www.squawchamois.com; 1970 Squaw Valley Rd; mains $8-16; ⊙11am-6pm Mon-Fri, to 8pm Sat & Sun, bar open to 9pm or 10pm; 🍴) For a social bite after shedding your bindings, this slope-side favorite is handily positioned between the cable-car building and the rental shop. Slide on over to devour a hot sammy or pizza and a beer with eye-pleasing mountain views.

Wildflour Baking Company   BAKERY, TAKEOUT $
(http://wildfloursquaw.com; items $2-10; ⊙7am-7pm or later; 🍴) Fresh-baked bread sandwiches and bagels make great breakfasts or afternoon snacks at this to-go counter in the cable-car building. Baristas whip up Scharffenberger hot chocolate and brew Peet's coffee and teas.

❶ Getting There & Away

The village at Squaw Valley, at the base of the mountain cable-car, is about a 20-minute drive from Tahoe City or Truckee via Hwy 89 (turn off at Squaw Valley Rd).

Tahoe Area Rapid Transit (TART; ☑530-550-1212, 800-736-6365; www.laketahoetransit. com; single/day pass $2/4) buses between Truckee and Tahoe City, Kings Beach and Crystal Bay stop at Squaw Valley every hour or so between 7am and 5pm daily, with a free morning ski shuttle from December to April.

Truckee & Donner Lake

Cradled by mountains and the Tahoe National Forest, Truckee is a thriving town steeped in Old West history. It was put on the map by the railroad, grew rich on logging and ice harvesting, and even had its brush with Hollywood during the 1924 filming of Charlie Chaplin's *The Gold Rush*. Today tourism fills much of the city's coffers, thanks to a well-preserved historical downtown and its proximity to Lake Tahoe and

no fewer than six downhill and four cross-country ski resorts (see p365).

◎ Sights

The aura of the Old West still lingers over Truckee's teensy one-horse downtown, where railroad workers and lumberjacks once milled about in raucous saloons, bawdy brothels and shady gambling halls. Most of the late-19th-century buildings now contain restaurants and upscale boutiques. Donner Memorial State Park and three-mile-long Donner Lake, a busy recreational hub, are another 3 miles further west.

Donner Memorial State Park   PARK
(☎530-582-7892; www.parks.ca.gov; per car $8; ⊙seasonal park hr vary, museum 9am-4pm year-round) At the eastern end of Donner Lake, this state-run park occupies one of the sites where the doomed Donner Party got trapped during the fateful winter of 1846–47 (see the boxed text, p390). Though its history is gruesome, the park is gorgeous and has a sandy beach, picnic tables hiking trails and wintertime cross-country skiing and snowshoeing.

The entry fee includes admission to the excellent **Emigrant Trail Museum**, which has fascinating, if admittedly macabre historical exhibits and a 25-minute film reenacting the Donner Party's horrific plight. (In future years, it will be replaced by a newer, bigger and more multicultural High Sierra Crossing Museum.) Outside, the **Pioneer Monument** has a 22ft pedestal – the exact depth of the snow piles that horrendous winter. A short trail leads to a memorial at one family's cabin site.

Old Jail   HISTORIC BUILDING
(http://truckeehistory.org; 10142 Jiboom St, cnr Spring St; suggested donation $2; ⊙11am-4pm Sat & Sun late May & mid-Jun–mid-Sep) Continuously in use until the 1960s, this 1875 red-brick building is filled with relics from the wild days of yore. George 'Machine Gun' Kelly was reportedly once held here for shoplifting at a local variety store, and 'Baby Face' Nelson and 'Ma' Spinelli and her gang did time too.

🏃 Activities

For outdoor-sports equipment rentals and in-the-know local advice, try:

THE DOOMED DONNER PARTY

In the 19th century, tens of thousands of people migrated west along the Overland Trail with dreams of a better life in California. Among them was the ill-fated Donner Party.

When the families of George and Jacob Donner and their friend James Reed departed Springfield, Illinois, in April 1846 with six wagons and a herd of livestock, they intended to make the arduous journey as comfortable as possible. But the going was slow and, when other pioneers told them about a cutoff that would save 200 miles, they jumped at the chance.

However, there was no road for the wagons in the Wasatch Mountains, and most of the livestock succumbed under the merciless heat of the Great Salt Lake Desert. Arguments and fights broke out. James Reed killed a man, was kicked out of the group and left to trundle off to California alone. By the time the party reached the eastern foot of the Sierra Nevada, near present-day Reno, morale and food supplies ran dangerously low.

To restore their livestock's energy and reprovision, the emigrants decided to rest here for a few days. But an exceptionally fierce winter came early, quickly rendering what later came to be called Donner Pass impassable and forcing the pioneers to build basic shelter near today's Donner Lake. They had food to last a month and the fervent hope that the weather would clear by then. It didn't.

Snow fell for weeks, reaching a depth of 22ft. Hunting and fishing became impossible. In mid-December a small group of people made a desperate attempt to cross the pass. They quickly became disoriented and had to ride out a three-day storm that killed some of them. One month later, less than half of the original 15 staggered into Sutter's Fort near Sacramento, having survived on one deer and their dead friends.

By the time the first rescue party arrived at Donner Lake in late February, the trapped pioneers were still surviving – barely – on boiled ox hides. But when the second rescue party, led by the banished James Reed, made it through in March, evidence of cannibalism was everywhere. Journals and reports tell of 'half-crazed people living in absolute filth, with naked, half-eaten bodies strewn about the cabins.' Many were too weak to travel.

When the last rescue party arrived in mid-April, only a sole survivor, Lewis Keseberg, was there to greet them. The rescuers found George Donner's body cleansed and wrapped in a sheet, but no sign of Tasmen Donner, George's wife. Keseberg admitted to surviving on the flesh of the dead, but denied charges that he had killed Tasmen for fresh meat. He spent the rest of his life trying to clear his name.

In the end, only 47 of the 89 members of the Donner Party survived. They settled in California, their lives forever changed by the harrowing winter at Donner Lake.

Back Country OUTDOOR OUTFITTER
(☎530-582-0909; www.thebackcountry.com; 11400 Donner Pass Rd; ☺8:30am-6pm, call ahead in winter & spring) Rents bicycles and snowshoes, and rents and sells new and used climbing gear, as well as backcountry ski gear.

Porters Tahoe OUTDOOR OUTFITTER
(☎530-587-1500; www.porterstahoe.com; 11391 Deerfield Dr; ☺10am-6pm; 🚻) In the Crossroads Center strip mall, Porters rents skis, snowboards and snowshoes on a first-come, first-served basis.

Truckee Sports Exchange OUTDOOR OUTFITTER
(☎530-582-4510; www.truckeesportsexchange. com; 10095 W River St; ☺call for seasonal hr) Big indoor climbing gym (day pass $5, shoe rental $5); rents kayaks and SUP gear.

🏄 Beaches & Water Sports

Warmer than Lake Tahoe, tree-lined **Donner Lake** is great for swimming, boating, fishing (license required), waterskiing and windsurfing. **West End Beach** (adult/child 1-17yr $4/3; 🚻) is a favorite of families for its roped-off swimming area, snack stand, volleyball nets and kayak, paddleboat and stand-up paddle boarding (SUP) rentals.

Tributary Whitewater Tours RIVER RUNNING
(☎530-346-6812, 800-672-3846; www.whitewatertours.com; half-day trip per adult/child 7-17yr $69/62; 🚻) From roughly mid-May through September, this long-running outfitter operates a 7-mile, half-day rafting run on the Truckee River over Class III+ rapids that

will thrill kids and their nervous parents alike.

Hiking & Climbing

Truckee is a great base for treks in the Tahoe National Forest, especially around Donner Summit. One popular 5-mile hike reaches the summit of 8243ft **Mt Judah** for awesome views of Donner Lake and the surrounding peaks. A longer, more strenuous ridge-crest hike links **Donner Pass** to **Squaw Valley** (15 miles each way) skirting the base of prominent peaks, but you'll need two cars for this shuttle hike.

Donner Summit is also a major rock-climbing mecca, with over 300 traditional and sport climbing routes. To learn the ropes, so to speak, take a class with **Alpine Skills International** (☏530-582-9170; www.alpineskills.com; 11400 Donner Pass Rd).

☞ Tours

Tahoe Adventure Company OUTDOOR SPORTS (☏530-913-9212, 866-830-6125; http://tahoeadventurecompany.com; tours per person from $50) A great option for guided high-Sierra adventures. Staff know the backcountry inside out and can customize any outing to your interest and skill level, from kayaking, hiking, mountain-biking and rock climbing to any combination thereof. They also offer full-moon snowshoe tours, and SUP lessons and guided lake paddles.

🛏 Sleeping

A few dependable midrange chain motels and hotels are also found off I-80 exits.

TOP CHOICE **Cedar House Sport Hotel** BOUTIQUE HOTEL $$$ (☏530-582-5655, 866-582-5655; www.cedarhousesporthotel.com; 10918 Brockway Rd; r incl breakfast $170-270; 🖥🐾) This chic, environmentally conscious contemporary lodge aims at getting folks out into nature. It boasts countertops made from recycled paper, 'rain chains' that redistribute water from the green roof garden, low-flow plumbing and in-room recycling. However, it doesn't skimp on plush robes, sexy platform beds with pillow-top mattresses, flat-screen TVs or the outdoor hot tub. Guided tours and multisport outdoor adventures can be arranged in-house. Pet fee $50 to $100.

Clair Tappaan Lodge HOSTEL $ (☏530-426-3632, 800-629-6775; www.sierraclub.org/outings/lodges/ctl; 19940 Donner Pass Rd; dm incl family-style meals per adult $50-60, child under 14yr $25-32; 🐾) About a mile west of Sugar Bowl, this cozy Sierra Club–owned rustic mountain lodge puts you near major ski resorts and sleeps up to 140 people in dorms and family rooms. Rates include family-style meals, but you're expected to do small chores and bring your own sleeping bag, towel and swimsuit (for the hot tub!). In winter, go cross-country skiing or snowshoeing (see p369), or careen down the sledding hill out back.

Larkspur Hotel Truckee-Tahoe HOTEL $$$ (☏530-587-4525, 800-824-6385; www.larkspurhotels.com; 11331 Brockway Rd; r incl breakfast $159-249; 🖥🐾) Forget about retro ski-lodge kitsch as you cozy up inside these crisp, earth-toned and down-to-earth hotel rooms that abound in sunny, natural woods. Sink back onto the feather-topped mattresses, refresh yourself with spa-quality bath amenities or hit the seasonal outdoor heated pool by the hot tub and cedar dry sauna. Continental breakfast buffet included. Pet fee $25 to $75.

Truckee Donner Lodge HOTEL $$ (☏530-582-9999, 877-878-2533; www.truckeedonnerlodge.com; 10527 Cold Stream Rd, off I-80 exit Donner Pass Rd; r incl breakfast $84-204; 🖥🐾) Just west of Hwy 89, this ex–Holiday Inn property gives you easy driving access to area ski resorts, shaving time off your morning commute to the slopes. No-nonsense, spacious hotel rooms come with microwaves and mini-fridges, and some have gas fireplaces. The hot-and-cold continental breakfast bar is complimentary.

Truckee Hotel HISTORIC HOTEL $$ (☏530-587-4444, 800-659-6921; www.truckeehotel.com; 10007 Bridge St; r with shared bath $49-169, with private bath $99-169, all incl breakfast; 🖥) Tucked behind an atmospheric red-brick street front arcade, Truckee's most historic abode has welcomed weary travelers since 1873. It's fully restored but still gives you that total Victorian immersion. Expect simply furnished rooms with drab, mismatched antiques and some train noise. Parking is inconvenient – ask first to avoid being towed.

River Street Inn B&B $$ (☏530-550-9290; http://riverstreetinntruckee.com; 10009 E River St; r incl breakfast $115-195) On the far side of the tracks, this sweet 1885 Victorian in Truckee's historic downtown has 11 rooms that blend nostalgic touches like clawfoot tubs with down comforters, but have few amenities other than TVs. Mingle with other guests over breakfast in the lounge. Bring earplugs to dull the occasional train noise.

Donner Memorial State Park Campground
CAMPGROUND $

(☑info 530-582-7894, reservations 800-444-7275; www.reserveamerica.com; tent & RV sites $35, hike-and-bike sites $7; ⊘late May-late Sep; 🅿🐾) Near Donner Lake, this family-oriented campground has 138 campsites with flush toilets and hot pay showers.

USFS Campgrounds
CAMPGROUND $

(☑877-444-6777; www.recreation.gov; tent & RV sites $17-38; ⊘mid-May–mid-Oct; 🐾) Conveniently located along Hwy 89 are three minimally developed riverside camping areas: Granite Flat, Goose Meadow and Silver Creek. All have potable water and vault toilets.

🍴 Eating & Drinking

TOP CHOICE Moody's Bistro & Lounge
CALIFORNIAN $$$

(☑530-587-8688; www.moodysbistro.com; 10007 Bridge St; lunch $12-16, dinner $20-34; ⊘11:30am-9:30pm Mon-Thu, 11:30am-10pm Fri, 11am-10pm Sat & 11am-9:30pm Sun) With its sophisticated supper-club looks and live jazz (Thursday to Saturday evenings), this gourmet restaurant in the Truckee Hotel oozes urbane flair. Only the freshest, organic and locally grown ingredients make it into the chef's perfectly pitched concoctions like pork lion with peach barbecue sauce, roasted beets with shaved fennel, or tempura-fried mozzarella with herbs.

Stella
ECLECTIC $$$

(☑530-582-5665; www.cedarhousesporthotel.com; 10918 Brockway Rd; mains $18-31; ⊘usually 5:30-8:30pm Wed-Sun) Housed at the trendy Cedar House Sport Hotel, this modern mountain-lodge dining room elevates Truckee's dining scene with Californian flair, harmonizing Asian and Mediterranean influences on its seasonal menu of housemade pastas, grilled meats and pan-roasted seafood. Bonuses: veggies grown on-site, housemade artisan bread and a killer wine list.

Squeeze In
DINER $$

(☑530-587-9814; www.squeezein.com; 10060 Donner Pass Rd; mains $8-13; ⊘7am-2pm; 🅿) Across

from the Amtrak station, this snug locals' favorite dishes up breakfasts big enough to feed a lumberjack. Over 60 varieties of humungous omelets – along with burgers, burritos and big salads – are dished up in this funky place crammed with silly tchotchkes and colorful handwritten notes plastered on the walls.

Burger Me
AMERICAN $$

(http://burgermetruckee.com; 10418 Donner Pass Rd; items $2-14; ⊘11am-9pm; 🅿) Getting two thumbs up from Food Network punk Guy Fieri may have gone to these guys' heads, but this fresh take on a burger shop still stocks all-natural meats and farm-fresh vegetables in the kitchen. Try the 'Truckee Trainwreck' – a beef patty topped with cheddar cheese, onion rings, turkey chili and a fried egg – if you dare.

Coffeebar
CAFE $

(www.coffeebartruckee.com; 10120 Jiboom St; items $2-8; ⊘6am-8pm; 🛜) Acid-orange molded chairs and electro tunes set the backdrop for this beatnik, bare-bones industrial coffee shop. Go for tantalizing breakfast crepes and overstuffed panini on herbed focaccia bread, or go for a jolt of organic espresso or an inspired specialty nectar like Vanilla Earl Cambric.

Fifty Fifty Brewing Co
BREWPUB $$

(www.fiftyfiftybrewing.com; 11197 Brockway Rd; mains $10-27; ⊘11:30am-2am, kitchen closes earlier) Inhale the aroma of toasting grains at this brewpub south of downtown, near the Hwy 267 intersection. Sip the popular Donner Party Porter or Eclipse barrel-aged imperial stout while noshing a huge plate of nachos, but skip the other so-so pub grub. Cozy Avec wine-tasting bar is nearby.

ⓘ Information

Tahoe Forest Hospital (☑530-587-6011; www.tfhd.com; 10121 Pine Ave, cnr Donner Pass Rd; ⊘24hr) Emergency room, specializing in sports injuries.

Truckee Donner Chamber of Commerce (☑530-587-2757, 866-443-2027; www.truckee.com; 10065 Donner Pass Rd; internet access per 15min $3; ⊘9am-6pm; @🛜) Inside the Amtrak train depot; free walking-tour maps and wi-fi.

USFS Truckee District Ranger Station (☑530-587-3558; 10811 Stockrest Springs Rd, off I-80 exit 188; ⊘8am-5pm Mon-Sat) Keeps shorter winter hours.

ⓘ Getting There & Around

Truckee straddles the I-80 and is connected to the lakeshore via Hwy 89 to Tahoe City or Hwy 267 to Kings Beach. The main drag through downtown Truckee is Donner Pass Rd, where you'll find the Amtrak train depot and metered on-street parking. Brockway Rd begins south of the river, connecting over to Hwy 267.

Though the Truckee Tahoe Airport has no commercial air service, **North Lake Tahoe Express** (☑866-216-5222; www.northlaketahoeexpress.com; one-way/round-trip per person $40/75) shuttles to the closest airport at Reno (see p452). Buses make several runs daily from 3:30am to midnight, serving multiple northern and western shore towns and Northstar-at-Tahoe and Squaw Valley ski resorts. Make reservations in advance.

Greyhound (☑800-231-2222; www.greyhound.com) has twice-daily buses to Reno ($18, one hour), Sacramento ($36, 2½ hours) and San Francisco ($34, 5½ to six hours). Greyhound buses stop at the train depot, as do **Amtrak** (☑800-872-7245; www.amtrak.com) Thruway buses and the daily *California Zephyr* train to Reno ($18, 1½ hours), Sacramento ($37, 4½ hours) and Emeryville/San Francisco ($41, 6½ hours).

The **Truckee Trolley** (☑530-587-7451; www.laketahoetransit.com; single/day pass $2/4) links the Amtrak train depot with Donner Lake hourly from 9am to 5pm daily. For Tahoe City and other towns on the lake's north, west or east shores, hop on the TART bus (p388) at the train depot. Single-ride TART tickets cost $2 (day pass $4). During ski season, additional buses run to many area ski resorts.

Northern Shore

Northeast of Tahoe City, Hwy 28 cruises through a string of cute, low-key towns, many fronting superb sandy beaches, with reasonably priced roadside motels and hotels all crowded together along the lakeshore. Oozing old-fashioned charm, the north shore is a blissful escape from the teeming crowds of South Lake Tahoe, Tahoe City and Truckee, but still puts you within easy reach of winter ski resorts and snow parks, summertime swimming, kayaking, hiking trails and more.

The **North Lake Tahoe Visitors' Bureau** (☑800-824-0348; www.gotahoenorth.com) can help get you oriented, although their closest walk-in office is at Incline Village, Nevada (see p395).

TAHOE VISTA

Pretty little Tahoe Vista has more **public beaches** (http://northtahoeparks.com) than any other lakeshore town. Sandy strands along Hwy 28 include small but popular **Moon Dunes Beach**, with picnic tables and firepits opposite the Rustic Cottages; **Tahoe Vista Recreation Area** (7010 N Lake Blvd), a locals' favorite with a small grassy area and marina; and **North Tahoe Beach** (7860 N Lake Blvd), near the Hwy 267 intersection, with picnic facilities, barbecue grills, beach volleyball courts and the **Tahoe Adventure Company** (☑530-913-9212, 866-830-6125; http://tahoeadventurecompany.com) for rental kayaks and SUP gear ($15 to $80).

Away from all the maddening crowds, **North Tahoe Regional Park** (http://northtahoeparks.com; 6600 Donner Rd; per car $3; ⧖) offers forested hiking and mountain-biking trails, an 18-hole disc-golf course, a children's playground and tennis courts lit-up for night play. In winter, a sledding hill and ungroomed cross-country ski and snowshoe tracks beckon. To find this hidden park, drive almost a mile uphill from Hwy 28 on National Ave, then go left on Donner Rd and follow the signs.

🛏 Sleeping

Rustic Cottages　　　　　　　　COTTAGE **$$**
(☑530-546-3523, 888-778-7842; www.rusticcottages.com; 7449 N Lake Blvd; cottages incl breakfast $75-229; ☎✿) These cottages consist of a cluster of about 20 little storybook houses in the pines, with nametags fashioned from hand saws. They sport beautiful wrought-iron beds and a bevy of amenities. Most cabins have full kitchens, and some have gas or real wood-burning fireplaces to warm your heart's cockles. Other perks: waffles and homemade muffins at breakfast, and free sleds and snowshoes to borrow in winter.

Franciscan Lakeside Lodge　CABIN, COTTAGE **$$**
(☑530-546-6300, 800-564-6754; http://franciscanlodge.com; 6944 N Lake Blvd; cabins, cottages & ste $85-345; ☎✿⧖) Spend the day on a private sandy beach or in the outdoor pool, then light the barbecue grill after sunset – ah, now that's relaxation. All of the simple cabins, cottages and suites have kitchenettes. Lakeside lodgings have better beach access and views, but roomier cabins near the back of the complex tend to be quieter and will appeal to families with younger kids in tow.

Cedar Glen Lodge INN $$

(☎530-546-4281; www.tahoecedarglen.com; 6589 N Lake Blvd; r, ste & cottages incl breakfast $89-199; 🐕📶🏊) Kids go nuts over all the freebies, from ping-pong tables, horseshoe pit, volleyball and croquet courts to an outdoor swimming pool and toasty firepit. Opposite the beach, some of these woodsy suites and cottages have kitchenettes and air-con, though standard-issue rooms look bland. Morning waffles and Bananas Foster on weekends help sleepyheads rise and shine. Pet fee $30.

✖ Eating & Drinking

TOP CHOICE **Wild Goose** CALIFORNIAN $$$

(☎530-546-3640; www.wildgoosetahoe.com; 7320 N Lake Blvd; mains $20-36; ⊙5:30-9pm Wed-Mon, bar from 2pm Wed-Thu & Sun-Mon, from 4pm Fri & Sat) Inhabiting a rehabbed ecofriendly lakefront building with inspirational panoramic windows, this New American bistro claims a globally inspired chef and a cellar that gets the nod from *Wine Spectator*. Leek and goat-cheese ravioli, oven-roasted chicken with fried artichoke and filet mignon with melted Maytag blue-cheese butter share a menu with Valhrona dark-chocolate fondue. Reservations are essential, but waterfront tables on the open-air deck are still first-come, first-served.

Gar Woods Grill & Pier AMERICAN $$$

(☎530-546-3366; www.garwoods.com; 5000 N Lake Blvd; mains lunch $12-18, dinner $18-37; ⊙noon-9:30pm Mon-Thu, noon-10pm Fri, 11:30am-10pm Sat, 11:30am-9:30pm Sun, bar till 11:30pm Sun-Thu, midnight Fri & Sat) A shoreline hot spot judging by the rowdy crowds, Gar Woods pays tribute to the era of classic wooden boats. Don't show up for the lackadaisical grill fare, but instead to slurp a Wet Woody cocktail while watching sunset over the lake. Be prepared to duke it out for a table on the no-reservations side of the beachfront deck out back.

Old Post Office Cafe DINER $

(5245 N Lake Blvd; mains $6-12; ⊙6:30am-2pm) Head west of town toward Carnelian Bay, where this always-packed, cheery wooden shack serves scrumptious breakfasts – buttery potatoes, crab-cake eggs Benedict, biscuits with gravy, fluffy omelettes with lotsa fillings and fresh-fruit smoothies. Waits for a table get long on summer and winter weekends, so roll up early.

El Sancho's MEXICAN, TAKEOUT $

(7019 N Lake Blvd; items $4-10; ⊙9am-9pm) Grab a big fat burrito or an order of *huaraches* – fried *masa* (cornmeal dough) topped with sauce, cheese and fried meat or beans – and a Mexican cane-sugar soda pop from this roadside *taqueria*.

KINGS BEACH

The utilitarian character of fetchingly picturesque Kings Beach lies in its smattering of back-to-basics retro motels all lined up along the highway. But in summer all eyes are on **Kings Beach State Recreation Area** (www.parks.ca.gov; 🅿), a seductive 700ft-long beach that often gets deluged with sun-seekers and leashed dogs. At the beach, you'll find picnic tables, barbecue grills and a fun kids' play structure, while nearby concessionaires rent kayaks, jet skis, paddleboats, SUP gear and more. **Adrift Tahoe** (☎530-546-1112, 888-676-7702; www.standuppaddletahoe.com; 8338 N Lake Blvd; ⊙call for seasonal hr) is one of several local outfitters offering kayak, outrigger canoe and SUP rentals, private lessons and tours, as well as yoga classes on the beach. Further inland, the nostalgic 1920s **Old Brockway Golf Course** (☎530-546-9909; www.oldbrockway.com; 7900 N Lake Blvd; green fee $25-40, club/cart rental from $18/20) is a quick par-36, nine-hole diversion with peekaboo lake views from along pine tree-lined fairways where Hollywood celebs hobnobbed back in the day.

✖ Eating & Drinking

Log Cabin Café DINER $$

(☎530-546-7109; www.logcabinbreakfast.com; 8692 N Lake Blvd; mains $8-15; ⊙7am-2pm) Come early (especially on weekends) to join the queue for the North Shore's best breakfast. Eggs Benedict, whole-wheat pancakes with hot fresh fruit and cranberry-orange waffles are just a few highlights from the huge menu. Tip: call ahead to put your name on the waitlist if you'd rather not wait an hour for a table.

Lanza's ITALIAN $$

(www.lanzastahoe.com; 7739 N Lake Blvd; mains $12-22; ⊙5-10pm, bar from 4:30pm) Next to the Safeway supermarket stands this beloved Italian trattoria where a tantalizing aroma of garlic, rosemary and 'secret' spices perfumes the air. Dinners, though undoubtedly not the tastiest you've ever had, are hugely filling and include salad and bread. Look for the owner's sepia-colored family photos in the entranceway.

Jason's Beachside Grille
BAR & GRILL $$
(www.jasonsbeachsidegrille.com; 8338 N Lake Blvd; mains lunch $8-13, dinner $13-25; ⊙11am-10pm) Looking for the party around sundown? Hit this waterfront deck with a schooner of microbrew. Never mind the unexciting American fare, like smoked chicken pasta, alongside an overflowing salad bar. On colder days, red-velvet sofas orbiting a sunken fireplace are the coziest, but in summer it's all about sunset views.

Char-Pit
AMERICAN $
(www.charpit.com; 8732 N Lake Blvd; items $2-8; ⊙11am-9pm; 🚹) No gimmicks at this 1960s fast-food stand, which grills juicy burgers and St Louis–style baby back ribs, and also fries up crispy onion rings and breaded mozzarella sticks. Somebody call an ambulance!

Grid Bar & Grill
PUB $
(www.thegridbarandgrill.com; 8545 N Lake Blvd; items $4-11; ⊙11am-2pm) This locals' dive bar looks rough round the edges, but happy hours are super-cheap and you can catch live music, from bluegrass to punk, DJs, dancing or karaoke, or trivia nights.

❶ Getting There & Around

Tahoe Area Rapid Transit (TART; ☎530-550-1212, 800-736-6365; www.laketahoetransit.com; single/day pass $2/4) buses between Tahoe City and Incline Village make stops in Tahoe Vista, Kings Beach and Crystal Bay every 30 minutes from approximately 6am until 6pm daily. Another TART route connects Crystal Bay and Kings Beach with the Northstar-at-Tahoe resort every hour or so from 8am until 5pm daily; in winter, this bus continues to Truckee (between May and November, you'll have to detour via Tahoe City first).

Eastern Shore

Lake Tahoe's eastern shore lies entirely within Nevada. Much of it is relatively undeveloped thanks to George Whittell Jr, an eccentric San Franciscan playboy who once owned a lot of this land, including 27 miles of shoreline. Upon his death in 1969, it was sold off to a private investor, who later wheeled and dealed most of it to the US Forest Service and Nevada State Parks. And lucky it was, because today the eastern shore offers some of Tahoe's best scenery and outdoor diversion. Hwy 28 rolls into Nevada at Crystal Bay and runs past Incline Village, heading along the eastern shore to intersect with Hwy 50, which rolls south to Zephyr Cove and Stateline casinos.

CRYSTAL BAY

Crossing into Nevada, the neon starts to flash and old-school gambling palaces pant after your hard-earned cash. The historic **Cal-Neva Resort** (ℹ️info 800-233-5551, reservations 800-225-6382; www.calnevaresort.com; 2 Stateline Rd; r $79-209; ❋🐾🐾🐾) literally straddles the California–Nevada border and has a colorful history involving ghosts, mobsters and Frank Sinatra, who once owned the joint. Shabby hotel rooms don't invite overnight stays (pet fee $50), but ask about the guided secret tunnel tours.

Also on the main drag, the **Tahoe Biltmore Lodge & Casino** (☎800-245-8667; www.tahoebiltmore.com; 5 Hwy 28; r $34-99; 🐾🐾), plays up its longevity with classic Tahoe photographs in the divey hotel rooms, though radiators give away the building's age. For greasy-spoon grill fare, duck under the mirrored ceilings into the artificial forest of the chintzy **Café Biltmore** (mains $8-15; ⊙7am-10pm Sun-Thu, to midnight Fri & Sat). Then catch a live-music show across the street at the **Crystal Bay Club Casino** (☎775-831-0512; www.crystalbaycasino.com; 14 Hwy 28).

For a breath of pine-scented air, flee the smoky casinos for the steep one-mile hike up paved Forest Service Rd 1601 to **Stateline Lookout**. Sunset views over Lake Tahoe and the snowy mountains are all around. A nature trail loops around the site of the former fire lookout tower – nowadays there's a split-level stone observation platform. To find the trailhead, drive up Reservoir Rd, just east of the Tahoe Biltmore parking lot, then take a quick right onto Lakeview Ave and follow it uphill just over a half-mile to the (usually locked) iron gate on your left.

INCLINE VILLAGE

One of Lake Tahoe's ritziest communities, Incline Village is the gateway to Diamond Peak and Mt Rose ski resorts (see p367). The latter is a 12-mile drive northeast via Hwy 431 (Mt Rose Hwy). During summer, the nearby **Mt Rose Wilderness** offers miles of unspoiled terrain, including a strenuous 10-mile round-trip to the summit of majestic **Mt Rose** (10,776ft). The trail starts from the deceptively named Mt Rose Summit parking lot, 9 miles uphill from Incline Village. For a more mellow meadow stroll that even young kids can handle, pull over a mile or so earlier at wildflower-strewn Tahoe Meadows. Stay on the nature loop trails to avoid trampling the fragile meadows; leashed dogs are allowed.

In summer, you can also visit George Whittell's mansion, Thunderbird Lodge (☑800-468-2463; www.thunderbirdlodge.org; adult/child 6-12yr $39/19; ⊙usually Tue-Sat Jun-Sep, reservations required), where he spent summers with his pet lion, Bill. Tours include a trip down a 600ft tunnel to the card house where George used to play poker with Howard Hughes and other famous recluses. The only way to get to the lodge is by shuttle bus, leaving from the helpful in-town Incline Village/Crystal Bay Visitors Bureau (☑775-832-1606, 800-468-2463; www.gotahoenorth.com; 696 Tahoe Blvd; ⊙8am-5pm Mon-Fri, 10am-4pm Sat & Sun; 🕿), or on a boat cruise or kayak tour ($110 to $135).

🛏 Sleeping

Hyatt Regency Lake Tahoe   HOTEL $$$
(☑775-832-1234, 800-633-7313; http://laketahoe.hyatt.com; 111 Country Club Dr; r from $305; ❄@ 🛜🏊🐾) Decorated like an Arts & Crafts–style mountain lodge, every room and lakeside cottage looks lavish, and the spa is even bigger than the casino. In summer you can sprawl on a private lakefront beach, or in winter let the heated outdoor swimming lagoon warm you up after a day on the slopes.

🍴 Eating & Drinking

Bite   CALIFORNIAN $$
(☑775-831-1000; www.bitetahoe.com; shared plates $5-18; ⊙5-10pm Sun-Wed, to 11pm Thu-Sat; 🍷) Don't let the strip-mall location stop you from rocking this creative, eclectic tapas and wine bar. Mix light, seasonal, veggie-friendly dishes with modern takes on rib-sticking comfort food like honeyed baby back ribs or green-chili mac 'n' cheese. An après-ski crowd turns up for happy hour.

Austin's   AMERICAN $$
(www.austinstahoe.com; 120 Country Club Dr; mains $7-22; ⊙11am-9pm, from 5pm Sat & Sun Sep-Jun; 🍴) A hearty welcome for the whole family is what you'll find at this wood-cabin diner with an outdoor deck. Buttermilk fries with jalapeño dipping sauce, chicken-fried steak, classic meatloaf, burgers, huge salad bowls and sandwiches will fill you up – and so will mountain-sized martinis.

Lone Eagle Grille   BAR
(http://laketahoe.hyatt.com; 111 Country Club Dr; ⊙11:30am-10pm Sun-Thu, to 11pm Fri & Sat) At the Hyatt's many-hearthed cocktail lounge, sip a divine orange-flavored margarita, then head outside for sunset and to flirt by the beach fire pit.

LAKE TAHOE-NEVADA STATE PARK

Back on the lake, heading south, is Lake Tahoe-Nevada State Park (☑775-831-0494; http://parks.nv.gov/lt.htm; Hwy 50; per car $7-12), which has beaches, lakes and miles of trails. Just 3 miles south of Incline Village is beautiful Sand Harbor, where two sand spits have formed a shallow bay with brilliant, warm turquoise water and white, boulder-strewn beaches. It gets very busy here, especially during July and August, when the Lake Tahoe Shakespeare Festival (☑800-747-4697; www.tahoebard.com) is underway.

At the park's southern end, just north of the Hwy 50/Hwy 28 junction, Spooner Lake is popular for catch-and-release fishing, picnicking, nature walks and cross-country skiing (p370). Spooner Lake is also the start of the famous 13-mile Flume Trail, a holy grail for experienced mountain-bikers. From the trail's end near Incline Village you can either backtrack 10 miles along the narrow, twisting shoulder of Hwy 28 or board a shuttle bus. Arrange shuttles and rent bikes by the trailhead inside the park at Flume Trail Mountain Bikes (☑775-749-5349; www.theflumetrail.com; mountain-bike rental per day $45-65, shuttle $10-15; ⊙8:30am-6pm Jun-Nov).

Yosemite & the Sierra Nevada

Best Places to Eat

» Mountain Room Restaurant (p411)

» Lakefront Restaurant (p440)

» Yosemite Bug Rustic Mountain Resort (p417)

» Convict Lake Resort (p442)

» Narrow Gauge Inn (p415)

Best Places to Stay

» Yosemite High Sierra Camps (p413)

» Ahwahnee Hotel (p409)

» Sierra Sky Ranch (p415)

» Evergreen Lodge (p411)

» Benton Hot Springs (p443)

Why Go?

An outdoor adventurer's wonderland, the Sierra Nevada is a year-round pageant of snow sports, white-water rafting, hiking, cycling and rock climbing. Skiers and snowboarders blaze through hushed pine-tree slopes, and wilderness seekers come to escape the stresses of modern civilization.

With fierce granite mountains standing watch over high-altitude lakes, the eastern spine of California is a formidable but exquisite topographical barrier enclosing magnificent natural landscapes. And interspersed between its river canyons and 14,000ft peaks are the decomposing ghost towns left behind by California's early white settlers, bubbling natural hot springs and Native American tribes that still call it home.

In the majestic national parks of Yosemite and Sequoia & Kings Canyon, visitors will be humbled by the groves of solemn giant sequoias, ancient rock formations and valleys, and the ever-present opportunity to see bears and other wildlife.

When to Go
Yosemite National Park

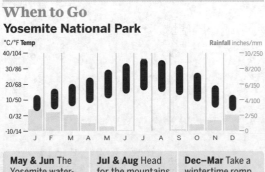

May & Jun The Yosemite waterfalls are gushing and spectacular in spring.

Jul & Aug Head for the mountains for wilderness adventures and glorious sunshine.

Dec–Mar Take a wintertime romp through snowy forests.

Yosemite & the Sierra Nevada Highlights

1 Marvel at the waterfall gush in spring at **Yosemite National Park** (p400)

2 Whoosh down the wintertime heights of snow-draped **Mammoth Mountain** (p436)

3 Gaze heavenward through the celestial sequoia canopies of **Sequoia & Kings Canyon National Parks** (p418)

4 Kayak the rapids at **Truckee River Whitewater Park** (p449) in Reno, Nevada

5 Amble around the evocative ghost town of **Bodie** (p432)

6 Canoe or kayak **Mono Lake** (p434) amid its haunting tufa

7 View the bizarre volcanic formation of **Devils Postpile** (p441)

8 Soak your troubles away at **hot spring pools** in Bridgeport (p429) and Benton (p443)

9 Visit the **Manzanar National Historic Site** (p446) where one of the darkest events in US history is memorialized

YOSEMITE NATIONAL PARK

The jaw-dropping head-turner of America's national parks, and a Unesco World Heritage site, Yosemite (yo-*sem*-it-ee) garners the devotion of all who enter. From the waterfall-striped granite walls buttressing emerald-green Yosemite Valley to the skyscraping giant sequoias catapulting into the air at Mariposa Grove, the place inspires a sense of awe and reverence – four million visitors wend their way to the country's third-oldest national park annually. But lift your eyes above the crowds and you'll feel your heart instantly moved by unrivalled splendors: the haughty profile of Half Dome, the hulking presence of El Capitan, the drenching mists of Yosemite Falls, the gemstone lakes of the high country's subalpine wilderness and Hetch Hetchy's pristine pathways.

History

The Ahwahneechee, a group of Miwok and Paiute peoples, lived in the Yosemite area for around 4000 years before a group of pioneers, most likely led by legendary explorer Joseph Rutherford Walker, came through in 1833. During the Gold Rush era, conflict between the miners and native tribes escalated to the point where a military expedition (the Mariposa Battalion) was dispatched in 1851 to punish the Ahwahneechee, eventually forcing the capitulation of Chief Tenaya and his tribe.

Tales of thunderous waterfalls and towering stone columns followed the Mariposa Battalion out of Yosemite and soon spread into the public's awareness. In 1855 San Francisco entrepreneur James Hutchings organized the first tourist party to the valley. Published accounts of his trip, in which he extolled the area's untarnished beauty, prompted others to follow, and it wasn't long before inns and roads began springing up. Alarmed by this development, conservationists petitioned Congress to protect the area – with success. In 1864 President Abraham Lincoln signed the Yosemite Grant, which eventually ceded Yosemite Valley and the Mariposa Grove of Giant Sequoias to California as a state park. This landmark decision paved the way for a national park system, of which Yosemite became a part in 1890, thanks to efforts led by pioneering conservationist John Muir.

Yosemite's popularity as a tourist destination continued to soar throughout the 20th century and, by the mid-1970s, traffic and congestion draped the valley in a smoggy haze. The General Management Plan (GMP), developed in 1980 to alleviate this and other problems, ran into numerous challenges and delays. Despite many improvements, and the need to preserve the natural beauty that draws visitors to Yosemite in the first place, the plan still hasn't been fully implemented.

◉ Sights

There are four main entrances to the park: South Entrance (Hwy 41), Arch Rock (Hwy 140), Big Oak Flat (Hwy 120 W) and Tioga Pass (Hwy 120 E). Hwy 120 traverses the park as Tioga Rd, connecting Yosemite Valley with the Eastern Sierra.

Visitor activity is concentrated in Yosemite Valley, especially in Yosemite Village, which has the main visitors center, a post office, a museum, eateries and other

---

ⓘ VISITING YOSEMITE

From late June to September, the entire park is accessible – all visitor facilities are open and everything from backcountry campgrounds to ice-cream stands are at maximum capacity. This is also when it's hardest – though not impossible – to evade the crush of humanity.

Crowds are smallest in winter but road closures (most notably of Tioga Rd, see p403, but also of Glacier Point Rd beyond Badger Pass Ski Area) mean that activity is concentrated in the valley and on Badger Pass. Visitor facilities are scaled down to a bare minimum and most campgrounds are closed and other lodging options limited. Note that 'winter' in Yosemite starts with the first heavy snowfall, which can be as early as October, and often lasts until May.

Spring, when the waterfalls are at their best, is a particularly excellent time to visit. Fall brings fewer people, an enchanting rainbow of foliage and crisp, clear weather (although waterfalls have usually dried to a trickle by then).

services. Curry Village is another hub. Notably less busy, Tuolumne (too-*ahl*-uh-*mee*) Meadows, toward the eastern end of Tioga Rd, primarily draws hikers, backpackers and climbers. Wawona, the park's southern focal point, also has good infrastructure. In the northwestern corner, Hetch Hetchy, which has no services at all, receives the smallest number of visitors.

YOSEMITE VALLEY

The park's crown jewel, spectacular meadow-carpeted Yosemite Valley stretches 7 miles long, bisected by the rippling Merced River and hemmed in by some of the most majestic chunks of granite anywhere on earth. The most famous are, of course, the monumental 7569ft **El Capitan** (El Cap; Map p404), one of the world's largest monoliths and a magnet for rock climbers, and 8842ft **Half Dome** (Map p404), the park's spiritual centerpiece – its rounded granite pate forms an unmistakable silhouette. You'll have great views of both from **Valley View** (Map p404) on the valley floor, but for the classic photo op head up Hwy 41 to **Tunnel View** (Map p404), which boasts a new viewing area. With a little sweat you'll have even better postcard panoramas – sans the crowds – from **Inspiration Point** (Map p404). The trail (2.6-mile round-trip) starts at the tunnel.

Yosemite's waterfalls mesmerize even the most jaded traveler, especially when the spring runoff turns them into thunderous cataracts. **Yosemite Falls** (Map p404) is considered the tallest in North America, dropping 2425ft in three tiers. A slick wheelchair-accessible trail leads to the bottom of this cascade or, if you prefer solitude and different perspectives, you can also clamber up the **Yosemite Falls Trail** (Map p408), which puts you atop the falls after a grueling 3.4 miles. No less impressive is nearby **Bridalveil Fall** (Map p404) and others scattered throughout the valley.

Any aspiring Ansel Adams should lug their camera gear along the 1-mile paved trail to **Mirror Lake** (off Map p408) early or late in the day to catch the ever-shifting reflection of Half Dome in the still waters. The lake all but dries up by late summer.

South of here, where the Merced River courses around two small islands, lies **Happy Isles**, a popular area for picnics, swimming and strolls. It also marks the start of the **John Muir Trail** (Map p408) and **Mist Trail** to several waterfalls and Half Dome.

FREE **Yosemite Museum** MUSEUM
(Map p408; ⊙9am-4:30pm or 5pm, closed for lunch) This museum has Miwok and Paiute artifacts, including woven baskets, beaded buckskin dresses and dance capes made from feathers. There's also an **art gallery** with paintings and photographs from the museum's permanent collection. Behind the museum, a self-guided interpretive trail winds past a reconstructed c 1870 **Indian village** with pounding stones, an acorn granary, a ceremonial roundhouse and a conical bark house.

Ahwahnee Hotel HISTORIC BUILDING
(Map p408) About a quarter-mile east of Yosemite Village, the **Ahwahnee Hotel** is a graceful blend of rustic mountain retreat and elegant mansion dating back to 1927. You don't need to be a guest to have a gawk and a wander. Built from local granite, pine and cedar, the building is splendidly decorated with leaded glass, sculpted tiles, Native American rugs and Turkish kilims. You can enjoy a meal in the baronial dining room or a casual drink in the piano bar. Around Christmas, the Ahwahnee hosts the **Bracebridge Dinner** (☎801-559-5000; www.bracebridgedinners. com; per person $425), sort of a combination banquet and Renaissance *faire*. Book early.

FREE **Nature Center at Happy Isles** MUSEUM
(Map p408; ⊙9:30am-4pm May-Sep; ⛀) A great hands-on nature museum, the Nature Center displays explain the differences between the park's various pinecones, rocks, animal tracks and (everyone's favorite subject) scat. Out back, don't miss an exhibit on the 1996 rock fall, when an 80,000-ton rock slab plunged 2000ft to the nearby valley floor, killing a man and felling about 1000 trees.

GLACIER POINT

A lofty 3200ft above the valley floor, 7214ft **Glacier Point** (Map p408) presents one of

ℹ MANDATORY HALF DOME PERMITS

To stem lengthy lines (and increasingly dangerous conditions) on the vertiginous cables of Half Dome, the park now requires that all-day hikers obtain an advance permit (☎877-444-6777; www.recreation.gov; per person $1.50) to climb the cables. Permits go on sale four months in advance, and the 300 available per day sell out almost immediately. Backpackers can obtain permits when they pick up wilderness permits, without having to reserve in advance. The process is still in development, so check www.nps.gov/yose/planyourvisit/hdpermits.htm for the latest information.

the park's most eye-popping vistas and practically puts you at eye level with Half Dome. To the left of Half Dome lies U-shaped, glacially carved Tenaya Canyon, while below you'll see Vernal and Nevada Falls. Glacier Point is about an hour's drive from Yosemite Valley via Glacier Point Rd off Hwy 41. Along the road, hiking trails lead to other spectacular viewpoints, such as Dewey Point (Map p404) and Sentinel Dome (Map p408). You can also hike up from the valley floor to Glacier Point via the thigh-burning Four Mile Trail (see p403). If you've driven up to Glacier Point and want to get away from the madding crowd, hiking down the Four Mile Trail for a bit will net you comparative solitude and more breathtaking views. Another way to get here is on the Glacier Point Hikers' Bus (p414). Many hikers take the bus one way and hike the other. Drivers should go in the morning to avoid the afternoon backup from the parking lot.

TIOGA ROAD & TUOLUMNE MEADOWS

Tioga Rd (or Hwy 120 E), the only road through the park, travels through 56 miles of superb high country at elevations ranging from 6200ft at Crane Flat to 9945ft at Tioga Pass. Heavy snowfall keeps it closed from about November until May. Beautiful views await after many a bend in the road, the most impressive being Olmsted Point (Map p404), where you can gawp all the way down Tenaya Canyon to Half Dome. Above the canyon's east side looms the aptly named

9926ft Clouds Rest (Map p404). Continuing east on Tioga Rd soon drops you at Tenaya Lake (Map p404), a placid blue basin framed by pines and granite cliffs.

Beyond here, about 55 miles from Yosemite Valley, 8600ft Tuolumne Meadows (Map p404) is the largest subalpine meadow in the Sierra. It provides a dazzling contrast to the valley, with its lush open fields, clear blue lakes, ragged granite peaks and domes, and cooler temperatures. If you come during July or August, you'll find a painter's palette of wildflowers decorating the shaggy meadows.

Tuolumne is far less crowded than the valley, though the area around the campground, lodge store and visitors center does get busy, especially on weekends. Some hiking trails, such as the one to Dog Lake (Map p404), are also well traveled. Remember that the altitude makes breathing a lot harder than in the valley, and nights can get nippy, so pack warm clothes.

The main meadow is about 2.5 miles long and lies on the north side of Tioga Rd between Lembert Dome (Map p404) and Pothole Dome (Map p404). The 200ft scramble to the top of the latter – preferably at sunset – gives you great views of the meadow. An interpretive trail leads from the stables to muddy Soda Springs (Map p404), where carbonated water bubbles up in red-tinted pools. The nearby Parsons Memorial Lodge (Map p404) has a few displays.

Hikers and climbers will find a paradise of options around Tuolumne Meadows, which is also the gateway to the High Sierra Camps (p413).

The Tuolumne Meadows Tour & Hikers' Bus (p414) makes the trip along Tioga Rd once daily in each direction, and can be used for one-way hikes. There's also a free Tuolumne Meadows Shuttle (p414), which travels between the Tuolumne Meadows Lodge and Olmsted Point, including a stop at Tenaya Lake.

WAWONA

Wawona, about 27 miles south of Yosemite Valley, is the park's historical center, home to the park's first headquarters (supervised by Captain AE Wood on the site of the Wawona Campground) and its first tourist facilities.

Mariposa Grove   FOREST
(Map p404) The main lure in this area of the park is the biggest and most impressive cluster of giant sequoias in Yosemite. The star

of the show – and what everyone comes to see – is the **Grizzly Giant**, a behemoth that sprang to life some 1800 years ago, or about the time the ancient Greeks held the first Olympic Games. You can't miss it – it's a half-mile walk along a well-worn path starting near the parking lot. Beyond here, crowds begin to thin out a bit, although for more solitude you should arrive early in the morning or after 6pm. Also nearby is the walk-through **California Tunnel Tree**, which continues to survive despite having its heart hacked out in 1895.

In the upper grove you'll find the **Fallen Wawona Tunnel Tree**, the famous drive-through tree that toppled over in 1969. For scenic views, take a 1-mile (round-trip) amble from the fallen tree to **Wawona Point**.

Also in the upper grove, the **Mariposa Grove Museum** (admission free; ☺10am-4pm May-Sep) has displays about sequoia ecology. The full hike from the parking lot to the upper grove is about 2.5 miles.

Parking can be very limited, so come early or late, or take the free shuttle bus from the Wawona Store or the park entrance. The grove can also be explored on a one-hour **guided tour** (☎209-375-1621; adult/child $25/18; ☺May-Sep) aboard a noisy open-air tram leaving from the parking lot.

FREE Pioneer Yosemite
History Center   MUSEUM
(Map p404; ☺24hr) In Wawona itself, about 6 miles north of the grove, take in the manicured grounds of the elegant Wawona Hotel (p411) and cross a covered bridge to this rustic center, where some of the park's oldest buildings were relocated. It also features stagecoaches that brought early tourists to Yosemite, and offers short **rides** (adult/child $4/3; ☺Wed-Sun Jun-Sep).

HETCH HETCHY
In the park's northwestern corner, Hetch Hetchy, which is Miwok for 'place of tall grass,' gets the least amount of traffic yet sports waterfalls and granite cliffs that rival its famous counterparts in Yosemite Valley. The main difference is that Hetch Hetchy Valley is now filled with water, following a long political and environmental battle in the early 20th century. It's a lovely, quiet spot and well worth the 40-mile drive from Yosemite Valley, especially if you're tired of the avalanche of humanity rolling through that area.

The 8-mile long **Hetch Hetchy Reservoir** (Map p404), its placid surface reflecting clouds and cliffs, stretches behind O'Shaughnessy Dam, site of a parking lot and trailheads. An easy 5.4-mile (round-trip) trail leads to the spectacular **Tueeulala** (*twee*-lala) and **Wapama Falls** (Map p404), which each plummet more than 1000ft over fractured granite walls on the north shore of the reservoir. **Hetch Hetchy Dome** (Map p404) rises up in the distance. This hike is best in spring, when temperatures are moderate and wildflowers poke out everywhere. Keep an eye out for rattlesnakes and the occasional bear, especially in summer.

There are no visitor services at Hetch Hetchy. The road is only open during daylight hours; specifics are posted at the Evergreen Rd turnoff.

🏃 **Activities**
Hiking
Over 800 miles of hiking trails cater to hikers of all abilities. Take an easy half-mile stroll on the valley floor; venture out all day on a quest for viewpoints, waterfalls and lakes; or go camping in the remote outer reaches of the backcountry.

IMPASSABLE TIOGA PASS

Hwy 120, the main route into Yosemite National Park from the Eastern Sierra, climbs through Tioga Pass, the highest pass in the Sierra at 9945ft. On most maps of California, you'll find a parenthetical remark – 'closed in winter' – printed on the map. While true, this statement is also misleading. Tioga Rd is usually closed from the first heavy snowfall in October to May, June or even July! If you're planning a trip through Tioga Pass in spring, you're likely to be out of luck. According to official park policy, the earliest date the road will be plowed is 15 April, yet the pass has been open in April only once since 1980. Other mountain roads further north, such as Hwys 108, 4 and 88/89, may also be closed due to heavy snow, albeit only temporarily. Call ☎800-427-7623 for road and weather conditions.

YOSEMITE & THE SIERRA NEVADA YOSEMITE NATIONAL PARK

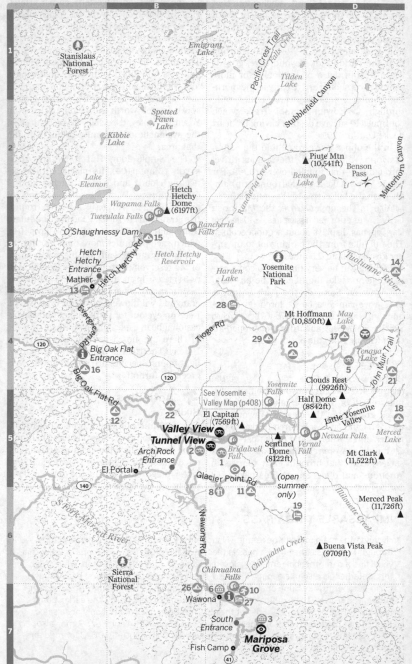

Some of the park's most popular hikes start right in Yosemite Valley, including to the top of Half Dome (17-mile round-trip), the most famous of all. It follows a section of the John Muir Trail and is strenuous, difficult and best tackled in two days with an overnight in Little Yosemite Valley. Reaching the top can only be done after rangers have installed fixed cables. Depending on snow conditions, this may occur as early as late May or as late as July, and the cables usually come down in mid-October. To whittle down the cables' notorious human logjams, the park now requires permits for day hikers (see the boxed text p402), but the route is still nerve-wracking as hikers must 'share the road.' The less ambitious or physically fit will still have a ball following the same trail as far as **Vernal Fall** (Map p404; 2.6-mile round-trip), the top of **Nevada Fall** (Map p404; 6.5-mile round-trip) or idyllic **Little Yosemite Valley** (Map p404; 8-mile round-trip). The **Four Mile Trail** (Map p408; 9.2-mile round-trip) to Glacier Point is a strenuous but satisfying climb to a glorious viewpoint (also see p401).

If you've got the kids in tow, nice and easy destinations include **Mirror Lake** (off Map p408; 2-mile round-trip, 4.5 miles via the Tenaya Canyon Loop) in the valley, the **McGurk Meadow** (Map p404; 1.6-mile round-trip) trail on Glacier Point Rd, which has a historic log cabin to romp around in, and the trails meandering beneath the big trees of the Mariposa Grove (p402) in Wawona.

Also in the Wawona area is one of the park's prettiest (and often overlooked) hikes to **Chilnualna Falls** (Map p404; 8.6-mile round-trip). Best done between April and June, it follows a cascading creek to the top of the dramatic overlook falls, starting gently, then hitting you with some grinding switchbacks before sort of leveling out again.

The highest concentration of hikes lies in the high country of Tuolumne Meadows, which is only accessible in summer. A popular choice here is the hike to **Dog Lake** (Map p404; 2.8-mile round-trip), but it gets busy. You can also hike along a relatively flat part of the John Muir Trail into lovely **Lyell Canyon** (Map p404; 17.6-mile round-trip), following the Lyell Fork of the Tuolumne River.

Backpacks, tents and other equipment can be rented from the **Yosemite Mountaineering School** (Map p408; ☏209-372-

Yosemite National Park

8344; www.yosemitemountaineering.com; Curry Village Mountain Shop). The school also offers two-day Learn to Backpack trips for novices and all-inclusive three- and four-day guided backpacking trips ($300 to $400 per person), which are great for inexperienced and

solo travelers. In summer, the school operates a branch from Tuolumne Meadows.

Rock Climbing

With its sheer spires, polished domes and soaring monoliths, Yosemite is rock-climbing nirvana. The main climbing season runs from April to October. Most climbers, including some legendary stars, stay at Camp 4 (p409) near El Capitan, especially in spring and fall. In summer, another base camp springs up at Tuolumne Meadows Campground (p410). Climbers looking for partners post notices on bulletin boards at either campground.

Yosemite Mountaineering School (p405) offers top-flight instruction for novice to advanced rock hounds, plus guided climbs and equipment rental. All-day group classes for beginners are $148 per person.

The meadow across from El Capitan and the northeastern end of Tenaya Lake (off Tioga Rd) are good for watching climbers dangle from granite (you need binoculars for a really good view). Look for the haul bags first – they're bigger, more colorful and move around more than the climbers, making them easier to spot. The **Yosemite Climbing Association** (www.yosemiteclimbing.org) began an 'Ask-a-Climber' program in 2011, where it sets up a telescope at El Capitan Bridge for a few hours a day (mid-May through mid-October) and answers visitors' questions.

Cycling

Mountain-biking isn't permitted within the park, but cycling along the 12 miles of paved trails is a popular and environmentally friendly way of exploring the valley. It's also the fastest way to get around when Valley traffic is at a standstill. Many families bring bicycles, and you'll often find kids doing laps through the campgrounds. See p414 for rental information.

Swimming

On a hot summer day, nothing beats a dip in the gentle Merced River, though if chilly water doesn't float your boat, you can always pay to play in the scenic outdoor swimming pools at Curry Village and Yosemite Lodge at the Falls (p413; adult/child $5/4). With a sandy beach, Tenaya Lake is a frigid but interesting option, though White Wolf's Harden Lake warms up to a balmy temperature by mid-summer.

Horseback Riding

Yosemite Stables (trips 2hr/half-/full day $64/85/128) runs guided trips to such scenic locales as Mirror Lake, Chilnualna Falls and the Tuolumne River from three bases: **Tuolumne Meadows** (Map p404; ☎209-372-8427), **Wawona** (Map p404; ☎209-375-6502) and **Yosemite Valley** (Map p408; ☎209-372-8348). The season runs from May to October, although this varies slightly by location. No experience is needed for the two-hour and half-day rides, but reservations are advised, especially at the Yosemite Valley stables. Some mounts are horses, but most likely you'll be riding a sure-footed mule.

Rafting

From around late May to July, floating the Merced River from Stoneman Meadow, near Curry Village, to Sentinel Bridge is a leisurely way to soak up Yosemite Valley views. Four-person **raft rentals** (☎209-372-4386; per adult/child over 50lbs $26/16) for the 3-mile trip are available from the concessionaire in Curry Village and include equipment and a shuttle ride back to the rental kiosk. Or bring your own and pay $5 to shuttle back.

River rats are also attracted to the fierce **Tuolumne River** (Map p404), a classic Class IV run that plunges and thunders through boulder gardens and cascades. See p416 for outfitters

Winter Sports

The white coat of winter opens up a different set of things to do, as the valley becomes a quiet, frosty world of snow-draped evergreens, ice-coated lakes and vivid vistas of gleaming white mountains sparkling against blue skies. Winter tends to arrive in full force by mid-November and peter out in early April.

Cross-country skiers can explore 350 miles of skiable trails and roads, including 90 miles of marked trails and 25 miles of machine-groomed track near Badger Pass. The scenic but grueling trail to Glacier Point (21-mile round-trip) also starts from here. More trails are at Crane Flat and the Mariposa Grove. The nongroomed trails can also be explored with snowshoes.

A free shuttle bus connects the Valley and Badger Pass. Roads in the Valley are plowed, and Hwys 41, 120 and 140 are usually kept open, conditions permitting. The Tioga Rd (Hwy 120 E), however, closes with the first snowfall (see boxed text, p403). Be sure to bring snow chains with you, as prices for them double once you hit the foothills.

Badger Pass Ski Area   SKIING, SNOWBOARDING
(Map p404; ☎209-372-8430; www.badgerpass.com; lift ticket adult/child $42/23; ☒) Most of the action converges on one of California's oldest ski resorts. The gentle slopes are perfect for families and beginner skiers and snowboarders. It's about 22 miles from the valley on Glacier Point Rd. There are five chairlifts, 800 vertical feet and 10 runs, a full-service lodge, equipment rental ($23 to $35 for a full set of gear) and the excellent **Yosemite Ski School**, where generations of novices have learned how to get down a hill safely (group lessons from $35).

Badger Pass Cross-Country Center & Ski School   SKIING
(Map p404; ☎209-372-8444) Located in the Badger Pass Ski Area, this school offers beginners' lesson and rental packages ($46), equipment rentals ($23) and guided tours. The center also runs overnight trips to **Glacier Point Ski Hut** (Map p408), a rustic stone-and-log cabin. Rates, including meals, are $350/120 guided/self-guided for one night or $550/240 for two nights.

Ostrander Ski Hut   SKIING
(Map p404; www.yosemiteconservancy.org) More experienced skiers can trek 10 miles out to the popular hut on Ostrander Lake, operated by Yosemite Conservancy. The hut is staffed all winter and open to backcountry skiers and snowshoers for $32 to $52

TOP FIVE THINGS TO DO IN WINTER

» Snowshoeing among the giants of Mariposa Grove (p402)

» Ice-skating at Curry Village (p408)

» Taking an overnight cross-country skiing trip to Glacier Point Ski Hut (p407)

» Toasting s'mores in the Mountain Room Lounge (p412)

» Feasting like royalty at the Bracebridge Dinner (p401) in the Ahwahnee Hotel

Yosemite Valley

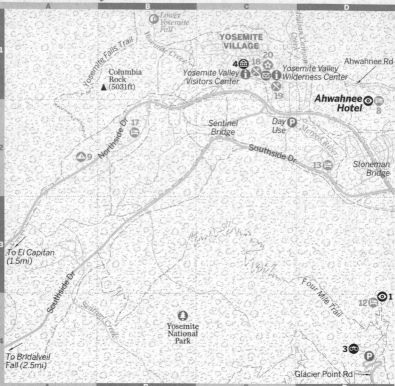

per person, per night. See the website for details.

Curry Village Ice Rink SKATING
(Map p408; per session adult/child $8/6, rental skates $3; ⊙Nov-Mar) A delightful winter activity is taking a spin on the outdoor rink, where you'll be skating under the watchful eye of Half Dome.

☞ Tours

The Yosemite Bug (see p417) runs handy tours to Yosemite year-round from San Francisco.

The nonprofit **Yosemite Conservancy** (yosemiteconservancy.org) has scheduled tours of all kinds, plus custom trips available.

First-timers often appreciate the two-hour **Valley Floor Tour** (per adult/child $25/13; ⊙year-round) run by DNC Parks & Resorts, which covers the valley highlights.

For other tour options stop at the tour and activity desks at Yosemite Lodge at the Falls (see p413), Curry Village or Yosemite Village, call ☎209-372-4386 or check www.yosemitepark.com.

⌸ Sleeping

Competition for campsites is fierce from May to September, when arriving without a reservation and hoping for the best is tantamount to getting someone to lug your Barcalounger up Half Dome. Even first-come, first-served campgrounds tend to fill by noon, especially on weekends and around holidays. Campsites can be reserved up to five months in advance. **Reservations** (☎877-444-6777, 518-885-3639; www.recreation.gov) become available from 7am PST on the 15th of every month in one-month blocks, and often sell out within minutes.

Without a booking, your only chance is to hightail it to an open first-come, first-

served campground or proceed to one of four campground reservation offices in Yosemite Valley, Wawona, Big Oak Flat and Tuolumne Meadows (the latter three are only open seasonally). Try to get there before 8am (when they open), put your name on a waiting list and then hope for a cancellation or early departure. Return when the ranger tells you to (usually 3pm) and if you hear your name, consider yourself very lucky indeed.

All campgrounds have flush toilets, except for Tamarack Flat, Yosemite Creek and Porcupine Flat, which have vault toilets and no potable water. Those at higher elevations get chilly at night, even in summer, so pack accordingly. The Yosemite Mountaineering School (p405) rents camping gear.

If you hold a wilderness permit, you may spend the nights before and after your trip in the backpacker campgrounds at Tuolumne Meadows, Hetch Hetchy, White Wolf and behind North Pines in Yosemite Valley. The cost is $5 per person, per night and reservations aren't necessary.

Opening dates for seasonal campgrounds vary according to the weather.

All noncamping reservations within the park are handled by **DNC Parks & Resorts** (☎801-559-4884; www.yosemitepark.com) and can be made up to 366 days in advance; reservations are absolutely critical from May to early September. Rates – and demand – drop from October to April.

YOSEMITE VALLEY

TOP CHOICE **Ahwahnee Hotel**　　HISTORIC HOTEL $$$
(Map p408; r from $449; ✳@🛜🏊) The crème de la crème of Yosemite's lodging, this sumptuous historic property dazzles with soaring ceilings, Turkish kilims lining the hallways and atmospheric lounges with mammoth stone fireplaces. It's the gold standard for upscale lodges, though if you're not blessed with bullion, you can still soak up the ambience during afternoon tea, a drink in the bar or a gourmet meal.

North Pines　　CAMPGROUND $
(Map p408; Yosemite Valley; tent & RV sites $20; ⏱Apr-Sep; 🏊) A bit off the beaten path (4000ft) with 81 sites near Mirror Lake; reservations required.

Upper Pines　　CAMPGROUND $
(Map p408; Yosemite Valley; tent & RV sites $20; ⏱year-round; 🏊) Busy, busy, busy – and big (238 sites, 4000ft); reservations required mid-March through November.

Lower Pines　　CAMPGROUND $
(Map p408; tent & RV sites $20; ⏱Mar-Oct; 🏊) Crammed and noisy with 60 sites at 4000ft; reservations required.

Camp 4　　CAMPGROUND $
(Map p408; per person $5; ⏱year-round) Walk-in campground at 4000ft, popular with climbers; sites are shared.

Housekeeping Camp　　CABIN $
(Map p408; 4-person tent cabin $93; ⏱Apr-Oct) This cluster of 266 cabins, each walled in by concrete on three sides and lidded by a canvas roof, is crammed and noisy, but the setting along the Merced River has its merits. Each unit can sleep up to six and has electricity, light, a table and chairs, and a covered patio with picnic tables.

Yosemite Valley

Yosemite Lodge at the Falls   MOTEL $$
(Map p408; r $191-218; @🛜🏊) Situated a short walk from Yosemite Falls, this multibuilding complex gets a thumbs up for its centrality, wide range of eateries, lively bar, big pool and other handy amenities. Rooms are fairly generic; the nicest are the upstairs units with beamed ceilings and Native American touches. All have cable TV, a telephone and, mostly, great panoramas unfolding from your patio or balcony.

Curry Village   CABINS, TENT CABINS $$
(Map p408; tent cabins $112-120, cabins with/without bath $168/127; 🏊) Founded in 1899 as a summer camp, Curry has hundreds of units squished tightly together beneath towering evergreens. The canvas cabins are basically glorified tents, so for more comfort, quiet and privacy get one of the cozy wood cabins, which have bedspreads, drapes and vintage posters. There are also 18 attractive motel-style rooms in the **Stoneman House** (r $191), including a loft suite sleeping up to six.

TIOGA ROAD
Tuolumne Meadows campers should note that the closest pay showers are located at Mono Vista RV Park (p434).

Tuolumne Meadows   CAMPGROUND $
(Map p404; tent & RV sites $20; ☉Jul-Sep; 🏊) Biggest campground in the park (8600ft) with 304 fairly well-spaced sites; half of these can be reserved.

Porcupine Flat   CAMPGROUND $
(Map p404; tent & RV sites $10; ☉Jul-Sep) Primitive 52-site area, at 8100ft; some sites near the road.

Tamarack Flat   CAMPGROUND $
(Map p404; tent sites $10; ☉Jul-Sep) Quiet, secluded, primitive at 6315ft; the 52 tent sites are a rough 3-mile drive off Tioga Rd.

White Wolf   CAMPGROUND $
(Map p404; tent & RV sites $14; ☉Jul-early Sep; 🏊) Attractive setting at 8000ft, but the 74 sites are fairly boxed in.

Yosemite Creek   CAMPGROUND $
(Map p404; tent sites $10; ☉Jul–mid-Sep; 🏊) The most secluded and quiet campground (7659ft) in the park, reached via a rough 4.5-mile road. There are 75 primitive sites.

Tuolumne Meadows Lodge   TENT CABINS $$
(Map p404; tent cabins $107; ☉mid-Jun–mid-Sep) In the high country, about 55 miles from the valley, this option attracts hikers to its 69

canvas tent cabins with four beds, a wood-burning stove and candles (no electricity). Breakfast and dinner are available.

White Wolf Lodge   CABINS, TENT CABINS $$

(Map p404; tent cabins $99, cabins with bath $120; ☉Jul–mid-Sep) This complex enjoys its own little world a mile up a spur road, away from the hubbub and traffic of Hwy 120 and the Valley. There are 24 spartan four-bedded tent cabins without electricity and four very-in-demand hard-walled cabins that feel like rustic motel rooms. The generator cuts out at 11pm, so you'll need a flashlight until early morning. There's also a dining room and a tiny counter-service store.

HETCH HETCHY & BIG OAK FLAT RD

TOP CHOICE **Evergreen Lodge**   RESORT $0

(Map p404; ☎209-379-2606, 800-935-6343; www.evergreenlodge.com; 33160 Evergreen Rd; tents $75-110, cabins $175-350; @🛜🐾) Outside the park near the entrance to Hetch Hetchy, this classic 90-year-old resort lets roughing-it guests cheat with comfy, prefurnished tents and rustic to deluxe mountain cabins with private porches but no phone or TV. Outdoor recreational activities abound, many of them family-oriented, with equipment rentals available. There's a **general store**, **tavern** with a pool table and a **restaurant** (dinner mains $18-28) serving three hearty meals every day.

Crane Flat   CAMPGROUND $

(Map p404; Big Oak Flat Rd; tent & RV sites $20; ☉Jun-Sep; 🐾) Large family campground at 6192ft, with 166 sites.

Hodgdon Meadow   CAMPGROUND $

(Map p404; Big Oak Flat Rd; tent & RV sites $14-20; ☉year-round; 🐾) Utilitarian and crowded 105-site campground at 4872ft; reservations required mid-April to mid-October.

WAWONA & GLACIER POINT RD

Bridalveil Creek   CAMPGROUND $

(Map p404; Glacier Point Rd; tent & RV sites $14; ☉Jul-early Sep; 🐾) Quieter than the Valley campgrounds, with 110 sites at 7200ft.

Wawona   CAMPGROUND $

(Map p404; Wawona; tent & RV sites $14-20; ☉year-round; 🐾🐾) Idyllic riverside setting at 4000ft with 93 well-spaced sites; reservations required April to September.

Wawona Hotel   HISTORIC HOTEL $$

(Map p404; Wawona; r with/without bath incl breakfast $217/147; ☉mid-Mar–Dec; 🛜🐾🐾) This National Historic Landmark, dating from 1879, is a collection of six graceful, whitewashed New England–style buildings flanked by wide porches. The 104 rooms – with no phone or TV – come with Victorian–style furniture and other period items, and about half the rooms share bathrooms, with nice robes provided for the walk there. The grounds are lovely, with a spacious lawn dotted with Adirondack chairs.

✕ Eating

You can find food options for all budgets and palates within the park, from greasy slabs of fast food to swanky cuts of top-notch steak.

Bringing in or buying your own food saves money but remember that you *must* remove it all from your car (or backpack or bicycle) and store it overnight in a bear box or canister. The **Village Store** (Map p408) in Yosemite Village has the best selection (including toiletries, health-food items and some organic produce), while stores at Curry Village, Wawona, Tuolumne Meadows, Housekeeping Camp and the Yosemite Lodge are more limited.

TOP CHOICE **Mountain Room Restaurant**   STEAKHOUSE $$

(Map p408; ☎209-372-1281; Yosemite Lodge; mains $17-35; ☉5:30-9:30pm, shorter winter hours; 🍴🐾) With a killer view of Yosemite Falls, the window tables at this casual and elegant contemporary steakhouse are a hot commodity. The chefs at the lodge whip up the best meals in the park, with flat-iron steak and locally caught mountain trout wooing diners under a rotating display of nature photographs. Reservations accepted only for groups larger than eight, and casual dress is okay.

🍴 **Ahwahnee Dining Room**   CALIFORNIAN $$$

(Map p408; ☎209-372-1489; Ahwahnee Hotel; mains breakfast $7-16, lunch $16-23, dinner $26-46; ☉7-10:30am, 11:30am-3pm & 5:30-9pm) The formal ambience (mind your manners) may not be for everybody, but few would not be awed by the sumptuous decor, soaring beamed ceiling and palatial chandeliers. The menu is constantly in flux, but most dishes have perfect pitch and are beautifully presented. There's a dress code at dinner, but otherwise shorts and sneakers are okay. Sunday brunch ($39.50; 7am to 3pm) is amazing. Reservations highly recommended for brunch and dinner.

Wawona Hotel Dining Room
AMERICAN $$

(Map p404; Wawona Hotel; mains breakfast & lunch $11-15, dinner $19-30; ⏱7:30-10am, 11:30am-1:30pm & 5:30-9pm Easter-Dec; 🖊🐾) Beautiful sequoia-painted lamps light this old-fashioned white-tablecloth dining room, and the Victorian detail makes it an enchanting place to have an upscale (though somewhat overpriced) meal. 'Tasteful, casual attire' is the rule for dinner dress, and there's a barbecue on the lawn every Saturday during summer. The Wawona's wide, white porch makes a snazzy destination for evening cocktails, and listen for veteran pianist Tom Bopp in the lobby.

Yosemite Lodge Food Court
CAFETERIA $

(Map p408; Yosemite Lodge; mains $7-12; ⏱6:30am-8:30pm Sun-Thu, to 9pm Fri & Sat; 🖊) This self-service restaurant has several tummy-filling stations serving pastas, burgers, pizza and sandwiches, either made to order or served from beneath heat lamps. Proceed to the cashier and find a table inside or on the patio.

Curry Village Pizza Patio
PIZZERIA $

(Map p408; Curry Village; pizzas from $8; ⏱noon-10pm, shorter winter hours) Enjoy tasty pizza at this buzzing eatery that becomes a chatty après-hike hangout in the late afternoon.

Degnan's Loft
PIZZERIA $

(Map p408; Yosemite Village; mains $8-10; ⏱5-9pm Mon-Fri Nov-Mar, daily Apr-Oct) Head upstairs to this convivial place with high-beamed ceilings and a many-sided fireplace, and kick back under the dangling lift chair for decent salads, veggie lasagna and pizza.

Curry Village Dining Pavilion
CAFETERIA $$

(Map p408; Curry Village; mains breakfast adult/child $11.50/7.75, dinner adult/child $15.25/8.25; ⏱7-10am & 5:30-8pm Apr-Nov) Although the cafeteria-style setting has all the charm of a train-station waiting room, the mediocre all-you-can-eat breakfast and dinner buffets are great for families, gluttons and the undecided.

Degnan's Deli
DELI $

(Map p408; Yosemite Village; sandwiches $6-8; ⏱7am-5pm) Excellent made-to-order sandwiches, breakfast items and snack foods.

Curry Village Coffee Corner
CAFE $

(Map p408; Curry Village; pastries $2-4; ⏱6am-10pm, shorter winter hours) For a coffee jolt or sugar fix.

Curry Village Taqueria
MEXICAN $

(Map p408; Curry Village; mains $4.50-10; ⏱11am-5pm spring-fall) Tacos and big burritos on a deck near the parking area.

Tuolumne Meadows Grill
FAST FOOD $

(Map p404; Tuolumne Meadows; mains under $10; ⏱8am-5pm Jul–mid-Sep) Scarf down burgers and grill items at the outdoor picnic tables.

Village Grill
FAST FOOD $

(Map p408; Yosemite Village; items $5-7; ⏱Apr-Oct) Fight the chipmunks for burgers and tasty fries alfresco.

🍷 Drinking

No one will mistake Yosemite for nightlife central, but there are some nice spots to relax with a cabernet, cocktail or cold beer. Outside the park, the Yosemite Bug Rustic Mountain Resort (p417) and the Evergreen Lodge (p411) both have lively lounges.

Mountain Room Lounge
BAR

(Map p408; Yosemite Lodge, Yosemite Valley) Catch up on the latest sports news while knocking back draft brews at this large bar that buzzes in wintertime. Order a s'mores kit (graham crackers, chocolate squares and marshmallows) to roast in the open-pit fireplace. Kids welcome until 9pm.

Ahwahnee Bar
BAR

(Map p408; Ahwahnee Hotel, Yosemite Valley) The perfect way to experience the Ahwahnee without dipping too deep into your pockets; settle in for a drink at this cozy bar, complete with pianist. Appetizers and light meals ($9.50 to $23) provide sustenance.

⭐ Entertainment

At the Yosemite Theater (Map p408; Yosemite Village; adult/child $8/4) take your pick from a rotating cast of performers, including Wawona Hotel pianist Tom Bopp, actor Lee Stetson, who portrays the fascinating life and philosophy of John Muir, and Park Ranger Shelton Johnson, who re-creates the experiences of a Buffalo Soldier (see the boxed text, p418). There are also special children's shows.

Other activities scheduled year-round include campfire programs, children's photo walks, twilight strolls, night-sky watching,

HIGH SIERRA CAMPS

In the backcountry near Tuolumne Meadows, the exceptionally popular **High Sierra Camps** (Map p404) provide shelter and sustenance to hikers who'd rather not carry food or a tent. The camps – called **Vogelsang**, **Merced Lake**, **Sunrise**, **May Lake** and **Glen Aulin** – are set 6 to 10 miles apart along a loop trail. They consist of dormitory-style canvas tent cabins with beds, blankets or comforters, plus showers (at May Lake, Sunrise and Merced Lake – subject to water availability) and a central dining tent. Guests bring their own sheets and towels. The rate is $151 per adult ($91 for children seven to twelve) per night, including breakfast and dinner. Organized hiking or saddle trips led by ranger naturalists are also available (from $901).

A short season (roughly late June to September) and high demand mean that there's a lottery for reservations. **Applications** (801-559-4909; www.yosemitepark.com) are currently accepted in September and October only. If you don't have a reservation, call from February to check for cancellations. Dates vary year to year, so watch the website for updates.

ranger talks and slide shows, while the tavern at the Evergreen Lodge (p411) has live bands some weekends. Scan the *Yosemite Guide* for full details.

❶ Information

Yosemite's entrance fee is $20 per vehicle or $10 for those on bicycle or foot and is valid for seven consecutive days. Upon entering the park, you'll receive an NPS map, an illustrated booklet and, most importantly, a copy of the seasonal *Yosemite Guide* newspaper, which includes an activity schedule and current opening hours of all facilities.

For recorded park information, campground availability, and road and weather conditions, call 209-372-0200.

Dangers & Annoyances

Yosemite is prime black bear habitat. To find out how to protect the bears and yourself from each other, see p765. Mosquitoes can be pesky in summer, so bug spray's not a bad idea. And please don't feed those squirrels. They may look cute but they've got a nasty bite.

Internet Access

Curry Village Lounge (Curry Village, behind registration office) Free wi-fi.

Degnan's Cafe (Yosemite Village, per min 25¢) Pay terminals in this cafe adjacent to Degnan's Deli.

Mariposa County Public Library Yosemite Valley (Girls Club Bldg, 58 Cedar Ct, Yosemite Valley; 8:30-11:30am Mon, 2-5pm Tue, 8:30am-12:30pm Wed, 4-7pm Thu); Bassett Memorial Library (Chilnualna Falls Rd, Wawona; 1-6pm Mon-Fri, 10am-3pm Sat, shorter hours fall-spring) Free internet terminals available.

Yosemite Lodge at the Falls (Yosemite Valley; per min 25¢) Pay terminals are in the lobby. Wi-fi costs $6 per day for nonguests.

Internet Resources

Yosemite Conservancy (www.yosemiteconservancy.org) Information and educational programs offered by the nonprofit park support organization.

Yosemite National Park (www.nps.gov/yose) Official Yosemite National Park Service site with the most comprehensive and current information.

Yosemite Park (www.yosemitepark.com) Online home of DNC Parks & Resorts, Yosemite's main concessionaire. Has lots of practical information and a lodging reservations function.

Medical Services

Yosemite Medical Clinic (209-372-4637; Ahwahnee Dr, Yosemite Valley; approx 9am-5pm) Twenty-four hour emergency service available. A **dental clinic** (209-372-4200) is also available next door.

Money

Stores in Yosemite Village, Curry Village and Wawona all have ATMs, as does the Yosemite Lodge at the Falls.

Post

The main post office is in Yosemite Village, but Wawona and Yosemite Lodge also have year-round services. A seasonal branch operates in Tuolumne Meadows.

Telephone

There are pay phones at every developed location throughout the park. Cell-phone reception is sketchy, depending on your location; AT&T, Verizon and Sprint have the best coverage.

Tourist Information

Extended summer hours may apply.

Big Oak Flat Information Station (Map p404; 209-379-1899; 8am-5pm May-Sep) Also has a wilderness permit desk.

Tuolumne Meadows Visitor Center (Map p404; 209-372-0263; 9am-6pm late spring-early fall)

Tuolumne Meadows Wilderness Center (Map p404; 209-372-0309; approx 8am-4:30pm spring & fall, 7:30am-5pm Jul & Aug) Issues wilderness permits.

Valley Wilderness Center (Map p408; 209-372-0745; Yosemite Village; 7:30am-5pm May-Sep) Wilderness permits, maps and backcountry advice.

Wawona Information Station (Map p404; 209-375-9531; 8:30am-5pm May-Sep) Issues wilderness permits.

Yosemite Valley Visitor Center (Map p408; 209-372-0299; Yosemite Village; 9am-7:30pm summer, shorter hours year-round) The main office, with exhibits and free film screenings of *Spirit of Yosemite*.

Getting There & Away

Car

Yosemite is accessible year-round from the west (via Hwys 120 W and 140) and south (Hwy 41), and in summer also from the east (via Hwy 120 E). Roads are plowed in winter, but snow chains may be required at any time. In 2006 a mammoth rockslide buried part of Hwy 140, 6 miles west of the park; traffic there is restricted to vehicles under 45ft.

Gas up year-round at Wawona and Crane Flat inside the park or at El Portal on Hwy 140 just outside its boundaries. In summer, gas is also sold at Tuolumne Meadows. You'll pay dearly.

Public Transportation

Yosemite is one of the few national parks that can be easily reached by public transportation. **Greyhound** buses and **Amtrak** trains serve Merced, west of the park, where they are met by buses operated by **Yosemite Area Regional Transportation System** (YARTS; 209-388-9589, 877-989-2787; www.yarts.com), and you can buy Amtrak tickets that include the YARTS segment all the way into the park. Buses travel to Yosemite Valley along Hwy 140 several times daily year-round, stopping along the way.

In summer, another YARTS route runs from Mammoth Lakes along Hwy 395 to Yosemite Valley via Hwy 120. One-way tickets to Yosemite Valley are $13 ($9 child and senior, three hours) from Merced and $15 ($10 child and senior, 3½ hours) from Mammoth Lakes, less if boarding in between.

YARTS fares include the park entrance fee, making them a super bargain.

Getting Around

Bicycle

Bicycling is an ideal way to take in Yosemite Valley. You can rent a wide-handled cruiser (per hour/day $10/28) or a bike with an attached child trailer (per hour/day $16.50/54) at the Yosemite Lodge at the Falls or Curry Village.

Car

Roadside signs with red bears mark the many spots where bears have been hit by motorists, so think before you hit the accelerator. Glacier Point and Tioga Rds are closed in winter.

Public Transportation

The free, air-conditioned **Yosemite Valley Shuttle Bus** is a comfortable and efficient way of traveling around the park. Buses operate year-round at frequent intervals and stop at 21 numbered locations, including parking lots, campgrounds, trailheads and lodges. For a route map, see the *Yosemite Guide*.

Free buses also operate between Wawona and the Mariposa Grove (spring to fall), and Yosemite Valley and Badger Pass (winter only). The **Tuolumne Meadows Shuttle** runs between Tuolumne Lodge and Olmsted Point in Tuolumne Meadows (usually mid-June to early September), and the **El Capitan Shuttle** runs a summertime valley loop from Yosemite Village to El Capitan.

Two fee-based hikers' buses also travel from Yosemite Valley. For trailheads along Tioga Rd, catch the **Tuolumne Meadows Tour & Hikers' Bus** (209-372-4386; Jul-early Sep), which runs once daily in each direction. Fares depend on distance traveled; the trip to Tuolumne Meadows costs $14.50/23 one way/round-trip. The **Glacier Point Hikers' Bus** (209-372-4386; one way/return $25/41; mid-May–Oct) is good for hikers as well as for people reluctant to drive up the long, windy road themselves. Reservations are required.

YOSEMITE GATEWAYS

Fish Camp

Fish Camp, just south of the park on Hwy 41, is more of a bend in the road, but it does have some good lodging options as well as the ever-popular **Sugar Pine Railroad** (559-683-7273; www.yosemitesteamtrains.com; rides adult/child $18/9; Mar-Oct;), a historic steam train that chugs through the woods on a 4-mile loop.

🛏️ Sleeping & Eating

TOP CHOICE **Narrow Gauge Inn** INN **$$**
(☎559-683-7720, 888-644-9050; www.narrow gaugeinn.com; 48571 Hwy 41; r incl breakfast Nov-Mar $79-109, Apr-Oct $120-220; ❇️🐾🛜❄️🏊) Next door to the railroad, this friendly, beautiful and supremely comfortable 26-room inn counts a hot tub, small bar, and the finest **restaurant** (mains $19-37, ⏰5:30-9pm Wed-Sun Apr-Oct) in the area. Each tastefully appointed room features unique decor and a pleasant deck facing the trees and mountains, and all have flat-screen TVs.

White Chief Mountain Lodge MOTEL **$$**
(☎559-683-5444; www.whitechiefmountainlodge. com; 7776 White Chief Mountain Rd; r $125-190; ⏰Apr-Oct) The cheapest and most basic option in town is this 1950s-era motel with simple kitchenette rooms. It's located a few hundred yards east of Hwy 41; watch for the sign and go up the wooded country road.

Summerdale Campground CAMPGROUND **$**
(☎877-444-6677; www.recreation.gov; tent & RV sites $21; ⏰May-Sep; 🐾) Has 28 well-dispersed United States Forest Service (USFS) sites along Big Creek.

Oakhurst

At the junction of Hwys 41 and 49, about 15 miles south of the park entrance, Oakhurst functions primarily as a service town. This is your last chance to stock up on reasonably priced groceries, gasoline and camping supplies.

🛏️ Sleeping & Eating

TOP CHOICE **Sierra Sky Ranch** LODGE **$$**
(☎559-683-8040; www.sierraskyranch.com; 50552 Rd 632; r incl breakfast $145-225; ❇️🛜🐾❄️) This former ranch dates back to 1875 and has numerous outdoor activities available on 14 attractive acres. The homespun rooms are phone-free and pet-friendly, with oversized wooden headboards and double doors that open onto shady verandas. The rambling and beautiful old lodge features a **restaurant** (dinner mains $12-41) and a rustic saloon, and has loads of comfortable lounging areas. With a storied history including previous uses as a TB hospital and a bordello, its past guests include Marilyn Monroe and John Wayne. Many swear that it's cheerfully haunted by former residents.

WILDERNESS PERMITS FOR OVERNIGHT CAMPING

Shedding the high-season crowds is easiest when you set foot into Yosemite's backcountry wilderness. Start by identifying a route that matches your schedule, skill and fitness level. Then secure a **wilderness permit** (☎209-372-0740; fax 209-372-0739; www.nps.gov/yose/planyourvisit/wpres.htm; advance reservation fee $5, plus $5 per person, free for walk-ins; ⏰8:30am-4:30pm Mon-Fri late Nov-Oct), which is mandatory for overnight trips. To prevent tent cities sprouting in the woods, a quota system limits the number of people leaving from each trailhead each day. For trips between mid-May and September, 60% of the quota may be reserved by fax, phone, or mail from 24 weeks to two days before your trip. Faxes received between 5pm (the previous day) and 7:30am (the first morning you can reserve) get first priority.

The remainder are distributed by the office closest to the trailhead on a first-come, first-served basis (beginning at 11am one day before your planned hike) at Yosemite Valley Wilderness Center (p414), Tuolumne Meadows Wilderness Center (p414), the information stations at Wawona (Map p404) and Big Oak Flat (Map p404), and the Hetch Hetchy Entrance Station (Map p404). Hikers who turn up at the wilderness center nearest the trailhead get priority over those at another wilderness center. For example, if a person who's been waiting for hours in the valley wants the last permit left for Lyell Canyon, the Yosemite Valley Wilderness Center calls the Tuolumne Meadows Wilderness Center to see if any hikers in Tuolumne want it. If a hiker waltzing into the Tuolumne office says 'yes!', they get priority over the person in the Valley.

Reservations are not available from October to April, but you'll still need to get a permit.

At night you must be sure to store all scented items in bear-resistant containers, which may be rented for $5 per week at the wilderness and visitors centers. For locations and details, check www.nps.gov/yose/planyourvisit/bearcanrentals.htm.

SCENIC DRIVE: SIERRA VISTA NATIONAL SCENIC BYWAY

Set entirely within Sierra National Forest, this scenic route (www.sierravistascenicbyway. org) follows USFS roads in an 83-mile loop that takes you from 3000ft to nearly 7000ft. Along the way are dramatic vistas, excellent fishing, and camping almost anywhere you like (dispersed camping is allowed in most areas). It's a great way for car campers – and curious day trippers – to lose themselves within the mountains.

From its start in **North Fork**, the route takes a half-day to complete, emerging on Hwy 41 a few miles north of **Oakhurst**. Open from June to November, the road is paved most of the way, but narrow and laced with curves. See www.byways.org/explore/by ways/2300 for a map and information on sights and the best overlooks.

Château du Sureau　BOUTIQUE HOTEL **$$$**
(☎559-683-6860; www.chateaudusureau.com; r incl breakfast $385-585, 2-bedroom villa $2950; ❄@🛜🏊) Never in a billion years would you expect to find this in Oakhurst. A luxe and discreet full-service European-style hotel and world-class spa, this serene destination property boasts an exceptional level of service. With wall tapestries, oil paintings and ornate chandeliers, its **restaurant** (prix fixe dinner $95) could be a countryside castle.

Hounds Tooth Inn　B&B **$$**
(☎559-642-6600; www.houndstoothinn.com; 42071 Hwy 41; r incl breakfast $95-179; ❄🛜) A few miles north of Oakhurst, this gorgeous garden B&B is swimming in rosebushes and Victorian-esque charm. Its 12 airy rooms, some with spas and fireplaces, feel a bit like an English manor house. Complimentary wine and hot drinks are available in the afternoon.

Oakhurst Lodge　MOTEL **$$**
(☎559-683-4417, 800-655-6343; www.oakhurst lodge.com; 40302 Hwy 41; r $145-160; ❄🛜🏊🐾) Right in the center of town, this 58-unit motel presents a fine no-frills budget option, with quiet, clean rooms, some with kitchenettes.

Merced River Canyon

The approach to Yosemite via Hwy 140 is one of the most scenic, especially the section that meanders through Merced River Canyon. The springtime runoff makes this a spectacular spot for **river rafting**, with many miles of class III and IV rapids. Age minimums vary with water levels.

Outfitters include **Zephyr Whitewater Expeditions** (☎209-532-6249, 800-431-3636; www.zrafting.com; half-day/1-day trips per person from $105/125), a large, reputable outfitter with a seasonal office in El Portal, and **OARS**

(☎209-736-4677, 800-346-6277; www.oars.com; 1-day trips per person $144-170), a worldwide rafting operator with a solid reputation.

Mariposa

About halfway between Merced and Yosemite Valley, Mariposa (Spanish for 'butterfly') is the largest and most interesting town near the park. Established as a mining and railroad town during the Gold Rush, it has the oldest courthouse in continuous use (since 1854) west of the Mississippi and a friendly feel.

Rock hounds should drive to the **Mariposa County Fairgrounds**, 2 miles south of town on Hwy 49, to see the 13-pound 'Fricot Nugget' – the largest crystallized gold specimen from the California Gold Rush era – and other gems and machinery at the **California State Mining & Mineral Museum** (☎209-742-7625; www.parks.ca.gov/?page_id=588; admission $4; ⏰10am-5pm Thu-Sun May-Sep, to 4pm Oct-Apr). An exhibit on glow-in-the-dark minerals is also very cool.

At the junction of Hwy 49s and 140 is the info-laden **Mariposa County Visitor Center** (☎209-966-7081, 866-425-3366; www.home ofyosemite.com; ⏰8am-8pm mid-May–mid-Oct, to 5pm mid-Oct–mid-May), which has friendly staff and racks of brochures.

YARTS (☎209-388-9589, 877-989-2787; www. yarts.com) buses run year-round along Hwy 140 into Yosemite Valley (adult/child $12/8 round-trip, 1¾ hours one way) stopping at the Mariposa visitor center. Tickets include park admission.

🛏 Sleeping & Eating

TOP CHOICE **River Rock Inn**　MOTEL **$$**
(☎209-966-5793; www.riverrockncafe.com; 4993 7th St; r incl breakfast $109-159; ❄🛜🐾) A bold splash of psychedelic purple and dusty or-

ange paint spruces up what claims to be the oldest motel in town. Rooms done up in artsy earth tones have TVs but no phones, and calming ceiling fans resemble lily pads. A block removed from Hwy 140 on a quiet side street, it features a small courtyard deck and deli cafe serving beer and wine, with live acoustic music some summer evenings.

Mariposa Lodge   MOTEL $$
(209-966-3607, 800-966-8819; www.mariposalodge.com; 5052 Hwy 140; r $119-159; ※🛜🐾🏊) More of a generic motel, the simple, well-kept Mariposa sports clean, quiet rooms (with TVs and phones) and friendly staff. It earns pluses for the good-sized rooms and for the blooming flowers that border the grounds.

Happy Burger   DINER $
(www.happyburgerdiner.com; Hwy 140 at 12th St; mains $6-10; ⏱5:30am-9pm; 🅿🛜🚸) Boasting the largest menu in the Sierra, this buzzing roadside joint decorated with old LP album covers serves the cheapest meals in Mariposa. Its all-American cuisine means burgers, sandwiches, Mexican food and a ton of sinful ice-cream desserts.

Savoury's   NEW AMERICAN $$
(209-966-7677; www.savouryrestaurant.com; 5034 Hwy 140; mains $15-30; ⏱5-9pm Thu-Tue;🅿) Now in a roomier location, upscale yet casual Savoury's is still the best restaurant in town. Black lacquered tables and contemporary art create a tranquil window dressing for dishes like apricot- and miso-glazed pork chops, hearty pastas and Steak Diane.

Midpines

The highlight of this almost nonexistent town is the folksy 🏠Yosemite Bug Rustic Mountain Resort (209-966-6666, 866-826-7108; www.yosemitebug.com; dm $25, tent cabins $45-75, r $75-155, cabins without bath $65-100; ◎🛜🐾🏊), tucked away on a forested hillside about 25 miles from Yosemite National Park. It's more like a convivial mountain retreat than a hostel: at night, friendly folks of all ages and backgrounds share stories, music and delicious freshly prepared meals in the woodsy cafe (mains $8.50-18; ⏱7am-9pm; 🅿) before retreating to their beds. Dorm dwellers have access to a communal kitchen, and the resort has a spa with a hot tub; yoga lessons and massages are also available.

The YARTS bus stops a quarter mile up the driveway, and the resort's Bug Bus tours offer a range of hiking trips (including overnights) to Yosemite year-round. A two-night package including transportation, lodging, meals and a park tour starts at $245. See details at www.yosemitebugbus.com.

Briceburg

Some 20 miles outside the park, right where the Merced River meets Hwy 140, the town of Briceburg consists of a visitors center (209-379-9414; www.blm.gov/ca/st/en/fo/folsom/mercedriverrec.html; ⏱1-5pm Fri, from 9am Sat & Sun late Apr-early Sep) and three primitive Bureau of Land Management (BLM)

SCENIC DRIVE: EBBETTS PASS SCENIC BYWAY

For outdoor fanatics, a scenic 61-mile section of Hwys 4 and 89 called the Ebbetts Pass Scenic Byway (www.scenic4.org) is a road trip through paradise. Heading northeast from Arnold, gaze up at the giant sequoias of Calaveras Big Trees State Park (www.parks.ca.gov/?page_id=551; per vehicle $8), and in winter stop at the family-friendly ski resort of Bear Valley (209-753-2301; www.bearvalley.com; lift tickets adult/child $62/15; 🚡). Continuing east, the stunningly beautiful Lake Alpine is skirted by slabs of granite, several great beaches and a handful of campgrounds, and boasts excellent watersports, fishing and hiking.

The next stretch is the most dramatic, when the narrow highway continues past picturesque Mosquito Lake and the Pacific Grade Summit (8060ft) before slaloming through historic Hermit Valley and finally winding up and over the 8730ft summit of Ebbetts Pass. North on Hwy 89 and just west of Markleeville, visit the two developed pools and seasonal campground at Grover Hot Springs State Park (530-694-2249; www.parks.ca.gov/?page_id=508; parking $8, pool admission adult/child $5/3, tent & RV sites $35; ⏱variable hours year-round).

From San Francisco, it's a three-hour drive north to Arnold, via Hwy 108 and Hwy 49. Ebbetts Pass closes after the first major snowfall and doesn't reopen until June, but Hwy 4 is usually plowed from the west as far as Bear Valley.

THE BUFFALO SOLDIERS

After the creation of the national parks in 1890, the US Army was called in to safeguard these natural resources. In the summer of 1903, troops from the 9th Cavalry – one of four well-respected (though segregated) African American regiments, known as the 'Buffalo Soldiers' – were sent to patrol here and in Yosemite. In Sequoia and what was then General Grant National Park, the troops had an impressively productive summer – building roads, creating a trail system and setting a high standard as stewards of the land.

The troops were commanded by Captain (later Colonel) Charles Young. At the time, Young was the only African American captain in the Army; his post as Acting Superintendent made him the first African American superintendent of a national park.

campgrounds (tent & RV sites $10) with a to-die-for location right on the river. To reach them, you cross a beautiful 1920s wooden suspension bridge, so long trailers and large RVs are not recommended.

El Portal

Right outside the Arch Rock entrance, and primarily inhabited by park employees, El Portal makes a convenient Yosemite base. YARTS buses run to Yosemite Valley (adult/child round-trip $7/5, one hour).

Primarily an inexpensive private campground, **Indian Flat RV Park** (☑209-379-2339; www.indianflatrvpark.com; 9988 Hwy 140; tent sites $25, RV sites $37-42, tent cabins $59, cottages $109; ☉year-round; ❋❋) also has a number of interesting housing options, including two pretty stone cabin cottages with air-conditioning. Guests can use the pool and wi-fi at its sister property next door, and nonguests can pay to shower.

Less than 2 miles from the park entrance, **Yosemite View Lodge** (☑209-379-2681, 888-742-4371; www.stayyosemiteviewlodge.com; 11136 Hwy 140; r $164-254, ste $304-714; ❋❋❋❋) is a big, modern complex with hot tubs, two restaurants and four pools. All the 336 rooms feature kitchenettes, some have gas fireplaces and views of the Merced River, and the ground-floor rooms have big patios. The souped-up 'majestic suites' are massive, with opulent bathrooms featuring waterfall showers and plasma-TV entertainment centers.

Groveland

From the Big Oak Flat entrance, it's 22 miles to Groveland, an adorable town with restored Gold Rush–era buildings.

A friendly 10-room 1918 confection with beds adorned in patchwork quilts, the **Ho-**tel Charlotte (☑209-962-6455; www.hotelcharlotte.com; 18736 Main St; r incl breakfast $129-225; ❋@❋❋) keeps the vintage flair alive. The cute **restaurant** (mains $12-20) serves a creative international menu.

Across the street from the Hotel Charlotte, the historic **Groveland Hotel** (☑209-962-4000, 800-273-3314; www.groveland.com; 18767 Main St; r incl breakfast $135-349; ❋@❋) dates from 1850 and now houses a small **bar**, an upscale **restaurant** (mains $14-21) and 17 bright, lovingly decorated rooms with wrap-around verandas and resident teddy bears.

SEQUOIA & KINGS CANYON NATIONAL PARKS

The twin parks of Sequoia & Kings Canyon dazzle with superlatives, though they're often overshadowed by Yosemite, their smaller neighbor to the north (a three-hour drive away). With towering forests of giant sequoias containing some of the largest trees in the world, and the mighty Kings River careening through the depths of Kings Canyon, one of the deepest chasms in the country, the parks are lesser-visited jewels where it's easier to find quiet and solitude. Throw in opportunities for cave spelunking, rock climbing and backcountry hiking through granite-carved Sierra landscapes, and backdoor access to Mt Whitney – the tallest peak in the lower 48 states – and you have all the ingredients for two of the best parks in the country.

The two parks, though distinct, are operated as one unit with a single admission (valid for seven consecutive days) of $20 per carload. For 24-hour recorded information, including road conditions, call ☑559-565-3341 or visit www.nps.gov/seki, the parks' comprehensive website. At either entrance station (Big Stump or Ash Mountain), you'll receive an NPS map and a copy of the parks' *The Guide* newspaper, with information on seasonal activities, camping and special programs, including those in the surrounding national forests and the Giant Sequoia National Monument.

Cell-phone coverage is nonexistent except for limited reception at Grant Grove, and gas is available at Hume Lake and Stony Creek Lodge, both on USFS land.

History
In 1890 Sequoia became the second national park in the USA (after Yellowstone). A few days later, the 4 sq miles around Grant Grove were declared General Grant National Park and, in 1940, absorbed into the newly created Kings Canyon National Park. In 2000, to protect additional sequoia groves, vast tracts of land in the surrounding national forest became the Giant Sequoia National Monument.

Dangers & Annoyances
Air pollution wafting up from the Sequoia Central Valley and Kings Canyon often thwarts long-range visibility, and people with respiratory problems should check with a visitors center about current pollution levels. Black bears are common and proper food storage is always required. Heed park instructions on wildlife procedures and see p765 for more information.

Kings Canyon National Park

With a dramatic cleft deeper than the Grand Canyon, Kings Canyon offers true adventure to those who crave seemingly endless trails, rushing streams and gargantuan rock formations. The camping, backcountry exploring and climbing here are all superb.

⊙ Sights & Activities
Kings Canyon National Park has two developed areas with markets, lodging, showers and visitor information. Grant Grove Village is only 4 miles past the Big Stump entrance (in the park's west), while Cedar Grove Village is 31 miles east at the bottom of the canyon. The two are separated by the Giant Sequoia National Monument and are linked by Kings Canyon Scenic Byway/Hwy 180.

GRANT GROVE
General Grant Grove   FOREST
This sequoia grove is nothing short of magnificent. The paved half-mile **General Grant Tree Trail** is an interpretive walk that visits a number of mature sequoias, including the 27-story **General Grant Tree**. This giant

---

SCENIC DRIVE: KINGS CANYON SCENIC BYWAY (HIGHWAY 180)

The 31-mile rollercoaster road connecting Grant Grove and Cedar Grove ranks among the most dazzling in all of California. It winds past the **Converse Basin Grove**, which once contained the world's largest grove of mature sequoias until loggers turned it into a sequoia cemetery in the 1880s. A half-mile loop trail leads to the 20ft-high **Chicago Stump**, the remains of the 3200-year-old tree that was cut down, sectioned and reassembled for the 1893 World Columbian Exposition in Chicago. North of here, a second side road goes to **Stump Meadow**, where stumps and fallen logs make good picnic platforms, and to the **Boole Tree Trail**, a 2.5-mile loop to the only 'monarch' left to live.

The road then begins its jaw-dropping descent into the canyon, snaking past chiseled rock walls, some tinged by green moss and red iron minerals, others decorated by waterfalls. Turnouts provide superb views, especially at **Junction View**.

Eventually the road runs parallel with the gushing Kings River, its thunderous roar ricocheting off granite cliffs soaring as high as 8000ft, making Kings Canyon even deeper than the Grand Canyon. Stop at **Boyden Cavern** (☎888-965-8243; www.boydencavern.com; tours adult/child from $13/8; ⊙10am-5pm late May-Sep, 11am-4pm late Apr-late May & Oct–mid-Nov) for a tour of its whimsical formations. While beautiful, they are smaller and less impressive than those in Crystal Cave (p425) in Sequoia National Park, but no advance tickets are required. About 5 miles further east, **Grizzly Falls** can be torrential or drizzly, depending on the time of year.

On your return trip, consider a detour via **Hume Lake**, created in 1908 as a dam for logging operations and now offering boating, swimming and fishing. Facilities include a small market and a gas station.

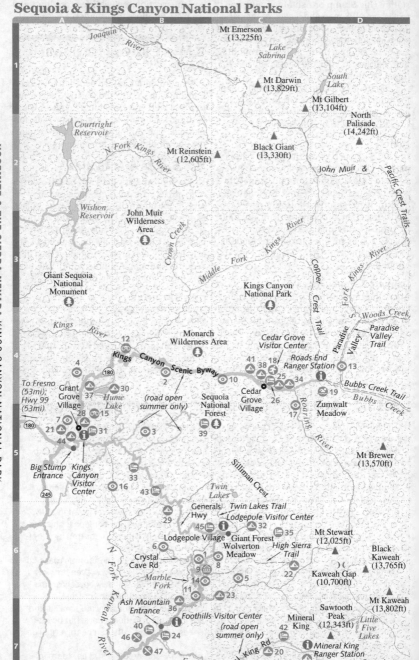

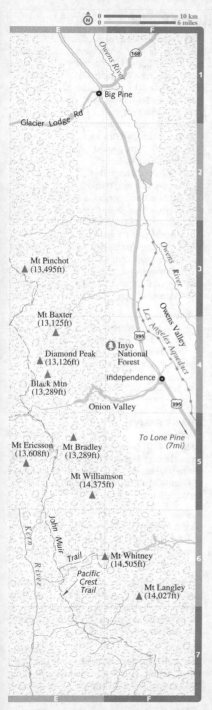

holds triple honors as the world's third-largest living tree, a memorial to US soldiers killed in war, and as the nation's Christmas tree. The nearby **Fallen Monarch**, a massive, fire-hollowed trunk that you can walk through, has been a cabin, hotel, saloon and stables for US Cavalry horses.

Panoramic Point LOOKOUT

For a breathtaking view of Kings Canyon, head 2.3 miles up narrow, steep and winding Panoramic Point Rd (trailers and RVs aren't recommended), which branches off Hwy 180. Follow a short paved trail uphill from the parking lot to the viewpoint, where precipitous canyons and the snowcapped peaks of the Great Western Divide unfold below you. Snow closes the road to vehicles during winter, when it becomes a cross-country ski and snowshoe route.

Redwood Canyon CANYON

South of Grant Grove Village, more than 15,000 sequoias cluster in this secluded and pristine corner of the park, making it the world's largest such grove. Relatively inaccessible, this area lets you enjoy the majesty of the giants away from the crowds on several moderate-to-strenuous trails. The trailhead is at the end of an unsigned, 2-mile bumpy dirt road across from the Hume Lake/Quail Flat sign on Generals Hwy, about 6 miles south of the village.

CEDAR GROVE & ROADS END

At Cedar Grove Village, a simple lodge and snack bar provide the last outpost of civilization before the rugged grandeur of the backcountry takes over. Pretty spots around here include **Roaring River Falls**, where water whips down a sculpted rock channel before tumbling into a churning pool, and the 1.5-mile **Zumwalt Meadow Loop**, an easy nature trail around a verdant green meadow bordered by river and granite canyon. A short walk from Roads End, **Muir Rock** is a large flat river boulder where John Muir often gave talks during Sierra Club field trips. The rock now bears his name, and the lazy river abounds with gleeful swimmers in summer.

The trail to **Mist Falls** (8-mile round-trip) is an easy to moderate hike to one of the park's larger waterfalls. The first 2 miles are fairly exposed, so start early to avoid the midday heat. Continuing past Mist Falls, the trail eventually connects with the John Muir/Pacific Crest Trail to form the 42-mile **Rae Lakes Loop**, the most popular long-

Sequoia & Kings Canyon National Parks

distance hike in Kings Canyon National Park (a wilderness permit is required, see p426).

For guided horse trips, both day and overnight, check with **Cedar Grove Pack Station** (☎559-565-3464).

🛏 Sleeping & Eating

Unless noted, all campsites are first-come, first-served. Showers are available at Grant Grove Village and Cedar Grove Village.

Potential campers should also keep in mind that there are great free uncrowded and undeveloped campgrounds off Big Meadows Rd in the Sequoia National Forest. They're some of the only empty campsites in the Sierra Nevada during peak summer season. Free roadside camping is also allowed in the forest, but no campfires without a permit (available from the Grant Grove Visitor Center).

Markets in Grant Grove Village and Cedar Grove Village have a limited selection of groceries.

GRANT GROVE

Princess CAMPGROUND $
(☎877-444-6777; www.recreation.gov; Giant Sequoia National Monument; tent & RV sites $18; ☺mid-May–late Sep; 🐾) About 6 miles north of Grant Grove, with vault toilets and 90 reservable sites.

Azalea CAMPGROUND $
(tent & RV sites $10-18; ☺year-round; 🐾) Flush toilets, 110 sites; the nicest sites border a meadow. Close to Grant Grove Village (elevation 6500ft).

Crystal Springs CAMPGROUND $
(tent & RV sites $18; ☺mid-May–mid-Sep; 🐾) Fifty wooded, well-spaced sites with flush toilets; the smallest campground in the Grant Grove area and generally very quiet.

Sunset CAMPGROUND $
(tent & RV sites $18; ☺late May-early Sep; 🐾🐾) Flush toilets, 157 sites, some overlooking the western foothills and the Central Valley. Close to Grant Grove Village.

Hume Lake
CAMPGROUND $

(📞877-444-6777; www.recreation.gov; Hume Lake Rd, Giant Sequoia National Monument; tent & RV sites $20; ⏱late May-early Sep; 🐾🏊) Flush toilets, 74 reservable and uncrowded shady campsites, a handful with lake views; on the lake's northern shore about 10 miles northeast of Grant Grove.

John Muir Lodge
LODGE $$$

(📞559-335-5500, 866-522-6966; www.sequoia-kingscanyon.com; Grant Grove Village, off Generals Hwy; r $69-190) An atmospheric wooden building hung with historical black-and-white photographs, this year-round hotel is a place to lay your head and still feel like you're in the forest. Wide porches have wooden rocking chairs, and homespun, if thin-walled, rooms contain rough-hewn wood furniture and patchwork bedspreads (no TVs). Cozy up to the big stone fireplace on chilly nights with a board game.

Grant Grove Cabins
CABINS $$

(📞559-335-5500, 866-522-6966; www.sequoia-kingscanyon.com; Grant Grove Village, off Generals Hwy; cabins $65-140) Set amid towering sugar pines, around 50 cabins range from decrepit tent-top shacks (open from early June until early September) to rustic but comfortable heated duplexes (a few are wheelchair-accessible) with electricity, private bathrooms and double beds. For lovebirds, number 9 is the lone hard-sided, free-standing 'Honeymoon Cabin' with a queen bed, and can book up to a year in advance.

Grant Grove Restaurant
AMERICAN $$

(Grant Grove Village, off Generals Hwy; mains $7-16; ⏱7-10:30am, 11am-4pm & 5-9pm late May-early Sep, reduced hours early Sep-late May; 🐾🍴) More of a diner, this is where most visitors to Grant Grove Village chow down, and there can be a wait at times. There's a breakfast buffet, lunch sandwiches and filling full dinners.

Pizza Parlor
PIZZERIA $$

(pizza $12-22; ⏱2-9pm 9pm late May-early Sep, variable hours otherwise; 🍴) Excellent crisp-crust pizzeria hidden off the back porch of the Grant Grove Restaurant; shows movies.

CEDAR GROVE
Cedar Grove's **Sentinel** campground, next to the village area, is open whenever Hwy 180 is open; **Sheep Creek**, **Canyon View** (tent only) and **Moraine** are opened as overflow when needed. These campgrounds are usually the last to fill up on busy summer weekends and are also good bets early and late in the season thanks to their comparatively low elevation (4600ft). All have flush toilets and $18 sites. Other facilities in the village don't start operating until mid-May.

Cedar Grove Lodge
LODGE $$

(📞559-335-5500, 866-522-6966; www.sequoia-kingscanyon.com; Cedar Grove Village, Hwy 180; r $119-135; ⏱mid-May-mid-Oct; 🌀🐾) The only indoor sleeping option in the canyon, the riverside lodge offers 21 motel-style rooms, some with air-con. Hallways tend toward dingy, bathrooms are cramped and the bedspreads scream frumpy. But the three ground-floor rooms with shady furnished patios have spiffy river views and kitchenettes. All rooms have phones but no TVs.

Cedar Grove Restaurant
FAST FOOD $

(Cedar Grove Village; mains under $10; ⏱7-10:30am, 11am-2pm & 5-8pm mid-May-mid-Oct; 🐾🍴) A basic grill with hot and greasy fare.

ℹ Information

ATMs exist at Grant Grove Village and Cedar Grove Village. There's free wi-fi near the lodging check-in desk inside the Grant Grove Restaurant building in Grant Grove Village.

Cedar Grove Visitor Center (📞559-565-3793; ⏱9am-5pm late May-early Sep) Small visitor center in Cedar Grove Village. The Roads End Ranger Station, which dispenses wilderness permits and rents bear canisters, is 6 miles further east.

Kings Canyon Visitor Center (📞559-565-4307; ⏱8am-7pm early Jul-late Aug, variable hours otherwise) In Grant Grove Village. Has exhibits, maps and wilderness permits.

ℹ Getting There & Around

From the west, Kings Canyon Scenic Byway (Hwy 180) travels 53 miles east from Fresno to the Big Stump entrance. Coming from the south, you're in for a long 46-mile drive through Sequoia National Park along sinuous Generals Hwy. Budget about two hours' driving time from the Ash Mountain entrance to Grant Grove Village. The road to Cedar Grove Village is only open from around April or May until the first snowfall.

Sequoia National Park

Picture unzipping your tent flap and crawling out into a 'front yard' of trees as high as a 20-story building and as old as the Bible. Brew some coffee as you plan your day in this extraordinary park with its soul-sustain-ing forests and gigantic peaks soaring above 12,000ft.

◉ Sights & Activities

Nearly all of the park's star attractions are conveniently lined up along the Generals Hwy, which starts at the Ash Mountain entrance and continues north into Kings Canyon. Tourist activity concentrates in the Giant Forest area and in Lodgepole Village, which has the most facilities, including a visitors center and market. The road to remote Mineral King veers off Hwy 198 in the town of Three Rivers, just south of the park's Ash Mountain entrance.

GIANT FOREST

Named by John Muir in 1875, this area is the top destination in the parks, and about 2 miles south of Lodgepole Village. By volume the largest living tree on earth, the massive **General Sherman Tree** rockets 275ft to the sky. Pay your respects via a short descent from the Wolverton Rd parking lot, or join the **Congress Trail**, a paved 2-mile pathway that takes in General Sherman and other notable named trees, including the **Washington Tree**, the world's second biggest sequoia, and the see-through **Telescope Tree**. To lose the crowds, set off on the 5-mile **Trail of the Sequoias**, which puts you into the heart of the forest.

Open in the warmer months, Crescent Meadow Rd heads east from the Giant Forest Museum for 3 miles to **Crescent Meadow**, a relaxing picnic spot, especially in spring when it's ablaze with wildflowers. Several short hikes start from here, including the 1-mile trail to **Tharp's Log**, where the area's first white settler spent summers in a fallen tree. The road also passes **Moro Rock**, a landmark granite dome whose top can be reached via a quarter-mile carved staircase for breathtaking views of the Great

Western Divide, a chain of mountains running north to south through the center of Sequoia National Park.

FREE **Giant Forest Museum** MUSEUM
(☏559-565-4480; ⏰9am-7pm summer, to 5 or 6pm spring & fall, to 4pm winter) For a primer on the intriguing ecology, fire cycle and history of the 'big trees,' drop in at this excellent museum, then follow up your visit with a spin around the paved (and wheelchair-accessible) 1.2-mile interpretive **Big Trees Trail**, which starts from the museum parking lot.

FREE **Beetle Rock Education Center** EDUCATION CENTER
(☏559-565-4480; ⏰1-4pm late Jun–mid-Aug; ⛹) Bugs, bones and artificial animal scat are just some of the cool things children get to play with at this bright and cheerful cabin with activity stations galore. Here inquisitive kiddos can scan bugs with digital microscopes, touch a taxidermied bobcat, put on a puppet show and paint ecology posters. Tents are set up for inside play, and binoculars lure youngsters outside to spot animals.

FOOTHILLS

From the Ash Mountain entrance in Three Rivers, the Generals Hwy ascends steeply through this southern section of Sequoia National Park. With an average elevation of about 2000ft, the Foothills are much drier and warmer than the rest of the park. Hiking here is best in spring when the air is cool and wildflowers put on a colorful show. Summers are buggy and muggy, but fall again brings moderate temperatures and lush foliage.

The Potwisha people lived in this area until the early 1900s, relying primarily on acorn meal. Pictographs and grinding holes still grace the **Hospital Rock** picnic

---

GIANT SEQUOIAS: KINGS OF THE FOREST

In California you can stand under the world's oldest trees and its tallest, but the record for biggest in terms of volume belongs to the giant sequoias (Sequoiadendron giganteum). They grow only on the Sierra's western slope and are most abundant in Sequoia & Kings Canyon and Yosemite National Parks. John Muir called them 'nature's forest masterpiece' and anyone who's ever craned their neck to take in their soaring vastness has done so with the awe usually reserved for Gothic cathedrals. Trees can grow to 300ft tall and over 100ft in circumference, with bark over 2ft thick. The Giant Forest Museum (p424) in Sequoia National Park has excellent exhibits about their fascinating history and ecology.

DON'T MISS

CRYSTAL CAVE

Discovered in 1918 by two fishermen, Crystal Cave (☑559-565-3759; www.sequoiahistory. org; Crystal Cave Rd; adult/child/senior $13/7/12; ☉tours 10:30am-4:30pm mid-May–late Oct) was carved by an underground river and has formations estimated to be 10,000 years old. Stalactites hang like daggers from the ceiling, and milky white marble formations take the shape of ethereal curtains, domes, columns and shields. The cave is also a unique biodiverse habitat for spiders, bats and tiny aquatic insects that are found nowhere else on earth. The 45-minute tour covers a half-mile of chambers, though adults can also sign up for more in-depth lantern-lit cave explorations and full-day spelunking adventures.

Tickets are *only* sold at the Lodgepole and Foothills visitors centers (see p427) and *not* at the cave. Allow about one hour to get to the cave entrance, which is a half-mile walk from the parking lot at the end of a twisty 7-mile road; the turnoff is about 3 miles south of the Giant Forest. Bring a sweater or light jacket, as it's a huddle-for-warmth 48°F inside.

area, once a Potwisha village site. Swimming holes abound along the Marble Fork of the Kaweah River, especially near Potwisha Campground. Be careful, though – the currents can be deadly, especially when the river is swollen from the spring runoff.

MINERAL KING

A scenic, subalpine valley at 7500ft, Mineral King is Sequoia's backpacking mecca and a good place to find solitude. Gorgeous and gigantic, its glacially sculpted valley is ringed by massive mountains, including the jagged 12,343ft Sawtooth Peak. The area is reached via Mineral King Rd – a slinky, steep and narrow 25-mile road, not suitable for RVs or speed demons; the road is usually open from late May through October. Plan on spending the night unless you don't mind driving three hours round-trip.

Hiking anywhere from here involves a steep climb out of the valley along strenuous trails, so be aware of the altitude, even on short hikes. Enjoyable day hikes go to Crystal, Monarch, Mosquito and Eagle Lakes. For long trips, locals recommend the Little Five Lakes and, further along the High Sierra Trail, Kaweah Gap, surrounded by Black Kaweah, Mt Stewart and Eagle Scout Peak– all above 12,000ft.

In spring and early summer, hordes of hungry marmots terrorize parked cars at Mineral King, chewing on radiator hoses, belts and wiring of vehicles to get the salt they crave after their winter hibernation. If you're thinking of going hiking during that time, you'd be a fool not to protect your car by wrapping the underside with chicken wire or a diaper-like tarp.

From the 1860s to 1890s, Mineral King witnessed heavy silver mining and lumber activity. There are remnants of old shafts and stamp mills, though it takes some exploring to find them. A proposal by the Walt Disney Corporation to develop the area into a massive ski resort was thwarted when Congress annexed it to the national park in 1978. The website of the Mineral King Preservation Society (www.mineralking.org) has all kinds of info on the area, including its rustic and still-occupied historic mining cabins.

🛏 Sleeping & Eating

The market at Lodgepole Village is the best stocked in either park, but basic supplies are also available at the small store in Stony Creek Lodge (closed in winter).

GENERALS HIGHWAY

A handful of campgrounds line the highway and rarely fill up, although space may get tight on holiday weekends. Those in the Foothills area are best in spring and fall when the higher elevations are still chilly, but they get hot and buggy in summer. Unless noted, sites are available on a first-come, first-served basis. Free dispersed camping is possible in the Giant Sequoia National Monument. Stop by a visitors center or ranger station for details or a fire permit. Lodgepole Village and Stony Creek Lodge have pay showers.

Stony Creek   CAMPGROUND $
(☑877-444-6777; www.recreation.gov; tent & RV sites $20; ☉mid-May–late Sep; ✤) USFS-operated with 49 comfortable wooded sites, including some right on the creek, and flush

BACKPACKING IN SEQUOIA & KINGS CANYON NATIONAL PARKS

With over 850 miles of marked trails, the parks are a backpacker's dream. **Cedar Grove** and **Mineral King** offer the best backcountry access. Trails are usually open by mid to late May.

For overnight backcountry trips you'll need a **wilderness permit** (per group $15), which is subject to a quota system in summer; permits are free and available by self-registration outside the quota season. About 75% of spaces can be reserved, while the rest are available in person on a first-come, first-served basis. Reservations can be made from March 1 until two weeks before your trip. For details see www.nps.gov/seki/planyourvisit/wilderness_permits.htm. There's also a dedicated wilderness desk at the Lodgepole Visitor Center (see p427).

All ranger stations and visitors centers carry topo maps and hiking guides. Note that you need to store your food in park-approved bearproof canisters, which can be rented at markets and visitors centers (from $5 per trip).

toilets. Smaller, primitive **Upper Stony Creek campground** is across the street but not reservable.

Lodgepole — CAMPGROUND $
(✆877-444-6777; www.recreation.gov; tent & RV sites $10-20; ☺year-round; ⚑🐾) Closest to the Giant Forest area with over 200 closely packed sites and flush toilets; this place fills quickly because of proximity to Lodgepole Village amenities.

Buckeye Flat — CAMPGROUND $
(tent sites $18; ☺Apr-Sep; 🐾) This campground is in the Foothills area, in an open stand of oaks about 6 miles north of the Ash Mountain entrance. There are 28 tent-only sites and flush toilets. Can be somewhat rowdy.

Potwisha — CAMPGROUND $
(tent & RV sites $18; ☺year-round; 🐾) Also in the Foothills, and blazing in summertime, this campground has decent shade and swimming spots on the Kaweah River. It's 3 miles north of the Ash Mountain entrance, with 42 sites and flush toilets.

Dorst Creek — CAMPGROUND $
(✆877-444-6777; www.recreation.gov; tent & RV sites $20; ☺late Jun-early Sep; 🐾) Big and busy campground with 204 sites and flush toilets; quieter back sites are tent-only.

Stony Creek Lodge — LODGE $$
(✆559-335-5500, 866-522-6966; www.sequoia-kingscanyon.com; 65569 Generals Hwy; r $109-189; ☺mid-May-mid-Oct; 🐾⚑) About halfway between Grant Grove Village and Giant Forest, this lodge has a big river-rock fireplace in its lobby and 11 aging but folksy motel rooms with telephone but no TV.

Wuksachi Lodge — HOTEL $$$
(✆559-565-4070, 866-807-3598; www.visitsequoia.com; 64740 Wuksachi Way, off Generals Hwy; r $90-335; 🐾) Built in 1999, the Wuksachi Lodge is the most upscale lodging and dining option in the park. But don't get too excited – the wood-paneled atrium lobby has an inviting stone fireplace and forest views, but charmless motel-style rooms with oak furniture and thin walls have an institutional feel. The lodge's location, however, just north of Lodgepole Village, can't be beat.

Sequoia High Sierra Camp — CABINS $$$
(✆877-591-8982; www.sequoiahighsierracamp.com; r without bath incl all meals per adult/child $250/100; ☺mid-Jun-early Oct) Accessed via a 1-mile hike deep into the Sequoia National Forest, off General's Hwy, this off-the-grid, all-inclusive resort is nirvana for active, sociable people who don't think 'luxury camping' is an oxymoron. Canvas cabins are spiffed up by pillow-top mattresses, down pillows and cozy wool rugs, with shared restrooms and a shower house. Reservations are required.

Lodgepole Village — MARKET $
(Generals Hwy; mains $6-10; ☺market & snack bar 9am-6pm mid-Apr-late May & early Sep-mid-Oct, 8am-8pm late May-early Sep, deli 11am-6pm mid-Apr-mid-Oct; ⚑) The park's most extensive market sells all kinds of groceries, camping supplies and snacks. Inside, a fast-food snack bar slings burgers and grilled sandwiches and dishes up breakfast. The adjacent deli is a tad more upscale and healthy, with focaccia sandwiches, veggie wraps and picnic salads.

BACKCOUNTRY

Bearpaw High Sierra Camp CABINS $$$
(✆reservations 801-559-4930, 866-807-3598; www.visitsequoia.com; tent cabin per person $175; ⊙mid-Jun–mid-Sep) About 11.5 miles east of Giant Forest on the High Sierra Trail, this tent hotel is ideal for exploring the backcountry without lugging your own camping gear. Rates include showers, dinner and breakfast, as well as bedding and towels. Bookings start at 7am every January 2 and sell out almost immediately, though you should always check for cancellations.

MINERAL KING

Mineral King's two pretty campgrounds, **Atwell Mill** (tent sites $12; ⊙late May-Oct; 🐾) and **Cold Springs** (tent sites $12; ⊙late May-Oct; 🐾), often fill up on summer weekends. Pay showers available at the Silver City Mountain Resort.

Silver City Mountain Resort CABINS $$
(✆559-561-3223; www.silvercityresort.com; Mineral King Rd; cabins with/without bathroom $195/120, chalets $250-395; ⊙late May-late Oct; 🐾📶) The only food and lodging option anywhere near these parts, this rustic, old-fashioned and family-friendly place rents everything from cute and cozy 1950s-era cabins to modern chalets (one is wheelchair-accessible) that sleep up to eight. There's a ping-pong table, outdoor swings, and nearby ponds to splash around in. All guests must bring their own sheets and towels. Most cabins don't have electricity, and the property's generator usually shuts off around 10pm. Its **restaurant** (mains $6 to $10; ⊙8am-8pm Thu-Mon, pie & coffee only 8am-5pm Tue-Wed) serves delicious homemade pies and simple fare on wooden picnic tables under the trees. It's located 3.5 miles west of the ranger station.

THREE RIVERS

Named for the nearby convergence of three Kaweah River forks, Three Rivers is a friendly small town populated mostly by retirees and artsy newcomers. The town's main drag, Sierra Dr (Hwy 198), is sparsely lined with motels, eateries and shops.

Sequoia Village Inn CABINS, COTTAGES $$
(✆559-561-3652; www.sequoiavillageinn.com; 45971 Sierra Dr; d $120-235; 🅿️🐾📶📺🌳) These 10 pretty modern cottages, cabins and chalets (many with kitchens), border the park and are great for families or groups. Most have outdoor woodsy decks and BBQs, and the largest can sleep 12.

Buckeye Tree Lodge MOTEL $$
(✆559-561-5900; www.buckeyetreelodge.com; 46000 Sierra Dr; d incl breakfast $125-150; 🅿️📶🐾📺) Sit out on your grassy back patio or perch on the balcony and watch the river case through a maze of boulders. Modern white-brick motel rooms, some with kitchenettes, feel airy and bright.

We Three Bakery & Restaurant CAFE $
(43368 Sierra Dr; mains $6-11; ⊙7am-4pm; 📶) Cinnamon French toast, biscuits with gravy and diner-style coffee lure in the breakfast crowd, while hot and cold sandwiches on blindingly bright Fiesta-ware make it a delish lunch spot. Chow down on the outdoor patio under a shady oak.

River View Restaurant & Lounge AMERICAN $$
(42323 Sierra Dr; mains lunch $6-12, dinner $12-26; ⊙6:30am-9pm, to 10pm Fri & Sat, bar open late) Colorful honky-tonk with great back patio; live music Fridays and Saturdays.

ⓘ Information

Lodgepole Village has an ATM, and there's free wi-fi at Wuksachi Lodge.

Foothills Visitor Center (✆559-565-3135; ⊙8am-4:30pm, to 6pm late May-early Sep) One mile north of the Ash Mountain entrance.

Lodgepole Visitor Center (✆559-565-4436; ⊙9am-4:30pm mid-Apr–mid-May, from 8am mid-May–late Jun & early Sep–mid-Oct, 7am-

---

DON'T MISS

BUCK ROCK LOOKOUT

Built in 1923, this active **fire lookout** (www.buckrock.org; ⊙9:30am-6pm Jul-Oct) is one of the finest restored watchtowers you could ever hope to visit. Staffed in fire season, its 172 stairs lead to a dollhouse-sized wooden cab on a dramatic 8500ft granite rise with panoramic forest views. To reach it from General Hwy, go about 1 mile north of the Montecito Lake Resort and then east onto Big Meadows Rd (FS road 14S11). At approximately 2.5 miles, turn north on the signed dirt road (FS road 13S04) and follow signs another 3 miles to the lookout parking area.

WINTER FUN

In winter, a thick blanket of snow drapes over trees and meadows, the pace of activity slows and a hush falls over the roads and trails. Note that snow often closes Generals Hwy between Grant Grove and Giant Forest and that tire chains may be required at any time. These can usually be rented near the parks' entrances, although you're not supposed to put them on rental cars. For up-to-date road conditions call ☎559-565-3341 or check www.nps.gov/seki.

Snowshoeing and cross-country skiing are both hugely popular activities, with 50 miles of marked but ungroomed trails crisscrossing the Grant Grove and Giant Forest areas. Winter road closures also make for excellent cross-country skiing and snowshoeing on Sequoia's Moro Rock–Crescent Meadow Rd, Kings Canyons' Panoramic Point Rd and the Sequoia National Forest's Big Meadows Rd. Trail maps are available at the visitors centers, and park rangers lead free snowshoe tours (equipment included). Tree-marked trails connect with those in the Giant Sequoia National Monument and the 30 miles of groomed terrain maintained by the private **Montecito Lake Resort** (☎559-565-3388, 800-227-9900; www.montecitosequoia.com; 8000 Generals Hwy). Equipment rentals are available at Grant Grove Village, the Wuksachi Lodge and the Montecito Lake Resort. There are also snow-play areas near Columbine and Big Stump in the Grant Grove region and at Wolverton Meadow in Sequoia.

In winter, cross-country skiers with reservations can sleep in one of the 10 bunks at **Pear Lake Ski Hut** (☎559-565-3759; www.sequoiahistory.org; dm $40; mid-Dec–late Apr), a 1940-era pine-and-granite building run by the Sequoia Natural History Association. You'll be glad to see it after the strenuous 6-mile cross-country ski or snowshoe trek from Wolverton Meadow. Reservations are assigned by lottery in November. Call or check the website for details.

6pm late Jun-early Sep) Maps, information, exhibits, Crystal Cave tickets and wilderness permits.

Mineral King Ranger Station (☎559-565-3768; 8am-4pm late May-early Sep) Twenty-four miles east of Generals Hwy; wilderness permits and campground availability info.

ℹ Getting There & Around

Coming from the south, Hwy 198 runs north from Visalia through Three Rivers past Mineral King Rd to the Ash Mountain entrance. Beyond here the road continues as the Generals Hwy, a narrow and windy road snaking all the way into Kings Canyon National Park, where it joins the Kings Canyon Scenic Byway (Hwy 180) near the western Big Stump entrance. Vehicles over 22ft long may have trouble negotiating the steep road with its many hairpin curves. Budget about one hour to drive from the entrance to the Giant Forest/Lodgepole area and another hour from there to Grant Grove Village in Kings Canyon.

Sequoia Shuttle (☎877-287-4453; www. sequoiashuttle.com; one way/round-trip $7.50/15; late May-late Sep) buses run five times daily between Visalia and the Giant Forest Museum (2½ hours) via Three Rivers; reservations required.

Shuttle buses run every 15 minutes from the Giant Forest Museum to Moro Rock and Crescent Meadow or to the General Sherman Tree parking areas and Lodgepole Village. Another route links Lodgepole, Wuksachi Lodge and Dorst Creek Campground every 30 minutes. All routes are free and currently operate from late May to late September.

EASTERN SIERRA

Cloud-dappled hills and sun-streaked mountaintops dabbed with snow typify the landscape of the Eastern Sierra, where slashing peaks – many over 14,000ft – rush abruptly upward from the arid expanses of the Great Basin and Mojave deserts. It's a dramatic juxtaposition that makes for a potent cocktail of scenery. Pine forests, lush meadows, ice-blue lakes, simmering hot springs and glacier-gouged canyons are only some of the beautiful sights you'll find in this region.

The Eastern Sierra Scenic Byway, officially known as Hwy 395, runs the entire length of the range. Turnoffs dead-ending at the foot of the mountains deliver you to pristine wilderness and countless trails, including the famous Pacific Crest Trail, John Muir Trail and main Mt Whitney Trail. The most important portals are the towns of Bridgeport, Mammoth Lakes, Bishop and Lone Pine. Note that in winter, when traffic thins, many facilities are closed.

Locally produced and available throughout the region, Sierra Maps' *Eastern Sierra: Bridgeport to Lone Pine* recreation and road map shows hot springs, ghost towns, hiking trails and climbing areas. Check out www.thesierraweb.com for area events and links to local visitor information.

❶ Getting There & Around

The Eastern Sierra is easiest to explore under your own steam, although it's possible to access the area by public transportation. Buses operated by **Eastern Sierra Transit Authority** (☎760-872-1901, 800-922-1930; www.easternsierratransitauthority.com) make round-trips between Lone Pine and Reno ($54, six hours) on Monday, Tuesday, Thursday and Friday, stopping at all Hwy 395 towns in between. Fares depend on distance, and reservations are recommended. There's also an express bus between Mammoth and Bishop ($6.50, one hour, three times daily) that operates Monday through Friday.

In the summer, connect to Yosemite via YARTS bus (see p414) in Mammoth Lakes or Lee Vining.

Mono Lake Area

BRIDGEPORT

Barely three blocks long, set amid open high valley and in view of the peaks of Sawtooth Ridge, Bridgeport flaunts classic western flair with charming old storefronts and a homey ambience. Most everything shuts down or cuts back hours for the brutal winters, but the rest of the year the town is a magnet for anglers, hikers, climbers and hot-spring devotees. Stop by the **Bridgeport Ranger Station & Visitor Center** (☎760-932-7070; www.fs.usda.gov/htnf; Hwy 395; ☺8am-4:30pm daily Jul & Aug, 8am-4:30pm Mon-Fri

Sep-Jun) for maps, information and Hoover Wilderness permits.

◉ Sights & Activities

Mono County Courthouse   HISTORIC BUILDING
(☺9am-5pm Mon-Fri) The gavel has been dropped since 1880 at the courthouse, an all-white Italianate dreamboat surrounded by a gracious lawn and a wrought-iron fence. On the street behind it, look for the Old County Jail, a spartan facility fashioned with iron latticework doors and stone walls 2ft thick. Unlucky inmates overnighted in its six cells from 1883 until 1964.

Mono County Museum   MUSEUM
(☎760-932-5281; www.monocomuseum.org; Emigrant St; adult/child $2/1; ☺9am-4pm Tue-Sat Jun-Sep) Two blocks away from the courthouse, in a schoolhouse of the same age, this museum has mining artifacts on display from all the local ghost towns, plus a room of fine Paiute baskets.

Travertine Hot Spring   HOT SPRING
A bit south of town, head here to watch a panoramic Sierra sunset from three hot pools set amid impressive rock formations. To get there, turn east on Jack Sawyer Rd just before the ranger station, then follow the dirt road uphill for about 1 mile.

If you're trolling for trout, try the **Bridgeport Reservoir** and the **East Walker River**. For information and fishing gear, stop by **Ken's Sporting Goods** (☎760-932-7707; www.kenssport.com; 258 Main St; ☺7am-8pm Mon-Thu, to 9pm Fri & Sat mid-Apr–mid-Nov, 9am-4pm Tue-Sat mid-Nov–mid-Apr).

🛏 Sleeping & Eating

Redwood Motel   MOTEL $
(☎760-932-7060, 888-932-3292; www.redwoodmotel.net; 425 Main St; d from $59-89; ☺Apr-Nov; ❄️🐾❓) A bucking bronco, an ox in a Ha

---

TIRED OF TAHOE?

To throw a few snowballs without blowing your family's budget or plodding along in weekend traffic, aim for some of California's 19 maintained **sno-parks** (http://ohv.parks.ca.gov/?page_id=1233; day pass/season permit per vehicle $5/25). Clustered along Sierra highways, these inexpensive winter activity parks offer opportunities for raucous sledding, serene cross-country ski touring or unhurried snowperson construction.

Or consider some of the smaller ski resorts. In addition to cheaper lift tickets, **Bear Valley** (Map p398; www.bearvalley.com; Hwy 4) has its own snow play area, **Dodge Ridge** (Map p398; www.dodgeridge.com; Hwy 108) has extensive get-to-know-the-snow lessons for kids, and **China Peak** (Map p398; www.skichinapeak.com; Hwy 168) gets sparse crowds and is nowhere near the congested Tahoe-bound freeways.

Mono Lake Area

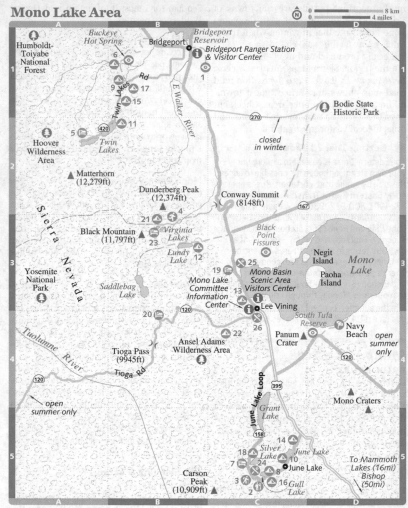

waiian shirt and other wacky farm animal sculptures provide a cheerful welcome to this little motel. Rooms are spotless and your dog-friendly host is super helpful in dispensing local area tips.

Bodie Victorian Hotel HISTORIC HOTEL **$**
(☎760-932-7020; www.bodievictorianhotel.com; 85 Main St; r $50-90; ⊙May-Oct) Go back to the 1800s in this curious building transplanted from Bodie (p432) that's completely furnished with antiques and rumored to be haunted. The bold Victorian wallpaper and striking bordello accoutrements more than make up for the slightly run-down feel. If

no one's there, poke your head inside the Sportsmens Bar & Grill next door to rustle up an employee.

Rhino's Bar & Grille AMERICAN **$**
(247 Main St; mains $9-20; ⊙10am-9pm Sun-Thu, to 10pm Fri & Sat May-Oct, 11am-8pm Nov-Dec & Mar-Apr) Folks seek out Rhino's freshly ground burgers and its smoldering chicken wings in nitro sauce. A local favorite decorated with license plates and beer taps suspended from the ceiling, it has good prices and a big selection of sandwiches, salads, steaks and pizzas (dinner only). Also has a bar and pool table.

Mono Lake Area

Hays Street Cafe AMERICAN $
(www.haysstreetcafe.com; 21 Hays St; mains under $10; ⊙6am-2pm May-Oct, 7am-1pm Nov-Apr) On the south end of town, this country-style place prides itself on its many homemade items, including its biscuits and gravy, and cinnamon rolls as big as bricks.

Pop's Galley AMERICAN $
(www.popsgalley.com; 247 Main St; mains $6-10; ⊙7am-9pm late May-early Sep, otherwise variable hours) Finger-lickin' fish and chips.

TWIN LAKES
Eager anglers line the shoreline of Twin Lakes, a gorgeous duo of basins cradled by the fittingly named Sawtooth Ridge. The area's famous for its fishing – especially since some lucky guy bagged the state's largest ever brown trout here in 1987 (it weighed in at a hefty 26lb). Lower Twin is quieter, while Upper Twin allows boating and waterskiing. Other activities include mountain-biking and, of course, hiking in the Hoover Wilderness Area and on into the eastern, lake-riddled reaches of Yosemite National Park. The main trailhead is at the end of Twin Lakes Rd just past Annett's Mono Village; weekly overnight parking is $10 per vehicle.

Twin Lakes Rd (Rte 420) runs through pastures and foothills for about 10 miles before reaching Lower Twin Lake. The road is a satisfying route for moderately fit cyclists, with mostly level terrain and heavenly scenery.

A stroll down a loose hillside brings you to out-of-the-way **Buckeye Hot Spring**, though it can get crowded. The water emerges piping hot from a steep hillside and cools as it trickles down into several rock pools right by the side of lively Buckeye Creek, which is handy for taking a cooling dip. One pool is partially tucked into a small cave made from a rock overhang. Clothing is optional.

To get there, turn right at Doc & Al's Resort (7 miles from Hwy 395), driving 3 miles on a (momentarily paved and then) graded dirt road. Cross the bridge at Buckeye Creek (at 2.5 miles), and bear right at the Y-junction, following signs to the hot spring. Go uphill a half mile until you see a flattish parking area on your right. Follow a trail down to the pools.

If you go left at the signed Y-junction instead, a road goes 2 miles to **Buckeye Campground** (tent & RV sites $17; ⊙May–mid-Oct), with tables, fire grates, potable water and toilets. You can also camp for free in undeveloped spots along Buckeye Creek on both sides of the creek bridge.

Honeymoon Flat, Robinson Creek, Paha, Crags and Lower Twin Lakes are all **USFS campgrounds** (☏800-444-7275; www.recreation.gov; tent & RV sites $17-20; ⊙mid-May–Sep) set among Jeffrey pine and sagebrush along Robinson Creek and Lower Twin Lake. All have flush toilets except for Honeymoon Flat, which has vault toilets.

WILDERNESS PERMITS: EASTERN SIERRA

Free wilderness permits for overnight camping are required year-round in the Ansel Adams, John Muir, Golden Trout and Hoover Wilderness areas. For the first three, trailhead quotas are in effect from May through October and about 60% of the quota may be reserved for a $5 fee (per person) from the Inyo National Forest Wilderness Permit Office (760-873-2483). From November to April, you can pick up permits at any ranger station mentioned in this section. If you find the station closed, look for self-issue permits outside the office. Permits are expected to be available online by the time you read this, so call or check www.fs.fed.us/r5/inyo for the latest.

Permits for the Hoover Wilderness (part of both the Inyo and the Humboldt-Toiyabe National Forests) can also be obtained at the Tuolumne Meadows Wilderness Center (p414) and the Bridgeport Ranger Station and Visitor Center (p429).

Twin Lakes Rd dead-ends at Annett's Mono Village (760-932-7071; www.monovillage.com; tent sites $18, RV sites with hookups $29, r $68, cabin $80-185; late Apr-Oct;), a huge and rather chaotic tumbledown resort on Upper Twin Lake. It has cheap but cramped lodging, and a kitschy low-ceilinged cafe (mains $8-16) studded with taxidermied fish. Pay showers available.

BODIE STATE HISTORIC PARK

For a time warp back to the Gold Rush era, swing by Bodie (760-647-6445; www.parks.ca.gov/?page_id=509; Hwy 270; adult/child $7/5; 9am-6pm Jun-Aug, to 3pm Sep-May), one of the West's most authentic and best-preserved ghost towns. Gold was first discovered here in 1859, and within 20 years the place grew from a rough mining camp to an even rougher boomtown with a population of 10,000 and a reputation for unbridled lawlessness. Fights and murders took place almost daily, the violence no doubt fueled by liquor dispensed in the town's 65 saloons, some of which did double duty as brothels, gambling halls or opium dens. The hills disgorged some $35 million worth of gold and silver in the 1870s and '80s, but when production plummeted, so did the population, and eventually the town was abandoned to the elements.

About 200 weather-beaten buildings still sit frozen in time in this cold, barren and windswept valley heaped with tailing piles. Peering through dusty windows you'll see stocked stores, furnished homes, a schoolhouse with desks and books, and workshops filled with tools. The jail is still there, as are the fire station, churches, a bank vault and many other buildings. The former Miners' Union Hall now houses a museum and visitors center (9am to one hour before park closes). Rangers conduct free general tours. In summertime, they also offer tours of the landscape and the cemetery; call for details. The second Saturday of August is Friends of Bodie Day (www.bodiefoundation.org), with stagecoach rides, history presentations and lots of devotees in period costumes.

Bodie is about 13 miles east of Hwy 395 via Rte 270; the last 3 miles are unpaved. Although the park is open year-round, the road is usually closed in winter and early spring, so you'd have to don snowshoes or cross-country skis to get there.

VIRGINIA LAKES

South of Bridgeport, Hwy 395 gradually arrives at its highest point, Conway Summit (8148ft), where you'll be whipping out your camera to capture the awe-inspiring panorama of Mono Lake, backed by the Mono Craters, and June and Mammoth Mountains.

Also at the top is the turnout for Virginia Lakes Rd, which parallels Virginia Creek for about 6 miles to a cluster of lakes flanked by Dunderberg Peak (12,374ft) and Black Mountain (11,797ft). A trailhead at the end of the road gives access to the Hoover Wilderness Area and the Pacific Crest Trail. The trail continues down Cold Canyon through to Yosemite National Park. Check with the folks at the Virginia Lakes Resort (760-647-6484; www.virginialakesresort.com; cabins from $107; mid-May–mid-Oct;), opened in 1923, for maps and tips about specific trails. The resort itself has snug cabins, a cafe and a general store. Cabins sleep two to 12 people, and usually have a minimum stay.

There's also the option of camping at Trumbull Lake Campground (800-444-7275; www.recreation.gov; tent & RV sites $17; mid-Jun–mid-Oct). The shady sites here are located among lodgepole pines.

Nearby, **Virginia Lakes Pack Station** (☎760-937-0326; www.virginialakes.com) offers horseback riding trips.

LUNDY LAKE

After Conway Summit, Hwy 395 twists down steeply into the Mono Basin. Before reaching Mono Lake, Lundy Lake Rd meanders west of the highway for about 5 miles to Lundy Lake. This is a gorgeous spot, especially in spring when wildflowers carpet the canyon along Mill Creek, or in fall when it is brightened by colorful foliage. Before reaching the lake, the road skirts first-come, first-served **Lundy Canyon Campground** (tent & RV sites $12; ☺mid-April–mid-Nov), with vault toilets but no water. At the end of the lake, there's a ramshackle resort on the site of an 1880s mining town, plus a small store and boat rentals.

Past the resort, a dirt road leads into **Lundy Canyon** where, in 2 miles, it dead-ends at the trailhead for the Hoover Wilderness Area. A moderate 1.5-mile hike follows Mill Creek to the 200ft-high **Lundy Falls**. Ambitious types can continue on via Lundy Pass to Saddlebag Lake.

LEE VINING

Hwy 395 skirts the western bank of Mono Lake, rolling into the gateway town of Lee Vining where you can eat, sleep, gas up (for a pretty penny) and catch Hwy 120 to Yosemite National Park when the road's open. A superb base for exploring Mono Lake, Lee Vining is only 12 miles (about a 30-minute drive) from Yosemite's Tioga Pass entrance. **Lee Vining Canyon** is a popular location for **ice climbing**.

In town, take a quick look at the **Upside-Down House**, a kooky tourist attraction created by silent film actress Nellie Bly O'Bryan. Originally situated along Tioga Rd, it now resides in a park in front of the tiny **Mono Basin Historical Society Museum** (www.monobasinhs.org; donation $2; ☺10am-4pm Thu-Mon, from noon Sun mid-May–early Oct). To find it, turn east on 1st St and go one block to Mattley Ave.

🛏 Sleeping & Eating

Lodging rates drop when Tioga Pass is closed.

TOP CHOICE **Whoa Nellie Deli** DELI $$
(www.whoanelliedeli.com; near junction of Hwys 120 & 395; mains $8-19; ☺7am-9pm mid-Apr–Oct) Great food in a gas station? Come on... No, really, you gotta try this amazing kitchen where chef Matt 'Tioga' Toomey feeds delicious fish tacos, wild buffalo meatloaf and other tasty morsels to locals and clued-in passersby.

El Mono Motel MOTEL $
(☎760-647-6310; www.elmonomotel.com; 51 Hwy 395; r $69-99; ☺May-Oct; 🛜) Grab a board game or soak up some mountain sunshine in this friendly flower-ringed place attached to an excellent cafe. In operation since 1927, and often booked solid, each of its 11 simple rooms (a few share bathrooms) is unique, decorated with vibrant and colorful art and fabrics.

Historic Mono Inn CALIFORNIAN $$$
(☎760-647-6581; www.monoinn.com; 55620 Hwy 395; dinner mains $8-25; ☺11am-9pm May-Dec) A restored 1922 lodge owned by the family of photographer Ansel Adams, this is now an elegant lakefront restaurant with outstanding California comfort food, fabulous wine and views to match. Browse the 1000-volume cookbook collection upstairs, and stop in for music on the creekside terrace. It's located about 5 miles north of Lee Vining. Reservations recommended.

Tioga Lodge CABINS $$
(☎760-647-6423; www.tiogalodgeatmonolake.com; cabin $129-159; ☺mid-May–mid-Oct; @🛜) About 2 miles north of Lee Vining, this cluster of cheery cabins has verandas overlooking Mono Lake. The **restaurant** (dinner mains $13-25) and registration buildings were moved here from Bodie in 1897.

Tioga Pass Resort CABINS $$
(tiogapassresortllc@gmail.com; Hwy 120; r $125, cabin $160-240; ☺May–mid-Oct) Founded in 1914 and located 2 miles east of Tioga Pass, this resort attracts a fiercely loyal clientele to its basic and cozy cabins beside Lee Vining Creek. The thimble-sized **cafe** (mains lunch $8-9, dinner $15) serves excellent fare all day at a few tables and a broken horseshoe counter, with a house pastry chef concocting dozens of freshly made desserts. Reserve lodging via email.

USFS campgrounds CAMPGROUNDS $
(www.fs.usda.gov/inyo; tent & RV sites $15-19) Towards Yosemite, there are a handful of first-come, first-served campgrounds along Tioga Rd (Hwy 120) and Lee Vining Creek, most with vault toilets and about half with potable water.

Mono Vista RV Park CAMPGROUND $
(☎760-647-6401; Hwy 395; showers $2.50; ⊘9am-6pm Apr-Oct) This campground has the closest pay showers to Tuolumne Meadows.

MONO LAKE

North America's second-oldest lake is a quiet and mysterious expanse of deep blue water, whose glassy surface reflects jagged Sierra peaks, young volcanic cones and the unearthly tufa (too-fah) towers that make the lake so distinctive. Jutting from the water like drip sand castles, tufas form when calcium bubbles up from subterranean springs and combines with carbonate in the alkaline lake waters.

In *Roughing It,* Mark Twain described Mono Lake as California's 'dead sea.' Hardly. The brackish water teems with buzzing alkali flies and brine shrimp, both considered delicacies by dozens of migratory bird species that return here year after year. So do about 85% of the state's nesting population of California gulls, which takes over the lake's volcanic islands from April to August. Mono Lake has also been at the heart of an environmental controversy (see boxed text, p435).

◉ Sights & Activities

South Tufa Reserve NATURE RESERVE
(☎office 760-647-6331; adult/child $3/free) Tufa spires ring the lake, but the biggest grove is on the south rim with a mile-long interpretive trail. Ask about ranger-led tours at the Mono Basin Scenic Area Visitors Center (p434). To get to the reserve, head south from Lee Vining on Hwy 395 for 6 miles, then east on Hwy 120 for 5 miles to the dirt road leading to a parking lot.

Navy Beach BEACH
The best place for swimming is at Navy Beach, just east of the reserve. It's also the best place to put in canoes or kayaks. From late June to early September, the **Mono Lake Committee** (☎760-647-6595; www.monolake.org/visit/canoe; tours $25; ⊘8am, 9:30am & 11am Sat & Sun) operates one-hour canoe tours around the tufas. Half-day kayak tours along the shore or out to Paoha Island are also offered by **Caldera Kayaks** (☎760-934-1691; www.calderakayak.com; tours $75; ⊘mid-May–mid-Oct). Both require reservations.

Panum Crater NATURAL FEATURE
Rising above the south shore, Panum Crater is the youngest (about 640 years old), smallest and most accessible of the craters that string south toward Mammoth Mountain. A panoramic trail circles the crater rim (about 30 to 45 minutes), and a short but steep 'plug trail' puts you at the crater's core. A dirt road leads to the trailhead from Hwy 120, about 3 miles east of the junction with Hwy 395.

Black Point Fissures NATURAL FEATURE
On the north shore of the lake are the Black Point Fissures, narrow crags that opened when lava mass cooled and contracted about 13,000 years ago. Access is from three places: east of Mono Lake County Park, from the west shore off Hwy 395, or south off Hwy 167. Check at the Mono Basin Scenic Area Visitors Center (p434) for specific directions.

❶ Information

Mono Basin Scenic Area Visitors Center
(☎760-647-3044; www.fs.usda.gov/inyo; Hwy 395, ⊘8am-5pm mid-Apr–Nov) Half a mile north of Lee Vining, this center has maps, interpretive displays, wilderness permits, bear-canister rentals, a bookstore and a 20-minute movie about Mono Lake.

Mono Lake Committee Information Center
(☎760-647-6595; www.monolake.org; cnr Hwy 395 & 3rd St; ⊘9am-5pm late Oct–mid-Jun, 8am-9pm mid-Jun–Sep) Internet access ($2 per 15 minutes), maps, books, free 30-minute video about Mono Lake and passionate, preservation-minded staff. Public restroom too.

JUNE LAKE LOOP

Under the shadow of massive Carson Peak (10,909ft), the stunning 14-mile June Lake Loop (Hwy 158) meanders through a picture-perfect horseshoe canyon, past the relaxed resort town of June Lake and four sparkling, fish-rich lakes: Grant, Silver, Gull and June. It's especially scenic in fall when the basin is ablaze with golden aspens. Catch the loop a few miles south of Lee Vining.

🏃 Activities

June Lake is backed by the Ansel Adams Wilderness area, which runs into Yosemite National Park. **Rush Creek Trailhead** has a day-use parking lot, posted maps and self-registration permits. Gem and Agnew Lakes make spectacular day hikes, while Thousand Island and Emerald Lake (both on the Pacific Crest/John Muir Trail) are stunning overnight destinations.

Boat and tackle rentals, as well as fishing licenses, are available at five marinas.

June Mountain Ski Area SKIING
(☎24hr snow info 760-934-2224, 888-586-3686; www.junemountain.com; lift tickets adult/child

WATER FOR A THIRSTY GIANT: A TALE OF TWO LAKES

Los Angeles may be 250 miles away, but its history and fate are closely linked with that of the Eastern Sierra. When LA's population surged around the turn of the 20th century, it became clear that groundwater levels would soon be inadequate to meet the city's needs, let alone sustain future growth. Water had to be imported, and Fred Eaton, a former LA mayor, and William Mulholland, head of the LA Department of Water & Power (LADWP), knew just how and where to get it: by aqueduct from the Owens Valley, which receives enormous runoff from the Sierra Nevada.

The fact that the Owens Valley itself was settled by farmers who needed the water for irrigation didn't bother either of the two men. Nor did it cause qualms in the least with the federal government, which actively supported the city's less-than-ethical maneuvering in acquiring land and securing water rights in the valley area. Voters gave Mulholland the $24.5 million he needed to build the aqueduct and work began in 1908. An amazing feat of engineering – crossing barren desert as well as rugged mountain terrain – the aqueduct opened to great fanfare on November 5, 1913. The Owens Valley, though, would never be the same.

With most of its inflows diverted, Owens Lake, which had once been 30ft deep and an important stopover for migrating waterfowl, quickly shriveled up. A bitter feud between local farmers and ranchers and the city grew violent when some of the opponents tried to sabotage the aqueduct by blowing up a section of it. All to no avail. By 1928 LA owned 90% of the water in Owens Valley and agriculture was effectively dead. These early water wars formed the basis for the 1974 movie *Chinatown*.

But as LA kept burgeoning, its water needs also grew. In the 1930s, the LADWP bought up water rights in the Mono Basin and extended the aqueduct by 105 miles, diverting four of the five streams feeding into Mono Lake. Not surprisingly, the volume of water in the lake dropped significantly, doubling the salinity and posing a major threat to its ecological balance.

In 1976 environmentalist David Gaines began to study the concerns surrounding the lake's depletion and found that, if left untouched, it would totally dry up within about 20 years. To avert this certain disaster, he formed the Mono Lake Committee in 1978 and enlisted the help of the National Audubon Society. Years of lobbying and legal action followed, but eventually the committee succeeded. In 1994 the California State Water Resources Control Board mandated the LADWP to substantially reduce its diversions and allow the lake level to rise by 20ft. In July 2011 its surface stood at 6383ft, still about 8ft short of the goal.

The Owens Lake, meanwhile, was not as lucky. It remains a mostly barren lakebed and the site of alkali dust storms, which are especially harmful to people with respiratory problems. A plan finalized in 1999, however, saw 30 sq miles of the lake (out of 100) shallow flooded, and by 2006 this had largely cleared the dust storms and re-created an important habitat for waterfowl.

Though conditions and habitat have improved, the Owens Valley Committee (www.ovcweb.org) and Sierra Club continue to closely monitor the LADWP, bringing the department to court regularly to force its compliance on mitigation agreements.

$69/35) Winter fun concentrates in this area, which is smaller and less crowded than nearby Mammoth Mountain and perfect for beginner and intermediate skiers. Some 35 trails crisscross 500 acres of terrain served by seven lifts, including two high-speed quads. Boarders can get their adrenaline flowing at three terrain parks with a kick-ass superpipe.

Ernie's Tackle & Ski Shop OUTDOOR EQUIPMENT (☏760-648-7756; www.erniestackleandski.com; 2604 Hwy 158) One of the most established outfitters in June Lake village.

🛏 Sleeping & Eating

Double Eagle Resort & Spa RESORT $$$ (☏760-648-7004; www.doubleeagleresort.com; 5587 Hwy 158; r incl breakfast $199, cabins $349; 🖵❄🐾) A swanky spot for these parts. The sleek two-bedroom log cabins and balconied hotel rooms lack no comfort, while worries disappear at the elegant spa. Its **restaurant** (dinner mains $15-30; ⊘8am-9pm) exudes rustic elegance, with cozy booths, a high ceiling and a huge fireplace.

June Lake Motel MOTEL $$
(✆760-648-7547, www.junelakemotel.com; 2716 Hwy 158; r with/without kitchen $115/105; @⊚) Enormous rooms – most with full kitchens – catch delicious mountain breezes and sport attractive light-wood furniture. There's a fish-cleaning sink and BBQs, plus a book library and a friendly resident Newfoundland dog.

USFS Campgrounds CAMPGROUNDS $
(✆800-444-7275; www.recreation.gov; tent & RV sites $20; ⊘mid-Apr–Oct) These include: June Lake, Oh! Ridge, Silver Lake, Gull Lake and Reversed Creek. The first three accept reservations; Silver Lake has gorgeous mountain views.

Carson Peak Inn AMERICAN $$
(✆760-648-7575; Hwy 158 btwn Gull & Silver Lakes; meals $19-34; ⊘5-10pm, shorter winter hours) Inside a cozy house with a fireplace, this restaurant is much beloved for its tasty old-time indulgences, such as beef brochette, pan-fried trout and chopped sirloin steak. Portion sizes can be ordered for regular or 'hearty' appetites.

Tiger Bar AMERICAN $$
(www.thetigerbarcafe.com; 2620 Hwy 158; mains $8-17; ⊘8am-10pm) After a day on slopes or trails, people gather at the long bar or around the pool table of this no-nonsense, no-attitude place. The kitchen feeds all appetites, with burgers, salads, tacos and other tasty grub, including homemade fries.

eastsierra.net CAFE $
(2775 Hwy 158; ⊘6am-5pm; ⊚) Internet cafe with organic coffees and teas.

Mammoth Lakes

This is a small mountain resort town endowed with larger-than-life scenery – active outdoorsy folks worship at the base of its dizzying 11,053ft Mammoth Mountain. Everlasting powder clings to these slopes, and when the snow finally fades, the area's an outdoor wonderland of mountain-bike trails, excellent fishing, endless alpine hiking and blissful hidden spots for hot-spring soaking. The Eastern Sierra's commercial hub and a four-season resort, outdoorsy Mammoth is backed by a ridgeline of jutting peaks, ringed by clusters of crystalline alpine lakes and enshrouded by the dense Inyo National Forest.

◉ Sights

TOP CHOICE **Earthquake Fault** NATURAL FEATURE
(Map p437) On Minaret Rd, about 1 mile west of the Mammoth Scenic Loop, detour to gape at Earthquake Fault, a sinuous fissure half a mile long gouging a crevice up to 20ft deep into the earth. Ice and snow often linger at the bottom until late summer, and Native Americans and early settlers used it to store perishable food.

Mammoth Museum MUSEUM
(Map p438; ✆760-934-6918; 5489 Sherwin Creek Rd; suggested donation $3; ⊘10am-6pm mid-May–Sep) For a walk down memory lane, stop by this little museum inside a historic log cabin.

⚐ Activities

Skiing & Snowboarding

There's free cross-country skiing along the 19 miles of nongroomed trails of the **Blue Diamond Trails System**, which winds through several patches of scenic forest around town. Pick up a map at the Mammoth Lakes Welcome Center (p441) or check out www.mammothnordic.com.

Mammoth Mountain SKIING
(Map p437; ✆760-934-2571, 800-626-6684, 24hr snow report 888-766-9778; www.mammothmountain.com; lift tickets adult/senior & child $92/46) This is a skiers' and snowboarders' dream resort, where sunny skies, a reliably long season (usually from November to June) and over 3500 acres of fantastic tree-line and open-bowl skiing are a potent cocktail. At the top you'll be dealing with some gnarly, nearly vertical chutes. The other stats are just as impressive: 3100 vertical feet, 150 trails, 29 lifts (including 10 quads). Boarders, meanwhile, will find world-class challenges in nine terrain parks with three intense superpipes and urban-style jibs.

There are five hubs at the base of the mountain: **Main Lodge** (Map p437), **Canyon Lodge** (Map p438), **Eagle Lodge** (Map p438), the **Mill Cafe** (Map p437) and the **Mountain Center** (Map p438), each with ticket offices and parking lots. Free ski shuttles pick up throughout town. Alternatively, hop on the **Village Gondola** (Map p438),

Mammoth Lakes Area

which whisks you up to Canyon Lodge – the base of several chair lifts – in six minutes.

Tamarack Cross-Country Ski Center
SKIING
(Map p437; ☏760-934-2442; Lake Mary Rd; all-day trail pass adult/child/senior $27/15/21; ⏱8:30am-5pm) Let the town shuttle take you to the Tamarack Lodge, which has almost 20 miles of meticulously groomed track around Twin Lakes and the lakes basin. The terrain is also great for snowshoeing. Rentals and lessons are available.

Cycling & Mountain-Biking
Stop at the Mammoth Lakes Welcome Center (p441) for a free map with area route descriptions and updated trail conditions.

Lakes Basin Path
CYCLING
(Map p438; www.mammothtrails.org) A local recreational umbrella group has been developing a fantastic new system of bicycle paths.

One completed segment is the 5.3-mile Lakes Basin Path, which begins at the southwest corner of Lake Mary and Minaret Rds and heads uphill (at a 5% to 10% grade) to Horseshoe Lake, skirting lovely lakes and accessing open mountain views. For a one-way ride, use the free Lakes Basin Trolley, which tows a 12-bicycle trailer.

Mammoth Mountain Bike Park
MOUNTAIN-BIKING
(Map p437; ☏800-626-6684; www.mammothmountain.com; day pass adult/child $43/22; ⏱9am-4:30pm Jun-Sep) Come summer, Mammoth Mountain morphs into the massive Mammoth Mountain Bike Park, with more than 80 miles of well-kept single-track trails. Several other trails traverse the surrounding forest. In general, Mammoth-style riding translates into plenty of hills and soft, sandy shoulders, which are best navigated with big knobby tires.

Mammoth Lakes

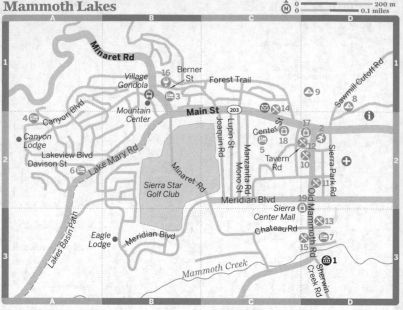

But you don't need wheels (or a medic) to ride the vertiginous **gondola** (adult/senior $23/12) to the apex of the mountain, where there's a cafe and an interpretive center with scopes pointing toward the nearby peaks. And for kids 13 and under, there's a fun **zip line** (1 zip $12, additional $7, ☺summer) behind the Adventure Center.

When the park's open, it runs a free **mountain-bike shuttle** (☺9am-5:30pm) from the Village area to the Main Lodge. Shuttles depart every 30 minutes, and mountain-bikers with paid mountain passes get priority over pedestrians.

Hiking

Mammoth Lakes rubs up against the **Ansel Adams Wilderness** and **John Muir Wilderness** areas, both laced with fabulous trails leading to shimmering lakes, rugged peaks and hidden canyons. Major trailheads leave from the Mammoth Lakes Basin, Reds Meadow and Agnew Meadows; the latter two are accessible only by shuttle (see p441). **Shadow Lake** (off Map p437) is a stunning 7-mile day hike from Agnew Meadows.

Fishing & Boating

From the last Saturday in April, the dozens of lakes that give the town its name lure in fly and trout fishers from near and far.

California fishing licenses are available at sporting goods stores throughout town. For equipment and advice, head to **Troutfitter** (Map p438; ☏760-934-2517; cnr Main St & Old Mammoth Rd) or **Rick's Sports Center** (Map p438; ☏760-934-3416; cnr Main & Center Sts).

The **Pokonobe Store and Marina** (Map p437; ☏760-934-2437; www.pokonoberesort. com), on the north end of Lake Mary, rents motor boats ($20 per hour), rowboats ($10), canoes ($16) and kayaks ($16 to $20). **Caldera Kayaks** (☏760-935-1691; www. calderakayak.com) has single ($30 for a half-day) and double kayaks ($50) for use on Crowley Lake.

🛏 Sleeping

Mammoth B&Bs and inns rarely sell out midweek, when rates tend to be lower. During ski season, reservations are a good idea on weekends and essential during holidays. Many properties offer ski-and-stay packages. Condo rentals often work out cheaper for groups.

Stop by the Mammoth Lakes Welcome Center (p441) or check its website for a full list of campgrounds, dispersed free camping locations (don't forget to pick up a free but mandatory fire permit) and public showers.

Mammoth Lakes

YOSEMITE & THE SIERRA NEVADA MAMMOTH LAKES

Mammoth Creek Inn   INN **$$**
(Map p438; ☑760-934-6162, 800-466-7000; www.
mammothcreekinn.com; 663 Old Mammoth Rd; r
$190-235, with kitchen $277-356; @🐾🛰) It's amen-
ities galore at this pretty inn at the end of
a commercial strip, with down comforters
and fluffy terry robes, as well as a sauna, a
hot tub and a fun pool table loft. The best
rooms overlook the majestic Sherwin Moun-
tains, and some have full kitchens and can
sleep up to six.

TOP
CHOICE Tamarack Lodge & Resort   RESORT **$$**
(Map p437; ☑760-934-2442, 800-626-6684; www.
tamaracklodge.com; lodge r $99-169, cabins $169-
599; @🐾🛰🏊) Kind people run this charming
year-round resort on the shore of Lower
Twin Lake. In business since 1924, the cozy
lodge includes a fireplace, bar, excellent restaurant, 11 rustic rooms and 35 cabins. The
cabins range from very simple to simply
deluxe, and come with full kitchen, private
bathroom, porch and wood-burning stove.
Some can sleep up to 10 people.

Cinnamon Bear Inn   B&B **$$**
(Map p438; ☑760-934-2873, 800-845-2873; www.
cinnamonbearinn.com; 133 Center St; r incl break-
fast $79-179; @🛰) At this down-to-earth inn
you'll sleep like a log in four-poster beds,
and most rooms have cozy gas fireplaces.
Swap stories about the day's adventures
with other guests over homemade refresh-
ments in the afternoon, or soak away sore-
ness in the small outdoor Jacuzzi.

Austria Hof Lodge   LODGE **$$**
(Map p438; ☑760 934 2764; www.austriahof.com;
924 Canyon Blvd; r incl breakfast $130-215; 🛰)
Close to Canyon Lodge, rooms here have
modern knotty pine furniture, thick down
duvets and DVD players. Ski lockers and
a sundeck hot tub make winter stays here
even sweeter. The lodge **restaurant** (dinner
mains $24-37) serves meaty gourmet German
fare in an evocative stained-glass dining
room.

Alpenhof Lodge   HOTEL **$$**
(Map p438; ☑760-934-6330, 800-828-0371; www.
alpenhof-lodge.com; 6080 Minaret Rd; r $159-239;
@🐾🛰) This Euro-flavored inn is a snow-
ball's toss away from the Village and has
fairly nondescript yet comfortable lodge
rooms, plus more luxurious accommoda-
tions with gas fireplaces or kitchens.

Davison Street Guest House   HOSTEL **$**
(Map p438; ☑760-924-2188, reservations 858-
755-8648; www.mammoth-guest.com; 19 Davison
St; dm $35-49, d $75-120; 🛰) A cute, five-room
A-frame chalet hostel on a quiet residential
street, this place has a stocked kitchen, plus
mountain views from the living room with
fireplace or sun deck. There's self-registra-
tion when the manager isn't around.

USFS campgrounds   CAMPGROUNDS **$**
(Maps p437 & p438; ☑877-444-6777; www.recrea
tion.gov; tent & RV sites $20-21; 🐾; ⊘approx mid-
Jun–mid-Sep) About 15 USFS campgrounds
(see 'Recreation' at www.fs.usda.gov/inyo)
are scattered in and around Mammoth

Lakes, all with flush toilets but no showers. Many sites are available on a first-come, first-served basis, and some are reservable. Note that nights get chilly at these elevations, even in July. Campgrounds include: New Shady Rest, Old Shady Rest, Twin Lakes, Lake Mary, Pine City, Coldwater, Lake George, Reds Meadow, Pumice Flat, Minaret Falls, Upper Soda Springs and Agnew Meadows.

✕ Eating & Drinking

Lakefront Restaurant   CALIFORNIAN, FRENCH **$$$**
(Map p437; ☎760-934-3534; www.tamaracklodge. com/lakefront-restaurant; Lakes Loop Rd, Twin Lakes; mains $28-38; ⊙5-9:30pm year-round, plus 11am-2pm summer, closed Tue & Wed in fall & spring) The Tamarack Lodge has an intimate and romantic dining room overlooking Twin Lakes. The chef crafts French–Californian specialties like elk medallions au poivre and heirloom tomatoes with Basque cheese, and the staff are superbly friendly. Reservations recommended.

TOP CHOICE **Skadi**   EUROPEAN **$$$**
(Map p438; ☎760-934-3902; www.skadirestau rant.com; 587 Old Mammoth Rd; mains $24-32; ⊙5:30-9:30pm Wed-Sun) Upstairs in a nondescript office complex, Skadi's 'alpine cuisine' includes dishes like roasted salmon and sausage made from its own ranch-raised venison. Sample its excellent European and California wines and gaze out at the dreamy Sherwin Range vistas. Reservations recommended.

Petra's Bistro & Wine Bar   CALIFORNIAN, FRENCH **$$$**
(Map p438; ☎760-934-3500; www.petrasbistro. com; 6080 Minaret Rd; mains $19-34; ⊙5-9:30pm Tue-Sun) Settle in here for seasonal cuisine and wines recommended by the three staff sommeliers. In wintertime, the best seats in the house are the cozy fireside couches. Start the evening with a cheese course and choose from 28 wines available by the glass or 250 vintages by the bottle. Reservations recommended.

Good Life Cafe   CALIFORNIAN **$**
(Map p438; www.mammothgoodlifecafe.com; Mammoth Mall, 126 Old Mammoth Rd; mains $8-10; ⊙6:30am-3pm; ☑) Healthy food, generously filled veggie wraps and big bowls of salad make this a perennially popular place. The front patio is blissful for a long brunch on a warm day.

☑ **Stellar Brew**   CAFE **$**
(Map p438; www.stellarbrewnaturalcafe.com; 3280 B Main St; salads & sandwiches $5.50; ⊙5:30am-8pm; ☑☑) Proudly locavore and mostly organic, settle into a comfy sofa here for your daily dose of locally roasted coffee, homemade granola and scrumptious vegan (and some gluten-free) pastries.

Roberto's Cafe   MEXICAN **$$**
(Map p438; www.robertoscafe.com; 271 Old Mammoth Rd; mains $7-15; ⊙11am-8pm, to 10pm winter & summer) Serving Mammoth's hands-down best Mexican food and a selection of more than 30 brands of tequila, this fun restaurant is usually bustling. Locals pack the outdoor deck to look out on a beautiful wildflower garden, or quaff margaritas in the tropical-themed upstairs cantina.

Stove   CAFE **$**
(Map p438; www.thestoverestaurant.com; 644 Old Mammoth Rd; breakfast mains $6-10; ⊙6:30am-2pm & 5-9pm) Great coffee and carbs; try the cinnamon-bread French toast.

Sierra Sundance Whole Foods   HEALTH FOOD **$**
(Map p438; 26 Old Mammoth Rd; ☑) Self-catering vegetarians can stock up on organic produce, bulk foods and tofu at this handy store and deli.

Clocktower Cellar   PUB
(Map p438; www.clocktowercellar.com; 6080 Minaret Rd) In the winter especially, locals throng this half-hidden basement of the Alpenhof Lodge. The ceiling is tiled with a swirl of bottle caps, and the bar stocks 31 beers on tap (in particular German brews) and about 50 bottled varieties.

FREE **Mammoth Brewing Company Tasting Room**   BREWERY
(Map p438; ☎760-934-7141; www.mammothbrew ingco.com; 94 Berner St; ⊙10am-6pm) Free samples anyone? Try some of the dozen brews on tap, then buy some IPA 395 or Double Nut Brown to go.

🛍 Shopping

For outdoor equipment sales and rentals, in-town shops are usually cheaper than at Mammoth Mountain.

Footloose   OUTDOOR EQUIPMENT
(Map p438; ☎760-934-2400; www.footloosesports. com; cnr Main St & Old Mammoth Rd) Full range

DON'T MISS

DEVILS POSTPILE

The most fascinating attraction in Reds Meadow is the surreal volcanic formation of **Devils Postpile National Monument** (Map p437). The 60ft curtains of near-vertical, six-sided basalt columns formed when rivers of molten lava slowed, cooled and cracked with perplexing symmetry. This honeycomb design is best appreciated from atop the columns, reached by a short trail. The columns are an easy, half-mile hike from the **Devils Postpile Ranger Station** (Map p437; ☎760-934-2289; www.nps.gov/depo; ☺9am-5pm summer).

From the monument, a 2.5-mile hike passing through fire-scarred forest leads to the spectacular **Rainbow Falls** (Map p437), where the San Joaquin River gushes over a 101ft basalt cliff. Chances of actually seeing a rainbow forming in the billowing mist are greatest at midday. The falls can also be reached via an easy 1.5-mile walk from the Reds Meadow area, which also has a cafe, store, the **Reds Meadow campground** (Map p437) and a pack station.

of footwear and seasonal equipment; local biking info.

Mammoth Mountaineering Supply
OUTDOOR EQUIPMENT
(Map p438; ☎760-934-4191; www.mammothgear.com; 3189 Main St) Offers friendly advice, topo maps and all-season equipment rentals.

Mammoth Sporting Goods
OUTDOOR EQUIPMENT
(Map p438; ☎760-934-3239; www.mammothsportinggoods.com; Sierra Center Mall, Old Mammoth Rd) Bikes, boards and skis; across from Von's supermarket.

ℹ Information

The **Mammoth Lakes Welcome Center** (☎760-934-2712, 888-466-2666; www.visitmammoth.com; ☺8am-5pm) and the **Mammoth Lakes Ranger Station** (☎760-924-5500; www.fs.fed.us/r5/inyo; ☺8am-5pm) share a building on the north side of Hwy 203. This one-stop information center issues wilderness permits, helps find accommodations and campgrounds, and provides road and trail condition updates. From May through October, when trail quotas are in effect, walk-in wilderness permits are released at 11am the day before; permits are self-issue the rest of the year.

Mammoth Hospital (☎760-934-3311; 85 Sierra Park Rd; ☺24hr) Emergency room.

Mammoth Times (www.mammothtimes.com) Free weekly tabloid.

ℹ Getting There & Away

Mammoth's updated airport **Mammoth Yosemite** (MMH) has a daily nonstop flight to San Francisco, operating winter through to spring on **United** (www.united.com). **Alaska Airlines** (www.alaskaair.com) runs a similar seasonal (and cheaper) San Jose flight and year-round service to Los Angeles. All flights are about an hour. Taxis meet incoming flights, and some lodgings provide free transfers. **Mammoth Taxi** (☎760-934-8294; www.mammoth.taxi.com) does airport runs as well as hiker shuttles throughout the Sierra.

Mammoth is a snap to navigate by public transportation year-round. In the summertime, **YARTS** (☎877-989-2787; www.yarts.com) runs buses to and from Yosemite Valley, and the **Eastern Sierra Transit Authority** (☎800-922-1930; www.easternsierratransitauthority.com) has year-round service along Hwy 395, north to Reno and south to Lone Pine. See p429 for details.

Within Mammoth, a year-round system of free and frequent **bus shuttles** connects the whole town with the Mammoth Mountain lodges; in summer, routes with bicycle trailers service the Lakes Basin and Mammoth Mountain Bike Park.

Around Mammoth Lakes

REDS MEADOW

One of the beautiful and varied landscapes near Mammoth is the Reds Meadow Valley, west of Mammoth Mountain. Drive on Hwy 203 as far as **Minaret Vista** (Map p437) for eye-popping views (best at sunset) of the Ritter Range, the serrated Minarets and the remote reaches of Yosemite National Park.

The road to Reds Meadow is only accessible from about June until September, weather permitting. To minimize impact when it's open, the road is closed to private vehicles beyond Minaret Vista unless you are camping, have lodge reservations or are disabled, in which case you must pay a $10 per car fee. Otherwise you must use a mandatory shuttle bus (Map p437; per adult/child $7/4). It leaves from a lot in front of the Adventure Center approximately every 30 minutes between 7:30am and 7pm (last bus out leaves Reds Meadow at 7:45pm), and you must buy tickets inside before joining the queue. There are also a half dozen direct departures from the Village (on Canyon Blvd, under the gondola) in the morning. The bus stops at trailheads, viewpoints and campgrounds before completing the one-way trip to Reds Meadow (45 minutes to an hour).

The valley road provides access to six campgrounds along the San Joaquin River. Tranquil willow-shaded **Minaret Falls Campground** (Map p437; tent & RV sites $20; 🐾) is a popular fishing spot where the best riverside sites have views of its namesake cascade.

HOT CREEK GEOLOGICAL SITE
For a graphic view of the area's geothermal power, journey a few miles south of Mammoth to where chilly Mammoth Creek blends with hot springs and continues its journey as Hot Creek. It eventually enters a small gorge and forms a series of steaming, bubbling cauldrons, with water shimmering in shades of blue and green reminiscent of the tropics. Until recently, soakers reveled in the blissful but somewhat scary temperate zones where the hot springs mixed with frigid creek water. But in 2006 a significant increase in geothermal activity began sending violent geysers of boiling water into the air, and the site is off-limits for swimming until the danger has subsided.

To reach the site, turn off Hwy 395 about 5 miles south of town and follow signs to the Hot Creek Fish Hatchery. From here, it's another 2 miles on gravel road to the parking area, and a short hike down into the canyon and creek.

For a soak that *won't* cook your goose, take Hwy 395 about 9 miles south of Mammoth to Benton Crossing Rd, which accesses a trove of primitive **hot spring pools**. Locals call this 'Green Church Rd,' because of the road's unmistakable marker. For detailed directions and maps, pick up the bible – Matt Bischoff's excellent *Touring California and Nevada Hot Springs*. And keep in mind these three golden rules: no glass, no additives to the water and, if you can, no bathing suit.

CONVICT LAKE
Located just southeast of Mammoth, Convict Lake is one of the area's prettiest lakes, with emerald water embraced by massive peaks. A hike along the gentle trail skirting the lake, through aspen and cottonwood trees, is great if you're still adjusting to the altitude. A trailhead on the southeastern shore gives access to Genevieve, Edith, Dorothy and Mildred Lakes in the John Muir Wilderness. To reach the lake, turn south from Hwy 395 on Convict Lake Rd (across from the Mammoth airport) and go 2 miles.

In 1871 Convict Lake was the site of a bloody shoot-out between a band of escaped convicts and a posse that had given chase. Posse leader, Sheriff Robert Morrison, was killed during the gunfight and the taller peak, Mt Morrison (12,268ft), was later named in his honor. The bad guys got away only to be apprehended later near Bishop.

The **campground** (📞877-444-6777; www.recreation.gov; tent & RV sites $20; ⊘mid-Apr–Oct) has flush toilets and nicely terraced sites. Otherwise your only option is **Convict Lake Resort** (📞760-934-3800, 800-992-2260; www.convictlake.com; cabins from $189; 🐾🌐), whose three houses and 27 cabins with kitchens sleep from two to 34 and range from rustic to ritzy. Foodies with deep pockets flock to the elegant **restaurant** (📞760-934-3803, mains lunch $8-15, dinner $23-42; ⊘5:30-9pm daily, plus 11am-2:30pm Jul & Aug), which many consider the best within a 100-mile radius.

Bishop
The second-largest town in the Eastern Sierra, Bishop is about two hours from Yosemite's Tioga Pass entrance. A major recreation hub, Bishop offers access to excellent fishing in nearby lakes, climbing in the Buttermilks just west of town, and hiking in the John Muir Wilderness via Bishop Creek Canyon and the Rock Creek drainage. The area is especially lovely in fall when dropping temperatures cloak aspen, willow and cottonwood in myriad glowing shades.

The earliest inhabitants of the Owens Valley were Paiute and Shoshone Native Americans, who today live on four reservations. White settlers came on the scene in the 1860s and began raising cattle to sell to nearby mining settlements.

👁 Sights

TOP
CHOICE⟩ **Laws Railroad Museum**   MUSEUM
(📞760-873-5950; www.lawsmuseum.org; requested donation $5; ⊘10am-4pm; 👶) Railroad

BENTON HOT SPRINGS

Soak in your own hot springs tub and snooze beneath the moonlight at **Benton Hot Springs** (☎760-933-2287; www.historicbentonhotsprings.com; Hwy 120, Benton; tent & RV sites for 2 people $40-50, d with/without bath incl breakfast $129/109; 🐾🏠), a small historic resort in a 150-year-old former silver mining town nestled along the White Mountains. Choose from nine well-spaced campsites with private tubs or one of the themed antique-filled B&B rooms with semi-private tubs. Daytime dips ($10 hourly per person) are also available, and reservations are essential for all visits.

It's reachable from Mono Lake via Hwy 120 (in summer), Mammoth Lakes by way of Benton Crossing Rd, or Hwy 6 from Bishop; the first two options are undulating drives with sweeping red-rock vistas that glow at sunset, and all take approximately one hour. An **Eastern Sierra Transit Authority bus** (☎800-922-1930; www.easternsierratransitauthority.com) connects Bishop and Benton ($5, one hour) on Tuesday and Friday, stopping right at the resort.

If you have time, ask for directions to the **Volcanic Tablelands petroglyphs** off Hwy 6, where ancient drawings decorate scenic rock walls.

and Old West aficionados should make the 6-mile detour north on Hwy 6 to this museum. It re-creates the village of Laws, an important stop on the route of the *Slim Princess,* a narrow-gauge train that hauled freight and passengers across the Owens Valley for nearly 80 years. The original 1883 train depot is here, as are a post office, a schoolhouse and other rickety old buildings. Many contain funky and eclectic displays (dolls, bottles, fire equipment, antique stoves etc) from the pioneer days.

FREE **Owens Valley Paiute Shoshone Cultural Center** CULTURAL BUILDING (☎760-873-3584; www.bishoppaiutetribe.com/culturalcenter.html; 2300 W Line St; ☺9am-5pm) A mile west of Hwy 395, this tribal cultural center is fronted by a native plant garden and includes exhibits on local basketry and the use of medical herbs.

FREE **Mountain Light Gallery** GALLERY (☎760-873-7700; 106 S Main St; ☺10am-6pm) To see the Sierra on display in all its majesty, pop into this gallery, which features the stunning outdoor images of the late Galen Rowell. His work bursts with color, and the High Sierra photographs are some of the best in existence.

🏃 Activities

Bishop is prime **bouldering** and **rock climbing** territory, with terrain to match any level of fitness, experience and climbing style. The main areas are the granite Buttermilk Country, west of town on Buttermilk

Rd, and the stark Volcanic Tablelands and Owens River Valley to the north. For details, consult with the staff at **Wilson's Eastside Sports** (☎760-873-7520; 224 N Main St), which rents equipment and sells maps and guidebooks. Another excellent resource is **Mammoth Mountaineering Supply** (☎760-873-4300; 298 N Main St), which also sells used gear, including shoes. The tablelands are also a wellspring of Native American petroglyphs – tread lightly.

Hikers will want to head to the high country by following Line St (Hwy 168) west along Bishop Creek Canyon, past Buttermilk Country and on to several lakes, including Lake Sabrina and South Lake. Trailheads lead into the John Muir Wilderness and on into Kings Canyon National Park. Check with the White Mountain Ranger Station (p444) for suggestions, maps and wilderness permits for overnight stays.

Fishing is good in all lakes but North Lake is the least crowded.

For hot springs, try **Keough's Hot Springs** (☎760-872-4670; www.keoughshotsprings.com; 800 Keough Hot Springs Rd; adult/conc $8/6; ☺11am-7pm Wed-Fri & Mon, 9am-8pm Sat & Sun, longer summer hours). About 8 miles south of Bishop, this historic institutional-green outdoor pool (dating from 1919) is filled with bathwater-warm water from local mineral springs and doused with spray at one end. A smaller and sheltered 104°F soaking pool sits beside it. Camping and tent cabins also available.

🛏 Sleeping

For a scenic night, stretch out your sleeping bag beneath the stars. The closest **USFS campgrounds** (tent & RV sites $21; ⊙May-Sep), all but one first-come, first-served, are between 9 miles and 15 miles west of town on Bishop Creek along Hwy 168, at elevations between 7500ft and 9000ft.

Joseph House Inn Bed
& Breakfast   B&B $$
(☑760-872-3389; www.josephhouseinn.com; 376 W Yaney St; r incl breakfast $143-178; ✳🐾🌐) A beautiful restored ranch-style home, this place has a patio overlooking a tranquil 3-acre garden, and six nicely furnished rooms, some with fireplaces, all with TV and VCR. Guests enjoy a complimentary gourmet breakfast and afternoon wine and snacks.

Chalfant House   B&B $$
(☑760-872-1790, 800-641-2996; www.chalfanthouse.com; 213 Academy; d incl breakfast $80-110; ✳🌐🐾) Lace curtains and Victorian accents swirl through the six rooms of this restored historic home. Originally built by the editor and publisher of Owens Valley's first newspaper, some of the rooms are named after Chalfant family members.

🍴 Eating & Drinking

Raymond's Deli   DELI $
(www.raymondsdeli.com; 206 N Main St; sandwiches $7-9; ⊙10am-6pm; 🐾) A sassy den of kitsch, pinball and Pac-man, Raynod's serves heaping sandwiches with names like 'When Pigs Fly,' 'Flaming Farm' and 'Soy U Like Tofu.' Kick back with a Lobotomy Bock and watch your food order get flung to the cook along a mini zip line.

Looney Bean   CAFE $
(399 N Main St; pastries $3; ⊙6am-7pm; 🌐) The combination of really fine coffee, a comfortable modern space and free wi-fi guarantee the popularity of this central cafe. It carries some organic brews, and lots of tasty scones and pastries for snacking.

Erick Schat's Bakery   BAKERY $
(www.erickschatsbakery.com; 763 N Main St; sandwiches $5-8.50; ⊙6am-6pm Sun-Thu, to 8pm Fri) A much-hyped tourist mecca filled to the rafters with racks of fresh bread, it has been making its signature shepherd bread and other baked goodies since 1938. The bakery also features a popular sandwich bar.

Whiskey Creek   AMERICAN $$
(www.whiskeycreekbishop.com; 524 N Main St; mains $11-29; ⊙11am-9pm, to 10:30pm Fri & Sat) This country dining room has comfort food like meatloaf and chicken pot pie, and a smattering of seafood and pastas.

ℹ Information

Public showers are available in town at **Wash Tub** (☑760-873-6627; 236 Warren St; ⊙approx 5pm & 8-10pm), and near South Lake at **Bishop Creek Lodge** (☑760-873-4484; www.bishopcreekresort.com; 2100 South Lake Rd; ⊙May-Oct) and **Parchers Resort** (☑760-873-4177; www.parchersresort.net; 5001 South Lake Rd; ⊙late May–mid-Oct).

Bishop Area Visitors Bureau (☑760-873-8405; www.bishopvisitor.com; 690 N Main St; ⊙10am-5pm Mon-Fri, to 4pm Sat & Sun)

Inyo County Free Library (☑760-873-5115; 210 Academy) Free internet access.

Spellbinder Books (☑760-873-4511; 124 S Main St; 🌐) Great indie bookstore with attached cafe and wi-fi.

White Mountain Ranger Station (☑760-873-2500; www.fs.usda.gov/inyo; 798 N Main St; ⊙8am-5pm daily May-Oct, Mon-Fri rest of year) Wilderness permits, trail and campground information for the entire area.

Big Pine

This blink-and-you-missed-it town has a few motels and basic eateries. It mainly functions as a launch pad for the Ancient Bristlecone Pine Forest (see the boxed text, p445) and to the granite **Palisades** in the John Muir Wilderness, a rugged cluster of peaks including six above 14,000ft. Stretching beneath the pinnacles is **Palisades Glacier**, the southernmost in the USA and the largest in the Sierra.

To get to the trailhead, turn onto Glacier Lodge Rd (Crocker Ave in town), which follows trout-rich Big Pine Creek up Big Pine Canyon, 10 miles west into a bowl-shaped valley. The strenuous 9-mile hike to Palisades Glacier via the North Fork Trail skirts several lakes – turned a milky turquoise color by glacial runoff – and a stone cabin built by horror-film actor Lon Chaney in 1925.

An ear-popping ascent up Glacier Lodge Rd passes by a trio of **USFS campgrounds** (☑877-444-6777; www.recreation.gov; tent & RV sites $20; ⊙May–mid-Oct) – Big Pine Creek, Sage Flat and Upper Sage Flat. Showers are available for $5 at **Glacier Lodge** (☑760-

DON'T MISS

ANCIENT BRISTLECONE PINE FOREST

For encounters with some of the earth's oldest living things, plan at least a half-day trip to the Ancient Bristlecone Pine Forest. These gnarled, otherworldly looking trees thrive above 10,000ft on the slopes of the seemingly inhospitable White Mountains, a parched and stark range that once stood even higher than the Sierra. The oldest tree – called Methuselah – is estimated to be over 4700 years old, beating even the Great Sphinx of Giza by about two centuries.

To reach the groves, take Hwy 168 east 12 miles from Big Pine to White Mountain Rd, then turn left (north) and climb the curvy road 10 miles to **Schulman Grove**, named for the scientist who first discovered the trees' biblical age in the 1950s. The entire trip takes about one hour. There's access to self-guided trails, and a new solar-powered **visitors center** (☏760-873-2500; www.fs.usda.gov/inyo; admission $5 per vehicle; ☺late May-Oct) is scheduled to open in summer 2012. White Mountain Rd is usually closed from November to April. It's nicest in August when wildflowers sneak out through the rough soil.

A second grove, the **Patriarch Grove**, is dramatically set within an open bowl and reached via a 12-mile graded dirt road. Four miles further on you'll find a locked gate, which is the departure point for day hikes to the **White Mountain Peak** – at 14,246ft it's the third-highest mountain in California. The round-trip is about 14 miles via an abandoned road, soon passing through the **Barcroft High Altitude Research Station**. Some ride the route on mountain bikes: the nontechnical and marmot-laden road winds above the tree line, though naturally, high elevation makes the going tough. Allow plenty of time, bring at least two quarts of water per person. For maps and details, stop at the White Mountain Ranger Station (p444) in Bishop.

For altitude adjustment or some good star gazing, spend a night at the **Grandview Campground** (donation $5) at 8600ft. It has awesome views, tables and vault toilets, but no water.

938-2837; www.jewelofthesierra.com; tent & RV sites $35, cabins $125; ☺mid-Apr–mid-Nov; ☻), a bunch of rustic cabins with kitchens, as well as a campground, with a two-night minimum stay; it was one of the earliest Sierra getaways when built in 1917.

Independence

This sleepy highway town has been a county seat since 1866 and is home to the **Eastern California Museum** (☏760-878-0364; www.inyocounty.us/ecmuseum; 155 N Grant St; donation requested; ☺10am-5pm). It contains one of the most complete collections of Paiute and Shoshone baskets in the country, as well as artifacts from the Manzanar relocation camp (see the boxed text, p447) and historic photographs of primitively equipped local rock climbers scaling Sierra peaks, including Mt Whitney.

Fans of **Mary Austin** (1868–1934), renowned author of *The Land of Little Rain* and vocal foe of the desertification of the Owens Valley, can follow signs leading to her former house at 253 Market St.

West of town via Onion Valley Rd (Market St in town), pretty **Onion Valley** harbors the trailhead for the **Kearsarge Pass** (9.4 miles round-trip), an old Paiute trade route. This is also the quickest eastside access to the Pacific Crest Trail and Kings Canyon National Park.

In addition to a few small motels in town, Onion Valley has a couple of **campgrounds** (☏877-444-6777; www.recreation.gov; tent & RV sites $16; ☺May-Sep) along Independence Creek.

Inexplicably located in a town otherwise inhabited by greasy spoon diners, **Still Life Cafe** (☏760-878-2555; 135 S Edward St; mains lunch $10-16, dinner $20-25; ☺11am-3pm & 6-9:30pm Wed-Mon), a French gourmet bistro, pops out like an orchid in a salt flat. Escargot, duck-liver mousse, steak au poivre and other French delectables are served with Gallic charm in this bright, artistic dining room.

Next to the courthouse, bustling **Jenny's Cafe** (246 N Edwards St; mains lunch $7-9, dinner $12-22; ☺6am-9pm Thu-Tue) serves rib-sticking fare like burgers, sandwiches and steaks in a country kitchen setting of rooster-print curtains and old teapots.

Manzanar National Historic Site

A stark wooden guard tower alerts drivers to one of the darkest chapters in US history, which unfolded on a barren and windy sweep of land some 5 miles south of Independence. Little remains of the infamous war concentration camp, a dusty square mile where more than 10,000 people of Japanese ancestry were corralled during WWII following the attack on Pearl Harbor (see the boxed text, p447). The camp's lone remaining building, the former high-school auditorium, houses a superb **interpretive center** (☎760-878-2194; www.nps.gov/manz; ⊙9am-4:30pm Nov-Mar, to 5:30pm Apr-Oct). A visit here is one of the historical highlights of the state and should not be missed.

Watch the 20-minute documentary, then explore the thought-provoking exhibits chronicling the stories of the families that languished here yet built a vibrant community. Afterwards, take a self-guided 3.2-mile driving tour around the grounds, which includes a re-created mess hall and barracks, vestiges of buildings and gardens, as well as the haunting camp cemetery.

Lone Pine

A tiny town, Lone Pine is the gateway to big things, most notably Mt Whitney (14,505ft), the loftiest peak in the contiguous USA, and Hollywood. In the 1920s cinematographers discovered that nearby Alabama Hills were a picture-perfect movie set for Westerns, and stars from Gary Cooper to Gregory Peck could often be spotted swaggering about town.

◎ Sights & Activities

A few basic motels, a supermarket, restaurants and stores (including gear and equipment shops) flank Hwy 395 (Main St in town). Whitney Portal Rd heads west at the lone stoplight, while Hwy 136 to Death Valley veers away about 2 miles south of town.

Mt Whitney   MOUNTAIN
West of Lone Pine, the jagged incisors of the Sierra surge skyward in all their raw and fierce glory. Cradled by scores of smaller pinnacles, Mt Whitney is a bit hard to pick out from Hwy 395, so for the best views, take a drive along Whitney Portal Rd through the Alabama Hills. As you get a fix

on this majestic megalith, remember that the country's lowest point is only 80 miles (as the crow flies) east of here: Badwater in Death Valley. Climbing to Mt Whitney's summit is among the most popular hikes in the entire country (see the boxed text p448).

TOP CHOICE Alabama Hills   NATURAL FEATURE
Located on Whitney Portal Rd, the warm colors and rounded contours of the Alabama Hills stand in contrast to the jagged snowy Sierras just behind. The setting for countless ride-'em-out movies and the popular *Lone Ranger* TV series, the stunning orange rock formations are a beautiful place to experience sunrise or sunset. You can drive, walk or mountain-bike along dirt roads rambling through the boulders, and along Tuttle and Lone Pine creeks. A number of graceful rock arches are within easy hiking distance of the roads. Head west on Whitney Portal Rd and either turn left at Tuttle Creek Rd, after a half-mile, or north on Movie Rd, after about 3 miles. The websites of the Lone Pine Chamber of Commerce (p447) and the Museum of Lone Pine Film History have excellent movie location maps.

Museum of Lone Pine Film History   MUSEUM
(☎760-876-9909; www.lonepinefilmhistorymuseum.org; 701 S Main St; admission $5; ⊙10am-6pm Mon-Wed, to 7pm Thu-Sat, to 4pm Sun) Over 450 movies have been shot in the area, and this museum contains exhibits of paraphernalia from locally set films. Don't miss the 7pm screenings in its theater every Thursday and Friday or the tricked-out Cadillac convertible in its foyer.

⌂ Sleeping & Eating

Dow Hotel & Dow Villa Motel   MOTEL, HOTEL $$
(☎760-876-5521, 800-824-9317; www.dowvillamotel.com; 310 S Main St; hotel r with/without bath $70/54, motel r $104-140; ❋⊛⊜⊛) John Wayne and Errol Flynn are among the stars who have stayed at this venerable hotel. Built in 1922, the place has been restored but retains much of its rustic charm. The rooms in the newer motel section are more comfortable and bright, but also more generic.

Whitney Portal Hostel   HOSTEL $
(☎760-876-0030; www.whitneyportalstore.com; 238 S Main St; dm $20, q $60; ❋@⊛⊛) A popu-

CAMP OF INFAMY

On December 7, 1941 – a day that, according to President Roosevelt, would forever live in infamy – Japanese war planes bombed Pearl Harbor. The attack plunged the US into WWII and fanned the flames of racial prejudice that had been fomenting against Japanese Americans for decades. Amid fears of sabotage and espionage, bigotry grew into full-blown hysteria, prompting Roosevelt to sign Executive Order 9066 in February 1942; another day that now lives in infamy. The act stated that all West Coast Japanese – most of them American-born citizens – were to be rounded up and moved to relocation camps.

Manzanar was the first of 10 such camps, built among pear and apple orchards in the dusty Owens Valley near Independence. Between 1942 and 1945, up to 10,000 men, women and children lived crammed into makeshift barracks pounded by fierce winds and the blistering desert sun, enclosed by barbed wire patrolled by military police.

After the war the camp was leveled and its dark history remained buried beneath the dust for decades. Recognition remained elusive until 1973, when the site was given landmark status; in 1992 it was designated a national historic site, and in 2004 a long-awaited interpretive center opened. On the last Saturday of every April, former internees and their descendants make a pilgrimage (www.manzanarcommittee.org) to honor family members who died here, keeping alive the memory of this national tragedy. For a vivid and haunting account of what life was like at the camp, read Jean Wakatsuki Houston's classic *Farewell to Manzanar*.

lar launching pad for Whitney trips and for post-hike wash-ups (public showers available), the carpeted bunk-bed rooms have towels and TVs to reacclimatize the weary, plus there's free coffee in the communal kitchenette (no stove). Reserve two months ahead for July and August.

Lone Pine Campground　　CAMPGROUND **$**
(☑518-885-3639, 877-444-6777; www.recreation.gov; Whitney Portal Rd; tent & RV sites $15-17; ☺mid-Apr–Oct) About midway between Lone Pine and Whitney Portal, this popular creekside USFS campground (elevation 6000ft) offers flush toilets and potable water.

Alabama Hills Cafe　　DINER **$**
(111 W Post St; mains $8-12; ☺6am-2pm Mon-Fri, from 7am Sat & Sun; ☑) Everyone's favorite breakfast joint, the portions here are big, the bread fresh-baked, and the hearty soups and scratch-made fruit pies make lunch an attractive option too.

Seasons　　NEW AMERICAN **$$**
(☑760-876-8927; 206 N Main St; mains $17-29; ☺5-10pm daily Apr-Oct, to 9pm Mon-Sat Nov-Mar) Seasons has everything you fantasized about the last time you choked down freeze-dried rations. Sauteed trout, roasted duck, filet mignon and plates of carb-replenishing pasta will revitalize your ap-

petite, and nice and naughty desserts will leave you purring.

ℹ Information

Eastern Sierra InterAgency Visitor Center (☑760-876-6222; www.fs.fed.us/r5/inyo; ☺8am-5pm, extended summer hours) USFS information central for the Sierra, Death Valley and Mt Whitney; about 1.5 miles south of town at the junction of Hwys 395 and 136.

Lone Pine Chamber of Commerce (☑760-876-4444; www.lonepinechamber.org; 120 S Main St; ☺8:30am-4:30pm Mon-Fri)

RENO (NEVADA)

A soothingly schizophrenic city of big-time gambling and top-notch outdoor adventures, Reno resists pigeonholing. 'The Biggest Little City in the World' has something to raise the pulse of adrenaline junkies, hardcore gamblers and city people craving easy access to wide open spaces.

◉ Sights

National Automobile Museum　　MUSEUM
(☑775-333-9300; www.automuseum.org; 10 S Lake St; adult/child/senior $10/4/8; ☺9:30am-5:30pm Mon-Sat, 10am-4pm Sun; ☀) Stylized street scenes illustrate a century's worth of automobile history at this engaging car

HIKING MT WHITNEY

The mystique of Mt Whitney captures the imagination, and conquering its hulking bulk becomes a sort of obsession for many. The main **Mt Whitney Trail** (the easiest and busiest one) leaves from Whitney Portal, about 13 miles west of Lone Pine via the Whitney Portal Rd (closed in winter), and climbs about 6000ft over 11 miles. It's a super strenuous, really, *really* long walk that'll wear out even experienced mountaineers, but doesn't require technical skills if attempted in summer or early fall. Earlier or later in the season, you'll likely need an ice axe and crampons.

Many people in good physical condition make it to the top, although only superbly conditioned, previously acclimatized hikers should attempt this as a day hike. Breathing becomes difficult at these elevations and altitude sickness is a common problem. Rangers recommend spending a night or two camping at the trailhead and another at one of the two camps along the route: **Outpost Camp** at 3.5 miles or **Trail Camp** at 6 miles up the trail.

When considering an ascent, do your homework. One recommended book is *Mt Whitney: The Complete Trailhead-to-Summit Hiking Guide* by Paul Richins Jr. When you pick up your permit and pack-out kits (hikers must pack out their poop) at the Eastern Sierra Interagency Visitor Center in Lone Pine, get the latest info on weather and trail conditions.

Near the trailhead, the **Whitney Portal Store** (www.whitneyportalstore.com; ☺May-Oct) sells groceries and snacks. It also has public showers ($3) and a **cafe** with enormous burgers and pancakes. Its excellent website is a comprehensive starting point for Whitney research.

The biggest obstacle in getting to the peak may be to obtain a **wilderness permit** (per person $15), which is required for all overnight trips and for day hikes past Lone Pine Lake (about 2.8 miles from the trailhead). A quota system limits daily access to 60 overnight and 100 day hikers from May through October. Because of the huge demand, permits are distributed via the **Mt Whitney lottery**. Historically, lottery applications have been accepted only by mail in February (and mixed up by a leaf blower in the stairwell!), but may be migrating online. Check www.fs.fed.us/r5/inyo for current procedures.

Want to avoid the hassle of getting a permit for the main Mt Whitney Trail? Consider ascending this popular pinnacle from the west, using the backdoor route from Sequoia & Kings Canyon National Parks. It takes about six days from Crescent Meadow via the High Sierra Trail to the John Muir Trail – with no Whitney Zone permit required – and wilderness permits are much easier to secure. See p426 for park permit information.

museum. The collection is enormous and impressive, with one-of-a-kind vehicles – including James Dean's 1949 Mercury from *Rebel Without a Cause*, a 1938 Phantom Corsair and a 24-karat gold-plated DeLorean – and rotating exhibits bringing in all kinds of souped-up or fabulously retro rides.

Nevada Museum of Art　　　MUSEUM
(☎775-329-3333; www.nevadaart.org; 160 W Liberty St; adult/child $10/1; ☺10am-5pm Wed-Sun, to 8pm Thu) In a sparkling building inspired by the geological formations of the Black Rock Desert, north of town, a floating staircase leads to galleries showcasing temporary exhibits and images related to

the American West. Great **cafe** for postcultural refueling.

FREE **Fleischmann Planetarium & Science Center**　　　SCIENCE CENTER
(☎775-784-4811; http://planetarium.unr.nevada.edu; 1650 N Virginia St; ☺noon-5pm Mon & Tue, to 9pm Fri, 10am-9pm Sat, to 5pm Sun) Pop into this flying saucer–shaped building, at the University of Nevada, for a window on the universe during star shows and feature presentations (adult/child $6/4).

Nevada Historical Society Museum　　　MUSEUM
(☎775-688-1190; www.museums.nevaculture.org; 1650 N Virginia St; adult/child $4/free;

⊘10am-5pm Wed-Sat) Near the science center, this museum includes permanent exhibits on neon signs, local Native American culture and the presence of the federal government.

🏃 Activities

Reno is a 30- to 60-minute drive from Lake Tahoe ski resorts, and many hotels and casinos offer special stay-and-ski packages.

For extensive information on regional hiking and mountain-biking trails, including the Mt Rose summit trail and the Tahoe-Pyramid Bikeway, download the **Truckee Meadows Trails guide** (www.reno.gov/Index. aspx?page=291).

Mere steps from the casinos, the Class II and III rapids at the **Truckee River Whitewater Park** are gentle enough for kids riding inner tubes, yet sufficiently challenging for professional freestyle kayakers. Two courses wrap around Wingfield Park, a small river island that hosts free concerts in summertime. **Tahoe Whitewater Tours** (☏775-787-5000; www.gowhitewater.com) and **Wild Sierra Adventures** (☏866-323-8928; www.wildsierra.com) offer kayak trips and lessons.

The **Historic Reno Preservation Society** (☏775-747-4478; www.historicreno.org; tours $10) will help you dig deeper with a walking or cycling tour of the city, highlighting subjects including architecture, politics and literary history.

✨ Festivals & Events

Reno River Festival   SPORTS
(www.renoriverfestival.com) The world's top freestyle kayakers compete in a mad paddling dash through Whitewater Park in mid-May. Free music concerts as well.

Tour de Nez   SPORTS
(www.tourdenez.com) Called the 'coolest bike race in America,' the Tour de Nez brings together pros and amateurs for five days of races and partying in July.

Hot August Nights   CULTURAL
(www.hotaugustnights.net) Catch the *American Graffiti* vibe during this seven-day celebration of hot rods and rock 'n' roll in early August. Hotel rates skyrocket to their peak.

🛏 Sleeping

Lodging rates vary widely depending on the day of the week and local events. Sunday through Thursday are generally the least expensive; Friday is somewhat more expensive and Saturday can be as much as triple the midweek rate.

Peppermill   CASINO HOTEL $$
(☏775-826-2121, 866-821-9996; www.peppermill reno.com; 2707 S Virginia St; r Sun-Thu $50-140, Fri & Sat $70-200; ❄@🛜≋) Now awash in Vegas-style opulence, the popular Peppermill boasts Tuscan-themed rooms in its newest 600-room tower, and has almost completed a plush remodel of its older rooms. The three sparkling pools (one indoor) are dreamy, with a full spa on hand. Geothermal energy powers the resort's hot water and heat.

Sands Regency   CASINO HOTEL $
(☏775-348-2200, 866-386-7829; www.sandsregency.com; 345 N Arlington Ave; r Sun-Thu, Fri & Sat from $29/89; ❄🛜≋≋) With some of the largest standard digs in town, rooms here are decked out in a cheerful tropical palette of upbeat blues, reds and greens – a visual relief from standard-issue motel decor. The 17th-floor gym and Jacuzzi are perfectly positioned to capture your eyes with drop-dead panoramic mountain views. Empress Tower rooms are best.

Wildflower Village   MOTEL $
(☏775-747-8848; www.wildflowervillage.com; 4395 W 4th St; r $50-75, B&B $100-125; ❄@🛜) Perhaps more of a state of mind than a motel, this artists colony on the west edge of town has a tumbledown yet creative vibe. Individual murals decorate the facade of each room, and you can hear the freight trains rumble on by.

GREAT BALLS OF FIRE!

For one week at the end of August, **Burning Man** (www.burningman.com; admission $210-320) explodes onto the sunbaked Black Rock Desert, and Nevada sprouts a third major population center – Black Rock City. An experiential art party (and alternative universe) that climaxes in the immolation of a towering stick figure, Burning Man is a whirlwind of outlandish theme camps, dust-caked bicycles, bizarre bartering, costume-enhanced nudity and a general relinquishment of inhibitions.

WORTH A TRIP

VIRGINIA CITY

Virginia City, about 23 miles south of Reno, was the site of the legendary Comstock Lode, a massive silver bonanza that began in 1859 and stands as one of the world's richest strikes. Some of the silver barons went on to become major players in California history, among them Leland Stanford of university fame and Bank of California founder William Ralston. Much of San Francisco was built with the treasure dug up from the soil beneath the town.

At its peak, Virginia City had over 30,000 residents and, as befits a mining town, was a wild and raucous place. A young local newspaper writer captured the shenanigans in a book called *Roughing It*, published under his pen name Mark Twain. A National Historic Landmark since 1961, Virginia City draws big crowds in search of Old West icons and lore. Though it sometimes has the feel of a frontier theme park, it's still a fun place to while away a few hours.

On the main drag, C street, you'll find the **visitors center** (www.virginiacity-nv.org; 86 South C St; ⊗10am-4pm), vintage buildings restored into wacky saloons, cheesy souvenir shops and small museums ranging from hokey to intriguing. To see how the mining elite lived, stop by the **Mackay Mansion** (D St) and the **Castle** (B St).

Drink like an old-time miner at one of the many Victorian-era watering holes that line C street. The longtime family-run **Bucket of Blood Saloon** (www.bucketofbloodsaloonvc.com; 1 South C St; ⊗2-7pm) serves up beer and 'bar rules' ('If the bartender doesn't laugh, you are not funny') at its antique wooden bar, and the **Palace Restaurant & Saloon** (www.palacerestaurant1875.com; 1 South C St; mains $6-10; ⊗hours vary) is full of town memorabilia and has tasty breakfasts and lunches.

The drive to Virginia City from Reno offers great views of the mountain. Take Hwy 395 south for about 10 miles, then Hwy 341 east for 13 miles.

Mt Rose   CAMPGROUND $
(📞877-444-6777; www.recreation.gov; Hwy 431; RV & tent sites $16) In the summer months, there's gorgeous high altitude camping here.

🍴 Eating & Drinking

Reno's dining scene goes far beyond the casino buffets.

TOP CHOICE Old Granite Street Eatery   AMERICAN $$
(📞775-622-3222; www.oldgranitestreeteatery.com; 243 S Sierra St; dishes $9-24; ⊗11am-10pm Mon-Thu, variable hours otherwise) A lovely well-lit place for organic and local comfort food, old-school artisanal cocktails and seasonal craft beers, this antique-strewn hotspot enchants diners with its stately wooden bar, water served in old liquor bottles and lengthy seasonal menu. Forgot to make a reservation? Check out the iconic rooster and pig murals and wait for seats at a community table fashioned from a barn door.

Pneumatic Diner   VEGETARIAN $
(2nd fl, 501 W 1st St; dishes $6-9; ⊗noon-10pm Mon, 11am-11pm Tue-Sat, 8am-10pm Sun; 📶) Consume a garden of vegetarian delights under salvaged neon lights. This groovy little place near the river has meatless and vegan comfort food and desserts to tickle your inner two-year-old, like the ice-cream laden Cookie Bomb. It's attached to the Truckee River Terrace apartment complex; use the Ralston St entrance.

Silver Peak Restaurant & Brewery   PUB $$
(www.silverpeakbrewery.com; 124 Wonder St; mains lunch $8-10, dinner $9-21; ⊗11am-midnight) Casual and pretense-free, this place hums with the chatter of happy locals settling in for a night of microbrews and great eats, from pizza with roasted chicken to shrimp pasta and filet mignon.

Peg's Glorified Ham & Eggs   DINER $
(www.pegsglorifiedhamneggs.com; 420 S Sierra St; dishes $7-10; ⊗6:30am-2pm; 📶) Locally regarded as the best breakfast in town, Peg's offers tasty grill food that's not too greasy.

Jungle Java & Jungle Vino   CAFE, WINE BAR
(www.javajunglevino.com; 246 W 1st St; ⊗6am-midnight; 📶) A side-by-side coffee shop and wine bar with a cool mosaic floor and an internet cafe all rolled into one. The wine bar has

weekly tastings, while the cafe serves breakfast bagels and lunchtime sandwiches ($8) and puts on diverse music shows.

Imperial Bar & Lounge   BAR
(www.imperialbarandlounge.com; 150 N Arlington Ave; ☺11am-2am Thu-Sat, to midnight Sun-Wed) A classy bar inhabiting a relic of the past – this building was once an old bank, and in the middle of the wood floor you can see cement where the vault once stood. Sandwiches and pizzas go with 16 beers on tap and a buzzing weekend scene.

St James Infirmary   BAR
(445 California Ave) With an eclectic menu of 120 bottled varieties and 18 on tap, beer aficionados will short circuit with delight. Red lights blush over black-and-white retro banquettes and a wall of movie and music stills. The bar hosts sporadic events, including jazz and bluegrass performances.

☆ Entertainment

The free weekly *Reno News & Review* (www.newsreview.com) is your best source for listings.

Wedged between the I-80 and the Truckee River, downtown's N Virginia St is casino central. South of the river it continues as S Virginia St. All of the hotel casinos listed are open 24 hours.

Edge   CLUB
(www.edgeofreno.com; Peppermill, 2707 S Virginia St; admission $10-20; ☺Thu-Sun) The Peppermill reels in the nighthounds with a big glitzy dance club, where go-go dancers, smoke machines and laser lights may cause sensory overload. If so, step outside to the lounge patio and relax in front of cozy fire pits.

Knitting Factory   LIVE MUSIC
(☑775-323-5648; http://re.knittingfactory.com; 211 N Virginia St) This midsized venue opened in 2010, filling a gap in Reno's music scene with mainstream and indie favorites.

Circus Circus   CASINO
(www.circusreno.com; 500 N Sierra St; 🅰) The most family-friendly of the bunch, Circus Circus has free circus acts to entertain kids beneath a giant, candy-striped big top, which also harbors a gazillion carnival and video games that look awfully similar to slot machines.

Silver Legacy   CASINO
(www.silverlegacyreno.com; 407 N Virginia St) A Victorian-themed place, the Silver Legacy is easily recognized by its white landmark dome, where a giant mock mining rig periodically erupts into a fairly tame sound-and-light spectacle.

Eldorado   CASINO
(www.eldoradoreno.com; 345 N Virginia St) The Eldorado has a kitschy Fountain of Fortune that probably has Italian sculptor Bernini spinning in his grave.

Harrah's   CASINO
(www.harrahsreno.com; 219 N Center St) Founded by Nevada gambling pioneer William Harrah in 1946, this is still one of the biggest and most popular casinos in town.

Peppermill   CASINO
(www.peppermillreno.com; 2707 S Virginia St) Dazzles with a 17-story Tuscan-style tower. About 2 miles south of downtown.

Atlantis   CASINO
(www.atlantiscasino.com; 3800 S Virginia St) Now more classy than zany, with an extensive spa, the remodeled casino retains a few tropical flourishes like indoor waterfalls and palm trees.

❶ Information

An information center sits near the baggage claim at **Reno-Tahoe International Airport**, which also has free wi-fi.

Java Jungle (246 W 1st St; per hr $2; ☺6am-midnight; 🛜) Great riverfront cafe with a few computers and free wi-fi.

Reno-Sparks Convention & Visitors Authority (☑800-367-7366; www.visitrenotahoe.com; 2nd

---

WORTH A TRIP

PYRAMID LAKE

A piercingly blue expanse in an otherwise barren landscape, 25 miles north of Reno on the Paiute Indian Reservation, Pyramid Lake is popular for recreation. Permits for **camping** (primitive campsites per vehicle per night $9) and **fishing** (per person $9) are available at outdoor suppliers and CVS drugstore locations in Reno, and at the **ranger station** (☑775-476-1155; www.pyramidlake.us; ☺8am-6pm) on SR 445 in Sutcliffe.

fl, Reno Town Mall, 4001 S Virginia St; ⊗8am-5pm Mon-Fri)

ⓘ Getting There & Away

About 5 miles southeast of downtown, the **Reno-Tahoe International Airport** (RNO; www.renoairport.com; 🛜) is served by most major airlines.

The **North Lake Tahoe Express** (🗹866-216-5222; www.northlaketahoeexpress.com) operates a shuttle ($40, six to eight daily, 3:30am to midnight) to and from the airport to multiple North Shore Lake Tahoe locations including Truckee, Squaw Valley and Incline Village. Reserve in advance.

The **South Tahoe Express** (🗹866-898-2463; www.southtahoeexpress.com; adult/child one way $27/15, round-trip $48/27) operates several daily shuttle buses from the airport to Stateline casinos; the journey takes 75 minutes up to two hours.

To reach South Lake Tahoe (weekdays only), take the wi-fi-equipped **RTC Intercity bus** (www.rtcwashoe.com) to the Nevada DOT stop in Carson City ($4, one hour, five daily Monday to Friday) and then the **BlueGo** (www.bluego.org) 21X bus ($2 with RTC Intercity transfer, one hour, seven to eight daily) to the Stateline Transit Center.

Greyhound (🗹775-322-2970; www.greyhound.com; 155 Stevenson St) buses run daily service to Truckee, Sacramento and San Francisco ($34, five to seven hours), as does the once-daily westbound *California Zephyr* route operated by Amtrak (🗹775-329-8638, 800-872-7245; 280 N Center St). The train is slower and more expensive, but also more scenic and comfortable, with a bus connection from Emeryville for passengers to San Francisco ($46, 7½ hours).

ⓘ Getting Around

Casino hotels offer frequent free airport shuttles for their guests (and don't ask to see reservations).

The local **RTC Ride buses** (🗹775-348-7433; www.rtcwashoe.com; per ride/all day $2/4) blanket the city, and most routes converge at the RTC 4th St station downtown. Useful routes include the RTC Rapid line for S Virginia St, 11 for Sparks and 19 for the airport.

The free **Sierra Spirit bus** loops around all major downtown landmarks – including the casinos and the university – every 15 minutes from 7am to 7pm.

Central Coast

Best Places to Eat

» Passionfish (p474)

» Cracked Crab (p507)

» Cass House Restaurant
(p489)

» San Luis Obispo Farmers
Market (p499)

» Bouchon (p519)

Best Places to Stay

» Post Ranch Inn (p482)

» Inn of the Spanish Garden
(p518)

» Cass House Inn (p488)

» El Capitan Canyon (p518)

» Dream Inn (p457)

Why Go?

Too often forgotten or dismissed as 'flyover' country between San Francisco and LA, this fairytale stretch of California coast is packed with wild Pacific beaches, misty redwood
forests where hot springs hide, and rolling golden hills of
fertile vineyards and farm fields.

Here Hwy 1 pulls out all the stops, scenery-wise. Flower-
power Santa Cruz and the historic port town of Monterey
are gateways to the rugged wild lands of the bohemian Big
Sur coast. It's an epic journey snaking down to vainglorious
Hearst Castle, past lighthouses and cliffs over which condors soar.

Or get acquainted with California's agricultural heartland
along inland Hwy 101, called El Camino Real (the King's
Highway) by Spanish conquistadors and Franciscan friars.
Then soothe your nature-loving soul between laid-back San
Luis Obispo and idyllic seaside Santa Barbara, just a short
hop from the Channel Islands.

When to Go
Santa Barbara

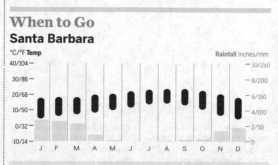

Apr Balmy
temperatures and
fewer tourists
than summer.
Wildflowers
bloom.

Jul Summer va-
cation and beach
season kick off;
SoCal ocean
waters warm up.

Oct Sunny blue
skies, yet smaller
crowds. Wine
country harvests
celebrated.

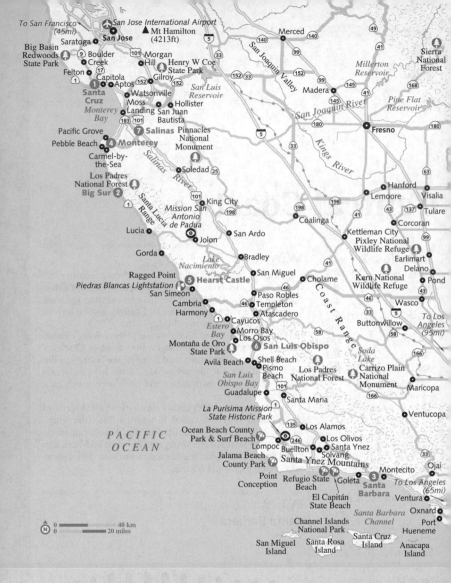

Central Coast Highlights

1 Scream your head off aboard the Giant Dipper on the beach boardwalk, then learn to surf in **Santa Cruz** (p455)

2 Cruise Hwy 1, where the sky touches the sea, along the rocky coastline of fairytale **Big Sur** (p477)

3 Soak up the chic atmosphere of whitewashed, red-tiled **Santa Barbara** (p513) before making your wine-country escape

4 Brings the kids to gawk at the aquatic denizens of the 'indoor ocean' at the **Monterey Bay Aquarium** (p464)

5 Marvel in disbelief at the grandiosity of **Hearst Castle** (p485) after meeting the neighbors: ginormous elephant seals

6 Hang loose in college-town **San Luis Obispo** (p498), surrounded by bodacious beaches and parklands

7 Explore down-to-earth novelist John Steinbeck's blue-collar world in the agricultural valley town of **Salinas** (p493)

ALONG HIGHWAY 1

Teeming with richly varied marine life, lined with often deserted beaches, and home to towns full of character and idiosyncratic charm all along its half-moon shore, Monterey Bay is anchored by Santa Cruz to the north. On the 125-mile stretch south of the Monterey Peninsula, you'll snake along an unbelievably picturesque coast until Hwy 1 joins with Hwy 101 at San Luis Obispo.

Santa Cruz

Santa Cruz has marched to its own beat since long before the Beat Generation. It's counterculture central, a touchy-feely, new-agey city famous for its leftie-liberal politics and live-and let-live ideology – except when it comes to dogs (rarely allowed off-leash), parking (meters run seven days a week) and Republicans (allegedly shot on sight). It's still cool to be a hippie or a stoner here (or better yet, both), although some far-out–looking freaks are just slumming Silicon Valley millionaires and trust-fund babies underneath.

Santa Cruz is a city of madcap fun, with a vibrant but chaotic downtown. On the waterfront is the famous beach boardwalk, and in the hills redwood groves embrace the University of California, Santa Cruz (UCSC) campus. Plan to spend at least half a day here, but to appreciate the aesthetic of jangly skirts, crystal pendants and Rastafarian dreadlocks, stay longer and plunge headlong into the rich local brew of surfers, students, punks and eccentric characters.

⦿ Sights

One of the best things to do in Santa Cruz is simply stroll, shop and people-watch along **Pacific Ave** downtown. A 15-minute walk away is the beach and the **Municipal Wharf**, where seafood restaurants, gift shops and barking sea lions compete for attention. Ocean-view **West Cliff Dr** follows the waterfront southwest of the wharf, paralleled by a paved recreational path.

Santa Cruz Beach
Boardwalk   AMUSEMENT PARK
(Map p458; ☎831-423-5590; www.beachboardwalk.com; 400 Beach St; per ride $3-5, all-day pass $30; ⊙from 10am or 11am daily May-Sep; ♿) The West Coast's oldest beachfront amusement park, this 1907 boardwalk has a glorious old-school Americana vibe, with the smell of cotton candy mixing with the salt air, punctuated by the squeals of kids hanging upside down on carnival rides. Famous thrills include the Giant Dipper, a 1924 wooden roller coaster, and the 1911 Looff carousel, both National Historic Landmarks. On summer Friday nights, catch free concerts by rock veterans you may have thought were already dead. For kid-friendly train rides up into the redwoods, see p463. Closing times and off-season hours vary.

Seymour Marine
Discovery Center   MUSEUM
(Map p462; www2.ucsc.edu/seymourcenter; end of Delaware Ave; adult/child 4-16yr $6/4; ⊙10am-5pm Tue-Sat, noon-5pm Sun, also 10am-5pm Mon Jul & Aug; ♿) Near Natural Bridges State Beach, this kids' educational center is part of UCSC's Long Marine Laboratory. Interactive natural-science exhibits include tidal touch pools and aquariums, while outside you can gawk at the world's largest blue-whale skeleton. Guided tours are usually given at 1pm, 2pm and 3pm daily; sign up in person an hour in advance (no reservations).

Santa Cruz Surfing Museum   MUSEUM
(Map p462; www.santacruzsurfingmuseum.org; 701 W Cliff Dr; admission by donation; ⊙noon-4pm Thu-Mon Sep-Jun, 10am-5pm Wed-Mon Jul & Aug) A mile south of the wharf along the coast, the old lighthouse is packed with memorabilia, including vintage redwood surfboards. Fittingly, Lighthouse Point overlooks two popular surf breaks.

University of California,
Santa Cruz   UNIVERSITY
(UCSC; Map p462; www.ucsc.edu) Check it: the school mascot is a banana slug! Established

---

FAST FACTS

» **Population of Santa Barbara** 88,410

» **Average temperature low/high in Santa Barbara** Jan 42/65°F, Jul 57/77°F

» **Los Angeles to Santa Barbara** 95 miles, 1¾ to 2½ hours

» **Monterey to San Luis Obispo** 140 miles, 2½ to three hours

» **San Francisco to Santa Cruz** 75 miles, 1½ to two hours

MYSTERY SPOT

A kitschy, old-fashioned tourist trap, Santa Cruz's **Mystery Spot** (☎831-423-8897; www.mysteryspot.com; 465 Mystery Spot Rd; admission $5, parking $5; ⏰10am-6pm Sun-Thu & 9am-7pm Fri & Sat late May-early Sep, 10am-4pm Sun-Thu & 10am-5pm Fri & Sat early Sep-late May; ⛪) has scarcely changed since it opened in 1940. On a steeply sloping hillside, compasses seem to point crazily, mysterious forces push you around and buildings lean at odd angles. Make reservations, or risk being stuck waiting for a tour. It's 3 miles north of downtown: take Water St to Market St, turn left and continue on Branciforte Dr into the hills.

in 1965 in the hills above town, this youthful university is known for its creative, liberal bent. The rural campus has fine stands of redwoods and architecturally interesting buildings – some made with recycled materials – designed to blend in with rolling pastureland. Peruse two top-notch art galleries, a peaceful **arboretum** (http://arboretum.ucsc.edu/; 1156 High St; adult/child 6-17yr $5/2, free 1st Tue of the month; ⏰9am-5pm) and picturesquely decaying 19th-century structures from Cowell Ranch, upon which the campus was built.

Santa Cruz Museum of Natural History   MUSEUM
(Map p462; www.santacruzmuseums.org; 1305 E Cliff Dr; adult/child under 18yr $4/free; ⏰10am-5pm Wed-Sun late May-early Sep, 10am-5pm Tue-Sat early Sep-late May; ⛪) The collections at this pint-sized museum include cultural artifacts from Ohlone tribespeople and a touch-friendly tidepool that shows off sea critters living along the beach right across the street.

Museum of Art & History   MUSEUM
(Map p458; www.santacruzmah.org; McPherson Center, 705 Front St; adult/child 12-17yr $5/2; ⏰11am-5pm Tue-Sun, to 9pm 1st Fri of the month) Downtown, this smart little museum is worth a look for its rotating displays by contemporary California artists and exhibits exploring offbeat local history.

🏖 Beaches
Sun-kissed Santa Cruz has warmer beaches than often-foggy Monterey. *Baywatch* it isn't, but 29 miles of coastline reveal a few Hawaii-worthy beaches, craggy coves, some primo surf spots and big sandy stretches where your kids will have a blast. Too bad fog ruins many a summer morning; it often burns off by the afternoon.

West Cliff Dr is lined with scramble-down-to coves and plentiful parking. If you don't want sand in your shoes, park yourself on a bench and watch enormous pelicans dive for fish. You'll find bathrooms and showers at the lighthouse parking lot.

Locals favor less-trampled **East Cliff Dr** beaches, which are bigger and more protected from the wind, making calmer waters. Except at a small metered lot at 26th Ave, parking is by permit only on weekends (buy a $7 per day permit at 9th Ave).

Less crowded **state beaches** (www.parks.ca.gov; per car $10; ⏰8am-sunset) await off Hwy 1 southbound. In Aptos, **Seacliff State Beach** (☎831-685-6442) harbors a 'cement boat,' a quixotic freighter built of concrete that floated OK, but ended up here as a coastal fishing pier. Further south near Watsonville, the La Selva Beach exit off Hwy 1 leads to **Manresa State Beach** (☎831-761-1975) and **Sunset State Beach** (☎831-763-7062), for miles of sand and surf practically all to yourself.

🏃 Activities
Surfing
Year-round, water temperatures average less than 60°F, meaning that without a wetsuit, body parts quickly turn blue. Surfing is incredibly popular, especially at experts-only **Steamer Lane** and beginners' **Cowell's**, both off West Cliff Dr. Other favorite surf spots include **Pleasure Point Beach**, on East Cliff Dr toward Capitola, and South County's **Manresa State Beach** off Hwy 1.

Santa Cruz Surf School   SURFING
(Map p458; ☎831-426-7072; www.santacruzsurfschool.com; 322 Pacific Ave; 2hr lesson incl equipment rental $80-90) Wanna learn to surf? Near the wharf, friendly male and female instructors will have you standing and surfing on your first day out.

O'Neill Surf Shop   SURFING
(Map p462; ☎831-475-4151; www.oneill.com; 1115 41st Ave; wetsuit/surfboard rental from $10/20; ⏰9am-8pm Mon-Fri, 8am-8pm Sat & Sun) Head east to Capitola to worship at this internationally renowned surfboard maker's flagship store. Also on the beach boardwalk and downtown.

Cowell's Beach Surf Shop   SURFING
(Map p458; ☏831-427-2355; 30 Front St; 2hr lesson $80; ⊘8am-6pm; ✸) Rent surfboards, boogie boards, wetsuits and other beach gear near the wharf, where veteran staff offer heaps of local tips and teach surfing too.

Kayaking

Kayaking lets you discover the craggy coastline and kelp beds where sea otters float.

Venture Quest   KAYAKING
(Map p458; ☏831-427-2267; www.kayaksantacruz.com; Municipal Wharf; kayak rentals $30-100, tours $30-70; ✸) Convenient rentals on the wharf, with whale-watching and sea-cave tours, including moonlight paddles.

Kayak Connection   KAYAKING
(Map p462; ☏831-479-1121; www.kayakconnection.com; Santa Cruz Harbor, 413 Lake Ave; kayak rentals $35-50, tours & lessons $50-100; ✸) Rents kayaks and offers lessons and tours, including sunrise, sunset and full-moon trips on Monterey Bay.

Whale-Watching & Fishing

Winter whale-watching trips run from December to April, though there's plenty of marine life to see on a summer bay cruise, too. Many fishing trips depart from the wharf, where a few shops rent fishing tackle and poles, if you're keen to join locals waiting patiently for a bite.

Stagnaro's   CRUISES, TOURS
(☏800-979-3370; www.stagnaros.com) This longstanding tour operator offers scenic and sunset cruises around Monterey Bay (adult/child under 14 years from $20/13), whale-watching tours (adult/child under 14 years

$45/31) and fishing trips (adult/child under 16 years from $50/40).

✸ Festivals & Events

Woodies on the Wharf   CULTURAL
(www.santacruzwoodies.com) A classic car show featuring vintage surf-style station wagons in late June.

Shakespeare Santa Cruz   THEATER
(www.shakespearesantacruz.org) Damn good productions of the Bard at UCSC and in a redwood grove during July, August and September.

Open Studio Art Tour   CULTURAL
(www.ccscc.org) Explore local artists' creative workshops over three weekends in October.

🛏 Sleeping

Santa Cruz does not have not enough beds to satisfy demand: expect outrageous prices at peak times for nothing-special rooms. Places near the boardwalk run the gamut from friendly to frightening. If you're looking for a straightforward motel, check out Ocean St further inland or Mission St (Hwy 1) near the UCSC campus.

TOP **Dream Inn**   BOUTIQUE HOTEL $$$
CHOICE
(Map p458; ☏831-426-4330, 866-774-7735; www.dreaminnsantacruz.com; 175 W Cliff Dr; r $200-380; ✲◉✶⊛) Overlooking the wharf from a spectacular hillside perch, this retro-chic boutique-on-the-cheap hotel is as stylish as Santa Cruz gets. Rooms have all mod cons, while the beach is just steps away. Don't miss happy hour at Aquarius restaurant's ocean-view bar.

CENTRAL COAST SANTA CRUZ

DON'T MISS

TOP SANTA CRUZ BEACHES

» **Main Beach** *The* scene, with a huge sandy stretch, volleyball courts and swarms of people. Park on East Cliff Dr and walk across the *Lost Boys* trestle to the boardwalk.

» **Its Beach** The only official off-leash beach for dogs (before 10am and after 4pm) is just west of the lighthouse. The field across the street is another good romping ground.

» **Natural Bridges State Beach** Best for sunsets, this family favorite has lots of sand, tidepools and monarch butterflies from mid-October through late February. It's at the far end of West Cliff Dr; parking costs $10.

» **Twin Lakes State Beach** Big beach with bonfire pits and a lagoon, good for kids and often fairly empty. It's off East Cliff Dr around 7th Ave.

» **Moran Lake County Park** With a good surf break and bathrooms, this pretty all-around sandy spot is further east at 26th Ave off East Cliff Dr.

Santa Cruz

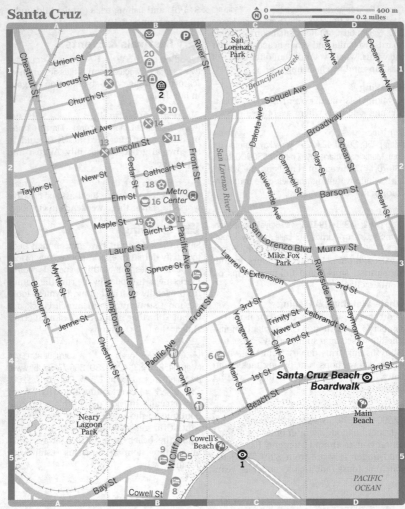

Adobe on Green B&B   B&B $$
(Map p462; ☎831-469-9866; www.adobeongreen.com; 103 Green St; r incl breakfast $149-199; ☎)
Peace and quiet are the mantras at this place, a short walk from Pacific Ave. The hosts are practically invisible, but their thoughtful touches are everywhere, from boutique-hotel amenities in spacious, stylish and solar-powered rooms to breakfast spreads from their organic gardens.

Pleasure Point Inn   INN $$$
(Map p462; ☎831-475-4657; www.pleasurepointinn.com; 23665 E Cliff Dr; r incl breakfast $225-295; ☎)
Live out your fantasy of California beachfront living in four clean-lined, contemporary rooms with hardwood floors, tiled bathrooms with Jacuzzi tubs, kitchenettes and private patios. Climb to the rooftop hot-tub deck for drop-dead ocean views.

Pacific Blue Inn   B&B $$
(Map p458; ☎831-600-8880; http://pacificblueinn.com; 636 Pacific Ave; r incl breakfast $170-240; ☎)
This downtown courtyard B&B is an eco-conscious gem, with water-saving fixtures and both renewable and recycled building materials. Refreshingly sleek rooms have

Santa Cruz

pillowtop beds, fireplaces and flat-screen TVs with DVD players. Free loaner bikes.

West Cliff Inn INN $$$
(Map p458; ☎831-457-2200; www.westcliffinn.com; 174 W Cliff Dr; r incl breakfast $175-400; 📶) In a classy Victorian house west of the wharf, this boutique inn's quaint rooms mix seagrass wicker, dark wood and jaunty striped curtains. The most romantic suites have gas fireplaces and let you spy on the breaking surf.

Sea & Sand Inn MOTEL $$$
(Map p458; ☎831-427-3400; www.santacruzmotels.com; 201 W Cliff Dr; r $109-429; 📶) With a grassy lawn at the cliff's edge, this spiffy, if overpriced motel overlooks Main Beach and the wharf. Fall asleep to braying sea lions! Rooms are smallish, but ocean views can be stellar.

Pelican Point Inn INN $$
(Map p462; ☎831-475-3381; www.pelicanpointinn-santacruz.com; 21345 E Cliff Dr; ste $99-199; 👪) Ideal for families, these roomy apartments near a kid-friendly beach are equipped with everything you'll need for a lazy vacation, from kitchenettes to high-speed internet. Weekly rates available.

Sunny Cove Motel MOTEL $$
(Map p462; ☎831-475-1741; www.sunnycovemotel.com; 21610 E Cliff Dr; r $90-200; 🏊🐾) It's nothing fancy, but this tidy little hideaway east of downtown is a staunch budget fave. The long-time Santa Cruzian owner rents retro beach-house rooms and kitchenette suites.

HI Santa Cruz Hostel HOSTEL $
(Map p458; ☎831-423-8304; www.hi-santacruz.org; 321 Main St; dm $25-28, r $55-105, all with shared bath; ⏰check-in 5-10pm; @) Budget overnighters dig this cute hostel at the century-old Carmelita Cottages surrounded by flowering gardens, just two blocks from the beach. Cons: 11pm curfew, three-night maximum stay. Reservations essential.

State Park Campgrounds CAMPGROUND $
(☎reservations 800-444-7275; www.reserveamerica.com; tent & RV sites $35-50) Book well ahead to camp by the beaches and in the cool Santa Cruz Mountains. Terrific spots include Henry Cowell Redwoods and Big Basin Redwoods State Parks, in the redwood forests off Hwy 9 (see p463); New Brighton State Beach, near Capitola; and Manresa and Sunset State Beaches farther south off Hwy 1 (see p516).

Best Western Plus Capitola By-the-Sea Inn & Suites MOTEL $$
(Map p462; ☎831-477-0607; www.bestwesterncapitola.com; 1435 41st Ave; r incl breakfast $90-240; ❄@📶🏊👪) Dependable motel away from the beach. Impeccably clean rooms, spacious enough for families.

Mission Inn MOTEL $$
(Map p462; ☎831-425-5455, 800-895-5455; www.
mission-inn.com; 2250 Mission St (Hwy 1); r incl
breakfast $80-140; ❀⛱☙) Serviceable motel
with a sauna and garden courtyard, near
UCSC. Away from the beach.

✕ Eating

Alas, Santa Cruz's food scene lacks luster.
Downtown is chockablock with just-okay
cafes. If you're looking for seafood, wander
among the wharf's takeout counter joints.
Mission St near UCSC and neighboring Cap-
itola offer cheap, casual eats.

Soif BISTRO $$$
(Map p458; ☎831-423-2020; www.soifwine.com;
105 Walnut Ave; small plates $5-17, mains $19-28;
☉5-10pm Sun-Thu, to 11pm Fri & Sat) Downtown
is where bon vivants flock for a heady selection of 50 international wines by the glass,
paired with a sophisticated, seasonally driv-
en Euro-Cal menu. Expect tastebud-ticklers
like wild arugula salad with roasted apricot
and curry-honey vinaigrette or baby back
ribs with coffee-barbecue sauce. Live music
some nights.

⬛ Cellar Door CALIFORNIAN $$$
(Map p462; ☎831-425-6771; www.bonnydoon
vineyard.com; 328 Ingalls St; small plates $5-22,
prix-fixe dinner $25-40; ☉noon-2pm Sat & Sun,
5:30-9pm Thu-Sun, community dinner 6:30pm
Wed) At Bonny Doon Vineyard's tasting
room, this hideaway cafe packs organic,
biodynamic and seasonal farm-to-table
goodness into tidy tapas plates and hosts
barrel-tasting winemakers' dinners. Linger
over a glass of whimsically named *Le Cig-
are Volant*, a wicked Rhone blend.

Engfer Pizza Works PIZZERIA $$
(Map p462; www.engferpizzaworks.com; 537
Seabright Ave; pizzas $8-23; ☉4-9:30pm Tue-Sun;
⬛) Detour to find this old factory, where
wood-fired oven pizzas are made from scratch
with love – the no-name specialty is like a giant salad on roasted bread. Play ping-pong
and down draft microbrews while you wait.

El Palomar MEXICAN $$
(Map p458; ☎831-425-7575; 1336 Pacific Ave;
mains $7-27; ☉11am-11pm; ⬛) Always packed
and consistently good (if not great), El Palo-
mar serves tasty Mexican staples – try the
seafood *ceviches* – and fruity margaritas.
Tortillas are made fresh by charming wom-
en in the covered courtyard.

Zachary's AMERICAN $
(Map p458; 819 Pacific Ave; mains $6-11; ☉7am-
2:30pm Tue-Sun) At the scruffy brunch spot
that locals don't want you to know about,
huge portions of sourdough pancakes and
blueberry cream-cheese coffee cake will
keep you going all day. 'Mike's Mess' is the
kitchen-sink standout.

Tacos Moreno MEXICAN $
(Map p462; www.tacosmoreno.com; 1053 Water
St; dishes $2-6; ☉11am-8pm) Who cares how
long the line is at lunchtime when every
hungry surfer in town is here? Aficionados
find taquería heaven, from marinated pork,
chicken and beef soft tacos and quesadillas
to supremely stuffed burritos.

Buttery BAKERY $
(Map p462; http://butterybakery.com; 702 Soquel
Ave; snacks $4-8; ☉7am-7pm; ⬛) For more than
two decades, this bustling bakery has been
baking such old-world confections as choco-
late croissants and fruit tarts. Squeeze your-
self into the corner cafe for deli sandwiches
and soups.

Bagelry DELI $
(Map p458; 320a Cedar St; items $3-6; ☉6:30am-
5:30pm Mon-Fri, 7:30am-4:30pm Sat, 6:30am-4pm
Sun; ⬛) The bagels here are twice-cooked
(boiled, then baked), and come with fantas-
tic crunchy spreads, like hummus and egg
salad. Check out the bulletin board for com-
munity goings-on.

⬛ Penny Ice Creamery ICE CREAM $
(Map p458; http://thepennyicecreamery.com; 913
Cedar St; ice cream $2-4; ☉noon-9pm Sun-Wed, to
11pm Thu-Sat) With a cult following, this arti-
san ice-cream shop makes its zany flavors,
like avocado, cherry-balsamic or roasted
barley, from scratch using local, organic and
even wild ingredients.

Donnelly Fine Chocolates CANDY $
(Map p462; www.donnellychocolates.com; 1509
Mission St; candy $2-5; ☉10:30am-6pm Tue-Fri,
noon-6pm Sat & Sun) The Willy Wonka of
Santa Cruz makes stratospherically priced
chocolates on par with the big city. This
guy is an alchemist! Try the cardamom
truffles.

**⬛ New Leaf Community
Market** GROCERIES $
(Map p458; www.newleaf.com; 1134 Pacific Ave;
☉9am-9pm) Organic local produce, natural-
foods groceries and deli take-out downtown.

Santa Cruz Farmers Market   MARKET $

(Map p458; www.santacruzfarmersmarket.org; cnr Lincoln & Center Sts; ⊘2:30-6:30pm Wed) For organic produce and an authentic taste of the local vibe.

🍷 Drinking

Downtown overflows with bars, hookah lounges and coffee shops.

Caffe Pergolesi   CAFE

(Map p458; www.theperg.com; 418 Cedar St; ⊘7am-11pm; 🛜) Discuss conspiracy theories over stalwart coffee, tea or beer at this way-popular landmark cafe in a Victorian house with a big ol' tree-shaded veranda overlooking the street. Local art hangs on the walls, with live musicians some evenings.

Santa Cruz Mountain Brewing   BREWPUB

(Map p462; www.santacruzmountainbrewing.com; Swift Street Courtyard, 402 Ingalls St; ⊘noon-10pm) Bold organic brews are poured at this tiny brewpub, squeezed between Santa Cruz Mountains wine-tasting rooms just west of town off Mission St (Hwy 1). Oddest flavor? Olallieberry cream ale.

Vino Prima   WINE BAR

(Map p458; www.vinoprimawines.com; Municipal Wharf; ⊘2-8pm Mon-Tue, 2-10pm Wed-Fri, noon-10pm Sat, noon-8pm Sun) Near the far end of the wharf, with dreamy ocean views, this spot pours California boutique wines, including hard-to-find bottles from Santa Cruz and Monterey Counties.

Surf City Billiards & Cafe   BAR

(Map p458; www.surfcitybilliards.com; 931 Pacific Ave; ⊘4-11pm Mon-Thu, 4pm-1am Fri & Sat, 10am-11pm Sun) A relief from downtown's dive bars, this upstairs pool hall has Brunswick Gold Crown tables for shooting stick, pro dartboards, big-screen TVs and pretty good pub grub.

Verve Coffee Roasters   CAFE

(Map p462; www.vervecoffeeroasters.com; 816 41st Ave; ⊘6am-7:30pm Mon-Fri, 7am-8:30pm Sat, 7am-7:30pm Sun; 🛜) To sip freshly roasted artisan espresso, join the surfers and internet hipsters at this industrial-zen cafe. Single-origin brews and house-made blends rule.

Firefly Coffee House   CAFE

(Map p458; 131 Front St; ⊘5:30am-6pm Mon-Sat, 7am-2pm Sun; 🛜) Bohemian indoor/outdoor people's coffeeshop brews organic, fair-trade java and delish chai flavored with orange zest and an Indian bazaar's worth of spices.

☆ Entertainment

Free weeklies *Metro Santa Cruz* (www.metrosantacruz.com) and *Good Times* (www.gtweekly.com) cover the music, arts and nightlife scenes.

Catalyst   LIVE MUSIC

(Map p458; ☎831-423-1336; www.catalystclub.com; 1011 Pacific Ave) Over the years, this venue for local bands has seen big-time national acts perform, from Queens of the Stone Age to Snoop Dogg. When there's no music, hang in the upstairs bar and pool room.

Moe's Alley   LIVE MUSIC

(Map p462; ☎831-479-1854; www.moesalley.com; 1535 Commercial Way; ⊘Tue-Sun) Hidden in an industrial wasteland, this casual place puts on live sounds almost every night, from jazz and blues to reggae, roots, salsa and acoustic world-music jams.

Kuumbwa Jazz Center   LIVE MUSIC

(Map p458; ☎831-427-2227; www.kuumbwajazz.org; 320 Cedar St) Hosting jazz luminaries since 1975, this nonprofit theater is for serious jazz cats who come for the famous-name performers in an electrically intimate room.

🔒 Shopping

Wander Pacific Ave and downtown's side streets to find one-of-a-kind, locally owned boutiques (not just head shops, we promise).

Annieglass   ART

(Map p458; www.annieglass.com; 110 Cooper St; ⊘11am-6pm Mon-Sat, to 5pm Sun) Handcrafted sculptural glassware sold in ultrachic New York department stores and displayed in the Smithsonian American Art Museum are made right here in wackadoodle Santa Cruz. Go figure.

O'Neill Surf Shop   SURFBOARDS, CLOTHING

(Map p458; www.oneills.com; 110 Cooper St; ⊘10am-6pm) For Santa Cruz' own internationally popular brand of surf wear and gear, from hoodies to board shorts. Also on the beach boardwalk and in Capitola.

Bookshop Santa Cruz   BOOKS

(Map p458; www.bookshopsantacruz.com; 1520 Pacific Ave; ⊘9am-10pm Sun-Thu, to 11pm Fri & Sat) Vast selection of new books, a few used ones, and popular and unusual magazines.

Around Santa Cruz

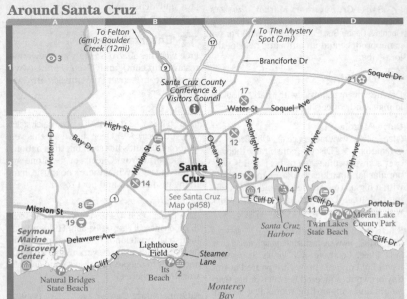

Around Santa Cruz

Buy 'Keep Santa Cruz Weird' bumper stickers here.

ℹ Information

FedEx Office (Map p458; 712 Front St; per min 20-30¢; ⊗24hr Mon-Thu, midnight-11pm Fri, 9am-9pm Sat, 9am-midnight Sun; @🖥) Pay-as-you-go internet workstations and free wi-fi.

KPIG 107.5FM Plays the classic Santa Cruz soundtrack (think Bob Marley, Janis Joplin and Willie Nelson).

Post office (Map p458; www.usps.com; 850 Front St; ⊗9am-5pm Mon-Fri)

Public library (Map p458; www.santacruzpl. org; 224 Church St; ⊗10am-7pm Mon-Thu,

Soquel

To Aptos (3mi);
Moss Landing (20mi);
Monterey (38mi)

Capitola

Capitola Chamber
of Commerce

Capitola
Ave

Capitola Rd

New Brighton
State Beach

PACIFIC
OCEAN

Pleasure
Point Beach

10am-5pm Sat, 1-5pm Sun; @🤶) Free wi fi and public internet terminals.

Santa Cruz County Conference & Visitors Council (Map p462; ☏831-425-1234; www. santacruz.org; 1211 Ocean St; ⊙9am-5pm Mon-Fri, 10am-4pm Sat & Sun; @) Free brochures, maps and internet-terminal access.

⊙ Getting There & Around

Santa Cruz is 75 miles south of San Francisco via Hwy 17, a nail-bitingly narrow, winding mountain road. Monterey is about an hour's drive further south via Hwy 1.

Greyhound (www.greyhound.com; Metro Center, 920 Pacific St) has a few daily buses to San Francisco ($16, three hours), Salinas ($14, 65 minutes), Santa Barbara ($50, six hours) and Los Angeles ($57, nine hours).

Santa Cruz Metro (☏831-425-8600; www. scmtd.com; single-ride/day pass $1.50/4.50) operates local and countywide bus routes that converge on downtown's **Metro Center** (Map p458; 920 Pacific Ave). Frequent Hwy 17 express buses link Santa Cruz with San Jose's Amtrak/ CalTrain station ($5, 50 minutes).

Santa Cruz Airport Shuttles (☏831-421-9883; http://santacruzshuttles.com) runs shared shuttles to/from the airports at San Jose ($45), San Francisco ($75) and Oakland ($75); prices are the same for one or two passengers (credit-card surcharge $5).

Around Santa Cruz
SANTA CRUZ MOUNTAINS

Winding between Santa Cruz and Silicon Valley, Hwy 9 is a 40-mile backwoods byway through the Santa Cruz Mountains, passing tiny towns, towering redwood forests and fog-kissed vineyards (estate-bottled pinot noir is a specialty). Many wineries are only open on 'Passport Days' on the third Saturday of January, April, July and November. The **Santa Cruz Mountains Winegrowers Association** (www.scmwa.com) publishes a free winery map, available at tasting rooms, including those that have relocated to Santa Cruz itself, west of downtown off Hwy 1.

Heading north from Santa Cruz, it's **7** miles to Felton, passing **Henry Cowell Redwoods State Park** (☏831-335-4598; www. parks.ca.gov; 101 N Big Trees Park Rd; per car $10; ⊙sunrise-sunset), which has miles of hiking trails through old-growth redwood groves and camping along the San Lorenzo River. In Felton, **Roaring Camp Railroads** (☏831-335-4484; www.roaringcamp.com; 5401 Graham Hill Rd; tours adult/child 2-12yr from $24/17, parking $8; ⊙call for schedules) operates narrow-gauge steam trains up into the redwoods and a standard-gauge train down to the Santa Cruz Beach Boardwalk (p455).

Seven miles further north on Hwy 9, you'll drive through the pretty town of **Boulder Creek**, a good place to grab a bite. Roadside **Boulder Creek Brewery & Cafe Company** (www.bouldercreekbrewery.net; 13040 Hwy 9; mains $7-15; ⊙11:30am-10pm Sun-Thu, to 10:30pm Fri & Sat) is a local institution.

Follow Hwy 236 northwest for nine twisting miles to **Big Basin Redwoods State Park** (☏831-338-8860; www.bigbasin.org, www. parks.ca.gov; 21600 Big Basin Way; per car $10), where nature trails loop past giant old-growth redwoods. A 12.5-mile one-way section of the exhilarating **Skyline to the Sea Trail** ends at Waddell Beach on the coast, almost 20 miles northwest of Santa Cruz. On weekends, if you check Santa Cruz Metro schedules carefully, you may be able to ride up to Big Basin on bus 35A in the morning and get picked up by bus 40 at the beach in the afternoon.

CAPITOLA

Six miles east of Santa Cruz, the little seaside town of Capitola, nestled quaintly between ocean bluffs, attracts affluent crowds and families. Downtown is laid out for strolling, with arty shops and touristy restaurants

CENTRAL COAST AROUND SANTA CRUZ

inside seaside houses. Show up for mid-September's **Capitola Art & Wine Festival**, or the famous **Begonia Festival**, held over Labor Day weekend, with a flotilla of floral floats along Soquel Creek.

Catch an organic, shade-grown and fairly traded caffeine buzz at **Mr Toots Coffeehouse** (Map p462; http://tootscoffee.com; 2nd fl, 231 Esplanade; ☉7am-10pm; ☏), which has an art gallery and live music. Head inland to **Gayle's Bakery & Rosticceria** (Map p462; www.gaylesbakery.com; 504 Bay Ave; ☉6:30am-8:30pm; ▣), with its fresh deli where you can assemble beach picnics, or **Dharma's** (Map p462; www.dharmaland.com; 4250 Capitola Rd; mains $7-14; ☉8am-9pm; ✍), a global-fusion fast-food vegetarian and vegan restaurant.

The **Capitola Chamber of Commerce** (Map p462; ☎800-474-6522; www.capitolachamber.com; 716g Capitola Ave; ☉10am-4pm) offers travel tips. Driving downtown can be a nightmare in summer and on weekends; try the parking lot behind City Hall, off Capitola Ave by Riverview Dr.

MOSS LANDING & ELKHORN SLOUGH

Hwy 1 swings back toward the coast at Moss Landing, just south of the Santa Cruz County line, and almost 20 miles north of Monterey. From the working fishing harbor, **Sanctuary Cruises** (☎831-917-1042; www.sanctuarycruises.com; tours adult/child under 3yr/child 3-12yr $48/10/38) operates year-round whale-watching and dolphin-spotting cruises aboard biodiesel-fueled boats (reservations essential). Devour dock-fresh seafood down at warehouse-sized **Phil's Fish Market** (www.philsfishmarket.com; 7600 Sandholdt Rd; mains $10-20; ☉10am-8pm Sun-Thu, to 9pm Fri & Sat) or, after browsing the antiques shops, lunch at the **Haute Enchilada** (www.hauteenchilada.com; 7902 Moss Landing Rd; mains $11-26; ☉10am-8pm), an inspired Mexican restaurant inside a Frida Kahlo–esque art gallery.

Just east, **Elkhorn Slough National Estuarine Research Reserve** (☎831-728-2822; www.elkhornslough.org; 1700 Elkhorn Rd; adult/child under 16yr $2.50/free; 1700 Elkhorn Rd, Watsonville; ☉9am-5pm Wed-Sun) is popular with bird-watchers and hikers. Docent-led tours are typically offered at 10am and 1pm on Saturday and Sunday. Kayaking is a fantastic way to see the slough, though not on a windy day or when the tide is against you. Reserve ahead for kayak rentals ($35 to $70) or guided tours ($30 to $120) with **Kayak Connection** (☎831-724-5692; www.kayakconnection.com; 2370 Hwy 1) or **Monterey Bay**

Kayaks (☎831-373-5357; www.montereybaykayaks.com; 2390 Hwy 1).

Monterey

Working-class Monterey is all about the sea. What draws many tourists is the world-class aquarium, overlooking **Monterey Bay National Marine Sanctuary**, which protects dense kelp forests and a sublime variety of marine life, including seals and sea lions, dolphins and whales. The city itself possesses the best-preserved historical evidence of California's Spanish and Mexican periods, with many restored adobe buildings. An afternoon's wander through downtown's historic quarter promises to be more edifying than time spent in the tourist ghettos of Fisherman's Wharf and Cannery Row.

👁 Sights

🌿 **Monterey Bay Aquarium**   AQUARIUM
(Map p470; ☎831-648-4888, tickets 866-963-9645; www.montereybayaquarium.org; 886 Cannery Row; adult/child 3-12yr $30/20; ☉9:30am-6pm Mon-Fri, 9:30am-8pm Sat & Sun Jun-Aug, 10am-5pm or 6pm daily Sep-May; ☏▣) Monterey's most mesmerizing experience is its enormous aquarium, built on the former site of the city's largest sardine cannery. All kinds of aquatic creatures are on proud display, from kid-tolerant sea stars and slimy sea slugs to animated sea otters and surprisingly nimble 800lb tuna. The aquarium is much more than an impressive collection of glass tanks – thoughtful placards underscore the bay's cultural and historical contexts.

Every minute, upwards of 2000 gallons of seawater is pumped into the three-story **kelp forest**, re-creating as closely as possible the natural conditions you see out the windows to the east. The large fish of prey are at their charismatic best during mealtimes; divers hand-feed at 11:30am and 4pm. More entertaining are the sea otters, which may be seen basking in the **Great Tide Pool** outside the aquarium, where they are readied for reintroduction to the wild.

Even new-agey music and the occasional infinity-mirror illusion don't detract from the astounding beauty of jellyfish in the **Jellies Gallery**. To see fish – including hammerhead sharks and green sea turtles – that outweigh kids many times over, ponder the awesome **Open Sea** tank. Upstairs and downstairs you'll find **touch pools**, where you can get close to sea cucumbers, bat rays and tidepool creatures. Younger kids will love the interactive, bilingual **Splash Zone**, with penguin feedings at 10:30am and 3pm.

A visit can easily become a full-day affair, so get your hand stamped and break for lunch. To avoid long lines in summer and on weekends and holidays, buy tickets in advance. Metered on-street parking is limited, but parking lots and garages offering daily rates are plentiful uphill from Cannery Row.

Cannery Row   HISTORIC SITE

(Map p470) John Steinbeck's novel *Cannery Row* immortalized the sardine-canning business that was Monterey's lifeblood for the first half of the 20th century. Back in Steinbeck's day, it was a stinky, hardscrabble, working-class melting pot, which the novelist described as 'a poem, a stink, a grating noise, a quality of light, a tone, a habit, a nostalgia, a dream.' Sadly, there's precious little evidence of that era now. Overfishing and climatic changes caused the industry's collapse in the 1950s.

A bronze **bust** of the Pulitzer Prize-winning writer sits at the bottom of Prescott Ave, just steps from the unabashedly commercial experience his row has devolved into, chockablock with chain restaurants and souvenir shops hawking saltwater taffy. Check out the **Cannery Workers Shacks** at the base of flowery Bruce Ariss Way, which have sobering explanations of the hard lives led by the Filipino, Japanese, Spanish and other immigrant laborers.

Monterey State Historic Park   HISTORIC SITE

(☑cellphone audiotour 831-998-9458; www.parks.ca.gov) Old Monterey is home to an extraordinary assemblage of 19th-century brick and adobe buildings, administered as Monterey State Historic Park, all found along a 2-mile self-guided walking tour portentously called the Path of History. You can inspect dozens of buildings, many with charming gardens; expect some to be open while others aren't, according to a capricious schedule dictated by severe state-park budget cutbacks.

Pacific House Museum

(Map p470; ☑831-649-7118; 20 Custom House Plaza; donations welcome; ☻10am-4:30pm) Grab a free map, find out what's currently open and buy guided tour tickets for individual historic houses inside this 1847 adobe building, which has in-depth exhibits covering the state's multinational history. Nearby are a few more of the park's highlights, includ-

ing an **old whaling station**, California's first **theater** and a short walk further afield, the **old Monterey jail** featured in John Steinbeck's novel *Tortilla Flat*.

Custom House

(Map p470; Custom House Plaza; ☻10am-4pm Sat & Sun) In 1822 newly independent Mexico ended the Spanish trade monopoly and stipulated that any traders bringing goods to Alta California must first unload their cargoes here for duty to be assessed. In 1846 when the US flag was raised over the Custom House, *voilà!* California was formally annexed from Mexico. Restored to its 1840s appearance, today the house displays an exotic selection of goods that traders brought to exchange for California cowhides.

Casa Soberanes

(Map p470; 336 Pacific St) A beautiful garden with meandering walkways paved with abalone shells, bottle glass and even whalebones fronts, this adobe house was built in the 1840s during the late Mexican period. The interior is adorned with an eclectic mix of New England antiques, 19th-century goods imported on Chinese trading ships and modern Mexican folk art. Opening hours vary.

Across Pacific St, the large and colorful **Monterey Mural**, a contemporary mosaic on the exterior of the Monterey Conference Center, illustrates the city's history.

Stevenson House

(Map p470; 530 Houston St; ☻1-4pm Sat) Scottish writer Robert Louis Stevenson came to Monterey in 1879 to court his wife-to-be, Fanny Osbourne. This building, then the French Hotel, was where he stayed while reputedly devising his novel *Treasure Island*. The boarding-house rooms were primitive and Stevenson was still a penniless unknown. Today the house displays a superb collection of the writer's memorabilia.

Cooper-Molera Adobe

(Map p470; 525 Polk St; ☻store 10am-4pm daily, to 5pm May-Sep, tour schedules vary) In 1827, this stately adobe home was built by John Rogers Cooper, a New England sea captain, and three generations of his family resided here until 1968. Over time, the adobe buildings were partitioned and expanded, gardens were added, and it was later willed to the National Trust. Worth a browse, the bookshop also sells nostalgic toys and household goods.

Monterey Peninsula

N
0 — 2 km
0 — 1 mile

PACIFIC OCEAN

Enlargement:
17 ✕
18
8
ℹ
Lighthouse Ave
3
Central Ave
Park St
Forest Ave
Pine Ave
0 — 200 m
0 — 0.1 miles

Ocean View Blvd
Point Pinos
Pacific Grove
Point Pinos Lighthouse
4
Asilomar State Beach
13
Ridge Rd
Lover's Point
Spanish Bay
Sunset Dr
Asilomar Blvd
11
Alder St
Monarch Grove Sanctuary
5
Shoreline Park
Sinex Ave
Forest Ave
Pine Ave
See Enlargement
Gate (toll)
Sunset Dr
David Ave
Prescott Ave
See Monterey Map (p470)
The Links at Spanish Bay
Spanish Bay Rd
Point Joe
17-Mile Dr
Monterey Bay
Lighthouse Ave
Monterey
Monterey State Beach
Forest Lodge Rd
Gate (toll)
68
Presidio of Monterey
Del Monte Beach
16
Congress Rd
Veterans Memorial Park
14
Del Monte Ave
7
Ocean Rd
Stevenson Dr
Slack Rd
Lopez Rd
Gate (toll)
Pacific St
Del Monte Ave
1
To Sanctuary Beach Resort (9mi); Moss Landing (18mi)
Bird Rock
Forest Lake
Botanical Reserve
Skyline Dr
Fremont St
68
Forest Lake Rd
Bird Rock Rd
Sunridge Rd
Skyline Forest Dr
1
To Monterey Peninsula Airport (2mi); Salinas (17mi)
Cypress Point
Spyglass Hill Golf Course
Gate (toll)
Scenic Dr
68
Cypress Point Golf Course
Ronda Rd
Sunridge Rd
Portola Rd
Pebble Beach Golf Course
Pebble Beach
1
17-Mile Dr
17-Mile Dr
Sunset Point
2
Cypress Dr
9
Stillwater Cove
Carpenter St
Pescadero Point
2nd Ave
19
7
Cabrillo Hwy
Carmel Beach
15
ℹ
20
Scenic Rd
San Antonio Ave
12
Juniper Ave
Carmel-by-the-Sea
Carmel Bay
Carmel Point
Tor House
10
San Carlos Borroméo de Carmelo Mission
Carmel Valley Rd
PACIFIC OCEAN
6
Rio Rd
Carmel River Lagoon & Natural Preserve
Carmel River State Park
Carmel River
Carmel River State Beach
Point Lobos
Whalers Cove
Carmel Valley
Point Lobos State Natural Reserve
1
To Big Sur (20mi); Hearst Castle (85mi)

CENTRAL COAST MONTEREY

Monterey Peninsula

Monterey History & Maritime Museum
MUSEUM

(Map p470; ☑831-372-2608; http://montereyhistory.org; 5 Custom House Plaza; admission $5, free after 3pm on 1st Tue of the month; ☉10am-5pm Tue-Sun) Near the waterfront, this voluminous modern exhibition hall illuminates Monterey's salty past, from early Spanish explorers to the roller-coaster–like rise and fall of the local sardine industry that brought Cannery Row to life in the mid-20th century. Highlights include a ship-in-a-bottle collection and the historic Fresnel lens from Point Sur Lightstation.

Monterey Museum of Art
MUSEUM

(MMA; www.montereyart.org; adult/child under 13 $10/free; ☉11am-5pm Wed-Sat & 1-4pm Sun) Downtown, **MMA Pacific Street** (Map p470; ☑831-372-5477; 559 Pacific St) is particularly strong in California contemporary art and modern landscape painters and photographers, including Ansel Adams and Edward Weston. Temporary exhibits fill **MMA La Mirada** (Map p470; ☑831-372-3689; 720 Via Mirada), a silent-film-star's villa, whose humble adobe origins are exquisitely concealed. Visit both locations on the same ticket.

Royal Presidio Chapel
CHURCH

(Map p470; www.sancarloscathedral.net; San Carlos Cathedral, 500 Church St; admission by donation; ☉10am-noon Wed, 10am-3pm Fri, 10am-2pm Sat, 1-3pm Sun, also 10am-noon & 1:15-3:15pm 2nd & 4th Mon of the month) Built of sandstone in 1794, this graceful chapel is California's oldest continuously functioning church. The original 1770 mission church stood here before being moved to Carmel. As Monterey expanded under Mexican rule in the 1820s, older buildings were gradually destroyed, leaving behind this National Historic Landmark as the strongest reminder of the defeated Spanish colonial presence.

FREE Presidio of Monterey Museum
MUSEUM

(Map p470; www.monterey.org; Bldg 113, Corporal Ewing Rd; ☉10am-1pm Mon, 10am-4pm Thu-Sat, 1-4pm Sun) On the grounds of the original Spanish fort, this minor museum treats Monterey's history from a military perspective, looking at the Native American, Mexican and American periods.

🕊 Activities

Like its larger namesake in San Francisco, **Fisherman's Wharf** is a tacky tourist trap at heart, and a jumping-off point for deep-sea fishing trips. On the flip side, the authentic **Municipal Wharf II** is a short walk east. There fishing boats bob and sway, painters work on their canvases and seafood purveyors hawk fresh catches.

FREE **Dennis the Menace Park** PLAYGROUND
(Map p470; 777 Pearl St; ⊙10am-dusk, closed
Tue Sep-May; 🚸) A must for fans of kick-ass
playgrounds, this park was the brainchild
of Hank Ketcham, the creator of the classic comic strip. This ain't your standard
dumbed-down playground, suffocated
by Big Brother's safety regulations. With
lightning-fast slides, a hedge maze and
towering climbing walls, even some adults
can't resist playing here.

Cycling & Mountain-Biking

Along a former railway line, the **Monterey Peninsula Recreational Trail** travels 18
car-free miles along the waterfront, passing Cannery Row en route to Lovers Point
in Pacific Grove. Road-cycling enthusiasts
with nerves of steel can make the round trip
to Carmel along the **17-Mile Drive** (see the
boxed text, p475). Mountain-bikers head to
Fort Ord for 50 miles of single-track and fire
roads; the **Sea Otter Classic** (www.seaotter
classic.com) races there in mid-April.

Adventures by the Sea CYCLING
(Map p470; ☎831-372-1807; www.adventuresbythe
sea.com; 299 Cannery Row; rental per hr/day $7/25)
Beach cruiser and hybrid mountain-bike
rentals on Cannery Row and **downtown**
(210 Alvarado St).

Bay Bikes CYCLING
(Map p470; ☎831-655-2453; www.baybikes.com;
585 Cannery Row; per hr/day from $8/32) Cruiser,
tandem, hybrid and mountain bike rentals
near the aquarium.

Whale-Watching

You can spot whales off the coast of
Monterey Bay year-round. The season for
blue and humpback whales runs from late
April to early December, while gray whales
pass by from mid-December to mid-April.
Tour boats depart from downtown's Fisherman's Wharf and also Moss Landing (see
p464). Reserve trips at least a day in advance; be prepared for a bumpy, cold ride.

Monterey Whale Watching BOAT TOURS
(Map p470; ☎831-372-2203; tickets 800-979-3370;
www.montereywhalewatching.com; 96 Fisherman's
Wharf; 2½hr tour adult/child 3-12yr $40/30) Several daily departures.

Monterey Bay Whale Watch BOAT TOURS
(Map p470; ☎831-375-4658; www.monterey
baywhalewatch.com; 84 Fisherman's Wharf; 2½hr

tour adult/child 4-12yr from $38/27) Morning
and afternoon departures.

Diving & Snorkeling

Monterey Bay offers world-renowned diving
and snorkeling, including off **Lovers Point**
in Pacific Grove and at **Point Lobos State
Natural Reserve** near Carmel-by-the-Sea.
You'll want a wetsuit year-round. In summer upwelling currents carry cold water
from the deep canyon below the bay, sending a rich supply of nutrients up toward the
surface level to feed the bay's diverse marine life. These frigid currents also account
for the bay's chilly water temperatures and
summer fog that blankets the peninsula.

Monterey Bay Dive Charters SCUBA DIVING
(☎831-383-9276; www.mbdcscuba.com; scuba
rental per day $79-89, shore/boat dive from
$49/199) Rent a full scuba kit with wetsuit,
arrange small-group shore or boat dives or
take a virgin undersea plunge by booking a
three-hour beginners' dive experience ($159,
no PADI certification required).

Kayaking & Surfing

Monterey Bay Kayaks KAYAKING
(Map p470; ☎800-649-5357; www.monterey
baykayaks.com; 693 Del Monte Ave; rental per day
$30-50, tours adult/child from $50/40; 🚸) Rents
kayaks and stand-up paddle boarding (SUP)
equipment and leads kayaking lessons and
guided tours of Monterey Bay, including full-
moon, sunrise and sunset trips, and family
adventures.

Sunshine Freestyle Surf SURFING
(Map p470; ☎831-375-5015; http://sunshinefree
style.com; 443 Lighthouse Ave; rental per half/full
day surfboard $20/30, wetsuit $10/15, boogie board
$7/10) Monterey's oldest surf shop rents and
sells all the gear you'll need. Staff grudgingly
dole out tips.

🎭 Festivals & Events

**AT&T Pebble Beach National
Pro-Am** GOLF
(www.attpbgolf.com) Famous golf tournament mixes pros with celebrities; in early
February.

Castroville Artichoke Festival FOOD
(www.artichoke-festival.org) North of Monterey,
features 3D 'agro art' sculptures, cooking
demos, a farmers market and field tours; in
mid-May.

Strawberry Festival at Monterey Bay FOOD
(www.mbsf.com) Berry-licious pie-eating contests and live bands in Watsonville, north of Monterey, in early August.

Concours d'Elegance STREET
(www.pebblebeachconcours.net) Classic cars roll onto the fairways at Pebble Beach in mid-August.

Monterey County Fair CULTURE
(www.montereycountyfair.com) Old-fashioned fun, carnival rides, horse-riding and livestock competitions, wine tasting and live music in late August and early September.

TOP CHOICE **Monterey Jazz Festival** MUSIC
(www.montereyjazzfestival.org) One of the world's longest-running jazz festivals (since 1958), held in mid-September.

🛌 Sleeping

Book ahead for special events and summer visits. To avoid the tourist congestion and jacked-up prices of Cannery Row, consider staying in Pacific Grove (p474). Cheaper chain and indie motels line Munras Ave, south of downtown, and N Fremont St, east of Hwy 1.

InterContinental–The Clement HOTEL $$$
(Map p470; 831-375-4500, 888-424-6835; www. intercontinental.com; 750 Cannery Row; r $200-455; ❋@🛜🏊🐾) Like an upscale version of a New England millionaire's seaside compound, this all-encompassing resort presides over Cannery Row. For the utmost luxury and romance, book an ocean-view suite with a balcony and private fireplace, then breakfast in bayfront C Restaurant downstairs. Parking $18.

Sanctuary Beach Resort HOTEL $$$
(831-883-9478, 877-944-3863; www.thesanctu arybeachresort.com; 3295 Dunes Dr, Marina; r $179-329; ❋@🛜🏊🐾) Be lulled to sleep by the surf at this low-lying retreat hidden in the sand dunes north of Monterey. Townhouses harbor petite rooms with gas fireplaces and binoculars to borrow for whale-watching. The beach is an off-limits nature preserve, but there are plenty of other beaches and walking trails nearby.

Jabberwock B&B $$$
(Map p470; 831-372-4777, 888-428-7253; www. jabberwockinn.com; 598 Laine St; r incl breakfast $169-309; @🛜) High atop a hill and barely visible through a shroud of foliage, this 1911 Arts and Crafts house hums a playful *Alice in Wonderland* tune through its seven immaculate rooms. Over afternoon tea and cookies or evening wine and hors d'oeuvres, ask the genial hosts about the house's many salvaged architectural elements.

Casa Munras BOUTIQUE HOTEL $$
(Map p470; 831-375-2411; www.hotelcasamun ras.com; 700 Munras Ave; r $185-279; @🛜🏊🐾) Built around an adobe hacienda once owned by a 19th-century Spanish colonial don, chic modern rooms come with lofty beds and some gas fireplaces, all inside two-story motel-esque buildings. Splash in a heated outdoor pool, unwind at the tapas bar or take a sea-salt scrub in the tiny spa. Pet fee $50.

Hotel Abrego BOUTIQUE HOTEL $$
(Map p470; 831-372-7551; www.hotelabrego. com; 755 Abrego St; r $140-270; 🛜🏊🐾) Another downtown boutique hotel, albeit with slightly fewer amenities, where most of the spacious, clean-lined contemporary rooms have gas fireplaces and chaise longues. Take a dip in the outdoor pool or warm up in the hot tub. Pet fee $30.

Monterey Hotel HISTORIC HOTEL $$
(Map p470; 831-375-3184, 800-966-6490; www. montereyhotel.com; 406 Alvarado St; r $70-310; 🛜) In the heart of downtown and a short walk from Fisherman's Wharf, this 1904 edifice harbors five dozen small, somewhat noisy, but freshly renovated rooms with Victorian-styled furniture and plantation shutters. No elevator. Parking $17.

Colton Inn MOTEL $$
(Map p470; 831-649-6500; www.coltoninn.com; 707 Pacific St; r $109-199; ❋🛜) Downtown, this champ of a motel prides itself on cleanliness and friendliness. There's no pool and zero view, but staff loan out DVDs, some rooms have real log-burning fireplaces, hot tubs or kitchenettes, and there's even a dry sauna for guests.

HI Monterey Hostel HOSTEL $
(Map p470; 831-649-0375; www.montereyhostel. org; 778 Hawthorne St; dm $25-28, r $59-75, all with shared bath; ⊘check-in 4-10pm; @) Four blocks from Cannery Row and the aquarium, this simple, clean hostel lets budget backpackers stuff themselves silly with make-your-own waffle breakfasts. Reservations strongly

Monterey

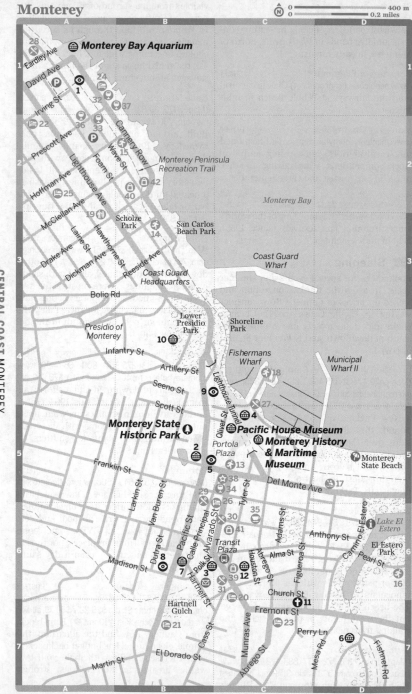

N

0 ——————— 400 m
0 ——————— 0.2 miles

Monterey Bay Aquarium

Eardley Ave

David Ave

Irving St

28

1

Cannery Row

24

32

37

22

36

33

Prescott Ave

Lighthouse Ave

Foam St

Wave St

15

Hoffman Ave

McClellan Ave

Laine St

Hawthorne St

Drake Ave

Dickman Ave

Reeside Ave

25

19

Scholze Park

14

40

42

*Monterey Peninsula
Recreation Trail*

Monterey Bay

San Carlos
Beach Park

*Coast Guard
Wharf*

Bolio Rd

*Presidio of
Monterey*

Infantry St

Lower
Presidio
Park

10

Artillery St

Seeno St

Scott St

9

*Coast Guard
Headquarters*

Shoreline
Park

*Fishermans
Wharf*

*Municipal
Wharf II*

18

27

**Monterey State
Historic Park**

Lighthouse Tunnel

Olivier St

4

Pacific House Museum

**Monterey History
& Maritime
Museum**

Portola
Plaza

2

5

13

38

Monterey
State Beach

Franklin St

Larkin St

Van Buren St

Pacific St

Calle Principal

Del Monte Ave

17

34

29

26

35

Tyler St

Adams St

Anthony St

Lake El
Estero

El Estero
Park

30

41

Transit
Plaza

Alma St

Abrego St

Houston St

Figueroa St

Camino El Estero

Pearl St

Madison St

Dutra St

8

7

Polk St

Alvarado St

Hartnell St

3

39

12

16

31

20

Cass St

Hartnell
Gulch

21

Church St

11

23

Fremont St

Munras Ave

Abrego St

Perry Ln

Mesa Rd

6

Fishnet Rd

Martin St

El Dorado St

Monterey

recommended. Take MST bus 1 from downtown's Transit Plaza.

Veterans Memorial Park CAMPGROUND $
(Map p466; ☑831-646-3865; www.monterey.org; Veterans Memorial Park, off Skyline Dr; tent & RV sites $25-30) Tucked into the forest, this municipal campground has 40 well-kept, grassy, nonreservable sites near nature-preserve hiking trails. Amenities include coin-op hot showers, flush toilets, drinking water, firepits and BBQ picnic areas. Three-night maximum stay.

✗ Eating

Uphill from Cannery Row, Lighthouse Ave is lined with budget-friendly, multiethnic eateries, from Japanese sushi to Hawaiian barbecue to Middle Eastern kebabs. Alternatively, keep going west to Pacific Grove (p474).

First Awakenings BRUNCH $
(Map p470; www.firstawakenings.net; American Tin Cannery Mall, 125 Oceanview Blvd; mains $5-12; ☺7am-2pm Mon-Fri, to 2:30pm Sat & Sun; 🖶) Sweet and savory, all-American breakfasts and lunches and bottomless pitchers of coffee merrily weigh down outdoor tables at this hideaway cafe. Order creative dishes like 'bluegerm' pancakes or the spicy 'Viva Carnita' egg scramble.

Monterey's Fish House SEAFOOD $$$
(Map p466; ☑831-373-4647; 2114 Del Monte Ave; mains $12-35; ☺11:30am-2:30pm Mon-Fri, 5-9:30pm daily) Watched over by photos of Sicilian fishermen, dig into dock-fresh seafood with an occasional Asian twist. Reservations are essential (it's so crowded), but the vibe is island-casual: Hawaiian shirts seem to be de rigueur for men. Try the barbecued oysters

or, for those stout of heart, the Mexican squid steak.

Montrio Bistro
CALIFORNIAN $$$

(Map p470; ☎831-648-8880; www.montrio.com; 414 Calle Principal; mains $14-29; ☺5-10pm Sun-Thu, to 11pm Fri & Sat; 🎨) Inside a 1910 firehouse, Montrio looks dolled up with leather walls and iron trellises, but the tables have butcher paper and crayons for kids. The seasonal New American menu mixes local, organic fare with California flair, including tapas-style small bites.

RG Burgers
DINER $

(Map p470; www.rgburgers.com; 570 Munras Ave; items $4-12; ☺11am-8:30pm Sun-Thu, to 9pm Fri & Sat) Next to Trader Joe's supermarket, where you can stock up on trail mix and take-out salads, this locally owned burger shop slings beef, bison, turkey, chicken and veggie patties, sweet tater fries and thick milkshakes.

🍃 Old Monterey Marketplace
FARMERS MARKET $

(Map p470; www.oldmonterey.org; Alvarado St, btwn Del Monte Ave & Pearl St; ☺4-7pm Tue Sep-May, to 8pm Jun-Aug) Rain or shine, head downtown for farm-fresh fruit and veggies, artisan cheeses and baked goods, and multiethnic takeout.

Crêpes of Brittany
SNACKS $

(Map p470; www.crepesofbrittany.com; 6 Old Fisherman's Wharf; snacks $4-9; ☺8am-3pm Mon, Thu-Fri, 8am-4pm Sat-Sun) Find authentic savory and sweet crepes swirled by a French expat – the homemade caramel is a treat. Expect long lines on weekends. Hours are reduced in winter.

🍷 Drinking & Entertainment

Prowl downtown's Alvarado St, touristy Cannery Row and locals-only Lighthouse Ave for more watering holes. For comprehensive entertainment and nightlife listings, check the free tabloid *Monterey County Weekly* (www.montereycountyweekly.com).

A Taste of Monterey
WINE BAR

(Map p470; www.atasteofmonterey.com; 700 Cannery Row; tasting fee $5-20; ☺11am-6pm) Sample medal-winning Monterey County wines from as far away as the Santa Lucia Highlands while soaking up dreamy sea views, then peruse thoughtful exhibits on barrel-making and cork production.

East Village Coffee Lounge
CAFE

(Map p470; www.eastvillagecoffeelounge.com; 498 Washington St; ☺6am-late Mon-Fri, 7am-late Sat & Sun) Sleek coffeehouse on a busy downtown corner brews fair-trade, organic beans. At night, it pulls off a big-city lounge vibe with film, open-mic, live-music and DJ nights and an all-important booze license.

Cannery Row Brewing Co
BREWPUB

(Map p470; www.canneryrowbrewingcompany.com; 95 Prescott Ave; ☺11:30am-midnight Sun-Thu, to 2am Fri & Sat) Brews from around the world bring crowds to Cannery Row's microbrew bar, as does the enticing outdoor deck with roaring firepits. Decent brewpub menu of burgers, fries, salads, BBQ and more.

Crown & Anchor
PUB

(Map p470; www.crownandanchor.net; 150 W Franklin St; ☺11am-2am) Descend into the basement of this British pub and the first thing you'll notice is the red plaid carpeting. At least these blokes know their way around a bar, with plentiful draft beers and single-malt scotch, not to mention damn fine fish and chips.

Sly McFly's Fueling Station
LIVE MUSIC

(Map p470; www.slymcflys.net; 700 Cannery Row; ☺11:30am-2am) Rubbing shoulders with billiards halls, comedy shops and touristy restaurants, this waterfront dive shows live blues, jazz and rock bands nightly. Skip the food, though.

Sardine Factory
LOUNGE

(Map p470; www.sardinefactory.com; 701 Wave St; ☺5pm-midnight) The legendary restaurant's fireplace cocktail lounge pours wines by the glass, delivers filling appetizers to your table and features live piano some nights.

Osio Cinemas
CINEMA

(Map p470; ☎831-644-8171; www.osiocinemas.com; 350 Alvarado St) Downtown cinema screens indie dramas, cutting-edge documentaries and offbeat Hollywood films. Drop by Cafe Lumiere for decadent cheesecakes and loose-leaf or bubble teas.

🛍 Shopping

Cannery Row is jammed with touristy shops, while downtown side streets hide one-of-a-kind finds.

Monterey Peninsula Art Foundation Gallery
ART

(Map p470; www.mpaf.org; 425 Cannery Row; ☺11am-5pm) Inside a cozy sea-view house, over two dozen local artists sell their plein-air paintings and sketches, plus contemporary works in all media.

Cannery Row Antique Mall   ANTIQUES
(Map p470; http://canneryrowantiquemall.com; 471 Wave St; ⏰10am-5:30pm) Inside a historic 1920s canning company building, two floors are stacked high with beguiling flotsam and jetsam from decades past.

Book Haven   BOOKS
(Map p470; 559 Tyler St; ⏰10am-6pm Mon-Sat) Tall shelves of new and used books, including rare first editions and John Steinbeck titles.

Luna Blu   CLOTHING
(Map p470; 176 Bonifacio Pl; ⏰11am-7pm Tue-Sat, to 5pm Sun & Mon) Vintage and name-brand consignment clothing, bags, and jaunty hats for women and men.

ⓘ Information

Doctors on Duty (Map p470; ☑831-649-0770; http://doctorsonduty.com; 501 Lighthouse Ave; ⏰8am-8pm Mon-Sat, 8am-6pm Sun) Walk-in, nonemergency medical clinic.

FedEx Office (Map p470; www.fedex.com; 799 Lighthouse Ave; per min 20-30¢; ⏰7am-11pm Mon-Fri, 9am-9pm Sat & Sun; @🖥) Pay-as-you-go internet workstations and free wi-fi.

Monterey County Convention & Visitors Bureau (Map p470; ☑831-657-6400, 877-666-8373; www.seemonterey.com; 401 Camino El Estero; ⏰9am-6pm Mon-Sat, to 5pm Sun) Ask for a free *Monterey County Film & Literary Map*. Closes one hour earlier November to March.

Post office (Map p470; www.usps.com; 565 Hartnell St; ⏰8:30am-5pm Mon-Fri, 10am-2pm Sat)

Public library (Map p470; www.monterey. org; 625 Pacific St; ⏰noon-8pm Mon-Wed, 10am-6pm Thu-Sat; @🖥) Free wi-fi and public internet terminals.

ⓘ Getting There & Around

A few miles east of downtown off Hwy 68, **Monterey Peninsula Airport** (MRY; www. montereyairport.com; 200 Fred Kane Dr, off Olmsted Rd) has flights with United (LA, San Francisco and Denver), American (LA), Allegiant Air (Las Vegas) and US Airways (Phoenix).

Monterey Airbus (☑831-373-7777; www. montereyairbus.com) links Monterey with airports in San Jose ($35, 90 minutes) and San Francisco ($45, 2¼ hours) almost a dozen times daily.

If you don't fly or drive to Monterey, first take a Greyhound bus or Amtrak train to Salinas, then catch a local Monterey-Salinas Transit bus (for details, see p494).

Monterey-Salinas Transit (☑888-678-2871; www.mst.org) operates local and regional buses; one-way fares cost $1 to $3 (day pass $8). Routes converge on downtown's **Transit Plaza** (Map p470; cnr Pearl & Alvarado Sts).

From late May until early September, MST's free **trolley** loops around downtown, Fisherman's Wharf and Cannery Row from 10am to 7pm daily.

Pacific Grove

Founded as a tranquil Methodist summer retreat in 1875, PG maintained a quaint, holier-than-thou attitude well into the 20th century – the selling of liquor was illegal up until 1969, making it California's last 'dry' town. Today, leafy streets are lined by stately Victorian homes. The charming, compact downtown orbits Lighthouse Ave.

⊙ Sights & Activities

Aptly named **Ocean View Blvd** affords views from Lover's Point west to Point Pinos, where it becomes **Sunset Dr**, offering tempting turnouts where you can stroll by pounding surf, rocky outcrops and teeming tidepools. This seaside route is great for cycling too. Some say it even rivals the famous 17-Mile Drive for beauty, and it's free.

Point Pinos Lighthouse   LIGHTHOUSE
(Map p466; www.ci.pg.ca.us/lighthouse; off Asilomar Ave; adult/child $2/1; ⏰1-4pm Thu-Mon) On the tip of the Monterey Peninsula, the West Coast's oldest continuously operating lighthouse has been warning ships off this hazardous point since 1855. Inside are modest exhibits on the lighthouse's history and, alas, its failures – local shipwrecks.

FREE **Monarch Grove Sanctuary**   PARK
(Map p466; www.ci.pg.ca.us/monarchs; off Ridge Rd, Pacific Grove; ⏰dawn-dusk) Between October and February, over 25,000 migratory monarch butterflies cluster in this thicket of tall eucalyptus trees, secreted inland from Lighthouse Ave. Volunteers are on hand to answer all of your questions.

Museum of Natural History   MUSEUM
(Map p466; www.pgmuseum.org; 165 Forest Ave; suggested donation per person/family $3/5; ⏰10am-5pm Tue-Sat; 🛝) With a gray whale sculpture out front, this small kids' museum has old-fashioned exhibits about sea otters,

coastal bird life, butterflies, the Big Sur coast and Native American tribes.

Pacific Grove Golf Links
GOLF

(Map p466; ☑831-648-5775; www.pggolflinks.com; 77 Asilomar Blvd; greens fees $42-65) Can't afford to play at famous Pebble Beach? This historic 18-hole municipal course, where black-tailed deer freely range, has impressive sea views, and it's a lot easier (not to mention cheaper) to book a tee time.

🛏 Sleeping

B&Bs have taken over many stately Victorian homes around downtown and by the beach. Motels cluster at the peninsula's western end, off Lighthouse and Asilomar Aves.

TOP
CHOICE Asilomar Conference Grounds
LODGE $$

(Map p466; ☑831-372-8016, 888-635-5310; www. visitasilomar.com; 800 Asilomar Ave, Pacific Grove; r incl breakfast $115-175; 🖩🌀🐾) Sprawling over more than 100 acres of sand dunes and pine forests, this state-park lodge is a find. Skip ho-hum motel rooms for historic houses designed by early-20th-century architect Julia Morgan (of Hearst Castle fame) – the thin-walled, hardwood-floored rooms may be small, but share a sociable fireplace lounge. The lobby rec room has ping-pong and pool tables, and wi-fi. Bike rentals available.

Centrella Inn
B&B $$$

(Map p466; ☑831-372-3372, 800-233-3372; www. centrellainn.com; 612 Central Ave; d incl breakfast $119-399; @🌀) For a romantic night inside a Victorian seaside mansion, this turreted National Historic Landmark beckons with enchanting gardens and a player piano. Some of the stately rooms have fireplaces, clawfoot tubs and kitchenettes, while private cottages welcome honeymooners and families. Rates include afternoon fresh-baked cookies and evening wine and hors d'oeuvres.

Sunset Inn Hotel
MOTEL $$$

(Map p466; ☑831-375-3529; www.gosunsetinn. com; 133 Asilomar Blvd; r $139-400; 🌀) At this small motor lodge near the golf course and the beach, attentive staff check you into crisply redesigned rooms that have hard-wood floors, king-sized beds with cheery floral-print comforters and some hot tubs and fireplaces. Ask about guest access to the top-notch Spa at Pebble Beach.

Pacific Gardens Inn
MOTEL $$

(Map p466; ☑831-646-9414, 800-262-1566; www. pacificgardensinn.com; 701 Asilomar Blvd; d $105-225; @🌀) A hospitable owner and a communal lobby make all the difference at this welcoming, wood-shingled motor lodge sheltered among tall oak trees. For chilly nights, some comfy rooms have wood-burning fireplaces. It's an easy stroll over to the beach.

🍴 Eating

Make reservations for these popular downtown eateries.

TOP
CHOICE Passionfish
SEAFOOD $$$

(Map p466; ☑831-655-3311; www.passionfish. net; 701 Lighthouse Ave; mains $16-28; ☺5-10pm) Fresh, sustainable seafood is artfully presented in any number of inventive ways, and the seasonally inspired menu also carries slow-cooked meats and vegetarian dishes. The earth-tone decor is spare, with tables squeezed a tad too close together. But an ambitious world-ranging wine list is priced near retail, and there are twice as many Chinese teas as wines by the glass.

Red House Cafe
CAFE $$

(Map p466; ☑831-643-1060; www.redhousecafe. com; 662 Lighthouse Ave; mains $5-16; ☺8-11am Sat & Sun, 11am-2:30pm & 5-9pm Tue-Sun; 🐾) Crowded with locals, this 1895 shingled house dishes up comfort food with delightful haute touches, from cinnamon-brioche French toast for breakfast to blue-cheese soufflés and roast chicken at dinner. Haute French tea list. Cash only.

ℹ Information

Pacific Grove Chamber of Commerce (Map p466; ☑831-373-3304, 800-656-6650; www.pa cificgrove.org; 584 Central Ave; ☺9:30am-5pm Mon-Fri, 10am-3pm Sat) Tourist information.

ℹ Getting There & Around

MST (☑888-678-2871; www.mst.org) bus 1 connects downtown Monterey, Cannery Row and Pacific Grove every half hour from 6:15am to 10:45pm daily.

Carmel-by-the-Sea

With borderline fanatical devotion to its canine citizens, quaint Carmel-by-the-Sea has the well-manicured feel of a country club. Simply plop down in any cafe and watch

SCENIC DRIVE: 17-MILE DRIVE

What to See

Pacific Grove and Carmel are linked by the spectacularly scenic, if overhyped 17-Mile Drive (Map p466), which meanders through Pebble Beach, a wealthy private resort. It's no chore staying within the 25mph limit – every curve in the road reveals another postcard vista, especially when wildflowers bloom. Cycling the drive is enormously popular, but try to do it during the week, when traffic isn't as heavy, and ride with the flow of traffic, from north to south.

Using the self-guided touring map provided upon entry, you can easily pick out landmarks such as **Spanish Bay**, where explorer Gaspar de Portolá dropped anchor in 1769; treacherously rocky **Point Joe**, which in the past was often mistaken for the entrance to Monterey Bay and thus became the site of several shipwrecks; and **Bird Rock**, also a haven for harbor seals and sea lions. The ostensible pièce de résistance is the trademark **Lone Cypress**, which has perched on a seaward rock for more than 250 years.

Besides the coastal scenery, star attractions at Pebble Beach include world-famous **golf courses**, where a celebrity and pro tournament happens every February – just imagine Tiger Woods driving down the spectacular 18th-hole fairway for a victory. The luxurious **Lodge at Pebble Beach** (☑831-624-3811, 800-654-9300; www.pebblebeach. com; 1700 17-Mile Drive; r $715-995; ❋@☎☒) embraces a spa and designer shops where the most demanding of tastes are catered to. Even if you're not a trust-fund baby, you can still soak up the rich atmosphere in the resort's art-filled public spaces or at the cocktail bar.

The Route

Operated as a toll road by the **Pebble Beach Company** (www.pebblebeach.com; per vehicle/bicycle $9.50/free), 17-Mile Drive is open from sunrise to sunset. The toll can be refunded later as a discount on a $25 minimum food purchase at Pebble Beach restaurants.

Time & Mileage

There are five separate gates for the 17-Mile Drive; how far you drive and how long you take is up to you. For the most scenery, enter at Pacific Grove (off Sunset Dr) and exit at Carmel.

the parade of behatted ladies toting fancy-label shopping bags to lunch and dapper gents driving top-down convertibles along Ocean Ave, the village's slow-mo main drag. Fairy-tale Comstock cottages, with their characteristic stone chimneys and pitched gable roofs, dot the town. Even payphones, garbage cans and newspaper vending boxes are shingled, and local bylaws forbid neon signs and billboards.

Founded as a seaside resort in the 1880s – fairly odd, given that its beach is often blanketed in fog – Carmel quickly attracted famous artists and writers, such as Sinclair Lewis and Jack London, and their hangers-on. An artistic flavor survives in the more than 100 galleries that line the town's immaculate streets, but sky-high property values have long obliterated any salt-of-the-earth bohemia.

⊙ Sights

Escape downtown's harried shopping streets and stroll tree-lined neighborhoods on the lookout for domiciles charming and peculiar. The Hansel and Gretel houses on Torres St, between 5th and 6th Avenues, are just how you'd imagine them. Another wicked cool house in the shape of a ship, made from stone and salvaged ship parts, is near 6th Ave and Guadalupe St, about three blocks east of Torres St.

San Carlos Borroméo de Carmelo Mission CHURCH
(Map p466; www.carmelmission.org; 3080 Rio Rd; adult/child $6.50/2; ⊙9:30am-5pm Mon-Sat, 10:30am-5pm Sun) The original Monterey mission was established by Spanish priest Junípero Serra in 1770, but poor soil and the corrupting influence of Spanish soldiers

forced the move to Carmel two years later. Today this is one of the most strikingly beautiful missions in California, an oasis of solemnity bathed in flowering gardens.

The mission's adobe (formerly wooden) chapel was later replaced with an arched basilica made of stone quarried in the Santa Lucia Mountains. Museum exhibits are scattered throughout the meditative complex. The spartan cell attributed to Serra looks like something out of *The Good, the Bad and the Ugly*, while a separate chapel houses his memorial tomb. Don't overlook the gravestone of 'Old Gabriel,' a Native American convert whom Serra baptized, and whose dates put him at 151 years old when he died. People say he smoked like a chimney and outlived seven wives. There's a lesson in there somewhere.

Tor House   HISTORIC BUILDING
(Map p466; ☎831-624-1813; www.torhouse.org; 26304 Ocean View Ave; tour adult/child 12-17yr $10/5; ⊙10am-3pm Fri & Sat) Even if you've never heard of 20th-century poet Robinson Jeffers, a pilgrimage to this house, which was built with his own hands, offers fascinating insights into both the man and the bohemian ethos of Old Carmel. A porthole in the Celtic-inspired Hawk Tower reputedly came from the wrecked ship that carried Napoleon from Elba. The only way to visit the property is to reserve space on a tour (children under 12 not allowed), although the tower can be glimpsed from the street.

☂ Activities

Not always sunny, Carmel Beach is a gorgeous white-sand crescent, where pampered pups excitedly run off-leash.

TOP CHOICE Point Lobos State
Natural Reserve   PARK
(Map p466; www.parks.ca.gov, www.pointlobos.org; per car $10; ⊙8am-30min after sunset; ⓓ) They bark, they bathe and they're fun to watch – sea lions are the stars here at Punta de los Lobos Marinos (Point of the Sea Wolves), 4 miles south of Carmel, where a dramatically rocky coastline offers excellent tide-pooling.

The full perimeter hike is 6 miles, but shorter walks take in wild scenery too, including Bird Island, shady Piney Woods, the historic Whaler's Cabin and Devil's Cauldron, a whirlpool that gets splashy at high tide. The kelp forest at Whalers Cove is popular with snorkelers and divers;

reservations for scuba-diving permits (☎831-624-8413; per two-person team $10) are required.

Arrive early on weekends; parking is limited. Don't skip paying the entry fee by parking along Hwy 1; California's state parks are chronically underfunded, and need your help!

★ Festivals & Events

Carmel Art Festival   CULTURE
(www.carmelartfestival.org) Meet plein-air painters and local sculptors in Devendorf Park over a long weekend in mid-May.

Carmel Bach Festival   MUSIC
(www.bachfestival.org) In July, classical and chamber-music performances and open rehearsals take place around town.

Harvest Farm-to-Table   FOOD, WINE
(www.harvestcarmel.com) Chefs' cooking demos, gardening and BBQ workshops, and wine and artisan-cheese tasting in the neighboring Carmel Valley in late September.

⌂ Sleeping

Seriously overpriced boutique hotels, inns and B&Bs fill up quickly, especially in summer; expect a two-night minimum on weekends. Ask at the chamber of commerce about last-minute lodging deals. For better-value lodgings, head north to Monterey.

Mission Ranch   INN $$$
(Map p466; ☎831-624-6436, 800-538-8221; www.missionranchcarmel.com; 26270 Dolores St; r incl breakfast $135-285; ⓢ) If woolly sheep grazing on green fields within view of the Pacific don't convince you to stay here, perhaps knowing that actor and director Clint Eastwood restored this historic ranch will. Accommodations range from shabby-chic rooms inside a converted barn to a family-sized 1850s farmhouse.

Sea View Inn   B&B $$
(Map p466; ☎831-624-8778; www.seaviewinncarmel.com; Camino Real btwn 11th & 12th Aves; r incl breakfast $135-265; ⓢ) At the Sea View – an intimate retreat away from downtown's hustle – fireside nooks are tailor-made for reading or taking afternoon tea. The cheapest rooms with slanted ceilings are short on cat-swinging space, but the beach is nearby.

Carmel River Inn
INN $$$

(Map p466; ☎831-624-1575, 800-966-6490; www.carmelriverinn.com; 26600 Oliver Rd; d $159-319; ❄❂❀☎) Tucked off Hwy 1, this peaceful garden retreat south of Carmel's mission rents white-picket fenced honeymooner and family cottages, many with fireplaces and kitchenettes, and simple country-style rooms. Pet fee $20.

Carmel Village Inn
MOTEL $$

(Map p466; ☎831-624-3864, 800-346-3864; www.carmelvillageinn.com; cnr Ocean & Junípero Aves; d incl breakfast buffet $80-250; ☎) With cheerful flowers decorating its exterior, this centrally located motel across from Devendorf Park has pleasant rooms, some with gas fireplaces, and nightly quiet hours.

✕ Eating

Carmel's restaurant scene is more about old-world sidewalk atmosphere than sustenance. Most places open early for breakfast, and stop serving dinner before 9pm.

La Bicyclette
FRENCH, ITALIAN $$$

(Map p466; www.labicycletterestaurant.com; Dolores St at 7th Ave; lunch mains $7-16, 3-course prix-fixe dinner $28; ⊗11:30am-4pm & 5-10pm) Rustic European comfort food using seasonal local ingredients packs canoodling couples into this bistro, with an open kitchen baking wood-fired oven pizzas. Excellent local wines by the glass.

Mundaka
TAPAS $$

(Map p466; www.mundakacarmel.com; San Carlos St btwn Ocean & 7th Aves; small plates $4-19; ⊗5:30-10pm Sun-Wed, 5:30-11pm Thu-Sat) This stone courtyard hideaway is a svelte escape from Carmel's stuffy 'newly wed and nearly dead' crowd. Take Spanish tapas plates for a spin and sip the house-made sangria while DJs or flamenco guitars play.

Carmel Belle
CALIFORNIAN $$

(Map p466; www.carmelbelle.com; Doud Craft Studios, cnr Ocean Ave & San Carlos St; brunch mains $5-12; ⊗8am-5pm) Fresh, often organic ingredients flow from Carmel Valley farms onto mini-mall tables at this charcuterie, cheese and wine shop.

Bruno's Market & Deli
DELI, GROCERIES $

(Map p466; www.brunosmarket.com; cnr 6th & Junípero Aves; sandwiches $5-8; ⊗7am-8pm) This small supermarket deli counter makes a saucy tri-trip beef sandwich and stocks all the accoutrements for a beach picnic, including Sparky's root beer from Pacific Grove.

🍷 Drinking & Entertainment

Forest Theater
THEATER

(Map p466; ☎831-626-1681; www.foresttheaterguild.org; cnr Mountain View Ave & Santa Rita St; ⊗May-Jul) Founded in 1910 and now the oldest community theater west of the Rockies, here musicals, drama, comedies and film screenings take place under the stars by flickering firepits.

Jack London's
PUB

(Map p466; www.jacklondons.com; Su Vecino Court, Dolores St, btwn 5th & 6th Aves; ⊗11am-late) Knock back a few drinks with the caddies from Pebble Beach next to the crackling fireplace at this Carmel institution.

ℹ️ Information

Downtown buildings have no street numbers, so addresses specify the street and nearest intersection only.

Carmel Chamber of Commerce (☎831-624-2522, 800-550-4333; www.carmelcalifornia.org; San Carlos St, btwn 5th & 6th Aves; ⊗10am-5pm) Free maps and information, including about local art galleries.

Carmel Pine Cone (www.pineconearchive.com) Free weekly newspaper packed with local personality and color – the police log is a comedy of manners.

ℹ️ Getting There & Around

Carmel is 5 miles south of Monterey via Hwy 1. Find free unlimited parking in a **municipal lot** (cnr 3rd & Junípero Aves) behind the Vista Lobos building.

MST (☎888-678-2871; www.mst.org) bus 5 ($2, every 30 minutes) and bus 7 ($2, hourly) connect Carmel with Monterey. Bus 4 runs between downtown Carmel and the mission ($1, every 30 minutes). Bus 22 ($3) passes through en route to/from Big Sur three times daily between late May and early September, and twice daily on Saturday and Sunday only the rest of the year.

Big Sur

Big Sur is more a state of mind than a place you can pinpoint on a map. There are no traffic lights, banks or strip malls, and when the sun goes down, the moon and the stars are the only streetlights – if summer's dense fog hasn't extinguished them, that is. Much ink has been spilled extolling the raw beauty

Big Sur

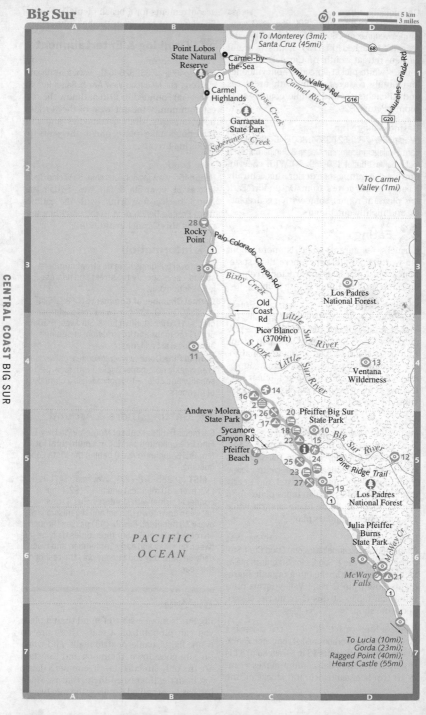

and energy of this precious piece of land shoehorned between the Santa Lucia Range and the Pacific Ocean, but nothing quite prepares you for your first glimpse of the craggy, unspoiled coastline.

In the 1950s and '60s, Big Sur – so named by Spanish settlers living on the Monterey Peninsula, who referred to the wilderness as *el país grande del sur* ('the big country to the south') – became a retreat for artists and writers, including Henry Miller and Beat Generation visionaries such as Lawrence Ferlinghetti. Today Big Sur attracts self-proclaimed artists, new-age mystics, latter-day hippies and city slickers seeking to unplug and reflect more deeply on this emerald-green edge of the continent.

◉ Sights & Activities

All of the following places are listed north to south. Most parks are open from a half-hour before sunrise until a half-hour after sunset, with 24-hour campground access. At state parks, your parking fee ($10) receipt is valid for same-day entry to all except Limekiln; don't skip paying the entry fee by parking illegally outside along Hwy 1.

Bixby Bridge
LANDMARK

Under 15 miles south of Carmel, this landmark spanning Rainbow Canyon is one of the world's highest single-span bridges. Completed in 1932, it was built by prisoners eager to lop time off their sentences. There's a perfect photo-op pull-off on the bridge's north side. Before Bixby Bridge was constructed, travelers had to trek inland on what's now called the **Old Coast Rd**, which heads off opposite the pull-off, reconnecting after 11 miles with Hwy 1 near Andrew Molera State Park. When the weather is dry enough, this route is usually navigable by 4WD or a mountain bike.

Point Sur State Historic Park
LIGHTHOUSE

(☎831-625-4419; www.pointsur.org; adult/child 6-17yr $10/5, moonlight tour $15/10; ☺tour schedules vary) Just over 6 miles south of Bixby Bridge, Point Sur rises like a green velvet fortress. This imposing volcanic rock looks like an island, but is actually connected to land by a sandbar. Atop the rock is the 1889 stone lightstation, which operated until 1974. Ocean views and tales of the lighthouse keepers' family lives are engrossing. Meet your tour guide at the locked gate a ¼-mile north of Point Sur Naval Facility, usually at 10am

Big Sur

Saturday and Sunday year-round, and 1pm Wednesday from November through March. Tours also depart at 2pm Wednesday and Saturday from April to October, when monthly full-moon tours are also available. Call ahead to confirm tour schedules. Arrive early because space is limited (no reservations).

Andrew Molera State Park PARK
(📞831-667-2315; www.parks.ca.gov; per vehicle $10) Named after the farmer who first planted artichokes in California, this oft-overlooked park is a trail-laced pastiche of grassy meadows, waterfalls, ocean bluffs and rugged beaches offering excellent wildlife watching. Look for the turn-off just over 8 miles south of Bixby Bridge.

From the parking lot, a half-mile walk along the beach-bound trail leads to a first-come, first-served campground, from where a gentle quarter-mile spur trail leads past the 1861 redwood **Cooper Cabin**, Big Sur's oldest building. Otherwise, keep hiking on the main trail out toward a beautiful beach where the Big Sur River runs into the ocean and condors can occasionally be spotted circling overhead.

South of the parking lot, learn all about endangered California condors at the park's **Big Sur Discovery Center** (📞831-620-0702; www.ventananaws.org; admission free; ⏰9am-4pm Fri-Sun late May–mid-Sep). At the nearby bird banding lab, inside a small shed which operates when funding allows, the public is welcome to watch naturalists at work carrying out long-term species monitoring programs.

Across Hwy 1 from the park entrance, **Molera Horseback Tours** (📞831-625-5486, 800-942-5486; http://molerahorsebacktours.com; per person $40-70; 🐴) offers guided trail rides on the beach. Walk-ins and novices are welcome; children must be at least six years old.

Pfeiffer Big Sur State Park PARK
(📞831-667-2315; www.parks.ca.gov; per vehicle $10) Named after Big Sur's first European settlers, who arrived in 1869, Pfeiffer Big Sur is the largest state park in Big Sur. Hiking trails loop through redwood groves and head into the adjacent Ventana Wilderness. The most popular trail – to 60ft-high **Pfeiffer Falls**, a delicate cascade hidden in the forest, which usually runs from December to May – is an easy 1.4-mile round-trip. Built in the 1930s by the Civilian Conservation Corps (CCC), the rustic Big Sur Lodge is near the park entrance, about 13 miles south of Bixby Bridge.

Pfeiffer Beach BEACH
(www.fs.usda.gov; per vehicle $5; ⏰9am-8pm; 🐕) This phenomenal, crescent-shaped and dog-friendly beach is known for its huge double rock formation, through which waves crash with life-affirming power. It's often windy, and the surf is too dangerous for swimming. But dig down into the wet sand – it's purple! That's because manganese garnet washes down from the craggy hillsides above.

To get here from Hwy 1, make a sharp right onto Sycamore Canyon Rd, marked by a small yellow sign that says 'narrow road' at the top. It's about half a mile south of Big Sur Station, or 2 miles south of Pfeiffer Big Sur State Park. From the turnoff, it's two more narrow, twisting miles (RVs and trailers prohibited) down to the beach.

Henry Miller Library ARTS CENTER
(📞831-667-2574; www.henrymiller.org; admission by donation; ⏰11am-6pm Wed-Mon; @🌐) 'It was here in Big Sur I first learned to say Amen!' wrote Henry Miller, a Big Sur denizen for 17 years. More of a living memorial, alt-cultural venue and bookshop, this community gathering spot was never Miller's home. The house belonged to Miller's friend, painter Emil White, until his death and is now run by a nonprofit group. Inside are copies of all of Miller's written works, many of his paintings and a collection of Big Sur and Beat Generation material, including copies of the top 100 books Miller said most influenced him. Stop by to browse and hang out on the front deck. It's about 0.4 miles south of Nepenthe restaurant.

Partington Cove BEACH
A raw and breathtaking spot where crashing surf salts your skin, this hidden cove is named for a settler who built a dock here in the 1880s. Originally used for loading freight, Partington Cove allegedly became a landing spot for Prohibition-era bootleggers. On the steep, half-mile dirt hike down to the cove, you'll cross a cool bridge and go through an even cooler tunnel. The water in the cove is unbelievably aqua and within it grow tangled kelp forests. There's no real beach access and ocean swimming isn't safe, but some people scamper on the rocks and look for tidepools as waves splash ominously.

Look for the unmarked trailhead turnoff inside a large hairpin turn on the west side of Hwy 1, about 6 miles south of Nepenthe restaurant or 2 miles north of Julia Pfeiffer

Burns State Park. The trail starts just beyond the locked vehicle gate.

Julia Pfeiffer Burns State Park PARK
(☎831-667-2315; www.parks.ca.gov; per vehicle $10) Named for another Big Sur pioneer, this park hugs both sides of Hwy 1. The big attraction is California's only coastal waterfall, **McWay Falls**, which drops 80ft straight into the sea – or onto the beach, depending on the tide. This is *the* classic Big Sur postcard shot, with tree-topped rocks jutting above a golden, crescent-shaped beach next to swirling blue pools and crashing white surf. To reach this spectacular viewpoint, take the short Overlook Trail west from the parking lot and cross underneath Hwy 1 via a tunnel. From trailside benches, you might spot migrating gray whales between mid-December and mid-April.

The park entrance is on the east side of Hwy 1, about 8 miles south of Nepenthe restaurant.

Esalen Institute HOT SPRINGS
(☎ 888-837-2536; www.esalen.org; 55000 Hwy 1; ☏) Marked only by a lighted sign reading 'Esalen Institute . By Reservation Only,' this infamous spot is like a new-age hippie camp for adults. Esoteric workshops treat anything 'relating to our greater human capacity,' from shapeshifting to Thai massage. Things have sure changed a lot since Hunter S Thompson was the gun-toting caretaker here in the 1960s.

Esalen's famous **baths** (☎831-667-3047; per person $20, credit cards only; ⊙public entry 1-3am nightly, reservations accepted 8am-8pm Mon-Thu & Sat, 8am-noon Fri & Sun) are fed by a natural hot spring and sit on a ledge above the ocean. Dollars to donuts you'll never take another dip that compares panorama-wise with the one here, especially on stormy winter nights. Only two small outdoor pools perch directly over the waves, so once you've stripped down (bathing is clothing-optional) and taken a quick shower, head outside immediately to score the best views. Otherwise, you'll be stuck with a tepid, no-view pool or even worse, a rickety bathtub.

Esalen is just over 11 miles south of Nepenthe restaurant and 10 miles north of Lucia.

Limekiln State Park PARK
(☎831-667-2403; www.parks.ca.gov; per vehicle $8; ⊙8am-sunset) Two miles south of Lucia, this petite park gets its name from the four remaining wood-fired kilns originally built here in the 1870s and '80s to smelt quar-

DRIVING HIG...
Driving this narrow two-la... through Big Sur and beyon... slow going. Allow about thre... to cover the distance betwee... Monterey Peninsula and San L... po, much more if you want to e... the coast. Traveling after dark can be risky and more to the point, it's futile, since you'll miss out on the seascapes. Watch out for cyclists and always use signposted roadside pullouts to let faster-moving traffic pass.

ried limestone into powder, a key ingredient in cement used to construct buildings from Monterey to San Francisco. Tragically, pioneers chopped down the steep canyon's old-growth redwood forests to fuel the kilns' fires. A one-mile round-trip trail through a redwood grove leads to the historic site, passing a quarter-mile spur trail to a gorgeous 100ft-high waterfall.

At press time, the future of this park was uncertain – it may close in 2012.

Los Padres National Forest FOREST
The tortuously winding 40-mile stretch of Hwy 1 south of Lucia to Hearst Castle is even more sparsely populated, rugged and remote, mostly running through national forest lands. Make sure you've got at least enough fuel in the tank to reach the expensive gas station at Gorda, around 11 miles south of Limekiln State Park.

About 5 miles south of Nacimiento-Fergusson Rd, almost opposite Plaskett Creek Campground, is **Sand Dollar Beach Picnic Area** (www.fs.usda.gov; per vehicle $5; ⊙9am-8pm), from where it's a five-minute walk down to southern Big Sur's longest sandy beach, a crescent-shaped strip of sand protected from winds by high bluffs.

In 1971, in the waters of **Jade Cove**, local divers recovered a 9000lb jade boulder that measured 8ft long and was valued at $180,000. People still comb the beach today. The best time to find jade, which is black or blue-green and looks dull until you dip it in water, is during low tide or after a big storm. Keep an eye out for hang gliders flying in for a dramatic landing on the beach. Trails down to the water start from roadside pulloffs immediately south of Plaskett Creek Campground.

CALIFORNIA'S COMEBACK CONDORS

When it comes to endangered species, one of the state's biggest success stories is the California condor. These gigantic, prehistoric birds weigh over 20lb with a wingspan of up to 10ft, letting them fly great distances in search of carrion. They're easily recognized by their naked pink head and large white patches on the underside of each wing.

This big bird became so rare that in 1987 there were only 27 left in the world – all were removed from the wild to special captive-breeding facilities. There are almost 400 California condors alive today, with increasing numbers of captive birds being released back into the wild, where it's hoped they will begin breeding naturally.

Pinnacles National Monument (p495) and the Big Sur coast both offer excellent opportunities to view this majestic bird.

If you have any sunlight left, keep trucking down the highway to **Salmon Creek Falls**, which usually flows from December through May. Tucked up a forested canyon, the double-drop waterfall can be glimpsed from the hairpin turn on Hwy 1, about 8 miles south of Gorda. Roadside parking gets very crowded, as everyone takes the 10-minute walk up to the falls to splash around in the pools, where kids shriek and dogs happily yip and yap.

Ragged Point   LANDMARK

Your last – or first – taste of Big Sur's rocky grandeur comes at this craggy cliff outcropping with fabulous views of the coastline in both directions, about 15 miles north of Hearst Castle. Once part of the Hearst empire, it's now taken over by a sprawling, ho-hum resort with a pricey gas station. Heading south, the land grows increasingly wind-swept as Hwy 1 rolls gently down to the water's edge.

🛏 Sleeping

With few exceptions, Big Sur's lodgings do not have TVs and rarely have telephones. This is where you come to escape the world. There aren't a lot of rooms overall, so demand often exceeds supply and prices can be outrageous. Bigger price tags don't necessarily buy you more amenities either. In summer and on weekends, reservations are essential, whether for resort rooms or campsites.

Post Ranch Inn   TOP CHOICE   RESORT $$$

(☎831-667-2200, 888-524-4787; www.postranchinn.com; 47900 Hwy 1; d from $595; 🐾📶) The last word in luxurious coastal getaways, the legendary Post Ranch pampers guests with exclusive accommodations featuring slate spa tubs, fireplaces, private decks and walking

sticks for coastal hikes. Ocean-view rooms celebrate the sea, while the treehouses without views have a bit of sway. Paddle around the clifftop infinity pool after your shamanic healing session in the spa or a group yoga, meditation or tai chi chuan class. One sour note: disappointing food from the panoramic sea-view restaurant.

Ventana Inn & Spa   RESORT $$$

(☎831-667-2331, 800-628-6500; www.ventanainn.com; 48123 Hwy 1; d from $450; 🐾📶) Almost at odds with Big Sur's hippie-alternative vibe, Ventana manages to inject a little soul into its luxury digs. Honeymooning couples and paparazzi-fleeing celebs pad from yoga class to the Japanese baths and clothing-optional pool, or hole up all day next to the wood-burning fireplace in their villa or ocean-view cottage.

Glen Oaks Motel   MOTEL $$$

(☎831-667-2105; www.glenoaksbigsur.com; Hwy 1; d $175-350; 🐾) At this 1950s redwood-and-adobe motor lodge, rustic rooms and cabins seem effortlessly chic. Dramatically transformed by eco-conscious design, these snug romantic hideaways all have gas fireplaces. The woodsy studio cottage has a kitchenette and walk-in shower built for two, or retreat to the one-bedroom house equipped with a full kitchen.

Treebones Resort   YURTS $$$

(☎877-424-4787; www.treebonesresort.com; 71895 Hwy 1; d $170-285; 📶🚲) Don't let the word 'resort' throw you. Yes, they've got an ocean-view hot tub, heated pool and massage treatments available. But noisy yurts with polished pine floors, quilt-covered beds, sink vanities and redwood decks are actually like 'glamping,' with little privacy. Bathrooms and showers are a short stroll away. Rates include a make-your-own waffle breakfast.

Look for the signposted turnoff a mile north of Gorda.

Big Sur Lodge
LODGE $$$

(☎831-667-3100, 800-424-4787; www.bigsurlodge. com; 47225 Hwy 1; d $189-369; ☒) What you're really paying for is a peaceful location, right inside Pfeiffer Big Sur State Park. Fairly rustic duplexes each have a deck or balcony looking out into the redwood forest, while family-sized rooms may have kitchens or wood-burning fireplaces. The outdoor swimming pool is usually open from March until October.

Big Sur Campground & Cabins
CABINS, CAMPGROUND $$

(☎831-667-2322; www.bigsurcamp.com; 47000 Hwy 1; cabins $90-345, tent/RV sites from $40/50; ☻☒) Right on the Big Sur River and shaded by redwoods, cozy housekeeping cabins come with full kitchens and fireplaces, while canvas-sided tent cabins are dog-friendly (pet fee $15). The riverside campground is especially popular with RVs. There are hot showers, a coin-op laundry, playground and general store.

Ripplewood Resort
CABINS $$

(☎831-667-2242; www.ripplewoodresort.com; 47047 Hwy 1; cabins $95-195; ☎) North of Pfeiffer Big Sur State Park, Ripplewood has struck a blow for fiscal equality by asking the same rates year-round. Throwback Americana cabins all have kitchens and private baths, while some sport fireplaces. Quiet riverside cabins are surrounded by redwoods, but roadside cabins can be noisy. Wi-fi works in the restaurant only.

Deetjen's Big Sur Inn
LODGE $$

(☎831-667-2377; www.deetjens.com; 48865 Hwy 1; d $90-250) Nestled among redwoods and wisteria, this creekside conglomeration of rustic, thin-walled rooms and cottages was built by Norwegian immigrant Helmuth Deetjen in the 1930s. Some rooms are warmed by wood-burning fireplaces, while cheaper ones share bathrooms.

Ragged Point Inn
MOTEL $$

(☎805-927-4502; www.raggedpointinn.net; 19019 Hwy 1; r $129-269; ☎☒) Split-level motel rooms are nothing special, except for ocean views; pet fee $50.

Lucia Lodge
MOTEL $$

(☎831-688-4884, 866-424-4787; www.lucialodge. com; 62400 Hwy 1; d $150-275; ☎) Dreamy clifftop views from tired 1930s cabin rooms.

Public Campgrounds

Camping is currently available at four of Big Sur's **state parks** (☎reservations 916-638-5883, 800-444-7275; www.reserveamerica.com) and two **United States Forest Service (USFS) campgrounds** (☎reservations 518-885-3639, 877-444-6777; www.recreation.gov) along Hwy 1.

Pfeiffer Big Sur State Park
CAMPGROUND $

(www.parks.ca.gov; Hwy 1; tent & RV sites $35-50, hike-and-bike sites $5) Over 200 sites nestle in a redwood-shaded river valley. Facilities include drinking water, coin-op showers and laundry, but no RV hookups.

Andrew Molera State Park
CAMPGROUND $

(www.parks.ca.gov; Hwy 1; tent sites $25) Two dozen first-come, first-served primitive walk-in sites with fire pits and drinking water, but no ocean views.

Julia Pfeiffer Burns State Park
CAMPGROUND $

(www.parks.ca.gov; Hwy 1; tent sites $30) Two small walk-in campsites on a semi-shaded ocean bluff; register at Big Sur Station (10.5 miles north) or Pfeiffer Big Sur State Park (11 miles north).

Limekiln State Park
CAMPGROUND $

(www.parks.ca.gov; Hwy 1; tent & RV sites $35) Near the park entrance, two dozen sites huddle under a Hwy 1 bridge next to the ocean; showers are available.

USFS Kirk Creek Campground
CAMPGROUND

(www.campone.com; Hwy 1; tent & RV sites $22) Over 30 beautiful, if exposed ocean-view blufftop campsites with drinking water and BBQ grills, 2 miles south of Limekiln.

USFS Plaskett Creek Campground
CAMPGROUND

(www.campone.com; Hwy 1; tent & RV sites $22) Almost 40 spacious, shaded campsites with drinking water in a forested meadow near Sand Dollar Beach, about 5 miles south of Nacimiento-Fergusson Rd.

✗ Eating

Like Big Sur's lodgings, restaurants and cafes are often overpriced, overcrowded and underwhelming.

Restaurant at Ventana
CALIFORNIAN $$$

(☎831-667-4242; www.ventanainn.com; 48123 Hwy 1; lunch mains $10-18, dinner mains $29-38; ☺11:30am-9pm; ☎) The old truism about the better the views, the worse the food just doesn't seem to apply here. The resort's ocean-view terrace restaurant and cocktail bar is hands down the happiest place for foodies anywhere along Hwy 1. Dig into tender bison steaks with truffled mac 'n cheese, curried chicken salad or roasted vegetable pastas flavored with herbs grown in the garden right outside.

Nepenthe & Café Kevah CALIFORNIAN $$$

(☑831-667-2345; www.nepenthebigsur.com 48510 Hwy 1; cafe mains $11-17, restaurant mains $15-39; ☺restaurant 11:30am-10pm, cafe 9am-4pm; 🚲) Nepenthe comes from a Greek word meaning 'isle of no sorrow', and indeed, it's hard to feel blue while sitting by the firepit on this clifftop terrace. Just-okay California bistro cuisine (try the renowned Ambrosia burger) takes a backseat to the views and Nepenthe's history – Orson Welles and Rita Hayworth briefly owned a cabin here in the 1940s. Downstairs, Café Kevah serves light, casual brunches and has head-spinning ocean views from its own outdoor patio (closed in winter and bad weather).

Big Sur Bakery & Restaurant CALIFORNIAN $$$

(☑831-667-0520; www.bigsurbakery.com; 47540 Hwy 1; snacks & drinks from $4, mains $14-36; ☺bakery from 8am daily, restaurant 11am-2:30pm Tue-Fri, 10:30am-2:30pm Sat & Sun, dinner from 5:30pm Tue-Sat) Behind the Shell station, this warmly lit, funky house has seasonally changing menus; wood-fired pizzas share space with more refined dishes like butter-braised halibut. Fronted by a pretty patio, the bakery pours Big Sur's priciest espresso. Expect long waits and standoffish service.

Deetjen's Big Sur Inn CALIFORNIAN $$$

(☑831-667-2377; www.deetjens.com; 48865 Hwy 1; breakfast mains $10-12, dinner mains $24-36; ☺8-11:30am & 6-9pm) This quaint yesteryear lodge has a cozy, candle-lit dining room serving up steaks, cassoulets and other hearty country fare from a daily changing menu, primarily sourced from organic local produce, hormone-free meat and sustainable seafood. Breakfast is a much better bet than dinner.

Big Sur Lodge AMERICAN, GROCERIES $$$

(☑831-667-3100; www.bigsurlodge.com; 47225 Hwy 1; breakfast & lunch mains $8-15, dinner mains $8-27; ☺restaurant 7:30am-9pm, general store 8am-9pm; 🚲) Inside Pfeiffer Big Sur State Park, pull up a wooden table in this cabinesque dining room and fill up on rainbow trout, pasta primavera, roast chicken and

trail-mix salads, all made with hungry hikers in mind. The lodge's small general store stocks camping supplies, snacks, drinks and ice-cream treats.

Big Sur River Inn AMERICAN, GROCERIES $$$

(☑831-667-2700; www.bigsurriverinn.com; Hwy 1; mains $9-29; ☺restaurant 8am-9pm, general store 11am-7pm; 🛜🚲) Woodsy old supper club with a deck overlooks a creek teeming with throaty frogs. The wedding reception–quality food is mostly classic American seafood, grilled meats and pastas, but diner-style breakfasts and lunches – from berry pancakes to BLT sandwiches – satisfy. The nearby general store has limited packaged foods and produce, but also a made-to-order fruit smoothie and burrito bar at the back.

Big Sur Roadhouse MEXICAN, AMERICAN $$

(☑831-667-2264; www.bigsurroadhouse.com; 47080 Hwy 1; mains $14-26; ☺5:30-9pm Wed-Mon) This Latin-flavored roadhouse fairly glows with its coppertop bar and corner fireplace. At outdoor riverside tables, fork into hearty adobo-marinated skirt steak, stuffed pasilla peppers or barbecue chicken with jicama salad.

🍷 Drinking & Entertainment

Henry Miller Library PERFORMING ARTS

(☑831-667-2574; www.henrymiller.org; Hwy 1) Just south of Nepenthe, this nonprofit performance space hosts a bohemian carnival of live-music concerts, author readings, open-mic nights and indie film screenings outdoors.

Maiden Publick House BAR

(☑831-667-2355; Hwy 1) Near the Big Sur River Inn, this dive has an encyclopedic beer bible and motley local musicians jamming, mostly on weekends.

Rocky Point BAR

(www.rocky-point.com; 36700 Hwy 1; ☺9am-9pm) Come for the dizzying ocean-view terrace, where Bloody Marys are served all day, 2.5 miles north of Bixy Bridge.

ℹ️ Information

Visitors often wander into businesses along Hwy 1 and ask, 'How much further to Big Sur?' In fact, there is no town of Big Sur as such, though you may see the name on maps. Commercial activity is concentrated along the stretch north of Pfeiffer Big Sur State Park. Sometimes called 'the Village,' this is where you'll find most of the lodging, restaurants and shops, some of which offer free wi-fi, although cellphone reception is rare.

Big Sur Chamber of Commerce (☏831-667-2100; www.bigsurcalifornia.org; ⊘9am-1pm Mon, Wed & Fri) Pick up the free *Big Sur Guide* newspaper (also downloadable online) at local businesses.

Big Sur Station (☏831-667-2315; www.parks.ca.gov; Hwy 1; ⊘8am-4pm, closed Mon & Tue Nov-Mar) About 1.5 miles south of Pfeiffer Big Sur State Park, this multiagency ranger station has information and maps for state parks, Los Padres National Forest and Ventana Wilderness.

Henry Miller Library (www.henrymiller.org; Hwy 1; ⊘11am-6pm Wed-Mon; @🛜) Free wi-fi and public internet terminals (donation requested).

Pacific Valley Station (☏805-927-4211; www.fs.usda.gov; Hwy 1; ⊘8am-4:30pm) South of Nacimiento-Fergusson Rd, USFS ranger station has limited visitor information.

Post office (www.usps.com; 47500 Hwy 1; ⊘10:30am-2:30pm Mon-Fri) Just north of Big Sur Bakery.

❶ Getting There & Around

Big Sur is best explored by car, since you'll be itching to stop frequently and take in the rugged beauty and vistas that reveal themselves after every hairpin turn. Even if your driving skills are up to these narrow switchbacks, others' aren't: expect to average 35mph or less along the route. Parts of Hwy 1 are battle-scarred, evidence of a continual struggle to keep them open after landslides and washouts. Call ☏800-427-7623 to check current highway conditions, and fill up your gas tank beforehand.

MST (☏888-678-2871; www.mst.org) bus 22 ($3, 1¼ hours) travels from Monterey via Carmel as far south as Nepenthe restaurant three times daily between late May and early September, and twice daily on Saturdays and Sundays only the rest of the year.

Point Piedras Blancas

Many lighthouses still stand along California's coast, but few offer such a historically evocative seascape. Federally designated an outstanding natural area, the jutting, wind-blown grounds of this 1875 lightstation (☏805-927-7361; www.piedrasblancas.org; tour adult/child 6-17yr $10/5; ⊘tour schedules vary) – one of the tallest on the West Coast – have been laboriously replanted with native flora. Picturesquely, everything looks much the way it did when the first lighthouse keepers helped ships find safe harbor at the whaling station at San Simeon Bay. Guided tours currently meet at 9:45am on Tuesdays, Thursdays and Saturdays at the old Piedras Blancas Motel, about 1.5 miles north of the lightstation. No reservations are taken, but call ahead to check tour schedules.

At a signposted vista point 4.5 miles north of Hearst Castle, you can observe a colony of elephant seals bigger than the one at Año Nuevo State Reserve. During peak winter season, about 16,000 seals seek shelter in the coves and beaches along this stretch of coast. On sunny days the seals usually 'lie around like banana slugs,' in the words of one docent. Interpretative panels and blue-jacketed **Friends of the Elephant Seal** (www.elephantseal.org) docents demystify the behavior of these beasts.

Hearst Castle

The most important thing to know about William Randolph Hearst (1863–1951) is that he did not live like *Citizen Kane*. Not that Hearst wasn't bombastic, conniving and larger than life, but the moody recluse of the movie he was definitely not. Hearst also didn't call his 165-room monstrosity a castle, preferring its official name, *La Cuesta Encantada* ('The Enchanted Hill'), or more often calling it simply 'the ranch.' From the 1920s into the '40s, Hearst and Marion Davies, his longtime mistress (Hearst's wife refused to grant him a divorce), adored entertaining a steady stream of the era's biggest movers and shakers. Invitations were highly coveted, but Hearst had his quirks – he despised drunkenness, and guests were forbidden to speak of death.

Hearst Castle is a wondrous, historic (Winston Churchill penned anti-Nazi essays here in the 1930s), over-the-top homage to material excess, perched high on a hill; a visit is practically a must. Architect Julia Morgan based the main building, Casa Grande, on the design of a Spanish cathedral, and over the decades catered to Hearst's every design whim, deftly integrating the spoils of his fabled European shopping sprees (ancient artifacts, monasteries etc). The estate sprawls across acres of lushly landscaped gardens, accentuated by shimmering pools and fountains, statues from ancient Greece and Moorish Spain and the ruins of what was in Hearst's day the world's largest private zoo (drivers along Hwy 1 can sometimes still spot the remnant zebra herd).

WORTH A TRIP

VENTANA WILDERNESS

The 200,000-acre **Ventana Wilderness** (www.ventanawild.org) is Big Sur's wild back-country. It lies within the northern Los Padres National Forest, which straddles the Santa Lucia Range and runs parallel to the coast. Most of this wilderness is covered with oak and chaparral, though canyons cut by the Big Sur and Little Sur Rivers support virgin stands of coast redwoods. The endemic Santa Lucia fir grows upslope in rocky outcroppings.

Partly reopened after devastating wildfires in 2008, the wilderness remains popular with adventurous backpackers. A favorite overnight destination is **Sykes Hot Springs**, natural 100°F (35°C) mineral pools framed by redwoods, but don't expect solitude during peak season (April through September). It's a moderately strenuous 10-mile one-way hike along the **Pine Ridge Trail**, starting from **Big Sur Station** (☑831-667-2315; www.parks.ca.gov; Hwy 1; ☺8am-4pm, closed Mon & Tue Nov-Mar), where you can get free campfire permits and pay for overnight trailhead parking ($5).

Much like Hearst's construction budget, the castle will devour as much of your time and money as you let it. To see anything of this **state historic monument** (☑info 805-927-2020, reservations 800-444-4445; www.hearstcastle.org; tours adult/child from $25/12; ☺daily, hr vary), you have to take a tour. In peak summer months, show up early enough and you might be able to get a same-day ticket for later that afternoon. For special holiday and evening tours, book at least two weeks in advance.

Tours usually start daily at 8:20am, with the last leaving the visitor center for the 10-minute ride to the hilltop at 3:20pm (later in summer and during December). There are three main tours: the guided portion of each lasts about 45 minutes, after which you're free to wander the gardens and terraces, photograph the iconic Neptune and Roman Pools and soak up views. Tour guides are almost preternaturally knowledgeable – just try and stump 'em. Best of all are Christmas holiday evening tours, featuring living-history reenactors who escort you back in time to the castle's 1930s heyday.

Facilities at the visitor center (no eating or drinking is allowed on the hilltop) are geared for industrial-sized mobs of visitors. It's better to grab lunch at Sebastian's General Store by the beach across Hwy 1, or in Cambria. Before you leave the castle, take a moment to visit the often-overlooked museum area at the back of the visitors center. The center's five-story-high **theater** shows a 40-minute historical film (admission included with tour tickets) about the castle and the Hearst family.

Dress with plenty of layers: gloomy fog at the sea-level visitors center can turn into sunny skies at the castle's hilltop location, and vice versa. **RTA** (☑805-541-2228; www.slorta.org) bus 12 makes three or four daily round-trips to Hearst Castle from San Luis Obispo ($3, two hours) via Morro Bay, Cayucos and Cambria.

San Simeon

Little San Simeon Bay sprang to life as a whaling station in 1852. Shoreline whaling was practiced to catch gray whales migrating between Alaskan feeding grounds and birthing waters in Baja California, while sea otters were hunted here by Russian fur traders. In 1865 Senator George Hearst purchased 45,000 acres of ranch land and established an oceanfront settlement on the western side of Hwy 1. Designed by architect Julia Morgan, the historic 19th-century houses are now rented to employees of the Hearst Corporation's 80,000-acre free-range cattle ranch.

⊙ Sights & Activities

FREE **William Randolph Hearst Memorial State Beach**   BEACH (www.parks.ca.gov; ☺dawn-dusk) Across Hwy 1 from Hearst Castle, this bayfront beach has a pleasant sandy stretch with rock outcroppings, kelp forests, a rickety wooden pier (fishing permitted) and picnic areas with barbecue grills.

Sea for Yourself Kayak Tours   KAYAKING (☑805-927-1787, 800-717-5225; www.kayakcambria.com; rentals $20-65, tours from $50) Right on the beach, you can rent sea kayaks, wetsuits, bodyboards and surfboards, or take a guided paddle around San Simeon Cove.

FREE **Coastal Discovery Center** MUSEUM
(☑805-927-6575; Hwy 1; ☺11am-5pm Fri-Sun mid-Mar–Oct, 10am-4pm Fri-Sun Nov–mid-Mar; ☖) Educational displays include a talking artificial tidepool that kids can touch and videos of deep-sea diving and a WWII-era shipwreck just offshore.

🛏 Sleeping & Eating

A few miles south of the original whaling station, the modern town of San Simeon is nothing more than a strip of unexciting motels and restaurants. There are better places to stay in Cambria and beach towns further south like Cayucos.

San Simeon State Park CAMPGROUND $
(☑reservations 800-444-7275; www.reservecameri ca.com; Hwy 1; tent & RV sites $20-35) About 4.5 miles south of Hearst Castle are two popular campgrounds: **San Simeon Creek**, with hot showers and flush toilets; and undeveloped **Washburn**, located along a dirt road. Drinking water is available at both.

Sebastian's General Store DELI, GROCERIES $
(442 San Simeon Rd, off Hwy 1; mains $7-12; ☺11am-5pm Tue-Sun, kitchen to 4pm) Down a side road across Hwy 1 from the castle, this tiny historic market sells cold drinks, Hearst Ranch beef burgers, giant deli sandwiches and salads for beach picnics at San Simeon Cove. Hearst Ranch Winery tastings are available at the copper-top bar.

Cambria

With a whopping dose of natural beauty, the coastal idyll of Cambria is a lone pearl cast along the coast. Built on lands that once belonged to Mission San Miguel, one of the village's first nicknames was Slabtown, after the rough pieces of wood pioneer buildings were constructed from. Today, just like at neighboring Hearst Castle, money is no object in this wealthy retirement community, whose motto 'Pines by the Sea' is affixed to the back of BMWs that toodle around town.

👁 Sights & Activities

Although its milky-white moonstones are long gone, **Moonstone Beach** still attracts romantics with its oceanfront boardwalk and truly picturesque rocky shoreline. For solitude, take the Windsor Rd exit off Hwy 1 and drive down to where the road dead-ends, then follow a 2-mile round-trip blufftop hiking trail across **East West Ranch**.

A 10-minute drive south of Cambria, past the Hwy 46 turnoff to Paso Robles' wine country, tiny **Harmony** is a slice of rural Americana, with an 1865 creamery now housing local artists' workshops and a hillside winery, **Harmony Cellars** (www.harmo nycellars.com; 3255 Harmony Valley Rd; ☺10am-5pm).

🛏 Sleeping

Cambria's choicest motels and hotels line Moonstone Beach Dr, while quaint B&Bs cluster around the village.

Blue Dolphin Inn HOTEL $$$
(☑805-927-3300, 800-222-9157; www.cam briainns.com; 6470 Moonstone Beach Dr; d incl breakfast basket $159-239; ☎☖☀) This sand-colored two-story, slat-sided building may not look as upscale as other oceanfront motels, but rooms do have romantic fireplaces, pillowtop mattresses and rich linens. Pet fee $25.

Fogcatcher Inn HOTEL $$$
(☑805-927-1400, 800-425-4121; www.fogcatch erinn.com; 6400 Moonstone Beach Dr; d incl breakfast $129-379; ☎☀) Motels along Moonstone Beach Dr are nearly identical, but this one is a standout for its hot tub. Faux English Tudor–style cottages harbor luxurious modern rooms, some with fireplaces and ocean views.

Cambria Shores Inn MOTEL $$$
(☑805-927-8644, 800-433-9179; www.cambri ashores.com; 6276 Moonstone Beach Dr; d incl breakfast $150-290; ☎☀) A stone's throw from Moonstone Beach, this ocean-view motel offers pampering amenities for pooches (pet fee $15), including a welcome doggie basket. Rates include a breakfast basket delivered to your door.

Bluebird Inn MOTEL $$
(☑805-927-4634, 800-552-5434; http://bluebird motel.com; 1880 Main St; d $70-220; ☎) With peaceful gardens, this friendly East Village motel offers basic, budget-conscious rooms, some with fireplaces and private creekside patios or balconies. Wi-fi in lobby only.

HI Cambria Bridge Street Inn HOSTEL $
(☑805-927-7653; www.bridgestreetinncambria.com; 4314 Bridge St; dm $22-25, r $45-80; ☺check-in

5-9pm; 🖥) Inside a 19th-century parsonage, this tiny hostel sleeps more like a grandmotherly B&B. It has floral charm and a communal kitchen, but the shabby-chic rooms are thin-walled. Book ahead.

🍴 Eating & Drinking

It's a short walk between several cafes and eateries in the East Village.

Indigo Moon CALIFORNIAN $$
(www.indigomooncafe.com; 1980 Main St; lunch mains $6-13, dinner mains $13-29; ⊙10am-4pm & 5-9pm Mon-Sat, 10am-3pm & 5-9pm Sun) Inside this artisan cheese and wine shop, breezy bistro tables complement market-fresh salads, toasty sandwiches and sweet-potato fries. Local luminaries gossip over lunch on the back patio, while dinner dates order lemon risotto, crab-stuffed trout or coriander-encrusted chicken.

Sow's Ear AMERICAN $$$
(☑805-927-4865; www.thesowsear.com; 2248 Main St; dinner mains $11-30; ⊙5-9pm) For over a decade, the old-school Sow's Ear has been whipping up haute comfort food inside a cozy house on the East Village's main drag. Make reservations to dine on traditional lobster pot pie, pork tenderloin with olallieberry chutney and fresh bread baked in terracotta flowerpots.

Linn's Easy as Pie Cafe DELI, BAKERY $
(www.linnsfruitbin.com; 4251 Bridge St; items $4-10; ⊙10am-6pm Oct-Apr, to 7pm May-Sep; 🖐) If you don't have time to visit Linn's Fruit Bin, the original farm store out on Santa Rosa Creek Rd (a 20-minute drive east via Main St), you can fork into their famous olallieberry pies and preserves at this take-out counter delivering salads, sandwiches and comfort fare to a sunny East Village patio.

Wild Ginger FUSION $$
(www.wildgingercambria.com; 2380 Main St; mains $12-17; ⊙11am-2:30pm Mon-Wed, Fri & Sat & 5-9pm Fri-Wed; 🖋) This bright, cheery chef-owned cafe dishes up garden-fresh, pan-Asian fare, perfectly seasoned and presented, plus housemade sorbets in exotic flavors like pomegranate and pineapple-coconut. Expect long waits.

Lily's Coffeehouse CAFE $
(www.lilyscoffee.com; 2028 Main St; coffee & snacks $2-8; ⊙8:30am-5pm Wed-Mon; 🖥) Francophilic Lily's has a peaceful garden patio and brews robust coffees and teas. Drop in on Saturday between 11am and 4pm for made-to-order crepes.

ℹ Information

Cambria has three distinct parts: the tourist-choked East Village, a half-mile from Hwy 1, where antiques shops, art galleries and coffeehouses line Main St; the newer West Village, further west along Main St, is where you'll find the **chamber of commerce** (☑805-927-3624; www.cambria-chamber.org; 767 Main St; ⊙9am-5pm Mon-Fri, noon-4pm Sat & Sun); and motel-lined Moonstone Beach, off Hwy 1.

ℹ Getting There & Around

From San Luis Obispo, **RTA** (☑805-541-2228; www.slorta.org) bus 12 makes three or four daily round trips via Morro Bay and Cayucos to Cambria ($3, 1¾ hours), running along Moonstone Beach Dr and Main St through the East and West Villages.

Cayucos

With its historic storefronts housing antiques shops and eateries, the main drag of amiable, slow-paced Cayucos calls to mind an Old West frontier town. But just one block west of Ocean Ave, surf's up!

⊙ Sights & Activities

At downtown's north end, fronting a broad white-sand beach, Cayucos' long wooden pier is popular with fishers – it's also a sheltered spot for beginning surfers.

Cayucos Surf Company SURFING
(☑805-995-1000; www.surfcompany.com; 95 Cayucos Dr; board & wetsuit rental $8-38, 2hr lesson $80-100; ⊙9am-6pm) Near the pier, this fun local surf shop rents surfboards, boogie boards and wetsuits. Call ahead for learn-to-surf lessons.

🛏 Sleeping

Cayucos doesn't lack for motels or beachfront inns, most higher-priced than in Morro Bay, 6 miles south.

⬛TOP CHOICE Cass House Inn B&B $$$
(☑805-995-3669; www.casshouseinn.com; 222 N Ocean Ave; d incl breakfast $165-325; 🖥) Inside a charmingly renovated 1867 Victorian inn, five truly luxurious rooms await, some with ocean views, deep-soaking tubs and antique fireplaces to ward off chilly coastal fog. All have plush beds, flat-screen TVs with DVD

players and tasteful, romantic accents. Reservations are essential.

Seaside Motel
MOTEL $$

(☑805-995-3809, 800-549-0900; www.seaside
motel.com; 42 S Ocean Ave; d $80-160; 🐾) Expect
a warm welcome from the hands-on owners
of this vintage motel. Country-kitsch rooms
may be on the small side, but some have
kitchenettes. Cross your fingers for quiet
neighbors.

Cayucos Beach Inn
MOTEL $$

(☑805-995-2828, 800-482-0555; www.cayu
cosbeachinn.com; 333 S Ocean Ave; d $85-175;
🐾🐾🐾🐾) A remarkably pet-friendly motel,
where even the doors have special peepholes
for your canine (pet fee $10). Spacious rooms
are nothing special, but you'll find invitingly
grassy picnic areas and BBQ grills out front.

Cypress Tree Motel
MOTEL $$

(☑805-995-3917, 800-241-4289; www.cypresstree
motel.com; 125 S Ocean Ave; d $50-120; 🐾🐾)
Retro motor court has lovingly cared-for,
but kinda hokey theme rooms, like 'Nautical Nellie' with a net of seashells suspended
behind the bed. Pet fee $10.

✖ Eating

TOP CHOICE Cass House Restaurant
EURASIAN $$$

(☑805-995-3669; www.casshouseinn.com; 222 N
Ocean Ave; 4-course prix-fixe dinner $64, incl wine
pairings $92; ⊙5-9pm Thu-Mon) The inn's flawless
chef-driven restaurant defies expectations. Linger over the locally sourced, seasonally inspired
menu that ambitiously ranges from finger-
lime snapper ceviche and artisan cheeses to
heritage pork loin in cherry jus and black cod
with lemongrass beurre blanc, all paired with
top-notch regional wines.

Hoppe's Bistro & Wine Bar
CALIFORNIAN $$$

(☑805-995-1006; www.hoppesbistro.com; 78 N
Ocean Ave; dinner mains $18-35; ⊙11am-10pm
Wed-Sun) This slightly kitschy dining rooms
features fresh seafood on its respectable
coastal, often organic menu – don't skip the
incredible red-abalone dishes. The somme-
lier really knows local wines.

Ruddell's Smokehouse
SEAFOOD $

(www.smokerjim.com; 101 D St; items $5-12;
⊙11am-6pm; 🐾🐾) 'Smoker Jim' transforms
fresh-off-the-boat seafood into succulently
smoked slabs and sandwiches, while fish ta-
cos come slathered in a unique apple-celery
relish. Squeeze yourself in the door to order.
Dogs allowed at sidewalk tables.

Sea Shanty
DINER $

(www.seashantycayucos.com; 296 S Ocean Ave;
mains $7-25; ⊙8am-9pm Sep-May, to 10pm Jun-
Aug; 🐾) At this family joint, where a bazillion
baseball caps hang from the ceiling, just-OK
breakfasts and fish and chips take a back
seat to killer desserts.

Brown Butter Cookie Co
BAKERY $

(www.brownbuttercookies.com; 250 N Ocean Ave;
snacks from $2; ⊙10am-5pm) Seriously addic-
tive cookies, worth the shocking price.

Schooner's Wharf
BAR & GRILL $$

(www.schoonerswharf.com; 171 N Ocean Ave; mains
$9-42; ⊙11am-9pm Sun-Thu, to 10pm Fri & Sat)
Come for the ocean-view bar, not necessarily the food.

❶ Getting There & Away

From San Luis Obispo, **RTA** (☑805-541-2228;
www.slorta.org) bus 12 travels three or four times
daily along Hwy 1 to Cayucos ($2.50, one hour)
via Morro Bay, continuing north to Cambria ($2,
25 minutes) and Hearst Castle ($2, 40 minutes).

Morro Bay

Home to a commercial fishing fleet, Morro
Bay's biggest claim to fame is Morro Rock,
a volcanic peak jutting dramatically from
the ocean floor. It's one of the Nine Sisters, a
21-million-year-old chain of rocks stretching
all the way south to San Luis Obispo. Morro
Bay's less boast-worthy landmark comes courtesy of the power plant, which threw up three
cigarette-shaped smokestacks by the bay.
Along this humble, working-class stretch of
coast are fantastic opportunities for kayaking,
hiking and camping, all within easy reach of
San Luis Obispo, where Hwy 1 meets Hwy 101.

◉ Sights & Activities

This town harbors natural riches, easily
worth a half day's exploration. The bay itself
is a deep inlet separated from the ocean by
a 5-mile-long sand spit. Leading south from
Morro Rock is the Embarcadero, a small
waterfront boulevard jam-packed with seafood eateries and souvenir shops that's also
a launching point for boat trips.

Morro Rock
LANDMARK

Chumash tribespeople are the only people
legally allowed to climb this volcanic rock,
now the protected nesting ground of peregrine falcons. You can laze at the small
beach on the rock's north side, but you

can't drive all the way around – instead, rent a kayak. The waters below are a giant estuary inhabited by two dozen threatened and endangered species, including brown pelicans, snowy plovers and sea otters.

Morro Bay State Park   PARK
(☑info 805-772-2560, museum 805-772-2694; www.parks.ca.gov; Morro Bay State Park Rd; park entry free, museum adult/child $2/free; ☉park sunrise-sunset, museum 10am-5pm; ⊛) Inside this woodsy waterfront park, a small natural-history museum has cool interactive exhibits geared toward kids that demonstrate how the forces of nature affect us all. Just north of the museum is a eucalyptus grove harboring one of California's last remaining great blue heron rookeries.

Kayak Horizons   KAYAKING
(☑805-772-6444; www.kayakhorizons.com; 551 Embarcadero; kayak & canoe rentals $12-44, tours & lessons $65) One of several places on the Embarcadero offering kayak rentals and tours for novices. When paddling out on your own, be aware of the tide schedules. Ideally, you'll want to ride the tide out and then back in. Winds are generally calmest in the mornings.

Morro Bay Golf Course   GOLF
(☑805-782-8060; www.slocountyparks.com; green fees $15-50) South of the Embarcadero, adjacent to the state park, this 18-hole golf course boasts tree-lined fairways and ocean views. A driving range and rental clubs and carts are available.

☞ Tours

Sub-Sea Tours   BOAT TRIPS
(☑805-772-9463; www.subseatours.com; 699 Embarcadero; 45min tour adult/child 3-12yr $14/7; ☉hourly departures 10am-4pm Jun-Sep, 11am-3pm Sat & Sun & 1pm Mon-Fri Oct-May; ⊛) For pint-sized views of kelp forests and schools of fish, take the kids on a spin on a yellow semi-submersible.

Virg's Landing   FISHING
(☑805-772-1222, 800-762-5263; www.morrobaysportfishing.com; 1169 Market St; tours $65-250) Salty dogs ready for a little sportfishing can book half-day or all-day trips with this long-running local outfit.

Central Coast Outdoors   OUTDOOR SPORTS
(☑805-528-1080, 888-873-5610; www.centralcoastoutdoors.com; tours $65-150) Leads kayaking tours (including sunset and full-moon paddles), guided hikes and cycling

trips along the coast and in nearby wine countries.

☆ Festivals & Events

Morro Bay Winter Bird Festival   OUTDOORS
(www.morrobaybirdfestival.org) Every January, bird-watchers flock together for guided hikes, kayaking trips and naturalist-led events, during which over 200 species can be spotted along the Pacific Flyway.

⊟ Sleeping

Dozens of motels cluster along Hwy 1 and around Harbor and Main Sts, between downtown and the Embarcadero.

Anderson Inn   INN $$$
(☑805-772-3434, 866-950-3434; www.andersoninnmorrobay.com; 897 Embarcadero; d $239-349; ☏) Like a small boutique hotel, this waterfront inn has just a handful of spacious, soothingly earth-toned rooms with flat-screen TVs, mini-fridges and if you're lucky, a gas fireplace, your own hot tub and harbor views.

La Serena Inn   MOTEL $$
(☑805-772-5665, 800-248-1511; www.laserenainn.com; 990 Morro Ave; d $89-169; ☏) Large, well-kept rooms at this bland three-story motel each have a microwave and minifridge. If you're feeling flush, request one with views of Morro Rock and a private balcony to hear the gentle clank-clank of boats in the harbor below.

Morro Bay State Park Campground   CAMPGROUND $
(☑reservations 800-444-7275; www.reserveamerica.com; tent & RV sites without/with hookups $35/50) Less than 2 miles south of downtown and the Embarcadero, over 115 woodsy sites are fringed by eucalyptus and cypress trees, with trails leading down to the beach. Facilities include fire pits, showers and an RV dump station.

Beach Bungalow Inn & Suites   MOTEL $$
(☑805-772-9700; www.morrobaybeachbungalow.com; 1050 Morro Ave; d $100-250; ☏☀) This butter-yellow motor court's chic, contemporary rooms have mod-cons; pet fee $20.

Inn at Morro Bay   MOTEL $$
(☑805-772-5651, 800-321-9566; www.innatmorrobay.com; 60 State Park Rd; d $115-275; ☒) Dated two-story waterfront lodge inside the state park set for renovations.

✕ Eating & Drinking

More predictable seafood shacks line the Embarcadero.

Taco Temple CALIFORNIAN $$
(2680 Main St, off Hwy 1; mains $7-13; ⊘11am-9pm Mon & Wed-Sat, to 8:30pm Sun; 🖼) Overlook the frontage-road location for huge helpings of Cal-Mex fusion flavor. At the next table, there might be fishers talking about the good ole' days or starving surfer buddies. Try one of the specials – they deserve the name. Cash only.

Giovanni's Fish Market & Galley SEAFOOD $$
(www.giovannisfishmarket.com; 1001 Front St; mains $7-13; ⊘9am-6pm; 🖼) This family-run joint on the Embarcadero is a classic California seafood shack. Folks line up for batter-fried fish and chips and killer garlic fries. Inside there's a market with all the fixin's for a beach campground fish fry.

Shine Cafe & Sunshine Health Foods VEGETARIAN $
(www.sunshinehealthfoods-shinecafe.com; 415 Morro Bay Blvd; mains $5-14; ⊘11am-5pm Mon-Fri, 9am-5pm Sat, 10am-4pm Sun; 🖼) Hidden inside a small natural-foods market, the mostly organic Shine Cafe serves karma-cleansing grub like tempeh tacos, garden-fresh salads and blueberry smoothies.

Stax Wine Bar TAPAS $$
(www.staxwine.com; 1099 Embarcadero; shared plates $6-10; ⊘noon-8pm Sun-Thu, to 10pm Fri & Sat) Perch on barstools in front of the harbor-view windows for a hand-selected tasting flight of local California wines. Tapas-sized bites such as artisan cheese and cured-meat plates keep revelers fueled, especially on live-music nights.

Last Stage West BARBECUE $$
(www.laststagewest.net; 15050 Morro Rd, Atascadero; mains $6-20; ⊘noon-9pm) At this Old West roadhouse and boot-stomping live-music venue, say 'Howdy, pardner!' to smoked tri-tip barbecue, slow-cooked pork ribs and rib-eye steak. To get here, drive Hwy 41 about 10 miles northeast of its intersection with Hwy 1 in Morro Bay.

ℹ Information

Morro Bay Chamber of Commerce (☎805-772-4467, 800-231-0592; www.morrobay.org; 845 Embarcadero; ⊘9am-5pm Mon-Fri, 10am-4pm Sat, 10am-2pm Sun) is in the thick of everything. A few blocks uphill, Main St is the less touristy downtown.

ℹ Getting There & Around

From San Luis Obispo, **RTA** (☎805-541-2228; www.slorta.org) bus 12b travels hourly on weekdays and a few times daily on weekends along Hwy 1 to Morro Bay ($2.50, 40 minutes). Three or four times daily, bus 12b continues north from Morro Bay to Cayucos ($1.50, 15 minutes), Cambria ($2, 45 minutes) and Hearst Castle ($2, one hour). From late May to early October, a **trolley** (single ride $1.25, day pass $3) loops around the waterfront and downtown, operating varying hours (no service Tuesday to Thursday).

Montaña de Oro State Park

In spring the hillsides are blanketed by bright California native poppies, wild mustard and other wildflowers, giving this park its Spanish name, meaning 'mountain of gold.' Wind-tossed coastal bluffs with wild, wide-open sea views make it a favorite spot with hikers, mountain bikers and horseback riders. The northern half of the park features sand dunes and an ancient marine terrace visible due to seismic uplifting. Spooner's Cove, once used by smugglers, is now a postcard-perfect sandy beach and picnic area. If you go tidepooling, remember to only touch the marine creatures like sea stars, limpets and crabs with the back of one hand to avoid disturbing them, and never remove them from their aquatic homes. You can hike along the beach and the grassy ocean bluffs, or drive uphill past the visitors center to the start of the exhilarating 7-mile loop trail tackling **Valencia** and **Oats Peaks**.

🛏 Sleeping

Montaña de Oro State Park Campground CAMPGROUND $
(☎reservations 800-444-7275; www.reserveamerica.com; tent & RV sites $20-25, hike-and-bike sites $5) Tucked into a small canyon by the visitor center, this minimally developed campground has pleasantly cool drive-up and environmental walk-in sites. Limited amenities include vault toilets, drinking water and firepits.

ℹ Information

Montaña de Oro State Park (☎805-772-7434; www.parks.ca.gov; 3550 Pecho Valley Rd, Los Osos; admission free; ⊘sunrise-sunset)

ⓘ Getting There & Away

From the north, exit Hwy 1 in Morro Bay at South Bay Blvd; after 4 miles, turn right onto Los Osos Valley Rd (which runs into Pecho Valley Rd) for 6 miles. From the south, exit Hwy 101 in San Luis Obispo at Los Osos Valley Rd, then drive northwest 16 miles.

ALONG HIGHWAY 101

Driving inland along Hwy 101 is a quicker way to travel between the Bay Area and Southern California. Although it lacks the striking scenery of coastal Hwy 1, the historic El Camino Real (the King's Highway), established by Spanish conquistadors and missionaries, has a beauty of its own, ranging from the fertile fields of Salinas, immortalized by novelist John Steinbeck, to the oak-dappled golden hills of San Luis Obispo and beyond to seaside Santa Barbara. Along the way are ghostly missions, jaw-dropping Pinnacles National Monument and standout wineries.

Gilroy

About 30 miles south of San Jose, the self-proclaimed 'garlic capital of the world' puts on the jam-packed **Gilroy Garlic Festival** (www.gilroygarlicfestival.com) over the last full weekend in July. Show up for carnival-quality chow – garlicky fries, garlic-flavored ice cream and more – and for cooking contests under the blazing-hot sun.

Unusual **Gilroy Gardens** (✆408-840-7100; www.gilroygardens.org; 3050 Hecker Pass Hwy/Hwy 152; adult/child 3-10yr $45/35; ⊙11am-5pm Mon-Fri mid-Jun–mid-Aug, 11am-6pm Sat & Sun late Mar-Nov; ⓐ) is a nonprofit family-oriented theme park focused on food and plants rather than Disney-esque cartoon characters. You've got to really love flowers, fruit and veggies to get your money's worth. Rides like the 'Mushroom Swing' are mostly tame.

Heading east on Hwy 152 toward I-5, **Casa de Fruta** (✆408-842-7282; www.casadefruta.com; 10021 Pacheco Pass Hwy, Hollister; admission free; ⓐ) is a commercialized farm stand with some hokey, old-fashioned rides ($2.50 to $4) for youngsters, including carousels and choo-choo trains. Opening hours vary.

San Juan Bautista

In atmospheric old San Juan Bautista, where you can practically hear the whispers of the past, California's 15th mission is fronted by the only original Spanish plaza remaining in the state. Along 3rd St, evocative historic buildings mostly shelter antiques shops and petite garden restaurants. Hark! That cock you hear crowing is one of the town's roosters, which are allowed by tradition to stroll the streets at will.

◉ Sights

Mission San Juan Bautista   MISSION
(www.oldmissionsjb.org; 406 2nd St; adult/child 5-17yr $4/2; ⊙9:30am-4:30pm) Founded in 1797, this mission has the largest church among California's original 21 missions. As it was unknowingly built directly atop the San Andreas Fault, the mission has been rocked by earthquakes. Bells hanging in the tower today include chimes that were salvaged after the 1906 San Francisco earthquake toppled the original mission. Parts of Alfred Hitchcock's thriller *Vertigo* were shot here, although the bell tower in the climactic scene is just a special effect. Below the cemetery, a section of El Camino Real, the Spanish colonial road built to link the missions, can still be seen.

WHAT THE...?

'Oh, my!' is one of the more printable exclamations overheard from visitors at the **Madonna Inn** (✆805-543-3000, 800-543-9666; www.madonnainn.com; 100 Madonna Rd; r $179-449; ❄❂), a garish confection visible from Hwy 101. You'd expect outrageous kitsch like this in Las Vegas, not SLO, but here it is, in all its campy extravagance. Japanese tourists, vacationing Midwesterners and hipster, irony-loving urbanites all adore the 110 themed rooms – including Yosemite Rock, Caveman and hot-pink Floral Fantasy. Check out photos of the different rooms online, or wander the halls and spy into the ones being cleaned. The urinal in the men's room is a bizarre waterfall. But the most irresistible reason to stop here? Old-fashioned cookies from the storybook-esque bakery.

San Juan Bautista State Historic Park

PARK

(☑831-623-4881; www.parks.ca.gov; 2nd St, btwn Washington & Mariposa Sts; park entry free, museum adult/child $3/free; ⊙10am-4:30pm) Buildings around the old Spanish plaza opposite the mission anchor this historical park. The large plaza stables hint at San Juan Bautista in its 1860s heyday as a stagecoach stop. In 1876 the railroad bypassed the town, which has been a sleepy backwater ever since.

Across 2nd St is the 1858 Plaza Hotel, which started life as a single-story adobe building, and now houses a little historical museum. Next door, the Castro-Breen Adobe once belonged to Mexican general José Castro, who led a successful revolt against an unpopular governor. In 1848 it was bought by the Breen family, survivors of the Donner Party disaster.

🛏 Sleeping

Fremont Peak State Park

CAMPGROUND $

(☑831-623-4255; www.parks.ca.gov; San Juan Canyon Rd, off Hwy 156; pcr car $6, tent & RV sites $25; ⊙park 8am-30min after sunset, campground 24hr) Eleven miles south of town, this park has a pretty, but primitive, 20-site campground shaded by oak trees on a hilltop with distant views of Monterey Bay. Equipped with a 30in telescope, the park's astronomical observatory (☑831-623-2465; 🖐) is usually open to the public on moonless Saturday nights between April and October, starting around 8pm.

🍴 Eating & Drinking

Jardines de San Juan

MEXICAN $$

(www.jardinesrestuarant.com; 115 3rd St; mains $8-18; ⊙11:30am-9pm Sun-Thu, to 10pm Fri & Sat; 🖐) Here at the longest-running contender in the town's long lineup of touristy Mexican eateries, it's all about the pretty outdoor garden, not necessarily authentic food. Sunday dinner brings out *pollos borrachos* ('drunken chickens').

San Juan Bakery

BAKERY $

(319 3rd St; snacks $2-4; ⊙7:30am-3pm) Pick up fresh loaves of cinnamon bread, hot-cross buns and guava turnovers to sustain you during the long drive south. Get there early, as it often sells out.

Vertigo Coffee

COFFEESHOP $

(www.vertigocoffee.com; 81 4th St; snacks & drinks $2-5; ⊙6:30am-4pm Mon, 6:30am-5:30pm Tue-Thu, 6:30am-7pm Fri, 8am-7pm Sat, 8am-4pm Sun) Rich espresso, pour-over brews and sticky bear claws make this coffee roaster's cafe a find.

ℹ Getting There & Away

San Juan Bautista is on Hwy 156, a 3.5-mile detour east of Hwy 101, south of Gilroy en route to Monterey or Salinas. Further south, Hwy 101 enters the sun-dappled eucalyptus grove that James Stewart and Kim Novak drove through in *Vertigo*.

Salinas

Best known as the birthplace of John Steinbeck and nicknamed the 'Salad Bowl of the World,' Salinas is a working-class agricultural center with down-and-out, even mean streets. It makes a thought-provoking contrast with the affluence of the Monterey Peninsula, a fact of life that helped shape Steinbeck's novel *East of Eden*. The historic center stretches along Main St, with the National Steinbeck Center at its northern end.

◉ Sights

National Steinbeck Center

MUSEUM

(☑831-775-4721; www.steinbeck.org; 1 Main St; adult/child 6-12yr/youth 13-17yr $11/6/8; ⊙10am-5pm; 🖐) This museum will enthrall almost anyone, even if you don't know a lick about Salinas' Nobel Prize–winning native son, John Steinbeck (1902–68), a Stanford University dropout. Tough, funny and brash, he sensitively portrayed the troubled spirit of rural, working-class Americans in such novels as *The Grapes of Wrath*. Interactive, kid-accessible exhibits and short video clips chronicle the writer's life and works in an engaging way. Gems include Rocinante, the customized camper in which Steinbeck traveled around America while researching *Travels with Charley*. Take a moment and listen to Steinbeck's Nobel acceptance speech – it's grace and power combined.

Admission also includes the small Rabobank Agricultural Museum, which takes visitors on a journey through the modern agricultural industry, from water to pesticides to transportation – it's way more interesting than it sounds, trust us.

Steinbeck House

HISTORIC BUILDING

(132 Central Ave) Steinbeck was born and spent much of his boyhood in this house, three blocks west of the center. It's now a twee lunch cafe; we're not sure he'd approve.

Garden of Memories Memorial Park CEMETERY
(768 Abbott St, west of Hwy 101 exit Sanborn Rd)
Steinbeck is buried in the Hamilton family plot, about 2 miles south of the center via Main, John and Abbott Sts.

☞ Tours

Farm TOURS
(☏831-455-2575; www.thefarm-salinasvalley.com; admission free, tours adult/child 2-15yr $8/6; ⏰10am-5pm early Nov–mid-Mar, to 6pm mid-Mar–early Nov) This family-owned organic fruit-and-veggie stand offers educational 45-minute walking tours of its fields, usually at 1pm on Tuesdays and Thursdays. On the drive in, watch for the kinda-creepy giant sculptures of farm workers by local artist John Cerney, which also stand along Hwy 101. The farm is off Hwy 68 at Spreckels Blvd, about 3.5 miles south of the center.

Ag Venture Tours TOURS
(☏831-761-8463; http://agventuretours.com; half-day minivan tours from adult/child 7-20yr $70/55) Take a more in-depth look at commercial and organic farm fields and vineyards around the Salinas Valley and Monterey County.

✿ Festivals & Events

California Rodeo Salinas RODEO
(www.carodeo.com) Bull riding, calf roping, horse shows and cowboy poetry in late July.

Steinbeck Festival CULTURE
(www.steinbeck.org) Four-day festival in early August features films, lectures, guided bus and walking tours, music and a literary pub crawl.

California International Airshow OUTDOORS
(www.salinasairshow.com) Professional stunt flying and vintage and military aircraft take wing in late September.

🛏 Sleeping

Salinas has plenty of budget motels off Hwy 101, including at the Market St exit.

Best Western Plus Salinas Valley Inn & Suites MOTEL $$
(☏831-751-6411, 800-780-7234; www.bestwestern.com; 187 Kern St; r incl breakfast $99-299; ❄🛜🏊🐾🍳) As posh as you can get next to the freeway, this chain has newer, tasteful rooms (pet fee $20) and an outdoor pool and hot tub. Don't confuse it with the less appealing Best Western Salinas Monterey Hotel.

Laurel Inn MOTEL $
(☏831-449-2474, 800-354-9831; www.laurelinnmotel.com; 801 W Laurel Dr; r $60-100; ❄🛜🏊) If chains don't do it for you, this sprawling, family-owned cheapie has predictable motel rooms that are nevertheless spacious. There's a swimming pool, whirlpool tub and dry sauna for relaxing.

🍴 Eating & Drinking

Habanero Cocina Mexicana MEXICAN $$
(157 Main St; mains $5-15; ⏰11am-9pm Sun-Thu, to 10pm Fri & Sat) On downtown's Restaurant Row just south of the National Steinbeck Center, this storefront Mexican kitchen gets a stamp of approval for its handmade tortillas, a rainbow of fresh salsas and chile-spiked carne asada tacos.

First Awakenings DINER $$
(www.firstawakenings.net; 171 Main St; mains $5-12; ⏰7am-2pm; 🍴) Fork into oversized diner breakfasts of fruity pancakes and egg crepes, or turn up later in the day for hand-crafted deli sandwiches, BBQ bacon burgers and market-fresh salads.

Monterey Coast Brewing Co BREWPUB $$
(165 Main St; mains $8-25; ⏰11am-11pm Tue-Sun, to 9pm Mon) This microbrewery is a welcome sign of life downtown; the nine-beer tasting sampler costs just 10 bucks.

A Taste of Monterey WINE BAR
(www.atasteofmonterey.com; tasting fee $5; 127 Main St; ⏰11am-5pm Mon-Wed, to 6pm Thu-Sat) This downtown tasting room pours Monterey Co wines. Ask for a free map to find local vineyards along Hwy 101.

ℹ Information

Salinas Valley Chamber of Commerce
(☏831-751-7725; www.salinaschamber.com; 119 E Alisal St; ⏰8am-5pm Mon & Wed-Fri, 9:30am-5pm Tue) Hands out free tourist information and maps, five blocks east of Main St.

ℹ Getting There & Away

Amtrak (www.amtrak.com; 11 Station Pl, off W Market St) runs daily trains on the Seattle–LA *Coast Starlight* route via Oakland ($16, three hours), Paso Robles ($24, two hours), San Luis Obispo ($31, 3½ hours) and Santa Barbara ($49, 6½ hours).

Greyhound (www.greyhound.com; 19 W Gabilan St, cnr Salinas St) has a few daily buses to Santa Cruz ($14, 65 minutes), and along Hwy 101 north to San Francisco ($25, four hours) or south to San Luis Obispo ($30, 2½ hours) and Santa Barbara ($50, 4¾ hours).

From the nearby **Salinas Transit Center** (110 Salinas St), **MST** (☎888-678-2871; www.mst. org) buses 20 and 21 leave every 30 to 60 minutes daily for Monterey ($3, one hour).

Pinnacles National Monument

Named for the towering spires that rise abruptly out of the chaparral-covered hills east of Salinas Valley, this off-the-beaten-path park (☎831-389-4486; www.nps.gov/pinn; per vehicle $5) protects the remains of an ancient volcano. A study in stunning geological drama, its craggy monoliths, sheer-walled canyons and twisting caves are the result of millions of years of erosion.

◉ Sights & Activities

Besides rock climbing (for route information, surf www.pinnacles.org), the park's biggest attractions are its two talus caves, formed by piles of boulders. **Balconies Cave** is always open for exploration. Scrambling through it is not an exercise recommended for claustrophobes, as it's pitch-black inside, making a flashlight essential. Be prepared to get lost a bit, too. The cave is found along a 2.5-mile hiking loop from the west entrance. Nearer the east entrance, **Bear Gulch Cave** is closed seasonally, so as not to disturb a resident colony of Townsend's big-eared bats.

To really appreciate Pinnacles' stark beauty, you need to hike. Moderate loops of varying lengths and difficulty ascend into the High Peaks and include thrillingly narrow clifftop sections. In the early morning or late afternoon, you may spot endangered California condors (see p482) soaring overhead. Rangers lead guided full-moon and dark-sky hikes, as well as cool bat-viewing and star-gazing programs, on select Friday and Saturday nights from spring through fall. Reservations are required for these programs; call ☎831-389-4486, ext 243.

⌂ Sleeping

Pinnacles Campground   CAMPGROUND $
(☎info 831-389-4485, reservations 877-444-6777; www.recreation.gov; tent & RV sites without/with hookups $23/36; ▣▥) On the park's east side, this popular family-oriented campground has over 130 sites (some with shade), plus drinking water, firepits and a seasonal outdoor pool.

❶ Information

The best time to visit Pinnacles National Monument is during spring or fall; summer's heat is extreme. Information, maps, books and bottled water are available on the park's east side from the small **NPS visitor center** (◷9:30am-5pm) inside the **campground store** (◷3-6pm Mon-Fri, 9am-6pm Sat & Sun).

❶ Getting There & Away

There is no road connecting the two sides of the park. To reach the less-developed **west entrance** (◷7:30am-8pm mid-Mar–early Nov, to 6pm early Nov–mid-Mar), exit Hwy 101 at Soledad and follow Hwy 146 northeast for 14 miles. The **east entrance** (◷24hr), where you'll find the visitor center and campground, is accessed via lonely Hwy 25 in San Benito County, southeast of Hollister and northeast of King City.

Mission San Antonio De Padua

Remote, tranquil and evocative, this mission (☎831-385-4478; www.missionsanantonio. net; end of Mission Rd, Jolon; adult/child under 13yr $5/3; ◷10am-4pm) sits in the Valley of the Oaks, once part of the sprawling Hearst Ranch land holdings. It's now inside the boundaries of active Fort Hunter Liggett.

The mission was founded in 1771 by Franciscan priest Junípero Serra. Built with Native American labor, the church has been restored to its early 19th-century appearance, with a wooden pulpit, canopied altar and decorative flourishes on whitewashed walls. A creaky door leads to a cloistered garden anchored by a fountain. The museum has a small collection of such utilitarian items as an olive press and a weaving loom once used in the mission's workshops. Around the grounds, you can inspect the remains of a grist mill and irrigation system with aqueducts.

It's seldom crowded here, and you may have this vast site all to yourself, except during Mission Days in late April and La Fiesta on the second Sunday of June. Pick up a visitor's pass from a military checkpoint on the way in; bring photo ID and proof of your vehicle's registration. From the north, take the Jolon Rd exit off Hwy 101 before King City and follow Jolon Rd (County Rte G14) about 18 miles south to Mission Rd. From the south, take the Jolon Rd (County Rte G18) exit off Hwy 101 and drive 22 miles northwest to Mission Rd.

San Miguel

San Miguel is a small farming town right off Hwy 101, where life seems to have remained almost unchanged for decades. **Mission San Miguel Arcángel** (☎805-467-3256; www.missionsanmiguel.org; 775 Mission St; suggested donation per person/family $2/5; ⏰10am-4:30pm) suffered heart-breaking damage during the 2003 Paso Robles earthquake. Although repairs are still underway, the restored mission church, cemetery, museum and gardens have since re-opened. An enormous cactus out front was planted around the same time as the mission was built in 1818.

Hungry? Inside a retro converted gas station downtown, **Station 3** (1199 Mission St; items $2-6; ⏰6am-2:30pm Mon-Fri, 7am-2:30pm Sat & Sun) vends live-wire espresso and cups o' coffee, breakfast burritos, pulled-pork sandwiches and whopping good brownies.

Paso Robles

In northern San Luis Obispo County, Paso Robles is the heart of an agricultural region where grapes are now the biggest money-making crop. Scores of wineries along Hwy 46 produce a brave new world of more-than-respectable bottles. The Mediterranean climate is yielding another bounty, too: a fledgling olive-oil industry. Paso's historic downtown centers on Park and 12th Sts, where boutique shops and wine-tasting rooms await.

◉ Sights & Activities

You could spend days wandering country back roads off Hwy 46, both east and west of Hwy 101. Most wineries have tasting rooms and a few offer vineyard tours. For anything else you might want to know, check www.pasowine.com.

EASTSIDE

FREE **Tobin James Cellars**   WINERY
(www.tobinjames.com; 8950 Union Rd; ⏰10am-6pm) Boisterous Old West saloon pours bold reds, including an outlaw 'Ballistic' zinfandel and 'Liquid Love' late-harvest dessert wine. No tasting fee.

FREE **Eberle**   WINERY
(www.eberlewinery.com; 3810 E Hwy 46; ⏰10am-5pm Oct-Mar, 10am-6pm Apr-Sep) Offers lofty vineyard views, bocce ball courts and daily tours of its wine caves. No-fee tastings run

the gamut of white and red varietals and blends, plus port.

Clautiere   WINERY
(www.clautiere.com; 1340 Penman Springs Rd; ⏰noon-5pm Thu-Mon) Don't let the fantastical tasting room, where you can try on Dr Seuss-ian hats, fool you: serious Rhône-style blends will delight connoisseurs.

Cass   WINERY
(www.casswines.com; 7350 Linne Rd; ⏰noon-5pm Mon-Fri, 11am-6pm Sat & Sun) All that rich Rhône wine-tasting, from Roussanne to Syrah, going straight to your head? Light lunches are served in the market cafe until 4pm daily.

WESTSIDE

Tablas Creek   WINERY
(www.tablascreek.com; 9339 Adelaida Rd; ⏰10am-5pm) Breathe easy at this organic estate vineyard in the rolling hillsides. Known for their Rhône varietals, signature blends also rate highly. Tours are usually offered at 10:30am and 2pm daily (reservations advised).

Castoro   WINERY
(www.castorocellars.com; 1315 N Bethel Rd; ⏰10am-5:30pm) Husband-and-wife team produces 'dam fine wine' (the mascot is a beaver, get it?), including from custom-crushed and organic grapes. Outdoor vineyard concerts in summer.

Zenaida   WINERY
(www.zenaidacellars.com; 1550 W Hwy 46; ⏰11am-5pm) Rustic tasting room that's simply zen for sampling estate zins and a signature 'Fire Sign' blend. Overnight vineyard accommodations (from $250 per night) are tempting too.

Dark Star   WINERY
(www.darkstarcellars.com; 2985 Anderson Rd; ⏰10:30am-5pm Fri-Sun) If you're lucky, you might meet the winemaker in this family-run tasting room, pouring big, bold red varietals and blends like 'Left Turn.'

🎉 Festivals & Events

Wine Festivals   FOOD & WINE
(www.pasowine.com) Oenophiles crowd the Zinfandel Festival in mid-March, Wine Festival in mid-May and Harvest Wine Weekend in mid-October.

California Mid-State Fair   CULTURE
(www.midstatefair.com) In late July and early August, 12 days of live rock and country-

and-western concerts, farm exhibits, carnival rides and a rodeo draw huge crowds.

🛏 Sleeping

Chain motels and hotels line Hwy 101. B&Bs and vacation rentals are scattered among the vineyards outside town.

Hotel Cheval BOUTIQUE HOTEL $$$
(☎805-226-9995, 866-522-6999; www.hotelcheval.com; 1021 Pine St; d incl breakfast $300-400; ✲@🛜🏊🐾) Cocoon with your lover inside an art-splashed aerie downtown. A dozen stylish, modern rooms all come with California king beds, spa-worthy amenities and plantation shutters; some have gas fireplaces and sundecks with teak furniture. Staff can be snobby. Pet fee $30.

Wild Coyote Estate Winery B&B $$$
(☎805-610-1311; www.wildcoyote.biz; 3775 Adelaida Rd; d incl breakfast $225-275; ✲) Steal yourself away among the stellar vineyards of Paso Robles' west side, where just five romantic adobe-walled casitas echo the Southwest and a complimentary bottle of wine awaits by your kiva-style fireplace. There's an outdoor hot tub and barbecue grills too.

Inn Paradiso B&B $$
(☎805-239-2800; www.innparadiso.com; 975 Mojave Ln; d incl breakfast from $265; 🛜) At an intimate B&B with only three contemporary rooms, amiable hosts pull out all the luxury stops, with gas fireplace sitting areas, deep soaking tubs, canopy king-sized beds and French balcony doors. Vegetarian breakfasts available.

Melody Ranch Motel MOTEL $
(☎805-238-3911, 800-909-3911; 939 Spring St; r $63-78; ✲🛜🏊) There's just one story and only 19 basic rooms at this small, family-owned, 1950s motor court downtown, which translates into prices that are almost as small as the outdoor pool.

Courtyard Marriott HOTEL $$
(☎805-239-9700, 888-236-2427; www.courtyardpasorobles.com; 120 S Vine St, off Hwy 101; r $129-259; ✲@🛜🏊🐾) Contemporary hotel with immaculate rooms and full amenities.

Adelaide Inn MOTEL $$
(☎805-238-2770, 800-549-7276; www.adelaideinn.com; 1215 Ysabel Ave, off Hwy 101; r $85-135; ✲@🛜🏊🐾) Fresh-baked cookies and mini golf keep kids happy at this family motel.

JAMES DEAN MEMORIAL

In Cholame, about 25 miles east of Paso Robles via Hwy 46, there's a memorial near the spot where *Rebel Without a Cause* star James Dean fatally crashed his Porsche on September 30, 1955, at the age of 24. Ironically, the actor had recently filmed a public-safety campaign TV spot, in which he said, 'The road is no place to race your car. It's real murder. Remember, drive safely. The life you save might be mine.' Look for the shiny silver memorial wrapped around an oak tree outside the truck-stop Jack Ranch Cafe, which has old photographs and movie-star memorabilia inside.

🍴 Eating & Drinking

Restaurants, cafes and bars surround downtown's City Park, a grassy central square off Spring St between 11th and 12th Sts.

Artisan CALIFORNIAN $$$
(☎805-237-8084; www.artisanpasorobles.com; 1401 Park St; lunch mains $10-22, dinner mains $26-31; ⏱11am-9pm Sun-Thu, to 10pm Fri & Sat) Eco-conscious chef Chris Kobayashi often ducks out of the kitchen just to make sure you're loving his impeccable contemporary renditions of modern American cuisine, featuring sustainably farmed meats, wild-caught seafood and artisan California cheeses. Make reservations and expect long waits.

🌿Thomas Hill Organics Market Bistro ECLECTIC $$$
(☎805-226-5888; www.thomashillorganics.com; 1305 Park St; mains $18-26; ⏱lunch 11am-3pm Mon & Wed-Sat, 10am-3pm Sun, dinner 5-9pm Wed, Thu, Sun & Mon, to 10pm Fri & Sat) Hidden down a side alley, this farm-fresh gourmands' kitchen has only a few tables, so book ahead. On the eclectic fusion menu, which ranges from Vietnamese pork sandwiches to roasted duck breast with harissa sauce, most ingredients are locally sourced. Service is slooooow.

Villa Creek CALIFORNIAN $$$
(☎805-238-3000; 1144 Pine St; mains $22-35; ⏱5:30-10pm) Perch casually at the wine bar and spin tapas plates or dine like a don in the formal restaurant, which marries early Spanish-colonial mission cooking traditions

with sustainable, organic ingredients in shepherd's plates of artisan cheese, sausages and olives, or rancho-style cassoulet with duck. Reservations recommended.

Firestone Walker Brewing Co   BREWERY
(www.firestonebeer.com; 1400 Ramada Dr; ⊘noon-7pm) Bring your buddies to the taproom to sample famous brews like Double Barrel Ale.

Vinoteca   WINE BAR
(www.vinotecawinebar.com; 835 12th St; ⊘4-9pm Mon-Thu, to 11pm Fri & Sat) Sends you soaring with its wine flights and Wednesday meet-the-winemaker nights.

ⓘ Information

Paso Robles Chamber of Commerce (☎805-238-0506; www.pasorobleschamber.com; 1225 Park St; ⊘8:30am-4:30pm Mon-Fri, 10am-2pm Sat) Information and free winery maps.

ⓘ Getting There & Away

With **Amtrak** (www.amtrak.com; 800 Pine St), daily *Coast Starlight* trains head north to Salinas ($19, two hours) and Oakland ($29, five hours) or south to Santa Barbara ($26, 4¾ hours) and Los Angeles ($45, 7½ hours). Several daily Thru-way buses link to more-frequent regional trains, including the *Pacific Surfliner*.

From the train station, **Greyhound** (www.grey hound.com; 800 Pine St) runs a few daily buses along Hwy 101 south to Santa Barbara ($40, three hours) and LA ($58, six hours) or north to San Francisco ($54, 6½ hours) via Santa Cruz ($40, 3¼ hours).

RTA (☎805-541-2228; www.slorta.org) bus 9 travels between San Luis Obispo and Paso Robles ($2.50, 70 minutes) hourly on weekdays, and three or four times daily on weekends.

San Luis Obispo

Almost halfway between LA and San Francisco, San Luis Obispo is the classic stopover point for road trippers. With no must-see attractions, SLO might not seem to warrant much of your time. That said, this lively yet low-key town has an enviably high quality of life – in fact, talk-show diva Oprah once deemed it America's happiest city. For travelers, SLO's proximity to beaches, state parks and Hearst Castle make it a convenient coastal hub. CalPoly university students inject a healthy dose of hubbub into the city's streets, pubs and cafes throughout the school year. Nestled at the base of the Santa Lucia foothills, SLO is just a grape's throw

from thriving Edna Valley wineries, known for their crisp chardonnays and subtle syrahs and pinot noirs.

◉ Sights

San Luis Obispo Creek, once used to irrigate mission orchards, flows through downtown. Uphill from Higuera St, **Mission Plaza** is a shady oasis with restored adobe buildings and fountains overlooking the creek. Look for the **Moon Tree**, a coast redwood grown from a seed that journeyed on board Apollo 14's lunar mission.

Mission San Luis Obispo de Tolosa   MISSION
(www.missionsanluisobispo.org; 751 Palm St; suggested donation $2; ⊘9am-4pm) Those satisfyingly reverberatory bells heard around downtown emanate from this active parish. The fifth California mission, it was established in 1772 and named for a 13th-century French saint. Nicknamed the 'Prince of the Missions,' its modest church has an unusual L-shape and whitewashed walls depicting Stations of the Cross. An adjacent building contains an old-fashioned museum about daily life during the Chumash tribal and Spanish colonial periods.

FREE **San Luis Obispo Museum of Art**   MUSEUM
(www.sloma.org; 1010 Broad St; ⊘11am-5pm, closed Tue Sep-Jun) Near the creek, this small gallery showcases local painters, sculptors, printmakers and fine-art photographers, as well as traveling California art exhibitions.

Bubblegum Alley   QUIRKY
(off 700 block of Higuera St) SLO's weirdest sight is colorfully plastered with thousands of wads of ABC ('already been chewed') gum. Watch where you step!

🏃 Activities

The most popular local hiking trail summits **Bishop Peak** (1546ft), the tallest of the Nine Sisters, a chain of volcanic peaks that stretches north to Morro Bay. The 2.2-mile one-way trail starts in a grove of live oaks (watch out for poison oak, too) and heads uphill along rocky, exposed switchbacks. Scramble up boulders at the tippy-top for panoramic views. To get to the trailhead, drive northwest from downtown on Santa Rosa St (Hwy 1), turn left onto Foothill Dr, then right onto Patricia Dr; after 0.8 miles,

TOP FIVE EDNA VALLEY WINERIES

For a winery map and more vineyards to explore, visit www.slowine.com.

» **Edna Valley Vineyard** (ednavalleyvineyard.com; 2585 Biddle Ranch Rd; ⏰10am-5pm)
Sip Paragon Vineyard estate chardonnay by panoramic windows.

» **Kynsi** (www.kynsi.com; 2212 Corbett Canyon Rd; ⏰11am-5pm Thu-Mon) Small, family-run
vineyard pours cult-worthy pinot noirs.

» **Niven Family Wine Estates** (www.baileyana.com; 5828 Orcutt Rd; ⏰10am-5pm)
Tastings from five premium labels inside an early-20th-century wooden schoolhouse.

» **Talley** (www.talleyvineyards.com; 3031 Lopez Dr; ⏰10:30am-4:30pm) Unpretentious,
value-priced wines set among rolling hillsides, with vineyard tours daily.

» **Tolosa** (www.tolosawinery.com; 4910 Edna Rd; ⏰11am-4:45pm) Classic no-oak chardonnay, soft pinot noir and bold red blends; guided tours and barrel tastings by
appointment.

look for three black posts with a trailhead sign on your left.

For more peak hikes with ocean views, visit nearby Montaña de Oro State Park (p491).

⭐ Festivals & Events

San Luis Obispo [TOP CHOICE]
Farmers Market   FOOD, CULTURE
(www.downtownslo.com; ⏰6-9pm Thu) The coun-ty's biggest and best weekly farmers market turns downtown's Higuera St into a giant street party, with smokin' barbecues, over-flowing fruit and veggie stands, live music of all stripes and free sidewalk entertainment, from salvation peddlers to wackadoodle po-litical activists. It's one of the liveliest eve-nings out anywhere along the Central Coast.

Concerts in the Plaza   MUSIC, FOOD
(www.downtownslo.com) From early June until early September, Friday night concerts in downtown's Mission Plaza rock out with lo-cal bands and food vendors.

Savor the Central Coast   FOOD, WINE
(www.savorcentralcoast.com) Behind-the-scenes farm and ranch tours, wine-tasting competi-tions and celebrity chefs' dinners happen in late September and early October.

🛏 Sleeping

Motels cluster off Hwy 101, especially at the northeast end of Monterey St and around Santa Rosa St (Hwy 1).

San Luis Creek Lodge   HOTEL $$
(☏805-541-1122, 800-593-0333; www.sanluis creeklodge.com; 1941 Monterey St; r incl breakfast $139-239; ❄@🛜👶) Although it rubs shoul-ders a little too closely with neighboring motels, this boutique inn has fresh, spacious rooms with divine beds (some with gas fire-places and jetted tubs) in three whimsically mismatched buildings built in Tudor, Arts and Crafts, and Southern Plantation styles. Fluffy robes, DVDs, chess sets and board games are free to borrow.

Peach Tree Inn   MOTEL $$
(☏805-543-3170, 800 227-6396; www. peachtreeinn.com; 2001 Monterey St; r incl breakfast $79-200; ❄@🛜) The folksy, nothing-fancy motel rooms here are inviting, especially those right by the creek or with rocking chairs on wooden porches overlooking grassy lawns, eucalyptus trees and rose gar-dens. A hearty breakfast features homemade breads.

Petit Soleil   INN $$
(☏805-549-0321; www.petitsoleilslo.com; 1473 Monterey St; r incl breakfast $159-299; 🛜) This French-themed, gay-friendly 'bed et break-fast' is a mostly charming retrofit of a court-yard motel. Each room is tastefully deco-rated with Provençal flair, and breakfast is a gourmet feast. The front rooms catch some street noise, though.

HI Hostel Obispo   HOSTEL $
(☏805-544-4678; www.hostelobispo.com; 1617 Santa Rosa St; dm $24-27, r from $45; ⏰check-in 4:30-10pm; @🛜) On a tree-lined street near the train station, this solar-empowered, avocado-colored hostel inhabits a converted Victorian, which gives it a bit of a B&B feel. Amenities include a kitchen and bike rentals (from $10 per day); BYOT (bring your own towel). No credit cards.

San Luis Obispo

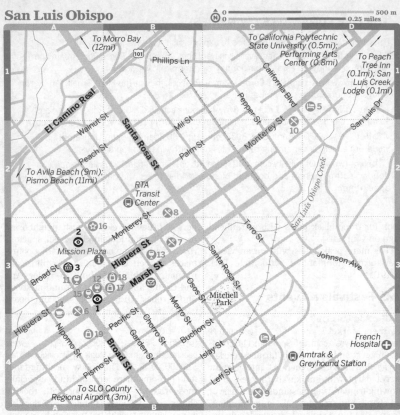

✗ Eating

Luna Red　　　　　　　　FUSION $$$
(☎805-540-5243; www.lunaredslo.com; 1009
Monterey St; small plates $4-15, dinner mains $18-
26; ⊙11am-9pm Mon-Thu, 11am-10pm Fri, 4-10pm
Sat, 5-9pm Sun) An inspired chef spins recher-
ché Californian, Mediterranean and Asian
tapas, with a keen eye towards freshness
and spice. Local bounty from the land and
sea rules the menu, including house-smoked
salumi and artisan cheeses. Stiff cocktails
enhance the sophisticated ambience, with
glowing lanterns and polished parquet
floors.

🍴Big Sky Café　　　　　CALIFORNIAN $$
(www.bigskycafe.com; 1121 Broad St; mains $6-22;
⊙7am-9pm Mon-Wed, 7am-10pm Thu-Fri, 8am-
10pm Sat, 8am-9pm Sun; 🖉) Big Sky is a big
room, and still the wait can be long – its
tagline is 'analog food for a digital world.'

Vegetarians have almost as many options
as carnivores, and many of the ingredients
are sourced locally. Big-plate dinners can be
bland, but breakfast (until 1pm daily) gets
top marks.

Meze Wine Café & Market　　MEDITERRANEAN $$
(www.mezemarket.com; 1880 Santa Barbara Ave;
sandwiches $8-10, shared plates $5-25; ⊙10am-
9:30pm Mon-Sat, 11:30am-8:30pm Sun) Hidden
downhill from the Amtrak station, this tiny
Mediterranean and North African epicurean
market, wine shop and tapas bar is an ec-
lectic gem. Gather with friends around the
cheese and charcuterie board, or stop in for
a hand-crafted sandwich accompanied by
couscous salad.

Firestone Grill　　　　　　BARBECUE $
(www.firestonegrill.com 1001 Higuera St; mains $5-
12; ⊙11am-10pm Sun-Wed, 11am-11pm Thu-Sun; 🖷)
If you can stomach huge lines, long waits for

San Luis Obispo

◎ Sights

⊜ Sleeping

⊗ Eating

◎ Drinking

⊛ Entertainment

⊜ Shopping

a table and sports bar–style service, you'll get to sink your teeth into an authentic Santa Maria–style tri-tip steak sandwich on a toasted garlic roll, or a rack of succulent pork ribs.

Splash Cafe CAFE $
(www.splashbakery.com; 1491 Monterey St; dishes $3-10; ☺7am-8:30pm Sun-Thu, to 9:30pm Fri & Sat; 🖼) Fresh soups and salads, sandwiches on house-made bread and tempting bakery treats are reason enough to kick back inside this airy uptown cafe, not far from motel row. The organic, hand-made Sweet Earth Chocolates shop is nearby.

🖉 New Frontiers Natural Marketplace GROCERIES, FAST FOOD $
(http://newfrontiers.com; 1531 Froom Ranch Way, off Hwy 101 exit Los Osos Valley Rd; ☺8am-9pm) For organic groceries, deli picnic meals and a hot-and-cold salad bar. It's a 15-minute

drive from downtown via Hwy 101 southbound.

SLO Donut Company SNACKS $
(www.slodonutcompany.com; 793 E Foothill Blvd; snacks from $2; ☺24hr; 🖼) Home of bizarrely tasty donuts like bacon-maple or PB&J and organic, fair-trade, locally roasted coffee. It's a five-minute drive north of downtown off Santa Rosa St (Hwy 1).

Bel Frites SNACKS $
(www.belfrites.com; 1127 Garden St; snacks $4-8; ☺3pm-2:30am Tue-Thu, noon-2:30am Fri & Sat, noon-6pm Sun) Belgian fries with New World seasonings and dipping sauces for late-night bar hoppers.

🍷 Drinking

Downtown, Higuera St is littered with college student–jammed bars and clubs.

Downtown Brewing Co BREWPUB
(www.slobrew.com; 1119 Garden St) More often called just SLO Brew, this study in rafters and exposed brick has plenty of craft beers to go with filling pub grub. Downstairs, you'll find DJs spinning or live bands with names like 'Atari Teenage Riot' playing most nights.

Creekside Brewing Co BREWPUB
(www.creeksidebrewing.com; 1040 Broad St) Kick back at a breezy patio overhanging the bubbling creek. It has got its own fairly respectable brews on tap, plus bottled Belgian beers. On Mondays, all pints are usually just three bucks.

Kreuzberg COFFEE SHOP
(www.kreuzbergcalifornia.com; 685 Higuera St; ☺6:30am-midnight; 🖼) SLO's newest coffeehouse has earned a fervent following, with comfy couches, sprawling bookshelves, local art splashed on the walls and occasionally live music.

Mother's Tavern BAR
(www.motherstavern.com; 729 Higuera St; 🖼) Cavernous two-story 'MoTav' pub that draws in the party-hardy CalPoly student masses with its no-cover DJ-driven dance floor and frequent live-music shows.

Granada Bistro LOUNGE
(www.granadabistro.com; 1126 Morro St; ☺Thu-Sun) Like a celebutante's living room, this swank lounge classes up the downtown scene, with imported wines and beers and live acoustic tunes.

☆ Entitlement Entertainment

Palm Theatre   CINEMA
(☎805-541-5161; www.thepalmtheatre.com; 817 Palm St) In SLO's blink-and-you'll-miss-it Chinatown, this small-scale movie house showing foreign and indie flicks happens to be the USA's first solar-powered cinema. Look for the San Luis Obispo International Film Festival in mid-March.

Sunset Drive-In   CINEMA
(☎805-544-4475; www.fairoakstheatre.net; 255 Elks Lane, off S Higuera St; 🚗) Recline your seat, put your feet up on the dash and munch on bottomless bags of popcorn at this classic Americana drive-in. Sticking around for the second feature (usually a B-list Hollywood blockbuster) doesn't cost extra. It's off Higuera St, about a 10-minute drive south of downtown.

Performing Arts Center   PERFORMING ARTS
(PAC; ☎805-756-2787, 888-233-2787; www.pacslo.org; 1 Grand Ave) On the CalPoly campus, this state-of-the-art theater is SLO's biggest cultural venue, presenting a variety of concerts, theater, dance recitals, stand-up comedy and other shows by big-name performers. Event parking costs $6.

🛍 Shopping

Downtown, Higuera and Marsh Sts, along with all of the arcades and cross streets in between, are stuffed full of unique boutiques. Take a wander and find something wonderful.

Hands Gallery   ART, JEWELRY
(www.handsgallery.com; 777 Higuera St; ⊙10am-6pm Mon-Wed, 10am-8pm Thu, 10am-7pm Fri & Sat, 11am-5pm Sun) Brightly lit gallery sells fine contemporary craftwork by vibrant California artisans, including jewelry, fiber arts, metal sculptures, ceramics and blown glass, perfect for gifts or souvenirs.

Mountain Air Sports   OUTDOORS
(www.mountainairsports.com; 667 Marsh St; ⊙10am-6pm Mon-Sat, to 8pm Thu, 11am-4pm Sun) Almost the only outdoor outfitter between Monterey and Santa Barbara, here you can pick up anything from campstove fuel and tents to brand-name active clothing and hiking boots.

Finders Keepers   CLOTHING
(www.finderskeepersconsignment.com; 1124 Garden St; ⊙10am-5pm) Seriously stylish second-hand women's fashions that match SLO's breezy, laid-back coastal lifestyle, plus hand-picked handbags, coats and jewelry.

ℹ Information

SLO's compact downtown is bisected by the parallel one-way arteries of Higuera St and Marsh St. Banks with 24-hour ATMs are off Marsh St, near the post office. Most downtown coffee shops offer free wi-fi.

FedEx Office (www.fedex.com; 1127 Chorro St; per min 20-30¢; ⊙7am-11pm Mon-Fri, 9am-9pm Sat & Sun; @🛜) Pay-as-you-go internet workstations and free wi-fi.

French Hospital (☎805-543-5353; www.frenchmedicalcenter.org; 1911 Johnson Ave; ⊙24hr) Emergency room.

Public library (www.slolibrary.org; 995 Palm St; ⊙10am-5pm Wed-Sat, to 8pm Tue; @🛜) Free wi-fi and public internet terminals.

San Luis Obispo Chamber of Commerce (☎805-781-2777; www.visitslo.com; 1039 Chorro St; ⊙10am-5pm Sun-Wed, 10am-7pm Thu-Sat) Free maps and information.

ℹ Getting There & Around

Off Broad St, over 3 miles southeast of downtown, **SLO County Regional Airport** (SBP; www.sloairport.com; 🛜) offers commuter flights with United (LA and San Francisco) and US Airways (Phoenix).

Amtrak (www.amtrak.com; 1011 Railroad Ave) runs daily Seattle–LA *Coast Starlight* and twice-daily SLO–San Diego *Pacific Surfliner* trains. Both routes head south to Santa Barbara ($29, 2¾ hours) and Los Angeles ($34, 5½ hours). Only the *Coast Starlight* connects north to Salinas ($31, 3½ hours) and Oakland ($34, six hours). Several daily Thruway buses link to more regional trains.

From the train station, about 0.6 miles east of downtown, **Greyhound** (www.greyhound.com; 1023 Railroad Ave) operates a few daily buses along Hwy 101 south to Los Angeles ($38, 5¼ hours) via Santa Barbara ($26, 2¼ hours) and north to San Francisco ($48, 6½ hours) via Santa Cruz ($39, four hours).

San Luis Obispo's **Regional Transit Authority** (RTA; ☎805-541-2228; www.slorta.org) operates daily county-wide buses with limited weekend services; one-way fares are $1.50 to $3 (day pass $5). All buses are equipped with two-bicycle racks. Lines converge on downtown's **transit center** (cnr Palm & Osos Sts).

SLO Transit (☎805-541-2877; www.slocity.org) runs local city buses and the downtown trolley (50¢), which loops around every 15 to 20 minutes between 3pm and 10pm on Thursday

CARRIZO PLAIN NATIONAL MONUMENT

Hidden in eastern SLO County, **Carrizo Plain National Monument** (www.ca.blm. gov/bakersfield; admission free; ☺24hr) is a geological wonderland, where you can walk or drive atop the San Andreas Fault. This peaceful wildlife preserve also protects a diversity of species including endangered California condors and jewel flowers, tule elk, pronghorn antelope and the San Joaquin kit fox. Pick up 4WD and hiking maps at the **Goodwin Education Center** (☑805-475-2131; ☺9am-4pm Thu-Sun Dec-May), past the dazzling white salt flats of Soda Lake, near the trailhead for Painted Rock, which displays Native American pictographs. The monument is about 55 winding miles east of Hwy 101, or 55 miles west of the I-5 Freeway, via Hwy 58 and Soda Lake Rd. Two primitive **Bureau of Land Management (BLM) Campgrounds** offer free, first-come, first-served campsites.

year-round, and 3pm to 10pm Friday and 1pm to 10pm Saturday from April through October.

Avila Beach

Quaint, sunny Avila Beach lures crowds with its strand of golden sand and a freshly built seafront commercial district lined by restaurants, shops and cafes. Two miles west of downtown, Port San Luis is a working fishing harbor.

◉ Sights & Activities

For a lazy summer day at the beach, rent beach chairs and umbrellas, surfboards, boogie boards and wetsuits underneath **Avila Pier**, off downtown's waterfront promenade. At the port, the barking of sea lions accompanies you as you stroll **Harford Pier**, one of the Central Coast's most authentic fishing piers.

Point San Luis Lighthouse LIGHTHOUSE
(Map p504; www.sanluislighthouse.org; lighthouse admission adult/family $5/10; trolley tour incl lighthouse admission per person $20; ☺guided hikes 9am-1pm Wed & Sat, trolley tours noon, 1pm & 2pm on 1st & 3rd Sat of the month) Just getting to this scenic 1890 lighthouse, overshadowed by Diablo Canyon nuclear power plant, is an adventure. The cheapest way to reach the lighthouse is via a rocky, crumbling, 3.75-mile trail. Weather permitting, it's open only for guided hikes (☑805-541-8735) led by Pacific Gas & Electric docents. Children under nine years old are not allowed to hike; call for reservations at least two weeks in advance and bring plenty of water. If you'd rather take it easy and ride out to the lighthouse, which harbors an original Fresnel lens and authentic Victo-

rian period furnishings, join a Saturday afternoon **trolley tour** (☑805-540-5771). Reservations are required.

Avila Valley Barn FARM
(Map p504; http://avilavalleybarn.com; 560 Avila Beach Dr; ☺9am-6pm daily Jun-Oct, 9am-5pm Thu-Mon Nov-May; ◉) At this rural farmstand and pick-your-own berry farm, park alongside the sheep and goat pens, lick an ice-cream cone, then grab a basket and walk out into the fields to harvest jammy olallieberries and strawberries in late spring, midsummer peaches and nectarines or apples and pumpkins in autumn.

Sycamore Mineral Springs HOT SPRINGS
(Map p504; ☑805-595-7302, 800-234-5831; www. sycamoresprings.com; 1215 Avila Beach Dr; per person per hr $12.50-17.50; ☺8am-midnight, last reservation 10:45pm) Make time for a luxuriant soak, where private redwood hot tubs are discreetly laddered up a woodsy hillside. Call in advance for reservations, as it's often fully booked, especially during summer and on weekends after dark.

Avila Hot Springs HOT SPRINGS
(Map p504; ☑805-595-2359; www.avilahotsprings. com; 250 Avila Beach Dr; adult/child under 16yr $10/8; ☺8am-9pm Sun-Thu, to 10pm Fri & Sat; ◉) For families, this slightly sulfuric, lukewarm public swimming pool has a pretty cool waterslide (open noon to 5pm daily).

Central Coast Kayaks KAYAKING
(Map p504; ☑805-773-3500; www.central coastkayaks.com; 1879 Shell Beach Rd, Shell Beach; kayak or SUP rentals $20-60, 2hr kayaking tour $70) Paddle out among sea otters and seals and through mesmerizing sea caves, arches and kelp forests.

San Luis Obispo Bay

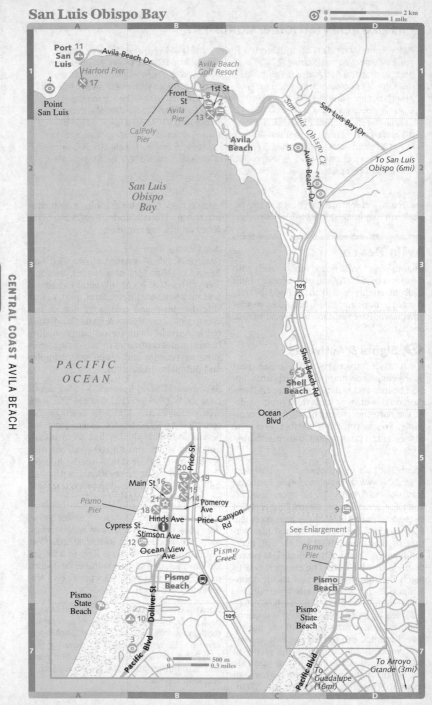

0 — 2 km
0 — 1 mile

Port San Luis 11
Harford Pier 17
4
Point San Luis
Avila Beach Dr
Avila Beach Golf Resort
1st St
Front St 8
7
Avila Pier 13
CalPoly Pier
Avila Beach
5
San Luis Obispo Ck
San Luis Bay Dr
2
1
Avila Beach Dr
To San Luis Obispo (6mi)

San Luis Obispo Bay

PACIFIC OCEAN

101
1

Shell Beach Rd
6
Shell Beach
Ocean Blvd

9

See Enlargement
Pismo Pier
Pismo Beach
Pismo State Beach

Price St
20
Main St 16
19
15
21
14
18
Pomeroy Ave
Pismo Pier
Hinds Ave
Price Canyon Rd
Cypress St
Stimson Ave
12
Ocean View Ave
Pismo Creek
Pismo Beach
Pismo State Beach
10
Dolliver St
3
Pacific Blvd
101
500 m
0.3 miles

Pacific Blvd
To Guadalupe (16mi)
To Arroyo Grande (3mi)

San Luis Obispo Bay

Patriot Sportfishing BOAT TOURS
(Map p504; ☏805-595-7200, 800-714-3474; www.patriotsportfishing.com; Harford Pier, off Avila Beach Dr; tours adult/child 4-12yr/child under 4yr from $35/15/10) This long-running local biz organizes deep-sea fishing trips and tournaments, as well as whale-spotting cruises between December and April.

⊜ Sleeping

Avila La Fonda BOUTIQUE HOTEL $$$
(Map p504; ☏805-595-1700; www.avilalafonda.com; 101 San Miguel St; ste $250-800; @🛜🏊) Downtown, this small inn evinces a harmonious mix of Mexican and Spanish colonial styles, with hand-painted tiles, stained-glass windows, wrought iron and rich wood. The deck has barbecue grills, a wet bar and a sociable fireplace for nightly wine and hors d'oeuvres. With vibrant colors, the sprawling rooms and suites have all mod cons (except air-con), plus hot tubs and some kitchens. Pet fee $50.

Avila Lighthouse Suites HOTEL $$$
(Map p504; ☏805-627-1900, 800-372-8452; www.avilalighthousesuites.com; 550 Front St; ste incl breakfast $229-479; ✳@🛜♿🐾) Any closer to the ocean, and your bed would actually be sitting on the sand. Made with families in mind, this apartment-style hotel offers suites and villas with kitchenettes. But it's the giant heated outdoor pool, ping-pong

tables, putting green and life-sized checkers board that keeps kids amused.

Port San Luis CAMPGROUND $
(Map p504; RV sites without/with hookups from $30/45) First-come, first-served parking spaces by the side of the road have ocean views; RVs only (no tents).

Avila Hot Springs Campground CAMPGROUND $
(Map p504; ☏805-595-2359; www.avilahotsprings.com; 250 Avila Beach Dr; tent & RV sites without/with hookups from $30/45) Crowded campground off Hwy 101 has hot showers and flush toilets; reservations essential in summer.

⊗ Eating
At Port San Luis, Harford Pier is home to seafood shops that sell rockfish, sole, salmon and other fresh catch right off the boats.

Avila Beach Fish & Farmers Market MARKET $
(Map p504; www.avilabeachpier.com; ⊙4-8pm Fri Apr–mid-Sep) With finger-lickin' food booths (seafood is a specialty, of course) and live music and entertainment, this outdoor street party takes over downtown's oceanfront promenade weekly in spring and summer.

Avila Grocery & Deli
AMERICAN, FAST FOOD $
(Map p504; http://avilagrocery.com; 354 Front St; mains $5-11; ⊙7am-7pm;) Gather everything you'll need for a beach picnic at this family-owned deli and general store on the ocean-front promenade. The chipotle tri-tip steak wrap is a gold-medal winner; so are bang-up breakfasts.

Pete's Pierside Cafe
SEAFOOD, FAST FOOD $
(Map p504; www.petespiersidecafe.com; Harford Pier, off Avila Beach Dr; mains $5-12; ⊙11am-5pm) Hit this unpretentious seafood shack for crispy fish and chips, fresh oysters and crab legs, and an excellent salsa bar to doctor your fish taco with.

Olde Port Inn
SEAFOOD $$$
(Map p504; ☎805-595-2515; www.oldeportinn. com; Harford Pier, off Avila Beach Dr; mains $10-38; ⊙11:30am-9pm Sun-Thu, to 10pm Fri & Sat) Clam chowder and cioppino are standouts at this seriously old-school seafood restaurant at the tip of Harford Pier. A few tables have glass tops, so lucky diners can peer down into the ocean.

ℹ Getting There & Around
From late May through September, a free **trolley** loops around downtown Avila Beach and Port San Luis, and out to Hwy 101. It usually operates hourly from 10am to 8pm on Saturday and 10am to 5pm on Sunday. In Shell Beach, the trolley connects with **South County Regional Transit** (SCAT; ☎805-781-4472; www.slorta.org) bus 21, which runs hourly to Pismo Beach ($1.25, 15 minutes).

Pismo Beach

The largest of San Luis Obispo Bay's 'Five Cities,' this 1950s-retro California beach town fronts a more commercial pier than neighboring Avila, but its beach is invitingly wide and sandy. Backed by a wooden pier that stretches toward the setting sun, here James Dean once trysted with Pier Angeli, and Pismo Beach today still feels like somewhere straight out of *Rebel Without a Cause* or *American Graffiti*. If you're looking for a sand-and-surf respite from road tripping, break your journey here.

◎ Sights & Activities
Pismo likes to call itself the 'Clam Capital of the World,' but these days the beach is pretty much clammed out. You'll have better luck catching something fishy off the pier,

where you can rent rods. To rent a wetsuit, boogie board or surfboard, cruise the nearby surf shops.

FREE Monarch Butterfly Grove
PARK
(Map p504; www.monarchbutterfly.org; ⊙sunrise-sunset) From late October until February, over 25,000 black-and-orange monarchs make their winter home here. Forming dense clusters in the tops of eucalyptus trees, they might easily be mistaken for leaves. Volunteers can tell you all about the insects' incredible journey, which outlasts any single generation of butterflies. Look for a gravel parking pull-out on the west side of Pacific Blvd (Hwy 1), just south of Pismo State Beach's North Beach Campground.

✺ Festivals & Events
Classic at Pismo Beach
CULTURE
(www.thepismobeachclassic.com) Show up in mid-June when hot rods and muscle cars line the main drags off Hwy 1.

Clam Festival
FOOD
(www.classiccalifornia.com) In mid-October, celebrate the formerly abundant and still tasty mollusk with a clam dig, chowder cookoff, food vendors and live music.

🛏 Sleeping
Pismo Beach has dozens of motels, but rooms fill up quickly and prices skyrocket in summer, especially on weekends. Resort hotels roost on cliffs north of town via Price St and Shell Beach Rd, while motels cluster near the beach and along Hwy 101.

Pismo Lighthouse Suites
HOTEL $$$
(Map p504; ☎805-773-2411, 800-245-2411; www. pismolighthousesuites.com; 2411 Price St; ste incl breakfast $149-329; ❄@☎☀) With everything a vacationing family needs – from in-room Nintendo and kitchenettes, to a life-sized outdoor chessboard, a putting green, table tennis and badminton courts – this contemporary all-suites hotel is hard to tear yourself away from.

Sandcastle Inn
HOTEL $$$
(Map p504; ☎805-773-2422, 800-822-6606; www.sandcastleinn.com; 100 Stimson Ave; r incl breakfast $169-435; ☎) Many of these Eastern Seaboard–styled rooms are mere steps from the sand. The best suite in the house is perfect for getting engaged after cracking open a bottle of wine at sunset on the ocean-view patio. Wi-fi in lobby only.

GUADALUPE

Hwy 1 ends its brief relationship with Hwy 101 just south of Pismo Beach, as it veers off toward the coast. Over 15 miles further south, you almost expect to have to dodge Old West tumbleweeds as you drive into the one-road agricultural town of Guadalupe.

In 1923 a huge Hollywood crew descended on this remote outpost for the filming of the silent version of the *Ten Commandments*. Enormous Egyptian sets were constructed in Guadalupe's oceanfront sand dunes, complete with huge sphinxes and more. Afterward, director Cecil B DeMille saved money by leaving the magnificent sets – albeit ones constructed of hay, plaster and paint – in place and simply burying them in the sand. Over the following decades knowledge of the exact location of the vast sets was lost.

In 1983 film and archaeology buffs started looking for the 'Lost City of DeMille.' Many artifacts have been found and the locations of main structures pinpointed. Learn loads more about these oddball archaeological excavations online at www.lostcitydemille.com.

Back in town, inspect some of the recovered movie-set pieces at the tiny **Dunes Visitor Center** (www.dunescenter.org; 1055 Guadalupe St; admission by donation; ☉10am-4pm Tue-Sat), which has exhibits about the ecology of North America's largest coastal dunes and also about the Dunites, mystical folks who called the dunes home during the 1930s.

The dunes preserve, which is a state-protected archaeological site (no digging or taking away souvenirs, sorry!) is about 5 miles west of town via Hwy 166. More recent movies shot here include *Pirates of the Caribbean: At World's End* (2007).

Pismo State Beach CAMPGROUND $
(Map p504; ☏reservations 800-444-7275; www.reserveamerica.com; tent & RV sites $25-35) About a mile south of downtown, off Dolliver St (Hwy 1), the state park's North Beach Campground has over 100 well-spaced, grassy sites, in the shade of eucalyptus trees. The campground offers easy beach access, flush toilets and hot showers.

✗ Eating

TOP CHOICE **Cracked Crab** SEAFOOD $$$
(Map p504; www.crackedcrab.com; 751 Price St; mains $9-50; ☉11am-9pm Sun-Thu, 11am-10pm Fri & Sat; ⚐) Fresh seafood is the staple at this super-casual, family-owned grill. When the famous bucket o'seafood, full of flying bits of fish, Cajun sausage, red potatoes and cob corn, gets dumped on your butcher-paper-covered table, make sure you're wearing one of those silly-looking plastic bibs. Excellent regional wine list.

Giuseppe's ITALIAN $$$
(Map p504; www.guiseppesrestaurant.com; 891 Price St; lunch mains $9-15, dinner mains $12-32; ☉lunch 11:30am-3pm Mon-Fri, dinner 4:30-10pm Sun-Thu, to 11pm Fri & Sat) Occasionally outstanding Southern Italian fare is served at this date-worthy *cucina,* which brims with the owner's personality – just eyeball the lineup of Vespa scooters parked out front. Safe bets are wood-fired pizzas and tradi-

tional pastas like spicy prawn spaghettini. Show up early, or expect a long wait (no reservations).

Splash Cafe SEAFOOD $
(Map p504; www.splashcafe.com; 197 Pomeroy Ave; dishes $4-10; ☉8am-9pm; ⚐) Uphill from the pier, lines go out the door to wrap around this scruffy surf-style hole-in-the-wall, famous for its award-winning clam chowder in a home-baked sourdough bread bowl, and a long lineup of grilled and fried briny fare. It keeps shorter hours in winter.

Klondike Pizza PIZZA $$
(www.klondikepizza.com; 104 Bridge St; pizzas $12-26; ☉11am-9pm Sun-Thu, to 10pm Fri & Sat; ⚐) Across Hwy 101 in small-town Arroyo Grande, this subterranean Alaskan-run pizzeria is littered with peanut shells and has checkers and other board games to play while you wait for your reindeer-sausage pie. Hum along with a kazoo during twice-monthly Saturday-night sing-alongs.

Doc Burnstein's Ice Cream Lab ICE CREAM $
(www.docburnsteins.com; 114 W Branch St; snacks $3-8; ☉11am-9:30pm Sun-Thu, to 10:30pm Fri & Sat; ⚐) On Arroyo Grande's main drag, Doc's scoops up fantastical flavors like Petite Syrah sorbet and the 'Elvis Special' (peanut butter with banana swirls). Live ice-cream lab shows start at 7pm sharp on Wednesday.

Old West Cinnamon Rolls
BAKERY $

(Map p504; www.oldwestcinnamon.com; 861 Dolliver St; snacks & drinks $2-5; ⊙6:30am-5:30pm) Really, the name says it all at this gobsmacking bakery by the beach.

Utopia Bakery Cafe
BAKERY $

(Map p504; www.utopiabakery.com; 950 Price St; snacks & sandwiches $2-8; ⊙6am-6pm) Corner stop for cookies, croissants, chocolate-chip scones and espresso drinks.

⚲ Drinking & Entertainment

Taste of the Valleys
WINE BAR

(Map p504; www.pismowineshop.com; 911 Price St; ⊙noon-9pm Mon-Thu, to 10pm Fri & Sat, to 8pm Sun) Inside a quiet wine shop stacked floor to ceiling with California vintages; ask for a taste of anything they've got open today, or sample from the astounding list of 500 wines poured by the glass.

Pismo Bowl
BOWLING ALLEY

(Map p504; www.pismobeachbowl.com; 277 Pomeroy Ave; ⊙noon-10pm Sun-Thu, to midnight Fri & Sat; 🖪) Epitomizing Pismo Beach's retro vibe, this old-fashioned bowling alley is just a short walk uphill from the pier. Rockin' blacklight 'cosmic bowling' rules on Friday and Saturday nights.

ⓘ Information

Pismo Beach Visitors Information Center (📞805-773-4382, 800-443-7778; www.classic california.com; 581 Dolliver St, cnr Hinds Ave; ⊙9am-5pm Mon-Fri, 11am-4pm Sat) Free tourist maps and brochures.

ⓘ Getting There & Around

Operating hourly on weekdays, and a few times daily on weekends, **RTA** (📞805-541-2228; www. slorta.org) bus 10 links Pismo's Premium Outlets mall, about a mile from the beach, with San Luis Obispo ($2, 25 minutes). **South County Regional Transit** (SCAT; 📞805-781-4472; www. slorta.org) runs hourly local buses ($1.25) connecting Pismo Beach with Shell Beach and Arroyo Grande.

La Purísima Mission State Historic Park

Surrounded by colorful commercial flower fields, this pastoral valley mission (www. lapurisimamission.org, www.parks.ca.gov; 2295 Purisima Rd, Lompoc; per car $6; ⊙9am-5pm) was extensively restored by the Civilian Conservation Corps (CCC) in the 1930s. Today it's one of the most evocative of California's original 21 Spanish colonial missions, with atmospheric adobe buildings that include a church, living quarters and shops. The mission's fields still support grazing livestock, while nearby flowering gardens are planted with medicinal plants used by Chumash tribespeople.

The mission is 15 miles west of Hwy 101 via Hwy 246. Past the golf course, take the turnoff for Purisima Rd on the north (right) side of the highway, then drive about another mile.

Santa Barbara Wine Country

Oak-dotted hillsides, winding country lanes, rows of sweetly heavy grapevines stretching as far as the eye can see – it's hard not to gush about the Santa Maria and Santa Ynez Valleys. Maybe you've been inspired to visit by the Oscar-winning film *Sideways*, an ode to the joys and hazards of wine-country living, as seen through the misadventures of middle-aged buddies Miles and Jack. The movie is like real life in one respect: this wine country is ideal for do-it-yourself-exploring with friends.

With more than 100 wineries spread out across the landscape, it can seem daunting at first. But the wine country's five small towns – Buellton, Solvang, Santa Ynez, Ballard and Los Olivos – are all clustered within 10 miles of one another, so it's easy to stop, shop and eat whenever and wherever you happen to feel like it. Don't worry about sticking to a regimented plan or following prescriptive wine guides. Just soak up the scenery and pull over where the signs look welcoming and the vibe feels right.

⦿ Sights & Activities

Nearer the coast, pinot noir – a particularly fragile grape – flourishes in the fog. Further inland, sun-loving Rhône varietals like Syrah thrive. Tasting fees average $10, and some wineries give vineyard tours (reservations may be required).

FOXEN CANYON

The pastoral Foxen Canyon Wine Trail (www.foxencanyonwinetrail.com) runs north from Hwy 154, just west of Los Olivos, into the rural Santa Maria Valley.

WORTH A TRIP

HIDDEN BEACHES OFF HIGHWAY 1

West of Lompoc lie some truly wild beaches worth the trouble of visiting.

Ocean Beach County Park (www.countyofsb.org/parks; ☺8am-sunset) and Surf Beach, with its remote Amtrak train stop, are really one beach sidling up to Vandenberg Air Force Base. During the 10-mile drive west of Lompoc via Ocean Ave, you'll pass mysterious-looking structures supporting spy and commercial satellite launches. The dunes are untrammeled and interpretive signs explain the estuary's ecology. Because endangered snowy plovers nest here, vast areas of the beach are often closed between March and September.

Leaving Hwy 1 around 5 miles east of Lompoc, Jalama Rd follows 14 miles of twisting tarmac across ranch and farmlands, leading to Jalama Beach County Park (www.countyofsb.org/parks; per car/dog $10/3; 🚻🅿️). Utterly isolated, it's home to a crazy-popular campground (📞805-736-3504; www.jalamabeach.com; tent & RV sites without/with hookups from $25/40, cabins $100-220; ☺campground store & cafe 7am-9pm) that only accepts reservations for its newly built cabins. Otherwise, you should arrive by 8am to get on the waiting list for a campsite – look for the 'campground full' sign, a half-mile south of Hwy 1, to avoid a wasted trip.

Firestone
WINERY
(📞805-688-3940; www.firestonewine.com; 5000 Zaca Station Rd; tour $5; ☺tasting room 10am-5pm, tour schedules vary) Firestone Vineyard is Santa Barbara's oldest estate winery, founded in 1972. Sweeping views of the vineyard from the sleek, wood-paneled tasting room are as impressive as the value-priced Syrah, pinot noir and Bordeaux-style blends.

Foxen
WINERY
(www.foxenvineyard.com; 7600 Foxen Canyon Rd; ☺11am-4pm) Crafts full-fruited pinot noirs, steel-cut chardonnays and Rhône-style reds inside a solar-powered tasting room on a former cattle ranch. Down the road, its rustic tin-roofed 'shack' pours Bordeaux-style and Cal-Ital varietals under the boutique 'Foxen 7200' label.

Zaca Mesa
WINERY
(www.zacamesa.com; 6905 Foxen Canyon Rd; ☺10am-4pm, to 5pm Fri & Sat late May-early Sep) Known not only for its sustainably-grown estate Rhône varietals and signature Z Cuvée red blend, but also a life-sized outdoor chessboard, shady picnic area and walking trails overlooking the vineyards.

Kenneth Volk
WINERY
(www.volkwines.com; 5230 Tepusquet Rd; ☺10:30am-4:30pm) Only an established cult winemaker could convince oenophiles to drive this far out of their way to taste standard-bearing pinot noir and heritage varietals like floral-scented Malvasia or inky Negrette.

SANTA RITA HILLS

The Santa Rita Hills Wine Trail (www.santaritahillswinetrail.com) shines brightly when it comes to ecoconscious farming practices and top-notch pinot noir. Country tasting rooms line a scenic loop west of Hwy 101 via Santa Rosa Rd and Hwy 246.

Alma Rosa
WINERY
(www.almarosawinery.com; 7250 Santa Rosa Rd; ☺11am-4:30pm) Cacti and cobblestones welcome you to the ranch, reached via a long, winding gravel driveway. Knock-out vineyard-designated pinot noirs and a fine pinot blanc made with California-certified organic grapes are poured.

Melville
WINERY
(www.melvillewinery.com; 5185 E Hwy 146; ☺11am-4pm) Mediterranean hillside villa offers estate-grown, small-lot bottled pinot noir, Syrah and chardonnay made by folks who believe in talking about pounds per plant, not tons per acre. Over a dozen different clones of pinot noir alone grow here.

Babcock
WINERY
(www.babcockwinery.com; 5175 E Hwy 146; ☺10:30am-4pm, to 5pm Apr-Oct) Family-owned vineyards overflowing with different varietals – chardonnay, sauvignon blanc, pinot noir, Syrah, cabernet sauvignon and more – let an innovative small-lot winemaker be the star. The Fathom red blend is pilgrimage-worthy.

Santa Barbara Wine Country

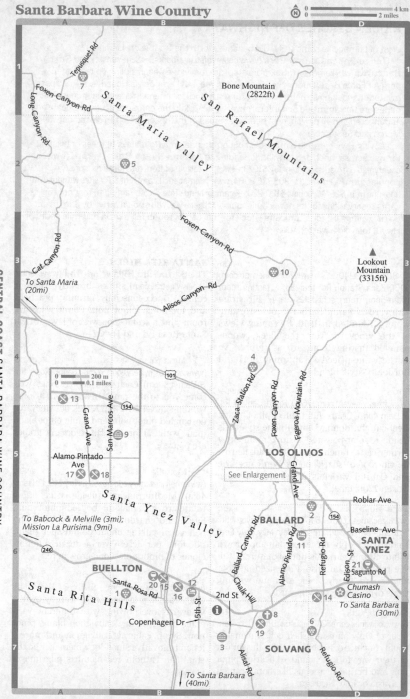

Santa Barbara Wine Country

SANTA YNEZ VALLEY

You'll find dozens of wineries inside the triangle of Hwys 154, 246 and 101, including in downtown Los Olivos and Solvang. Noisy tour groups, harried staff and stingy pours too often disappoint at many popular places, but not at these welcoming wineries.

Beckmen WINERY
(www.beckmenvineyards.com; 2670 Ontiveros Rd; ⊙11am-5pm) Bring a picnic to the duckpond gazebos at this tranquil winery, where biodynamically farmed, estate-grown Rhône varietals flourish on the unique terroir of Purisima Mountain. Follow Roblar Ave west of Hwy 154.

Kalyra WINERY
(www.kalyrawinery.com; 343 Refugio Rd; ⊙11am-5pm Mon-Fri, 10am-5pm Sat & Sun) An Australian surfer traveled halfway around the world to combine his two loves: surfing and wine making. Try his unique Shiraz–cabernet sauvignon blend made from Australian grapes or more locally grown varietals, all in bottles with Aboriginal art–inspired labels.

AROUND THE WINE COUNTRY TOWNS

Cap'n, we've hit a windmill! Solvang is a touristy Danish village founded in 1911 on what was once a 19th-century Spanish colonial mission, later a Mexican *rancho* land grant. With its knickknack stores and cutesy motels, the town is almost as sticky-sweet as the Scandinavian pastries foisted upon the wandering hordes. Solvang's Elverhøj Museum (www.elverhoj.org; 1624 Elverhoy Way; adult/child under 13 $3/free; ⊙1-4pm Wed & Thu,

noon-4pm Fri-Sun) uncovers the roots of real Danish life in the area, while Mission Santa Inés (www.missionsantaines.org; 1760 Mission Dr; adult/child under 12 $5/free; ⊙9am-4:30pm) witnessed an 1824 Chumash revolt against Spanish colonial cruelty.

Farther northwest, the posh ranching town of Los Olivos has a four-block-long main street lined with wine-tasting rooms and bars, art galleries, cafes and surprisingly fashionable shops seemingly airlifted straight out of Napa. The petite Wilding Art Museum (www.wildingmuseum.org; 2928 San Marcos Ave; admission by donation; ⊙11am-5pm Wed-Sun) exhibits nature-themed California and American Western art.

ALONG HIGHWAY 154 (SAN MARCOS PASS RD)

The Los Padres National Forest (www.r5.fs. fed.us/lospadres) offers several good hiking trails off Paradise Rd, which crosses Hwy 154 north of San Marcos Pass. Try the 2-mile round-trip Red Rock Trail, where the Santa Ynez River deeply pools among rocks and waterfalls, a tempting spot for swimming and sunbathing. En route to the trailhead, which lies beyond the river crossing, drop by the ranger station (☎805-967-3481; 3505 Paradise Rd; ⊙8:30am-4:30pm Mon-Fri) for posted trail maps and information and a National Forest Adventure Pass for parking ($5 per day).

Just northwest, Cachuma Lake Recreation Area (www.cachuma.com; per car $10; ⊙sunrise-sunset) is a county-park haven for fishers, canoers and kayakers, with wildlife-watching cruises (☎805-686-5050/5055; adult/child 4-12yr $15/7) and a kid-friendly nature center ([phone]805-693-0691; 2265 Hwy 154; [hours]daily Jun-Aug, weekends only Sep-May; [parking]).

Tours

Sustainable Vine
Wine Tours
WINERY TOURS

([phone]805-698-3911; www.sustainablevine.com; full-day tour incl lunch $125) Biodiesel van tours of wineries implementing organic and sustainable agricultural practices.

Santa Barbara Wine Country Cycling
Tours
WINERY TOURS

([phone]888-557-8687; www.winecountrycycling.com; bike rentals per day $45-85, half-/full-day tours from $70/135) Cycling tours leave from Santa Ynez; quality road and hybrid mountain bike rentals also available.

Sleeping

Avoid the price-gouging by taking a day trip from Santa Barbara. Otherwise, Buellton has bland chains right off Hwy 101. A few miles east along Hwy 246, Solvang has many more motels and hotels, but don't expect any bargains, especially not on weekends. Smaller wine-country towns offer a handful of historic inns.

Ballard Inn & Restaurant
B&B $$$

([phone]805-688-7770, 800-638-2466; www.ballardinn.com; 2436 Baseline Ave, Ballard; r incl breakfast $269-345; [wifi]) For honeymooners and romantics, this contemporary-built inn awaits in the 19th-century stagecoach town of Ballard, flung between Los Olivos and Solvang. Wood-burning fireplaces make private ensuite rooms even more cozy. Rates include wine tastings. Reservations essential.

Hadsten House Inn
BOUTIQUE HOTEL $$

([phone]805-688-3210, 800-457-5373; www.hadstenhouse.com; 1450 Mission Dr; r incl breakfast $150-255; [wifi][pool]) This revamped motel has glammed up everything except an uninspiring exterior. Inside, you'll find a heated pool and rooms that are surprisingly plush, with flatscreen TVs, triple-sheeted beds and L'Occitane bath products. Rates include afternoon wine-and-cheese tasting.

Cachuma Lake
Recreation Area
CAMPGROUND, CABINS $

([phone]info 805-686-5055, yurt & cabin reservations 805-686-5050; www.cachuma.com; tent & RV sites without/with hookups from $20/40, yurts $80-105, cabins $100-220) First-come, first-served campsites with access to hot showers fill quickly, especially in summer and on weekends. Book ahead for ecofriendly canvas-sided yurts and knotty pine-paneled cabins (no air-con).

Los Padres National Forest
CAMPGROUND $

([phone]reservations 877-444-6777; www.recreation.gov; tent & RV sites $19-35) First-come, first-served and reservable sites include Fremont, Paradise and Los Prietos before the ranger station and Upper Oso at the end of Paradise Rd, off Hwy 154.

Eating

Petros
MEDITERRANEAN $$$

([phone]805-686-5455; www.petrosrestaurant.com; Fess Parker Wine Country Inn & Spa, 2860 Grand Ave, Los Olivos; shared plates $6-18, dinner mains $22-36; [hours]7am-10pm Sun-Thu, to 11pm Fri & Sat) In a sunny, modern clean-lined dining room, sophisticated Greek cuisine makes for a refreshing change from Italianate wine-country kitsch. Grilled pita with sweet-and-savory dips, flatbread pizzas and feta-crusted rack of lamb will satisfy even picky foodies. Reservations recommended.

Los Olivos Café
CALIFORNIAN $$$

([phone]805-688-7265; www.losolivoscafe.com; 2879 Grand Ave, Los Olivos; mains $12-30; [hours]11:30am-8:30pm) With white canopies and a wisteria-covered trellis, this Cal-Mediterranean bistro swirls up a casual-chic ambience that adds a nice finish to a long day of touring. The menu gets mixed marks; stick with antipasto platters, hearty salads and crispy pizzas, and wine flights at the bar. Reservations essential.

Brothers Restaurant at
Mattei's Tavern
AMERICAN $$$

([phone]805-688-4820; www.matteistavern.com; 2350 Railway Ave, Los Olivos; mains $18-44; [hours]5-9pm) You half expect a stagecoach to come thundering up in time for dinner at this authentic late-19th-century tavern. At checkered-tablecloth tables, dine on bold American country flavors like hickory-smoked salmon and oven-roasted rack of lamb. Get gussied up, pardner! Reservations advisable.

Hitching Post II
STEAKHOUSE $$$

([phone]805-688-0676; www.hitchingpost2.com; 406 E Hwy 246, Buellton; mains $22-48; [hours]5-9:30pm Mon-Fri, 4-9:30pm Sat & Sun) You'll be hard-pressed to find better steaks and chops than at this legendary, old-guard country steakhouse, which serves oak-grilled steaks and baby back ribs and makes its own pinot noir (which is damn good, by the way). Reservations essential.

El Rancho Market

FAST FOOD, GROCERIES $

(www.elranchomarket.com; 2886 Mission Dr (Hwy 246), Solvang; ☺6am-10pm) If you want to fill a picnic basket, not to mention reintegrate into society after a day of windmills, clogs and *abelskiver*, this supermarket has a fantastic deli case; take-out barbecue, soups and salads; bargain wine racks; and an espresso bar.

Ellen's Danish Pancake House

BREAKFAST $$

(www.ellensdanishpancakehouse.com; 272 Ave of the Flags, Buellton; mains $6-12; ☺6am-8pm Tue-Sun, to 2pm Mon; ⊞) Who needs Solvang? Locals know to come here for the wine country's best Danish pancakes, Danish sausages and not-so-Danish Belgian waffles.

Solvang Bakery

BAKERY $

(www.solvangbakery.com; 460 Alisal Rd, Solvang; items from $2; ☺7am-6pm) Solvang's bakeries prove an irresistible draw, but most aren't especially good. This tasty exception vends Danish cookies, iced almond butter rings and more.

🍷 Drinking & Entertainment

Avant Tapas & Wine

WINE BAR

(www.avantwines.com; 35 Industrial Way, Buellton; ☺11am-8pm Thu & Sun, to 10pm Fri & Sat) Hidden upstairs in an industrial-chic space, this under-the-radar gathering spot tempts with hot and cold tapas, pizzas and DIY tastes of over 30 boutique wines barreled on-site.

Maverick Saloon

BAR, NIGHTCLUB

(www.mavericksaloon.org; 3687 Sagunto St, Santa Ynez; ☺noon-2am) In the one-horse town of Santa Ynez, en route to Chumash Casino, this Harley-friendly honky-tonk stages live country-and-western and rock bands, late-night DJs and dancing on weekends.

ℹ Information

The **Santa Barbara County Vintners' Association** (www.sbcountywines.com) publishes a self-guided winery touring map, available free at tasting rooms and the **Solvang Visitors Center** (☑805-688-6144, 800-468-6765; www.solvangusa.com; 1639 Copenhagen Dr, Solvang; ☺9am-5pm).

ℹ Getting There & Around

The wine country is northwest of Santa Barbara; drive there in under an hour via Hwy 101 or more scenic, narrow and winding Hwy 154 (San Marcos Pass Rd). Hwy 246 runs east–west across the bottom of the Santa Ynez Valley, passing Solvang (where it's called Mission Dr) between Santa Ynez (off Hwy 154) and Buellton (off Hwy 101).

Santa Barbara

Frankly put, this area is damn pleasant to putter around. Just a 90-minute drive north of Los Angeles, tucked between mountains and the Pacific, Santa Barbara basks smugly in its near-perfection. Founded by a Spanish mission, the city's signature red-tile roofs, white stucco buildings and Mediterranean vibe have long given credence to its claim to the title of the 'American Riviera.' Santa Barbara is blessed with almost freakishly good weather, and no one can deny the appeal of those beaches that line the city tip to toe either. Just ignore those pesky oil derricks out to sea.

History

For hundreds of years before the arrival of the Spanish, the Chumash people thrived here, setting up trading routes over to the Channel Islands, which they reached in redwood canoes called *tomols*. In 1542 explorer Juan Rodríguez Cabrillo sailed into the channel and claimed it for Spain, then quickly met his doom on a nearby island.

The Chumash had little reason for concern until the permanent return of the Spanish in the late 1700s, when priests and soldiers arrived to establish military outposts and convert the tribe to Christianity. The Spaniards forced the Chumash to evacuate the Channel Islands, construct the missions and presidios and provide subsequent labor. Many Native Americans changed their diet and clothing, and died of European diseases, ill treatment and culture shock.

Mexican ranchers arrived after wining independence from Spain in 1821. Easterners began arriving en masse with the 1849 Gold Rush, and by the late 1890s the city was an established vacation spot for the wealthy. After a massive earthquake in 1925, laws were passed requiring much of the city to be rebuilt in its now characteristic faux-Spanish style of white-stucco buildings with red-tiled roofs.

◎ Sights

Mission Santa Barbara

MISSION

(www.sbmission.org; 2201 Laguna St; adult/child 6-15yr $5/1; ☺9am-4:30pm) Reigning from a hilltop above town, the 'Queen of the Missions' became the 10th California mission

Downtown Santa Barbara

Mission St

To Mission Santa
Barbara (0.25mi)

Orpet
Park

W Valerio St   16

18

W Arrellaga St

W Micheltorena St

W Sola St   Alameda
Park

20

E Victoria St

36   **Santa Barbara
Museum of Art**

W Anapamu St   1   E Anapamu St

33   **Santa Barbara
County Courthouse**

W Figueroa St

Greyhound   MTD Transit
Center

W Carrillo St

13   **El Presidio de Santa Barbara
State Historic Park**

W Cañon Perdido St

15

Paseo
Nuevo   30

W De La Guerra St   29   31   **Santa Barbara
Historical Museum**

34

W Ortega St   E Ortega St   Ortega
Park

39

W Cota St   27   E Cota St

26

W Haley St   37   E Haley St

22   40

24   E Gutierrez St

Ladera St

Cliff Dr   12   Montecito St   25

32

Plaza
del Mar
Park   19   Yanonali St

Natoma Ave   10

17   14   Mason St   38

11   Cabrillo Blvd

Ambassador
Park   9

8   West Beach

5

6

2   Sand
Bar   3   East
Beach

7

4

21   Santa Barbara
Harbor   Chase
Palm Park

28

Santa Barbara
Channel

To Motel 6 Santa Barbara (1mi);
Blue Sands Motel (1mi)

0   500 m
0   0.25 miles

Downtown Santa Barbara

on the feast day of Saint Barbara in 1786. Occupied by Catholic priests ever since, the mission escaped Mexico's policy of forced secularization. Today it functions as a Franciscan friary, parish church and historical museum. The 1820 stone church has Chumash artwork and beautiful cloisters; its imposing Doric facade, an homage to a chapel in ancient Rome, is topped by twin bell towers. Behind the church is an extensive cemetery – look for skull carvings over the door leading outside – with 4000 Chumash graves and the elaborate mausoleums of early settlers.

El Presidio de Santa Barbara State Historic Park HISTORIC SITE
(☏805-965-0093; www.sbthp.org; 123 E Cañon Perdido St; adult/child under 17yr $5/free; ☺10:30am-4:30pm) Founded in 1782 to protect missions between San Diego and Monterey, this fort

was Spain's last military stronghold in Alta California. But its mission wasn't solely to protect – the presidio also served as a social and political hub, and as a stopping point for traveling Spanish military. Today this small urban park shelters some of the city's oldest structures, which seem to be in constant need of propping up and restoring. Be sure to stop by the chapel, its interior radiant with kaleidoscopic color. Tickets also include admission to **Casa de la Guerra** (15 E De La Guerra St; ☺noon-4pm Sat & Sun), a 19th-century colonial adobe displaying Spanish-American heritage exhibits.

FREE **Santa Barbara County Courthouse** HISTORIC BUILDING
(1100 Anacapa St; ☺8:30am-4:45pm Mon-Fri, 10am-4:45pm Sat & Sun) Built in Spanish-Moorish Revival style, it's an absurdly beautiful place to be on trial. The magnificent 1929

courthouse features hand-painted ceilings, wrought-iron chandeliers and tiles from Tunisia and Spain. Step inside the hushed 2nd-floor mural room depicting Spanish colonial history, then climb the 85ft clocktower for arch-framed panoramas of the city, ocean and mountains. Docent-led tours are usually offered at 2pm daily and 10:30am on Monday, Tuesday, Wednesday and Friday.

Santa Barbara Historical Museum
MUSEUM

(www.santabarbaramuseum.com; 136 E De La Guerra St; admission by donation; ☺10am-5pm Tue-Sat, noon-5pm Sun) Embracing a romantic cloistered adobe courtyard, this off-the-beaten-path museum has an endlessly fascinating collection of local memorabilia, ranging from simply beautiful, like Chumash woven baskets and colonial-era textiles, to intriguing, such as an intricately carved coffer once belonging to Junípero Serra. Learn about Santa Barbara's involvement in toppling the last Chinese monarchy, among other interesting footnotes in local history.

Santa Barbara Botanic Garden
GARDEN

(www.sbbg.org; 1212 Mission Canyon Rd; adult/child 2-12yr/student $8/4/6; ☺9am-5pm Nov-Feb, to 6pm Mar-Oct; ⚹🌳) Take a soul-satisfying jaunt around this 40-acre botanic garden, devoted to California's native flora. Over 5 miles of partly wheelchair-accessible trails meander through cacti, redwoods and wildflowers past the old mission dam, originally built by Chumash tribespeople. Guided tours are available at 2pm daily and 11am on Saturday and Sunday. Ask for a 'Family Discovery Sheet' from the admission kiosk. Leashed dogs are welcome. See the website or call ahead for directions; it's about a 10-minute drive uphill from the mission.

Santa Barbara Museum of Art
MUSEUM

(www.sbma.net; 1130 State St; adult/child 6-17yr $9/6; ☺11am-5pm Tue-Sun; ⚹) Culture vultures delight in these downtown galleries, which hold an impressive, well-edited collection of contemporary Californian artists, modern masters like Matisse and Chagall, 20th-century photography and Asian art, with provocative special exhibits, an interactive children's gallery and a cafe. Sundays are pay-what-you-wish admission.

Santa Barbara Maritime Museum
MUSEUM

(www.sbmm.org; 113 Harbor Way; adult/child 1-5yr/youth 6-17yr $7/2/4, all free 3rd Thu of the month; ☺10am-5pm Thu-Tue Sep-May, to 6pm Jun-Aug; ⚹)

Even li'l cap'ns will get a kick out of this museum by the yacht harbor. A two-level exhibition hall celebrates Santa Barbara's briny history with historical artifacts and memorabilia, hands-on and virtual-reality exhibits, and a small theater for documentary videos.

FREE Karpeles Manuscript Library
MUSEUM

(www.rain.org/~karpeles; 21 W Anapamu St; ☺10am-4pm) Stuffed with historical written artifacts, this museum is an embarrassment of riches for history nerds, science geeks and literary and music lovers. Rotating exhibits often spotlight literary masterworks, from Shakespeare to Sherlock Holmes.

Stearns Wharf
LANDMARK

(www.stearnswharf.org) At its southern end, State St runs into Stearns Wharf, once co-owned by tough-guy actor Jimmy Cagney. Built in 1872, it's the West Coast's oldest continuously operating wooden pier. There's 90 minutes of free parking with validation from any shop or restaurant, but it's more fun to walk atop the very bumpy wooden slats.

🏖 Beaches

The long, sandy stretch between Stearns Wharf and Montecito is East Beach, Santa Barbara's largest and most crowded. At its far end, near the Biltmore hotel, Armani swimsuits and Gucci sunglasses abound at chic, but narrow Butterfly Beach.

Between Stearns Wharf and the harbor, West Beach is popular with tourists. There Los Baños del Mar (☎805-966-6110; 401 Shoreline Dr; admission $6; ⚹), a municipal heated outdoor pool complex, is good for recreational and lap swimming, plus a kids' wading pool. Call for opening hours. West of the harbor, Leadbetter Beach is the spot for beginning surfers and windsurfers. Climbing the stairs on the west end takes you to Shoreline Park, with picnic tables and awesome kite-flying conditions.

Further west, near the junction of Cliff Dr and Las Positas Rd, family-friendly Arroyo Burro (Hendry's) Beach has free parking and a restaurant and bar. Above the beach is the Douglas Family Preserve, offering cliffside romps for dogs.

Outside town off Hwy 101 you'll find even more spacious, family-friendly state beaches (☎805-958-1033; www.parks.ca.gov; per car $10; ☺sunrise-sunset; ⚹), including Carpinteria State Beach, about 12 miles southeast of

TOP 5 SANTA BARBARA SPOTS FOR CHILDREN

Museum of Natural History (www.sbnature.org; 2559 Puesta del Sol; adult/child 3-12yr/youth 13-17yr $11/7/8; ⊙10am-5pm; ⓗ) Stuffed wildlife mounts, glittering gems and a pitch-dark planetarium captivate kids' imaginations. It's about a 10-minute drive uphill from the mission.

Arroyo Burro (Hendry's) Beach (p516) Wide sandy beach, away from the tourist crowds, popular with local families.

Ty Warner Sea Center (www.sbnature.org/seacenter; 211 Stearns Wharf; adult/child 2-12yr/youth 13-17yr $8/5/7; ⊙10am-5pm; ⓗ) Gawk at a gray whale skeleton, touch tide-pool critters and crawl through a 1500-gallon surge tank.

Santa Barbara Sailing Center (below) Short, one-hour harbor sails let young 'uns see sea lions up close.

Santa Barbara Maritime Museum (p516) Peer through a periscope, reel in a virtual fish or check out the gorgeous model ships.

Santa Barbara, and **Refugio & El Capitán State Beaches**, over 20 miles west in Goleta.

🏃 Activities

Surfing, Kayaking, Sailing & Whale-Watching

Santa Barbara's proximity to the wind-breaking Channel Islands makes it a good spot to learn how to ride the waves. Unless you're a novice, conditions are too mellow in summer; swells kick back up in winter. Pro-level **Rincon Point** in Carpinteria has long, glassy, point-break waves, while **Leadbetter Point** is best for beginners. From spring through fall, kayakers can paddle the calm waters of the harbor or the coves of the Gaviota coast, or hitch a ride out to the Channel Islands for more solitude and sea caves. Meanwhile, stand-up paddle boarders can get their feet wet in the city's harbor.

Santa Barbara Sailing Center KAYAKING, SAILING
(☎805-962-2826, 800-350-9090; www.sbsail.com; 133 Harbor Way; rental per hr single/double kayak $10/15, kayaking lessons & tours $55-95, catamaran cruises $10-65) Rents kayaks and leads guided paddles, teaches sailing and offers sunset cocktail and wildlife-watching cruises.

Santa Barbara Adventure Co KAYAKING, SURFING
(☎805-884-9283; www.sbadventureco.com; kayaking tours $50-105, surfing & SUP lessons $99-125) Offers traditional board-surfing and SUP lessons, and leads guided coastal kayaking tours – ask about stargazing floats.

Paddle Sports KAYAKING, SURFING
(☎805-899-4925; www.kayaksb.com; 117b Harbor Way; surfboard rentals $10-30, kayak rentals $25-120, SUP rentals $40-65, 1hr SUP lesson $65, 2hr kayak tour $50) Friendly community-based outfitter, conveniently positioned right at the harbor.

Condor Express BOAT TOURS
(☎805-882-0088, 888-779-4253; www.condorcruises.com; 301 W Cabrillo Blvd; adult/child 5-12yr from $48/25) Runs year-round narrated whale-watching tours, including out to the Channel Islands, aboard a smooth-sailing catamaran.

Cycling

A paved recreational path stretches for 3 miles along the waterfront between Leadbetter Beach and Andrée Clark Bird Refuge, passing Stearns Wharf. **Santa Barbara Bicycle Coalition** (www.sbbike.org) offers free cycling tour maps online.

Wheel Fun CYCLING
(www.wheelfunrentals.com; ⊙8am-8pm) Cabrillo (23 E Cabrillo Blvd); State St (22 State St) Rents beach cruisers, hybrid mountain bikes and cheesy pedal-powered surreys with the fringe on top (local kids like to bomb 'em with water balloons!).

Hang-Gliding & Paragliding

For condor's-eye ocean views, **Eagle Paragliding** (☎805-968-0980; www.eagleparagliding.com) and **Fly Above All** (☎805-965-3733; www.flyaboveall.com) offer paragliding lessons (from $200) and tandem flights ($60 to $200). For hang-gliding lessons and tandem flights, contact **Fly Away** (☏805-403-8487; www.flyawayhanggliding.com).

☞ Tours

🚶 Architectural Foundation of Santa Barbara

WALKING TOURS

(☏805-965-6307; www.afsb.org; adult/child under 12yr $10/free) Nonprofit organization offers 90-minute fascinating guided small-group walking tours of downtown's art, history and architecture, usually on Saturday and Sunday mornings.

🚶 Santa Barbara Trolley

BUS TOURS

(☏805-965-0353; www.sbtrolley.com; adult/child 3-12yr $19/8; ⊙10am-5:30pm) Biodiesel trolley buses make a narrated 90-minute one-way loop around major tourist attractions, starting at Stearns Wharf (last departure 4pm). Hop-on, hop-off tickets are valid all day and qualify for small discounts at select attractions.

✸✸ Festivals & Events

First Thursday

CULTURE

(www.santabarbaradowntown.com) On the first Thursday evening of every month, downtown art galleries, museums and theaters come alive for a big street party with live entertainment.

Santa Barbara International Film Festival

CINEMA

(http://sbiff.org) Film buffs arrive in droves for screenings of independent US and foreign films in late January and early February.

I Madonnari Italian Street Painting Festival

CULTURE

(www.imadonnarifestival.com) Chalk drawings adorn Santa Barbara's mission sidewalks over Memorial Day weekend.

Summer Solstice Celebration

CULTURE

(www.solsticeparade.com) Wacky, wildly popular – and just plain wild – performance-art parade and outdoor fun in late June.

Old Spanish Days Fiesta

CULTURE

(www.oldspanishdays-fiesta.org) The city gets packed in early August for this long-running but slightly overrated heritage festival featuring rodeos, music and dancing.

Avocado Festival

FOOD

(www.avofest.com) In small-town Carpinteria, witness the world's largest guacamole vat in early October, with food and arts-and-crafts vendors and live bands.

🛏 Sleeping

Prepare for sticker shock: basic motel rooms by the beach command over $200 in summer. Don't show up without reservations, especially on weekends. Cheaper motels and hotels cluster along upper State St and Hwy 101 between Goleta and Carpinteria.

TOP CHOICE Inn of the Spanish Garden

BOUTIQUE HOTEL $$$

(☏805-564-4700, 866-564-4700; http://spanishgardeninn.com; 915 Garden St; d incl breakfast $259-519; ✱@🔊🏊) At this elegant Spanish Revival-style downtown hotel, two dozen romantic rooms and suites have balconies and patios overlooking a gracious fountain courtyard. Beds have luxurious linens, bathrooms boast deep soaking tubs and concierge service is top-notch.

Four Seasons Resort – The Biltmore

RESORT $$$

(☏805-969-2261, 800-819-5053; www.fourseasons.com/santabarbara; 1260 Channel Dr; d from $595; ✱@🔊🏊🐾) Wear white linen and live like Jay Gatsby at the oh-so-cushy 1927 Biltmore, Santa Barbara's iconic Spanish Colonial–style hotel and spa, overlooking Butterfly Beach. Every detail is perfect, from bathrooms with Mediterranean tiles to hideaway garden cottages for honeymooners. Wi-fi in lobby and poolside only. The resort is a 15-minute drive from downtown via Hwy 101 southbound.

El Capitan Canyon

CABINS, CAMPGROUND $$

(☏805-685-3887, 866-352-2729; www.elcapitancanyon.com; 11560 Calle Real, off Hwy 101; safari tents $155, cabins $225-350; 🔊🏊🐾) Go 'glamping' in this woodsy car-free zone near El Capitán State Beach, a 20-mile drive west of Santa Barbara via Hwy 101. Enjoy the great outdoors by day, and rustic safari tents or creekside cedar cabins with heavenly mattresses, gas fireplaces and backyard firepits by night.

Canary Hotel

HOTEL $$$

(☏805-884-0300, 877-468-3515; www.canarysantabarbara.com; 31 W Carrillo St; d from $299; @🔊🏊🐾) Downtown's sleekest multi-story hotel has a rooftop pool and a sunset-watching perch for cocktails. Posh accommodations have four-poster Spanish-framed beds and all mod cons, but 'suites' are just oversized rooms. Ambient street noise may leave you sleepless. Pet fee $35.

James House B&B $$$
(☑805-569-5853; www.jameshousesantabarbara.com; 1632 Chapala St; r incl breakfast $190-240; �ি) For a traditional B&B experience, revel in this stately Queen Anne Victorian run by a charmingly hospitable owner. All of the antique-filled rooms are sheer elegance, with lofty ceilings, some fireplaces and none of that shabby-chic look. Full sit-down breakfast served.

Harbor House Inn MOTEL $$
(☑805-962-9745, 888-474-6789; www.harborhouseinn.com; 104 Bath St; r $129-335; �ি🐾) All of these brightly lit studios inside a converted motel have hardwood floors, small kitchens and a cheery design scheme. Rates include a welcome basket of breakfast goodies, a DVD library and three-speed bikes to borrow. Pet fee $15.

Agave Inn MOTEL $$
(☑805-687-6009; www.agaveinnsb.com; 3222 State St; r $79-209; ✳ি🐾) While it's still just a motel at heart, this boutique-on-a-budget property's 'Mexican pop meets modern' motif livens things up with a color palette out of a Frieda Kahlo painting. Family-sized rooms come with kitchenettes and pull-out sofabeds. It's a 10-minute drive north of downtown.

Presidio Motel MOTEL $$
(☑805-963-1355; http://thepresidiomotel.com; 1620 State St; r incl breakfast $119-220; ✳ি) Presidio is to lodging what H&M is to shopping: a cheap, trendy alternative. Just north of downtown, these crisp, modern motel rooms have panache, with dreamy bedding and art-splashed walls. Noise can be an issue, though. Free loaner beach cruisers.

Brisas del Mar HOTEL $$
(☑805-966-2219, 800-468-1988; www.sbhotels.com; 223 Castillo St; r incl breakfast $145-290; ✳@ি🐾) Big kudos for the freebies (DVDs, wine and cheese, milk and cookies) and the Mediterranean-style front section, although the motel wing is unlovely. Its sister properties away from the beach may be lower-priced.

State Park Campgrounds CAMPGROUND $
(☑reservations 800-444-7275; www.reserveamerica.com; tent & RV sites $35-50, hike-and-bike sites $10) Under a 30-minute drive from Santa Barbara, Carpinteria, Refugio and

---

ⓘ SANTA BARBARA'S URBAN WINE TRAIL

No wheels to head up to Santa Barbara's wine country? No problem! Walk between almost a dozen wine-tasting rooms (and a killer microbrewery, too) near the beach, southeast of downtown. You can join the burgeoning **Urban Wine Trail** (www.urbanwinetrailsb.com) anywhere along its route. Most wine-tasting rooms are open from 11am to 6pm daily.

El Capitán State Beaches each offer a jam packed, popular campground with flush toilets, hot showers, BBQ grills and picnic tables. Reserve ahead.

Marina Beach Motel MOTEL $$
(☑805-963-9311, 877-627-4621; www.marinabeachmotel.com; 21 Bath St; r $115-289; ✳@ি🐾) Flower-festooned, one-story motor lodge by the sea, with some kitchenettes; pet fee $10.

Blue Sands Motel MOTEL $$
(☑805-965-1624; www.thebluesands.com; 421 S Milpas St; r $99-259; ি✳🐾) Kinda kitschy two-story motel just steps from East Beach, with some kitchens; pet fee $10.

Motel 6 Santa Barbara MOTEL $$
(☑805-564-1392, 800-466-8356; www.motel6.com; 443 Corona del Mar; r $85-185; ি✳🐾) The very first Motel 6, remodeled with Ikea-esque design; pet fee $10.

Santa Barbara Tourist Hostel HOSTEL $
(☑805-963-0154; www.sbhostel.com; 134 Chapala St; dm $25-43, r $79-139; ⏲check-in 2:30-11:15pm; @ি) Traveling strangers, trains rumbling by and a rowdy bar just steps from your door – it's either the perfect country-and-western song or this low-slung, tattered hostel.

🍴 Eating

TOP CHOICE **Bouchon** FRENCH $$$
(☑805-730-1160; www.bouchonsantabarbara.com; 9 W Victoria St; mains $28-36; ⏲5:30-9pm Sun-Thu, to 10pm Fri & Sat) Flavorful French cooking with a seasonal California influence is on the menu at convivial Bouchon (meaning 'wine cork'). Locally grown farm produce and ranched meats marry beautifully with more than 30 regional wines by the glass. Lovebirds, book a table on the candlelit patio.

TOP CHOICE Santa Barbara Shellfish Company

SEAFOOD $$

(www.sbfishhouse.com; 230 Stearns Wharf; dishes $5-19; ⊙11am-9pm) 'From sea to skillet to plate' best describes this end-of-the-wharf crab shack that's more of a counter joint. Great lobster bisque, ocean views and the same location for 25 years.

Olio Pizzeria

ITALIAN $$

(☎805-899-2699; www.oliopizzeria.com; 11 W Victoria St; dishes $3-24; ⊙11:30am-2pm Mon-Sat, 5-10pm Sun-Thu, to 11pm Fri & Sat) Cozy, high-ceilinged pizzeria and enoteca with a happening wine bar. It proffers a tempting selection of crispy pizzas, imported cheeses and meats, traditional antipasti and *dolci* (desserts).

Palace Grill

SOUTHERN $$$

(www.palacegrill.com; 8 E Cota St; lunch mains $8-15, dinner mains $16-30; ⊙11:30am-3pm daily, 5:30-10pm Sun-Thu, to 11pm Fri & Sat; 🖬) With all the exuberance of Mardi Gras, this N'awlins grill dishes up delectable biscuits and ginormous (if only so-so) plates of jambalaya, gumbo ya-ya and blackened catfish. Act unsurprised if the staff lead diners in a rousing sing-along.

Silvergreens

HEALTHY $$

(www.silvergreens.com; 791 Chapala St; dishes $4-10; ⊙7:30am-10pm Mon-Fri, 11am-10pm Sun; 🖬🖉) Who says fast food can't be fresh and tasty? With the tag line 'Eat smart, live well,' this sun-drenched cafe makes nutritionally sound (check the calorie counts on your receipt) salads, soups, sandwiches and breakfast burritos.

Brophy Bros

SEAFOOD $$

(www.brophybros.com; 119 Harbor Way; mains $9-20; ⊙11am-10pm Sun-Thu, to 11pm Fri & Sat) A longtime favorite for its fresh-off-the-dock seafood, rowdy atmosphere, salty harborside setting and sunset-view deck. Skip the long lines for a table and start knocking back oyster shooters and Bloody Marys at the bar.

El Buen Gusto

MEXICAN $

(836 N Milpas St; dishes $3-8; ⊙8am-9pm) While waiting for authentic south-of-the-border tacos, kick back at plasticky booths with an *agua fresca* or cold Pacifico as Mexican music videos and soccer games blare on TVs. *Menudo* (tripe soup) and *birria* (spicy stew) are weekend specials.

D'Angelo Pastry & Bread

CAFE $

(25 W Gutierrez St; dishes $2-8; ⊙7am-2pm) This retrolicious downtown bakery with shiny-silver sidewalk bistro tables is a perfect quick breakfast or brunch spot, whether for a buttery croissant and rich espresso or Iron Chef Cat Cora's favorite 'Eggs Rose.'

Sojourner

HEALTH FOOD $$

(www.sojournercafe.com; 134 E Cañon Perdido St; mains $8-15; ⊙11am-11pm Mon-Sat, to 10pm Sun; 🖉) This granola-flavored favorite has been doing its all-natural, mostly meatless magic since 1978. Chili-spiced tempeh tacos and ginger tofu wonton pillows are tasty. Fair-

---

WORTH A TRIP

OJAI

Hollywood director Frank Capra chose the Ojai Valley to represent mythical Shangri-La in his 1937 movie *Lost Horizon*. Today Ojai (pronounced 'oh-hi', meaning 'moon' to the Chumash) attracts artists, organic farmers, spiritual seekers and anyone ready to indulge in spa-style pampering. Start by wandering around Arcade Plaza, a maze of Mission Revival–style buildings on Ojai Ave (downtown's main drag), alive with arty boutiques and cafes.

Ojai is famous for the rosy glow that emanates from its mountains at sunset, the so-called 'Pink Moment.' The ideal vantage point for catching it is the peaceful lookout **Meditation Mount** (www.meditationmount.org; 10340 Reeves Rd; admission free). Head east of downtown on Ojai Ave (Hwy 150), then take a left at Boccali's farm-stand pizzeria. For hiking trail maps to hot springs, waterfalls and more mountaintop viewpoints, visit the **Ojai Ranger Station** (☎805-646-4348; www.fs.fed.us/r5/lospadres; 1190 E Ojai Ave; ⊙8am-4:30pm Mon-Fri).

Ojai is about 35 miles east of Santa Barbara via Hwys 101 and 150, or 15 miles inland from Ventura via Hwy 33.

trade coffee, local beers and wines and delish desserts.

Lilly's Taquería
MEXICAN $
(www.lillystacos.com; 310 Chapala St; dishes from $2; ⊙11am-9pm Mon & Wed-Thu, to 10pm Fri & Sat, to 9:30pm Sun) Almost always a line out the door for *adobada* (marinated pork) tacos.

Metropulos
DELI $
(www.metrofinefoods.com; 216 E Yanonali St; dishes $6-10; ⊙8:30am-5:30pm Mon-Fri, 10am-4pm Sat) Artisan breads, cheeses and cured meats, hand-crafted sandwiches and market-fresh salads.

Santa Barbara Farmers Market
MARKET $
(www.sbfarmersmarket.org; cnr Santa Barbara & Cota Sts; ⊙8:30am-1pm Sat) Farmers and food vendors also set up along lower State St on Tuesday afternoons.

Drinking

Santa Barbara's after-dark scene revolves around college-age bars and nightclubs on lower State St. Saturday nights here get rowdy.

Brewhouse
BREWPUB
(www.brewhousesb.com; 229 W Montecito St; ⊙11am-11pm Sun-Thu, to midnight Fri & Sat; ☎) This rowdy dive down by the railroad tracks crafts its own unique small-batch beers (Saint Bar's Belgian-style rules!) and has cool art and rockin' live music Wednesday to Saturday nights.

Press Room
PUB
(http://pressroomsb.com; 15 E Ortega St) This downtown pub attracts a slew of students and European travelers. There's no better place to watch the footie, stuff quarters in the jukebox and be jovially abused by the British bartender.

French Press
COFFEE SHOP
(1101 State St; ⊙6am-7pm Mon-Fri, 7am-7pm Sat, 8am-5pm Sun; ☎) This State St coffee shop shames the chains with beans roasted in Santa Cruz, shiny silver espresso machines from Italy and baristas that know how to pull their shots and mix spicy chais.

Blenders in the Grass
JUICE, SMOOTHIES $
(www.drinkblenders.com; 720 State St; drinks $3-6; ⊙7am-9pm Mon-Thu, 7am-10pm Fri, 8am-10pm Sat, 8am-9pm Sun) For a quick, healthy burst of energy, pop by this locally owned juice and smoothie bar for a wheatgrass shot or date milkshake.

Hollister Brewing Co
BREWPUB
(www.hollisterbrewco.com; Camino Real Marketplace, 6980 Marketplace Dr, off Hwy 101 exit Glen Annie Rd; ⊙11am-10pm) Beer geeks won't regret making the trip out near the UCSB campus to sample unique brews like White Star XPA or Hip Hopimperial ale. It's about a 20-minute drive from downtown via Hwy 101 northbound.

☆ Entertainment

For a calendar of events and live shows, including in downtown's historic movie palaces and theaters, pick up the free weekly *Santa Barbara Independent* (www.independent.com) or Friday's 'Scene' guide from the *Santa Barbara News-Press* (www.sbnewspress.com).

Santa Barbara Bowl
MUSIC, COMEDY
(☎805-962-7411; www.sbbowl.org; 1122 N Milpas St) Built by the 1930s New Deal–era WPA labor, this outdoor stone amphitheater grants ocean views from the highest cheap seats. Kick back in the summer sunshine or under the stars during live rock, jazz and folk concerts and stand-up comedy shows, including big-name acts.

Soho
MUSIC
(☎805-962-7776; www.sohosb.com; 1221 State St, 2nd level) An unpretentious brick room hosts live music almost nightly, upstairs inside a downtown office complex. Lineups range from indie rock, jazz, folk, funk and world beats to DJs.

Velvet Jones
MUSIC, COMEDY
(☎805-965-8676; www.velvet-jones.com; 423 State St) Long-running downtown punk and indie dive for rock, hip-hop, comedy and 18+ DJ nights for the city's college crowd. Many bands stop here between gigs in LA and San Francisco.

Zodo's Bowling & Beyond
BOWLING, BILLIARDS
(☎805-967-0128; www.zodos.com; 5925 Calle Real, off Hwy 101 exit Fairview Rd; ☎) With over 40 beers on tap, pool tables and a video arcade (Skee-Ball!), this bowling alley near UCSB is good ol' family fun. Call for schedules of open-play lanes and 'glow bowling' nights. It's a 15-minute drive from downtown via Hwy 101 northbound.

ⓘ CAR-FREE SANTA BARBARA

If you use public transportation to get to Santa Barbara, you can get valuable hotel discounts, plus get a nice swag bag of coupons for various activities and attractions, all courtesy of Santa Barbara Car Free (www.santabarbaracarfree.org).

🛍 Shopping

Downtown's State St is packed with shops, from vintage clothing to brand-name boutiques; cheapskates stick to lower State St, while trust-fund babies head uptown. For indie shops, dive into the Funk Zone, east of State St, just south of Hwy 101.

Channel Islands Surfboards OUTDOORS
(www.cisurfboards.com; 36 Anacapa St) Dying to take home a handcrafted, authentic SoCal surfboard? Down in the Funk Zone, this contempo surf shack turns out innovative pro-worthy board designs, cool surfer threads and beanie hats.

CRSVR SHOES, CLOTHING
(www.crsvr.com; 632 State St) Check this downtown sneaker boutique run by DJs, not just for rare, limited-edition Nikes and other athletic-shoe brands, but also trendy T-shirts, hats and other men's urban styles.

REI OUTDOORS
(www.rei.com; 321 Anacapa St; 10am-9pm Mon-Fri, 10am-7pm Sat, 11am-6pm Sun) West Coast's biggest independent co-op outdoor retailer is the place to pick up active clothing, shoes, sports gear and topographic recreational maps.

ⓘ Information

Several downtown coffee shops offer free wi-fi.

FedEx Office (www.fedex.com; 1030 State St; per min 20-30¢; 7am-11pm Mon-Fri, 9am-9pm Sat & Sun; @🖥) Pay-as-you-go internet workstations and free wi-fi.

Post office (www.usps.com; 836 Anacapa St; 9:30am-6pm Mon-Fri, 10am-2pm Sat) Full-service.

Public library (www.sbplibrary.org; 40 E Anapamu St; 10am-8pm Mon-Thu, 10am-5:30pm Fri & Sat, 1-5pm Sun; @🖥) Public internet terminals and free wi-fi.

Santa Barbara Cottage Hospital (805-682-7111; http://cottagehealthsystemc.org; cnr Pueblo & Bath Sts; 24hr) Emergency room.

Visitor center (805-965-3021; www.santabarbaraca.com; 1 Garden St; 9am-5pm Mon-Sat, 10am-5pm Sun) Maps, brochures and tourist information at the waterfront.

ⓘ Getting There & Away

About 10 miles west of downtown off Hwy 101, small **Santa Barbara Airport** (SBA; www.flysba.com; 500 Fowler Rd) is served by American (LA), Frontier (Denver), Horizon (Seattle), United (Denver, LA and San Francisco) and US Airways (Phoenix).

Santa Barbara Airbus (805-964-7759, 800-423-1618; www.sbairbus.com) shuttles between Los Angeles International Airport (LAX) and Santa Barbara (one way/round trip $48/90, 2½ to three hours, eight daily).

Amtrak (www.amtrak.com; 209 State St) is a stop on the daily Seattle–LA *Coast Starlight*. Regional *Pacific Surfliner* trains head south to LA ($25, three hours, six daily) and San Diego ($35, six hours, four daily), or north to San Luis Obispo ($29, 2¾ hours, twice daily). Connecting Amtrak Thruway buses also head north along Hwy 101 via San Luis Obispo and Paso Robles to the San Francisco Bay Area.

Greyhound (www.greyhound.com; 34 W Carrillo St) has a few daily services along Hwy 101 south to LA ($18, three hours) or north to San Francisco ($53, nine hours) via San Luis Obispo ($26, 2¼ hours).

ⓘ Getting Around

Equipped with front-loading bicycle racks, local buses operated by **Metropolitan Transit District** (MTD; 805-963-3366; www.sbmtd.gov; 1020 Chapala St) cost $1.75 per ride; ask for a free transfer when boarding.

MTD's electric **Downtown Shuttle** runs along State St to Stearns Wharf every 10 to 15 minutes, while the **Waterfront Shuttle** travels from Stearns Wharf west to the harbor and east to the zoo every 15 to 30 minutes. Both routes operate 10am to 6pm daily (also from 6pm to 10pm on Fridays and Saturdays between late May and early September). The fare is 25¢ (transfers free).

In 10 municipal lots and garages around downtown parking is free for the first 75 minutes; each additional hour costs $1.50.

Channel Islands National Park

Don't let this remote park, part of an island chain lying off the SoCal coast, loiter too long on your bucket list. Imagine hiking, kayaking, scuba diving, camping and whale-watching, all amid a raw, end-of-the-world landscape. Rich in unique species of flora and fauna, tide pools and kelp forests, the islands are home to 145 species found nowhere else in the world, earning them the nickname 'California's Galapagos.'

⊙ Sights & Activities

Most tourists arrive during summer, when island conditions are hot, dusty and bone-dry. Better times to visit are during the spring wildflower bloom or in early fall, when the fog clears and kayaking conditions are ideal. Winter can be stormy, but it's also great for wildlife watching, especially whales.

Before you shove off from the mainland, stop by Ventura Harbor's NPS Visitor Center (p524) for educational natural-history exhibits, a short video and ranger-led family activity programs on weekends and holidays.

Anacapa Island   ISLAND
If you're short on time, Anacapa Island, which is actually three separate islets, gives a memorable introduction to the islands' ecology. Boats dock on the East Island and after a short climb you'll find 2 miles of trails offering fantastic views of island flora, a historic lighthouse, and rocky Middle and West Islands. Kayaking, diving, tidepooling and seal-watching are popular activities here. After checking out the small museum at the visitors center, ask about ranger-led programs. In summer, scuba divers with videocameras may broadcast live images to TV monitors you can watch.

Santa Cruz Island   ISLAND
The park's largest island (96 sq mi) boasts two mountain ranges. The western three-quarters of the island is managed by the Nature Conservancy and can only be accessed with a permit (apply online at www.nature.org/cruzpermit). But the remaining eastern quarter, managed by the NPS, packs a wallop – ideal if you want an action-packed day trip or overnight camping trip. You can swim, snorkel, scuba dive and kayak. There are rugged hikes too, which are best not attempted midday – there's little shade. It's a 1-mile climb to captivating, but windy Cavern Point.

Santa Rosa Island   ISLAND
Snowy white-sand beaches and a chance to spot hundreds of bird and plant species are among the highlights of Santa Rosa, where seals and sea lions haul out. Hiking trails through grasslands and canyons and along beaches abound, but high winds typically make swimming, diving and kayaking tough for everyone but experts.

San Miguel Island   ISLAND
The most remote of the park's northern islands offers solitude and a wilderness experience, but it's often shrouded in fog and is very windy. Some sections are off-limits to prevent disruption of the fragile ecosystem, which includes a ghostly caliche forest (made of the hardened calcium-carbonate castings of trees and vegetation) and seasonal colonies of seals and sea lions.

Santa Barbara Island   ISLAND
Only 1 sq mile in size, this isolated island is for nature lovers. Big, blooming coreopsis, cream cups and chicory are just a few of the island's memorable plant species. It's also a thriving playground for seabirds and marine wildlife, including humongous elephant

PARADISE LOST & FOUND

Humans have left a heavy footprint on the Channel Islands, originally inhabited by Chumash and Gabrieleño tribespeople. In the 19th century, ranching livestock overgrazed, causing erosion, while rabbits fed on native plants. The US military even used San Miguel as a mid-20th–century practice bombing range. In 1969, an offshore oil spill engulfed the northern islands in an 800-sq-mi slick, killing off uncountable seabirds and mammals. Meanwhile, deep-sea fishing has caused the destruction of three-quarters of the islands' kelp forests.

Despite past abuses, the islands' future is not bleak. Brown pelicans, once decimated by the effects of DDT and reduced to one chick on Anacapa in 1970, have rebounded, and bald eagles were recently reintroduced. On San Miguel, native vegetation has returned a half century after overgrazing sheep were removed. On Santa Cruz, the National Park Service (NPS) and the Nature Conservancy have implemented ambitious multi-year plans to eliminate invasive plants and feral pigs. Information is available from the NPS (☎805-658-5730; www.nps.gov/chis; 1901 Spinnaker Dr, off Harbor Blvd, Ventura; ☺8:30am-5pm;) and from Nature Conservancy (www.nature.org)..

seals and Xantus' murrelets, a bird that nests in cliff crevices. Ask at the island's visitor center about the best diving, snorkeling and kayaking spots.

☞ Tours

Most trips require a minimum number of participants, and may be canceled due to surf and weather conditions.

Island Packers   WHALE-WATCHING
(☑805-642-1393; www.islandpackers.com; 1691 Spinnaker Dr, Ventura Harbor; adult/child 3hr cruise from $33/24, full-day trip from $72/54) Offers whale-watching excursions from late December to early April (gray whales) and in summer (blue and humpback whales).

Paddle Sports of Santa Barbara   KAYAKING, HIKING
(☑805-899-4925, 888-254-2094; www.kayaksb.com; 117b Harbor Way, Santa Barbara; day trips from $175) Organizes kayaking and hiking excursions to all five islands.

Santa Barbara Adventure Co   KAYAKING
(☑805-899-4925, 888-254-2094; www.kayaksb.com; 720 Bond Ave, Santa Barbara; day trips adult/child from $170/150; ☻) Offers both day and overnight sea-kayaking trips to the islands.

🛏 Sleeping

Each island has a primitive year-round **campground** (☑reservations 518-885-3639, 877-444-6777; www.recreation.gov; tent sites $15) with pit toilets and picnic tables. Water is available on Santa Cruz and Santa Rosa islands only. Campers must pack everything in and out, including trash. Due to fire danger, campfires are not allowed (enclosed gas campstoves are OK). Advance camping reservations are required.

ℹ Information

NPS Visitor Center (☑805-658-5730; www.nps.gov/chis; 1901 Spinnaker Dr, off Harbor Blvd, Ventura; ⊙8:30am-5pm; ☻) On the mainland, at the far end of Ventura Harbor, it's a one-stop shop for books, maps and trip-planning information.

ℹ Getting There & Away

Trips may be canceled anytime due to surf and weather conditions. Reservations are essential for weekends, holidays and summer trips.

AIR Channel Islands Aviation (☑805-987-1301; www.flycia.com; day trips adult/child from $160/135, campers from $300) runs half-day beach excursions, surf-fishing trips and camper shuttles to Santa Rosa Island, departing from Camarillo or Santa Barbara.

BOAT Island Packers (☑805-642-1393; www.islandpackers.com; 1691 Spinnaker Dr, Ventura Harbor; day trips adult/child from $56/39) provides regularly scheduled boat service to all of the islands; campers pay extra. Some departures from Oxnard.

Ventura

The primary departure point for Channel Islands trips, Ventura may not look at first like the most enchanting coastal city, but it has its seaside charms, especially along the beaches and in the historic downtown corridor along Main St, north of Hwy 101.

CHANNEL ISLANDS NPS CAMPGROUNDS

CAMPGROUND NAME	NO OF SITES	ACCESS FROM BOAT LANDING AREA	DESCRIPTION
Anacapa	7	0.5-mile walk with 154 stairs	High, rocky, sun-exposed & isolated
San Miguel	9	Steep 1-mile walk uphill	Windy, often foggy with volatile weather
Santa Barbara	10	Steep 0.5-mile walk uphill	Large, grassy & surrounded by trails
Santa Cruz (Scorpion Ranch)	40	Flat, 0.5-mile walk	Popular with groups, often crowded & partly shady
Santa Rosa	15	Flat, 1.5-mile walk	Eucalyptus grove in a windy canyon

◉ Sights & Activities

San Buenaventura State Beach   BEACH
(☎805-968-1033; www.parks.ca.gov; per car $10; ☺dawn-dusk; ♿) Off Hwy 101, this long, golden strand is perfect for swimming, surfing or just lazing on the sand. Recreational cycling paths connect to more nearby beaches.

Mission San Buenaventura   MISSION
(www.sanbuenaventuramission.org; 211 E Main St; adult/child $2/50¢; ☺10am-5pm Mon-Fri, 9am-5pm Sat, 10am-4pm Sun) Ventura's Spanish colonial roots are in evidence at the final California mission founded by Junípero Serra in 1782. A stroll around this petite parish church is a tranquil experience, leading through a small museum, past statues of saints, centuries-old religious paintings and unusual wooden bells, and around a garden courtyard.

Limoneira   AGROTOURISM
(☎805-525-5541; www.limoneira.com; 1141 Cummings Rd, Santa Paula; tours $20-40) A 20-minute drive outside town, this working ranch and farm is the place to get up close and smell the citrus that Ventura is famous for: lemons. Drop by the historical ranch store and play bocce ball on outdoor courts, or reserve a guided tour of the ranch, the modern packing house and the sea-view fruit and avocado orchards. Call for opening hours.

California Oil Museum   MUSEUM
(☎805-933-0076; www.oilmuseum.net; 1001 E Main St, off Hwy 126, Santa Paula; adult/child 6-17yr/senior $4/1/3; ☺10am-4pm Wed-Sun) If you've seen the Oscar-winning movie *There Will Be Blood*, then you already know that SoCal's early oil boom was a bloodthirsty business. Examine SoCal's 'black bonanza' with modest historical exhibits that include an authentic 1890s drilling rig and vintage gas pumps. To reach downtown Santa Paula, drive about 13 miles east of Ventura via Hwy 126.

🛏 Sleeping & Eating

Midrange motels and high-rise beachfront hotels cluster off Hwy 101 and by Ventura Harbor. Alternatively, keep driving on Hwy 101 southbound to Camarillo, where cheaper roadside chains abound. Back in downtown Ventura, Main St is chock-a-block with taco shops, healthy SoCal-style cafes and globally flavored kitchens.

Brooks   CALIFORNIAN $$$
(☎805-652-7070; www.restaurantbrooks.com; 545 E Thompson Blvd; mains $17-34; ☺5-9pm Tue-Thu & Sun, to 10pm Fri & Sat) Just off Hwy 101, this chef-driven restaurant serves such high-flying New American cuisine as cornmeal-fried oysters, jalapeño cheddar grits and Maytag blue cheesecake with seasonal berries.

Anacapa Brew Pub   BREWPUB $$
(www.anacapabrewing.com; 472 E Main St; mains $9-20; ☺11:30am-9pm Sun-Wed, to midnight Thu-Sun) Right downtown, this casual brewpub crafts its own microbrews – props to the Pierpoint IPA – and makes a fine pulled-pork sandwich too.

Mary's Secret Garden   VEGETARIAN $
(☎805-641-3663; 100 S Fir St; mains $5-12; ☺4-9:30pm Tue-Thu, 11am-9:30pm Fri & Sat; ♪) Two blocks east of California St by a pretty park, this internationally spiced vegan haven mixes up fresh juices, smoothies and out-of-this-world cakes.

🍸 Drinking

Wine Rack   WINE BAR
(www.weaverwines.com; 14 S California St; ☺4-9pm Mon & Tue, 2-9pm Wed & Thu, noon-10pm Fri & Sat, 2-8pm Sun) At this upbeat wine shop, novices can sidle up to the unpretentious tasting bar, loiter over a tasty cheese plate and listen to live music.

Zoey's Café   CAFE $$
(☎805-652-1137; www.zoeyscafe.com; 185 E Santa Clara St; mains $9-15; ☺6-9pm Tue-Sat, later on show nights) Cozy coffeehouse that makes pizzas and paninis, and showcases live acts almost nightly, mostly bluegrass, folk and acoustic singer-songwriters.

🛍 Shopping

Downtown on Main St, you'll find a terrific assortment of antiques, vintage, secondhand thrift and indie boutique shops.

Patagonia   OUTDOOR EQUIPMENT
(www.patagonia.com; 235 W Santa Clara St; ☺10am-6pm Mon-Sat & 11am-5pm Sun) Ventura is the birthplace of this pioneering outdoor-gear and clothing outfitter, known for its commitment to sustainable, environmentally progressive practices.

Real Cheap Sports   OUTDOOR EQUIPMENT
(www.realcheapsports.com; 36 W Santa Clara St; ☺10am-6pm Mon-Sat, to 5pm Sun) Shh, don't

tell anyone but you can get that brand-name outdoors stuff for less here, including Patagonia factory seconds.

Camarillo Premium Outlets   MALL
(www.premiumoutlets.com; 740 E Ventura Blvd, Camarillo; ☻10am-9pm Mon-Sat & 10am-8pm Sun) For steeply discounted designer duds, drive about 20 minutes from downtown via Hwy 101 southbound to this mall.

ℹ Information

Ventura Visitors & Convention Bureau (☎805-648-2075, 800-483-6214; www.ven

tura-usa.com; 101 S California St; ☻8:30am-5pm Mon-Fri, 9am-5pm Sat, 10am-4pm Sun) Free information and maps downtown.

ℹ Getting There & Away

Ventura's unstaffed **Amtrak station** (www.amtrak.com; cnr Harbor Blvd & Figueroa St) has five daily trains north to Santa Barbara ($12, 40 minutes) and south to Los Angeles ($20, 2¼ hours). **Vista** (☎800-438-112; www.goventura.org) runs several daily Coastal Express buses between Ventura and Santa Barbara ($3, 35 minutes).

Los Angeles

Best Places to Eat

» Bottega Louie (p559)

» Osteria Mozza & Pizzeria Mozza (p559)

» Ivy (p561)

» Bazaar (p561)

» Gjelina (p562)

Best Places to Stay

» Standard Downtown LA (p556)

» Hollywood Roosevelt Hotel (p556)

» Beverly Hills Hotel (p557)

» Casa Del Mar (p558)

» Queen Mary Hotel (p558)

Why Go?

Ah, Los Angeles, land of starstruck dreams and Tinseltown magic. You may think you know what to expect from LA: celebrity worship, plastic surgery junkies, endless traffic, earthquakes, wildfires...And true, your waitress today might be tomorrow's starlet and you may well encounter artificially enhanced blondes and phone-clutching honchos weaving lanes at 80mph, but LA is intensely diverse and brimming with fascinating neighborhoods and characters that have nothing to do with the 'Industry' (entertainment, to the rest of us). Its innovative cooking has pushed the boundaries of American cuisine for generations. Arts and architecture? Frank Lloyd Wright to Frank Gehry. Music? The Doors to Dr Dre and Dudamel.

So do yourself a favor and leave your preconceptions in the suitcase. LA's truths are not doled out on the silver screen or gossip rags; rather, you will discover them in everyday interactions. Chances are, the more you explore, the more you'll enjoy.

When to Go
Los Angeles

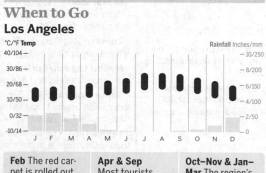

Feb The red carpet is rolled out for the Academy Awards. Prime time for celebspotting.

Apr & Sep Most tourists visit when the sun shines the brightest on LA's golden sands.

Oct–Nov & Jan–Mar The region's two distinct wet seasons.

Fast Facts

» **Population of LA** 3.8 million

» **Average temperature low/high in LA** Jan 47/66°F, July 62/82°F

» **LA to Disneyland** 26 miles

» **LA to San Diego** 120 miles

» **LA to Palm Springs** 110 miles

Planning Your Trip

Reserve hotels in prime locations at least three weeks out, especially for summer weekends. Two weeks out, make reservations for popular restaurants. Weekends are toughest, but primo nights for celeb sightings at dining hot spots are actually Tuesday through Thursday.

Resources

» California Division of Tourism (www.visitcalifornia.com)

» California Department of Transportation (✆800-427-7623; www.dot.ca.gov/

Actually, Some People do Walk in LA

'No one walks in LA,' the '80s band Missing Persons famously sang. That was then. Fed up with traffic, smog and high gas prices, the region that defined car culture is developing a foot culture. Angelenos are moving into more densely populated neighborhoods and are walking, cycling and taking public transportation.

You may not need a car during your visit if you stay near one of the arty stations on the Metro Red Line, which connects Union Station in Downtown LA to the San Fernando Valley via Koreatown, Hollywood and Universal Studios. Unlimited-ride passes ($5 per day, via stored-value TAP cards) are a downright bargain, and given LA's legendary traffic it's often faster to travel below ground than above. Light-rail lines connect Downtown with Long Beach, Pasadena and East LA. A Culver City line was due to open as we went to press, to be extended to Santa Monica by 2015.

In 2011, the city of Los Angeles authorized construction of an eventual 1,680 miles of bikeways, in addition to those in other cities around the county. Bicycles are permitted on Metro trains and buses are fitted with bike racks.

While eventual plans call for a 'Subway to the Sea' in Santa Monica, for now you'll be busing, biking or – gasp! – driving to Mid-City, Beverly Hills and the beaches.

GRAUMAN'S CHINESE THEATRE

Yes, every other tourist goes there too, but even the most jaded may thrill to matching hand- or footprints with those of the stars, enshrined forever in concrete in front of Grauman's Chinese Theatre in Hollywood (p539).

Top Five LA Beaches

» **El Matador** (off Map p574) Hideaway hemmed by battered rock cliffs and strewn with giant boulders. Wild surf; not suitable for children.

» **Zuma** (p546) Gorgeous 2-mile ribbon of sand for swimming, body surfing and tight bodies.

» **Malibu Lagoon/Surfrider** (p546) Legendary surf beach with superb swells and a lagoon for bird-watching.

» **Santa Monica** (p547) Families escape inland heat on this extra-wide beach, home to the Santa Monica Pier and South Bay Bicycle Trail (p553).

» **Venice** (p547) provides a nonstop parade of friends and freaks. Drum circle in the sand on Sundays.

History

Los Angeles' human history began as early as 6000 BC, as home to the Gabrieleño and Chumash tribespeople. Their hunter-gatherer existence ended in the late 18th century with the arrival of Spanish missionaries and pioneers, led by Padre Junípero Serra. Established in 1781, the civilian settlement of El Pueblo de la Reina de Los Angeles (Village of the Queen of the Angels) became a thriving farming community but remained an isolated outpost for decades.

Spain lost its hold on the territory to Mexico in 1821 and, following the Mexican-American War (1846–48), California came under US rule. The city was incorporated on April 4, 1850.

A series of seminal events caused LA's population to swell to two million by 1930: the collapse of the Northern California Gold Rush in the 1850s, the arrival of the railroad in the 1870s, the birth of the citrus industry in the late 1800s, the discovery of oil in 1892, the launch of San Pedro Harbor in 1907, the arrival of the motion picture industry in 1908 and the opening of the LA Aqueduct in 1913. Beginning in WWI, aviation and defense industries helped drive the city's economy through the end of the Cold War. The 10th Summer Olympic Games, held here in 1932, marked LA's coming of age as a world city (10th St was renamed Olympic Blvd in their honor).

After WWII, a deluge of new residents, drawn by reasonably priced housing, seemingly boundless opportunity and reliably fabulous weather, shaped LA into the megalopolis of today. Culturally, LA's freewheeling, free-thinking, free-living lifestyle defined the American consciousness of the 1960s and '70s, a boom culminating in a second Summer Olympics held here in 1984.

LA's growth has not been without its problems, including suburban sprawl and air pollution, though smog levels have fallen annually since records have been kept. Major riots in 1965 and 1992 created distrust between the city's police department and various ethnic groups. Violent crime has since dropped significantly, and in May 2005 Angelenos elected Antonio Villaraigosa, the city's first mayor of Latino descent since 1872.

In the new millennium, traffic, a teetering national economy, struggling public education system and fluctuating real-estate mar-

ket continue to cloud LA's sunny skies. But all things considered, LA's a survivor.

DON'T MISS

ANGELS FLIGHT

Part novelty act, part commuter train for the lazy, Angels Flight (1901; Map p534; www.angelsflight.com; per ride 25¢; ⊙6:45am-10pm) is a funicular billed as the 'shortest railway in the world' (298 feet). The adorable cars chug up and down the steep incline connecting Hill and Olive Sts.

◉ Sights

Los Angeles may be vast and amorphous, but the areas of visitor interest are fairly well defined. About 12 miles inland, Downtown LA is the region's hub, combining great architecture and culture with global-village pizzazz. Northwest of Downtown, there's sprawling Hollywood and nearby hip 'hoods Los Feliz and Silver Lake. West Hollywood is LA's center of urban chic and the gay and lesbian community, while Long Beach, at six o'clock from Downtown, is a bustling port with big city sophistication. Most TV and movie studios are north of Hollywood in the San Fernando Valley, and to its east Pasadena feels like an all-American small town writ large.

South of Hollywood, Mid-City's main draw is Museum Row, while further west are ritzy Beverly Hills and the Westside communities of Westwood and Brentwood. Santa Monica is the most tourist- and pedestrian-friendly beach town; others include swish-but-low-key Malibu and bohemian Venice.

DOWNTOWN & AROUND

For decades, Downtown was LA's historic core and main business and government district – and empty nights and weekends. No more. Crowds fill Dowtown's performance and entertainment venues, and young professionals and artists have moved by the thousands into new lofts, attracting bars, restaurants and galleries. Don't expect Manhattan just yet, but for adventurous urbanites, now is an exciting time to be Downtown.

Downtown is easily explored on foot or by subway or DASH minibus. Parking is cheapest (about $6 all day) around Little Tokyo and Chinatown.

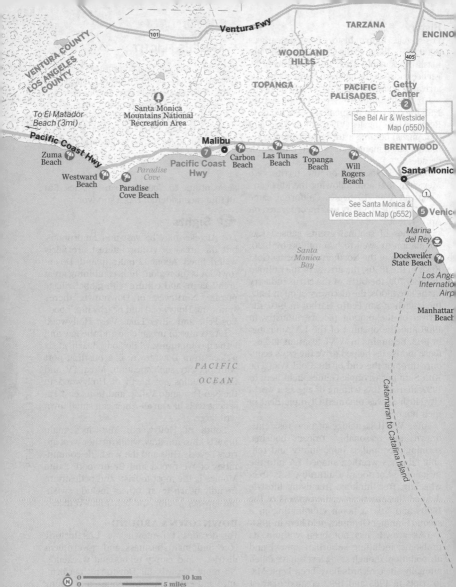

Ventura Fwy

101

TARZANA

ENCINO

WOODLAND
HILLS

405

VENTURA COUNTY
LOS ANGELES
COUNTY

TOPANGA

PACIFIC
PALISADES

Getty
Center
2

Santa Monica
Mountains National
Recreation Area

See Bel Air & Westside
Map (p550)

To El Matador
Beach (3mi)

Pacific Coast Hwy

BRENTWOOD

Malibu
7

Pacific Coast
Hwy

Carbon
Beach

Las Tunas
Beach

Topanga
Beach

Will
Rogers
Beach

Santa Monica

Zuma
Beach

Paradise
Cove

1

Westward
Beach

Paradise
Cove Beach

See Santa Monica &
Venice Beach Map (p552)

5 Venice

Marina
del Rey

Santa
Monica
Bay

Dockweiler
State Beach

Los Angeles
International
Airport

Manhattan
Beach

PACIFIC
OCEAN

Catamaran to Catalina Island

N

| 0 | 10 km |
| 0 | 5 miles |

Los Angeles Highlights

1 Go behind the scenes on a **studio tour** (p540)

2 Visit world-famous venues such as the **Walt Disney Concert Hall** (p532), the **Los Angeles County Museum**

of Art (p542) and the **Getty Center** (p544)

3 Discover the perfect taco, shrimp dumpling or Korean barbecue at one of thousands of **ethnic restaurants** (p559)

4 Enjoy a picnic and a concert under the stars at the venerable **Hollywood Bowl** (p568)

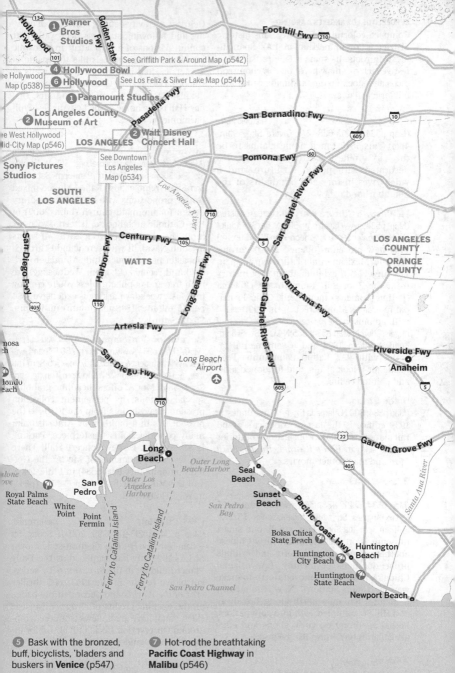

134 **Hollywood Fwy**
1 Warner Bros Studios
Golden State Fwy
Foothill Fwy **210**
101
See Griffith Park & Around Map (p542)
4 Hollywood Bowl
See Los Feliz & Silver Lake Map (p544)
ee Hollywood Map (p538)
6 Hollywood
1 Paramount Studios
Pasadena Fwy
San Bernadino Fwy **10**
Los Angeles County Museum of Art
2
Walt Disney Concert Hall
2
ee West Hollywood Mid-City Map (p546)
LOS ANGELES
Pomona Fwy **60**
605
See Downtown Los Angeles Map (p534)
Sony Pictures Studios
Los Angeles River
SOUTH LOS ANGELES
710
San Gabriel River Fwy
5
LOS ANGELES COUNTY
ORANGE COUNTY
Century Fwy **105**
Harbor Fwy
San Diego Fwy
405
WATTS
Long Beach Fwy
110
San Gabriel River Fwy
Santa Ana Fwy
Artesia Fwy
Long Beach Airport
Riverside Fwy
Anaheim
5
San Diego Hwy
710
605
1
22
Garden Grove Fwy
405
nosa ch
Long Beach
Outer Long Beach Harbor
Seal Beach
Santa Ana River
San Pedro
Outer Los Angeles Harbor
Sunset Beach
Pacific Coast Hwy
londo each
Royal Palms State Beach
White Point
Point Fermin
San Pedro Bay
Bolsa Chica State Beach
Huntington City Beach **7**
Huntington Beach
lone ve
Ferry to Catalina Island
Ferry to Catalina Island
Huntington State Beach **7**
San Pedro Channel
Newport Beach

5 Bask with the bronzed, buff, bicyclists, 'bladers and buskers in **Venice** (p547)

6 Mingle with the beau monde in a hip **Hollywood** bar or club (p566)

7 Hot-rod the breathtaking **Pacific Coast Highway** in **Malibu** (p546)

Compact, colorful and car-free, this historic district is an immersion in LA's Spanish-Mexican roots. Its spine is Olvera Street, a festive tack-o-rama where you can chomp on tacos and stock up on handmade candy and folkloric trinkets.

FREE Avila Adobe HISTORIC HOME
(Map p534; 🖉213-628-1274, Olvera St; 🕑9am-4pm) This 1818 ranch home claims to be the city's oldest existing building. It's decorated with period furniture, and a video gives history and highlights of the neighborhood.

La Plaza de Cultura y Artes CULTURAL MUSEUM
(Map p534; www.lapca.org; 501 Main St; adult/student/senior $9/5/7; 🕑noon-7pm Wed-Sun; P) This new museum (opened 2010) chronicles the Mexican–American experience in Los Angeles, in exhibits about city history from the Zoot Suit Riots to the Chicana (Latina women's) movement. Calle Principal re-creates Main Street in the 1920s.

It adjoins La Placita (Our Lady Queen of Angels Church; Map p534; 535 N Main St; 🕑8am-8pm), built in 1822 and a sentimental favorite with LA's Latino community. Peek inside for a look at the gold-festooned altar and painted ceiling.

Union Station LANDMARK
(Map p534; 800 N Alameda St; P) This majestic 1939 edifice is the last of America's grand rail stations; its glamorous art deco interior can be seen in *Blade Runner*, *Bugsy*, *Rain Man* and many other movies.

Chinese American
Museum CULTURAL MUSEUM
(Map p534; 🖉213-485-8567; www.camla.org; 425 N Los Angeles St; adult/student/senior $3/2/2; 🕑10am-3pm Tue-Sun) This small but smart museum is on the site of an early Chinese apothecary and general store, and exhibits probe questions of identity. LA's original Chinatown was here (moved north to make way for Union Station). 'New' Chinatown is about a half-mile north along Broadway and Hill St, crammed with dim sum parlors, herbal apothecaries, curio shops and edgy art galleries on Chung King Road.

FREE Walt Disney
Concert Hall CONCERT HALL, ARCHITECTURE
(Map p534; www.laphil.com; 111 S Grand Ave) This gleaming concert venue, designed by Frank Gehry, is a gravity-defying sculpture of curving and billowing stainless-steel walls that conjure visions of a ship adrift in a cosmic sea. The auditorium feels like the inside of a finely crafted instrument clad in walls of smooth Douglas fir. Check the website for details of free guided and audio tours. Disney Hall is the home of the Los Angeles Philharmonic (p568).

Cathedral of Our Lady of
the Angels CHURCH
(Map p534; www.olacathedral.org; 555 W Temple St; 🕑6:30am-6pm Mon-Fri, 9am-6pm Sat, 7am-6pm Sun) Architect José Rafael Moneo mixed Gothic proportions with bold contemporary design for the main church (built 2002) of LA's Catholic archdiocese. It teems with art (note the contemporary tapestries of saints by John Nava), lit with serene light through alabaster panes. Tours (1pm, Monday to Friday) and recitals (12:45pm Wednesday) are both free and popular. Unless you're coming for Mass, weekday parking is expensive – $4 per 15 minutes ($18 maximum) until 4pm, $5 on Saturday.

Museum of Contemporary Art ART MUSEUM
(MoCA; Map p534; www.moca.org; 250 S Grand Ave; adult/child/student & senior $10/free/5, 5-8pm Thu free; 🕑11am-5pm Mon & Fri, to 8pm Thu, to 6pm Sat & Sun) MoCA offers headline-grabbing special exhibits; its permanent collection presents heavy hitters from the 1940s to the present. It's in a building by Arata Isozaki; many consider it his masterpiece. Parking is $9, at Walt Disney Concert Hall. There are two other branches of MoCA: the Geffen Contemporary (Map p534) in Little Tokyo and the MoCA Pacific Design Center (p541) in West Hollywood.

FREE City Hall ARCHITECTURE
(Map p534; 🖉213-978-1995; 200 N Spring St; 🕑8am-5pm Mon-Fri) The ziggurat-style crown of LA's 1928 city hall cameoed as the Daily Planet Building in the *Superman* TV series, got blown to bits in the 1953 sci-fi thriller *War of the Worlds* and decorated the badge on the opening credits of *Dragnet*. In clear skies, you'll have great views from the wraparound Observation Deck. Call ahead for information on guided tours.

FREE Wells Fargo History
Museum MUSEUM
(Map p534; www.wellsfargohistory.com; 333 S Grand Ave; 🕑9am-5pm Mon-Fri) Continuing south

10 DOWNTOWN LA GLAMOUR BUILDINGS

In addition to Walt Disney Concert Hall and the Cathedral of Our Lady of the Angels, architecture buffs shouldn't leave Downtown without checking out some of the following gems.

» **Richard J Riordan Central Library** (1922; 630 W 5th St) Bertram Goodhue, inspired by the discovery of King Tut's tomb the same year, incorporated numerous Egyptian motifs. The Tom Bradley Wing is an eight-story glass atrium added in 1993 and named for a former mayor.

» **US Bank Tower** (1989; 633 W 5th St) The tallest building west of Chicago has 73 floors and juts 1017 feet up. Designed by Henry Cobb, an architect from the New York firm of IM Pei, the tower was attacked by an alien spaceship in the 1996 movie *Independence Day*.

» **Caltrans Building** (2004; 100 S Main St) Headquarters of District 7 of the California Department of Transportation. Santa Monica-based architect Thom Mayne won the 2005 Pritzker Prize, the Oscar of architecture, for this futuristic design. Neon stripes on the facade recall head- and tail-lights whizzing along a freeway, and the windows open or close depending on the outside temperature and angle of the sun.

» **One Bunker Hill** (1931; 601 W 5th St) The reliefs above the entrance to this 12-story art deco moderne office tower recall the building's former occupant, the Southern California Edison company, depicting energy, light and power. In the 40ft-high lobby are 17 types of marble, gold-leaf ceilings and a mural by Hugo Ballin, a set designer for Cecil B DeMille.

» **Millenium Biltmore Hotel** (1923; 515 S Olive St) Overlooking Pershing Square, this is one of LA's grandest hotels. Designed by the team that also created New York's Waldorf Astoria, it has hosted presidents, political conventions and eight Academy Awards ceremonies. It boasts carved and gilded ceilings, marble floors, grand staircases and styles from Renaissance to Baroque to Neoclassical.

» **Oviatt Building** (1928; 617 S Olive St) This art deco gem was conceived by the mildly eccentric James Oviatt, owner of a men's clothing store here (now Cicada restaurant). Oviatt fell in love with art deco on a visit to Paris and had carpets, draperies and fixtures shipped from France, including the purportedly largest shipment of etched decorative glass by René Lalique ever to cross the Atlantic.

» **Fine Arts Building** (1927; 811 W 7th St) This 12-story Walker & Eisen structure is a visual feast inside and out. The facade is awash in floral and animal ornamentation, and sculptures peer down from arcaded upstairs windows. The cathedral-like lobby is especially striking. Built in Spanish Renaissance style, it has a galleried mezzanine from which large sculptures representing the arts gaze down.

» **High School for the Visual and Performing Arts** (2008; aka High School No. 9; cnr N Grand Ave & W Cesar Chavez Blvd) The metal cladding on the exterior – by Austrian architecture firm Coop Himmelb(l)au – echoes the Walt Disney Concert Hall a few blocks away, as if to inspire the students. Look for a spiral ramp protruding skyward from the roof.

» **Historic Movie Theaters** Until eclipsed by Hollywood in the mid-1920s, Broadway was LA's entertainment hub, with a dozen-plus movie palaces in a riot of styles – beaux arts to East Indian to Spanish Gothic – on the National Register of Historic Places. Standouts include the 1931 **Los Angeles Theater** (Map p534; 615 S Broadway), where Charlie Chaplin's *City Lights* premiered, and the 1926 **Orpheum Theater** (Map p534; 842 S Broadway), which more recently has hosted *American Idol* auditions. See them on one of the excellent tours offered by the Los Angeles Conservancy (p555), or through its Last Remaining Seats film series of Hollywood classics on their big screens.

Downtown Los Angeles

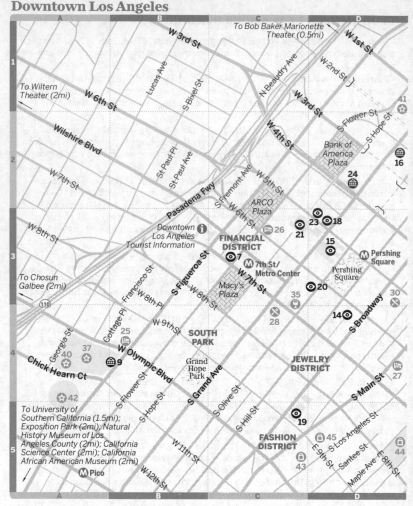

LOS ANGELES SIGHTS

along Grand Ave is this small but intriguing museum, which relives the Gold Rush era with an original Concord stagecoach, a 100oz gold nugget and a 19th-century bank office.

Dodger Stadium BASEBALL STADIUM
(Map p534; losangeles.dodgers.mlb.com; 1000 Elysian Park Ave; tour adult/child 4-14yr/senior $15/10/10; ⊗tours 10am & 11:30am except during day games) Just north of Chinatown sits this beloved, 56,000-seat baseball park, home of the Los Angeles Dodgers (see p569). Tours

(up to 90 minutes) visit the press box, dugout, field, Dugout Club and training center.

LITTLE TOKYO
Little Tokyo is a contemporary but attractive mix of Buddhist temples and Japanese shops and eateries, as you'd expect. There's also an increasingly lively **Arts District** drawing a young, adventurous crowd who live and work in makeshift studios in abandoned warehouses and support a growing number of restaurants nightspots. Stop into the **Little Tokyo Koban** (Map p534; ☎213-

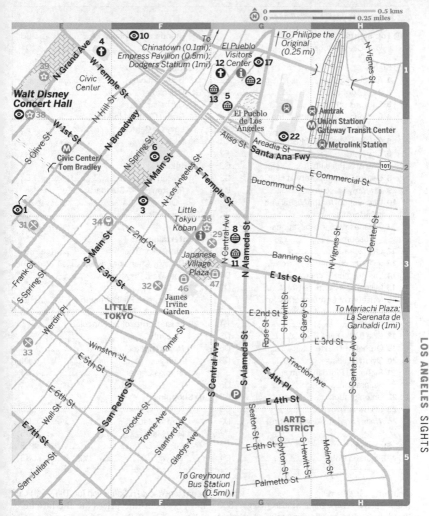

613-1911; 307 E 1st St; ⊘10am-6pm Mon-Sat) visitors center for maps and information.

Japanese American National Museum

MUSEUM

(Map p534; www.janm.org; 369 E 1st St; adult/seniors & students $9/5; ⊘11am-5pm Tue, Wed & Fri-Sun, to 8pm Thu) Brims with objects of work and worship, photographs, art and even a uniform worn by *Star Trek* actor (and Japanese-American) George Takei. Special focus is given to the painful chapter of the WWII internment camps.

SOUTH PARK

The southwestern corner of Downtown, South Park isn't a park but an emerging neighborhood, including Staples Center arena (p569), LA's Convention Center and LA Live, which includes a dozen restaurants, live-music venues, a 54-story hotel tower and the 7100-seat Nokia Theatre, home to the MTV Music Awards and *American Idol* finals. This is also where you'll find the Fashion District (see p571).

Parking is in private lots ($8 to $20). South Park is near the Metro Blue Line light-rail.

Downtown Los Angeles

Grammy Museum   MUSEUM
(Map p534; www.grammymuseum.org; 800 W Olympic Blvd; adult/child/senior & student $12.95/10.95/11.95; ⏱11:30am-7:30pm Mon-Fri, 10am-7:30pm Sat & Sun) The highlight of LA Live. Music lovers will get lost in interactive exhibits, which define, differentiate and link musical genres, while live footage strobes from all corners. You can glimpse GnR's bass drum, Lester Young's tenor, Yo Yo Ma's cello and Michael's glove. Interactive sound chambers allow you and your friends to try your hand at mixing and remixing, singing and rapping.

Downtown LA Flower Market   MARKET
(Map p534; www.laflowerdistrict.com; Wall St btwn 7th & 8th Sts; admission Mon-Fri $2, Sat $1; ⏱8am-

noon Mon, Wed & Fri, 6am-noon Tue, Thu & Sat) Cut flowers at cut-rate prices are the lure here, where a few dollars gets you armloads of Hawaiian ginger or sweet roses, a potted plant or elegant orchid. The market is busiest in the wee hours when florists stock up. Bring cash.

EXPOSITION PARK
A couple miles south of Downtown, family-friendly Exposition Park (off Map p534) started as an agricultural fairground in 1872 and now contains three fine museums, a lovely **Rose Garden** (admission free; ⏱9am-sunset mid-Mar–Dec) and the 1923 **Los Angeles Memorial Coliseum**, best known as venue for the 1932 and 1984 Summer Olympic Games. The **University of Southern California**

(USC; www.usc.edu) is just north of the museums. Famous alumni include George Lucas, John Wayne and Neil Armstrong.

DASH minibus 'F' (p573) and the Metro Expo light rail line serve South Park from Downtown. Parking lots start at around $6.

Natural History Museum of Los Angeles County   SCIENCE MUSEUM

(off Map p534; www.nhm.org; 900 Exposition Blvd; adult/child/senior & student $12/5/8; ☺9:30am-5pm; ⊛) Take a spin around the world and back in time at this popular museum, inside a baronial building corner (it stood in for Columbia University in the first *Spider-Man* movie). The Dino Hall was due to reopen as we went to press. Other crowd-pleasers include stuffed African elephants and the giant megamouth, one of the world's rarest sharks. Historical exhibits include prized Navajo textiles, baskets and jewelry in the Hall of Native American Cultures. The Gem & Mineral Hall, meanwhile, is a glittering spectacle with a walk-through gem tunnel and more gold than any other such collection in the US. Kids love the hands-on Discovery Center and the Insect Zoo with its tarantulas, hissing cockroaches and other creepy-crawlies.

FREE California Science Center   SCIENCE MUSEUM

(off Map p534; www.californiasciencecenter.org; 700 State Dr; ☺10am-5pm; ⊛) At this un-stuffy museum, experience a simulated earthquake, watch baby chicks hatch in an incubator, play virtual reality games, push buttons, switch lights and pull knobs. As we went to press, the museum was preparing to become the permanent home of the Space Shuttle Endeavour. Other flying machines include the 1902 *Wright Glider* and the Soviet-made *Sputnik*, the first human-made object to orbit the earth in 1957.

Of the three main exhibition areas, World of Life focuses mostly on the human body. You can 'hop on' a red blood cell for a computer fly-through of the circulatory system, ask Gertie how long your colon really is and meet Tess, a giant techno-doll billed as '50 feet of brains, beauty and biology.' The Science Center's IMAX theater (☎213-744-7400; adult/child/senior & student $8.25/5/6; ⊛) caps off an action-filled day.

Avoid weekday mornings during the school year, when the center typically crawls with school kids.

California African American Museum   CULTURAL MUSEUM

(off map p534; www.caamuseum.org; 600 State Dr; admission free; ☺10am-5pm Tue-Sat, 11am-5pm Sun) This acclaimed museum documents African and African American art and history, especially in California and other western states, further illuminated by an active lecture and performance schedule.

SOUTH LOS ANGELES

The area south of Exposition Park was long known as South Central, a name that quietly went away after the 1992 riots had their epicenter here. Gangs, drugs, poverty, crime and drive-by shootings are just a few of the negative images – not entirely undeserved – associated with this district. This is too bad because South Central (named for Central Ave, which runs through it) was once the proud and prosperous heart of LA's African American community. The upscale shops and restaurants of Leimert (luh-*murt*) Park Village reflect this heritage, particularly around the intersection of Degnan and 43rd Sts.

Watts Towers   MONUMENT

(www.wattstowers.org; 1727 E 107th St; tours adult/child/senior & teen $7/free/3; ☺tours every 30 mins 11am-3pm Thu & Fri, 10:30am-3pm Sat, 12:30-3pm Sun Oct-Jun, 10:30am-3pm Thu-Sat & 12:30-3pm Sun Jul-Sep; P) South LA's beacon of pride, the towers rank among the world's greatest monuments of folk art. Italian immigrant Simon Rodia spent 33 years (from 1921 to 1954) cobbling together this whimsical free-form sculpture from a motley assortment of found objects – from green 7-Up bottles to sea shells, rocks to pottery.

HOLLYWOOD, LOS FELIZ & SILVER LAKE

Aging movie stars know that a facelift can quickly pump up a drooping career, and the same has been done with the legendary Hollywood Blvd (Map p538), preened and spruced up in recent years. Though it still hasn't recaptured its Golden Age (1920s–1940s) glamour, much of its late-20th-century seediness is gone.

Historic movie palaces bask in restored glory, Metro Rail's Red Line makes access easy, some of LA's hottest bars and nightclubs have sprung up here, and even 'Oscar' has found a permanent home in the Kodak Theatre, part of the vast shopping and entertainment complex called Hollywood & Highland.

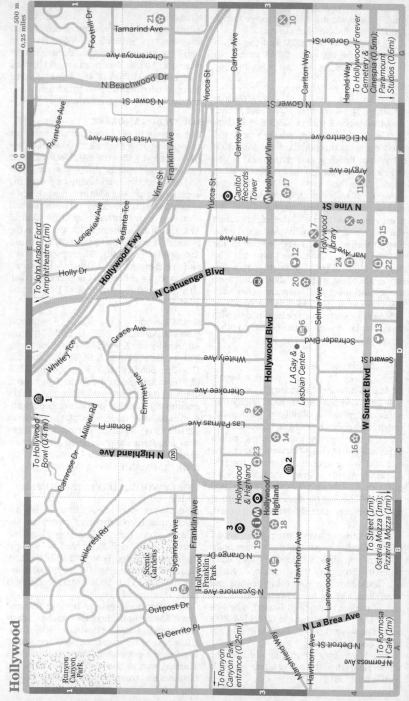

Hollywood

Hollywood

The most interesting mile runs between La Brea Ave and Vine St, along the **Hollywood Walk of Fame**, which honors more than 2000 celebrities with brass stars embedded in the sidewalk. For interesting historical tidbits about local landmarks, keep an eye out for the sign markers along here, or join a guided walking tour operated by Red Line Tours.

Following Hollywood Blvd east beyond Hwy 101 (Hollywood Fwy) takes you to the neighborhoods of **Los Feliz** (los *fee*-liss) and **Silver Lake**, both boho-chic enclaves with offbeat shopping, funky bars and a hopping cuisine scene.

The Metro Red Line serves central Hollywood (Hollywood/Highland and Hollywood/ Vine stations) and Los Feliz (Vermont/Sunset station) from Downtown LA and the San Fernando Valley. Pay-parking lots abound in the side streets. The Hollywood & Highland parking garage charges $2 for four hours with validation (no purchase necessary) from any merchant within the mall or the Hollywood Visitors Center (Map p538).

HOLLYWOOD BOULEVARD

Grauman's Chinese Theatre   CINEMA
(Map p538; 6925 Hollywood Blvd) Even the most jaded visitor may thrill in the Chinese Theater's famous forecourt at the heart of the Hollywood Walk of Fame, where generations of screen legends have left their imprints in cement: feet, hands, dreadlocks (Whoopi Goldberg), and even magic wands (the young *Harry Potter* stars). Actors dressed as Superman, Marilyn Monroe and the like pose for photos (for tips), and you may be offered free tickets to TV shows.

El Capitan Theatre   CINEMA
(Map p538; ☎323-467-7674; 6838 Hollywood Blvd) Flamboyant theatre hosts Disney Studios first-runs.

Egyptian Theatre   CINEMA
(Map p538; ☎323-466-3456; www.egyptiantheatre. com; 6712 Hollywood Blvd) Home of the non-profit American Cinematheque (p567).

Kodak Theatre   THEATER
(Map p538; www.kodaktheatre.com; adult/child & senior $15/10; ◎10:30am-4pm; closed irregularly) Real-life celebs sashay along the Kodak's red carpet for the Academy Awards – columns with names of Oscar-winning films line the entryway. Pricey 30-minute tours take you inside the auditorium, VIP room and past an actual Oscar statuette. Cirque du Soleil presents **Iris** (www.cirquedusoleil.com; tickets $43-253) here, a new film-themed performance. FYI, the first Academy Awards ceremony was held diagonally across the street in the 1927 Hollywood Roosevelt Hotel.

Hollywood Sign   LANDMARK
(Map p542) LA's most recognizable landmark first appeared atop its hillside perch in 1923 as an advertising gimmick for a real-estate development called Hollywood Land. Each letter is 50 feet tall and made of sheet metal. It's illegal to hike up to the sign, but there are many places where you can catch good views, including the Hollywood & Highland shopping and entertainment complex, Griffith Park and the top of Beachwood Dr.

BEHIND THE CURTAIN

Did you know it takes a week to shoot a half-hour sitcom? Or that you rarely see ceilings on TV because the space is filled with lights and lamps? You'll learn these and other fascinating nuggets about the world of film and TV production while touring a working studio. Action is slowest (and star-sighting potential lowest) during 'hiatus' (May to August). Reservations recommended; bring photo ID.

Paramount Studios (off Map p538; ☑323-956-1777; www.paramountstudios.com/special -events/tours.html; 5555 Melrose Ave, Hollywood; tours $45; ⊘Mon-Fri by reservation) The only studio in Hollywood proper runs two-hour tram tours of its historic lot. Group size is limited to eight per tram, leaving ample opportunity to pepper your guide with questions. No two tours are alike, and access to stages varies daily, but they might include the sets of *Dr Phil* or *Nip/Tuck*. Minimum age 12.

Sony Pictures Studios (☑310-244-868; www.sonypicturesstudiostours.com; 10202 W Washington Blvd, Culver City; tour $33; ⊘tours 9:30am, 10:30am, 1:30pm & 2:30pm Mon-Fri; ℗) Two-hour walking tours include possible visits to sound stages where *Men in Black*, *Spider-Man*, *Charlie's Angels* and other blockbusters were filmed. Munchkins hopped along the Yellow Brick Road in the *Wizard of Oz*, filmed when this was the venerable MGM studio. You might even pop in on the set of *Jeopardy!* Minimum age 12.

Warner Bros Studios (Map p542; ☑818-972-8687; www.wbstudiotour.com; 3400 Riverside Dr, Burbank; tours $45; ⊘8:30am-4pm Mon-Fri, extended hr Mar-Sep) This 2¼-hour, fun-yet-authentic look behind the scenes kicks off with a video of WB's greatest hits (*Rebel Without a Cause*, *Harry Potter*, etc) before you travel by mini-tram to sound stages, backlot sets and technical departments, including costumes and set building. The studio museum is a treasure trove of props and memorabilia, including Hogwarts' Sorting Hat. Tours leave roughly every half-hour. Minimum age eight. Parking $7.

Hollywood Museum MUSEUM
(Map p538; www.thehollywoodmuseum.com; 1660 N Highland Ave; adult/student/senior/child $15/12/12/5; ⊘10am-5pm Wed-Sun) The slightly musty museum is a 35,000-sq-ft shrine to the stars, crammed with kitsch, costumes, knickknacks and props from Charlie Chaplin to *Glee*.

Hollywood Bowl & Around AMPHITHEATER
(off Map p538; ☑323-850-2000; www.hollywoodbowl.com; 2301 N Highland Ave; ⊘concerts late Jun-Sep) Summer concerts at the Hollywood Bowl have been a great LA tradition since 1922. This 18,000-seat hillside amphitheater is the summer home of the LA Philharmonic, and is also host to big-name rock, jazz and blues acts. Many concertgoers come early to enjoy a pre-show picnic on the parklike grounds or in their seats (alcohol is allowed). For insight into the Bowl's storied history, visit the **Hollywood Bowl Museum** (off Map p538; www.hollywoodbowl.com/visit/museum.cfm; 2301 N Highland Ave; admission free; ⊘10am-8pm Tue-Sat, 4-7pm Sun mid-Jun–mid-Sep, 10am-5pm Tue-Fri mid-Sep– mid-Jun). The Bowl grounds are open to the public daytimes.

Hollywood Heritage Museum MUSEUM
(Map p538; www.hollywoodheritage.org; 2100 N Highland Ave; adult/child $7/free; ⊘noon-4pm Wed-Sun; ℗) Across from the Bowl, this museum is inside the horse barn used by the movie pioneer Cecil B DeMille in 1913 and 1914 to shoot *The Squaw Man,* Hollywood's first feature-length film. Inside are exhibits on early filmmaking, including costumes, projectors and cameras, as well as a replica of DeMille's office.

Griffith Park PARK
(Map p542; www.laparks.org/dos/parks/griffithpk; admission free; ⊘6am-10pm, trails close at dusk; ℗♿) America's largest urban park is five times the size of New York's Central Park. It embraces an outdoor theater, zoo, observatory, museum, antique trains, golf, tennis, playgrounds, bridle paths, 53 miles of hiking trails, Batman's caves and the Hollywood Sign. The **Ranger Station** (Map p542; 4730 Crystal Springs Dr) has maps.

Kids particularly love the 1926 **Griffith Park Merry-Go-Round** (Map p542; rides $1; ☺11am-5pm daily May-Sep, 11am-5pm Sat & Sun Oct-Apr; ♿), with beautifully carved and painted horses sporting real horse-hair tails and vintage railcars and steam locomotives of the **Travel Town Museum** (Map p542; 5200 W Zoo Dr; admission free; ☺10am-5pm Mon-Fri, to 6pm Sat & Sun; ♿). **Griffith Park & Southern Railroad** (Map p542; 4400 Crystal Springs Dr; tickets $2.50; ☺10am-4:30pm Mon-Fri, to 5pm Sat & Sun; ♿) is a miniature train chugging through a re-created old Western town and a Native American village.

Griffith Observatory   OBSERVATORY
(Map p542; www.griffithobservatory.org; 2800 Observatory Rd; admission free, planetarium shows adult/child/senior $7/3/5; ☺noon-10pm Tue-Fri, 10am-10pm Sat & Sun, closed occasional Tue; P♿) Above Los Feliz loom the iconic triple domes of this 1935 observatory, which boasts a super-techie planetarium and films in the Leonard Nimoy Event Horizon Theater. During clear night-time skies, you can often peer through the telescopes at heavenly bodies.

Los Angeles Zoo & Botanical Gardens   ZOO
(Map p542; www.lazoo.org; 5333 Zoo Dr; adult/child/senior $14/9/11; ☺10am-5pm; P♿) Make friends with 1100 finned, feathered and furry creatures, including in the Campo Gorilla Reserve and the Sea Cliffs, which replicate the California coast complete with harbor seals.

Museum of the American West   MUSEUM
(Map p542; www.autrynationalcenter.org; 4700 Western Heritage Way; adult/child/students & seniors $10/4/6, free 2nd Tue each month; ☺10am-4pm Tue-Fri, to 5pm Sat & Sun; P♿) Exhibits on the good, the bad and the ugly of America's westward expansion rope in even the most reluctant of cowpokes. Star exhibits include an original stagecoach, a Colt firearms collection and a nymph-festooned saloon. Its affiliated **Southwest Museum of the American Indian** (234 Museum Dr) is scheduled to reopen in 2013.

Hollyhock House   ARCHITECTURE
(1919; Map p544; www.hollyhockhouse.net; Barnsdall Art Park; adult/student/child $7/3/free; ☺tours hourly 12:30-3:30pm Wed-Sun; P) An early masterpiece by Frank Lloyd Wright, this house marks the famous architect's first attempt at creating an indoor-outdoor living space in harmony with LA's sunny climate, a style he later referred to as California Romanza. Admission is by tour only.

Hollywood Forever Cemetery   CEMETERY
(off Map p538; www.hollywoodforever.com; 6000 Santa Monica Blvd; ☺8am-5pm; P) Next to Paramount Studios, this cemetery is crowded with famous 'immortals,' including Rudolph Valentino, Tyrone Power, Jayne Mansfield and Cecil B DeMille. Pick up a map ($5) at the flower shop near the entrance. See p567 for details of **film screenings** here. No, really.

FREE 826 LA Time Travel Mart   GALLERY
(off map p544; www.826la.org; 1714 W Sunset Blvd; noon-8pm Mon-Fri, to 6pm Sat & Sun) At first glance, this is a convenience store stocked with products from the past and the future: whale oil (not really) and spice rubs (really), suction-cup clocks and the correct answer in a can ('That looks great on you!'). In reality, proceeds fund a center in the back room specializing in homework help and writing workshops, brainchild of author, screenwriter and McSweeney's founder, Dave Eggers.

WEST HOLLYWOOD
Rainbow flags fly proudly over Santa Monica Blvd. Celebs keep gossip rags happy by misbehaving at clubs on the fabled Sunset Strip. Welcome to the city of West Hollywood (WeHo), 1.9 sq miles of pure personality.

Boutiques on Robertson Blvd and Melrose Ave purvey the sassy and chic for Hollywood royalty, Santa Monica Blvd is gay central, WeHo's eastern precincts are filled with Russian speaking émigrés, and Sunset Blvd bursts with clubs, chichi hotels and views across LA. WeHo's also a hotbed of cutting-edge interior design, particularly along the **Avenues of Art and Design** around Beverly Blvd and Melrose Ave.

Pacific Design Center   DESIGN CENTER
(Map p546; www.pacificdesigncenter.com; 8687 Melrose Ave; ☺9am-5pm Mon-Fri) Some 130 galleries fill the monolithic blue and green 'whales' of the Cesar Pelli–designed Pacific Design Center (a red whale should open by 2012). Visitors are welcome to window-shop, though most sales are to the trade. There's a small offshoot of the **Museum of Contemporary Art** (Map p546, admission free). Parking is $6 per hour.

Griffith Park & Around

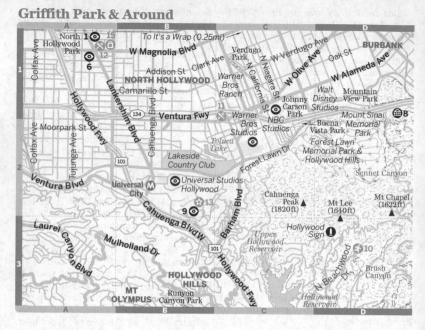

Schindler House   ARCHITECTURE
(Map p546; www.makcenter.org; 835 N Kings Rd; adult/senior & student $7/6, 4-6pm Fri free; ⏰11am-6pm Wed-Sun) A point of pilgrimage, which pioneering modernist architect Rudolph Schindler (1887–1953) made his home. It houses changing exhibits and lectures.

Parking lot rates vary widely. Use caution when parking on the street as parking is quite restricted and fervently enforced. WeHo is also served by the DASH bus.

Sunset Strip   NEIGHBORHOOD
The famed Sunset Strip – Sunset Blvd between Laurel Canyon Blvd and Doheny Dr – has been a favorite nighttime playground since the 1920s. The **Chateau Marmont** and clubs such as Ciro's (now the **Comedy Store**; p569), Mocambo and the Trocadero (both now defunct) were favorite hangouts for Hollywood high society, from Bogart to Bacall, Monroe to Sinatra. The 1960s saw the opening of **Whisky-a-Go-Go** (☎310-652-4202; 8901 W Sunset Blvd), America's first discotheque, the birthplace of go-go dancing and a launch pad for The Doors, who were the club's house band in 1966. Nearby is the **AN-dAZ** (Map p546; ☎323-656-1234; 8401 W Sunset Blvd), which, in its previous incarnation as the Hyatt Hotel, earned the moniker 'Riot House' during the 1970s, when it was the hotel of choice for raucous rock royalty such as Led Zeppelin. At one time, the band rented six floors and raced motorcycles in the hallways.

Today the strip is still nightlife central, although it's lost much of its cutting edge. It's a visual cacophony dominated by billboards and giant advertising banners draped across building facades. More recent places include the **House of Blues** (Map p557); the jet-set **Mondrian hotel** (Map p557); the **Sky Bar** (p566); and the **Viper Room** (Map p557), until recently owned by Johnny Depp, where Tommy Lee attacked a paparazzo and, in 1993, actor River Phoenix overdosed.

MID-CITY
Mid-City encompasses an amorphous area east of West Hollywood, south of Hollywood, west of Koreatown and north of I-10 (Santa Monica Fwy). A historic farmers market and a row of top-notch museums are its main attractions. There's plenty of street parking and validated parking at the farmers market and the adjacent Grove shopping mall. The main sights are served by DASH buses on the Fairfax route.

Los Angeles County Museum of Art   ART MUSEUM
(Map p546; www.lacma.org; 5905 Wilshire Blvd; adult/child under 17yr/student & senior $15/

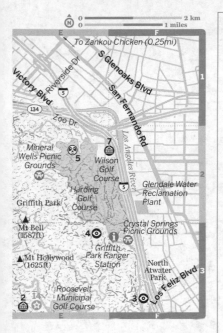

free/10; ◷noon-8pm Mon, Tue & Thu, noon-9pm Fri, 11am-8pm Sat & Sun) One of the country's top art museums and the largest in the western USA. The collection in the new Renzo Piano–designed **Broad Contemporary Art Museum** (B-CAM) includes seminal pieces by Jeff Koons, Roy Lichtenstein and Andy Warhol, and two gigantic works in rusted steel by Richard Serra.

Other LACMA pavilions brim with paintings, sculpture and decorative arts: Rembrandt, Cézanne and Magritte; ancient pottery from China, Turkey and Iran; photographs by Ansel Adams and Henri Cartier-Bresson; and a jewel box of a Japanese pavilion. There are often headline-grabbing touring exhibits. Parking is $10.

La Brea Tar Pits   HISTORIC SITE
Between 10,000 and 40,000 years ago, tarlike bubbling crude oil trapped saber-toothed cats, mammoths and other now-extinct Ice Age critters, which are still being excavated at La Brea Tar Pits. Check out their fossilized remains at the **Page Museum** (Map p546; www.tarpits.org; 5801 Wilshire Blvd; adult/child/senior & student $11/5/8, free first Tue each month; ◷9:30am-5pm; ⓟ). New fossils are being discovered all the time, and an active staff of archaeologists works behind glass. Parking is $7.

Petersen Automotive Museum   MUSEUM
(Map p546; www.petersen.org; 6060 Wilshire Blvd; adult/child/student/senior $10/3/5/8; ◷10am-6pm Tue-Sun; ⓟ) A four-story ode to the auto, the museum exhibits shiny vintage cars galore, plus a fun LA streetscape showing how the city's growth has been shaped by the automobile. Parking is $8.

BEVERLY HILLS & WESTSIDE
The mere mention of Beverly Hills conjures up images of fame and wealth, reinforced by film and TV. Opulent mansions flank manicured grounds on palm-lined avenues, especially north of **Sunset Blvd**, while legendary **Rodeo Drive** is three solid blocks of style for the Prada and Gucci brigade.

These days much of Beverly Hills' wealth is new money, brought here by Iranian émigrés who've been settling here since the fall of the Shah in the late 1970s. About 25% of the 35,000 residents are of Iranian descent, spawning the nickname 'Tehrangeles.'

Several city-owned parking lots and garages offer up to two hours free parking.

West of Beverly Hills to the Santa Monica city line, the well-to-do LA neighborhoods of

Brentwood, Bel Air, Westwood and the separate city Culver City are collectively referred to as the Westside.

Getty Center ART MUSEUM
(off Map p550; www.getty.edu; 1200 Getty Center Dr; admission free; ⊙10am-5:30pm Sun & Tue-Thu, to 9pm Fri & Sat) Triple delights: stellar art collection (Renaissance to David Hockney), Richard Meier's soaring architecture and Robert Irwin's ever-evolving gardens. On clear days, add breathtaking views of the city and ocean to the list. Visit in the late afternoon after the crowds have thinned. See also Getty Villa (p547). Parking is $15, or Metro bus 761 stops here.

Paley Center for Media MUSEUM
(www.paleycenter.org; 465 N Beverly Dr; suggested donation adult/child/senior/student $10/5/8/8; ⊙noon-5pm Wed-Sun) TV and radio addicts can indulge their passion at this mind-boggling archive of TV and radio broadcasts

from 1918 through the internet age. Pick your faves, grab a seat at a private console and enjoy. There's an active program of lectures and screenings. It's just south of Little Santa Monica Blvd.

Museum of Tolerance
MUSEUM
(www.museumoftolerance.com; 9786 W Pico Blvd; adult/child/student & senior $15/12/11; ⊙10am-5pm Mon-Thu, to 3:30pm Fri, 11am-5pm Sun; P⊕) This museum uses interactive technology to make visitors confront racism and bigotry. There's a particular focus on the Holocaust, including Nazi-era artifacts and letters by Anne Frank. A history wall celebrates diversity, exposes intolerance and champions rights in America. Reservations recommended.

FREE Annenberg Space for Photography
MUSEUM
(www.annenbergspaceforphotography.org; 2000 Ave of the Stars, No 10; admission free; ⊙11am-6pm Wed-Sun) This fine museum shows special exhibits in a camera-shaped building just west of Beverly Hills, in the skyscraper village known as Century City. Parking is $3.50 from Wednesday to Friday, or $1 on Saturday and Sunday or after 4:30pm daily.

Museum of Jurassic Technology
MUSEUM
(www.mjt.org; 9341 Venice Blvd, Culver City; suggested donation adult/student & senior/under 12yr $5/3/free; ⊙2-8pm Thu, noon-6pm Fri-Sun) It has nothing to do with dinosaurs and even less with technology. Instead, madness nibbles at your synapses as you try to read meaning into displays about Cameroonian stink ants, a tribute to trailer parks or a sculpture of the Pope squished into the eye of a needle. It may all be a mind-bending spoof. Or not.

University of California, Los Angeles
UNIVERSITY
(Map p550; ☑campus tour reservations 310-825-8764; www.ucla.edu; 405 Hilgard Ave) Westwood is practically synonymous with UCLA, alma mater of Francis Ford Coppola, James Dean, Jim Morrison and multiple Nobel Prize laureates. Campus parking: $11 per day.

Excellent, university-run museums include the Hammer Museum (Map p550; www.hammer.ucla.edu; 10899 Wilshire Blvd; adult/child/senior $10/free/5, free Thu; ⊙11am-7pm Tue, Wed, Fri & Sat, to 9pm Thu, to 5pm Sun) with cutting-edge contemporary art exhibits and a court-yard cafe (Hammer parking is $3), and the Fowler Museum of Cultural History (Map p550; www.fowler.ucla.edu; admission free; ⊙noon-5pm Wed & Fri-Sun, to 8pm Thu) presenting a rich variety of arts, crafts and artifacts from non-Western cultures.

Gardens include the sprawling Franklin D Murphy Sculpture Garden (Map p550), with dozens of works by Rodin, Moore, Calder and other American and European artists, and tranquil Mildred E Mathias Botanical Garden (Map p550).

Westwood Village Memorial Park
CEMETERY
(Map p550; 1218 Glendon Ave, Westwood; admission free; ⊙8am-5pm) Tucked among Westwood's high-rises, this postage-stamp-sized park is packed with such famous 6-feet-under residents as Marilyn Monroe, Burt Lancaster and Rodney Dangerfield.

Sawtelle Blvd
NEIGHBOURHOOD
Can't make it all the way to Little Tokyo? The smaller Japanese neighborhood around Sawtelle Blvd, between Olympic and Santa Monica Blvds and just west of I-405, is sometimes called Little Osaka, after Japan's second city. It's easy to spend an hour or two browsing shops selling *manga*, Japanese trinkets and housewares, going 'hmm?' in the groceries and, of course, enjoying the restaurants. The largest concentration is within a few blocks north of Olympic Blvd.

Skirball Cultural Center
MUSEUM
(☑tickets 877-722-4849; www.skirball.org; 2701 N Sepulveda Blvd; adult/child 2-12yr/student/senior $10/5/7/7, Thu free; ⊙noon-5pm Tue, Wed & Fri, to 9pm Thu, 10am-5pm Sat & Sun, closed major Jewish holidays; P⊕) This museum in the Sepulveda Pass beyond the Getty Center has two main attractions. The preschool set can climb the gigantic wooden Noah's Ark by noted architect Moshe Safdie, an indoor playground of imaginative creatures made from car mats, couch springs, metal strainers and other recycled items. Entry to Noah's Ark is by timed tickets, which also cover museum admission; advance reservations are recommended. For grown-ups, the permanent exhibit is an engaging view of 4000 years of history, traditions, trials and triumphs of the Jewish people, including replicas of a mosaic floor from an ancient Galilee synagogue and Hitler's racist rant *Mein Kampf.*

West Hollywood & Mid-City

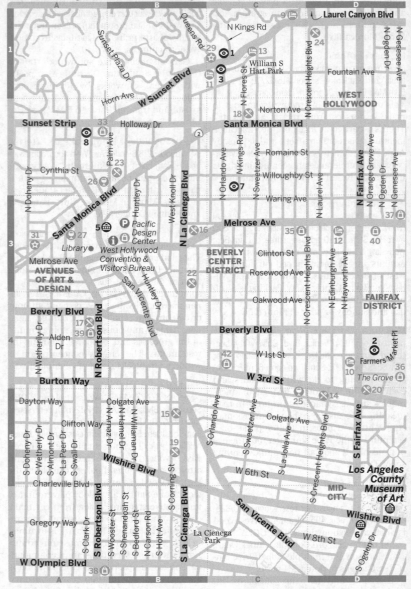

MALIBU

Malibu has been synonymous with celebrities since the early 1930s. Clara Bow and Barbara Stanwyck were the first to stake out their turf in what became known as the **Malibu Colony** and the earliest Hollywood elite to Barbra and Leo have lived here ever since.

Along Malibu's spectacular 27-mile stretch of the Pacific Coast Hwy, where the Santa Monica Mountains plunge into the ocean, are some fine beaches, including **Las**

but you'll find the greatest concentration of restaurants and shops near the century-old **Malibu Pier**. The most likely star-spotting venue is the **Malibu Country Mart shopping center** (3835 Cross Creek Rd).

Getty Villa
ART MUSEUM

(www.getty.edu; 17985 Pacific Coast Hwy; admission free; ☺10am-5pm Wed-Mon; Ⓟ) Malibu's cultural star – a replica Roman villa that's a fantastic showcase of Greek, Roman and Etruscan antiquities. Admission is by timed ticket (no walk-ins). See also the Getty Center. Parking is $15.

SANTA MONICA

Santa Monica is the belle by the beach, mixing urban cool with a laid-back vibe.

Tourists, teens and street performers make car-free, chain-store-lined **Third Street Promenade** (Map p552) the most action-packed zone. For more local flavor, shop celeb-favored **Montana Avenue** or down-home **Main Street** (Map p552), backbone of the neighborhood once nicknamed 'Dogtown' as birthplace of skateboard culture. Rent bikes or in-line skates from many outlets along the beach.

There's free two hour parking in public garages on 2nd and 4th Sts ($3 flat rate after 6pm), and most lines of Santa Monica's Big Blue Bus converge around the Promenade.

Santa Monica Pier
AMUSEMENT PARK

(Map p552; www.santamonicapier.org; admission free, unlimited rides under/over age 7 $16/22; ☺24hr; ⓐ) Kids love the venerable 1908 pier, where attractions include a quaint 1922 carousel, a tiny aquarium with touch tanks and the **Pacific Park** (www.pacpark. com) amusement park crowned by a solar-powered Ferris wheel.

Bergamot Station Arts Center
ART GALLERIES & MUSEUM

(2525 Michigan Ave; ☺10am-6pm Tue-Sat; Ⓟ) Art fans gravitate inland toward this avant-garde center, a former trolley stop that now houses 35 galleries and the progressive **Santa Monica Museum of Art** (www.smmoa.org; 2525 Michigan Ave; suggested donation $5; ☺11am-6pm Tue-Sat).

VENICE

Venice was created in 1905 by eccentric tobacco heir Abbot Kinney as an amusement park, called 'Venice of America,' complete with Italian *gondolieri* who poled visitors around canals. Most of the waterways have

Tunas, **Point Dume**, **Zuma** and the world-famous surfing spot **Surfrider**. Rising behind Malibu is **Malibu Creek State Park**, part of the Santa Monica Mountains National Recreation Area and laced with hiking trails (see p553). Malibu has no real center,

West Hollywood & Mid-City

since been paved over, but those that remain are flanked by flower-festooned villas, easily accessed from either Venice or Washington Blvds.

The hippest Westside strip is funky, sophisticated **Abbot Kinney Boulevard** (Map p552), a palm-lined mile of restaurants, yoga studios, art galleries and eclectic shops selling mid-century furniture and handmade fashions.

There's street parking around Abbot Kinney Blvd, and parking lots ($6 to $15) on the beach.

SOUTH BAY & PALOS VERDES

South of LAX, Santa Monica Bay is lined by a trio of all-American beach towns – **Manhattan Beach, Hermosa Beach** and **Redondo Beach** – with a distinctive laid-back vibe. Pricey, if not lavish, homes come all the way down to the gorgeous white beach, which is the prime attraction here and paralleled by the **South Bay Bicycle Trail** (p553).

The beaches run into the **Palos Verdes Peninsula**, a rocky precipice that's home to some of the richest and most exclusive communities in the LA area. A drive along Palos Verdes Dr takes you along some spectacular rugged coastline with sublime views of the ocean and Catalina Island.

Wayfarers Chapel   CHURCH
(www.wayfarerschapel.org; 5755 Palos Verdes Dr S; ⊙8am-5pm) Enchanting modernist hillside structure built in 1949 and surrounded by mature redwood trees and gardens. The work of Lloyd Wright (Frank's son), it is almost entirely made of glass and is one of LA's most popular spots for weddings.

SAN PEDRO

While other LA beachside communities primp, tempt and put on airs, San Pedro (*pee*-droh) feels like what it is: a working port, albeit in the shadow of ritzy Palos Verdes. It began as a lumber port and grew on an influx of Croatian, Italian, Greek, Japanese and Scandinavian fishers. Today their descendants populate this 90,000-strong enclave, part of the largest container port in North America (nearby Long Beach is the second largest).

San Pedro's symbol is the 1874 **Point Fermin Lighthouse** (www.pointferminlighthouse.org; 807 W Paseo del Mar; admission free, donations welcome; ☺tours 1pm, 2pm, 3pm Tue-Sun), unusually built of wood, like a Victorian home. The impressive WWII-era **Fort MacArthur**(www.ftmac.org; 3601 S Gaffey St; suggested donation adult/child $3/1; ☺noon-5pm Tue, Thu, Sat & Sun) displays military history through artifacts and weaponry inside a maze-like battery built into the cliffs.

If you enjoy clambering around old ships, head a mile north to the **SS Lane Victory** (www.lanevictory.org; Berth 94; adult/child $3/1; ☺9am-3pm), a museum vessel that sailed the seven seas from 1945 to 1971. Self-guided tours take in the engine room and the cargo holds. See the website for directions.

Further south, you'll be besieged by shrieking gulls and excited children at **Ports O'Call Village** (Berth 77; admission free; ☺11am-10pm). Skip the trinket stores and fill up on fresh fish and shrimp at the raucous **San Pedro Fish Market & Restaurant**. Afterwards, hop on a port cruise or join a whale-watching trip (January to March).

Pedro's surfer-sophisticate **Arts District** (6th St, btwn Pacific Ave & Palos Verdes St) perks with coffee shops, art galleries, army-surplus stores and restaurants, many in art deco buildings, including the fabulous 1931 **Warner Grand Theatre** (www.warnergrand.org; 478 W 6th St).

San Pedro is most easily reached by car. Take the 110 Fwy from either Downtown LA or the 405 Fwy.

LONG BEACH

While San Pedro still retains some of its port city edge, Long Beach's has worn smooth in its humming downtown and restyled waterfront. Pine Ave is chockablock with restaurants and clubs popular with everyone from coiffed conventioneers to the testosterone-fuelled frat pack.

The Metro Blue Line (55 minutes) connects Long Beach with Downtown LA, and Passport minibuses (www.lbtransit.org) shuttle you around the major sights for free ($1.25 elsewhere in town).

Queen Mary OCEAN LINER
(www.queenmary.com; 1126 Queens Hwy; adult/child/senior from $25/13/22; ☺10am-6pm) Long Beach's 'flagship' is this grand (and supposedly haunted!) British ocean liner, permanently moored here. Larger and fancier than the *Titanic,* it transported royals, dignitaries, immigrants and troops during its 1001 Atlantic crossings between 1936 and 1964. Parking is $12.

Aquarium of the Pacific AQUARIUM
(www.aquariumofpacific.org; 100 Aquarium Way; adult/child/senior $25/13/22; ☺9am-6pm; ●) Kids will probably have a better time here a high-tech romp through an underwater world in which sharks dart, jellyfish dance and sea lions frolic. Imagine the thrill of petting a shark! Parking is $8 to $15. *Queen Mary* and aquarium combination tickets cost $36/20 for adult/child three to 11 years.

Museum of Latin American Art ART MUSEUM
(www.molaa.org; 628 Alamitos Ave; adult/child/student & senior $9/free/6, Sun free; ☺11am-5pm Wed-Sun; ●) The only museum in the western USA specializing in contemporary art from south of the border. The permanent collection highlights spirituality and landscapes, and special exhibits are first-rate.

Gondola Getaway BOAT RIDES
(www.gondo.net; 5437 E Ocean Blvd; per couple $85; ☺11am-11pm) About three miles east of

YOUR 15 MINUTES OF FAME

Come on, haven't you always dreamed of seeing your silly mug on TV? Well, LA has a way of making dreams come true, but you have to do your homework before coming to town. Here are some leads to get you started.

Sitcoms and game shows usually tape between August and March before live audiences. To nab free tickets, check with **Audiences Unlimited** (☎818-260-0041; www.tvtickets.com). For tickets to the *Tonight Show* at **NBC Studios** (Map p542; 3000 W Alameda Ave, Burbank), check www.nbc.com/nbc/footer/Tickets.shtml.

Although many game shows tape in LA, the chances of becoming a contestant are greatest on *The Price is Right*, at **CBS Television City** (Map p546; www.cbs.com/daytime/price; 7800 Beverly Blvd, Mid-City).

Bel Air & Westside

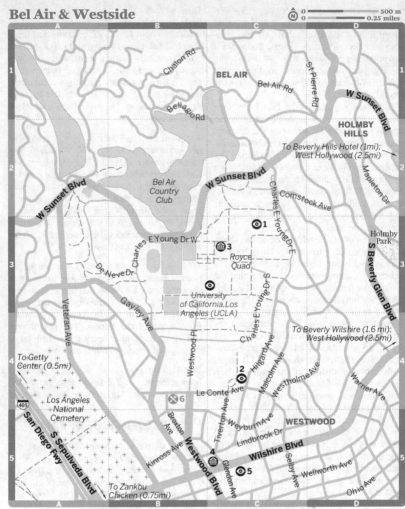

Downtown Long Beach, the upscale neighborhood of canal-laced Naples can be explored via hour-long cruises aboard authentic gondolas.

SAN FERNANDO VALLEY

The sprawling grid of suburbia known simply as 'the Valley' is home to most of the major movie studios, which makes it prime hunting grounds for 'Industry' fans. It's also the world capital of the porn movie industry. An arts district in North Hollywood (NoHo) has given the Valley a hip, artsy side.

Universal Studios Hollywood   THEME PARK
(Map p542; www.universalstudioshollywood.com; 100 Universal City Plaza; admission over/under 48in $77/69; ⊘open daily, hours vary; ⛎) One of the world's oldest and largest continuously operating movie studios, Universal first opened to the public in 1915, when studio head Carl Laemmle invited visitors at a quaint 25¢ each (including a boxed lunch) to watch silent films being made.

Your chances of seeing an actual movie shoot are approximately nil at Universal's current theme park incarnation, yet generations of visitors have had a ball here. Start with the 45-minute narrated **Studio Tour** aboard a giant, multicar tram that takes you past working soundstages and outdoor sets such as *Desperate Housewives*. Also prepare to survive a shark attack à la *Jaws* and an 8.3-magnitude earthquake. It's hokey but fun.

Among the dozens of other attractions, **King Kong in 3-D** scares the living daylights, the **Simpsons Ride** is a motion-simulated romp 'designed' by Krusty the Klown, and you can splash down among the dinos of **Jurassic Park**, while **Special Effects Stages** illuminate the craft of movie-making. **Water World** may have bombed as a movie, but the live action show based on it is a runaway hit, with stunts including giant fireballs and a crash-landing seaplane. Note: the single-digit set may be too short or too easily spooked for many attractions.

Allow a full day, especially in summer, as lines can easily take 45 minutes for top attractions. To beat the crowds, invest in the Front of Line Pass ($149).

The adjacent **Universal City Walk** is an unabashedly commercial (yet also entertaining) fantasy promenade of restaurants, shops, bars and entertainment venues. Get your hand stamped if you'd like to return to the park.

Parking is $12, or arrive via Metro Red Line.

NoHo Arts District   NEIGHBORHOOD
(www.nohoartsdistrict.com) At the end of the Metro Red Line, **North Hollywood** (NoHo) was a down-on-its-heels neighborhood of artists, but thanks to a redevelopment effort it now boasts some 20 stage theaters in 1 square mile and a burgeoning community of art galleries, restaurants, gyms and vintage clothing stores around them. Most of the theaters are 'Equity waiver houses' – 99 seats or fewer – where members of the Actors' Equity union (some quite famous) can perform at below regular wages, for example to showcase work or talent before heading to larger venues.

The Hall of Fame Plaza at the **Academy of Television Arts & Sciences** (Map p542; ☎818-754-2000; www.emmys.tv; 5200 Lankershim Blvd, North Hollywood; admission free) bursts with busts and life-size bronzes of TV legends (Johnny Carson, Bill Cosby, Lucille Ball et al) and a giant, gleaming Emmy award. **Millennium Dance Complex** (Map p542; www.millenniumdancecomplex.com; 5113 Lankershim Blvd, North Hollywood; classes from $15) trains many of the world's top hip-hop dancers and is open to the public. Vintage clothing stores (many with celebrity clients) line Magnolia Blvd east of Lankershim Blvd.

NoHo is best visited late afternoon through early evening, Thursday through Sunday, when the streets are buzzing with activity around the theaters.

PASADENA

Resting below the lofty San Gabriel Mountains, Pasadena is a genteel city with old-time mansions, superb Arts and Crafts architecture and fine-art museums. Every New Year's Day, it is thrust into the national spotlight during the **Rose Parade**.

The main fun zone is **Old Town Pasadena**, a bustling 20-block shopping and entertainment district in handsomely restored historic Spanish colonial buildings along Colorado Blvd, west of Arroyo Pkwy. Pick up information at the **Pasadena Convention & Visitors Bureau** (☎626-795-9311, 800-307-7977; www.pasadenacal.com; 171 S Los Robles Ave; ◷8am-5pm Mon-Fri, 10am-4pm Sat). Outside the town center is the **California Institute of Technology** (Caltech; www.caltech.edu; 551 S Hill Ave), one of the world's leading scientific universities and operator of the **Jet Propulsion Laboratory** (JPL; www.jpl.nasa.gov), NASA's main center for robotic exploration of the solar system.

Pasadena is served by the Metro Gold Line from Downtown LA. Pasadena ARTS buses (fare 50¢) plough around the city on seven different routes.

TOP CHOICE Huntington Library MUSEUM, GARDENS
(www.huntington.org; 1151 Oxford Rd; adult/child
$15/6 Tue-Fri, $20/6 Sat & Sun; ⊙10:30am-
4:30pm Tue-Sun Jun-Aug, noon-4:30pm Tue-Fri,
plus 10:30am-4:30pm Sat & Sun, Sep-May; P) LA's
biggest understatement does have a library
of rare books, including a Gutenberg Bible,
but it's the collection of great British and
French art (most famously Thomas Gains-
borough's *Blue Boy*) and exquisite gardens
that make it special. The Rose Garden boasts
more than 1200 varieties (and a lovely high
tea; reserve ahead, adult/child $28/15), the
Desert Garden has a Seussian quality, and
the Chinese garden has a small lake crossed
by a stone bridge.

Norton Simon Museum ART MUSEUM
(www.nortonsimon.org; 411 W Colorado Blvd; adult/
child & student/senior $10/free/5; ⊙noon-6pm
Wed-Thu & Sat-Mon, to 9pm Fri; P) Stroll west
and you'll see Rodin's *The Thinker,* a mere
overture to the full symphony of European
art at this museum. Don't skip the basement, with fabulous Indian and Southeast
Asian sculpture.

Gamble House ARCHITECTURE
(www.gamblehouse.org; 4 Westmoreland Pl; adult/
child/student & senior $10/free/7; ⊙admission by
tour only noon-3pm Thu-Sun; P) A masterpiece
of California craftsman architecture, this
1908 house by Charles and Henry Greene
was Doc Brown's home in the movie *Back to
the Future.* Admission is by one-hour guided
tour.

Pacific Asia Museum ART MUSEUM
(www.pacificasiamuseum.org; 46 N Los Robles
Ave; adult/student & senior $9/7; ⊙10am-6pm
Wed-Sun; P) This re-created Chinese palace
houses nine galleries, which rotate a stellar collection of ancient and contemporary
art and artifacts from Asia and the Pacific
Islands: Himalayan Buddhas to Chinese
porcelain and Japanese costumes.

**Pasadena Museum of
California Art** ART MUSEUM
(www.pmcaonline.org; 490 E Union St; adult/stu-
dent & senior/child $7/5/free, 1st Fri of month free;
⊙noon-5pm Wed-Sun; P) A progressive gallery
dedicated to art, architecture and design created by California artists since 1850. Shows
change every few months. Also swing by the
Kosmic Kavern, a former garage done over
by spray-mural pop artist Kenny Scharf.

Santa Monica & Venice Beach

Santa Monica & Venice Beach

Rose Bowl & Brookside Park   STADIUM
(www.rosebowlstadium.com; 1001 Rose Bowl Dr)
One of LA's most venerable landmarks, the 1922 Rose Bowl Stadium can seat up to 93,000 spectators, and every New Year's hosts the famed Rose Bowl Game between two top-ranked college football teams. At other times, concerts, special events and the huge monthly **Rose Bowl Flea Market** (p570) bring in the crowds.

The Rose Bowl is surrounded by **Brookside Park**, a broadening of the Arroyo Seco, a now-dry riverbed that runs from the San Gabriel Mountains to Downtown LA. It's a nice spot for hiking, cycling and picnicking. South of the stadium is the **Kidspace Children's Museum** (p554).

🏃 Activities

Cycling & In-line Skating

Anyone who's ever watched tourism footage of LA (or the opening of *Three's Company*) knows about skating or riding on the **South Bay Bicycle Trail**. This paved path parallels the beach for 22 miles, from just north of Santa Monica to the South Bay, with a detour around the yacht harbor at Marina del Rey. Mountain-bikers will find the **Santa Monica Mountains** (Map p574)a suitably challenging playground. You'll find lots of good information at www.labikepaths.com.

There are numerous bike-rental shops, especially along the beaches. Prices range from about $6 to $10 per hour and $10 to $30 per day (more for high-tech mountain bikes).

Perry's Cafe & Rentals   BICYCLE RENTALS
(Map p552; ☎310-939-0000; www.perryscafe.com; Ocean Front Walk; bikes per hr/day $10/25; ☺9:30am-5:30pm) Several locations on the bike path. They also rent body boards ($8/17 per hour/day). Cash only.

Hiking

Trails surprisingly close to the city provide instant getaways from the nation's second-largest metropolis.

For a quick ramble, head to **Griffith Park** (Map p542) or **Runyon Canyon** (Map p542; www.runyon-canyon.com), both just a hop, skip and jump from frenzied Hollywood Blvd. The latter is a favorite playground of hip and fitness-obsessed locals and their dogs, which roam mostly off-leash. You'll have fine views of the Hollywood Sign, the city and, on clear days, all the way to the beach. Runyon's southern trailhead is at the end of Fuller St, off Franklin Ave.

Runyon Canyon is on the eastern edge of the 150,000-acre **Santa Monica Mountains National Recreation Area** (Map p574; ☎805-370-2301; www.nps.gov/samo). This hilly, tree- and chaparral-covered park follows the outline of Santa Monica Bay from just north of Santa Monica all the way north across the Ventura County line to Point

VENICE BOARDWALK

Freak show, human zoo and wacky carnival, the **Venice Boardwalk** (Ocean Front Walk; Map p552) is an essential LA experience. This cauldron of counterculture is the place to get your hair braided or a *qi gong* back massage, or pick up cheap sunglasses or a woven bracelet. Encounters with bodybuilders, hoop dreamers, a Speedo-clad snake charmer or an in-line-skating Sikh minstrel are pretty much guaranteed, especially on hot summer afternoons. Alas, the vibe gets a bit creepy after dark.

Mugu. **Will Rogers State Historic Park**, **Topanga State Park** and **Malibu Creek State Park** are popular hikes here. The latter has a great trail leading to the set of the hit TV series *M*A*S*H*, where an old Jeep and other leftover relics rust serenely in the sunshine. The trailhead is in the park's main parking lot on Malibu Canyon Rd, which is called Las Virgenes Rd if coming from Hwy 101 (Hollywood Fwy). Parking is $8. For more ideas, consult the Santa Monica Mountains Conservancy (http://smmc.ca.gov).

Horseback Riding

Leave the urban sprawl behind on the forested bridle trails of Griffith Park or Topanga Canyon. All rides are accompanied by an experienced equestrian wrangler. Rates vary, and a 20% tip is customary.

Los Angeles Horseback Riding HORSEBACK RIDING
(☎818-591-2032; www.losangeleshorsebackriding.com; 2661 Old Topanga Canyon Rd, Topanga Canyon) Sunset, day and full-moon rides in the Santa Monica Mountains with fabulous views all around. Reservations required.

Sunset Ranch Hollywood HORSEBACK RIDING
(Map p542; ☎323-469-5450; www.sunsetranchhollywood.com; 3400 N Beachwood Dr, Hollywood) Guided tours, including popular Friday-night dinner rides.

Swimming & Surfing

LA pretty much defines beach culture, yet be prepared: the Pacific is generally pretty chilly; in colder months you'll definitely want a wet suit. Water temperatures peak at about 70°F in August and September. Water quality varies; for updated conditions check the 'Beach Report Card' at www.healthebay.org.

For a list of LA's top beaches, see p528.

Surfing novices can expect to pay up to $120 for an up to two-hour private lesson or $65 to $75 for a group lesson, including board and wet suit. Contact the following surfing schools for details:

Learn to Surf LA SURF SCHOOL
(www.learntosurfla.com)

Malibu Long Boards SURF SCHOOL
(www.malibulongboards.com)

Surf Academy SURF SCHOOL
(www.surfacademy.org)

Los Angeles for Children

Keeping the rug rats happy is child's play in LA.

The sprawling Los Angeles Zoo (p541) in family-friendly Griffith Park is a sure bet. Dino fans dig the Page Museum at the La Brea Tar Pits (p543) and Natural History Museum (p537), while budding scientists love the California Science Center (p537) next door. For live sea creatures, head to the Aquarium of the Pacific (p549); teens might get a kick out of the ghost tours of the *Queen Mary* (p549). Special mention goes to Noah's Ark at the Skirball Cultural Center (p545).

Among LA's amusement parks, Santa Monica Pier (p547) is meant for kids of all ages. Activities for younger children are more limited at Universal Studios Hollywood (p550). See the Orange County chapter for Disneyland and Knott's Berry Farm (p593).

Kidspace MUSEUM
(www.kidspacemuseum.org; 480 N Arroyo Blvd, Pasadena; admission $8, ☺9:30am-5pm Mon-Fri, 10am-5pm Sat & Sun; ℗☷) Hands-on exhibits, outdoor learning areas and gardens lure the single-digit set. It's best after 1pm, when the field-trip crowd has left.

Bob Baker Marionette Theater PUPPET THEATER
(off Map p534; www.bobbakermarionettes.com; 1345 W 1st St, near Downtown; admission $15, reservations required; ☺10:30am Tue-Fri, 2:30pm Sat & Sun; ℗☷) Adorable singing and dancing marionettes have enthralled generations of wee Angelenos.

☞ Tours

Esotouric HISTORY, LITERATURE
(☏323-223-2767; www.esotouric.com; bus tours $58) Hip, offbeat, insightful and entertaining walking and bus tours themed around literary lions (Chandler to Bukowski), famous crime sites (Black Dahlia) and historic neighborhoods.

Los Angeles Conservancy ARCHITECTURE, WALKING
(☏213-623-2489; www.laconservancy.org; tours $10) Architectural walking tours, mostly of Downtown LA. Check the website for self-guided tours.

Melting Pot Tours CULINARY, WALKING
(☏800-979-3370; www.meltingpottours.com; tours from $58; ⊙Wed-Sun) Snack your way through the Original Farmers Market and the aromatic alleyways of Old Town Pasadena.

Six Taste CULINARY, WALKING
(☏888-313-0936; www.sixtaste.com; tours $55-65) Walking tours of restaurants in LA neighborhoods, including Downtown, Little Tokyo, Chinatown, Thai Town and Santa Monica.

Out & About GAY, LESBIAN
(www.outandabout-tours.com; tours $60; ⊙Sat & Sun) Enthusiastic guides show landmarks of LA's gay and lesbian history – there's a lot more than you think!

Red Line Tours WALKING, BUS
(☏323-402-1074; www.redlinetours.com; tours from $25) 'Edutaining' walking tours of Hollywood and Downtown using headsets that cut out traffic noise.

Starline Tours BUS
(☏323-463-333, 800-959-3131; www.starlinetours.com; tours from $39) Narrated bus tours of the city, stars' homes and theme parks.

Bikes & Hikes LA CYCLING
(☏323-796-8555; www.bikesandhikesla.com; cycling tours from $44-158) Tours of Hollywood, celebrity homes and the signature, six-hour 'LA in One Day' tour ($158) from WeHo to the beaches.

✹ Festivals & Events

In addition to the following annual events, monthly street fairs include the gallery and shop open houses and food truck meetups of **Downtown LA Art Walk** (www.downtownartwalk.com; ⊙2nd Thu each month) and **First Fridays** (⊙1st Fri each month) on Abbot Kinney Blvd in Venice.

Tournament of Roses PARADE
(☏626-449-4100; www.tournamentofroses.com) New Year's Day cavalcade of flower-festooned floats along Pasadena's Colorado Blvd, followed by the Rose Bowl football game.

Toyota Grand Prix of Long Beach AUTO RACE
(☏888-827-7333; www.longbeachgp.com) Week-long auto-racing spectacle in mid-April drawing world-class drivers.

Fiesta Broadway STREET FAIR
(☏310-914-0015; www.fiestabroadway.la) Mexican-themed fair along historic Broadway in Downtown, with performances by Latino stars. Last Sunday in April.

West Hollywood Halloween Carnival STREET FAIR
(☏323-848-6400; www.visitwesthollywood.com) Eccentric, and often NC-17-rated, costumes fill Santa Monica Blvd, on October 31.

🛏 Sleeping

For seaside life, base yourself in Santa Monica, Venice or Long Beach; Long Beach is also convenient to Disneyland and Orange

RONALD REAGAN LIBRARY & MUSEUM

No matter how you feel about Ronald Reagan (1911–2004), his **presidential library** (www.reaganlibrary.com; 40 Presidential Dr; adult/teen/senior $12/6/9; ⊙10am-5pm; P) is quite fascinating. Galleries cover the arc of the man's life from his childhood in Dixon, Illinois, through his early days in radio and acting to his years as governor of California, although the focus is obviously on his stint as president (1980–88) in the waning years of the Cold War. The museum features re-creations of the Oval Office and the Cabinet Room, Reagan family memorabilia, gifts from heads of state, a nuclear cruise missile and even a graffiti-covered chunk of the Berlin Wall. His grave is on the grounds as well. Get there via the I-405 (San Diego Fwy) north to the 118 (Ronald Reagan Fwy) west; exit at Madera Rd South, turn right on Madera and continue straight for 3 miles to Presidential Dr.

SCENIC DRIVE: MULHOLLAND DRIVE

What to See

The legendary road winds and dips for 24 miles through the Santa Monica Mountains, skirting the mansions of the rich and famous (Jack Nicholson's is at No 12850, Warren Beatty's at No 13671) and delivering iconic views of Downtown, Hollywood and the San Fernando Valley at each bend. Named for its creator, California aqueduct engineer William Mulholland, it's especially pretty just before sunset (go west to east, though, to avoid driving into the setting sun) and on clear winter days when the panorama opens up from the snowcapped San Gabriel Mountains (Map p574) to the shimmering Pacific Ocean.

At the very least, drive up to the Hollywood Bowl Overlook (off Map p538) for classic views of the Hollywood Sign (Map p542) and the beehive-shaped bowl below. Other pullouts offer hiking-trail access, for instance to Runyon Canyon (p553). Note that pulling over after sunset is verboten.

Time & Route

Driving the entire route takes about an hour, but even a shorter spin is worth it. Mulholland Dr runs from the US-101 Fwy (Hollywood Fwy; take the Cahuenga exit, then follow signs) to about 2 miles west of the I-405 (San Diego Fwy). About 8 miles of dirt road, closed to vehicles but not to hikers and cyclists, links it with Mulholland Hwy, which continues a serpentine route through the mountains for another 23 miles as far as Leo Carrillo State Beach.

County. Cool-hunters and party people will be happiest in Hollywood or WeHo; culture-vultures, in Downtown. Expect a lodging tax of 12% to 14%; always inquire about discounts. Rates quoted here are for high season.

DOWNTOWN

TOP CHOICE Standard Downtown LA HOTEL $$
(Map p534; 213-892-8080; www.standardhotel.com; 550 S Flower St; r from $165; ❉@🛜🏊) This 207-room design-savvy hotel in a former office building goes for a young, hip and shag-happy crowd – the rooftop bar fairly pulses – so don't come here with kids or to get a solid night's sleep. Mod, minimalist rooms have platform beds and peek-through showers. Parking is $33.

Figueroa Hotel HISTORIC HOTEL $$
(Map p534; 213-627-8971, 800-421-9092; www.figueroahotel.com; 939 S Figueroa St; r $148-184, ste $225-265; ❉@🛜🏊) A rambling 1920s oasis across from LA Live, the Fig welcomes guests with a richly tiled Spanish-style lobby that segues to a sparkling pool and buzzy outdoor bar. Rooms, furnished in a world-beat mash-up of styles (Morocco, Mexico, Zen...), are comfy but varying in size and configuration. Parking is $12.

Stay HOSTEL $
(Map p534; 213-213-7829; www.stayhotels.com; 636 S Main St; dm $35, r with/without bath $80/60; P@🛜🏊🐾) Occupying the first three floors of Hotel Cecil, Stay has groove factor, with marble floors, baby-blue walls and a frosted-glass, faux-flower wall in the wired lobby. Rooms have retro furnishings and bedspreads, iPod docks and safety-orange accent walls. Most accommodations have shared baths with marble showers.

HOLLYWOOD

Hollywood Roosevelt Hotel HOTEL $$$
(Map p538; 323-466-7000, 800-950-7667; www.hollywoodroosevelt.com; 7000 Hollywood Blvd; r from $269; ❉@🛜🏊) This venerable hotel has hosted elite players since the first Academy Awards were held here in 1929. It pairs a palatial Spanish lobby with sleek Asian contemporary rooms, a busy pool scene and rockin' restos: Public and 25 Degrees burger bar. Parking is $33.

Magic Castle Hotel HOTEL $$
(Map p538; 323-851-0800, 800-741-4915; www.magiccastlehotel.com; 7025 Franklin Ave; r $154-304; ❉🛜🏊🐾) Walls are thin, but this renovated former apartment building around a courtyard boasts contemporary furniture, attractive art, comfy bathrobes and fancy bath amenities. Most rooms have a separate

living room. For breakfast: freshly baked goods and gourmet coffee on your balcony or poolside. Ask about access to the namesake private club for magicians. Parking is $10.

USA Hostels Hollywood   HOSTEL $

(Map p538; ☑323-462-3777, 800-524-6783; www.usahostels.com; 1624 Schrader Blvd; incl breakfast & tax dm from $30-40, r from $70-85; ✳@ 🛜) Not for introverts, this energetic hostel puts you within steps of Hollywood's party circuit. Make new friends during staff-organized barbecues, comedy nights and tours, or during free pancake breakfast in the guest kitchen.

WEST HOLLYWOOD & MID-CITY

Mondrian   HOTEL $$$

(Map p546; ☑323-650-8999; www.mondrian hotel.com; 8440 W Sunset Blvd; r $295-375, ste $405-495; ✳@ 🛜≋) This Ian Schrager hotel has been the place to be since the attached Sky Bar's '90s heyday, with sleek wood floors and billowy white linens, dangling chandeliers, tinted orange and pink glass accents, rain showers and down duvets. And let's not forget the model-licious staff. Parking is $32.

Standard Hollywood   HOTEL $$

(Map p546; ☑323-650-9090; www.standardhotel. com; 8300 W Sunset Blvd; r $165-250, ste from $350; ✳@ 🛜≋) This white-on-white property on the Sunset Strip is a scene with Astroturf-fringed pool offering a view across LA and sizable shagadelic rooms with silver beanbag chairs, orange-tiled bathrooms and Warhol poppy-print curtains. Parking is $29.

Farmer's Daughter Hotel   MOTEL $$

(Map p546; ☑323-937-3930; www.farmers daughterhotel.com; 115 S Fairfax Ave; r $219-269; ✳@ 🛜≋🐾) Opposite the Original Farmers Market, Grove and CBS Studios, this perennial pleaser gets high marks for its sleek 'urban cowboy' look. Adventurous lovebirds should ask about the No Tell Room… Parking is $18.

Chateau Marmont   HISTORIC HOTEL $$$

(Map p546; ☑323-656-1010; www.chateaumar mont.com; 8221 W Sunset Blvd; r $415, ste $500-875; ✳🛜≋) Its French-flavored indulgence may look dated, but this faux-chateau has long attracted A-listers – from Greta Garbo to Bono – with its legendary discretion. The garden cottages are the most romantic. Parking is $28.

Orbit Hotel & Hostel   HOSTEL $

(Map p546; ☑323-655-1510; www.orbithotel.com; 7950 Melrose Ave; dm $35, r$75-85; P✳@ 🛜) Fun-seekers should thrive at this retro-styled hostel within staggering distance of hip shopping, boozing and dancing. Meet up with fellow travelers over movie nights, Sunday barbecues and clubbing (shuttle available). Dorms sleep six in full-size beds, while private rooms have a TV and bathroom.

BEVERLY HILLS & WESTSIDE

TOP CHOICE Beverly Hills Hotel   HOTEL $$$

(Map p550; ☑310-276-2251, 800-283-8885; www. beverlyhillshotel.com; 9641 Sunset Blvd; r from $530; ✳@ 🛜≋) The legendary Pink Palace from 1912 oozes opulence. The pool deck is classic, the grounds are lush, and the Polo Lounge remains a clubby lunch spot for the well heeled and well dressed. Rooms are comparably old-world, with gold accents and marble tiles. Parking is $33.

Avalon Hotel   HOTEL $$

(Map p550; ☑310-277-5221; www.avalonbever lyhills.com; 9400 W Olympic Blvd; r $228-370; ✳@ 🛜≋) Mid-Century Modern gets a 21st-century spin at this fashion-crowd fave – Marilyn Monroe's old pad in its days as an apartment building. The beautiful, moneyed and metrosexual now vamp it up in the chic restaurant-bar overlooking a sexy hourglass-shaped pool. Rooms facing the other direction are quieter. Parking is $30. It's near the corner of Olympic Blvd and Beverly Dr.

Beverly Wilshire   HOTEL $$$

(off Map p550; ☑310-275-5200; www.foursea sons.com/beverlywilshire; 9500 Wilshire Blvd; r $495-545, ste $695-1795; ✳@ 🛜≋🐾) It has anchored the corner of Wilshire Blvd and Rodeo Dr since 1928, yet amenities are very much up-to-the-minute, both in the original Italian Renaissance wing and in the newer addition. And yes, this is the very hotel from which Julia Roberts first stumbled then strutted in *Pretty Woman*. Parking costs $33.

MALIBU

Malibu Beach Inn   INN $$$

(☑310-456-6444; www.malibubeachinn.com; 22878 Pacific Coast Hwy; r from $325; 🛜) If you want to live like a billionaire, stay with one. Hollywood mogul David Geffen has plunked megabucks into this intimate hacienda near his home on Carbon Beach. Its 47 super-deluxe ocean-facing rooms are sheathed in soothing browns and outfitted with fireplaces, a handpicked wine selection and Dean & Deluca gourmet goodies. Parking is $23. It's just west of Sweetwater Canyon Dr.

Leo Carrillo State Beach Campground
CAMPING $

(☎800-444-7275; www.reserveamerica.com; 35000 W Pacific Coast Hwy; campsite $35; 🖥️👪) This shady, kid-friendly site gets busy in summer, so book early, especially on weekends. It has 140 sites, flush toilets and coin-operated hot showers. A long sandy beach, offshore kelp beds and tide pools are all great for exploring. Enter about 0.3 of a mile west of Malibu Pier.

SANTA MONICA & VENICE

Casa Del Mar
HOTEL $$$

(Map p552; ☎310-581-5533; www.hotecasadelmar.com; 1910 Ocean Way, Santa Monica; r $425-1275; 🖥️@🖥️👪) A historic brick hotel built beachside in 1926. Powder-blue rooms have wood-floor entryways, four-poster beds and marble bathrooms with soaker tubs. The lobby bar gets a good crowd in both summer and winter when the fireplace roars. Parking is $34.

Viceroy
HOTEL $$$

(Map p552; ☎310-260-7500, 800-622-8711; www.viceroysantamonica.com; 1819 Ocean Ave, Santa Monica; r from $370; 🖥️@🖥️👪) Ignore the highrise eyesore exterior and plunge headlong into *Top Design*'s Kelly Wearstler's campy 'Hollywood Regency' decor and color palette from dolphin gray to mamba green. Look for poolside cabanas, Italian designer linens, and a chic bar and restaurant. Parking is $33.

Hotel Erwin
HOTEL $$

(Map p552; ☎310-452-1111; www.jdvhotels.com; 1679 Pacific Ave, Venice; r from $169; 🖥️@🖥️) A worthy emblem of Venice. Rooms aren't the biggest and in most there's a low traffic hum, but you're steps from the beach and your room features graffiti- or anime-inspired art and honor bar containing sunglasses and '70s-era soft drinks. The rooftop bar offers spellbinding coastal vistas. Parking is $28.

Embassy Hotel Apartments
BOUTIQUE HOTEL $$

(Map p552; ☎310-394-1279; www.embassyhotelapts.com; 1001 3rd St, Santa Monica; r $169-390; P@) This hushed 1927 Spanish-colonial hideaway delivers charm by the bucket. A rickety elevator takes you to units oozing old-world flair and equipped with internet. Kitchens make many rooms well suited to do-it-yourselfers. No air-con.

HI Los Angeles-Santa Monica
HOSTEL $

(Map p552; ☎310-393-9913; www.lahostels.org; 1436 2nd St, Santa Monica; r $26-30; 🖥️@🖥️) Near the beach and Promenade, the location is the envy of much fancier places. Its 200 beds in single-sex dorms and bed-in-a-box doubles with shared bathrooms are clean and safe; party people are better off in Hollywood.

LONG BEACH

Queen Mary Hotel
CRUISE SHIP $$

(☎562-435-3511; www.queenmary.com; 1126 Queens Hwy, Long Beach; r $110-395; 🖥️@🖥️) Take a trip without leaving the dock aboard this grand ocean liner (p549). Staterooms brim with original art deco details – avoid the cheapest ones that are on the inside. Rates include admission to guided tours. Parking is $12 to $15.

Hotel Varden
BOUTIQUE HOTEL $$

(☎562-432-8950, 877-382-7336; www.thevardenhotel.com; 335 Pacific Ave; r from $109; 🖥️@🖥️) The designers clearly had a field day with their modernist renovation of the 35 diminutive rooms in this 1929 hotel: tiny desks, tiny sinks, lots of right angles, cushy beds, white, white and more white. Rates include a simple continental breakfast and wine hour. It's a block from Pine Avenue's restaurants and night spots. Parking is $10.

PASADENA

Bissell House B&B
B&B $$

(☎626-441-3535; www.bissellhouse.com; 201 S Orange Grove Blvd; r $155-255; P🖥️👪) Sumptuous antiques, sparkling hardwood floors and a crackling fireplace make this romantic, six-room 1887 Victorian B&B on 'Millionaire's Row' a bastion of warmth and hospitality. If you don't like flowery decor, book the Prince Albert room. The Garden Room comes with a Jacuzzi for two.

Saga Motor Hotel
HISTORIC MOTEL $$

(☎626-795-0431; www.thesagamotorhotel.com; 1633 E Colorado Blvd; r $79-135 incl breakfast; P🖥️👪) One of the best bets on Pasadena's 'motel row' on historic Route 66, this well-kept vintage inn (built in 1957) has comfortable, spotless rooms. The nicest are near the good-sized pool orbited by plenty of chaises and chairs for soaking up the SoCal sunshine. Extra-large units available for families.

✕ Eating

LA's culinary scene is one of the world's most vibrant and eclectic. You'll have no trouble finding high-profile restaurants helmed by celebrity chefs, whipping up farmers-market-fresh California fare, and ethnic neighborhoods covering huge swaths also mean authentic international cooking.

Reservations are recommended for dinner, especially at top-end places.

DOWNTOWN

Downtown's restaurant scene has exploded in the past few years. Great neighborhoods for browsing include 7th St east of Grand Ave, Little Tokyo (not just for Japanese cuisine anymore), LA Live (Map p534), and the food stalls of the Grand Central Market (Map p534; 317 S Broadway; ⊙9am-6pm).

Bottega Louie   ITALIAN $$
(Map p534; ☑213-802-1470; www.bottegalouie.com; 700 S Grand Ave; mains $11-18, ⊙breakfast, lunch & dinner) The wide marble bar has become a magnet for the artsy loft set and office workers alike. The open-kitchen crew, in chef's whites, grills house-made sausage and wood-fires thin-crust pizzas in the white-on-white, big-as-a-gym dining room. Always busy, always buzzy.

Lazy Ox Canteen   GASTROPUB $$
(Map p534; ☑213-626-5299; www.lazyoxcanteen.com; 241 S San Pedro St; appetizers $4-16, mains $21-21; ⊙lunch & dinner) Where Little Tokyo is headed, culinarily: contemporary tapas in post-industrial digs. Think grilled squid with garbanzo beans, brick-roast mussels and fantastic burgers and vegetarian dishes. Pair them with something from the creative beer and wine list.

Gorbals   NEW AMERICAN $$
(Map p534; ☑213-488-3408; www.thegorbalsla.com; 501 S Spring St; small plates $8-17; ⊙6pm-midnight Mon-Wed, 6pm-2am Thu-Sat) Top Chef winner Ilan Hall tweaks traditional Jewish comfort food: bacon-wrapped matzoh balls, potato latkes with smoked applesauce, gribenes (fried chicken fat) served BLT style. It's hidden in the back of the Alexandria Hotel lobby.

Nickel Diner   DINER $
(Map p534; www.5cdiner.com; 524 S Main St; mains $8-14; ⊙8am-3:30pm Tue-Sun, 6pm-11pm Tue-Sat) In Downtown's boho historic district, this red-vinyl joint feels like a throwback to the 1920s. Ingredients are 21st century, though:

artichokes stuffed with quinoa salad, burgers piled with poblano chiles. Must-try dessert: maple-glazed bacon donut.

Philippe the Original   DINER $
(off Map p534; www.philippes.com; 1001 N Alameda St; sandwiches $6-7.50; ⊙6am-10pm; [P]) LAPD hunks, stressed-out attorneys and Midwestern vacationers all flock to this legendary 'home of the French dip sandwich,' dating back to 1908 at the edge of Chinatown. Order your choice of meat on a crusty roll dipped in au jus, and hunker down at the tables on the sawdust-covered floor. Coffee is just 10¢ (no misprint). Cash only.

HOLLYWOOD, LOS FELIZ & SILVER LAKE

Osteria Mozza & Pizzeria Mozza   ITALIAN $$$
(off Map p546; ☑323-297-0100; www.mozza-la.com; 6602 Melrose Ave, Mid-City; mains Osteria $17-29, Pizzeria $10-18; ⊙lunch & dinner) Reserve weeks ahead at LA's hottest Italian eatery, run by celebrity chefs Mario Batali and Nancy Silverton. Two restaurants share the same building: a wide-ranging menu at the Osteria, and precision-made pizzas baked before your eyes at the Pizzeria (☑323-297-0101, 641 N Highland Ave).

Musso & Frank Grill   BAR, GRILL $$
(Map p538; ☑323-467-7788; 6667 Hollywood Blvd; mains $12-35; ⊙11am-11pm Tue-Sat) Hollywood history hangs thickly in the air at the boulevard's oldest eatery. Waiters balance platters of steaks, chops, grilled liver and other

---

LA'S MOVEABLE FEASTS

In 2009, Korean-born, LA-raised chef Roy Choi began roving the streets of LA in a food truck, selling Korean grilled beef inside Mexican tacos and tweeting the locations, and a trend was born. His Kogi truck spawned some of LA's most creative mobile kitchens – Brazilian to Singaporean, southern BBQ, Vietnamese banh mi sandwiches and grilled cheese sandwiches topped with short ribs and mac and cheese. Now hundreds of gourmet food trucks plough the city streets (standouts include Kogi, the Grilled Cheese Truck and the Dim Sum Truck), and no street fair, lunch break or pub crawl is complete without them. Check out www.trucktweets.com for each day's locations.

EATING LA: ESSENTIAL ETHNIC NEIGHBORHOODS

Taking nothing away from LA's top-end eateries, some of the city's greatest food treasures are its ethnic restaurants. With some 140 nationalities in the county, we can just scratch the surface, but here are some of the most prominent neighborhoods for authentic cuisine and fun things to do nearby.

» **Little Tokyo** Downtown LA; Essential dish: steaming bowl of ramen at **Daikokuya** (Map p534; www.daikoku-ten.com; 327 E 1st St; ⏰11am-2.30pm & 5pm-midnight Mon-Sat). While there: shop for J-pop culture at Tokyo (114 Japanese Village Plaza).

» **Chinatown** Downtown LA; Essential dish: dim sum at **Empress Pavilion** (off Map p534; www.empresspavilion.com; 2nd fl, 988 N Hill St; dim sum per plate $2-6, most mains $10-25; ⏰10am-2:30pm & 5:30-9pm, to 10pm Sat & Sun). While there: view contemporary art in galleries along Chung King Rd.

» **Boyle Heights (Mexican)** East LA; Essential dish: gourmet tortilla soup at **La Serenata de Garibaldi** (off Map p534; www.laserenataonline.com; 1842 E 1st St; mains $10-25; ⏰11:30am-10:30pm Mon-Fri, 9am-10:30pm Sat & Sun). While there: listen to mariachis at Mariachi Plaza.

» **Koreatown** West of Downtown LA; Essential dish: barbecue cooked at your table with lots of *banchan* (side dishes) at **Chosun Galbee** (www.chosungalbee.com; 3300 Olympic Blvd; mains $12-24; ⏰11am-11pm). While there: browse the giant Koreatown Galleria mall (Olympic Blvd and Western Ave) for housewares and more food.

» **Thai Town** East Hollywood; Essential dish: curries with accompaniment by an Elvis impersonator at **Palms Thai** (Map p538; www.palmsthai.com; 5900 Hollywood Blvd; mains $6-19; ⏰11am-midnight Sun-Thu, to 2am Fri & Sat). While there: pick up a flower garland at Thailand Plaza shopping center (5321 Hollywood Blvd).

dishes harking back to the days when cholesterol wasn't part of our vocabulary. Service is smooth, so are the martinis.

Street   FUSION $$
(off Map p538; ☎323-203-0500; www.eatatstreet. com; 742 N Highland Ave; dishes $7-17; ⏰lunch & dinner) From Singapore's *kaya* toast (with coconut jam and a soft fried egg) to Ukrainian spinach dumplings and Syrian lamb kafta meatballs, celeb chef Susan Feniger's hot spot offers small plates of global street food in upmarket environs.

Hungry Cat   SEAFOOD $$
(Map p538; ☎323-462-2155; www.thehungrycat. com; 1535 Vine St, Hollywood; mains $10-27; ⏰lunch & dinner; P) This kitty is small and sleek and hides out in the heart of Hollywood. It fancies fresh seafood and will have you salivating for hunky lobster roll, portly crab cakes and savory fish-*du-jour* specials. The Pug Burger – slathered with avocado, bacon and blue cheese – is a worthy meaty alternative. There's a second location by the beach in Santa Monica (☎310-459-3337, 100 W Channel Rd, Santa Monica; ⏰dinner nightly, brunch Sat & Sun).

Waffle   NEW AMERICAN $
(Map p538; ☎323-465-6901; www.thewaffle.us; 6255 W Sunset Blvd; most mains $9-12; ⏰6:30am-2:30am Sun-Thu, to 4:30am Fri & Sat) After a night out clubbing, do you really feel like filling yourself with garbage? Us, too. But the Waffle's 21st-century diner food – cornmeal-jalapeño waffles with grilled chicken, carrot cake waffles, mac and cheese, samiches, heaping salads – is organic and locally sourced, so it's (almost) good for you.

Umami Burger   BURGERS $$
(Map p544; www.umamiburger.com; 4655 Hollywood Blvd; burgers $9-17; ⏰lunch & dinner; P) With a spacious brick interior framed by rusted iron, this is by far the grooviest Umami in the fledgling empire. It does the staples everyone loves (the Umami, the So-Cal and the Truffle), as well as a *carnitas* (Mexican braised pork) and a Jurky (jerk turkey) burger. The wine bar offers $4 artisan drafts or glasses of wine, and $5 'smash burgers' at happy hour (3pm to 7pm). Other locations include the Space 1520 shopping mall and the Fred Segal fashion boutique in Santa Monica.

Yuca's
TAQUERIA $

(Map p544; www.yucasla.com; 2056 Hillhurst Ave, Los Feliz; tacos $1.75-2, burritos $2.50-4, tortas $3.50; ⊘lunch & dinner Mon-Sat; ℗) Location, location, location...is definitely not what lures people to this parking-lot snack shack. But the tacos, *tortas*, burritos and other Mexi faves have earned the Herrera family the coveted James Beard Award.

El Conquistador
MEXICAN $$

(Map p544; ☎323-666-5136; www.elconquistador restaurant.com; 3701 W Sunset Blvd, Silver Lake; mains $9-16.50; ⊘lunch Tue-Sun, dinner daily) Wonderfully campy Mexican cantina that's perfect for launching yourself into a night on the razzle. The margaritas are potent, so be sure to fill your belly with tasty nachos, *chiles rellenos* (stuffed peppers, usually with cheese, but anything goes) and quesadillas to sustain your stamina.

WEST HOLLYWOOD & MID-CITY

Ivy
AMERICAN $$$

(Map p546; ☎310-274-8303; www.theivyla.com; 113 N Robertson Blvd; mains $20-38; ⊘11:30am-11pm Mon-Fri, 11am-11pm Sat, 10am-11pm Sun) In the heart of Robertson's fashion frenzy, the Ivy's picket-fenced porch and rustic cottage are *the* power lunch spot. Chances of catching B-lister (possibly A-lister) babes nibbling on a carrot stick or studio execs discussing sequels over the lobster omelet are excellent.

Original Farmers Market
MARKET $

(Map p546; cnr 3rd St & S Fairfax Ave; ♠) The market hosts a dozen worthy, budget-priced eateries, most *alfresco*. Try the classic diner Du-par's, Cajun-style cooking at the Gumbo Pot, ¡Loteria! Mexican grill or Singapore's Banana Leaf.

Comme Ça
FRENCH $$

(Map p546; ☎323-782-1178; www.commecares taurant.com; 8479 Melrose Ave, West Hollywood; mains breakfast $8-14, lunch $12-25, dinner $19-28; ⊘8am-midnight) 'Bistro cooking' way understates the case at this vibrant, all-day Francophile eatery. Look for *croque madame, moules frites,* a cheese bar and a raw bar, all from Michelin-starred chef David Myers. Plus there's old-world bartending; the penicillin cocktail will cure what ails you with scotch, ginger, lemon and honey.

AOC
WINE BAR $$$

(Map p546; ☎323-653-6359; www.aocwinebar.com; 8022 W 3rd St, Mid-City; mains $4-14; ⊘dinner) The small-plate menu at this stomping ground of the rich, lithe and silicone-enhanced will have you noshing happily on sweaty cheeses, homemade charcuterie and such richly nuanced morsels as braised pork cheeks. Huge list of wines by the glass.

Marix Tex Mex
MEXICAN $

(Map p546; www.marixtexmex.com; 1108 N Flores St; mains $9-19; ⊘11:30am-11pm) Many an evening in Boystown has begun with flirting on Marix's patios over kick-ass margaritas, followed by fish tacos, fajitas, chipotle chicken sandwiches, and all-you-can-eat on Taco Tuesdays.

Veggie Grill
VEGETARIAN $

(Map p546; www.veggiegrill.com; 8000 W Sunset Blvd; mains $7-9.50; ⊘11am-11pm; ℗) If Santa Fe crispy chickin' or a carne asada sandwich don't sound vegetarian, know that this cheery local chain uses seasoned vegetable proteins (mostly tempeh). Try sides of 'sweetheart' sweet potato fries or steamin' kale with miso dressing.

Pink's
HOT DOGS $

(Map p546; www.pinkshollywood.com; 709 N La Brea Ave, Mid-City; dishes $3.45-6.20; ⊘9:30am-2am Sun-Thu, to 3am Fri & Sat) Folks have been queuing at this corner hot-dog stand since 1939, the specialty is gut-busting chili dogs ($3.45); lines are long all day, especially after nights on the prowl.

BEVERLY HILLS & WESTSIDE

TOP CHOICE Bazaar
SPANISH $$$

(Map p546; ☎310-246-5555; 465 S La Cienega Blvd; dishes $8-18; ⊘brunch 11am-3pm Sat & Sun, 6pm-11pm daily) In the SLS Hotel, the Bazaar dazzles with over-the-top design by Philippe Starck and 'molecular gastronomic' tapas by José Andrés. Caprese salad pairs cherry tomatoes with mozzarella balls that explode in your mouth, or try cotton-candy foie gras or a Philly cheesesteak on 'air bread.' Caution: those small plates add up.

Spago
CALIFORNIAN, FUSION $$$

(☎310-385-0880; www.wolfgangpuck.com; 176 N Cañon Dr, Beverly Hills; mains $43-150; ⊘lunch Mon-Sat, dinner daily) Wolfgang Puck practically defined California cuisine for SoCal, and his flagship emporium has long been tops for A-list celebrity-spotting and fancy eating. Try to score a table on the lovely patio and prepare your taste buds to do cartwheels over fusion pork chops, porcini, pasta and pizzas. Reservations essential. It's north of Wilshire Blvd.

Matsuhisa

JAPANESE $$$

(Map p546; ☎323-659-9639; www.nobumatsuhisa.com; 129 S La Cienega Blvd; dishes $5-36; ☻lunch Mon-Fri, dinner Mon-Sun) Chef Nobu Matsuhisa has gone on to conquer the world with Nobu restaurants in major food capitals. The legend began here on La Cienega's Restaurant Row. There's always something fresh and innovative alongside old standbys such as lobster ceviche and sushi adorned with cilantro and jalapeño.

Yakitoriya

JAPANESE $$

(☎310-479-5400; 11301 W Olympic Blvd, West LA; dishes $2.50-27; ☻dinner; ☛) Simple and real, this chef-owned and family-operated *yakitori* (Japanese grilled chicken) joint crafts tender and savory grilled-chicken skewers. It's one of several tasty Japanese spots north of Olympic Blvd on Sawtelle Blvd.

Nate 'n Al's

DELI $$

(www.natenal.com; 414 N Beverly Dr, Beverly Hills; dishes $6.50-13; ☻breakfast, lunch & dinner) Dapper seniors, chatty girlfriends, financial planners and even Larry King have kept this New York–style deli busy since 1945. The huge menu boasts what may quite possibly be the best pastrami on rye, lox and bagels and chicken soup this side of Manhattan.

✏ Tender Greens

ORGANIC $

(www.tendergreensfood.com; 9523 Culver Blvd, Culver City; dishes $10.50; ☻lunch & dinner; ☛) Herbivore or meathead, your tastebuds will be doing somersaults when treated to the carefully composed salads, tossed as you move down the line. The ahi tuna niçoise and grilled flatiron steak are fabulous, and the chicken soup is soul-restoring. Ingredients are sourced from local providers. See website for other locations in Hollywood, WeHo (Map p546) and Pasadena.

Shamshiri

PERSIAN $$

(www.shamshiri.com; 1712 Westwood Blvd, Westwood; appetizers $4.-16, mains $13-24; ☻lunch & dinner; ☛) One of a string of Persian kitchens in Westwood, these guys bake their own flatbread for wrapping chicken, beef and lamb shwarma, kebabs and falafel. They also do salad and vegan stews. Great-value lunch specials.

Versailles

CUBAN $

(www.versaillescuban.com; 10319 Venice Blvd, Culver City; mains $11-15; ☻lunch & dinner; ☛) There's nothing fancy about this country-style Cuban eatery, but that barely matters when the garlic sauce (served with everything from roast chicken to fish) is so celestial. Many dishes come with rice, beans and fried plantains. Also at 1415 S La Cienega Blvd in West LA (☎310-289-0392).

Diddy Riese Cookies

DESSERT $

(Map p550; ☎310-208-0448; www.diddyriese.com; 926 Broxton Ave, Westwood; cookies 35¢; ☻10am-midnight Mon-Thu, to 1am Fri, noon-1am Sat, to midnight Sun) No night out in Westwood is complete without Diddy's bargain-priced ice-cream sandwiches ($1.50). Choose from over a dozen ice-cream flavors between 10 fresh-baked cookie options.

MALIBU

Reel Inn

SEAFOOD $$

(www.reelinnmalibu.com; 18661 Pacific Coast Hwy; fresh grilled fish $12-25; ☻lunch & dinner; ☛) Across PCH from the ocean, this shambling shack with counter service and picnic tables serves up fish and seafood for any budget and many styles, including grilled, fried or Cajun. The coleslaw, potatoes and Cajun rice (included in most meals) have fans from Harley riders to beach bums and families. It's an easy detour from Topanga State Park or the Getty Villa (p547).

✏ Inn of the Seventh Ray

ORGANIC $$$

(☎310-455-1311; www.innoftheseventhray.com; 128 Old Topanga Canyon Rd; mains $24-55; ☻lunch & dinner; ☛☛) If you've lived through the '60s, you might experience flashbacks at this New Agey hideaway in an impossibly idyllic setting in Topanga Canyon. All of the food is organic, much of it raw, most of it meat-free and some rather esoteric. Crispy vegan duck anyone?

SANTA MONICA & VENICE

Santa Monica's Third Street Promenade and Main St, as well as Abbot Kinney Blvd in Venice, are all happy hunting grounds for browsing.

TOP CHOICE Gjelina

CALIFORNIAN $$

(Map p552; ☎310-450-1429; www.gjelina.com; 1429 Abbot Kinney Blvd, Venice; dishes $8-25; ☻lunch & dinner) Whether you carve out a slip on the communal table between the hipsters and yuppies or get your own slab of wood on the rustic stone terrace, you will dine on delicious and imaginative small plates (think chanterelles and gravy on toast or raw yellowtail spiced with chili and mint,

LA'S FABULOUS FARMERS MARKETS

In a city as big as LA, it's easy to forget that California is America's most productive agricultural state. Nearby farmers, top-name chefs and locavore home-cooks come together at dozens of certified farmers markets. Here are just some standouts.

Santa Monica (Map p552; www01.smgov.net/farmers_market; ⊙8:30am-1pm Wed & Sat cnr 3rd St Promenade & Arizona Ave, 9:30am-1pm Sun cnr Main St & Ocean Park Blvd) Cream of the crop. Serious gourmets and high profile chefs gather over everyday produce and exotica from Asian vegetables to heirloom tomatoes, herbs and lotions and potions made from them, raw cheeses and organically raised meat.

Hollywood (Map p538; www.farmernet.com; cnr Ivar & Selma Aves; ⊙8am-1pm Sun) Some 90 farmers set up stalls alongside vendors of prepared foods, including Mexican, Caribbean and espresso. Artisans and street musicians round out the experience.

and drenched in olive oil and blood orange), and sensational thin-crust, wood-fired pizza.

3 Square Café & Bakery CALIFORNIAN $
(Map p552; ☎310-399-6504; 1121 Abbot Kinney Blvd, Venice; mains $8-20; ⊙cafe 8am-10pm Mon-Thu, to 11pm Fri, 9am-11pm Sat, to 10pm Sun, bakery 7am-7pm) Tiny, modernist cafe at which you can devour Hans Röckenwagner's German-inspired pretzel burgers, gourmet sandwiches and apple pancakes. Bakery shelves are piled high with rustic breads and fluffy croissants.

Library Alehouse PUB $$
(Map p552; www.libraryalehouse.com; 2911 Main St, Santa Monica; mains $12-20; ⊙11:30am-midnight) Locals gather as much for the food as the 29 beers on tap, in the wood-paneled dining room or cozy back patio. Angus burgers, fish tacos and hearty salads sate the 30-something regulars.

Real Food Daily VEGETARIAN $
(www.realfood.com; Map p552; 514 Santa Monica Blvd, Santa Monica; mains $10-14; ⊙lunch & dinner; ☎) Are you tempted by tempeh? Salivating for seitan? Vegan cooking queen Ann Gentry sure knows how to give these meat substitutes the gourmet treatment. Start things off with lentil-walnut pâté, move on to the vegan club sandwich with Caesar salad, then finish up with a rich tofu cheesecake. Also in West Hollywood (Map p546; 414 N La Cienega Blvd).

Father's Office PUB $$
(off 1018 Montana Ave; dishes $6-16; ⊙5pm-1am Mon-Thu, 4pm-2am Fri, noon-2am Sat, to midnight Sun) This elbow-to-elbow pub packs 'em in for LA's chic-est burger: a dry-aged beef number dressed in smoky bacon, sweet caramelized onion and an ingenious combo of Gruyère and blue cheese. Pair it with fries served in a mini-shopping cart and a mug of handcrafted brew chosen from three dozen on tap. Downside: service can be snooty. Also in Culver City (☎310-736-2224; 3229 Helms Ave).

Joe's CALIFORNIAN $$$
(Map p552; www.joesrestaurant.com; 1023 Abbot Kinney Blvd, Venice; mains lunch $13-18, dinner $26-30; ⊙lunch Tue-Sun, dinner daily) Like a good wine, this charmingly unpretentious restaurant only seems to get better with age, and has a new Michelin star to prove it. Owner-chef Joe Miller consistently serves great and gimmick-free seasonal Cal-French food. Choicest tables are out on the patio with the waterfall fountain. Three-course lunch menus are a steal at $18.

Santa Monica Place SHOPPING CENTER $$
(Map p552; www.santamonicaplace.com; 3rd fl, Cnr Third St & Broadway, Santa Monica; ☎) We wouldn't normally eat at a mall, but the indoor-outdoor dining deck sets standards: Latin-Asian fusion at Zengo (think Peking duck tacos), sushi at Ozumo, wood-oven-baked pizzas at Antica. Most restaurants have seating with views across adjacent rooftops – some to the ocean. Stalls in the market do *salumi* to soufflés.

LONG BEACH & SAN PEDRO

San Pedro Fish Market & Restaurant SEAFOOD $$
(www.sanpedrofishmarket.com; 1190 Nagoya Way, San Pedro; meals $13.50; ⊙breakfast, lunch & dinner; ☎) Seafood feasts don't get any more rootsy and decadent than at this family-run, harbor-view institution. Pick from the day's catch, have it spiced and cooked to order with potatoes, tomatoes and peppers,

lug your tray to a picnic table, fold up your sleeves and devour meaty crabs, plump shrimp, slimy oysters, melty yellowtail and tender halibut. Don't forget to ask for buttery garlic bread and a pile of extra napkins.

Number Nine   VIETNAMESE $

(www.numberninenoodles.com; 2118 E 4th St, Long Beach; mains $7-9; noon-midnight) Maximalist portions of Vietnamese noodles and five-spice chicken with egg roll, in minimalist surrounds on Retro Row. Meats and poultry are sustainably raised.

George's Greek Café   GREEK $$

(www.georgesgreekcafe.com; 135 Pine Ave, Long Beach; mains $8-19; 11am-10pm Sun-Thu, to 11pm Fri & Sat) George himself may greet you at the entrance on the generous patio, heart of the Pine Ave restaurant row, both geographically and spiritually. Locals cry *'Opa!'* for the *saganaki* (flaming cheese) and lamb chops.

Alegria   SPANISH $$

(www.alegriacocinalatina.com; 115 Pine Ave, Long Beach; tapas $5-11, mains $7-20;) Long Beach's busy Pine Ave nightlife district, trippy, technicolor mosaic floor, trompe l'oeil murals and an eccentric art nouveau bar form an appropriately spirited backdrop to Alegria's vivid Latino cuisine. The tapas menu is great for grazers and the paella a feast for both eyes and stomach. There's even live flamenco some nights.

SAN FERNANDO VALLEY

Asanebo   SUSHI $$$

(818-760-3348; 11941 Ventura Blvd, Studio City; dishes $3-21; lunch Tue-Fri, dinner Tue-Sun) Ventura Blvd in Studio City is Sushi Row, which locals will tell you has the highest concentration of sushi restaurants in America. Asanebo stands out and has a Michelin star to prove it; think halibut sashimi with fresh truffle or kanpachi with miso and Serrano chilies.

Zankou Chicken   ARMENIAN $

(off Map p542; www.zankouchicken.com; 1001 N San Fernando Rd, Burbank; mains $8-11; 10am-10pm) Lip-smacking Armenian-style rotisserie chicken, best paired with vampire-repellent garlic sauce. Also in Westwood (off Map p550; 310-444-0550; 1716 Sepulveda Blvd).

Eclectic   CALIFORNIA-ITALIAN $$

(Map p542; www.eclecticwinebarandgrille.com; 5156 Lankershim Blvd, North Hollywood; mains $8-32; lunch & dinner) An anchor of NoHo's

Arts District (p551), this loft-style space is as diverse as its name suggests (though trends Italian) with pasta and pizza to BLTs and rack of lamb. It's best, though, for people-watching after a show, when the casts come in and hold court.

Bob's Big Boy   DINER $

(Map p542; www.bigboy.com; 4211 Riverside Dr, Burbank; mains $6-9; 24hr; P) This landmark 1950s coffee shop has been doing comfort food (patty melts, half-pound burgers, mac and cheese, great fries and shakes) since way before it became retro-fashionable.

PASADENA & SAN GABRIEL VALLEY

Saladang Song   THAI $$

(www.saladangsong.com; 383 S Fair Oaks Ave; dishes $10-18; breakfast, lunch & dinner; P) Soaring concrete walls with artsy, cut-out steel insets hem in the outdoor dining room of this modern Thai temple. Even simple curries become extraordinary at Saladang Song, and look for unusual breakfast soups.

Burger Continental   MIDDLE EASTERN $

(626-792-6634; www.burgercontinental.com; 535 S Lake Ave, Pasadena; mains $9-14; breakfast, lunch & dinner; P) What sounds like a patty-and-bun joint is in reality Pasadena's most beloved Middle Eastern nosh spot. Nibble on classic hummus, dig into sizzling kebab dinners or go adventurous with the Moon of Tunis platter (chicken, gyros and shrimp in filo). Live bands and belly dancers provide candy for ears and eyes. Great patio.

Drinking

Hollywood has been legendary sipping territory since before the Rat Pack days. Nowadays bartenders are as creative as they were back then, even if your taste is Budweiser. Hollywood Blvd and the Sunset Strip are classic bar-hopping grounds, but there's plenty of good drinking going on in the beach cities and Downtown as well.

DOWNTOWN

Edison   BAR

(Map p534; www.edisondowntown.com; 108 W 2nd St, enter off Harlem Alley; 5pm-2am Wed-Fri, 6pm-2am Sat) *Metropolis* meets *Blade Runner* at this industrial-chic basement boîte, where you'll sip mojitos surrounded by turbines from Edison's days as a boiler room. It's all tarted up nicely with cocoa leather couches and three cavernous bars. No athletic wear, flip-flops or baggy jeans.

OUT & ABOUT IN LA

The rainbow flag flies especially proudly in 'Boystown,' along Santa Monica Blvd in West Hollywood, which is lined with dozens of high-energy bars, cafes, restaurants, gyms and clubs, and is especially busy Thursday through Sunday. Most places cater to gay men. Beauty reigns supreme here and the intimidation factor can be high unless you're buff, bronzed and styled...or a 'fag hag.'

Elsewhere, the gay scenes are considerably more laid-back. Silver Lake, LA's original gay enclave, has evolved from largely leather and Levi's to encompass both cute hipsters of all ethnicities and an older contingent. Long Beach also has a significant gay neighborhood.

If nightlife isn't your scene, the gay community has plenty of ways to meet, greet and engage. **Will Rogers Beach** ('Ginger Rogers' to her friends) in Santa Monica is LA's unofficial gay beach. Run with **Frontrunners** (www.lafrontrunners.com), take a tour of gay history (p555), hike with **Great Outdoors** (www.greatoutdoorsla.org), catch a show at the **Celebration Theatre** or a concert by the amazing **Gay Men's Chorus of Los Angeles** (www.gmcla.org).

Long Beach Pride Celebration (www.longbeachpride.com; ⊘late May), is a warm-up for **LA Pride** (www.lapride.org; ⊘mid-Jun), a weekend of nonstop partying and a parade down Santa Monica Blvd, attended by hundreds of thousands.

Following are some nightlife classics to get you started. For more, consult free listings mags or www.losangeles.gaycities.com.

LA's essential gay bar and restaurant is **The Abbey** (Map p546; www.abbeyfoodandbar.com; 692 N Robertson Blvd; mains $9-24; ⊘9am-2am). Take your pick of preening and partying spaces spanning from a leafy patio to a slick lounge, and enjoy flavored martinis, mojitos and upscale pub grub.

Eleven (Map p546; www.eleven.la; 8811 Santa Monica Blvd; mains $13-29; ⊘6-10pm Tue-Sun, 11am-3pm Sat & Sun) This glam spot occupies a historic building, serves New American cuisine and offers different theme nights, from Musical Mondays to high-energy dance parties; check the website for club nights.

Akbar (Map p544; www.akbarsilverlake.com; 4356 W Sunset Blvd) Best jukebox in town, a casbah atmosphere, and a crowd that's been known to change from hour to hour – gay, straight or just hip, but not too-hip-for-you. Some nights, the back room's a dance floor; other nights, you'll find comedy, craft-making or 'Bears in Space'.

MJ's (Map p544; www.mjsbar.com; 2810 Hyperion Ave) Popular contempo hangout for dance nights, 'porn star of the week' and cruising. Young but diverse crowd.

Oil Can Harry's (www.oilcanharrysla.com; 11502 Ventura Blvd, Studio City) If you've never been country-and-western dancing, you'll be surprised at just how sexy it can be, and Oil Can's is the place to do it, three nights a week, with lessons for the uninitiated. Saturday night: retro disco.

Roosterfish (Map p552; www.roosterfishbar.com; 1302 Abbot Kinney Blvd, Venice) The Westside's last remaining gay bar, the 'Fish has been serving the men of Venice for over three decades, but still feels current and chilled, with a pool table and back patio. Friday nights are busiest.

Silver Fox (www.silverfoxlongbeach.com; 411 Redondo Ave, Long Beach) Despite its name, all ages frequent this mainstay of gay Long Beach, especially on karaoke nights. It is a short drive from shopping on Retro Row.

Seven Grand BAR
(Map p534; www.sevengrand.la; 515 W 7th St) It's as if hipsters invaded mummy and daddy's hunt club, amid the tartan-patterned carpeting and deer heads on the walls. Whiskey is the drink of choice: choose from over 100 from Scotland, Ireland and even Japan.

Rooftop Bar@Standard Downtown LA BAR
(Map p534; 550 S Flower St; ⊘noon-1:30am) The scene at this outdoor lounge, swimming in a sea of skyscrapers, is libidinous, intense and more than a bit surreal. There are vibrating waterbed pods for lounging, hot-bod servers and a pool for cooling off if it all gets too steamy. Velvet rope on weekends.

LOS ANGELES DRINKING

HOLLYWOOD, LOS FELIZ & SILVER LAKE

Formosa Cafe
BAR

(off Map p538; ☎323-850-9050; 7156 Santa Monica Blvd, Hollywood) Bogie and Bacall used to knock 'em back at this watering hole, and today you can use all that nostalgia to soak up mai tais and martinis.

Dresden
PIANO BAR

(Map p544; www.thedresden.com; 1760 N Vermont Ave, Los Feliz; 4pm-2am Mon-Sat, to midnight Sun) If Formosa had Bogie and Bacall, Dresden has the songster duo Marty & Elayne, who've been there for almost as long. They're an institution (watch them perform 'Muskrat love') – you saw them singing 'Stayin' alive' in *Swingers*.

Good Luck Bar
BAR

(Map p544; ☎323-666-3524; 1514 Hillhurst Ave, Los Feliz; 7pm-2am Mon-Fri, 8pm-2am Sat & Sun) The clientele is cool, the jukebox loud and the drinks seductively strong at this cultish watering hole decked out in Chinese opium–den carmine red. The baby-blue Yee Mee Loo and Chinese herb-based whiskey are popular choices.

Cat & Fiddle
PUB

(Map p538; www.thecatandfiddle.com; 6530 Sunset Blvd; ⏰11:30am-2am; Ⓟ) From Morrissey to Frodo, you never know who might be popping by for Boddingtons or Sunday-night jazz. Still, this Brit pub with leafy beer garden is more about friends and conversation than faux-hawks and deal-making.

Beauty Bar
BAR, NAIL SALON

(Map p538; www.beautybar.com; 1638 N Cahuenga Blvd; ⏰9pm-2am Sun-Wed, 6pm-2am Thu-Sat) Still beautilicious after all these years, this pint-sized, retro cocktail bar is the place for having your nails painted in lurid pink while catching up on gossip and getting liquefied on martinis ($10, 7pm to 11pm Thursday to Saturday).

WEST HOLLYWOOD

WeHo is the epicenter of LA's gay scene (see the boxed text, p565), but there's a cluster of other venues frequented by hipsters of all sorts.

Sky Bar
BAR

(Map p546; ☎323-848-6025; 8440 W Sunset Blvd, West Hollywood) The poolside bar at the Mondrian hotel has made a virtue out of snobbery. Unless you're exceptionally pretty, rich or are staying at the hotel, chances are relatively slim that you'll be imbibing expensive drinks (from plastic cups no less, because of the pool) with the ultimate in-crowd.

El Carmen
TEQUILA BAR

(Map p546; ☎323-852-1552; 8138 W 3rd St, Mid-City; ⏰5pm-2am Mon-Fri, 7pm-2am Sat & Sun) Beneath mounted bull heads and *lucha libre* (Mexican wrestling) masks, this tequila temple dispenses cocktails based on over 100 tequilas. Industry-heavy crowd.

SANTA MONICA & VENICE

Copa d'Oro
LOUNGE

(Map p552; www.copadoro.com; 217 Broadway; ⏰6pm-2am Mon-Fri, 8pm-2am Sat & Sun) Oldschool, handcrafted cocktails from a well of top-end liquors and a produce bin of fresh herbs, fruits, juices and a few veggies too. The rock tunes and the smooth, dark ambience don't hurt.

Ye Olde King's Head
PUB

(Map p552; ☎310-451-1402; www.yeoldekingshead. com; 116 Santa Monica Blvd, Santa Monica; ⏰8am-2am) Unofficial headquarters of Santa Monica's big British expat community, complete with darts, soccer (er, football) on the TV (er, telly), traditional English breakfast and the best fish and chips in town.

Otherroom
BAR

(Map p552; ☎310-396-6230; 1201 Abbot Kinney Blvd, Venice; ⏰5pm-2am) Dark, loud and industrial, this loftlike lounge screams 'Soho transplant' but is actually a laid-back lair for local lovelies, artists and professionals. Only beer and wine are served, but the selection is tops and handpicked; sometimes the crowd is too.

For bars that ooze history, pop into **Chez Jay** (Map p552; ☎310-395-1741; 1657 Ocean Ave, Santa Monica) or the **Galley** (Map p552; ☎310-452-1934; 2442 Main St, Santa Monica), both classic watering holes with campy nautical themes.

☆ Entertainment

LA's nightlife is lively, progressive and multifaceted. You can hobnob with hipsters at a trendy dance club, groove to experimental sounds in an underground bar, skate along the cutting edge at a multimedia event in an abandoned warehouse or treat your ears to a concert by the LA Philharmonic. Mainstream and fringe theater, performance art and comedy clubs all thrive. Even seeing a movie can be a deluxe event.

The freebie *LA Weekly* and the *Los Angeles Times* Calendar section are your best sources for plugging into the local scene. Buy tickets at box offices or through **Ticketmaster** (☎213-480-3232; www.ticketmaster.com). Half-price tickets to many shows are sold online by **LAStageTIX** (www.theatrela.org).

Cinemas

Moviegoing is serious business in LA; it's not uncommon for viewers to sit through the end credits, out of respect for friends and neighbors. In addition to the classic Hollywood theaters like Grauman's Chinese and El Capitan, venues listed here are noteworthy for their upscale atmosphere. Movie ticket prices run between $12 and $15, a little less before 6pm. Tickets for most theaters can be booked online or through **Moviefone** (☎from any LA area code 777-3456).

ArcLight   CINEMA
(Map p544; ☎323-464-4226; www.arclightcinemas.com; 6360 W Sunset Blvd, Hollywood) This cineastes' favorite multiplex offers plush seating and no commercials before films (only trailers). Look for the landmark geodesic Cinerama Dome.

American Cinematheque   CLASSIC CINEMA
(☎323-466-3456; www.americancinematheque.com) Hollywood (Map p538; Egyptian Theatre, 6712 Hollywood Blvd); Santa Monica (off Map p552; Aero Theatre, 1328 Montana Ave) Eclectic film fare from around the world for serious cinephiles, often followed by chats with the actors or director.

Cinespia   OUTDOOR SCREENINGS
(off Map p538; www.cemeteryscreenings.com; 6000 Santa Monica Blvd, Hollywood; ☺Sat & Sun May-Oct) Screenings 'to die for,' projected on the wall of the mausoleum at Hollywood Forever Cemetery (p541). Bring a picnic and cocktails (yes, alcohol is allowed!) to watch classics with a hipster crowd. A DJ spins until showtime.

Live Music

Following are some of our favorite live-music clubs. Cover charges vary widely. Unless noted, venues are open nightly and only open to those 21 or older.

Troubadour   LIVE MUSIC
(Map p546; www.troubadour.com; 9081 Santa Monica Blvd, West Hollywood; ☺Mon-Sat) The Troub did its part in catapulting the Eagles and Tom Waits to stardom, and it's still a great place

BIG-NAME ACTS

» **Staples Center** (Map p534; www.staplescenter.com; 1111 S Figueroa St, Downtown)

» **Nokia Theatre** (Map p534; www.nokiatheatrelive.com; 1111 S Figueroa St, Downtown)

» **Gibson Amphitheatre** (Map p542; ☎818-622-4440; www.hob.com; 100 Universal City Plaza, Universal City)

» **Wiltern Theater** (off Map p534; www.livenation.com; 3790 Wilshire Blvd)

» **Greek Theatre** (Map p542; www.greektheatrela.com; 2700 N Vermont Ave, Griffith Park)

» **John Anson Ford Amphitheatre** (off Map p538; www.fordtheatres.org; 2580 E Cahuenga Blvd, Hollywood; ☺May-Oct)

to catch tomorrow's headliners. The all-ages policy ensures a mixed crowd that's refreshingly low on attitude. Mondays are free.

Spaceland   LIVE MUSIC
(Map p544; www.clubspaceland.com; 1717 Silver Lake Blvd, Silver Lake) Mostly local alt-rock, indie, skate-punk and electrotrash bands take the stage here in the hopes of making it big. Beck and the Eels played some of their early gigs here.

Catalina Bar & Grill   JAZZ
(Map p544; www.catalinajazzclub.com; 6725 W Sunset Blvd, Hollywood; cover $12-35, plus dinner or 2 drinks; ☺Tue-Sun) LA's premier jazz club has a ho-hum location but top-notch acts, including Ann Hampton Calloway and Karen Akers.

McCabe's Guitar Shop   ACOUSTIC
(off Map p552; www.mccabes.com; 3101 Pico Blvd; tickets $8-22; ☺8pm Fri & Sat, 11am & 7pm Sun) This mecca of musicianship sells guitars and other instruments, and in the postage-stamp-sized back room the likes of Jackson Browne and Liz Phair have performed live and unplugged. It hosts a popular Matinee Kids' Show Sundays at 11am.

Hotel Cafe   LIVE MUSIC
(Map p538; www.hotelcafe.com; 1623-1/2 N Cahuenga Blvd; tickets $10-15) The 'it' place for handmade music sometimes features big-timers such as Suzanne Vega, but it's

really more of a stepping stone for message-minded newbie balladeers. Get there early and enter from the alley.

Babe & Ricky's
BLUES

(www.bluesbar.com; 4339 Leimert Blvd, Leimert Park) Mama Laura has presided over LA's oldest blues club for nearly four decades. The Monday-night jam session, with free food, often brings the house down.

Nightclubs

To confirm all your clichés about Los Angeles, look no further than a nightclub in Hollywood or West Hollywood. Come armed with a hot bod, a healthy attitude or a fat wallet in order to impress the armoire-sized goons presiding over the velvet rope. Clubs in other neighborhoods are considerably more laid-back, but most require you to be at least 21 (bring picture ID). Cover ranges from $5 to $20. Doors are usually open from 9pm to 2am.

Drai's
CLUB

(Map p538; www.draishollywood.com; 6250 Hollywood Blvd; ⊘10pm-3am Tue-Sat) The W Hotel rooftop is the domain of this classic Vegas after-hours club. If you dig bling and surgical enhancements, hip-hop and the sweaty pulse of a packed dance floor, you will be in Shangri La. Wednesday and Friday are the big nights.

Little Temple
CLUB

(Map p544; www.littletemple.com; 4519 Santa Monica Blvd; ⊘9pm-2am Wed-Sun) This Buddha-themed lounge still brings global grooves to the people via live acts and local DJs. Fans of good reggae, funk and Latin rhythms shake their collective ass here. Admission prices vary.

Zanzibar
WORLD MUSIC

(Map p552; www.zanzibarlive.com; 1301 5th St, Santa Monica; cover $7-10; ⊘Tue-Sun) Beat freaks will be in heaven at this groovetastic den dressed in a sensuous Indian-African vibe with a shape-shifting global DJ lineup that goes from Arabic to Latin to African depending on the night. The crowd is just as multiculti.

Performance Arts

Hollywood Bowl
AMPHITHEATER

(off Map p538; ☎323-850-2000; www.hollywoodbowl.com; 2301 N Highland Ave, Hollywood; tickets $1-105; ⊘late Jun-Sep) One of those quintessential LA summer experiences, the Bowl is the LA Phil's summer home and also a stellar place to catch big-name rock, jazz, blues and pop acts. Come early for a preshow picnic (alcohol is allowed).

Los Angeles Philharmonic
ORCHESTRA

(Map p534; www.laphil.org; 111 S Grand Ave, Downtown) The world-class LA Phil performs classics and cutting-edge works at the Walt Disney Concert Hall, under the baton of Venezuelan phenom Gustavo Dudamel.

Redcat
THEATER

(Map p534; ☎213-237-2800; www.redcat.org; 631 W 2nd St, Downtown) Part of the Walt Disney Concert Hall complex, this venue presents a global feast of avant-garde and experimental theater, performance art, dance, readings, film and video.

Theater

Believe it or not, there are more live theaters in LA than in New York. Venues range from a 1000-plus seats down to 99-seat-or-less 'Equity waiver' houses, so named because actors can showcase themselves or new works free of the rules of the Actors' Equity union. Following are some of the leaders:

Music Center of Los Angeles County
THEATER

(Map p534; ☎213-628-2772; www.musiccenter.org; 135 N Grand Ave) This blocks-long triple-threat comprises the Dorothy Chandler Pavilion, home of the LA Opera led by Placido Domingo, the multiple Tony and Pulitzer award winning horseshoe-shaped Mark Taper Forum and the Ahmanson Theatre known for big Broadway road shows. Phone for $20 'Hot Tix.' Parking is $9.

Actors' Gang
THEATER

(www.theactorsgang.com; 9070 Venice Blvd, Culver City) Cofounded by Tim Robbins, this socially mindful troupe has won many awards for its bold and offbeat interpretations of classics and new works pulled from ensemble workshops.

East West Players
THEATER

(Map p534; www.eastwestplayers.org; 120 N Judge John Aiso St, Little Tokyo; tickets $23-38) Founded in 1965, this pioneering Asian American ensemble presents modern classics as well as premieres by local playwrights. Alumni have gone on to win Tony, Emmy and Academy awards.

Will Geer Theatricum Botanicum
AMPHITHEATER

(www.theatricum.com; 1419 N Topanga Canyon Blvd, Malibu) Enchanting summer repertory in the woods. It's up Topanga Canyon Blvd, about 6.3 miles from Pacific Coast Highway.

Celebration Theatre
GAY, LESBIAN

(Map p546; www.celebrationtheatre.com; 7051 Santa Monica Blvd, West Hollywood) One of the nation's leading producers of gay and lesbian plays, winning dozens of awards.

Comedy

Little surprise that LA is one of the world's comedy capitals. If the club serves dinner and you're not eating, many clubs require a two-drink minimum order on top of the cover charge (usually $5 to $20). Except where noted, you must be 21 or older to get in.

Upright Citizens Brigade
COMEDY

(Map p538; www.ucbtheatre.com; 5919 Franklin Ave; admission up to $10) Founded in New York by *SNL* alums including Amy Poehler, this sketch-comedy group cloned itself in Hollywood in 2005 and is arguably the best improv theater in town.

Groundlings
COMEDY

(Map p546; www.groundlings.com; 7307 Melrose Ave, Mid-City) This improv school and company launched the careers of Lisa Kudrow, Jon Lovitz, Will Ferrell and other top talent. Improv night on Thursday brings together the main company, alumni and surprise guests. All ages.

Comedy Store
COMEDY

(Map p546; www.thecomedystore.com; 8433 W Sunset Blvd, West Hollywood) From Chris Tucker to Whoopi Goldberg, there's hardly a famous comic alive that has not at some point performed at this classic, which was a gangster hangout in an earlier life.

Comedy & Magic Club
COMEDY

(www.comedyandmagicclub.com; 1018 Hermosa Ave, Hermosa Beach) Best known as the place where Jay Leno tests out his *Tonight Show* shtick most Sunday nights. Reservations required; 18 and over.

Sports

Dodger Stadium
BASEBALL

(off Map p534; www.dodgers.com; 1000 Elysian Park Dr, Downtown) LA's Major League Baseball team plays from April to October in this legendary stadium.

Staples Center
BASKETBALL, ICE HOCKEY

(Map p534; www.staplescenter.com; 1111 S Figueroa St, Downtown) All the high-tech trappings fill this flying-saucer-shaped home to the Lakers, Clippers and Sparks basketball teams, and the Kings ice hockey team. Headliners – Britney Spears to Katy Perry – also perform here.

🛍 Shopping

Fashion-forward fashionistas (and paparazzi) flock to Robertson Blvd (between Beverly Blvd and W 3rd St) or Melrose Ave (between San Vicente and La Brea) in West Hollywood, while bargain hunters haunt Downtown's Fashion District (see the boxed text, p571). If money is no object, Beverly Hills beckons with international couture, jewelry and antiques, especially along Rodeo Dr, which is ground central for groovy tunes. East of here Silver Lake has cool kitsch and collectibles, especially around Sunset Junction (Hollywood and Sunset Blvds). Santa Monica has good boutique shopping on high-toned Montana Ave and eclectic Main St, while the chain store brigade (H&M to Banana Republic) has taken over Third Street Promenade. In nearby Venice, you'll find cheap and crazy knickknacks along the Venice Boardwalk, although locals prefer Abbot Kinney Blvd with its fun mix of art, fashion and new-age emporiums.

Fahey/Klein Gallery
GALLERY

(Map p546; www.faheykleingallery.com; 148 S La Brea Ave; ☺10am-6pm Tue-Sat) Vintage and contemporary fine-art photography by icons such as Annie Leibovitz, Bruce Weber and the late, great rock and roll shutterbug, Jim Marshall.

Ten Women
GALLERY

(Map p552; www.tenwomengallery.com; 1237 Abbot Kinney Blvd) This bright, whimsical gallery is a collective of two dozen female artists and craftswomen who paint, weave wire, blow glass and create beautiful material magic. They also take turns behind the counter.

Fred Segal
CLOTHING

West Hollywood (Map p546; 📞323-651-4129; 8100 Melrose Ave; 🅿️); Santa Monica (Map p552; 📞310-458-9940; 500 Broadway; 🅿️) Cameron and

---

IT'S A WRAP

Dress like a movie star – in their actual clothes! Packed-to-the-rafters It's a Wrap Mid-City (Map p546; www.itsawrap.com; 1164 S Robertson Blvd) and Burbank (Map p542; 3315 W Magnolia Blvd) sells wardrobe castoffs – tank tops to tuxedos – worn by actors and extras working on TV or movie shoots. Tags are coded, so you'll know whose clothing you can brag about wearing.

Gwyneth are among the stars kitted out at this kingpin of LA fashion boutiques, where you can also stock up on beauty products, sunglasses, gifts and other essentials.

Kitson   CLOTHING
(Map p546; ☑310-859-2652; 115 S Robertson Blvd, West Hollywood) If you like to stay ahead of the fashion curve, pop into this hip haven chock-full of tomorrow's outfits and accessories, many of them by local labels. It's a major stop for celebs on a shopping prowl.

American Rag Cie   VINTAGE
(Map p546; www.amrag.com; 150 S La Brea; ☉10am-9pm Mon-Sat, noon-7pm Sun; ℗) This industrial-flavored warehouse-sized space has kept trend-hungry stylistas looking fabulous since 1985. Join the vintage vultures in their hunt for second-hand leather, denim, T-shirts and shoes. It also has some new gear. It's not cheap, but it is one hell of a browse. We particularly enjoyed the period homewares in the Maison Midi wing.

RIF   SHOES
(Map p534; www.rif.la; 334 E 2nd St; ☉noon-7pm) A hip-hop spiced consignment shoe store and your one-stop shop for new and used limited edition, imported and old-school sneaks.

Jewelry District   JEWELRY
(Map p534; www.lajd.net; Hill St, Downtown) For bargain bling head to this bustling downtown district, between 6th & 8th Sts, where you can snap up watches, gold, silver and gemstones at up to 70% off retail, even if they're unlikely to be seen on the red carpet.

Rose Bowl Flea Market   FLEA MARKET
(www.rgcshows.com; 1001 Rose Bowl Dr, Pasadena; admission $8-20; ☉5am-4:30pm 2nd Sun of the month) The 'mother' of all flea markets with more than 2500 vendors; held monthly.

Melrose Trading Post   FLEA MARKET
(Map p546; www.melrosetradingpost.com; Fairfax High School, 7850 Melrose Ave, West Hollywood; admission $2; ☉9am-5pm Sun) Good weekly flea market that brings out hipsters in search of retro treasure.

Amoeba Music   MUSIC
(Map p538; www.amoeba.com; 6400 W Sunset Blvd, Hollywood; ☉10:30am-11pm Mon-Sat, 11am-9pm Sun; ℗) Our friends call it 'Hot-moeba' for good reason: all-star staff and listening stations help you sort through over half a mil-

lion new and used CDs, DVDs, videos and vinyl, and there are free in-store live shows.

Head Line Records   MUSIC
(Map p546; www.headlinerecords.com; 7706 Melrose Ave, Mid-City; ☉noon-8pm) The ultimate source for punk and hardcore.

Bar Keeper   MIXOLOGY
(Map p544; www.barkeepersilverlake.com; 3910 W Sunset Blvd; ☉noon-6pm Mon-Thu, 11am-7pm Fri & Sat, to 6pm Sun) Eastside mixologists now have their dream habitat. Here are all manner of stemware, absinthe fountains, shakers, mixers and vessels needed to pour fine cocktails.

Puzzle Zoo   TOYS
(Map p552; www.puzzlezoo.com; 1413 Third St Promenade, Santa Monica; ☉10am-9pm Sun-Thu, to 11pm Fri & Sat) Encyclopedic selection of puzzles, board games and toys, including every imaginable *Star Wars* figurine this side of Endor.

Wacko/Soap Plant   POP CULTURE
(Map p544; www.soapplant.com; 4633 Hollywood Blvd, Los Feliz; ☉11am-7pm Mon-Wed, to 9pm Thu-Sat, noon-6pm Sun) Billy Shire's emporium of camp and kitsch has been a fun browse since 1976. Pick up hula-girl swizzle sticks, a Frida Kahlo mesh bag, an inflatable globe or other, well, wacky stuff.

Meltdown Comics & Collectibles   COMICS
(Map p546; ☑323-851-7283; www.meltcomics.com; 7522 W Sunset Blvd, West Hollywood; ☉11am-9pm, 10am-10pm Wed) LA's coolest comics store beckons with indie and mainstream books, from Japanese manga to graphic novels by Daniel Clowes of *Ghost World* fame. The Baby Melt department stocks rad stuff for kids.

Frederick's of Hollywood   LINGERIE
(Map p538; www.fredericks.com; 6751 Hollywood Blvd; ☉10am-9pm Mon-Sat, 11am-7pm Sun) This legendary inventor of the cleavage-enhancing push-up bra and the G-string also sells everything from chemises to crotchless panties, all tastefully displayed with no need to blush.

Space 1520   MALL
(Map p538; www.space1520.com; 1520 N Cahuenga Blvd; ☉11am-9pm Mon-Fri, 10am-10pm Sat, to 9pm Sun; ℗) The hippest mini-mall in Hollywood, this designer construct of brick, wood, concrete and glass is home to classic and trendsetting mini-chains such as Umami Burger and the Hennesy & Ingalls art and design bookstore.

LA'S FASHION DISTRICT DEMYSTIFIED

Nordstrom's semiannual sale? Barney's warehouse blowout? Mere child's play to serious bargain shoppers, who save their best game for Downtown LA's **Fashion District** (Map p534; ☑213-488-1153; www.fashiondistrict.org), a frantic, 90-block trove of stores, stalls and showrooms where discount shopping is an Olympian sport. Basically, the district is sub-divided into specialty areas:

Designer knockoffs (Santee & New Alleys) Enter on 11th St between Maple Ave and Santee St.

Children (Wall St) Between 12th St and Pico Blvd.

Jewelry and accessories (Santee St) Between Olympic Blvd and 11th St.

Men and bridal (Los Angeles St) Between 7th and 9th Sts.

Textiles (8th St) Between Santee and Wall Sts.

Women (Los Angeles St) Between Olympic and Pico Blvds; also at 11th St between Los Angeles and San Julian Sts.

Shops with signs reading 'Wholesale Only' or 'Mayoreo' are off-limits to the public. Haggling is OK, but don't expect more than 10% or 20% off, and most vendors accept only cash. Refunds or exchanges are rare, so choose carefully; many items are 'seconds,' meaning they're slightly flawed. Most stores don't have dressing rooms. Hours are generally 9am to 5pm Monday to Saturday; many stores are closed on Sunday except on Santee Alley.

On the last Friday most months (except during trade shows or around holidays; call to confirm), snap up amazing deals when dozens of designer showrooms open to the public for 'sample sales,' 9am to 3pm in and around the **New Mart** (Map p534; ☑213-627-0671; 127 E 9th St, Downtown), which specializes in contemporary and young designers, and the **California Mart** (Map p534, ☑213-630-3600; 110 E 9th St, Downtown), one of the largest apparel marts in the country, with 1500 showrooms.

ℹ Information

Dangers & Annoyances

Despite what you see in the movies, walking around LA is generally safe. Crime rates are lowest in Westside communities such as Westwood through Beverly Hills, as well as in the beach towns (except parts of Venice) and Pasadena.

Downtown's Skid Row, an area roughly bounded by 3rd, Alameda, 7th and Main Sts, has plenty of homeless folks, as does Santa Monica, though they usually avoid you if you avoid them.

Bookstores

$1 Bookstore (www.odbstore.com; 248 Pine Ave, Long Beach; ☺10am-9pm Sun-Thu, 9am-10pm Fri, 10am-10pm Sat) Groovy warehouse of fiction and non, comics, textbooks and magazines. And, yes, everything is $1.

Book Soup (Map p546; www.booksoup.com; 8818 W Sunset Blvd, West Hollywood) Frequent celeb sightings.

Distant Lands (www.distantlands.com; 56 S Raymond Ave, Pasadena) Treasure chest of travel books, guides and gadgets.

Traveler's Bookcase (Map p546; www.travelersbookcase.com; 8375 W 3rd St, Mid-City) Just what it says.

Vroman's (www.vromansbookstore.com; 695 E Colorado Blvd, Pasadena) SoCal's oldest bookstore (since 1894) and a favorite with local literati.

Emergency

Emergency number (☑911) For police, fire or ambulance service.

Rape & Battering Hotline (☑800-656-4673)

Internet Access

Coffee shops, including the local chain **Coffee Bean & Tea Leaf** (www.cbtl.com), offer wi-fi with a purchase. Libraries offer free access. Below are some main branches; phone or surf for branch locations.

Los Angeles Public Library (☑213-228-7000; www.lapl.org; 630 W 5th St, Downtown; 🛜)

Santa Monica Public Library (☑310-458-8600; www.smpl.org; 601 Santa Monica Blvd; 🛜)

Internet Resources

Daily Candy LA (www.dailycandy.com) Little bites of LA style.

Discover Los Angeles (http://discoverlosangeles.com) Official tourist office site.

Gridskipper LA (www.gridskipper.com/travel/los-angeles) Urban travel guide to the offbeat.

LA Observed (www.laobserved.com) News blog that rounds up – and often scoops – other media.

LA.com (www.la.com) Clued-in guide to shopping, dining, nightlife and events.

Thrillist (www.thrillist.com) A *DailyCandy* for guys.

Media

For entertainment listings magazines, see p566.

KCRW 89.9 fm (www.kcrw.org) Santa Monica-based National Public Radio (NPR) station with cutting-edge music and well-chosen public affairs programming.

KPCC 89.3 fm (www.kpcc.org) Pasadena-based NPR station with intelligent local talk shows.

LA Weekly (www.laweekly.com) Free alternative news and listings magazine.

Los Angeles Magazine (www.losangelesmagazine.com) Glossy lifestyle monthly with useful restaurant guide.

Los Angeles Times (www.latimes.com) The west's leading daily and winner of dozens of Pulitzer Prizes. Embattled but still useful.

Medical Services

Cedars-Sinai Medical Center (☑310-423-3277; 8700 Beverly Blvd, West Hollywood; ☺24hr emergency)

Rite-Aid pharmacies (☑800-748-3243; ☺some 24hr) Call for the nearest branch.

Money

Travelex (☑310-659-6093; US Bank, 8901 Santa Monica Blvd, West Hollywood; ☺9am-5pm Mon-Thu, to 6pm Fri, to 1pm Sat)

Post

Call ☑800-275-8777 or visit www.usps.com for the nearest branch.

Telephone

LA County is covered by 10 area codes (some shared with neighboring counties). Dial 1 plus the area code before the final seven digits, even when calling within the same area code.

Tourist Information

Beverly Hills (☑310-248-1015, 800-345-2210; www.lovebeverlyhills.org; 239 S Beverly Dr, Beverly Hills; ☺8:30am-5pm Mon-Fri)

Downtown LA (☑213-689-8822; http://discoverlosangeles.com; 685 S Figueroa St; ☺8:30am-5pm Mon-Fri)

Hollywood (☑323-467-6412; http://discoverlosangeles.com; Hollywood & Highland complex, 6801 Hollywood Blvd; ☺10am-10pm Mon-Sat, to 7pm Sun)

Long Beach (☑562-628-8850; www.visitlongbeach.com; 3rd fl, One World Trade Center; ☺11am-7pm Sun-Thu, 11:30am-7:30pm Fri & Sat Jun-Sep, 10am-4pm Fri-Sun Oct-May)

Santa Monica (☑310-393-7593, 800-544-5319; www.santamonica.com) Visitor center (1920 Main St; ☺9am-6pm); Information kiosk (☑1400 Ocean Ave; ☺9am-5pm Jun-Aug, 10am-4pm Sep-May)

ℹ Getting There & Away

Air

Los Angeles International Airport (LAX; www.lawa.org; 1 World Way, Los Angeles) is one of the world's busiest, located on the coast between Venice and the South Bay city of Manhattan Beach. Of its eight terminals, most international airlines operate out of Tom Bradley International Terminal. Free shuttles to other terminals and hotels stop outside each terminal on the lower level. A free minibus for the mobility-impaired can be ordered by calling ☑310-646-6402.

Locals love **Bob Hope Airport** (BUR; www.bobhopeairport.com; 2627 N Hollywood Way, Burbank), commonly called Burbank Airport, in the San Fernando Valley. It has delightful art deco style, easy-to-use terminals and proximity to Hollywood, Downtown and Pasadena.

To the south, on the border with Orange County, **Long Beach Airport** (LGB; www.longbeach.gov/airport; 4100 Donald Douglas Dr, Long Beach) is convenient for Disneyland. **Ontario International Airport** (ONT; www.lawa.org/ont; 2900 E Airport Dr, Ontario), is approximately 35 miles east of Downtown LA.

Bus

LA's hub for **Greyhound** (☑213-629-8401, 800-231-2222; www.greyhound.com; 1716 E 7th St) is in an unsavory part of Downtown, so avoid arriving after dark. Bus 18 makes the 10-minute trip to the 7th St metro station with onward service across town, including Metro Rail's Red Line to Hollywood; bus 620 Rapid takes you across town to Santa Monica via Wilshire Blvd.

Greyhound buses serve San Diego approximately hourly ($19, 2¼ to 3¾ hours). They also have about four daily buses to/from Santa Barbara ($18, 2¼ to 2¾ hours), about a dozen to/from San Francisco ($56.50, 7¼ to 12¼ hours), and about a half-dozen to Anaheim ($11, one hour). Some northbound buses stop at the terminal in **Hollywood** (☑323-466-6381; 1715 N Cahuenga Blvd), and a few southbound buses also pass through **Long Beach** (☑562-218-3011; 1498 Long Beach Blvd).

For more information, see p770 and p771.

Car & Motorcycle

All the major international car-rental agencies have branches at airports and throughout Los

Angeles (see p773 for central reservation numbers). If you haven't booked, use the courtesy phones in airport arrival areas at LAX. Offices and lots are outside the airport, reached by free shuttles.

Eagle Rider (☑888-600-6020; www.eagleri der.com; 11860 S La Cienega Blvd, Hawthorne; ☺9am-5pm), just south of LAX, and **Route 66** (☑310-578-0112, 888-434-4473; www. route66riders.com; 4161 Lincoln Blvd, Marina del Rey; ☺9am-6pm Tue-Sat, 10am-5pm Sun & Mon) rent Harleys. Rates start from $140 per day, with discounts for longer rentals.

Train

Amtrak trains roll into Downtown's historic **Union Station** (☑800-872-7245; www.amtrak. com; 800 N Alameda St) from across California and the country. The *Pacific Surfliner* travels daily to San Diego ($36, 2¾ hours), Santa Barbara ($29, 2¾ to 3¼ hours) and San Luis Obispo ($40, 5½ hours). See p776 for full details.

❶ Getting Around
To/From Airports

LOS ANGELES INTERNATIONAL AIRPORT

At LAX, door-to-door shared-ride vans operated by **Prime Time** (☑800-473-3743; www.prime timeshuttle.com) and **Super Shuttle** (☑310 782-6600; www.supershuttle.com) leave from the lower level of all terminals. Typical fares to Santa Monica, Hollywood or Downtown are $20, $25 and $16, respectively. **Disneyland Express** (☑714-978-8855; www.grayline.com) travels at least hourly between LAX and Disneyland-area hotels for one way/round trip $22/$32.

Curbside dispatchers will summon a taxi for you. There's a flat fare of $46.50 to Downtown LA. Otherwise, metered fares ($2.85 at flag fall plus $2.70 per mile) average $30 to Santa Monica, $42 to Hollywood and up to $90 to Disneyland. There is a $4 surcharge for taxis departing LAX.

LAX Flyaway Buses (☑866-435-9529; www. lawa.org/flyaway) depart LAX terminals every 30 minutes, from about 5am to midnight, nonstop to both Westwood ($5, 30 min) and Union Station ($7, 45 min) in Downtown LA.

Other **public transportation** is slower and less convenient but cheaper. From the lower level outside any terminal, catch a free shuttle bus to parking lot C, next to the LAX Transit Center, hub for buses serving all of LA. You can also take shuttle bus G to Aviation Station and the Metro Green Line light rail, from where you can connect to the Metro Blue Line and Downtown LA or Long Beach (40 minutes).

Popular routes (trip times given are approximate and depend on traffic):

DOWNTOWN Metro Buses 42a or 439 West ($1.50, 1½ hours)

HOLLYWOOD Metro bus 42a West to Overhill/ La Brea, transfer to Metro bus 212 North ($3, 1½ hours)

VENICE & SANTA MONICA Big Blue Bus 3 or Rapid 3 ($1, 30 to 50 minutes)

BOB HOPE AIRPORT

Typical shuttle fares are Hollywood $23, Downtown $24 and Pasadena $23. Cabs charge about $20, $30 and $40, respectively. Metro Bus 222 goes to Hollywood (30 minutes), while Downtown is served by Metro Bus 94 South (one hour).

LONG BEACH AIRPORT

Shuttle services cost $35 to the Disneyland area, $40 to Downtown LA and $29 to Manhattan Beach. Cabs cost $45, $65 and $40, respectively. Long Beach Transit Bus 111 makes the trip to the Transit Mall in downtown Long Beach in about 45 minutes. From here you can catch the Metro Blue Line to Downtown LA and points beyond.

Bicycle

Most buses have bike racks and bikes ride for free, although you must securely load and unload it yourself. Bikes are also allowed on Metro Rail trains except during rush hour (6:30am to 8:30am and 4:30pm to 6:30pm, weekdays). For rental places, see p553.

Car & Motorcycle

Unless time is no factor or money is extremely tight, you'll probably find yourself behind the wheel. Driving in LA doesn't need to be a hassle (a GPS device helps), but be prepared for some of the worst traffic in the country during rush hour (roughly 7:30am to 9am and 4pm to 6:30pm).

Parking at motels and cheaper hotels is usually free, while fancier ones charge from $8 to $36. Valet parking at nicer restaurants, hotels and nightspots is commonplace, with rates ranging from $2.50 to $10.

For local parking recommendations, see each of the neighborhoods in the Sights section.

Public Transportation

Trip-planning help is available via LA's **Metro** (☑800-266-6883; www.metro.net), which operates about 200 bus lines and six subway and light-rail lines:

BLUE LINE Downtown (7th St/Metro Center) to Long Beach.

EXPO LINE Downtown (7th St/Metro Center) to Culver City, via Exposition Park (scheduled opening: winter 2011–12).

GOLD LINE Union Station to Pasadena and East LA.

GREEN LINE Norwalk to Redondo Beach, with shuttle to LAX.

PURPLE LINE Downtown to Koreatown.

RED LINE Union Station to North Hollywood, via Downtown, Hollywood and Universal Studios.

Tickets cost $1.50 per boarding (get a transfer when boarding if needed). There are no free transfers between trains and buses, but 'TAP card' unlimited ride passes cost $5/20/75 (plus $1 for the reusable card) per day/week/month. Purchase train tickets and TAP cards at vending machines in stations, or visit www.metro.net for other vendors.

Local **DASH minibuses** (☏your area code + 808-2273; www.ladottransit.com; 50¢) serve Downtown and Hollywood. Santa Monica-based **Big Blue Bus** (☏310-451-5444; www.bigb luebus.com, $1) serves much of the Westside and LAX. Its Line 10 Freeway Express connects Santa Monica with Downtown LA ($2; one hour).

Taxi

Except for taxis lined up outside airports, train stations, bus stations and major hotels, it's best to phone for a cab. Fares are metered: $2.85 at flag fall plus $2.70 per mile. Taxis serving the airport accept credit cards, though sometimes grudgingly. Some recommended companies:

Checker (☏800-300-5007)

Independent (☏800-521-8294)

Yellow Cab (☏800-200-1085)

AROUND LOS ANGELES

Six Flags Magic Mountain & Hurricane Harbor

Velocity rules at **Six Flags Magic Mountain** (Map p574; www.sixflags.com/parks/magic mountain; 26101 Magic Mountain Parkway, Valencia; adult/child under 4ft $62/37; ⏱check website; ♿) about 30 miles north of LA off I-5 (Golden State Fwy), an amusement park with dozens of baffling ways to go up, down and inside out, fast to faster.

Teens and college kids get their jollies on the 16 bone-chilling roller coasters, including the aptly named **Scream**, which goes through seven loops, including a zero-gravity roll and a dive loop, with you sitting in a floorless chair. If you've got a stomach of steel, don't miss **X2**, where cars spin 360 degrees while hurtling forward and plummeting all at once. Many rides have height restrictions ranging from 36in to 58in, but there are tamer rides for the elementary-school set, plus shows, parades and concerts for all ages.

On hot summer days, little ones might be more in their element next door at **Six Flags Hurricane Harbor** (www.sixflags.com/parks/hurricaneharborla; 26101 Magic Mountain Parkway;

Around Los Angeles

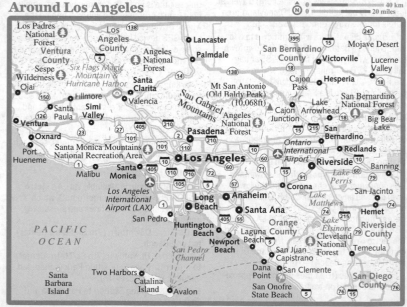

adult/child under 4ft $35/25; ◙), a jungle-themed 22-acre water park with a tropical lagoon, churning wave pools and wicked high-speed slides.

Check the website for discounts. If you don't have your own transport, look for organized tour flyers in hotels. Parking is $15.

Catalina Island

Mediterranean-flavored Catalina is just '26 miles across the sea,' as the old song by The Four Preps goes, but it feels an ocean away from LA. Even if it sinks under the weight of day-trippers in summer, stay overnight and you'll feel the ambience go from frantic to romantic.

Part of the Channel Islands, Catalina has a unique ecosystem and history. Until the late 19th century, it was alternately a hangout for sea-otter poachers, smugglers and Union soldiers. Chewing-gum magnate William Wrigley Jr purchased it in 1919 and brought his Chicago Cubs baseball team here for spring training. In 1924, bison were imported for the shooting of a western (*The Vanishing American*); today their descendants form a managed herd of about 250. Of the island's sun-baked hillsides, valleys and canyons, 88% is owned by the Santa Catalina Island Conservancy, ensuring that most of it remains free of development, though open for visitors.

For more information, see the **Catalina Visitors Bureau** (☑310-510-1520; www.catalina. com; Green Pier, Avalon).

◉ Sights & Activities

Most tourist activity concentrates in the pint-sized port town of Avalon, where a yacht-studded harbor hems in a tiny downtown with shops, hotels and restaurants. The only other settlement is remote Two Harbors in the backcountry, which has a general store, dive and kayak center, snack bar and lodge.

Avalon's most recognizable landmark is the 1929 art deco hall **Casino** (☑310-510-0179; 1 Casino Way), not a gambling casino but a cinema and ballroom still in use. Fabulous murals, a twinkling domed ceiling and history can be seen via an amusing one-hour tour (adult/child two to 12 $17.50/14.25). Tour tickets also include admission to the **Catalina Island Museum** (www.catalinamuseum.org; 1 Casino Way; adult/child/senior $5/2/4;

◷10am-5pm) downstairs, which has modest exhibits about island history.

Catalina's protected, hilly interior, filled with flora, fauna and memorable vistas of the rugged coast, sandy coves and LA coastline, may only be explored on foot, mountain bike or organized tour. Pick up maps and compulsory permits at the **Catalina Island Conservancy** (☑310-510-2595; www.catalinaconservancy.org; 125 Claressa Ave; biking permit adult/student $35/25, hiking permit free; ◷8:30am-4:30pm, closed for lunch). Hikers might hop on the **Airport Shuttle** (☑310-510-0143; adult/child round-trip $25/20, reservations required; ◷from 5 times daily) to the hilltop airport, a popular starting point as you're hiking downhill virtually the whole 10 miles back to Avalon. There's very little shade so bring a hat, sunscreen and plenty of water.

Avalon's sliver of a beach along Crescent Ave gets packed, and it's not much better at palm-tree-lined **Descanso Beach** (admission $2), a beach club with a bar and restaurant that's a short walk north of the Casino. Nearby, though, is some of SoCal's finest kayaking.

There's good **snorkeling** at Lovers' Cove and at Casino Point Marine Park, a marine reserve that's also the best shore dive. Rent gear at any of these locations or on Green Pier.

☞ Tours

Discovery Tours (☑310-510-2500; www.visit catalinaisland.com) and **Catalina Adventure Tours** (☑310-510-2888; www.catalinaadventuretours.com) both offer scenic tours ($16 to $79) of Avalon, the coastline, the interior countryside and the fish-rich underwater gardens from a glass-bottom boat. A two-hour **zip-line tour** ($113) takes you on five separate lines, up to 600 feet above ground and as fast as 55mph. This popular attraction can book out a month or more in advance, so make reservations as soon as you have your travel dates set.

⌸ Sleeping & Eating

Rates soar on weekends and between May and September, but at other times they're about 30% to 60% lower than what's listed here.

Hotel Metropole BOUTIQUE HOTEL $$$
(☑800-300-8528; www.hotel-metropole.com; 205 Crescent Ave; r from $249) The newest and grooviest spot in Avalon. Oceanfront rooms are huge, with wood floors, fireplaces,

soaker tubs and sea views. Its M restaurant does creative fusion such as duck breast and oyster mushrooms coated in blood orange molasses.

Hermosa Hotel & Cottages COTTAGES $
(☑310-510-1010, 877-453-1313; www.hermosa hotel.com; 131 Metropole St; r without bath $45-75, cottage with bath $65-170) Tidy, central, home-style and diver-friendly collection of compact wooden rooms and cottages (some dating back to 1896). Some rooms have kitchenettes and air-con.

Campgrounds CAMPING $
(☑310-510-8368; www.visitcatalinaisland.com/ camping; tent sites per adult/child $14/7) The best way to get up close and personal with the island's natural beauty and possibly bison. There are several campgrounds, including one about 1.5 miles from central Avalon (Hermit Gulch); Little Harbor is especially scenic. Reservations required.

Ristorante Villa Portofino ITALIAN $$
(☑310-510-2009; 101 Crescent Ave; mains $15-35; ⏲dinner) The restaurant at the Villa Portofino hotel serves Italian specialties that would be at home at top LA restaurants, such as *mezzaluna di pollo* (chicken-filled pasta) and *vitello al marsala* (veal in mushroom and marsala wine sauce). All served with a view of the harbor.

Cottage DINER $
(www.menu4u.com/thecottage; 603 Crescent Ave; sandwiches & burgers $8-11; ⏲breakfast, lunch & dinner) Huge breakfasts, sandwiches and American, Italian and Mexican favorites are served here.

Casino Dock Cafe CAFE $
(www.casinodockcafe.com; 1 Casino Way; appetizers $6-12, sandwiches, burgers & hot dogs $4-10; ⏲breakfast & lunch) Casual waterfront hangout, good for a beer and a simple meal.

ℹ Getting There & Around

It takes about 1½ hours to get to Catalina from any of several coastal ports.
Catalina Express (☑800-481-3470; www. catalinaexpress.com; adult/child round-trip $69.50/54) Ferries to Avalon from San Pedro, Long Beach and Dana Point in Orange County and to Two Harbors from San Pedro. Up to 30 services daily.
Catalina Marina del Rey Flyer (☑310-305-7250; adult/child round-trip $54/42) Catama-

ran to Avalon and Two Harbors from Marina del Rey in LA. Schedules vary seasonally.
Catalina Passenger Service (☑800-830-7744; www.catalinainfo.com; adult/child round-trip $68/51) Catamaran to Avalon from Newport Beach in Orange County.
Most places in Avalon are within a 10-minute walk. The Avalon Trolley (single ride/day pass $2/6) operates along two routes, passing all major sights and landmarks.

Big Bear Lake

Big Bear Lake and the towns in its surrounding valley (total population 21,000) are family-friendly and versatile holiday destinations, drawing ski bums and boarders in winter, and hikers, mountain-bikers and water-sports enthusiasts the rest of the year. About 99 miles northeast of LA, it's a popular getaway.

Big Bear is approached by Rim of the World Drive (Hwy 18), which climbs, curves and meanders through 37 miles of the San Bernardino National Forest to the town of San Bernardino. Views are spectacular on clear days. The forest is hugely popular with weekend warriors, but from Monday to Thursday you'll often have trails and facilities to yourself, and can also benefit from lower accommodation prices.

🏃 Activities

Most of Big Bear is sandwiched between the lake's south shore and the mountains. The main thoroughfare, Big Bear Blvd (Hwy 18), is lined with motels, cabins and businesses. It skirts the pedestrian-friendly 'Village,' which has cutesy shops, restaurants and the Big Bear Lake Resort Association. The ski resorts are east of the Village. North Shore Blvd (Hwy 38) is quieter and provides access to campgrounds.

Hiking
In summer, people trade their ski boots for hiking boots and hit the forest trails. If you only have time for one short hike, make it the Castle Rock Trail, which is a 2.4-mile round-trip offering superb views. The first half-mile is pretty steep but the trail flattens out somewhat after that. The trailhead is off Hwy 18 on the western end of the lake. Also popular is the moderate Cougar Crest Trail (5 miles round trip), starting near the Discovery Center, which links up with the Pacific Crest Trail (PCT) after about 2 miles and offers views of the lake and Holcomb

Valley. Most people continue eastward for another half-mile to the top of **Bertha Peak** (8502ft) for a 360-degree view of Bear Valley, Holcomb Valley and the Mojave Desert.

Mountain-Biking

Big Bear is a mountain-biking mecca, with over 100 miles of trails and fire roads. It hosts several pro and amateur races each year. A good place to get your feet in gear is along the aptly named 9-mile **Grandview Loop**, which starts at the top of Snow Summit, easily reached via the **Scenic Sky Chair** (one way/round trip without bike $8/12, with bike one way/day pass $12/25). One of the best single-track rides is the intermediate 13-mile **Grout Bay Trail**, which starts on the north shore.

Bear Valley Bikes (☑909-866-8000; 40298 Big Bear Blvd; half-/full day from $30/40), near the Alpine Slide amusement park, is a good rental place.

Skiing

With an 8000ft ridge rising above the lake's southern side, Big Bear usually gets snow between mid-December and March or April, and has two ski mountains with the same parent: **Bear Mountain** (☑909-585-2519; www.bearmountain.com) and **Snow Summit** (☑909-866-5766; www.snowsummit.com), both off Hwy 18. Bear Mountain, the higher of the two, has a vertical drop of 1665 feet (1200 feet at Snow Summit), and is an allmountain freestyle park, while Snow Summit focuses on traditional downhill skiing. Altogether the mountains are laced by over 60 runs and served by 26 lifts, including four high-speed quads. An adult lift ticket costs half-/full day $46/56 Monday to Friday, $59/69 on Saturday and Sunday. One ticket buys access to both resorts, which are linked by a free shuttle. Ski and boot rentals cost around $25.

Water Sports

Swim Beach, near the Village, has lifeguards and is popular with families. For a bit more privacy, rent a boat, kayak or waverunner and get out on the water. A pretty destination is **Boulder Bay** near the lake's western end. Rent boats at **Holloway's** (☑909-866-5706; www.bigbearboating.com; 398 Edgemoor Rd).

Cantrell Guide Service   FISHING
(☑909-585-4017) Cantrell guarantees a catch – or your money back. You'll need a fishing license, available at sporting stores around town, and there's a three-hour minimum for boat hire (per hour $75).

Alpine Slide   AMUSEMENT PARK
(www.alpineslidebigbear.com; 800 Wild Rose Ln; prices vary; ⊙vary) Great for families, this small fun park has a water slide (day pass $12), a wheeled downhill bobsled ride, a go-cart track and a miniature golf course.

☞ Tours

Take a 20-mile self-guided tour through the Holcomb Valley, the site of Southern California's biggest Gold Rush in the early 1860s on the Gold Fever Trail. The dirt road is negotiable by mountain bikes and practically all vehicles. Budget two to four hours, stops included. The Big Bear Discovery Center has a free pamphlet describing 12 sites of interest along this route.

Guided tours are offered by **Off-Road Adventures** (☑909-585-1036; www.offroadadventure.com) to a variety of landscapes including Butler Peak, a mountaintop crowned by a historic fire lookout tower for panoramic views.

🛏 Sleeping

Rates are highest in the winter peak and lowest in summer. Big Bear Lake Resort Association books accommodations for $20 per reservation.

Big Bear has five **US Forest Service campgrounds** (☑800-444-6777; www.recreation.gov), open spring to fall (dates vary), most on the North Shore, with potable water and flush toilets.

Knickerbocker Mansion   B&B $$
(☑909-878-9190, 800 388-4179; www.knickerbockermansion.com; 869 Knickerbocker Rd; r $125-280; P@🛒) Secluded from the tourist fray of the Village, innkeepers Thomas and Stanley have poured their hearts into this ornate B&B with nine rooms and two suites inside a hand-built 1920s log home and a converted carriage house. Breakfasts are to die for, and fine dinners are served on Fridays and Saturdays (make reservations).

Grey Squirrel Resort   CABINS $$
(☑909-866-4335, 800-381-5569; www.greysquirrel.com; 39372 Big Bear Blvd; r $94-218; P@🛒) On the main road into town, amid pines, this delightful throwback, built in 1927, has an assortment of classic mountain cabins named for woodland creatures and sleeping

two to 14. All have kitchen and the nicest come with fireplace, sundeck and Jacuzzi.

Northwoods Resort
HOTEL $$

(☎909-866-3121, 800-866-3121; www.northwoodsresort.com; 40650 Village Dr; r $139-169; P@🖥❄☲) 'Resort' may be a bit overblown, but this 148-room inn is your best bet in town for mod-cons. Mineshaft-style timber beamed hallways lead to motel-style rooms (warning: thin walls). The large pool is heated year-round. The restaurant (mains lunch $10 to $15, dinner $10 to $32) has sandwiches, steaks, pizzas and tables on the pond-adjacent patio.

Castlewood Theme Cottages
COTTAGES $$

(☎909-866-2720; www.castlewoodcottages.com; 547 Main St; r $49-319; P🖥) Bored with bland motel rooms? Your fantasies can go wild in these well-crafted, clean and amazingly detailed cabins, complete with Jacuzzi tubs and costumes. Let your inner Tarzan roar, fancy yourselves Robin and Marian or Antony and Cleopatra, or cavort among woodland fairy-folk or an indoor waterfall. It's cheesy, wacky and, oddly, fun. Kids are not allowed.

Big Bear Hostel
HOSTEL $

(☎909-866-8900; www.bigbearhostel.com; 541 Knickerbocker Rd; dm $25-30, r per person from $35; P@🖥) Grayson, a mountain-biker and snowboarder enthusiast, and a fount of local info, oversees this 49-bed inn. Furnishings and bedding are standard-issue – but hey, man, it's a hostel – and there's a deck for lounging with views of the lake. Linens are provided, though BYOT (towel).

✖ Eating & Drinking

Grizzly Manor Cafe
DINER $

(☎909-866-6226; 41268 Big Bear Blvd; mains $3-9; ☉breakfast & lunch; 🖥) You'll feel like you've stepped into a backwoods sitcom at this buzzy locals' hangout, about a quarter mile east of the Village. Breakfasts are bear-sized (look for pancakes bigger than the plate), staff irreverent, walls covered with whacky stickers and prices small.

Himalayan
SOUTH ASIAN $

(www.himalayanbigbear.com; 672 Pine Knot Ave; mains $8-16; ☉lunch & dinner; 🖋) Homey spot for authentic dishes from Nepal and India. Momo (Tibetan-style dumplings) are a refreshing start, while chicken soup is thick with garlic, onion and tomato. Tandoori chicken and chicken *saag* (with pureed spinach) are also popular.

Peppercorn Grille
ITALIAN-AMERICAN $$

(www.peppercorngrille.com; 553 Pine Knot Ave; mains $12-34; ☉lunch & dinner) Locals and visitors alike swear by the Italian-inspired American fare for a fancy meal at this cute cottage in the Village: brick-oven baked pizzas, pastas, chicken breast stuffed with artichoke and spinach, steak, lobster and homemade desserts such as tiramisu.

❶ Information

Drivers need to obtain a National Forest Adventure Pass if parking on forest land. Passes are available at the Big Bear Discovery Center.

Tourist Information

Big Bear Discovery Center (☎909-382-2790; www.bigbeardiscoverycenter.com; 40971 North Shore Dr (Hwy 38), Fawnskin; ☉8:30am-4:30pm Thu-Mon) Operated in cooperation with the US Forest Service, the center offers outdoor information, exhibits & guided tours.

Big Bear Lake Resort Association (☎909-866-7000, 800-424-4232; www.bigbear.com; 630 Bartlett Rd; ☉8am-5pm Mon-Fri, 9am-5pm Sat & Sun) Maps, information and room reservations.

❶ Getting There & Away

From I-10 take I-210 and CA-330 (in Highland) to CA-18 (in Running Springs). To avoid serpentine mountain roads, CA 38 near Redlands is longer but relatively easy on the queasy.

Mountain Area Regional Transit Authority (MARTA; www.marta.cc) buses connect Big Bear with the Greyhound bus station in San Bernardino ($10; three times Monday to Friday, once Saturday), with connections to LA ($13, 1¼ hours).

Disneyland & Orange County

Best Places to Eat

» Bluewater Grill (p600)

» French 75 Bistro & Champagne Bar (p604)

» Sabatino's Sausage Company (p600)

» Napa Rose (p590)

» Nick's Deli (p595)

Best Places to Stay

» Shorebreak Hotel (p596)

» Disney's Grand Californian Hotel & Spa (p588)

» Newport Channel Inn (p600)

» Casa Laguna Inn (p603)

» Montage (p603)

Why Go?

Once upon a time, long before the *Real Housewives* threw lavish pool parties and the rich teens of MTV's *Laguna Beach* screamed at each other on our TV screens, Orange County's public image was defined by an innocent animated mouse. Even in his wildest imagination, Walt Disney couldn't have known that Mickey would one day share the spotlight with Botoxed socialites and rich kids driving Porsches along the sunny Pacific Coast Hwy. But Walt might have imagined the bigger picture – those same catfighting teens will someday grow up, get married and bring their little ones to Disneyland, too.

These seemingly conflicting cultures, plus a growing population of Vietnamese and Latino immigrants seeking the American dream, form the county's diverse population of more than three million. And while there's truth to the televised stereotypes, look closer – there are also deep pockets of individuality and open-mindedness keeping the OC real.

When to Go
Anaheim

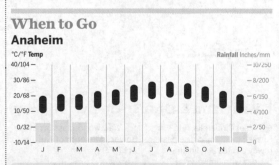

May Spring break draws crowds, then numbers drop until Memorial Day. Sunny and balmy days.

Jul & Aug Summer vacation and beach season peak. Surfing and art festivals by the coast.

Sep Blue skies, cooler temperatures inland, fewer crowds at the theme parks.

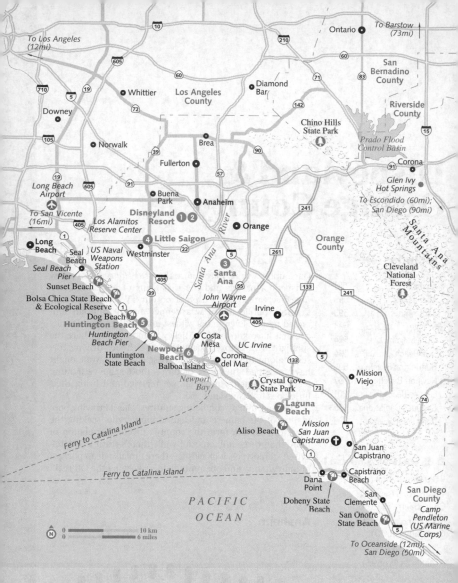

Disneyland & Orange County Highlights

❶ Meet Cinderella, ride Space Mountain, cruise past rowdy pirates and finish the day with fireworks at **Disneyland park** (p583)

❷ Join an eager crowd of Pixar enthusiasts and visit **Cars Land** (p588), a brand-new section of Disney California Adventure park

❸ View world-class art at the **Bowers Museum of Cultural Art** (p593)

❹ Go for pho in the Vietnamese enclave of **Little Saigon** (p594)

❺ Watch the pros hit the waves in Surf City, USA, also known as **Huntington Beach** (p595)

❻ Shop the boutiques, ride a bicycle along beach paths and watch beautiful people in **Newport Beach** (p597)

❼ Check out the bohemian-chic art scene of Laguna Beach with the **First Thursdays Art Walk** (p603) or, in summer, at the **Festival of the Arts** (p604)

❶ Getting There & Around

Air

If you're heading to Disneyland or the Orange County beaches, avoid always-busy Los Angeles International Airport (LAX) by flying in to the easy-to-navigate **John Wayne Airport** (SNA; ☑949-252-5200; 18601 Airport Way; www.ocair.com) in Santa Ana. The airport is 8 miles inland from Newport Beach, via Hwy 55, near the junction of I-405 (San Diego Fwy). Airlines serving Orange County include Alaska, American, Continental, Delta, Frontier, Northwest, Southwest, United and US Airways.

Long Beach Airport (LGB; ☑562-570-2600; www.longbeach.gov/airport; 4100 Donald Douglas Dr), to the north just across the county line, is a handy alternative.

From John Wayne Airport, Orange County bus 76 runs west to South Coast Plaza and Huntington Beach, and southeast to Fashion Island in Newport Beach. To get to Orange County from Long Beach Airport, take Long Beach bus 111 to the Long Beach Transit Center. Catch Orange County bus 60 to 7th and Channel and transfer to Orange County bus 1, which travels along the Orange County coast.

For information on shuttle services, see p592.

Bus

The **Orange County Transportation Authority** (OCTA; ☑714-636-7433; www.octa.net; ◷info line 7am-8pm Mon-Fri, to 7pm Sat & Sun) runs county-wide bus service. Buses generally run from about 5am to 10pm weekdays, with shorter hours on weekends. The fare is $1.50 per ride or $4 for a day pass. You can buy both types of tickets onboard, and you'll need exact change. Look for OCTA bus system maps and schedules at train stations and online. To get schedule information by phone, call during the hours noted above; there is no after hours automated phone service.

Although it would not be time efficient to explore all of Orange County by bus, hopping on OCTA bus 1 – which runs along the coast between Long Beach and San Clemente – is a cheap and easy way to visit the county's oceanfront communities. Bus 1 runs roughly every half-hour on weekdays (4:30am to 10pm) and every hour on weekends (5:30am to 7:20pm).

Car

The easiest way to get around is by car, but avoid driving on the freeways during the morning and afternoon rush hours (7am to 10am and 3pm to 7pm).

Train

Fullerton, Anaheim, Orange, Santa Ana, Irvine, Laguna Niguel, San Juan Capistrano and San Clemente are all served by Amtrak's Pacific Surfliner (p776).

A one-way trip from LA to Anaheim ($14) takes about 40 minutes, and the trip to San Juan Capistrano from LA ($20) is one hour and 20 minutes. From San Diego, it takes one hour and 20 minutes to get to San Juan Capistrano ($21), and two hours to get to Anaheim ($27). The Pacific Surfliner runs about every hour between 6am and 5pm weekdays and between 7am and 5pm on weekends.

DISNEYLAND & ANAHEIM

Mickey is one lucky mouse. Created by animator Walt Disney in 1928, he caught a ride on a multimedia juggernaut (film, TV, publishing, music, merchandising and theme parks) that's made him an international superstar. Plus, he lives in the Happiest Place on Earth, a slice of 'imagineered' hyperreality where the streets are always clean, the employees – called cast members – are always upbeat and there's a parade every day of the year. It would be easy to hate the guy but since opening the doors to his Disneyland home in 1955, he's been a thoughtful host to millions of guests.

But there are grounds for discontent. Every ride seems to end in a gift store, prices are high and there are grumblings that management could do more to ensure affordable local housing for employees as well as cover health insurance for more workers at its hotels. (With 20,000 workers on payroll, Disneyland Resort is the largest private employer in Orange County.) But the parade marches on and for the millions of kids and

IS IT A SMALL WORLD AFTER ALL?

Pay attention to the cool optical illusion along Main Street, USA. As you look from the entrance up the street toward Sleeping Beauty Castle, everything seems far away and larger-than-life. When you're at the castle looking back, everything seems closer and smaller. This technique is known as forced perspective, a trick used on Hollywood sets where buildings are constructed at a decreasing scale to create an illusion of height or depth. Welcome to Disneyland.

FASTPASS: THE INS AND OUTS

Even if you don't have a smartphone app (p592) to update you with current wait times at the theme parks' rides and attractions, you can still significantly cut your time in line with FASTPASS.

Walk up to a FASTPASS ticket machine – located near the entrance to select theme park rides – and insert your park entrance ticket or annual passport. You'll receive a slip of paper showing the 'return time' for boarding (always at least 40 minutes later). Then show up within the window of time printed on the ticket and join the ride's FASTPASS line, where a cast member will check your FASTPASS ticket. There'll still be a wait, but it's shorter (typically 15 minutes or less). Hang on to your FASTPASS ticket until you board the ride, just in case another cast member asks to see it.

Even if you're running late and miss the time window printed on your FASTPASS ticket, you can still try joining the FASTPASS line. Cast members are rarely strict about enforcing the end of the time window, but showing up before your FASTPASS time window is a no-no.

You're thinking, 'what's the catch,' right? When you get a FASTPASS, you will have to wait at least two hours before getting another one (check the 'next available' time printed at the bottom of your ticket). So make it count. Before getting a FASTPASS, check the display above the machine, which will tell you what the 'return time' for boarding is. If it's much later in the day, or doesn't fit your schedule, a FASTPASS may not be worth it. Ditto if the ride's current wait time is just 15 to 30 minutes.

Some Disneyland fans have developed strategies for taking advantage of the FAST-PASS system. For example, for now there's nothing to prevent you from simultaneously getting FASTPASSes at both Disneyland Park and Disney's California Adventure. As long as you have a Park Hopper ticket and don't mind doing a *lot* of walking between the two parks, you can bounce back and forth between a dozen or so of the most popular rides and attractions all day long.

families who visit every year, Disneyland remains a magical experience.

History

Having celebrated its 55th anniversary, Disneyland still aims to be the 'Happiest Place on Earth,' an expression coined by Walt Disney himself when the 'theme park' (another Disney-ism) first opened on July 17, 1955. Carved out of Anaheim's orange and walnut groves, the park's construction took just one year. But Disneyland's opening day was a disaster. Temperatures over 100°F (about 40°C) melted asphalt underfoot, leaving women's high heels stuck in the tar. There were plumbing problems, which made all of the drinking fountains quit working. Hollywood stars didn't show up on time, and more than twice the number of expected guests – some 28,000 by the day's end – crowded through the gates, some holding counterfeit tickets. But none of this kept eager Disney fans away for long; more than 50 million tourists visited in its first decade alone.

During the 1990s, Anaheim, the city surrounding Disneyland, undertook a staggering $4.2 billion revamp and expansion, cleaning up run-down stretches and establishing the first US police force specifically for guarding tourists. (They call it 'tourist-oriented policing.') The cornerstone of the five-year effort was the addition of a second theme park in 2001, Disney California Adventure (DCA). Adjacent to the original Disneyland Park, DCA was designed to pay tribute to the state's most famous natural landmarks and cultural history. More recently Downtown Disney, an outdoor pedestrian mall, was added and at the time of writing, major construction was underway at DCA. This ever-expanding ensemble is called the Disneyland Resort.

Nearby roads have been widened, landscaped and given the lofty name 'the Anaheim Resort.' In 2008, Anaheim GardenWalk opened on Katella Ave within walking distance of the park. This outdoor mall, though lacking personality, brings a welcome array of sit-down restaurants to the Disney-adjacent neighborhood.

Sights & Activities

You can see either Disneyland park or DCA in a day, but going on all the rides requires at least two days (three if visiting both parks), as waits for top attractions can be an hour or more. To minimize wait times, especially in summer, arrive midweek before the gates open and use the Fastpass system (p582), which assigns boarding times for selected attractions. A variety of multiday passes are available. Check the website for discounts and seasonal park hours. Parking is $15.

DISNEYLAND PARK

As you push through the turnstiles (note the giant floral Mickey) at the entrance of **Disneyland park** (☏714-781-4565/4400; www.disneyland.com; 1313 Harbor Blvd, Anaheim; 1-day pass Disneyland Park or DCA adult/child 3-9yr $80/74, both parks $105/99; ⌖), look for the sign above the nearby archway leading to Main Street, USA. It reads, 'Here you leave today and enter the world of yesterday, tomorrow and fantasy,' an apt but slightly skewed greeting that's indicative of the upbeat, slightly skewed 'reality' of the park itself. But it's a reality embraced by the millions of children who visit every year.

Spotless, wholesome Disneyland is still laid out according to Walt's original plans: **Main Street, USA**, a pretty thoroughfare lined with old-fashioned ice-cream parlors and shops, is the gateway into the park.

Main Street, USA

Fashioned after Walt's hometown of Marceline, MO, bustling Main Street, USA resembles a classic turn-of-the-20th-century all-American town. It's an idyllic, relentlessly cheerful representation complete with a barbershop quartet, penny arcades, ice-cream shops and a steam train.

If you're visiting on a special occasion, stop by City Hall to pick up oversized buttons celebrating birthdays, anniversaries and those 'Just Married.' There's also an Information Center here. Nearby there's a station for the **Disneyland Railroad**, a steam train that loops the park and stops at four different locations.

There's plenty of shopping along Main Street, but you can save that for the evening as the stores remain open after the park's attractions close. The same goes for the antique photos and history exhibit at **Disneyland Story: Presenting Great Moments with Mr. Lincoln**, on your right as you enter the park – younger children won't be interested, but adults will enjoy learning more about Walt's ambitions, plans and personal history.

Main Street ends in the **Central Plaza**, the hub of the park from which the eight different lands (such as Frontierland and Tomorrowland) can be reached. **Sleeping Beauty Castle** lords over the plaza, its towers and turrets fashioned after Neuschwanstein, a Bavarian castle owned by Mad King Ludwig. One difference? The roof here was placed on backward.

Tomorrowland

What did the future look like to Disney's 1950s imagineers? Visiting Tomorrowland suggests a space-age community where monorails and rockets are the primary forms of transportation. In 1998 this 'land' was revamped to honor three timeless futurists – Jules Vern, HG Wells, and Leonardo da Vinci – while major corporations like Microsoft and HP sponsor futuristic robot shows and interactive exhibits in the **Innoventions** pavilion.

The retro high-tech **monorail** glides to a stop in Tomorrowland, its rubber tires traveling a 13-minute, 2.5-mile round-trip route to Downtown Disney. Right away, kiddies will want to shoot laser beams on **Buzz Lightyear's Astro Blaster** adventure. Then jump aboard the **Finding Nemo Submarine Voyage** to search for Nemo from within a refurbished submarine and rumble through an underwater volcanic eruption.

The recently reimagineered **Star Tours** clamps you into a Starspeeder shuttle for a wild and bumpy 3D ride through the desert canyons of Tatooine on a space mission with several alternate storylines, so you can ride it again and again. **Space Mountain**, Tomorrowland's signature attraction and one of the USA's best roller coasters, hurtles you into complete darkness at frightening speed.

Another classic is **Captain EO**, a short 3D sci-fi film starring a young Michael Jackson. The film was shown at Disneyland in the late '80s and into the '90s; after the superstar's death, Disney started rescreening the film as a tribute. Catch this one if you can; adults in particular will get a kick out of

---

TOP FIVE THEME-PARK AREAS FOR YOUNG KIDS

» Fantasyland (p585)
» Mickey's Toontown (p585)
» Paradise Pier (p588)
» Critter Country (p586)
» Cars Land (p588)

Disneyland Resort

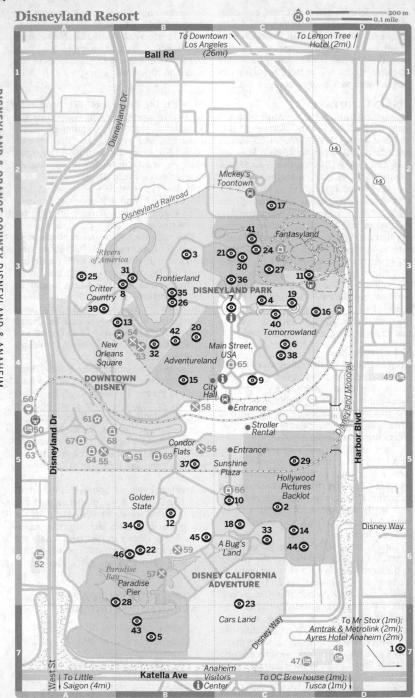

Disneyland Resort

watching a still-innocent Michael – kids will like his adorable animated pals – under the direction of Francis Ford Coppola. Look for Anjelica Huston in a delightful cameo.

Fantasyland

Behind Sleeping Beauty Castle, Fantasyland is filled with the characters of classic children's stories – it's also your best bet for meeting princesses and other characters in costume. If you only see one attraction in Fantasyland, visit **"it's a small world"**, a boat ride past hundreds of creepy Audio-Animatronics children from different cultures, now joined by Disney characters, all singing the annoying theme song in an astounding variety of languages. Another classic, the **Matterhorn Bobsleds** is a steel-frame roller coaster that mimics a bobsled ride down a mountain. The **Storybook Land Canal Boats** is a narrated boat cruise past hand-crafted miniatures of famous Disney stories, including straw and brick houses from *Three Little Pigs,* the Alpine village from *Pinocchio* and the royal city of Agrabah from *Aladdin.*

Fans of old-school attractions will also get a kick out of the *Wind in the Willows*–inspired **Mr. Toad's Wild Ride**, a loopy jaunt in an open-air jalopy through London. Younger kids love whirling around the **Mad Tea Party** teacup ride and the **King Arthur Carrousel**, then cavorting with characters in nearby **Mickey's Toontown**, a topsy-turvy minimetropolis where kiddos can traipse through Mickey's and Minnie's houses.

Frontierland
In the wake of the successful *Pirates of the Caribbean* movies, Tom Sawyer Island – the only attraction in the park personally designed by Uncle Walt – was re-imagined as **Pirate's Lair on Tom Sawyer Island** and now honors Tom in name only. After a raft ride to the island, wander among roving pirates, cannibal cages, ghostly apparitions and buried treasure. Or just cruise around the island on the 18th-century replica **Sailing Ship Columbia** or the **Mark Twain Riverboat**, a Mississippi-style paddle wheeler. The rest of Frontierland gives a nod to the rip-roarin' Old West with a shooting gallery and the **Big Thunder Mountain Railroad**, a mining-themed roller coaster.

Adventureland
Adventureland loosely derives its style from Southeast Asia and Africa. The hands-down highlight is the jungle-themed **Indiana Jones Adventure**. Enormous Humvee-type vehicles lurch and jerk their way through the wild for spine-tingling encounters with creepy crawlies and scary skulls in re-creations of stunts from the famous film trilogy. (Look closely at Indy during the ride: is he real or Audio-Animatronics?) If you can, get a seat in the front of the car.

Nearby, little ones love climbing the stairways of **Tarzan's Treehouse**. Cool down with a **Jungle Cruise** where exotic Audio-Animatronics animals from the Amazon, Ganges, Nile and Irrawaddy Rivers jump out and challenge your boat's skipper. The cruise narration's somewhat forced humor can be grating, but kids don't mind.

New Orleans Square
Chicory coffee, jazz bands, wrought-iron balconies, mint juleps and beignets – must be New Orleans. (It's Walt Disney's version, of course, so the drinks are alcohol-free and the beignets are shaped like Mickey Mouse.) New Orleans was Walt and his wife Lilian's favorite city, and he paid tribute to it by building this charming square. **Pirates of the Caribbean**, the longest ride in Disneyland (17 minutes) and the inspiration for the movies, opened in 1967 and was the first addition to the original park. Today, you'll float through the subterranean haunts of tawdry pirates where artificial skeletons perch atop mounds of booty, cannons shoot across the water, wenches are up for auction and the mechanical Jack Sparrow character is creepily lifelike. At the **Haunted Mansion**, '999 happy haunts' – spirits and goblins, shades and ghosts – evanesce while you ride the Doom Buggy through web-covered graveyards of dancing skeletons. The Disneyland Railroad stops at New Orleans Square.

Critter Country
Tucked behind the Haunted Mansion, Critter Country's main attraction is **Splash Mountain**, a flume ride that transports you through the story of Brer Rabbit and Brer Bear, based on the controversial 1946 film *Song of the South.* Right at the big descent, a camera snaps your picture. Some visitors lift their shirts, earning the ride the nickname 'Flash Mountain,' though R-rated pics are destroyed. Just past Splash Mountain, hop in a mobile beehive on the **Many Adventures of Winnie the Pooh**. Nearby on the Rivers of America, you can paddle **Davy Crockett's Explorer Canoes** on summer weekends.

DISNEY CALIFORNIA ADVENTURE
'The other park,' Disney California Adventure (DCA; ☎714-781-4565/4400; www.disneyland.com; 1313 Harbor Blvd, Anaheim; 1-day pass Disneyland Park or DCA adult/child 3-9yr $80/74, both parks $105/99; ♿), which opened in 2001, is located just across the plaza from Disneyland's mon-

DON'T MISS

DISNEYLAND FIREWORKS, PARADES & SHOWS

Magical, the fireworks spectacular above Sleeping Beauty Castle, happens nightly around 9:30pm in summer; for the rest of the year, check the online schedule to find out when and where evening fireworks are happening. In winter, artificial snow falls on Main Street, USA after the fireworks. However, the extremely short **Celebrate! A Street Party** parade down Main Street, USA is forgettable – there's no need to plan around it.

At the **Princess Fantasy Faire** in Fantasyland, your little princesses and knights can join the Royal Court and meet some Disney princesses. Storytelling and coronation ceremonies happen throughout the day in summer. Younglings can learn to harness 'The Force' at Tomorrowland's **Jedi Training Academy**, which accepts Padawans several times daily in peak season.

Fantasmic!, an outdoor extravaganza on Disneyland's Rivers of America, may be the best show of all, with its full-size ships, lasers and pyrotechnics. Arrive early to snag the best seats, which are down front by the water, or splurge and reserve **balcony seating** (📞714-781-4400; adult/child $59/49) upstairs in New Orleans Square, which includes premium show seating, coffee and desserts . Book up to 30 days in advance.

Verify all show times once you arrive in the park; also see p589 for events at Disney's California Adventure.

---

ument to fantasy and make-believe. An ode to Californian geography, history and culture – or at least a sanitized G-rated version of it – DCA covers more acres than Disneyland and feels less crowded, even on summer weekend afternoons. If the original theme park leaves you feeling claustrophobic and jostled or, gasp!, bored – you'll like this park better, with its more modern rides and attractions. DCA's critics, on the other hand, say that the newer park feels a lot less magical than Disneyland park.

Even though the park is only a decade old, the Disney honchos are pushing to expand and improve it. At the moment, DCA is undergoing a $1.1 billion building spree that's set to finish in 2012. The park remains open during construction. Some of the brand-new attractions have already rolled out, like the epic **World of Color** water show and the **Little Mermaid – Ariel's Undersea Adventure** ride, while others, like **Cars Land** (based on the Disney/Pixar classic), are hotly anticipated.

SUNSHINE PLAZA

The entrance to DCA was designed to look like an old-fashioned painted-collage postcard. As you pass through the turnstiles, note the gorgeous mosaics on either side of the entrance. One represents Northern California, the other Southern California. After passing under the Golden Gate Bridge, you'll arrive at Sunshine Plaza, where a 50ft-tall sun made of gold titanium 'shines' all the time (heliostats direct the rays of the real

sun onto the Disney sun). According to the plans, Sunshine Plaza will soon be replaced by an homage to a 1920s Los Angeles streetscape, complete with a red trolley running down the street into what will be renamed 'Hollywoodland.'

Hollywood Pictures Backlot

With its soundstages, movable props and studio store, Hollywood Pictures Backlot is designed to look like the backlot of a Tinseltown studio. If you're early you'll have an unobstructed view of the forced-perspective **mural** at the end of the street, a sky-and-land backdrop that looks, at least in photographs, like the street keeps going.

The big attraction, however, is **The Twilight Zone Tower of Terror**, a 13-story drop down an elevator chute situated in a haunted hotel – which eerily resembles the historic Hollywood Roosevelt Hotel in Los Angeles. From the upper floors of the tower, you'll have views of the Santa Ana Mountains, if only for a few heart-pounding seconds. Less brave children can navigate a taxicab through 'Monstropolis' on the **Monsters, Inc: Mike & Sulley to the Rescue!** ride heading back toward the street's beginning.

In the air-conditioned **Animation Building** you can have a live conversation with Crush, the animated sea turtle from Finding Nemo. In addition, aspiring artists can learn how to draw like Disney in the Animation Academy, discover how cartoon artwork becomes 3D at the Character Close-Up or simply be amazed by the interactive Sorcerer's Workshop.

Changes are ahead, but not all have been announced to the public; this theme-park area will soon be reimagineered as 'Hollywoodland'.

A Bug's Land

Giant clover, rideable insects and oversized pieces of fake litter give kids a view of the world from a bug's perspective. Attractions here, which were designed in conjunction with Pixar Studios' film *A Bug's Life* in mind, include the 3D It's Tough to Be a Bug! – kids will love putting on a pair of 'bug eyes.' Princess Dot Puddle Park, where guests can splash around and enjoy the spray of sprinklers and drenching fountains, is a relief on a sweltering summer's day.

Golden State

On first impression, the concept behind this part of the park – celebrating California's cultural and scientific achievements – doesn't sound too thrilling. But Golden State is home to one of DCA's coolest attractions, Soarin' over California, a virtual hang-gliding ride, which uses Omnimax technology that lets you float over landmarks such as the Golden Gate Bridge, Yosemite Falls, Lake Tahoe and Malibu. (It's part of Condor Flats, a nod to the state's aerospace industry.) Enjoy the winds on your face as you soar and keep your nostrils open for smells of the sea, orange groves and pine forests. Grizzly River Run takes you 'rafting' down a faux Sierra Nevada river; you *will* get wet so try it on a warm day.

Nearby, kids can tackle the Redwood Creek Challenge Trail, with its 'Big Sir' redwoods, wooden towers and lookouts, and rock slide and climbing traverses. You can also get a behind-the-scenes look at what's in the works next for Disneyland's theme parks inside the Walt Disney Imagineering Blue Sky Cellar.

Paradise Pier

The brand-new attraction here is the Little Mermaid – Ariel's Undersea Adventure ride, in which guests board giant clam shells and descend below the waves (so to speak, with the help of elaborate special effects) into a colorful underwater world. The wicked Ursula, more than 7ft tall and 12ft wide, is a force to be reckoned with.

This section of the park was designed to look like a combination of all the beachside amusement piers in California. The state-of-

the-art California Screamin' roller coaster resembles an old wooden coaster, but it's got a smooth-as-silk steel track: it feels like you're being shot out of a cannon. Awesome. Just as popular is Toy Story Mania!, a 4D ride with lots of old-fashioned arcade games. Want a bird's-eye view of the park? Head to Mickey's Fun Wheel, a 15-story Ferris wheel where gondolas pitch and yaw (unless you've requested one of the stationary ones).

Cars Land

Look for this brand-new area of DCA, designed around the popular Disney/Pixar movie *Cars* and expected to open sometime in 2012. Take a tractor ride through Mater's Junkyard Jamboree, steer your bumper car through Luigi's Flying Tires or ride along with the wacky Radiator Springs Racers. Route 66–themed gift shops and diners will take on that special glow of nostalgia underneath neon lights in the evening.

DOWNTOWN DISNEY

This quarter-mile-long pedestrian mall feels longer than it is, mostly because it's packed with stores, restaurants, entertainment venues and, in summer, hordes of people. The shops and restaurants are mostly chains and there are very few stores with individual character. On summer evenings, musicians perform outside.

🛏 Sleeping

Anaheim gets most of its hotel business from Disneyland tourism, but the city is also a year-round convention destination. Room rates spike accordingly, so the following rates fluctuate. Most properties offer packages combining lodging with tickets to Disneyland or other local attractions, and some run shuttles to the park. Prices listed are for standard double rooms during high season. Many hotels have family rooms that sleep up to six people.

For the full Disney experience, splurge and stay right at the resort (☑reservations 714-956-6425; www.disneyland.com). Be aware that the three Disney hotels charge an additional resort fee of $14 per day, which covers parking, internet access and other amenities. The Disneyland Hotel is nothing special but is currently under renovation (stay tuned).

TOP CHOICE Disney's Grand Californian Hotel & Spa LUXURY HOTEL $$$
(☑714-635-2300; http://disneyland.disney.go.com/grand-californian-hotel; 1600 S Disneyland Dr; d $384-445; ❄🛜🐾🚗) Along the prom-

DON'T MISS

DCA SHOWS & PARADES

Disney California Adventure (DCA) has one major advantage over the original Disneyland park – the live entertainment here is more varied and often more impressive. The premier show is **World of Color**, a dazzling nighttime display of lasers, lights and animation projected over Paradise Bay. It's so popular, you'll need a FASTPASS ticket (see p582). Otherwise, **reserved seating** (714-781-4400; per person $15) includes a picnic meal; make reservations up to 30 days in advance. Tip: if you're here in summer and have a Park Hopper ticket, see World of Color first, then head over to Disneyland Park for the fireworks and to catch the later show of Fantasmic!

During the day, don't miss the **Pixar Play Parade**, led by race car Lightning McQueen from *Cars* and featuring energetic, even acrobatic appearances by characters from other popular animated movies like *Monsters, Inc, The Incredibles, Ratatouille, Finding Nemo* and *Toy Story*. Be prepared to get squirted by aliens wielding water hoses.

Also popular is **Disney's Aladdin – A Musical Spectacular**, a 40-minute one-act extravaganza based on the movie of the same name. It's in the Hyperion Theater on the Hollywood Studios Backlot. Sit in the mezzanine for the best view of the Magic Carpet. Teens will prefer the nearby **ElecTRONica**, a street party–style show with live DJs, lasers, martial artists and dancing. Check the online calendar for dates and times.

---

enade of Downtown Disney, you'll see the entrance to this splurgeworthy craftsman-style hotel offering family-friendly scavenger hunts, swimming pools bordered by private cabanas and its own entrance to DCA. Non-guests can soak up some of the hotel's glamour by stopping for lunch or a glass of wine at **Napa Rose**, the onsite wine bar and eatery – **Disney Dining** (714-781-3463) handles reservations.

Disney's Paradise Pier Hotel HOTEL $$
(714-999-0990; www.disneyland.com; 1717 S Disneyland Dr; r $290-370; @⊛⊛) From some rooms at Paradise Pier, you can see fireworks and DCA's fabulous World of Color show – a major perk for those traveling with small children with early bedtimes. Sunbursts, surfboards and a giant superslide are all on deck at the Paradise Pier Hotel, the cheapest, but maybe the most fun, of the Disney hotel trio. Kids will love the beachy decor, not to mention the rooftop pool and the tiny-tot video room filled with mini Adirondack chairs. Rooms are just as spotlessly kept as at the other hotels and are decorated with colorful fabrics and custom furniture. The hotel connects directly to DCA.

Candy Cane Inn MOTEL $$
(714-774-5284; www.candycaneinn.net; 1747 S Harbor Blvd; r $123-144; ⊛⊛) Bright bursts of flowers, tidy grounds and a cobblestone drive welcome guests to this cute motel, which is also adjacent to the main gate at Disneyland. Rooms have all the mod cons,

plus down comforters and plantation shutters. It's a top choice and booking well ahead of time is strongly advised.

Carousel Inn & Suites HOTEL $$
(714-758-0444; www.carouselinnandsuites.com; 1530 S Harbor Blvd; r $139-239; ⊛⊛) Recently remodeled, this four-story hotel makes an effort to look stylish, with upgraded furniture and pots of flowers hanging from the wrought-iron railings of its exterior corridors. The rooftop pool has great views of Disneyland parks' fireworks.

Alpine Inn MOTEL $$
(714-535-2186; www.alpineinnanaheim.com; 715 W Katella Ave; r $86-189; ⊛⊛) Connoisseurs of kitsch will love this snow-covered motel with its A-frame exterior and glistening 'icicles' – framed by palm trees of course. On the border of DCA, the inn has views of the Ferris wheel and is close to a shuttle stop. Rooms are on the older side but clean, and there are five family-friendly suites.

Lemon Tree Hotel HOTEL $$
(866-311-5595; http://lemon-tree-hotel.com; 1600 E Lincoln Ave; r $89-119, ste $159; ⊛⊛) Disneygoers and road-trippers appreciate the great value and communal BBQ facilities at this Aussie-owned inn. The simple but appealing accommodations include studios with kitchenettes and a two-room, three-bed suite with a kitchen that's ideal for families.

Ayres Hotel Anaheim HOTEL $$
(☎714-634-2106; www.ayreshotels.com/anaheim; 2550 E Katella Ave; r $129-149; ❀@☎☎) For something a bit more upscale but still affordable, try this French country-style hotel where amenities include complimentary evening receptions, large flat-screen TVs and pillow top beds.

✕ Eating

For both parks, call Disney Dining (☎714-781-3463; ☉7am-9pm) if you need to make dining reservations, have dietary restrictions or want to inquire about character dining (Disney characters work the dining room and greet the kids). For a birthday, call to ask about decorate-your-own-cake parties and birthday meals (you'll need to order 48 hours ahead).

There are dozens of dining options inside the theme parks; it's part of the fun to hit the walk-up food stands for treats like huge dill pickles, turkey legs and sugar-dusted churros. Park maps use the red apple icon to indicate restaurants where you can find healthy foods and vegetarian options.

DISNEYLAND PARK
Blue Bayou CAJUN $$$
(☎714-781-3463; New Orleans Sq; lunch $22-40; ☉11:30am-park closure) Surrounded by the 'bayou' inside Pirates of the Caribbean, this place is famous for its Monte Cristo sandwiches at lunch and Creole and Cajun specialties at dinner. Make reservations. Whatever the time of day, you'll feel like you're dining outside under the stars, while the ride's boats floating peacefully by.

Café Orleans SOUTHERN $
(New Orleans Sq; mains $11-20; ☉11am-park closure) Jambalaya and virgin mint juleps served cafeteria-style. Have lunch under the pavilion while listening to live music.

DISNEY CALIFORNIA ADVENTURE
In addition to the following option, there is a good food court at Pacific Wharf.

Wine Country Trattoria ITALIAN $$
(Golden Vine Winery, Golden State; mains $12-25; ☉11am-6pm) DCA's best place for a relaxing sit-down lunch serves wonderfully appetizing Italian pasta, salads, gourmet sandwiches and wines by the glass.

DOWNTOWN DISNEY
La Brea Bakery BAKERY, CAFE $
(1556 Disneyland Dr; breakfast $5-20; ☉8am-11pm) This branch of one of LA's top bakeries serves up great sandwiches and salads. Express items under $10.

Napa Rose CALIFORNIAN $$$
(☎714-781-3463; Disney's Grand Californian Hotel & Spa, 1600 S Disneyland Dr; mains $32-45; ☉5:30-10pm) Disney's – and one of the OC's – finest restaurants occupies a soaring Arts and Crafts–style dining room overlooking DCA's Grizzly Peak. There's a special emphasis on pairing native ingredients with native wines. Enter from Downtown Disney or through DCA. Reservations strongly recommended.

Catal Restaurant CALIFORNIAN, ITALIAN $$$
(☎714-774-4442; www.patinagroup.com/catal; 1580 S Disneyland Dr; breakfast $9-14, dinner $23-38; ☉8am-10pm; ⓕ) The chef cooks up a fusion of Californian and Mediterranean cuisines (squid-ink pasta with lobster, grilled ahi with curry sauce) at this airy two-story restaurant decorated in a sunny Mediterranean-Provençal style with exposed beams and lemon-colored walls. Reserve ahead for balcony seating.

ANAHEIM
The 2008 opening of Anaheim GardenWalk (☎714-635-7400; www.anaheimgardenwalk.com; 321 W Katella Ave), an outdoor mall on Katella Ave one block east of Harbor Blvd, brought a welcome influx of sit-down eateries within walking distance of the park. Yes, it's heavy on chain restaurants and it's a long walk away, but dining options beyond Downtown Disney are so scarce we won't complain. Other nearby options are listed here.

✿ Tusca CALIFORNIAN, ITALIAN $$
(www.tusca.com; Hyatt Regency Orange County, 11999 Harbor Blvd, Garden Grove; mains $11-24; ☉6:30am-2pm & 5-10pm) You know Anaheim's dining scene isn't too exciting when we recommend dining inside a chain hotel. But Tusca's crispy handmade pizzas and seasonally inspired pastas prepared by a northern Italian chef – with herbs and veggies grown on the hotel's rooftop – justify the detour. Meanwhile, lobby-level OC Brewhouse pours California microbrews.

Mr Stox CALIFORNIAN $$
(☎714-634-2994; www.mrstox.com; 1105 E Katella Ave; mains lunch $12-20, dinner $20-42; ☉11:30am-2:30pm Mon-Fri, 5:30pm-10pm Mon-Sat, to 9pm Sun) For country club ambience, settle into one of the oval booths and savor some of Anaheim's best California Cuisine. Mains include prime rib, duck and rack of

lamb, plus a fair number of seafood and vegetarian options. Wear nice shoes and make reservations.

🍷 Drinking & Entertainment
DISNEYLAND RESORT
After a long day of waiting in lines and snapping pictures with princesses, harried parents might be wondering where they can get a drink in this town. You can't buy any alcohol in Disneyland Park, but you can at DCA, Downtown Disney and Disney's trio of resort hotels.

Uva Bar   WINE BAR
(www.patinagroup.com/catal; 1580 S Disneyland Dr; ⊙11am-10pm; 🚇) Named after the Italian word for grape, this bar resembling a Paris metro station is Downtown Disney's best outdoor spot to tipple wine, nibble Cal-Mediterranean tapas and people-watch. There are 40 wines available by the glass.

Golden Vine Winery   WINE BAR
(Golden State; ⊙11am-park closure) This centrally located terrace is a great place for relaxing and regrouping in DCA. Nearby at Pacific Wharf, walk-up window **Rita's Baja Blenders** whips up frozen cocktails.

Napa Rose Lounge   WINE BAR
(Disney's Grand Californian Hotel & Spa, 1600 S Disneyland Dr; ⊙5:30-10pm) Raise a glass to Napa as you nosh on pizzettas, artisan cheese plates and Scharffen Berger chocolate truffle cake.

ESPN Zone   SPORTS BAR
(www.espnzone.com; 1545 Disneyland Dr; ⊙11am–11pm Sun-Thu, to 12am Fri-Sat) Show up early and score a personal leather recliner at this sports and drinking emporium with 175 TVs. Ball-park food and couch-potato classics make up an all-American menu.

House of Blues   LIVE MUSIC
(☎714-778-2583; www.houseofblues.com; 1530 S Disneyland Dr; ⊙11am – 1:30am) House of Blues occasionally gets some heavy-hitting rock, pop, jazz and blues concerts. Call or check online for showtimes and tickets.

🛍 Shopping
DISNEYLAND PARK & DISNEY CALIFORNIA ADVENTURE
Every section of the Disney parks has its own shopping options tailored to its own particular themes – Davy Crockett, New Orleans, the Old West, Route 66 or a seaside amusement park. The biggest theme-park stores – Disneyland Park's **Emporium** (Main Street, USA) and DCA's **Greetings from California** – have a mind-boggling variety of souvenirs, clothing and Disneyana, from T-shirts to mouse ears. Girls go wild at the **Bibbidi Bobbidi Boutique** (☎reservations 714-781-7895; Fantasyland; ⊙open by reservation only), where princess makeovers – including hairstyle, makeup and gown – don't come cheap.

Don't bother carrying your purchases around all day; store them at the Newsstand (Main Street, USA), Star Trader (Tomorrowland), Pioneer Mercantile (Frontierland) or Engine Ear Toys (DCA). If you're staying at Disneyland, have packages sent directly to your hotel – you can even pay for your purchases with your keycard.

DOWNTOWN DISNEY
Most shops in Downtown Disney open and close with the parks.

Disney Vault 28   CLOTHING, GIFTS
Hipster gear from distressed T-shirts with edgy Cinderella prints to black tank tops patterned with white skulls. Features Disney boutique lines like Kingdom Couture and Disney Vintage.

LittleMissMatched   CLOTHING, GIFTS
Quirky-cool apparel for girls; the specialty is colorful mismatched socks sold in packs of three, so it'll never matter if you lose one.

Lego Imagination Center   CLOTHING, GIFTS
Just what it says. Featuring hands-on exhibits and all the latest Lego building sets.

World of Disney   SOUVENIRS
Pirates and princesses are hot at this mini-metropolis of merchandising. Don't miss the special room dedicated to Disney's villains.

Compass Books   BOOKS
Decorated in the style of an old-school NYC Explorers' Club, this shop stocks best sellers, manga paperbacks and travel tomes from an independent local bookseller.

ⓘ Information
FASTPASS & Single Riders
With a bit of preplanning, you can significantly cut your wait time for popular attractions. One option is using the FASTPASS system (p582). If you're traveling solo, ask the greeter at the entrance to the ride if there's a single-rider line;

you can often head to the front of the queue. Availability may depend on the crowd size.

Internet Resources

Mouse Wait (www.mousewait.com) This free iPhone app offers up-to-the-minute updates on ride wait times and what's happening in the parks.

Touring Plans (www.touringplans.com) The 'unofficial guide to Disneyland' since 1985, this online resource offers no-nonsense advice, a crowd calendar and a 'lines app' for most mobile devices.

Medical Services

Western Medical Center Anaheim (714-533-6220; www.westernmedanaheim.com; 1025 S Anaheim Blvd; 24hr) Emergency room available 24/7.

Stroller Rental

Rent a stroller for $15 per day ($25 for two strollers) outside the main entrance of Disneyland park. Rental strollers may be taken into both theme parks.

Tickets & Opening Hours

Both parks are open 365 days a year, but park hours depend on the marketing department's projected attendance numbers. You can access the **current calendar** (recorded info 714-781-4565, live assistance 714-781-7290; www.disneyland.com) by phone or online. During peak season (mid-June to early September) Disneyland Park's hours are usually 8am to midnight. The rest of the year it's open from 10am to between 8pm and 11pm. DCA closes at 9pm in summer, earlier in the low season.

One-day admission to either Disneyland or DCA costs $80 for adults and $74 for children aged three to nine. To visit both parks in one day costs $105/99 per adult/child. Multiday Park Hopper Tickets cost $173/161 for two days, $214/198 for three days, $234/216 for four days and $246/226 for five days. Ticket prices increase annually, so check the website for the latest information. You may also be able to buy discounted tickets online.

For parking, see p592.

Tourist Information

Anaheim Visitors Center (714-765-8888; www.anaheimoc.org; 800 W Katella Ave; 8am-5pm Mon-Fri) Just south of DCA at the Anaheim Convention Center. Offers information on county-wide lodging, dining and transportation. No public internet access. Best to walk here to avoid a parking fee of $10 per day.

Central Plaza Information Board (714-781-4565; Main Street, USA, Disneyland park) One of several information centers in the theme parks.

ⓘ Getting There & Away

Air

See p581 for information on air connections.

Southern California Gray Line/Coach America (714-978-8855; www.graylineanaheim.com) runs the Disneyland Resort Express between LAX and Disneyland-area hotels at least hourly (one way/round-trip to LAX $20/30). It also serves John Wayne Airport (SNA) in Santa Ana ($15/25).

Bus

Frequent departures are available with **Greyhound** (714-999-1256; 100 W Winston Rd) to and from downtown LA ($8 to $15, about one hour) and to San Diego ($14 to $27, 2½ hours).

Car

Disneyland Resort is just off I-5 on Harbor Blvd, about 30 miles south of downtown LA. The park is roughly bordered by Ball Rd, Disneyland Dr, Harbor Blvd and Katella Ave. Giant, easy-to-read overhead signs indicate which ramps you need to take for the theme parks, hotels or Anaheim's streets.

All-day parking costs $15. Enter the 'Mickey & Friends' parking structure from southbound Disneyland Dr at Ball Rd. (It's the largest parking structure in the world, with a capacity of 10,300 vehicles.) Take the tram to reach the parks; follow the signs. The lots stay open one hour after the parks close.

The parking lots for Downtown Disney are reserved for shoppers and have a different rate structure: the first three hours are free, with an additional two more free hours if you have a validation from a table-service restaurant or the movie theater. After that it's $6 per hour, up to $30 a day. Downtown Disney also has valet parking for an additional $6, plus tip.

Train

If you're arriving by train, you'll stop at the **depot** (2150 E Katella Ave) next to Angel Stadium, a quick shuttle or taxi ride east of Disneyland. **Amtrak** (714-385-1448; www.amtrak.com) and **Metrolink** (800-371-5465; www.metrolinktrains.com) commuter trains connect Anaheim to LA's Union Station ($14, 50 minutes) and San Diego ($27, two hours).

ⓘ Getting Around

Bus

The bus company **Anaheim Resort Transit** (ART; 714-563-5287, 888-364-2787; www.rideart.org) provides frequent service between Disneyland and hotels in the immediate area, saving headaches parking and walking. An all-day pass costs $4 per adult and $1 per child aged three to nine. You must buy the pass before boarding; pick one up at one of a dozen kiosks (exact cash or credit card) or online. If you hop on without a pass, you can pay $3 onboard for a one-way trip. Service starts one hour before Disneyland opens and ends half an hour after it closes.

Many hotels and motels have free shuttles to Disneyland and other area attractions; ask before booking.

Monorail

Take the monorail from Tomorrowland to the Disneyland Hotel, across from Downtown Disney, and save about 20 minutes of walking time. It's free if you've bought a park admission ticket.

AROUND DISNEYLAND

If the relentless cheeriness of Disneyland starts to grate on your nerves, there are several entertaining – even kitschy – alternatives within 5 miles of the parks. Anaheim's streets are laid out in an easy-to-navigate grid, with most neighborhoods flowing seamlessly from one to another.

Buena Park

Knott's Berry Farm   AMUSEMENT PARK

(☏714-220-5200; www.knotts.com; 8039 Beach Blvd; adult/child 3-11yr & senior $57/25; ☺from 10am, closing hours vary; ♿) They drop off kids by the busload at this Old West–themed park. Just 4 miles northwest of Anaheim off the I-5, Knott's is smaller and less frenetic than the Disneyland parks, but it can be fun, especially for roller coaster fanatics, young teens and kids who love the *Peanuts* gang. Opening hours vary seasonally so call ahead or check online. Also check the website for the latest discounts; some can be substantial. Parking costs $14.

The park opened in 1940 when Mr Knott's boysenberries (a blackberry-raspberry hybrid) and Mrs Knott's fried-chicken dinners attracted crowds of local farmhands. Mr Knott built an imitation ghost town to keep them entertained. Eventually they hired local carnival rides and charged admission. Mrs Knott kept frying chicken but the rides and Old West buildings became the main attraction.

Today the park keeps the Old West theme alive with shows and demonstrations in Ghost Town, but it's the thrill rides that draw the crowds. Nearby, the suspended, inverted **Silver Bullet** screams through a corkscrew, a double spiral and an outside loop. From the ground, look up to see the dirty socks and bare feet of suspended riders

who've removed their shoes. The **Xcelerator** is a '50s-themed roller coaster that blasts you from 0mph to 82mph in only 2.3 seconds. There's a hair-raising twist at the top. One of the tallest wooden roller coasters in the world – and the largest attraction in the park's history – is the 118ft-tall **GhostRider**, in which riders climb into 'mining cars' for a thrilling journey. **Camp Snoopy** is a kiddie wonderland populated by the Peanuts characters and family-friendly rides.

In October Knott's hosts what is regarded as SoCal's best and scariest Halloween party. On select dates from late September to Halloween, the park closes at 5:30pm and reopens at 7pm as Knott's Scary Farm. Terrifying mazes and creepy shows – not to mention 1000 roaming monsters – keep things scary.

Next to Knott's is the affiliated water park **Knott's Soak City USA** (☏714-220-5200; www.knotts.com; adult/child 3-11yr & senior $27/22; ☺mid-May–Sep; ♿).

Medieval Times Dinner & Tournament   SPECTATOR SPORT

(☏714-521-4740; www.medievaltimes.com; 7662 Beach Blvd; adult/child $58/36; ☺daily, show times vary; ♿) Hear ye, hear ye! Gather ye clans and proceed forthwith to Medieval Times for an evening of feasting and performance in 12th-century style. Guests root for various knights as they joust, fence and show off their horsemanship (on real live Andalusian horses). Dinner is OK; the show's the thing.

Santa Ana

Discovery Science Center   MUSEUM

(☏714-542-2823; www.discoverycube.org; 2500 N Main St; adult/child & senior $18/13; ☺10am-5pm; ♿) This fantastic science center has more than 100 interactive displays in exhibit areas that include Dynamic Earth, The Body and Dino Quest. Step into the eye of a hurricane – you hair will get mussed – or grab a seat in the Shake Shack for a 6.9 quake. Heading south on the I-5 from Disneyland (about 5 miles), look for the 10-story cube seemingly balanced on one of its points. Parking costs $4.

Bowers Museum of Cultural Art   MUSEUM

(☏714-567-3600; www.bowers.org; 2002 N Main St; permanent collection adult/child $12/9; ☺10am-4pm Tue-Sun) The Bowers may be small, but the place draws major crowds with its tantalizing, high-quality special exhibits; at the time of writing, offerings included 'The Art and Craft of the American Whaler' and a collection of Chinese objects borrowed from the Shanghai Museum. This Mission-style museum also has a rich permanent collection of pre-Columbian, African, Oceanic and Native American art. Special exhibits may require separate tickets, which have cost as much as $27 per adult; the museum is free on the first Sunday of each month.

Orange

For a pleasant dose of small-town life complete with a wide selection of mom-and-pop restaurants and shops, drive 1.5 miles south from Disneyland on S Harbor Blvd then turn left on Chapman Ave, following it east about 3.5 miles to Old Towne Orange in the City of Orange. Old Towne was originally laid out by Alfred Chapman and Andrew Glassell who, in 1869, received the 1-sq-mile piece of real estate in lieu of legal fees. Built around a pretty plaza at the intersection of Chapman Ave and Glassell St, it's got the most concentrated collection of antiques shops in Orange County.

You can enjoy breakfast inside a former gas station at the Filling Station (www.fillingstationcafe.com; 201 N Glassell St; mains $4-12; ☺9am-5pm), now serving gourmet scrambles and pancake sandwiches instead of unleaded. For lunch or dinner, nab a patio table at Felix Continental Cafe (www.felixcontinentalcafe.com; 36 Plaza Sq; mains lunch $5-12, dinner $7-14; ☺11am-10pm Mon-Fri, from 8am Sat & Sun). This longtime favorite serves spiced-just-right Caribbean, Cuban and Spanish dishes, most accompanied by a hefty serving of black beans or rice. Disneyland's imagineered Main Street, USA will lose a little luster after you slurp a chocolate malt at the counter inside Watson Drug & Soda Fountain (www.watsonsdrugs.com; 116 E Chapman Ave; ☺6:30am-9pm Mon-Sat, 8am-8pm Sun), a 100-year-old diner and soda shop.

Little Saigon

If you head a few miles southwest of Disneyland, you'll drive into the city of Westminster near the junction of I-405 and Hwy 22. Home to a large Vietnamese population, the community has carved out its own vibrant commercial district around the intersection of Bolsa and Brookhurst Aves. At its heart is the Asian Garden Mall (www.asiangardenmall.com; 9200 Bolsa Ave), a behemoth of a structure packed with 400 ethnic boutiques, including herbalists and jade jewelers. On weekend evenings in summer, there's a night market from 7pm to midnight with vendors, food and live entertainment.

If you're here at lunchtime, browse the photo menus at the casual eateries on the lower level toward the mall's north entrance. The mini food court offers a variety of noodle and vegetable dishes and the *pho ga* (chicken noodle soup) is superb.

Another popular restaurant is Brodard (www.brodard.net; 9892 Westminster Ave, Garden Grove; mains under $13; ☺8am-9pm, closed Tue), where half the fun is finding the place. The restaurant is known for its *nem nuong cuon,* rice paper wrapped tightly around a Spam-like pork paste and served with a light special sauce. It's oddly addictive. From Disneyland, follow Harbor Blvd south for 3.5 miles. Turn right at W 17th St, which becomes Westminister Ave, and cross Brookhurst Ave. At the mall on your left, drive behind the 99 cent store and continue to the restaurant's red awning.

ORANGE COUNTY BEACHES

An inviting string of beaches and coastal communities lines Orange County's 42-mile coast, each of them boasting a distinctly different set of charms. The six major towns, starting with Seal Beach in the north, are linked by the Pacific Coast Hwy (PCH; Hwy 1) and grow increasingly scenic – and some may say ritzy – as you continue south.

From Seal Beach, PCH passes scruffy Sunset Beach, surfing-crazed Huntington Beach, ritzy Newport Beach and Corona del Mar before rolling into the cliff-and-cove-dotted artists' enclave of Laguna Beach. Just south, Dana Point draws the yacht crowd, while end-of-the-county San Clemente returns to the small-town vibe – and one awesome, border-hugging surf spot.

In summer, accommodations book up far in advance, prices rise and some properties impose minimum two- or three-night stays.

Seal Beach

In the pageant for charming small towns, Seal Beach enjoys an unfair advantage over the competition: 1.5 miles of pristine beach glittering like an already won crown. And that's without mentioning its three-block Main St – a lineup of locally owned restaurants, mom-and-pop stores and indie coffeehouses that are refreshingly low on attitude and high on welcoming charm.

Main St spills into **Seal Beach Pier**, which extends 1885ft out over the ocean. The beach faces south here and, except for the offshore oil rigs (which locals seem to easily tune out), it's very pleasant. The mild waves make it a great place to learn how to surf before heading to more challenging waves further south. Good thermal winds make the coast here a prime spot for kite-surfing. For surfing lessons, look for the marked van owned by **M&M Surfing School** (☑714-846-7873; www.mmsurfingschool.com; 3hr group lesson $65) usually parked in the lot north of the pier.

The one hotel that's within walking distance of the beach is **Pacific Inn** (☑562-493-7501, 866-466-0300; www.pacificinn-sb.com; 600 Marina Dr; r from $159; ❉@🐾📶🐾). The recently renovated rooms have down comforters and complimentary wi-fi; there's also a sunny central pool.

As for food, most of the restaurants on Main St are worthy of recommendation. In the morning, we suggest **Nick's Deli** (223 Main St; mains $5-8; ⊘7am-7pm Mon-Fri, to 4pm Sat & Sun) for the county's best breakfast burritos (they sell about one per minute). Everybody's favorite for fresh fish is **Walt's Wharf** (www.waltswharf.com; 201 Main St; mains lunch $8-15, dinner $13-27; ⊘11am-3:30pm & 4-9pm); some people even drive here from LA. Walt's gets packed on weekends and you can't make reservations for dinner, but it's worth the long wait for the oak-fire-grilled seafood and steaks, served with delicious sauces.

Huntington Beach

In June 2011, the mayor of Huntington Beach (HB) presented the 'key to the city' to surfing legend Kelly Slater – an event that tells you everything you need to know about this beach community. HB has been a surf mecca for nearly a century, starting in 1914 when Hawaiian-Irish surfing star George Freeth (brought to California by pioneer developer Henry Huntington) gave demonstrations of the exotic sport off the coast. In recent years, HB's surfing image has been heavily marketed, with city fathers even getting a bit aggro (surfer slang for 'territorial') in their efforts to ensure exclusive rights to the now-trademarked nickname 'Surf City, USA.' The moniker originally came from Jan and Dean's 1963 pop hit by the same name. But

the sport is big business, with buyers for major retailers coming here to see what surfers are wearing and then marketing the look.

Commercial development along Main St has left downtown with a vaguely prefab feel, but the bland facades are frequently enlivened by sidewalk-surfing skateboarders and inebriated barflies whooping it up from the street's numerous bars. Just look around at the beautiful blonde people playing volleyball on the sand or skating along the beach paths – HB is still the quintessential place to celebrate the coastal SoCal lifestyle.

In late July, the city hosts the **US Open of Surfing** (www.usopenofsurfing.com), a six-star competition drawing more than 600 surfers, 400,000 spectators and a minivillage of concerts, motocross demos and skater jams.

◉ Sights & Activities

Surfing in Huntington Beach is competitive; control your longboard or draw the ire of territorial locals. Surf north of the pier and consider **M&M Surfing School** (☑714-846-7873; www.mmsurfingschool.com; 3hr group lesson $65) for lessons (and a bodyguard). For kite-surfing instruction, try **Kitesurfari** (☑714-964-5483; www.kitesurfari.com; 18822 Beach Blvd; 3hr lesson from $180). If you just want to watch surfers in action, walk down to **Huntington City Beach** at the foot of the pier. Just south is **Huntington State Beach**, the place to build a beach bonfire. Buy wood at nearby concessionaires then stake out a concrete fire ring. Romp with your dog in the surf at **Dog Beach**, northwest of Goldenwest St. Huntington Beach prides itself on being a dog-friendly community: the visitors center has full listings of the city's dog parks and cafes and shops that cater to canines.

International Surfing Museum   MUSEUM
(☑714-960-3483; www.surfingmuseum.org; 411 Olive Ave; suggested donation $2; ⊘noon-5pm Mon & Wed-Fri, to 9pm Tue, 11am-6pm Sat & Sun) A small but interesting collection of surf-related memorabilia can be found at this museum just off Main St. Exhibits chronicle the sport's history with photos, surfboards and surf music. The museum also hosts film screenings and special events; check the website for details.

Bolsa Chica State Ecological Reserve   NATURE RESERVE
(☑714-846-1114; ⊘sunrise-sunset) Just north of HB, PCH looks out onto Bolsa Chica State Ecological Reserve. At first glance it may

look rather desolate (especially with the few small oil wells scattered about), but this restored salt marsh is an environmental success story teeming with bird life – according to reports, 321 of Orange County's 420 bird species have been spotted here in the past decade. These 1700 acres have been saved from numerous development projects over the years by a band of determined locals. A 1.5-mile loop trail starts from the parking lot on PCH. There's a small **interpretative center** (3842 Warner Ave; ⊘9am-4pm Tue-Fri, 10am-3pm Sat & Sun) near the intersection of PCH and Warner.

🛏 Sleeping

There aren't many budget option in HB, especially in summer when nothing-special motels hike their prices to ridiculous levels. If you want budget accommodation, head inland toward I-405.

TOP CHOICE **Shorebreak Hotel**   LUXURY HOTEL $$$
(☑714-861-4470; www.shorebreakhotel.com; 500 Pacific Coast Hwy; r from $224; ✸@🛜🏊) Stunning and sleek, the brand-new Shorebreak – the latest from Joie de Vivre, the popular California boutique hotel chain – is the hands-down winner for the coolest place to stay near the water. There's an airy patio with several fire pits, a state-of-the-art fitness center, an evening wine reception for guests, and 157 rooms with flat-screen TVs and decks or balconies (some of which face the sea). There's even a 'Beach Butler' to book your surfing lessons for you.

Hotel Huntington Beach   HOTEL $
(☑714-891-0123, 877-891-0123; www.hotelhb.com; 7667 Center Ave; r from $85; ✸@🛜🏊) This eight-story hotel, which looks like an office building, is decidedly sans personality and a bit worn, but the rooms are clean and perfect for get-up-and-go travelers (the hotel's adjacent to I-405).

Comfort Suites   HOTEL $$
(☑714-841-1812; www.comfortsuiteshuntington beach.com; 16301 Beach Blvd (Hwy 39); r $100-120; ✸@🛜🏊) Hot breakfast items such as scrambled eggs and bacon, plus free parking and complimentary wi-fi, make this chain worth a mention. The rates are pretty reasonable for comfortable, if not particularly distinctive, rooms. Closer to I-405 than the beach: you'll have to drive away from the water for about 10 minutes to reach the hotel.

Sun 'n Sands   MOTEL $$
(☑714-536-2543, www.sunnsands.com; 1102 Pacific Coast Hwy; r $149-189, mini-ste $229-269; 🛜🏊) This mom-and-pop motel would cost well under $100 a night anywhere east of town, but its location across from the beach lets it get away with absurdly high rates. The place offers views of the Huntington Beach Pier, but it probably goes without saying that it can get pretty loud here at night.

✖ Eating & Drinking

It's easy to find a bar in HB. (Walk up Main Street in the early evening and it might seem like there's nothing *but* bars in this town.)

Sugar Shack   BREAKFAST $
(www.hbsugarshack.com; 213 1/2 Main St; mains $5-10; ⊘6am-4pm Mon, Tue & Thu, to 8pm Wed, to 5pm Fri-Sun) The sidewalk patio is the place to sit at this Main St stalwart for some of HB's best people-watching. And if you're here really early, you might catch surfer dudes donning their wetsuits. The $5.55 breakfast special comes with two pancakes, an egg and bacon or a sausage. Sign up for a table at the clipboard on the outside wall.

Chronic Tacos   MEXICAN $
(www.eatchronictacos.com; 328 11th St; mains under $8; ⊘8am-9pm) For surfer haute cuisine, mosey into this sticker-covered shack and request a made-to-order Fatty Taco, then settle in for one of the best Mexican meals around. With the Dead playing on the stereo, a couple of surf bums shooting pool and chatty, laid-back staff, you might just never leave. You'll see other locations scattered across SoCal.

Park Bench Cafe   BREAKFAST, CAFE $
(www.parkbenchcafe.com; 17732 Goldenwest St; mains breakfast $6-10, lunch $9-11; ⊘7:30am-2pm Tue-Fri, to 3pm Sat & Sun; 🐾🏊) A short drive east on Goldenwest St from PCH lands you at this shady outdoor cafe in Huntington Central Park. If you're traveling with Fido, he can order the Hound Dog Heaven patty off the dog menu.

RA Sushi   SUSHI $$
(www.rasushi.com; 155 5th St; mains $10-18; ⊘11am-11pm Tue-Fri) The sushi is so-so at this stylish clublike eatery across the street from the beach; the real draw is the budget-friendly happy hour (3pm to 7pm Monday through Saturday) with a long menu of discounted appetizers and Asian-style tapas from pork gyoza and crunchy calamari rolls

(each $5) to hot sake ($2) and vodka martinis ($5).

Deville
PUB, BURGERS $

(424 Olive Ave; mains $4-9; ⊙11am-11pm Mon-Fri, from 10am Sat & Sun) This dark, down-to-earth pub – across the street from the International Surfing Museum – is a local favorite, thanks to delicious $5 burgers and $1 beers. It's on the small side, so it stays a little quieter than some of the loud bars on Main St.

Duke's
AMERICAN $$

(www.dukeshuntington.com; 317 Pacific Coast Hwy; lunch $9-15, dinner $20-30; ⊙noon-10pm Tue-Sat, 5-10pm Mon; ⓐ) It's definitely touristy, but this Hawaiian-themed restaurant – named after surfing legend Duke Kahanamoku – is also fun and offers up some of the best views around. Start things off with the poke-roll appetizer then pick your fish and seasoning from a long list of choices. If you're just in the mood for drinks, try the Barefoot Bar downstairs.

Beachfront 301
AMERICAN $$

(www.beachfront301.com; 301 Main St; mains $8-18; ⊙10am-late; ⓐ) This laid-back corner bar and grill is renowned for its lively happy hour (all day Monday and 3pm to 9pm Tuesday through Friday) with bargain food and drink specials. Offerings include $3 Baja-style chicken tacos and onion rings; $5 will buy you a veggie pizza, Santa Fe chicken wrap or double cheeseburger.

ℹ️ Information

Huntington Beach Convention and Visitors Bureau (☎714-969-3492; www.surfcityusa.com; Suite 208, 301 Main St; ⊙9am-5pm Mon-Fri) provides tourist maps and other information.

Newport Beach & Around

Pop culture representations of Newport Beach – rich kids driving sports cars on *The OC*, an earnest George Michael Bluth working at the frozen banana stand on *Arrested Development* – are surprisingly realistic. Indeed, Orange County's ritziest beach community is filled with beautiful, moneyed people. The locals, almost uniformly fresh-faced and sun-kissed, are the last word in resort wear – you'll be hard-pressed to find even one brooding, pimply-faced smoker in a too-large sweater. And yes, there are frozen bananas (though Newport's classic summertime treat is actually the Balboa Bar,

a square of vanilla ice cream dipped into chocolate and served on a stick).

So why visit Newport? Because the local environment is particularly lovely. The city surrounds a pretty natural harbor that's one of the largest for pleasure craft in the US. Balboa Peninsula, which faces the harbor on one side and the open ocean on the other, offers fantastically wide beaches. At almost any hour of the day, you'll see a steady stream of cyclists, joggers and skaters on paved beach paths that extend as far as the eye can see. Just southeast of Newport is the chichi beach community of Corona del Mar and the historic Crystal Cove State Park.

For a more down-to-earth vibe, follow Hwy 55 south onto Balboa Peninsula. Six miles long and a quarter-mile wide, the peninsula is home to white-sand beaches, a number of hotels, seafood restaurants and stylish homes – and lots of surfers catching oceanside waves.

Hotels, restaurants and bars cluster around the peninsula's two piers: **Newport Pier**, near its western end, and **Balboa Pier**, at the eastern end. The oceanfront strip teems with beachgoers and the people-ogling is great

⊙ Sights & Activities

Lovell House
HISTORIC BUILDING

(1242 W Ocean Front) One of Newport Beach's most architecturally significant homes, this 1926 house sits beside the beach bike path. Designed by seminal modernist architect Rudolph Schindler, it was built using site-cast concrete frames and wood.

Balboa Fun Zone
AMUSEMENT PARK

(www.thebalboafunzone.com; 603 E Bay Ave; ⊙11am-9pm Sun-Thu, to 10pm Fri & Sat) Opposite the Balboa Pier on the harbor side of the peninsula, visitors can hop aboard the iconic Ferris wheel (you'll catch great views of the sea from the top) or take a spin on the carousel, which has been around since 1936.

Newport Harbor Nautical Museum MUSEUM

(☎949-675-8915; www.nhnm.org; Balboa Fun Zone, 600 E Bay Ave; adult/child $4/2; ⊙11am-6pm Sun-Thu, to 7pm Sat) This lively nautical museum features model ships, maritime memorabilia and a kid-friendly wing with a 'Touch Tank' where visitors can interact with sea creatures (sea stars, bat stars, sea urchins) found in the region's tidepools. The nearby **Balboa Pavilion**, a landmark dating from 1905, is beautifully illuminated at night.

Newport Beach

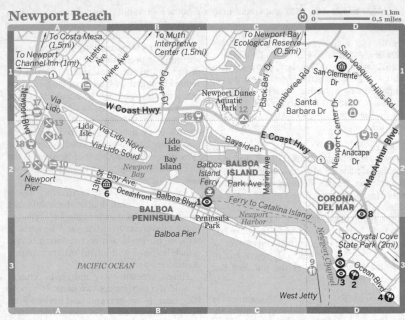

Wedge
SURFING

At the very tip of the peninsula, by the West Jetty, the Wedge is a bodysurfing and knee-boarding spot famous for its perfectly hollow waves that can get up to 30ft high. Look for the small crowd watching the high-octane action from the shore. But beware venturing in yourself – the waves are shore-breakers and regularly smash bodysurfers against the sand like rag dolls.

Balboa Island
ISLAND

In the middle of the harbor sits the island that time forgot. Its streets are still largely lined with tightly clustered cottages built in the 1920s and '30s when this was a summer getaway from LA. The 1.5-mile promenade that circles the island makes a terrific car-free stroll or jog. Near the Ferris wheel on the harbor side, the **Balboa Island Ferry** (www. balboaislandferry.com; 410 S Bayfront; adult/child/car & driver $1/0.50/2; ☺6:30am-midnight) shuttles passengers across the bay. The ferry lands at Agate Ave, about 11 blocks west of Marine Ave, which is lined with swimwear boutiques, Italian trattorias and cocktail bars.

Orange County Museum of Art
MUSEUM

(☎949-759-1122; www.ocma.net; 850 San Clemente Dr; adult/child under 12yr $12/free; ☺11am-5pm Wed & Fri-Sun, to 8pm Thu) Less than a mile from Fashion Island, this engaging museum highlights California art and cutting-edge contemporary artists with exhibits rotating through its two large gallery areas every four to six months. There's also a sculpture garden, an eclectic gift shop and a theater screening classic, foreign and art-related films.

Corona del Mar
NEIGHBORHOOD

This ritzy bedroom community, perched on the privileged eastern bluffs of the Newport Channel, has some of the best coastal views in SoCal. It also includes a high-end stretch of PCH, with trendy shops and restaurants, as well as **Corona del Mar State Beach** (☎949-644-3151; www.parks.ca.gov; ☺5am-10pm), which lies at the foot of rocky cliffs. Parking costs $15, even more on peak summer holidays. If you're early (or lucky), try to nab a free parking spot above the beach on Ocean Blvd.

Lookout Point sits above the beach along Ocean Blvd near Heliotrope Ave. Locals throw sunset cocktail parties here, but be discreet with your chardonnay: technically, open containers are illegal. Stairs lead to **Pirate's Cove**, which has a great, wave-less beach and is ideal for families. Scenes from *Gilligan's Island* were shot here. A bit further east on Ocean Blvd is **Inspiration Point**, another nice spot to enjoy the view.

Newport Beach

Children love the tide pool just east at **Little Corona del Mar Beach**.

Corona del Mar's prize attraction is the compact **Sherman Library & Gardens** (☏949-673-2261; www.slgardens.org; 2647 E Coast Hwy; adult/child $3/1, Mon admission free; ⊙gardens 10:30am-4pm daily, library 9am-4:30pm Tue-Thu). The gardens are manicured, lush and bursting with color. The small, noncirculating research library holds a wealth of California historical documents, as well as paintings by early California landscape artists. If you're here around lunchtime, dine in full view of the gardens at the French-inspired **Café Jardin** (☏949-673-0033; ⊙11:30am-2pm Mon-Fri; set menu $20-25).

Crystal Cove State Park PARK (☏949-494-3539; www.crystalcovestatepark.com; Pacific Coast Hwy; ⊙6am-sunset) Once you get past the parking lots ($15), it's easy to forget you're in a crowded metropolitan area at this state park, where visitors are treated to 2000 acres of undeveloped woodlands and 3.5 miles of coastline. Everyone thought the hilltops were part of the state park too, until the Irvine Company, the actual landowner, bulldozed them to make room for McMansions that are the dream of many OC residents. For a more discreet, short-term stay, reserve one of the park's inland campsites (it's a 3-mile hike each way) with **Reserve America** (☏800-444-7275; www.reservecamerica.com; tent sites $20).

Newport Bay Ecological Reserve NATURE RESERVE Inland from the harbor, where runoff from the San Bernardino Mountains meets the sea, the brackish water of the Newport Bay Ecological Reserve supports more than 200 species of birds. This is one of the few estuaries in Southern California that has been preserved, and it's an important stopover on the Pacific Flyway. The **Muth Interpretive Center** (☏949-923-2290; www.ocparks.com/unbic; 2301 University Dr; ⊙10am-4pm Tue-Sun; ♿), near Irvine Ave and just out of view of the parking lot, is made from sustainable materials. Inside, you'll find displays and information about the 752-acre reserve, as well as a kid-friendly activity room with a number of small, snake-and-spider-filled terraria. For guided tours with naturalists and weekend kayak tours of the Back Bay (from $20 per person) contact the **Newport Bay Naturalists & Friends** (☏949-640-6746; www.newportbay.org).

🛏 Sleeping

Rates drop by as much as 40% (or more) in winter. Those listed here are for high season.

Newport Dunes Waterfront Resort & Marina CAMPGROUND $ (☏949-729-3863; www.newportdunes.com; 1131 Back Bay Dr; tent & RV sites with hookups from $64, cottages from $146; ◉⊛⊛⊛) Welcome to RV heaven. Besides hookups, Newport Dunes has a pool, a spa, game rooms and a small beach on one of Newport's brackish lagoons. For those without a Winnebago, the tiny cottages are a good deal, especially in the low season. There are a few campsites. In the lobby, look for the concrete handprints of several cast members from the now-canceled show *The OC;* the memorial was booted from its former spot of glory at the visitors bureau.

Newport Channel Inn MOTEL $$
(☎800-255-8614; www.newportchannelinn.com; 6030 W Coast Hwy; r $109-200; ❋🐾) Cyclists love this two-story motel's proximity to the beach bike path, which is just across the street. Other perks include large rooms, a big common sundeck and genuinely friendly owners. The large A-framed room 219 sleeps up to seven. Top budget choice that works well for traveling groups.

Bay Shores Peninsula Hotel HOTEL $$
(☎949-675-3463, 800-222-6675; www.thebestinn. com; 1800 W Balboa Blvd; d $179-300; ❋@🐾) *Endless Summer* surf murals. Freshly baked cookies. Shelves of free movies. This three-story hotel has a fun, beach-minded hospitality that makes the surfing lifestyle seem accessible – even if you're a middle-aged landlubber who's never touched a board in your life.

Holiday Inn Express MOTEL $$
(☎800-308-5401; www.hienewportbeach.com; 2300 W Coast Hwy; r $190-219; ❋@❋🐾) There's not much in the way of local charm, but this Holiday Inn branch is good value. Rooms have up-to-date furnishings and extras such as microwaves and refrigerators. Centrally located on PCH between major attractions.

✕ Eating

TOP CHOICE **Bluewater Grill** SEAFOOD $$
(www.bluewatergrill.com; 630 Lido Park Dr; mains $8-30; ⊙11am-10pm Mon-Thu, to 11pm Fri & Sat, 10am-10pm Sun) This casual yet elegant New England–style seafood eatery, occupying a quiet spot on the edge of the bay, is a hit with locals thanks to the spacious patio seating, raw oyster bar, fresh grilled swordfish and the famous house clam chowder. Try the ceviche lettuce wraps at lunchtime or come for happy hour (3:30pm to 6:30pm Monday through Friday) at the nautical-themed bar.

Sabatino's Sausage Company ITALIAN $$
(www.sabatinoschicagosausage.com; 251 Shipyard Way; mains $10-27; ⊙11am-10pm Mon-Fri, from 8:30am Sat & Sun) Around the corner from Bluewater Grill is this pleasantly rustic Italian restaurant with checkered tablecloths and free-flowing red wine. Famous for

Sicilian-style sausage – you'll see a stream of locals coming in to buy it at the central deli counter – Sabatino's also turns out savory seafood stews and pasta tossed with fresh clams and mussels. If you're with a few people, be sure to order the sizzling sausage platter (grilled with sauteed peppers and onions) to start. Note that Sabatino's is tucked away on the bayside; though it's not far from the beach, it's also not on the way anywhere.

Sol Grill SEAFOOD, AMERICAN $
(www.solgrill.com; 110 McFadden Pl; mains $5-25; ⊙5-10pm Tue-Sun; ❋) This down-to-earth bar and eatery, specializing in ahi chowder, lobster ravioli and fruity sangria, has brightly painted walls and an unpretentious atmosphere. There's live music and candlelight in the evenings. The place feels refreshingly bohemian – especially considering the location just across the street from the Newport Pier – and the prices are more than fair.

☕ Drinking

Ruby's Crystal Cove Shake Shack CAFE, JUICE BAR
(☎949-464-0100; 7703 E Coast Hwy; shakes under $5; ⊙10am-sunset) This been-here-forever wooden milkshake stand is now owned by the Ruby's Diner chain, but the shakes and the ocean view are just as good as ever. It's located just east of the Crystal Cove/Los Trancos entrance to the state park.

Alta Coffee Warehouse COFFEE SHOP
(www.altacoffeeshop.com; 506 31st St; ⊙7am-11pm Sun-Thu, to midnight Fri & Sat) Regulars hang their mug on the wall at this cozy coffee shop housed in an inviting bungalow. Try the iced toffee coffee or come for a lunchtime salad on the patio.

Muldoon's PUB
(www.muldoonspub.com; 202 Newport Center Dr; ⊙11:30am-late Tue-Sat, 10:30am-3pm Sun) The SoCal Irish tradition continues at lively Muldoon's, which anchors a small strip mall across the street from Fashion Island.

Cassidy's Bar & Grill BAR
(2603 Newport Blvd; ⊙11am-late) This centrally located dive bar does cheap, strong drinks, addictive cheeseburgers (add its signature hot pepper sauce for a kick) and specials like juicy ribs or chicken. By noon – even on a weekday – most of the barstools are already taken. Located at the intersection of Balboa and Newport Blvds.

COSTA MESA

It takes a lot to drag Newport Beach locals away from their beloved sand and sea. But if there's one thing they love even more than sailing, biking and stand-up paddleboarding, it's looking fabulous – so they all make frequent pilgrimmages to the land-locked suburb of Costa Mesa to do some serious credit card damage at South Coast Plaza (☑800-782-8888; www.southcoastplaza.com; 3333 Bristol St). This sprawling shopping complex is home to 300 luxury stores – it attracts 25 million visitors a year and reports annual sales approaching $1.5 billion. Boutiques such as Chanel and Rolex do their part to keep the numbers high.

If you're not ready to drop a thousand dollars on a bikini and sandals, consider a visit to the Lab (☑714-966-6660; www.thelab.com; 2930 Bristol St; ☺10:30am-9pm Mon-Sat, 11am-6pm Sun), an ivy-covered, outdoor 'anti-mall' where indie shoppers can sift through vintage clothing, trendy styles and eclectic tennis shoes. Pop into the Lab's sultry Cuban-inspired eatery Habana for mojitos, or head next door to the '60s-style bar and Southern-inspired small plates at Memphis Cafe (www.mcmphiscafe.com). You'd be hard-pressed to find a place this moody and stylish anywhere in sunny Newport.

3-Thirty-3 Waterfront
BAR, LOUNGE

(www.3thirty3nb.com; 333 Bayside Dr; ☺11:30am-2am Mon-Fri, from 9am Sat & Sun) Perfect for a low-key happy hour with friends (try the gourmet sliders and fries), this stylish harborside lounge morphs into the stereotypical Newport 'scene' as the night rolls on – think Botoxed former beauties and overtanned yachtsmen, all on a midnight prowl. On weekend mornings, there's a happening brunch with a mix-your-own Bloody Mary bar and gigantic breakfast burritos.

🛍 Shopping

A string of tiny boutiques lines PCH in Corona del Mar. On Balboa Island, Marine Ave is lined with unassuming (but not cheap) shops in a village-like atmosphere.

Fashion Island
MALL

(www.shopfashionisland.com; 401 Newport Center Dr; ☺10am-9pm Mon-Fri, to 7pm Sat, 11am-6pm Sun) Sometimes referred to as Fascist Island, this chic mall has nearly 200 stores and is the draw here for serious shopping. Its breezy, Mediterranean-style walkways are lined with specialty stores, national chains, upscale kiosks, restaurants and the occasional koi pond and fountain. Anchor stores include Bloomingdales, Macy's and Neiman Marcus. There's a small indoor section, Atrium Court, with a Barnes & Noble.

ℹ Information

Your best bet for information? Order the visitors guide from the website before arrival from the **Newport Beach Conference and Visitors'** Center (☑949-719-6100; www.newportbeach-cvb.com; Suite 120, 1200 Newport Center Dr; ☺9am-5pm).

ℹ Getting Around

OCTA (☑714-560-6282; www.octa.net) bus 71 stops at the corner of PCH and Hwy 55, and goes south to Palm St beside the Balboa Pier. It departs about every 45 minutes and the trip between Newport Pier and Balboa Pier is about eight minutes. Bus 57 goes north to South Coast Plaza in Costa Mesa. It runs roughly every 30 minutes daily from the Newport Transportation Center on San Nicolas Dr (near Fashion Island) to South Coast Plaza. The trip takes about 25 minutes.Check current schedules online.

The local fare is $1.50 per trip, cash only. It can be purchased from OCTA fareboxes or the bus driver – you'll need exact change. A one-day pass, available from the driver, costs $4.

Laguna Beach

If you've ever wanted to step into a painting, a sunset stroll through Laguna Beach might be the next best thing. But hidden coves, romantic cliffs, azure waves and waterfront parks aren't the only aesthetic draw. Public sculptures, arts festivals and gallery nights imbue the city with an artistic sensibility you won't find elsewhere in SoCal. Most locals here, though wealthy, are also live-and-let-live, and there's a palpable artistic *joie de vivre* in the air that increases the sense of fun (the kids of MTV's *Laguna Beach* being the one troubling exception).

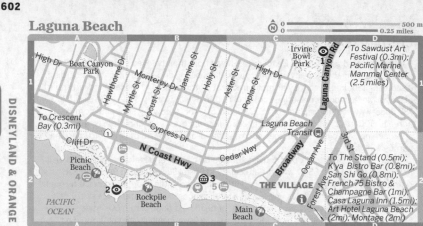

Laguna Beach

The city's natural beauty was a siren's call for San Francisco artist Norman St Clair, who discovered Laguna around 1910 and stayed on to paint its surf, cliffs and hills. His enthusiasm attracted other artists who, influenced by French impressionism, came to be known as the 'plein air' (open air) school.

Partly tucked into canyons and partly arrayed on oceanfront bluffs, Laguna is also a refreshing change from the OC's beige-box architecture, with a combination of classic Arts and Crafts cabins and bold (if at times garish) modern homes. There's even a distinct downtown, known as the Village, with shops, art galleries and restaurants.

While Laguna swells with tourists on summer weekends, there are plenty of uncrowded beaches once you move away from downtown and the adjacent Main Beach.

⊙ Sights & Activities

Laguna stretches for about 7 miles along Pacific Coast Hwy. Shops, restaurants and bars are concentrated along a quarter-mile stretch in the Village, along three parallel streets: Broadway, Ocean Ave and Forest Ave.

Laguna Art Museum   MUSEUM
(☎949-494-8971; www.lagunaartmuseum.org; 307 Cliff Dr; adult/child under 12yr/student $12/free/10; ☉11am-5pm, later in summer) This breezy museum has changing exhibits, usually featuring one or two California artists, plus a permanent collection heavy on California landscapes, vintage photographs and works by early Laguna artists. The museum also makes an effort to support new artists and runs an excellent foreign film series.

The museum is a centrally located stop on the **First Thursdays Art Walk** (☎949-683-6871; www.firstthursdaysartwalk.com; museum admission free; ☉5-9pm). During this convivial monthly event, numerous galleries open their doors for an evening of art, music and special exhibits.

🖼 **Pacific Marine Mammal Center**   NATURE CENTER
(www.pacificmmc.org; 20612 Laguna Canyon Rd; ☉10am-4pm; 🚼) A nonprofit organization dedicated to rescuing and rehabilitating injured or ill marine mammals, this center northeast of town has a small staff and many volunteers who help nurse rescued pinnipeds – mostly sea lions and seals – before releasing them back into the wild. There are several outside pools and holding

pens – but remember, this is a rescue center, not SeaWorld. Still, it's educational and heart-warming. Admission is by donation and anything you buy in the gift shop (say, a stuffed animal) helps.

🦜 Beaches

With 30 public beaches and coves, Laguna is perfect for do-it-yourself exploring. Although many beaches are hidden from view by multimillion-dollar homes, a sharp eye will reveal one of the numerous stairways leading to the sand. Traveling south from the Village on PCH, pick an oceanside cross street and see what you can find.

Located at the western end of Broadway, Main Beach has benches, tables, restrooms and volleyball and basketball courts. It's also the best beach for swimming. Northwest of Main Beach, it's too rocky to surf; tidepooling is best. (Tidepool etiquette: tread carefully and don't pick up any living thing that you find in the rocks.)

Just northwest of Main Beach, follow the path to the grassy, bluff-top Heisler Park for sweeping views of the craggy coves and deep blue sea. Bring your camera. Drop down below the park to Diver's Cove, a deep, protected inlet popular with snorkelers and, of course, divers. Northwest of town, Crescent Bay has big hollow waves good for bodysurfing, but parking is difficult here; try the bluffs atop the beach.

👉 Tours

The visitors center has brochures detailing self-guided tours. *The Heritage Walking Companion* is a tour of the city's architecture with an emphasis on bungalows and cottages. The self-guided *Tour Laguna by Bus* gives a more general overview.

First Thursdays Art Walk WALKING
(📞949-683-6871; www.firstthursdaysartwalk.com; admission free) On the first Thursday of the month, downtown gets festive during these walks, which includes 40 local galleries and the Laguna Art Museum from 6pm to 9pm. Shuttles run from the museum to various clusters of galleries.

🛏 Sleeping

Most hotels in Laguna are on PCH, and traffic can be loud. If you're sensitive ask for a room away from the street or use earplugs. There are no budget lodgings in summer, but it's the best place in the OC for charm-

ing, noncorporate digs. Summer rates are listed. Come fall, they drop significantly.

📍 Casa Laguna Inn B&B $$$
(📞800-233-0449; www.casalaguna.com; 2510 S Coast Hwy; r from $300; 🅿@🛜🐾) Laguna's B&B gem is built around a historic 1920s Mission-revival house surrounded by lush, manicured, mature plantings. Rooms are inside former artists' bungalows built in the 1930s and '40s; all have delicious beds, some have Jacuzzi tubs. There's a full breakfast, and evening wine and cheese.

Laguna Cliffs Inn INN $$$
(📞949-497-6645; www.lagunacliffsinn.com; 475 N Coast Hwy; r $209-379; 🅿🛜) Be it good feng shui, friendly staff, comfy beds or proximity to the ocean, something just feels right at this 36-room inn. From the big green pillows on the bed and the flat-screen TVs to the hardwood floors, the decor is a nice mix of new, comfy and clean. For a relaxing close to the day, settle in to the outdoor Jacuzzi with your honey as the sun drops over the ocean. Formerly known as By the Sea Inn.

Montage RESORT $$$
(📞949-715-6000, 866-271-6953, www.montagelagunabeach.com; 30801 S Coast Hwy; d from $580; @🛜🐾) Widely regarded as the most luxurious and fashionable resort in the area, Montage is an indulgent place to hide away with your lover in a secluded bungalow. Even if you're not staying, come for a spa treatment or a cocktail and check out the lobby art and the spectacular sunburst-inlaid swimming pool. At the resort's southern end, there's underground public parking and a public walkway that loops around the grounds atop the bluffs overlooking the sea, and grants access to the sandy shore.

📍 Art Hotel Laguna Beach HOTEL $$
(📞877-363-7229; www.arthotellagunabeach.com; 1404 N Coast Hwy; r from $154; @🛜🐾) One mile north of downtown near Crystal Cove State Park, this simply furnished 28-room hotel boasts appealing extras like free wi-fi, free parking, a handful of oceanview rooms and a deck with a brand-new Jacuzzi.

Inn at Laguna Beach HOTEL $$$
(📞949-497-9722; www.innatlagunabeach.com; 211 N Coast Hwy; r $199-599; @🛜🐾) This three-story white concrete hotel at the north end of Main Beach walks the fine line between hip and homey, with personable finesse. All

DON'T MISS

LAGUNA ART FESTIVALS

With a 6-acre canyon as its backdrop, Laguna's landmark event is the Festival of Arts (☎949-494-1145; www.foapom.com; 650 Laguna Canyon Rd; adult/student & senior $7/4; ⏰from 10am Jul & Aug), a two-month celebration of original artwork in almost all its forms. The 140 exhibiting artists – all approved pursuant to a juried selection process – display art ranging from paintings to handcrafted furniture to scrimshaw. Started in the 1930s by local artists who needed to drum up buyers, the festival now attracts patrons and tourists from around the world. In addition to the art, there are free daily artists workshops, docent tours and live entertainment. For a slightly more indie-minded art show, look for the Sawdust Art Festival (☎949-494-3030; www.sawdustartfestival.org; 935 Laguna Canyon Rd; adult/child/senior $7.75/3.25/6.25; ⏰10am-10pm Jul & Aug) across the street.

The most thrilling part of the main festival is the Pageant of the Masters (☎949-497-6582; www.pageanttickets.com; admission $15-100; ⏰8:30-11:30pm nightly Jul & Aug), where human models blend seamlessly into re-creations of famous paintings. It began in 1933 as a sideshow to the main festival. Tickets generally go on sale around the beginning of December the previous year and sell out before the year ends. You may be able to snag last-minute cancellations at the gate.

rooms have a fresh, clean look enhanced by French blinds and thick featherbeds. Some have balconies overlooking the water. Watch the extra charges – parking costs $20 per day, the resort fee is another $25.

✕ Eating

French 75 Bistro & Champagne Bar   FRENCH $$
(☎949-494-8444; www.french75.net; 1464 S Coast Hwy; mains $19-35; ⏰4:30-11pm) Fantastic coq au vin, chocolate souffle, and icy champagne cocktails (half-price at the bar everyday from 4:30pm to 6:30pm) are the main draws at this refined but friendly bistro. It's a choice spot for a romantic evening out; reservations recommended.

San Shi Go   SUSHI $$
(1100 S Coast Hwy; mains $10-25; ⏰11.30am-2pm Tue-Fri, 5-10pm Mon-Thu, 5-11pm Fri & Sat) This slightly hidden sushi spot has ocean views from some of the tables; more importantly, the rainbow roll and lemon salmon roll practically melt in your mouth. For a more authentic experience, sit at the sushi bar and ask the chef to make you something special (ie a roll that's not on the menu).

The Stand   VEGAN $
(238 Thalia St; mains $6-12; ⏰7am-7pm; ✍) This tiny tribute to vegan cuisine reflects what's best about Laguna living – it's friendly, unassuming and filled with indie spirit. The long menu includes hummus-and-guac sandwiches, sunflower-sprout salads and bean-and-rice burritos. For a snack, try a

smoothie or the corn tortilla chips and salsa. Grab a spot on the wooden patio.

☕ Drinking & Entertainment

K'ya Bistro Bar   COCKTAIL BAR
(www.kyabistro.com; 1287 S Coast Hwy) This chic rooftop bar does killer cocktails (strawberry balsamic martini, anyone?) and tasty small plates. Perched atop the La Casa del Camino Hotel, the bar is noteworthy for its beautiful coastal views and friendly vibe. Follow the crowds through the hotel lobby and take the elevator to the top. As for mojitos, there are five on the cocktail menu, including mango and wild berry.

Las Brisas   COCKTAIL BAR
(☎949-497-5434; www.lasbrisaslagunabeach.com; 361 Cliff Dr) Locals roll their eyes at the mere mention of this tourist-heavy spot, but out-of-towners flock here for a good reason: the blufftop view of the beach. Sip margaritas while you stare at the crashing waves from the glassed-in patio; the image of the coast will leave an indelible impression. Cocktail hour gets packed; make reservations.

❶ Information

Laguna Beach Library (☎949-497-1733; www.ocpl.org; 363 Glenneyre St; ⏰10am-8pm Mon-Wed, to 6pm Thu, 10am-5pm Fri & Sat; @📶) Free wi-fi and walk-in computer and internet access.

Laguna Beach Visitors Center (☎949-497-9229; www.lagunabeachinfo.org; 381 Forest Ave; ⏰10am-4pm Mon-Fri) The staff at this visitors center is very helpful, and one wall here is filled with maps, brochures, bus schedules and coupons.

❶ Getting There & Around

To reach Laguna Beach from the I-405, take Hwy 133 (Laguna Canyon Rd) southwest. Laguna is served by OCTA (☎714-560-6282; www.octa. net) bus 1, which runs along the coast from Long Beach to San Clemente.

Number one piece of advice? Bring lots of quarters to feed the meters. Laguna is hemmed in by steep canyons, and parking is a perpetual problem. In and around the Village you'll find a few outdoor change machines (there's one on Cliff Dr by Heisler Park). If you're spending the night, leave your car at the hotel and ride the local bus. Parking lots in the Village charge $10 to $20 or more per entry and fill up early during summer.

Laguna Beach Transit (www.lagunabeachc ity.net; 375 Broadway) has its central bus depot on Broadway, just north of the visitors center in the heart of the Village. It operates three routes at hourly intervals (approximately 7am to 6pm Monday through Friday, 9am to 6pm Saturday). Routes are color-coded and easy to follow but subject to change. For tourists, the most important route is the one that runs along PCH. Pick up a brochure and schedule at your hotel or the visitors center. Rides cost 75¢ (exact change). All routes are free during July and August. No Sunday service.

San Juan Capistrano

Famous for the swallows that annually return here from their winter migration on March 19 (though sometimes they arrive a bit early), San Juan Capistrano is also home to the 'jewel of the California missions.'

◉ Sights & Activities

Mission San Juan Capistrano   HISTORIC SITE
(☎949-234-1300; www.missionsjc.com; 31882 Camino Capistrano, cnr Ortega Hwy; adult/child/sen ior $9/5/8; ☉8:30am-5pm) Located about 10 miles southeast and inland of Laguna Beach, this beautiful mission was built around a series of 18th-century arcades, all of which enclose photogenic fountains and lush gardens. The charming Serra Chapel – whitewashed outside and decorated with vivid frescoes inside – is considered the oldest building in California. It's the only chapel still standing in which Padre Junípero Serra gave Mass. He founded the mission on November 1, 1776 and tended it personally for many years. Particularly moving are the remains of the Great Stone Church, almost completely destroyed by an earthquake in 1812 that killed 42 Native Americans worshipping inside. Plan to spend at least an hour looking around. Admission includes a worthwhile free audio tour with interesting stories narrated by locals.

To celebrate the swallows' return from their South American sojourn, the city puts on the Festival of the Swallows every year. The birds nest in the walls of the mission until around October 23. They're best observed at feeding time, usually early in the morning and late afternoon to early evening.

Los Rios Historic District   DISTRICT
One block west, next to the Capistrano train depot, is this picturesque assemblage of cottages and adobes housing cafes and gift shops.

✖ Eating

Ramos House Cafe   CAFE $$
(www.ramoshouse.com; 31752 Los Rios St; mains $13-17, weekend brunch $35; ☉8:30am-3pm Tue-Sun; ☑) Famous for earthy comfort food flavored with herbs from the nearby garden, Ramos House is the best spot for breakfast or lunch near the Mission. To find it, walk across the railroad tracks at the end of Verdugo St and turn right. Promptly reward yourself with cinnamon-apple beignets, basil-cured salmon or pulled-pork sandwiches with sweet-potato fries.

Tea House on Los Rios   CAFE $$
(www.theteahouseonlosrios.com; 31731 Los Rios St; mains $13-27; ☉11am-5pm Wed-Fri, 10am-5pm Sat & Sun) Made for ladies who lunch – or sip tea – and their significant others. Think flower-covered trellis, a table-dotted porch and dainty settings, but the menu isn't all cucumber sandwiches. There's also prime rib, shepherd's pie and beer on offer.

☆ Entertainment

Coach House   LIVE MUSIC
(☎949-496-8930; www.thecoachhouse.com; 33157 Camino Capistrano) Long-running live-music venue which features a roster of local and national rock, indie, alternative and retro bands; expect a cover charge of $15 to $40 depending on who's playing. Recent performers include Robben Ford, Aimee Mann and the Gin Blossoms.

SCENIC DRIVE: CRYSTAL COVE TO DOHENY STATE BEACH

This quiet stretch of the Pacific Coast Highway (PCH) offers gorgeous ocean views, a classic roadside milkshake stand, dramatic cliffs, Orange County's (the OC) prettiest beach town, and options to get out of the car and hit the hiking trails.

What to See

Start at the forested coastal paradise of Crystal Cove State Park (p599) and head south on the PCH, stopping for a chocolate milkshake at Ruby's Crystal Cove Shake Shack (p600). The stand, though now owned by a chain, is an old-fashioned OC classic. Enjoy sea views as you continue south towards Laguna Beach. Stop for mango ceviche or chips and salsa with stunning views at Las Brisas (p604), then continue driving through the Village. Continue along the PCH towards Dana Point and the family-friendly Ocean Institute (p606) before ending up at Doheny State Beach (p606) to splash around the tidepools, set up an afternoon picnic or ride bikes along the beach paths.

The Route

The Pacific Coast Highway (Hwy 1) from Crystal Cove State Park south to Doheny State Beach.

Time & Mileage

Fifteen miles, 35 minutes without stops and one to two hours or more if you pull over frequently.

Worthy Detours

Hike the trails high above the ocean in Crystal Cove State Park or head inland from Laguna Beach to tour the beautiful Mission San Juan Capistrano (p605).

❶ Getting There & Away

From Laguna Beach, ride **OCTA** (☏714-560-6282; www.octa.net) bus 1 south to Dana Point. At the intersection of PCH and Del Obispo St, catch bus 91 northbound toward Mission Viejo. Buses run every 30 to 60 minutes and the trips takes about an hour. You'll have to pay the one-way fare ($1.50, exact change) twice.

The Amtrak depot is one block south and west of the mission; you could arrive by train from LA or San Diego in time for lunch, visit the mission and be back in the city for dinner.

Drivers should exit I-5 at Ortega Hwy and head west for about a quarter of a mile.

Dana Point & Around

Nineteenth-century adventurer Richard Dana called Dana Point 'the only romantic spot on the coast.' Nowadays its yacht-filled marinas don't inspire immediate thoughts of romance, but it is a pleasant place to wander if you enjoy maritime history and family-oriented attractions. Most of the action occurs around the man-made harbor on Dana Point Harbor Dr, just off PCH.

The kid-friendly **Ocean Institute** (☏949-496-2274; www.ocean-institute.org; 24200 Dana Pt Harbor Dr; adult/child $6.50/4.50, extra for cruises; ⊙10am-3pm Sat & Sun; ⓓ) includes replicas of historic tall ships, maritime-related exhibits and a floating research lab. Specific trips include a marine-wildlife cruise aboard the RV *Sea Explorer* (adult/child $35/22) and a Pyrate Adventure Sail – with a cast of pirates – on the 118ft *Spirit of Dana Point* tall ship.

Just as fun may be nearby **Doheny State Beach** (☏949-496-6172; www.parks.ca.gov, www.dohenystatebeach.org; ⊙6am-8pm Nov-Feb, to 10pm Mar-Oct; ☕ⓓ), where you'll find picnic tables, grills, volleyball courts, a bike path and surf that's good for swimming, surfing and diving. They also allow **beach camping** (☏800-444-7275, international callers 916-638-5883; www.reserveamerica.com; tent & RV sites $25-45). Day-use parking is $15.

Dedicated surfers won't mind the 1-mile hike to world-renowned **Trestles**, just south of the town of **San Clemente** and north of San Onofre State Beach, bordering the San Diego County line. It's a natural surfbreak that consistently churns out perfect waves. Check out www.surfrider.org for more information on the potential extension of a nearby toll road that could affect the waves. Exit off I-5 at Los Christianos Rd.

San Diego

Best Places to Eat

» Prado (p635)

» Puerto La Boca (p634)

» George's at the Cove (p637)

» Bread & Cie (p635)

Best Places to Stay

» Hotel del Coronado (p632)

» Hotel Indigo (p632)

» La Pensione Hotel (p632)

» Inn at Sunset Cliffs (p633)

» Crystal Pier Hotel (p633)

Why Go?

There's a certain arrogance that comes with living on the SoCal coast, a breezy confidence that springs from the assumption that your life is just, well, *better* than everyone else's. No offense – it just is. But as far as coastal snobs go, San Diegans are the ones we like the most. Whether it's a battle-tested docent sharing stories on the USS *Midway* or a no-worries surf diva helping you catch a wave, folks here are pretty willing to share the good life.

The only problem is that with 70 miles of coastline and a near-perfect climate, it's tough to decide where to start. Exploring maritime history, biking the beach paths, microbrewery hopping, ball games, horse races, Japanese gardens? Killer whales? When in doubt, do as the locals do and just take it easy – grab a fish taco and a surfboard and head for the beach.

When to Go

San Diego

Jun–Aug High season. Temperatures and hotel rates are highest. Beware of cloudy weather.

Sep–Oct & Mar–May Shoulder seasons; moderate hotel rates. Chilly evenings and sunny days.

Nov–Feb Low season. But it's still sunnier in San Diego than almost anywhere else in the USA.

Fast Facts

» **Population** 1.3 million

» **Average high temperature in San Diego** Jan 65°F, Jul 76°F

» **San Diego to Tijuana** 18 miles

Planning Your Trip

As your San Diego visit approaches, look online for coupons and special promotions for SeaWorld and the Zoo. If you'd rather skip the stress of southern California traffic, book a hotel room downtown – you can take the trolleys to get around instead.

Resources

» www.sandiego.org – the official San Diego resource for travelers

» www.signonsandiego.com – the city's major daily

» www.sdreader.com – an alt-weekly covering the city's music, art and theater scenes

Green San Diego: the 'finest city on earth?'

San Diegans hold their fair city in high esteem. And by the looks of it, they're devoted to protecting their beautiful beaches and clear, sunny skies: sustainable building and ecofriendly businesses are on the rise, and the laid-back metropolis recently became the home of North America's first all-electric car-sharing program.

GOURMET SAN DIEGO

Though wine connoisseurs and foodies often head elsewhere in California to taste, swirl and sip, San Diego is a gourmet destination in its own right. Local chefs, farmers and brewmasters have slowly but steadily added flavor to a culinary scene that, thanks to the city's location near the border, has long been associated with one-dimensional Mexican food.

On almost any day of the week, you'll find organic farmers selling their plump avocados, strawberries and basil at **farmers markets** scattered throughout San Diego's neighborhoods. While you pick out your peaches and parsley, you'll likely bump shoulders with the kitchen staff from stylish but down-to-earth eateries like **JRDN** (p637) of Pacific Beach or **whisknladle** (p637) of La Jolla. Meanwhile, at **microbreweries** around the city, brewmasters are turning out award-winning India Pale Ales and barley wine. Taste their concoctions at any bar downtown, or drive out to the microbreweries' onsite **tasting rooms**; we recommend **AleSmith** or **The Lost Abbey** (p638). Go ahead, raise your glass to the city's underrated food and drink scene – the secret's not out yet.

San Diego's Best Beach Moments

» **Coronado** Walk barefoot in the soft white sand in front of the glamorous old Hotel del Coronado, then sit on the terrace with an ice-cold cocktail and stare out at the ocean.

» **La Jolla** Kayak around sea caves, snorkel near the shore or just pretend like you're in the Mediterranean along this stunning stretch of coastline.

» **Mission Beach** Rent a bike and ride along the endless beach paths, go for a ride on a vintage roller coaster or just kick back on the sand at this lively, family-friendly beach.

History

Evidence of human habitation in the region dates back to 18,000 BC. By the time the Spanish explorer Juan Rodriguez Cabrillo sailed into San Diego Bay in 1542 – the first European to do so – the region was divided peaceably between the Kumeyaay and Lu- iseño/Juaneño peoples. Their way of life continued undisturbed until Junípero Serra and Gaspar de Portolá arrived in 1769. They founded a mission and a military fort on the hill now known as the Presidio, making it the first permanent European settlement in California.

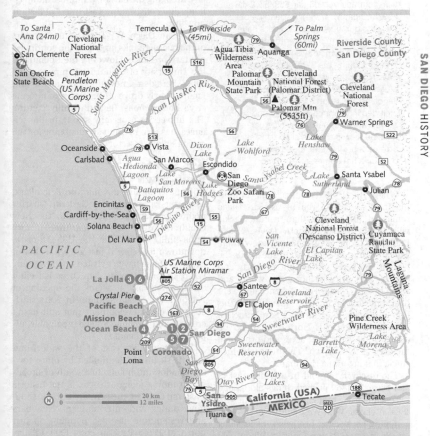

San Diego Highlights

❶ Explore the nation's largest urban cultural park, **Balboa Park** (p612), then go for margaritas on the lively Spanish-style patio of the **Prado** (p635)

❷ Wander the 4-acre flight deck and get lost in the snaking corridors of the **USS Midway** (p612), an impressive aircraft carrier parked along the Embarcadero

❸ Kayak through the eerily beautiful sea caves along the coast of **La Jolla Cove** (p630)

❹ Eat your way through **Ocean Beach** (p636), feasting on fish tacos, juicy burgers and other classic SoCal street foods

❺ Come face-to-face with the King of the Jungle at the **San Diego Zoo Safari Park** (p614)

❻ Learn to hang ten off **La Jolla Shores** (p629).

❼ Bar-hop through the happening nightlife scene of the **Gaslamp** (p637), stopping for a drink at rooftop lounges and down-to-earth dive bars

GO SAN DIEGO CARD

If you're planning on doing significant sightseeing in San Diego, it's wise to pick up the Go San Diego Card (☎866-628-9032; www.smartdestina tions.com; adult/child 1-day $69/58, 2-day $99/87, 3-day $174/134). Depending on the pass purchased, cardholders have steeply discounted entry into their choice of 50 of the city's top attractions, including the San Diego Zoo and Safari Park, the Midway Aircraft Carrier Museum, the Air and Space Museum, Legoland and Knott's Berry Farm. Also included in the price are kayak and bike rentals at select outfitters, plus permission to skip the line at the busiest attractions. (Trust us, that's a serious perk on a hot summer afternoon.)

When the United States took California from Mexico in the 1840s, San Diego remained little more than a ramshackle village. But William Heath Davis, a San Francisco property speculator, knew there was a fortune to be made. In the 1850s, he bought 160 acres of bayfront property and erected prefabricated houses, a wharf and warehouses. 'Davis' Folly' eventually went bust, but only because he was ahead of his time. A decade later, another San Francisco speculator, Alonzo E Horton, snapped up almost 1000 waterfront acres and promoted the area as 'New Town.' This time, the idea stuck, making him a rich man.

The discovery of gold in the hills east of San Diego in 1869 pushed things along, and the ensuing rush brought the railroad here in 1884. A classic Wild West culture of saloons, gambling houses and brothels thrived along 5th St in the Gaslamp Quarter. When gold played out, the economy took a nosedive, and the city's population plummeted yet again.

When San Francisco hosted the successful Panama-Pacific International Exposition (1914), San Diego responded with its own Panama-California Exposition (1915–16), hoping to attract investment to a city with a deepwater port, a railroad hub and a perfect climate – but virtually no industry. To give San Diego a unique image, boosters built exhibition halls in the romantic, Spanish colonial style that still defines much of the city today.

However, it was the bombing of Pearl Harbor in 1941 that made San Diego. The US Pacific Fleet needed a mainland home for its headquarters. The top brass quickly settled on San Diego, whose excellent deepwater port affords protection in almost all weather. The military literally reshaped the city, dredging the harbor, building landfill islands and constructing vast tracts of instant housing.

For San Diego, WWII was only the start of the boom, thanks largely to the continued military presence. However, the opening of the University of California campus in the 1960s heralded a new era, as students and faculty slowly drove a liberal wedge into the city's homogenous, flag-and-family culture. The university, especially strong in the sciences, has also become an incubator for the region's biotech sector.

◎ Sights

DOWNTOWN

With baseball fans flowing into Petco Park, scenesters cramming into Gaslamp Quarter nightclubs, kids scrambling into the New Children's Museum and maritime history buffs lining up outside the USS *Midway*, downtown feels like it just gulped a shot of caffeine. If you haven't visited in a few years, you're in for a surprise. San Diego is feeling a little, well, hip. It seems the opening of Petco Park baseball stadium in 2004 started a wave of development that still hasn't crested, and the energy here is palpable, especially on weekends.

Downtown lies east of the waterfront, and its skyline is dominated by office towers, condos and hotels. Just south of Broadway, running along 5th Ave, is the historic Gaslamp Quarter, the primary hub for shopping, dining and entertainment. New bars and restaurants are also popping up just north of Petco Park in edgy East Village. To the west lies the Embarcadero district, a nice spot for a bayfront jog or a stroll through historic sea-faring vessels. A short walk north lands you in Little Italy, where mom-and-pop eateries alternate with high-end design stores.

Soon after his arrival in San Diego in 1867, San Francisco speculator Alonzo Horton purchased 960 acres of land stretching south from Broadway to the waterfront and east to 15th St – for a grand total of $265. While respectable businesses went up along Broadway, the 5th Ave area became known as The Stingaree, a notorious red-light district filled with saloons, bordellos, gambling halls and opium dens.

By the 1960s it had declined to a skid row of flophouses and bars, but the neighborhood's very seediness made it so unattractive to developers that many of the older buildings survived when others around town were being razed. When developers turned their eyes toward the area in the early 1980s, preservationists organized to save the old brick and stone facades from the wrecking ball. The city stepped up, contributing trees, benches, wide brick sidewalks and replica 19th-century gas lamps. Restored buildings (built between the 1870s and the 1920s) became home to restaurants, bars, galleries, shops and theaters. The 16-acre area south of Broadway between 4th Ave and 6th Ave is designated a National Historic District and development is strictly controlled.

These days, the Gaslamp Quarter is enjoying a second, post-Petco wave of revitalization and growth, one characterized by a youthful, stylish energy. Upscale hotels and sleek restaurants are making ever-more-frequent debuts, while new rooftop bars and velvet-rope clubs are fending off (or creating) long lines of martini-craving scenesters. The neighborhood isn't a total hipster haven – yet – and a smattering of dive bars are working hard to keep things real.

The commercial focal point of downtown is Westfield Horton Plaza (Map p616; Broadway & 4th Sbr; P), a five-story mall designed by Los Angeles architect Jon Jerde, who also designed Universal City Walk. Inside, toytown arches, post-modern balconies and an asymmetrical floor plan – all surrounding an open-air atrium – are reminiscent of an MC Escher drawing.

William Heath Davis House HISTORIC BUILDING
(Map p616; 619-233-4692; www.gaslampquarter.org; 410 Island Ave; adult/senior $5/4; 10am-6pm Tue-Sat, 9am-3pm Sun) For a taste of local history, peruse the exhibits inside this museum; the saltbox house was the onetime home of William Heath Davis, the man credited with starting the development of modern San Diego. Upstairs, look for the hidden prohibition-era still. Self-guided tours are available and the foundation also offers **guided walking tours** (adult/student & senior $10/8; 11am Sat) of the quarter.

San Diego Chinese Historical Museum MUSEUM
(Map p616; 619-338-9888; www.sdchm.org; 404 3rd Ave; admission $2; 10:30am-4pm Tue-Sat, from noon Sun) This was the heart of San Diego's former Chinatown. The museum occupies the attractive Chinese Mission Building, built in the 1920s, as well as a contemporary annex completed in 2004. Exhibits include a former warlord's 40-piece wood-carved bed – assembled without nails – as well as the ornate, ultratiny slippers worn by women with bound feet.

Museum of Contemporary Art MUSEUM
(Map p616; 858-454-3541; www.mcasd.org; 1001 & 1100 Kettner Blvd; adult/student/senior $10/free/5; 11am-5pm Thu-Tue, to 7pm third Thu each month, with free admission 5-7pm) This modern art museum emphasizes minimalist and pop art, conceptual works and cross-border art. The original branch, open since the 1960s, is in La Jolla (p627). Tickets are valid for seven days in all locations.

New Children's Museum MUSEUM
(Map p616; 619-233-8792; www.thinkplaycreate.org; 200 W Island Ave; adult & child/senior/child under 1yr $10/5/free; 10am-4pm Mon, Tue, Fri & Sat, to 6pm Thu, noon-4pm Sun) With concrete

HAUNTED SAN DIEGO

Don't let the sunshine and happy people fool you: San Diego has an unnerving number of haunted homes and hotels. (Do the ghosts know something we don't about this shiny coastal city?) Take the **Horton Grand Hotel** (p632), built on the site of the 19th-century Seven Buckets of Blood Saloon. According to hotel lore, a local troublemaker was shot in a room above the saloon, and his ghost now haunts the hotel's Room 309, playing tricks on maids and causing some guests to check out at 2am. A jilted woman allegedly walks the halls at the **Hotel del Coronado** (p622) and appears on the TV screen in the room where her heart was broken. Then there's the **Whaley House** (p619), certified haunted by the US Department of Commerce, where staff and guests claim to have seen apparitions, even in the daytime.

floors, soaring walls, and mod furnishings and decor, this revamped interactive museum is engaging for kids and adults; it earns kudos for its environmentally sustainable features. Part art studio, part children's museum, and part modern art gallery, the museum displays artist-created exhibits that encourage kids of all ages to think about art, react to it, and create it.

LITTLE ITALY

Like any 'Little Italy' worth its salt, San Diego's version offers friendly pizzerias with red and white checkered tablecloths, unpretentious espresso bars, mom-and-pop delis, and family-friendly businesses. It's a place where San Diegans come to while away a sunny afternoon. The pedestrian-friendly neighborhood is perched on a small rise of land east of the Embarcadero, north of Ash St.

The neighborhood's always been community minded, beginning in the mid-19th century, when Italian immigrants, mostly fishermen and their families, first started settling here. The tight-knit neighborhood had its heyday in the 1920s, when Prohibition opened up new business opportunities (read 'bootlegging').

The construction of I-5 in 1962 – right beside Little Italy – disrupted the community. The hardiest of the old family businesses survived, mingling easily beside the chichi restaurants and specialty shops. You'll find the busiest patio tables on the eastern side of India Street (Map p616), a prime spot for a glass of Chianti.

EMBARCADERO

Heading west from downtown, cross the tram tracks to enter a 500yd-wide stretch of landfill that culminates with the Embarcadero. This wide pedestrian strip hugs the bay, offering breezy views of the water and an impressive line-up of ships and vessels, not to mention a few overpriced restaurants. It's also the launch point for the ferry to Coronado, the site of a public fishing pier, and the home of the San Diego Convention Center. Designed by Canadian avant-garde architect Arthur Erickson, the building – which some say was inspired by an ocean liner – stretches for a half-mile.

Maritime Museum MUSEUM
(Map p616; ☎619-234-9153; www.sdmaritime.com; 1492 N Harbor Dr; adult/child/senior $14/8/11; ⊙9am-8pm, to 9pm late May-early Sep; ⊕) The 100ft masts of the square-rigger tall ship *Star of India* – one of seven vessels open to the public here – make this museum easy to find. Built on the Isle of Man and launched in 1863, the restored ship plied the England-India trade route, carried immigrants to New Zealand, became a trading ship based in Hawaii and, finally, worked the Alaskan salmon fisheries. Nowadays she's taken out once a year for a sail, making her the oldest active ship in the world.

Kids can learn the Pirate's Code at the small but engaging pirate's exhibit below deck on the HMS *Surprise*. For the highest wow-per-square-foot factor, squeeze into the museum's B-39 Soviet attack submarine. (Take note: the sub is a claustrophobe's nightmare.) If you do venture in, check out the torpedo tubes. In a last-ditch attempt to escape a crippled sub, sailors would blast from these tubes as human torpedoes. Metered parking and $10 day lots are nearby.

USS Midway Museum MUSEUM
(Map p616; ☎619-544-9600; www.midway.org; Navy Pier; adult/child/senior & student $18/10/15; ⊙10am-5pm; ⊕) A short walk south is the Embarcadero's heavyweight attraction, the USS *Midway*, clocking in with a total weight of 69,000 tons. Commissioned in 1945, the ship is the Navy's longest-serving aircraft carrier, seeing action in Vietnam and the first Gulf War. It opened as a museum in 2004. An engaging self-guided audio tour – filled with first person accounts from former crewmen – takes visitors on a maze-like climb through the engine room, the brig, the galley and the 4-acre flight deck, where an impressive lineup of fighter jets – including an F-14 Tomcat – await up-close inspection. For an eagle-eye view of the flight deck and San Diego Bay, take the docent-led tour of the Island Superstructure, which includes stops in the bridge and flight control. Parking costs $5 to $7.

Seaport Village PLAZA
(Map p616; ☎619-235-4014; www.seaportvillage.com; ⊙10am-10pm summer) Continue south to this open-air tourist promenade which is technically neither a Seaport nor a Village. Filled with outdoor restaurants and knick-knack shops (if you need a coffee mug or T-shirt, come here), it's a pretty place to relax, listen to live music or look at the water.

BALBOA PARK

The rumors are true: Balboa Park is, in fact, the largest urban cultural park in the US. While we're spouting statistics, it's also the

Metropolitan San Diego

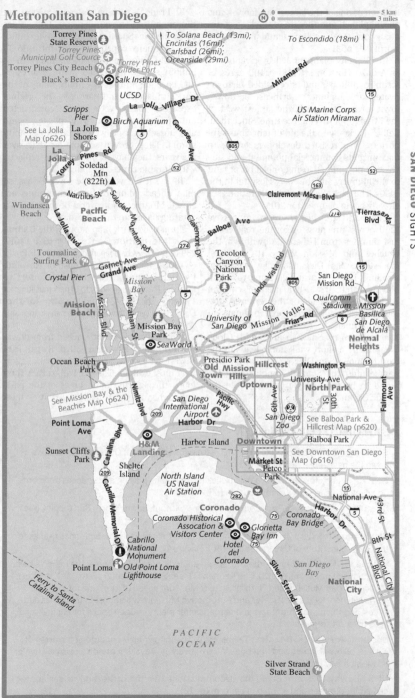

Torrey Pines State Reserve
Torrey Pines Municipal Golf Course
Torrey Pines City Beach
Torrey Pines Glider Port
Black's Beach
Salk Institute
UCSD
To Solana Beach (13mi); Encinitas (16mi); Carlsbad (26mi); Oceanside (29mi)
To Escondido (18mi)
Miramar Rd
La Jolla Village Dr
US Marine Corps Air Station Miramar
Scripps Pier
Birch Aquarium
Genesee Ave
See La Jolla Map (p626)
La Jolla Shores
La Jolla
Torrey Pines Rd
Soledad Mtn (822ft)
Clairemont Mesa Blvd
Nautilus St
Soledad Mountain Rd
Tierrasanta Blvd
Windansea Beach
La Jolla Blvd
Pacific Beach
Balboa Ave
Tourmaline Surfing Park
Garnet Ave
Grand Ave
Mission Bay
Clairemont Dr
Tecolote Canyon National Park
San Diego Mission Rd
Qualcomm Stadium
Mission Basilica San Diego de Alcalá
Crystal Pier
Mission Beach
Mission Blvd
Ingraham St
Mission Bay Park
SeaWorld
University of San Diego
Mission Valley
Friars Rd
Linda Vista Rd
Normal Heights
Ocean Beach Park
Nimitz Blvd
Presidio Park
Old Town
Mission Hills
Hillcrest
Uptown
Washington St
University Ave
North Park
6th Ave
30th St
Fairmount Ave
See Mission Bay & the Beaches Map (p624)
Point Loma Ave
San Diego International Airport
Harbor Dr
Pacific Hwy
San Diego Zoo
See Balboa Park & Hillcrest Map (p620)
Sunset Cliffs Park
Catalina Blvd
H&M Landing
Harbor Island
Downtown
Balboa Park
Shelter Island
North Island US Naval Air Station
Market St
Petco Park
See Downtown San Diego Map (p616)
Cabrillo Memorial Dr
Coronado
Coronado Historical Association & Visitors Center
Glorietta Bay Inn
Coronado Bay Bridge
National Ave
Cabrillo National Monument
Hotel del Coronado
San Diego Bay
Harbor Dr
8th St
National City Blvd
43rd St
Point Loma
Old Point Loma Lighthouse
Ferry to Santa Catalina Island
Silver Strand Blvd
National City
PACIFIC OCEAN
Silver Strand State Beach

location of one of the largest outdoor organs on the planet, and the site of the largest annual (and free) environmental fair in the world (see p631).

In 1868 city planners, led by civic booster Alonzo Horton, set aside 1400 acres of scrubby hilltops and steep-sided arroyos (water-carved gullies) northeast of downtown for use as a park, the largest west of the Mississippi River at the time. Since then, Balboa Park – with the aid of tenacious supporters – has resisted developers' efforts to maximize its commercial potential and survived almost intact, losing only a bit of land to the highway and the Navy Hospital in the 1950s. The park's centennial celebrations are already being planned for 2015.

The park stretches over an impressive 1200 acres, preening on prime real estate just minutes from Hillcrest, downtown, the beaches and Mission Valley. It's an ideal place to see San Diegans at play – jogging, strolling, in-line skating, catching rays and playing catch. It's also a premier cultural center, with a cluster of theaters and museums arrayed along the extraordinary El Prado promenade. Nearby is a faithful reconstruction of Shakespeare's Old Globe theater, and a short walk north leads to the world-famous San Diego Zoo. The park is named after the Spanish conquistador believed to be the first European to see the Pacific Ocean.

El Prado is the park's main pedestrian thoroughfare, surrounded on both sides by romantic Spanish colonial-style buildings originally constructed for the 1915–16 Panama-California Exposition. Today, these buildings – ornamented with beaux-arts and baroque flourishes – house many of the park's museums and gardens. The original exposition halls were mostly constructed out of stucco, chicken wire, plaster, hemp and horsehair, and were meant to be temporary. They proved so popular that, over the years, they have been gradually replaced with durable concrete replicas.

To see it all would take several days, so plan ahead. Many of the 15 museums are closed Monday, and several per week (on a rotating basis) are free Tuesday.

For a good park map, stop by the **Balboa Park Information Center** (Map p620; ☎619-239-0512; www.balboapark.org; 1549 El Prado; ◷9:30am-4:30pm) in the House of Hospitality. Helpful staff here sell the **Passport to Balboa Park** (single entry to 14 park museums for 1 wk adult/child $45/24) and the **Stay-for-the-Day Pass** (your choice of 5 museums in the same day for $35).

Balboa Park is easily reached from downtown on bus 7 along Park Blvd. By car, Park Blvd provides easy access to free parking lots near most exhibits. The free Balboa Park Tram loops through the main areas of the park, although you don't really need it – most

---

SAN DIEGO FOR CHILDREN

San Diego Zoo From pandas to koalas, flamingos to Elephant Odyssey, this is paws-down the best zoo in America (p615).

SeaWorld Look for Shamu and pals frolicking, penguins playing and specials and combo tickets to keep your expenses down (p624).

San Diego Zoo Safari Park Journey to Africa without leaving North San Diego County (p614).

Birch Aquarium La Jolla Aquarium that's as entertaining as it is educational, thanks to the Scripps Institute of Oceanography (p627).

Balboa Park After exploring the zoo, spend an additional day at one of the nation's best collections of museums (p612). The Reuben H Fleet Science Center (with IMAX theater), Model Railroad Museum and Natural History Museum are all tailor-made for kids, the Marie Hitchcock Puppet Theater and Automotive Museum will appeal to particular audiences, and the plazas, fountains and gardens offer plenty of open space for children of all ages to let off some steam.

Mission and Pacific Beaches Teenagers will be in their element among the array of surfers, bikers, 'bladers and buff bods. Alternatively, go kayaking or ride a paddle wheeler on Mission Bay (p625).

USS Midway Museum Board this decommissioned aircraft carrier and gain an appreciation for our men and women in uniform (p612).

SAN DIEGO ZOO SAFARI PARK

How close can you get to the animals at this 1800-acre **open-range zoo** (☎760-747-8702; www.sandiegozoo.org; 15500 San Pasqual Valley Rd, Escondido; general admission incl tram adult/child $40/30; ☉opens 9am, closing times vary; 🚹) just 30 miles northeast of downtown? Consider this sign near the Lowlands Gorilla Habitat: 'In gorilla society prolonged eye contact is not only impolite, but it's considered a threat. Please respect the social signals of our gorillas and do not stare at them directly.' Seems we're so close we need to be reminded of our manners. But the sign is indicative of the experience here, where protecting and preserving wild animals and their habitats – while educating guests in a soft-handed manner – is the primary goal.

For a minisafari, hop aboard The Journey into Africa biodiesel tram for a drive through the world's second-largest continent. Sit on the left-hand side for slightly better views of the rhinos, giraffes, ostriches and other herbivores (by law, predators can't share space with prey). To enjoy close-up views of big cats, follow signs to the 33,000 sq ft Lion Camp and the Safari Walk Backcountry – and pray there's not a park-disrupting earthquake. Combination tickets with the San Diego Zoo are $76/56.

And for the wildlife lover who has everything? Book the **Roar & Snore** (☎619-718-3000; tickets adult/child $180/150; ☉seasonal) camping experience on a hilltop where families sleep in canvas tents overlooking the East African–style plains and their wild inhabitants.

To get to the park take the freeway to the Via Rancho Parkway exit, turn right and continue to San Pasqual Rd. Turn right and follow signs to the park. Parking costs $10. For bus information contact **North San Diego County Transit District** (☎619-233-3004, from northern San Diego 800-266-6883; www.gonctd.com).

attractions are within an easy stroll of each other.

California Building & Museum of Man
MUSEUM

From the west, El Prado passes under an archway and into an area called the California Quadrangle, with the **Museum of Man** (Map p620; ☎619-239-2001; www.museumofman. org; Plaza de California; adult/child 3-12yr/youth 13-17yr/senior $12.50/5/8/10; ☉10am-4:30pm) on its northern side. This was the main entrance for the 1915 exposition, and the building was said to be inspired by the churrigueresque church of Tepotzotlán near Mexico City. California Building's single tower, sometimes called the **Tower of California**, is richly decorated with blue and yellow tiles, and has become a symbol of San Diego itself. Inside, the museum specializes in anthropology, with a focus on Native American cultures, particularly those in the American Southwest.

San Diego Zoo
ZOO

(Map p620; ☎619-231-1515; www.sandiegozoo.org; 2920 Zoo Dr; adult/child with guided bus tour & aerial tram ride $40/30; ☉opens 9am, closing times vary; 🚹) If it slithers, crawls, stomps, swims, leaps or flies, chances are you'll find it in this world-famous zoo in northern Balboa Park. Since its opening in 1916, the zoo has also pioneered ways to house and display animals that mimic their natural habitat, leading to a revolution in zoo design and, so the argument goes, to happier animals. In its efforts to re-create those habitats, the zoo has also become one of the country's great botanical gardens. Experts trick San Diego's near-desert climate to yield everything from bamboo to eucalyptus to Hawaiian koa. The plants don't just provide pleasant cover for cages and fences; many are grown specifically to feed the zoo's more finicky eaters.

Today, the zoo is home to thousands of animals representing 800-plus species in a beautifully landscaped setting. Perennial favorite **Polar Bear Plunge** (just remodeled) wows crowds with up-close, underwater views of the bears through thick glass walls. Other hotspots are **Elephant Odyssey** and **Panda Canyon**, where a live narrator shares facts about pandas at the outdoor viewing area here and, more importantly, keeps the line moving.

Arboreal orangutans and siamangs peacefully coexist in the **Lost Forest**. Don't miss the vast **Scripps Aviary** and **Owens Rain Forest Aviary**, where carefully placed feeders (and remarkably fearless birds) allow for close-up viewing. To note: if you didn't like Hitchcock's *The Birds*, the aviaries might be

Downtown San Diego

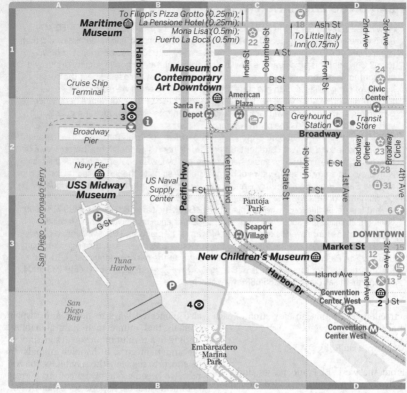

a less than enjoyable experience. The koalas in the **Outback** have proved so popular that Australians may be surprised to find them an unofficial symbol of San Diego. Less cuddly is the Komodo dragon in the reptile house, an Indonesian lizard that grows up to 10ft long.

At **Discovery Outpost**, youngsters can pet small critters and watch animal shows. Visitors of all ages will enjoy viewing 'zoo babies,' the park's newest arrivals.

Arrive early, when the animals are most active. There's a large, free parking lot off Park Blvd that starts filling fast right at opening time. Write down where you parked, as it can be confusing at the end of the day. Bus 7 will get you there from downtown. If you would like to leave the zoo and return, staff will stamp your hand. If you're not in a hurry, take the 35-minute double-decker bus tour first thing in the morning to get oriented. You'll also pick up intriguing facts about the animals – grizzlies can run the length of a football field in six seconds!

San Diego Natural History Museum

MUSEUM

(Map p620; ☑619-232-3821; www.sdnhm.org; 1788 El Prado; adult/child/senior $17/11/15; ☺10am-5pm; ▣) Seventy-five million years of SoCal fossils are the subject of one of the museum's newer permanent exhibits, Fossil Mysteries, which opened at the museum in 2006. Ongoing and upcoming exhibits cover climate change in polar regions and the ancient bond between horses and humans. At the time of writing, the museum had just received a $7 million state grant to build a permanent exhibit about the natural habitats of southern California.

San Diego Air & Space Museum

MUSEUM

(Map p620; ☑619-234-8291; www.sandiegoairand space.org; 2001 Pan American Plaza; adult/child/ student & senior $16.50/6/13.50; ☺10am-5:30pm

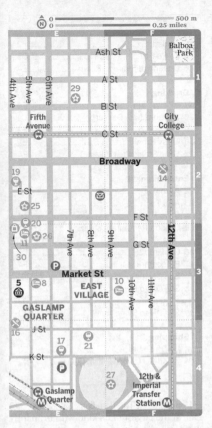

verwork. The permanent collection holds a number of paintings by European masters (a few of the Spanish old masters are represented by sculptures on the building's facade), as well as noteworthy American landscape paintings and a fine collection of Asian art. The Sculpture Garden has pieces by Alexander Calder and Henry Moore. Check the website to see if a 'Cocktail & Culture' night is coming up – the evening event ($15) features cocktails, DJs, and a pre-tour of upcoming exhibits.

FREE Timken Museum of Art MUSEUM
(Map p620; ☑619-239-5548; www.timkenmuseum.org; 1500 El Prado; ◷10am-4:30pm Tue-Sat, from 1:30pm Sun) It's not just the impressive collection of European old masters that makes the Timken stand out from its Balboa Park peers. The Timken is special because its simple exterior stands in bold contrast to the park's ubiquitous Spanish colonial style. It's also free. Paintings are from the Putnam Foundation collection and include works by Europeans Rembrandt, Rubens, El Greco, Cézanne and Pissarro, and Americans John Singleton Copley and Eastman Johnson.

Balboa Park Gardens GARDENS
(Map p620) Balboa Park is home to nine gardens, most clustered just south of El Prado. The Alcazar Garden, a formal Spanish-style garden, is tucked in a courtyard across from the Old Globe, south of El Prado, while the Palm Canyon, which has more than 50 species of palms, is a short stroll south. For a tranquil stroll or a bit of meditation, the Japanese Friendship Garden (☑619-232-2721; www.niwa.org; adult/student & senior $4/3; ◷10am-4pm Tue-Sun, to 5pm in summer), just north of Spreckels Organ Pavilion, is a convenient retreat. A short path winds past a koi pond, rippling water and the Exhibit House with a glass-walled meditation room overlooking the Zen Garden.

Spreckels Organ Pavilion LANDMARK
(Map p620) South of Plaza de Panama, an extravagantly curved colonnade provides shelter for one of the world's largest outdoor organs. Donated by the Spreckels family of sugar fortune and fame, the pipe organ – which has more than 4500 pipes – came with the stipulation that San Diego must always have an official organist. Free concerts are held at 2pm every Sunday.

Jun-Aug, to 4:30pm Sep-May) One look at the banged-up silver pod inside the rotunda of this museum, at the end of Pan American Plaza, and you'll be glad you chose not to become an astronaut. The pod, known as Gumdrop, is the Apollo 9 command module used in a 1969 mission to test the lunar module before the first moon landing. Exhibits here trace the history of aviation, providing plenty of close-up views of planes with dangerous names – Flying Tiger, Cobra and Skyhawk – plus a few reproductions. Moon rocks and a space suit are also cool.

San Diego Museum of Art MUSEUM
(Map p620; ☑619-232-7931; www.sdmart.org; 1450 El Prado, Plaza de Panama; adult/child/senior $12/4.50/9; ◷10am-5pm Tue-Sat, noon-5pm Sun, to 9pm Thu Jun-Sep) The building's architect, San Diegan William Templeton Johnson, chose the 16th-century Spanish plateresque style, which gets its name from heavy ornamentation that resembles decorated sil-

Downtown San Diego

Reuben H Fleet Science Center MUSEUM
(Map p620; ☎619-238-1233; www.rhfleet.org; 1875 El Prado; adult/child & senior $10/8.75; ◎10am-varies; ♿) Family-oriented hands-on museum and **Imax theater** (incl Science Center adult/child $14:50/11.75). The exhibits at this hands-on science center include the energy-focused So Watt! and the galaxy-minded Origins in Space, where colorful Hubble images of colliding galaxies are particularly mesmerizing.

Mingei International Museum MUSEUM
(Map p620; ☎619-239-0003; www.mingei.org; 1439 El Prado; adult/child/senior $7/4/5; ◎10am-4pm Tue-Sun) Exhibits folk art from around the globe; don't miss the lovely museum store here.

Museum of Photographic Arts MUSEUM
(Map p620; ☎619-238-7559; www.mopa.org; 1649 El Prado; adult/child/senior $8/free/6; ◎10am-5pm Tue-Sun) Exhibits fine-art photography and hosts an ongoing film series.

San Diego Model Railroad Museum MUSEUM
(Map p620; ☎619-696-0199; www.sdmrm.org; 1649 El Prado; adult/senior/student $7/6/3;

◎11am-4pm Tue-Fri, 11am-5pm Sat & Sun; ♿) One of the largest of its kind with brilliantly 'landscaped' train sets.

San Diego Automotive Museum MUSEUM
(Map p620; ☎619-231-2886; www.sdautomuseum.org; 2080 Pan-American Plaza; adult/child/senior $8/4/6; ◎10am-5pm) It's all about polished chrome and cool tailfins at this museum.

OLD TOWN

In 1769 Padre Junípero Serra and Gaspar de Portola established the first Spanish settlement in California on Presidio Hill, overlooking the valley of the San Diego River. Spanish soldiers built adobe homes and started families at the southwestern base of the hill, and in 1821 the community, with 600 citizens, became the first official civilian Spanish settlement – called a pueblo – in California. It remained the city center until a devastating fire in 1872, after which the city's main body moved to the downtown.

Today, this area below Presidio Hill is called Old Town, and it presents life as it was between 1821 and 1872. Although it is neither very old (most of the buildings are reconstructions), nor exactly a town (more like a leafy suburb), it's a more-or-less faithful copy of San Diego's original nucleus, offering a pedestrian plaza surrounded by historic buildings, shops, a number of restaurants and cafes, and a good opportunity to explore San Diego's early days.

The Old Town Transit Center, on the trolley line off Taylor St just east of Congress St at the western edge of Old Town, is a stop for the *Coaster* commuter train, the San Diego Trolley (blue and green lines) and buses. Old Town Trolley tours stop southeast of the plaza on Twiggs St.

Old Town State Historic Park visitor center
MUSEUM

(☑619-220-5422; www.parks.ca.gov; Robinson-Rose House, 4002 Wallace St; ☺10am-5pm; ℗) At the western end of the Plaza de las Armas close to the entrance of the Old Town State Historic Park. It houses memorabilia and books about the era as well as a diorama depicting the pueblo in 1872. If you're really interested in the historical background, take a guided tour, which leaves from the visitors center at 11am and 2pm. A row of small, historical-looking buildings (only one is authentically old) line the southern border of the plaza and some house souvenir and gift shops. There's plenty of free parking next to the Old Town Transit Center, about a block away.

Whaley House
HISTORICAL BUILDING

(☑619-297-7511; www.whaleyhouse.org; 2476 San Diego Ave; adult/child/senior $6/4/5; ☺10am-9:30pm Jun-Aug, 10am-5pm Mon & Tue, 10am-9:30pm Thu-Sat Sep-May) We can't guarantee what you'll see at this lovely Victorian home (and the city's oldest brick building), two blocks northeast of the Old Town perimeter. It's served as a courthouse, theater and private residence, but that's not the cool part. What's intriguing is that the house was *officially* certified as haunted by the US Department of Commerce. Guides here claim ghostly encounters occur even during the day, from observing figures with no faces to hearing talking behind them (when no one's there) to learning that a visitor's camera batteries have drained while in the house. Ask the informative guides to share their stories.

Presidio Hill
PARK

(Map p613) The walk from Old Town east along Mason St to the top of Presidio Hill rewards you with excellent views of San Diego Bay and Mission Valley – just don't depend on the most horribly marked trail in all of California to get you there! At the end of Mason St, if you obey the arrow pointing left, you'll follow a series of historic trail markers that *supposedly* end up at the Serra Museum. If you follow the arrow pointing up Presidio Hill, turn left at the dirt trail at the top and you might stumble upon the **Fort Stockton Memorial**. American forces occupied the hill in 1846, during the Mexican-American War, and named it for American commander Robert Stockton. A flagpole, cannon, some plaques and earthen walls form the memorial. If you turn right at the top of the hill, the path leads to Presidio Dr. Follow it to the **El Charro Statue**, a bicentennial gift to the city from Mexico depicting a Mexican cowboy on horseback. Nothing remains of the original Presidio structures.

Junípero Serra Museum
MUSEUM

(☑619-232-6203; www.sandiegohistory.org; 2777 Presidio Dr; adult/child/student & senior $6/2/4; ☺10am-5pm Sat & Sun, varying hours Mon-Fri; ℗) A Spanish colonial–style structure designed by William Templeton Johnson in 1929. The museum has a small but interesting collection of artifacts and pictures from the mission and rancho periods.

Mission Basilica San Diego de Alcalá
MISSION

(Map p613; ☑619-281-8449; www.missionsandiego. com; 10818 San Diego Mission Rd; adult/child/student & senior $3/1/2; ☺9am-4:45pm) Though the first California mission was established on Presidio Hill near Old Town, Padre Junípero Serra decided in 1773 to move upriver several miles, closer to a better water supply and more arable land. In 1784 the missionaries built a solid adobe and timber church, but it was destroyed by an earthquake in 1803. The church was promptly rebuilt, and at least some of it still stands on a slope overlooking Mission Valley. With the end of the mission system in the 1830s, the buildings were turned over to the Mexican government. The buildings were later used as US army barracks before falling into disrepair. Some accounts say that they were reduced to a facade and a few crumbling walls by the 1920s. Extensive reconstruction began in 1931, and the pretty white church

Balboa Park & Hillcrest

Balboa Park & Hillcrest

and the buildings you see now are the result of the thorough restoration.

Inside, a bougainvillea-filled garden offers a tranquil spot for meditation, and nearby tile panels that depict the crucifixion are moving in their simplicity. In the museum, a glass case holds items unearthed at the site, ranging from old spectacles to buttons to medicine bottles. In fact, don't be surprised if you see an archaeologist sifting through the dirt just outside. Look for old photographs and artifacts set up beside their dig site – currently across from the visitors center – when they're working. Come at sunset for glowing views over the valley and the ocean beyond.

The mission is two blocks north of I-8 via the Mission Gorge Rd exit just east of I-15. After exiting, take a left just past Roberto's at San Diego Mission Rd (on the right it's called Twain Ave) and follow it to the mission. You can take the trolley to the Mission stop, walk two blocks north and turn right onto San Diego Mission Rd.

UPTOWN

Just east of Old Town, between Mission Valley to the north and downtown to the south, is Uptown. As you head north from down-town along the west side of Balboa Park, you arrive at a series of bluffs that, in the late 19th century, became San Diego's most fashionable neighborhood – only those who owned a horse-drawn carriage could afford to live here. Known as Bankers Hill after some of the wealthy residents, these upscale heights had unobstructed views of the bay and Point Loma before I-5 went up.

Spruce Street Footbridge & Quince Street Bridge
BRIDGE

(Map p620) As you head northward toward Hillcrest consider a detour across the 375ft **Spruce Street Footbridge**. Note that the 1912 suspension bridge, built over a deep canyon between Front St and Brant St, wriggles beneath your feet. But don't worry; it was designed that way. The nearby **Quince Street Bridge**, between 4th Ave and 3rd Ave, is a wood-trestle structure built in 1905 and refurbished in 1988 after community activists vigorously protested its slated demolition.

HILLCREST

Just up from the northwestern corner of Balboa Park, you hit Hillcrest (Map p620), the heart of Uptown. The neighborhood began its life in the early 20th century as a

WORTH A TRIP

NORTH PARK

The hip-right-now neighborhood of North Park, a gentrifying, Bohemian-light enclave just east of Hillcrest, is getting press for its eco-friendly dining and drinking scene. The big North Park sign at 30th and University Aves marks the center of the action. Carnivores with a conscience flock to **The Linkery** (www.thelinkery.com; 3794 30th St; mains $10-25; 5-11pm Mon-Thu, noon-midnight Fri, 11am-midnight Sat, 11am-10pm Sun) for a vast selection of local microbrews and a daily changing menu of housemade sausages and hand-cured meats from sustainably raised animals. Nearby, **Alchemy** (www.alchemysandiego.com; 1503 30th St; mains $13-25; 4pm-midnight Sun-Thu, 4pm-1am Fri & Sat, 10am-2pm Sat & Sun) features a spin-the-globe menu of local ingredients from small plates – try the Parmesan frites with garlic aioli – in an art-filled blondwood room.

For something sweeter, there's **Heaven Sent Desserts** (www.heavensentdesserts. com; 3001 University Ave; 11am-11pm Tue-Thu, to midnight Fri & Sat, to 10pm Sun) for tarts, tiramisu and chunky chocolate chip cookies. For a great indie coffeehouse, walk a block west to high-ceilinged **Caffé Calabria** (www.caffecalabria.com; 3933 30th St; 6am-3pm Mon & Tue, to 11pm Wed-Fri, 7am-11pm Sat & Sun), which has freshly roasted coffee and wood fire-baked Neapolitan pizzas. You'll see North Park's energy and diversity if you spend an hour or two sitting at one of the cafe's sunny patio tables.

modest middle-class suburb. Today, it's San Diego's most bohemian district, with a decidedly urban feel, despite the suburban visuals. It's also the headquarters of the city's gay and lesbian community. University Ave and 5th Ave are lined with coffeehouses, fashion-forward thrift shops and excellent restaurants in all price ranges.

For a tour, begin at the **Hillcrest Gateway** (Map p620), which arches over University Ave at 5th Ave. On 5th Ave between University Ave and Washington St is the multiplex **Landmark Hillcrest Cinemas** (Map p620) and lots of restaurants and shops. Go east on University Ave to see the 1919 **Kahn Building** (Map p620) at No 535; it is an original Hillcrest commercial building with a kitschy facade. Then head south on 5th Ave to find a variety of cafes, friendly gay bars, vintage clothing shops and independent bookstores, many with a good selection of nonmainstream publications.

CORONADO

In 1885 Coronado Island wasn't much more than a scrappy patch of land sitting off the coast of what's now downtown San Diego. Home to jackrabbits and the occasional tycoon that rowed over to shoot them, Coronado was not a postcard-worthy destination. But what a difference three years makes. In February 1888, the Hotel del Coronado – at the time the largest hotel west of the Mississippi – welcomed its very first guests. Today, the hotel and its stunning surroundings are

the primary reasons to visit this well-manicured community.

The city of **Coronado** (Map p613) is now connected to the mainland by the graceful 2.12-mile Coronado Bay Bridge (opened in 1969), as well as by a narrow spit of sand known as the Silver Strand, which runs south to Imperial Beach and connects Coronado to the mainland. The large North Island US Naval Air Station occupies a northern tip of the island.

The **Coronado Visitors Center** (Map p613; 619-437-8788; www.coronadovisitorcenter. com; 1100 Orange Ave; 9am-5pm Mon-Fri, 10am-5pm Sat & Sun) conducts a walking tour ($12), starting from the **Glorietta Bay Inn** (Map p613; 1630 Glorietta Blvd), near Silver Strand Blvd, at 11am Tuesday, Thursday and Saturday. The visitors center also has information on special-interest tours (Coronado Tree Tour, Coronado by gondola, etc). We recommend picking up the pamphlet for a self-guided tour of Coronado's public artworks.

The **Coronado Historical Assocation**, housed in the same space as the visitors center, runs 90-minute **tours** (619-437-8788; $15; 10:30am Tue & Fri, 2pm Sat & Sun) of the historic Hotel del Coronado. Reserve ahead.

Hotel del Coronado   HISTORIC BUILDING
(1500 Orange Ave) This iconic hotel, familiar today with its whitewashed exterior, red conical towers, cupolas and balconies, sprang from the vision of two of the aforementioned jackrabbit hunters, Elisha Babcock and HL Story, who bought the island

for $110,000. They cooked up the idea of building a grand hotel as a gimmick to entice people to buy parcels of land on the island. Coronado land sales were a booming success and construction began on the hotel in 1887. Craftsmanship and innovation were strong points – the Del was the first hotel to have electric lights – as was sheer determination to finish it. The hotel had its grand opening, with 399 completed rooms, in February 1888 (although work on the property continued for two more years). Though the hotel was a success, Babcock and Story couldn't keep up with the bills and by 1900 millionaire John D Spreckels bankrolled the island into one of the most fashionable getaways on the west coast.

Guests have included 11 US presidents and world royalty – pictures are displayed in the history gallery downstairs from the lobby. The hotel, affectionately known as The Del, achieved its widest exposure in the 1959 movie *Some Like It Hot*, which earned its lasting association with Marilyn Monroe. Today, the hotel still exudes a snappy, look-at-me exuberance that makes guests and day-trippers alike feel as though they've been invited to the jazziest party in town.

Coronado Ferry FERRY
(Map p613; ☑619-234-4111; www.sdhe.com; each way $4.25; ⊙9am-10pm) Hourly ferry shuttles between the Broadway Pier on the Embarcadero to the Coronado Ferry Landing at the foot of First Street, where **Bikes & Beyond** (☑619-435-7180; rental per 1-2 hrs $25; ⊙9am-8pm, call for seasonal hours) rents bicycles.

POINT LOMA

Cabrillo National Monument MONUMENT
(Map p613; ☑619-557-5450; www.nps.gov/cabr; per car $5, per person $3; ⊙9am-5pm; 🅿) For spectacular views of downtown San Diego, Coronado and San Diego Bay, take a half-day to visit on the southern tip of Point Loma, the handily placed peninsula that provides shelter to the bay. This hilltop monument is also the best place in San Diego to see the gray whale migration (January to March) from land. Historically, this is the spot where Portuguese conquistador Juan Rodriguez Cabrillo landed in 1542 – making him the first European to step on the United States' western shores. A small museum highlights his travels. The 1854 **Old Point Loma Lighthouse**, atop the point, is furnished with typical lighthouse furniture from the 1880s. Displays reveal the lonely, hard life (endless

maintenance, sleepless nights) of the lighthouse keeper. Gearheads will want to check out the massive 5ft 2in 3rd Order Fresnel lens weighing 1985lb. On the ocean side of the point, drive or walk down to the **tide pools** to look for anemones and starfish.

OCEAN BEACH

In Ocean Beach, the beach bums and the restaurants are a little scruffier than those in coastal communities to the north. And the pier? It just doesn't seem to care that it's not all that photogenic. But therein lies the charm of this Bohemian neighborhood just south of I-8 and Mission Beach. You can get tattooed, shop for antiques, and walk into a restaurant shirtless and barefoot and nobody cares. You can also enjoy the best cheap eats in town and maybe grab a nice sunset or a little surfing. All with a minimum of surf-god pretension.

Newport Ave, which runs perpendicular from the beach, is the main drag, passing surf shops, bars, music stores, java joints, and used-clothing and secondhand furniture stores. The street ends a block from the half-mile-long **Ocean Beach Pier** (Map p624), an excellent spot for fishing or a breath of fresh air.

Just north of the pier, near the end of Newport Ave, is the central beach scene, with volleyball courts and sunset barbecues. A bit further north is **Dog Beach** (Map p624), where Fido can run unleashed around the marshy area where the San Diego River meets the sea. A few blocks south of the pier is **Sunset Cliffs Park**, a great spot to watch the sun dipping below the horizon.

There are good surf breaks at the cliffs and, to the south, off Point Loma. Under the pier, the brave slalom the pilings. If you're new to the area, beware of the rips and currents, which can be deadly.

MISSION BAY

While San Diego is famous generally as a watersports mecca, the actual heart of the sailing, windsurfing and kayaking scene is Mission Bay, shimmering in sun-dappled glory at the end of the San Diego River just west of the I-5.

In the 18th century, the mouth of the river formed a shallow bay when the river flowed, and a marshy swamp when it didn't; the Spanish called it False Bay. After WWII, a combination of civic vision and coastal engineering turned the swamp into a 7 sq mile playground, with 27 miles of shoreline and 90 acres of public parks. With financing from public bonds and expertise from the Army Corps of Engineers, the river was channeled to the sea, the bay was dredged, and millions of tons of sludge were used to build islands, coves and peninsulas. A quarter of the land created has been leased to hotels, boatyards and other businesses, providing ongoing city revenue. Today, Mission Bay Park, at 4235 acres, is the largest man-made aquatic park in the US.

SeaWorld AQUARIUM, AMUSEMENT PARK
(Map p613; ☎800-257-4268, 619-226-3901; www.seaworld.com/seaworld/ca; 500 SeaWorld Dr; adult/child 3-9yr $70/62; ☺9am-10pm Jul–mid-Aug, to 11pm Fri-Sun, shorter hours rest of year; ⊛) Along with the zoo, SeaWorld is one of San Diego's most popular attractions, and Shamu has become an unofficial mascot for the city itself (not to be a spoilsport, but for the record, several killer whales here perform under the name Shamu). SeaWorld has a shamelessly commercial feel, but it's undoubtedly entertaining and even educational. Its popularity means you should plan on long waits for rides, shows and exhibits during peak seasons.

SeaWorld's claim to fame is its live shows, which feature trained dolphins, seals, sea lions and killer whales. Current hits are **Blue Horizons**, a bird and dolphin extravaganza, and **One Ocean**, featuring Shamu and his killer whale amigos leaping, diving and gliding. At the time of writing, the aquatic (and acrobatic) show **Cirque de la Mer** was scoring rave reviews. There are also zoolike animal exhibits and a few amusement-park-style rides.

In **Penguin Encounter**, you'll smell the 250 tuxedoed show-offs before you see them. Here, penguins share a habitat that faithfully simulates Antarctic living conditions. Nearby, dozens of sharks glide overhead as you walk through a 57ft acrylic tube at **Shark Encounter**. Species include reef sharks and sand tiger sharks, some impressively large. Word of warning: the shark habitat gets very crowded.

Amusement-park-style rides – there aren't too many – include **Wild Arctic**, a simulated helicopter flight, and **Journey to Atlantis**, a combination flume ride and roller coaster that ends with a 60ft plunge – you'll get wet if you sit in the front seat.

Discount coupons are available, and you can find deals by buying tickets online, but

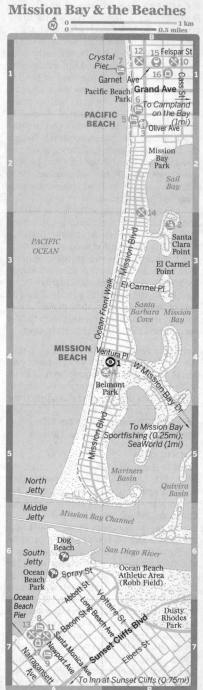

Mission Bay & the Beaches

Mission Bay & the Beaches

the extras add up – parking costs $14 and food is expensive ($2.79 for a regular soda). Ways to get the best value: a re-entry stamp (you can go out for a break and return later – good during late-opening hours in summer) or buy a combination ticket. Check the Sea World website for promotions.

The park is easy to find by car – take Sea World Dr off I-5 less than a mile north of where it intersects with I-8. Take bus 9 from downtown. Tickets sales end 90 minutes before closing time.

MISSION BEACH & PACIFIC BEACH
If you want to enjoy a quintessential California beach day, the 3 mile-long swath of sand between the South Mission Jetty and Pacific Beach Point is the best place. The wide beach fills fast on summer weekends with determined sun-worshippers, families and surfers.

Planning-wise, be prepared for 'June Gloom' cloud cover early in the summer, when a stubborn marine layer typically hides the sun and makes June the least sunny month here.

Up in Pacific Beach (or PB) the activity spreads further inland, especially along Garnet Ave (Map p624), where hordes of 20-somethings toss back brews and gobble cheap tacos. It gets hoppin' on Taco Tuesdays. At the ocean end of Garnet Ave, Crystal Pier (Map p624) is worth a look. Built in the 1920s, it's home to San Diego's quirkiest hotel (p633), which consists of a cluster of Cape Cod–style cottages built out over the waves. Surfing is more demanding around Crystal Pier, where the waves are steep and fast.

Ocean Front Walk BOARDWALK
(Map p624) The beachfront boardwalk teems year-round with joggers, in-line skaters, cyclists and a few brave dog-walkers. It's a primo spot for people-watching. One block off the beach, Mission Blvd, which runs up and down the coast, consists of block after block of surf shops, burger joints, beach bars and '60s-style motels. The surf is a beach break, good for beginners, bodyboarders and bodysurfers.

Belmont Park AMUSEMENT PARK
(Map p624; ☏858-488-1549; www.belmontpark. com; admission free, rides $2-6, unlimited rides adult/child $27/16; ⊙from 11am; P⊛) The family-style amusement park in the heart of Mission Beach has been here since 1925. When the park was threatened with demolition in the mid-1990s, concerted community action saved the large indoor pool known as the Plunge (Map p624) and the classic wooden Giant Dipper roller coaster (Map p624; per person $6; ⊙from 11am), which might just shake the teeth right out of your mouth. Other rides include bumper cars, a tilt-a-whirl, a carousel and the popular FlowRider, a wave machine for simulated surfing.

Cheap Rentals BICYCLE RENTAL, WATER SPORTS
(☏858-488-9070; www.cheap-rentals.com; 3689 Mission Blvd) To get around, consider renting a bike or in-line skates. This place, at the corner of Santa Clara Pl, rents everything from bicycles, skates and baby joggers (all per hour/day $5/12) to surfboards ($15 per day) and kayaks ($40 per day); it also accepts advance reservations, crucial in summer for late sleepers.

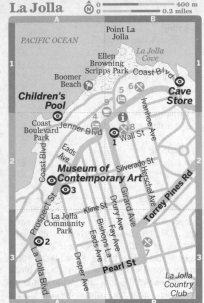

La Jolla

N 0 — 400 m / 0 — 0.2 miles

LA JOLLA

Locals like to say that the name La Jolla (la hoya) is derived from the Spanish for 'the jewel.' One look at the tidy parks, upscale boutiques and glitzy restaurants clustered downtown and the appropriateness of this explanation is immediately apparent. Some challenge this claim, however, saying that the indigenous people who lived in the area until the mid-19th century called it 'Mut la Hoya, la Hoya' – the place of many caves. It's this second explanation that's more intriguing to outdoor enthusiasts and fun-loving families because the sea caves, sandy coves and marine life here make it a fantastic place to kayak, dive, snorkel and tide-pool.

Technically part of San Diego, La Jolla feels like a world apart, both because of its radical affluence as well as its privileged location above San Diego's most photogenic stretch of coast. The community – generally stretching from Pacific Beach north past Torrey Pines to Del Mar – first became fashionable when Ellen Browning Scripps moved here in 1897. The newspaper heiress acquired much of the land along Prospect St, which she then donated to various community uses, including Bishop's School (Map p626; cnr Prospect St & La Jolla Blvd) and the La Jolla Woman's Club (Map p626; 715 Silverado St). She also hired Irving Gill to set the architectural tone – an elegant if unadorned Mediterranean style noted by its arches, colonnades, palm trees, red-tile roofs and pale stucco.

Bus 30 connects La Jolla to downtown via the Old Town Transit Center.

LA JOLLA VILLAGE & THE COAST

La Jolla Village, known locally as 'the Village,' sits atop a bluff lapped by the Pacific on three sides. There's little interaction between the compact downtown and the sea, although you can catch lovely glimpses of Pacific blue from a few of the fancy rooftop restaurants. The main thoroughfares, Prospect St and Girard Ave, are lined with boutiques, galleries and jewelry stores.

For a camera-worthy stroll, take the half-mile bluff-top path that winds above the shoreline a few blocks west of the Village. Near the path's western end is the Children's Pool (see boxed text, p629), off Coast Dr near Jenner Blvd. Here, a jetty funded by Ellen Browning Scripps protects the beach from big waves.

Continuing northeast, you'll reach Point La Jolla, at the path's eastern end, and Ellen Browning Scripps Park (Map p626), a tidy expanse of green lawns and palm trees. It's a great place to read, relax with your kids or watch the sunset. A short walk north leads to picnic tables and grills plus views of **La Jolla Cove** just below the path. This gem of a beach provides access to some of the best snorkeling around; it's also popular with rough-water swimmers.

Athenaeum Music & Arts Library
LIBRARY

(Map p626; ☎858-454-5872; www.ljathenaeum. org; 1008 Wall St; ⏰10am-5:30pm Tue-Sat, to 8:30pm Wed; ℗) Housed in a small but graceful Spanish renaissance structure near the intersection of Prospect St and Girard Ave, the library hosts small art exhibits and concerts. There's also a good selection of art and music books in the library plus a few used books (including current fiction) for sale.

Museum of Contemporary Art
MUSEUM

(MCASD; Map p626; ☎858-454-3541; www. mcasd.org; 700 Prospect St; adult/student/senior $10/free/5; ⏰11am-5pm Thu-Tue, to 7pm third Thu each month, with free admission 5-7pm) The La Jolla branch of the small but excellent museum shows world-class exhibitions that rotate every six months. Originally designed by Irving Gill in 1916 as the home of Ellen Browning Scripps, the building was renovated by Philadelphia's postmodern architect Robert Venturi. Overall, MCASD holds more than 4000 works of art created after 1950 in its collection. Inside, the Krichman Family Gallery offers a superb view of the ocean below. Outside, Nancy Rubin's *Pleasure Point* sculpture bursts with boats – from kayaks to canoes to paddleboards. Tickets are good for one week at all museum locations.

San Diego-La Jolla Underwater Park Ecological Reserve
DIVING, SNORKELING

Look for the white buoys offshore from Point La Jolla north to Scripps Pier that mark this protected zone with a variety of marine life, kelp forests, reefs and canyons (see p629). Waves have carved caves into the sandstone cliffs east of the cove.

Cave Store
CAVE

(Map p626; ☎858-459-0746; www.cavestore.com; 1325 Coast Blvd; adult/child $4/3; ⏰10am-5pm) For a spooky mini-adventure, continue walking north on Coast Blvd. Here, 145 wooden steps descend a dank, man-made tunnel (completed in 1905) to the largest of the caves, Sunny Jim Cave. From its marine-ripe interior, you can watch kayakers paddling off-shore.

Windansea Beach
BEACH

(Map p613) A popular, not-for-beginners surf spot, 2 miles south of downtown (take La Jolla Blvd south and turn west on Nautilus St). Locals here can be aggressive toward outsiders. If you brave their ire, you'll find that the surf's consistent peak – a powerful reef break – works best at medium to low tide. Immediately south at **Big Rock**, at the foot of Palomar Ave, is California's version of Hawaii's Pipeline, which has steep, hollow tubes. The name comes from the large chunk of reef protruding just offshore – a great spot for tide pooling at low tide.

LA JOLLA SHORES

Called 'the Shores,' this area northeast of La Jolla Cove is where La Jolla's cliffs meet the wide, sandy beaches that stretch north to Del Mar. To reach the **beach** (Map p613), take La Jolla Shores Dr north from Torrey Pines Rd and turn west onto Ave de la Playa. The waves here are gentle enough for beginner surfers, and kayakers can launch from the shore without much problem.

Some of the best beaches in the county are north of the Shores at **Torrey Pines City Beach** (Map p613). At extreme low tides (about twice a year), you can walk from the Shores north to Del Mar along the beach. The **Torrey Pines Glider Port** (Map p613) at the end of Torrey Pines Scenic Dr is the place for hang gliders and paragliders to launch themselves into the sea breezes that rise over the high cliffs. It's a beautiful sight – tandem flights are available if you can't resist trying it (p631). Below, **Black's Beach** (Map p613), is a storied clothing-optional venue – though bathing suits are technically required, most folks don't seem to know that; there's a gay section at the far (north) end.

Birch Aquarium
AQUARIUM

(Map p613; ☎858-534-3474; http://aquarium.ucsd. edu; 2300 Exhibition Way; adult/child/student & senior $12/8.50/9; ⏰9am-5pm; ℗🚇) Off N Torrey Pines Rd, this aquarium has brilliant displays about the marine sciences and marine life. The **Hall of Fishes** has more than 60 fish tanks simulating marine environments from the Pacific Northwest to the tropics of Mexico and the Caribbean. Divers feed leopard sharks, garibaldi, sea bass and eels in the 70,000-gallon kelp tank during half-hour shows; check the website for times. The 13,000-gallon shark tank holds white-tip and black-tip reef sharks and others native to tropical reef habitats. There's a small touch-tank tide pool in back.

From downtown San Diego and La Jolla, take bus 30.

FREE **Salk Institute** ARCHITECTURE
(Map p613; ☎858-453-4100 ext 1287; www.salk. edu; 10010 N Torrey Pines Rd; ☺architectural tours noon-Mon-Fri, reservations required) Jonas Salk, the pioneer of polio prevention, founded the Salk Institute in 1960 for biological and biomedical research. San Diego County donated 27 acres of land, the March of Dimes provided financial support and Louis Kahn designed the building. Completed in 1965, it is a masterpiece of modern architecture, with its classically proportioned travertine marble plaza and cubist, mirror-glass laboratory blocks framing a perfect view of the Pacific. The Salk Institute attracts the best scientists to work in a research-only environment. The facilities have been expanded, with new laboratories designed by Jack McAllister, a follower of Kahn's work. Bus 101 follows N Torrey Pines Rd from the University Town Center (UTC) transit center.

Torrey Pines State Natural Reserve WILDLIFE RESERVE
(Map p613; ☎858-755-2063; www.torreypine.org; 12600 N Torrey Pines Rd; car $10; ☺8am-dusk) Birders, whale-watchers, hikers and those seeking great coastal views will want to amble through this tree-studded reserve that preserves the last mainland stands of the Torrey pine (Pinus torreyana), a species adapted to sparse rainfall and sandy, stony soils that's only found here and on Santa Rosa Island in Channel Islands National Park. Steep sandstone gullies are eroded into wonderfully textured surfaces, and the views over the ocean and north to Oceanside are superb, especially at sunset. The reserve is on the Pacific Flyway, making it a popular pit stop for migrating birds.

The main access road, Torrey Pines Park Rd, off N Torrey Pines Rd (bus 101) at the reserve's northern end, winds its way up to a simple adobe – built as a lodge in 1922 by (drum roll) Ellen Browning Scripps – which is now a **visitors center** (☺9am-6pm mid-March–Oct, to 4pm Nov–mid-Mar) – with displays on the local flora and fauna. Rangers lead nature walks from here at 10am and 2pm on weekends.

Admission is free if you enter on foot. Several walking trails wind through the reserve and down to the beach. For a good sampling of reserve highlights, plus good whale-watching spots, staff recommend the ⅔-mile Guy Fleming loop trail.

Torrey Pines Municipal Golf Course GOLF
(Map p613) Crowds swarmed the area for the historic, Tiger Woods–winning US Open golf tournament in June 2008. Located just north of the glider port, Torrey Pines is only the second public course to ever host the event.

University of California, San Diego UNIVERSITY
(UCSD; Map p613) The 1200-acre campus of the University of California San Diego was established in 1960 and now enrolls more than 22,000 undergraduates. Known for its math and science programs, the respected university lies on rolling coastal hills in a park-like setting, with many tall and fragrant eucalyptus trees shading the campus. Its most distinctive structure is the space-agey **Geisel Library**, a visually stunning upside-down pyramid of glass and concrete whose namesake, Theodor Geisel, is better known as Dr Seuss, creator of the *Cat in the Hat*. He and his wife, longtime residents of La Jolla, contributed substantially to the library. A collection of his drawings and books are displayed on the ground level in March.

For an engaging fusion of art and exercise, stroll the **Stuart Collection** of outdoor sculptures dotting the campus. Pick up the Stuart Collection brochure and map from the library's helpful information desk. From the eastern side of the library's 2nd level, an allegorical snake created by artist Alexis Smith winds around a native California plant garden, past an enormous marble copy of John Milton's *Paradise Lost*. Other works include Niki de Saint Phalle's *Sun God*, Bruce Nauman's *Vices & Virtues* (which spells out seven of each in huge neon letters), and a forest containing poem-reciting and music-singing trees. Most installations are near the Geisel Library.

The **UCSD bookstore**, located at the Price Center, has helpful staff and excellent stock that includes travel, religion, arts, sci-fi and California history. Inside the Mandell Weiss Center for the Performing Arts, the **La Jolla Playhouse** (☎858-550-1010; www. lajollaplayhouse.org) is known for high-quality productions.

The best access to campus is off La Jolla Village Dr or N Torrey Pines Rd (bus 30 from downtown). Pick up a campus map at Gil-

SEALS VS SWIMMERS

The **Children's Pool** (Map p626) was created in the early 1930s when the state deeded the area to the city with the proviso that it be used as a public park and children's pool. As part of the arrangement, Ellen Browning Scripps paid for a protective 300ft seawall. Then came the seals, drawing tourists but gradually nudging out swimmers. Animal rights groups want to protect the cove as a rookery while some swimmers and divers want the seals – whose presence raises bacteria levels in the water to unsafe levels – removed. In 2005 the California Superior Court ruled that the seals had to go. The US Appeals Court refused to hear an appeal by animal activists in 2008, and the California Supreme Court has done the same. In the last few years, it's been a constant battle between animal activists, City Council and the State Court – the State Court ordered the seals to be removed in 2009, then City Council called for the seals' habitat to be roped off, a temporary solution that was ended due to an insufficient budget. Activists keep up the fight, manning an information table near the pool's entrance. Visit www.savesandiegoseals.com to learn more.

man Dr Visitor Center. Parking is free on weekends. During the week, look for a metered spot just north of the library.

🏃 Activities

Surfing

San Diego has great surf spots for all skill levels, but the water can get crowded. Several spots, particularly Sunset Cliffs and Windansea, get especially territorial and you could get taunted unless you're an awesome surfer.

Fall brings the strong swells and offshore Santa Ana winds. In summer, swells come from the south and southwest, and in winter from the west and northwest. Spring brings more frequent onshore winds, but the surfing can still be good.

Beginners looking for classes and board rentals should try Mission or Pacific Beaches, where the waves are gentle. North of the Crystal Pier, Tourmaline Surfing Park (Map p613) is an especially good place to take your first strokes.

The best surf breaks, from south to north, are at Imperial Beach (south of Coronado, especially in winter); Point Loma (reef breaks, which are less accessible but less crowded; best in winter); Sunset Cliffs in Ocean Beach (a bit territorial); Pacific Beach; Big Rock (California's Pipeline); Windansea (hot reef break, best at medium to low tide; locals can be territorial); La Jolla Shores (beach break, best in winter); and Black's Beach (a fast, powerful wave). In North County (Map p644), there are breaks at Cardiff State Beach, San Elijo State Beach, Swami's, Carlsbad State Beach and Oceanside.

Bodysurfing is good at Coronado, Mission Beach, Pacific Beach and La Jolla Shores.

Pacific Beach Surf School   SURFING
(Map p624; ☎858-373-1138; www.pacificbeachsurfschool.com; 4150 Mission Blvd, Suite 161; private/semi-private lessons per person $80/65) Learn to hang 10 at surf school or just rent a board and wetsuit (half-day $25) at San Diego's oldest surf shop.

Surf Diva   SURFING
(☎858-454-8273; www.surfdiva.com; 2160 Avenida de la Playa) In La Jolla, the wonderful women here offer two-day weekend workshops for gals of all ages ($165 per person) and private classes for gals and guys ($60 per 90 minutes per person, price decreases with added students). They take newbies into the easygoing waves at nearby La Jolla Shores.

Diving & Snorkeling

Divers will find kelp beds, shipwrecks (including the *Yukon,* a WWII destroyer) and deep canyons just off the coast of San Diego County.

A number of commercial outfits teach scuba courses, sell or rent equipment, fill tanks and run boat trips to nearby wrecks and islands.

San Diego-La Jolla Underwater Park Ecological Reserve   SNORKELING, DIVING
For some of the state's best and most accessible (no boat needed) diving and snorkeling, just a few kicks from La Jolla Cove. With an average depth of 20ft, the 6000 acres of look-but-don't-touch underwater real estate are home to the bright orange garibaldi,

HIKE TO CITYWIDE VIEWS

A popular trail leads to the top of 1592ft **Cowles Mountain** (www.mtrp. org) near San Diego State University. On this two-hour summit bagger (3 miles round trip), you'll pass joggers, dog-walkers and moms with toddlers, all hoping to catch sweeping views that can stretch from La Jolla south to Coronado on a clear day. From I-8, take the College Ave north exit, following College Ave to Navajo Rd. Take a right onto Navajo Rd and drive almost 2 miles, turning left onto Goldcrest Dr then enter the parking lot.

California's protected state fish (there's a fine for poaching one). Further out, you'll see forests of giant California kelp (which can increase its length by up to 2ft per day) and the 100ft-deep La Jolla Canyon.

OEX Dive & Kayak   WATER SPORTS
(☎858-454-6195; www.oexcalifornia.com; 2243/2132 Avenida de la Playa, La Jolla) For gear or instruction, including spearfishing seminars and stand-up paddleboard lessons, head to this one-stop resource.

Fishing

If you're over 16 years of age, you'll need a state fishing license, except when fishing from an ocean pier (one/two/10 days $14/22/43). Call a recorded service on ☎619-465-3474 for fishing information. An ocean enhancement stamp ($5) is currently required for 10-day trips but not one- or two-day trips.

The most popular public fishing piers are Imperial Beach Municipal Pier, Embarcadero Fishing Pier at the Marina Park, Shelter Island Fishing Pier, Ocean Beach Pier and Crystal Pier at Pacific Beach. The best time of year for pier fishing is from about April to October. Offshore catches can include barracuda, bass and yellowtail. In summer albacore is a special attraction.

For guided fishing try the following outfitters. Prices do not include license and tackle (about $10 to $15).

H&M Landing   FISHING
(Map p613; ☎619-222-1144; www.hmlanding.com; 2803 Emerson St, Shelter Island) Half-day trips just off the coast cost $46 per person. See

the website for full day-trip and multiday trip options.

Mission Bay Sportfishing   FISHING
(off Map p624; ☎619-222-1164; 1551 West Mission Bay Dr) This friendly outfitter offers half-day trips from around $40 per adult (less for children). See website for overnight tuna fishing trips and boat rental information.

Boating

Rent power and sailboats, sailboards, kayaks and Waverunners on Mission Bay. Experienced sailors can charter yachts and sailboats for trips on San Diego Bay and out into the Pacific. You'll find the following charter companies on Harbor Islands (on the west side of San Diego Bay near the airport).

Family Kayak   KAYAKING
(☎619-282-3520; www.familykayak.com) Ocean kayaking is a good way to see sealife and explore cliffs and caves inaccessible from land. This company offers a guided tour of San Diego Bay (per adult/child $42/17).

Mission Bay Sportcenter   KAYAKING, BOATING
(Map p624; ☎858-488-1004; www.missionbay sportcenter.com; 1010 Santa Clara Pl). A sailboat costs $24/72/96 per hour/four hours/full day and a single kayak is $13/39/44.

Whale-Watching

From mid-December to late February, gray whales pass San Diego on their way south to Baja California and again in mid-March on their way back to Alaskan waters. Their 12,000-mile round-trip journey is the longest migration of any mammal on earth.

There's a bluff-top viewing area at Cabrillo National Monument (Map p613), the best place to observe the whales from land. You'll also find whale-related film and exhibits year-round and, seasonally, whale-centric ranger programs. Southwest of the Old Point Loma Lighthouse is a small glass-walled shelter, where you can watch the whales breach (bring binoculars). Further north, Torrey Pines State Reserve (p628) and La Jolla Cove (p626) are also good whale-watching spots.

H&M Landing   CRUISE
(p630) Three-hour whale-watching boat trips (adult/child $25/17.50) and six-hour blue whale–watching cruises (adult/child $80/55) are offered seasonally.

Hornblower Cruises
CRUISE
(Map p616; ☑888-467-6256; www.hornblower.com; tour per adult/child/senior $40/20/33) Offers a seasonal 3½-hour tour.

Hang Gliding

Torrey Pines Glider Port ADVENTURE SPORTS
(Map p613; ☑858-452-9858; www.flytorrey.com; 2800 Torrey Pines Scenic Dr; tandem paraglider flights/hang glider flights per person $150/200) Don't let age keep you from a tandem paraglide with an instructor. Instructors have lifted off with three-years-olds and 99-year-olds at this world-renowned gliding center by the sea, where most rides last between 20 and 25 minutes. The difference between paragliding and hang gliding? With paragliding, the instructor and passenger remain in a seated position under a soft 'wing,' while hang gliders fly in a prone position under a triangular wing.

Experienced pilots can fly here if they are USHGA members and/or have on them a temporary 30-day USGHA membership card.

☞ Tours

Look for brochures with discounts or check online for deals.

Another Side of San Diego WALKING, BOAT
(Map p616; ☑619-239-2111; www.anothersideof sandiegotours.com; 300 G St) This highly rated tour company does Segway tours of Balboa park, horseback riding on the beach and Gaslamp food tours.

Hike, Bike, Kayak San Diego CYCLING
(☑858-551-9510, 866-425-2925; www.hikebikekay ak.com; 2246 Avenida de la Playa, La Jolla) Just what it says.

Old Town Trolley Tours TROLLEY
(☑619-298-8687; www.trolleytours.com; adult/child $34/17) Not to be confused with the Metropolitan Transit System's rail trolleys, these open-air, hop-on-hop-off buses loop to the main attractions in and around downtown and in Coronado. Tickets for the orange-and-green trolleys are good for unlimited all-day travel. Board in Old Town. Tours run every 30 minutes.

San Diego Harbor Excursion
BOAT
(Map p616; ☑619-234-4111; www.sdhe.com; 1050 N Harbor Dr; adult/child from $22/11) A variety of bay and harbor cruises.

🎊 Festivals & Events

For the most current list, contact the San Diego Convention & Visitors Bureau.

Kiwanis Ocean Beach Kite Festival KITES
(www.oceanbeachkiwanis.org) Kite-making, decorating, flying and competitions at Ocean Beach on the first Saturday in March.

EarthFair FAIR
(www.earthdayweb.org/EarthFair.html) The world's largest annual – and free – environmental fair draws upwards of 60,000 visitors each year on April's Earth Day. Don't miss the fantastic Food Pavilion.

San Diego County Fair FAIR
(www.sdfair.com) Over 1.4 million attended this huge county fair in 2011, held from mid June to July 4; features headline acts and hundreds of carnival rides and shows at the Del Mar Fairgrounds in Del Mar.

San Diego Gay Pride GAY, LESBIAN
(www.sdpride.org) The city's gay community celebrates in Hillcrest and Balboa Park at the end of July.

Comic-Con International COMICS
(www.comic-con.org) America's largest event for collectors of comic, pop culture and movie memorabilia at the San Diego Convention Center. Late July.

December Nights CAROLS
(www.balboapark.org) Festival in Balboa Park includes crafts, carols and a candlelight parade in the park.

Harbor Parade of Lights CULTURAL
(www.sdparadeoflights.org) More than 100 decorated, illuminated vessels float in procession on the harbor on two Sunday evenings in December.

🛏 Sleeping

High-season summer rates for double-occupancy rooms are listed in this section. The prices drop significantly between September and June, often by 40% or more. Budget travelers should consider cheaper lodgings in neighboring Mission Valley.

DOWNTOWN

Despite its recent popularity, downtown still has some great, quirky budget options. It's also where you'll find several independently run midrange lodgings, from boutique hotels to B&Bs, and the bulk of the city's high-end palaces.

USA Hostels San Diego
HOSTEL $

(Map p616; ☎619-232-3100, 800-438-8622; www.usahostels.com; 726 5th Ave; dm/d incl breakfast from $28/72; ✳@⊙) In a former Victorian-era hotel, this convivial Gaslamp hostel has cheerful rooms, a full kitchen and an inviting movie room. Rates include a pancake breakfast and laundry facilities; the nightly family-style dinner costs $5.

HI San Diego Downtown Hostel
HOSTEL $

(Map p616; ☎619-525-1531; www.sandiegohostels.org/downtown; 521 Market St; incl breakfast dm $29-32, d with/without bath $93/77; @⊙) Friendly, helpful staff coordinate lots of activities and tours at this bustling, mazelike hostel. Located in the heart of the Gaslamp Quarter, this former Victorian-era hotel is close to public transportation and nightlife. Rates include a pancake breakfast, 24-hour access (including kitchen facilities), a laundry room and lockers (bring your own lock).

La Pensione Hotel
BOUTIQUE HOTEL $

(off Map p616; ☎800-232-4683; www.lapensionehotel.com; 606 W Date St; r $100; P✳⊙) At this four-story Little Italy hotel, rooms are built around a frescoed courtyard – a pleasant place to sip coffee from the adjacent cafe. Thanks to extensive renovations in 2010, the hotel looks fresh and stylish, even if rooms are on the small side. The location can hardly be beat, but if you have a car, there's complimentary parking under the building.

Little Italy Inn
B&B $$

(off Map p616; ☎619-230-1600; www.littleitalyhotel.com; 505 W Grape St; incl breakfast r with shared/private bath $89/109, 2-room apt from $149; ⊙) If you can't get enough of Little Italy's charm, this pretty B&B is an ideal place to hang your hat. The 23-room Victorian-style inn boasts comfortable beds, cozy bathrobes in each room, a casual European-style breakfast and wine socials on weekend evenings.

Hotel Indigo
BOUTIQUE HOTEL $$

(Map p616; ☎619-727-4000; www.hotelsandiegodowntown.com; 509 9th Ave; r from $146; P✳@⊙✱⊙) The first LEED-certified hotel in San Diego, Hotel Indigo is smartly designed and ecofriendly. The design is contemporary but colorful; guest rooms feature huge floor-to-ceiling windows, spa-style baths and large flat-screen TVs. Parking is $35.

500 West Hotel
HOSTEL, GUESTHOUSE $

(Map p616; ☎619-231-4092; www.500westhotelsd.com; 500 W Broadway; s/d with shared bath from $50/62; @⊙) Budget-minded hipsters go for the tiny rooms, bright decor and communal kitchen inside this 1920s beaux arts YMCA building.

Horton Grand Hotel
HISTORIC HOTEL $$

(Map p616; ☎619-544-1886, 800-542-1886; www.hortongrand.com; 311 Island Ave; r $149-269; ✳@⊙) This Gaslamp classic, dating from 1886 and once the home of Wyatt Earp, has Victorian-era furnishings and marble fireplaces.

CORONADO

Hotel del Coronado
LUXURY, HISTORIC HOTEL $$$

(Map p613; ☎619-435-6611, 800-468-3533; www.hoteldel.com; 1500 Orange Ave; r from $325; P✳@⊙✱) You probably don't *need* to take the antique elevator – complete with uniformed operator – to your 2nd-floor room but 'the Del' is so darn charming you won't want to miss a bit of its history. The 120-year old hotel combines tradition (p622), luxury and access to the city's most stunning beach. Amenities include two pools, a full-service spa, fitness center, shops, restaurants and manicured grounds. Note that half the accommodations are not in the main Victorian-era hotel, but in an adjacent seven-story building constructed in the 1970s. For a sense of place, book a room in the original hotel. Watch the fees, though. There's a $25 daily resort fee that includes use of the broadband in your room, local phone calls and access to the fitness center. Parking is another $25.

Coronado Inn
MOTEL $$

(☎619-435-4121, 800-598-6624; www.coronadoinn.com; 266 Orange Ave; r $119-159, ste with kitchen $179-199; P✳@⊙✱) It feels like home – in a good way – at this tidy, motel-style property wrapped around a small parking lot on Orange Ave near the ferry. Relax under the palm trees by the pool or grill your own fish on the communal barbecue.

OCEAN BEACH & POINT LOMA

Inn at Sunset Cliffs
HOTEL $$

(Map p624; ☎619-222-7901, 866-786-2543; www.innatsunsetcliffs.com; 1370 Sunset Cliffs Blvd, Point Loma; r from $175; P❉@🕸⊠) Hear the surf crashing onto the rocky shore at this breezy charmer wrapped around a flower-bedecked courtyard. Newly renovated rooms are light-filled but on the small side; recent efforts to decrease the hotel's water and plastic consumption have made the place greener.

Ocean Beach Hotel
HOTEL $$

(Map p624; ☎619-223-7191; www.obhotel.com; 5080 Newport Ave, Ocean Beach; d from $129; ❉@🕸) This recently remodeled hotel is just across the street from the beach. Spotless guest rooms are on the smaller side; the French provincial look is a bit dated but all feature refrigerators and complimentary wi-fi.

Ocean Beach International Hostel
HOSTEL $

(Map p624; ☎800-339-7263; www.californiahostels.com; 4961 Newport Ave; dm incl breakfast $35; @🕸) A large peace sign signals the cheapest sleeping option in the neighborhood, only a couple of blocks from the ocean. It's a fun, slightly rundown place reserved for international travelers and students, with bonfires, barbecues, free linens, and surfboard rentals. They'll arrange free transportation from the airport, train station or bus terminal.

MISSION BAY & PACIFIC BEACH

Crystal Pier Hotel
QUIRKY, HISTORIC HOTEL $$$

(Map p624; ☎800-748-5894; www.crystalpier.com; 4500 Ocean Blvd; d cottage from $300, 3-night minimum; P🕸) White clapboard cottages with flower boxes and blue shutters are the draw at this popular hotel, and not just because they're picturesque. The cottages – dating from 1936 – are special because they sit atop the pier itself, offering one-of-a-kind views of coast and sea. Newer, larger cottages sleep more people, but the older units are the best. Book well in advance for summer reservations.

Banana Bungalow
HOSTEL $

(Map p624; ☎858-273-3060; www.bananabungalow.com; 707 Reed Ave; dm/r $35/150; @🕸) The Bungalow has a top beachfront location that's just a few blocks from the Garnet Ave bar scene. It's reasonably clean, though pretty basic, and it gets rowdy. A communal, made-for-keggers patio overlooks the boardwalk and Mission Beach. It's more of a party scene than other city hostels.

Campland on the Bay
CAMPGROUND $

(Map p624; ☎800-422-9386; www.campland.com; 2211 Pacific Beach Dr; tent & RV sites $52-142; P🕸⊠🐾) This kid-friendly campground, with more than 40 acres fronting Mission Bay, also has a restaurant, two pools, a small grocery, a marina, boating rentals and full RV hook-ups. The location is great, but the tent area can be pretty sorry – try to avoid the shadeless, dusty sites.

Beach Cottages
HOTEL, BUNGALOWS $$$

(Map p624; ☎858-483-7440; www.beachcottages.com; 4255 Ocean Blvd; r from $285, cottages from $300; P🕸@🕸⊠🐾) This picturesque family-owned complex comprises 17 cozy, 1940s-era beachfront cottages, plus motel-style rooms in the main building.

OLD TOWN

Old Town Inn
HOTEL $$

(☎800-643-3025; www.oldtown-inn.com; 4444 Pacific Hwy; incl breakfast r $90-135, with kitchen $145-155; P❉@🕸⊠) Rooms look a bit dark when compared to those in the shiny hipster hotels downtown, but otherwise this simple, mission-style motel has a lot to recommend it. Centrally located off the I-5, on the opposite side of the interstate from the Old Town Transit Center, it's an easy walk to Old Town. Sturdy mattresses, an on-site laundry, and complimentary wi-fi, parking and continental breakfast round out the appeal.

LA JOLLA

It's hard to find a cheap room here, even on weekdays off-season. Less expensive options, including a handful of midrange chains and the occasional family-run motel, can be found south of town along La Jolla Blvd. Longer stays yield lower rates.

La Valencia
HISTORIC HOTEL $$$

(Map p626; ☎858-454-0771, 800-451-0772; www.lavalencia.com; 1132 Prospect St, La Jolla; r $285-515, ste $695; P❉@🕸⊠) For Old Hollywood style, book a room at this pink 1926 Mediterranean-style palace. The 116 rooms are compact – befitting the era – but the hotel wins for Old Hollywood romance; recent ecofriendly efforts add to the charm. Even if you can't afford to sleep with the ghosts of Depression-era Hollywood, have a drink in La Sala, the elegant Spanish revival lounge. Parking is $32.

DON'T MISS

FISH TACOS

The ingredients of this SoCal staple are always the same: a soft tortilla topped with fish, salsa, cabbage and special sauce. It's the preparation that makes San Diego's addition to the culinary lexicon – the fish taco – so interesting. Ralph Rubio, who founded his namesake fish-centric fast-food chain **Rubio's Fresh Mexican Grill** (www.rubios.com) in 1983, is credited with popularizing the dish. Who serves the city's best version? Perennial frontrunners include the piled-high bad boys at **South Beach Bar & Grille** (p636) in Ocean Beach, where the lightly fried mahi mahi is the fish of choice. Then there are the uber-fresh grilled fish tacos at **Blue Water Seafood Market & Grill** (www.bluewater. sandiegan.com; 3667 India St). The deep-fried fish taco at longtime chain **Roberto's** (www. robertos.us) is a corndog-sized piece of fried fish that is sure to ruin any diet. Minichain **Brigantine** (www.brigantine.com; 1333 Orange Ave) also has a devoted following.

Grande Colonial Hotel   LUXURY HOTEL $$$
(Map p626; ☎888-828-5498; www.thegrandeco lonial.com; 910 Prospect St; r $255-500, ste from $325;❄☞✿) Warm colors, simple prints and classic furnishings set a conservative but sophisticated mood at the popular Grande Colonial, demure step-sister to the pink palace just down the road. There's been a hotel on the site for almost a century, and its central location makes it a perfect home base for exploring. Accommodating staff add to the ambience. Parking is $22 a day.

✖ Eating

San Diego's not a foodie capital like some California cities, though the dining scene is becoming increasingly dynamic. As a rule of thumb, you'll find haute cuisine and fine steakhouses in the Gaslamp, casual seafood along the beaches, ethnic food in and around Hillcrest, and tacos and margaritas, well, everywhere. For full listings of sustainable San Diego eating options, look for a free copy of the seasonal magazine *Edible San Diego*.

DOWNTOWN & EMBARCADERO
It seems new restaurants are opening weekly in the Gaslamp Quarter, particularly in and around the trendy hotels surrounding nearby Petco Park – reservations are recommended. If you're in the mood for Italian, just take a stroll along Little Italy's India Street and choose the most inviting sidewalk table.

Café 222   BREAKFAST $
(Map p616; ☎619-236-9902; www.cafe222.com; 222 Island Ave; mains $7-11; ☺7am-1:45pm; ▣) This small, airy breakfast spot is renowned for pumpkin waffles, orange pecan pancakes and farm-fresh egg scramblers. The French toast stuffed with peanut butter and bananas was featured on the Food Network.

TOP CHOICE Puerto La Boca   ARGENTINE $$
(off Map p616; ☎619-234-4900; www.puertolaboca. com; 2060 India St; mains lunch $8-12; dinner $15-45; ☺11am-10pm Mon-Thu, to 11pm Fri, noon-11pm Sat, 1-8:30pm Sun; ▣) This classy, new-on-the-scene Argentine eatery in Little Italy is surprisingly authentic: come for grilled chorizo and steak, fried empanadas, garlicky mussels, and a glass of Malbec or Torrontés. Happy hour food and wine specials (4:30 to 7:30pm Monday to Saturday and all day Sunday) are a bargain.

C Level   SEAFOOD $$
(☎619-298-6802; www.islandprime.com; 880 Harbor Island Dr; mains $14-30; ☺from 11am-late) The food is as aesthetically pleasing as the view from this Harbor Island patio lounge with sweeping vistas of the bay and downtown. Here, carefully crafted salads, sandwiches and light seafood fare are winning rave reviews. The uber-rich lobster and fontina BLT – dunked in lobster bisque – is a top choice. The Social Hour (3:30 to 5:30pm Monday to Friday) offers $5 'bites and libations.' C Level is located on the tip of Harbor Island, which juts into the bay near the airport; to get here, take N Harbor Dr north from the Gaslamp Quarter and Embarcadero.

Filippi's Pizza Grotto   PIZZERIA $$
(Map p616; www.realcheesepizza.com; 1747 India St; mains $11-20; ☺11am-10pm Sun-Thu, to 11:30pm Fri & Sat) Regularly lauded by locals for its pizza, this old-school Italian joint – think red-and-white checked tablecloths, tiny booths, small deli up front – often has a line out the door. Look for a **second location** (Map p624; 962 Garnet Ave) in Pacific Beach.

Candelas
MEXICAN $$$

(Map p616; ☑619-702-4455; www.candelas-sd. com; 416 3rd Ave; mains $18-53; ⊙5-11pm) Upscale 'rustic' decor, flattering lighting, attentive waiters and savory Mexican specialties – from beef tenderloin au gratin (with blue cheese) to jumbo prawns flamed with tequila – make Candelas one of downtown's most romantic dining experiences. Don't be surprised if someone pops the question at the adjacent table. Now there's a **second location** (1201 1st St) in Coronado.

The Oceanaire Seafood Room
SEAFOOD $$$

(Map p616; ☑619-858-2277; www.theoceanaire. com; 400 J St; mains $24-40; ⊙5-10pm Sun-Thu, to 11pm Fri & Sat) The look is art-deco ocean liner and the service is just as refined, with an oyster bar (get them for a buck during happy hour, 5 to 6pm Monday to Friday) and inventive creations, including Maryland blue crab cakes and horseradish-crusted Alaskan halibut.

La Puerta
MEXICAN $

(Map p616; www.taco619.com; 560 4th Ave; mains $7-10; ⊙11:30am-2am Mon-Sat, from 10am Sun) Toss back Coronas, enchiladas and fresh guacamole at this shadowy Mexican bar that looks like the inside of a vampire's lair.

Mona Lisa
DELI, ITALIAN $

(Map p616; www.monalisalittleitaly.com; 2061 India St; mains lunch $6-9, dinner $12-18; ⊙11am-10pm Mon-Sat, from 3pm Sun) This traditional Italian eatery and deli is the place to dig into veal piccata or pick up picnic fixings.

BALBOA PARK

TOP CHOICE **Prado**
MEDITERRANEAN, AMERICAN $$

(Map p620; ☑619-557-9441; www.pradobalboa. com; 1549 El Prado; mains lunch $10-15, dinner $21-34; ⊙11:30am-3pm Mon-Fri & from 5pm Tue-Sun, 11am-3pm Sat & Sun; ⊛) This classic lunch spot in the museum district of Balboa Park serves up fresh Mediterranean cuisine like steamed mussels, shrimp paella and grilled portobello sandwiches. Breezy outdoor seating and the Mexican-tiled interior are equally inviting; happy hour food and drink specials (4 to 6pm Tuesday to Friday) are a steal.

Tea Pavilion
ASIAN $

(Map p620; 2215 Pan American Way; mains $5-10; ⊙10am-5pm, later in summer) Enjoy a quick and spicy noodle bowl – or a simple cup of tea – under an umbrella at this low-key eatery next to the Japanese Garden.

OLD TOWN

Old Town overflows with lively Mexican restaurants, but only a few are reasonably authentic. Still, the pretty outdoor seating and ice-cold margaritas can make for a fun lunch or evening out.

Old Town Mexican Café
MEXICAN $

(☑619-297-4330; www.oldtownmexcafe.com; 2489 San Diego Ave; mains $4-15; ⊙7am-2am; ⊛) Watch the staff turn out fresh tortillas in the window while waiting for a table. Besides breakfast (great *chiluquiles* – soft tortilla chips covered with mole), there's *pozole* (spicy pork stew), avocado tacos and margaritas at the festive central bar.

HILLCREST & MISSION HILLS

You'll find lots of ethnic dining options in and around Hillcrest: wander around University Ave and 5th Ave for an overview. Restaurants here tend to be more casual than downtown – and better value.

Bread & Cie
BAKERY $

(Map p620; www.breadandciecatering.com; 350 University Ave; mains $6-10; ⊙7am-7pm Mon-Fri, to 6pm Sat, 9am-6pm Sun; ⊛) A delightful sensory overload of aromatic fresh bread, chattering locals and pastry-filled trays awaits inside this bustling Hillcrest crossroads. Daily breads include black olive and walnut raisin. Try the almond croissant or the ridiculously rich and oversized *pain au chocolat*.

Kous Kous
MOROCCAN $$

(Map p620; www.kouskousrestaurant.com; 3940 4th Ave; mains $14-20; ⊙5pm-late; ☑) Entering this otherworldly Moroccan eatery is like stepping onto another continent: the dining room is seductively illuminated by glowing lanterns, dinner guests sit on jewel-toned cushions drinking exotic cocktails, the aroma of ginger, nutmeg and foreign spices hangs in the air. Don't miss the lamb sausage or the B'stila roll (saffron chicken baked with honey, cinnamon and almonds in phyllo dough).

Khyber Pass
MIDDLE EASTERN $$

(Map p620; www.khyberpasssandiego.com; 523 University Ave; mains $14-30; ⊙11:30am-10pm; ☑) Afghan tapestries and moody photos set the tone in this tall-ceilinged space, with adventuresome Afghan cooking. Never had it? Think Indian meets Middle Eastern, with yogurt curries, kababs and stews.

TO MARKET, TO MARKET

Swinging by the local farmers market to pick up your eggs and basil is *so Californian*. So it's no surprise that San Diego has a street market (or two or three) for almost every day of the week. For full listings of where the hipsters are eating tamales and foodies shop for avocados and ginger root, visit the San Diego Farm Bureau website at www.sdfarmbureau.org.

» Tuesday – **Coronado Farmers Market** (1st St & B Ave, Ferry Landing; ⊙2:30-6pm) and **UCSD La Jolla Farmers Market** (Town Square; ⊙10am-2pm)

» Wednesday – **Ocean Beach Farmers Market** (4900 Newport Ave, ⊙4-8pm) and **Carlsbad Farmers Market** (Roosevelt St & Carlsbad Village Dr, ⊙1-5pm)

» Thursday – **North Park Farmers Market** (3151 University & 32nd St, ⊙3-7pm) and **SDSU Farmers Market** (Campanile Walkway near Love Library, ⊙10am-3pm)

» Friday – **Imperial Beach Farmers Market** (Seacoast Dr, Pier Plaza; ⊙2-7:30pm) and **Mission Hills Farmers Market** (Falcon St & W Washington; ⊙3-7pm)

» Saturday – **Little Italy Mercato** (Date St & Kettner; ⊙9am-1:30pm) and **Del Mar Farmers Market** (1050 Camino del Mar; ⊙1-4pm)

» Sunday – **Gaslamp Farmers Market** (400 block of 3rd Ave, ⊙9am-1pm), **Hillcrest Farmers Market** (3960 Normal & Lincoln Sts; ⊙9am-2pm), **Point Loma Farmers Market** (Cañon & Rosecrans; ⊙9:30am-2:30pm) and **Solana Beach Farmers Market** (410 S Cedros Ave; ⊙1-5pm)

Saigon on Fifth   VIETNAMESE $$
(Map p620; 3900 5th Ave; mains $11-16; ⊙11am-midnight; P) For good Vietnamese, try this elegant but not overbearing place.

Hash House a Go Go   BREAKFAST $$
(Map p620; www.hashhouseagogo.com; 3628 5th Ave; mains breakfast & lunch $8-17, dinner $15-39; ⊙7:30am-2pm daily, 5:30-9pm Tue-Sun) Does this fantastically popular breakfast joint merit the hype (and long lines)? One way to find out – the portions are massive, so consider sharing your flapjacks.

CORONADO

Coronado Brewing Company   PUB $$
(www.coronadobrewingcompany.com; 170 Orange Ave; mains $10-22; ⊙10:30am-late) The delicious house brew (the Pilsner-style Coronado Golden) goes well with the pizzas, pastas, sandwiches and fries at this good-for-your-soul, bad-for-your-diet bar and grill near the ferry. Try the $9 beer tasting.

1500 Ocean   SEAFOOD $$$
(Map p613; 619-522-8490; www.dine1500ocean.com; Hotel del Coronado; 1500 Orange Ave; mains $18-45; ⊙5:30-9pm Tue-Thu, to 10pm Fri-Sun) Bright marigolds border the veranda at the Del's most romantic restaurant, adding a cheerful splash of color to palm-framed views of the sea. Come here to impress someone, celebrate or simply revel in your good fortune over duck confit or seared scallops.

OCEAN BEACH

OB is the place to go for the city's best cheap eats. Most places are on Newport Ave.

Hodad's   BURGERS $
(Map p624; www.hodadies.com; 5010 Newport Ave, Ocean Beach; burgers $4-9; ⊙5am-10pm) If there was a glossy magazine called *Beach Bum Living*, then legendary Hodad's, with its surfboards- and-license-plates decor, communal wooden tables and baskets of burgers and fries, would score the very first cover. Many say the succulent burgers are the best in town. Add an order of onion rings and you'll go home happy. A **second location** (Map p616; 945 Broadway Ave) recently opened downtown.

South Beach Bar & Grille   MEXICAN, CALIFORNIAN $
(Map p624; www. southbeachob.com; 5059 Newport Ave; mains $8-10; ⊙11am-1am Sun-Thu, to 2am Fri & Sat) Maybe it's the lightly fried mahi mahi. Or the kickin' white sauce. Or the layer of cabbage and salsa. Whatever the secret, the fish tacos at this beachside bar and grill stand out in a city of awesome fish tacos. On Fridays, follow the noise to this festive watering hole in a nondescript building at the end of Newport Ave.

MISSION BAY & PACIFIC BEACH
You can eat well on a tight budget in these two coastal communities. Both have a young, mostly local scene; PB has the bulk of the restaurants, especially along Garnet Ave.

The Mission   BREAKFAST, LATIN AMERICAN $
(Map p624; 3795 Mission Blvd; dishes $7-11; ☺7am-3pm; 🖉🖼) Savor the famously delicious coffee or homemade cinnamon bread for breakfast – or kick back with Chino-Latino lunch specialties that include ginger sesame wraps and rosemary potatoes with salsa and eggs. Other locations have popped up around town: **The Mission SoMa** (1250 J St) and **The Mission North Park** (2801 University Ave).

🖉**JRDN**   SEAFOOD, CALIFORNIAN $$$
(Map p624; www.jrdn.com; Tower 23, 723 Felspar St; mains breakfast $10-18, lunch $9-18, dinner $23-46; ☺7am-11am Mon-Fri, 9am-4pm Sat & Sun, 5-10pm daily) Sustainably farmed meats and seafood join local veggies for a plate topping farmers market at chic, vowel-disdaining JRDN, where you can choose futuristic decor indoors or ocean views outdoors. Try dry scallops with crabmeat risotto, miso halibut and green-onion creamers (aka mashed potatoes).

LA JOLLA
La Jolla is a major haute-cuisine outpost, but there are some good budget and mid-range options, too.

Harry's Coffee Shop   DINER $
(Map p626; www.harryscoffeeshop.com; 7545 Girard Ave; dishes $5-12; ☺6am-3pm; 🖼) Classic coffee shop serving all-American fare with vinyl booths and a posse of regulars, from blue-haired socialites to sports celebs.

🖉**whisknladle**   MODERN AMERICAN $$
(Map p626, 🖉858-551-7575; www.whisknladle.com; 1044 Wall St; mains brunch & lunch $12-19, dinner $15-30; ☺11:30am-9:30pm Mon-Fri, from 10am Sat & Sun) whisknladle serves up carefully selected and seasoned 'slow food' – fresh fare simply prepared. The breezy covered patio is the main dining area, and there's only a small bar – and artsy wall of empty wine bottles – inside. Dinner menu favorites include chorizo date fritters and charred bone marrow (tastes far better than it sounds). For lunch, try the locally harvested mussels with fries.

George's at the Cove   MODERN AMERICAN $$
(Map p626; 🖉858-454-4244; www.georgesatthecove.com; 1250 Prospect St; mains $11-48; ☺11am-11pm) Chef Trey Foshee's Euro-Cal cuisine is as dramatic as this eatery's oceanfront location. George's has graced just about every list of top restaurants in California. Three venues allow you to enjoy it at different price points: **George's Bar** (lunch mains $9-16), **Ocean Terrace** (lunch mains $11-18) and **George's California Modern** (dinner mains $28-48). Walk-ins welcome at the bar, but reservations are recommended for the latter two.

🍷 **Drinking**

If you want to explore the city's alive and kicking bar scene, head to the Gaslamp for rooftop bars atop fashionable hotels, Hillcrest for bohemian and gay friendly watering holes, and the beaches for casual bars where surfers and college kids down cheap beers and tacos.

TOP CHOICE **Wine Steals**   WINE BAR
(Map p620; 🖉619-295-1188; www.winestealssd.com; 1243 University Ave, Hillcrest) Laid-back wine tastings (go for a flight or choose a bottle off the rack in the back), live music, gourmet pizzas and cheese platters bring in a nightly crowd to this low-lit wine bar. Look for two newer branches in San Diego, **Wine Steals East Village** (Map p616; 793/5 J Street, Downtown) and **Lounge-Point Loma** (2970 Truxtun Rd, Point Loma).

TOP CHOICE **Cafe 1134**   CAFE $
(1134 Orange Ave, Coronado; mains $8-10; ☺9am-7pm) This cool coffeeshop on Coronado's main drag offers more than your morning fix: think delicious Greek-style egg scramblers, grilled panini, spinach salads, high-end teas and a wine and beer list. Prices are slashed as part of the 'Money Wise Menu' on Sunday, Monday and Tuesday evenings.

🖉**Starlite**   COCKTAIL BAR
(www.starlitesandiego.com; 3175 India St, Mission Hills) Slightly out of the way – don't worry, the drive is worthwhile – is this hipster cocktail haven with top-notch house creations and a lively central bar. The list changes frequently: just try anything made with ginger beer. From the Gaslamp/downtown, take I-5 N to exit 17B, then follow India St for 0.5 miles. Starlite will be on your right.

SAN DIEGO MICROBREWERIES

San Diegans take their craft beers seriously – even at a dive bar, you might overhear local guys talking about hops and cask conditioning. Various microbreweries on the city outskirts specialize in India Pale Ale (IPA) and Belgian-style brews; the following venues are beer-enthusiast favorites.

Stone Brewing Company (☑760-471-4999; www.stonebrew.com; 1999 Citracado Pkwy, Escondido; ⊙11am-9pm). Take a free tour before a guided tasting of Oaked Arrogant Bastard Ale and Stone Barley Wine.

Lost Abbey (☑800-918-6816; www.lostabbey.com; 155 Mata Way 104, San Marcos; ⊙1-6pm Wed-Thu, 3-9pm Fri, noon-6pm Sat & Sun). More than 20 brews ($1 per taste) are on tap in the tasting room – try Lost and Found Abbey Ale.

AleSmith (☑858-549-9888; www.alesmith.com; 9368 Cabot Dr; ⊙2-7pm Thu-Fri, noon-6pm Sat, to 4pm Sun). Wee Heavy and the potent Old Numbskull ($1 per taste) are the standout brews.

Living Room Coffeehouse
COFFEE SHOP
(Map p626; www.livingroomcafe.com; 1010 Prospect St, La Jolla; ⊙6am-midnight) This popular cafe serves spinach salads, quiche lorraine, and apricot strudel and has a great central position in the heart of the Village. There's a **second location** (2541 San Diego Ave) in Old Town and several others around town.

Extraordinary Desserts
CAFE
(Map p620; ☑619-294-2132; www.extraordinarydesserts.com; 2929 5th Ave, Hillcrest; ⊙8:30am-11pm Mon-Thu, to midnight Fri, 10am-midnight Sat, 10am-11pm Sun; 🐾) For those with a sweet tooth, Karen Krasne's treasure trove of stylishly decadent pastries – fruit-topped tarts, chunky cookies, creamy chocolate cheesecake and unforgettable bread pudding, to name a few – is heaven. There's organic coffee and wine, too, and cozy couches where you can share your treats with friends. There's a **second location** (1430 Union St) with a full bar in Little Italy.

Altitude Sky Lounge
COCKTAIL BAR
(Map p616; www.altitudeskylounge.com; 660 K St) The Marriott's rooftop bar is our favorite. It may have the *de rigueur* firepits and sleek decor, but unlike other open-air lounges, the vibe is friendly, not hipper-than-thou. Sightlines to Petco Park are superb.

Tipsy Crow
BAR, LOUNGE
(Map p616; www.thetipsycrow.com; 770 5th Ave, Downtown) There are three distinct levels at this historic Gaslamp building that's been turned into an atmospheric watering hole: the main floor with its long mahogany bar, the lounge-like 'Nest' (thought to be the site of a former brothel), and the brick-walled 'Underground' with a dance floor and live music acts.

Nunu's Cocktail Lounge
COCKTAIL BAR
(Map p620; www.nunuscocktails.com; 3537 5th Ave, Hillcrest) Dark and divey, this hipster haven started pouring when JFK was president and still looks the part with its curvy booths, big bar and lovably kitsch decor.

Cosmopolitan Restaurant & Hotel
BAR
(www.oldtowncosmo.com; 2660 Calhoun St, Old Town) The service is spotty, but the historic Old Town atmosphere (the house dates from the 1820s) makes the 3pm to 6pm happy hour appealing.

Pacific Beach Bar & Grill
BAR
(Map p624; ☑858-272-4745; 860 Garnet Ave, Pacific Beach) This classic attracts a young, party-hearty crowd to its long wooden tables, patios and big central bar.

Star Bar
BAR
(Map p616; ☑619-234-5575; 423 E St) Down-and-divey Star Bar: the place where dreams come to die.

☆ Entertainment

The Thursday editions of the free weekly *San Diego Reader* and the Night & Day section of the San Diego *Union Tribune* list the latest movies, theater shows, gallery exhibits and music gigs in the area. From a kiosk outside Horton Plaza, **Arts Tix** (Map p616; ☑858-381-5595; www.sdartstix.com; 3rd Ave & Broadway, Downtown; ⊙9:30am-5pm Tue-Thu, 9:30am-6pm Fri & Sat), sells half-price tickets for same-day evening performances as well as discounts tickets to other events.

There's a thriving theater culture in San Diego. Book tickets at the box office or with Arts Tix.

TOP
CHOICE **Cinema Under the Stars**   CINEMA
(off Map p620; 619-295-4221; www.topspresents.com; 4040 Goldfinch St, Mission Hills;) Catch classic films, both new and old – from *An Affair to Remember* to the latest Harry Potter installment – at this family-friendly outdoor theater. Heatlamps, reclining chairs and fleece blankets are provided.

San Diego Opera   OPERA
(Map p616; 619-533-7000; www.sdopera.com; Civic Theatre, cnr 3rd Ave & B St) This fine company presents high quality, eclectic programming under the direction of maestro Karen Keltner.

Anthology   LIVE MUSIC
(Map p616; 619-595-0300; www.anthologysd.com; 1337 India St; cover free-$60) Near Little Italy, Anthology presents live jazz, blues and Indie music in a swank supper-club setting, from both up-and-comers and big-name performers.

San Diego Symphony   CLASSICAL MUSIC
(Map p616; 619-235-0804; www.sandiegosymphony.com; 750 B St) Nearly a century old, this accomplished symphony presents classical and family concerts at the Copley Symphony Hall. Starting in June, performances move to the Embarcadero Marina Park South for the lively outdoor Summer Pops season.

Casbah   LIVE MUSIC
(Map p620; 619-232-4355; www.casbahmusic.com; 2501 Kettner Blvd; cover free-$20) Liz Phair, Alanis Morissette and the Smashing Pumpkins all rocked this funky Casbah on their way up the charts; catch local acts and headliners like Bon Iver.

La Jolla Playhouse   THEATER
(619-550-1010; www.lajollaplayhouse.com; UCSD, 2910 La Jolla Village Dr) Classic and contemporary plays.

Landmark Hillcrest Cinemas   CINEMA
(Map p620; 619-819-0236; www.landmarktheatres.com; 3965 5th Ave, Hillcrest) Regularly shows new arthouse, foreign films and classics in the boxy, postmodern Village Hillcrest Center.

Croce's Restaurant & Jazz Bar   JAZZ, LIVE MUSIC
(Map p616; www.croces.com; cnr 5th Ave & F St) Ingrid Croce's tribute to her late husband Jim, this busy restaurant and club hosts great nightly jazz, blues and R&B performers.

Gaslamp Stadium 15   CINEMA
(Map p616; 619-232-0400; www.readingcinemasus.com; 701 5th Ave) A downtown cinema showing current-release movies.

Old Globe Theatre   THEATER
(Map p620; 619-234-5623; www.theoldglobe.org; Balboa Park) Three venues stage Shakespeare, classics and contemporary plays.

San Diego Repertory Theatre   THEATER
(Map p616; 619-544-1000; www.sdrep.org; Lyceum Theatre, 79 Horton Plaza) Avant-garde, multicultural and a musical or two.

Petco Park   STADIUM
(Map p616; 619-795-5011, tickets 877-374-2784; www.padres.com; 100 Park Blvd) Home of the San Diego Padres Major League Baseball team. The season lasts from April to early October. Behind-the-scenes stadium **tours** (10:30am, 12:30pm & 2:30pm Tue-Sun May-Aug, 10:30am & 12:30pm Apr & Sep, subject to game schedule) are possible year-round.

Qualcomm Stadium   STADIUM
(Map p613; 619-280-2121; www.chargers.com; 9449 Friars Rd, Mission Valley) The San Diego Chargers National Football League team plays here: the season runs August through January.

🔒 Shopping

Though San Diego isn't known for shopping, you'll find plenty to purchase in this town if you're so inclined. Local fashionistas head to the upscale boutiques of La Jolla, shoppers in search of colorful housewares like the museum stores at Balboa Park and the Mexican artisan stands of Old Town, hipsters hit the secondhand clothing racks in Hillcrest and Ocean Beach, and kids find stuffed Shamus at SeaWorld. Surf shops and bikini boutiques dot the coastal communities.

The San Diego Trolley green line (or your car) takes you to each of three large malls in Mission Valley, visible just north of I-8 and bordering Hotel Circle.

TOP
CHOICE **Bazaar del Mundo Shops**   HOMEWARES, HANDICRAFTS
(www.bazaardelmundo.com; 4133 Taylor St, Old Town) Housed in a romantic hacienda-style building in Old Town, these lively shops specialize in high-quality Latin American

GAY & LESBIAN NIGHTLIFE

Interestingly, many historians trace the roots of San Diego's thriving gay community to the city's strong military presence. During WWII, amid the enforced intimacy of military life, gay men from around the country were suddenly able to create strong (if clandestine) social networks. After the war, many stayed.

In the late 1960s, a newly politicized gay community began to make the Hillcrest neighborhood its unofficial headquarters. Here you'll find the highest concentration of bars catering to lesbians and gays. The scene is generally more casual and friendly than in San Francisco and LA.

Baja Betty's (Map p620; www.bajabettyssd.com; 1421 University Ave) Gay owned and straight friendly, this restaurant-bar is always a party with a just-back-from Margarita-ville vibe (and dozens of tequilas to take you back there) alongside dishes like Mexi-queen queso dip & You Go Grill swordfish tacos.

Brass Rail (Map p620; www.thebrassrailsd.com; 3796 5th Ave) The city's oldest gay bar has a different music style nightly, from Latin to African to Top 40.

Urban Mo's (Map p620; www.urbanmos.com; 308 University Ave) Equal parts bar and restaurant, Mo's isn't particularly known for great food, service or prices, but it's popular nonetheless for its thumping club beats, casual vibe, dance floor and happy hours.

artisan wares, folk art, Mexican jewelry and home accessories.

✐ United Nations International Gift Shop
HOMEWARES, HANDICRAFTS
(p620; United Nations Bldg, 2171 Pan American Plaza, Balboa Park) Fair-trade gifts and housewares from Africa and Latin America.

Pangaea Outpost
MARKET
(Map p624; www.pangaeaoutpost.com; 909 Garnet Ave, Pacific Beach) This funky indoor marketplace features 70 funky miniboutiques and craft stores – think surf-baby tanks, hand-painted wine glasses and bright Oaxacan figurines.

Westfield Horton Plaza Center
MALL
(Map p616; Broadway & 4th St, Downtown; P) For general shopping downtown, Horton Plaza has the highest concentration of shops and a variety of casual eateries.

Fashion Valley
MALL
(off Map p620; www.simon.com; 7007 Friars Rd) Furthest west, home to Tiffany & Co, Burberry, Louis Vuitton, Kiehl's, Restoration Hardware, and department stores Neiman Marcus, Saks Fifth Avenue, Macy's and Nordstrom.

South Coast Surf Shop
CLOTHING, OUTDOOR EQUIPMENT
(Map p624; www.southcoast.com; 5023 Newport Ave) Surf dudes staff the counter at this beach apparel and surf-gear shop in Ocean Beach that carries a good selection of Quiksilver, Hurley, Billabong and O'Neill for men and women.

Le Travel Store
BOOKS
(Map p616; 745 4th Ave) Excellent selection of maps, travel guides and accessories.

ℹ Information

Dangers & Annoyances

San Diego is fairly safe, though you should be cautious venturing east of 6th Ave in downtown – especially after dark. Hostile panhandling is the most common problem.

Emergency & Medical Services

Scripps Mercy Hospital (☎619-294-8111; www.scripps.org; 4077 5th Ave, Hillcrest; ⏰24hr) Has a 24-hour emergency room.

Internet Access

All city-operated libraries provide free internet and wireless access; no library card is required. Check www.sandiego.gov/public-library to see various use policies.

Media

KPBS 89.5FM (www.kpbs.org) Public radio, high-quality news and information.

San Diego Reader (www.sdreader.com) On Thursdays, look for this alt-weekly with the latest on the active music, art and theater scenes.

San Diego Union-Tribune (www.signonsandiego.com) The city's major daily.

Money

You'll find ATMs throughout San Diego.

Travelex (☎619-235-0901; 177 Horton Plaza, Downtown; ☺10am-7pm Mon-Fri, to 6pm Sat, 11am-4pm Sun) For foreign-currency exchange.

Post

For local post office locations, call ☎800-275-8777 or log on to www.usps.com.

Downtown post office (Map p616; ☎619-232-8612; 815 E St; ☺8:30am-5pm Mon-Fri)

Tourist Information

Balboa Park Visitors Center (Map p620; ☎619-239-0512; www.balboapark.org; 1549 El Prado; ☺9:30am-4:30pm) In the House of Hospitality. Sells park maps and the Passport to Balboa Park (adult/child $45/24, with zoo admission $77/42), which allows one-time entry to 14 of the park's museums within seven days.

San Diego Visitor Information Centers (☎619-236-1212, 800-350-6205; www.sandiego.org) Downtown (Map p616; cnr W Broadway & Harbor Dr; ☺9am-5pm Jun-Sep, 9am-4pm Oct-May); La Jolla (7966 Herschel Ave; ☺11am-5pm, possible longer hr Jun-Sep & Sat & Sun) The downtown location is designed for international visitors.

Old Town State Historic Park Visitor Center (☎619-220-5422; www.parks.ca.gov; Robinson-Rose House, Old Town ☺10am-5pm; P) For information about state parks in San Diego County, head to the Robinson-Rose House at the western end of the plaza.

ℹ Getting There & Away

Air

San Diego International Airport-Lindbergh Field (SAN; Map p613; ☎619-231-2100; www.san.org; 3225 N Harbor Dr) Because of the limited length of runways, most flights into this airport are domestic. It sits just 3 miles from downtown and plane-spotters will be thrilled watching planes come in over Balboa Park for landing. Coming from overseas, you'll likely change flights – and clear US Customs – at one of the major US gateway airports, such as LA, Chicago or Miami.

Bus

Greyhound (Map p616; ☎619-515-1100; www.greyhound.com; 120 W Broadway, Downtown) Serves San Diego from cities all over North America. There are hourly direct buses to Los Angeles (one way/round-trip $19/31, two to three hours). Service between San Diego and San Francisco (one way $72 to $90, 11 to 13 hours, six to eight daily) requires a transfer in LA.

Car & Motorcycle

The region's main north-south highway is I-5, which parallels the coast from the Camp Pendle-ton Marine Corps Base in the north to the Mexican border at San Ysidro in the south. The I-8 runs east from Ocean Beach, through Mission Valley, past suburbs including El Cajon, and on to the Imperial Valley and, eventually, Arizona.

Train

Amtrak (☎800-872-7245; www.amtrak.com) Runs the *Pacific Surfliner* several times daily to Los Angeles ($36, three hours) and Santa Barbara ($41, 5½ hours) from the **Santa Fe Depot** (Map p616; 1055 Kettner Blvd, Downtown). Amtrak and **Metrolink** (☎800-371-5465; www.metrolinktrains.com) commuter trains connect Anaheim to San Diego ($27, two hours).

ℹ Getting Around

While many people get around by car (and the city's fairly easy to navigate), it's possible to enjoy an entire vacation here using buses, trolleys and trains operated by the **Metropolitan Transit System** (MTS; ☎619-233-3004; www.sdmts.com).

To/From the Airport

Bus 992 ('the Flyer,' $2.25) operates at 10- to 15-minute intervals between the airport and Downtown, with stops along Broadway. Airport shuttles such as **Super Shuttle** (☎800-974-8885; www.supershuttle.com) charge about $8 to $10 to Downtown. A taxi fare to Downtown from the airport is $10 to $15.

Bicycle

Some areas around San Diego are great for biking, particularly Pacific Beach, Mission Beach, Mission Bay and Coronado.

All public buses are equipped with bike racks and will transport two-wheelers free. Inform the driver before boarding, then stow your bike on the rack on the tail end of the bus. For more information telephone ☎619-685-4900.

For rentals try Cheap Rentals (p625).

Boat

San Diego Harbor Excursion operates a **water taxi** (☎619-235-8294; www.sdhe.com; per person one way $7; ☺9am-9pm Sun-Thu, to 11pm Fri & Sat) serving Harbor Island, Shelter Island, Downtown and Coronado. It also runs the hourly **Coronado Ferry** (☎619-234-4111; www.sdhe.com; per person one way $4.25; ☺9am-10pm) shuttling between Broadway Pier on the Embarcadero to the ferry landing at the northern end of First St. Headed to a Padres game? Park at the Coronado ferry landing and take SDHE's **PETCO Shuttle** (one way $4.25, game days) across the water to the stadium.

TIJUANA, MEXICO

Times are tough in Tijuana. For years 'TJ' has been a cheap, convivial destination just south of the border, popular with hard-partying San Diegans, Angelenos and sailors. Drug-related violence and too-frequent fatal shoot-outs, however, have turned once-bustling tourist areas into near ghost towns.

The government has taken steps to turn things around, but efforts haven't met with much success. Indeed, the heavy presence of armed soldiers clad in bulletproof vests tends to inspire fear, not confidence, in foreign guests. On the other hand, intrepid tourists who stay low-key (avoid flashy jewelry and stay aware of your surroundings) will find authentic dining experiences, great cultural attractions and an otherwise welcoming populace.

After descending from the pedestrian bridge at the border, stop by the San Ysidro Border crossing **visitor center** (www.tijuanaonline.org; ⊙9am-6pm) for a map. Pass through the turnstile and follow the street toward the **Tijuana Arch**. After a 10-minute walk, you'll arrive at the blocks-long Av Revolution (La Revo). La Revo's once-raucous streets are decidedly light on revelers, although you'll still find plenty of souvenir shops, low-priced pharmacies and liquor stores. There's no need to change your money, as nearly all businesses accept US dollars.

A short drive away is **Centro Cultural Tijuana** (CECUT; ☎01-664-687-9600; www.cecut.gob.mx; cnr Paseo de los Heroes & Av Independencia), a modern cultural center showcasing highbrow concerts, theater, readings, conferences and dance recitals. Inside the Centro Cultural the **Museo de las Californias** provides an excellent history of Baja California from prehistoric times to the present, including the earliest Spanish expeditions, the mission period, the Treaty of Guadalupe Hidalgo, irrigation of the Colorado River and the advent of the railroad. Signage is in English.

Travelers really interested in Tijuana can book a down-to-earth day tour through **Turista Libre** (www.turistalibre.com), an offbeat travel agency whose slogan is 'No narco warfare. No strolls down hooker row. No donkey shows. No gringo stereotypes. Lo mejor del alternaturismo.'

An easy way to get to Tijuana is via the San Diego Trolley on the blue line, which runs from Old Town to downtown to San Ysidro ($2.50, about 30 minutes). From the San Ysidro stop, follow the pedestrian bridge mentioned above. You can also drive to the border, but it's better to leave your car on the US side. Traffic in Tijuana is frenetic, parking is competitive, and there will likely be a long wait to cross back into the States. If you do drive, buy daily Mexican car insurance at a US office on Via San Ysidro and Camino de la Plaza.

US citizens not planning to go past the border zone (ie beyond Ensenada, or 20km to 30km/12.4 miles to 18.6 miles from the border, depending on location), or planning to stay in the border zone more than 72 hours, don't need a visa. All visitors, however, must bring their passport and US visa (if needed) for re-entry to the US.

Public Transportation

BUS

The MTS covers most of the metropolitan area, North County, La Jolla and the beaches. It's most convenient if you're staying downtown and not partying until the wee hours. Get a free *Regional Transit Map* from the Transit Store.

For route and fare information, call **MTS** (☎619-233-3004, 24hr recorded info 619-685-4900, in San Diego 511). For online route planning, visit www.sdmts.com. Fares are $2.25 for most trips; express routes cost $2.50. Exact fare is required on all buses; drivers cannot make change. The **Transit Store** (Map p616; ☎619-234-1060; Broadway & 1st Ave; ⊙9am-5pm Mon-Fri) has route maps, tickets and Day Tripper passes for $5/9/12/15 for one/two/three/four days. Single-day passes are available for purchase on board buses.

Useful routes to/from downtown and Old Town:

ROUTE 3 Hillcrest, UCSD Medical Center, Balboa Park

ROUTE 7 Balboa Park, Zoo

ROUTE 30 Old Town, Pacific Beach, La Jolla

ROUTE 35 Old Town, Ocean Beach

ROUTE 901 Coronado, PETCO Park

Car

All the big-name rental companies have desks at the airport, but lesser-known ones may be cheaper. Shop around – prices vary widely. Check the company's policy before taking the car into Mexico.

For contact information for the big-name rental companies, see p773. Smaller, independent companies in Little Italy like **West Coast Rent A Car** (☎619-544-0606; www. westcoastrentacar.net; 834 W Grape St) offer cheaper rates for older rental cars; a one-day rental goes for about $35.

Taxi

Taxi fares start at $2.20 for the first one-tenth mile and $2.30 for each additional mile. Some established companies:

Orange Cab (☎619-291-3333; www.orange cabsandiego.com)

Yellow Cab (☎619-234-6161; www.driveu.com)

Train

Coaster commuter trains ($4.50 to $5.50) run from downtown's **Santa Fe train depot** (Map p616) up the coast to North County, stopping in Solana Beach, Encinitas, Carlsbad and Oceanside. Before entering North County, it stops at the Old Town Transit Center and Sorrento Valley, where there are Coaster Connections throughout Torrey Pines. Buy self-validating tickets from Coaster stations. Machines accept cash and credit cards.

There are 11 daily trains in each direction Monday to Friday; the first trains leave Oceanside at 5:15am and the Santa Fe depot at 6:31am; the last ones depart at 5:35pm and 7:03pm, respectively. Six trains run on Saturdays, four on Sundays and holidays.

For information, contact **North San Diego County Transit District** (☎619-233-3004, from North County 800-266-6883; www.gonctd.com).

Trolley

San Diego's trolleys are an efficient, convenient and typically safe way to travel. They're also fun, especially for kids. There are three lines – blue, orange and green. Blue Line trolleys head south to San Ysidro (last stop, just before Tijuana, Mexico) and north to Old Town Transit Center. The Green Line runs east through Mission Valley, past Fashion Valley to Qualcomm Stadium and Mission San Diego de Alcala. The Orange Line connects the Convention Center and Seaport Village with downtown.

Trolleys run between about 4:15am and midnight at roughly 15-minute intervals during the day and half-hour intervals in the evening. A one-way trolley route costs $2.50; buy tickets at vending machines on station platforms.

NORTH COUNTY COAST

The North County Coast feels like summer camp: loads of outdoor activities, gorgeous natural surroundings and a laid-back approach to daily life. If there's a real emergency, the big city is less than an hour away.

'North County,' as locals call it, begins at pretty Del Mar, just north of La Jolla and Torrey Pines, and continues up the coast through Solana Beach, Encinitas and Carlsbad (home of Legoland) before hitting Oceanside, largely a bedroom community for Camp Pendleton Marine Base. The communities hug the shore and overlook fantastic beaches (with lots of good surf spots). They also offer a variety of unique attractions, including the Del Mar Racetrack, the Chopra Center and Legoland.

As you drive north on Hwy 101, coastal cliffs and coves gradually give way to wide sandy shores. A constant companion is the railroad tracks, and though the trains can be distracting, they do make it easy to glide up here for a day trip. By car via I-5 in nonrush-hour traffic, Del Mar is only 20 to 30 minutes from San Diego, Oceanside 45 to 60 minutes.

ⓘ Getting There & Around

For the most scenic approach, take N Torrey Pines Rd to Del Mar. Driving north along the coast, S21 changes its name from Camino del Mar to Coast Hwy 101 to Old Hwy 101 to Carlsbad Blvd. If you're in a hurry or headed to Los Angeles, the parallel I-5 is quicker. Traffic can snarl everywhere during rush hour, however, as well as during race or fair season when heading toward the Del Mar Racetrack.

Bus 101 departs from University Towne Centre near La Jolla and follows the coastal road to Oceanside; for information call the **North County Transit District** (NCTD; ☎760-966-6500; www.gonctd.com).

The NCTD also operates the *Coaster* commuter train, which originates at the Santa Fe Depot in downtown San Diego and travels north, stopping in Old Town, Solana Beach, Encinitas, Carlsbad and Oceanside. Train travel is an easy and convenient way to visit the north coast communities because most stations are right in town and close to the beach. See p643.

Del Mar

North County's ritziest seaside suburb, Del Mar has good, if pricey, restaurants, high-end boutiques and a fabled horse-racing track that's also the site of the annual county fair in June. Downtown Del Mar (sometimes

North County Coast

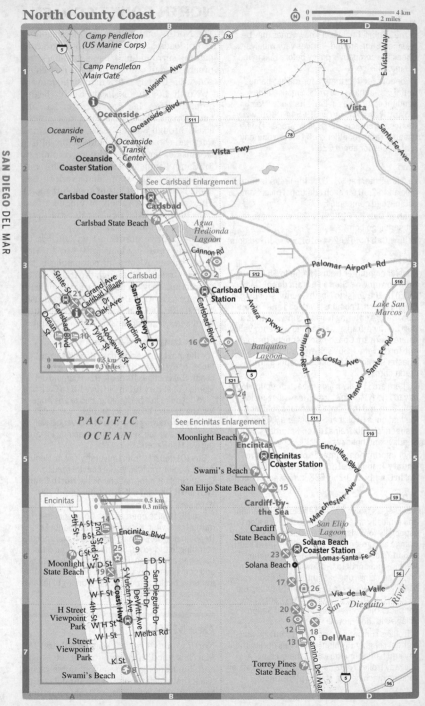

Camp Pendleton
(US Marine Corps)

Camp Pendleton
Main Gate

Oceanside

Oceanside
Pier

Oceanside
Transit
Center

Oceanside
Coaster Station

Carlsbad Coaster Station

Carlsbad

Carlsbad State Beach

Agua
Hedionda
Lagoon

Cannon Rd

Carlsbad Poinsettia
Station

Batiquitos
Lagoon

PACIFIC
OCEAN

See Carlsbad Enlargement

See Encinitas Enlargement

Moonlight Beach

Encinitas

Encinitas
Coaster Station

Swami's Beach

San Elijo State Beach

Cardiff-by-
the Sea

Cardiff
State Beach

San Elijo
Lagoon

Solana Beach
Coaster Station

Solana Beach

Lomas Santa Fe Dr

Via de la Valle

Del Mar

Torrey Pines
State Beach

Vista

Mission Ave

Oceanside Blvd

Vista Fwy

Carlsbad Blvd

Aviara Pkwy

El Camino Real

La Costa Ave

Rancho Santa Fe Rd

Palomar Airport Rd

Lake San
Marcos

E Vista Way

Santa Fe Ave

Encinitas Blvd

Manchester Ave

Camino Del Mar

San Dieguito River

Carlsbad

State St

Grand Ave
Carlsbad Village
Dr

Oak Ave

San Diego Fwy

Carlsbad Blvd

Ocean
St

Roosevelt St

Tyler St

Harding St

0   0.5 km
0   0.3 miles

Encinitas

5th St

A St

2nd St

3rd St

B St

Encinitas Blvd

C St

Moonlight
State Beach

W D St

E D St

W E St

S Vulcan Ave

San Dieguito Dr

Cornish Dr

DeWitt Ave

W F St

H Street
Viewpoint
Park

4th St

W H St

W I St

Melba Rd

S Coast Hwy

I Street
Viewpoint
Park

K St

Swami's Beach

0   0.5 km
0   0.3 miles

North County Coast

called 'the Village') extends for about a mile along Camino del Mar. Fifteenth St crosses Camino del Mar at the tasteful **Del Mar Plaza**, the city's unofficial hub, where you'll find restaurants, shops and upper-level terraces that look out to sea.

◉ Sights & Activities

Seagrove Park   PARK
At the beach end of 15th St, this park overlooks the ocean. Despite the occasional whooshing train on the adjacent train tracks, this little stretch of tidy beachfront lawn is a favorite gathering place for locals and a good spot for a picnic.

Del Mar Racetrack & Fairgrounds   HORSE RACING
(☑858-755-1141; www.dmtc.com; 2260 Jimmy Durante Blvd; admission $5-20) Founded in 1937 by a number of Hollywood luminaries, including Bing Crosby and Jimmy Durante. The lush gardens and pink, Mediterranean-style architecture are a visual delight. Get gussied up for the horse races, which run from mid-July to early September.

California Dreamin'   BALLOONING
(☑800-373-3359; www.californiadreamin.com; per person from $178) Brightly colored hot-air balloons are a trademark of the Del Mar's northern skies. Come here for a sunset flight.

🛏 Sleeping

L'Auberge del Mar   LUXURY HOTEL $$$
(☑800-245-9757; www. laubergedelmar.com; 1540 Camino Del Mar; r from $450; P❋❄) This ecofriendly beachfront resort offers chic but simple guest rooms in shades of sand, sea and sky. The sunset view from the terrace and swimming pool – where an outdoor cocktail bar opens to the public – is probably the finest in Del Mar.

Les Artistes Inn   QUIRKY, INN $$
(☑858-755-4646; www.lesartistesinn.com; 944 Camino del Mar; r from $105; ❋P) One of the less expensive options (comparatively speaking) in Del Mar is this bohemian inn with Southwestern-style adobe architecture, Buddha statues in the courtyard, and a rustic central fireplace. Each of the 12 rooms is inspired by, and named for, a different famous artist.

🍴 Eating

Jake's del Mar   SEAFOOD $$
(☑858-755-2002; www.jakesdelmar.com; 1660 Coast Blvd; mains lunch $10-18, dinner $10-37; ◷11:30am-9pm, from 4pm Mon) Just north of

SCENIC DRIVE: CARLSBAD TO DEL MAR

This pretty coastal drive takes you through the quaint towns of San Diego's North County, past a few notable geographic landmarks, past a design-minded shopping district, and ends up on a terrace with (you guessed it) a stunning ocean view.

What to See

Start in the village of Carlsbad (p647). Drive south along Carlsbad Blvd towards the Batiquitos Lagoon (p648), one of California's last remaining tidal wetlands. Continue south to Encinitas and stop for your caffeine fix at Pannikin Coffee and Tea (p647) along the PCH. Follow Hwy 101 past the San Elijo Lagoon and onto Solana Beach and the colorful Cedros Design District (p646) where you can pull over and browse the design books and home decor. While you're there, pick up a bottle of locally produced wine at Carruth Cellars (p646). Finish heading south on the dramatic downhill slope into Del Mar, stopping for sunset cocktails on the terrace at ecofriendly L'Auberge del Mar (p645)

The Route

Carlsbad Blvd south to Vulcan Ave, continuing south to North Coast Hwy 101 to Camino del Mar in Del Mar – the trick is to stay on the coastal road and never exit onto the freeway.

Time & Mileage

17 miles, 22 minutes without stops and one to two hours or more if you pull over frequently.

Seagrove Park is ever-popular Jake's, exuding a clubby feel with its wood-planked ceiling, historic photos, and rich old guys enjoying seafood chowder, crusted sea bass, filets and lobster tail. Great views of kids and volleyball players on the beach.

Harvest Ranch Market   MARKET $
(www.harvestranchmarkets.com; 1555 Camino Del Mar; ☺8am-9pm) To craft your own meal, try this place in the Del Mar Plaza for high-quality groceries and sandwiches for the beach. Check the sign outside for upcoming **wine tastings** ($10-20 per person; ☺usually 4-6pm Thu & Fri, from 3pm Sat).

Solana Beach

Solana Beach may not be as posh as its southern neighbor, but it has lovely beaches as well as the **Cedros Design District** (Cedros Ave), a blocks-long avenue filled with home-furnishing stores, art and architecture studios, antiques shops and handcrafted-clothing boutiques.

Beach Grass Cafe (www.beachgrasscafe.com; 159 S Hwy 101; mains $6-15; ☺7am-3pm daily, 5-9pm Sun-Thu; ✍) A local favorite for breakfast, Beach Grass Cafe's bestsellers include pineapple pancakes and macacha taco omelets.

Pizza Port (www.pizzaport.com; 135 N Hwy 101; mains $8-15) This branch of the popular local pizza and microbrew chain is across the street from the train station.

🍷**Carruth Cellars** (☎858-847-9463; www.carruthcellars.com; 320 S Cedros Ave; ☺noon-9pm Mon-Sat, to 6pm Sun) Taste Sonoma syrah and locally produced cheeses at this friendly urban winery.

Cardiff-by-the-Sea

The stretch of restaurants, surf shops and new age–style businesses just south of Encinitas (and technically part of that city) on the Pacific Coast Hwy – called 'Cardiff' by locals – is known for its surfing and laid-back crowds.

Cardiff is also home to **San Elijo Lagoon** (☎760-436-3944; www.sanelijo.org), an ecological preserve (almost 1000 acres) popular with bird-watchers for herons, coots, terns, ducks, egrets and about 250 more species. Nearly 7 miles of trails lead through the area. The nature center is at 2710 Manchester Ave.

At **Cardiff State Beach** (☎760-753-5091; www.parks.ca.gov; ☺7am-sunset), just south of Cardiff-by-the-Sea, the surf break on the reef is mostly popular with longboarders. A little further north, **San Elijo State Beach** has good winter waves.

San Elijo State Beach Campground (☎760-753-5091; reservations 800-444-7275; www.parks.ca.gov,reserveamerica.com; tent/RV sites $26/39; ☎) Overlooks the surf at the end of Birmingham Dr.

Encinitas

Golden lotus domes mark the southern border of Encinitas on South Coast Hwy 101, setting an offbeat tone that permeates this funky little beach town. Since Paramahansa Yoganada founded his **Self-Realization Fellowship Retreat & Hermitage** here in 1937, the town has been a magnet for healers, seekers and hardcore surfers. The gold lotus domes of the hermitage also border the turnout for **Swami's**, a powerful reef break favored by territorial locals. If you practice yoga, meditation or just want a nice place to stretch your legs, stroll the hermitage's **Meditation Garden** (215 K St; www.yogananda-srf. org; ☺9am-5pm Tue-Sat, 11am-5pm Sun), which has wonderful ocean vistas.

The heart of Encinitas lies north of the hermitage between E and D Sts. Apart from the outdoor cafes, bars, restaurants and surf shops, the town's main attraction is **La Paloma Theatre** (☎760-436-7469; www.lapalomatheatre.com; 471 S Coast Hwy 101), built in 1928. La Paloma shows current movies nightly and *The Rocky Horror Picture Show* every Friday at midnight.

🛏 Sleeping

Moonlight Beach Motel MOTEL $$
(☎760-753-0623; www.moonlightbeachmotel. com; 233 2nd St; r $135-170; P☀☎⊕) Upstairs rooms have private decks and partial ocean views at this mom-and-pop motel, 1½ blocks from the sea and the kiddie-minded park at Moonlight Beach. Some furnishings could use upgrading, but rooms are clean, quiet and have furnished kitchens.

Best Western Encinitas Inn & Suites HOTEL $$
(☎760-942-7455; www.bwencinitas.com; 85 Encinitas Blvd; r $160-210; P☀☎☎) With an exterior caught somewhere between treehouse-modern and adobe-mission, it's a nice surprise to find well-appointed, spacious rooms boasting all modern conveniences and up-to-date furnishings.

✗ Eating & Drinking

El Q'ero PERUVIAN $$$
(☎760-753-9050; www.qerorestaurant.com; 564 S Coast Hwy; mains lunch $10-18, dinner $32-48; ☺11:30am-3pm & from 5pm Tue-Sun) Inside this tiny Peruvian charmer, red-tile floors, bright print tablecloths and boldly colored paintings set a convivial mood, but ah, it's the food that makes us happiest. Perfectly seasoned dishes like papa *lomo saltado* (flatiron steak with garlic, cracked pepper and sautéed onions) and *aji gallina* (tender chicken in toasted walnut and chili sauce) bring out the best flavors of Peru. And yes, 'slow food' aptly describes the cooking process, but it's well worth the wait. Make reservations for dinner.

Pannikin Coffee & Tea CAFE $
(www.pannikincoffeeandtea.com; 510 N Coast Hwy; ☺6am-6pm) As far as indie coffee shops go, this yellow former train station is a prime example of what works. Large patio dotted with Adirondack chairs? Check. Chalkboard list of coffee and teas? Check. Lots of muffins and desserts on display? Check. Quirky decor plus a well-planted inspirational quote or two? Check.

Carlsbad

While Carlsbad may be known for Legoland, a theme park built on our love for joinable plastic blocks, it's the natural attractions here that may be the most stunning, from long, sandy beaches to a 50-acre flower field to a flora-and-fauna filled lagoon.

WHAT THE ...?

Discretion may be the better part of small talk when it comes to the much-maligned 'Magic Carpet Ride' statue erected on the west side of Hwy 101 at Chesterfield Dr in 2007. The intent was to commission a statue celebrating the surfing lifestyle – presumably something cool. The $120,000 result? A gangly young man with his arms awkwardly outstretched, trying to maintain his balance on the board. An object of derision and pranksters ever since, he's been draped in a Mexican wrestling mask and a bikini top. Judge for yourself: he's holding tight beside San Elijo State Beach.

The community got its start when train service arrived in the 1880s, building up a solid four square block downtown rather than stretching along the highway like most North County towns. Early homesteader John Frazier, a former ship's captain, sank a well and found water with a high mineral content, supposedly identical to that of spa water in Karlsbad, Bohemia (now the Czech Republic). He built a grand spa hotel that prospered until the 1930s.

Carlsbad is bordered by I-5 and Carlsbad Blvd, which run north-south. You'll find many of the community's hotels and restaurants clustered on or near Carlsbad Village Dr, the east-west road connecting I-5 and Carlsbad Blvd.

◎ Sights & Activities

Legoland California   AMUSEMENT PARK
(☏760-918-5346; www.california.legoland.com; 1 Legoland Dr; adult/child $69/59; ☺opens 10am, closing hours vary; ⊞). Modeled loosely after the original in Denmark, Legoland California is a fantasy environment built on the backs of an army of joinable plastic building blocks. Geared toward younger kids, expect to spend most of the day here.

In the **Land of Adventure** area of the park, a 16ft Pharaoh made from 300,000-plus Legos guards the new Lost Kingdom Adventure. Inside, families can laser-blast targets from a moving car. A longtime highlight includes **Miniland**, where the skylines of major metropolitan cities have been spectacularly re-created entirely of Legos. Elsewhere, many activities are geared specifically to kids, such as face painting, boat rides and scaled-down roller coasters. Combination passes are available to the adjacent water park and aquarium.

From I-5, take the Legoland/Cannon Rd and follow the signs. From downtown Carlsbad or downtown San Diego, take the *Coaster* to the Carlsbad Village Station and hop on bus 344 straight to the park. Parking costs $12.

Carlsbad Ranch   GARDENS
(☏760-431-0352; www.theflowerfields.com; 5704 Paseo del Norte; adult/senior/child $10/9/5; ☺9am-6pm) From early March to early May, nearly 50 acres of flower fields of Carlsbad Ranch come ablaze in a vibrant sea of carmine, saffron and snow-white ranunculus blossoms. The fields are two blocks east of I-5; take the Palomar Airport Rd exit, go east, then left on Paseo del Norte Rd.

Batiquitos Lagoon   NATURE RESERVE
(☏760-931-0800; www.batiquitosfoundation.org; 7380 Gabbiano Ln; ☺9am-12:30pm Mon-Fri, to 3pm Sat & Sun) One of the last remaining tidal wetlands in California, Batiquitos Lagoon separates Carlsbad from Encinitas. A self-guided tour lets you explore area plants, including the prickly pear cactus, coastal sage scrub and eucalyptus trees, as well as lagoon birds, such as the great blue heron and the snowy egret. To get to the Nature Center follow Poinsettia Lane east past the I-5 turn and go right onto Batiquitos Dr, then turn right onto Gabbiano Lane, taking it to the end.

Chopra Center for Wellbeing   SPIRITUAL
(☏760-494-1600; www.chopra.com; 2013 Costa del Mar; ☺7am-8pm Mon-Fri, to 6pm Sat & Sun) This den of tranquility and personal empowerment offers free tea to those browsing several shelves of books by alternative-health guru Deepak Chopra and acolyte David Simon. The welcoming (but no-pressure) center, located on the lush grounds of La Costa Resort & Spa, offers Ayurveda-based programs and workshops as well as yoga classes and personal consultations.

⊨ Sleeping & Eating

South Carlsbad State Park
Campground   CAMPGROUND $
(☏760-438-3143, reservations 800-444-7275; www.parks.ca.gov; 7201 Carlsbad Blvd; tent & RV sites $35-50; ☜) Three miles south of downtown, this campground has 222 tent and RV sites and a bluff-top perch above the beach. Spots go fast; start calling months before your desired date.

Best Western Plus Beach
View Lodge   HOTEL $$
(☏760-729-1151; www.beachviewlodge.com; 3180 Carlsbad Blvd; d $152-215; P☜❄☻) An Arts and Crafts–style lobby with great ocean views welcomes guests to this small, friendly Best Western that's just across Hwy 101 (called Carlsbad Blvd here) from the beach. Three floors wrap around a small courtyard and pool. (The 'Plus' means the place is nicer than your average Best Western.)

Carlsbad Inn Beach Resort   LUXURY HOTEL $$$
(☏760-434-7020, 800-235-3939; www.carlsbadinn.com; 3075 Carlsbad Blvd; d from $240; P❄@☻❋) This upscale Tudor-style hotel and time-share property sits just across from the beach. Guests have access to an elaborate calendar of events and activities from stand-up paddle-

boarding ($15 per person) to yoga ($5), wine tasting ($5) and sailing ($45 per person).

Pizza Port   PIZZERIA, PUB $
(www.pizzaport.com; 571 Carlsbad Village Dr; mains $8-20; ⊙11am-10pm Sun-Thu, to midnight Fri & Sat; 🚻) Pizza Port is like the general store of yore, an easygoing hub where everybody seems to swing by at some point. The main draw inside this surfboard-adorned mini-warehouse are the homebrewed beers and thick, buttery, almost fluffy slices, ranging from standard pepperoni to 'anti-wimpy' gourmet pies (margherita, garlic veggie).

Le Passage   FRENCH $$
(www.lepassagefrenchbistro.net; 2961 State St; mains lunch $10-16, dinner $16-32; ⊙11:30am-3pm & 5pm-late Tue-Fri, noon-3pm & 5pm-late Sat) This welcoming country French bistro is a retreat from the ocean fray and a nice place to bump it up a notch (just a bit) from T-shirts and flip-flops. There's a rustic exposed-brick interior and cozy back patio where guests can enjoy baked brie and lavender roasted chicken.

Oceanside

Just outside the giant Camp Pendleton Marine Base, Oceanside lacks the charm of Encinitas and Carlsbad, but the wide beaches and fine surf continue unabated. Amtrak, Greyhound, the *Coaster* and MTS buses stop at the **Oceanside Transit Center** (235 S Tremont St). Another crowd-getter is the

---

WORTH A TRIP

TEMECULA

According to the menu at the Swing Inn Cafe, 'Temecula' was a Native American word meaning 'The Valley of Joy.' That label certainly holds true today, with tourists flocking here for weekends filled with wine tasting, gambling and a bit of Old West-style shopping.

Located in Riverside County, about one hour north from downtown San Diego, the area was a ranching outpost for Mission San Luis Rey in the 1820s, later becoming a stop along the Butterfield stagecoach line. But perhaps most interesting is the region's recent history. Marketing itself as a stylish wine country community, the town successfully lured newcomers with its small-town charms.

Tourists come to wander five-block Front St, the heart of Old Town Temecula, where faux Old West facades front a line-up of restaurants, antique dealers and wine shops. This is motorcycle country, so don't be surprised to hear Harleys rumbling up behind you. For cheap diner-style eats check out the aforementioned **Swing Inn Cafe** (www.swinginncafe; 28676 Old Town Front St; ⊙5am-9pm), where two eggs, two hotcakes and two strips of bacon will set you back six bucks. The hickory-smoked pork at nearby **Sweet Lumpy's BBQ** (www.sweetlumpys.com; 41915 3rd St; mains $7-20; ⊙11am-8pm Tue-Fri, from 8am Sat & Sun) was voted best barbecue in the Inland Empire. As for Old Town shopping, you'll find flavored olive oils and free samples at **Temecula Olive Oil Company** (www.temeculaoliveoil.com; 28653 Old Town Front St). Next door at **Temecula House of Jerky** (www.getmyjerky.com; 28655 Old Town Front St) look for ostrich, buffalo and venison jerky in addition to the usual teeth-pulling suspects. **Country Porch** (28693 Old Town Front St) is an atmospheric antiques market where you can shop for vintage sunglasses or cowboy boots.

Wine tasting is popular in the rolling hills about 10 minutes east of Old Town. **Wilson Creek** (📞951-699-9463; www.wilsoncreekwinery.com; 35960 Rancho California Rd; tastings $12-15; ⊙10am-5pm) makes almond champagne (infused with almond oil in the fermentation process) and a chocolate-infused port. Further afield, **Leonesse Cellars** (📞951-302-7601; www.leonessecellars.com; 38311 De Portola Rd; tastings $14; ⊙11am-5pm) offers award-winning viognier and Melange des Reves, plus sweeping views from its Tudor-esque tower. For a tour, try **Grapeline Temecula** (📞888-894-6379; www.gogrape.com; tasting-inclusive tour $98 per person). Visit www.temeculawines.org for links to the wineries' websites – many offer two-for-one tasting coupons.

To see Temecula by air, contact **California Dreamin'** (📞800-373-3359; www.californiadreamin.com) for an air balloon ride (from $178 per person). Of course, you could just blow off the wine, jerky and balloons and head straight to California's largest casino, **Pechanga Resort & Casino** (📞877-711-2946; www.pechanga.com; 45000 Pechanga Pkwy) where your perception of the Valley of Joy may depend on the spin of the wheel.

California Welcome Center (☎760-721-1101, 800-350-7873; www.oceansidechamber.org, www.californiawelcomecenter.org; 928 N Coast Hwy; ☺9am-5pm), which has loads of brochures and coupons for local attractions, as well as maps and information about the San Diego area and the entire state.

Nearby, stretch your legs on the wooden **Oceanside Pier**, which extends 1942ft out to sea. **Mission San Luis Rey de Francia** (☎760-757-3651; www.sanluisrey.org; 4050 Mission Ave; adult/child/senior $5/3/4; ☺9am-5pm Mon-Fri, from 10am Sat & Sun), lies 4 miles inland. Founded in 1798, it was the 18th of the 21 California missions and, as the largest

California mission, was dubbed 'King of the Missions.' It was also the most successful in recruiting Native American converts. After the Mexican government secularized the missions, San Luis fell into ruin; only the adobe walls of the 1811 church are original. Inside, exhibits highlight work and life in the mission, with some original religious art and artifacts. Ruins of the *lavanderia* (the Luiseno Indian laundry) and mission soldiers' barracks are visible in front. From I-5, follow Hwy 76 about 4 miles east. The mission is on the left at the Rancho del Oro exit.

Palm Springs & the Deserts

Best Places to Eat

» Trio (p661)

» Cheeky's (p661)

» C'est Si Bon (p693)

» Ricochet Gourmet (p672)

» Pastels Bistro (p694)

Best Places to Stay

» Riviera Palm Springs (p659)

» El Morocco Inn & Spa (p661)

» Palms at Indian Head (p677)

» Mandalay Bay (p701)

Why Go?

There's something undeniably artistic in the way the landscape unfolds in the California desert. Weathered volcanic peaks stand sentinel over singing sand dunes and mountains shimmering in hues from mustard yellow to vibrant pink. Hot mineral water spurts from the earth's belly to feed palm oases and soothe aching muscles in stylish spas. Tiny wildflowers push up from the hard-baked soil to celebrate springtime.

But it's not just nature that has shaped the desert. The riches of its soil have lured prospectors and miners, while its beauty and spirituality has tugged at the hearts of artists, visionaries and wanderers. Eccentrics, misfits and the military are drawn by its vastness and solitude. Hipsters and celebs come for the climate and retro flair. And through it all threads iconic Route 66, still lined with moodily rusting roadside relics. No matter what your trail, the desert will creep into your consciousness and never fully leave.

When to Go
Palm Springs

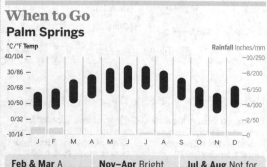

Feb & Mar A painter's palette of wildflowers drenches the desert floor in a riot of color.

Nov–Apr Bright and warm days lure the sun-starved. Perfect time for outdoor activities.

Jul & Aug Not for the faint of heart. Temperatures soar, but room rates plunge.

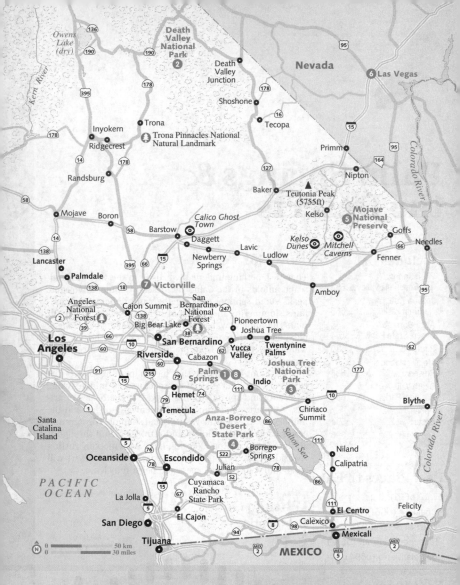

Palm Springs & the Deserts Highlights

1 Ascend through five distinct zones in less than 15 minutes aboard the **Palm Springs Aerial Tramway** (p653)

2 Poke around mining ghost towns in **Death Valley National Park** (p686)

3 Navigate smooth boulders in **Hidden Valley** (p666) at Joshua Tree National Park

4 Hunt rare elephant trees and scramble around the wind caves of vast **Anza-Borrego Desert State Park** (p674)

5 Hide out at **Hole-in-the-Wall** (p684) in the forgotten Mojave National Preserve

6 Lose yourself (but hopefully not your money) on the **Las Vegas Strip** (p696)

7 Revel in the mythology of the Mother Road at the **California Route 66 Museum** (p681) in Victorville

8 Feel fabulous stretched out next to the kidney-shaped pool in a **Mid-Century Modern boutique hotel** (p659) in Palm Springs

PALM SPRINGS & THE COACHELLA VALLEY

The Rat Pack is back, baby, or at least its hangout is. In the 1950s and '60s, Palm Springs, some 100 miles east of LA, was the swinging getaway of Sinatra, Elvis and dozens of other stars, partying the night away in fancy estate homes. Once the Rat Pack packed it in, though, the 300-sq-mile Coachella Valley surrendered to retirees in golf clothing. That is, until the mid-1990s, when a new generation fell in love with the city's retro-chic charms: steel-and-glass bungalows designed by famous modernist architects, boutique hotels with vintage decor and kidney-shaped pools, and hushed piano bars serving the perfect martini. In today's Palm Springs, retirees mix comfortably with hipsters and a significant gay and lesbian contingent.

Palm Springs is the principal city of the Coachella Valley, a string of desert towns ranging from ho-hum Cathedral City to glamtastic Palm Desert and America's date capital of Indio, all linked by Hwy 111. North of Palm Springs, Desert Hot Springs is garnering its share of visitors thanks to a slew of new chic boutique hotels built on top of those soothing springs.

The valley is a delightful playground for body and mind. Relax by the pool, hike in a palm-oasis canyon and snowshoe in the mountains all in the same day. Hunt down Mid-Century Modern architecture or tour a windmill farm. See where Elvis lived or straddle an earthquake fault line. Play golf, tennis or shop. Boredom, here, is an alien concept.

History

Cahuilla (ka-*wee*-ya) tribespeople have occupied the canyons on the southwest edge of the Coachella Valley for over 1000 years. Early Spanish explorers called the hot springs beneath Palm Springs *agua caliente* (hot water), which later became the name of the local Cahuilla band.

In 1876 the federal government carved the valley into a checkerboard of various interests. The Southern Pacific Railroad received odd-numbered sections, while the Agua Caliente were given even-numbered sections as their reservation. Formal boundaries were not established until the 1940s and by then much of the Native American land had been built on. Since the tribes own the local casinos, they're actually quite wealthy today.

The town of Indio, about 20 miles southeast of Palm Springs, began as a railway construction camp and its artesian water was tapped to irrigate crops. Date palms were imported from French-held Algeria in 1890 and have become the valley's major crop, along with citrus fruit and table grapes.

⊙ Sights

In Palm Springs' compact downtown, Hwy 111 runs one way south as Palm Canyon Dr and is paralleled by northbound Indian Canyon Dr. Tahquitz Canyon Way, dividing addresses north from south, heads east to Palm Springs' airport.

Many of the area's most fascinating attractions are not in downtown Palm Springs but spread out across the Coachella Valley. Though convenient, travel on Hwy 111 can be extremely slow thanks to dozens of traffic lights. Depending on where in the valley you're headed, it may be quicker to take I-10, then cut over on roads named for Frank Sinatra, Bob Hope, Gerald Ford, Dinah Shore and the like.

TOP CHOICE **Palm Springs Aerial Tramway**   CABLE CAR
(Map p660; ☑760-325-1449; www.pstramway.com; 1 Tram Way; round-trip adult/child $23.95/16.95; ⊙10am-8pm Mon-Fri, 8am-8pm Sat & Sun, last tram down 9:45pm; ⓐ) North of downtown, this rotating cable car is a highlight of any Palm Springs trip. It climbs nearly 6000 vertical feet through five different vegetation zones, from the Sonoran desert floor to the San Jacinto Mountains, in less than 15 minutes. The 2.5-mile ascent is said to be the temperature equivalent of driving from Mexico to Canada. It's 30°F to 40°F (up to 4°C) cooler as you step out into pine forests at the top, so bring warm clothing. Snow is not uncommon, even in the spring and fall.

The **Mountain Station** (8516ft), at the top of the tramway, has a bar, cafeteria, observation area and a theater that shows

> PALM SPRINGS & THE DESERTS PALM SPRINGS & THE COACHELLA VALLEY

FAST FACTS

» **Population of Palm Springs** 44,500
» **Population of Las Vegas** 583,750
» **Los Angeles to Palm Springs** 110 miles, two to three hours
» **San Diego to Borrego Springs** 95 miles, 1½ to two hours
» **Los Angeles to Las Vegas** 280 miles, four to five hours

DON'T MISS

ELVIS' LOVE NEST

One of the most spectacular Mid-Century Modern houses in Palm Springs was designed in the early 1960s by local developer Robert Alexander for his wife Helene. It consists of four circular rooms built on three levels, accented with glass and stone throughout. *Look* Magazine called it the 'House of Tomorrow' and featured it in an eight-page spread, making the Alexanders national celebrities. Sadly the entire family died in a plane crash in 1965, but the estate gained even greater fame a year later when Elvis Presley moved in. On May 1, 1967 he carried his new bride Priscilla over the threshold to begin their honeymoon. The **Elvis Honeymoon Hideaway** (Map p656; ☑760-322-1192; www.elv ishoneymoon.com; 1350 Ladera Circle; tours daily by appointment per person $25) has been authentically restored and can be rented for events and visited on daily tours. Tickets are sold over the phone and online.

documentary films. There's also a restaurant, cafe and cocktail bar (ask about dinner packages). Beyond here sprawls the wilderness of **Mt San Jacinto State Park**, which is crisscrossed by hiking trails.

The turnoff for the tram is about 3 miles north of downtown Palm Springs.

Palm Springs Art Museum   MUSEUM
(Map p656; ☑760-322-4800; www.psmuseum. org; 101 Museum Dr; adult/child $12.50/5, free 4-8pm Thu; ☺10am-5pm Tue, Wed & Fri-Sun, noon-8pm Thu) This art beacon is a good place for keeping tabs on the evolution of American painting, sculpture, photography and glass art over the past century or so. Alongside well-curated temporary exhibitions, the permanent collection is especially strong when it comes to modern painting and sculpture and includes works by Henry Moore, Ed Ruscha, Mark di Suvero and other heavy hitters. There's also stunning glass art by Dale Chihuly and William Morris.

Village Green Heritage Center   HISTORIC SITE
(Map p656; 219-221 S Palm Canyon Dr) Arranged around this grassy little downtown square are three exhibits in historic buildings.

Palm Springs Historical Society (www.pshistoricalsociety.org; adult/child $1/free; ☺10am-4pm Wed-Sat, noon-3pm Sun Oct-May) delves into Palm Springs' rich past in a small but classy exhibit of photos and memorabilia in the town's oldest building, the 1884 McCallum Adobe. An edutaining video plays nonstop.

FREE **Agua Caliente Cultural Museum** (www.accmuseum.org; ☺10am-5pm Wed-Sat, noon-5pm Sun mid-Sep–mid-May, Fri-Sun only mid-May–mid-Sep) is a small exhibit – a grand new museum is still on the drawing board – introducing aspects of the local tribe's history through changing exhibits and special events.

Ruddy's General Store (adult/child 95¢/ free; ☺10am-4pm Thu-Sun Oct-Jun, 10am-4pm Sat & Sun Jul-Sep) is a reproduction of a 1930s general store.

Moorten Botanical Garden   GARDENS
(Map p656; ☑760-327-6555; www.moortengarden. com; 1701 S Palm Canyon Dr; adult/child $4/2; ☺9am-4:30pm Mon, Tue & Thu-Sat, 10am-4pm Sun) Chester 'Cactus Slim' Moorten, one of the original Keystone Cops, and his wife Patricia channeled their passion for plants into this compact garden founded in 1938. Today, their son Clark, an expert on low-water vegetation, curates this enchanting symphony of cacti, succulents and other desert flora.

Palm Springs Air Museum   MUSEUM
(Map p660; ☑760-778-6262; www.air-museum. org; 745 N Gene Autry Trail; adult/child $15/8; ☺10am-5pm, last entry 4pm; ⓐ) Adjacent to the airport, this museum has an exceptional collection of WWII aircraft and flight memorabilia, a movie theater and occasional flight demonstrations.

Living Desert   ZOO
(Map p660; ☑760-346-5694; www.livingdesert.org; 47900 Portola Ave; adult/child $14.25/7.75; ☺8am-1:30pm (last entry 1pm) Jun-Sep, 9am-5pm (last entry 4pm) Oct-May; ⓐ) This amazing, wide-open zoo, located in Palm Desert, shows off a variety of desert plants and animals, along with exhibits on desert geology and Native American culture. It's educational fun and worth the 30-minute drive down-valley. Highlights include a walk-through wildlife hospital and an African-themed village with a fair-trade market and storytelling grove. Camel rides,

a spin on the endangered species carousel and a hop-on, hop-off shuttle that stops at 11 key locations cost extra.

Cabot's Pueblo Museum MUSEUM
(Map p660; ☑760-329-7610; www.cabotsmuseum. org; 67616 E Desert Ave, at Miracle Hill; tour adult/child $10/8; ☺tours 9:30am, 10:30am, 11:30am, 1:30pm & 2:30pm Tue-Sun Oct-May, 9:30am Jun-Sep) Cabot Yerxa, a wealthy East Coaster who traded high society for desert solitude, hand built this rambling 1913 adobe in Desert Hot Springs from reclaimed and found objects, including telephone poles and wagon parts. Today it's a quirky museum displaying Native American basketry and pottery, as well as a photo collection from Cabot's turn-of-the-century travels to Alaska. Call ahead to confirm tour schedules.

🏃 Activities

🖋Tahquitz Canyon HIKING
(Map p656; ☑760 416 7044; www.tahquitzcanyon. com; 500 W Mesquite Ave; adult/child $12.50/6; ☺7:30am-5pm daily Oct-Jun, 7:30am-5pm Fri-Sun Jul-Sep, last entry 3:30pm) A historic and sacred centerpiece for the Agua Caliente people, this canyon featured in the 1937 Frank Capra movie *Lost Horizon*. In the 1960s it was taken over by teenage squatters and soon became a point of contention between tribespeople, law-enforcement agencies and the squatters, who claimed the right to live in its rock alcoves and caves. After the squatters were booted out, it took the tribe years to haul out trash, erase graffiti and get the canyon back to its natural state.

The visitors center has natural and cultural history exhibits and also shows a video about the legend of Tahquitz, a shaman of the Cahuilla people. Rangers lead educational 2-mile, 2½-hour hikes that visit a seasonal 60ft-high waterfall, an ancient irrigation system and rock art. Tours leave from the visitors center at 8am, 10am, noon and 2pm every day the canyon's open (call ahead for reservations). Self-guided hiking is available until 3:30pm.

🖋Indian Canyons HIKING
(Map p660; ☑760-323-6018; www.indian-canyons.com; adult/child $9/5, guided hikes $3/2; ☺8am-5pm daily Oct-Jun, 8am-5pm Fri-Sun Jul-Sep) Streams flowing from the San Jacinto Mountains sustain a rich variety of plants in oases around Palm Springs. Home to Native American communities for hundreds of years and now part of the Agua Caliente Indian Reservation, these canyons, shaded by fan palms and surrounded by towering cliffs, are a delight for hikers.

Closest to the entrance gate is **Andreas Canyon** with a pleasant picnic area. Nearby are imposing rock formations where you can find Native American mortar holes, used for grinding seeds, and some rock art. The

---

TOP FIVE SPAS

Get your stressed-out self to these pampering shrines to work out the kinks and turn your body into a glowing lump of tranquility. Choices are plentiful (heck, there's even a pet spa; see www.aquapaws.net, if you must know!), but here are our five faves. Reservations are de rigueur.

» **Estrella Spa at Viceroy Palm Springs** (Map p656; ☑760-320-4117; www.viceroypalmsprings.com; 415 S Belardo Rd) Stylish boutique-hotel spa for massages in poolside cabanas.

» **Feel Good Spa at Ace Hotel & Swim Club** (Map p656; ☑760-329-8791; www.acehotel.com/palmsprings/spa; 701 E Palm Canyon Dr) At Palm Springs' newest hipster spa you can get a treatment inside a yurt.

» **Spa Resort Casino** (Map p656; ☑760-778-1772; www.sparesortcasino.com; 100 N Indian Canyon Dr) Try a five-step 'taking of the waters' course through the valley's original hot springs.

» **Spa Terre at Riviera Palm Springs** (Map p656; ☑760-778-6690; www.psriviera.com; 1600 N Indian Canyon Dr) The ultimate in swanky pampering, with Watsu pool and exotic spa rituals.

» **Palm Springs Yacht Club** (Map p660; ☑760-770-5000; www.theparkerpalmsprings.com/spa; Parker Palm Springs, 4200 E Palm Canyon Dr) This newly renovated spa is again the ritzy, glitzy fave of celebs and society ladies.

Palm Springs

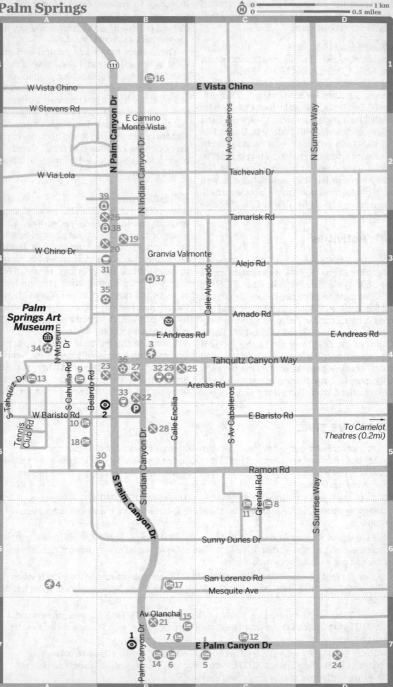

Palm Springs

PALM SPRINGS & THE DESERTS PALM SPRINGS & THE COACHELLA VALLEY

trail up the canyon is an easy walk. About a 20-minute traipse south from Andreas Canyon is **Murray Canyon**, which is popular with bird-watchers. With luck, you might even spot an elusive bighorn sheep on the slopes above the canyon. At the end of the winding access road is 15-mile-long **Palm Canyon**, the most extensive canyon, with good trails and a store selling snacks. In the morning, look for animal tracks in the sandy patches.

From downtown Palm Springs, head south on Palm Canyon Dr (continue straight when the main road turns east) for about 2 miles to the reservation entrance. From here, it's 3 miles up to the Trading Post, which sells hats, maps, water and knick-knacks. Trail posts at the entrance to each canyon have maps and hiking info.

🏕 **Mt San Jacinto State Park**   HIKING
(Map p660; ☎951-659-2607; www.parks.ca.gov) The wilderness unfolding beyond the Palm Springs Aerial Tramway mountain station is crisscrossed by 54 miles of hiking trails, including a nontechnical route up Mt San Jacinto (10,834ft). The state park visitors center in the station sells books, maps and nature-themed gifts. If you're heading into the backcountry (whether for overnight camping or even just for a few hours of hiking), you must self-register for a wilderness permit at the ranger station downhill from the mountain station.

SUNNY LIVING AT SUNNYLANDS

Sunnylands (Map p660; ☎760-328-2829; www.sunnylands.org; 70177 Hwy 111, Rancho Mirage) is the retro-glam Mid-Century Modern estate of the Annenbergs, one of America's 'first families.' Designed by A Quincy Jones and surrounded by superb grounds incorporating a nine-hole golf course and 11 stocked lakes, it was set to open to the public by the time you read this. Walter Annenberg (1908–2002) was an American publisher, US ambassador and philanthropist. At their winter estate in Rancho Mirage, he and his wife entertained seven US presidents, royalty and international celebrities. The new center was created using the latest sustainable technology, including low-water-use plants and a solar field. Inside will be historic and art galleries and a cafe; tours will be available with advance reservation. Ask at the Palm Springs Official Visitor Center or check the website for updates.

Winter Adventure Center SNOW SPORTS
(☉10am-4pm Thu-Mon mid-Nov–mid-Apr, snow conditions permitting, last rental 2:30pm) Outside the Palm Springs Aerial Tramway mountain station, this outfit gets you into the snowy backcountry on snowshoes ($18) and cross-country skis ($21), available on a first-come, first-served bases to anyone over 18

Smoke Tree Stables HORSEBACK RIDING
(Map p660; ☎760-327-1372; www.smoketrees tables.com; 2500 S Toledo Ave; 1/2hr guided ride $50/90) Near the Indian Canyons, this outfit arranges trail rides, from one-hour outings to all-day treks, for both novice and experienced riders. Reservations required.

Knott's Soak City WATER PARK
(Map p660; ☎760-327-0499; www.knotts.com/public/park/soakcity; 1500 S Gene Autry Trail; adult/child $32/22, after 3pm $22/12; ☉mid-Mar–Sep, hours vary; 👶) A great place to keep cool on hot days, Knott's boasts a massive wave pool, thunderous water slides and tube rides. Parking costs $8. Call or check the website for current opening hours.

Stand By Golf GOLF
(☎760-321-2665; www.standbygolf.com) Golf is huge here, with more than 100 public, semi-private, private and resort golf courses scattered around the valley. This outfit books tee times for discounted same-day or next-day play at a few dozen local courses.

☞ Tours

The visitors center has brochures for self-guided tours, including public art and historic sites (free), modernism ($5) and stars' homes ($5).

Best of the Best Tours GENERAL
(☎760-320-1365; www.thebestofthebesttours.com; tours from $25) Extensive program includes windmill tours and bus tours of celebrity homes.

Desert Adventures GENERAL
(☎760-340-2345; www.red-jeep.com; 90min/3hr tours $85/125) Four-wheel-drive tours of the Joshua Tree backcountry and the San Andreas Fault.

Historic Walking Tours WALKING
(☎760-323-8297; www.pshistoricalsociety.org; tour $10; ☉10am Thu & Sat) Just what it says. Organized by the Palm Springs Historical Society.

Palm Springs Modern Tours HISTORICAL
(☎760-318-6118; psmoderntours@aol.com; tours $75) Three-hour minivan tour of Mid-Century Modern architectural jewels by such masters as Albert Frey, Richard Neutra and John Lautner.

✸✸ Festivals & Events

Palm Springs International Film Festival FILM
(www.psfilmfest.org) Early January brings a Hollywood-star-studded film festival, showing more than 200 films from over 60 countries. A short-film festival follows in June.

Modernism Week CULTURAL
(www.modernismweek.com) A 10-day celebration of all things Mid-Century Modern, with architecture and home tours, films, lectures, a design show and lots of parties; in mid-February.

Coachella Music & Arts Festival MUSIC
(www.coachella.com; 1/3 day passes around $100/300) Held at Indio's Empire Polo Club over two weekends in April, this is one of the hottest indie-music festivals of its kind. Get tickets early or forget about it.

Stagecoach Festival
MUSIC

(www.stagecoachfestival.com; 1/3 day passes from $100/250) The weekend after Coachella, at the same venue, this festival celebrates new and established country-music artists.

Restaurant Week
FOOD

(www.palmspringsrestaurantweek.com) Discounted prix-fixe menus at top restaurants throughout the valley; in June.

🛏 Sleeping

Palm Springs and the Coachella Valley offer an astonishing variety of lodging options, including fine vintage-flair boutique hotels, full-on luxury resorts and chain motels. We've quoted high-season (November to April) rack rates; summer savings can be significant. Generally speaking, midweek rates are lower than weekend rates. Continental breakfast is often included, although standards vary widely. Campers should head to Joshua Tree National Park or Mt San Jacinto State Park. Pets are welcome at most properties, although usually an extra fee is charged.

PALM SPRINGS

TOP CHOICE **Riviera Palm Springs** LUXURY HOTEL $$$
(Map p656; ☎760-327-8311; www.psriviera.com; 1600 Indian Canyon Dr; r $240-260, ste $290-540; ❄◉☎≋) If you're lusting for luxury, check into this famous Rat Pack playground that just emerged from a big-bucks renovation and is sparkling brighter than ever. Expect the full range of fancy mod-cons amid luscious gardens and cute '60s accents like shag rugs, classily campy crystal chandeliers and Warhol art.

Ace Hotel & Swim Club
HOTEL $$

(Map p656; ☎760-325-9900; www.acehotel.com/palmsprings; 701 E Palm Canyon Dr; r $120-190, ste $200-440; ❄☎≋🐾) Palm Springs goes Hollywood – with all the sass but sans attitude – at this former Howard Johnson motel turned hipster hangout. Rooms (many with patio) sport a glorified tent-cabin look and are crammed with lifestyle essentials (big flat-screens, MP3 plugs). Happening on-site restaurant and bar to boot.

Parker Palm Springs
RESORT $$$

(Map p660; ☎760-770-5000; www.theparkerpalmsprings.com; 4200 E Palm Canyon Dr; r from $255; ❄☎≋🐾) Featured in the Bravo TV series *Welcome to the Parker*, this posh full-service resort boasts whimsical decor by Jonathan Adler. Drop by for a cocktail at Mister Parker's or a posh brunch at Norma's five-star coffee shop. The grounds boast hammocks, *boules* (lawn bowling) and a fabulous spa.

Caliente Tropics
MOTEL $

(Map p656; ☎760-327-1391; www.calientetropics.com; 411 E Palm Canyon Dr; d $66-111; ❄☎🐾🏊) Elvis once frolicked poolside at this premier budget pick, a nicely kept 1950s tiki-style motor lodge. Drift off to dreamland on quality mattresses in rooms that are spacious and dressed in warm colors.

Orbit In
BOUTIQUE HOTEL $$

(Map p656; ☎760-323-3585; www.orbitin.com; 562 W Arenas Rd; d incl breakfast $149-259; ❄☎≋) Swing back to the '50s – pinkie raised and all – during the 'Orbitini' happy hour at this fabulously retro property, with high-end Mid-Century Modern furniture (Eames, Noguchi et al) in rooms set around a quiet saline pool with a Jacuzzi and fire pit. The long list of freebies includes bike rentals and daytime sodas and snacks.

Palm Springs Travelodge
MOTEL $

(Map p656; ☎760-327-1211; www.palmcanyonhotel.com; 333 E Palm Canyon Dr; r incl breakfast $60-140; ❄☎≋) Save cash without sacrificing style or comfort at...wait a minute...a Travelodge? This 2.0 version welcomes you to a sleek lobby, beds you down in rooms sporting mod black furniture and keeps you chillin' poolside with barbecue, fire pits and canopied lounge beds. Not the motel your parents knew.

Viceroy
BOUTIQUE HOTEL $$$

(Map p656; ☎760-320-4117; www.viceroypalmsprings.com; 415 S Belardo Rd; d $310-400; ❄☎≋🏊) Wear a Pucci dress and blend right in at this 1960s-chic miniresort done up in black, white and lemon-yellow (think Austin Powers meets Givenchy). There's a

---

DON'T MISS

VILLAGEFEST

The best day to be in Palm Springs is Thursday when Palm Canyon Dr morphs into a fun street fair with farmers market, food vendors, live music and arts and handicrafts booths. Called Villagefest, the weekly partly is held from 6pm to 10pm (from 7pm June to September) between Amado and Baristo Rds and brings out locals and visitors in droves.

Coachella Valley

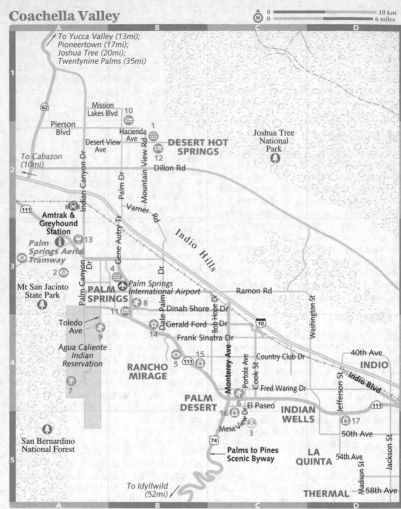

PALM SPRINGS & THE DESERTS PALM SPRINGS & THE COACHELLA VALLEY

full-service spa (see the boxed text, p655), a fab but pricey Cal-French restaurant for a white-linen luncheon or swanky supper, and free town-cruiser bikes to borrow. Booking at least three weeks in advance can save you big bucks.

Chase Hotel at Palm Springs MOTEL **$$**
(Map p656; ☎760-320-8866; www.chasehotel palmsprings.com; 200 W Arenas Rd; d incl breakfast $120-210; ❋☎☎❂) A classic Mid-Century Modern motel complex with large open spaces, the Chase has immaculately kept, oversized rooms that are cozy while exuding

designer-sleek. It's great value, with friendly service and free afternoon cookies.

Del Marcos Hotel BOUTIQUE HOTEL **$$**
(Map p656; ☎760-325-6902; www.delmarcosho tel.com; 225 W Baristo Rd; r $140-200; ❋☎☎❂) At this 1947 gem, designed by William F Cody, groovy lobby tunes usher you to a saltwater pool and ineffably chic rooms. Extra pet-friendly (free bones, toys and treats).

Horizon Hotel BOUTIQUE HOTEL **$$**
(Map p656; ☎760-323-1858; www.thehorizonhotel. com; 1050 E Palm Canyon Dr; r $140-220; ❋☎❂)

Coachella Valley

Another Cody creation, this intimate retreat saw Marilyn Monroe and Betty Grable lounging by the poolside bar back in the day. Treat yourself to alfresco showers, a chemical-free swimming pool and private patios. Adult-only.

DESERT HOT SPRINGS

TOP CHOICE El Morocco Inn & Spa   BOUTIQUE HOTEL $$$

(Map p660; ☏760-288-2527; www.elmoroccoinn.com; 66814 4th St; r incl breakfast $169-249; ❄️🛜🏊) Heed the call of the Kasbah at this drop-dead gorgeous hideaway where the scene is set for romance. Ten exotically furnished rooms wrap around a pool deck where your enthusiastic host serves free 'Moroccotinis' during happy hour. Other perks: the on-site spa, a huge DVD library and delicious homemade mint ice tea. Check out the original sultan's tent in the spa garden.

The Spring   BOUTIQUE HOTEL $$$

(☏760-251-6700; www.the-spring.com; 12699 Reposo Way; r incl breakfast $179-279; ❄️🛜🏊) Splash out in this humble 1950s motel morphed into a chic, whisper-quiet spa retreat where natural hot mineral water feeds three pools. The 10 rooms are minimalist in design but not in amenities (rich duvets, fluffy robes, small kitchens). Achieve a state of bliss while enjoying a treatment or simply calming valley and mountain views.

✕ Eating

TOP CHOICE Trio   MODERN AMERICAN $$

(Map p656; ☏760-864-8746; www.triopalmsprings.com; 707 N Palm Canyon Dr; mains $13-28; ⏱4-10pm) The winning formula in this '60s modernist space: updated American comfort food (awesome Yankee pot roast!), eye-catching artwork and picture windows. The $19 'early bird' three-course dinner (served 4pm to 6pm) is a steal.

TOP CHOICE Cheeky's   MODERN AMERICAN $$

(Map p656; ☏760-327-7595; www.cheekysps.com; 622 N Palm Canyon Dr; mains $6-13; ⏱8am-2pm Wed-Mon; 🎬) Waits can be long and service only so-so, but the farm-to-table menu dazzles with witty inventiveness. Dishes change weekly, but custardy scrambled eggs, arugula pesto frittata and bacon bar 'flights' keep making appearances.

Tyler's Burgers   BURGERS $

(Map p656; http://tylersburgers.com; 149 S Indian Canyon Dr; burgers $4.50-9; ⏱11am-4pm Mon-Sat; 🎬🏊) The best burgers in town, bar none. Waits are practically inevitable, which is presumably why there's an amazingly well-stocked magazine rack.

Sherman's   DELI $$

(Map p656; ☏760-325-1199; www.shermansdeli.com; 401 E Tahquitz Canyon Way; sandwiches $9-12; ⏱7am-9pm; 🎬🏊) With a breezy sidewalk patio, this 1950s kosher-style deli pulls in an all-ages crowd with its 40 sandwich varieties (great hot pastrami!), finger-lickin' rotisserie chicken and to-die-for pies. Walls are festooned with head shots of celebrity regulars, including Don Rickles.

Fisherman's Market & Grill   SEAFOOD $$

(Map p656; ☏760-327-1766; www.fishermans.com; 235 S Indian Canyon Dr; mains $8-15; ⏱11am-9pm Mon-Sat, noon-8pm Sun; 🎬🏊) At this no-frills counter-service shack, the seafood is so fresh you half expect to see fishing boats bobbing outside. Fish and chips is a classic, as are the fish tacos and the seafood gumbo. Call ahead for takeout.

El Mirasol
MEXICAN $$

(Map p656; ☑760-323-0721; http://elmirasolcoci namexicana.menutoeat.com; 140 E Palm Canyon Dr; mains $10-19; ☺11am-10pm; 🎦) There are showier Mexican places around town, but everyone ends up back at El Mirasol, with its earthy decor, generous margaritas and snappy dishes. The chicken in mole or in *pipián* sauce (made from ground pumpkin seeds and chilis) are menu stars.

🌱 Native Foods
VEGAN $

(Map p656; ☑760-416-0070; www.nativefoods. com; Smoke Tree Village, 1775 E Palm Canyon Dr; mains $8-11; ☺11:30am-9:30pm Mon-Sat; 🎦🎦) Vegan cooking guru Tanya Petrovna does an amazing job at injecting complex flavors into meat and dairy substitutes. The creative sandwiches, Southwestern salads, sizzling-hot rice bowls and tasty pizzas and burgers feed both body and soul.

Matchbox
BISTRO $$

(Map p656; ☑760-778-6000; www.matchboxpalm springs.com; 2nd level, 155 S Palm Canyon Dr; pizza from $13, mains $18-30; ☺5-11pm Sun-Thu, 5pm-1am Fri & Sat) This buzzy bistro with a plaza-view patio is famous for pizzas with pizzazz. Think lots of mouth-watering toppings such as spiced artichoke hearts, homemade meatballs and roasted garlic. Fabulous happy hour until 6:30pm.

King's Highway
AMERICAN $$

(Map p656; ☑760-325-9900; www.acehotel.com; Ace Hotel & Swim Club, 701 E Palm Canyon Dr; mains $8-30; ☺7am-1am Sun-Wed, to 3am Thu-Sat; 🎦🎦) A fine case of creative recycling, this former Denny's is now a diner for the 21st century where the tagliatelle is handmade, the sea bass wild-caught, the beef grass-fed, the vegetables organic and the cheeses artisanal. Great breakfast, too.

Wang's in the Desert
ASIAN $$

(Map p656; ☑760-325-9264; www.wangsinth edesert.com; 424 S Indian Canyon Dr; mains $12-20; ☺5-9:30pm Sun-Thu, to 10:30pm Fri & Sat) This mood-lit gay fave with indoor koi pond delivers creatively crafted Chinese classics and has a busy daily happy hour.

Copley's
AMERICAN $$$

(Map p656; ☑760-327-9555; www.copleyspalm springs.com; 621 N Palm Canyon Dr; mains $27-38; ☺6pm-late Jan-Apr, closed Jul & Aug and Mon May, Jun & Sep-Dec) After stints in the UK, Australia and Hawaii, chef Copley now concocts swoon-worthy American fare on the former Cary Grant estate. The Oh My Lobster Pot Pie is unlikely to ever go out of fashion. Bring your sweetie and your credit card.

🍷 Drinking

Many of the restaurants have hugely popular happy hours, including Wang's, Matchbox and Azul, and there are happening hotel bars at Parker, Riviera and Ace.

Birba
BAR

(Map p656; www.birbaps.com; 622 N Palm Canyon Dr; ☺6-11pm Wed-Fri, from 9:30am Sat & Sun) It's cocktails and pizza at this fabulous indoor-outdoor space where floor-to-ceiling sliding glass doors separate the long marble bar from a hedge-fringed patio with sunken fire pits.

Shanghai Red's
BAR

(Map p656; www.fishermans.com/shanghaireds. php; 235 S Indian Canyon Dr; ☺5pm-late) Part of Fisherman's Market & Grill (p661), this joint has a busy courtyard, an inter-generational crowd and live blues on Friday and Saturday nights.

Melvyn's
LOUNGE

(Map p656; www.inglesideinn.com; 200 W Ramon Rd; ☺10am-2am) Join the Bentley pack for stiff martinis and quiet jazz at this former Sinatra haunt at the Ingleside Inn. Sunday afternoon jazz is a long-standing tradition. Shine your shoes.

Palm Springs Koffi
CAFE

(Map p656; www.kofficoffee.com; 515 N Palm Canyon Dr; ☺5:30am-8pm; 🎦) Tucked among the art galleries on N Palm Canyon Dr, this coolly minimalist, indie java bar serves strong organic coffee.

Village Pub
PUB

(Map p656; www.palmspringsvillagepub.com; 266 S Palm Canyon Dr; 🎦) This casual dive is perfect for kicking back with your posse over beers, darts, loud music and the occasional live band.

☆ Entertainment

Azul
MUSIC

(Map p656; ☑760-325-5533; www.azultapaslounge. com; 369 N Palm Canyon Dr; mains $11-24; ☺11am-late) Popular with gays and their friends, the Azul restaurant has almost nightly enter-

GAY & LESBIAN PALM SPRINGS

Nicknamed 'Provincetown in the Desert' and 'Key West of the West,' Palm Springs is one of America's great gay destinations. For background, surf www.palmspringsgayinfo.com or www.visitgaypalmsprings.com and pick up the *Official Gay & Lesbian Visitors Guide* from the visitors center.

In early April, **Dinah Shore Weekend** (www.dinahshoreweekend.com) hosts lesbian comedy, pool parties, mixers and more during the Nabisco (ex-Dinah Shore) LPGA golf tournament. Over Easter weekend, the **White Party** (www.jeffreysanker.com) is one of the USA's biggest gay dance events. Show up in early November for **Palm Springs Pride** (www.pspride.org).

Resorts

Men's resorts are concentrated in the Warm Sands neighborhood, just southeast of downtown Palm Springs, or on San Lorenzo Rd, about a mile away. Most men's resorts are clothing-optional. Lesbian resorts (fewer in number) are scattered throughout town.

» **Hacienda at Warm Sands** (Map p656; ☎760-327-8111; www.thehacienda.com; 586 Warm Sands Dr; r incl breakfast & lunch $150-400; ❄@☎☂) With Indonesian teak and bamboo furnishings, the Hacienda raises the bar for luxury and has genial innkeepers who are never intrusive, but always available.

» **Triangle Inn** (Map p656; ☎760-322-7993; www.triangle-inn.com; 555 E San Lorenzo Rd; r incl breakfast $125-205; ❄@☎☂) At this intimate clothing-optional Mid-Century Modern retreat you'll be staying in homey suites outfitted with kitchenettes, large baths and an alphabet soup of entertainment tools (DVD, TV, VCR, CD). Days start with poolside breakfast against a backdrop of bougainvillea and birds of paradise.

» **Century Palm Springs** (Map p656; ☎760-323-9966; www.centurypalmsprings.com; 598 Grenfall Rd; r incl breakfast $180-300; ❄@☎☂☂) At the small Century, designed by William Alexander in 1955, rooms are hued in cheerful orange and olive and furnished with plush bedding and pieces by Starck, Eames and Noguchi. Soak up cocktails and serene mountain views from the minimalist pool deck.

» **Casitas Laquita** (Map p656; ☎760-416-9999; www.casitaslaquita.com; 450 E Palm Canyon Dr; r $155-195; ❄☎☂) This newly made-over, Southwest-flavored compound for lesbians has rooms and suites with kitchens; some even have kiva-style fireplaces. Afternoon tapas and drinks are complimentary, as is continental breakfast. Free wi-fi poolside.

» **Queen of Hearts** (Map p656; ☎760-322-5793; www.queenofheartsps.com; 435 Avenida Olancha; r incl breakfast $145-165, ste $185-350; ❄☎☂☂) Palm Springs' original lesbian hotel counts many regulars among its guests, thanks, in large part, to its super-friendly owner Michelle. It's in a quiet neighborhood with nine rooms encircling a swimming pool and patios framed by fruit trees.

Drinking & Entertainment

The bars at Azul (p662) and Wang's (p662) are also buzzy stops on the gay party circuit.

» **Toucan's Tiki Lounge** (Map p660; www.toucanstikilounge.com; 2100 N Palm Canyon Dr; ☉noon-2am) A couple of miles north of Arenas, this locals' hangout has something for everyone: tropical froufrou, bingo mavens, karaoke, drag revues, smoking patio and dance floor. Packed on weekends.

» **Hunters** (Map p656; www.huntersnightclubs.com; 302 E Arenas Rd; ☉10am-2am) Wildly diverse male clientele, lots of TV screens, a cruisy dance scene and pool tables.

» **Streetbar** (Map p656; www.psstreetbar.com; 244 E Arenas Rd) Congenial mix of locals, long-time visitors and occasional drag performers. There's a cozy streetside patio for watching the crowds saunter by.

PALM SPRINGS & THE DESERTS PALM SPRINGS & THE COACHELLA VALLEY

A BLAST FROM THE PAST

Downtown's 1936 Plaza Theater hosts the **Palm Springs Follies** (☑760-327-0225; www.psfollies.com; 128 S Palm Canyon Dr; tickets $50-93; ☺Nov-May), a three-hour Ziegfeld Follies–style revue of music, dancing, showgirls and off-color comedy. The twist? Many of the performers are as old as the theater – all are over 50, and some are octogenarians. But this is no amateur hour: in their heyday these old-timers hoofed it alongside Hollywood and Broadway's biggest, who occasionally guest star.

tainment in its piano bar, plus the wickedly funny **Judy Show** (www.thejudyshow.com; incl dinner $35) on Sundays, starring impersonator Michael Holmes as Judy Garland, Mae West and other campy legends of yore.

Annenberg Theater   PERFORMING ARTS
(Map p656; ☑760-325-4490; www.psmuseum.org) This intimate theater at the Palm Springs Art Museum presents an eclectic schedule of films, lectures, theater, ballet and music performances.

Spa Resort Casino   CASINO
(Map p656; www.sparesortcasino.com; 401 E Amado Rd; ☺24hr) There's this perfectly legal Native American–owned den of vice right in the heart of downtown Palm Springs, as well as other gambling halls off I-10. Vegas they ain't.

Camelot Theatres   CINEMA
(Off Map p656; www.camelottheatres.com; 2300 Baristo Rd; adult/child $10/7, before 2pm $7/6.50) The desert's premier art-house cinema has a full bar and cafe.

Desert IMAX Theatre   CINEMA
(Map p660; www.desertimax.org; 68510 E Palm Canyon Dr, Cathedral City; tickets $8-12; 🔊) Big-screen Hollywood and 3D movies, as well as virtual-reality IMAX ride-films, screen here.

🛍 Shopping

Trina Turk   CLOTHING
(Map p656; www.trinaturk.com; 891 N Palm Canyon Dr) Trina makes form-flattering 'California-chic' fashions that are beautifully presented amid shag carpeting and floral foil wallpaper in her original boutique in a 1960s Al-

bert Frey building. Her Mr Turk menswear line is also available here.

Angel View   THRIFT SHOP
(Map p656; www.angelview.org; 462 N Indian Canyon Dr; ☺9am-6pm Mon-Sat, 10am-5pm Sun) At this well-established thrift store, today's hipsters can shop for clothes and accessories as cool as when they were first worn a generation or two ago.

Collectors Corner   VINTAGE
(Map p660; 71280 Hwy 111, Rancho Mirage) Antiques, vintage clothing, jewelry and furniture draw enthusiastic shoppers to this store next to the Eisenhower Medical Center, about 12 miles southeast of Palm Springs.

El Paseo   MALL
(Map p660; www.elpaseo.com; El Paseo, Palm Desert) For serious shopping, head to Palm Desert where the elegant El Paseo shopping strip has been dubbed the 'Rodeo Drive of the Desert'. It's one block south and parallel to Hwy 111, 14 miles southeast of Palm Springs.

Desert Hills Premium Outlets   MALL
(www.premiumoutlets.com; 48400 Seminole Dr, Cabazon; ☺10am-8pm Sun-Thu, to 9pm Fri, 9am-9pm Sat) Bargain hunters might get lucky ferreting through the offerings at dozens of outlet stores: Gap to Gucci, Polo to Prada, plus department stores like Off 5th and Barneys New York. Wear comfortable shoes – this mall is huge! It's off I-10 (exit at Fields Rd), 20 minutes west of Palm Springs.

Modern Way   FURNITURE
(Map p656; www.psmodernway.com; 745 N Palm Canyon Dr) The oldest and most stylin' consignment shop for collectors of modern furniture.

ℹ Information

High season is October to April, but Palm Springs (population 44,500, elevation 487ft) stays reasonably busy even in summer, when hotel rates drop and temperatures spike above 100°F (37°C). Between June and August many businesses keep shorter hours or even close, so call ahead to check.

Desert Regional Medical Center (☑800-491-4990; 1150 N Indian Canyon Dr) Twenty-four-hour emergency room and physician referral.

Palm Springs Official Visitors Center (☑760-778-8418; www.visitpalmsprings.com; 2901 N Palm Canyon Dr; ☺9am-5pm) This well-stocked and well-staffed visitors center is 3 miles north of downtown, in a 1965 Albert

Frey–designed gas station at the tramway turnoff.

Palm Springs Police (☎760-323-8116) For nonemergency situations.

Palm Springs Post Office (Map p656; 333 E Amado Rd; ⊙8am-5pm Mon-Fri, 9am-3pm Sat)

Palm Springs Public Library (300 S Sunrise Way; ⊙9am-8pm Tue-Wed, to 6pm Thu-Sun) Free wi-fi and internet terminals.

❶ Getting There & Away

Air

A 10-minute drive northeast of downtown, **Palm Springs International Airport** (Map p660; www.palmspringsairport.com; 3400 E Tahquitz Canyon Way) is served year-round by Alaska, Allegiant, American, Delta, Horizon, United, US Airways and Westjet, and seasonally by Sun Country.

Bus

Greyhound has a few daily buses to/from LA ($32.50, three hours). The terminus is at Palm Springs' train station.

Car & Motorcycle

From LA, the trip to Palm Springs and the Coachella Valley takes about two to three hours via I-10.

Train

Amtrak serves the unstaffed and kinda-creepy – it's deserted and in the middle of nowhere – North Palm Springs station (Map p660), 5 miles north of downtown Palm Springs. *Sunset Limited* trains run to/from LA ($37, 2½ hours) on Sunday, Wednesday and Friday; trains are often late.

❶ Getting Around

To/From the Airport

Many area hotels provide free airport transfers. Otherwise a taxi to downtown Palm Springs costs about $12. If you're staying in another Coachella Valley town, rides on shared shuttle vans will likely be more economical. Try **Desert Valley Shuttle** (☎760-251-4020; www.palmsspringshuttle.com) or **Skycap Shuttle** (☎760-272-5988; www.skycapshuttle.com). Fares depend on distance and reservations are advised. SunLine bus 24 stops at the airport but doesn't go all the way to downtown Palm Springs.

Bicycle

Many hotels have loaner bicycles for free or a small fee. Otherwise **Funseekers** (Map p660; ☎760-340-3861; www.palmdesertbikerentals.com; 73-865 Hwy 111, Palm Desert; bicycles per 24hr/3 day/week from $25/50/65, delivery & pick up from $30) rents and sells bikes for city and mountain use, plus mopeds and Segways.

Bus

Alternative-fuel-powered **SunLine** (www.sunline.org; single ride/day pass $1/3) is the local bus service that travels around the valley, albeit slowly, from around 5am to 10pm. The most useful route is bus 111, which links Palm Springs with Palm Desert (one hour) and Indio (1½ hours) via Hwy 111. Buses have air-con, wheel-

---

THE PERFECT DATE

The Coachella Valley is the ideal place to find the date of your dreams – the kind that grows on trees, that is. Some 90% of US date production happens here, with dozens of permutations of shape, size and juiciness, and species with exotic-sounding names like halawy, deglet noor and golden zahidi.

Date orchards let you sample different varieties for free, an act of shameless but delicious self-promotion. A signature taste is the date shake: crushed dates mixed into a vanilla milk shake. They're much richer than they look!

» **Shields Date Gardens** (Map p660; www.shieldsdates.com; cnr Hwy 111 & Jefferson St, Indio; ⊙9am-5pm) In business since 1924 this is where you can watch *The Romance and Sex Life of the Date*, with the chirpy feel of a 1950s educational film.

» **Oasis Date Gardens** (www.oasisdate.com; 59-111 Grapefruit Blvd, Thermal; ⊙9am-4pm) En route to the Salton Sea, this certified-organic date garden is handy for picking up gift boxes and yummy date shakes.

» **Hadley Fruit Orchards** (www.hadleyfruitorchards.com; 48980 Seminole Dr, Cabazon; ⊙9am-7pm Mon-Thu, 8am-8pm Fri-Sun) This landmark claims to have invented trail mix and makes a good grab-and-go stop on your way to or from LA.

» **National Date Festival** (www.datefest.org; Riverside County Fairgrounds, 82-503 Hwy 111, Indio; adult/child $8/6, parking $7; ⊞) For old-fashioned carnival fun, come in February for outrageous camel and ostrich races. From I-10, exit at Monroe St.

WHAT THE...?

West of Palm Springs, you may do a double take when you see the **World's Biggest Dinosaurs** (☎951-922-0076; www.cabazondinosaurs.com; 50770 Seminole Dr, Cabazon, off I-10 exit Main St; adult/child $7/6; ⊙varies by season, usually 10am-6pm). Claude K Bell, a sculptor for Knott's Berry Farm, spent over a decade crafting these concrete behemoths, now owned by Christian creationists who contend that God created the original dinosaurs in one day, along with the other animals. In the gift shop, alongside the sort of dino-swag you might find at science museums, you can read about the alleged hoaxes and fallacies of evolution and Darwinism.

chair lifts and a bicycle rack. Cash only (bring exact change).

Car & Motorcycle

Though you can walk to most sights in downtown Palm Springs, you'll need a car to get around the valley. Major rental-car companies have airport desks. **Scoot Palm Springs** (☎760-413-2883; www.scootpalmsprings.com), based at the Ace Hotel & Swim Club (p659), rents scooters from $50 per half day. For motorcycles try **Eaglerider** (☎877-736-8243; www.eaglerider.com), where rates start at $94 per day for a Sportster, not including insurance.

JOSHUA TREE NATIONAL PARK

Taking a page from a Dr Seuss book, the whimsical Joshua trees (actually tree-sized yuccas) welcome visitors to this 794,000-acre park at the convergence of the Colorado and Mojave Deserts. It was Mormon settlers who named the trees because the branches stretching up toward heaven reminded them of the biblical prophet Joshua pointing the way to the promised land.

Rock climbers know 'JT' as the best place to climb in California, but kids and the young at heart also welcome the chance to scramble up, down and around the giant boulders. Hikers seek out hidden, shady, desert-fan-palm oases fed by natural springs and small streams, while mountain bikers are hypnotized by the desert vistas seen from dirt 4WD roads.

The park is especially lovely in springtime when the Joshua trees send up a huge single cream-colored flower and the octopus-like tentacles of the ocotillo cactus shoot out crimson flowers. The mystical quality of this stark, boulder-strewn landscape has inspired many artists, most famously the band U2, which named its 1987 album *The Joshua Tree.*

Unless you're day-tripping from Palm Springs, you can base yourself in the trio of desert communities linked by the Twentynine Palms Hwy (Hwy 62) along the park's northern perimeter. Of these, Yucca Valley is the most commercial, with banks, supermarkets and big stores. Joshua Tree is favored by artists and writers and has the best eateries along the highway. Twentynine Palms, home to the country's largest US marine base, is more down-to-earth.

Sights & Activities

Joshua Tree has three park entrances. Access the west entrance from the town of Joshua Tree, the north entrance from Twentynine Palms and the south entrance from I-10. The park's northern half harbors most of the attractions, including all of the Joshua trees.

TOP CHOICE Hidden Valley OUTDOORS

Some 8 miles south of the West Entrance, this whimsically dramatic cluster of rocks is a rock climbers' mecca, but just about anyone can enjoy a clamber on the giant boulders. An easy 1-mile trail loops through it and back to the parking lot and picnic area.

TOP CHOICE Keys View LOOKOUT

From Park Blvd, it's an easy 20-minute drive up to Keys View (5185ft), where breathtaking views take in the entire Coachella Valley and extend as far as the Salton Sea and – on a good day – Mexico. Looming in front of you are Mt San Jacinto (10,834ft) and Mt San Gorgonio (11,500ft), two of Southern California's highest peaks, while down below you can spot a section of the San Andreas Fault.

Desert Queen Ranch HISTORIC SITE

(☎reservations 760-367-5555; tour adult/child $5/2.50; ⊙tours 10am & 1pm daily year-round, 7pm Tue & Thu-Sat Oct-May) Anyone interested in local history and lore should take the 90-minute guided tour of this ranch that's also known as Keys Ranch after its builder, Russian immigrant William Keys. He built a homestead here on 160 acres in 1917 and over the next 60 years turned it into a full working ranch, school, store and workshop. The buildings stand much as they did when Keys died in 1969.

Tour reservations are highly recommended; remaining tickets may be available one day in advance at the Cottonwood, Joshua Tree and Oasis park visitors centers (p673).

The ranch is about 2 miles northeast of Hidden Valley Campground, up a dirt road. Drive as far as the locked gate where your guide will meet you.

Oasis of Mara   OASIS

Behind the Oasis visitors center in Twentynine Palms, this natural oasis encompasses the original 29 palm trees for which the town is named. They were planted by members of the Serrano tribe, who named this 'the place of little springs and much grass.' The Pinto Mountain Fault, a small branch of the San Andreas, runs through the oasis, as does a 0.5-mile, wheelchair-accessible nature trail with labeled desert plants.

Geology Tour Road   DRIVING TOUR

East of Hidden Valley, travelers with 4WD vehicles or mountain bikes can take this 18-mile field trip into and around Pleasant Valley, where the forces of erosion, earthquakes and ancient volcanoes have played out in stunning splendor. Before setting out pick up a self-guided tour brochure and an update on road conditions at any park visitors center.

Covington Flats   DRIVING TOUR

Joshua trees grow throughout the northern section of the park, including right along Park Blvd, but some of the biggest trees are found in this area accessed via La Contenta Rd, south off Hwy 62 between the towns of Yucca Valley and Joshua Tree. For photogenic views, follow the dirt road 3.8 miles up Eureka Peak (5516ft) from the picnic area.

Pinto Basin Road   DRIVING TOUR

To see the natural transition from the high Mojave Desert to the low Colorado Desert, wind down to Cottonwood Spring, a 30-mile drive from Hidden Valley. Stop at **Cholla Cactus Garden**, where a 0.25-mile loop leads around waving ocotillo plants and jumping 'teddy bear' cholla. Near the Cottonwood visitors center, **Cottonwood Spring** is an oasis with a natural spring that Cahuilla tribespeople depended on for centuries. Look for *morteros*, rounded depressions in the rocks used by Native Americans for grinding seeds. Miners came searching for gold here in the late 19th century.

Hiking

Leave the car behind to appreciate Joshua Tree's trippy lunar landscapes. Staff at the visitors centers can help you match your time and fitness level to the perfect trail. Distances given are round-trip.

49 Palms Oasis Escape the crowds on this 3-mile up-and-down trail starting near Indian Cove.

Barker Dam A 1.1-mile loop that passes a little lake and a rock incised with Native American petroglyphs; starts at Barker Dam parking lot.

Lost Horse Mine A strenuous 4-mile climb that visits the remains of an au-

SCENIC DRIVE: PALMS TO PINES SCENIC BYWAY

What to See

This day trip from Palm Springs ascends to piney forests and descends back to the desert floor in a mere couple of hours. As the road climbs the landscape quickly changes to ponderosa-blanketed mountains. Look for bald eagles above and bobcats below, and when you're done ferret for bargains at Desert Hills Premium Outlets (p664).

The Route

From Palm Springs take Hwy 111 southeast to Palm Desert, and turn right onto Palms to Pines Scenic Byway (CA74), across from Monterey Ave. At Mountain Center connect with Rte 243 north, also called the Banning-Idyllwild Panoramic Hwy. It's about 28 winding miles to Banning, where you can connect back to I-10 east toward Palm Springs.

Time & Mileage

It's about 68 miles one way between Palm Desert and Banning. With time for twists, turns, oohs and aahs, allow about 1¾ hours' drive time.

Joshua Tree National Park

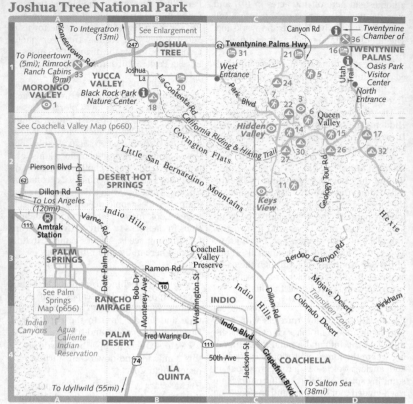

thentic Old West silver and gold mine, in operation until 1931.

Lost Palms Oasis Reach this remote canyon filled with desert fan palms on a fairly flat 7.2-mile hike starting from Cottonwood Spring.

Mastodon Peak Enjoy views of the Eagle Mountains and the Salton Sea from an elevation of 3371ft on this 3-mile hike from Cottonwood Spring.

Ryan Mountain For more bird's-eye park views, tackle the 3-mile hike up this 5458ft-high peak.

Skull Rock This easy 1.7-mile trail around evocatively eroded rocks starts at Jumbo Rocks campground.

Backpacking routes, such as the 16-mile, out-and-back **Boy Scout Trail** and a 35-mile one-way stretch of the **California Riding & Hiking Trail**, present a challenge because of

the need to carry gallons of water per person per day. No open fires are allowed in the park, so you'll also have to bring a camping stove and fuel. Overnight backcountry hikers must register (to aid in census-taking, fire safety and rescue efforts) at one of 13 backcountry boards located at trailhead parking lots throughout the park. Unregistered vehicles left overnight may be cited or towed.

Cycling

Cycling is only permitted on paved and dirt public roads; bikes are not allowed on hiking trails. **Village Bicycle** ([📞] 760-808 4557; Hallee Rd; [🕐] 10am-6pm Mon-Fri, 9am-9pm Sat, 9am-2pm Sun), behind Sam's in Joshua Tree, rents basic mountain bikes for $45 per day. The owner also does repairs.

Popular riding routes include challenging **Pinkham Canyon Rd**, starting from the Cottonwood visitors center, and the long-distance **Black Eagle Mine Rd**, which starts

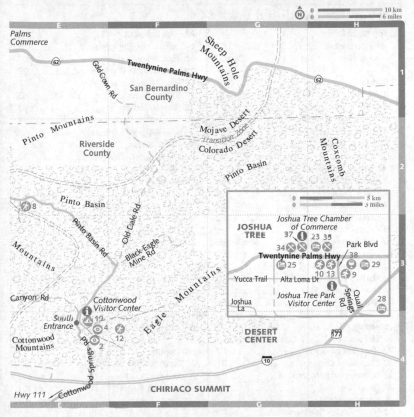

6.5 miles further north. **Queen Valley** has a gentler set of trails with bike racks found along the way, so people can lock up their bikes and go hiking, but it's busy with cars, as is the bumpy, sandy and steep **Geology Tour Rd** (p667). There's a wide-open network of dirt roads at **Covington Flats** (p667).

Rock Climbing

JT's rocks are famous for their rough, high-friction surfaces, and from boulders to cracks to multipitch faces, there are more than 8000 established routes, many right off the main road. The longest climbs are not much more than 100ft or so, but there are many challenging technical routes, and most can be easily top-roped for training. Some of the most popular climbs are in the Hidden Valley area.

Shops catering to climbers with quality gear, advice and tours include the following:

Joshua Tree Outfitters (☎760-366-1848; www.joshuatreeoutfitters.com; 61707 Twentynine Palms Hwy, Joshua Tree; ☺usually 9am-5pm)

Nomad Ventures (☎760-366-4684; www.nomadventures.com; 61795 Twentynine Palms Hwy, Joshua Tree; ☺8am-6pm Mon-Thu, to 8pm Fri & Sat, to 7pm Sun Oct-Apr, 9am-7pm daily May-Sep)

Coyote Corner (☎760-366-9683; www.joshuatreevillage.com/546/546.htm; 6535 Park Blvd, Joshua Tree; ☺9am-7pm)

The following outfits offer guided climbs and climbing instruction starting at $135 for a one-day introduction.

Joshua Tree Rock Climbing School (☎760-366-4745; www.joshuatreerockclimbing.com)

Vertical Adventures (☎949-854-6250; www.verticaladventures.com)

Uprising Adventure (☎888-254-6266; www.uprising.com)

Joshua Tree National Park

✵✵ Festivals & Events

National Park Art Festival   ART
(www.joshuatree.org) This nonprofit festival shows desert-themed paintings, sculpture, photography, ceramics and jewelry in early April.

Joshua Tree Music Festival   MUSIC
(www.joshuatreemusicfestival.com; 2-day pass $60) Over a long weekend in May, this family-friendly indie-music fest grooves out at Joshua Tree Lake Campground. It's followed by a soulful roots celebration in mid-October. No dogs.

Pioneer Days   CULTURAL
(www.visit29.org) Twentynine Palms' Old West–themed carnival on the third October weekend has a parade, an arm-wrestling competition and a chili dinner.

Hwy 62 Art Tours   ART
(www.mbcac.org) Tour artists' studios, galleries and workshops over two weekends in October.

🛏 Sleeping

Inside the park there are only campgrounds but there are plenty of lodging options along Hwy 62. Twentynine Palms has the biggest selection of accommodations, including national chain motels (check their websites), but pads in Joshua Tree have more character and charm.

TOP CHOICE Hicksville Trailer Palace   MOTEL $$
(☏310-584-1086; www.hicksville.com; r $75-200; ✽🌐🐾🏊) Fancy sleeping among glowing wigs, in a haunted house, or in a horse stall? Check in at Hicksville, where 'rooms' are eight outlandishly decorated vintage trailers set around a kidney-shaped saltwater swim-

ming pool. Spawned by the vision of LA writer and director Morgan Higby Night, each offers a journey into a unique, surreal and slightly wicked world. All but two share facilities. To keep out looky-loos, you'll only be given directions after making reservations.

Desert Lily   B&B $$
(☑760-366-4676; www.thedesertlily.com; Joshua Tree Highlands; s/d incl breakfast $140/155; ⊙closed Jul & Aug; @🉑) The charming Carrie presides over this three-room adobe retreat with Old West–meets-Southwest decor. Days start with scrumptious breakfasts and there's always a tray of fresh cookies in the common area anchored by a fireplace. Rooms are a bit snug, but there are also four private cabins with full kitchens should you need more elbow space. Well-behaved pets considered.

Sacred Sands   B&B $$$
(☑760-424-6407; www.sacredsands.com; 63155 Quail Springs Rd, Joshua Tree; d incl breakfast $269-299; ❄🉑) In an isolated, pin-drop-quiet spot, these two luxurious suites, each with a private outdoor shower, hot tub, sundeck and sleeping terrace under the stars, are the ultimate romantic retreat. Owners Scott and Steve are gracious hosts and killer breakfast cooks.

Spin & Margie's Desert Hide-a-Way   BOUTIQUE INN $$
(☑760-366-9124; www.deserthideaway.com; Sunkist Rd, off Twentynine Palms Hwy; ste $125-175; ❄🉑) This handsome hacienda-style inn is perfect for restoring calm after a long day on the road. The five boldly colored suites are an eccentric symphony of corrugated tin, old license plates and cartoon art. Each has its own kitchen and flat-screen TV with DVD and CD player. Knowledgeable, gregarious owners ensure a relaxed visit. It's down the dirt Sunkist Rd, about 3 miles east of downtown Joshua Tree.

Joshua Tree Inn   MOTEL $
(☑760-366-1188; www.joshuatreeinn.com; 61259 Twentynine Palms Hwy, Joshua Tree; d/tr/q incl breakfast $95/110/125; ❄🉑🉑) This pleasant motel has spacious rooms behind turquoise doors leading off from a desert garden courtyard. It gained notoriety in 1973 when rock legend Gram Parsons overdosed in Room 8, which is now decorated with photos and posters in tribute to the man. The communal area features a rock fireplace. Reception is open from 3pm to 8pm only.

Safari Motor Inn   MOTEL $
(☑760-366-1113; www.joshuatreemotel.com; 61959 Twentynine Palms Hwy, Joshua Tree; r $55-75; ❄🉑🉑) This one's an excellent choice for modern nomads not keen on dropping bunches of cash for a roof over their heads. Most of the well-worn standard rooms have microwaves and mini refrigerators. It's a short walk to eateries and outdoor outfitters. Pets OK.

Harmony Motel   MOTEL $
(☑760-367-3351; www.harmonymotel.com; 71161 Twentynine Palms Hwy, Twentynine Palms; s/d $70/77; ❄@🉑🉑) This 1950s motel, where U2 once stayed, has a small pool and large, cheerfully painted rooms; some have kitchenettes.

High Desert Motel   MOTEL $
(☑760-366-1978; www.highdesertmotel.com; 61310 Twentynine Palms Hwy, Joshua Tree; r $50-70; ❄🉑🉑) Plain-Jane rooms with mini fridges and microwaves but still a decent budget pick.

29 Palms Inn   HOTEL $$
(☑760-367-3505; www.29palmsinn.com; 73950 Inn Ave, Twentynine Palms, r & cottages incl breakfast $95-260; ❄@🉑🉑) History oozes from every nook and cranny in these old-timey adobe-and-wood cabins dotted around a palm oasis.

Camping

Of the park's nine **campgrounds** (tent & RV sites $10-15), only Cottonwood and Black Rock have potable water, flush toilets and dump stations. Indian Cove and Black Rock accept **reservations** (☑877-444-6777; www.recreation.gov). The others are first-come, first-served and have pit toilets, picnic tables and fire grates. None have showers but there are some at Coyote Corner (p673) in Joshua Tree, which charges $4. During the springtime wildflower bloom, campsites fill by noon, if not earlier.

Backcountry camping (no campfires) is allowed 1 mile from any trailhead or road and 100ft from water sources; free self-registration is required at the park's 13 staging areas. **Joshua Tree Outfitters** (☑760-366-1848; 61707 Twentynine Palms Hwy, Joshua Tree) rents and sells quality camping gear.

Along Park Blvd, Jumbo Rocks has sheltered rock alcoves that act as perfect sunset- and sunrise-viewing platforms. Belle and White Tank also have boulder-embracing views. Hidden Valley is always busy. Sheep

Pass and Ryan are also centrally located campgrounds. Family-friendly Black Rock is good for camping novices; more remote Indian Cove also has 100-plus sites. Cottonwood, near the park's southern entrance, is popular with RVs.

✗ Eating

Yucca Valley has several large supermarkets, as well as the tiny **Earth Wise Organic Farms**, at the turnoff to Pioneertown Rd, a co-op that sells produce grown by local farmers. On Saturday mornings, locals gather for gossip and groceries at the **farmers market** in a parking lot near Joshua Tree Health Foods, just west of Park Blvd in Joshua Tree.

Ricochet Gourmet　　INTERNATIONAL $
(www.ricochetjoshuatree.com; 61705 Twentynine Palms Hwy, Joshua Tree; mains $8-15; ⊗7am-5pm Mon-Sat, 8am-5pm Sun; 🛜🍷) At this neighborhood-adored cafe-cum-deli the menu bounces from breakfast frittatas to curry chicken salad and fragrant soups, all of them homemade with organic and seasonal ingredients.

Restaurant at 29 Palms Inn　　AMERICAN $$
(☎760-367-3505, www.29palmsinn.com; 73950 Inn Ave, Twentynine Palms; mains lunch $7.50-10, dinner $9-21; 🛜) This well-respected restaurant has its own organic garden and does burgers and salads at lunchtime and grilled meats and toothsome pastas for dinner.

WORTH A TRIP

BIG MORONGO CANYON PRESERVE

Named as one of California's most important bird habitat areas by no less an authority than the Audubon Society, **Big Morongo Canyon Preserve** (☎760-363-7190; 11055 East Dr, Morongo Valley; admission free; ⊗7:30am-sunset) encloses a natural spring-fed desert oasis that's a native riparian habitat where cottonwoods and willows grow. Even bighorn sheep are occasionally attracted to its watering holes. From the interpretive kiosk at the entrance, wooden boardwalks pleasantly meander through marshy woodlands. The entrance is in Morongo Valley, off Hwy 62, about a 25-minute drive west of Joshua Tree, towards I-10.

JT's Country Kitchen　　BREAKFAST, ASIAN $
(☎760-366-8988; 61768 Twentynine Palms Hwy, Joshua Tree; mains $4-10; ⊗6am-3:30pm) This roadside shack serves down-home cookin': eggs, pancakes, biscuits with gravy, sandwiches and...what's this? Cambodian noodles and salads? Delish.

Sam's　　PIZZA, INDIAN $
(☎760-366-9511; 61380 Twentynine Palms Hwy, Joshua Tree; mains $8-11; ⊗11am-9pm Mon-Sat, 3-8pm Sun; 🍴) Sure, there's pizza but clued-in locals flock to Sam's for the flavor-packed Indian curries, many of them meatless and also available for takeout.

Crossroads Cafe　　AMERICAN $
(☎760-366-5414; 61715 Twentynine Palms Hwy, Joshua Tree; ⊗7am-9pm daily) Following a total makeover, the much-loved Crossroads may have a new look but is still the go-to place for carbo-loaded breakfasts, fresh sandwiches and dragged-through-the-garden salads that make both omnivores and vegans happy.

Pie for the People　　PIZZA $
(☎760-366-0400; 61740 Twentynine Palms Hwy, Joshua Tree; slices $3-4, pies from $11; ⊗11am-9pm Mon & Thu, to 10pm Fri & Sat, to 8pm Sun) Yummy pizzas for takeout and delivery.

Mango Hut　　FILIPINO $$
(☎760-367-4488; www.themangohut.com; 6427 Mesquite Ave #A, Twentynine Palms; mains $7-16; ⊗10am-9pm Sun, Mon, Wed & Thu, 8am-10pm Fri & Sat) American and Filipino breakfasts, burgers and meat platters.

☿ Drinking & Entertainment

There's also live music at Pappy & Harriet's in Pioneertown (p674).

Joshua Tree Saloon　　BAR
(http://thejoshuatreesaloon.com; 61835 Twentynine Palms Hwy, Joshua Tree; mains $9-17; ⊗8am-late; 🛜) This watering hole with jukebox, pool tables and cowboy flair serves bar food along with rib-sticking burgers and steaks. Most people come here for the nightly entertainment, such as open-mike Tuesdays, karaoke Wednesdays and DJ Fridays. Over 21 only.

🛍 Shopping

Wind Walkers　　CRAFT
(http://windwalkershoppe.com; 61731 Twentynine Palms Hwy, Joshua Tree) This neat place has an entire courtyard with pottery large and small as well as a hand-picked selection of

WHAT THE...?

In 1947 former aerospace engineer George van Tassel moved his family to a patch of dusty desert north of Joshua Tree. The land included a freestanding boulder, beneath which local desert rat Frank Critzer had excavated a series of rooms. Van Tassel started meditating in these rooms and, as the story goes, was visited in August 1953 by a flying saucer from Venus. The aliens invited him aboard and taught him the technique for rejuvenating living cells. Van Tassel used his otherworldly knowledge to build the **Integratron** (☏760-364-3126; www.integratron.com; 2477 Belfield Blvd, Landers; sound baths from $10, private tours from $60), a wooden domed structure that he variously called a time machine, an antigravity device and a rejuvenation chamber. Judge for yourself by taking a personal tour or a sonic healing bath, in which crystal bowls are struck under the acoustically perfect dome. Check the website for special events like UFO symposiums. Public sound baths are conducted at noon on two weekends a month (the website has dates). All other visits are by appointment only.

Native American crafts, silver jewelry, blankets and knickknacks.

Red Arrow Gallery   ART
(www.theredarrowgallery.com; 61597 Twentynine Palm Hwy, Joshua Tree; ⊙5-8pm Fri, noon-5pm Sat & Sun) It's always worth dropping by to see what's up on the walls of this well-respected gallery that often showcases local artists.

Funky & Darn Near New   VINTAGE
(55812 Twentynine Palms Hwy, Yucca Valley) At her large store just west of the Pioneertown Rd turnoff, Evelyn sells immaculate hand-picked vintage dresses and hand-tailored new clothing at fair prices.

Ricochet Wears   VINTAGE
(61705 Twentynine Palms Hwy, Joshua Tree; ⊙11am-3pm Fri & Mon, 10am-3pm Sat & Sun) Great assortment of recycled clothing and accessories, including cowboy shirts and boots along with some neat old aprons.

ℹ Information

Joshua Tree National Park (☏760-367-5500; www.nps.gov/jotr) is flanked by I-10 in the south and by Hwy 62 (Twentynine Palms Hwy) in the north. Entry permits ($15 per vehicle) are valid for seven days and come with a map and the seasonally updated *Joshua Tree Guide*.

There are no facilities inside the park other than restrooms, so gas up and bring drinking water and whatever food you need. Potable water is available at the Oasis of Mara, the Black Rock and Cottonwood campgrounds, the West Entrance and the Indian Cove ranger station.

Cell phones don't work in the park, but there's an emergency-only telephone at the Intersection Rock parking lot near the Hidden Valley Campground.

Pets must be kept on leash and are prohibited on trails.

Internet Access
Coyote Corner (6535 Park Blvd, Joshua Tree; ⊙9am-7pm) Free wi-fi for customers.
Joshua Tree Outfitters (61707 Twentynine Palms Hwy, Joshua Tree; per 15min $2; ⊙usually 9am-5pm)
San Bernardino County Library Joshua Tree (6465 Park Blvd; ⊙10am-6pm Mon-Fri, to 2pm Sat); Twentynine Palms (6078 Adobe Rd; ⊙noon-8pm Mon & Tue, 10am-6pm Wed-Fri, 9am-5pm St) Free wi-fi and internet terminals.

Medical Services
Hi-Desert Medical Center (☏760-366-3711; 6601 Whitefeather Rd, Joshua Tree; ⊙24hr)

Tourist Information
Black Rock Park Nature Center (9800 Black Rock Canyon Rd, south of Hwy 62; ⊙8am-4pm Sat-Thu, noon-8pm Fri Oct-May) At the Black Rock Campground.
Cottonwood Visitor Center (Cottonwood Spring Rd, north of I-10; ⊙9am-3pm) Just inside the park's south entrance.
Joshua Tree Chamber of Commerce (☏760-366-3723; www.joshuatreechamber.org; 6448 Hallee Rd; ⊙10am-4pm Tue, Thu & Sat) Near Sam's in Joshua Tree.
Joshua Tree Park Visitor Center (Park Blvd, Joshua Tree; ⊙8am-5pm) Outside the west entrance.
Oasis Park Visitor Center (National Park Blvd, at Utah Trail, Twentynine Palms; ⊙8am-5pm) Outside the north entrance.
Twentynine Palms Chamber of Commerce (☏760-367-3445; www.visit29.org; 73484 Twentynine Palms, Twentynine Palms; ⊙9am-5pm Mon-Fri, 10am-4pm Sat & Sun)

WORTH A TRIP

TURN BACK THE CLOCK AT PIONEERTOWN

Turn north off Hwy 62 onto Pioneertown Rd in Yucca Valley and drive 5 miles straight into the past. Looking like an 1870s frontier town, Pioneertown (www.pioneertown.com; admission free; ◎) was actually built in 1946 as a Hollywood Western outdoor movie set. Gene Autry and Roy Rogers were among the original investors and more than 50 movies and several TV shows were filmed here in the 1940s and '50s. These days the Pioneertown Posse stages free mock gunfights on 'Mane St' at 2:30pm on Saturdays and Sundays from April to October.

For local color, toothsome BBQ, cheap beer and kick-ass live music, drop in at Pappy & Harriet's Pioneertown Palace (☏760-365-5956; www.pappyandharriets.com; 53688 Pioneertown Rd; burgers $5-12, mains $16-30; ◎11am-2am Thu-Sun, 5pm-midnight Mon), a textbook honky-tonk. Monday's open-mike nights are legendary and often bring out astounding talent.

Within staggering distance is the atmospheric Pioneertown Motel (☏760-365-7001; www.pioneertown-motel.com; 5040 Curtis Rd; r $50-100; ❋☎), where yesteryear's silver-screen stars once slept during filming and whose rooms are now filled with eccentric Western-themed memorabilia; some have kitchenettes.

About 4.5 miles north of here, Rimrock Ranch Cabins (☏760-228-1297; www.rimrock ranchcabins.com; 50857 Burns Canyon Rd, Pioneertown; cabins $90-140; ❋❋❋) is a cluster of four vintage 1940s cabins with kitchens and private patios perfect for stargazing.

ℹ Getting There & Around

Rent a car in Palm Springs or LA. From LA, the trip takes about 2½ to three hours via I-10 and Hwy 62. From Palm Springs it takes about an hour to reach the park's west (preferable) or south entrances.

Bus 1, operated by Morongo Basin Transit Authority (www.mbtabus.com), runs frequently along Twentynine Palms Hwy (one-way fares $1 to $2, day pass $3). Bus 12 to Palm Springs from Joshua Tree and Yucca Valley (one way/round-trip $7/11) has fewer departures. Many buses are equipped with bicycle racks.

ANZA-BORREGO DESERT STATE PARK

Shaped by an ancient sea and tectonic forces, enormous and little-developed Anza-Borrego covers 640,000 acres, making it the largest state park in the USA outside Alaska. Human history here goes back more than 10,000 years, as recorded by Native American pictographs and petroglyphs. The park is named for Spanish explorer Juan Bautista de Anza, who arrived in 1774, pioneering a colonial trail from Mexico and no doubt running into countless *borregos,* the wild peninsular bighorn sheep that once ranged as far south as Baja California. (Today only a few hundred of these animals survive, having been endangered by drought, disease,

poaching and off-highway driving.) In the 1850s Anza-Borrego became a stop along the Butterfield stagecoach line, which delivered mail between St Louis and San Francisco.

Winter and spring are the high seasons here. Depending on winter rains, wildflowers bloom brilliantly, albeit briefly, starting in late February, making a striking contrast to the subtle earth tones of the desert. Summers are extremely hot; the daily average temperature in July is 107°F (41°C), but it can reach 125°F (51°C).

◉ Sights & Activities

The park's main town, Borrego Springs (population 3429) has a handful of restaurants and lodgings. On the outskirts of town you'll find the park visitors center and easy-to-reach sights, such as Borrego Palm Canyon and Fonts Point, that are fairly representative of the park as a whole. The Split Mountain area, east of Ocotillo Wells, is popular with off-highway vehicles (OHVs), but also contains interesting geology and spectacular wind caves. The desert's southernmost region is the least visited and, aside from Blair Valley, has few developed trails and facilities. Besides solitude its attractions include historic sites and hot springs.

Many of the most awesome sights are accessible only by dirt roads. To find out which roads require 4WD vehicles, or are currently impassable, check the signboard inside the park visitors center.

Peg Leg Smith Monument MONUMENT
The pile of rocks by the road northeast of Borrego Springs, where County Rte S22 takes a 90-degree turn east, is actually a monument to Thomas Long 'Peg Leg' Smith – mountain man, fur trapper, horse thief, con artist and Wild West legend. He passed through Borrego Springs in 1829 and allegedly picked up some rocks that were later found to be pure gold. Strangely, when he returned during the Gold Rush era, he was unable to locate the lode. Nevertheless, he told lots of prospectors about it (often in exchange for a few drinks) and many came to search for the 'lost' gold and add to the myths.

Fonts Point LOOKOUT
East of Borrego Springs, a 4-mile dirt road, sometimes passable without 4WD (check at the visitors center), diverges south from County Rte S22 out to Fonts Point (1249ft). From up here a spectacular panorama unfolds over the Borrego Valley to the west and the Borrego Badlands to the south. You'll be amazed when the desert seemingly drops from beneath your feet.

Vallecito County Park HISTORIC SITE
(☑760-765-1188; www.co.san-diego.ca.us/parks; 37349 County Rte S2; admission per car $3; ☺Sep-May) This pretty little park in a refreshing valley in the southern part of the park centers on a replica of a historic Butterfield Stage Station. It's 36 miles south of Borrego Springs via County Rte S2. See p678 for camping information.

Agua Caliente County Park HOT SPRINGS
(☑760-765-1188; www.co.san-diego.ca.us/parks; 39555 County Rte S2; admission per car $3; ☺Sep-May) In a lovely park 4 miles from Vallecito, you can take a dip in indoor and outdoor pools fed by hot natural mineral springs. See p678 for camping information.

Hiking

Borrego Palm Canyon Trail HIKING
This popular 3-mile loop trail starts at the top of Borrego Palm Canyon Campground, 1 mile north of the visitors center, and goes past a palm grove and waterfall, a delightful oasis in the dry, rocky countryside. Keep an eye out for bighorn sheep.

Maidenhair Falls Trail HIKING
This plucky trail starts from the Hellhole Canyon Trailhead, 2 miles west of the visitors center on County Rte S22, and climbs for 3 miles past several palm oases to a seasonal waterfall that supports bird life and a variety of plants.

Ghost Mountain Trail HIKING
A steep 2-mile round-trip trail climbs to the remains of the 1930s adobe homestead built by desert recluse Marshall South and his family. Pick it up in Blair Valley, at the Little Pass primitive campground.

Pictograph/Smuggler's Canyon Trail HIKING
In Blair Valley this 2-mile round-trip trail skirts boulders covered in Native American pictographs and also offers a nice view of the Vallecito Valley. Take the Blair Valley turnoff on County Rte S2, and continue on the dirt road for about 3.8 miles to the turnoff for a parking area reached in another 1.5 miles.

Elephant Tree Trail HIKING
The rare elephant trees get their name from their stubby trunks, which are thought to resemble elephant legs. Unfortunately only one living elephant tree remains along this 1.5-mile loop trail but it's still a nice, easy hike through a rock wash. The turnoff is on Split Mountain Rd, about 6 miles south of Hwy 78 and Ocotillo Wells.

Split Mountain Wind Caves HIKING
Four miles south of the Elephant Tree Trail, on Split Mountain Rd, is the dirt-road turnoff for Fish Creek primitive campground; another 4 miles brings you to Split Mountain, where a popular 4WD road goes right between 600ft-high walls created by earthquakes and erosion. At the southern end of this 2-mile-long gorge, a steep 1-mile trail leads up to delicate wind caves carved into sandstone outcrops.

Blair Valley OUTDOORS
In the west of the park, about 5 miles southeast of Scissors Crossing (where County Rte S2 crosses Hwy 78), is Blair Valley, known for its Native American pictographs and *morteros* (hollows in rocks used for grinding seeds). The valley and its hiking trailheads lie a few miles east of County Rte S2, along a dirt road. Over on the north side of the valley, a monument at Foot and Walker Pass marks a difficult spot on the Butterfield Overland Stage Route. In Box Canyon you can see the marks where wagons had to hack through the rocks to widen the Emigrant Trail.

Anza-Borrego Desert State Park

0 ____ 10 km
0 ____ 6 miles

Hoberg Rd 0 ____ 2 km
0 ____ 1 mile

Anza-Borrego Desert State Visitor Center
20 Borrego Desert Nature Center
Christmas Circle
26
24
Palm Canyon Dr
19 25
27 Borrego Springs Chamber of Commerce
21

Coyote Creek

Clark Dry Lake

Borrego Springs

4

S22

To Salton Sea (20mi)

San Ysidro Peak (6147ft)
22
18
7
See Enlargement
S3
Borrego Palm Canyon
13
10
23
Palm Canyon Dr

2
Anza Trail
Borrego Badlands

Pinyon Ridge
Grapevine Canyon

S22

Borrego Sink

San Felipe Creek

Ocotillo Wells State Vehicular Recreation Area

Buttes Pass Rd

Pacific Crest Trail

S2

9
17
6
S3
Yaqui Pass Rd

78

Old Kane Springs Rd

Ocotillo Wells

To Julian (8mi)
78

14

Vallecito Mountains

11

Split Mountain Rd

Granite Mtn (5633ft)

Pinyon Mtn Rd
3
Blair Valley
15
12
Whale Peak (5320ft)

Fish Creek Primitive Campground

Split Mtn (519ft)
16

8
S2

5

Garnet Peak (5905ft)

1

Carrizo Badlands

S1

Vallecito Creek

Carrizo Creek

Canyon Sin Nombre

Pacific Crest Trail

8

Bow Willow Campground

Jacumba Mountains

S2

To San Diego (50mi)

To I-8 (8mi)

Anza-Borrego Desert State Park

Cyoling

Over 500 miles of the park's dirt and paved roads (but never hiking trails) are open to bikes. Popular routes are Grapevine Canyon off Hwy 78 and Canyon Sin Nombre in the Carrizo Badlands. Flatter areas include Blair Valley and Split Mountain. Get details at the visitors center. **Carrizo Bikes** (☑760-767-3872; 3278 Wagon Rd, Borrego Springs) rents bikes and does repairs.

🎉 Festivals & Events

Peg Leg Smith Liars Contest   CULTURAL
In this hilarious event on the first Saturday of April, amateur liars compete in the Western tradition of telling tall tales. Anyone can enter, so long as the story is about gold and mining in the Southwest, is less than five minutes long and is anything but the truth.

🛏 Sleeping

Free backcountry camping is permitted anywhere that's off-road and at least 100ft from water. There are also several free primitive campgrounds with pit toilets but no water in the park. All campfires must be in metal containers. Gathering vegetation (dead or alive) is strictly prohibited.

Room rates drop significantly in summer; some places close altogether.

TOP CHOICE **Palms at Indian Head**   BOUTIQUE HOTEL **$$**
(☑760-767-7788; www.thepalmsatindianhead.com; 2220 Hoberg Rd, Borrego Springs; r $170-250; ❋❄) This former haunt of Cary Grant, Marilyn Monroe and other old-time celebs has been reborn as a chic Mid-Century Modern retreat. Connect with the era over martinis and chicken cordon bleu at the on-site bar and grill while enjoying mesmerizing desert views.

TOP CHOICE **Borrego Valley Inn**   BOUTIQUE HOTEL **$$**
(☑760-767-0311; www.borregovalleyinn.com; 405 Palm Canyon Dr, Borrego Springs; r incl breakfast $185-275; ❋❄❅❄) This petite, immaculately kept inn, filled with Southwestern knickknacks and Native American weavings, is an intimate spa-resort, perfect for adults. One pool is clothing-optional. Most rooms have kitchenettes. The grounds are entirely non-smoking.

Palm Canyon Resort   MOTEL **$$**
(☑760-767-5341; www.palmcanyonresort.com; 221 Palm Canyon Dr, Borrego Springs; r $90-215; ❄❅❄) For that Old West flair, check into this welcoming motel, but don't be fooled: the place was only built in the '80s! It's about a mile from the park's visitors center

and has two pools for unwinding and a restaurant and saloon for sustenance.

Hacienda del Sol HOTEL $

(☎760-767-5442; www.haciendadelsol-borrego. com; 610 Palm Canyon Dr, Borrego Springs; r/duplex/cottages $75/120/160; ☎❄❖) Bask in the retro glow of this small hotel that's been put through some upgrades and now sports new beds and DVD players (free DVD rentals). Choose from hotel rooms, cottages and duplex units. The pool is great for relaxing or socializing.

Borrego Palm Canyon Campground CAMPGROUND $

(☎reservations 800-444-7275; www.reserveam erica.com; tent/RV sites with hookups $25/35) Near the visitors center this campground has award-winning toilets, close-together campsites and an amphitheater with ranger programs.

Agua Caliente County Park CAMPGROUND $

(☎reservations 858-565-3600; www.co.san-diego. ca.us/parks; 39555 County Rte S2; tent sites $19, RV sites with partial/full hookups $24/28; ☺Sep-May; ❖) A good choice for sociable RVers, with natural hot-spring pools.

Vallecito County Park CAMPGROUND $

(☎reservations 858-565-3600; www.co.san-diego. ca.us/parks; 37349 County Rte S2; tent & RV sites $19; ☺Sep-May; ❖) Has more tent-friendly sites, in a cool, green valley refuge.

✖ Eating & Drinking

In summer many places keep shorter hours or close additional days. Self-caterers can stock up at the **Center Market** (590 Palm Canyon Dr; ☺8:30am-6:30pm Mon-Sat, to 5pm Sun) in Borrego Springs.

TOP CHOICE French Corner FRENCH $$

(☎760-767-5713; 721 Avenida Sureste, Borrego Springs; mains $15-25; ☺11am-2:30pm & 5-9pm Wed-Sun Oct-May) For a taste of Europe stop by this antique shop–cum-bistro where owners Yves and Elyan will tempt you with hearty beef bourguignonne, light quiches, sweet and salted crepes, and even garlic-drenched escargot (snails). Be sure to try their homemade pâté and don't skip dessert (the crème brûlée rocks).

Red Ocotillo AMERICAN $$

(☎760-767-7788; 2220 Hobert Rd; mains $10-36; ☺7am-9pm; ❖) Thumbs up for the unfussy fare at this popular restaurant at the Palms

at Indian Head hotel. Regulars swear by the eggs benedict and finger-lickin' herbed home fries but the plump burgers also get our vote. Fabulous desert views, especially from the patio.

Carmelita's Bar & Grill MEXICAN $$

(575 Palm Canyon Dr; breakfast $5-9, lunch & dinner $9.50-14; ☺10am-9pm Mon-Fri, 8am-9pm Sat & Sun; ❖) This lively joint with its cheerful decor serves the best Mexican food in town, including delicious huevos rancheros. The bar staff knows how to whip up a good margarita.

Arches AMERICAN $$

(☎760-767-5700; 1112 Tilting T Dr, Borrego Springs; mains $9-25; ☺7am-9pm) Enjoy sweeping views of the golf course from your linen-draped table at this fine-dining restaurant at the Borrego Springs Resort. The eclectic menu mixes Tex-Mex with salads and meaty mains, including prime rib on weekend nights. The Fireside Lounge is a fine place to wrap up the day.

Carlee's Place AMERICAN $$

(☎760-767-3262; 660 Palm Canyon Dr, Borrego Springs; mains lunch $7-14, dinner $12-23; ☺11am-9pm) Even though the decor feels like it hasn't been updated since the 1970s, locals pick Carlee's for its burgers, pastas and steak dinners. The pool table, live music and karaoke are big draws, too.

ⓘ Information

Driving through the park is free but if you camp, hike or picnic, a day fee of $8 per car applies. You'll need a 4WD to tackle the 500 miles of backcountry dirt road.

Borrego Springs has stores, ATMs, banks, gas stations, a post office and a public library with free internet access and wi-fi. Cell phones may work in Borrego Springs but nowhere else.

Borrego Desert Nature Center (☎760-767-3098; www.california-desert.org; 652 Palm Canyon Dr, Borrego Springs; ☺9am-5pm daily Sep-Jun, 9am-3pm Fri & Sat Jul & Aug) An excellent bookshop run by the Anza-Borrego Desert Natural History Association, which also organizes tours, lectures, guided hikes and outdoor-skills courses.

Chamber of Commerce (☎760-767-5555; www.borregospringschamber.com; 786 Palm Canyon Dr, Borrego Springs; ☺9am-4pm Mon-Sat) Tourist information.

Visitors center (☎760-767-4205; www.parks. ca.gov; 200 Palm Canyon Dr, Borrego Springs; ☺9am-5pm daily Oct-May, Sat & Sun only Jun-Sep, subject to change because of budget cuts)

EASY HIKES IN ANZA-BORREGO

» **Bill Kenyon Overlook** This 1-mile loop from Yaqui Pass primitive campground rolls out to a viewpoint over the San Felipe Wash, the Pinyon Mountains and, on clear days, the Salton Sea.

» **Yaqui Well Trail** A 2-mile trail that leads past labeled desert plants and a natural water hole that attracts a rich variety of birds; starts opposite Tamarisk Grove campground.

» **Narrows Earth Trail** Some 4.5 miles east of Tamarisk Grove along Hwy 78, this 0.5-mile path is an amateur geologist's dream walk through a fault zone. Look for low-lying, brilliant-red chuparosa shrubs, which attract hummingbirds.

» **Cactus Loop Trail** A self-guided 1-mile round-trip past a great variety of cacti; starts across from Tamarisk campground and delivers nice views of San Felipe Wash.

Built partly underground, the stone walls of the park visitors center blend beautifully with the mountain backdrop, while inside are top-notch displays and audiovisual presentations. Two miles west of Borrego Springs.

Wildflower Hotline (☑760-767-4684)

ℹ Getting There & Around

There is no public transport to Anza-Borrego Desert State Park. From Palm Springs (1½ hours) take I-10 to Indio, then Hwy 86 south along the Salton Sea and west onto S22. From LA (three hours) and Orange County (via Temecula) take I-15 south to Hwy 79 to County Rtes S2 and S22. From San Diego (two hours) I-8 to County Rte S2 is easiest but if you want a more scenic ride, take twisty Hwy 79 from I-8 north through Cuyamaca Rancho State Park and into Julian, then head east on Hwy 78.

AROUND ANZA-BORREGO

Julian

The mountain hamlet of Julian, with its three-block main street, is a favorite getaway for city folk who love its quaint 1870s streetscape, gold-mining lore and famous apple pies. Prospectors, including many Confederate veterans, arrived here after the Civil War, but the population did not explode until the discovery of flecks of gold in 1869. Today, apples are the new gold. There are nearly 17,000 trees in the orchards flanking Hwy 78 outside town. The harvest takes place in early fall when some farmers may let you pick your own apples. At any time, at least taste a slice of delicious apple pie, sold at bakeries all over town.

Julian sits at the junction of Hwys 78 and 79. It's about 1¼ hours from San Diego (via I-8 east to Hwy 79 north) and 40 minutes from Borrego Springs Head (south over Yaqui Pass on County Rte S3, then Hwy 78 west).

For more information, contact the **Chamber of Commerce** (☑760-765-1857; www.julianca.com; 2129 Main St; ☉10am-4pm).

◉ Sights

Eagle & High Peak Mine   MINE
(☑760-765-0036; end of C St; adult/child $10/5; ☉call for hours; ♿) Be regaled with tales of the hardscrabble life of the town's early pioneers during an hour-long underground tour through these former gold mines.

🛏 Sleeping & Eating

Julian Gold Rush Hotel   HOTEL $$
(☑760-765-0201; www.julianhotel.com; 2032 Main St; r $135-210) At this 1897 antique-filled B&B, lace curtains, claw-foot tubs and other paraphernalia painstakingly evoke a bygone era.

Orchard Hill Country Inn   B&B $$$
(☑760-765-1700; www.orchardhill.com; 2502 Washington St; r $195-250, cottage $295-375, all incl breakfast; @🕏) Turn back the clock at this romantic B&B where rooms are spread across a Craftsman lodge and a dozen cozy cottages, all furnished with impeccable taste. Each is decorated differently but all feature a fireplace or patio; some also have whirlpool tubs.

Julian Pie Company   PIES $
(2225 Main St; ☉9am-5pm) This popular joint churns out apple cider, cinnamon-dusted cider donuts and classic apple-filled pies and pastries.

WHAT THE...?

Southeast of the Salton Sea, **Salvation Mountain** (www.salvationmountain.us) is a mighty strange sight indeed: a 100ft-high hill of concrete and hand-mixed adobe slathered in colorful paint and found objects (hay bales, tires, telephone poles) and inscribed with religious messages. The vision of Leonard Knight, it's been three decades in the making and has become one of the great works of American folk art that's even been recognized as a national treasure in the US Senate. It's in Niland, about 3 miles off Hwy 111, via Main St.

Salton Sea

Driving along Hwy 111 southeast of Indio, it's a most unexpected sight: California's largest lake in the middle of its largest desert. The Salton Sea has a fascinating past, complicated present and uncertain future.

Geologists say that the Gulf of California once extended 150 miles north of the present-day Coachella Valley, but millions of years' worth of rich silt flowing through the Colorado River gradually cut it off, leaving a sink behind. By the mid-1800s the sink was the site of salt mines and geologists realized that the mineral-rich soil would make excellent farmland. Colorado River water was diverted into irrigation canals.

In 1905 the Colorado River breached, giving birth to the Salton Sea. It took 18 months, 1500 workers and 500,000 tons of rock to put the river back on course, but with no natural outlet, the water was here to stay. Today, the Salton Sea is about 35 miles long and 15 miles wide and has water that is 30% saltier than the Pacific Ocean.

By mid-century the Salton Sea was stocked with fish and marketed as the 'California Riviera'; vacation homes lined its shores. The fish, in turn, attracted birds, and the sea remains a prime spot for bird-watching, including migratory and endangered species such as snow geese, eared grebes, ruddy ducks, white and brown pelicans, bald eagles and peregrine falcons.

These days, if you've heard of the Salton Sea at all, it's probably due to annual fish die-offs, which are caused by phosphorous and nitrogen in agricultural runoff from nearby farmland. The minerals cause algal blooms, and when the algae die they deprive the water – and fish – of oxygen. Even if farming were to stop tomorrow, there are still generations' worth of minerals in the soil, waiting to reach the sink.

One solution would seem to be to cut off the water to the sea and let it die, but that carries its own dilemma. A dry Salton Sea would leave a dust bowl with a potential dust cloud that could widely devastate the local air quality. The debate rages on.

Alas, at the time of writing, the **Salton Sea State Recreation Area** (☎760-393-3052; www.parks.ca.gov), on the north shore, was slated for closure due to budget cuts. Further south, **Sonny Bono Salton Sea National Wildlife Refuge** (www.fws.gov/saltonsea; 906 W Sinclair Rd, Calipatria; ⏲sunrise-sunset, visitors center 7am-3:15pm Mon-Fri year-round, 10am-2pm Sat & Sun Oct-Feb) is a major migratory stopover along the Pacific Flyway and has a visitors center, a short self-guided trail, an observation tower and a picnic area. It's about 4 miles west of Hwy 111, between Niland and Calipatria.

ROUTE 66

Completed in 1926, iconic Route 66 connected Chicago and Los Angeles across the heartland of America. What novelist John Steinbeck called the 'Mother Road' came into its own during the Depression, when thousands of migrants escaped the Dust Bowl by slogging westward in beat-up old jalopies painted with 'California or Bust' signs, *Grapes of Wrath*–style. After WWII Americans took their newfound wealth and convertible cars on the road to get their kicks on Route 66.

As traffic along the USA's post-WWII interstate highway system boomed, many small towns along Route 66, with their neon-signed motor courts, diners and drive-ins, eventually went out of business. Every year another landmark goes up for sale, but more get rescued from ruin.

In California Route 66 mostly follows the National Old Trails Hwy, which is prone to potholes and dangerous bumps. From the beach in Santa Monica, it rumbles through the LA basin, crosses over the Cajon Pass to the railroad towns of Barstow and Victorville and runs a gauntlet of Mojave Desert ghost towns, arriving in Needles near the Nevada stateline.

Los Angeles to Barstow

Route 66 kicks off in Santa Monica, at the intersection of Ocean Ave and Santa Monica Blvd. Follow the latter through Beverly Hills and West Hollywood, turn right on Sunset Blvd and pick up the 110 Fwy north to Pasadena. Take exit 31B and drive south on Fair Oaks Ave for an egg cream at the Fair Oaks Pharmacy (☑626-799-1414; www.fairoakspharmacy.net; 1526 Mission St, South Pasadena; mains $4.50-10; ☺9am-9pm Mon-Sat, 10am-7pm Sun; ♨), a nostalgic soda fountain from 1915. Turn around and follow Fair Oaks Ave north, then turn right on Colorado Blvd, where the vintage Saga Motor Hotel (☑626-795-0431; www.thesagamotorhotel.com; 1633 E Colorado Blvd, Pasadena; r $92-135; ❋❀☎♨) still hands out quaint metal room keys to its guests.

Continue east on Colorado Blvd to Colorado Pl and Santa Anita Park (☑626-574-7223, tour reservations 626-574-6677; www.santaanita.com; 285 W Huntington Dr, Arcadia; ☺racing 26 Dec-20 Apr), where the Marx Brothers' *A Day at the Races* was filmed and legendary thoroughbred Seabiscuit ran. During the live racing season, free tram tours take you behind the scenes into the jockeys' room and training areas; weekends only, reservations required.

Colorado Pl turns into Huntington Dr E, which you'll follow to 2nd Ave, where you turn north, then east on Foothill Blvd. This older alignment of Route 66 follows Foothill Blvd through Monrovia, where the 1925 Mayan Revival–style architecture of the allegedly haunted Aztec Hotel (311 W Foothill Blvd, Monrovia) is worth a look. In May 2011, however, the building went into foreclosure and its fate remained uncertain at the time of writing.

Continue east on W Foothill Blvd, then jog south on S Myrtle Ave and hook a left on E Huntington Dr through Duarte, which puts on a Route 66 parade (http://duarteroute66parade.com) every September, with boisterous marching bands, old-fashioned carnival games and a classic-car show. In Azusa, Huntington turns into E Foothill Blvd, which becomes Alosta Blvd in Glendora where The Hat (☑626-857-0017; 611 W Rte 66, Glendora; mains $3-7.50; ☺10am-11pm Sun-Thu, to 1am Fri & Sat; ♨) has made piled-high pastrami sandwiches since 1951.

Continue east on Foothill Blvd, where two campily retro steakhouses await in Rancho Cucamonga. First up is the 1955 Magic Lamp Inn (☑909-981-8659; 8189 Foothill Blvd, Rancho Cucamonga; lunch $11-17, dinner $15-42; ☺11:30am-2:30pm Tue-Fri, 5-11pm Tue-Thu, 5-10:30pm Fri & Sat, 4-9pm Sun), easily recognized by its fabulous neon sign. There's dancing Wednesday through Saturday nights. Up the road, the rustic Sycamore Inn (☑909-982-1104; www.thesycamoreinn.com; 8318 Foothill Blvd, Rancho Cucamonga; mains $22-49; ☺5-9pm Mon-Thu, to 10pm Fri & Sat, 4-8:30pm Sun) has been dishing up juicy steaks since 1848.

Cruising on through Fontana, birthplace of the notorious Hells Angels biker club, you'll see the now-boarded-up Giant Orange (15395 Foothill Blvd, Fontana), a 1920s juice stand of the kind that was once a fixture alongside SoCal's citrus groves.

Foothill Blvd continues on to Rialto where you'll find the Wigwam Motel (☑909-875-3005; www.wigwammotel.com; 2728 W Foothill Blvd, San Bernardino; r $65-82; ❋❀☎) whose kooky concrete faux tipis date from 1949. Continue east, then head north on N East St to the First McDonald's Museum (☑909-885-6324; 1398 N E St, San Bernadino; admission by donation; ☺10am-5pm), which has interesting historic Route 66 exhibits. Continue north, then turn left on W Highland Ave and pick up the I-215 Fwy to I-15 and exit at Cleghorn for Cajon Blvd to trundle north on an ancient section of the Mother Road. Get back onto I-15 and drive up to the Cajon Pass. At the top, take the Oak Hill Rd exit (No 138) to the Summit Inn Cafe (☑760-949-8688; 5960 Mariposa Rd, Oak Hills; mains $5-12; ☺6am-8pm Mon-Thu, to 9pm Fri & Sat), a 1950s roadside diner with antique gas pumps, a retro jukebox and a lunch counter that serves ostrich burgers and date shakes.

Get back on I-15 and drive downhill to Victorville, exiting at 7th St and driving past the San Bernardino County Fairgrounds, home of the Route 66 Raceway. Follow 7th St to D St and turn left for the excellent

ⓘ **NAVIGATING THE MOTHER ROAD**

For Route 66 enthusiasts who want to drive every mile of the old highway, free turn-by-turn driving directions are available online at www.historic66.com. Also surf to www.cart66pf.org and www.route66ca.org for more historical background, photos and info about special events.

California Route 66 Museum (www.calif rt66museum.org; 16825 South D St, Victorville; donations welcome; ⊙10am-4pm Thu-Sat & Mon, 11am-3pm Sun), inside the old Red Rooster Cafe opposite the train station. There you'll discover a wonderfully eclectic collection of 1930s teardrop trailers, sparkling red naughahyde booths with tabletop mini-jukeboxes and bits and pieces from the Roy Rogers Museum that used to be in Victorville before moving to Branson, Missouri, where it closed in 2010.

Follow South D St north under I-15 where it turns into the National Trails Hwy. Beloved by Harley bikers, this rural stretch to Barstow is like a scavenger hunt for Mother Road ruins, such as antique filling stations and tumbledown motor courts.

In Oro Grande, the Iron Hog Saloon (20848 National Old Trails Hwy, Oro Grande; ⊙8am-10pm Mon-Thu & Sun, to 2am Fri & Sat) is an old-time honky-tonk dripping with memorabilia and character(s). It's hugely popular with bikers and serves large portions of rib-stickers, including rattlesnake and ostrich. Further north, Elmer's Place is a colorful roadside folk-art collection of glass bottles artfully arranged on telephone poles along with weathered railroad signs.

Barstow

At the junction of I-40 and I-15, nearly halfway between LA and Las Vegas, down-and-out Barstow (population 22,639) has been a desert travelers' crossroads for centuries. In 1776 Spanish colonial priest Francisco Garcés caravanned through, and in the mid-19th century the Old Spanish Trail passed nearby, with pioneer settlers on the Mojave River selling supplies to California immigrants. Meanwhile, mines were founded in the hills outside town. Barstow, named after a railway executive, got going as a railroad junction after 1886. After 1926 it became a major rest stop for motorists along Route 66. Today it exists to serve nearby military bases and is still a busy pit stop for travelers.

◉ Sights

Barstow is well known for its history-themed murals that spruce up often empty and boarded-up downtown buildings, mostly along Main St between 1st and 6th Sts.

FREE Route 66 'Mother Road' Museum   MUSEUM
(www.route66museum.org; 681 N 1st St; ⊙10am-4pm Fri-Sun) Inside the beautifully restored Casa del Desierto, a 1911 Harvey House designed by famed Western architect Mary Colter, this museum documents life along the historic highway with some great old black-and-white photographs alongside eclectic relics, including a 1915 Ford Model T and a 1913 telephone switchboard. The excellent gift shop stocks Route 66 driving guides, maps and books. The museum is north of Main St, across the train tracks.

Western America Railroad Museum   MUSEUM
(http://barstowrailmuseum.org; 685 N 1st St; ⊙11am-4pm Fri-Sun) Rail buffs make a beeline to another section of the Casa del Desierto to marvel at a century's worth of railroad artifacts, including old timetables, uniforms and the amazing Dog Tooth Mountain model railroad. Outside you can see historic locomotives, bright-red cabooses and even a car used to ship racehorses.

FREE Desert Discovery Center   MUSEUM
(www.discoverytrails.org; 831 Barstow Rd; ⊙11am-4pm Tue-Sat; ⊕) The star exhibit in this kid-oriented, educational center in an adobe building near I-15 is the Old Woman Meteorite, the second-largest ever found in the USA, weighing in at a hefty 6070 pounds.

Calico Ghost Town   GHOST TOWN
(☑800-862-2542; www.calicotown.com; 36600 Ghost Town Rd, Yermo; adult/child $6/5; ⊙9am-5pm; ⊕) This endearingly hokey Old West attraction consists of a cluster of reconstructed pioneer-era buildings amid the ruins of a late-19th-century silver mining town. You'll pay extra to go gold panning, tour the Maggie Mine, ride a narrow-gauge railway or see the 'mystery shack.' Old-timey heritage celebrations include Civil War reenactments and a bluegrass 'hootenanny.' There's also a campground (tent/RV sites with full hookup $25/30). Take the Ghost Town Rd exit off I-15.

🛏 Sleeping & Eating

Only when the Mojave freezes over will there be no rooms left in Barstow. Just drive along E Main St and take your pick from the string of national chain motels, many with doubles from $40.

Oak Tree Inn
MOTEL $

(☏760-254-1148; www.oaktreeinn.com; 35450 Yermo Rd, Yermo; r incl breakfast $53-74; ✦✦✦✦) For more class and comfort, steer towards this three-story motel, where rooms have black-out draperies and triple-paned windows. It's 11 miles east of town (exit Ghost Town Rd off I-15), near Calico Ghost Town. Breakfast is served at the 1950s-style diner, which is also a 24-hour truck stop.

Lola's Kitchen
MEXICAN $

(1244 E Main St; mains $5-12; ⊘4am-7:30pm Mon-Fri, to 4:30pm Sat; ✦) Interstate truckers, blue-collar workers and Vegas-bound hipsters all gather at this simple Mexican *cocina*, tucked away inside a strip mall and run by two sisters who make succulent *carne asada* burritos, *chile verde* enchiladas and more. Hot, fresh tortilla chips with spicy salsa are served while you wait.

Idle Spurs Steakhouse
STEAKHOUSE $$

(☏760-256-8888; 690 Old Hwy 58; mains lunch $8-21, dinner $13-40; ⊘11am-9pm Mon-Fri, 4-9pm Sat & Sun; ✦) In the saddle since 1950, this Western-themed spot, ringed around an atrium and a full bar, is a fave with locals and RVers. Surrender helplessly to your inner carnivore with slow-roasted prime rib, hand-cut steaks and succulent lobster tail. Kids menu available.

Texas Style BBQ
BARBECUE $

(208 E Main St; sandwiches $5.50-8.50, dinner $9-14; ⊘10am-10pm) Talk about hot! From the Lone Star state, this down-home takeout shack slow cooks succulent beef brisket, tri-tip, pork ribs, chicken and spicy sausage with baked beans and potatoes. Try its sweet-potato pie for dessert.

☆ Entertainment

Skyline Drive-In
CINEMA

(☏760-256-3333; 31175 Old Hwy 58; adult/child $6/2; ✦) One of the few drive-ins left in California, this 1960s movie theater shows one or two flicks nightly.

❶ Information

Barstow Area Chamber of Commerce (☏760-256-8617; www.barstowchamber.com; 681 N 1st Ave; ⊘8:30am-5:30pm Mon-Fri, 10am-2pm Sat) At the train station, just north of downtown.

Barstow Community Hospital (☏760-256-1761; 555 S 7th Ave; ⊘emergency room 24hr)

❶ Getting There & Around

You'll need a car to get around Barstow and to drive Route 66. A few major car-rental agencies have in-town offices.

Frequent Greyhound buses from LA ($33.50, 2½ to 5¼ hours), Las Vegas ($29, 2¾ hours) and Palm Springs ($40, 3¾ hours) arrive at the main **bus station** (1611 E Main St) east of downtown, near I-15.

Amtrak's *Southwest Chief* runs to/from LA ($51, 3¾ hours) daily but is often late. There's no staffed ticket office at Barstow's historic **train station** (685 N 1st Ave).

Barstow to Needles

Leave Barstow on I-40 east and exit at Daggett, site of the California inspection station once dreaded by Dust Bowl refugees. Drive north on A St, cross the railroad tracks and turn right on Santa Fe St. On your left, just past the general store, you'll see the moodily crumbling late-19th-century **Daggett Stone Hotel**, where desert adventurers like Death Valley Scotty (see p687) used to stay.

Continue on Santa Fe, take your first right, then turn left to pick up the National Trails Hwy going east. This potholed, crumbling backcountry stretch of Route 66 crawls through ghostly desert towns once perfectly named in backward alphabetical order.

Shortly after the highway ducks under I-40, you're in Newberry Springs, where the grizzled **Bagdad Cafe** (www.bagdadcafethereal.com; 46548 National Old Trails Hwy, Newberry Springs; mains $7-10; ⊘7am-7pm) was the main filming location of the eponymous 1987 indie flick starring CCH Pounder and Jack Palance, which was a cult hit in Europe. The interior is chockablock with posters, movie stills and memorabilia, while outside, the old water tower and airstream trailer are slowly rusting away.

The National Trails Hwy runs south along the freeway, crosses it at Lavic and continues east along the northern side of I-40. In Ludlow turn right on Crucero Rd, cross I-40 again and pick up the highway by turning left.

Beyond Ludlow Route 66 veers away from the freeway and runs past haunting ruins spliced into the majestic landscape. Only a few landmarks interrupt the limitless horizon, most famously the sign of **Roy's Motel & Cafe**, east of **Amboy Crater**, an almost perfectly symmetrical volcanic cinder cone

PALM SPRINGS & THE DESERTS ROUTE 66

that went dormant 600 years ago. You can scramble up its west side (don't attempt it in high winds or summer heat).

Past Essex the Mother Road leaves the National Trails Hwy and heads north on Goffs Rd through Fenner, where it once more crosses I-40. In Goffs the one-room 1914 Mission-style **Goffs Schoolhouse** (☑760-733-4482; www.mdhca.org; 37198 Lanfair Rd, Goffs; donations welcome; ⊘by prior arrangement) remains part of the best-preserved historic settlement in the Mojave Desert.

Continue on Goffs Rd (US Hwy 95) to I-40 East and follow it to **Needles**. Named after nearby mountain spires, it's the last Route 66 stop before the Arizona border, where the Old Trails Arch Bridge carried the Joad family across the Colorado River in *The Grapes of Wrath*.

Exit at J St and turn left, follow J St to W Broadway, turn right and then left on F St, which runs into Front St, paralleling the railway track. Go past the old mule-train wagon and 1920s Palm Motel to **El Garces**, a 1908 Harvey House that's been undergoing restorations for years.

MOJAVE NATIONAL PRESERVE

If you're on a quest for the 'middle of nowhere,' you'll find it in the wilderness of the **Mojave National Preserve** (☑760-252-6100; www.nps.gov/moja; admission free), a 1.6-million-acre jumble of sand dunes, Joshua trees, volcanic cinder cones and habitats for bighorn sheep, desert tortoises, jackrabbits and coyotes. Solitude and serenity are the big draws. Daytime temperatures hover above 100°F (37°C) during summer, then hang around 50°F (10°C) in winter, when snowstorms are not unheard of. Strong winds will practically knock you over in spring and fall. No gas is available within the preserve.

◉ Sights & Activities

You can spend an entire day or just a few hours driving around the preserve, taking in its sights and exploring some of them on foot.

Cima Dome   MOUNTAIN
Visible to the south from I-15, Cima Dome is a 1500ft hunk of granite spiked with volcanic cinder cones and crusty outcrops of basalt left by lava. Its slopes are smothered in Joshua trees that collectively make up the largest such forest in the world. For close-ups, tackle the 3-mile round-trip hike up **Teutonia Peak** (5755ft), starting on Cima Rd, 6 miles northwest of Cima.

Kelso Dunes   DUNES
Rising up to 600ft high, these beautiful 'singing' dunes are the country's third-tallest sand dunes. Under the right conditions they emanate low humming sounds that are caused by shifting sands. Running downhill sometimes jump-starts the effect. The dunes are 3 miles along a graded dirt road west of Kelbaker Rd, 7.5 miles south of Kelso Depot.

Hole-in-the-Wall   OUTDOORS
These vertical walls of rhyolite tuff (pronounced toof), which look like Swiss-cheese cliffs made of unpolished marble, are the result of a powerful prehistoric volcanic eruption that blasted rocks across the landscape. On the 0.5-mile **Rings Trail**, metal rings lead down through a narrow slot canyon, once

---

SLOW: DESERT TORTOISE X-ING

The Mojave is the home of the desert tortoise, which can live for up to 80 years, munching on wildflowers and grasses. Its canteen-like bladder allows it to go for up to a year without drinking. Using its strong hind legs, it burrows to escape the summer heat and freezing winter temperatures, and also to lay eggs. The sex of the hatchlings is determined by temperature: cooler for males, hotter for females.

Disease and shrinking habitat have decimated the desert tortoise population. They do like to rest in the shade under parked cars (take a quick look around before just driving away), and are often hit by off-road drivers. If you see a tortoise in trouble (eg stranded in the middle of a road), call a ranger.

It's illegal to pick one up or even approach too closely, and for good reason: a frightened tortoise may urinate on a perceived attacker, possibly dying of dehydration before the next rains come.

used by Native Americans to escape 19th-century ranchers. **Wild Horse Canyon Rd**, an incredibly scenic 9.5-mile backcountry drive up to Mid Hills, also starts at Hole-in-the-Wall. Ask at the visitors center if it's currently passable. Hole-in-the-Wall is on Black Canyon Rd, east of Kelso-Cima Rd via unpaved Cedar Canyon Rd. Coming from I-40, exit at Essex Rd.

Mitchell Caverns   CAVERNS
(☑760-928-2586) In the Providence Mountains in the eastern part of the reserve, these splendid caverns unlock a world of quirky limestone formations. Unfortunately, tours were suspended until further notice at press time. Call ahead for updates.

🛏 Sleeping & Eating

Baker, north of the preserve along I-15, has plenty of cheap and largely charmless motels and takeout restaurants. Southeast of the preserve, along Route 66, Needles (p684) has slightly better options.

Camping

First-come, first-served sites with pit toilets and potable water are available at two small, developed **campgrounds** (tent & RV sites $12): Hole-in-the-Wall, surrounded by rocky desert landscape; and Mid Hills (no RVs), set among pine and juniper trees. Free backcountry and roadside camping is permitted throughout the preserve in areas already used for the purpose, such as the Rainy Day Mine Site and Granite Pass off the Kelbaker Rd, and Sunrise Rock off the Cima Rd. Ask for details and directions at the visitors centers. There's no camping along paved roads, in day-use areas or within 200yd of any water source.

ℹ Information

Hole-in-the-Wall visitors center (☑760-252-6104; ⏲9am-4pm Wed-Sun Oct-Apr, Fri-Sun May-Sep) Seasonal ranger programs, backcountry information and road condition updates. It's about 20 miles north of I-40 via Essex Rd.
Kelso Depot visitors center (☑760-252-6108; Kelbaker Rd, Kelso; ⏲9am-5pm) The preserve's main visitors center is in a gracefully restored 1920s Spanish Mission revival railway depot. It is staffed with knowledgeable rangers who can help you plan your day. There are also excellent natural and cultural history exhibits as well as an old-fashioned **lunch counter** (dishes $3.50-8.50).

ℹ Getting There & Away

Mojave National Preserve is hemmed in by I-15 in the north and I-40 in the south. The main entrance off I-15 is at Baker, from where it's about 30 miles south to the central Kelso Depot visitors center via Kelbaker Rd, which links up with I-40 after another 23 miles. Cima Rd and Morning Star Mine Rd near Nipton are two other northern access roads. From I-40 Essex Rd leads to the Black Canyon Rd and Hole-in-the-Wall.

AROUND MOJAVE NATIONAL PRESERVE

Nipton

On the northeastern edge of the preserve, the teensy, remote outpost of **Nipton** (www.nipton.com) got its start in 1900 as a camp for workers in a nearby gold mine. The railway has passed through here since 1905 en route from Salt Lake City to Los Angeles. In 2010 the settlement made news when it opened a solar plant that generates 85% of its electrical needs.

The charismatic **Hotel Nipton** (☑760-856-2335; www.nipton.com; 107355 Nipton Rd; tent cabins d $65, r without bath $80, all incl breakfast; ⏲reception 8am-6pm; ❄🐾) also dates to the first decade of the 20th century. There are five rooms sharing two baths in an adobe hotel with wraparound porch, as well as 'eco-lodges' (tented cabins) equipped with electricity, fans, woodstoves and platform beds. All guests may unwind in the two outdoor hot tubs.

Check-in is at the well-stocked **trading post** (⏲8am-6pm), which has maps, books, groceries, beverages and souvenirs. Next door is the **Whistle Stop Oasis** (dishes $7-10; ⏲11am-6pm, dinner by reservation). No alcohol is served but you're welcome to purchase beer or wine at the trading post and bring it with you.

There's also an **RV park** (sites $25).

Primm

At the Nevada state line, next to an outlet shopping mall off I-15, **Terrible's Primm Valley Casino Resorts** (☑02-386-7867; www.primmvalleyresorts.com; 31900 Las Vegas Blvd S; r from $25; ❄@🐾) is a trio of casino hotels linked by a tram. Rooms are basic and long in the tooth but fine for a night. Family-friendly Buffalo Bill's is best and has its own amusement park, including a white-knuckle roller coaster and a log flume ride, as well as a buffalo-shaped swimming pool. Whiskey Pete's accepts pets ($15 fee). Primm Valley Hotel & Casino, across the freeway, has a spa and updated fitness center. Each has the gamut of casino-style dining options, including fast-food courts, all-you-can-eat buffets and 24-hour coffee shops.

DEATH VALLEY NATIONAL PARK

The name itself evokes all that is harsh, hot and hellish – a punishing, barren and lifeless place of Old Testament severity. Yet closer inspection reveals that in Death Valley nature is putting on a truly spectacular show: singing sand dunes, water-sculpted canyons, boulders moving across the desert floor, extinct volcanic craters, palm-shaded oases and plenty of endemic wildlife. This is a land of superlatives, holding the US records for hottest temperature (134°F, or 57°C), lowest point (Badwater, 282ft below sea level) and largest national park outside Alaska (over 5000 sq miles).

Peak seasons are winter and the springtime wildflower bloom. From late February until early April, lodging within a 100-mile radius is usually booked solid and campgrounds fill before noon, especially on weekends. In summer, when the mercury climbs above 120°F (49°C), a car with reliable aircon is essential and outdoor explorations in the valley should be limited to the early morning and late afternoon. Spend the hottest part of the day by a pool or drive up to the higher – and cooler – elevations.

◉ Sights

FURNACE CREEK
Furnace Creek is Death Valley's commercial hub, with a general store, park visitors center, gas station, post office, ATM, internet access, golf course, lodging and restaurants. Cleverly concealed by a date palm grove is a solar power plant that currently generates one-third of Furnace Creek's energy needs.

FREE Borax Museum (◷9am-9pm Oct-May, variable in summer) is great for finding out what all the fuss about borax was about. It also has a great collection of pioneer-era stagecoaches and wagons out back. A short drive north, an interpretive trail follows in the footsteps of late-19th-century Chinese laborers and through the adobe ruins of Harmony Borax Works, where you can take a side trip through twisting Mustard Canyon.

SOUTH OF FURNACE CREEK
If possible start out early in the morning to drive up to Zabriskie Point for spectacular valley views across golden badlands eroded into waves, pleats and gullies. Escape the heat by continuing on to Dante's View at 5475ft, where you can simultaneously see the highest (Mt Whitney) and lowest (Badwater) points in the contiguous USA. The drive there takes about 1½ to two hours round-trip.

Badwater itself, a foreboding landscape of crinkly salt flats, is a 17-mile drive south of Furnace Creek. Here you can walk out onto a boardwalk above a constantly evaporating bed of salty, mineralized water that's otherworldly in its beauty. Along the way, you may want to check out narrow Golden Canyon, easily explored on a 2-mile round-trip walk, and Devil's Golf Course, where salt has piled up into saw-toothed miniature mountains. A 9-mile one-way scenic loop along Artists Drive is best done in the late afternoon when exposed minerals and volcanic ash make the hills erupt in fireworks of color.

STOVEPIPE WELLS & AROUND
Stovepipe Wells, about 26 miles northwest of Furnace Creek, was Death Valley's original 1920s tourist resort. Today it has a small store, gas station, ATM, motel, campground and bar. En route, look for the roadside pull-off where you can walk out onto the powdery, Sahara-like sand dunes. The dunes are at their most photogenic when the sun is low in the sky and especially magical during full moon. Across the road, look for the Devil's Cornfield, full of arrow weed clumps. Some 2.5 miles southwest of Stovepipe Wells, a 3-mile gravel side road leads to Mosaic Canyon, where you can hike and scramble along the smooth multihued rock walls. Colors are sharpest at midday.

ALONG EMIGRANT CANYON RD
Some 6 miles southwest of Stovepipe Wells, Emigrant Canyon Rd veers off Hwy 190 and travels south to the park's higher elevations. En route you'll pass the turnoff to Skidoo, a mining ghost town where the silent movie

CALLING DEATH VALLEY HOME

Timbisha Shoshone tribespeople lived in the Panamint Range for centuries, visiting the valley every winter to gather acorns, hunt waterfowl, catch pupfish in marshes and cultivate small areas of corn, squash and beans. After the federal government created Death Valley National Monument in 1933, the tribe was forced to move several times and was eventually restricted to a 40-acre village site near Furnace Creek, which it still occupies. In 2000 President Clinton signed an act transferring 7500 acres of land back to the Timbisha Shoshone tribe, creating the first Native American reservation inside a US national park. Learn more at http://timbisha.org.

Greed was filmed in 1923. It's an 8-mile trip on a graded gravel road suitable for high-clearance vehicles only to get to the ruins and jaw-dropping Sierra Nevada views.

Further south Emigrant Canyon Rd passes the turnoff for the 7-mile dirt road leading past the **Eureka Mines** to the vertiginous **Aguereberry Point** (high-clearance vehicles only), where you'll have fantastic views into the valley and out to the colorful Funeral Mountains from a lofty 6433ft. The best time to visit is in the late afternoon.

Emigrant Canyon Rd now climbs steeply over Emigrant Pass and through Wildrose Canyon to reach the **charcoal kilns**, a lineup of large, stone, beehive-shaped structures historically used by miners to make fuel for smelting silver and lead ore. The landscape is subalpine, with forests of piñon pine and juniper; it can be covered with snow, even in spring.

PANAMINT SPRINGS

About 30 miles west of Stovepipe Wells, on the edge of the park, Panamint Springs is a tiny enclave with a motel, campground, pricey gas station and small store. Several often overlooked but wonderful hidden gems are easily accessed from here. **Father Crowley Point**, for instance, peers deep into Rainbow Canyon, created by lava flows and scattered with colorful volcanic cinders. In spring DIY adventurers attempt the 2-mile graded gravel road, followed by a mile-long cross-country hike out to **Darwin Falls**, a spring-fed cascade that plunges into a gorge, embraced by willows that attract migratory birds. You could also take roughshod Saline Valley Rd out to **Lee Flat**, where Joshua trees thrive.

SCOTTY'S CASTLE & AROUND

About 55 miles north of Furnace Creek, **Scotty's Castle** (adult/child $11/6; ☺grounds 7:30am-5:30pm May-Oct, 7:30am-6pm Nov-Apr) is named for Walter E Scott, alias 'Death Valley Scotty', a gifted tall-tale teller who captivated people with his fanciful stories of gold. His most lucrative friendship was with Albert and Bessie Johnson, insurance magnates from Chicago. Despite knowing that Scotty was a freeloading liar, they bankrolled the construction of this elaborate Spanish-inspired villa. Restored to its 1930s glory appearance, the historic house has sheepskin drapes, carved California redwood, handmade tiles, elaborately wrought iron, woven Shoshone baskets and a bellowing pipe organ upstairs.

Costumed guides recount Scotty's apocryphal story in colorful detail on the **Living History Tour** (☺at least hourly 9:30am-4pm May-Oct, 9am-5pm Nov-Apr). More technically minded **Underground Tours** (adult/child $11/6; ☺Nov-Apr, as staffing permits at other times) and ranger-guided hiking tours to Scotty's cabin at **Lower Vine Ranch** (adult/child $15/8; ☺2pm Wed & Sat year-round, 10am Sat Jan-Apr) are also offered on a more limited schedule.

Advance tickets are available at ☎877-444-6777 or www.recreation.gov at least one day before your visit. On the day of the tour, tickets are sold on a first-come, first-served basis at the Scotty's Castle visitors center, which has some introductory exhibits. Waits of two hours or more for the next available tour are not uncommon on busy weekends.

Three miles west of Scotty's pad, a rough 5-mile dirt road leads to 770ft-deep **Ubehebe Crater**, formed by the explosive meeting of fiery magma and cool groundwater. Hikers can loop around its half-mile-wide rim and over to younger **Little Hebe Crater**.

It's slow going for another 27 miles on a tire-shredding dirt road (high-clearance required) to the eerie **Racetrack**, where you can ponder the mystery of faint tracks that slow-moving rocks have etched into the dry lakebed.

Death Valley & Around

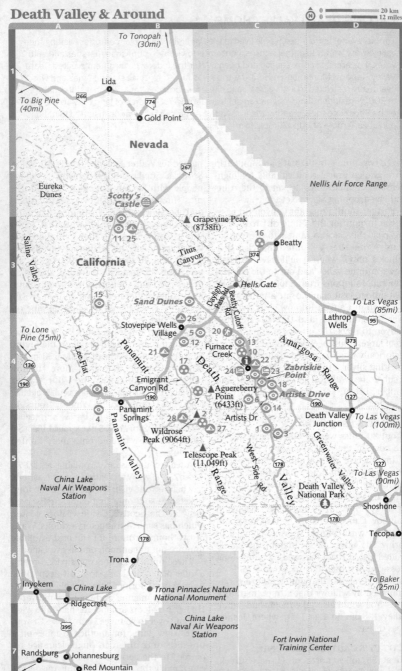

Death Valley & Around

There's a snack bar but no gas station at Scotty's.

TOWARDS BEATTY

Driving north from Furnace Creek, Hwy 374 veers off Hwy 190 and runs 22 miles east to Beatty, across the Nevada state line. About 2 miles outside the park boundary is the turnoff to one-way **Titus Canyon Rd**, one of the most spectacular backcountry roads, leading back to Death Valley in about 27 miles of unpaved track. The road climbs, dips and winds to a crest in the Grapevine Mountains then slowly descends back to the desert floor past a ghost town, petroglyphs and dramatic canyon narrows. The best light conditions are in the morning. High-clearance vehicles are recommended. Check road conditions at the visitors center.

Rhyolite (www.rhyolitesite.com; Hwy 374; ☉sunrise-sunset), a ghost town a few miles beyond the Titus Canyon turnoff, epitomizes the hurly-burly, boom-and-bust story of Western gold-rush mining towns. Don't overlook the 1906 'bottle house' or the skeletal remains of a three-story bank. Also here is the bizarre **Goldwell Open Air Museum** (www.goldwellmuseum.org; admission free; ☉24hr), a trippy art installation begun by Belgian artist Albert Szukalski in 1984.

🏃 Activities

Families can pick up fun-for-all-ages **junior ranger program** activity books at the Furnace Creek visitors center, which has info-packed handouts on all kinds of activities, including hiking trails and mountain-biking routes.

Farabee's Jeep Rentals   DRIVING TOUR
(☏760-786-9872; www.deathvalleyjeeprentals.com; 2-/4-door Jeep incl 200 miles $175/195; ☉mid-Sep–mid-May) If you don't have a 4WD but would like to explore the park's backcountry, you can rent a Jeep from this outfit, provided you're over 25 years old, have a valid driver's license, credit card and proof of insurance. The office is next to the Furnace Creek Inn.

Furnace Creek Cyclery   MOUNTAIN-BIKING
(☏760-786-3372, ext 372; bike hire 1/24hr $10/49; ☉year-round) Another way to get off the asphalt is by renting a mountain bike from the Cyclery at Furnace Creek Ranch. Cycling is allowed on all established paved and dirt roads, but never on trails. Ask at the visitors center for recommended routes. Staff at the Cyclery also organize the 2½-hour **Hells Gate Downhill Bike Tour** (tour $49; ☉10am & 2pm), which transports you up to a 2200ft elevation for a 10-mile downhill ride back to the valley floor. The minimum age is 18.

Furnace Creek Golf Course　　GOLF
(☎760-786-3373; Hwy 190, Furnace Creek; greens fees summer/winter $30/55; ⊙year-round) For novelty's sake you can play a round at the world's lowest-elevation golf course (18 holes, par 70), redesigned by Perry Dye in 1997. It's also been certified by the Audubon society as a Cooperative Sanctuary for its environment-friendly management; see http://acspgolf.auduboninternational.org for details.

Furnace Creek Stables　　HORSEBACK RIDING
(☎760-614-1018; www.furnacecreekstables.net; Hwy 190, Furnace Creek; 1/2hr rides $45/65; ⊙mid-Oct–mid-May) Saddle up to see what Death Valley looks like from the back of a horse on these guided rides. The monthly full-moon rides are the most memorable.

**Furnace Creek Ranch
Swimming Pool**　　SWIMMING
This huge spring-fed pool is kept at a steady 84°F (29°C) and cleaned with a nifty flow-through system that uses minimal chloride. It's primarily for Furnace Creek Ranch guests, but a limited number of passes are available to visitors ($5).

Hiking

Avoid hiking in summer, except on higher-elevation mountain trails, which may be snowed in during winter.

On Hwy 190, just north of Beatty Cutoff Rd, is the half-mile **Salt Creek Interpretive Trail**; in late winter or early spring, rare pupfish splash in the stream alongside the boardwalk. A few miles south of Furnace Creek is **Golden Canyon**, where a self-guided interpretive trail winds for a mile up to the now-oxidized iron cliffs of **Red Cathedral**. With a good sense of orientation, you can keep going up to **Zabriskie Point**, for a hardy 4-mile round-trip. Before reaching Badwater, stretch your legs with a 1-mile round-trip walk to the **Natural Bridge**.

Off Wildrose Canyon Rd, starting by the charcoal kilns, **Wildrose Peak** (9064ft) is an 8.4-mile round-trip trail. The elevation gain is 2200ft, but great views start about halfway up.

The park's most demanding summit is **Telescope Peak** (11,049ft), with views that plummet down to the desert floor, which is as far below as two Grand Canyons deep! The 14-mile round-trip climbs 3000ft above Mahogany Flat, off upper Wildrose Canyon

Rd. Get full details from the visitors center before setting out.

Festivals & Events

Death Valley '49ers　　CULTURAL
(www.deathvalley49ers.org) In early or mid-November, Furnace Creek hosts this historical encampment, featuring cowboy poetry, campfire sing-alongs, a gold-panning contest and a Western art show. Show up early to watch the pioneer wagons come thunderin' in.

Badwater Ultramarathon　　SPORTS
(www.badwater.com) The 'world's toughest foot race,' Badwater is a 135-mile ultramarathon from Badwater Basin up to Whitney Portal (p448), staged in the suicidal summer heat in mid-July.

Sleeping

In-park lodging is pricey and often booked solid in springtime but there are several gateway towns with cheaper lodging. The closest is Beatty (p692) but choices are more plentiful in Las Vegas (p701) and Ridgecrest (p696).

Stovepipe Wells Village　　MOTEL $$
(☎760-786-2387; www.escapetodeathvalley. com; Hwy 190, Stovepipe Wells Village; RV sites with hookups $31, r $80-155; ✸🛜🐾🛗) Newly spruced-up rooms feature quality linens beneath cheerful Native American–patterned bedspreads as well as coffeemakers. The small pool is cool and the cowboy-style restaurant (mains $5 to $25) delivers three square meals a day.

Furnace Creek Ranch　　RESORT $$
(☎760-786-2345; www.furnacecreekresort.com; Hwy 190, Furnace Creek; cabins $130-162, r $162-213; ✸🛜🐾🛗) Tailor-made for families, this rambling resort has been subjected to a vigorous facelift, resulting in spiffy rooms swathed in desert colors, updated bathrooms, new furniture and French doors leading to porches with comfortable patio furniture. The grounds encompass a playground, a spring-fed swimming pool and tennis courts.

Furnace Creek Inn　　HOTEL $$$
(☎760-786-2345; www.furnacecreekresort.com; Hwy 190, Furnace Creek; r $335-455, ste $440-470; ⊙mid-Oct–mid-May; ✸🛜🐾) Roll out of bed and count the colors of the desert as you pull back the curtains in your room at this elegant 1927 mission-style hotel. After a day

CAMPING IN DEATH VALLEY

Of the park's nine campgrounds, only **Furnace Creek** (☎877-444-6777; www.recreation. gov) accepts reservations and only from mid-April to mid-October. All other camp-grounds are first-come, first-served. At peak times, such as weekends during the spring wildflower bloom, campsites fill by mid-morning.

Backcountry camping (no campfires) is allowed 2 miles off paved roads and away from developed and day-use areas, and 100yd from any water source; pick up free per-mits at the visitors center.

Furnace Creek Ranch and Stovepipe Wells Village offer public showers ($5, including swimming-pool access).

CAMPGROUND	SEASON	LOCATION	FEE	CHARACTERISTICS
Furnace Creek	year-round	valley floor	$18 mid-Oct–mid-Apr, $12 other times	pleasant grounds, some shady sites
Sunset	Oct-Apr	valley floor	$12	huge, RV-oriented
Texas Spring	Oct-Apr	valley floor	$14	good for tents
Stovepipe Wells	Oct-Apr	valley floor	$12	parking-lot style, close to dunes
Mesquite Springs	year-round	1800ft	$12	close to Scotty's Castle
Emigrant	year-round	2100ft	free	tents only
Wildrose	year-round	4100ft	free	seasonal water
Thorndike	Mar-Nov	7400ft	free	may need 4WD, no water
Mahogany Flat	Mar-Nov	8200ft	free	may need 4WD, no water

of sweaty touring, you can enjoy languid val-ley views while lounging by the spring-fed swimming pool, cocktail in hand. The lobby has a 1930s retro look, but rooms are per-haps a little less sumptuous than one might expect.

Panamint Springs Resort   MOTEL, CAMPGROUND $
(☎760-482-7680; www.deathvalley.com/psr; Hwy 190, Panamint Springs; tent site $7.50, RV partial/ full hookup $15/30, r $80-110; ❋🐾🏊🐕) At these prices you know you're not getting the Ritz, but rooms, while simple and aging, are clean and decent-sized. Not a bad spot for launch-ing a Death Valley exploration.

✖ Eating & Drinking

Furnace Creek and Stovepipe Wells have gen-eral stores stocking basic groceries and camp-ing supplies. Scotty's Castle has a snack bar.

Toll Road Restaurant   AMERICAN $$
(Stovepipe Wells Village, Hwy 190; full breakfast buf-fet $12, dinner $12-25; ⊗7-9:30am & 7-10pm mid-May–mid-Oct, 7-10am & 5-9pm mid-Oct–mid-May; 🏊🐕) Above-par cowboy cooking happens at

this ranch house, which gets Old West flair from a rustic fireplace and rickety wooden chairs and tables. Many of the mostly meaty mains are made with local ingredients, such as mesquite honey, prickly pear and piñons. Food, including late-night snacks, is also served next door at the **Badwater Saloon** (⊗from 11am) along with cold draft beer and Skynyrd on the jukebox.

49'er Cafe   AMERICAN $$
(Furnace Creek Ranch, Hwy 190, Furnace Creek; mains $8-25; ⊗7am-9pm; 🐕) This family-friendly tummy filling station serves only average American food, yet it's always crowded. Portions are huge.

Wrangler Restaurant   STEAKHOUSE $$$
(Furnace Creek Ranch, Hwy 190, Furnace Creek; breakfast/lunch buffet $11/15, dinner mains $28-39; ⊗6-9am, 11am-2pm & 5:30-9pm Oct-May, 6-10am & 6-9:30pm May-Oct) The ranch's main restau-rant serves belly busting buffets at break-fast and lunchtime (when tour bus groups invade) and turns into a pricey steakhouse at night.

Corkscrew Saloon AMERICAN $$

(Furnace Creek Ranch, Hwy 190, Furnace Creek; mains $6-23, barbecue $28-36; ⊙11:30am-midnight) This gregarious joint has darts, draft beer and dynamite barbecue at dinner time, as well as pretty good but pricey pizzas and pub grub like onion rings and burgers.

19th Hole Bar & Grill AMERICAN $

(mains $8-11; ⊙lunch Oct-May) On the golf course, this place has the juiciest burgers in the park.

Furnace Creek Inn INTERNATIONAL $$$

(☑760-786-2345; mains lunch $13-17, dinner $24-38; ⊙7:30-10:30am, noon-2:30pm & 5:30-9:30pm mid-Oct–mid-May) Views of the Panamint Mountains are stellar from this formal dining room with a dress code (no shorts or T-shirts, jeans ok), where the menu draws inspiration from continental, southwestern and Mexican cuisine. Afternoon tea in the lobby lounge and Sunday brunch are longstanding hoity-toity affairs. The nicest place for sunset cocktails is the outdoor patio.

Panamint Springs Resort AMERICAN $$

(Hwy 190, Panamint Springs; dishes from $10; ⊙breakfast, lunch & dinner; 🐾) This friendly outback cafe on the park's western edge serves up pizzas, burgers, salads, steaks and other standards. Toast the panoramic views from the front porch with one of its 100 bottled beers from around the world.

ℹ Information

Entry permits ($20 per vehicle) are valid for seven days and sold at self-service pay stations throughout the park. For a free map and newspaper, show your receipt at the visitors center.

Cell-phone reception is poor to nonexistent in the park, but there are pay phones at Furnace Creek, Stovepipe Wells Village and Scotty's Castle; phone cards are sold at the general stores in Stovepipe Wells and Furnace Creek. The latter also has credit-card activated **internet access** (per hr/24hr $5/11; ⊙7am-10pm).

Furnace Creek visitors center (☑760-786-3200; www.nps.gov/deva; Hwy 190, Furnace Creek; ⊙8am-5pm) Under construction at press time, the renovated main visitors center should have reopened by the time you're reading this. New exhibits were expected to come online by this book's publication. Check schedules for ranger-led activities, given daily between November and March.

Scotty's Castle visitors center (☑760-786-2392, ext 231; North Hwy; ⊙8:45am-4:30pm May-Oct, 8:30am-5:30pm Nov-Apr) Has exhibits from the castle's museum-worthy collection.

ℹ Getting There & Away

Gas is expensive in the park, so fill up your tank beforehand.

Furnace Creek can be reached via Baker (115 miles, two to 2½ hours), Beatty (45 miles, one to 1½ hours), Las Vegas (via Hwy 160, 120 miles, 2½ to three hours), Lone Pine (105 miles, two hours), Los Angeles (300 miles, five to 5½ hours) and Ridgecrest (via Trona, 120 miles, 2½ to three hours).

AROUND DEATH VALLEY NATIONAL PARK

Beatty, Nevada

Around 45 miles north of Furnace Creek, this historic Bullfrog mining district boomtown (population 1154) has certainly seen better days but makes a good and reasonably inexpensive launch pad for visiting Death Valley. You'll find an ATM, 24-hour gas station, public library with internet access and a teensy museum with artifacts from the Old West mining days all along Hwy 95, here called Main St.

🛏 Sleeping & Eating

🌿 Atomic Inn MOTEL $

(☑775-553-2250; www.atomic-inn.com; 350 S 1st St; r incl breakfast $52-60; ✳🐾) This nicely updated motel opened in 1980 as a home base for military personnel working at nearby Nellis Air Force Base, home to a nuclear testing site and planned nuclear-waste repository. Get a deluxe room to enjoy flat-screen TVs and DVD players; there's a movie library near reception. Classic movies also play in the lobby nightly. Kudos for the solar water-heating system and xeriscaped grounds.

Motel 6 MOTEL $

(☑775-553-9090; www.motel6.com; 550 US Hwy 95 N; r $53-59; ✳🐾) It's a cookie-cutter Motel 6, so don't expect any frills. This is, however, an admirably well-maintained, rather modern and super-clean property and thus good value for money.

Stagecoach Hotel & Casino HOTEL $

(☑775-553-2419; 900 Hwy 95 N; r $60-110; ✳🐾🐾) Rooms are pretty bland but comfy enough for an overnight stay, while the pool is a nice place to lounge away a dusty day in Death Valley. Rita's Cafe serves three square

LIFE AT DEATH VALLEY JUNCTION

The spot where Hwys 127 and 190 collide, about 30 miles east of Furnace Creek, is known as Death Valley Junction (population 3, plus a few resident ghosts) and home to one of California's kookiest roadside attractions: the **Amargosa Opera House** (www. amargosaoperahouse.com; shows adult/child $15/12; ⊙2pm Sun). Built by the Pacific Borax Company, this 1920s Mexican colonial-style courtyard building was once the social hub of Death Valley Junction but fell into disrepair after 1948. Then, in 1967, New York dancer Marta Becket's car broke down nearby. Marta fell in love with the place and decided to inject new life into it by opening – what else? – an opera house. Until recently Marta entertained the curious with heartbreakingly corny dance-and-mime shows in an auditorium whose walls she personally adorned with fanciful murals showing an audience she imagined might have attended an opera in the 16th century, including nuns, gypsies and royalty.

Now over 80 years old, Marta's high-stepping days may be over but she continues to regale fans with singing and story-telling Sunday matinees. In 2010 she also starred in a 70-minute documentary called *The Ghosts of Death Valley Junction* and, at press time, she was hoping to premiere her new show called 'Life is a Three Ring Circus'. Tours of the opera house cost $5; enquire at the reception of the attached **motel** (☎775-852-4441; r $65-85; ❀🛜☎). To complete the eccentric experience, consider spending the night in one of its seriously faded rooms with boudoir lamps and murals but no TVs or phones. The **cafe** (dishes $6.50-16, pie per slice $3; ⊙7am-3pm Sun-Thu, to 8pm Fri & Sat) has delicious homemade pies.

meals a day, while the Alexander does a roaring trade in steaks and other meaty mains. There's live music on weekends

Exchange Club Motel MOTEL $
(☎775-553-2333; 119 W Main St; r $60; ❀🛜) The 44 rooms here have been put through a recent makeover, resulting in new carpets and neutrally hued furniture.

KC's Outpost Saloon AMERICAN $
(100 Main St; dishes $3.50-8; ⊙10am-10pm Sun-Thu, to 11pm Fri & Sat; 👪) KC's yummy burgers and bulging sandwiches (including vegetarian options) – on homemade bread no less! – have garnered rave reviews. The potato salad makes a delish side dish.

Shoshone

Just a blip on the desert map, Shoshone (population 31) is 55 miles from Furnace Creek via Death Valley Junction, though most folks elect to follow the 20-mile-longer, but more scenic, Hwy 178 through Badwater Basin instead. It has a gas station, store, lodging and free public wi-fi access.

Look for an old Chevy parked outside the **Shoshone Museum** (admission by donation; ⊙9am-3pm), which houses quirky and well-meaning exhibits as well the local **visitors**

center (☎760-852-4524; www.deathvalleychamber.org; ⊙10am-4pm).

Across the street the 1950s **Shoshone Inn** (☎760-852-4335; www.shoshonevillage.com; Hwy 127; d $96-105, cabins $113; ❀🛜🏊) has updated cabins and a dozen basic courtyard rooms, all with satellite TV, that were getting a sprucing up during our visit. Some have a refrigerator and microwave. Bonus: the small warm-springs pool. **Shoshone RV Park** (☎760-852-4569; RV site with full hookup $25) is just north of town.

TOP CHOICE **Cafe C'est Si Bon** (Hwy 127; mains $7-10; ⊙usually 8am-5pm Wed-Mon; 🛜📶👪) is an always-delightful, solar-powered place where the genial chef-owner makes a mean espresso, gourmet baked goods, and 'flexitarian' breakfasts and lunches (think homemade crepes and quiche). World music plays soothingly in the background, occasionally interrupted by the happy oinks of Pizza, the pet pig. Also check out the sculpture garden.

Tecopa

Some 8 miles south of Shoshone, this old mining town (population 150) was named after a peace-making Paiute chief and is home to some wonderfully soothing hot natural mineral springs.

🏃 Activities

There are two places where you can take a dip.

Delight's Hot Springs Resort   HOT SPRINGS
(🕿760-852-4343; www.delightshotspringsresort.
com; 368 Tecopa Hot Springs Rd; hot springs 10am-
5pm $10, 10am-10pm $15, RV sites with hookups
$39, r $79, cabins $89-125) There are four private hot-springs tubs for splashing around
in as well as a handful of 1930s cabins with
kitchenette and newer motel rooms, in case
you want to spend the night.

Tecopa Hot Springs   HOT SPRINGS
(🕿760-852-4420; www.tecopahotsprings.org; 860
Tecopa Hot Springs Rd; bathhouse $10, tent/RV site
$20/30, r $70-85; ⊙7am-9pm Oct-May) This outfit
has two simple but clean men's and women's
bathhouses, where tribal elders, snowbird RVers and curious tourists soak together. There
are also private pools ($25) for up to six people. Camping rates include the bathhouse fee.

China Ranch Date Farm   FARM
(🕿760-852-4415; www.chinaranch.com; ⊙9am-
5pm) Just outside Tecopa, this family-run organic date farm is a lush oasis in the middle
of the blistering desert. You can go hiking
or bird-watching and, of course, stock up
on luscious dates or try its yummy date nut
bread. To get here, follow the Old Spanish
Trail Hwy east of Tecopa Hot Springs Rd,
turn right on Furnace Creek Rd and look for
the signs.

🛏 Sleeping & Eating

Cynthia's   HOSTEL & B&B $
(🕿760-852-4580; www.discovercynthias.com;
2001 Old Spanish Trail Hwy; dm $22-25, d/tipi
$98/148; ❉❀) Match your budget to the bed
at this congenial inn helmed by the friendly
Cynthia. Your choices: a colorful and eclectically decorated private room in a vintage
trailer, a bed in a dorm, or a Native American-style tipi with thick rugs, fire pits and
comfy king-size beds. The tipis are a short
drive away at China Ranch. Coffee and tea
are free and there's access to a communal
kitchen. Reservations are essential, even if
that means just calling ahead from the road.

TOP
CHOICE **Pastels Bistro**   CALIFORNIAN $
(mains $12-26; ⊙usually 9am-9pm) This is as
gourmet as things get in the desert. The
California fusion menu, often made with
organic ingredients, is always changing, and
the bread is house-baked fresh daily.

UPPER MOJAVE DESERT

The Mojave Desert covers a vast region,
from urban areas on the northern edge of
LA County to the remote, sparsely populated country of the Mojave National Preserve
(p684). The upper Mojave is a harsh land,
with sporadic mining settlements and vast
areas set aside for weapons and aerospace
testing. Most of the traffic here consists of
big rigs making their way between Bakersfield and Barstow on Hwy 58, and heading
up to the Sierras on US Hwy 395 – these
highways cross each other at Kramer Junction. But there are a few things out here
worth stopping for, too.

Lancaster-Palmdale

The Antelope Valley is dead flat. It's difficult
to see a valley, much less an antelope. But
in spring it's spectacularly carpeted with
bright-orange fields of California poppies,
like a vision out of *The Wizard of Oz*.

West of Lancaster the **Antelope Valley
California Poppy Reserve** (🕿661-724-1180;
www.parks.ca.gov; 15101 Lancaster Rd, at 170th St
W; per vehicle $10; ⊙sunrise-sunset) offers hillside walks among the wildflowers. To get
there take Hwy 14 south of Mojave for about
25 miles, exit at Ave I in Lancaster and drive
15 miles west, following the signs.

Also at the poppy preserve, the **Mojave
Desert Information Center** (🕿661-724-1206;
⊙8am-5pm Mon-Fri) dispenses brochures,
maps and advice about sights in and around
the Antelope Valley.

FREE **Arthur B Ripley Desert Woodland State Park** (Lancaster Rd, at 210th St
W; ⊙sunrise-sunset), 5 miles west, has an
untrammeled interpretive trail leading
through precious stands of Joshua trees.

East of Lancaster, **Antelope Valley Indian Museum** (🕿661-942-0662; http://avim.
parks.ca.gov; Ave M; adult/child under 12yr $3/free;
⊙11am-4pm Sat & Sun) displays Native American artifacts from around California and
across the Southwest but, at press time, was
slated for closure due to budget cuts. Call
ahead to confirm.

There is first-come, first-served camping among Joshua trees and desert-tortoise
habitat at nearby **Saddleback Butte State
Park** (🕿661-942-0662; 170th St E, south of Ave J;
tent & RV sites $20), although it too is threatened with closure.

Budget motels line the Sierra Hwy, east of downtown Lancaster and Hwy 14. The retro 1950s **Town House Motel** (☑661-942-1195; 44125 Sierra Hwy; r $60-70; ✳🛜🏊) has clean, simple rooms. Chain motels and hotels cluster further south near LA/Palmdale Regional Airport.

A wonderful find in downtown Lancaster is **Lemon Leaf Cafe** (http://thelemonleaf.com; 653 W Lancaster Blvd; mains $10-17; ⊙7am-9pm Mon-Thu & Sat, to 10pm Fri), a culinary oasis making market-fresh Mediterranean salads, grilled panini sandwiches, pasta and pizza as well as a nicely tangy lemon tart.

Mojave

Driving north on Hwy 14, Mojave (population 4238) is the first stop on the 'Aerospace Triangle' that also includes Boron (p695) and Ridgecrest (p696). The modest town is home to a huge air force base as well as the country's first commercial space port and has witnessed major moments in air and space flight history.

The storied **Edwards Air Force Base** (☑661-277-8707; www.edwards.af.mil) is a flight-test facility for the US Air Force, NASA and civilian aircraft, and a training school for test pilots with the 'right stuff'. It was from here that Chuck Yeager piloted the world's first supersonic flight and where the first space shuttles glided in after their missions. Free five-hour tours of the on-base flight museum and NASA flight research center are usually given on the first and third Fridays of the month. Reservations are essential and must be made at least 14 days in advance (30 days for non-US citizens). See the website (link to 'Questions') for full details.

Created in 2003, the **Mojave Air & Space Port** (www.mojaveairport.com) was the first commercial space port in the US, making history a few months later with the launch of **Space-ShipOne**, the plane that made the first privately funded human space flight, thus laying the groundwork for commercial space tourism. Dozens of aerospace companies are hard at work here developing the latest aeronautical technologies, including SpaceShipTwo for Richard Branson's Virgin Galactic.

A replica of SpaceShipOne is on display in the airport's small **Legacy Park**, along with a huge Rotary Rocket, which was an early reusable civilian space vehicle developed here in the late '90s. The **Voyager Cafe** has some great old photographs.

The air and space port is also home to a huge **airplane graveyard**, where retired commercial airplanes are roosting in the dry desert air waiting to be scavenged for spare parts.

Boron

Off Hwy 58, about midway between Mojave and Barstow, this tiny town (population 2253) catapulted onto the map in 1927 with the discovery of one of the world's richest borax deposits. Today, it is home to California's **largest open pit mine**, operated by the massive global mining concern called Rio Tinto Borax. At 1 mile wide, 1.5 miles long and up to 650ft deep, the gash looks like a man-made Grand Canyon and supplies 40% of the world's demand for this versatile mineral. Historically, Boron was where Death Valley's famous 20-mule teams deposited their huge loads of borax, hauled from over 165 miles away, at a dusty desert railway station.

⊙ Sights

Borax Visitors Center   MUSEUM
(☑760-762-7588; www.borax.com; Borax Rd, off Hwy 58; per car $3; ⊙9am-5pm) Up on a hilltop on the grounds of the mining complex, this modern facility reeks of corporate advertising but also has some fine exhibits and a film explaining the process of borax mining, processing and distribution as well as the mineral's many uses in such everyday products as detergent and fertilizer. Views of the mine from up here are stupendous.

Saxon Aerospace Museum   MUSEUM
(☑760-762-6600; www.saxonaerospacemuseum.com; 26922 Twenty Mule Team Rd; admission by donation; ⊙usually 10am-4pm) This modest, volunteer-run museum recounts milestones in experimental flight testing in the surrounding desert, including the first breaking of the sound barrier, the first hypersonic flight and the first space shuttle landing.

Twenty Mule Team Museum   MUSEUM
(☑760-762-5810; www.20muleteammuseum.com; 26962 Twenty Mule Team Rd; admission by donation; ⊙10am-4pm) Next door to Saxon Aerospace Museum, this low-budget museum is a haphazardly organized treasure trove of historic knick-knacks, including a 1930s beauty shop, products made with locally mined borax, and movie stills and magazine stories about the 2000 movie *Erin Brockov-*

ich, which was filmed nearby and employed many locals as extras.

✕ Eating

Domingo's   MEXICAN **$$**
(☎760-762-6266; 27075 Twenty Mule Team Rd; mains $6-18; ☉11am-10pm; 🖷) Autographed photos of astronauts and air-force test pilots hang on the walls of this casual joint that's packed with lunchtime crowds from the nearby military base.

Ridgecrest

Ridgecrest (population 27,616) is a service town where you find gas, supplies, information and cheap lodging en route to Death Valley or the Eastern Sierra Nevada. Its main raison d'être is the China Lake US Naval Air Weapons Station that sprawls for a million acres (one third the size of Delaware!) north of the town.

FREE **US Naval Museum of Armament & Technology** (☎760-939-3530; www.china lakemuseum.org; ☉10am-4pm Mon-Sat), right on the base, is an unapologetic celebration of US military might that is likely to fascinate technology, flight, history and military buffs – and perhaps even utter pacifists.

Many of the rockets, guided missiles, torpedoes, guns, bombs, cluster weapons etc on display were developed or tested on this very base before seeing action in wars from WWII to Afghanistan. If you ever wanted to touch a Tomahawk missile or have your picture taken with a 'Fat Man' (the atomic bomb that was dropped on Japan, that is), this is the place to do it. A documentary takes you on a helicopter flight of the base for bird's-eye views of the 4-mile-long supersonic research track and the anti-missile testing grounds.

In order to get to the museum, you need to stop at the base's visitors center on China Lake Blvd (near Inyokern Rd), fill out a form and present your driver's license, car registration and vehicle insurance. Foreign visitors must also show their passport.

Trona Pinnacles

What do the movies *Battlestar Galactica, Star Trek V: The Final Frontier* and *Planet of the Apes* have in common? Answer: they were all filmed at Trona Pinnacles, an awesome national natural landmark where tufa spires rise out of an ancient lakebed in alien fashion.

Look for the turnoff from Rte 178, about 18 miles east of Ridgecrest. From there it's another 5 miles south along a rutted dirt road to the scenic driving loop and short walking trails. Free primitive campsites are available.

Randsburg

About 20 miles south of Ridgecrest, off US Hwy 395, Randsburg is a 'living ghost town,' where you can visit a tiny historical museum, antiques shops, a saloon and an opera house cafe (where old-timey melodramas are occasionally performed). You can even stay overnight in the yesteryear hotel and hear the coyotes howling outside at night.

LAS VEGAS

It's three in the morning in a smoky casino when you spot an Elvis lookalike sauntering by arm in arm with a glittering showgirl just as a bride in a long white dress shrieks 'Blackjack!'

Vegas is Hollywood for the everyman. It's the only place in the world you can see ancient hieroglyphics, the Eiffel Tower, the Brooklyn Bridge and the canals of Venice in a few short hours. Sure, they're all reproductions, but in a slice of desert that's transformed itself into one of the most lavish places on earth, nothing is halfway – even the illusions.

Las Vegas is the ultimate escape. Time is irrelevant here. There are no clocks, just never-ending buffets and ever-flowing drinks. This is a city of multiple personalities, constantly reinventing herself since the days of the Rat Pack. Sin City aims to infatuate, and its reaches are all-inclusive. Hollywood bigwigs gyrate at A-list ultralounges, while college kids seek cheap debauchery and grandparents whoop it up at the penny slots. You can sip designer martinis as you sample the apex of world-class cuisine or wander the casino floor with a 3ft-high cocktail tied around your neck.

If you can dream up the kind of vacation you want, it's already a reality here. Welcome to the dream factory.

◉ Sights

Roughly four miles long, the Strip, aka Las Vegas Blvd, is the center of gravity in Sin City. Circus Circus caps the north end of the Strip and Mandalay Bay is at the south end, near the airport. Whether you're walking or driving, distances on the Strip are deceiving; a walk to what looks like a nearby casino usually takes longer than expected.

Downtown Las Vegas is the original town center and home to the city's oldest hotels and casinos: expect a retro feel, cheaper drinks and lower table limits. Its main drag is fun-loving Fremont St, four blocks of which are a covered pedestrian mall that runs a groovy light show every night.

Major tourist areas are safe. However, Las Vegas Blvd between downtown and the Strip gets shabby, and Fremont St east of downtown is rather unsavory.

Casinos

TOP CHOICE Cosmopolitan   CASINO
(www.cosmopolitanlasvegas.com; 3708 Las Vegas Blvd S) Hipsters who have long thought they were too cool for Vegas finally have a place to go where they don't need irony to endure – much less enjoy – the aesthetics. Like the new Hollywood 'It girl,' the Cosmo looks good at all times of the day or night, full of ingenues and entourages, plus regular folks who enjoy contemporary design. With a focus on pure fun, it avoids utter pretension, despite the constant wink-wink, retro moments: the Art-o-Matics (vintage cigarette machines hawking local art rather than nicotine), and possibly the best buffet in town, the **Wicked Spoon**.

TOP CHOICE Encore   CASINO
(www.encorelasvegas.com; 3121 Las Vegas Blvd S) Steve Wynn has upped the wow factor, and the skyline, yet again with the Encore, a slice of the French Riviera in Las Vegas – and classy enough to entice any of the Riviera's regulars. Filled with indoor flower gardens, a butterfly motif and a dramatically luxe casino, it's an oasis of bright beauty. **Botero**, the restaurant headed by Mark LoRusso, is centered on a large sculpture by Fernando Botero himself. Encore is attached to its sister property, the $2.7-billion **Wynn Las Vegas** (www.wynnlasvegas.com; 3131 Las Vegas Blvd S). The entrance is obscured from the Strip by a $130-million artificial mountain, which rises seven stories tall in some places. Inside, the Wynn resembles a natural paradise – with mountain views, tumbling waterfalls, fountains and other special effects.

TOP CHOICE Hard Rock   CASINO
(www.hardrockhotel.com; 4455 Paradise Rd) Beloved by SoCal visitors, this trés-hip casino

hotel is home to one of the world's most impressive collections of rock and roll memorabilia, including Jim Morrison's handwritten lyrics to one of the Door's greatest hits, and leather jackets from a who's who of famous rock stars. The Joint concert hall, Vanity Nightclub and 'Rehab' summer pool parties attract a pimped-out, sex-charged crowd flush with celebrities.

Bellagio   CASINO
(www.bellagio.com; 3600 Las Vegas Blvd S) The Bellagio dazzles with Tuscan architecture and an 8-acre artificial lake, complete with don't-miss choreographed dancing fountains. Look up as you enter the lobby: the stunning ceiling adorned with a backlit glass sculpture composed of 2000 hand-blown flowers by world-renowned artist Dale Chihuly. The **Bellagio Gallery of Fine Art** (adult/child $13/free; ◷10am-6pm Sun, Mon, Tue & Thu, 10am-7pm Wed, Fri & Sat) showcases temporary exhibits by top-notch artists. The **Bellagio Conservatory & Botanical Gardens** (admission free; ◷daily) features changing exhibits throughout the year.

Venetian
(www.venetian.com; 3355 Las Vegas Blvd S) Hand-painted ceiling frescoes, roaming mimes, gondola rides and full-scale reproductions of famous Venice landmarks are found at the romantic Venetian. Next door, the **Palazzo** (www.palazzo.com; 3325 Las Vegas Blvd S) exploits a variation on the Italian theme to a less interesting effect: despite the caliber of the **Shoppes at the Palazzo** and the star-studded dining – including exhilarating ventures by culinary heavyweights Charlie Trotter, Emeril Legasse and Wolfgang Puck – the luxurious casino floor and common areas somehow exude a lackluster brand of excitement.

Caesars Palace   CASINO
(www.caesarspalace.com; 3570 Las Vegas Blvd S) Quintessentially Las Vegas, Caesars Palace is a Greco-Roman fantasyland featuring marble reproductions of classical statuary, including a not-to-be-missed 4-ton Brahma shrine near the front entrance. Towering fountains, goddess-costumed cocktail waitresses and the swanky haute-couture **Forum Shops** all ante up the glitz.

Paris Las Vegas   CASINO
(www.parislasvegas.com; 3655 Las Vegas Blvd S) Evoking the gaiety of the City of Light, Paris Las Vegas strives to capture the essence of the grand dame by re-creating her land-

Las Vegas

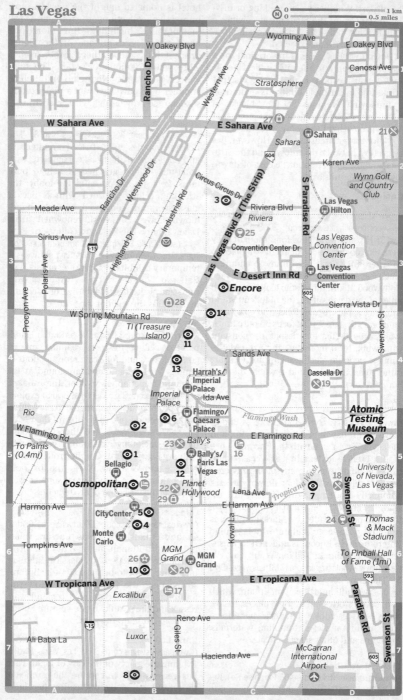

Las Vegas

marks. Fine likenesses of the Opéra, the Arc de Triomphe, the Champs-Élysées, the soaring Eiffel Tower and even the Seine frame the property.

Mirage CASINO
(www.mirage.com; 3400 Las Vegas Blvd S) With a tropical setting replete with a huge atrium filled with jungle foliage and soothing

cascades, the Mirage captures the imagination. Circling the atrium is a vast Polynesian-themed casino, which places gaming areas under separate roofs to evoke intimacy, including a popular high-limit poker room. Don't miss the 20,000-gallon saltwater aquarium, with 60 species of critters hailing from Fiji to the Red Sea. Out front in the lagoon, a fiery faux volcano erupts hourly after dark until midnight.

Flamingo   CASINO
(www.flamingolasvegas.com; 3555 Las Vegas Blvd S) The Flamingo is quintessential vintage Vegas. Weave through the slot machines to the Wildlife Habitat (admission free; ⊙daily) to see the flock of Chilean flamingos that call these 15 tropical acres home.

New York New York   CASINO
(www.nynyhotelcasino.com; 3790 Las Vegas Blvd S) A mini metropolis featuring scaled-down replicas of the Empire State Building, the Statue of Liberty, ringed by a September 11 memorial, and the Brooklyn Bridge.

Mandalay Bay   CASINO
(M-Bay; www.mandalaybay.com; 3950 Las Vegas Blvd S) Not trying to be any one fantasy, the tropically themed Mandalay Bay is worth a walkthrough. Standout attractions include the multilevel Shark Reef (www.sharkreef.com; adult/child $18/12; ⊙10am-8pm Sun-Thu, 10am-10pm Fri & Sat; ⊛), an aquarium home to thousands of submarine beasties with a shallow pool where you can pet pint-sized sharks.

Palms   CASINO
(www.palms.com; 4321 W Flamingo Rd) Equal parts sexy and downright sleazy, the Palms attracts loads of notorious celebrities (think Paris Hilton and Britney Spears) as well as a younger, mostly local crowd. Its restaurants and nightclubs are some of the hottest in town. Other highlights include a 14-screen cinema with IMAX capabilities, and a live-music club, the Pearl. Just don't take the elevator to the Playboy Club expecting debauchery à la Hef's mansion: while a few bunny-eared, surgically enhanced ladies deal blackjack in a stylishly appointed lounge full of mostly men, the sexiest thing about it is the stunning skyline view.

Golden Nugget   CASINO
(www.goldennugget.com; 129 E Fremont St) Looking like a million bucks, this casino hotel has set the downtown benchmark for extravagance since opening in 1946. No brass or cut glass was spared inside the swanky casino, known for its nonsmoking poker room; the RUSH Lounge, where live local bands play; the utterly lively casino and some of downtown's best restaurants. Don't miss the gigantic 61lb Hand of Faith, the world's largest gold nugget, around the corner from the hotel lobby.

Other Attractions

TOP CHOICE **Atomic Testing Museum**   MUSEUM
(www.atomictestingmuseum.org; 755 E Flamingo Rd; adult/child $14/11; ⊙10am-5pm Mon-Sat, noon-5pm Sun) Recalling an era when the word 'atomic' conjured modernity and mystery, the Smithsonian-run Atomic Testing Museum remains an intriguing testament to the period when the fantastical – and destructive – power of nuclear energy was tested just outside of Las Vegas. Don't skip the deafening Ground Zero Theater, which mimics a concrete test bunker.

TOP CHOICE **Neon Museum**   MUSEUM
(☎702-387-6366; www.neonmuseum.org; 821 Las Vegas Blvd N; displays free, guided tours $15; ⊙displays 24hr, guided tours noon & 2pm Tue-Sat) Experience the outdoor displays through a fascinating walking tour ($15) of the newly unveiled Neon Boneyard Park, where irreplaceable vintage neon signs – the original

---

LAS VEGAS FOR CHILDREN

State law prohibits people under 21 years of age from loitering in gaming areas.

The Circus Circus (www.circuscircus.com; 2880 Las Vegas Blvd S; ⊛) hotel complex is all about the kids, and its Adventuredome (adult/child $27/17; ⊙10am-7pm Sun-Thu, 10am-midnight Fri & Sat; ⊛) is a 5-acre indoor theme park with fun ranging from laser tag to bumper cars and a roller coaster. The Midway (admission free; ⊙11am-midnight; ⊛) features animals, acrobats and magicians performing on center stage.

The Pinball Hall of Fame (www.pinballmuseum.org; 1610 E Tropicana Ave; admission free, games 25-50¢; ⊙11am-11pm Sun-Thu, to midnight Fri & Sat; ⊛) is an interactive museum that's more fun than any slot machines.

art form of Las Vegas – spend their retirement. At press time, the museum was expanding its digs and hoped to add a self-guided component; until this is in place, be sure to reserve your tour at least a few weeks in advance.

Stroll around downtown come evening (when the neon comes out to play) to discover the free, self-guided component of the 'museum.' You'll find delightful al-fresco galleries of restored vintage neon signs, including sparkling genie lamps, glowing martini glasses and 1940s motel marquees. The biggest assemblages are found on the 3rd St cul-de-sac just north of Fremont St.

Fremont Street Experience   STREET
(www.vegasexperience.com; Fremont St; ⊙hourly 7pm-midnight) A four-block pedestrian mall topped by an arched steel canopy and filled with computer-controlled lights, the Fremont Street Experience, between Main St and Las Vegas Blvd, has brought life back to downtown. Every evening, the canopy is transformed into a six-minute light-and-sound show enhanced by 550,000 watts of wraparound sound.

Downtown Arts District   ARTS CENTER
On the **First Friday** (www.firstfriday-lasvegas. org) of each month, a carnival of 10,000 art-lovers, hipsters, indie musicians and hangers-on descend on Las Vegas' downtown arts district. These giant monthly block parties feature gallery openings, performance art, live bands and tattoo artists. The action revolves around the **Arts Factory** (101-109 E Charleston Blvd), **Commerce Street Studios** (1551 S Commerce St) and the **Funk House** (1228 S Casino Center Blvd).

CityCenter   SHOPPING CENTER
(www.citycenter.com; 3780 Las Vegas Blvd S) We've seen this symbiotic relationship before (think giant hotel anchored by a mall 'concept') but the way that this futuristic-feeling complex places a small galaxy of hypermodern, chichi hotels in orbit around the glitzy **Crystals** (www.crystalsatcitycenter. com; 3720 Las Vegas Blvd S) shopping center is a first. The uber-upscale spread includes the subdued, stylish **Vdara** (www.vdara.com; 2600 W Harmon Ave), the hush-hush opulent **Mandarin Oriental** (www.mandarinoriental. com; 3752 Las Vegas Blvd) and the dramatic architectural showpiece **Aria** (www.arialasvegas. com; 3730 Las Vegas Blvd S), whose sophisticated casino provides a fitting backdrop to its many drop-dead gorgeous restaurants.

🏃 Activities

TOP CHOICE **Qua Baths & Spa**   SPA
(☑702-731-7776; www.harrahs.com/qua; Caesars Palace, 3570 Las Vegas Blvd S; ⊙6am-8pm) Social spa going is encouraged in the tea lounge, herbal steam room and arctic ice room, where dry-ice snowflakes fall.

Desert Adventures   KAYAKING, HIKING
(☑702-293-5026; www.kayaklasvegas.com; 1647 Nevada Hwy, Suite A, Boulder City; trips from $149) With Lake Mead and Hoover Dam just a few hours' drive away, would-be river rats should check out Desert Adventures for lots of half-, full- and multiday kayaking adventures. Hiking and horseback-riding trips, too.

Escape Adventures   MOUNTAIN-BIKING
(☑800-596-2953; www.escapeadventures.com; 8221 W Charleston Blvd; trips incl bike from $120) The source for guided mountain-bike tours of Red Rock Canyon State Park.

🛏 Sleeping

Rates rise and fall dramatically. Check hotel websites, which usually feature calendars listing day-by-day room rates.

THE STRIP

TOP CHOICE **Mandalay Bay**   CASINO HOTEL $$
(☑702-632-7777; www.mandalaybay.com; 3950 Las Vegas Blvd S; r $100-380; ❋@🛜☀) The ornately appointed rooms here have a South Seas theme, and amenities include floor-to-ceiling windows and luxurious bathrooms. Swimmers will swoon over the sprawling pool complex, with a sand-and-surf beach.

TOP CHOICE **Tropicana**   CASINO HOTEL $
(☑702-739-2222; www.troplv.com; 3801 Las Vegas Blvd S; r/ste from $40/140; ❋@🛜☀) As once-celebrated retro properties go under, the Tropicana – keeping the Strip tropical vibe going since 1953 – just got (surprise!) cool again. The multimillion-dollar renovation shows, from the airy casino to the lush, relaxing gardens with their newly unveiled pool and beach club. The earth-toned, breezy rooms and bi-level suites are bargains.

Cosmopolitan   CASINO HOTEL $$$
(☑702-698-7000; www.cosmopolitanlasve gas.com; 3708 Las Vegas Blvd S; r $200-400; ❋@🛜☀) Are the too-cool-for-school, hip rooms worth the price tag? The indie set seems to think so. The rooms are impressive exercises in mod design, but the real

delight of staying here is to stumble out of your room at 1am to play some pool in the upper lobbies before going on a mission to find the 'secret' pizza joint.

Bill's Gamblin' Hall & Saloon   CASINO HOTEL $

(☎702-737-2100; www.billslasvegas.com; 3595 Las Vegas Blvd S; r $70-200; ✴@☎) Set slap-bang mid-Strip with affordable rooms nice enough to sport plasma TVs, Bill's is great value, so book far ahead. Rooms feature Victorian-themed decor, and guests can use the pool next door at the Flamingo without charge.

Encore   CASINO HOTEL $$$

(☎702-770-8000; www.encorelasvegas.com; 3121 Las Vegas Blvd S; r $199-850; ✴@☎✱) Classy and playful more than overblown and opulent – even people cheering at the roulette table clap with a little more elegance. The rooms are studies in subdued luxury.

Caesars Palace   CASINO HOTEL $$

(☎866-227-5938; www.caesarspalace.com; 3570 Las Vegas Blvd S; r from $99; ✴@✱) Send away the centurions and decamp in style – Caesars' standard rooms are some of the most luxurious you will find in town.

Paris Las Vegas   CASINO HOTEL $$

(☎702-946-7000; www.parislasvegas.com; 3655 Las Vegas Blvd S; r from $80; ✴@✱) Nice rooms with a nod to classic French design; the newer Red Rooms are a study in sumptuous class.

DOWNTOWN & OFF THE STRIP

Downtown hotels are generally less expensive than those on the Strip.

TOP CHOICE Hard Rock   CASINO HOTEL $$

(☎702-693-5000; www.hardrockhotel.com; 4455 Paradise Rd; r $69-450; @☎✱) Everything about this boutique hotel spells stardom. French doors reveal skyline and palm tree views, and brightly colored Euro-minimalist rooms feature souped-up stereos and plasma-screen TVs. While we dig the jukeboxes in the HRH All-Suite Tower, the standard rooms are nearly as cool. The hottest action revolves around the lush Beach Club.

TOP CHOICE Artisan Hotel   BOUTIQUE HOTEL $

(☎800-554-4092; www.artisanhotel.com; 1501 W Sahara Ave; r from $40; ✴@☎✱) A Gothic baroque fantasy with a decadent dash of rock and roll, each suite is themed around the work of a different artist. Yet with one of Vegas' best after-parties raging on weekend nights downstairs (a fave with the local alternative set), you may not spend much time in your room. The libidinous, mysterious vibe here isn't for everyone, but if you like it, you'll love it. Artisan's sister hotel, Rumor (☎877-997-8667; www.rumorvegas.com; 455 E Harmon Ave; ste from $69; ✴@☎✱) is across from the Hard Rock and features a carefree, Miami-cool atmosphere; its airy suites overlook a palm-shaded courtyard pool area dotted with daybeds and hammocks perfect for lounging.

El Cortez Cabana Suites   BOUTIQUE HOTEL $

(☎800-634-6703; www.eccabana.com; 651 E Ogden Ave; ste $45-150; ✴@☎) You probably won't recognize this sparkling little boutique hotel for its brief movie cameo in Scorcese's *Casino* (hint: Sharon Stone was murdered here) and that's a good thing, because a massive makeover has transformed it into a vintage oasis downtown. Mod suites decked out in mint green include iPod docking stations and retro tiled bathrooms. Plus the coolest vintage casino in town – the El Cortez – is right across the street.

Platinum Hotel   BOUTIQUE HOTEL $$

(☎702-365-5000; www.theplatinumhotel.com; 211 E Flamingo Rd; r from $120; ✴@☎✱) Just off the Strip, the coolly modern rooms at this spiffy, non-gaming property are comfortable and full of nice touches – many have fireplaces and they all have kitchens and Jacuzzi tubs.

Red Rock Resort   RESORT $$$

(☎702-797-7878; www.redrocklasvegas.com; 11011 W Charleston Blvd; r $110-625; ✴@☎✱) Red Rock touts itself as the first off-Strip billion-dollar gaming resort, and most people who stay here eschew the Strip forever more. There's free transportation between the Strip, and outings to the nearby Red Rocks State Park and beyond. Rooms are well appointed and comfy.

✗ Eating

Sin City is an unmatched eating adventure. Reservations are a must for fancier restaurants; book in advance.

THE STRIP

On the Strip itself, cheap eats beyond fast-food joints are hard to find.

DON'T MISS

COOL POOLS

» **Hard Rock** (p697) Seasonal swim-up blackjack and killer 'Rehab' pool parties at the beautifully landscaped and uberhip Beach Club.

» **Mirage** (p699) The lush tropical pool is a sight to behold, with waterfalls tumbling off cliffs, deep grottoes and palm-tree-studded islands for sunbathing.

» **Mandalay Bay** (p700) Splash around an artificial sand-and-surf beach built from imported California sand and boasting a wave pool, lazy-river ride, casino and DJ-driven topless Moorea Beach Club.

» **Caesars Palace** (p697) Corinthian columns, overflowing fountains, magnificent palms and marble-inlaid pools make the Garden of the Gods Oasis divine. Goddesses proffer frozen grapes in summer, including at the topless Venus pool lounge.

» **Golden Nugget** (p700) Downtown's best pool offers lots of fun and zero attitude. Play poolside blackjack, or sip on a daiquiri in the Jacuzzi and watch the sharks frolic in the adjacent aquarium.

Sage
AMERICAN $$$

(☎877-230-2742; www.arialasvegas.com; Aria, 3730 Las Vegas Blvd S; mains $25-42; ☺5-11pm Mon-Sat) Acclaimed chef Shawn McClain meditates on the seasonally sublime with global inspiration and artisanal, farm-to-table ingredients in one of Vegas' most drop-dead gorgeous dining rooms. Don't miss the inspired seasonal cocktails doctored with housemade liqueurs, French absinthe and fruit purees.

TOP CHOICE Joël Robuchon
FRENCH $$$

(☎702-891-7925; MGM Grand, 3799 Las Vegas Blvd S; menus per person $120-420; ☺5:30-10pm Sun-Thu, to 10:30pm Fri & Sat) A once-in-a-lifetime culinary experience; block off a solid three hours and get ready to eat your way through the multicourse seasonal menu of traditional French fare. **L'Atelier de Joël Robuchon**, next door, is where you can belly up to the counter for a slightly more economical but still delicious meal.

TOP CHOICE DOCG Enoteca
ITALIAN $$

(☎702-698-7920; Cosmopolitan, 3708 Las Vegas Blvd S; mains $13-28; ☺10am-5pm) Among the Cosmopolitan's alluring dining options, this is one of the least glitzy – but most authentic – options. That's not to say it isn't loads of fun. Order up to-die-for fresh pasta or a wood-fired pizza in the stylish *enoteca* (wine shop)–inspired room that feels like you've joined a festive dinner party. Or head next door to sexy **Scarpetta**, which offers a more intimate, upscale experience by the same fantastic chef, Scott Conant.

Social House
JAPANESE $$$

(☎702-736-1122; www.socialhouselv.com; Crystals at CityCenter, 3720 Las Vegas Blvd S; mains $24-44; ☺5pm-10pm Mon-Thu, noon-11pm Fri & Sat, noon-10pm Sun) Nibble on creative dishes inspired by Japanese street food in one of the Strip's most serene yet sultry dining rooms. Watermarked scrolls, wooden screens, and loads of dramatic red and black conjure visions of Imperial Japan, while the sushi and steaks are totally contemporary.

RM Seafood
SEAFOOD $$$

(☎702-632-9300; www.rmseafood.com; Mandalay Place, 3930 Las Vegas Blvd S; lunch $13-36, dinner $20-75; ☺11:30am-11pm, restaurant 5-11pm) From ecoconscious chef Rick Moonen, modern American seafood dishes, such as Cajun popcorn and Maine lobster, come with comfort-food sides (like gourmet mac 'n' cheese), a raw shellfish and sushi bar, and a 'biscuit bar' serving savory salads.

Fiamma
ITALIAN $$$

(☎702-891-7600; www.mgmgrand.com; MGM Grand, 3799 Las Vegas Blvd S; meals $50-60; ☺5:30-10pm Sun & Mon, to 10:30pm Tue-Thu, to 11pm Fri & Sat) Fiamma is set in a row of outstanding restaurants at MGM Grand, but what sets it apart is that it's a top-tier dining experience you won't be paying off for the next decade. You haven't had spaghetti until you've had Fiamma's take on it, made with Kobe beef meatballs.

WORTHY INDULGENCES: BEST BUFFETS

» **Wicked Spoon Buffet** (www.cosmo politanlasvegas.com; Cosmopolitan, 3708 Las Vegas Blvd S)

» **Le Village Buffet** (www.parislasve gas.com; Paris Las Vegas, 3655 Las Vegas Blvd S)

» **Spice Market Buffet** (Planet Hollywood, 3667 Las Vegas Blvd S)

» **Sterling Brunch at Bally's** (☎702-967-7999; Bally's, 3645 Las Vegas Blvd S; ◷Sun)

» **Buffet Bellagio** (☎702-693-7111; www.bellagio.com; Bellagio, 3600 Las Vegas Blvd S)

» **Sunday Gospel Brunch** (☎702-632-7600; www.hob.com; House of Blues, Mandalay Bay, 3950 Las Vegas Blvd S)

Victorian Room CAFE $$
(www.billslasvegas.com; Bill's Gamblin' Hall & Saloon, 3595 Las Vegas Blvd S; mains $8-25; ◷24hr) A hokey old-fashioned San Francisco theme belies one of the best deals in sit-down restaurants in Las Vegas. The steak and eggs special ($7) is delicious around the clock.

Olives MEDITERRANEAN $$$
(☎702-693-8865; www.bellagio.com; Bellagio, 3600 Las Vegas Blvd S; mains $16-52; ◷lunch & dinner) Bostonian chef Todd English dishes up homage to the life-giving fruit. Flatbread pizzas, housemade pastas and flame-licked meats get top billing, and patio tables overlook Lake Como. Try his rollicking new CityCenter venture, **Todd English PUB** (www.toddenglishpub.com; Crystals at CityCenter, 3720 Las Vegas Blvd S; mains $13-24; ◷lunch & dinner), a strangely fun cross between a British pub and a frat party, with creative sliders, English pub classics and an interesting promotion: if you drink your beer in less than seven seconds, it's on the house.

Society Cafe CAFE $$
(www.wynnlasvegas.com; Encore, 3121 Las Vegas Blvd S; mains $14-30; ◷7am-midnight Sun-Thu, 7am-1am Fri & Sat) A slice of reasonably priced culinary heaven in the midst of Encore's loveliness. The basic cafe here is equal to fine dining at other joints.

'wichcraft SANDWICHES $
(www.mgmgrand.com; MGM Grand, 3799 Las Vegas Blvd S; sandwiches $8-11; ◷10am-5pm) This designy little sandwich shop, the brain-child of celebrity chef Tom Colicchio, is one of the best places to taste gourmet on a budget.

DOWNTOWN & OFF THE STRIP

Traditionally off the culinary radar, downtown's restaurants offers better value than those on the Strip, whether a casino buffet or a retro steakhouse.

Just west of the Strip, the Asian restaurants on Spring Mountain Rd in Chinatown are also good budget options, with lots of vegetarian choices.

TOP CHOICE Ferraro's ITALIAN $$
(www.ferraroslasvegas.com, 4480 Paradise Rd; mains $10-39; ◷11:30am-2am Mon-Fri, 4pm-2am Sat & Sun) The photos on the wall offer testimony to the fact that locals have been flocking to classy, family-owned Ferraro's for 85 years to devour savory Italian classics. These days, the fireplace patio and the amazing late night happy hour draw an eclectic crowd full of industry and foodie types at the friendly bar. To-die-for house-made pastas compete for attention with legendary osso buco, and a killer antipasti menu served til midnight.

TOP CHOICE Firefly TAPAS $$
(www.fireflylv.com; 3900 Paradise Rd; small dishes $4-10, large dishes $11-20; ◷11:30am-2am Sun-Thu, to 3am Fri & Sat) Locals seem to agree on one thing about the Vegas food scene: a meal at Firefly can be twice as fun as an overdone Strip restaurant, and half the price. Is that why it's always hopping? Nosh on traditional Spanish tapas, while the bartender pours sangria and flavor-infused *mojitos.*

Lotus of Siam THAI $$
(www.saipinchutima.com; 953 E Sahara Ave; mains $9-29; ◷11:30am-2pm Mon-Fri, 5:30-9:30pm Mon-Thu, 5:30-10pm Fri & Sat) The top Thai restaurant in the US? According to *Gourmet Magazine,* this is it. One bite of simple pad Thai – or any of the exotic northern Thai dishes – nearly proves it.

N9NE STEAKHOUSE $$$
(☎702-933-9900; www.palms.com; Palms, 4321 W Flamingo Rd; mains $26-43; ◷dinner) At this hip steakhouse heavy with celebs, a

dramatic dining room centers on a champagne-and-caviar bar. Chicago-style aged steaks and chops keep coming, along with everything from oysters Rockefeller to Pacific sashimi.

Pink Taco MEXICAN $$

(www.hardrockhotel.com; Hard Rock, 4455 Paradise Rd; mains $8-24; ☉7am-11am Mon-Thu, to 3am Fri & Sat) Whether it's the 99-cent taco and margarita happy hour, the leafy poolside patio, or the friendly rock and roll clientele, Pink Taco always feels like a worthwhile party.

Golden Gate SEAFOOD $

(www.goldengatecasino.com; 1 E Fremont St; ☉11am-3am) Famous $1.99 shrimp cocktails (super-size them for $3.99).

🍸 Drinking

For those who want to mingle with the locals and drink for free, check out **SpyOnVegas** (www.spyonvegas.com). It arranges an open bar at a different venue every weeknight.

THE STRIP

TOP CHOICE Mix LOUNGE

(www.mandalaybay.com; 64th fl, THEhotel at Mandalay Bay, 3950 Las Vegas Blvd S; cover after 10pm $20-25) THE place to grab sunset cocktails. The glassed-in elevator has amazing views, and that's before you even glimpse the mod interior design and soaring balcony.

TOP CHOICE Gold Lounge LOUNGE, CLUB

(www.arialasvegas.com; Aria, 3730 Las Vegas Blvd S; cover after 10pm $20-25) You won't find watered-down Top 40 at this luxe ultralounge, but you will find gold, gold and more gold. It's a fitting homage to Elvis: make a toast in front of the giant portrait of the King himself.

Chandelier BAR

(www.cosmopolitanlasvegas.com; Cosmopolitan, 3708 Las Vegas Blvd S; ☉5pm-2am) In a city full of lavish hotel lobby bars, this one pulls out all the stops. Kick back with the Cosmopolitan hipsters and enjoy the curiously thrilling feeling that you're tipsy inside a giant crystal chandelier.

LAVO LOUNGE, CLUB

(www.palazzo.com; Palazzo, 3325 Las Vegas Blvd S) One of the sexiest new restaurant-lounge-nightclub combos for the see-and-be seen set, Lavo's terrace is the place to be at happy hour. Sip a Bellini in the dramatically lit bar or stay to dance among reclining Renaissance nudes in the club upstairs.

Parasol Up – Parasol Down BAR, CAFE

(www.wynnlasvegas.com; Wynn Las Vegas, 3131 Las Vegas Blvd S; ☉11am-4am Sun-Thu, to 5am Fri & Sat) Unwind with a fresh fruit *mojito* by the soothing waterfall at the Wynn to experience one of Vegas' most successful versions of paradise.

Red Square BAR

(www.mandalaybay.com; Mandalay Bay, 3950 Las Vegas Blvd S) Heaps of Russian caviar, a solid ice bar and over 200 frozen vodkas, infusions and cocktails. Don a Russian army coat to sip vodka in the subzero vault.

DOWNTOWN & OFF THE STRIP

Want to chill out with the locals? Head to one of their go-to favorites.

TOP CHOICE Fireside Lounge COCKTAIL BAR

(www.peppermilllasvegas.com; Peppermill, 2985 Las Vegas Blvd S; ☉24hr) The Strip's most unlikely romantic hideaway is inside a retro coffee shop. Courting couples flock here for the low lighting, sunken fire pit and cozy nooks built for supping on multistrawed tiki drinks and for acting out your most inadvisable 'what happens in Vegas, stays in Vegas' moments.

TOP CHOICE Double Down Saloon BAR

(www.doubledownsaloon.com; 4640 Paradise Rd; no cover; ☉24hr) You can't get more punk rock than a dive whose tangy, blood-red house

---

EMERGENCY ARTS

A coffee shop, an art gallery, studios, and a de facto community center of sorts, all under one roof and right smack downtown? The **Emergency Arts** (www.emergencyartslv.com; 520 Fremont St) building, also home to **Beat Coffeehouse** (www.thebeatlv.com; sandwiches $6-7; ☉7am-midnight Mon-Fri, 9am-midnight Sat, 9am-3pm Sun) is a friendly bastion of laid-back cool and strong coffee where vintage vinyl spins on old turntables. If you're aching to meet some savvy locals who know their way around town, this is your hangout spot.

drink is named 'Ass Juice' and where happy hour means everything in the bar is two bucks. (Ass Juice and a Twinkie for $5: one of Vegas' bizarrely badass bargains.) Killer Juke box, cash only.

Beauty Bar   COCKTAIL BAR
(www.thebeautybar.com; 517 E Fremont St; cover $5-10) At the salvaged innards of a 1950s New Jersey beauty salon, swill a cocktail while you get a makeover demo or chill out with the hip DJs and live local bands. Then walk around the corner to the Downtown Cocktail Room, a speakeasy.

Frankie's Tiki Room   THEME BAR
(www.frankiestikiroom.com; 1712 W Charleston Blvd; ⊗24hr) At the only round-the-clock tiki bar in the US, the drinks are rated in strength by skulls and the top tiki sculptors and painters in the world have their work on display.

☆ Entertainment

Las Vegas has no shortage of entertainment on any given night, and Ticketmaster (☎702-474-4000; www.ticketmaster.com) sells tickets for pretty much everything.

Tix 4 Tonight   BOOKING SERVICE
(☎877-849-4868; www.tix4tonight.com; Bill's Gamblin' Hall & Saloon, 3595 Las Vegas Blvd S; ⊗10am-8pm) Offers half-price tix for a limited lineup of same-day shows and small discounts on 'always sold-out' shows.

Nightclubs & Live Music

Admission prices to nightclubs vary wildly based on the mood of door staff, male-to-female ratio and how crowded the club is that night.

TOP CHOICE Marquee   CLUB
(www.cosmopolitanlasvegas.com; Cosmopolitan, 3708 Las Vegas Blvd) When someone asks what the coolest club in Vegas is, Marquee is the undisputed answer. Celebrities (we spotted Macy Gray as we danced through the crowd), an outdoor beach club, hot DJs and that certain *je ne sais quoi* that makes a club worth waiting in line for.

TOP CHOICE Tryst   CLUB
(www.trystlasvegas.com; Wynn Las Vegas, 3131 Las Vegas Blvd S) All gimmicks aside, the flowing waterfall makes this place ridiculously (and literally) cool. Blood-red booths and plenty of space to dance ensure that you can have a killer time even without splurging for bottle service.

Drai's   CLUB
(www.drais.net; Bill's Gamblin' Hall & Saloon, 3595 Las Vegas Blvd S; ⊗1-8am Thu-Mon) Feel ready for an after-hours scene straight outta Hollywood? Things don't really get going here until 4am, when DJs spinning progressive discs keep the cool kids content. Dress to kill.

Stoney's Rockin' Country   LIVE MUSIC
(www.stoneysrockincountry.com; 9151 Las Vegas Blvd S; cover $5-10; ⊗7pm-late Thu-Sun) An off-Strip place that's worth the trip. Friday and Saturday features all-you-can-drink draft beer specials and free line-dancing lessons. The mechanical bull is a blast.

Moon   CLUB
(www.n9negroup.com; Palms, 4321 W Flamingo Rd; cover from $20; ⊗11pm-4am Tue & Thu-Sun) Stylishly outfitted like a nightclub in outer space; the retractable roof opens for dancing to pulsating beats under the stars. Admission includes entry to the only Playboy Club in the world.

Production Shows

There are hundreds of shows to choose from in Vegas. Any Cirque du Soleil show tends to be an unforgettable experience.

TOP CHOICE Steel Panther   LIVE MUSIC
(☎702-617-7777; www.greenvalleyranchresort. com; Green Valley Resort, 2300 Paseo Verde Pkwy, Henderson; admission free; ⊗11pm-late Thu) A hair-metal tribute band makes fun of the audience, themselves and the 1980s with sight gags, one-liners and many a drug and sex reference.

TOP CHOICE LOVE   PERFORMING ARTS
(☎702-792-7777; www.cirquedusoleil.com; tickets $99-150) At the Mirage is a popular addition to the Cirque du Soleil lineup; locals who have seen many a Cirque production come and go say it's the best one yet.

O   PERFORMING ARTS
(☎702-796-9999; www.cirquedusoleil.com; tickets $99-200) Still a favorite is Cirque du Soleil's aquatic show, O, performed at the Bellagio.

Zumanity   PERFORMING ARTS
(☎702-740-6815; www.cirquedusoleil.com; tickets $69-129) A Sensual and sexy adult-only show at New York New York.

VEGAS CLUBBING 101

Brave the velvet rope – or skip it altogether – with these nightlife survival tips we culled from the inner circle of Vegas doormen, VIP hosts and concierges.

» Avoid waiting in that long line by booking ahead with the club VIP host. Most bigger clubs have someone working the door during the late afternoon and early evening hours.

» Ask the concierge of your hotel for clubbing suggestions – he or she will almost always have free passes for clubs, or be able to make you reservations with the VIP host.

» If you hit blackjack at the high-roller table or just want to splurge, think about bottle service. Yes, it's expensive (starting at around $300 to $400 and upwards for a bottle, including mixers, plus tax and tip), but it usually waives cover charge (and waiting in line) for your group, plus you get to chill out at a table – valuable 'real estate' in club speak.

🔒 Shopping

Bonanza Gifts   GIFTS
(2440 Las Vegas Blvd S) The best place for only-in-Vegas kitsch souvenirs.

The Attic   VINTAGE
(www.atticvintage.com; 1018 S Main St; ⊙10am-6pm, closed Sun) Be mesmerized by fabulous hats and wigs, hippie-chic clubwear and lounge-lizard furnishings at Vegas' best vintage store.

Fashion Show Mall   MALL
(www.thefashionshow.com; 3200 Las Vegas Blvd S) Nevada's biggest and flashiest mall.

Forum Shops   MALL
(www.caesarspalace.com; Caesars Palace, 3570 Las Vegas Blvd S) Upscale stores in an air-conditioned version of Ancient Rome.

Grand Canal Shoppes   MALL
(www.thegrandcanalshoppes.com; Venetian, 3355 Las Vegas Blvd S) Italianate indoor luxury mall with gondolas.

Shoppes at Palazzo   MALL
(Palazzo, 3327 Las Vegas Blvd S) Sixty international designers, from Tory Burch to Jimmy Choo, flaunt their goodies.

Miracle Mile Shops   MALL
(www.miraclemileshopslv.com; Planet Hollywood, 3663 Las Vegas Blvd S) A staggering 1.5 miles long; get a tattoo, drink and duds.

ℹ Information

Emergency & Medical Services
Gamblers Anonymous (☎702-385-7732) Assistance with gambling concerns.
Police (☎702-828-3111)

Sunrise Hospital & Medical Center (☎702-731-8000; 3186 S Maryland Pkwy)
University Medical Center (☎702-383-2000; 1800 W Charleston Blvd)

Internet Access
Wi-fi is available in most hotel rooms (about $10 to $25 per day, sometimes included in the 'resort fee') and there are internet kiosks with attached printers in most hotel lobbies.

Internet Resources & Media
Cheapo Vegas (www.cheapovegas.com) Good for a run-down of casinos with low table limits and their insider's guide to cheap eating.
Las Vegas Review-Journal (www.lvrj.com) Daily paper with a weekend guide, *Neon*, on Friday.
Las Vegas Tourism (www.onlyinvegas.com) Official tourism website.
Las Vegas Weekly (www.lasvegasweekly.com) Free weekly with good entertainment and restaurant listings.
Las Vegas.com (www.lasvegas.com) Travel services.
Lasvegaskids.net (www.lasvegaskids.net) The lowdown on what's up for the wee ones.
Vegas.com (www.vegas.com) Travel information with booking service.

Money
Every hotel-casino and bank and most convenience stores have an ATM. The ATM fee at most casinos is around $5. Best to stop at off-Strip banks if possible.
American Express (☎702-739-8474; Fashion Show Mall, 3200 Las Vegas Blvd S; ⊙10am-9pm Mon-Fri, 10am-8pm Sat, noon-6pm Sun) Changes currencies at competitive rates.

Post
Post office (☎702-382-5779; 201 Las Vegas Blvd S) Downtown.

Tourist Information
Las Vegas Visitor Information Center (☎702-847-4858; www.visitlasvegas.com; 3150 Paradise Rd; ⊙8am-5pm) Free local calls, internet access and maps galore.

❶ Getting There & Around

Just south of the major Strip casinos and easily accessible from I-15, **McCarran International Airport** (www.mccarran.com) has direct flights from most US cities, and some from Canada and Europe. **Bell Trans** (☎702-739-7990; www.bell-trans.com) offers a shuttle service ($6.50) between the airport and the Strip. Fares to downtown destinations are slightly higher. At the airport, exit door 9 near baggage claim to find the Bell Trans booth.

All of the attractions in Vegas have free self-parking and valet parking available (tip $2). Fast, fun and fully wheelchair accessible, the **monorail** (☎702-699-8299; www.lvmonorail. com) connects the Sahara to the MGM Grand, stopping at major Strip megaresorts along the way, and operating from 7am to 2am Monday to Thursday and until 3am Friday through Sunday. A single ride is $5, a 24-hour pass is $12 and a three-day pass is $28. The **Deuce** (☎702-228-7433; www.rtcsouthernnevada.com), a local double-decker bus, runs frequently 24 hours daily between the Strip and downtown (two-/24-hour pass $5/7).

Understand California

>

population per sq mile

USA California Los Angeles

≈ 80 people

California Today

California Dreamin' vs Reality

Even if you've seen it in movies or on TV, California still comes as a shock to the system. Venice Beach skateboarders, Santa Cruz hippies, Rodeo Drive–pillaging trophy wives and Silicon Valley millionaires aren't on different channels; they all live here, where tolerance for other people's beliefs, be they conservative, liberal or just plain wacky, is the social glue.

Recently, the most divisive political hot-potato topic has been same-sex marriage, and the proposed constitutional amendment to ban it, which remains tied up in legal battles. Medical marijuana is old news for Californians, who approved a state proposition allowing its use back in 1996 – although the proliferation of marijuana clubs and rumors of Mexican cartel intervention have raised eyebrows lately.

Roots of Environmentalism

There's no denying that California's culture of conspicuous consumption is exported via Hollywood flicks and reality TV (hello, *The Hills* and *Real Housewives of Orange County*). But since the 1960s, Californians have trailblazed another way by choosing more sustainable foods and low-impact lifestyles, preserving old-growth forests with tree-sitting activism, declaring nuclear-free zones, pushing for environmentally progressive legislation and establishing the USA's biggest market for hybrid vehicles.

That shouldn't come as a surprise. It was Californians who originally helped kick-start the world's conservation movement in the midst of the industrial revolution, with laws curbing industrial dumping, swaths of prime real estate set aside as urban greenspace, and pristine wilderness protected by national and state parks. Today, even conservative California politicians prioritize environmental issues. That said, the state's current budget crisis has resulted in deep cuts in environmental protections.

Natural Wonders

» Highest point: Mt Whitney (14,497ft)

» Lowest point: Death Valley (-282ft)

» Area of national and state parks: 6.5 million acres

» Miles of coast-line: 1100

Top Films

» *Maltese Falcon* (1941)
» *Vertigo* (1958)
» *The Graduate* (1967)
» *Chinatown* (1974)
» *Bladerunner* (1982)
» *Pulp Fiction* (1994)
» *Sideways* (2004)

Top Downloads

» 'California Dreaming' – Mamas and the Papas
» 'Surfer Girl' – Beach Boys
» 'Californication' – Red Hot Chili Peppers
» 'California Love' – 2Pac
» 'California Gurls' – Katy Perry

Dos and Don'ts

» Do slather on the sunblock, even on cloudy days.
» Do leave tips where appropriate.
» Don't smoke indoors.
» Don't get tanked while wine-tasting.

belief systems
(% of population)

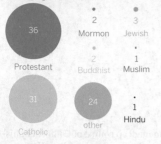

36 Protestant

2 Mormon

3 Jewish

2 Buddhist

1 Muslim

31 Catholic

24 other

1 Hindu

if California were 100 people

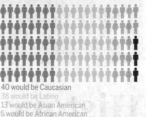

40 would be Caucasian
38 would be Latino
13 would be Asian American
6 would be African American
3 would be other

Fast Companies

California's technological innovations need no introduction by anyone. Perhaps you've heard of PCs, iPods, Google and the internet? The home of Silicon Valley and a burgeoning biotech industry, Northern California is giving Southern California's gargantuan entertainment industry a run for its money as the state's main economic engine.

Slow Food

You may notice Californians tend to proselytize about their food and idolize homegrown chefs like rock stars. After a few bites, you may begin to understand their obsession. Mulling over menus also means taking a stand on issues close to many Californian's hearts: organic and non-GMO crops, veganism, grass-fed versus grain-fed meat, biodynamic vineyards, fair-trade coffee, and the importance of buying local food. It's no accident that the term 'locavore' – meaning people who eat food grown locally – was invented here.

New World Religions

Despite their proportionately small numbers, California's alternative religions and utopian communities dominate the popular imagination, from modern-day pagans to new-age healers. California made national headlines in the 1960s with gurus from India, in the 1970s with Jim Jones' People's Temple and Erhard Seminars Training (EST), in the 1990s with Heaven's Gate doomsday UFO cult in San Diego, and in 2011 when Oakland radio minister Harold Camping proselytized that the Rapture was about to happen. Around since 1954, the controversial Church of Scientology is still seeking acceptance with celebrity proponents from movie-star Tom Cruise to musician Beck.

California by the Numbers

» Population: 37.3 million

» Proportion of US GDP: 13% ($1.9 trillion)

» Annual taxes earned from medical marijuana sales: $105 million

Go Outside

If you want to do like locals do, get back to nature. Over 60% of Californians say they've hugged a tree, nearly 25% have tried surfing and at least one out of every five skinny dips on occasion.

Rural Life

Less than 10% of Californians live in rural areas, yet they're responsible for one of the state's major industries: agriculture. The Central Valley still produces almost 50% of all fruit harvested in the US.

Tribal Casinos

Though Native Californian tribal reservations account for less than 1% of the total land in the state, voter-approved 1998 state Proposition 5, allowing gambling on reservations, generates almost $7 billion annually.

History

Gold is the usual reason given for the madcap course of Californian history, but it all actually started with a dazzling pack of lies. Have you heard the one about the sunny island of Amazon women armed with gold weapons, who flew griffins fed with their own sons? No, this isn't a twisted Hollywood *Wonder Woman* remake. It's the plot of Garcí Ordóñez de Montalvo's 16th-century Spanish novel *Las Sergas de Esplanadíans* which inspired Spanish adventurers, including Hernán Cortés, who said in a 1524 letter from Meoxico he hoped to find the island a couple of days' sail to the northwest.

Apart from the mythical bird-beasts and filicidal Wonder Women, Montalvo and Cortés weren't entirely wrong. Across the water from mainland Mexico was a peninsula that Spanish colonists called Baja (lower) California, after Queen Calafía, Montalvo's legendary queen of the Amazons. Above it was Alta California – not exactly an island, though certainly rich in gold. But in Montalvo's tale, the warrior Queen Calafía willingly changed her wild ways, settled down and converted to Christianity – not quite how it happened in California.

Before the Ghosts

For starters, indigenous Californians weren't as easily characterized as Montalvo's Amazons. By AD 1500 more than 300,000 Native Americans in the California area spoke some 100 distinct languages. Most political leaders were men, but women shamans summoned dreamworld powers to cure illness, control the weather and bring victories in hunting and war. Central-coast fishing communities such as the Ohlone, Miwok and Pomo built subterranean roundhouses and saunas, where they held ceremonies, told stories and gambled for fun. Northwest hunting communities such as the Hupa, Karok and Wiyot constructed big houses and redwood dugout canoes, while southwest Californian Yumaand Mojave

TIMELINE	6000–10,000 BC	AD 1542–43	1769
	Native American communities get settled across the state, from the Yurok in gabled redwood houses in the North to the Tipai-Ipai in thatched domed dwellings in Southern California.	Juan Rodríguez Cabrillo becomes the first European explorer to navigate the California coast. After stumbling against a jagged rock, his journey ends with a gangrenous wound that causes his death.	Padre Junípero Serra and Captain Gaspar de Portolá lead a Spanish expedition to establish missions, rounding up Native Americans as converts and conscripted labor.

made sophisticated pottery and developed irrigation systems that made farming in the desert possible.

Unlike Montalvo's Amazons, Native Americans did not hoard gold or attack offensively. Native Americans in California had no written language but observed oral contracts and zoning laws, and expected that newcomers would likewise make good on their word. For all these reasons, the 1542 arrival of Juan Rodríguez Cabrillo's Spanish exploratory mission to Alta California did not immediately spark a war.

When English pirate Sir Francis Drake harbored briefly on Miwok land north of San Francisco, the English were taken to be the dead returned from the afterworld, and shamans saw the arrival as a warning of apocalypse. Story and gift exchanges eased tensions between Native Americans and Spanish and English adventurers, but the omens weren't entirely wrong. Within a century of the arrival of Spanish colonists in 1769, California's Native American population would be decimated to 20,000 by European diseases, conscripted labor regimes and famine.

Spain's Mission Impossible

When 18th-century Russian and English trappers began trading valuable otter pelts from Alta California, Spain concocted a plan for colonization. For the glory of God and the tax coffers of Spain, missions would be built across the state, and within 10 years these would be going concerns run by local converts. This 'Sacred Expedition' was approved by Spain's quixotic Visitor-General José de Gálvez of Mexico, who was full of grand schemes – including controlling Sonora province with a trained army of apes.

Almost immediately after Spain's missionizing plan was approved in 1769, it began to fail. When Franciscan Padre Junípero Serra and Captain Gaspar de Portolá made the overland journey to establish Mission San Diego de Alcalá, only half the sailors on their supply ships survived the ocean journey. Portolá had heard of a fabled cove to the north, but failing to recognize Monterey Bay in the fog, he gave up and turned back.

Portolá reported to Gálvez that if the Russians or English wanted California, they were welcome to it. But Padre Serra wouldn't give up, and secured support to set up presidios (military posts) alongside missions in 1775 in Monterey, in 1776 in San Francisco and in 1782 in Santa Barbara. When soldiers weren't paid regularly, they looted and pillaged local communities. Clergy objected to this treatment of potential Native American converts, but relied on soldiers to round up conscripts to build missions. In exchange for their labor, Native Americans were allowed one meal a day (when available) and a place in God's kingdom – which came much

Native Californians
- » Cahuilla
- » Hupa
- » Karok
- » Miwok
- » Mojave
- » Ohlone
- » Paiute
- » Pomo
- » Wiyot
- » Yuma

HISTORY SPAIN'S MISSION IMPOSSIBLE

1821	1826–32	1835	1846
Mexican independence ends Spanish colonization of California. Mexico inherits 21 missions, along with unruly Californio cowboys and a decimated Native American population.	Teenager Kit Carson blazes the Santa Fe Trail to Los Angeles through 900 miles of rattlesnake-filled high desert and plains vigilantly guarded by the Apache and Comanche.	An emissary of President Andrew Jackson makes a formal offer to buy Northern California, but Mexico tries to unsuccessfully sell California as a package deal to England instead.	Sierra Nevada blizzards strand the Donner Party of settlers who avoid starvation by cannibalism. Five women and two men snowshoe 100 miles for help; half the party of 87 survives.

THE BEAR FLAG REPUBLIC

In June 1846, American settlers tanked up on liquid courage declared independence in the town of Sonoma. Not a shot was fired – instead, they captured the nearest Mexican official and hoisted a hastily made flag. Locals awoke to discover they were living in the independent 'Bear Republic', under a flag with a grizzly that looked like a drunken dog (p185). The Bear Flag Republic lasted an entire month before US orders arrived to stand down.

sooner than expected, due to the smallpox the Spanish brought with them.

Native Americans often rebelled against the 21 Spanish missions. Only a month after the mission was established in San Diego, escaped converts attacked it. After Yuma villagers found soldiers' cattle munching their winter bean supply in 1781, they launched a surprise attack, killing 30 soldiers and four priests and holding others for ransom. Spain wasn't prepared to handle losses on an already unprofitable venture, and after Padre Serra passed away in 1784 only a handful of skittish soldiers were left on duty.

California Under Mexico

Spain wasn't sorry to lose California to Mexico in the 1810–21 Mexican war for independence. As long as missions had the best grazing land, *rancheros* (ranchers) couldn't compete in the growing market for cowhides and tallow (for use in soap). But Spanish, Mexican and American settlers who had intermarried with Native Americans were now a sizable constituency, and together these 'Californios' convinced Mexico to secularize the missions in 1834.

Californios quickly snapped up deeds to privatized mission property. Only a few dozen Californios were literate in the entire state, so boundary disputes that arose were settled with muscle, not paper. By law, half the lands were supposed to go to Native Americans who worked at the missions, but few Native American mission workers actually received their entitlements.

Through marriage and other mergers, most of the land and wealth in California was held by just 46 *ranchero* families by 1846. The average *rancho* (ranch) was now 16,000 acres, having grown from cramped shanties to elegant haciendas where women were supposedly confined to quarters at night. But *rancheras* (ranch women) weren't so easily bossed around: women owned 13% of Californian ranches, rode horses

1848	1850	1851	May 10, 1869
Gold is discovered near present-day Placerville by mill employees. Sometime San Francisco newspaper publisher and full-time bigmouth Sam Brannan lets word out, and the Gold Rush is on.	With hopes of solid-gold tax revenues, the US dubs California the 31st state. When miners find tax loopholes, SoCal ranchers are left carrying the tax burden, creating early north–south rivalries.	The discovery of gold in Australia means cheering in the streets of Melbourne and panic in the streets of San Francisco, as the price for California gold plummets.	The Golden Spike is nailed in place, completing the first transcontinental railroad and connecting California to the East Coast.

as hard as men and caused romantic scandals worthy of *telenovelas* (soap operas).

Meanwhile, Americans were arriving in the trading post of Los Angeles via the Santa Fe Trail. The northern passes through the Sierras were trickier, as the Donner Party (see p390) tragically discovered in 1846: stranded in a desolate mountain pass, they resorted to cannibalism. Still, the US saw potential in California, but when US president Andrew Jackson offered financially strapped Mexico $500,000 for the territory, the offer was tersely rejected. After the US annexed the Mexican territory of Texas in 1845, Mexico broke off diplomatic relations and ordered all foreigners without proper papers deported from California.

The Mexican–American War was declared in 1846, lasting two years with very little fighting in California. Hostilities ended with the Treaty of Guadalupe Hidalgo, ceding California and the present-day southwest to the USA. Mexico could not have had worse timing: within days of signing away California, gold was discovered.

Eureka!

The Gold Rush began with another bluff. Real estate speculator, lapsed Mormon and tabloid publisher Sam Brannan was looking to unload some California swampland in 1848 when he heard rumors of gold flakes found near Sutter's Mill, 120 miles from San Francisco. Figuring this news should sell some newspapers and raise real estate values, Brannan published the rumor as fact. Initially the story didn't generate excitement – gold flake had surfaced in southern California as far back as 1775. So Brannan ran another story, this time verified by Mormon employees at Sutter's Mill who had sworn him to secrecy. Brannan reportedly kept his word by running through the San Francisco streets, brandishing gold entrusted to him as tithes for the Mormon church, shouting, 'Gold on the American River!'

Other newspapers around the world weren't scrupulous about getting their facts straight either, hastily publishing stories of 'gold mountains' near San Francisco. By 1850, the year California was fast-tracked for admission as the 31st state, California's non-native population had ballooned from 15,000 to 93,000. Most arrivals weren't Americans, but Peruvians, Australians, Chileans and Mexicans, with some Chinese, Irish, native Hawaiian and French prospectors.

Early arrivals panned for gold side by side, slept in close quarters, drank firewater with Chinese takeout and splurged on French food and Australian wines. But with each wave of arrivals, profits dropped and gold became harder to find. In 1848 each prospector earned an average of about $300,000 in today's terms; by 1849, earnings were $95,000–

In her bestselling *The Joy Luck Club*, Amy Tan weaves the stories of four Chinese-born women and their American-born daughters into a textured history of immigration and aspiration in San Francisco's Chinatown.

1882

The US Chinese Exclusion Act suspends new immigration from China, denies citizenship to those already in the country and sanctions racially targeted laws that stay on the books until 1943.

1906

An earthquake levels entire blocks of San Francisco in 47 seconds flat, setting off fires that rage for three days. Survivors start rebuilding immediately.

SCIENCE PHOTO LIBRARY/GETTY ©

1927

After a year of tinkering, San Francisco inventor Philo Farnsworth transmits the first successful TV broadcast of...a straight line.

» San Francisco earthquake

145,000; by 1865 they dipped to $35,000. When surface gold became harder to find, miners picked, shoveled and dynamited through mountains. The work was grueling and dangerous, and with few doctors, injuries often proved lethal. The cost of living in cold, filthy camps was sky-high: in 1849 a cot in a drafty flophouse among men who rarely washed could run $10 a night (about $250 in today's terms), and such culinary abominations as a jelly omelette cost $2 (about $50 today). With one woman per 400 men in some camps, many turned to paid company, drink and opium for consolation.

Vigilantes & Robber Barons

Prospectors who did best arrived early and got out quick; those who stayed too long either lost fortunes searching for the next nugget or became targets of resentment. Successful Peruvians and Chileans were harassed and denied renewals to their mining claims, and most left California by 1855. Native American laborers who helped the '49ers strike it rich were denied the right to hold claims. Any wrongdoing was hastily pinned on Australians – from 1851 to 1856, San Francisco's self-appointed Vigilante Committee tried, convicted and hung 'Sydney Ducks' in hour-long proceedings known as 'kangaroo trials.' Australian boarding houses were torched six times by arsonists from 1849 to 1851, so when gold was found in Australia in 1851 many were ready to head home. Also at the receiving end of nativist hostility were the Chinese, the most populous group in California by 1860. Frozen out of mining claims, many Chinese opened service-based businesses that survived when mining ventures went bust – incurring resentment among miners.

Such rivalries obscured the real competitive threat posed not by fellow miners or service workers, but by those who controlled the means of production: California's 'robber barons.' These Californian speculators hoarded the capital and industrial machinery necessary for deep-mining operations at the Comstock silver lode, discovered in 1860. As mining became industrialized, fewer miners were needed, and jobless prospectors turned anger toward a convenient target: Chinese dockworkers. Discriminatory Californian laws restricting housing, employment and citizenship for anyone born in China were reinforced in the 1882 US Chinese Exclusion Act, which remained law until 1943.

Laws limiting work options for Chinese arrivals served the needs of robber barons, who needed cheap labor to build railroads to their claims and reach East Coast markets. To blast tunnels through the Sierras, workers were lowered down sheer mountain faces in wicker baskets, planted lit sticks of dynamite in rock crevices, and urgently tugged the rope to be hoisted out of harm's way. Those who survived the day's work were

Chinatown (1974) is the fictionalized yet surprisingly accurate account of the brutal water wars that were waged to build both Los Angeles and San Francisco.

WATER WARS

1928	1934	1942	July 17, 1955
The Jazz Singer, about a Jewish singer who rebels against his father and performs in blackface, is the first feature-length 'talkie' movie. Worldwide movie demand kicks off Hollywood's Golden Age.	A longshoremen's strike ends with 34 San Francisco strikers and sympathizers shot and 40 beaten by police. After mass funeral processions and citywide strikes, shipping magnates meet union demands.	Executive Order 9066 sends 120,000 Japanese Americans to internment camps. California's Japanese American Citizens' League files civil rights lawsuits, providing legal support for the 1964 Civil Rights Act.	Disneyland opens to guests and bad press. As crowds swarm the park, plumbing breaks and Fantasyland springs a gas leak. Walt Disney calls a do-over, relaunching successfully the next day.

confined to bunkhouses under armed guard in cold, remote mountain regions. With little other choice of legitimate employment, an estimated 12,000 Chinese laborers blasted through the Sierra Nevada, meeting the westbound end of the railroad in 1869.

Oil & Water

During the American Civil War (1861–65), California couldn't count on food shipments from the East Coast, and started growing its own. California recruited Midwestern homesteaders to farm the Central Valley with shameless propaganda. 'Acres of Untaken Government Land for a Million Farmers without Cyclones or Blizzards,' trumpeted one California-boosting poster, neglecting to mention earthquakes or ongoing land disputes with *rancheros* and Native American groups. It worked: more than 120,000 homesteaders came to California in the 1870s to 1880s.

Homesteaders discovered that California's gold rush had left the state badly tarnished. Hills were stripped bare, vegetation wiped out, streams silted up and mercury washed into water supplies. Cholera spread through open sewers of poorly drained camps claiming many lives, and smaller finds in southern California mountains diverted streams essential to dry valleys below. Because mining claims leased by the US government were granted significant tax exemptions, there were insufficient public funds for clean-up programs or public water works.

Frustrated Californian farmers south of San Luis Obispo voted to secede from California in 1859, but appeals for secession were shelved during the Civil War. In 1884 Southern Californians passed a pioneering law preventing dumping into Californian rivers and, with the support of budding agribusiness and real-estate concerns, passed bond measures to build aqueducts and dams that made large-scale farming and real-estate development possible. By the 20th century the lower one-third of the state took two-thirds of available water supplies, inspiring Northern Californian calls for secession.

Edward Doheny had gone broke speculating on real estate in Los Angeles by 1892, until he dug himself a hole that would change California. By the following year his oil well was yielding 40 barrels a day; by 1900 California was producing 4 million barrels of 'black gold.' Downtown Los Angeles sprang up around Doheny's well, becoming a hub of industry with 100,000 inhabitants.

While bucolic Southern California was urbanizing, Northern Californians who had witnessed devastation from mining and logging firsthand were forming the nation's first conservation movement. Naturalist John Muir founded the Sierra Club in 1892 and played a part in the establishment of the National Park Service. Dams and pipelines to

The Oscar-winning *There Will Be Blood* (2007), adapted from Upton Sinclair's book *Oil!*, depicts a Californian oil magnate and was based on real-life SoCal tycoon Edward Doheny.

HISTORY OIL & WATER

1957	1966	1967	June 5, 1968
At the height of McCarthyism, City Lights wins a landmark ruling against book banning over the publication of Allen Ginsberg's 'Howl'.	Ronald Reagan is elected governor, setting a career precedent for fading film stars. He served until 1975, and in 1981 became the 40th president of the United States.	The Summer of Love kicks off on January 14 at the Human Be-In in Golden Gate Park with blown conch shells and brain cells and draft cards used as rolling papers.	Presidential candidate, former US attorney-general, civil-rights ally and antipoverty campaigner Robert Kennedy is fatally shot moments after winning the critical California primary.

Oscar-winning film *LA Confidential* (1997) traces three cops' search for the truth amid the Hollywood deception and police corruption of postwar Los Angeles.

support communities in SoCal deserts and coastal cities were built over his objections – including Hetch Hetchy reservoir in Yosemite, which supplies Bay Area water today. In drought-prone California, tensions still regularly come to a boil between developers and conservationists, and NorCal drinking-water hoarders and SoCal lawn-water splurgers.

Reforming the Wild West

When the great earthquake and fire hit San Francisco in 1906, it signaled change for California. With public funds for citywide water mains and fire hydrants siphoned off by corrupt bosses, there was only one functioning water source in San Francisco. When the smoke lifted, one thing was clear: it was time for the Wild West to change its ways.

While San Francisco was rebuilt at a rate of 15 buildings a day, California's reformers set to work on city, state and national politics, one plank at a time. Californians concerned about public health and trafficking in women pushed for the passage of the 1914 statewide Red Light Abatement Act. Mexico's revolution from 1910 to 1921 brought a new wave of migrants and revolutionary ideas, including ethnic pride and worker solidarity. As California's ports grew, longshoremen's unions coordinated a historic 83-day strike in 1934 along the entire West Coast that forced concessions for safer working conditions and fair pay.

At the height of the Depression in 1935, some 200,000 farming families fleeing the drought-struck Dust Bowl in Texas and Oklahoma arrived in California, where they found scant pay and deplorable working conditions at major farming concerns. California's artists alerted middle America to the migrants' plight, and the nation rallied around Dorothea Lange's haunting documentary photos of famine-struck families and John Steinbeck's harrowing fictionalized account in his 1939 novel *The Grapes of Wrath*. The book was widely banned, and the 1940 movie version, its star Henry Fonda and Steinbeck himself were accused of harboring Communist sympathies. But Steinbeck won both the Pulitzer and Nobel Prizes for his masterwork, and the public sympathy he generated for farm workers helped launch the United Farm Workers' union.

The Hollywood Walk of Fame celebrates top talent with more than 2000 stars embedded in the sidewalk. With some peeling stars posing tripping hazards, the Walk is now undergoing restoration.

California's workforce permanently changed in WWII, when women and African Americans were recruited for wartime industries and Mexican workers were brought in to fill labor shortages. Contracts in military communications and aviation attracted an international elite of engineers, who would launch California's high-tech industry. Within a decade after the war, California's population had grown by 40%, reaching almost 13 million.

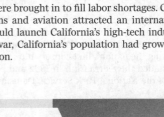

1969

UCLA links to Stanford Research Institute via ARPANET, a precursor to the internet. When an unsolicited group message about politics is sent across the network, spam is born.

1969

Native American activists symbolically reclaim Alcatraz as native land until ousted by the FBI in 1971. Public support for protesters strengthens self-rule concessions for Native American territories.

CHAD EHLERS/ALAMY ©

» Alcatraz (p79)

CALIFORNIA'S CIVIL RIGHTS MOVEMENT

Before the 1963 march on Washington, DC, the civil rights movement was well under way in California. When 110,000 Japanese Americans along the West Coast were ordered into internment camps by President Roosevelt in 1942, the San Francisco–based Japanese American Citizen's League immediately filed suits that advanced all the way to the Supreme Court. These lawsuits established groundbreaking civil rights legal precedents, and in 1992 internees received reparations and an official letter of apology for internment signed by George HW Bush. Adopting the non-violent resistance practices of Mahatma Gandhi and Martin Luther King Jr, labor leaders César Chávez and Dolores Huerta formed United Farm Workers in 1962 to champion the rights of under-represented immigrant laborers. While civil rights leaders marched on Washington, Chávez and Californian grape pickers marched on Sacramento, bringing the issue of fair wages and the health risks of pesticides to the nation's attention. When Bobby Kennedy was sent to investigate, he sided with Chávez, bringing Latinos into the US political fold.

Hollywood & Counterculture

Perhaps California's greatest export was the sunny, wholesome image it projected to the world through its homegrown film and TV industry. In 1908, California became a convenient movie location because of its consistent sunlight and versatile locations, although its role was limited to doubling for more exotic locales and providing backdrops for period piece productions like Charlie Chaplin's *Gold Rush* (1925). But gradually, California began stealing the scene in movies and iconic TV shows with waving palms and sunny beaches. Through the power of Hollywood, California tamed its Wild West image and adopted a more marketable image of beach boys and bikini-clad blondes.

Not all Californians saw themselves as extras in *Beach Blanket Bingo* (1965), however. WWII sailors discharged for insubordination and homosexuality in San Francisco found themselves at home in North Beach's bebop jazz clubs, Bohemian coffeehouses and City Lights Bookstore. San Francisco became the home of free speech and free spirits, and soon everyone who was anyone was getting arrested: Beat poet Lawrence Ferlinghetti for publishing Allen Ginsberg's epic poem 'Howl', comedian Lenny Bruce for uttering the F-word onstage and Carol Doda for going topless. When the CIA made the mistake of using writer and willing test-subject Ken Kesey to test psychoactive drugs intended to create the ultimate soldier, it inadvertently kicked off the psychedelic era. At the January 14, 1967 Human Be-In in Golden Gate Park, trip-master Timothy Leary urged a crowd of 20,000 hippies to dream a new American dream and 'turn on,

Erin Brockovich (2000) is based on the true story of a Southern Californian mom who discovered a small town being poisoned by industrial waste, and won a class-action lawsuit that raised the standard for corporate accountability.

1977	1989	1992	1994
San Francisco Supervisor Harvey Milk becomes the first openly gay man elected to US public office. Milk sponsors a gay-rights bill before his murder by political opponent Dan White.	On October 17, the Loma Prieta Earthquake hits 6.9 on the Richter scale near Santa Cruz, destroying a two-level section of the Interstate 880 and resulting in 63 deaths and thousands of injuries.	Three of four white police officers charged with beating African American Rodney King are acquitted by a predominantly white jury. Following the trial, Los Angeles endures six days of riots.	Orange County, one of the wealthiest municipalities in the US, declares bankruptcy after the county treasurer loses $1.5 billion investing in risky derivatives and pleads guilty to six felony charges.

tune in, drop out.' When Flower Power faded, other Bay Area rebellions grew in its place: Black Power, Gay Pride (see p72) and medical marijuana clubs.

But while Northern California had the more attention-grabbing counterculture in the 1940s to '60s, nonconformity in sunny Southern California shook America to the core. In 1947, when Senator Joseph McCarthy attempted to root out suspected Communists in the movie industry, 10 writers and directors who refused to admit to Communist alliances or to name names were charged with contempt of Congress and barred from working in Hollywood. The Hollywood Ten's impassioned defenses of the Constitution were heard nationwide, and major Hollywood players boldly voiced dissent and hired blacklisted talent until Californian lawsuits put a legal end to McCarthyism in 1962.

California is America's top technology hub, accounting for one-third of all US venture capitol, half of biotech employment, and half of all FDA-approved medical therapies since 1985.

Yet California's beach-paradise image – and its oil-industry dealings – would be permanently changed not by Hollywood directors, but Santa Barbara beachcombers. An oil rig dumped 200,000 gallons of oil into Santa Barbara Channel on January 28, 1969, killing dolphins, seals and some 3600 shore birds. Playing against type, the laid-back beach community organized a highly effective protest, spurring the establishment of the Environmental Protection Agency.

Geeking Out

When Silicon Valley introduced the first personal computer in 1968, advertisements breathlessly gushed that Hewlett-Packard's 'light' (40lb) machine could 'take on roots of a fifth-degree polynomial, Bessel functions, elliptic integrals and regression analysis' – all for just $4900 (about $29,000 today). Consumers didn't know quite what to do with computers, but in his 1969 *Whole Earth Catalog*, author (and former CIA LSD tester) Stewart Brand explained that the technology governments used to run countries could empower ordinary people. Hoping to bring computer power to the people, 21-year-old Steve Jobs and Steve Wozniak introduced the Apple II at the 1977 West Coast Computer Faire with unfathomable memory (4KB of RAM) and microprocessor speed (1MHz). But the question remained: what would ordinary people do with all that computing power?

By the mid-1990s an entire dot-com industry boomed in Silicon Valley with online start-ups, and suddenly people were getting everything – their mail, news, politics, pet food and, yes, sex – online. But when dot-com profits weren't forthcoming, venture funding dried up and fortunes in stock-options disappeared on one nasty Nasdaq-plummeting day: March 10, 2000. Overnight, 26-year-old vice-presidents and Bay Area service-sector employees alike found themselves jobless. But as online

1994	March, 2000	2003	2004
Los Angeles is the epicenter of a 6.7 quake with shocks felt in Las Vegas. The quake takes 72 lives and causes some $12 billion in damage.	The Nasdaq crashes ending the dot-com era. Traditional industry wonks gloat over the burst bubble, until knock-on effects lead to a devalued dollar and NYSE slide beginning in 2002.	Republican Arnold Schwarzenegger (aka The Governor) is elected governor of California. Schwarzenegger breaks party ranks on environmental issues and wins 2007 re-election.	Google's IPO raises a historic $1.67 billion at $85 per share. Share prices have since septupled and the company's worth is valued at $111 billion.

users continued to look for useful information – and one another – in those billions of web pages, search engines and social media boomed.

Meanwhile, California biotech has also been making strides. In 1976 an upstart company called Genentech was founded over beer at a San Francisco bar, and quickly got to work cloning human insulin and introducing the hepatitis B vaccine. California voters approved a $3 billion bond measure in 2004 for stem cell research, and by 2008 California had become the biggest funder of stem cell research and the focus of Nasdaq's new Biotech Index. Now all that's missing is the actual boom – but if history is any indication, California will make good on its talk, no matter how outlandish.

To read more about the garage-workshop culture of Silicon Valley go to www. folklore.org, which covers the crashes and personality clashes that made geek history.

October 2007	2008	2013	2013
Wildfires sweep drought-stricken Southern California forcing 900,000 people to evacuate homes. Local migrant workers, state prisoners and Tijuana firefighters volunteer to curb blazes.	California voters pass Proposition 8, defining legal marriage as between a man and a woman. Courts ruled the law unconstitutional, given California's civil rights protections; further appeals are pending.	Following bitter legal fights between Golden Gate Yacht Club and Geneva-based Société Nautique de Genève, the America's Cup held in San Francisco has the makings of a nautical grudge match.	The eastern span of the Bay Bridge is due for completion, including the final seismic retrofit, after the 1989 earthquake ,and commuter bike lanes.

California Cuisine

If you don't kiss the ground when you touch down in California, you might once you've tried the food. As you graze the Golden State from surfer-worthy fish tacos to foraged-ingredient chef's tasting menus, you'll often have cause to compliment the chef – but they're quick to share the compliment with local producers. Almost anything can and does grow in California's fertile Central Valley; north-coast pastures provide pristine grazing territory for California's luckiest livestock; and with 1000 miles of coastline, seafood doesn't get much fresher than this.

Pasadena native Julia Childs (1912–2004) gave America permission to enjoy food and the skills to cook it with *Mastering the Art of French Cooking* (1961).

Then & Now

'Let the ingredients speak for themselves!' is the rallying cry of California cuisine. With ingredients this fresh, heavy French sauces and fussy molecular-gastronomy foams need not apply to make meals memorable. Dishes are prepared with a light touch, often using kitchen craft borrowed from neighbors across the Pacific in East Asia and the distant Mediterranean where the climate and soil are similar to California's.

Fusion Soul Food

Beyond exceptionally rich dirt, California has another culinary advantage: an experimental attitude toward food that dates from its Wild West days. Most '49ers were men not accustomed to cooking for themselves, as seems obvious from such early mining-camp culinary experiments as jelly omelettes and chop suey, an American Chinese noodle dish with a name derived from the Cantonese expression 'odds and ends'. But the Gold Rush also introduced America to the hangtown fry (a scramble of eggs, bacon and cornbreaded oysters), dim sum (meaning 'small eats' in Cantonese) and the first US Italian restaurant, opened in San Francisco in 1886.

Slow Food Nation: Why Our Food Should Be Good, Clean and Fair (2007) is a manifesto for America's food revolution, written by California's own Alice Waters with Italian Slow Food founder Carlo Petrini.

Some 150 years later, fusion is not a fad but second nature in California, where chefs can hardly resist adding local twists to international flavors. California belonged to Mexico before it became a US state in 1850, and Californian takes on Mexican classics remain go-to comfort foods. Californian cross-pollination has yielded the burrito – a mega-meal in a flour tortilla – and the Korean taco: marinated beef, vegetables and rice in a seaweed wrapper.

Alice Waters' Food Revolution

Local, seasonal eating is hitting the US mainstream, but in California it started 40 years ago. As the turbulent 1960s wound down, many disillusioned idealists concluded that the revolution was not about to be delivered on a platter – but California's pioneering organic farmers weren't about to give up the idea. In 1971, Alice Waters opened Chez Panisse (p143) in a converted house in Berkeley with the then-radical notion of making

SLOW FOOD

the most of California's seasonal, all-natural, sustainably produced bounty. Waters combined French flourishes with Wild West imagination, and diners tasted the difference.

Today, Waters' credo of organic, seasonal, locally grown, pasture-raised cuisine has inspired the worldwide Slow Food movement. To taste the difference that local, organic, sustainably sourced ingredients make, try restaurants with the 🌿icon.

Food Fight: East Coast v West Coast

California's food fixations are easily exaggerated: not every Californian demands grass-fed burgers with heirloom tomato ketchup. But when New York chefs David Chang and Anthony Bourdain mocked California cuisine as merely putting an organic fig on a plate, Californian chefs turned the tables saying that New York needs to get out more often and actually try some Mission figs – one of hundreds of heirloom varietals developed by California horticulturalists since the 19th century.

East–West Coast rivalries have erupted not just in rap battles but also in culinary freestyling, with epicurean pundits tracking the James Beard Awards (the gastronomic Oscars) like sportscasters comparing teams. With a challenge from New York on the table, California chefs are combining fusion tendencies with organic ingredients, expanding beyond historic Cal-Mex and Cal-Italian to more organic, hyphenated cuisines: Cal-Vietnamese, Cal-Moroccan, Cal-Ecuadorian. Meanwhile, New York menus have been looking suspiciously Californian, citing local farms and introducing specialty organics from (where else?) California. With chefs on both coasts out to prove that reliance on fresh, seasonal ingredients doesn't necessarily make cuisine predictable, the ultimate winners in the East–West food fight have already emerged: diners.

Some Pacific marine species have been overfished to near-extinction, disrupting local aquaculture. For more information, check out Monterey Bay Aquarium's Seafood Watch (www.montereybayaquarium.org/cr/seafoodwatch.aspx).

Breakfast, Lunch & Dinner in California

No matter when you arrive, you're just in time for a fabulous meal. Here's what to expect, from brunches and food trucks through bistros and pop-up restaurants.

Breakfast

California is home to classic vinyl-booth diners that inspired movies from *American Graffiti* to *Swingers* and breakfast joints are still your best bet for daytime star sightings in Los Angeles. But now a farm-raised ingenue is stealing the scene: the farm egg. As everyone who's watched California-based Food Network knows, eggs represent the ultimate culinary challenge. California chefs use them as platforms for seasonal ingredients – Dungeness crab, morels, yellow peppers – but also grant them star treatment usually reserved for other proteins, serving eggs slow-cooked for smokiness or *sous-vide* (sealed in a bag and cooked in a water-bath) for maximum velvetiness. Don't miss weekend brunches when California chefs turn eggs and other farmer's market finds into feasts that will last you until dinner.

URBAN KITCHEN GARDENS

Not all the star ingredients on SF menus come from farmers' markets or specialty importers: increasingly, they're grown in urban backyards. With inspiration from SF's Green Festival urban-farming programs and the beehive-covered freeway on-ramp at Hayes Valley Farm, San Francisco chefs and home cooks alike are growing their own kitchen gardens. For tips on growing your own organic food, farming for kids, and urban composting (now mandated by law in SF), check out workshops at SF's sustainable gardening nonprofit, Garden for the Environment (www.gardenforhteenvironment.org).

Lunch

Weekday lunches may last only 30 minutes for Californians, and every minute counts. Californians torn between gourmet sit-down meals and enjoying sunshine outdoors no longer have to make a choice: food trucks deliver gourmet options to office hubs, from rotisserie chicken salads to clamshell buns packed with roast duck and fresh mango. To find trucks coming soon to a curb near you, search for 'food truck' and your location on Twitter. Come prepared with cash and sunblock: most trucks are cash-only, and lines for popular trucks can take 10-20 minutes. Look for prominently displayed permits as your guarantee of proper food preparation, refrigeration and regulated working conditions.

Dinner

The most lavish Californian meals are still served at dinner – though the idea of California cuisine is to savor, not gorge, so don't expect family-size portions. Most restaurants take a flexible, California-casual approach to dining: jeans are acceptable, dietary limitations cheerfully accommodated, and well-informed servers will help you discover your new favorite dish. Unlike the movie-version of California restaurants, most servers probably won't share their astrological signs, though they may gush about 'personal favorites' and chime in on dinner conversations. Reservations are recommended at restaurants with buzz; on weekends, they're practically mandatory, unless you want to eat before 6pm or after 9:30pm. At many upscale restaurants you'll find a lively scene and affordable menu at the bar – no reservations necessary.

Lately, dinner has also been popping up in unexpected places, including galleries, warehouses and storefronts. Chefs at pop-up restaurants prepare wildly creative meals around a theme, eg street foods, fundraisers and winemaker dinners. Foodies seek out these overnight taste sensations via Twitter, www.eater.com, and www.chowhound.com, but there are some downsides: pop-ups often charge restaurant prices, but without advance menus, quality control, health-inspected facilities or professional service. Bring cash and arrive early; most pop-ups don't accept credit cards and popular dishes run out fast.

Regional Specialties

So what are your best bets on the local menu? Given California's varied seasonal cuisine, that depends where you are and the time of year. Winter can be slim pickings in the Sierras, but ideal for SoCal citrus; for California seasonal food charts, see www.cuesa.org/page/seasonal -foods.

For coupons and deals on top California restaurants, check Open Table (www.opentable.com) and Blackboard Eats (http://blackboardeats.com).

VEGANS & VEGETARIANS WELCOME

To all you beleaguered vegetarians accustomed to making do with reheated vegetarian lasagna: relax, you're in California now. Your needs are not an afterthought in Californian cuisine, which revolves around seasonal produce instead of the usual American meat and potatoes. Long before actress Alicia Silverstone (of *Clueless* fame) championed a vegan diet in her cookbook *The Kind Diet* and website (www.thekindlife.com), LA, SF and North Coast restaurants were catering to vegans. Diners may not always cater to vegans, but bakeries, bistros and even mom-and-pop joints in the remote Sierras are ready for meat-free, dairy-free, eggless requests. To find vegetarian and vegan restaurants and health-food stores near you in California, consult the free online directory at Happy Cow (www.happycow.net).

SELF-CATERING

Cater your own fabulous meals in California directly from the produce stalls and artisan food stands at farmers markets across the state; to find a market near you, see www.cafarmersmarkets.com. A grocery store may sound like the last place you'd want to dine, but in California you'll find corner stores selling Bento boxes of sustainable sushi and Mexicatessans fragrant with fresh tamales (savory, filled corn-cakes) steaming in corn husks.

North Coast & the Sierras

Hippies and hedonism have turned remote NorCal regions into dining destinations. San Francisco hippies headed back to the land in the 1970s for a more self-sufficient lifestyle, reviving traditions of making breads and cheeses from scratch and growing their own *everything* (note: farms from Mendocino to Humboldt are serious about trespassing. Obey the signs). Early adopters of pesticide-free farming, hippie-homesteaders innovated hearty, organic cuisine that was health-minded yet satisfied the munchies.

Stop by roadside inns and saloons in the Sierras, and you'll taste NorCal cuisine that's catered to rugged appetites and downright lushes since the gold-mining days. One notable hangover from Gold Rush cuisine is Placerville's hangover-remedying hangtown fry, a scramble of eggs, bacon and cornbreaded oysters. This was the Gold Rush's richest dish: oysters were brought 100 miles overland packed in ice, salt-pork came from the East Coast, and the eggs cost $10 a dozen in 1849 California – the equivalent of $272 today.

On the North Coast, you can taste the influence of wildcrafted Ohlone and Miwok cuisine. In addition to fishing, hunting game and making bread from acorn flour, these Native Northern Californians also tended orchards and carefully cultivated foods along the coast. With such attentive stewardship, nature has been kind to this landscape, yielding bonanzas of wildflower honey and blackberries. Alongside traditional shellfish collection, sustainable caviar and oyster farms have sprung up along the coast. Fearless foragers have identified every edible plant from Sierras wood sorrel to Mendocino sea vegetables, though key spots for wild mushrooms remain closely guarded local secrets.

NorCal Wine Country: Napa and Sonoma

With international reputations for local wines in the 1970s (p728) came woozy Wine Country visitors in need of food, and Sonoma cheesemakers and Wine Country restauranteurs graciously obliged. Chef Thomas Keller transformed a Yountville 1900-saloon-turned-restaurant into an international foodie landmark in 1994, showcasing garden-grown organic produce and casual elegance in multicourse feasts at French Laundry (p173). Other chefs eager to make their names and fortunes among free-spending wine-tasters flocked to the area; those offering the best price-to-quality ratios are featured in the Napa & Sonoma Wine Country chapter. But Sonoma hasn't forgotten its origins as a Mexican colony, and you can still find respectable taco trucks among Napa vineyards.

San Francisco Bay Area

With miners converging here for the Gold Rush, San Francisco offered an unrivalled variety of novelties and cuisines, ranging from ubiquitous Chinese street food to struck-it-rich French fine dining. Today, San Francisco's adventurous eaters support the most award-winning chefs and

Top 5 North Coast & Sierras Ingredients

» Sustainably farmed oysters
» Ollalieberries
» Wild mushrooms
» Sustainably farmed abalone
» Venison Deer

restaurants per capita of any US city – five times more restaurants than New York, if anyone's keeping score – and 25 farmers markets in San Francisco alone, more than any other US city.

Some SF novelties have had extraordinary staying power, including ever-popular *cioppino* (Dungeness crab stew), chocolate bars invented by the Ghirardelli family, and sourdough bread, with original Gold Rush–era mother dough still yielding local loaves with that distinctive tang. Dim sum is Cantonese for what's known in Mandarin as *xiao che* (small eats) or *yum cha* (drink tea). There are dozens of places in San Francisco where you'll call it lunch with steaming baskets of dumplings, platters of garlicky sautéed greens and plates of sweet sesame balls.

Mexican, French and Italian food remain perennial local favorites, along with more recent SF ethnic food crazes: *izakaya* (Japanese bars serving small plates), Korean tacos (see p722), *banh mi* (Vietnamese sandwiches featuring marinated meats and pickled vegetables on French baguettes), and *alfajores* (Arabic-Argentine crème-filled shortbread cookies). Beyond the obvious Pacific Rim influences, no SF chef's tasting menu is complete without foraged ingredients – wild chanterelles found beneath California oaks, miner's lettuce from Berkeley hillsides or SF-backyard nasturtium flowers – and Daniel Patterson sets the standard at Coi (see p87).

> Castroville is the source of nearly all America's artichokes, and goes all out each May for the Artichoke Festival (www.artichoke-festival.org).

Central Coast & Central Valley

Most of California's produce is grown in the hot, irrigated Central Valley south of the Bay Area, but road-tripping foodies tend to bolt through this sunny stretch to reach Los Angeles in time for dinner – if only to make it past stinky cattle feed-lots without losing their appetites. Yet they're missing out on some of the state's freshest seafood around Monterey Bay, excellent wine-tasting from Santa Cruz Mountains to Santa Barbara (see p728) and worthy farmstand produce pitstops from Watsonville strawberries to Santa Barbara mangoes. Much of the region remains dedicated to large-scale agribusiness, but Central Valley farms that have converted to organic production have helped make California the top US producer of organics.

SoCal

Fake tans dot the Southern California landscape, but the food here is the real deal. Follow Los Angeles authenticity-trippers to Koreatown for flavor-bursting *kalbi* (marinated barbecued beef short ribs), East LA for tacos *al pastor* (marinated, fried pork), and Little Tokyo for ramen noodles made fresh daily. Surfers cruise Highway One beach towns from Laguna Beach to La Jolla in search of the ultimate wave and fish taco.

There's no telling which came first in LA: the chefs or the stars. True immortality isn't achieved with a star in a Michelin guide or on the Walk of Fame, but by having a dish named in your honor – Robert H. Cobb, celebrity-owner of Hollywood's Brown Derby Restaurant, is remembered as the namesake of the Cobb salad (lettuce, tomato, egg, chicken, bacon

COOKING COURSES

Take California's signature dishes home with leading California chefs sharing their secrets at workshops and courses at these culinary education institutions:

» **Culinary Institute of America** (p175)
» **Ramekins Sonoma Valley Culinary School** (p187)
» **Relish Culinary School** (p208)

TOP 5 SOCAL STAR-STUDDED FOOD EVENTS

» **Taste of the Nation** June heats up in Culver City with this fundraiser for Share Our Strength, the nonprofit to end child hunger, starring an ensemble cast of top chefs headed by *Top Chef* star Tom Colicchio (www.tasteofthenation.com).

» **American Wine & Food Festival** The star-studded foodie fundraising event is held on the backlot at Universal Studios (p550) each September (www.awff.org).

» **Dine LA** In September, 40 top restaurants and rising-star chefs celebrate California's bounty with creative pairing menus (http://discoverlosangeles.com/play/dining).

» **Santa Barbara Vintner's Fest** Toast California's other wine country, made famous in the movie *Sideways*, in April (www.santabarbara.com).

» **National Date Festival** Score a famous date at Indio's February festival, when Palm Springs' A-list abandons pool-loungers for sweet treats (p665).

and Roquefort). Wolfgang Puck launched the celebrity-chef trend with his Sunset Strip's star-spangled Spago restaurant in 1982. Reservations at private chef's tables are now as sought-after as entry into club VIP backrooms. As with certain Hollywood blockbusters, trendy LA bistros don't always live up to the hype – for LA's most brutally honest opinions, check www.laweekly.com and www.eater.com. When all else fails, make late-night raids on local food trucks and Hollywood diners that haven't changed since Technicolor was introduced.

Wine, Beer & Beyond

Powerful drink explains a lot about California. Mission vineyards planted in the 18th century gave California a taste for wine, which led settlers to declare an independent 'Bear Flag Republic' in the Mexican settlement of Sonoma one drunken night in 1846 (it lasted a month). The Gold Rush brought a rush on the bar. By 1850 San Francisco had one woman per 100 men, but 500 saloons shilling hooch. Today California's traditions of wine, beer and cocktails are converging in saloon revivals, wine-bar trends, and microbrewery booms – and, for the morning after, specialty coffee roasters.

Find the perfect wine to enjoy with your dinner using the interactive pairing guide at www.winean swers.com.

Wine

Mission communion wine was fine for Sundays and minor revolutions, but by the 1830s Californians were already importing premium varietals. When imported French wine was slow to arrive via Australia during the Gold Rush, two Czech brothers named Korbel started making their own bubbly in 1882 (today their winery is the biggest US distributor of sparkling wines). Drinkers began switching to the local stuff from Sonoma and Napa Valleys and, by the end of the century, vintages from California Wine Country were quietly winning medals at Paris expositions. Some California vines survived federal scrutiny during Prohibition on the grounds that the grapes were needed for sacramental wines back east – a bootlegging bonanza that kept West Coast speakeasies well supplied and saved old vinestock from being torn out by the authorities.

California's Prestige Wines

The movie *Bottle Shock* (2008) takes liberties with the true story of the Judgment of Paris – what was with that love triangle? – but it captures the flavor of winemaking in Sonoma and Napa in the 1970s.

By 1976 California had an established reputation for mass-market plonk and bottled wine spritzers when upstart wineries in Napa Valley and the Santa Cruz Mountains suddenly gained international status. At a landmark blind tasting by international critics, Stag's Leap Wine Cellars cabernet sauvignon, Chateau Montelena chardonnay and Ridge Monte Bello cabernet sauvignon beat venerable French wines to take top honors. This event became known as the Judgment of Paris. The tasting was repeated 30 years later with Stag's Leap and Ridge again taking top honors (Montelena had sold out of its original vintage).

Sonoma, Napa, the Santa Cruz area and Mendocino county continue to produce the state's most illustrious vintages. The exceptional combination of coastal fog, sunny valleys, rocky hillsides and volcanic soils in Napa and Sonoma Valleys mimic the wine-growing regions of France and Italy. Precious bottom-land sells for up to $20,000 an acre in skinny, 30-mile-long Napa, where many wineries understandably stick to established, marketable chardonnay and cabernet sauvignon. Neighboring

Sonoma and Mendocino have complex microclimates with morning fog cover to protect the thin-skinned, prized pinot noir grape.

But California's risk-taking attitude prevails even on prestigious Napa, Sonoma and Mendocino turf, with unconventional red blends and freak-factor pinots with 'forest floor' flavors claiming top honors in industry mags and the Superbowl of US wine competitions, the San Francisco Chronicle Wine Competition (http://winejudging.com); for top options, see p186.

Sustainable Wines

During the internet bubble of the late '90s, owning a vineyard became the ultimate Silicon Valley status symbol. Believing the dreaded phylloxera blight had been conquered with the development of resistant California rootstock AxR1, it seemed like a comparatively solid investment – until phylloxera made a catastrophic comeback and acres of infected vines across the state had to be dug out from the roots. But disaster brought breakthroughs: winemakers rethought their approach from the ground up, re-planting organically and trialing biodynamic methods to keep the soil healthy and pests at bay.

Today such sustainable winemaking processes have become wide-spread across California, with pioneering green wineries establishing the Lodi Rules for green winemaking (see www.lodiwine.com) and pursuing Demeter certification for biodynamic wines (http://demeter-usa.org). California's renegade winemakers are now experimenting with natural-process winemaking methods such as wild yeast fermentation, bringing the thrill of the unexpected to tasting rooms across the state. While you're visiting you may notice owl boxes for pest management, sheep for weed control and solar panels atop LEED certified winery buildings – all increasingly standard features of California's environmentally savvy wineries.

Other Wine Countries

There is no time like the present to wine-taste across California, with a broad variety of heirloom and imported varietals that are true expressions of this vibrant, varied landscape. California has 112 distinct AVAs, or American Viticulture Areas, which are known for different varietals and have developed distinct winemaking styles. The rugged, hot Sierra foothills from Amador County stretching toward Lodi in the Central Valley (p316) favor the steep, hearty zinfandel, while the steep, partly forested Santa Cruz Mountains AVA produces fine coastal chardonnay and complex cabernet sauvignon. The hot Central Valley generates 75% of the state's wine and though much of it is mass-market plonk, smaller growers are

The 2004 wine country road-trip movie *Sideways* was a critical hit, but California winemakers have a love/hate relationship with it for praising California pinot noir at merlot's expense.

AWARD-WINNING CALIFORNIA WINE TASTINGS

» **San Francisco Chronicle Wine Competition Grand Tasting** (http://winejudging.com) February in San Francisco.

» **Sonoma County Harvest Fair and Wine Competition** (www.harvestfair.org) October in Santa Rosa.

» **International Alsace Varietal Festival** (www.avwines.com) February in Mendocino.

» **Rhône Rangers Grand Tasting** (www.rhonerangers.org) San Francisco in March, Los Angeles and Paso Robles tasting events in August.

» **Santa Barbara Vintners' Festival** (http://sbcountywines.com/events/festival.html) Lompoc in April.

**Top 5
Indie Wine
Countries**

» Mendocino
(p223)

» Santa Ynez &
Santa Maria
Valleys (p508)

» Paso Robles
(p496)

» Lodi (p344)

» Santa Cruz
Mountains (p463)

making the most of the valley's sunny disposition in renegade syrah blends, especially around Paso Robles (p496). The 2004 film *Sideways* quite rightly celebrates Central Coast pinot noirs from the Santa Maria and Santa Ynez Valley AVAs around Santa Barbara, which are blessed with sun, cooling ocean breezes and morning mists.

Wine Bar Boom

VIP bottle service and Kristal are so the LA of the 1990s; these days there's no reason to get fancy just to get a decent glass of wine in California. Bartenders across the state are increasingly rolling out the barrels from local wineries and pouring the good stuff straight from the tap. Trendy wine bars and recession-minded restaurants have started to offer top-notch, small-production California wines *alla spina,* or on tap. *Alla spina* by the ounce or carafe is eco-friendlier than bottles and a better value than flights, which usually include a clunker or two. But in specialty wine bars and restaurants, definitely check out the wine list and ask your sommelier to point out cult wines rarely distributed outside California.

Beer

Drinking snobbery is often reversed in California. Wine drinkers are always game for a glass of something local and tasty, while beer drinkers fuss over their monk-brewed triple Belgians and debate relative hoppiness levels. California beer-drinkers are spoiled for choice. According to the Brewers' Association California has twice as many breweries than any other state. You won't get attitude for ordering beer with fancy food here – many California sommeliers are happy to suggest beer pairings with your meal and some spiffy NorCal saloons offer tasting plates specifically to accompany beer.

Steam Brewing

Blowing off steam took on new meaning during the Gold Rush when entrepreneurs trying to keep up with the demand for drink started brewing beer at higher temperatures, like ales. The result was an amber color, rich, malted flavor and such powerful effervescence that when a keg was

---

WINE-TASTING TIPS

» **Swirl** Before tasting a vintage red, swirl your glass to oxygenate the wine and release the flavors.

» **Sniff** Dip your nose (without getting it wet) into the glass for a good whiff. Your nose signals your taste buds what's coming.

» **Swish** Take a swig, and roll it over the front of your teeth and sides of your tongue to get the full effect of complex flavors and textures. After you swallow, breathe out through your nose to appreciate 'the finish'.

» **If you're driving or cycling, don't swallow** Sips are hard to keep track of at tastings, so perfect your graceful arc into the spit bucket.

» **You don't have to buy anything** No one expects you to buy, especially if you're paying to taste or take a tour. That said, it's customary to buy a bottle before winery picnics.

» **Take it easy** Wine tasting is not an Olympic sport, so there's no need for speed. Plan to visit three or four wineries a day maximum.

» **Don't smoke** Not in the gardens either. Wait until you're off the property.

» **Don't be afraid to ask questions** Most winemakers love helping visitors understand what they're tasting

CALIFORNIA BEER BLASTS

» **California Beer Festival** (www.californiabeerfestival.com) September in Ventura.

» **Sierra Brew Fest** (www.musicinthemountains.org/brewfest.php) August in Grass Valley.

» **San Francisco Beer Week** (www.sfbeerweek.org) February in San Francisco.

» **California Festival of Beers** (www.hospiceslo.org/beerfes) San Luis Obispo in May.

» **San Diego Festival of Beers** (http://sdbeerfest.org) San Diego in September.

tapped a mist would rise like steam. San Francisco's Anchor Brewing Company has made its signature Anchor Steam amber ale this way since 1896, using copper distilling equipment.

Where to Score California Beer

For quality small-batch brews you won't find elsewhere, seek out any of the microbreweries listed in the destination chapters – any self-respecting California city has at least one craft brewery or brewpub of note. For the broadest beer selection LA's Yard House has a selection of 160 draft beers, rivaled only by the selection of 400 brews available at San Francisco's Toronado (p99). But for instant relief on scorching summer days, craft beers are widely available at California corner stores in bottles and cans, in six-packs and singles. California's craft breweries are increasingly canning craft beer to make it cheaper, greener and more widely distributable across California. This also preserves the classic satisfaction of popping the tab on a cold one on a hot California beach day.

Spirits

Tonight you're gonna party like it's 1899. Before picking up their shakers at night, local bartenders have spent the day dusting off 19th century recipes. The highest honorific for a California bartender these days isn't mixologist (too technical) or artisan (too medieval), but 'drink historian'. Gone are the mad-scientist's mixology beakers of two years ago. California bartenders are now judged by their absinthe fountains and displays of swizzle sticks from long-defunct ocean liners. Just don't be surprised if your anachronistic cocktail comes served in cordial glass, punch bowl or Mason jar, instead of a tumbler, highball or martini glass. All that authenticity-tripping over happy hour may sound self-conscious, but after strong pours at California's vintage saloons and revived speakeasies, consciousness is hardly an issue.

Researched Cocktails

Cocktails have appeared on California happy hour menus since San Francisco's Barbary Coast days, when they were used to sedate sailors and shanghai them onto outbound ships. Now bartenders are researching old recipes and reviving California traditions. Don't be surpised to see absinthe poured from fountains into cordial glasses of Sazerac, including the traditional foamy egg whites in Pisco sours as though no one had ever heard of veganism or salmonella. Bartenders are apparently still trying to knock sailors cold with combinations of tawny port and Nicaraguan rum. Irish coffee (coffee, cream, sugar and Irish whiskey) is another California cocktail ideal for foggy, San Francisco noir-novel nights, while margaritas (made with tequila, lime, Cointreau, ice and salt) have fueled SoCal beach-bar crawls since the 1940s.

Every California bartender holds strong opinions on the martini, first mentioned in an 1887 bartending guide by Professor Jerry Thomas. Legend

Top 5 California Brews

» **Boont Amber Ale** Anderson Valley Brewery (Mendocino)

» **Baltic Porter** Uncommon Brewers (Santa Cruz)

» **Christmas Ale** Anchor Steam (San Francisco)

» **Racer 5 IPA** Bear Republic (Healdsburg)

» **Pale Ale** Sierra Nevada (Chico)

has it that the martini was invented when a boozehound walked into an SF bar and demanded something to tide him over until he reached Martinez across the bay – a likely story, but we'll drink to that. The original was made with vermouth, gin, bitters, lemon, maraschino cherry and ice, though by the 1950s the recipe was reduced to gin with vermouth vapors and an olive or a twist. Today's California drink historians offer variations on the original, as well as the Sinatra Rat Pack Hollywood version.

Coffee

When California couples break up, the thorniest issue is: who gets the cafe? Californians are fiercely loyal to specific roasts and baristas, and most first internet dates meet on neutral coffee grounds. Berkeley's Peet's Coffee kicked off the specialty coffee craze for espresso drinks made with single-origin beans back in 1966 (in 1971 they supplied beans to an offshoot known as Starbucks). Santa Cruz was another early adoptor of speciality coffee in 1978 – like Berkeley, it's a coffee-drinking college town – and Santa Cruz Coffee became one of the first US roasters and cafes to offer certified Fair Trade coffee beans.

Third & Fourth Wave Coffee

California has since become a hub for 'third wave' coffee. *LA Weekly*'s Jonathan Gold defines this as coffee directly sourced from small farms and medium-roasted to maximize bean characteristics, instead of being overroasted to the point of tar-like harshness. Los Angeles' third-wave cafes tend not to roast their own, but cherry-pick the best beans from micro-roasters along the West Coast and Chicago. San Francisco's Blue Bottle Coffee added a 'fourth wave' element of showmanship to coffee geekery, introducing a $20,000 Japanese coffee siphon to filter their brews. Meanwhile Sightglass Coffee has become the latest object of coffee cult worship with beans roasted in small batches in a vintage coffee roaster (p96).

Cafe Society

At some wi-fi–enabled California cafes that serve as workplaces for telecommuters, you may actually get a stern look for laughing too loud. But there's a backlash afoot. Third-wave cafes are limiting wi-fi usage, eliminating outlets and hosting events to revive California's more lively 1960s coffeehouse culture. When using free cafe wi-fi, remember: order something every hour, don't leave laptops unattended and deal with interruptions graciously.

Top 5 California Spirits

» **Old Potrero Hotaling's Whiskey** San Francisco

» **Hangar One Vodka** Alameda

» **209 Gin** San Francisco

» **Ballast Point Three Sheets Rum** San Diego

» **Takara Sake** Berkeley

Join the caffeinated conversation about third-wave coffee roasters – and the emerging fourth wave coffee bars opening across California – in the forums at www.coffeegeek.com.

The Way of Life

In the California of the dream world you wake up, have your shot of wheatgrass and roll down to the beach while the surf's up. Lifeguards wave to you as they go jogging by in their bathing suits. You skateboard down the boardwalk to your yoga class where everyone admires your downward dog. A taco truck pulls up with your favorite: low-carb, sustainable, line-caught tilapia fish tacos with organic mango chipotle salsa.

Napping on the beach afterwards, you awake to find a casting agent hovering over you, blocking your sunlight, imploring you to star in a movie based on a best-selling comic book. You say you'll have your lawyer look over the papers, and by your lawyer you mean your roommate who plays one on TV. The conversation is cut short when you get a text to meet up with some friends at a bar.

That casting agent was a stress case – she wanted an answer in, like, a month – so you swing by your medical pot dispensary and a tattoo parlor to get 'Peace' inscribed on your bicep in five languages as a reminder to yourself to stay chill. At the bar, you're called onstage to play a set with the band, and afterwards you tell the drummer how the casting agent harshed your mellow. She recommends a wine country getaway, but you're already doing that Big Sur primal scream colon-cleansing retreat this weekend.

You head back to your beach house to update your status on your social-networking profile, alerting your one million online friends to the major events of the day: 'Killer taco, solid downward dog, third peace tattoo, movie offer.' Then you repeat your nightly self-affirmations: 'I am a child of the universe...I am blessed, or at least not a New Yorker...tomorrow will bring sunshine and possibility...om.'

Regional Identity

Now for the reality check: any Northern Californian hearing your California dream is bound to get huffy. What, political protests and open-source software inventions don't factor in your dreams? Huh, typical SoCal slacker. But Southern Californians will also roll their eyes at the stereotypes: they didn't create NASA's Jet Propulsion Lab and almost half the world's movies by slacking off.

Still there is some truth to your California dreamscape. Some 80% of Californians live near the coast rather than inland, even though California beaches aren't always sunny or swimmable (the odds of that increase the further south you go, thus Southern California's inescapable associations with surf, sun and prime-time TV soaps like *Baywatch* and *The OC*). And there's truth in at least one other outdoorsy stereotype: over 60% of Californians admit to having hugged a tree.

Self-help, fitness and body modification are major industries throughout California, successfully marketed since the 1970s as 'lite' versions of religious experience – all the agony and ecstasy of the major religions, without all those heavy commandments. Exercise and good food help

SURFER SLANG

Riptionary (www. riptionary.com), the world's most definitive online lexicon of surfer slang, will help you translate stuff like 'The big mama is fully mackin' some gnarly grinders!'

SoCal inventions include the Space Shuttle, Mickey Mouse, whitening toothpaste, the hula hoop (or at least its trademark), Barbie, skateboard and surfboard technology, the Cobb salad and the fortune cookie.

keep Californians among the fittest in the nation. Yet almost 250,000 Californians are apparently ill enough to merit prescriptions for medical marijuana.

At least Northern and Southern Californians do have one thing in common: they are baffled by New Yorkers' delusion that the world revolves around the Big Apple, when everyone knows it doesn't, dude.

Lifestyle

The charmed existence you dreamed about is a stretch, even in California. Few Californians can afford to spend entire days tanning and incidentally networking, what with UVB rays and the rent to consider. According to a recent Cambridge University study, creativity, imagination, intellectualism and mellowness are all defining characteristics of Californians compared with inhabitants of other states.

If you're like most Californians, you effectively live in your car, not your house. Californians commute an average of 30 minutes each way to work and spend at least $1 out of every $5 earned on car-related expenses. But Californians have zoomed ahead of the national energy-use curve in their smog-checked cars, buying more hybrid and fuel-efficient cars than any other state. Despite California's reputation for smog, two of the 25 US cities with the cleanest air are in California (hello, San Luis Obispo and Salinas!).

Few Californians could afford a beach dream-home anyway, and most rent rather than own on a median household income of $56,134 per year. Eight of the 10 most expensive US housing markets are in California, and in the number-one most expensive area, suburban La Jolla, the average house price is $1.875 million. Almost half of all Californians reside in cities, but much of the other half live in the suburbs, where the cost of living is just as high, if not higher: Marin County outside San Francisco is currently the most costly place to live in America. Yet Californian cities (especially San Francisco and San Diego) consistently top national quality-of-life indexes.

As for those roommates you dreamed about: if you're a Californian aged 18 to 24, there's a 50/50 possibility that your roomies are your parents. Among adult Californians, one in four live alone, and almost 50% are unmarried. Of those who are currently married, 33% won't be in 10 years. Increasingly, Californians are shacking up: the number of unmarried cohabiting couples has increased 40% since 1990.

Homelessness is not part of the California dream, but it's a reality for at least 160,000 Californians. Some are teens who have run away or been kicked out by their families, but the largest contingent of homeless Californians are US military veterans – almost 30,000 in all. What's more, in the 1970s mental health programs were cut, and state-funded drug treat-

Southern California has thousands of believers in Santeria, a fusion of Catholicism and Yoruba beliefs practiced by West African slaves in the Caribbean and South America. Drop by a *botànica* (herbal folk medicine) shop for charms and candles.

MARRIAGE: EQUAL RIGHTS FOR ALL

Forty thousand Californians were already registered as domestic partners when, in 2004, San Francisco Mayor Gavin Newsom issued marriage licenses to same-sex couples in defiance of a California same-sex marriage ban. Four thousand same-sex couples promptly got hitched. The state ban was nixed by California courts in June 2008, but then a proposition passed that November to amend the state's constitution to prohibit same-sex marriage. Civil-rights activists are challenging the constitutionality of the proposition, but meanwhile California's reputation as a haven of LGBT (lesbian/gay/bisexual/transgender) tolerance is lagging behind other states that have already legalized same-sex marriage, including Massachusetts, New Hampshire, Vermont, Connecticut, Iowa and New York, as well as the District of Columbia.

ment programs were dropped in the 1980s, leaving many Californians with mental illnesses and substance abuse problems with no place to go.

Also standing in line at homeless shelters are the working poor, unable to cover medical care and high rent on minimum-wage salaries. Rather than addressing the underlying causes of homelessness, some California cities have criminalized loitering, panhandling, even sitting on sidewalks. Since empathy has not yet been outlawed, feel free to give to local charities doing their part to keep California alive and dreaming.

Since 1988, California's prison population has increased by over 200%, mostly for drug-related crimes. More than four out of every 1000 Californians are currently in jail.

Population & Multiculturalism

With 37 million residents, California is the most populous US state: one in every nine Americans lives here. It's also one of the fastest growing states, with three of America's 10 biggest cities (Los Angeles, San Diego and San Jose) and over 350,000 newcomers very year. You still don't believe it's crowded here? California's population density is 217 people per sq mile – almost triple the national average.

If you were the average Californian, you'd be statistically likely to be Latina, aged about 34, living in densely populated LA, Orange or San Diego Counties, and you'd speak more than one language. There's a one in four chance you were born outside the US, and if you were born in the US the odds are 50/50 you moved here recently from another state.

One of every four immigrants to the US lands in California, with the largest segment coming from Mexico. Most legal immigrants to California are sponsored by family members who already live here. In addition, an estimated two million undocumented immigrants currently live in California. But this is not a radical new development: before California became a US state in 1850 it was a territory of Mexico and Spain, and historically most of the state's growth has come from immigration, legal or otherwise.

Most Californians see their state as an easygoing multicultural society that gives everyone a chance to live the American dream. No one is expected to give up their cultural or personal identity to become Californian: Chicano pride, gay pride and black power all built their bases here. But historically, California's Chinatowns, Japantowns and other ethnic enclaves were often created by segregationist sentiment, not by choice. While equal opportunity may be a shared goal, in practice it's very much a work in progress. Even racially integrated areas can be quite segregated in terms of income, language, education and perhaps most ironically, internet access. (This is the home of Silicon Valley after all.)

Californian culture reflects the composite identity of the state. California's Latino and Asian populations are steadily increasing. Over 30% of the USA's Asian American population currently lives in California, while the state's Latino population is expected to become California's majority ethnic group by 2020. Latino culture is deeply enmeshed with Californian culture, from J.Lo and Tejano tunes to burritos and margaritas and Governor Schwarzenegger's 1991 catchphrase in *Terminator II*: 'Hasta la vista, baby'. Despite being just 6.6% of the population, and relatively late arrivals with the WWII shipping boom, African Americans have also defined West Coast popular culture, from jazz and hip-hop to fashion and beyond.

The bond holding the Golden State together isn't a shared ethnic background, common language, ubiquitous cocktail or signature catchphrase: it's choosing to be Californian. Along with that comes the freedom to choose your religion, if any. Although Californians are less churchgoing than the American mainstream, and one in five Californians professes no

Over 200 different languages are spoken in California, with Spanish, Chinese, Tagalog, Persian and German in the top 10. In fact, almost 40% of state residents speak a language other than English at home.

In his column 'iAsk a Mexican!', *OC Weekly* columnist Gustavo Arellano tackles such questions as why Mexicans swim with their clothes on, alongside weighty social issues involving immigrants' rights. Read it at www.ocweekly.com.

CALLING ALL (NON) SPORTS FANS

Even if you're not a sports buff, you may find something that catches your eye in California:

» Surfing is the coastal spectator sport of choice, with waves reaching 100ft at the annual Mavericks competition near Half Moon Bay.

» Now an Olympic sport, professional beach volleyball started in Santa Monica in the 1920s. Tournaments are held in SoCal every summer, including at LA's Hermosa and Manhattan Beaches

» Motor sports are another obsession, especially at Bakersfield and Long Beach near LA.

religion at all, it remains one of the most religiously diverse states. About a third of Californians are Catholic, due in part to the state's large Latino population, while another third are Protestants. But there are also more than one million Muslims statewide, and LA has the second-largest Jewish community in North America. California also has the largest number of Buddhists anywhere outside of Asia.

Sports

California has more professional sports teams than any other state, and loyalties to local NFL football, NBA basketball and major-league baseball teams run deep. For proof that Californians do get excited about sports, go ahead and just try to find tickets before they sell out for an Oakland Raiders or San Diego Chargers football, San Francisco Giants baseball, Los Angeles Lakers basketball or Los Angeles Kings hockey game.

According to a recent study, Californians are less likely to be couch potatoes than other Americans, but when one Californian team plays another, the streets are deserted and all eyes glued to the tube. The biggest grudge matches are between the San Francisco '49ers and Oakland Raiders, LA Lakers and LA Clippers, San Francisco Giants and LA Dodgers, or baseball's Oakland A's and Anaheim's Angels. California college sports rivalries are equally fierce, especially UC Berkeley's Cal Bears against the Stanford University Cardinals or the USC Trojans versus the UCLA Bruins.

LA is one of only four cities to have hosted the summer Olympic Games twice, in 1932 and 1984. The others are Athens, London and Paris; London will host for a third time in 2012.

To see small but dedicated crowds of hometown fans (and score cheaper tickets more easily), watch pro men's or women's (WNBA) basketball in Sacramento, pro hockey in Anaheim and San Jose or pro soccer in San Jose or LA. Or catch minor-league baseball teams up and down the state, especially the winning San Jose Giants.

Except for championship play-offs, the regular season for major-league baseball runs from April to September, soccer from April to October, WNBA basketball from late May to mid-September, NFL football from September to early January, NHL ice hockey from October to March and NBA basketball from November to April.

On Location: Film & TV

Try to imagine living in a world without Orson Welles whispering 'Rosebud,' Judy Garland clicking her heels three times, John Travolta dancing in his white suit or the Terminator promising 'I'll be back.' California is where these iconic film and TV images hatched. From the moment movies – and later TV – became the dominant entertainment medium starting in the 20th century, California took center stage in the world of popular culture and has stood there ever since.

Shakespeare claimed that 'all the world's a stage,' but in California, it's actually more of a film set. Every palm-lined boulevard or beach seems to come with its own IMDB.com filming resume, and no wonder: in any given year some 40 TV shows and scores of movies use Californian locations, not including all of those shot on SoCal studio backlots.

The Industry

You might know it as TV and movie-making entertainment, but to Southern Californians it's simply 'The Industry'. The 'Industry grew out of the humble orchards of Hollywoodland, a residential neighborhood of Los Angeles, where entrepreneurial moviemakers established studios in the early 1900s. German-born Carl Laemmle built Universal Studios in 1915, selling lunch to curious guests coming to watch the magic of moviemaking; Polish immigrant Samuel Goldwyn joined with Cecil B DeMille to form Paramount Studios; and Jack Warner and his brothers, born to Polish parents, arrived a few years later from Canada.

SoCal's perpetually balmy weather (over 315 sunny days per year) meant that most outdoor scenes could be easily shot here, and moviemaking flourished in Los Angeles. What's more, the proximity of the Mexican border enabled filmmakers to rush their equipment to safety when challenged by the collection agents of patent holders such as Thomas Edison. Palm Springs became a favorite weekend getaway for Hollywood stars, partly because its distance from LA (just under 100 miles) was as far as they could then travel under their restrictive studio contracts.

Fans loved early silent-film stars like Charlie Chaplin and Harold Lloyd, and the first big Hollywood wedding occurred in 1920 when Douglas Fairbanks wed Mary Pickford, becoming Hollywood's first de-facto royal couple. The silent-movie era gave way to 'talkies' after 1927's *The Jazz Singer,* a Warner Bros musical starring Al Jolson, premiered in downtown LA, ushering in Hollywood's glamorous Golden Age.

Hollywood & Beyond

From the 1920s, Hollywood became the Industry's social and financial hub, but it's a myth that most movie production took place there. Of the major studios, only Paramount Pictures stood in Hollywood proper,

Top California Film Festivals

» AFI Fest (www. afi.com/afifest)

» LA Film Fest (www.lafilmfest. com)

» Outfest (www. outfest.org)

» Palm Springs International Film Festival (www. psfilmfest.org)

» San Francisco International Film Festival (www. sffs.org)

» Sonoma International Film Festival (www. sonomafilmfest. org)

albeit surrounded by block after block of production-related businesses like lighting and post-production.

Most movies have long been shot elsewhere around LA, for example, in Culver City (at MGM, now Sony Pictures), Studio City (at Universal Studios) and Burbank (at Warner Bros and later at Disney). Remember, too, that California's first big movie palaces were built not on Hollywood Blvd but on Broadway in downtown LA.

Moviemaking hasn't been limited to LA either. Founded in 1910, the American Film Manufacturing Company, aka Flying 'A' Studios, filmed box-office hits for years, first in San Diego and then Santa Barbara, while Balboa Studios in Long Beach was another major silent-era dream factory. Well known contemporary movie production companies based in the San Francisco Bay Area include Francis Ford Coppola's Zoetrope, George Lucas' Industrial Light & Magic and Pixar. Both San Francisco and LA remain creative hubs for emerging independent filmmakers.

The high cost of filming has sent location scouts far beyond LA's San Fernando Valley (where most movie and TV studios are found) all the way across the country and north of the border to Canada, where film production crews are welcomed with open arms (and pocketbooks) in 'Hollywood North', particularly in Vancouver, Toronto and Montréal. The Los Angeles Economic Development Council reports that only 2.5% of people living in LA County today are employed directly in film, TV and radio production.

For star gazers or movie buffs, however, LA is still a pilgrimage spot. Star-worthy experiences are infinite there: you can tour major movie studios, be part of a TV studio audience, shop at boutiques alongside today's hottest stars, see where celebrities live, dine out and go clubbing, or attend a star-studded film festival or awards gala ceremony.

Animated Magic

A young cartoonist named Walt Disney arrived in LA in 1923, and five years later he had his first breakout hit, *Steamboat Willie,* starring a mouse named Mickey. That film spawned the entire Disney empire, and dozens of other animation studios have followed with films, TV pro-

SCREEN WRITERS

During the 1930s, '40s and '50s, famous American writers F Scott Fitzgerald, Dorothy Parker, Truman Capote, William Faulkner and Tennessee Williams all did stints as Hollywood screenwriters.

CALIFORNIA ON CELLULOID

Images of California are distributed far beyond its borders, ultimately reflecting back upon the state itself. Hollywood films often feature California not only as a setting but as a topic and, in some cases, almost as a character. LA especially loves to turn the camera on itself, often with a dark film-noir angle. For classic California flicks from before the turn of the 21st century, here are our top picks:

» **The Maltese Falcon** (1941) John Huston directs Humphrey Bogart as Sam Spade, the classic San Francisco private eye.

» **Sunset Boulevard** (1950) Billy Wilder's classic stars Gloria Swanson and William Holden in a bonfire of Hollywood vanities.

» **Vertigo** (1958) The Golden Gate Bridge dazzles and dizzies in Alfred Hitchcock's noir thriller starring Jimmy Stewart and Kim Novak.

» **The Graduate** (1967) Dustin Hoffman flees status-obsessed California suburbia to search for meaning, heading across the Bay Bridge to Berkeley (in the wrong direction).

» **Chinatown** (1974) Roman Polanski's gripping version of the early 20th-century water wars that made and nearly broke LA.

» **Blade Runner** (1982) Ridley Scott's sci-fi cyberpunk thriller projects LA into the 21st century, with high-rise corporate fortresses and chaotic streets.

» **The Player** (1992) Directed by Robert Altman and starring Tim Robbins, this satire on the Industry features dozens of cameos by actors spoofing themselves.

grams and special effects. Among the most beloved are Warner Bros (Bugs Bunny et al in *Looney Tunes*), Hanna-Barbera (*The Flintstones, The Jetsons, Scooby-Doo*), DreamWorks (*Shrek, Madagascar, Kung-Fu Panda*) and Film Roman (*The Simpsons, King of the Hill*). Even if much of the hands-on work takes place overseas (in places such as South Korea), concept and supervision is still done in LA.

In San Francisco, George Lucas's Industrial Light & Magic is made up of a team of high-tech wizards who produce computer-generated special effects for such blockbusters as the *Star Wars, Raiders of the Lost Ark, Terminator* and the *Transformers* series. Pixar Animation Studios, located in the East Bay, has produced an unbroken string of animated hits including *Toy Story, Finding Nemo, Cars* and *Ratatouille*.

The Small Screen

The first TV station began broadcasting in Los Angeles in 1931. Through the next decades of the 20th century, iconic images of LA were beamed into living rooms across America in shows such as *Dragnet* (1950s), *The Beverly Hillbillies* (1960s), *The Brady Bunch* (1970s), *LA Law* (1980s), *Baywatch, Melrose Place* and *The Fresh Prince of Bel-Air* (1990s), through to teen 'dramedies' (drama-comedies) *Beverly Hills 90210* (1990s), which made that LA zip code into a status symbol, and *The OC* (2000s) set in Newport Beach, Orange County. If you're a fan of reality TV, you'll spot Southern California starring in everything from *Top Chef* to the *Real Housewives of Orange County* and MTV's *Laguna Beach* and *The Hills*, about rich, gorgeous twentysomethings cavorting in SoCal. Get a sneak peek of new TV shows by joining a live studio audience in LA (see p549).

Southern California is also a versatile backdrop for edgy cable TV dramas, from Showtime's *Weeds* – about a pot-growing SoCal widow with ties to Mexican drug cartels – to TNT's cop show *The Closer* about homicide detectives in LA, and FX's *The Shield*, which fictionalized police corruption in the City of Angels. HBO's *Six Feet Under* (2000s) examined modern LA through the eyes of an eccentric extended family running a funeral home. HBO's *Entourage* portrays the highs, the lows and the intrigues of the Industry through the eyes of a rising star and his posse, while Showtime's *Californication* shows, with no holds barred, what happens when a successful New York novelist goes Hollywood. More biting social satire about the Industry and life in LA (and now, NYC) is the fare of HBO's *Curb Your Enthusiasm*, by *Seinfeld* co-creator Larry David and often guest starring celebrities playing themselves, including Martin Scorsese, Julia Louis-Dreyfus and Wanda Sykes.

ON LOCATION: FILM & TV

MILESTONES IN CALIFORNIA FILM HISTORY

1913
The first full-length Hollywood feature movie, a silent Western drama called *The Squaw Man*, is shot by director Cecil B de Mille.

1927
The first talkie, *The Jazz Singer*, ends the silent film era. Sid Grauman opens his Chinese Theatre in Hollywood; stars have been leaving their hand- and footprints there ever since.

1939
The Wizard of Oz is the first wide-release movie shown in full color. Nonetheless, it loses the Oscar for Best Picture the next year to *Gone with the Wind*.

1950s
During the anticommunist Cold War era, the federal government's House Un-American Activities Committee investigates and subsequently blacklists many Hollywood actors, directors and screenwriters, some of whom leave for Europe.

1975
The age of the modern blockbuster begins with the thriller *Jaws*, by a young filmmaker named Steven Spielberg, whose later blockbusters include *E.T.* and *Jurassic Park*.

2001
In the Hollywood & Highland Complex on Hollywood Blvd, the new Kodak Theatre becomes the permanent home of the Academy Awards ceremony.

Music & the Arts

When Californians thank their lucky stars – or good karma, or the goddess – that they don't live in New York, they're not just talking about beach weather. California supports thriving music and arts scenes that aren't afraid to be completely independent, even outlandish at times. Even Californians acknowledge that their music is eclectic, ranging from pitch-perfect opera to off-key punk. Meanwhile, critics have tried and failed to find any consistency whatsoever to the styles and schools of music and art that have flourished here – but in the context of California, the most racially and ethnically diverse state in the country, that variety makes perfect sense.

Music

In your California dreamin', you jam with a band – so what kind of music did you play? Beach Boys covers, rap, bluegrass, hardcore, swing, classic soul, hard bop, heavy-metal riffs on opera or DJ mashups of all of the above? No problem: a walk down a city street here can sound like the world's most eclectic iPod set to shuffle.

Much of the recording industry is based in Los Angeles, and SoCal's film and TV industries have proven powerful talent incubators. But today's troubled pop princesses and airbrushed boy bands are only here thanks to the tuneful revolutions of all the decades of innovation that came before, from country folk to urban rap.

Early Eclectic Sounds

Chronologically speaking, Mexican folk music arrived in California even before the Gold Rush introduced Western bluegrass, bawdy dancehall ragtime and Chinese classical music, but, by the turn of the 20th century, opera had become California's favorite sound. The city of San Francisco alone had 20 concert and opera halls before the 1906 earthquake literally brought down the houses. Soon afterward, talented opera performers converged on the shattered city for free public performances that turned arias into anthems for the city's rebirth. Among San Francisco's first public buildings to be completed was the War Memorial Opera House, now home to the second-largest US opera company after New York's Metropolitan.

Swing Jazz, Blues & Soul

Swing was the next big thing to hit California, in the 1930s and '40s, as big bands sparked a lindy-hopping craze in LA and sailors on shore leave hit San Francisco's underground, integrated jazz clubs. California's African American community grew with the 'Great Migration' during the WWII shipping and manufacturing boom, and from this thriving scene emerged the West Coast blues sound. Texas-born bluesman T-Bone Walker worked in LA's Central Ave clubs before making hit records of his electric guitar stylings for Capitol Records. Throughout the 1940s and

When the 1906 earthquake hit San Francisco, the visiting Metropolitan opera lost all its costumes and tenor Enrico Caruso was thrown from his bed. Caruso never returned, but the Met played free shows in the rubble-choked streets.

In the 1950s, the hard-edged, honky-tonk Bakersfield Sound emerged inland in California's Central Valley, where Buck Owens and the Buckaroos and Merle Haggard performed their own twist on Nashville country hits for hard-drinkin' audiences of Dust Bowl migrants and cowboy ranchers.

'50s, the West Coast blues sound was nurtured in San Francisco and Oakland by guitarists such as Pee Wee Crayton from Texas and Oklahoma-born Lowell Fulson.

With Beat poets riffing over improvised bass-lines and audiences finger-snapping their approval, the cool, 1950s West Coast jazz of Chet Baker and Dave Brubeck emerged from San Francisco's North Beach neighborhood. In the African American cultural hub along LA's Central Avenue, the hard bop of Charlie Parker and Charles Mingus kept the SoCal scene alive and swinging. In 1950s and '60s California, doo-wop, rhythm and blues, and soul music were all in steady rotation at nightclubs in South Central LA, considered the 'Harlem of the West.' Soulful singer Sam Cooke ran his own hit-making record label here, attracting soul and gospel talent to Los Angeles.

Rockin' Out

The first homegrown rock-and-roll talent to make it big in the 1950s was Richie Valens, whose 'La Bamba' was a rockified version of a Mexican folk song. Dick Dale (aka 'The King of the Surf Guitar'), whose recording of 'Miserlou' featured in the movie *Pulp Fiction,* started experimenting with reverb effects in Orange County in the 1950s, then topped the charts with his band the Del-Tones in the early '60s, influencing everyone from the Beach Boys to Jimi Hendrix.

When Joan Baez and Bob Dylan had their Northern California fling in the early 1960s, Dylan plugged in his guitar and played folk rock. When Janis Joplin and Big Brother & the Holding Company developed their shambling musical stylings in San Francisco, folk rock splintered into psychedelia. Emerging from that same San Francisco melange, Jefferson Airplane remade Lewis Carroll's children's classic *Alice's Adventures in Wonderland* into the psychedelic hit 'White Rabbit.'

Meanwhile, Jim Morrison and The Doors and The Byrds blew minds on LA's famous Sunset Strip. The epicenter of LA's psychedelic rock scene was the Laurel Canyon neighborhood, just uphill from the Sunset Strip and the legendary Whisky A-Go-Go nightclub. Sooner or later, many of these 1960s rock-and-roll headliners wound up overdosing on drugs. Those that survived cleaned up and cashed out – though for the original jam-band, the Grateful Dead, the song remained the same until guitarist Jerry Garcia's passing in a Marin County rehabilitation clinic in 1995.

MUSIC HISTORY

MUSIC & THE ARTS MUSIC

Waiting for the Sun: Strange Days, Weird Scenes and the Sound of Los Angeles, by British rock historian Barney Hoskyns, follows the twists and turns of the SoCal music scene from Nat King Cole to NWA.

PUNK'S NOT DEAD IN CALIFORNIA

In the 1970s, American airwaves were jammed with commercial arena rock that record companies paid DJs to shill like laundry soap, much to the articulate ire of California rock critics Lester Bangs and Greil Marcus. California teens bored with prepackaged anthems started making their own with secondhand guitars, three chords and crappy amps that added a loud buzz to their unleashed fury.

LA punk paralleled the scrappy local skate scene with the hardcore grind of Black Flag from Hermosa Beach and the Germs. LA band X bridged punk and new wave from 1977 to 1986 with John Doe's rockabilly guitar, Exene Cervenka's angsty wail, and disappointed-romantic lyrics inspired by Charles Bukowski and Raymond Chandler. Local LA radio station KROQ rebelled against the tyranny of playlists, putting local punk on the airwaves and launching punk-funk sensation the Red Hot Chili Peppers.

San Francisco's punk scene was arty and absurdist, in rare form with Dead Kennedys singer (and future San Francisco mayoral candidate) Jello Biafra howling 'Holiday in Cambodia.' That was suitably anarchic for a city where local band the Avengers opened for the Sex Pistols' 1978 San Francisco show, which Sid Vicious celebrated with an OD in the Haight that broke up the band.

The country-influenced pop of The Eagles and Linda Ronstadt became America's soundtrack for the early 1970s, joined by the Mexican-fusion sounds of Santana from San Francisco and iconic funk bands War from Long Beach and Sly and the Family Stone, which got their groove on in the Bay area before moving to LA.

Post-Punk to Pop

The 1980s saw the rise of such influential LA crossover bands as Bad Religion (punk) and Suicidal Tendencies (hardcore/thrash), while more mainstream all-female bands The Bangles and The Go-Gos, new wavers Oingo Boingo, and rockers Jane's Addiction and Red Hot Chili Peppers took the world by storm. Bangin' out of Hollywood, Guns N' Roses was the '80s hard-rock band of choice. On avant-garde rocker Frank Zappa's 1982 single *Valley Girl,* his 14-year-old daughter Moon Unit taught the rest of America to say 'Omig*o*-o-o-od!' like an LA teenager.

By the 1990s alternative rock acts like Beck and Weezer had gained national presence. Los Lobos was king of the Latino bands, an honor that has since passed to Ozomatli. Another key '90s band was the ska-punk-alt-rock No Doubt, of Orange County (which later launched the solo career of lead singer Gwen Stefani). Berkeley revived punk in the '90s, including with Grammy Award–winning Green Day.

SoCal rock stars of the new millennium include the approachable hip-hop of the Black Eyed Peas, anchored by Fergie and will.i.am., San Diego-based pop-punksters Blink 182, Orange County's the Offspring, and indie-rockers Avi Buffalo out of Long Beach and Rilo Kiley from LA.

Rap & Hip-Hop Rhythms

Since the 1980s, LA has been a hotbed for West Coast rap and hip-hop. Eazy E, Ice Cube and Dr Dre released the seminal NWA (Niggaz With Attitude) album, *Straight Outta Compton,* in 1989. Death Row Records, cofounded by Dr Dre, has launched megawatt rap talents including Long Beach bad-boy Snoop Dog and the late Tupac Shakur, who began his rap career in Marin County of all places and was fatally shot in 1996 in Las Vegas in a suspected East Coast/West Coast rap feud. Feuds also once checkered the musical and legal career of LA rapper Game, whose 2009 *R.E.D Album* featured an all-star line-up of Diddy, Dr Dre, Snoop Dog and more.

Throughout the 1980s and '90s, California maintained a grassroots hip-hop scene closer to the streets in LA and in the heart of the black power movement in Oakland. In the late 1990s, the Bay Area birthed the 'hyphy movement,' a reaction against the increasing commercialization of hip-hop, and underground artists like E-40. Also from Oakland, Michael Franti & Spearhead blend hip-hop with funk, reggae, folk, jazz and rock stylings into messages for social justice and peace in 2010's *The Sound of Sunshine*. Meanwhile, Korn from Bakersfield and Linkin Park from LA County have combined hip-hop with rap and metal to popularize 'nu metal.'

Architecture

There's more to California than beach houses and boardwalks. Californians have adapted imported styles to the climate and available materials, building cool, adobe-inspired houses in San Diego and fog-resistant redwood-shingle houses in Mendocino. But after a century and a half of Californians grafting on inspired influences and eccentric details as the mood strikes them, the element of the unexpected is everywhere: tiled Maya deco facades in Oakland, Shinto-inspired archways in LA, English thatched roofs in Carmel, Chinoiserie streetlamps in San Francisco. California's architecture was postmodern before the word even existed.

Tune into the 'Morning Becomes Eclectic' show on Southern California's KCRW radio station (www.kcrw.com) for live in-studio performances and musician interviews.

In 1915, newspaper magnate William Randolph Hearst commissioned California's first licensed female architect Julia Morgan to build his Hearst Castle. The commission would take Morgan decades.

HEARST CASTLE

Spanish Missions & Victorian Queens

The first Spanish missions were built around courtyards, using materials that Native Californians and colonists found on hand: adobe, limestone and grass. Many missions crumbled into disrepair as the church's influence waned, but the style remained practical for the climate. Early California settlers later adapted it into the rancho adobe style, as seen at El Pueblo de Los Angeles and in San Diego's Old Town.

Once the mid-19th-century Gold Rush was on, California's nouveau riche imported materials to construct grand mansions matching European fashions, and raised the stakes with ornamental excess.

Many millionaires favored the gilded Queen Anne style. Outrageous examples of Victorian architecture, including 'Painted Ladies' and 'gingerbread' houses, can be found in such Northern California towns as San Francisco, Ferndale and Eureka.

Californian architecture has always had its contrarian streak, and many architects rejected frilly Victorian styles in favor of the simple, classical lines of Spanish colonial architecture. Mission revival details are restrained and functional: arched doors and windows, long covered porches, fountains, courtyards, solid walls and red tiled roofs. Several Southern California train depots showcase this style, as do stand-out buildings in San Diego's Balboa Park and downtown Santa Barbara.

Oddball California Architecture

» **Hearst Castle**
San Simeon

» **Tor House**
Carmel-by-the-Sea

» **Theme Building**
LAX Airport

» **Wigwam Motel**
San Bernardino

» **Integratron**
Landers

MUSIC & THE ARTS ARCHITECTURE

Art Deco & Arts and Crafts

Simplicity was the hallmark of California's Arts and Crafts style. Influenced by both Japanese design principles and England's Arts and Crafts movement, its woodwork and handmade touches marked a deliberate departure from the Industrial Revolution. SoCal architects Charles and Henry Greene and Bernard Maybeck in Northern California popularized the versatile one-story bungalow, which became trendy at the turn of the 20th century. Today you'll spot them in Pasadena and Berkeley with their overhanging eaves, terraces and sleeping porches harmonizing indoors and outdoors.

California was cosmopolitan from the start, and couldn't be limited to any one set of international influences. In the 1920s, the international art deco style took elements from the ancient world – Mayan glyphs, Egyptian pillars, Babylonian ziggurats – and flattened them into modern motifs to cap stark facades and outline streamlined skyscrapers, notably in LA and downtown Oakland. Streamline moderne kept decoration to a minimum and mimicked the aerodynamic look of ocean liners and airplanes.

Post-Modern Evolutions

True to its mythic nature, California couldn't help wanting to embellish the facts a little, veering away from strict high modernism to add unlikely postmodern shapes to the local landscape. Richard Meier made

CALIFORNIA'S NAKED ARCHITECTURE

Clothing-optional California has never been shy about showcasing its assets. Starting in the 1960s, California embraced the stripped-down, glass-wall aesthetics of the International Style championed by Bauhaus architects Walter Gropius and Ludwig Mies van der Rohe, and Le Corbusier. Open floor-plans and floor-to-ceiling windows were especially suited to the see-and-be-seen culture of Southern California, in a residential style adapted by Austrian-born Rudolph Schindler and Richard Neutra that can be spotted today in LA and Palm Springs. Neutra and Schindler were influenced by Frank Lloyd Wright, who designed LA's Hollyhock House in a style he dubbed 'California Romanza.' Neutra also contributed with Charles and Ray Eames to the experimental open-plan Case Study Houses, several of which jut out of the LA landscape and are still used as iconic filming locations, for example, in *LA Confidential*.

his mark on West LA with the Getty Center, a cresting white wave of a building atop a sunburned hilltop. Canadian-born Frank Gehry relocated to Santa Monica, and his billowing, sculptural style for LA's Walt Disney Concert Hall winks cheekily at shipshape Californian streamline moderne. Renzo Piano's signature inside-out industrial style can be glimpsed in the sawtooth roof and red-steel veins on the new Broad Contemporary Art Museum extension of the Los Angeles County Museum of Art.

San Francisco has lately championed a brand of postmodernism by Pritzker Prize-winning architects that magnifies and mimics California's great outdoors, especially in Golden Gate Park. Swiss architects Herzog & de Meuron clad the MH de Young Memorial Museum in copper, which will eventually oxidize green to match its park setting. Nearby, Renzo Piano literally raised the roof on sustainable design at the LEED platinum-certified California Academy of Sciences, capped by a living garden.

> To find museums, galleries, fine art exhibition spaces and calendars of upcoming shows throughout SoCal, check out *ArtScene* (www.artscenecal.com) or *Artweek LA* (www.artweek.la) magazines.

Visual Arts

Although the earliest European artists were trained cartographers accompanying Western explorers, their images of California as an island show more imagination than scientific rigor. This mythologizing tendency continued throughout the Gold Rush era, as Western artists alternated between caricatures of Wild West debauchery and manifest-destiny propaganda urging pioneers to settle the golden West. The completion of the Transcontinental Railroad in 1869 brought an influx of romantic painters, who produced epic California wilderness landscapes. In the early 1900s, homegrown colonies of California Impressionist plein-air painters emerged, particularly at Laguna Beach and Carmel-by-the-Sea.

With the invention of photography, the improbable truth of California's landscape and its inhabitants was revealed. Pirkle Jones saw expressive potential in California landscape photography after WWII, while San Francisco native Ansel Adams' sublime photographs had already started doing justice to Yosemite. Adams founded Group f/64 with Edward Weston from Carmel and Imogen Cunningham in San Francisco. Berkeley-based Dorothea Lange turned her unflinching lens on the plight of Californian migrant workers in the Great Depression and Japanese Americans forced to enter internment camps in WWII, producing poignant documentary photos.

As the postwar American West became crisscrossed with freeways and divided into planned communities, Californian painters captured the abstract forms of manufactured landscapes on canvas. In San Francisco Richard Diebenkorn and David Park became leading proponents of Bay Area Figurative Art, while San Francisco sculptor Richard Serra captured urban aesthetics in massive, rusting monoliths resembling ship prows and industrial Stonehenges. Meanwhile, pop artists captured the

LATINO MURALS: TAKING IT TO THE STREETS

Beginning in the 1930s, when the federal Works Progress Administration sponsored schemes to uplift and beautify cities across the country, murals came to define California cityscapes. Mexican muralists Diego Rivera, David Alfaro Siqueiros and José Clemente Orozco sparked an outpouring of murals across LA that today number in the thousands. Rivera was also brought to San Francisco for murals at the San Francisco Art Institute, and his influence is reflected in the interior of San Francisco's Coit Tower and scores of murals lining the Mission District preserved and expanded by **Precita Eyes** (www.precitaeyes.org). Murals gave voice to Chicano pride and protests over US Central American policies in the 1970s, notably in San Diego's Chicano Park and East LA murals by collectives such as East Los Streetscapers.

ethos of conspicuous consumerism, through Wayne Thiebaud's gumball machines, British émigré David Hockney's LA pools, and above all, Ed Ruscha's studies of SoCal pop culture. In San Francisco, artists showed their love for rough-and-readymade 1950s Beat collage, 1960s psychedelic Fillmore posters, earthy '70s funk and beautiful-mess punk, and '80s graffiti and skate culture.

Today's California contemporary art scene brings all these influences together with muralist-led social commentary, an obsessive dedication to craft and a new-media milieu pierced by California's cutting-edge technology. LA's Museum of Contemporary Art puts on provocative and avant-garde shows, as does LACMA's Broad Contemporary Art Museum and the Museum of Contemporary Art San Diego, which specializes in post-1950s pop and conceptual art. To see California-made art at its most experimental, browse the SoCal gallery scenes in downtown LA and Culver City, then check out independent NorCal art spaces in San Francisco's Mission District and the laboratory-like galleries of SOMA's Yerba Buena Arts District.

Timeless, rare Ansel Adams photographs are paired with excerpts from canonical Californian writers such as Jack Kerouac and Joan Didion in *California: With Classic California Writings*, edited by Andrea Gray Stillman.

MUSIC & THE ARTS THEATER

Theater

In your California dream you're discovered by a movie talent scout, but most Californian actors actually get their start in theater. Home to about 25% of the nation's professional actors, LA is the second-most influential city in America for theater, while San Francisco has been a US hub for experimental theater since the 1960s.

Spaces to watch around LA include the Geffen Playhouse close to UCLA, the Ahmanson Theatre and Mark Taper Forum in downtown LA, and the Actors' Gang Theatre, cofounded by actor Tim Robbins. Small theaters flourish in West Hollywood (WeHo) and North Hollywood (NoHo), the West Coast's answers to off- and off-off-Broadway. Influential multicultural theaters include Little Tokyo's East West Players, while critically acclaimed outlying companies include the innovative Long Beach Opera and Orange County's South Coast Repertory.

San Francisco's priorities have been obvious since the great earthquake of 1906, when survivors were entertained in tents set up amid the smoldering ruins, and its famous theaters were rebuilt well before City Hall. Major productions destined for the lights of Broadway and London premiere at the American Conservatory Theater, and San Francisco's answer to Edinburgh is the annual SF Fringe Festival at the Exit Theatre. The Magic Theatre gained a national reputation in the 1970s, when Sam Shepard was the theater's resident playwright, and still today it premieres innovative California playwrights. Across the Bay, the Berkeley Repertory Theatre has launched acclaimed productions based on such unlikely subjects as the rise and fall of Jim Jones' Peoples Temple.

Photography buffs can plan their California trip around the superb collections at SFMOMA and LA's Getty Center – California's Louvre of photography, with over 31,000 images.

By the Book

Californians make up the largest market for books in the US, and read much more than the national average. Skewing the curve is bookish San Francisco, with more writers, playwrights and book purchases per capita than any other US city. The entire West Coast has long attracted novelists, poets and storytellers, and California's resident literary community today is stronger than ever.

You've probably already read books by Californians without knowing it. Some of the best-known titles by resident writers aren't necessarily set in their home state. Take for example Ray Bradbury's 1950s dystopian classic *Fahrenheit 451*; Alice Walker's Pulitzer Prize–winning *The Color Purple;* Ken Kesey's quintessential '60s novel *One Flew Over the Cuckoo's Nest*; Isabel Allende's best-selling *House of the Spirits*; feminist poetry by Adrienne Rich; and Michael Chabon's Pulitzer Prize–winning *The Amazing Adventures of Kavalier and Clay*.

Early Voices of Social Realism

Arguably the most influential author to emerge from California was John Steinbeck, born in Salinas in 1902. Steinbeck focused attention on Central Valley farming communities. Published in the 1930s, his first California novel, *Tortilla Flat*, takes place in Monterey's Mexican American community, while his masterpiece, *The Grapes of Wrath*, tells of the struggles of migrant farm workers. Another social realist, Eugene O'Neill took his 1936 Nobel Prize money and transplanted himself near San Francisco, where he wrote the autographical play *Long Day's Journey into Night*.

Starting in the 1920s, many novelists looked at LA in political terms, often viewing it unfavorably as the ultimate metaphor for capitalism. Classics in this vein include Upton Sinclair's *Oil!*, a muckraking work of historical fiction with socialist overtones. Aldous Huxley's *After Many a Summer Dies the Swan* is based on the life of publisher William Randolph Hearst (also an inspiration for Orson Welles' film *Citizen Kane*). F Scott Fitzgerald's final novel, *The Last Tycoon*, makes scathing observations about the early years of Hollywood by following the life of a 1930s movie producer who is slowly working himself to death.

In Northern California, professional hell-raiser Jack London grew up and cut his teeth in Oakland. He turned out a massive volume of influential fiction, including tales of the late-19th-century Klondike Gold Rush. Oakland was famously scorned by 'Lost Generation' literary luminary Gertrude Stein (who lived there briefly) when she quipped, 'There is no there there,' although, to be fair, she was really only saying that she couldn't find her old house when she returned from Europe in the 1930s.

Pulp Noir & Science Fiction

In the 1930s, San Francisco and Los Angeles became the capitals of the pulp detective novel, examples of which were often made into noir crime films. Dashiell Hammett (*The Maltese Falcon*) made San Francisco's fog a

---

Taste a real slice of the state's heartland by reading *Highway 99: A Literary Journey Through California's Central Valley*, edited by Oakland-based writer Stan Yogi. It's full of multicultural perspectives, from early European settlers to 20th-century Mexican and Asian immigrant farmers.

For a memorable romp through California with contemporary authors from Pico Iyer to Michael Chabon, check out *My California: Journeys by Great Writers*. Proceeds from online purchases (www.angelcitypress.com/myca.html) support the California Arts Council.

sinister character. The king of hard-boiled crime writers was Raymond Chandler, who thinly disguised his hometown of Santa Monica as Bay City. Since the 1990s, a renaissance of California crime fiction has been masterminded by James Ellroy *(LA Confidential),* Elmore Leonard *(Get Shorty)* and Walter Mosley *(Devil in a Blue Dress),* whose Easy Rawlins detective novels are set in South Central LA's impoverished neighborhoods.

California has also proved fertile ground for the imaginations of sci-fi writers. Berkeley-born Philip K Dick is chiefly remembered for his science fiction, notably *Do Androids Dream of Electric Sheep?,* later adapted into the 1982 dystopian sci-fi classic *Blade Runner.* Dick's novel *The Man in the High Castle* presents the ultimate what-if scenario: imagine San Francisco circa 1962 if Japan and Nazi Germany had won WWII. Ursula K Le Guin *(The Left Hand of Darkness, A Wizard of Earthsea),* a lauded fantasy writer, feminist and essayist, also grew up in Berkeley in the 1940s.

Social Movers & Shakers

After the chaos of WWII, the Beat Generation brought about a provocative new style of writing: short, sharp, spontaneous and alive. Based in San Francisco, the scene revolved around Jack Kerouac *(On the Road),* Allen Ginsberg *(Howl)* and Lawrence Ferlinghetti, the Beats' patron and publisher. Poet-painter-playwright Kenneth Rexroth was instrumental in advancing the careers of several Bay Area writers and artists of that era and he shared an interest in Japanese traditions with Buddhist Gary Snyder, a Beat poet of deep ecology.

Few writers have nailed contemporary California culture as well as Joan Didion. She's best known for her collection of essays, *Slouching Towards Bethlehem,* which takes a caustic look at 1960s flower power and Haight-Ashbury. Tom Wolfe also put '60s San Francisco in perspective with *The Electric Kool-Aid Acid Test,* which follows Ken Kesey's band of Merry Pranksters, who began their acid-laced 'magic bus' journey near Santa Cruz. In the 1970s, Charles Bukowski's semiautobiographical novel *Post Office* captured down-and-out downtown LA, while Richard Vasquez's *Chicano* took a dramatic look at LA's Latino barrio.

For a frothy taste of 1970s San Francisco, the serial-style *Tales of the City,* by Armistead Maupin, collars the reader as the author follows the lives of several colorful, fictional characters, gay and straight. Zooming ahead, the mid-1980s brought the startling revelations of Bret Easton Ellis' *Less Than Zero,* about the cocaine-addled lives of wealthy Beverly Hills teenagers in SoCal.

POETRY

BY THE BOOK

California Poetry: From the Gold Rush to the Present, edited by Dana Gioia, Chryss Yost and Jack Hicks, is a ground-breaking anthology with enlightening introductions that give each poet their deserved context.

READING CALIFORNIA

Classics from some of California's less likely literary locations:

» **Central Coast** *Selected Poetry of Robinson Jeffers* – In the looming, windswept pines surrounding Tor House (p476), Jeffers found inspiration for staggering, twisted poems.

» **Central Valley** *Woman Warrior: Memoirs of a Girlhood Among Ghosts* (Maxine Hong Kingston) – A chronicle of growing up Chinese American, reflecting the shattered mirror of Californian identity.

» **Gold Country** *Roughing It* (Mark Twain) – The master of sardonic observation tells of earthquakes, silver booms and busts, and getting by for a month on a dime in the Wild West.

» **Sierra Nevada** *Riprap and Cold Mountain Poems* (Gary Snyder) – Influenced by Japanese and Chinese spirituality and classical literature, the Beat poet captures the meditative openness of wild mountain landscapes.

The Land & Wildlife

From soaring snowcapped peaks, to scorching deserts and misty coastal forests, California is home to a bewildering variety of ecosystems and animals. In fact this state has the highest biodiversity in North America. Its Mediterranean climate, characterized by dry summers and mild wet winters, is favored by scores of unique plants and animals. At the same time, California has the largest human population of any US state and the nation's highest projected growth rate, which puts a tremendous strain on its many precious natural resources.

Browse through over 1200 aerial photos covering almost every mile of California's gorgeously rugged coastline, from Oregon to the Mexican borders, at www.californiacoastline.org.

Lay of the Land

The third-largest state after Alaska and Texas, California covers more than 155,000 sq miles, making it larger than 85 of the world's smallest nations. It's bordered to the north by Oregon, to the south by Mexico, to the east by Nevada and Arizona, and by 840 miles of Pacific shoreline to the west.

Geology & Earthquakes

California is a complex geologic landscape formed from fragments of rock and earth crust scraped together as the North American continent drifted westward over hundreds of millions of years. Crumpled coast ranges, the downward-bowing Central Valley and the still-rising Sierra Nevada all provide evidence of gigantic forces exerted as the continental and ocean plates crushed together.

According to the US Geological Survey, the odds of a magnitude 6.7 or greater earthquake hitting California in the next 30 years is 99.7%.

Everything changed about 25 million years ago, when the ocean plates stopped colliding and instead started sliding against each other, creating the massive San Andreas Fault. Because this contact zone doesn't slide smoothly, but catches and slips irregularly, it rattles California with an ongoing succession of tremors and earthquakes.

In 1906 the state's most famous earthquake measured 7.8 on the Richter scale and demolished San Francisco, leaving more than 3000 people dead. The Bay Area made headlines again in 1989 when the Loma Prieta earthquake (7.1) caused a section of the Bay Bridge to collapse. Los Angeles' last 'big one' was in 1994, when the Northridge quake (6.7) caused parts of the Santa Monica Fwy to fall down, making it the most costly quake in US history...so far.

The Coast to the Central Valley

Much of California's coast is fronted by rugged coastal mountains that capture winter's water-laden storms. San Francisco divides the Coast Ranges roughly in half, with the foggy North Coast remaining sparsely populated, while the Central and Southern California coasts have a balmier climate and many more people.

EARTHQUAKE

Geography of California

Over 120in of rain a year fall in the northernmost reaches of the Coast Ranges and, in some places, persistent summer fog contributes another 12in of precipitation. Nutrient-rich soils and abundant moisture foster forests of giant trees (where they haven't been cut), including stands of towering coast redwoods growing as far south as Big Sur all the way north to Oregon.

On their eastern flanks, the Coast Ranges subside into gently rolling hills that give way to the sprawling Central Valley. Once an inland sea, this flat inland basin is now an agricultural powerhouse producing about half of America's fruits, nuts and vegetables valued at over $14 billion a year. Stretching about 450 miles long and 50 miles wide, the Central Valley gets about as much rainfall as a desert, but receives huge volumes of water running off the Sierra Nevada.

Before the arrival of Europeans the Central Valley was a natural wonderland – a region of vast marshes and home to flocks of geese that blackened the sky, not to mention grasslands carpeted with countless flowers and grazed by millions of antelopes, elk and grizzly bears. Virtually this entire landscape has been plowed under and replaced with alien weeds (including agricultural crops) and livestock.

Mountain Highs

On the eastern side of the Central Valley looms California's most prominent topographic feature, the world-famous Sierra Nevada, nicknamed 'The Range of Light' by conservationist John Muir. At 400 miles long and 50 miles wide, this is not only one of the largest mountain ranges in the world, but it's also the home of 13 peaks over 14,000ft. The vast wilderness of the High Sierra (lying mostly above 9000ft) presents an astounding landscape of glaciers, sculpted granite peaks and remote canyons, beautiful to look at but difficult to access, and one of the greatest challenges for 19th-century settlers attempting to reach California.

The soaring Sierra Nevada captures storm systems and drains them of their water, with most of the precipitation over 3000ft falling as snow. Snowfalls average almost 40ft at midelevations on the west slope, making this a premier skiing and winter sports destination. These waters eventually flow into a half dozen major river systems on the range's west and east slopes, providing the vast majority of water for agriculture in the Central Valley and helping meet the needs of major metropolitan areas from San Francisco to LA.

At its northern end the Sierra Nevada merges imperceptibly into the southern tip of the volcanic Cascade Mountains that continue north into Oregon and Washington. At its southern end, the Sierra Nevada makes a funny westward hook and connects via the Transverse Ranges (one of few examples of east–west mountains in the USA) to the southern Coast Ranges.

The Deserts & Beyond

With the west slope of the Sierra Nevada capturing the lion's share of water, all lands east of the Sierra crest are dry and desertlike, receiving less than 10in of rain a year. Surprisingly, some valleys at the eastern foot of the Sierra Nevada are well watered by creeks and support a vigorous economy of livestock and agriculture.

Areas in the northern half of California, especially on the elevated Modoc Plateau of northeastern California, are a cold desert at the western edge of the Great Basin, blanketed with hardy sagebrush shrubs and pockets of juniper trees. Temperatures increase as you head south, with a prominent transition as you descend from Mono Lake into the Owens Valley east of the Sierra Nevada. This southern hot desert (part of the Mojave Desert) includes Death Valley, one of the hottest places on earth.

The rest of Southern California is a hodgepodge of small mountain ranges and desert basins. Mountains on the eastern border of the Los Angeles Basin continue southward past San Diego and down the spine of northern Baja California. The Mojave Desert of the southern Sierra Ne-

HIGHS & LOWS

California claims both the highest point in contiguous US (Mt Whitney, 14,505ft) and the lowest elevation in North America (Badwater, Death Valley, 282ft below sea level) – and they're only 90 miles apart, as the condor flies.

ALMOST AN ISLAND

Much of California is a biological island cut off from the rest of North America by the soaring heights of the Sierra Nevada. As on other 'islands' in the world, evolution has created unique plants and animals under these biologically isolated conditions. As a result, California ranks first in the nation for its number of endemic plants, amphibians, reptiles, freshwater fish and mammals. Even more impressive: 30% of all the plant species found in the USA, 50% of all bird species and 50% of all mammal species occur in California.

EYEING E-SEALS

Northern elephant seals follow a precise calendar. In November and December, adult male 'bull seals' return to their colony's favorite California beaches and start the ritual struggles to assert superiority; only the largest, strongest and most aggressive 'alpha' males gather a harem. In January and February, adult females, already pregnant from last year's beach antics, give birth to their pups and soon mate with the dominant males, who promptly depart on their next feeding migration. The bull seals' motto seems to be 'love 'em and leave 'em"!

At birth an elephant seal pup weighs about 75lb, and while being fed by its mother it puts on about 10lb a day. But female seals leave the beach in March, abandoning their offspring. For up to two months the young seals, now known as 'weaners,' lounge around in groups, gradually learning to swim, first in tidal pools, then in the sea. Then they, too, depart by May, having lost 20% to 30% of their weight during this prolonged fast.

Between June and October, elephant seals of all ages and both sexes return in smaller numbers to the beaches to molt.

Always observe e-seals from a safe distance and do not approach or otherwise harass these unpredictable wild animals, who surprisingly can move faster on the sand than you can.

vada morphs into the Colorado Desert (part of Mexico's greater Sonoran Desert) around the Salton Sea.

Wild Things

Although the staggering numbers of animals that greeted the first European settlers are now a thing of the past, it is still possible to see wildlife thriving in California in the right places and at the right times of year. You're likely to spot at least a few charismatic species, such as coyotes, bobcats and eagles, during your travels. Unfortunately, some of these are but shadow populations, hovering at the edge of survival, pushed up against California's burgeoning human population.

Marine Superstars

Spend even one day along California's coast and you may spot pods of bottle-nosed dolphins and porpoises swimming and doing acrobatics in the ocean. Playful sea otters and harbor seals typically stick closer to shore, especially around public piers and protected bays. Since the 1989 earthquake, loudly barking sea lions have been piling up on San Francisco's Pier 39 (p65), much to the delight of ogling tourists. Other places to see wild pinnipeds include Point Lobos State Natural Reserve near Monterey and the Channel Islands National Park.

Once threatened by extinction, gray whales now migrate in growing numbers along California's coast. Adult whales live up to 50 years, are longer than a city bus and can weigh up to 40 tons, making quite a splash when they dive below or leap out of the water. In summer, the whales feed in Arctic waters between Alaska and Siberia. In the fall, they move south down the Pacific coast of Canada and the USA to sheltered lagoons in the Gulf of California, by the Mexican state of Baja California. During this 6000-mile migration, the whales pass by California between December and April.

Also almost hunted to extinction by the late 19th century, northern elephant seals have made a remarkable comeback along California's coast. Año Nuevo State Reserve, north of Santa Cruz, is a major breeding ground for northern elephant seals. But California's biggest elephant seal colony is found at Piedras Blancas (p485) near Hearst Castle, south of Big Sur. There's a smaller rookery at Point Reyes National Seashore (p127).

THE LAND & WILDLIFE WILD THINGS

Peak mating season for northern elephants seals along the Pacific coast just happens to coincide with Valentine's Day (February 14).

Mountain Kings

California's most symbolic animal – it graces the state flag – is the grizzly bear. Extirpated in the early 1900s after relentless persecution, grizzlies once roamed California's beaches and grasslands in large numbers, eating everything from whale carcasses to acorns. Grizzlies were particularly abundant in the Central Valley, but retreated upslope into the mountains as they were hunted out.

All that remains now are the grizzlies' smaller cousins, black bears, which typically weigh under 400lb. These burly omnivores feed on berries, nuts, roots, grasses, insects, eggs, small mammals and fish, but can become a nuisance around campgrounds and mountain cabins where food is not stored properly (for safety tips, see p765).

Mountain lions hunt throughout the mountains and forests of California, especially in areas teeming with deer. Solitary lions, which can grow 8ft in length and weigh 175lb, are formidable predators (see p765). Few attacks on humans have occurred, however, and mostly where encroachment has pushed hungry lions to their limits – for example, at the boundaries between wilderness and rapidly developing suburbs.

California's mountain forests are home to an estimated 25,000 to 35,000 black bears, whose fur actually ranges in color from black to dark brown, cinnamon or even blond.

More Mammals, Big & Small

As European settlers moved into California in the 1800s, many other large mammals fared almost as poorly as grizzlies. Immense herds of tule elk and antelope in the Central Valley were particularly hard hit, with antelope retreating in small numbers to the northeastern corner of the state, and elk hunted into near-extinction (a small remnant herd was moved to Point Reyes, where it has since rebounded).

Some smaller mammals have done well around the edges of towns. Bobcats, coyotes and foxes are prolific enough that you are almost guaranteed a sighting of these creatures when you travel through the wilder areas of the state, whether in mountain forests, in deserts or along the coast. Sharp-eyed visitors may even spot a weasel, a badger, a beaver, or one of the truly rare animals like a marten or a fisher.

Desert Critters

The desert is far from deserted, but most critters don't hang out in the daytime heat, coming out only at night like bats. Roadrunners, those black-and-white mottled ground cuckoos with long tails and punk-style mohawks, can often be spotted on roadsides. Other desert inhabitants include burrowing kit foxes, tree-climbing grey foxes, jackrabbits and kangaroo rats, slow-moving (and endangered) desert tortoises and a variety of snakes, lizards and spiders. Desert bighorn sheep and myriad birds flock to watering holes, often around seasonal springs and native fan-palm oases, especially in Joshua Tree National Park and Anza-Borrego Desert State Park.

The Audubon Society's free California chapter website (http://ca.audubon.org) has helpful birding checklists, a newsy blog, and descriptions of key species and important birding areas statewide.

Feathered Friends & Butterflies

California lies on major migratory routes for over 350 species of birds, which either pass through the state or linger through the winter. This is one of the top birding destinations in North America. Witness, for example, the congregation of one million ducks, geese and swans at the Klamath Basin National Wildlife Refuges (p294) in early every November. During winter, these waterbirds head south into the refuges of the Central Valley, another area to observe huge numbers of native and migratory species.

Year-round you can see birds at California's beaches, estuaries and bays, where herons, cormorants, shorebirds and gulls gather, including Point Reyes National Seashore and the Channel Islands. Monarch butterflies are gorgeous orange creatures that follow long-distance migration patterns in search of milkweed, their only source of food. They winter in California by the tens of thousands, mostly on the Central Coast including at Santa Cruz, Pacific Grove and Pismo Beach.

As you drive along the Big Sur coast, look skyward to spot endangered California condors (see the boxed text, p482), which also soar over inland Pinnacles National Monument. Also keep an eye out for regal bald eagles, which have regained a foothold on the Channel Islands (p522), and also sometimes spend their winters at Big Bear Lake near LA (p576).

Going Native: Wildflowers & Trees

California's 6000 kinds of plants are both flamboyant and subtle. Many species are so obscure and similar that only a dedicated botanist could tell them apart, but add them all together in the spring and you end up with riotous carpets of wildflowers that can take your breath away. The state flower is the orange-yellow native California poppy.

California is also a land of superlative trees: the tallest (coast redwoods approaching 380ft), the largest (giant sequoias of the Sierra Nevada over 36ft across at the base) and the oldest (bristlecone pines of the White Mountains that are almost 5000 years old, see boxed text, p445). The giant sequoia, which is unique to California, survives in isolated groves scattered on the Sierra Nevada's western slopes, including in Yosemite, Sequoia and Kings Canyon National Parks.

An astounding 20 native species of oak grow in California, including live, or evergreen, oaks with holly-like leaves and scaly acorns, which thrive in coastal ranges. More rare native species include Monterey pines and Torrey pines, gnarly trees that have adapted to harsh coastal conditions such as high winds, sparse rainfall and sandy, stony soils. The latter pine species only grows at Torrey Pines State Reserve near San Diego and in Channel Islands National Park, home to dozens more endemic plant species.

Heading inland, the Sierra Nevada has three distinct ecozones: the dry western foothills covered with oak and chaparral; conifer forests starting from about 2000ft; and an alpine zone above 8000ft. Twenty-three species of conifer occur in the Sierra Nevada, with midelevation forests home to massive Douglas firs, ponderosa pines and, biggest of all, the giant sequoia. Deciduous trees include the delightful quaking aspen, a white-trunked tree whose shimmering leaves brighten many mountain meadow edges. Its large rounded leaves turn pale yellow in the fall, creating some of the most spectacular scenery you'll see, notably around June Lake in the Eastern Sierra.

In 2006 the world's tallest tree was discovered in Redwood National Park (its location is being kept secret). It's named Hyperion and stands a whopping 379ft tall.

WILD ABOUT WILDFLOWERS

The famous 'golden hills' of California are actually the result of many plants drying up in preparation for the long dry summer. Many plants have adapted to long periods of almost no rain by growing prolifically during California's mild wet winters, springing to life with the first rains of autumn and blooming as early as February. Southern California's desert areas begin their peak blooming in March, with other lowland areas of the state producing abundant wildflowers in April. Visit Anza-Borrego Desert State Park, Death Valley National Park, Antelope Valley Poppy Preserve and Carrizo Plain National Monument for some of the most spectacular and predictable wildflower displays. As snows melt later at higher elevations in the Sierra Nevada, Yosemite National Park's Tuolumne Meadows is another prime spot for wildflower walks and photography, with peak blooms usually in late June or early July.

Cacti & Their Cousins

South of the Sierra Nevada, cacti and other desert plants have adapted to more arid climates with thin, spiny leaves that resist moisture loss (and deter grazing animals), and seed and flowering mechanisms that kick into gear during brief winter rains.

Among the most common and easy to identify is cholla, which appears so furry that it's nicknamed 'teddy-bear cactus.' But it's far from cuddly and instead will bury extremely sharp, barbed spines in your skin at the slightest touch. Also watch out for catclaw acacia, nicknamed 'wait-a-minute bush' because it's small, sharp, hooked thorny spikes can snatch clothing or skin as you brush past. The spiky ocotillo, which grows up to 20ft tall, has cane-like branches that produce blood-red flowers in spring.

Like figments from a Dr Seuss book, whimsical Joshua trees are the largest type of yucca and are related to lily plants, with heavy, creamy greenish-white flowers that erupt in spring. Joshua trees were named by emigrant Mormons, who thought the crooked branches resembled the outstretched arms of a biblical prophet. Joshua trees grow throughout the Mojave Desert, although their habitat and long-term survival is severely threatened by global warming.

National & State Parks

The majority of Californians rank outdoor recreation as vital to their quality of life, and the amount of preserved lands has steadily grown due to important pieces of legislation passed since the 1960s, including the landmark 1976 California Coastal Act, which saved the coastline from further development, and the controversial 1994 California Desert Protection Act, which angered many ranchers, miners and off-roaders. Today, **California State Parks** (www.parks.ca.gov) protect nearly a third of the state's coastline, along with redwood forests, mountain lakes, desert canyons, waterfalls, wildlife preserves and historical sites.

In recent years, both federal and state budget shortfalls and chronic underfunding have been partly responsible for widespread park closures, more limited visitor services and steadily rising park-entry and outdoor recreation fees. Even so, it's in California's economic best interests to protect wilderness, as recreational tourism consistently outpaces competing 'resource extraction' industries like mining.

Unfortunately, some of California's parks are also being loved to death. Overcrowding severely impacts the environment, and it's increasingly difficult to balance public access with conservation. Try visiting big-name parks like Yosemite in the shoulder seasons (ie not summer) to avoid the biggest crowds. Alternatively, lesser-known natural areas managed by the **National Park Service** (www.nps.gov/state/CA) may go relatively untouched most of the year, which means you won't have to reserve permits, campsites or accommodations months in advance.

There are 18 national forests in California run by the **US Forest Service** (USFS; www.fs.fed.us/r5/), including lands around Mt Whitney, Mt Shasta and Big Bear Lake, and many other areas worth exploring. National wildlife refuges (NWR), favored by bird-watchers, are managed by the **US Fish & Wildlife Service** (USFWS; www.fws.gov/refuges). More wilderness tracts are overseen by the **Bureau of Land Management** (BLM; www.blm.gov/ca/st/en.html).

Conserving California

Although California is in many ways a success story, development and growth have come at great environmental cost. Starting in 1849, Gold Rush miners tore apart the land in their frenzied quest for the 'big strike,' ultimately sending more than 1.5 billion tons of debris, and uncalculat-

---

California's Top Parks

» Channel Islands National Park (p522)

» Death Valley National Park (p686)

» Point Reyes National Seashore (p127)

» Redwood National & State Parks (p260)

» Yosemite, Sequoia & Kings Canyon National Parks (p400 & p418)

Both experts and enthusiasts will treasure www.calflora.org, a massive project with mapped locations and photos of over 2250 plant species in California, from desert cacti to rarely seen alpine wildflowers.

ed amounts of poisonous mercury, downstream into the Central Valley where rivers and streams became clogged and polluted.

Water, or the lack thereof, has long been at the heart of California's epic environmental struggles and catastrophes. Despite campaigning by California's greatest environmental champion, John Muir, in the 1920s the Tuolumne River was dammed at Hetch Hetchy (inside Yosemite National Park), so that San Francisco could have drinking water. Likewise, the diversion of water to LA has contributed to the destruction of Owens Lake and its fertile wetlands, and the degradation of Mono Lake (see boxed text, p435). Statewide, the damming of rivers and capture of water for houses and farms has destroyed countless salmon runs and drained marshlands. The Central Valley, for example, today resembles a dust bowl, and its underground aquifer is in poor shape.

Altered and compromised habitats, both on land and water, make easy targets for invasive species, including highly aggressive species that wreak havoc on both California's economy and ecosystems. In San Francisco Bay alone, one of the most important estuaries in the world, there are now over 230 alien species choking the aquatic ecosystem and in some areas they already comprise as much as 95% of the total biomass.

Although air quality in California has improved markedly in past decades, it's still among the worst in the country. Auto exhaust and fine particulates generated by the wearing down of vehicle tires, along with industrial emissions, are the chief culprits. An even greater health hazard is ozone, the principal ingredient in smog, which makes sunny days around LA and the Central Valley look hazy.

But there's hope. Low-emission vehicles are becoming one of the most sought-after types of car in the state, and rapidly rising fuel costs are keeping more gas guzzling SUVs off the road. Californians recently voted to fund construction of solar-power plants, and there's even talk of harnessing the tremendous tidal flows of the Pacific to generate more 'clean' energy. By law California's utilities must get 33 percent of their energy from renewable resources by 2020, the most ambitious target yet set by any US state.

Southern California would not exist as it does today without water. Marc Reisner's must-read *Cadillac Desert: The American West and Its Disappearing Water* examines the contentious, sometimes violent, water wars that gave rise to modern California.

Co-founded by John Muir in 1892, the Sierra Club (www.sierraclub.org) was the USA's first conservation group and it remains the nation's most active, offering educational programs, group hikes, organized trips and volunteer vacations.

Survival Guide

Directory A-Z

Accommodations

» Budget-conscious accommodations include campgrounds, hostels and motels. Because midrange properties generally offer better value for money, most of our accommodations fall into this category.

» At midrange motels and hotels, expect clean, comfortable and decent-sized double rooms with at least a private bathroom, and standard amenities such as cable TV, direct-dial telephone, a coffeemaker, and perhaps a microwave and mini fridge.

» Top-end lodgings offer top-notch amenities and perhaps a scenic location, edgy decor or historical ambience. Pools, fitness rooms, business centers, full-service restaurants and bars as well as other convenient facilities are all standard.

» Where an indoor or outdoor pool is available, the swimming icon (⊠) appears with the review.

» In Southern California, nearly all lodgings have air-conditioning, but in Northern California and in coastal areas as far south as Santa Barbara, where it rarely gets hot, the opposite is true, and even fans may not be provided. Where air-con is available, the ❄ icon appears.

» Accommodations offering online computer terminals for guests are designated with the internet icon (@). A fee may apply (eg at full-service business centers inside hotels).

» When wireless internet access is offered, the wi-fi icon (🛜) appears. There may be a fee, especially for in-room access. Look for free wi-fi hot spots in hotel public areas (eg lobby, poolside).

» Many lodgings are now exclusively nonsmoking. Where they still exist, smoking rooms are often left unrenovated and in less desirable locations. Expect a hefty 'cleaning fee' ($100 or more) if you light up in designated nonsmoking rooms.

Rates

» This guide lists accommodations in order of author recommendation. Rates are categorized as $ (under $100), $$ ($100 to $200) or $$$ (over $200). Unless noted, rates do not include taxes, which average more than 10%.

» Generally, midweek rates are lower except in hotels geared toward weekday business travelers, which then lure leisure travelers with weekend deals.

» Rates quoted in this book are for high season: June to August everywhere, except the deserts and mountain ski areas, where December through April are the busiest months.

» Demand and prices spike even higher around major holidays (p764) and for festivals (p26), when some properties may impose multiday minimum stays.

» Discount cards (p760) and auto-club membership (p772) may get you 10% or more off standard rates at participating hotels and motels.

» Look for freebie ad magazines packed with hotel and motel discount coupons at gas stations, highway rest areas, tourist offices and online at **Roomsaver.com** (www.roomsaver.com).

» You might get a better deal by booking through discount-travel websites like **Priceline** (www.priceline.com), **Hotwire** (www.hotwire.com) or **Hotels.com** (www.hotels.com).

» Bargaining may be possible for walk-in guests without reservations, especially during off-peak times.

BOOK YOUR STAY ONLINE

For more accommodations reviews by Lonely Planet authors, check out hotels.lonelyplanet.com/California. You'll find independent reviews, as well as recommendations on the best places to stay. Best of all, you can book online.

Reservations

» Reservations are recommended for weekend and holiday travel year-round, and every day of the week during high season.

» If you book a reservation by phone, always get a confirmation number and ask about the cancellation policy before you give out your credit-card information.

» If you plan to arrive late in the evening, call ahead on the day of your stay to let them know. Hotels overbook, but if you've guaranteed the reservation with your credit card, they should accommodate you somewhere else.

B&Bs

If you want an atmospheric or perhaps romantic alternative to impersonal motels and hotels, bed-and-breakfast inns typically inhabit fine old Victorian houses or other heritage buildings, bedecked with floral wallpaper and antique furnishings. However, people who like privacy may find California B&Bs too intimate.

Rates often include breakfast, but occasionally do not (never mind what the name 'B&B' suggests). Amenities vary widely, but rooms with TV and telephone are the exception; the cheapest units share bathrooms. Standards are high at places certified by the **California Association of Bed & Breakfast Inns** (www.cabbi.com).

Most require advance reservations, although some will accommodate the occasional drop-in. Smoking is generally prohibited and children are usually not welcome. Minimum-stay requirements are common, especially on weekends and in peak season.

Camping

In California, camping is much more than just a cheap way to spend the night. The best campsites will have you waking up on the beach, next to an alpine lake or underneath a canopy of redwood trees. For details, see p37.

PRACTICALITIES

» **DVDs** NTSC standard (incompatible with PAL or SECAM); DVDs coded region 1 (USA & Canada only)

» **Electricity** 110/120V AC, 50/60Hz

» **Newspapers** *Los Angeles Times* (www.latimes.com), *San Francisco Chronicle* (www.sfgate.com), *San Jose Mercury News* (www.mercurynews.com), *Sacramento Bee* (www.sacbee.com)

» **Radio** National Public Radio (NPR), lower end of FM dial

» **TV** PBS (public broadcasting); cable: CNN (news), ESPN (sports), HBO (movies), Weather Channel

» **Weights & Measures** Imperial

Hostels

California has 19 hostels affiliated with **Hostelling International USA** (HI-USA; ☎301-495-1240; www.hiusa.org). Dorms in HI hostels are typically gender-segregated and alcohol and smoking are prohibited. HI-USA membership cards (adult/senior $28/18 per year, free for under-18s) entitle you to $3 off per night.

California also has dozens of independent hostels, particularly in coastal cities. They generally have more relaxed rules, often no curfew and frequent guest parties and activities. Some hostels include a light breakfast in their rates, arrange local tours or offer pick-ups at transportation hubs. No two hostels are alike but facilities typically include mixed dorms, semi-private rooms with shared bathrooms, communal kitchens, lockers, internet access, laundry and TV lounges.

Some hostels say they accept only international visitors (basically to keep out homeless locals), but Americans who look like travelers (eg you're in possession of an international plane ticket) may be admitted, especially during slower times.

Dorm-bed rates average $20 to $40 per night, including tax. Reservations are always a good idea, especially in high season. Most hostels take reservations online or

by phone. Many independent hostels belong to reservation services like www.hostels.com, www.hostelz.com and www.hostelworld.com, which sometimes offer lower rates than the hostels directly.

Hotels & Motels

Rooms are often priced by the size and number of beds, rather than the number of occupants. A room with one double or queen-size bed usually costs the same for one or two people, while a room with a king-size bed or two double beds costs more.

There is often a small surcharge for the third and fourth person, but children under a certain age (this varies) may stay free. Cribs or rollaway cots usually incur a surcharge. Beware that suites or 'junior suites' may simply be oversized rooms; ask about the layout when booking.

Recently renovated or larger rooms, or those with a view, are likely to cost more. Descriptors like 'oceanfront' and 'oceanview' are often too liberally used, and may require a periscope to spot the surf. If you arrive without reservations, ask to see a room before paying for it, especially at motels.

Overnight rates may include breakfast, which could be just a stale donut and wimpy coffee, an all-you-can-eat hot and cold buffet, or anything in between.

GREEN HOTELS & MOTELS

Surprisingly, many of California's hotels and motels haven't yet jumped on the environmental bandwagon. Apart from offering you the option of reusing your towels and sheets, even such simple eco-initiatives as switching to bulk soap dispensers or replacing plastic and Styrofoam cups and dropping prepackaged breakfast items are pretty rare. However, some hotels and motels now put recycling baskets in guestrooms, and a few loan or rent bicycles to guests. The **California Green Lodging Program** (www.dgs.ca.gov/travel/Programs/GreenLodging \Directory.aspx) is a voluntary state-run certification program; look for properties denoted by two palm trees.

Business Hours

Unless otherwise noted in reviews, standard opening hours for listings in this guide are as follows.

Banks 8:30am-4:30pm Mon-Fri, some to 5:30pm Fri, 9am-12:30pm Sat

Bars 5pm-midnight daily

Business hours (general) 9am-5pm Mon-Fri

Nightclubs 10pm-2am Thu-Sat

Post offices 9am-5pm Mon-Fri, some 9am-noon Sat

Restaurants 7am-10:30am, 11:30am-2:30pm & 5-9:30pm daily, some later Fri & Sat

Shops 10am-6pm Mon-Sat, noon-5pm Sun (malls open later)

Customs

Currently, non-US citizens and permanent residents may import:

» 1L of alcohol (if you're over 21 years old)

» 200 cigarettes (one carton) or 50 (non-Cuban) cigars (if you're over 18)

» $100 worth of gifts

Amounts higher than $10,000 in cash, traveler's checks, money orders and other cash equivalents must be declared. Don't even think about bringing in illegal drugs.

For more complete, up-to-date information, check with **US Customs and Border Protection** (www.cbp.gov).

Discount Cards

For discounts for children and families, see p48.

American Association of Retired Persons (AARP; ☑888-687-2277; www.aarp. org; annual membership $16) Member discounts (usually 10%) for Americans 50 years and older.

American Automobile Association (AAA; ☑877-428-2277; www.aaa.com; annual membership from $48) Members of AAA and its foreign affiliates (eg CAA, AA) qualify for small discounts (usually 10%) on Amtrak trains, car rentals, motels and hotels, chain restaurants, shopping, tours and theme parks.

America the Beautiful Interagency Annual Pass (http://store.usgs.gov/pass; $80) Admits four adults and all children under 16 years for free to all national parks and federal recreational lands (eg USFS, BLM) for one year. Can be purchased online or at any national park entrance station. US citizens and permanent residents 62 years and older are eligible for a lifetime Senior Pass ($10) that grants free entry and 50% off some recreational-use fees like camping, as does the lifetime Access Pass (free to US citizens or permanent residents with a permanent disability); these passes are only available in person.

Go Los Angeles Card (one-day pass adult/child $60/50) and **Go San Diego Card** ($70/59) both include admission to major SoCal theme parks (but not Disneyland), while the **Go San Francisco Card** ($55/40) covers museums, bicycle rental and a bay cruise. Note that you've got to do *a lot* of sightseeing over multiple days to make these passes even come close to paying off. For the best prices, buy online in advance at www.smartdestinations.com.

International Student Identity Card (ISIC; www.isic.org; $22) Offers savings on airline fares, travel insurance and local attractions for full-time students. For nonstudents under 26 years of age, an **International Youth Travel Card** (IYTC; $22) grants similar benefits. Cards are issued by student unions, hostelling organizations and travel agencies.

Seniors People over 65 (sometimes 55 or 60) often qualify for the same discounts as students; an ID with your birthdate should suffice as proof of age.

Southern California City-Pass (www.citypass.com) If you're visiting SoCal theme parks, the CityPass costs from $276 per adult (child aged three to nine $229). It covers three-day admission to Disneyland and Disney California Adventure and one-day admission each to Universal Studios and Sea-World, with another day at either the San Diego Zoo or Safari Park. Passes are valid for 14 days from the day of the first use. Purchase in person at participating attractions or online in advance for the lowest prices.

Student Advantage Card (☑877-256-4672; www.studentadvantage.com; $23) For international and US students, offers 15% savings on Amtrak and 20% on Greyhound, plus discounts of 10% to 20% on some airlines and chain shops, hotels and motels.

Electricity

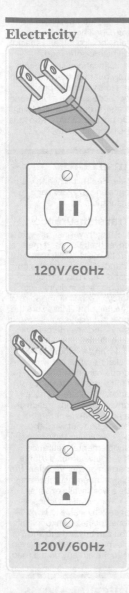

120V/60Hz

120V/60Hz

Food

Throughout this book, restaurant prices usually refer to an average main course at dinner:

Budget ($) Dinner mains under $10

Midrange ($$) Most dinner mains $10-20

Top End ($$$) Dinner mains over $20

These prices don't include drinks, appetizers, desserts, taxes or tip. Note the same dishes at lunch will usually be cheaper, maybe even half-price.

Lunch is generally served between 11:30am and 2:30pm, and dinner between 5:30pm and 9pm daily, though some restaurants close later, especially on Friday and Saturday nights. If breakfast is served, it's usually between 7am and 10:30am; some diners and coffee shops keep serving breakfast into the afternoon, or all day. Weekend brunch is a laidback affair, usually available from 10am until 3pm on Saturdays and Sundays. Full opening hours are given with all restaurant reviews in this book.

Like all things Californian, restaurant etiquette tends to be informal. Only a handful of restaurants require more than a dressy shirt, slacks and a decent pair of shoes; most places require far less. Here are more things to keep in mind:

» Tipping 15% to 20% is expected anywhere you receive table service.

» Smoking is illegal indoors; some restaurants have patios or sidewalk tables where lighting up is tolerated, though don't expect your neighbors to be happy about secondhand smoke.

» You can bring your own wine to most restaurants, but expect to pay a 'corkage' fee of $15 to $30. Lunches rarely include booze, though a glass of wine or beer, while uncommon, is usually acceptable.

» If you ask the kitchen to divide a plate between two (or more) people, there may be a small split-plate surcharge.

» Vegetarians and travelers with food allergies or restrictions are in luck – most restaurants are used to catering to specific dietary needs.

» If you're dining out with kids, see p48.

Gay & Lesbian Travelers

California is a magnet for LGBTQ travelers. The hot spots are the Castro in San Francisco (p98), West Hollywood (WeHo), Silver Lake and Long Beach in LA (p565), the Hillcrest area of San Diego (p640), the desert resort of Palm Springs (p663), and Guerneville (p201) and Calistoga (p177) in the Wine Country. Some scenes are predominantly male-oriented, but women usually won't feel too left out.

California offers gays and lesbians extensive domestic rights but currently stops short of the legalization of same-sex marriage and civil unions. Despite widespread tolerance, make no mistake: homophobic bigotry still exists. In small towns, especially away from the coast, tolerance often comes down to a 'don't ask, don't tell' policy.

Helpful Resources

Advocate (www.advocate.com/travel) Online news articles, gay travel features and destination guides.

Damron (www.damron.com) Classic, advertiser-driven international gay travel guides, including *Men's Travel Guide, Women's Traveller* and *Accommodations;* digital editions and 'Gay Scout' mobile app now available.

Gay.com Daily Travel (daily.gay.com/travel) City guides, blog-style travel news and special events.

Gay & Lesbian Yellow Pages (www.glyp.com) Includes ads for local restaurants, bars and clubs; 'Gay Yellow Pages' mobile app now available.

Gay & Lesbian National Hotline (888-843-4564;

www.glnh.org; ⏱1-9pm Mon-Fri, 9am-2pm Sat) For counseling and referrals of any kind.

Gay Travelocity (www.travelocity.com/gaytravel) LGBT travel articles with hotel, guided tour and activity bookings.

Out Traveler (www.outtraveler.com) Free online magazine, trip planner, destination guides and a mobile app.

Purple Roofs (www.purpleroofs.com) Online directory of LGBT accommodations.

Health

Healthcare & Insurance

» Medical treatment in the USA is of the highest caliber, but the expense could kill you. Many health-care professionals demand payment at the time of service, especially from out-of-towners or international visitors.

» Except for medical emergencies (in which case call ☑911 or go to the nearest 24-hour hospital emergency room, or ER), phone around to find a doctor who will accept your insurance.

» Keep all receipts and documentation for billing and insurance claims, and reimbursement purposes.

» Some health-insurance policies require you to get pre-authorization for medical treatment before seeking help.

» Overseas visitors with travel health-insurance policies may need to contact a call center for an assessment by phone before getting medical treatment.

» Carry any medications you may need in their original containers, clearly labeled. Bring a signed, dated letter from your doctor describing all medical conditions and medications (including generic names).

Dehydration, Heat Exhaustion & Heatstroke

» Take it easy as you acclimatize, especially on hot summer days and in Southern California's deserts. Drink plenty of water. A one gallon per person per day minimum is recommended when you're active outdoors.

» Dehydration or salt deficiency can cause heat exhaustion, often characterized by heavy sweating, pale skin, fatigue, lethargy, headaches, nausea, vomiting, dizziness, muscle cramps and rapid, shallow breathing.

» Long, continuous exposure to high temperatures can lead to possibly fatal heatstroke. Warning signs include altered mental status, hyperventilation and flushed, hot and dry skin (ie sweating stops).

» Hospitalization is essential. Meanwhile, get out of the sun, remove clothing that retains heat (cotton is OK), douse the body with water and fan continuously; ice packs can be applied to the neck, armpits and groin.

Hypothermia

» Skiers and hikers will find that temperatures in the mountains and desert can quickly drop below freezing, especially during winter. Even a sudden spring shower or high winds can lower your body temperature dangerously fast.

» Instead of cotton, wear synthetic or woolen clothing that retains warmth even when wet. Carry waterproof layers (eg Gore-Tex jacket, plastic poncho, rain pants) and high-energy, easily digestible snacks like chocolate, nuts and dried fruit.

» Symptoms of hypothermia include exhaustion, numbness, shivering, stumbling, slurred speech, dizzy spells, muscle cramps and irrational or even violent behavior.

» To treat hypothermia, get out of bad weather and change into dry, warm clothing. Drink hot liquids (no caffeine or alcohol) and snack on high-calorie food.

» In advanced stages, carefully put hypothermia sufferers in a warm sleeping bag cocooned inside a wind- and water-proof outer wrapping. Do not rub victims, who must be handled gently.

Insurance

See 'Health' for health insurance and p772 for car insurance.

Travel Insurance

Getting travel insurance to cover theft, loss and medical problems is highly recommended. Some policies do not cover 'risky' activities such as scuba diving, motorcycling and skiing so read the fine print. Make sure the policy at least covers hospital stays and an emergency flight home.

Paying for your airline ticket or rental car with a credit card may provide limited travel accident insurance. If you already have private health insurance or a homeowners or renters policy, find out what those policies cover and only get supplemental insurance. If you have prepaid a large portion of your vacation, trip cancellation insurance may be a worthwhile expense.

Worldwide travel insurance is available at www.lonelyplanet.com/bookings. You can buy, extend and claim online anytime – even if you're already on the road.

Internet Access

» Internet cafes listed throughout this guide typically charge $6 to $12 per hour for online access.

» With branches in most cities and towns, **FedEx Office** (☑800-254-6567; www.fedex.com) offers internet access at self-service computer workstations (20¢ to 30¢ per minute) and sometimes free wi-fi, plus digital-photo printing and CD-burning stations.

» Accommodations, cafes, restaurants, bars etc that provide guest computer terminals for going online are identified in this book by the internet icon (@); the wi-fi icon (☎) indicates that wireless access is available. There may be a charge for either service.

» Wi-fi hot spots (free or fee-based) can be found at major airports; many hotels, motels and coffee shops (eg Starbucks); and some tourist information centers, RV parks (eg KOA), museums, bars, restaurants (including fast-food chains such as McDonalds) and stores (eg Apple).

» Free public wi-fi is proliferating and even some state parks are now wi-fi–enabled (for a list, click to www.parks.ca.gov/wifi).

» To find more public wi-fi hot spots, search www.wififreespot.com/ca.html or www.jiwire.com.

» Public libraries have internet terminals, but online time may be limited, advance sign-up required and a nominal fee charged for out-of-network visitors. Increasingly, libraries offer free wi-fi access.

Legal Matters
Drugs & Alcohol

» Possession of under 1oz of marijuana is a misdemeanor in California. Possession of any other drug or more than an ounce of weed is a felony punishable by lengthy jail time. For foreigners, conviction of any drug offense is grounds for deportation.

» Police can give roadside sobriety checks to assess if you've been drinking or using drugs. If you fail, they'll require you to take a breath, urine or blood test to determine if your blood-alcohol is over the legal limit (0.08%).

Refusing to be tested is treated the same as if you had taken and failed the test.

» Penalties for driving under the influence (DUI) of drugs or alcohol range from license suspension and fines to jail time.

» It's illegal to carry open containers of alcohol inside a vehicle, even if they're empty. Unless they're full and still sealed, store them in the trunk.

» Consuming alcohol anywhere other than at a private residence or licensed premises is a no-no, which puts most parks and beaches off-limits (although many campgrounds allow it).

» Bars, clubs and liquor stores often ask for photo ID to prove you are of legal drinking age (ie 21). Being 'carded' is standard practice; don't take it personally.

Police & Security

» If you are stopped by the police, be courteous. Don't get out of the car unless asked. Keep your hands where the officer can see them (eg on the steering wheel).

» There is no system of paying fines on the spot. Attempting to pay the fine to the officer may lead to a charge of attempted bribery.

» For traffic violations the ticketing officer will explain the options to you. There is usually a 30-day period to pay a fine; most matters can be handled by mail.

» If you are arrested, you have the right to remain silent and are presumed innocent until proven guilty. Everyone has the right to make one phone call. If you don't have a lawyer, one will be appointed to you free of charge. Foreign travelers who don't have a lawyer, friends or family to help should call their embassy or consulate; the police can provide the number upon request.

» For police, fire and ambulance emergencies, dial

911. For nonemergency police assistance, call directory assistance (411) for the number of the nearest local police station.

» Due to security concerns about terrorism, never leave your bags unattended, especially not at airports or bus and train stations.

» Carrying mace or cayenne-pepper spray is legal in California, as long as the spray bottle contains no more than 2.5oz of active product. Federal law prohibits it from being carried on planes.

» In cases of sexual assault, rape crisis center and hospital staff can advocate on your behalf and act as a liaison to community services, including the police. Telephone books have listings of local crisis centers, or call the 24-hour **National Sexual Assault Hotline** (800-656-4673; www.rainn.org).

Smoking

» Smoking is generally prohibited inside all public buildings, including airports, shopping malls and train and bus stations.

» There is no smoking allowed inside restaurants, although lighting up may be tolerated at outdoor patio or sidewalk tables (ask first, however).

» At hotels, you must specifically request a smoking room, but note some properties are entirely nonsmoking by law.

» In some cities and towns, smoking outdoors within a certain distance of any public business is now forbidden.

Maps

Visitor centers distribute free (but often very basic) maps. If you're doing a lot of driving, you'll need a more detailed road map or map atlas, or a GPS, though GPS navigation cannot be relied upon 100%. Members of the **American Automobile Association** (AAA; 800-874-7532;

www.aaa.com) or its international affiliates (bring your membership card) can get free driving maps from any local AAA office. Benchmark Maps' comprehensive *California Road & Recreation Atlas* ($25) shows campgrounds, recreational areas and topographical land features, although it's less useful for navigating congested urban areas. For topographic hiking and wilderness maps, see p43.

Money

For US dollar exchange rates and setting your trip budget, see p18.

ATMs

» ATMs are available 24/7 at most banks, shopping malls, airports and grocery and convenience stores.

» Expect a minimum surcharge of $2 to $3 per transaction, in addition to any fees charged by your home bank.

» Most ATMs are connected to international networks

and offer decent foreign-exchange rates.

» Withdrawing cash from an ATM using a credit card usually incurs a hefty fee and high interest rates; check with your credit-card company for a PIN number.

Cash

» Most people do not carry large amounts of cash for everyday use, relying instead on credit amd debit cards. Some businesses refuse to accept bills over $20.

Credit Cards

» Major credit cards are almost universally accepted. In fact, it's almost impossible to rent a car, book a room or buy tickets over the phone without one. A credit card may also be vital in emergencies.

» Visa, MasterCard and American Express are the most widely accepted.

Moneychangers

» You can exchange money at major airports, some banks and all currency-exchange offices such as

American Express (www.americanexpress.com). Always enquire about rates and fees.

» Outside big cities, exchanging money may be a problem, so make sure you have a credit card and sufficient cash on hand.

Taxes

» A California state sales tax of 8.25% is added to the retail price of most goods and services (gasoline is an exception).

» Local and city sales taxes may tack on an additional 1.5% or more.

» Tourist lodging taxes vary statewide, but currently average over 10%.

Traveler's Checks

» Traveler's checks have pretty much fallen out of use.

» Larger restaurants, hotels and department stores will often accept traveler's checks (in US dollars only), but small businesses, markets and fast-food chains may refuse them.

» Visa and American Express are the most widely accepted issuers of traveler's checks.

Post

» The US Postal Service (USPS; ☎800-275-8777; www.usps.com) is inexpensive and reliable.

» Postcards and standard letters up to 1oz (about 28g) cost 44¢ within the US, 75¢ to Canada, 79¢ to Mexico and 98¢ to all other countries. Postal rates increase by a few pennies every couple of years.

» For sending important letters or packages overseas, try Federal Express (FedEx; ☎800-463-3339; www.fedex.com) or UPS (☎800-782-7892; www.ups.com).

Public Holidays

On the following national holidays, banks, schools and government offices (including post offices) are closed,

TIPPING

Tipping is *not* optional. Only withhold tips in cases of outrageously bad service.

Airport skycaps & hotel bellhops	$2 per bag, minimum $5 per cart
Bartenders	10% to 15% per round, minimum $1 per drink
Concierges	Nothing for simple information, up to $20 for securing last-minute restaurant reservations, sold-out show tickets etc
Housekeeping staff	$2 to $4 daily, left under the card provided; more if you're messy
Parking valets	At least $2 when handed back your car keys
Restaurant servers & room service	15% to 20%, unless a gratuity is already charged
Taxi drivers	10% to 15% of metered fare, rounded up to the next dollar

and transportation, museums and other services operate on a Sunday schedule. Holidays falling on a weekend are usually observed the following Monday.

New Year's Day January 1

Martin Luther King Jr Day Third Monday in January

Presidents' Day Third Monday in February

Easter Sunday March/April

Memorial Day Last Monday in May

Independence Day July 4 (aka Fourth of July)

Labor Day First Monday in September

Columbus Day Second Monday in October

Veterans' Day November 11

Thanksgiving Day Fourth Thursday in November

Christmas Day December 25

School Holidays

» Colleges take a one- or two-week 'spring break' around Easter, sometime in March or April. Some hotels and resorts, especially along the coast, near SoCal's theme parks and in the deserts, raise their rates during this time.

» School summer vacations run from early June to late August, making July and August the busiest travel months.

Safe Travel

Despite its seemingly apocalyptic list of dangers – guns, violent crime, riots, earthquakes – California is a reasonably safe place to visit. The greatest danger is posed by car accidents (buckle up – it's the law), while the biggest annoyances are city traffic and crowds. Wildlife poses some small threats, and of course there is the dramatic, albeit unlikely, possibility of a natural disaster.

Earthquakes

Earthquakes happen all the time but most are so tiny they are detectable only by sensitive seismological instruments. If you're caught in a serious shaker:

» If indoors, get under a desk or table or stand in a doorway.

» Protect your head and stay clear of windows, mirrors or anything that might fall.

» Don't head for elevators or go running into the street.

» If you're in a shopping mall or large public building, expect the alarm and/or sprinkler systems to come on.

» If outdoors, get away from buildings, trees and power lines.

» If you're driving, pull over to the side of the road away from bridges, overpasses and power lines. Stay inside the car until the shaking stops.

» If you're on a sidewalk near buildings, duck into a doorway to protect yourself from falling bricks, glass and debris.

» Prepare for aftershocks.

» Turn on the radio and listen for bulletins.

» Use the telephone only if absolutely necessary.

Riptides

If you find yourself being carried offshore by a dangerous ocean current called a riptide, the important thing is to just keep afloat. Don't panic or try to swim against the current, as this will quickly exhaust you and you could drown. Instead, swim parallel to the shoreline and once the current stops pulling you out, swim back to shore.

Wildlife

» Never feed or approach wild animals – it causes them to lose their innate fear of humans, which in turn makes them more aggressive.

» Disturbing or harassing specially protected species (eg many marine mammals) is a crime, subject to enormous fines.

» Black bears are often attracted to campgrounds, where they may find food, trash and any other scented items left out on picnic tables or stashed in tents and cars. Always use bear-proof containers where provided. Visit http://sierrawild.gov/bears for more bear-country travel tips.

» If you encounter a black bear in the wild, don't run. Stay together, keeping small children next to you and picking up little ones. Keep back at least 100yds. If the bear starts moving toward you, back away slowly off-trail and let it pass by, being careful not to block any of the bear's escape routes or to get caught between a mother and her cubs. Sometimes a black bear will 'bluff charge' to test your dominance. Stand your ground by making yourself look as big as possible (eg waving your arms above your head) and shouting menacingly.

» Mountain lion attacks on humans are rare. If you encounter one, stay calm, pick up small children, face the animal and retreat slowly. Try to appear larger by raising your arms or grabbing a stick. If the lion becomes aggressive, shout or throw rocks at it. If attacked, fight back aggressively.

» Snakes and spiders are common throughout California, not just in wilderness areas. Always look inside your shoes before putting them back on outdoors, especially when camping. Snake bites are rare, but occur most often when a snake is stepped on or provoked (eg picked up or poked with a stick). Antivenom is available at most hospitals.

Telephone

Cell (Mobile) Phones

» You'll need a multiband GSM phone in order to make calls in the US, which differs from most other countries. Popping in a US prepaid rechargeable SIM card is usually cheaper than using your network.

» SIM cards are sold at telecommunications and electronics stores. These stores also sell inexpensive prepaid phones, including some airtime.

» You can rent a cell phone in Los Angeles and San Francisco from **TripTel** (☎877-874-7835; www.triptel. com); pricing plans vary, but typically are expensive.

Dialing Codes

» US phone numbers consist of a three-letter area code followed by a seven-digit local number.

» When dialing a number within the same area code, use the seven-digit number; however, some places now require you to dial the entire 10-digit number even for a local call.

» If you are calling long distance, dial ☑1 plus the area code plus the phone number.

» Toll-free numbers begin with ☑800, ☑866, ☑877 or ☑888 and must be preceded by ☑1.

» For direct international calls, dial ☑011 plus the country code plus the area code (usually without the initial '0') plus the local phone number.

» For international call assistance, dial ☑00.

» If you're calling from abroad, the country code for the US is ☑1 (the same as Canada, but International rates apply between the two countries).

Payphones & Phonecards

» Where payphones still exist, they are usually coin-operated, although some may only accept credit cards (eg in national parks).

» Local calls usually cost 50¢ minimum.

» For long-distance calls, you're usually better off buying a prepaid phonecard, sold at convenience stores, supermarkets, newsstands and electronics stores.

Time

» California is on Pacific Standard Time (GMT minus eight hours). When it's noon in LA, it's 3pm in New York, 8pm in London and 5am (the next day) in Sydney.

» Daylight Saving Time (DST) starts on the second Sunday in March, when clocks are set one hour ahead, and ends on the first Sunday in November.

Tourist Information

» For pretrip planning, peruse the information-packed website of the **California Travel and Tourism Commission** (www.visitcalifornia. com).

» This state-run agency also operates several **California Welcome Centers** (www.visitcwc.com), where staff dispense maps and brochures and help find accommodations.

» Almost every city and town has a local visitor center or a chamber of commerce where you can pick up maps, brochures and information; these are listed in the destination chapters.

» For helpful tourist information websites, see p19.

Travelers with Disabilities

Southern California is reasonably well-equipped for travelers with disabilities.

Communications

» Telephone companies provide relay operators (dial ☑711) for the hearing impaired.

» Many banks provide ATM instructions in Braille.

Helpful Resources

Access Northern California (www.accessnca. com) Extensive links to accessible-travel resources, publications, tours and transportation, including outdoor recreation opportunities and car and van rentals, plus a searchable lodgings database and an events calendar.

Access San Francisco (www.onlyinsanfrancisco.com/ plan_your_trip/access_guide. asp) Free downloadable accessible travel info (somewhat dated, but still useful).

Access Santa Cruz County (www.sharedadven tures.com/access_guide.htm) Slightly outdated but still handy bilingual (English/ Spanish) accessible travel guide (US shipping $3).

Accessible San Diego (http://asd.travel) Downloadable city guide booklet ($3, print version $5) that's updated annually.

California Coastal Conservancy (www.wheel ingcalscoast.org) Free accessibility information covering beaches, parks and trails, plus downloadable wheelchair riders' guides to the San Francisco, Los Angeles and Orange County coasts.

California State Parks (http://access.parks.ca.gov) Online searchable map and database to find accessible features at parks statewide.

Disabled Sports Eastern Sierra (http://disabledsports easternsierra.org) Offers summer and winter outdoor activities around Mammoth Mountain and Lakes.

Disabled Sports USA Far West (www.dsusafw. org) Organizes summer and winter sports and outdoor recreation programs (annual membership $30).

Flying Wheels Travel (www. flyingwheelstravel.com) Full-service travel agency.

Los Angeles for Disabled Visitors (http://discov erlosangeles.com/guides/ la-living/) Tips for accessible sightseeing, entertainment, museums, theme parks and transportation.

MossRehab Resource Net (www.mossresourcenet.org/

travel.htm) Useful links and general advice about accessible travel.

Theme-Park Access Guide (www.mouseplanet. com/tag) An insider's view of Disneyland and other Southern California theme parks 'on wheels.'

Yosemite Access Guide (www.nps.gov/yose/plan yourvisit/upload/access.pdf) Detailed, if somewhat dated downloadable information for Yosemite National Park.

Mobility & Accessibility

» Most intersections have dropped curbs and sometimes audible crossing signals.

» The Americans with Disabilities Act (ADA) requires public buildings built after 1993 to be wheelchair accessible, including restrooms.

» Motels and hotels built after 1993 must have at least one Americans with Disabilities Act (ADA)–compliant accessible room; state your specific needs when making reservations.

» For nonpublic buildings built prior to 1993, including hotels, restaurants, museums and theaters, there are no accessibility guarantees; call ahead to find out what to expect.

» Most national and many state parks and some other outdoor recreation areas offer paved or boardwalk-style nature trails accessible by wheelchairs; for a free national parks pass, see p760.

Public Transportation

» All major airlines, Greyhound buses and Amtrak trains can accommodate people with disabilities, usually with 48 hours of advance notice (for details, see the Transportation chapter, p768).

» Major car-rental agencies offer hand-controlled vehicles and vans with wheelchair lifts at no extra charge,

but you must reserve these well in advance.

» For wheelchair-accessible van rentals, try **Wheelchair Getaways** (☎800-642-2042; www.wheelchairgetaways. com) in LA, San Diego and San Francisco or **Mobility Works** (☎877-275-4915; www. mobilityworks.com) in LA.

» Local buses, trains and subway lines usually have wheelchair lifts.

» Seeing-eye dogs are permitted to accompany passengers on public transportation.

» Taxi companies have at least one wheelchair-accessible van, but you'll usually need to call and then wait for one.

Visas

» All of the following information is highly subject to change. Depending on your country of origin, the rules for entering the USA keep changing. Double-check current visa requirements *before* coming to the USA.

» Currently, under the US Visa Waiver Program (VWP), visas are not required for citizens of 36 countries for stays up to 90 days (no extensions) as long as your passport meets current US standards (see p768).

» Citizens of VWP countries must also register with the Electronic System for Travel Authorization (ESTA; $14) online (https://esta.cbp.dhs. gov) at least 72 hours before travel. Once approved, the registration is valid for up to two years.

» Citizens from all other countries or whose passports don't meet US standards will need to apply for a visa in their home country. The process costs a nonrefundable $140, involves a personal interview and can take several weeks, so apply as early as possible.

» For more information, consult http://travel.state. gov/visa.

Volunteering

Casual drop-in volunteer opportunities are most common in cities, where you can socialize with locals while helping out nonprofit organizations. Browse upcoming projects and sign up online with local organizations such as **One Brick** (www.onebrick. org), **HandsOn Bay Area** (www.handsonbayarea.org), **LA Works** (www.laworks. com), **Volunteer San Diego** (www.volunteersandiego.org) or **OneOC** (www.oneoc.org). For more opportunities, check local alternative weekly newspapers and **Craigslist** (www.craiglist.org).

Helpful Resources

California Volunteers (www.californiavolunteers.org) State volunteer directory and matching service, with links to national service days and long-term programs.

Habitat for Humanity (www.habitat.org) Nonprofit organization helps build homes for impoverished families, including weekend and week-long projects.

Idealist.org (www.idealist. org) Free searchable database includes both short- and long-term opportunities.

Sierra Club (www.sierraclub. org) Day or weekend projects and longer volunteer vacations (including for families) focusing on conservation; annual membership $25.

TreePeople (www.treepeople. org) Organizes half- and full-day group tree-planting, invasive weed-pulling and habitat restoration projects around LA, from urban parks to wildfire-damaged forests.

Wilderness Volunteers (www.wildernessvolunteers. org) Week-long trips help maintain national parks, wildlands and outdoor recreation areas.

Worldwide Opportunities on Organic Farms (www. wwoofusa.org) Long-term opportunities on local organic farms.

Transportation

GETTING THERE & AWAY

Getting to California by air or overland by bus, car or train is easy, although it's not always cheap. Flights, tours and train tickets can be booked online at www.lonely planet.com/bookings.

Entering the Region

Under the US Department of Homeland Security (DHS) registration program, US-VISIT (www.dhs.gov/us-visit), almost all visitors to the US (excluding, for now, many Canadians, some Mexican citizens and children under age 14) will be digitally photographed and have their electronic (inkless) fingerprints scanned upon arrival; the process typically takes less than a minute.

Regardless of your visa status, US immigration officers have absolute authority to refuse entry to the USA. They may ask about your plans and whether you have sufficient funds; it's a good idea to list an itinerary, produce an onward or round-trip ticket and have at least one major credit card. Don't make too much of having friends, relatives or business contacts in the US – officers may decide this makes you more likely to overstay your visa. For more information on visas, see p767.

California is an important agricultural state. To prevent the spread of pests and diseases, certain food items (including meats, fresh fruit and vegetables) may not be brought into the state. Bakery items, chocolates and hard-cured cheeses are admissible. If you drive into California across the border from Mexico or from the neighboring states of Oregon, Nevada or Arizona, you may have to stop for a quick inspection and questioning by California Department of Food and Agriculture agents.

For Mexico land-border crossings, see p769.

Passports

» Under the Western Hemisphere Travel Initiative (WHTI), all travelers must have a valid machine-readable (MRP) passport when entering the USA by air, land or sea.

» The only exceptions are for most US citizens and some Canadian and Mexican citizens traveling *by land* who can present other WHTI-compliant documents (eg preapproved 'trusted traveler' cards). For details, check www.getyouhome.gov.

» All foreign passports must meet current US standards and be valid for at least six months longer than your intended stay.

» MRP passports issued or renewed after October 26, 2006 must be e-passports (ie have a digital photo and integrated chip with biometric data). For more information, consult www.cbp.gov/travel.

CLIMATE CHANGE & TRAVEL

Every form of transport that relies on carbon-based fuel generates CO_2, the main cause of human-induced climate change. Modern travel is dependent on aeroplanes, which might use less fuel per kilometer per person than most cars but travel much greater distances. The altitude at which aircraft emit gases (including CO_2) and particles also contributes to their climate change impact. Many websites offer 'carbon calculators' that allow people to estimate the carbon emissions generated by their journey and, for those who wish to do so, to offset the impact of the greenhouse gases emitted with contributions to portfolios of climate-friendly initiatives throughout the world. Lonely Planet offsets the carbon footprint of all staff and author travel.

Air

» To get through airport security checkpoints (30-minute wait times are standard), you'll need a boarding pass and photo ID.

» Some travelers may be required to undergo a secondary screening, involving hand pat-downs and carry-on bag searches.

» Airport security measures restrict many common items (eg pocket knives) from being carried on planes. Check current restrictions with the **Transportation Security Administration** (TSA; 866-289-9673; www.tsa.gov).

» Currently, TSA requires that all carry-on liquids and gels be stored in 3oz or smaller bottles placed inside a quart-sized clear plastic zip-top bag. Exceptions, which must be declared to checkpoint security officers, include medications.

» All checked luggage is screened for explosives. TSA may open your suitcase for visual confirmation, breaking the lock if necessary. Leave your bags unlocked or use a TSA-approved lock such as **Travel Sentry** (www.travelsentry.org).

Airports

California's primary international airports:

Los Angeles International Airport (LAX; www.lawa.org/lax) California's largest and busiest airport, 20 miles southwest of downtown LA, near the coast.

San Francisco International Airport (SFO; www.flysfo.com) Northern California's major hub, 14 miles south of downtown, on San Francisco Bay.

Regional airports that offer limited international services:

LA/Ontario International Airport (ONT; www.lawa.org/ont) In Riverside County, east of LA.

WARNING!

As of April 2011, the **US State Department** (http://travel.state.gov) has issued a travel warning about increasing drug-trafficking violence and crime along the US–Mexico border. Travelers should exercise extreme caution in Tijuana, avoid large-scale gatherings and demonstrations, and refrain from venturing out after dark, especially in cars with US license plates.

Mineta San José International Airport (SJC; www.flysanjose.com) In San Francisco's South Bay.

Oakland International Airport (OAK; www.flyoakland.com) In San Francisco's East Bay.

Palm Springs International Airport (PSP; www.palmspringsairport.com) In the desert, east of LA.

San Diego International Airport (SAN; www.san.org) Four miles northwest of downtown.

For more regional airports handling domestic flights, see p770.

Land

Border Crossings

It's relatively easy crossing from the USA into Canada or Mexico; it's crossing back into the USA that can pose problems if you haven't brought all of the required documents. Check the ever-changing passport (p768) and visa (p767) requirements with the **US Department of State** (http://travel.state.gov) beforehand.

US Customs & Border Protection (http://apps.cbp.gov/bwt) tracks current wait times at every Mexico border crossing. On the US–Mexico border between San Diego and Tijuana, San Ysidro is the world's busiest border crossing. US citizens and residents do not require a visa for stays of 72 hours or less within the border zone (ie as far south as Ensenada). For more

details about traveling to Tijuana, see p642.

BUS

» US-based **Greyhound** (800-231-2222; www.greyhound.com) and **Greyhound México** (800-010-0600; www.greyhound.com.mx) have cooperative service, with direct buses between main towns in Mexico and California.

» Northbound buses from Mexico can take some time to cross the US border, since US immigration may insist on checking every person on board.

» **Greyhound Canada** (800-661-8747; www.greyhound.ca) routes between Canada and the US usually require transferring buses at the border.

CAR & MOTORCYCLE

» If you're driving into the USA from Canada or Mexico, bring your vehicle's registration papers, liability insurance and driver's license; an International Driving Permit (IDP) is a good supplement but is not required.

» If you're renting a car or a motorcycle, ask if the agency allows its vehicles to be taken across the Mexican or Canadian border – chances are it doesn't.

To/from Canada

» Canadian auto insurance is typically valid in the USA and vice versa.

» If your papers are in order, taking your own car across the US–Canada border is usually quick and easy.

» On weekends and holidays, especially in summer, border-crossing traffic can be heavy and waits long.

» Occasionally the authorities of either country decide to search a car *thoroughly*. Remain calm and be polite.

To/from Mexico

» Unless you're planning an extended stay in Tijuana, taking a car across the Mexican border is more trouble than it's worth. Instead, take the trolley from San Diego (p642) or leave your car on the US side and walk across.

» If you do decide to drive across, you must buy Mexican car insurance either beforehand or at the border crossing.

» Expect long border-crossing waits, as security has tightened in recent years.

TRAIN

» **Amtrak** (☑800-872-7245; www.amtrak.com) operates twice-daily Cascades rail service and several daily Thruway buses from Vancouver, British Columbia in Canada to Seattle, Washington.

» US or Canadian customs and immigration inspections happen at the border, not upon boarding.

» From Seattle, Amtrak's Coast Starlight (p770) connects south to several destinations in California en route to LA.

» Currently, no train services connect California and Mexico.

Bus

» **Greyhound** (☑800-231-2222; www.greyhound.com) is the major long-distance bus company, with routes throughout the USA, including to/from California.

» Greyhound has recently stopped service to many small towns; routes trace major highways and stop at larger population centers.

» Greyhound's **Discovery Pass** (www.discoverypass.

com) is good for unlimited travel throughout the US and Canada for seven ($246), 15 ($356), 30 ($456) or 60 ($556) consecutive days.

» If you're starting your trip in the US, passes may be bought at Greyhound terminals or online (for terminal pickup) up to two hours before travel.

» For more details about Greyhound, including on-board amenities, costs and reservations, see p771.

Train

» **Amtrak** (☑800-872-7245; www.amtrak.com) operates a fairly extensive rail system throughout the USA.

» Fares vary according to the type of train and seating (eg reserved or unreserved coach seats, business class, sleeping compartments).

» Trains are comfortable, if a bit slow, and are equipped with dining and lounge cars on long-distance routes.

» Amtrak's **USA Rail Pass** (www.amtrak.com) is valid for coach-class travel for 15 ($389), 30 ($579) or 45 ($749) days; children aged two to 15 pay half-price.

» With a rail pass, actual travel is limited to eight, 12 or 18 one-way 'segments,' respectively.

» A rail pass segment is *not* the same as a one-way trip; if reaching your destination requires riding more than one train, you'll use multiple pass segments.

» Purchase rail passes online; make advance reservations for each travel segment.

» For Amtrak's California Rail Pass, see p776.

AMTRAK ROUTES TO/FROM CALIFORNIA

California Zephyr Daily service between Chicago and Emeryville (from $149, 52 hours), near San Francisco, via Denver, Salt Lake City, Reno and Sacramento.

Coast Starlight Travels the West Coast daily from Seattle to LA (from $104,

35 hours) via Portland, Sacramento, Oakland and Santa Barbara; wi-fi may be available.

Southwest Chief Daily departures between Chicago and LA (from $149, 44 hours) via Kansas City, Albuquerque, Flagstaff and Barstow.

Sunset Limited Thrice-weekly service between New Orleans and LA (from $138, 47 hours) via Houston, San Antonio, El Paso, Tucson and Palm Springs.

For more details about Amtrak trains, including costs, reservations, onboard amenities and intra-California routes, see p776.

GETTING AROUND

Most people drive around California, although you can also fly (if time is limited) or save money by taking buses or often scenic trains.

Air

Besides California's major international airports (see p769), domestic flights also depart from smaller regional airports, including the following:

Arcata/Eureka Airport (ACV; www.co.humboldt.ca.us/aviation) On the North Coast.

Bob Hope Airport (BUR; www.bobhopeairport.com) In Burbank, Los Angeles County.

Fresno Yosemite International Airport (FYI; www.flyfresno.org) In the Central Valley.

John Wayne Airport (SNA; www.ocair.com) In Santa Ana, Orange County.

Long Beach Airport (LGB; www.lgb.org) In Los Angeles County.

Monterey Peninsula Airport (MRY; www.montereyairport.com) On the Central Coast.

Redding Municipal Airport (RDD; http://ci.redding.ca.us/transeng/airports/rma.htm) In the Northern Mountains.

Sacramento International Airport (SMF; www.sacairports.org/int) In the Gold Country.

San Luis Obispo County Regional Airport (SBP; www.sloairport.com) On the Central Coast.

Santa Barbara Municipal Airport (SBA; www.flysba.com) On the Central Coast.

Several major US carriers fly within California. Flights are often operated by their regional subsidiaries, such as American Eagle, Delta Connection and United Express. Alaska Airlines and partner Horizon Air serve many regional airports, as do popular low-cost airlines Southwest and JetBlue. Virgin America currently flies out of San Francisco, Los Angeles and San Diego.

Bicycle

Although it's a nonpolluting 'green' way to travel, the distances involved in cycling around California demand a high level of fitness and make it hard to cover much ground. Forget about the deserts in summer or the mountains in winter.

Some helpful resources for cyclists:

Adventure Cycling Association (www.adventurecycling.org) Excellent online resource for purchasing bicycle-friendly maps, long-distance route guides and gadgets.

Better World Club (☑866-238-1137; www.betterworldclub.com) Annual membership ($40, plus $12 enrollment fee) entitles you to two 24-hour emergency roadside pickups with transportation to the nearest bike-repair shop within a 30-mile radius.

California Department of Transportation (www.dot.ca.gov/hq/tpp/offices/bike)

Road rules, safety tips and links to statewide bicycle advocacy groups.

Road Rules

» Cycling is allowed on all roads and highways – even along freeways if there's no suitable alternative, such as a smaller parallel road; all mandatory exits are marked.

» Some cities have designated bicycle lanes, but make sure you have your wits about you when venturing out into heavy traffic.

» Cyclists must follow the same rules of the road as vehicles. Don't expect drivers to always respect your right of way.

» Wearing a helmet is mandatory for riders under 18 years old.

» Ensure you have proper lights and reflective gear, especially if you're pedaling at night or in fog.

Rental & Purchase

» You can rent bikes by the hour, day or week in most cities and major towns.

» Rentals start around $10 per day for beach cruisers up to $45 or more for mountain bikes; ask about multiday and weekly discounts.

» Most rental companies require a credit-card security deposit of $200 or more.

» Buy new models from specialty bike shops, sporting-goods stores and discount-warehouse stores, or used from notice boards at hostels, cafes and universities.

» To buy or sell used bikes, check online bulletin boards such as **Craigslist** (www.craigslist.org).

Transporting Bicycles

» If you tire of pedaling, some local buses and trains are equipped with bicycle racks.

» Greyhound transports bicycles as luggage (surcharge $30 to $40), provided the bicycle is disassembled and

placed in a box ($10, available at some terminals).

» Most of Amtrak's *Cascades, Pacific Surfliner, Capital Corridor* and *San Joaquin* trains feature onboard racks where you can secure your bike unboxed; try to reserve a spot when making your ticket reservation (surcharge $5 to $10).

» On Amtrak trains without racks, bikes must be put in a box ($15) and checked as luggage (fee $5). Not all stations or trains offer checked-baggage service.

» Before flying, you'll need to disassemble your bike and box it as checked baggage; contact the airline directly for details, including applicable surcharges (typically $50 to $100, sometimes more).

Boat

Boats won't get you around California, although there are a few offshore routes, notably to Catalina Island off the coast of Los Angeles and Orange County, and to Channel Islands National Park from Ventura or Oxnard, north of LA. On San Francisco Bay, regular ferry routes operate between San Francisco and Sausalito, Larkspur, Tiburon, Angel Island, Oakland, Alameda and Vallejo.

Bus

Greyhound (☑800-231-2222; www.greyhound.com) buses are an economical way to travel between major cities and to points along the coast, but won't get you off the beaten path or to national parks. Frequency of service varies from 'rarely' to 'constantly,' but the main routes have service several times daily.

Greyhound buses are usually clean, comfortable and reliable. The best seats are typically near the front, away from the bathroom. Limited on-board amenities include freezing air-con (bring a sweater) and slightly reclining seats; select buses have electrical outlets and wi-fi. Smoking on board is prohibited. Long-distance buses stop for meal breaks and driver changes.

Bus stations are typically dreary places, often in dodgy areas; if you arrive at night, take a taxi into town. In small towns where there is no station, know exactly where and when the bus arrives, be obvious as you flag it down and pay the driver with exact change.

Costs

For lower fares, purchase tickets seven to 14 days in advance. Round-trips and Monday through Thursday travel may be cheaper.

Discounts (on unrestricted fares only) are available for seniors over 62 (5% off), students (20%) with a Student Advantage Card (p760) and children aged two to 11 (25%).

Special promotional discounts, such as 50% off companion fares, are often available on the Greyhound website, though they may come with restrictions or blackout periods.

Some sample Greyhound fares and times:

LA–San Francisco ($55, 7½ to 12¼ hours, 14 daily)

LA–San Diego ($18, 2½ to 3¼ hours, 19 daily)

LA–Santa Barbara ($18, 2¼ to 2¾ hours, four daily)

San Diego–Anaheim ($18, two to 2¼ hours, six daily)

San Francisco–Sacramento ($21, two to 2¾ hours, seven daily)

San Francisco–San Luis Obispo ($48, 6½ to 7¼ hours, five daily)

Reservations

It's easy to buy tickets online with a credit card, then pick them up (bring photo ID) at the terminal. You can also buy tickets over the phone or in person from a ticket agent. Greyhound terminal ticket windows also accept debit cards, traveler's checks and cash.

Most boarding is done on a first-come, first-served basis. Buying tickets in advance does not guarantee you a seat on any particular bus unless you also purchase priority boarding ($5 fee; available at some terminals). Otherwise, arrive at least one hour before the scheduled departure to secure a seat; allow extra time on weekends and around holidays.

Travelers with disabilities who need special assistance should call ☎800-752-4841 (TDD/TTY ☎800-345-3109) at least 48 hours before traveling. Wheelchairs are accepted as checked baggage and service animals are allowed on board.

Car, Motorcycle & RV

California's love affair with cars runs so deep it often verges on pathological, and it's here to stay for at least one practical reason: the state is so big, public transportation can't cover it. For flexibility and convenience, you'll want a car. Independence costs you, though: rental rates and gas prices can eat up a good chunk of your trip budget.

Automobile Associations

For 24-hour emergency roadside assistance, free maps and discounts on lodging, attractions, entertainment, car rentals and more:

American Automobile Association (AAA; ☎877-428-2277; www.aaa.com) Walk-in offices throughout California, add-on coverage for RVs and motorcycles, and reciprocal agreements with some international auto clubs (eg CAA in Canada, AA in the UK) – bring your membership card from home.

Better World Club (☎866-238-1137; www.betterworldclub.com) Ecofriendly alternative supports environmental causes and also offers cyclists emergency roadside assistance (see p771).

Driver's Licenses

» Visitors may legally drive a car in California for up to 12 months with their home driver's license.

» If you're from overseas, an International Driving Permit (IDP) will have more credibility with traffic police and simplify the car-rental process, especially if your license doesn't have a photo or isn't written in English.

» To drive a motorcycle, you'll need a valid US state motorcycle license or a specially endorsed IDP.

» International automobile associations can issue IDPs, valid for one year, for a fee. Always carry your home license together with the IDP.

Fuel

» Gas stations in California, nearly all of which are self-service, are ubiquitous, except in national parks and some sparsely populated desert and mountain areas.

» Gas is sold in gallons (one US gallon equals 3.78L). At press time, the cost for midgrade fuel ranged from $3.75 to $4.25.

Insurance

California law requires liability insurance for all vehicles. When renting a car, check your auto insurance policy from home or your travel insurance policy (p762) to see if you're already covered. If not, expect to pay about $20 per day.

Insurance against damage to the car itself, called Collision Damage Waiver (CDW) or Loss Damage Waiver (LDW), costs another $20 per day; the deductible may require you to pay the first $100 to $500 for any repairs. Some credit cards cover this, provided you charge the entire cost of the car rental to the card. If there's an accident you may have to

ROAD DISTANCES (miles)

	Anaheim	Arcata	Bakersfield	Death Valley	Las Vegas	Los Angeles	Monterey	Napa	Palm Springs	Redding	Sacramento	San Diego	San Francisco	San Luis Obispo	Santa Barbara	Sth Lake Tahoe
Arcata	680															
Bakersfield	135	555														
Death Valley	285	705	235													
Las Vegas	265	840	285	140												
Los Angeles	25	650	110	290	270											
Monterey	370	395	250	495	535	345										
Napa	425	265	300	545	590	400	150									
Palm Springs	95	760	220	300	280	110	450	505								
Redding	570	140	440	565	725	545	315	190	650							
Sacramento	410	300	280	435	565	385	185	60	490	160						
San Diego	95	770	230	350	330	120	465	520	140	665	505					
San Francisco	405	280	285	530	570	300	120	50	400	215	85	500				
San Luis Obispo	225	505	120	365	405	200	145	265	310	430	290	320	230			
Santa Barbara	120	610	145	350	360	95	250	370	205	535	395	215	335	105		
Sth Lake Tahoe	505	400	375	345	460	480	285	160	485	260	100	600	185	390	495	
Yosemite	335	465	200	300	415	310	200	190	415	325	160	430	190	230	345	190

pay the rental-car company first, then seek reimbursement from the credit-card company. Check your credit card's policy carefully before renting.

Parking

» Parking is usually plentiful and free in small towns and rural areas, but scarce and expensive in cities.

» Look for the free-parking icon (P) used in the San Francisco, Los Angeles and San Diego chapters of this book.

» You can pay municipal parking meters with coins (eg quarters) or sometimes credit cards.

» Expect to pay at least $25 to park overnight in a city lot or garage.

» Flat-fee valet parking at hotels and restaurants is common in major cities.

» When parking on the street, read all posted regulations and restrictions (eg street-cleaning hours, permit-only residential areas) and pay attention to colored curbs, or you may be ticketed and towed.

Rental

CARS

To rent your own wheels, you'll typically need to be at least 25 years old, hold a valid driver's license and have a major credit card, *not* a check or debit card. A few companies may rent to drivers under 25 but over 21 for a surcharge (around $25 per day). If you don't have a credit card, you may occasionally be able to make a large cash deposit instead.

With advance reservations, you can often get an economy-size vehicle with unlimited mileage from around $30 per day, plus insurance, taxes and fees. Weekend and weekly rates are usually more economical.

Airport locations may have cheaper rates but higher fees; if you get a fly-drive package, local taxes may be extra when you pick up the car. City-center branches may offer free pickups and drop-offs.

Rates generally include unlimited mileage, but expect surcharges for additional drivers and one-way rentals. Some rental companies let you pay for your last tank of gas upfront; this is rarely a good deal, as prices are higher than at gas stations and you'd need to bring the car back almost on empty. Child or infant safety seats are compulsory (reserve them when booking), and cost about $10 per day (maximum $50 per rental).

Major international car-rental companies:

Alamo (☎877-222-9075; www.alamo.com)

Avis (☎800-331-1212; www.avis.com)

Budget (☑800-527-0700; www.budget.com)

Dollar (☑800-800-3665; www.dollar.com)

Enterprise (☑800-261-7331; www.enterprise.com)

Fox (☑800-225-4369; www.foxrentacar.com)

Hertz (☑800-654-3131; www.hertz.com)

National (☑877-222-9058; www.nationalcar.com)

Thrifty (☑800-847-4389; www.thrifty.com)

You might get a better deal by booking through discount-travel websites such as **Priceline** (www.priceline.com) or **Hotwire** (www.hotwire.com), or by using online travel-booking sites, such as **Expedia** (www.expedia.com), **Orbitz** (www.orbitz.com) or **Travelocity** (www.travelocity.com).

If you'd like to minimize your carbon footprint, a few major car-rental companies (including Avis, Budget, Enterprise, Fox, Hertz and Thrifty) offer 'green' fleets of hybrid or biofuel rental cars, but they're in short supply. Reserve well in advance and expect to pay significantly more for these models. Also try:

Simply Hybrid (☑323-653-0011, 888-359-0055; www.simplyhybrid.com) In Los Angeles. Free delivery and pickup from some locations with a three-day minimum rental.

Zipcar (☑866-494-7227; www.zipcar.com) Currently available in 20 California cities (mostly along the coast), this car-sharing club charges usage fees (per hour or daily), including free gas, insurance (a damage fee of up to $500 may apply) and limited mileage. Apply online (foreign drivers OK); annual membership $50, application fee $25.

To find and compare independent car-rental companies, try **Car Rental Express** (www.carrentalexpress.com) – especially useful for searching out cheaper long-term rentals. Some independent companies may rent to drivers under 25:

Rent-a-Wreck (☑877-877-0700; www.rentawreck.com) Minimum rental age and surcharges vary by location. Ten locations, mostly around LA and the San Francisco Bay area.

Super Cheap Cars (www.supercheapcar.com) Normally a surcharge for drivers ages 21 to 24; daily fee applies for drivers aged 18 to 21. Three locations in San Francisco, Los Angeles and Orange Counties.

For wheelchair-accessible van rentals, see p767.

MOTORCYCLES

Motorcycle rentals and insurance are not cheap, especially if you have your eye on a Harley. Depending on the model, renting a motorcycle costs $100 to $200 per day plus taxes and fees, including helmets, unlimited miles and liability insurance; one-way rentals and collision insurance (CDW) cost extra. Discounts may be available for three-day and weekly rentals. Security deposits range from $1000 to $3000 (credit card required).

Motorcycle and scooter rental agencies:

Dubbelju (☑415-495-2774, 866-495-2774; www.dubbelju.com; 698a Bryant St, San Francisco) Harley-Davidson, BMW, Japanese-import and electric motorcycles for rent.

Eagle Rider (☑888-900-9901; www.eaglerider.com) Nationwide company with 12 locations in California, as well as Reno, Nevada. One-way rental surcharge $250.

Route 66 (☑310-578-0112, 888-434-4473; www.route66riders.com; 4161 Lincoln Blvd, Marina del Rey) Harley-Davidson rentals in LA's South Bay.

RECREATIONAL VEHICLES

It's easy to find campgrounds throughout California with electricity and water hookups for RVs, but in big cities RVs are a nuisance, since there are few places to park or plug them in. RVs are also cumbersome to drive and they burn fuel at an alarming rate. That said, they do solve transportation, accommodation and cooking needs in one fell swoop. Even so, there are many places in national and state parks and in the mountains that RVs can't go.

Book RV rentals as far in advance as possible. Rental costs vary by size and model, but you can expect to pay over $100 per day for a campervan or 25ft-long RV sleeping up to five people. Rates often don't include mileage (from 35¢ per mile), bedding or kitchen kits (rental fee $50 to $100), vehicle prep ($100 surcharge) or taxes. Pets may be allowed, sometimes for an additional surcharge.

RV rental agencies:

Cruise America (☑480-464-7300, 800-671-8042; www.cruiseamerica.com) Two dozen pickup locations statewide.

El Monte (☑562-483-4956, 888-337-2214; www.elmonterv.com) Ask about AAA discounts.

Happy Travel Campers (☑310-928-3980, 800-370-1262; www.camperusa.com) LA-based.

Moturis (☑877-297-3687; www.moturis.com) In LA, San Diego, San Francisco and Sacramento.

Road Bear (☑818-865-2925, 866-491-9853; www.roadbearrv.com) In LA and San Francisco.

Road Conditions & Hazards

For up-to-date highway conditions in California, including road closures and construction updates, dial ☑800-427-7623 or visit www.dot.ca.gov. For Nevada highways, call ☑877-687-6237 or check www.nvroads.com.

In places where winter driving is an issue, snow tires and

tire chains may be required in mountain areas. Ideally, carry your own chains and learn how to use them before you hit the road. Otherwise, chains can usually be bought (but not cheaply) on the highway, at gas stations or in the nearest town. Most car-rental companies don't permit the use of chains. Driving off-road, or on dirt roads, is also prohibited by most rental-car companies, and it can be dangerous in wet weather.

In rural areas, livestock sometimes graze next to unfenced roads. These areas are typically signed as 'Open Range,' with the silhouette of a steer. Where deer and other wild animals frequently appear roadside, you'll see signs with the silhouette of a leaping deer. Take these signs seriously, particularly at night. In coastal areas thick fog may impede driving – slow down and if it's too soupy, get off the road. Along coastal cliffs and in the mountains, watch out for falling rocks, mudslides and avalanches that could damage or disable your car if struck.

Road Rules
» Drive on the right-hand side of the road.
» Talking on a cell phone while driving is illegal.
» The use of seat belts is required for drivers, front-seat passengers and children under age 16.
» Infant and child safety seats are required for children under six years old or weighing less than 60lb.
» All motorcyclists must wear a helmet. Scooters are not allowed on freeways.
» High-occupancy (HOV) lanes marked with a diamond symbol are reserved for cars with multiple occupants, sometimes only during morning and afternoon rush hours.
» Unless otherwise posted, the speed limit is 65mph on freeways, 55mph on two-lane undivided highways, 35mph on major city streets and 25mph in business and residential districts and near schools.
» It's forbidden to pass a school bus when its rear red lights are flashing.
» Except where indicated, turning right at red lights after coming to a full stop is permitted, although intersecting traffic still has the right of way.
» At four-way stop signs, cars proceed in the order in which they arrived. If two cars arrive simultaneously, the one on the right has the right of way. When in doubt, politely wave the other driver ahead.
» When emergency vehicles (ie police, fire or ambulance) approach from either direction, carefully pull over to the side of the road.
» California has strict anti-littering laws; throwing trash from a vehicle may incur a $1000 fine. Like Woody says, 'Give a hoot, don't pollute.'
» Driving under the influence of alcohol or drugs is illegal (see p763).
» It's also illegal to carry open containers of alcohol inside a vehicle, even empty ones. Unless containers are full and still sealed, store them in the trunk.

Public Transportation
Except in cities, public transit is rarely the most convenient option, and coverage to outlying towns and suburbs can be sparse. However, it is usually cheap, safe and reliable. See the regional chapters for details.

Bicycle
» Cycling is a feasible way of getting around smaller cities and towns, but it's not much fun in traffic-dense areas such as LA.
» Davis, San Francisco, San Luis Obispo, Santa Barbara and Santa Cruz are among California's most bike-friendly communities, as rated by the **League of American Bicyclists** (www.bikeleague.org).
» Bicycles may be transported on many buses and trains (see p771), sometimes during non-commute hours only.
» For rentals or buying a bike, see p771.

Bus, Cable Car, Streetcar & Trolley
» Most cities and larger towns have reliable local bus systems (average $1 to $3 per ride), but they may be designed for commuters and provide only limited evening and weekend service.
» San Francisco's extensive Municipal Railway (MUNI) network includes not only buses and trains, but also historic streetcars and those famous cable cars.
» San Diego runs trolleys around some neighborhoods and to the Mexican border.

Train
» In LA, the Metro is a combined, ever-expanding network of subway and light-rail, while Metrolink commuter trains connect LA with surrounding counties.
» San Diego operates Coaster commuter trains along the coast between downtown and Oceanside in the North County.
» To get around the San Francisco Bay Area, hop aboard Bay Area Rapid Transit (BART) or Caltrain.

Taxi
» Taxis are metered, with flag-fall fees of $2.50 to $3.50 to start, plus $2 to $3 per mile. Credit cards may be accepted.
» Taxis may charge extra for baggage and airport pickups.
» Drivers expect a 10% to 15% tip, rounded up to the next dollar.
» Taxis cruise the busiest areas in large cities, but elsewhere you may need to call a cab company.

ALL ABOARD! CALIFORNIA'S SCENIC RAILWAYS

» **Napa Valley Wine Train** (p162)
» **California State Railroad Museum** (p329)
» **Railtown 1897 State Historic Park** (p324)
» **Roaring Camp Railroads** (p463)
» **Skunk Train** (p229)
» **Yosemite Mountain Sugar Pine Railroad** (p414)

Train

Amtrak (☎800-872-7245; www.amtrak.com) runs comfortable, if occasionally tardy, trains to major California cities and limited towns. At some stations Thruway buses provide onward connections. Smoking is prohibited on board trains and buses.

Amtrak routes within California:

California Zephyr Daily service from Emeryville (near San Francisco) via Davis and Sacramento to Truckee (near Lake Tahoe) and Reno, Nevada.

Capitol Corridor Links San Francisco's East Bay (including Oakland, Emeryville and Berkeley) and San Jose with Davis and Sacramento several times daily. Thruway buses connect west to San Francisco, north to Auburn in the Gold Country and east to Truckee (near Lake Tahoe) and Reno, Nevada.

Coast Starlight Chugs roughly north–south almost the entire length of the state. Daily stops include LA, Santa Barbara, San Luis Obispo, Paso Robles, Salinas, San Jose, Oakland, Emeryville, Davis, Sacramento, Chico, Redding and Dunsmuir. Wi-fi may be available.

Pacific Surfliner Over a dozen daily trains ply the San Diego–LA route (via Anaheim, home of Disneyland). Six trains continue north to Santa Barbara, with three going all the way to San Luis Obispo. The trip itself, which hugs the coastline for much of the route, is a visual treat.

San Joaquin Several daily trains between Bakersfield and Oakland or Sacramento. Thruway bus connections include San Francisco, LA, Palm Springs and Yosemite National Park.

Costs

Purchase tickets at train stations, by phone or online. Fares depend on the day of travel, the route, the type of seating and so on. Fares may be slightly higher during peak travel times (eg summer). Round-trip tickets cost the same as two one-way tickets.

Usually seniors over 62 and students with an ISIC or Student Advantage Card (p760) receive a 15% discount, while up to two children aged two to 15 who are accompanied by an adult get 50% off. AAA members save 10%. Special promotions can become available anytime, so check the website or ask.

Sample Amtrak fares and times:

Los Angeles–Oakland/San Francisco ($54, 12 hours)
Los Angeles–San Luis Obispo ($33, 5½ hours)
Los Angeles–Santa Barbara ($25, 2¾ hours)
San Diego–Los Angeles ($31, 2½ hours)
San Francisco/Emeryville–Sacramento ($28, 2¼ hours)
San Francisco/Emeryville–Truckee ($44, 5½ hours)

Reservations

Reservations can be made any time from 11 months in advance to the day of departure. In summer and around holidays, trains sell out quickly, so book tickets as early as possible. The cheapest coach fares are usually for unreserved seats; business-class fares typically come with reserved seats.

Travelers with disabilities who need special assistance, wheelchair space, transfer seats or accessible accommodations should call ☎800-872-7245 (TDD/TTY ☎800-523-6590), and inquire about discounted fares when booking.

Train Passes

» Amtrak's California Rail Pass costs $159 ($80 for children aged two to 15).
» The pass is valid on all trains (except certain long-distance routes) and most connecting Thruway buses for seven days of travel within a 21-day period.
» Passholders must make advance reservations for each leg of travel and obtain hard-copy tickets prior to boarding.
» For Amtrak's USA Rail Pass, see p770.

behind the scenes

SEND US YOUR FEEDBACK

We love to hear from travelers – your comments keep us on our toes and help make our books better. Our well-traveled team reads every word on what you loved or loathed about this book. Although we cannot reply individually to postal submissions, we always guarantee that your feedback goes straight to the appropriate authors, in time for the next edition. Each person who sends us information is thanked in the next edition – and the most useful submissions are rewarded with a free book.

Visit **lonelyplanet.com/contact** to submit your updates and suggestions or to ask for help. Our award-winning website also features inspirational travel stories, news and discussions.

Note: We may edit, reproduce and incorporate your comments in Lonely Planet products such as guidebooks, websites and digital products, so let us know if you don't want your comments reproduced or your name acknowledged. For a copy of our privacy policy visit lonelyplanet.com/privacy.

OUR READERS

Many thanks to the travelers who used the last edition and wrote to us with helpful hints, useful advice and interesting anecdotes:

Martina Alpeza, Gino Assaf, Hans ter Beek, Collette Beuther, Lalimarie Bhagwani, Dr Andrew Brandeis, Rob Brehant, Thor Brisbin, Scott Broc, Alison Cant, Dave Carlisle, Deric Carner, Roe Cheung, Michael Chien, Ted Choi, May Chu, Eileen Connery, Gerald Crosby, Christine Dauer, Jason Dibler, Silke Diedenhofen, Robert Douthit, Richard Edwards, Keith Endean, Kenneth Endo, Edgar Ennen, Damian Ennis, Behrooz Farahani, Gerhard Faul, Gentry Fischer, Judy Fried, Pierre Garapon, Peter Garvey, Marg Gibson, Sven Gold, Monica Griffin, Cindy de Groot, Michael Gullo, Caroline Hall, Chris Hardman, Henrik Hiltunen, Bobbi Lee Hitchon, TJ Huffman, Mary Jenn, Winnie Kaplan, Marijn Kastelein, S Keizer, Christine Klerian, Ali Komiha, Harish Kumar, April Kummrow, Jason Kwon, Tom Laufer, Jennifer Lee, Ali Lemer, Gillian Lomax, Bo Lorentzen, Diderik Lund, Megan MacDonald, Melissa MacNabb, Stephanie Magalhaes, Ara Martirosyan, Victoria Mascord, Trevor Mazzucchelli, Kevin McElroy, Jimmy McGill, Steve McInnes, Ben Miller, Molly Mitoma, Jacqui Monaghan, Heather Monell, Kirsty Moore, Bradford Nordeen, Junhui Park, Jerry Patel, Sudha Patel, Sheri Peters, Celeste Perez, Juliana Pesavento, Charlotte Pothuizen, Louisa Ramshaw, Mona Reed, Christine Rice, Bobby Richards, Raphael Richards, Julia Ringma, Daniel Roberts, Matthew Roder, Danny Roman, Elizabeth Saenger, Karen Sams, Art Sandoval, Elie Sasson, Matthew Scharpnick, Hannah Schmidt, Scott Schmidt, David Schnur, Geoff Shepherd, Joe Silins, Aimee Smith, Allie Smith, Mike Smith, Renee Stuart, Susan Sueiro, Estrella Tadeo, Emanuela Tasinato, Mona Telega, Amanda Thomas, Aaron Tomas, Carton Tsutomu, Christian Utzman, Ophelie Vantournout, Luka Vidovic, Lorna Visser, Ira Vouk, Gordon Waggoner, Cyndi Wish, Alex Wong, Dr Felix Z, Greta Zeit

AUTHOR THANKS

Sara Benson

Without everyone at Lonely Planet and all of my California co-authors, this book never would have had such smooth sailing. I'm grateful to those folks I met on the road who shared their local expertise and tips. Big thanks to all of my friends and family across the Golden State, especially the Picketts for their Lake Tahoe hospitality and Jai for road-tripping humor (cowbears!). PS to MSC Jr: Glad that avalanche didn't kill us. Whew! Here's hoping we're invincible.

Andrew Bender

Suki Gear, Alison Lyall and Sam Benson for the opportunity and their good cheer and advice. Thanks also to Adrienne Costanzo, Karen Grant, Corey Hutchison and Bella Li for their assistance on this book.

Alison Bing

Suki Gear and Sam Benson, whose guidance, insight and support make any tricky mental backbend possible. Shameless California bear hugs to John Vlahides and Robert Landon for setting giddily high writing standards for this book, to fearless leaders Brice Gosnell and Heather Dickson at Lonely Planet, to the Sanchez Writers' Grotto, and above all to Marco Flavio Marinucci, whose kindness and bracing espresso make everything possible.

Nate Cavalieri

Thanks to my partner Florence Chien for joining my research travels through Northern California and giving this text a careful read. Thanks to The Ben Calhoun and Catrin Einhorn for sheltering me while this book was completed. Thanks also to the lovely people at Lonely Planet, and particularly for the enthusiasm of commissioning editor and mentor Suki Gear.

Bridget Gleeson

Thank you to my lovely sister Molly, my brother-in-law Germán and my dear friend Starla Silver for their hospitality, and to all their friends for endless dining and drinking suggestions. Thanks, as well, to my mother Margaret, who always serves as my faithful travel companion.

Beth Kohn

All the usual suspects get thanks again, especially the fabulous multi-tasking Suki Gear and the dynamo known as Sam Benson. California cohorts and experts this time around included Agent 'Pedal-to-the-metal' Moller, Felix 'Hella Loves Oakland' Thomson, Jenny 'Stink' G, Dillon 'The Scientist' Dutton and Julia 'Wawona' Brashares, plus all the helpful and patient rangers at Yosemite National Park.

Andrea Schulte-Peevers

Big thanks to Suki Gear for letting me have another shot at California. A heartfelt thank you also to my husband David for being such good company while tooling around the desert. Big kudos to all the good folks who shared their local insights, steered me in the right direction and made helpful introductions, including Hillary Angel, Mark Graves, Cheryl Chipman and Christopher Vonloudermilk.

John Vlahides

I owe heartfelt thanks to my commissioning editor, Suki Gear, and co-authors, Sam Benson and Alison Bing, for their wonderful help and always-sunny dispositions. Kate Brady, Steven Kahn, Karl Soehnlein, Kevin Clarke, Jim Aloise and Adam Young – you kept me upbeat and laughing when things seemed impossible. And to you, readers: thank you for letting me be your guide to Wine Country. Have fun. I know you will.

ACKNOWLEDGMENTS

Climate map data adapted from Peel MC, Finlayson BL & McMahon TA (2007) 'Updated World Map of the Köppen-Geiger Climate Classification', Hydrology and Earth System Sciences, 11, 163344.

Cover photograph: Winery, Santa Maria, California, Brent Winebrenner.

Many of the images in this guide are available for licensing from Lonely Planet Images: www.lonelyplanetimages.com.

THIS BOOK

This 6th edition of California was researched and written by a fabulous author team (see Our Writers), with Sara Benson coordinating. The previous edition was also coordinated by Sara Benson. This guidebook was commissioned in Lonely Planet's Oakland office, and produced by the following:

Commissioning Editor Suki Gear

Coordinating Editor Bella Li

Coordinating Cartographers Corey Hutchison, Eve Kelly

Coordinating Layout Designer Kerrianne Southway

Managing Editors Bruce Evans, Annelies Mertens, Anna Metcalfe

Managing Cartographers Shahara Ahmed, David Connolly, Alison Lyall

Managing Layout Designers Chris Girdler, Jane Hart

Assisting Editors Holly Alexander, Andrew Bain, Judith Bamber, Elin Berglund, Adrienne Costanzo, Emma Gilmour, Carly Hall, Paul Harding, Pat Kinsella, Katie O'Connell, Kristin Odijk, Monique Perrin

Assisting Cartographers Ildiko Bogdanovits, Xavier Di Toro, Mick Garrett, Karen Grant, Valentina Kremenchutskaya, James Leversha, Marc Milinkovic

Cover Research Naomi Parker

Internal Image Research Sabrina Dalbesio

Thanks to Helen Christinis, Ryan Evans, Wayne Murphy, Susan Paterson, Julie Sherdian, Angela Tinson, Gerard Walker

index

000 Map pages
000 Photo pages

000 Map pages
000 Photo pages

how to use this book

These symbols will help you find the listings you want:

👁 Sights	👉 Tours	🍷 Drinking
🐋 Beaches	🎉 Festivals & Events	☆ Entertainment
🏃 Activities	🛏 Sleeping	🛍 Shopping
🎓 Courses	🍴 Eating	ℹ Information/Transport

These symbols give you the vital information for each listing:

☎ Telephone Numbers	📶 Wi-Fi Access	🚌 Bus
⏰ Opening Hours	🏊 Swimming Pool	⛴ Ferry
🅿 Parking	🌱 Vegetarian Selection	Ⓜ Metro
⊖ Nonsmoking	📋 English-Language Menu	Ⓢ Subway
❄ Air-Conditioning	👨‍👩‍👧 Family-Friendly	⊖ London Tube
@ Internet Access	🐾 Pet-Friendly	🚋 Tram
		🚆 Train

Reviews are organised by author preference.

Look out for these icons:

TOP CHOICE	Our author's recommendation
FREE	No payment required
🌿	A green or sustainable option

Our authors have nominated these places as demonstrating a strong commitment to sustainability – for example by supporting local communities and producers, operating in an environmentally friendly way, or supporting conservation projects.

Map Legend

Sights
- 🏖 Beach
- ☸ Buddhist
- 🏰 Castle
- ✝ Christian
- ॐ Hindu
- ☪ Islamic
- ✡ Jewish
- ⛲ Monument
- 🏛 Museum/Gallery
- 🏚 Ruin
- 🍷 Winery/Vineyard
- 🐾 Zoo
- 👁 Other Sight

Activities, Courses & Tours
- 🤿 Diving/Snorkelling
- 🛶 Canoeing/Kayaking
- ⛷ Skiing
- 🏄 Surfing
- 🏊 Swimming/Pool
- 🚶 Walking
- 🏄 Windsurfing
- ⊕ Other Activity/Course/Tour

Sleeping
- 🛏 Sleeping
- ⛺ Camping

Eating
- 🍴 Eating

Drinking
- ☕ Drinking
- ☕ Cafe

Entertainment
- ☆ Entertainment

Shopping
- 🛍 Shopping

Information
- ✉ Post Office
- ℹ Tourist Information

Transport
- ✈ Airport
- ⊗ Border Crossing
- 🚌 Bus
- 🚡 Cable Car/Funicular
- 🚲 Cycling
- ⛴ Ferry
- Ⓜ Metro
- 🚝 Monorail
- 🅿 Parking
- Ⓢ S-Bahn
- 🚕 Taxi
- 🚉 Train/Railway
- 🚋 Tram
- Ⓣ Tube Station
- Ⓤ U-Bahn
- • Other Transport

Routes
- Tollway
- Freeway
- Primary
- Secondary
- Tertiary
- Lane
- Unsealed Road
- Plaza/Mall
- Steps
-)(Tunnel
- Pedestrian Overpass
- Walking Tour
- Walking Tour Detour
- Path

Boundaries
- International
- State/Province
- Disputed
- Regional/Suburb
- Marine Park
- Cliff
- Wall

Population
- ✪ Capital (National)
- ◉ Capital (State/Province)
- ● City/Large Town
- ○ Town/Village

Geographic
- 🛖 Hut/Shelter
- 🗼 Lighthouse
- 👁 Lookout
- ▲ Mountain/Volcano
- 🌴 Oasis
- 🌳 Park
-)(Pass
- 🏕 Picnic Area
- 💧 Waterfall

Hydrography
- River/Creek
- Intermittent River
- Swamp/Mangrove
- Reef
- Canal
- Water
- Dry/Salt/Intermittent Lake
- Glacier

Areas
- Beach/Desert
- + + + Cemetery (Christian)
- × × × Cemetery (Other)
- Park/Forest
- Sportsground
- Sight (Building)
- Top Sight (Building)